CCNP TSHOOT 642-832
Official Certification Guide

Kevin Wallace, CCIE No. 7945

Cisco Press

800 East 96th Street

Indianapolis, IN 46240

MW00835421

CCNP TSHOOT 642-832 Official Certification Guide

Kevin Wallace, CCIE No. 7945

Copyright © 2010 Pearson Education, Inc.

Published by:
Cisco Press
800 East 96th Street
Indianapolis, IN 46240 USA

All rights reserved. No part of this book may be reproduced or transmitted in any form or by any means, electronic or mechanical, including photocopying, recording, or by any information storage and retrieval system, without written permission from the publisher, except for the inclusion of brief quotations in a review.

Printed in the United States of America

Sixth Printing: July 2012

Library of Congress Cataloging-in-Publication Data:

Wallace, Kevin, CCNP.
   CCNP TSHOOT 642-832 official certification guide / Kevin Wallace.
      p. cm.
   Includes index.
   ISBN-13: 978-1-58705-844-8
   ISBN-10: 1-58705-844-8
   1. Computer networks—Management—Examinations—Study guides. 2. Telecommunications engineers—Certification. 3. Cisco Systems, Inc.—Examinations—Study guides. I. Title.
   TK5105.8.C57W35 2010
   004.6076—dc22

Warning and Disclaimer

This book is designed to provide information about the CCNP TSHOOT Exam (Exam 642-832) for the CCNP Routing and Switching certification. Every effort has been made to make this book as complete and as accurate as possible, but no warranty or fitness is implied.

The information is provided on an "as is" basis. The authors, Cisco Press, and Cisco Systems, Inc. shall have neither liability nor responsibility to any person or entity with respect to any loss or damages arising from the information contained in this book or from the use of the discs or programs that may accompany it.

The opinions expressed in this book belong to the author and are not necessarily those of Cisco Systems, Inc.

Trademark Acknowledgments

All terms mentioned in this book that are known to be trademarks or service marks have been appropriately capitalized. Cisco Press or Cisco Systems, Inc., cannot attest to the accuracy of this information. Use of a term in this book should not be regarded as affecting the validity of any trademark or service mark.

Corporate and Government Sales

The publisher offers excellent discounts on this book when ordered in quantity for bulk purchases or special sales, which may include electronic versions and/or custom covers and content particular to your business, training goals, marketing focus, and branding interests. For more information, please contact: **U.S. Corporate and Government Sales**   1-800-382-3419   corpsales@pearsontechgroup.com

For sales outside the United States please contact: **International Sales**   international@pearsoned.com

Feedback Information

At Cisco Press, our goal is to create in-depth technical books of the highest quality and value. Each book is crafted with care and precision, undergoing rigorous development that involves the unique expertise of members from the professional technical community.

Readers' feedback is a natural continuation of this process. If you have any comments regarding how we could improve the quality of this book, or otherwise alter it to better suit your needs, you can contact us through e-mail at feedback@ciscopress.com. Please make sure to include the book title and ISBN in your message.

We greatly appreciate your assistance.

Publisher: Paul Boger

Business Operation Manager, Cisco Press: Anand Sundaram

Associate Publisher: Dave Dusthimer

Manager Global Certification: Erik Ullanderson

Executive Editor: Brett Bartow

Copy Editors: Gill Editorial Services and Water Crest Publishing, Inc.

Managing Editor: Patrick Kanouse

Technical Editor: Elan Beer

Senior Project Editor: Tonya Simpson

Proofreader: Williams Woods Publishing Services, LLC

Senior Development Editor: Christopher Cleveland

Editorial Assistant: Vanessa Evans

Book Designer: Louisa Adair

Composition: Mark Shirar

Indexer: Tim Wright

··|···|··
CISCO.

Americas Headquarters
Cisco Systems, Inc.
San Jose, CA

Asia Pacific Headquarters
Cisco Systems (USA) Pte. Ltd.
Singapore

Europe Headquarters
Cisco Systems International BV
Amsterdam, The Netherlands

Cisco has more than 200 offices worldwide. Addresses, phone numbers, and fax numbers are listed on the Cisco Website at **www.cisco.com/go/offices.**

CCDE, CCENT, Cisco Eos, Cisco HealthPresence, the Cisco logo, Cisco Lumin, Cisco Nexus, Cisco StadiumVision, Cisco TelePresence, Cisco WebEx, DCE, and Welcome to the Human Network are trademarks; Changing the Way We Work, Live, Play, and Learn and Cisco Store are service marks; and Access Registrar, Aironet, AsyncOS, Bringing the Meeting To You, Catalyst, CCDA, CCDP, CCIE, CCIP, CCNA, CCNP, CCSP, CCVP, Cisco, the Cisco Certified Internetwork Expert logo, Cisco IOS, Cisco Press, Cisco Systems, Cisco Systems Capital, the Cisco Systems logo, Cisco Unity, Collaboration Without Limitation, EtherFast, EtherSwitch, Event Center, Fast Step, Follow Me Browsing, FormShare, GigaDrive, HomeLink, Internet Quotient, IOS, iPhone, iQuick Study, IronPort, the IronPort logo, LightStream, Linksys, MediaTone, MeetingPlace, MeetingPlace Chime Sound, MGX, Networkers, Networking Academy, Network Registrar, PCNow, PIX, PowerPanels, ProConnect, ScriptShare, SenderBase, SMARTnet, Spectrum Expert, StackWise, The Fastest Way to Increase Your Internet Quotient, TransPath, WebEx, and the WebEx logo are registered trademarks of Cisco Systems, Inc. and/or its affiliates in the United States and certain other countries.

All other trademarks mentioned in this document or website are the property of their respective owners. The use of the word partner does not imply a partnership relationship between Cisco and any other company. (0812R)

About the Author

Kevin Wallace, CCIE No. 7945, is a certified Cisco instructor who holds multiple Cisco certifications, including CCSP, CCVP, CCNP, and CCDP, in addition to multiple security and voice specializations. With Cisco experience dating back to 1989 (beginning with a Cisco AGS+ running Cisco IOS 7.x), Kevin has been a network design specialist for the Walt Disney World Resort, a senior technical instructor for SkillSoft/Thomson NETg/KnowledgeNet, and a network manager for Eastern Kentucky University. Kevin holds a bachelor of science degree in electrical engineering from the University of Kentucky. Kevin has authored multiple books for Cisco Press, including *Routing Video Mentor* and *TSHOOT Video Mentor*, both of which target the current CCNP Routing and Switching certification. Kevin lives in central Kentucky with his wife (Vivian) and two daughters (Stacie and Sabrina).

About the Technical Reviewer

Elan Beer, CCIE No. 1837, CCSI No. 94008, is a senior consultant and Certified Cisco Instructor. His internetworking expertise is recognized internationally through his global consulting and training engagements. As one of the industry's top internetworking consultants and Cisco instructors, Elan has used his expertise for the past 17 years to design, implement, and deploy multiprotocol networks for a wide international clientele. As a senior instructor and course developer, Elan has designed and presented public and implementation-specific technical courses spanning many of today's top technologies. Elan specializes in MPLS, BGP, QoS, and other Internetworking technologies.

Dedications

This book is dedicated to my family. To my beautiful wife Vivian, you have an unbelievably giving spirit. To my daughter Sabrina, you have a keen business mind at only 12 years of age. You're destined for big things. To my daughter Stacie, at the age of 14, you radiate happiness and are maturing into a wonderful young lady.

Acknowledgments

My thanks go out to the team of professionals at Cisco Press. I'm proud to be associated with such a respected organization.

My family is unbelievably supportive of my writing efforts. Thank you to my wife, Vivian, and my daughters, Sabrina and Stacie. You all have been very understanding when I seclude myself to write. Also, I'm grateful to God for surrounding me with such quality people, both personally and professionally.

Contents at a Glance

CD-Only Appendixes

Contents

Icons Used in This Book

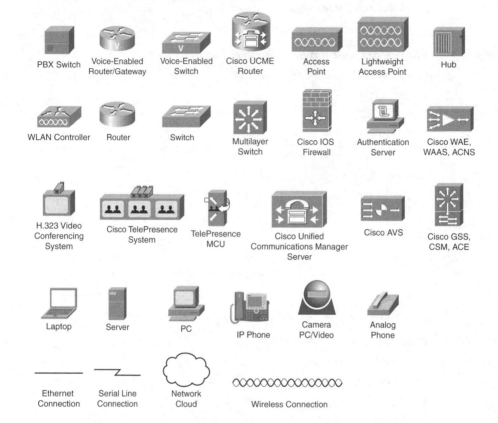

Command Syntax Conventions

The conventions used to present command syntax in this book are the same conventions used in the IOS Command Reference. The Command Reference describes these conventions as follows:

- **Boldface** indicates commands and keywords that are entered literally as shown. In actual configuration examples and output (not general command syntax), boldface indicates commands that are manually input by the user (such as a **show** command).

- *Italic* indicates arguments for which you supply actual values.

- Vertical bars (|) separate alternative, mutually exclusive elements.

- Square brackets ([ ]) indicate an optional element.

- Braces ({ }) indicate a required choice.

- Braces within brackets ([{ }]) indicate a required choice within an optional element.

Foreword

CCNP TSHOOT 642-832 Official Certification Guide is an excellent self-study resource for the CCNP TSHOOT exam. Passing this exam is a crucial step to attaining the valued CCNP Routing and Switching certification.

Gaining certification in Cisco technology is key to the continuing educational development of today's networking professional. Through certification programs, Cisco validates the skills and expertise required to effectively manage the modern enterprise network.

Cisco Press Certification Guides and preparation materials offer exceptional—and flexible—access to the knowledge and information required to stay current in your field of expertise or to gain new skills. Whether used as a supplement to more traditional training or as a primary source of learning, these materials offer users the information and knowledge validation required to gain new understanding and proficiencies.

Developed in conjunction with the Cisco certifications and training team, Cisco Press books are the only self-study books authorized by Cisco and offer students a series of exam practice tools and resource materials to help ensure that learners fully grasp the concepts and information presented.

Additional authorized Cisco instructor-led courses, e-learning, labs, and simulations are available exclusively from Cisco Learning Solutions Partners worldwide. To learn more, visit http://www.cisco.com/go/training.

I hope that you find these materials to be an enriching and useful part of your exam preparation.

Erik Ullanderson
Manager, Global Certifications
Learning@Cisco
January 2010

Introduction: Overview of Certification and How to Succeed

Professional certifications have been an important part of the computing industry for many years and will continue to become more important. Many reasons exist for these certifications, but the most popularly cited reason is that of credibility. All other considerations held equal, the certified employee/consultant/job candidate is considered more valuable than one who is not.

Objectives and Methods

The most important and somewhat obvious objective of this book is to help you pass the Cisco CCNP TSHOOT exam (Exam 642-832). In fact, if the primary objective of this book were different, the book's title would be misleading; however, the methods used in this book to help you pass the TSHOOT exam are designed to also make you much more knowledgeable about how to do your job. Although this book and the accompanying CD-ROM have many exam preparation tasks and example test questions, the method in which they are used is not to simply make you memorize as many questions and answers as you possibly can.

The methodology of this book helps you discover the exam topics about which you need more review, fully understand and remember exam topic details, and prove to yourself that you have retained your knowledge of those topics. So this book helps you pass not by memorization, but by helping you truly learn and understand the topics. The TSHOOT exam is just one of the foundation topics in the CCNP Routing and Switching certification, and the knowledge contained within is vitally important to consider yourself a truly skilled routing and switching engineer or specialist. This book would do you a disservice if it did not attempt to help you learn the material. To that end, the book can help you pass the TSHOOT exam by using the following methods:

- Covering all of the exam topics and helping you discover which exam topics you have not mastered

- Providing explanations and information to fill in your knowledge gaps

- Supplying multiple troubleshooting case studies with diagrams and diagnostic output that enhance your ability to resolve trouble tickets presented in the exam environment, in addition to real-world troubleshooting issues you might encounter

- Providing practice exercises on exam topics, presented in each chapter and on the enclosed CD-ROM

Who Should Read This Book?

This book is not designed to be a general networking topics book, although it can be used for that purpose. This book is intended to tremendously increase your chances of passing the Cisco TSHOOT exam. Although other objectives can be achieved from using this book, the book is written with one goal in mind: to help you pass the exam.

The TSHOOT exam is primarily based on the content of the Cisco TSHOOT course. You should have either taken the course, read through the TSHOOT course material or this book, or have a couple of years of troubleshooting experience.

Cisco Certifications and Exams

Cisco offers four levels of routing and switching certification, each with an increasing level of proficiency: Entry, Associate, Professional, and Expert. These are commonly known by their acronyms CCENT (Cisco Certified Entry Networking Technician), CCNA (Cisco Certified Network Associate), CCNP (Cisco Certified Network Professional), and CCIE (Cisco Certified Internetworking Expert). There are others as well, but this book focuses on the certifications for enterprise networks.

For the CCNP Routing and Switching certification, you must pass exams on a series of CCNP topics, including the SWITCH, ROUTE, and TSHOOT exams. For most exams, Cisco does not publish the scores needed for passing. You need to take the exam to find that out for yourself.

To see the most current requirements for the CCNP Routing and Switching certification, go to cisco.com and click Training and Events. There you can find out other exam details such as exam topics and how to register for an exam.

The strategy you use to prepare for the TSHOOT exam might be slightly different than strategies used by other readers, mainly based on the skills, knowledge, and experience you have already obtained. For example, if you have attended the TSHOOT course, you might take a different approach than someone who learned troubleshooting through on-the-job training. Regardless of the strategy you use or the background you have, this book is designed to help you get to the point where you can pass the exam with the least amount of time required.

How This Book Is Organized

Although this book can be read cover to cover, it is designed to be flexible and enable you to easily move between chapters to cover only the material that you need more work with. The chapters can be covered in any order, although some chapters are related and build upon each other. If you do intend to read them all, the order in the book is an excellent sequence to use.

Each core chapter covers a subset of the topics on the CCNP TSHOOT exam. The chapters are organized into parts, covering the following topics:

■ **Chapter 1, "Introduction to Network Maintenance":** This chapter discusses the importance of proactive maintenance tasks, as opposed to the reactive maintenance required to address a problem. Also discussed in this chapter is a collection of commonly used maintenance approaches.

Next, this chapter lists common maintenance tasks, emphasizes the importance of regularly scheduled maintenance, and summarizes critical areas of network performance. Finally, this chapter identifies how to compile a set of network maintenance tools that complement your network maintenance plan.

■ **Chapter 2, "Introduction to Troubleshooting Processes":** This chapter addresses troubleshooting fundamentals, discusses the benefits of having a structured troubleshooting model, and discusses several popular troubleshooting models.

Also discussed is each subprocess in a structured troubleshooting approach. Finally, this chapter shows how maintenance processes and troubleshooting process can work in tandem to complement one another.

■ **Chapter 3, "The Maintenance and Troubleshooting Toolbox":** This chapter shows how a few readily accessible Cisco IOS commands can be used to quickly gather information, as part of a structured troubleshooting process.

This chapter also introduces a collection of specialized features, such as SPAN, RSPAN, SMTP, NetFlow, and EEM, which can be used to collect information about a problem.

■ **Chapter 4, "Basic Cisco Catalyst Switch Troubleshooting":** This chapter reviews the basics of Layer 2 switch operation and demonstrates a collection of Cisco Catalyst **show** commands that can be used to quickly gather information, as part of a structured troubleshooting process.

Also, this chapter introduces spanning tree protocol (STP), which allows a Layer 2 topology to have redundant links while avoiding the side effects of a looped Layer 2 topology, such as a broadcast storm. You then learn strategies for troubleshooting an STP issue.

Finally, troubleshooting an EtherChannel connection is addressed. This chapter concludes with a trouble ticket and an associated topology. You are also given **show** command output (baseline output and output collected after the reported issue occurred). Based on the information provided, you hypothesize an underlying cause for the reported issue and develop a solution. You can then compare your solution with a suggested solution.

■ **Chapter 5, "Advanced Cisco Catalyst Switch Troubleshooting":** This chapter begins by contrasting Layer 3 switches and routers. Troubleshooting procedures are also compared for these platforms. Two approaches for routing packets using Layer 3 switches are also discussed. These approaches are using routed ports and using switched virtual interfaces (SVIs).

Next, this chapter discusses three approaches to providing first-hop router redundancy. Options include HSRP, VRRP, and GLBP. Troubleshooting strategies are discussed for HSRP with suggestions on how to modify those strategies for troubleshooting VRRP and GLBP. Examined next is the architecture of a Cisco Catalyst switch and the different architectural components that could become troubleshooting targets. You are presented with a series of **show** commands used to gather information about different aspects of a switch's performance.

Finally, this chapter presents you with a trouble ticket and an associated topology. You are also given **show** and **debug** command output (baseline output and output collected after a reported issue occurred). Based on the information provided, you hypothesize an underlying cause for the reported issue and develop a solution. You can then compare your solution with a suggested solution.

- **Chapter 6, "Introduction to Troubleshooting Routing Protocols":** This chapter begins by reviewing basic routing concepts. For example, you examine the changes to a frame's header as that frame's data is routed from one network to another. You see how Layer 2 information can be learned and stored in a router. Cisco Express Forwarding (CEF) is also discussed. Additionally, you are presented with a collection of **show** commands, useful for troubleshooting IP routing.

  Next, this chapter generically reviews how an IP routing protocol's data structures interact with a router's IP routing table. Then, EIGRP's data structures are considered, followed by a review of basic EIGRP operation. Again, you are presented with a collection of **show** and **debug** commands useful for troubleshooting various EIGRP operations.

  Finally, this chapter challenges you with a trouble ticket and an associated topology. You are also given **show** command output. Based on the information provided, you hypothesize an underlying cause for the reported issue and develop a solution. You can then compare your solution with a suggested solution.

- **Chapter 7, "OSPF and Route Redistribution Troubleshooting":** This chapter begins by introducing you to OSPF's routing structures, followed by a review of OSPF operation. You are then presented with a collection of **show** and **debug** commands useful for troubleshooting OSPF operations.

  This chapter next presents you with a trouble ticket and an associated topology. You are also given **show** command output. Based on the information provided, you hypothesize an underlying cause for the reported issues and develop solutions. You can then compare your solutions with the suggested solutions.

  This chapter also introduces the concept of route redistribution and discusses how a route from one routing process can be injected into a different routing process. Common route redistribution troubleshooting targets are identified, along with strategies for troubleshooting route redistribution.

  Finally, this chapter challenges you with another trouble ticket and an associated topology. You are also given **show** command output. Based on the information provided, you hypothesize an underlying cause for the reported issue and develop a solution. You can then compare your solution with a suggested solution.

- **Chapter 8, "Troubleshooting BGP and Router Performance Issues":** This chapter begins by introducing you to BGP's data structures, followed by a review of BGP operation. You are then presented with a collection of **show** and **debug** commands useful for troubleshooting BGP operations.

  This chapter next presents you with a trouble ticket and an associated topology. You are given **show** command output. Based on the information provided, you hypothesize an underlying cause for the reported issue and develop a solution. You can then compare your solutions with the suggested solutions.

  Finally, this chapter discusses how to troubleshoot performance issues on a router, focusing on CPU utilization, packet-switching modes, and memory utilization.

■ **Chapter 9, "Security Troubleshooting":** This chapter begins by reviewing various security measures that might be put in place on Cisco routers and switches to protect three different planes of network operation. These planes are the management plane, the control plane, and the data plane. Once you review these security measures, this chapter considers how your troubleshooting efforts might be impacted by having various layers of security in place.

Next, this chapter describes the basic operation and troubleshooting tips for Cisco IOS firewalls and AAA services. Although complete configuration details for Cisco IOS firewalls and AAA is beyond the scope of the TSHOOT curriculum, as a reference, this chapter does provide a couple of basic configuration examples with an explanation of the syntax used.

Finally, this chapter presents you with a trouble ticket and an associated topology. You are also given **show** command output and a syntax reference. Based on the information provided, you hypothesize how to correct the reported issues. You can then compare your solutions with the suggested solutions.

■ **Chapter 10, "IP Services Troubleshooting":** This chapter begins by reviewing the purpose and basic operation of Network Address Translation (NAT). As a reference, sample topologies are provided, along with their configurations. Common NAT troubleshooting targets are identified, and a syntax reference is provided to aid in troubleshooting NAT issues.

Next, this chapter reviews Dynamic Host Configuration Protocol (DHCP) operation and various types of DHCP messages. You are given three configuration examples corresponding to the three roles a router might play in a DHCP environment: DHCP relay agent, DHCP client, and DHCP server. Common DHCP troubleshooting targets are reviewed, along with recommended DHCP troubleshooting practices. This section also presents a collection of commands that could prove to be useful in troubleshooting a suspected DHCP issue.

Finally, this chapter presents you with a trouble ticket and an associated topology. You are also given **show** and **debug** command output, which confirms the reported issue. Then, you are challenged to hypothesize how to correct the reported issue. You can then compare your solution with a suggested solution.

■ **Chapter 11, "IP Communications Troubleshooting":** This chapter begins by introducing you to design and troubleshooting considerations that arise when adding voice traffic to a data network. Several protocols are involved when a Cisco IP Phone registers with its call agent in order to place and receive voice calls. You review the function of these protocols along with recommendations for troubleshooting voice issues. One of the major troubleshooting targets for voice networks involves quality of service. Therefore, this chapter provides overview of quality of service configuration, verification, and troubleshooting commands. Additionally, this chapter considers video traffic in an IP network, including video's unique design and troubleshooting challenges.

Also, video-based networks often rely on an infrastructure that supports IP multicasting. Because multicasting has not been addressed in any depth thus far in this book, this chapter serves as a primer to multicast technologies. Included in this primer are commands used to configure, monitor, and troubleshoot multicast networks. The chapter next considers common video troubleshooting issues and recommends resolutions for those issues.

Finally, this chapter presents you with two trouble tickets focused on unified communications. You are presented with a topology used by both trouble tickets, in addition to a collection of **show** command output. For each trouble ticket, you are challenged to hypothesize how to correct the reported issue. You can also compare your solutions with suggested solutions.

- **Chapter 12, "IPv6 Troubleshooting":** This chapter introduces the purpose and structure of IP version 6 (IPv6) addressing. You consider the various types of IPv6 addresses, routing protocols supporting IPv6, and basic syntax for enabling a router to route IPv6 traffic. A sample configuration is provided to illustrate the configuration of a router to support IPv6. Additionally, as an organization is migrating from IPv4 to IPv6, there might be portions of the network that are still running IPv4 with other portions of the network running IPv6. For IPv6 traffic to span an IPv4 portion of the network, one option is to create a tunnel spanning the IPv4 network. Then, IPv6 traffic can travel inside the tunnel to transit the IPv4 network. This section discusses the syntax and provides an example of tunneling IPv6 over an IPv4 tunnel.

This chapter also contrasts the characteristics of two versions of OSPF, specifically OSPFv2 and OSPFv3. OSPFv3 can support the routing of IPv6 networks, whereas OSPFv2 cannot. OSPFv3 configuration syntax is presented, along with a sample configuration. You are also provided with a collection of verification troubleshooting commands and a listing of common OSPFv3 issues.

Next, this chapter presents you with a trouble ticket addressing a network experiencing OSPF adjacency issues. You are presented with a collection of **show** and **debug** command output and challenged to resolve a series of misconfigurations. Suggested solutions are provided.

Also, this chapter contrasts the characteristics of RIP next generation (RIPng) with RIPv2. You are given a set of RIPng configuration commands along with a sample configuration. From a troubleshooting perspective, you compare RIPng troubleshooting commands with those commands used to troubleshoot RIPv1 and RIPv2. This chapter also discusses some of the more common RIPng troubleshooting issues you might encounter.

Finally, this chapter challenges you to resolve a couple of RIPng issues being observed in a network. Specifically, load balancing and default route advertisements are not behaving as expected. To assist in your troubleshooting efforts, you are armed with a collection of **show** and **debug** command output. Your proposed solutions can then be compared with suggested solutions.

- **Chapter 13, "Advanced Services Troubleshooting":** This chapter introduces you to Cisco's Application Network Services (ANS) architecture. Cisco ANS includes multiple pieces of dedicated equipment aimed at optimizing the performance of network-based applications (for example, improving the response time of a corporate web server for users at a remote office). Although this chapter introduces a collection of Cisco ANS components, the primary focus is on Cisco IOS features that can improve application performance. Specifically, the Cisco IOS features addressed are NetFlow, IP SLAs, NBAR, and QoS.

  Also, this chapter addresses the troubleshooting of wireless networks, and it begins by contrasting autonomous and split-MAC wireless network architectures. Wired network issues that could impact wireless networks are then highlighted. These issues include power, VLAN, security, DHCP, and QoS issues.

- **Chapter 14, "Large Enterprise Network Troubleshooting":** This chapter begins by identifying a collection of technologies that might become troubleshooting targets for a remote office network. The primary technologies focused on are Virtual Private Network (VPN) technologies. Sample syntax is provided for a VPN using IPsec and GRE. Also, several useful **show** commands are provided as a troubleshooting reference.

  Finally, this chapter discusses the troubleshooting of complex networks, and begins by identifying how multiple network technologies map to the seven layers of the OSI model. Also, you are given a list of resources a troubleshooter should have prior to troubleshooting a complex enterprise network. Finally, this chapter reviews key points from all trouble tickets previously presented.

- **Chapter 15, "Final Preparation":** This chapter identifies tools for final exam preparation and helps you develop an effective study plan.

Appendix A has the answers to the "Do I Know This Already" quizzes and an online appendix tells you how to find any updates should there be changes to the exam.

Each chapter in the book uses several features to help you make the best use of your time in that chapter. The features are as follows:

- **Assessment:** Each chapter begins with a "Do I Know This Already?" quiz that helps you determine the amount of time you need to spend studying each topic of the chapter. If you intend to read the entire chapter, you can save the quiz for later use. Questions are all multiple-choice, to give a quick assessment of your knowledge.

- **Foundation Topics:** This is the core section of each chapter that explains the protocols, concepts, configuration, and troubleshooting strategies for the topics in the chapter.

- **Exam Preparation Tasks:** At the end of each chapter, this section collects key topics, references to memory table exercises to be completed as memorization practice, key terms to define, and a command reference that summarizes any relevant commands presented in the chapter.

Finally, the companion CD-ROM contains practice CCNP TSHOOT questions to reinforce your understanding of the book's concepts. Be aware that the TSHOOT exam will primarily be made up of trouble tickets you need to resolve. Mastery of the topics covered by the CD-based questions, however, will help equip you with the tools needed to effectively troubleshoot the trouble tickets presented on the exam.

The CD also contains the Memory Table exercises and answer keys.

How to Use This Book for Study

Retention and recall are the two features of human memory most closely related to performance on tests. This exam-preparation guide focuses on increasing both retention and recall of the topics on the exam. The other human characteristic involved in successfully passing the exam is intelligence; this book does not address that issue!

This book is designed with features to help you increase retention and recall. It does this in the following ways:

- By providing succinct and complete methods of helping you determine what you recall easily and what you do not recall at all.

- By referencing the portions of the book that review those concepts you most need to recall, so you can quickly be reminded about a fact or concept. Repeating information that connects to another concept helps retention, and describing the same concept in several ways throughout a chapter increases the number of connectors to the same pieces of information.

- Finally, accompanying this book is a CD-ROM that has questions covering troubleshooting theory, tools, and methodologies. Familiarity with these troubleshooting resources can help you be more efficient when diagnosing and resolving a reported network issue.

When taking the "Do I Know This Already?" assessment quizzes in each chapter, make sure that you treat yourself and your knowledge fairly. If you come across a question that makes you guess at an answer, mark it wrong immediately. This forces you to read through the part of the chapter that relates to that question and forces you to learn it more thoroughly.

If you find that you do well on the assessment quizzes, it still might be wise to quickly skim through each chapter to find sections or topics that do not readily come to mind. Look for the Key Topics icons. Sometimes even reading through the detailed table of contents will reveal topics that are unfamiliar or unclear. If that happens to you, mark those chapters or topics, and spend time working through those parts of the book.

CCNP TSHOOT Exam Topics

Carefully consider the exam topics Cisco has posted on its website as you study, particularly for clues to how deeply you should know each topic. Also, you can develop a broader knowledge of the subject matter by reading and studying the topics presented in this book. Remember that it is in your best interest to become proficient in each of the CCNP subjects. When it is time to use what you have learned, being well rounded counts more than being well tested.

Table I-1 shows the official exam topics for the TSHOOT exam, as posted on cisco.com. Note that Cisco has occasionally changed exam topics without changing the exam number, so do not be alarmed if small changes in the exam topics occur over time. When in doubt, go to cisco.com and click Training and Events.

Table I-1   *CCNP TSHOOT Exam Topics*

Exam Topics	Chapters Where Exam Topics Are Covered
Maintain and monitor network performance	
Develop a plan to monitor and manage a network Perform network monitoring using IOS tools Perform routine IOS device maintenance Isolate sub-optimal internetwork operation at the correctly defined OSI Model layer	Chapters 1–3 and 14
Troubleshooting IPv4 and IPv6 routing protocols and IP services in a multiprotocol system network	
Troubleshoot EIGRP Troubleshoot OSPF Troubleshoot eBGP Troubleshoot routing redistribution solution Troubleshoot a DHCP client and server solution Troubleshoot NAT Troubleshoot first-hop redundancy protocols Troubleshoot IPv6 routing Troubleshoot IPv6 and IPv4 interoperability	Chapters 5–8, 10, and 12
Troubleshoot switch-based features	
Troubleshoot switch-to-switch connectivity for a VLAN-based solution Troubleshoot loop prevention for a VLAN-based solution Troubleshoot access ports for a VLAN-based solution Troubleshoot private VLANS Troubleshoot port security Troubleshoot general switch security Troubleshoot VACL and PACL Troubleshoot switch virtual interfaces (SVIs) Troubleshoot switch supervisor redundancy Troubleshoot switch support of advanced services Troubleshoot a VoIP support solution Troubleshoot a video support solution	Chapters 4–5, 11, and 13

Table I-1 *CCNP TSHOOT Exam Topics*   (*Continued*)

Exam Topics	Chapters Where Exam Topics Are Covered
Troubleshoot Cisco router and switch device hardening	
Troubleshoot Layer 3 security Troubleshoot issues related to ACLs used to secure access to Cisco routers Troubleshoot configuration issues related to accessing an AAA server for authentication purposes Troubleshoot security issues related to IOS services	Chapters 9 and 10

For More Information

If you have any comments about the book, you can submit those via the ciscopress.com website. Just go to the website, select Contact Us, and type your message. Cisco might make changes that affect the CCNP Routing and Switching certification from time to time. You should always check cisco.com for the latest details. Also, you can look to www.ciscopress.com/title/1587058448, where we publish any information pertinent to how you might use this book differently in light of Cisco's future changes. For example, if Cisco decided to remove a major topic from the exam, it might post that on its website; Cisco Press will make an effort to list that information as well via an online updates appendix.

This chapter covers the following subjects:

Understanding Maintenance Methods: This section discusses the importance of proactive maintenance tasks, as opposed to reactive maintenance, required to address a problem in a network. Also discussed in this section is a collection of commonly used maintenance approaches.

Identifying Common Maintenance Procedures: This section lists common maintenance tasks, emphasizes the importance of regularly scheduled maintenance, and summarizes critical areas of network performance.

The Network Maintenance Toolkit: This section identifies how to compile a set of network maintenance tools that complement your network maintenance plan.

CHAPTER 1

Introduction to Network Maintenance

Business operations are becoming increasingly dependent upon the reliable operation of business data networks (which might also carry voice and video traffic). A structured and systematic maintenance approach significantly contributes to the uptime for such networks.

Consider the purchase of a new car. Many excited owners of a new car peruse the owner's manual to find the recommended maintenance schedule and vow to perform the routine recommended maintenance. They instinctively know that adhering to a documented maintenance plan can reduce the occurrence of issues with their car. Similarly, the number of issues in a network can be reduced by following a documented schedule of maintenance.

This chapter discusses the importance of having a maintenance plan and introduces several popular models that can be adapted to your network. Next, you are introduced to specific maintenance tasks. Finally in this chapter, you identify the tools (for example, network monitoring and disaster recovery tools) you need in your virtual toolbox.

"Do I Know This Already?" Quiz

The "Do I Know This Already?" quiz helps you determine your level of knowledge on this chapter's topics before you begin. Table 1-1 details the major topics discussed in this chapter and their corresponding quiz sections.

Table 1-1 *"Do I Know This Already?" Section-to-Question Mapping*

Foundation Topics Section	Questions
Understanding Maintenance Methods	1–4
Identifying Common Maintenance Procedures	5–10
The Network Maintenance Toolkit	11–14

1. Which of the following are considered network maintenance tasks? (Choose the three best answers.)

    a. Troubleshooting problem reports

    b. Attending training on emerging network technologies

    c. Planning for network expansion

    d. Hardware installation

2. Network maintenance tasks can be categorized into one of which two categories? (Choose two.)

    a. Recovery tasks

    b. Interrupt-driven tasks

    c. Structured tasks

    d. Installation tasks

3. Identify the network maintenance model defined by the ITU-T for maintaining telecommunications networks.

    a. FCAPS

    b. ITIL

    c. TMN

    d. Cisco Lifecycle Services

4. Which letter in the FCAPS acronym represents the maintenance area responsible for billing end users?

    a. F

    b. C

    c. A

    d. P

    e. S

5. The lists of tasks required to maintain a network can vary widely, depending on the goals and characteristics of that network. However, some network maintenance tasks are common to most networks. Which of the following would be considered a common task that should be present in any network maintenance model?

    a. Performing database synchronization for a network's Microsoft Active Directory

    b. Making sure digital certificates used for PKI are renewed in advance of their expiration

    c. Using CiscoWorks to dynamically discover network device changes

    d. Performing scheduled backups

6. Which of the following statements is true regarding scheduled maintenance?

    a. Scheduled maintenance helps ensure that important maintenance tasks are not overlooked.

    b. Scheduled maintenance is not recommended for larger networks, because of the diversity of maintenance needs.

    c. Maintenance tasks should only be performed based on a scheduled maintenance schedule, in order to reduce unexpected workflow interruptions.

    d. Scheduled maintenance is more of a reactive approach to network maintenance, as opposed to a proactive approach.

7. Which of the following questions are appropriate when defining your change management policies? (Choose two.)

    a. What version of operating system is currently running on the device to be upgraded?

    b. What is the return on investment (ROI) of an upgrade?

    c. What measureable criteria determine the success or failure of a network change?

    d. Who is responsible for authorizing various types of network changes?

8. Which three of the following components would you expect to find in a set of network documentation? (Choose three.)

    a. Logical topology diagram

    b. Listing of interconnections

    c. License files

    d. IP address assignments

9. Which three of the following are components that would be most useful when recovering from a network equipment outage? (Choose three.)

    a. Backup of device configuration information

    b. Physical topology

    c. Duplicate hardware

    d. Operating system and application software (along with any applicable licensing) for the device

10. What type of agreement exists between a service provider and one of their customers, which specifies performance metrics for the link interconnecting the customer with the service provider?

    a. MTBF

    b. GoS

    c. TOS

    d. SLA

11. Which command would you use to view archival copies of a router's startup configuration?

    a. show backup

    b. show archive

    c. show flash: | begin backup

    d. show ftp: | begin archive

12. Which of the following would be appropriate for a collaborative web-based documentation solution?

    a. blog

    b. vlog

    c. wiki

    d. podcast

13. CiscoWorks Resource Manager Essentials (RME) is a component of what CiscoWorks product?

    a. LMS

    b. RWAN

    c. QPM

    d. IPM

14. Which of the following is a Cisco IOS technology that uses a collector to take data from monitored devices and present graphs, charts, and tables to describe network traffic patterns?

    a. NBAR

    b. Netflow

    c. QDM

    d. IPS

Foundation Topics

Understanding Maintenance Methods

Network maintenance is an inherent component of a network administrator's responsibilities. However, that network administrator might be performing maintenance tasks in response to a reported problem. This reactive approach is unavoidable, because unforeseen issues do arise. However, the occurrence of these interrupt-driven maintenance tasks can be reduced by proactively performing regularly scheduled maintenance tasks.

You could think of regularly scheduled tasks, such as performing backups and software upgrades, as *important* but not *urgent*. Spending more time on the important tasks can help reduce time spent on the urgent tasks (for example, responding to user connectivity issues or troubleshooting a network outage).

This section begins by identifying several network maintenance tasks. Common network maintenance models are discussed. However, an off-the-shelf network maintenance model might not be a perfect fit for your organization. So, this section concludes by discussing how a well-known model can be adapted to your needs.

Introducing Network Maintenance

Before discussing approaches to network maintenance, let us first spend a few moments defining network maintenance. Network maintenance, at its essence, is doing whatever is required to keep the network functioning and meeting the business needs of an organization.

Some examples of the tasks that fall under the umbrella of network maintenance are as follows:

Key Topic

- Hardware and software installation and configuration
- Troubleshooting problem reports
- Monitoring and tuning network performance
- Planning for network expansion
- Documenting the network and any changes made to the network
- Ensuring compliance with legal regulations and corporate policies
- Securing the network against internal and external threats

Obviously, this listing is only a sampling of network maintenance tasks. Also, keep in mind that the list of tasks required to maintain your network could be quite different from the list of tasks required to maintain another network.

Proactive Versus Reactive Network Maintenance

Network maintenance tasks can be categorized as one of the following:

- **Structured tasks:** Performed as a predefined plan.
- **Interrupt-driven tasks:** Involve resolving issues as they are reported.

As previously mentioned, interrupt-driven tasks can never be completely eliminated; however, their occurrence can be lessened through a strategic structured approach.

Not only does a structured maintenance approach offer reduced downtime (by fixing problems before they occur), it also proves to be more cost effective. Specifically, unplanned network outages can be resolved more quickly. Fewer resources are consumed responding to problems, because fewer problems occur. Also, because a structured maintenance approach includes planning for future network capacity, appropriate hardware and software purchases can be made early on, reducing obsolescence of relatively new purchases.

Because a structured approach considers underlying business goals, resources can be allocated that complement business drivers. Also, security vulnerabilities are more likely to be discovered through ongoing network monitoring, which is another component of a structured maintenance approach.

Well-Known Network Maintenance Models

The subtleties of each network should be considered when constructing a structured network maintenance model. However, rather than starting from scratch, you might want to base your maintenance model on one of the well-known maintenance models and make adjustments as appropriate.

The following is a sampling of some of the more well-known maintenance models:

- **FCAPS:** FCAPS (which stands for Fault management, Configuration management, Accounting management, Performance management, and Security management) is a network maintenance model defined by the International Organization for Standardization (ISO).

- **ITIL:** An IT Infrastructure Library (ITIL) defines a collection of best-practice recommendations that work together to meet business goals.

- **TMN:** The Telecommunications Management Network (TMN) network management model is the Telecommunications Standardization Sector's (ITU-T) variation of the FCAPS model. Specifically, TMN targets the management of telecommunications networks.

- **Cisco Lifecycle Services:** The Cisco Lifecycle Services maintenance model defines distinct phases in the life of a Cisco technology in a network. These phases are Prepare, Plan, Design, Implement, Operate, and Optimize. As a result, the Cisco Lifecycle Services model is often referred to as the PPDIOO model.

Adapting a Well-Known Network Maintenance Model

The maintenance model you use in your network should reflect business drivers, resources, and expertise unique to your network. Your maintenance model might, however, be based on one of the previously discussed well-known maintenance models.

As an example, imagine you have selected the ISO FCAPS model as the foundation for your maintenance model. To adapt the FCAPS model for your environment, for each element of the FCAPS model, you should identify specific tasks to perform on your network. Table 1-2 provides a sampling of tasks that might be categorized under each of the FCAPS management areas.

Table 1-2   *FCAPS Management Tasks*

Key
Topic

Type of Management	Examples of Management Tasks
Fault management	Use network management software to collect information from routers and switches. Send an e-mail alert when processor utilization or bandwidth utilization exceeds a threshold of 80 percent. Respond to incoming trouble tickets from the help desk.
Configuration management	Require logging of any changes made to network hardware or software configurations. Implement a change management system to alert relevant personnel of planned network changes.
Accounting management	Invoice IP telephony users for their long distance and international calls.
Performance management	Monitor network performance metrics for both LAN and WAN links. Deploy appropriate quality of service (QoS) solutions to make the most efficient use of relatively limited WAN bandwidth, while prioritizing mission critical traffic.
Security management	Deploy firewall, virtual private network (VPN), and intrusion prevention system (IPS) technologies to defend against malicious traffic. Create a security policy dictating rules of acceptable network use. Use an Authorization, Authentication, and Accounting (AAA) server to validate user credentials, assign appropriate user privileges, and log user activity.

By clearly articulating not just a theoretical methodology but actionable and measurable processes, you can reduce network downtime and more effectively perform interrupt-driven tasks. This structured approach to network management helps define what tools are needed in a toolkit prior to events requiring the use of those tools.

Identifying Common Maintenance Procedures

Although the listings of procedures contained in various network maintenance models vary, some procedures are common to nearly all network maintenance models. This section identifies common network maintenance tasks, discusses the importance of regularly scheduled maintenance, and summarizes critical network maintenance areas.

Routine Maintenance Tasks

Some routine maintenance tasks should be present in a listing of procedures contained in a network maintenance model. Following is a listing of such common maintenance tasks:

- **Configuration changes:** Businesses are dynamic environments, where relocation of users from one office space to another, the addition of temporary staffers, and new hires are commonplace. In response to organizational changes, network administrators need to respond by performing appropriate reconfigurations and additions to network hardware and software. These processes are often referred to as moves, adds, and changes.

- **Replacement of older or failed hardware:** As devices age, their reliability and comparable performance tend to deteriorate. Therefore, a common task is the replacement of older hardware, typically with better performing and more feature-rich devices. Occasionally, production devices fail, thus requiring immediate replacement.

- **Scheduled backups:** Recovery from a major system failure can occur much quicker if network data and device configurations have been regularly backed up. Therefore, a common network maintenance task is to schedule, monitor, and verify backups of selected data and configuration information. These backups can also be useful in recovering important data that were deleted.

- **Updating software:** Updates to operating system software (for servers, clients, and even network devices) are periodically released. The updates often address performance issues and security vulnerabilities. New features are also commonly offered in software upgrades. Therefore, performing routine software updates becomes a key network maintenance task.

- **Monitoring network performance:** The collection and interpretation of traffic statistics, bandwidth utilization statistics, and resource utilization statistics for network devices are common goals of network monitoring. Through effective network monitoring (which might involve the collection and examination of log files or the implementation of a high-end network management server), you can better plan for future expansion (that is, *capacity planning*), anticipate potential issues before they arise, and better understand the nature of the traffic flowing through your network.

Benefits of Scheduled Maintenance

After defining the network maintenance tasks for your network, those tasks can be ranked in order of priority. Some task will undoubtedly be urgent in nature and need a quick response (for example, replacing a failed router that connects a business to the Internet). Other tasks can be scheduled. For example, you might schedule weekly full backups of your network's file servers, and you might have a monthly maintenance window, during which time you apply software patches.

By having such a schedule for routine maintenance tasks, network administrators are less likely to forget an important task, because they were busy responding to urgent tasks. Also, users can be made aware of when various network services will be unavailable, due to maintenance windows, thus minimizing the impact on workflow.

Managing Network Changes

Making changes to a network often has the side effect of impacting the productivity of users relying on network resources. Additionally, a change to one network component might create a problem for another network component. For example, perhaps a firewall was installed to provide better security for a server farm. However, in addition to common protocols that were allowed to pass through the firewall (for example, DNS, SMTP, POP3, HTTP, HTTPS, and IMAP), one of the servers in the server farm acted as an FTP server, and the firewall configuration did not consider that server. Therefore, the installation of a firewall to better secure a server farm resulted in a troubleshooting issue, where users could no longer reach their FTP server.

The timing of network changes should also be considered. Rather than taking a router down in order to upgrade its version of Cisco IOS during regular business hours, such an operation should probably be performed during off hours.

Making different organization areas aware of upcoming maintenance operations can also aid in reducing unforeseen problems associated with routine maintenance. For example, imagine that one information technology (IT) department within an organization is re-sponsible for maintaining WAN connections that interconnect various corporate offices, whereas another IT department is charged with performing network backups. If the WAN IT department plans to upgrade the WAN link between a couple of offices at 2:00 AM next Tuesday, the IT department in charge of backups should be made aware of that planned upgrade, because a backup of remote data (that is, data accessible over the WAN link to be upgraded) might be scheduled for that same time period.

Some organizations have a formalized change management process, where one department announces online their intention to perform a particular maintenance task during a speci-fied time period. Other departments are then notified of this upcoming change, and deter-mine if the planned change will conflict with that department's operations. If a conflict is identified, the departments can work together to accommodate one another's needs.

Of course, some network maintenance tasks are urgent (for example, a widespread network outage). Those tasks need timely response, without going through a formalized change management notification process and allowing time for other departments to respond.

When defining a change management system for your organization, consider the following:

- Who is responsible for authorizing various types of network changes?

- Which tasks should only be performed during scheduled maintenance windows?

- What procedures should be followed prior to making a change (for example, backing up a router's configuration prior to installing a new module in the router)?

- What measureable criteria determine the success or failure of a network change?

- How will a network change be documented, and who is responsible for the documentation?

- How will a rollback plan be created, such that a configuration can be restored to its previous state if the changes resulted in unexpected problems?

■   Under what circumstances can formalized change management policies be overridden, and what (if any) authorization is required for an override?

Maintaining Network Documentation

Network documentation typically gets created as part of a network's initial design and installation. However, keeping that documentation current, reflecting all changes made since the network's installation, should be part of any network maintenance model. Keeping documentation current helps more effectively isolate problems when troubleshooting. Additionally, accurate documentation can prove to be valuable to designers who want to scale the network.

At a basic level, network documentation could consist of physical and logical network diagrams, in addition to a listing of network components and their configurations. However, network documentation can be much more detailed, including such components as formalized change management procedures, a listing of contact information (for example, for service providers and points of contact in an organization's various IT groups), and the rationale for each network change made.

Key Topic

While the specific components in a set of network documentation can vary, just as the procedures in a network maintenance model vary, the following list outlines common elements found in a set of network documentation:

■   **Logical topology diagram:** A logical topology diagram shows the interconnection of network segments, the protocols used, and how end users interface with the network. However, this diagram is not concerned with the physical locations of network components.

■   **Physical topology diagram:** Unlike a logical topology diagram, a physical topology diagram shows how different geographical areas (for example, floors within a building, buildings, or entire sites) interconnect. The diagram reflects where various network components are physically located.

■   **Listing of interconnections:** A listing of interconnections could be, for example, a spreadsheet that lists which ports on which devices are used to interconnect network components, or connect out to service provider networks. Circuit IDs for service provider circuits might be included in this documentation.

■   **Inventory of network equipment:** An inventory of network equipment would include such information as the equipment's manufacturer, model number, version of software, information about the licensing of the software, serial number, and an organization's asset tag number.

■   **IP address assignments:** An organization might use private IP address space internally and use network address translation (NAT) to translate those private IP address space numbers into publicly routable IP addresses. Alternately, an organization might have public IP addresses assigned to some or all of their internal devices. A classful IP address space (either public or private) might be subdivided within an organization, resulting in subnets with a non-default subnet mask. These types of IP addressing specifications would be included in a set of network documentation.

- **Configuration information:** When a configuration change is made, the current configuration should be backed up. With a copy of current configuration information, a device could be replaced quicker, in the event of an outage. Beyond having a backup of current configuration information, some network administrators also maintain archival copies of previous configurations. These older configurations could prove to be useful when attempting to roll back to a previous configuration state or when trying to duplicate a previous configuration in a new location. It is a good practice to name archival copies of previous configurations based on a certain format that makes sense to you. For example, some companies name their archival copies by date, others by function, and still others by a combination of both.

- **Original design documents:** Documents created during the initial design of a network might provide insight into why certain design decisions were made, and how the original designers envisioned future network expansion.

Larger network environments often benefit from having step-by-step guidelines for troubleshooting a given network issue. Such a structured approach to troubleshooting helps ensure that all troubleshooting personnel use a common approach. Although a network issue might be successfully resolved through various means, if different personnel troubleshoot using different approaches, at some point those approaches might conflict with one another, resulting in further issues.

For example, consider one network administrator that configures IEEE 802.1Q trunking on Cisco Catalyst switches by disabling Dynamic Trunk Protocol (DTP) frames and forcing a port to act as a trunk port. Another network administrator within the same company configures 802.1Q trunking by setting a port's trunk state to *desirable*, which creates a trunk connection only if it receives a DTP frame from the far end of the connection. These two approaches are not compatible, and if each of these two network administrators configured different ends of what they intended to be an 802.1Q trunk, the trunk connection would never come up. This example illustrates the criticality of having clear communication among IT personnel and a set of standardized procedures to ensure consistency in network configuration and troubleshooting practices.

Restoring Operation After Failure

Although most modern network hardware is very reliable, failures do occur from time to time. Aside from hardware failures, environmental factors could cause a network outage. As a few examples, the failure of an air conditioner unit could cause network equipment to overheat; water leakage due to flooding or plumbing issues could cause hardware failures; or a fire could render the network equipment unusable.

Planning and provisioning hardware and software for such outages before they occur can accelerate recovery time. To efficiently replace a failed (or damaged) device, you should be in possession of the following:

- Duplicate hardware

- Operating system and application software (along with any applicable licensing) for the device

- Backup of device configuration information

Measuring Network Performance

Network monitoring is a proactive approach to network maintenance, enabling you to be alerted to trends and utilization statistics (as a couple of examples), which can forecast future issues. Also, if you work for a service provider, network performance monitoring can ensure that you are providing an appropriate service level to a customer. Conversely, if you are a customer of a service provider, network monitoring can confirm that the service provider is conforming to the SLA for which you are paying.

The Network Maintenance Toolkit

After selecting the processes, and their corresponding tasks, that make up your network maintenance model, you next need to identify the tools required to carry out your maintenance processes. These tools should be targeted toward your specific processes and tasks, helping you focus your troubleshooting efforts without having to wade through reams of irrelevant information. This section provides examples of a few indispensible elements you should have in your network maintenance toolkit.

Basic Network Maintenance Tools

Network maintenance tools often range in expense from free to tens of thousands of dollars. Similarly, these tools vary in their levels of complexity and usefulness for troubleshooting specific issues. You need to select tools that balance your troubleshooting needs and budgetary constraints.

Regardless of budget, nearly all network maintenance toolkits can contain the command-line interface (CLI) commands executable from a router or switch prompt. Many network devices have a graphical user interface (GUI) to assist network administrators in their configuration and monitoring tasks. External servers (for example, backup servers, logging servers, and time servers) can also collect, store, or provide information useful for day-to-day network operation and for troubleshooting.

CLI Tools

Cisco IOS offers a wealth of CLI commands, which can be invaluable when troubleshooting a network issue. For example, a **show** command can display router configuration information and the routes that have been learned by a routing process. The **debug** command can provide real-time information about router or switch processes. To illustrate, consider Example 1-1, which shows router R2 receiving Open Shortest Path First (OSPF) link state updates from its OSPF neighbors as those updates occur.

Example 1-1 *Sample* debug *Output*

```
R2# debug ip ospf events
OSPF events debugging is on
R2#
*Mar  1 00:06:06.679: OSPF: Rcv LS UPD from 10.4.4.4 on Serial1/0.2 length 124
  LSA count 1
*Mar  1 00:06:06.691: OSPF: Rcv LS UPD from 10.3.3.3 on Serial1/0.1 length 124
  LSA count 1
```

```
*Mar  1 00:06:06.999: OSPF: Rcv LS UPD from 10.4.4.4 on Serial1/0.2 length 124
  LSA count 1
*Mar  1 00:06:07.067: OSPF: Rcv LS UPD from 10.3.3.3 on Serial1/0.1 length 156
  LSA count 2
```

A newer Cisco IOS feature, which allows a router to monitor events and automatically re-spond to a specific event (such as a defined threshold being reached) with a predefined ac-tion, is called Cisco IOS Embedded Event Manager (EEM). EEM policies can be created using Cisco's tool command language (Tcl).

GUI Tools

Although Cisco has some GUI tools, such as CiscoWorks, that can manage large enter-prise networks, several device-based GUI tools are freely available. Examples of these free tools from Cisco are the following:

- Cisco Configuration Professional (CCP)

- Cisco Configuration Assistant (CCA)

- Cisco Network Assistant (CNA)

- Cisco Security Device Manager (SDM)

Figure 1-1 shows the home screen of Cisco SDM.

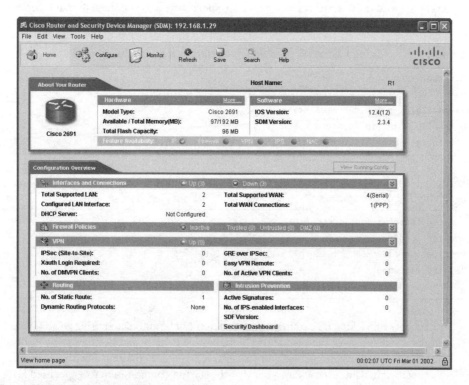

Figure 1-1 *Cisco Security Device Manager*

Backup Tools

External servers are often used to store archival backups of a device's operating system (for example, a Cisco IOS image) and configuration information. Depending on your network device, you might be able to back up your operating system and configuration information to a TFTP, FTP, HTTP, or SCP server. To illustrate, consider Example 1-2.

Example 1-2   *Backing Up a Router's Startup Configuration to an FTP Server*

```
R1# copy startup-config ftp://kevin:cisco@192.168.1.74
Address or name of remote host [192.168.1.74]?
Destination filename [r1-confg]?
Writing r1-confg !
1446 bytes copied in 3.349 secs (432 bytes/sec)
```

In Example 1-2, router R1's startup configuration is being copied to an FTP server with an IP address of 192.168.1.74. Notice that the login credentials (that is, username=kevin and password=cisco) for the FTP server are specified in the **copy** command.

If you intend to routinely copy backups to an FTP server, you can avoid specifying the login credentials each time (for security purposes), by adding those credentials to the router's configuration. Example 1-3 shows how to add username and password credentials to the router's configuration, and Example 1-4 shows how the startup configuration can be copied to an FTP server without explicitly specifying those credentials in the **copy** command.

Example 1-3   *Adding FTP Server Login Credentials to a Router's Configuration*

```
R1# conf term
Enter configuration commands, one per line.  End with CNTL/Z.
R1(config)# ip ftp username kevin
R1(config)# ip ftp password cisco
R1(config)# end
```

Example 1-4   *Backing Up a Router's Startup Configuration to an FTP Server Without Specifying Login Credentials*

```
R1# copy startup-config ftp://192.168.1.74
Address or name of remote host [192.168.1.74]?
Destination filename [r1-confg]?
Writing r1-confg !
1446 bytes copied in 3.389 secs (427 bytes/sec)
```

The process of backing up a router's configuration can be automated using an archiving feature, which is part of the Cisco IOS Configuration Replace and Configuration Rollback feature. Specifically, you can configure a Cisco IOS router to periodically (that is, at intervals specified in minutes) back up a copy of the startup configuration to a specified location (for example, the router's flash or an FTP server). Also, the archive feature can be configured to create an archive every time you copy a router's running configuration to the startup configuration.

Example 1-5 illustrates a router configured to back up its startup configuration every day (that is, every 1440 minutes) to an FTP server (with an IP address of 192.168.1.74, where the login credentials have already been configured in the router's configuration). In addition to regular daily backups, the **write-memory** command causes the router to archive a copy of the startup configuration whenever the router's running configuration is copied to the startup configuration.

Example 1-5 *Automatic Archive Configuration*

Key
Topic

```
R1#show run
Building configuration...
...OUTPUT OMITTED...
ip ftp username kevin
ip ftp password cisco
!
archive
 path ftp://192.168.1.74/R1-config
 write-memory
 time-period 1440
...OUTPUT OMITTED...
```

You can view the files stored in a configuration archive by issuing the **show archive** command, as demonstrated in Example 1-6.

Example 1-6 *Viewing a Configuration Archive*

Key
Topic

```
R1# show archive
The next archive file will be named ftp://192.168.1.74/R1-config-3
 Archive #  Name
   0
   1          ftp://192.168.1.74/R1-config-1
   2          ftp://192.168.1.74/R1-config-2 <- Most Recent
   3
   4
   5
   6
   7
   8
   9
   10
   11
   12
   13
   14
```

Example 1-7 shows the execution of the **copy run start** command, which copies a router's running configuration to the router's startup configuration. The **show archive** command is then reissued, and the output confirms that an additional configuration archive (named R1-config-3) has been created on the FTP server.

Example 1-7   *Confirming Automated Backups*

```
R1# copy run start
Destination filename [startup-config]?
Building configuration...
[OK]
Writing R1-config-3 !
R1# show archive
The next archive file will be named ftp://192.168.1.74/R1-config-4
 Archive #  Name
    0
    1        ftp://192.168.1.74/R1-config-1
    2        ftp://192.168.1.74/R1-config-2
    3        ftp://192.168.1.74/R1-config-3 <- Most Recent
    4
    5
    6
    7
    8
    9
   10
   11
   12
   13
   14
```

You can restore a previously archived configuration using the **configure replace** command. This command does not merge the archived configuration with the running configuration, but rather completely replaces the running configuration with the archived configuration. Example 1-8 shows the restoration of an archived configuration to a router. Notice that the router's hostname changes after the configuration restoration.

Key
Topic

Example 1-8   *Restoring an Archived Configuration*

```
Router# configure replace ftp://192.168.1.74/R1-config-3
This will apply all necessary additions and deletions
to replace the current running configuration with the
contents of the specified configuration file, which is
assumed to be a complete configuration, not a partial
configuration. Enter Y if you are sure you want to proceed. ? [no]: Y
Loading R1-config-3 !
[OK - 3113/4096 bytes]
```

```
Total number of passes: 1
Rollback Done

R1#
```

Logging Tools

Device logs often offer valuable information when troubleshooting a network issue. Many events that occur on a router are automatically reported to the router's console. For example, if a router interface goes down, a message is written to the console. However, this feedback is not provided to you, by default, if you are connected to a router via Telnet. If you are connected to a router via Telnet and want to see console messages, you can enter the command **terminal monitor.**

A downside of solely relying on console messages is that those messages can scroll off the screen, or you might close your terminal emulator, after which those messages would no longer be visible. Therefore, a step beyond console messages is logging those messages to a router's buffer (that is, in the router's RAM). To cause messages to be written to a router's buffer, you can issue the **logging buffered** command. As part of that command, you can specify how much of the router's RAM can be dedicated to logging. After the buffer fills to capacity, older entries will be deleted to make room for newer entries. This buffer can be viewed by issuing the **show logging history** command.

You might only want to log messages that have a certain level of severity. Severity levels range from 0–7, with corresponding names, as shown in Table 1-3. Notice that lower severity levels produce less logging output.

Table 1-3 *Severity Levels*

Severity Level	Name
0	Emergencies
1	Alerts
2	Critical
3	Errors
4	Warnings
5	Notifications
6	Informational
7	Debugging

Key
Topic

You might want to log messages of one severity level to a router's console and messages of another severity level to the router's buffer. That is possible, by using the **logging console** *severity_level* and **logging buffered** *severity_level* commands.

Another logging option is to log messages to an external syslog server. By sending log messages to an external server, you are able to keep a longer history of logging messages. You can direct your router's log output to a syslog server's IP address using the **logging** *ip_address* command.

Example 1-9 illustrates several of the logging configurations discussed here.

Example 1-9   *Logging Configuration*

```
R1# show run
...OUTPIT OMITTED...
Building configuration...
!
logging buffered 4096 warnings
logging console warnings
!
logging 192.168.1.50
...OUTPUT OMITTED...
```

In Example 1-9, events with a severity level of *warning* (that is, 4) or less (that is, 0–2) are logged to the router's buffer. This buffer can be viewed with the **show logging history** command. The router can use a maximum of 4096 bytes of RAM for the buffered logging. The console is configured for logging events of the same severity level. Additionally, the router is configured to log messages to a syslog server with an IP address 192.168.1.50. Figure 1-2 shows logging messages being collected by a Kiwi Syslog Server (available from www.kiwisyslog.com).

Network Time Protocol

Imagine that you are reviewing device logs collected in a router's buffer and are attempting to correlate the events in the device logs with an issue you are troubleshooting. To make that correlation, the logged events need to have accurate timestamps.

Although you could individually set the clock on each of your routers, those clocks might drift over time and not agree. You might have heard the saying that a man with one watch always knows what time it is, whereas a man with two watches is never sure. This implies that devices need to have a common point of reference for their time. Such a reference point is made possible by Network Time Protocol (NTP), which allows routers to point to a device acting as an NTP server. Because the NTP server might be referenced by devices in different time zones, each device has its own time zone configuration, which indicates how many hours its time zone differs from Greenwich Mean Time (GMT).

Example 1-10 shows an NTP configuration entered on a router located in the Eastern time zone, which is five hours behind GMT when daylight savings time is not in effect. The **clock summer-time** command defines when daylight savings time begins and ends. In this example, daylight savings time begins at 2:00 AM on the second Sunday in March and ends at 2:00 AM on the first Sunday in November. The **ntp server** command is used to point to an NTP server. Note that a configuration can have more than one **ntp server** command, for redundancy.

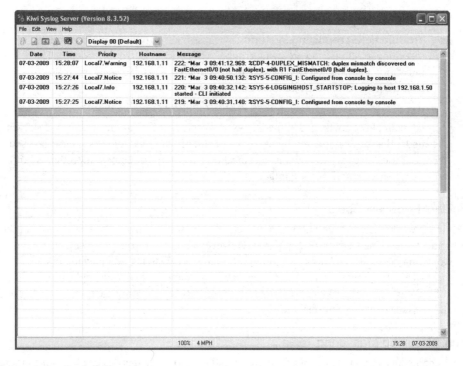

Figure 1-2 *Syslog Server*

Example 1-10 *Configuring a Router to Point to an NTP Server*

Key
Topic

```
R1# conf term
Enter configuration commands, one per line.   End with CNTL/Z.
R1(config)# clock timezone EST -5
R1(config)# clock summer-time EDT recurring 2 Sun Mar 2:00 1 Sun Nov 2:00
R1(config)# ntp server 192.168.1.150
R1(config)# end
```

Cisco Support Tools

Cisco has several other troubleshooting and maintenance tools available on its website:

http://www.cisco.com/en/US/support/tsd_most_requested_tools.html

Some of the tools available at this website require login credentials with appropriate privilege levels.

Network Documentation Tools

Earlier, we discussed the importance of network documentation. For this documentation to truly add value, however, it should be easy to retrieve and be current. To keep the documentation current, it should be easy to update.

A couple of documentation management system examples are as follows:

■ **Trouble ticket reporting system:** Several software applications are available for recording, tracking, and archiving trouble reports (that is, trouble tickets). These applications are often referred to as help desk applications. However, their usefulness extends beyond the help desk environment.

■ **Wiki:** A wiki can act as a web-based collaborative documentation platform. A popular example of a wiki is Wikipedia (www.wikipedia.com), an Internet-based encyclopedia that can be updated by users. This type of wiki technology can also be used on your local network to maintain a central repository for documentation that is both easy to access and easy to update.

Incident Recovery Tools

This section demonstrated how to automatically archive and manually restore router configurations using Cisco IOS commands. However, higher-end tools are available for automating backups, tracking configuration or hardware changes, and pushing out a centralized configuration to multiple devices. An example of such an application is CiscoWorks Resource Manager Essentials (RME). RME is a component of CiscoWorks LAN Management Solutions (LMS).

Monitoring and Measuring Tools

Keeping an eye on network traffic patterns and performance metrics can help you anticipate problems before they occur. As a result, you can address those issues proactively, rather than taking a reactive stance where you continually respond to problem reports.

Beyond basic **show** and **debug** commands, more advanced utilities are available for traffic and performance monitoring. For example, Cisco IOS Netflow can provide you with tremendous insight into your network traffic patterns. Several companies market Netflow collectors, which are software applications that can take the Netflow information reported from a Cisco router and convert that raw data into useful graphs, charts, and tables reflecting traffic patterns.

Simple Network Management Protocol (SNMP) allows a monitored device (for example, a router or a switch) to run an SNMP agent. An SNMP server can then query the SNMP agent running on a monitored device to collect data such as utilization statistics or device configuration information.

Reasons to monitor network performance include the following:

■ **Assuring compliance with an SLA:** If you work for a service provider or are a customer of a service provider, you might want to confirm that performance levels to and from the service provider's cloud are conforming to the agreed-upon SLA.

■ **Trend monitoring:** Monitoring resource utilization on your network (for example, bandwidth utilization and router CPU utilization) can help you recognize trends and forecast when upgrades will be required.

■ **Troubleshooting performance issues:** Performance issues can be difficult to troubleshoot in the absence of a baseline. By routinely monitoring network performance, you have a reference point (that is, a *baseline*) against which you can compare performance metrics collected after a user reports a performance issue.

Exam Preparation Tasks

Review All the Key Topics

Review the most important topics from inside the chapter, noted with the Key Topics icon in the outer margin of the page. Table 1-4 lists these key topics and the page numbers where each is found.

Key Topic

Table 1-4 *Key Topics for Chapter 1*

Key Topic Element	Description	Page Number
List	Network maintenance tasks	7
List	Well-known maintenance models	8
Table 1-2	FCAPS management tasks	9
List	Change management considerations	11
List	Common network documentation elements	12
Example 1-2	Backing up a router's startup configuration to an FTP server	16
Example 1-5	Automatic archive configuration	17
Example 1-6	Viewing configuration archive	17
Example 1-8	Restoring an archived configuration	18
Table 1-3	Severity levels	19
Example 1-9	Logging configuration	20
Example 1-10	Configuring a router to point to an NTP server	21

Complete the Tables and Lists from Memory

Print a copy of Appendix B, "Memory Tables" (found on the CD) or at least the section for this chapter, and complete the tables and lists from memory. Appendix C, "Memory Tables Answer Key," also on the CD, includes completed tables and lists to check your work.

Definition of Key Terms

Define the following key terms from this chapter, and check your answers in the Glossary:

interrupt-driven task, structured maintenance task, FCAPS, ITIL, TMN, Cisco Lifecycle Services, SLA, wiki

Command Reference to Check Your Memory

This section includes the most important configuration commands (see Table 1-5) and EXEC commands (see Table 1-6) covered in this chapter. To determine how well you have memorized the commands as a side effect of your other studies, cover the left side of the table with a piece of paper; read the descriptions on the right side; and see whether you remember the command.

Table 1-5 *Chapter 1 Configuration Command Reference*

Command	Description
archive	Global configuration mode command, used to enter archive configuration mode.
path ftp://*IP_address/ filename_prefix*	Archive configuration mode command that specifies the IP address of an FTP server and filename prefix a router uses to write its archival configuration files.
write-memory	Archive configuration mode command that causes an archival backup of a router's configuration to be written each time the router's running configuration is copied to its startup configuration.
time-period *seconds*	Archive configuration mode command that specifies the interval used by a router to automatically back up its configuration.
ip ftp username *username*	Global configuration mode command used to specify an FTP username credential, which no longer necessitates the user entering the username.
ip ftp password *password*	Global configuration mode command used to specify an FTP password credential, which no longer necessitates the user entering the password.
logging buffered [*max_buffer_size*] [*minimum_severity_level*]	Global configuration mode command used to log events to a router's internal buffer, optionally with a maximum number of bytes to be used by the buffer and optionally the minimum severity level of an event to be logged.
logging console [*minimum_severity_level*]	Global configuration mode command used to log events to a router's console, optionally with a minimum severity level of an event to be logged.
logging *IP_address*	Global configuration mode command used to specify the IP address of a syslog server to which a router's log files are written.

Table 1-5 *Chapter 1 Configuration Command Reference* *(Continued)*

Command	Description
clock timezone *time_zone_name* {+ | -} *hours*	Global configuration mode command used to specify a router's local time zone and number of hours the time zone varies from Greenwich Mean Time (GMT).
clock summer-time *time_zone_name* recurring {1-4} *beginning_day beginning_month time* {1-4} *ending_day ending_month time*	Global configuration mode command used to specify a router's time zone when daylight savings time is in effect, and when daylight savings time begins and ends.
ntp server *IP_address*	Global configuration mode command used to specify the IP address of an NTP server.

Table 1-6 *Chapter 1 EXEC Command Reference*

Command	Description
copy startup-config ftp://*username:password@IP_address*	Performs a backup of a router's startup configuration to an FTP server at the specified IP address, where the login credentials are provided by the username and password parameters.
copy startup-config ftp://*IP_address*	Performs a backup of a router's startup configuration to an FTP server at the specified IP address, where the login credentials have previously been added to the router's configuration.
show archive	Displays files contained in a router's configuration archive.
configure replace ftp://*IP_address/filename*	Replaces (as opposed to merges) a router's running configuration with a specified configuration archive.

This chapter covers the following subjects:

Troubleshooting Methods: This section addresses troubleshooting fundamentals, discusses the benefits of having a structured troubleshooting model, and discusses several popular troubleshooting models.

Using Troubleshooting Procedures: This section discusses each subprocess in a structured troubleshooting approach.

Including Troubleshooting in Routine Network Maintenance: This section shows how maintenance processes and troubleshooting processes can work in tandem to complement one another.

CHAPTER 2

Introduction to Troubleshooting Processes

Workflow within an organization can be severely impacted because of network problems. Therefore, troubleshooting those problems must be done efficiently, rather than haphazardly trying one potential solution after another.

As the size of a network increases, so does the complexity facing a network administrator attempting to resolve a network problem. Therefore, a structured troubleshooting process can help troubleshooters better focus their efforts, avoid duplication of efforts, and help other IT personnel to better assist in troubleshooting an issue.

This chapter defines troubleshooting and identifies the steps involved in a structured troubleshooting process. Additionally, this chapter emphasizes that network maintenance and network troubleshooting are not independent tasks, but rather overlap in several areas.

"Do I Know This Already?" Quiz

The "Do I Know This Already?" quiz helps you determine your level of knowledge of this chapter's topics before you begin. Table 2-1 details the major topics discussed in this chapter and their corresponding quiz questions.

Table 2-1 *"Do I Know This Already?" Section-to-Question Mapping*

Troubleshooting Methods	Questions
Understanding Troubleshooting Methods	1–4
Using Troubleshooting Procedures	5–11
Including Troubleshooting in Routine Network Maintenance	12–16

1. Identify the three steps in a simplified troubleshooting model. (Choose three.)

   a. Problem replication

   b. Problem diagnosis

   c. Problem resolution

   d. Problem report

2. Experienced troubleshooters with in-depth comprehension of a particular network might skip the *examine information* and *eliminate potential causes* steps in a structured troubleshooting model, instead relying on their own insight to determine the

most likely cause of a problem. This illustrates what approach to network troubleshooting?

   a.   Ad hoc

   b.   Shoot from the hip

   c.   Crystal ball

   d.   Independent path

3. Which of the following troubleshooting models requires access to a specific application?

   a.   Bottom-up

   b.   Divide and conquer

   c.   Comparing configurations

   d.   Top-down

4. Based on your analysis of a problem report and the data collected, you want to use a troubleshooting model that can quickly eliminate multiple layers of the OSI model as potential sources of the reported problem. Which of the following troubleshooting methods would be most appropriate?

   a.   Following the traffic path

   b.   Bottom-up

   c.   Top-down

   d.   Component swapping

5. Which of the following is the best statement to include in a problem report?

   a.   The network is broken.

   b.   User A cannot reach the network.

   c.   User B recently changed his PC's operating system to Microsoft Windows 7.

   d.   User C is unable to attach to an internal share resource of \\10.1.1.1\Budget, although he can print to all network printers, and he can reach the Internet.

6. What troubleshooting step should you perform after a problem has been reported and clearly defined?

   a.   Hypothesize underlying cause

   b.   Collect information

   c.   Eliminate potential causes

   d.   Examine collected information

7. What are the two primary goals of troubleshooters as they are collecting information? (Choose two answers.)

   a.   Eliminate potential causes from consideration.

   b.   Identify indicators pointing to the underlying cause of the problem.

   c.   Hypothesize the most likely cause for a problem.

   d.   Find evidence that can be used to eliminate potential causes.

8. When performing the *eliminate potential causes* troubleshooting step, which caution should the troubleshooter be aware of?

    a. The danger of drawing an invalid conclusion from the observed data

    b. The danger of troubleshooting a network component over which the troubleshooter does not have authority

    c. The danger of causing disruptions in workflow by implementing the proposed solution

    d. The danger of creating a new problem by implementing the proposed solution

9. A troubleshooter is hypothesizing a cause for an urgent problem, and her hypothesis involves a network device that she is not authorized to configure. The person who is authorized to configure the network device is unavailable. What should the troubleshooter do?

    a. Wait for authorized personnel to address the issue.

    b. Attempt to find a temporary workaround for the issue.

    c. Override corporate policy, based on the urgency, and configure the network device independently because authorized personnel are not currently available.

    d. Instruct the user to report the problem to the proper department that is authorized to resolve the issue.

10. What are two reasons why troubleshooters should document their steps as they attempt to verify their hypothesis? (Choose the two best answers.)

    a. The steps can be submitted to the proper authority prior to their implementation.

    b. The steps serve as a rollback plan if the attempted solution does not resolve the problem.

    c. The steps help ensure the troubleshooters do not skip a step in their solution.

    d. The steps help reduce duplication of efforts.

11. What two steps should be taken after a problem has been resolved? (Choose two answers.)

    a. For consistency, the same configuration should be implemented on all equipment of the same type.

    b. To accidentally prevent their reuse, previously archived configurations of the repaired device should be deleted from the archive server.

    c. Confirm that the user who reported the problem agrees that the problem is resolved.

    d. Make sure the implemented solution is integrated into the network's routine maintenance model.

12. What is the ideal relationship between network maintenance and troubleshooting?

    a. Networking maintenance and troubleshooting efforts should be isolated from one another.

    b. Networking maintenance and troubleshooting efforts should complement one another.

    c. Networking maintenance and troubleshooting efforts should be conducted by different personnel.

    d. Networking maintenance is a subset of network troubleshooting.

13. Which three of the following suggestions can best help troubleshooters keep in mind the need to document their steps? (Choose three.)

    a. Require documentation.

    b. Routinely back up documentation.

    c. Schedule documentation checks.

    d. Automate documentation.

14. What command can you use to display a router's CPU utilization averages?

    a. show processes cpu

    b. show cpu processes

    c. show cpu util

    d. show util cpu

15. Which three troubleshooting phases require clear communication with end users? (Choose three answers.)

    a. Problem report

    b. Information collection

    c. Hypothesis verification

    d. Problem resolution

16. What are two elements of a change management system? (Choose two answers.)

    a. Determine when changes can be made.

    b. Determine potential causes for the problem requiring the change.

    c. Determine who can authorize a change.

    d. Determine what change should be made.

Foundation Topics

Troubleshooting Methods

Troubleshooting network issues is implicit in the responsibilities of a network administrator. Such issues could arise as a result of human error (for example, a misconfiguration), equipment failure, a software bug, or traffic patterns (for example, high utilization or a network being under attack by malicious traffic).

Network issues can be successfully resolved using a variety of approaches. However, having a formalized troubleshooting method can prove more efficient than a haphazard approach to troubleshooting. A troubleshooter can select from several formalized troubleshooting approaches. Although these approaches vary in their effectiveness, based on the issue being addressed, a troubleshooter should have knowledge of several approaches to troubleshooting.

This section begins by introducing you to the basics of troubleshooting. Next, you learn the benefits of having a structured troubleshooting model, and then you are introduced to several popular troubleshooting models. Finally, this section provides guidance to help you select an appropriate combination of approaches for a given troubleshooting issue.

Defining Troubleshooting

The process of troubleshooting at its essence is the process of responding to a problem report (sometimes in the form of a trouble ticket), diagnosing the underlying cause of the problem, and resolving the problem. Although you normally think of the troubleshooting process beginning when a user reports an issue, realize that through effective network monitoring, you might detect a situation that could become a troubleshooting issue and resolve that situation before users are impacted.

After an issue is reported, the first step toward resolution is clearly defining the issue. When you have a clearly defined troubleshooting target, you can begin gathering information related to that issue. Based on the information collected, you might be able to better define the issue. Then you hypothesize likely causes of the issue. Evaluation of these likely causes leads to the identification of the suspected underlying root cause of the issue.

After you identify a suspected underlying cause, you next define approaches to resolving the issue and select what you consider to be the best approach. Sometimes the best approach to resolving an issue cannot be implemented immediately. For example, a piece of equipment might need replacing, or a business's workflow might be disrupted by implementing such an approach during working hours. In such situations, a troubleshooter might use a temporary fix until a permanent fix can be put in place.

As a personal example, when troubleshooting a connectivity issue for a resort hotel at a major theme park, we discovered that the supervisor engine in a Cisco Catalyst switch had an issue causing Spanning Tree Protocol (STP) to fail, resulting in a Layer 2 topological loop. This loop flooded the network with traffic, preventing the hotel from issuing keycards for guest rooms. The underlying cause was clear. Specifically, we had a bad supervisor engine. However, the time was about 4:00 PM, a peak time for guest registration. So, instead of immediately replacing the supervisor engine, we disconnected one of the redundant links, thus breaking the Layer 2 loop. The logic was that it was better to have the network function at this time without STP than for the network to experience an even longer outage while the supervisor engine was replaced. Late that night, someone came back to the switch and swapped out the supervisor engine, resolving the underlying cause while minimizing user impact.

Consider Figure 2-1, which depicts a simplified model of the troubleshooting steps previously described.

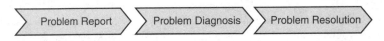

Figure 2-1   *Simplified Troubleshooting Flow*

This simplified model consists of three steps:

Step 1.   Problem report

Step 2.   Problem diagnosis

Step 3.   Problem resolution

Of these three steps, the majority of a troubleshooter's efforts are spent in the problem diagnosis step. Table 2-2 describes key components of this problem diagnosis step.

Table 2-2   *Steps to Diagnose a Problem*

Step	Description
Collect information	Because a typical problem report lacks sufficient information to give a troubleshooter insight into a problem's underlying cause, the troubleshooter should collect additional information, perhaps using network maintenance tools or by interviewing impacted users.
Examine collected information	After collecting sufficient information about a problem, the troubleshooter then examines that information, perhaps comparing the information against previously collected baseline information.
Eliminate potential causes	Based on the troubleshooter's knowledge of the network and his interrogation of collected information, he can begin to eliminate potential causes for the problem.
Hypothesize underlying cause	After the troubleshooter eliminates multiple potential causes for the problem, he is left with one or more causes that are more likely to have resulted in the problem. The troubleshooter hypothesizes what he considers to be the most likely cause of the problem.

Table 2-2   *Steps to Diagnose a Problem*   (*Continued*)

Step	Description
Verify hypothesis	The troubleshooter then tests his hypothesis to confirm or refute his theory about the problem's underlying cause.

The Value of a Structured Troubleshooting Approach

Troubleshooting skills vary from administrator to administrator. Therefore, although most troubleshooting approaches include collection and analysis of information, elimination of potential causes, hypothesizing of likely causes, and testing of the suspected cause, troubleshooters might spend different amounts of time performing these tasks.

If a troubleshooter does not follow a structured approach, the temptation is to move between the previously listed troubleshooting tasks in a fairly random way, often based on instinct. Although such an approach might lead to a problem resolution, it can become confusing to remember what you have tried and what you have not. Also, if another administrator comes to assist you, communicating to that other administrator the steps you have already gone through could be a challenge. Therefore, following a structured troubleshooting approach not only can help reduce the possibility of trying the same resolution more than once and inadvertently skipping a task, but aid in communicating to someone else possibilities you have already eliminated.

A structured troubleshooting method might look like the approach depicted in Figure 2-2.

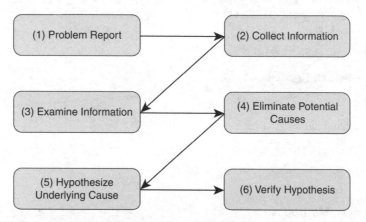

Figure 2-2   *Structured Troubleshooting Approach*

Some experienced troubleshooters, however, might have seen similar issues before and might be extremely familiar with the subtleties of the network they are working on. In such instances, spending time methodically examining information and eliminating potential causes might actually be less efficient than immediately hypothesizing a cause after they collect information about the problem. This method, illustrated in Figure 2-3, is often called the *shoot from the hip* method.

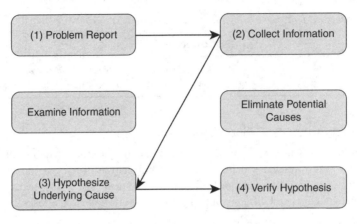

Figure 2-3 *Shoot from the Hip Troubleshooting Approach*

Notice that the major distinction between a structured approach and a shoot from the hip approach is examining information and eliminating potential causes based on that information. The danger with the shoot from the hip method is that if the troubleshooter's instincts are incorrect, valuable time is wasted. Therefore, a troubleshooter needs the perceptual acuity to know when to revert to a structured approach.

Popular Troubleshooting Methods

As noted previously, the elimination of potential causes is a key step in a structured troubleshooting approach. You can use several common approaches to narrow the field of potential causes:

- The Top-Down Method

- The Bottom-Up Method

- The Divide and Conquer Method

- Following the Traffic Path

- Comparing Configurations

- Component Swapping

The Top-Down Method

The top-down troubleshooting method begins at the top layer of the Open Systems Interconnection (OSI) seven-layer model, as shown in Figure 2-4. The top layer is numbered Layer 7 and is named the application layer.

The top-down method first checks the application residing at the application layer and moves down from there. The theory is, when the troubleshooter encounters a layer that is functioning, the assumption can be made that all lower layers are also functioning. For example, if you can ping a remote IP address, because ping uses Internet Control Message Protocol (ICMP), which is a Layer 3 protocol, you can assume that Layers 1–3 are functioning properly. Otherwise, your ping would have failed. A potential downside to this approach is that the troubleshooter needs access to the specific application experiencing a problem to test Layer 7.

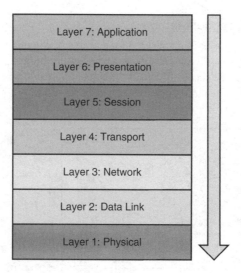

Figure 2-4 *Top-Down Troubleshooting Method*

The Bottom-Up Method

The reciprocal of the top-down method is the bottom-up method, as illustrated in Figure 2-5. The bottom-up method seeks to narrow the field of potential causes by eliminating OSI layers beginning at Layer 1, the physical layer.

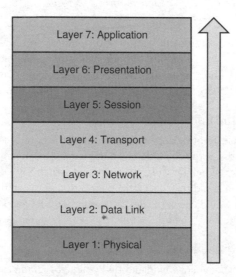

Figure 2-5 *Bottom-Up Troubleshooting Method*

Although this is a highly effective method, the bottom-up approach might not be efficient in larger networks because of the time required to fully test lower layers of the OSI model. Therefore, the bottom-up method is often used after employing some other method to narrow the scope of the problem.

The Divide and Conquer Method

After analyzing the information collected for a problem, you might not see a clear indication as to whether the top-down or bottom-up approach would be most effective. In such a situation, you might select the divide and conquer approach, which begins in the middle of the OSI stack, as shown in Figure 2-6.

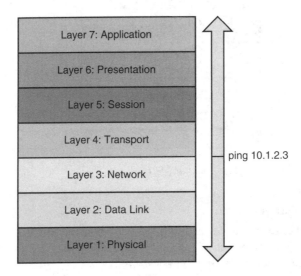

Figure 2-6   *Divide and Conquer Troubleshooting Method*

In the example shown in Figure 2-6, the network administrator issued the **ping 10.1.2.3** command. If the result was successful, the administrator could conclude that Layers 1–3 were operational, and a bottom-up approach could begin from that point. However, if the ping failed, the administrator could begin a top-down approach at Layer 3.

Following the Traffic Path

Another useful troubleshooting approach is to follow the path of the traffic experiencing a problem. For example, if the client depicted in Figure 2-7 is unable to reach its server, you could first check the link between the client and switch SW1. If everything looks good on that link, you could then check the connection between the switch SW1 and router R1. Next, you would check the link between router R1 and switch SW2 and finally the link between switch SW2 and the server.

Comparing Configurations

Did you ever go to the dentist as a kid and find yourself looking through a *Highlights* magazine? This magazine often featured two similar pictures, and you were asked to spot the differences. This childhood skill can also prove valuable when troubleshooting some network issues.

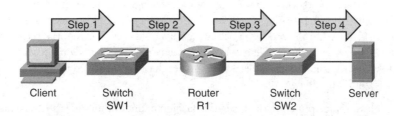

Figure 2-7   *Following the Path of Traffic*

For example, imagine you have multiple remote offices, each running the same model of Cisco router. Clients at one of those remote offices cannot obtain an IP address via DHCP. One troubleshooting approach is to compare that site's router configuration with the router configuration of another remote site that is working properly. This methodology is often an appropriate approach for a less experienced troubleshooter not well versed in the specifics of the network. However, the problem might be resolved without a thorough understanding of what caused the problem. Therefore, the problem is more likely to reoccur.

Component Swapping

Yet another approach to narrowing the field of potential causes of a problem is to physically swap out components. If a problem's symptoms disappear after swapping out a particular component (for example, a cable or a switch), you can conclude that the old component was faulty (either in its hardware or its configuration).

As an example, consider Figure 2-8. A problem report states that the connection between laptop A and switch SW1 is not bringing up a link light on either the laptop or the switch.

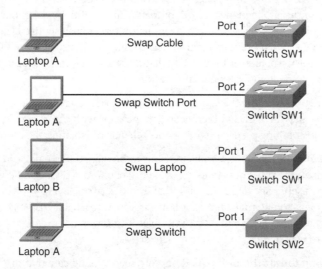

Figure 2-8   *Component Swapping*

As a first step, you might swap out the cable interconnecting these two devices with a known working cable.

If the problem persists, you will want to undo the change you made and then move the cable from switch port 1 to switch port 2. As a next step, you could connect a different laptop to switch SW1. If the problem goes away, you could conclude that the issue is with laptop A. However, if the problem continues, you could swap out switch SW1 with another switch: SW2 in this example. As you test each component and find it is not the problem, undo the change.

Although swapping out components in this fashion might not provide great insight into the specific problem, it could help focus your troubleshooting efforts. For example, if swapping out the switch resolved the issue, you could start to investigate the configuration of the original switch, checking for configuration or hardware issues.

Practice Exercise: Selecting a Troubleshooting Approach

As a troubleshooter, you might use one of the previously discussed troubleshooting methods or perhaps a combination of methods. To illustrate how you might select an appropriate troubleshooting approach, consider the following problem report:

> A computer lab at a university contains 48 PCs. Currently, 24 of the PCs cannot access the Internet, whereas the other 24 PCs can. The 24 PCs that cannot currently access the Internet were able to access the Internet yesterday.

Consider which of the previously discussed troubleshooting models might be appropriate for an issue such as the one reported. After you reach your own conclusions regarding which method or methods would be most appropriate, consider the following rationale:

- **Top-down:** Because the application is working on some PCs in the same location, starting at the application layer will probably not be effective. Although it is possible that 24 of the PCs have some setting in their Internet browser (for example, a proxy configuration) that prevents them from accessing the Internet, these PCs were working yesterday. Therefore, it is unlikely that these 24 PCs were all recently reconfigured with an incorrect application configuration.

- **Bottom-up:** Based on the symptom reported, it is reasonable to guess that there might be an issue with an Ethernet switch (perhaps with a port density of 24). Therefore, a bottom-up approach stands a good chance of isolating the problem quickly.

- **Divide and conquer:** The problem seems to be related to a block of PCs, and the problem is probably not application related. Therefore, a divide and conquer approach could be useful. Starting at Layer 3 (that is, the network layer), you could issue a series of pings to determine if a next-hop gateway is reachable. If the next-hop gateway is not reachable, you could start to troubleshoot Layer 2, checking the Cisco Catalyst switch to which these 24 PCs are attached.

- **Following the traffic path:** The symptom seems to indicate that these 24 PCs might share a common switch. Therefore, following the traffic path to the other end of the cabling (that is, to a switch) could prove useful. Perhaps the switch has lost power resulting in this connectivity issue for the 24 PCs.

- **Comparing configurations:** If a previous troubleshooting method (for example, bottom-up, divide and conquer, or following the traffic path) reveals that the 24 PCs that are not working are connected to one Cisco Catalyst switch, and the 24 PCs that are working are connected to another Cisco Catalyst switch, comparing the configuration of those two switches could be helpful.

- **Component swapping:** Because the 24 PCs are experiencing the same problem within a short time frame (since yesterday), it is unlikely that swapping cables would be useful. However, if these 24 PCs connect to the same Cisco Catalyst switch, swapping out the switch could help isolate the problem.

Using Troubleshooting Procedures

No single collection of troubleshooting procedures is capable of addressing all conceivable network issues, because too many variables (for example, user actions) are in play. However, having a structured troubleshooting approach can help ensure that an organization's troubleshooting efforts are following a similar flow, thus allowing one troubleshooter to more efficiently take over for or assist another troubleshooter.

The previous section, "Troubleshooting Methods," introduced a three-step troubleshooting flow consisting of the following:

Step 1.   Problem report

Step 2.   Problem diagnosis

Step 3.   Problem resolution

As mentioned, most troubleshooting efforts occur in the *problem diagnosis* step, which can again be dissected into its subcomponents:

A.   Collect information

B.   Examine collected information

C.   Eliminate potential causes

D.   Hypothesize underlying cause

E.   Verify hypothesis

By combining these components, you get the following listing of all subprocesses in the structured troubleshooting procedure:

Step 1.   Problem report

Step 2.   Collect information

Step 3.   Examine collected information

Key Topic

Step 4.   Eliminate potential causes

Step 5.   Hypothesize underlying cause

Step 6.   Verify hypothesis

Step 7.   Problem resolution

This section examines each of these subprocesses in more detail.

Problem Report

A problem report from a user often lacks sufficient detail for you to take that problem report and move on to the next troubleshooting process (that is, collect information). For example, a user might report, "The network is broken." If you receive such a vague report, you probably need to contact the user and ask him exactly what aspect of the network is not functioning correctly.

After your interview with the user, you should be able to construct a more detailed problem report that includes statements such as, when the user does X, she observes Y. For example, "When the user attempts to connect to a website on the Internet, her browser reports a 404 error. However, the user can successfully navigate to websites on her company's intranet."

After you have a clear articulation of the issue, you might need to determine who is responsible for working on the hardware or software associated with that issue. For example, perhaps your organization has one IT group tasked with managing switches and another IT group charged with managing routers. Therefore, as the initial point of contact, you might need to decide whether this issue is one you are authorized to address or if you need to forward the issue to someone else.

Collect Information

When you are in possession of a clear problem report, the next step is gathering relevant information pertaining to the problem. Efficiently and effectively gathering information involves focusing information gathering efforts on appropriate network entities (for example, routers, servers, switches, or clients) from which information should be collected. Otherwise, the troubleshooter could waste time wading through reams of irrelevant data.

Perhaps a troubleshooter is using a troubleshooting model where he follows the path of the affected traffic, and information needs to be collected from a network device over which he has no access. At that point, the troubleshooter might need to work with appropriate personnel who *do* have access to that device. Alternatively, the troubleshooter might switch troubleshooting models. For example, instead of following the traffic's path, he might swap components or use a bottom-up troubleshooting model.

Examine Collected Information

After collecting information regarding the problem report (for example, collecting output from **show** or **debug** commands, or performing packet captures), the next structured troubleshooting process is the analysis of the collected information.

A troubleshooter has two primary goals while examining the collected information:

■   Identify indicators pointing to the underlying cause of the problem.

■   Find evidence that can be used to eliminate potential causes.

Key Topic

To achieve these two goals, the troubleshooter attempts to find a balance between two questions:

■   What *is* occurring on the network?

■   What *should be* occurring on the network?

The delta between the responses to these questions might give the troubleshooter insight into the underlying cause of a reported problem. A challenge, however, is for the troubleshooter to know what currently should be occurring on the network.

If the troubleshooter is experienced with the applications and protocols being examined, she might be able to determine what is occurring on the network and how that differs from what should be occurring. However, if the troubleshooter lacks knowledge of specific protocol behavior, she still might be able to effectively examine her collected information by contrasting that information with baseline data.

Baseline data might contain, for example, the output of **show** and **debug** commands issued on routers when the network was functioning properly. By contrasting this baseline data with data collected after a problem occurred, even an inexperienced troubleshooter might be able to see the difference between the data sets, thus giving him a clue as to the underlying cause of the problem under investigation. This implies that as part of a routine network maintenance plan, baseline data should periodically be collected when the network is functioning properly.

Eliminate Potential Causes

Following an examination of collected data, a troubleshooter can start to form conclusions based on that data. Some conclusions might suggest a potential cause for the problem, whereas other conclusions eliminate certain causes from consideration.

A caution to be observed when drawing conclusions is not to read more into the data than what is actually there. As an example, a troubleshooter might reach a faulty conclusion based on the following scenario:

A problem report indicates that PC A cannot communicate with server A, as shown in Figure 2-9. The troubleshooter is using a troubleshooting method where she follows the path of traffic through the network. The troubleshooter examines output from the **show cdp neighbor** command on routers R1 and R2. Because those routers recognize each other as Cisco Discovery Protocol (CDP) neighbors, the troubleshooter leaps to the conclusion that these two routers see each other as OSPF neighbors and have mutually formed OSPF adjacencies. However, the **show cdp neighbor** output is insufficient to conclude that OSPF adjacencies have been formed between routers R1 and R2.

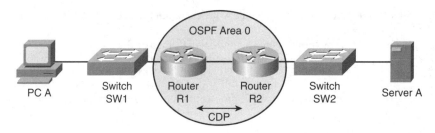

Figure 2-9 *Scenario Topology*

If time permits, explaining the rationale for your conclusions to a coworker can often help reveal faulty conclusions. Continuing your troubleshooting efforts based on a faulty conclusion can dramatically increase the time required to resolve a problem.

Hypothesize Underlying Cause

By eliminating potential causes of a reported problem, as described in the previous process, a troubleshooter should be left with one (or a few) potential cause. The troubleshooter should then select the potential cause she believes is most likely to be the underlying one for the reported problem. Her efforts then focus on addressing this hypothesized cause.

After hypothesizing an underlying cause, the troubleshooter might realize that he is not authorized to access a network device that needs to be accessed to resolve the problem report. In such a situation, the troubleshooter needs to assess whether the problem can wait until authorized personnel have an opportunity to resolve the issue. If the problem is urgent and no authorized administrator is currently available, the troubleshooter might attempt to at least alleviate the symptoms of the problem by creating a temporary workaround. Although this approach does not solve the underlying cause, it might help business operations continue until the main cause of the problem can be appropriately addressed.

Verify Hypothesis

After the troubleshooter has proposed what he believes to be the most likely cause of a problem, he needs to develop a plan to address the suspected cause. Alternatively, if the troubleshooter decided to implement a workaround, he needs to come up with a plan for deploying it.

Often, implementing a plan to resolve a network issue causes a temporary network outage for other users. Therefore, the troubleshooter must balance the urgency of the problem with the potential productivity impact resulting from deploying a planned solution at that time and network regulations regarding when and how changes can be made. If the impact on workflow outweighs the urgency of the problem, the troubleshooter might wait until after business hours to execute the plan.

A key component in deploying a solution is to have the steps documented. Not only does a documented list of steps help ensure the troubleshooter does not skip any, but such a document can serve as a rollback plan if the implemented solution fails to resolve the problem.

If the problem is not resolved after the troubleshooter implements the plan, or if the execution of the plan resulted in one or more additional problems, the troubleshooter should execute the rollback plan. After the network is returned to its previous state (that is, the state prior to deploying the proposed solution), the troubleshooter can then reevaluate her hypothesis.

Perhaps the troubleshooter still believes the underlying cause has been identified, even though the original solution failed to resolve that cause. In that case, the troubleshooter could create a different plan to address that cause. Alternatively, if the troubleshooter still knows of other potential causes that have not yet been ruled out, he can identify which of those causes is most likely resulting in the problem and create an action plan to resolve that cause.

This process can repeat itself until the troubleshooter has exhausted the list of potential causes. At that point, she might need to gather additional information or enlist the aid of a coworker or the Cisco Technical Assistance Center (TAC).

Problem Resolution

After the reported problem is resolved, the troubleshooter should make sure the solution becomes a documented part of the network. This implies that routine network maintenance will maintain the implemented solution. For example, if the solution involved reconfiguring a Cisco IOS router, a backup of that new configuration should be made part of routine network maintenance practices.

As a final task, the troubleshooter should report the problem resolution to the appropriate party or parties. Beyond simply notifying a user that a problem has been resolved, however, the troubleshooter should get user confirmation that the observed symptoms are now gone. This task confirms that the troubleshooter resolved the specific issue reported in the problem report, rather than a tangential issue.

Including Troubleshooting in Routine Network Maintenance

Troubleshooting occurs not only in response to a problem report, but as part of routine network maintenance. Similarly, ongoing network maintenance processes (for example, updating network documentation) often help troubleshoot future problems. This section addresses the mutually beneficial relationship between troubleshooting and maintenance.

The Relationship Between Maintenance and Troubleshooting Tasks

Chapter 1, "Introduction to Network Maintenance," pointed out that network maintenance is composed of multiple processes and tasks. Interestingly, network maintenance tasks often include troubleshooting tasks, and vice versa. For example, when installing a new network component as part of ongoing network maintenance, an installer is often required to troubleshoot the installation until the new network component is functioning properly. Also, when troubleshooting a network issue, the troubleshooter might use network documentation (for example, a physical topology diagram created as part of a network maintenance task) to help isolate a problem.

This interrelationship between maintenance and troubleshooting suggests that the effectiveness of your troubleshooting efforts is influenced by the effectiveness of your routine network management tasks. Because these tasks are so interrelated, you might want to take proactive measures to ensure your structured maintenance and troubleshooting processes complement one another. For example, both network troubleshooting and maintenance include a documentation component. Therefore, the value of a centralized repository of documentation increases as a result of its use for both maintenance and troubleshooting efforts.

Maintaining Current Network Documentation

A set of current network documentation can dramatically improve the efficiency of troubleshooting efforts. For example, if a troubleshooter is following the path that specific traffic takes through a network, a physical network topology diagram could help in quickly determining the next network component to check.

A danger with relying on documentation, however, is that if the documentation is dated, the troubleshooter could be led down an incorrect path because of her reliance on that documentation. Such a scenario is often worse than not having documentation at all, because in the absence of documentation, a troubleshooter is not aware of the need to collect updated and appropriate data.

Although few argue with the criticality of maintaining current documentation, in practice, documenting troubleshooting efforts often falls by the wayside. The lack of follow-through when it comes to documenting what happened during a troubleshooting scenario is understandable. The troubleshooter's focus is on resolving a reported issue in a timely manner (that is, an *urgent* task) rather than documenting what they are doing at the time (that is, an *important* task). Following are a few suggestions to help troubleshooters keep in mind the need to document their steps:

- **Require documentation:** By making documentation a component in the troubleshooting flow, troubleshooters know that before a problem report or a trouble ticket can be closed out, they must generate appropriate documentation. This knowledge often motivates troubleshooters to perform some level of documentation (for example, scribbling notes on the back of a piece of paper) as they are performing their tasks as opposed to later trying to recall what they did from memory, thus increasing the accuracy of the documentation.

- **Schedule documentation checks:** A structured maintenance plan could include a component that routinely requires verification of network documentation.

- **Automate documentation:** Because manual checks of documentation might not be feasible in larger environments, automated processes could be used to, for example, compare current and backup copies of device configurations. Any difference in the configurations indicates that someone failed to update the backup configuration of a device after making a configuration change to that device. To assist with the automation of backups, Cisco IOS offers the Configuration Archive and Rollback feature and the Embedded Event Manager.

Establishing a Baseline

As previously mentioned, troubleshooting involves knowing what should be happening on the network, observing what is currently happening on the network, and determining the difference between the two. To determine what should be happening on the network, a baseline of network performance should be measured as part of a routine maintenance procedure.

For example, a routine network maintenance procedure might require that a **show processes cpu** command be periodically issued on all routers in a network, with the output logged and archived. As shown in Example 2-1, the **show processes cpu** command demonstrates the 5-second, 1-minute, and 5-minute CPU utilization averages. When troubleshooting a performance problem on a router, you could issue this command to determine how a router is currently operating. However, without a baseline as a reference before troubleshooting, you might not be able to draw a meaningful conclusion based on the command output.

Example 2-1 *Monitoring Router CPU Utilization*

```
R1# show processes cpu
CPU utilization for five seconds: 18%/18%; one minute: 22%; five minutes: 22%

 PID Runtime(ms)    Invoked      uSecs   5Sec    1Min    5Min TTY Process
   1           0          1          0   0.00%   0.00%   0.00%   0 Chunk Manager
   2           4        167         23   0.00%   0.00%   0.00%   0 Load Meter
   3         821        188       4367   0.00%   0.13%   0.14%   0 Exec
   4           4          1       4000   0.00%   0.00%   0.00%   0 EDDRI_MAIN
   5       43026       2180      19736   0.00%   4.09%   4.03%   0 Check heaps
...OUTPUT OMITTED...
```

Communicating Throughout the Troubleshooting Process

Each of the troubleshooting phases described in the previous section, "Using Troubleshooting Procedures," requires clear communication. Table 2-3 describes how communication plays a role in each troubleshooting phase.

Table 2-3 *Importance of Clear Communication During Troubleshooting*

Troubleshooting Phase	The Role of Communication
Problem report	When a user reports a problem, clear communication with that user helps define the problem. For example, the user can be asked exactly what is not working correctly, if she made any recent changes, or when the problem started.

continues

Table 2-3 *Importance of Clear Communication During Troubleshooting* *(Continued)*

Troubleshooting Phase	The Role of Communication
Collect information	Some information collected might come from other parties (for example, a service provider). Clearly communicating with those other parties helps ensure collection of the proper data.
Examine collected information	Because a troubleshooter is often not fully aware of all aspects of a network, collaboration with other IT personnel is often necessary.
Eliminate potential causes	The elimination of potential causes might involve consultation with others. This consultation could provide insight leading to the elimination of a potential cause.
Hypothesize underlying cause	The consultation a troubleshooter conducts with other IT personnel when eliminating potential causes might also help the troubleshooter more accurately hypothesize a problem's underlying cause.
Verify hypothesis	Temporary network interruptions often occur when verifying a hypothesis; therefore, the nature and reason for an interruption should be communicated to the users impacted.
Problem resolution	After a problem is resolved, the user originally reporting the problem should be informed, and the user should confirm that the problem has truly been resolved.

Also, depending on the severity of an issue, multiple network administrators could be involved in troubleshooting a problem. Because these troubleshooters might be focused on different tasks at different times, it is possible that no single administrator can report on the overall status of the problem. Therefore, when managing a major outage, those involved in troubleshooting the outage should divert user inquiries to a manager who is in frequent contact with the troubleshooting personnel. As a side benefit, being able to quickly divert user requests for status reports to a manager helps minimize interruptions from users.

Change Management

Managing when changes can be made and by whose authority helps minimize network downtime. In fact, these two factors (that is, when a change is allowed and who can authorize it) are the distinguishing factors between making a change as part of a routine maintenance plan and making a change as part of a troubleshooting process.

The process of change management includes using policies that dictate rules regarding how and when a change can be made and how that change is documented. Consider the following scenario, which illustrates how a maintenance change could be a clue while troubleshooting a problem report:

> Last week, a network administrator attempted to better secure a Cisco Catalyst switch by administratively shutting down any ports that were in the down/down state (that is, no physical layer connectivity to a device). This morning a user reported that her PC could not access network resources. After clearly defining the problem, the troubleshooter asked if anything had changed, as part of the collect information troubleshooting phase. Even though the user was unaware of any changes, she mentioned that she had just returned from vacation, thus leading the troubleshooter to wonder if any network changes had occurred while the user was on vacation. Thanks to the network's change management system, the troubleshooter was able to find in the documentation that last week an administrator had administratively shut down this user's switch port.

The previous illustration points out the need for a troubleshooter to ask the question "Has anything changed?" By integrating a documentation requirement in a change management policy, someone troubleshooting a problem can leverage that documented change information.

Exam Preparation Tasks

Review All the Key Topics

Key Topic

Review the most important topics from inside the chapter, noted with the Key Topics icon in the outer margin of the page. Table 2-4 lists these key topics and the page numbers where each is found.

Table 2-4 *Key Topics for Chapter 2*

Key Topic Element	Description	Page Number
List	Simplified troubleshooting model	32
Table 2-2	Steps to diagnose a problem	32
List	Common approaches to troubleshooting	34
List	Structured troubleshooting procedure	39
List	Primary goals when collecting information	41
Example 2-1	Monitoring router CPU utilization	45
Table 2-3	The importance of clear communication	45

Complete the Tables and Lists from Memory

Print a copy of Appendix B, "Memory Tables," (found on the CD) or at least the section for this chapter, and complete the tables and lists from memory. Appendix C, "Memory Tables Answer Key," also on the CD, includes completed tables and lists to check your work.

Definition of Key Terms

Define the following key terms from this chapter, and check your answers in the Glossary:

shoot from the hip, top-down method, bottom-up method, divide and conquer method, following the traffic path, comparing configurations, component swapping, baseline

Command Reference to Check Your Memory

This section includes the EXEC command covered in this chapter. To determine how well you have memorized this command as a side effect of your other studies, cover the left side of the table with a piece of paper; read the description on the right side; and see whether you remember the command.

Table 2-5 *Chapter 2 EXEC Command Reference*

Command	Description
show processes cpu	Displays 5-second, 1-minute, and 5-minute CPU utilization statistics

This chapter covers the following subjects:

Cisco IOS Diagnostic Tools: This section shows how a few readily accessible Cisco IOS Software commands can be used to quickly gather information as part of a structured troubleshooting process.

Specialized Diagnostic Tools: This section introduces a collection of specialized features, such as Switched Port Analyzer (SPAN), Remote SPAN (RSPAN), Simple Mail Transfer Protocol (SMTP), NetFlow, and Embedded Event Manager (EEM), which can be used to collect information about a problem.

CHAPTER 3

The Maintenance and Troubleshooting Toolbox

Key to maintaining and troubleshooting a network is the collection of information about that network. Fortunately, Cisco IOS offers many commands that can be used for information gathering. Mastery of these basic tools can dramatically reduce the time a troubleshooter spends isolating the specific information needed for a troubleshooting task.

Beyond basic Cisco IOS commands, many network devices support features targeted toward the collection of information. Perhaps an event occurs on a network device, such as a router's processor utilization exceeding a defined threshold. The network device could report the occurrence of such an event. Alternatively, network devices might be periodically queried by a network management system for device and traffic statistics.

This chapter covers several basic Cisco IOS commands, in addition to specialized information collection features. These features not only help a troubleshooter collect information about a problem, but they can create a baseline of network performance. This baseline data can then be contrasted with data collected when a problem is occurring. The comparison of these two data sets often provides insight into the underlying cause of a problem.

"Do I Know This Already?" Quiz

The "Do I Know This Already?" quiz helps you determine your level of knowledge of this chapter's topics before you begin. Table 3-1 details the major topics discussed in this chapter and their corresponding quiz questions.

Table 3-1 *"Do I Know This Already?" Section-to-Question Mapping*

Foundation Topics Section	Questions
Cisco IOS Diagnostic Tools	1–3
Specialized Diagnostic Tools	4–7

1. Which of the following commands displays a router's running configuration, starting where the routing protocol configuration begins?

   a. show running-config | tee router

   b. show running-config | begin router

   c. show running-config | redirect router

   d. show running-config | append router

2. Which of the following is the ping response to a transmitted ICMP Echo datagram that needed to be fragmented when fragmentation was not permitted?

   a. U

   b. .

   c. M

   d. D

3. Which portion of the **show interfaces** command output indicates that a router received information faster than the information could be processed by the router?

   a. **input queue drops**

   b. **output queue drops**

   c. **input errors**

   d. **output errors**

4. The types of information collection used in troubleshooting fall into which three broad categories? (Choose three.)

   a. Troubleshooting information collection

   b. Baseline information collection

   c. QoS information collection

   d. Network event information collection

5. What features available on Cisco Catalyst switches allow you to connect a network monitor to a port on one switch to monitor traffic flowing through a port on a different switch?

   a. RSTP

   b. SPAN

   c. RSPAN

   d. SPRT

6. Which two of the following are characteristics of the NetFlow feature? (Choose the two best answers.)

   a. Collects detailed information about traffic flows

   b. Collects detailed information about device statistics

   c. Uses a pull model

   d. Uses a push model

7. Identify the Cisco IOS feature that allows you to create your own event definition for a network device and specify the action that should be performed in response to that event.

   a. SNMP

   b. EEM

   c. NetFlow

   d. syslog

Foundation Topics

Cisco IOS Diagnostic Tools

After a problem has been clearly defined, the first step in diagnosing that problem is collecting information, as described in Chapter 2, "Introduction to Troubleshooting Processes." Because the collection of information can be one of the most time consuming of the troubleshooting processes, the ability to quickly collect appropriate information becomes a valuable troubleshooting skill. This section introduces a collection of basic Cisco IOS commands useful in gathering information and discusses the filtering of irrelevant information from the output of those commands. Also included in this section are commands helpful in diagnosing connectivity and hardware issues.

Filtering the Output of **show** Commands

Cisco IOS offers multiple **show** commands useful for gathering information. However, many of these **show** commands produce a large quantity of output.

Consider the output shown in Example 3-1. The output from the **show processes cpu** command generated approximately 180 lines of output, making it challenging to pick out a single process.

Example: **show processes cpu** Command

Example 3-1   show processes cpu *Command Output*

Key
Topic

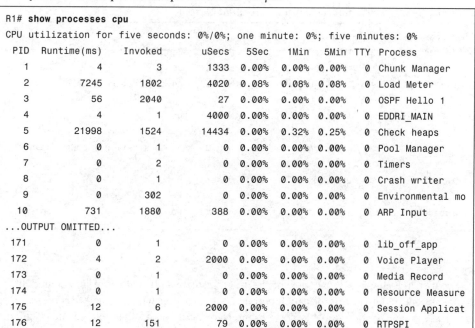

```
R1# show processes cpu
CPU utilization for five seconds: 0%/0%; one minute: 0%; five minutes: 0%
 PID  Runtime(ms)    Invoked     uSecs  5Sec    1Min   5Min TTY Process
   1            4          3      1333  0.00%  0.00%  0.00%   0 Chunk Manager
   2         7245       1802      4020  0.08%  0.08%  0.08%   0 Load Meter
   3           56       2040        27  0.00%  0.00%  0.00%   0 OSPF Hello 1
   4            4          1      4000  0.00%  0.00%  0.00%   0 EDDRI_MAIN
   5        21998       1524     14434  0.00%  0.32%  0.25%   0 Check heaps
   6            0          1         0  0.00%  0.00%  0.00%   0 Pool Manager
   7            0          2         0  0.00%  0.00%  0.00%   0 Timers
   8            0          1         0  0.00%  0.00%  0.00%   0 Crash writer
   9            0        302         0  0.00%  0.00%  0.00%   0 Environmental mo
  10          731       1880       388  0.00%  0.00%  0.00%   0 ARP Input
...OUTPUT OMITTED...
 171            0          1         0  0.00%  0.00%  0.00%   0 lib_off_app
 172            4          2      2000  0.00%  0.00%  0.00%   0 Voice Player
 173            0          1         0  0.00%  0.00%  0.00%   0 Media Record
 174            0          1         0  0.00%  0.00%  0.00%   0 Resource Measure
 175           12          6      2000  0.00%  0.00%  0.00%   0 Session Applicat
 176           12        151        79  0.00%  0.00%  0.00%   0 RTPSPI
```

```
177         4        17599        0   0.00%  0.00%  0.00%     0  IP NAT Ager
178         0            1        0   0.00%  0.00%  0.00%     0  IP NAT WLAN
179         8          314       25   0.00%  0.00%  0.00%     0  CEF Scanner
```

Perhaps you were only looking for CPU utilization statistics for the *Check heaps* process. Because you know that the content of the one line you are looking for contains the text **Check heaps,** you could take the output of the **show processes cpu** command and *pipe* that output (that is, use the | character) to the **include Check heaps** statement. The piping of the output causes the output to be filtered to only include lines that include the text **Check heaps,** as demonstrated in Example 3-2. This type of filtering can help troubleshooters more quickly find the data they are looking for.

Example 3-2   *Filtering the* **show processes cpu** *Command Output*

```
R1# show processes cpu | include Check heaps
   5       24710      1708       14467  1.14%  0.26%  0.24%    0 Check heaps
```

Example: **show ip interfaces brief** Command

Similar to piping output to the **include** option, you could alternatively pipe output to the **exclude** option. The **exclude** option can display all lines of the output *except* lines containing the string you specify. For example, the **show ip interfaces brief** command can display IP address and status information for all interfaces on a router, as shown in Example 3-3.

Example 3-3   **show ip interface brief** *Command Output*

```
R1# show ip interface brief
Interface           IP-Address      OK?  Method  Status                  Protocol
FastEthernet0/0     192.168.1.11    YES  NVRAM   up                      up
Serial0/0           unassigned      YES  NVRAM   administratively down   down

FastEthernet0/1     192.168.0.11    YES  NVRAM   up                      up

Serial0/1           unassigned      YES  NVRAM   administratively down   down

NVI0                unassigned      YES  unset   up                      up

Loopback0           10.1.1.1        YES  NVRAM   up                      up
```

Notice in Example 3-3 that some of the interfaces have an IP address of **unassigned.** If you want to only view information pertaining to interfaces with assigned IP addresses, you can pipe the output of the **show ip interface brief** command to **exclude unassigned,** as illustrated in Example 3-4.

Example 3-4   *Filtering Output from the* show ip interface brief *Command*

```
R1# show ip interface brief | exclude unassigned
Interface            IP-Address        OK?      Method      Status      Protocol
FastEthernet0/0      192.168.1.11      YES      NVRAM       up          up

FastEthernet0/1      192.168.0.11      YES      NVRAM       up          up

Loopback0            10.1.1.1          YES      NVRAM       up          up
```

Example: Jumping to the First Occurrence of a String in **show** Command Output

As another example, you might be troubleshooting a routing protocol issue and want to see the section of your running configuration where the routing protocol configuration begins. Piping the output of the **show running-config** command to **begin router**, as shown in Example 3-5, skips the initial portion of the **show running-config** output and begins displaying the output where the routing protocol configuration begins.

Example 3-5   *Filtering the Output from the* show running-config *Command*

```
R1# show running-config | begin router
router ospf 1
 log-adjacency-changes
 network 0.0.0.0 255.255.255.255 area 0
...OUTPUT OMITTED...
```

Example: The **show ip route** Command

Another command that often generates a lengthy output, especially in larger environments, is the **show ip route** command. As an example, consider the **show ip route** output presented in Example 3-6.

Example 3-6   *Sample* show ip route *Command Output*

```
R1# show ip route
Codes: C - connected, S - static, R - RIP, M - mobile, B - BGP
       D - EIGRP, EX - EIGRP external, O - OSPF, IA - OSPF inter area
       N1 - OSPF NSSA external type 1, N2 - OSPF NSSA external type 2
       E1 - OSPF external type 1, E2 - OSPF external type 2
       i - IS-IS, su - IS-IS summary, L1 - IS-IS level-1, L2 - IS-IS level-2
       ia - IS-IS inter area, * - candidate default, U - per-user static route
       o - ODR, P - periodic downloaded static route


Gateway of last resort is not set


     172.16.0.0/30 is subnetted, 2 subnets
O       172.16.1.0 [110/65] via 192.168.0.22, 00:50:57, FastEthernet0/1
```

```
O        172.16.2.0 [110/65] via 192.168.0.22, 00:50:57, FastEthernet0/1
      10.0.0.0/8 is variably subnetted, 6 subnets, 3 masks
O        10.2.2.2/32 [110/2] via 192.168.0.22, 00:50:57, FastEthernet0/1
O        10.1.3.0/30 [110/129] via 192.168.0.22, 00:50:57, FastEthernet0/1
O        10.3.3.3/32 [110/66] via 192.168.0.22, 00:50:57, FastEthernet0/1
O        10.1.2.0/24 [110/75] via 192.168.0.22, 00:50:58, FastEthernet0/1
C        10.1.1.1/32 is directly connected, Loopback0
O        10.4.4.4/32 [110/66] via 192.168.0.22, 00:50:58, FastEthernet0/1
C     192.168.0.0/24 is directly connected, FastEthernet0/1
C     192.168.1.0/24 is directly connected, FastEthernet0/0
```

Although the output shown in Example 3-6 is relatively small, some IP routing tables contain hundreds or even thousands of entries. If, for example, you wanted to determine if a route for network 172.16.1.0 were present in a routing table, you could issue the command **show ip route 172.16.1.0**, as depicted in Example 3-7.

Perhaps you were looking for all subnets of the 172.16.0.0/16 address space. In that event, you could specify the subnet mask and the **longer-prefixes** argument as part of your command. Such a command, as demonstrated in Example 3-8, shows all subnets of network 172.16.0.0/16, including the major classful network of 172.16.0.0/16.

Example 3-7 *Specifying a Specific Route with the* **show ip route** *Command*

```
R1# show ip route 172.16.1.0
Routing entry for 172.16.1.0/30
  Known via "ospf 1", distance 110, metric 65, type intra area
  Last update from 192.168.0.22 on FastEthernet0/1, 00:52:08 ago
  Routing Descriptor Blocks:
  * 192.168.0.22, from 10.2.2.2, 00:52:08 ago, via FastEthernet0/1
      Route metric is 65, traffic share count is 1
```

Example 3-8 *Filtering Output from the* **show ip route** *Command with the* **longer-prefixes** *Option*

```
R1#show ip route 172.16.0.0 255.255.0.0 longer-prefixes
Codes: C - connected, S - static, R - RIP, M - mobile, B - BGP
       D - EIGRP, EX - EIGRP external, O - OSPF, IA - OSPF inter area
       N1 - OSPF NSSA external type 1, N2 - OSPF NSSA external type 2
       E1 - OSPF external type 1, E2 - OSPF external type 2
       i - IS-IS, su - IS-IS summary, L1 - IS-IS level-1, L2 - IS-IS level-2
       ia - IS-IS inter area, * - candidate default, U - per-user static route
       o - ODR, P - periodic downloaded static route

Gateway of last resort is not set
```

```
        172.16.0.0/30 is subnetted, 2 subnets
O          172.16.1.0 [110/65] via 192.168.0.22, 00:51:39, FastEthernet0/1
O          172.16.2.0 [110/65] via 192.168.0.22, 00:51:39, FastEthernet0/1
```

Redirecting **show** Command Output to a File

Imagine that you are working with Cisco Technical Assistance Center (TAC) to troubleshoot an issue, and they want a file containing output from the **show tech-support** command issued on your router. Example 3-9 shows how you can use the **| redirect** option to send output from the **show tech-support** command to a file on a TFTP server.

Notice that directing output to a file suppresses the onscreen output. If you wanted both (that is, for the output to be displayed onscreen and stored to a file), you could pipe the output to the **tee** option, as demonstrated in Example 3-10.

Example 3-9 *Redirecting Output to a TFTP Server*

```
R1# show tech-support | redirect tftp://192.168.1.50/tshoot.txt
!
R1#
```

Example 3-10 *Redirecting Output While Also Displaying the Output Onscreen*

```
R1# show tech-support | tee tftp://192.168.1.50/tac.txt
!

--------------------show version--------------------

Cisco IOS Software, C2600 Software (C2600-IPVOICE_IVS-M), Version 12.4(3b), RELE
ASE SOFTWARE (fc3)
Technical Support: http://www.cisco.com/techsupport
Copyright (c) 1986-2005 by Cisco Systems, Inc.
Compiled Thu 08-Dec-05 17:35 by alnguyen
...OUTPUT OMITTED...
```

If you already have an output file created and you want to append the output of another **show** command to your existing file, you can pipe the output of your **show** command to the **append** option. Example 3-11 shows how to use the **append** option to append the output of the **show ip interface brief** command to a file named **baseline.txt**.

Example 3-11 *Appending Output to an Existing File*

```
R1# show ip interface brief | append tftp://192.168.1.50/baseline.txt
!
R1#
```

Key
Topic

Troubleshooting Connectivity

In addition to **show** command output, you can use many other Cisco IOS commands to troubleshoot network conditions. A common command, which can be used to check network connectivity, is the **ping** command. A basic **ping** command sends Internet Control Message Protocol (ICMP) Echo messages to a specified destination; for every ICMP Echo Reply received from that specified destination, an exclamation point appears in the output, as shown in Example 3-12.

Example 3-12 *Basic* ping *Command*

```
R1# ping 10.4.4.4



Type escape sequence to abort.
Sending 5, 100-byte ICMP Echos to 10.4.4.4, timeout is 2 seconds:
!!!!!
```

The **ping** command does have several options that can prove useful during troubleshooting. For example:

- **size:** Specifies the number of bytes per datagram

- **repeat:** Specifies the number of ICMP Echo messages sent (defaults to 5)

- **timeout:** Specifies the number of seconds to wait for an ICMP Echo Reply

- **source:** Specifies the source of the ICMP Echo datagrams

- **df-bit:** Sets the *do not fragment* bit in the ICMP Echo datagram

Not only can a **ping** command indicate that a given IP address is reachable, but the response to a **ping** command might provide insight into the nature of a problem. For example, if the **ping** results indicate alternating failures and successes (that is, **!.!.!**), a troubleshooter might conclude that traffic is being load-balanced between the source and destination IP addresses. Traffic flowing across one path is successful, whereas traffic flowing over the other path is failing.

You can also use the **ping** command to create a load on the network to troubleshoot the network under heavy use. Specifically, you can specify a datagram size of 1500 bytes, along with a large byte count and a timeout of zero seconds, as shown in Example 3-13.

Notice that all the pings failed. These failures occurred because of the zero-second timeout. Specifically, the router did not wait for any amount of time before considering the ping to have failed and sending another ICMP Echo message.

Example 3-13 *Creating a Heavy Load on the Network*

```
R1# ping 10.4.4.4 size 1500 repeat 9999 timeout 0


Type escape sequence to abort.
```

```
Sending 9999, 1500-byte ICMP Echos to 10.4.4.4, timeout is 0 seconds:
................................................................
................................................................
................................................................
...OUTPUT OMITTED...
```

Perhaps you suspect that an interface has a nondefault maximum transmission unit (MTU) size. You could send ICMP Echo messages across that interface using the **df-bit** and **size** options of the **ping** command to specify the size of the datagram to be sent. The **df-bit** option instructs a router to drop this datagram rather than fragmenting it if fragmentation is required.

Example 3-14 shows the sending of pings with the do not fragment bit set. Notice the **M** in the ping responses. An **M** indicates that fragmentation was required but could not be performed because the do not fragment bit was set. Therefore, you can conclude that a link between the source and destination is using a nonstandard MTU (that is, an MTU less than 1500 bytes).

Example 3-14 *Pinging with the Do Not Fragment Bit Set*

```
R1# ping 10.4.4.4 size 1500 df-bit

Type escape sequence to abort.
Sending 5, 1500-byte ICMP Echos to 10.4.4.4, timeout is 2 seconds:
Packet sent with the DF bit set
M.M.M
```

The challenge is how to determine the nondefault MTU size without multiple manual attempts. An extended ping can help with such a scenario. Consider Example 3-15, which issues the **ping** command without command-line parameters. This invokes the extended ping feature. The extended ping feature allows you to granularly customize your pings. For example, you could specify a range of datagram sizes to use in your pings to help determine the size of a nondefault MTU. Specifically, in Example 3-15, you could determine that the MTU across at least one of the links from the source to the destination IP address was set to 1450 bytes, because the **M** ping responses begin after 51 ICMP Echo datagrams were sent (with datagram sizes in the range of 1400 to 1450 bytes).

Example 3-15 *Extended Ping Performing a Ping Sweep*

Key
Topic

```
R1# ping
Protocol [ip]:
Target IP address: 10.4.4.4
Repeat count [5]: 1
Datagram size [100]:
Timeout in seconds [2]:
Extended commands [n]: y
```

```
Source address or interface:
Type of service [0]:
Set DF bit in IP header? [no]: yes
Validate reply data? [no]:
Data pattern [0xABCD]:
Loose, Strict, Record, Timestamp, Verbose[none]:
Sweep range of sizes [n]: y
Sweep min size [36]: 1400
Sweep max size [18024]: 1500
Sweep interval [1]:
Type escape sequence to abort.
Sending 101, [1400..1500]-byte ICMP Echos to 10.4.4.4, timeout is 2 seconds:
Packet sent with the DF bit set
!!!!!!!!!!!!!!!!!!!!!!!!!!!!!!!!!!!!!!!!!!!!!!!!!!!!!!M.M.M.M.M.M.M.M.M
.M.M.M.M.M.M.M.M.M.M.M.M.M.M.M.
Success rate is 50 percent (51/101), round-trip min/avg/max = 60/125/232 ms
```

Although the **ping** command can be useful for testing Layer 3 (that is, the network layer) connectivity, the **telnet** command is useful for troubleshooting Layer 4 (that is, the transport layer). Specifically, although Telnet typically uses TCP port 23, you can specify an alternate port number to see if a particular Layer 4 service is running on a destination IP address. Such an approach might be useful if you are using a divide and conquer approach, starting at Layer 3 (which was determined to be operational as a result of a successful ping), or a bottom-up approach (which has also confirmed Layer 3 to be operational).

To illustrate, notice the **telnet 192.168.1.50 80** command issued in Example 3-16. This command causes router R1 to attempt a TCP connection with 192.168.1.50 using port 80 (that is, the HTTP port). The response of **Open** indicates that 192.168.1.50 is indeed running a service on port 80.

Example 3-16   *Using Telnet to Connect to a Nondefault Port*

```
R1#telnet 192.168.1.50 80
Trying 192.168.1.50, 80 ... Open
```

Troubleshooting Hardware

In addition to software configurations, a network's underlying hardware often becomes a troubleshooting target. As a reference, Table 3-2 offers a collection of Cisco IOS commands used to investigate hardware performance issues.

Table 3-2   *Cisco IOS Commands for Hardware Troubleshooting*

Key
Topic

Command	Description
show processes cpu	Provides 5-second, 1-minute, and 5-minute CPU utilization statistics, in addition to a listing of processes running on a platform along with each process's utilization statistics
show memory	Displays summary information about processor and I/O memory, followed by a more comprehensive report of memory utilization
show interfaces	Shows Layer 1 and Layer 2 interface status, interface load information, and error statistics including the following: ■ **input queue drops:** Indicates a router received information faster than the information could be processed by the router ■ **output queue drops:** Indicates a router received information faster than the information could be sent out of the outgoing interface (perhaps because of an input/output speed mismatch) ■ **input errors:** Indicates frames were not received correctly (for example, a cyclic redundancy check (CRC) error occurred), perhaps indicating a cabling problem or a duplex mismatch ■ **output errors:** Indicates frames were not transmitted correctly, perhaps due to a duplex mismatch NOTE: Prior to collecting statistics, interface counters can be reset using the **clear counters** command.
show controllers	Displays statistical information for an interface (for example, error statistics), where the information varies for different interface types (for example, the type of connected cable might be displayed for a serial interface)
show platform	Provides detailed information about a router or switch hardware platform

Specialized Diagnostic Tools

The collection of network information occurs not just as part of a structured troubleshooting process but when gathering baseline data. Additionally, the occurrence of certain network events (for example, processor utilization on a network server exceeding a specified threshold) might be configured to trigger the writing of log information (for example, to a syslog server). Cisco offers network maintenance and troubleshooting tools targeted toward this type of data collection. This section introduces you to a sampling of these specialized tools, which can supplement the Cisco IOS commands used for data collection as discussed in the section "Cisco IOS Diagnostic Tools," earlier in this chapter.

Using Specialized Tools in the Troubleshooting Process

Chapter 2 introduced you to a series of processes (and subprocesses) that can work together in a structured troubleshooting process. Several of these processes involve the collection of information:

- **Difficulty report:** By proactively monitoring network devices, you might be alerted to impending performance issues before users are impacted.

- **Collect information:** The collection of information when troubleshooting a problem can often be made more efficient through the use of specialized maintenance and troubleshooting tools.

- **Examine collected information:** As troubleshooters investigate the information they collected while troubleshooting a problem, they need to know what normal network behavior looks like. They can then contrast that normal (that is, baseline) behavior against what they are observing in their collected data. Specialized maintenance and troubleshooting tools can be used in a network to collect baseline data on an ongoing basis.

- **Verify hypothesis:** Specialized maintenance and troubleshooting tools help a troubleshooter roll back an attempted fix, if that fix proves unsuccessful.

Most of the information collection tasks performed in the previous processes fall into one of three categories:

- **Troubleshooting information collection:** This information collection is conducted as part of troubleshooting a reported problem.

- **Baseline information collection:** This information collection is conducted when the network is operating normally, to form a frame of reference against which other data can be compared.

- **Network event information collection:** Some network devices can be configured to automatically generate alerts in response to specific conditions (for example, configured utilization levels on a switch, router, or server being exceeded).

Performing Packet Captures

You can use dedicated appliances or PCs running packet capture software to collect and store packets flowing across a network link. When troubleshooting, analysis of captured packets can provide insight into how a network is treating traffic flow. For example, a packet capture data file can show if packets are being dropped or if sessions are being reset. You can also look inside Layer 2, 3, and 4 headers using a packet capture application. For example, you can view a packet's Layer 3 header to determine that packet's Layer 3 quality of service (QoS) priority marking. An example of a popular and free packet capture utility you can download is Wireshark (www.wireshark.org), as shown in Figure 3-1.

Capturing and analyzing packets, however, presents two major obstacles. First, the volume of data collected as part of a packet capture can be so large that finding what you are looking for can be a challenge. Therefore, you should understand how to use your packet capture application's filtering features.

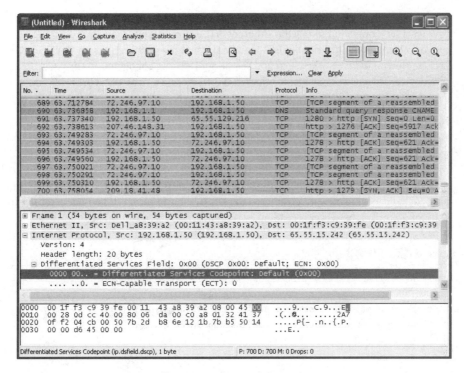

Figure 3-1 *Wireshark Packet Capture Application*

A second challenge is that if you want to monitor, for example, traffic flow between two network devices connected to a switch, the packets traveling between those two devices will not appear on your packet capture device's switch port. Fortunately, Cisco IOS supports a feature known as SPAN. SPAN instructs a switch to send copies of packets seen on one port (or one VLAN) to another port. You can connect your packet capture device to this other port, as shown in Figure 3-2.

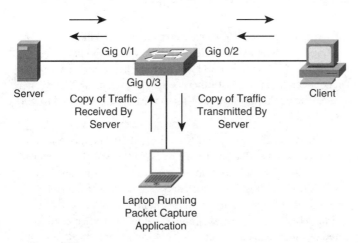

Figure 3-2 *Cisco Catalyst Switch Configured for SPAN*

Notice that Figure 3-2 depicts a client (connected to Gigabit Ethernet 0/2) communicating with a server (connected to Gigabit Ethernet 0/1). A troubleshooter inserts a packet capture device into Gigabit Ethernet 0/3. However, a switch's default behavior does not send packets flowing between the client and server out the port connected to the packet capture device. To cause port Gigabit Ethernet 0/3 to receive a copy of all packets sent or received by the server, SPAN is configured on the switch, as shown in Example 3-17.

Notice that Example 3-17 uses the **monitor session** *id* **source interface** *interface_id* command to indicate that a SPAN monitoring session with a locally significant identifier of **1** will copy packets crossing (that is, entering and exiting) port Gigabit Ethernet 0/1. Then the **monitor session** *id* **destination interface** interface_id command is used to specify port Gigabit Ethernet 0/3 as the destination port for those copied packets. A laptop running packet capture software connected to port Gigabit Ethernet 0/3 will now receive a copy of all traffic the server is sending or receiving.

Key
Topic

Example 3-17   *SPAN Configuration*

```
Cat3550# conf term
Enter configuration commands, one per line.  End with CNTL/Z.
Cat3550(config)# monitor session 1 source interface gig 0/1
Cat3550(config)# monitor session 1 destination interface gig 0/3
Cat3550(config)# end
Cat3550# show monitor
Session 1
-----------
Type                    : Local Session
Source Ports            :
    Both                : Gi0/1
Destination Ports       : Gi0/3
    Encapsulation       : Native
          Ingress : Disabled
```

In larger environments, a network capture device connected to one switch might need to capture packets flowing through a different switch. *Remote SPAN* (RSPAN) makes such a scenario possible. Consider Figure 3-3, where a troubleshooter has her laptop running a packet capture application connected to port Fast Ethernet 5/2 on switch SW2. The traffic that needs to be captured is traffic coming from and going to the server connected to port Gigabit Ethernet 0/1 on switch SW1.

A VLAN is configured whose purpose is to carry captured traffic between the switches. Therefore, a trunk exists between switches SW1 and SW2 to carry the SPAN VLAN in addition to a VLAN carrying user data. Example 3-18 shows the configuration on switch SW1 used to create the SPAN VLAN (that is, VLAN 20) and to specify that RSPAN should monitor port Gigabit Ethernet 0/1 and send packets sent and received on that port out of Gigabit Ethernet 0/3 on VLAN 20. The **show monitor** command is then used to verify the RSPAN source and destination. Also, note that by default the **monitor session** *id* **source** command monitors both incoming and outgoing traffic on the monitored port.

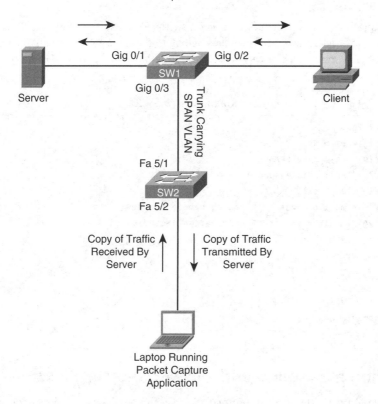

Figure 3-3 *Cisco Catalyst Switch Configured for RSPAN*

Example 3-18 *RSPAN Configuration on Switch SW1*

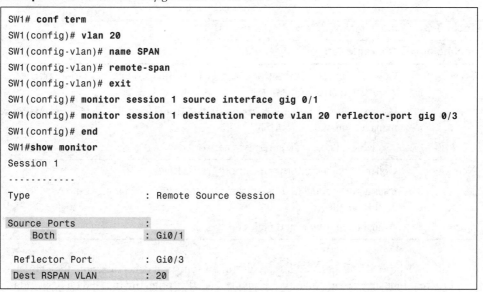

```
SW1# conf term
SW1(config)# vlan 20
SW1(config-vlan)# name SPAN
SW1(config-vlan)# remote-span
SW1(config-vlan)# exit
SW1(config)# monitor session 1 source interface gig 0/1
SW1(config)# monitor session 1 destination remote vlan 20 reflector-port gig 0/3
SW1(config)# end
SW1#show monitor
Session 1
------------
Type                     : Remote Source Session

Source Ports             :
   Both                  : Gi0/1

  Reflector Port         : Gi0/3
 Dest RSPAN VLAN         : 20
```

Example 3-19 shows the configuration on switch SW2 used to create the SPAN VLAN (which is not necessary if the switches belong to the same VTP domain), to specify that RSPAN should receive captured traffic from VLAN 20 and send it out port Fast Ethernet 5/2.

Example 3-19 *RSPAN Configuration on Switch SW2*

```
SW2# conf term
SW2(config)# vlan 20
SW2(config-vlan)# name SPAN
SW2(config-vlan)# remote-span
SW2(config-vlan)# exit
SW2(config)# monitor session 2 source remote vlan 20
SW2(config)# monitor session 2 destination interface fa 5/2
SW2(config)# end
SW2# show monitor
Session 2
-----------
Type                : Remote Destination Session
Source RSPAN VLAN : 20
Destination Ports : Fa5/2
```

Creating a Baseline with SNMP and NetFlow

Simple Network Management Protocol (SNMP) and NetFlow are two technologies available on some Cisco IOS platforms that can automate the collection statistics. These statistics can be used, for example, to establish a baseline in a troubleshooting scenario. Table 3-3 contrasts these two technologies.

Table 3-3 *Comparing SNMP and NetFlow*

Technology	Characteristics
SNMP	Collects device statistics (for example, platform resource utilization, traffic counts, and error counts)
	Uses a pull model (that is, statistics pulled from monitored device by a network management station [NMS])
	Available on nearly all enterprise network devices
NetFlow	Collects detailed information about traffic flows
	Uses a push model (that is, statistics pushed from the monitored device to a NetFlow collector)
	Available on routers and high-end switches

Although both SNMP and NetFlow are useful for statistical data collection, they target different fundamental functions. For example, SNMP is primarily focused on device statistics, whereas NetFlow is primarily focused on traffic statistics.

SNMP

A device being managed by SNMP runs a process called an *SNMP agent*. A Network Management System (NMS) can then query the agent for information, using the SNMP protocol. SNMP version 3 (that is, SNMPv3) supports encryption and authentication of SNMP messages; however, the most popular SNMP version deployed today is SNMPv2c. SNMPv2c uses *community strings* for security. Specifically, for an NMS to be allowed to read data from a device running an SNMP agent, the NMS must be configured with a community string that matches the managed device's read-only community string. For the NMS to change the information on the managed device, the NMS must be configured with a community string that matches the managed device's read-write community string. To enhance the security available with SNMPv2c, you can create an access list that determines valid IP addresses or network addresses for NMS servers.

Figure 3-4 shows a topology using SNMP. In the topology, router R1 is running an SNMP agent that the NMS server can query.

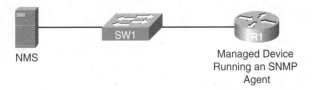

NMS   SW1   Managed Device
Running an SNMP
Agent

Figure 3-4   *SNMP Sample Topology*

Example 3-20 illustrates the SNMP configuration on router R1. The **snmp-server community** *string* [**ro** | **rw**] commands specify a read-only (that is, **ro**) community string of **CISCO** and a read-write (that is, **rw**) community string of **PRESS**. Contact and location information for the device is also specified. Finally, notice the **snmp-server ifindex persist** command. This command ensures that the SNMP interface index stays consistent during data collection, even if the device is rebooted. This consistency is important when data is being collected for baselining purposes.

Example 3-20   *SNMP Sample Configuration*

```
R1# conf term
R1(config)# snmp-server community CISCO ro
R1(config)# snmp-server community PRESS rw
R1(config)# snmp-server contact demo@ciscopress.local
R1(config)# snmp-server location 3rd Floor of Wallace Building
R1(config)# snmp-server ifindex persist
```

Key
Topic

NetFlow

Unlike SNMP, NetFlow can distinguish between different traffic flows. A *flow* is a series of packets, all of which have shared header information such as source and destination IP addresses, protocols numbers, port numbers, and Type of Service (TOS) field information. NetFlow can keep track of the number of packets and bytes observed in each flow. This information is stored in a *flow cache*. Flow information is removed from a flow cache if the flow is terminated, times out, or fills to capacity.

You can use the NetFlow feature as a standalone feature on an individual router. Such a standalone configuration might prove useful for troubleshooting because you can observe flows being created as packets enter a router. However, rather than using just a standalone implementation of NetFlow, entries in a router's flow cache can be exported to a *NetFlow collector* prior to the entries expiring. After the NetFlow collector has received flow information over a period of time, analysis software running on the NetFlow collector can produce reports detailing traffic statistics.

Figure 3-5 shows a sample topology in which NetFlow is enabled on router R4, and a Net-Flow collector is configured on a PC at IP address 192.168.1.50.

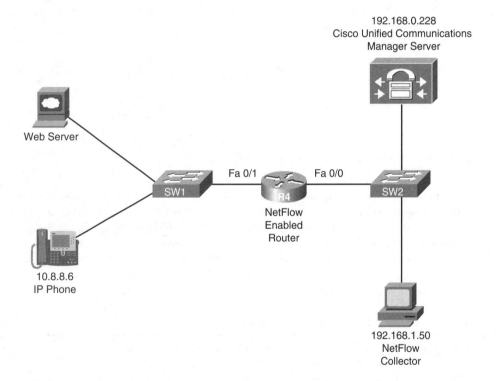

Figure 3-5 *NetFlow Sample Topology*

Example 3-21 illustrates the NetFlow configuration on router R4. Notice that the **ip flow ingress** command is issued for both the Fast Ethernet 0/0 and Fast Ethernet 0/1 interfaces. This ensures that all flows passing through the router, regardless of direction, can be monitored. Although not required, router R4 is configured to report its NetFlow information to a NetFlow collector at IP address 192.168.1.50. The **ip flow-export source lo 0/0** command indicates that all communication between router R4 and the NetFlow collector will be via interface Loopback 0. A NetFlow version of **5** was specified. Note that although version 5 is the most widely deployed, you should check the documentation for your

NetFlow collector software to confirm which version to configure. Finally, the **ip flow-export destination 192.168.1.50 5000** command is issued to specify that the NetFlow collector's IP address is **192.168.1.50**, and communication to the NetFlow collector should be done over UDP port **5000**. Because NetFlow does not have a standardized port number, please check your NetFlow collector's documentation when selecting a port.

Example 3-21 *NetFlow Sample Configuration*

```
R4# conf term
R4(config)# int fa 0/0
R4(config-if)# ip flow ingress
R4(config-if)# exit
R4(config)# int fa 0/1
R4(config-if)# ip flow ingress
R4(config-if)# exit
R4(config)# ip flow-export source lo 0
R4(config)# ip flow-export version 5
R4(config)# ip flow-export destination 192.168.1.50 5000
R4(conig)# end
```

Although an external NetFlow collector is valuable for longer-term flow analysis, you can issue the **show ip cache flow** command at a router's CLI prompt to produce a summary of flow information, as shown in Example 3-22. A troubleshooter can look at the output displayed in Example 3-22 and be able to confirm, for example, that traffic is flowing between IP address 10.8.8.6 (a Cisco IP Phone) and 192.168.0.228 (a Cisco Unified Communications Manager server).

Both syslog (discussed in Chapter 1, "Introduction to Network Maintenance") and SNMP (introduced in this section) are protocols that can report the occurrence of specific events on a network device. Although these protocols by themselves lack a mechanism to alert a network administrator (for example, via e-mail) when a network event is logged, third-party software is available that can selectively alert appropriate personnel when specific events are logged.

Earlier, this section discussed how a network device running an SNMP agent can be queried for information from an NMS. However, a network device running an SNMP agent can also initiate communication with an NMS. If an interface goes down, for example, the SNMP agent on a managed network device can send a message containing information about the interface state change to an NMS. Such notifications that a managed device sends to an NMS are called *traps*. These traps require an NMS to be interpreted because they are not in a readable format.

Example 3-22 *Viewing NetFlow Information*

```
R4# show ip cache flow
...OUTPUT OMITTED...
Protocol         Total     Flows   Packets   Bytes Packets Active(Sec) Idle(Sec)
```

- - - - - - - - - -	Flows	/Sec	/Flow	/Pkt	/Sec	/Flow	/Flow
TCP-Telnet	12	0.0	50	40	0.1	15.7	14.2
TCP-WWW	12	0.0	40	785	0.1	7.1	6.2
TCP-other	536	0.1	1	55	0.2	0.3	10.5
UDP-TFTP	225	0.0	4	59	0.1	11.9	15.4
UDP-other	122	0.0	114	284	3.0	15.9	15.4
ICMP	41	0.0	13	91	0.1	49.9	15.6
IP-other	1	0.0	389	60	0.0	1797.1	3.4
Total:	949	0.2	18	255	3.8	9.4	12.5

SrcIf	SrcIPaddress	DstIf	DstIPaddress	Pr	SrcP	DstP	Pkts
Fa0/0	10.3.3.1	Null	224.0.0.10	58	0000	0000	62
Fa0/1	10.8.8.6	Fa0/0	192.168.0.228	06	C2DB	07D0	2
Fa0/0	192.168.0.228	Fa0/1	10.8.8.6	06	07D0	C2DB	1
Fa0/0	192.168.1.50	Fa0/1	10.8.8.6	11	6002	6BD2	9166
Fa0/1	10.8.8.6	Fa0/0	192.168.1.50	11	6BD2	6002	9166
Fa0/0	10.1.1.2	Local	10.3.3.2	06	38F2	0017	438

Providing Notifications for Network Events

Whereas responding to problem reports from users is a reactive form of troubleshooting, monitoring network devices for significant events and responding to those events
is a proactive form of troubleshooting. For example, before a user loses connectivity
with the Internet, a router that is dual-homed to the Internet might report the event
of one of its Internet connections going down. The redundant link can then be
repaired, in response to the notification, thus resolving the problem without users
being impacted.

Example 3-23 demonstrates how to enable a router to send SNMP traps to an NMS.
The **snmp-server host 192.168.1.50 version 2c CISCOPRESS** command points router
R4 to an SNMP server (that is, an NMS) at IP address 192.168.1.50. The SNMP server is
configured for SNMP version **2c** and a community string of **CISCOPRESS**. The **snmp-
server enable traps** command attempts to enable all traps. Notice from the output,
however, that a couple of the traps are mutually exclusive, causing one of the traps to
not be enabled. You can view the enabled traps by using the **show run | include traps**
command. Rather than enabling all possible traps with the **snmp-server enable traps**
command, you can selectively enable traps using the **snmp-server enable traps** *trap-
name* command.

**Key
Topic**

Example 3-23   *Enabling SNMP Traps*

```
R4# conf term
R4(config)# snmp-server host 192.168.1.150 version 2c CISCOPRESS
R4(config)# snmp-server enable traps
% Cannot enable both sham-link state-change interface traps.
% New sham link interface trap not enabled.
R4(config)# end
R4# show run | include traps
```

```
snmp-server enable traps snmp authentication linkdown linkup coldstart warmstart
snmp-server enable traps vrrp
snmp-server enable traps ds1
snmp-server enable traps gatekeeper
snmp-server enable traps tty
snmp-server enable traps eigrp
snmp-server enable traps xgcp
snmp-server enable traps ds3
...OUTPUT OMITTED...
```

The messages received via syslog and SNMP are predefined within Cisco IOS. This large collection of predefined messages accommodates most any network management requirement; however, Cisco IOS supports a featured called EEM that allows you to create your own event definitions and specify custom responses to those events. An event can be defined based on syslog messages, SNMP traps, and entering specific Cisco IOS commands, as just a few examples. In response to a defined event, EEM can perform various actions, including sending an SNMP trap to an NMS, writing a log message to a syslog server, executing specified Cisco IOS commands, sending an e-mail to an appropriate party, or executing a tool command language (Tcl) script.

To illustrate the basic configuration steps involved in configuring EEM, consider Example 3-24. The purpose of the configuration is to create a syslog message, which will be displayed on the router console, when someone clears the router's interface counters using the **clear counters** command. The message should remind the administrator to update the network documentation, listing the rationale for clearing the interface counters.

Example 3-24 *EEM Sample Configuration*

```
R4# conf term
R4(config)# event manager applet COUNTER-RESET
R4(config-applet)# event cli pattern "clear counters" sync no skip no occurs 1
R4(config-applet)# action A syslog priority informational msg "Please update
  network documentation to record why the counters were reset."
R4(config-applet)# end
```

Key
Topic

The **event manager applet COUNTER-RESET** command creates an EEM applet named **COUNTER-RESET** and enters applet configuration mode. The **event** command specifies what you are looking for in your custom-defined event. In this example, you are looking for the CLI command **clear counters**. Note that the **clear counters** command would be detected even if a shortcut (for example, **cle co**) were used. The **sync no** parameter says that the EEM policy will run asynchronously with the CLI command. Specifically, the EEM policy will not be executed before the CLI command executes. The **skip no** parameter says that the CLI command will not be skipped (that is, the CLI command will be executed). Finally, the **occurs 1** parameter indicates that the EEM event is triggered by a single occurrence of the **clear counters** command being issued.

The **action** command is then entered to indicate what should be done in response to the defined event. In Example 3-24, the action is given a locally significant name of **A** and is assigned a syslog priority level of **informational.** The specific action to be taken is producing an informational message saying, **"Please update network documentation to record why the counters were reset."**

To verify the operation of the EEM configuration presented in Example 3-24, the **clear counters** command is executed in Example 3-25. Notice that entering the **clear counters** command triggers the custom-defined event, resulting in generation of a syslog message reminding an administrator to document the reason he cleared the interface counters.

Example 3-25   *Testing EEM Configuration*

```
R4# clear counters
Clear "show interface" counters on all interfaces [confirm]
R4#
*Mar  3 08:41:00.582: %HA_EM-6-LOG: COUNTER-RESET: Please update network docu-
  mentation to record why the counters were reset.
```

Exam Preparation Tasks

Review All the Key Topics

Review the most important topics from inside the chapter, noted with the Key Topics icon in the outer margin of the page. Table 3-4 lists these key topics and the page numbers where each is found.

Table 3-4 *Key Topics for Chapter 3*

Key Topic Element	Description	Page Number
Example 3-1	The **show processes cpu** command	53
Example 3-8	Filtering **show** output with the **longer-prefixes** option	56
Example 3-9	Redirecting output using the **redirect** option	57
Example 3-10	Redirecting output using the **tee** option	57
Example 3-11	Redirecting output using the **append** option	57
Example 3-15	Extended Ping performing a Ping sweep	59
Example 3-16	Using **telnet** to connect to a nondefault port	60
Table 3-2	Cisco IOS commands for hardware troubleshooting	61
List	How information collection plays a role in troubleshooting	62
List	Three categories of information collection	62
Example 3-17	SPAN configuration	64
Example 3-18	RSPAN configuration	65
Table 3-3	Comparing SNMP and NetFlow	66
Example 3-20	SNMP sample configuration	67
Example 3-21	NetFlow sample configuration	69
Example 3-22	Viewing NetFlow information	69
Example 3-23	Enabling SNMP traps	70
Example 3-24	EEM Sample configuration	71

Complete Tables and Lists from Memory

Print a copy of Appendix B, "Memory Tables" (found on the CD), or at least the section for this chapter, and complete the tables and lists from memory. Appendix C, "Memory Tables Answer Key," also on the CD, includes completed tables and lists to check your work.

Define Key Terms

Define the following key terms from this chapter, and check your answers in the Glossary:

input queue drops, output queue drops, input errors, output errors, SPAN, RSPAN, trap, NMS, NetFlow, EEM

Command Reference to Check Your Memory

This section includes the most important configuration and EXEC commands covered in this chapter. To determine how well you have memorized the commands as a side effect of your other studies, cover the left side of the table with a piece of paper; read the descriptions on the right side; and see whether you remember the command.

Table 3-5   *Chapter 3 Configuration Command Reference*

Command	Description
monitor session *id* {**source** | **destination**} **interface** *interface_id*	Global configuration mode command that configures SPAN, which specifies the source or destination interface for traffic monitoring
remote-span	VLAN configuration mode command that indicates a VLAN is to be used as an RSPAN VLAN
monitor session *id* **destination remote vlan** *VLAN_id* **reflector-port** *port_id*	Global configuration mode command that configures RSPAN on a monitored switch, where the RSPAN VLAN is specified in addition to the port identifier for the port being used to flood the monitored traffic to the monitoring switch
monitor session *id* **source remote vlan** *VLAN_id*	Global configuration mode command that configures RSPAN on a monitoring switch, where the RSPAN VLAN is specified
snmp-server community *community_string* {**ro** | **rw**}	Global configuration mode command that defines a read-only (**ro**) or read-write (**rw**) SNMP community string
snmp-server contact *contact_info*	Global configuration mode command that specifies SNMP contact information

Table 3-5   *Chapter 3 Configuration Command Reference*   (*Continued*)

Command	Description
snmp-server location *location*	Global configuration mode command that specifies SNMP location information
snmp-server ifindex persist	Global configuration mode command that forces an SNMP interface index to stay consistent during data collection, even if a device is rebooted
ip flow ingress	Interface configuration mode command that enables NetFlow for that interface
ip flow-export source *interface_id*	Global configuration mode command that specifies the interface used to communicate with an external NetFlow collector
ip flow-export version {1 | 5 | 9}	Global configuration mode command that specifies the NetFlow version used by a device
ip flow-export destination *IP_address port*	Global configuration mode command that specifies the IP address and port number of an external NetFlow collector
snmp-server host *IP_address* version {1 | 2c | 3} *community_string*	Global configuration mode command that specifies the IP address, SNMP version, and community string of an NMS
snmp-server enable traps	Global configuration mode command that enables all possible SNMP traps
event manager applet *name*	Global configuration mode command that creates an embedded event manager applet and enters applet configuration mode

Table 3-6   *Chapter 3 EXEC Command Reference*

Command	Description
show processes cpu	Displays 5-second, 1-minute, and 5-minute CPU utilization averages, in addition to a listing of running processes with their CPU utilization
show ip route *network_address subnet_mask* longer-prefixes	Shows all subnets within the specified address space

continues

Table 3-6   *Chapter 3 EXEC Command Reference   (Continued)*

Command	Description
ping *IP_address* **size** [*bytes*] **repeat** [*number*] **timeout** [*seconds*] [*df-bit*]	Sends ICMP Echo packets to the specified IP address, with options that include these: **size:** The number of bytes in the ICMP Echo packet **repeat:** The number of ICMP Echo packets sent **timeout:** The number of seconds the router waits for an ICMP Echo Reply packet after sending an ICMP Echo packet **df-bit:** Sets the do-not-fragment bit in the ICMP Echo packet
telnet IP_address [port]	Connects to a remote IP address via Telnet using TCP port 23 by default or optionally via a specified TCP port
show memory	Displays summary information about processor and I/O memory, followed by a more comprehensive report of memory utilization
show interfaces	Shows Layer 1 and Layer 2 interface status, interface load information, and error statistics including these: **input queue drops:** Indicates a router received information faster than the information could be processed by the router **output queue drops:** Indicates a router received information faster than the information could be sent out of the outgoing interface (perhaps because of an input/output speed mismatch) **input errors:** Indicates frames were not received correctly (for example, a CRC error occurred), perhaps indicating a cabling problem or a duplex mismatch **output errors:** Indicates frames were not transmitted correctly, perhaps due to a duplex mismatch **NOTE:** Prior to collecting statistics, interface counters can be reset using the **clear counters** command.
show controllers	Displays statistical information for an interface (for example, error statistics) where the information varies for different interface types (for example, the type of connected cable might be displayed for a serial interface)
show platform	Provides detailed information about a router or switch hardware platform

This chapter covers the following subjects:

VLAN Troubleshooting: This section reviews the basics of Layer 2 switching operation and shows how a few readily accessible Cisco IOS commands can be used to quickly gather information as part of a structured troubleshooting process.

Spanning Tree Protocol Troubleshooting: This section introduces Spanning Tree Protocol (STP), which allows a Layer 2 topology to have redundant links while avoiding the side effects of a looped Layer 2 topology, such as a broadcast storm. You then learn strategies for troubleshooting an STP issue. Finally, this section addresses troubleshooting an EtherChannel connection.

Trouble Ticket STP: This section presents you with a trouble ticket and an associated topology. You are also given **show** command output (baseline output and output collected after the reported issue occurred). Based on the information provided, you hypothesize an underlying cause for the reported issue and develop a solution. You can then compare your solution with a suggested solution.

CHAPTER 4

Basic Cisco Catalyst Switch Troubleshooting

Most enterprise LANs rely on some flavor of Ethernet technology (for example, Ethernet, Fast Ethernet, or Gigabit Ethernet). Therefore, an understanding of Ethernet switch operation at Layer 2 is critical to troubleshooting many issues. This chapter reviews basic Layer 2 switch operation. Beyond a review of basic operation, this chapter discusses potential troubleshooting issues involving Layer 2 switches and steps to troubleshoot these issues.

Maintaining high availability for today's enterprise networks is a requirement for many applications, such as voice and e-commerce, which can impact a business' bottom line if these applications are unavailable for even a short period. To improve availability, many enterprise networks interconnect Layer 2 switches with redundant connections, allowing a single switch or a single link to fail while still maintaining connectivity between any two network endpoints. Such a redundant topology, however, can result in Layer 2 loops, which can cause frames to endlessly circle a LAN (for example, broadcast frames creating a broadcast storm). Therefore, STP is frequently used to logically break these Layer 2 topological loops by strategically blocking ports, while being able to detect a link failure and bring up a previously blocked switch port to restore connectivity. This chapter reviews the operation of STP and focuses on troubleshooting STP issues.

Finally, you are introduced to the first in a series of trouble tickets, which provides a reported issue and its associated topology. Various **show** command output is provided to help you hypothesize the underlying cause of the issue being reported. This chapter's trouble ticket focuses on troubleshooting an STP issue.

"Do I Know This Already?" Quiz

The "Do I Know This Already?" quiz helps you determine your level of knowledge of this chapter's topics before you begin. Table 4-1 details the major topics discussed in this chapter and their corresponding quiz questions.

Table 4-1 *"Do I Know This Already?" Section-to-Question Mapping*

Foundation Topics Section	Questions
VLAN Troubleshooting	1–2
Spanning Tree Protocol Troubleshooting	3–6

1. Which two of the following statements are true of a Layer 2 switch? (Choose two.)

   a. Each switch port is in its own collision domain.

   b. Each switch port is in its own broadcast domain.

   c. Each VLAN is its own collision domain.

   d. Each VLAN is its own broadcast domain.

2. Which two Cisco Catalyst switch commands display to which VLAN each switch port belongs? (Choose two.)

   a. show mac address-table

   b. show interfaces trunk

   c. show vlan

   d. traceroute mac

3. What is the STP port type for all ports on a root bridge?

   a. Designated port

   b. Root port

   c. Nondesignated port

   d. Nonroot port

4. Which two of the following commands are most helpful in determining STP information for a Layer 2 switch? (Choose two.)

   a. show spanning-tree vlan

   b. debug spanning-tree state

   c. show spanning-tree interface

   d. show port span

5. What are two common issues that could result from an STP failure? (Choose two.)

   a. Tagged frames being sent into a native VLAN

   b. Broadcast storms

   c. MAC address table filling to capacity

   d. MAC address table corruption

6. Which switch feature allows multiple physical links to be bonded into a logical link?

   a. FRF.12

   b. EtherChannel

   c. Jumbo frames

   d. RPF

Foundation Topics

VLAN Troubleshooting

To effectively troubleshoot Ethernet-based LAN environments, you should be familiar with the basics of Layer 2 switch operation. Therefore, this section reviews switch fundamentals, including how a switch's MAC address table is populated, as well as the characteristics of VLANs and trunks. After a review of basic switch operation, this section highlights common issues in a switched environment and how to use Cisco IOS to troubleshoot such issues.

Reviewing Layer 2 Switching

Unlike Ethernet hubs, which take bits in one port and send those same bits out all other ports, Ethernet switches learn the devices connected to their ports. Therefore, when an Ethernet switch sees a frame destined for a particular MAC address, the switch can consult its MAC address table to determine out of which port to forward the newly arrived frame. This behavior results in more efficient bandwidth utilization on a LAN and eliminates the concern of collisions. Specifically, in a hubbed environment, if two endpoints each transmitted a data frame on the wire at the same time, those two frames would collide, resulting in both frames being corrupted. This collision would require each endpoint to retransmit its data frame. Every port on an Ethernet switch, however, is its own collision domain, whereas all ports on a hub are in a common collision domain.

Ethernet switches can dynamically learn the MAC addresses attached to various switch ports by looking at the source MAC address on frames coming into a port. For example, if switch port Gigabit Ethernet 1/1 received a frame with a source MAC address of DDDD.DDDD.DDDD, the switch could conclude that MAC address DDDD.DDDD.DDDD resided off of port Gigabit Ethernet 1/1. In the future, if the switch received a frame destined for a MAC address of DDDD.DDDD.DDDD, the switch would only send that frame out of port Gigabit Ethernet 1/1.

Initially, however, a switch is unaware of what MAC addresses reside off of which ports (unless MAC addresses have been statically configured). Therefore, when a switch receives a frame destined for a MAC address not yet present in the switch's MAC address table, the switch floods that frame out of all the switch ports, other than the port on which the frame was received. Similarly, broadcast frames (that is, frames with a destination MAC address of FFFF.FFFF.FFFF) are always flooded out all switch ports except the port on which the frame was received. The reason broadcast frames are always flooded is that no endpoint will have a MAC address of FFFF.FFFF.FFFF, meaning that the FFFF.FFFF.FFFF MAC address will never be learned in the MAC address table of a switch.

To illustrate how a switch's MAC address table becomes populated, consider an endpoint named PC1 that wants to form a Telnet connection with a server as shown in Figure 4-1. Also, assume that PC1 and its server reside on the same subnet (that is, no routing is required to get traffic between PC1 and its server). Before PC1 can send a Telnet segment to its server, PC1 needs to know the IP address (that is, the Layer 3 address) and the MAC address (that is, the Layer 2 address) of the server. The IP address of the server is typically known or is resolved via a Domain Name System (DNS) lookup. In this example, assume the server's IP address is known. To properly form a Telnet segment, however, PC1 needs to know the server's Layer 2 MAC address. If PC1 does not already have the server's MAC address in its ARP cache, PC1 can send an Address Resolution Protocol (ARP) request in an attempt to learn the server's MAC address.

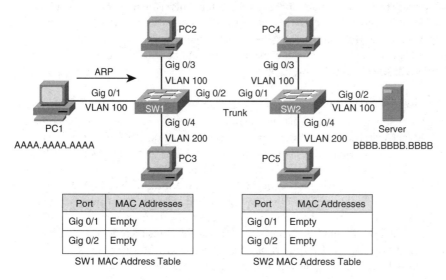

Figure 4-1   *Endpoint Sending an ARP Request*

When switch SW1 sees PC1's ARP request enter port Gigabit 0/1, the PC1 MAC address of AAAA.AAAA.AAAA is added to the MAC address table of switch SW1. Also, because the ARP request is a broadcast, its destination MAC address is FFFF.FFFF.FFFF. Because the MAC address of FFFF.FFFF.FFFF is unknown to switch SW1's MAC address table, switch SW1 floods a copy of the incoming frame out all switch ports except the port on which the frame was received, with one exception. Notice that port Gig 0/1 on switch SW1 belongs to VLAN 100, whereas port Gig 0/4 belongs to VLAN 200. Because a broadcast is constrained to a VLAN, this broadcast frame originating in VLAN 100 is not flooded out Gig 0/4 because Gig 0/4 is a member of a different VLAN. Port Gig 0/2, however, is a trunk port, and a trunk can carry traffic for multiple VLANs. Therefore, the ARP request is flooded out of port Gig 0/2, as illustrated in Figure 4-2.

When switch SW2 receives the ARP request over its Gig 0/1 trunk port, the source MAC address of AAAA.AAAA.AAAA is added to switch SW2's MAC address table. Also, similar to the behavior of switch SW1, switch SW2 floods the broadcast frame out of port Gig 0/3 (a member of VLAN 100) and out of port Gig 0/2 (also a member of VLAN 100), as depicted in Figure 4-3.

The server receives the ARP request and responds with an ARP reply, as seen in Figure 4-4. Unlike the ARP request, however, the ARP reply frame is not a broadcast frame. The ARP reply in this case has a destination MAC address of AAAA.AAAA.AAAA.

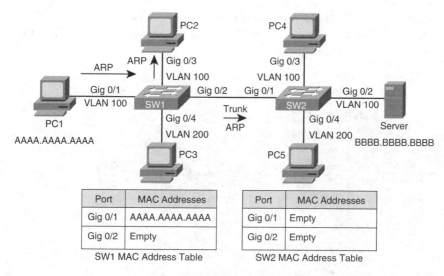

Figure 4-2 *Switch SW1 Flooding the ARP Request*

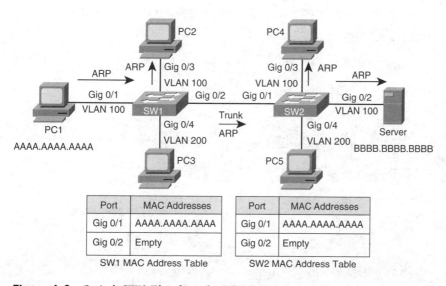

Figure 4-3 *Switch SW2 Flooding the ARP Request*

Upon receiving the ARP reply from the server, switch SW2 adds the server's MAC address of BBBB.BBBB.BBBB to its MAC address table, as shown in Figure 4-5. Also, the ARP reply is only sent out port Gig 0/1 because switch SW1 knows that the destination MAC address of AAAA.AAAA.AAAA is available off of port Gig 0/1.

When receiving the ARP reply in its Gig 0/2 port, switch SW1 adds the server's MAC address of BBBB.BBBB.BBBB to its MAC address table. Also, like switch SW2, switch SW1

now has an entry in its MAC address table for the frame's destination MAC address of
AAAA.AAAA.AAAA. Therefore, switch SW1 forwards the ARP reply out port Gig 0/1 to
the endpoint of PC1, as illustrated in Figure 4-6.

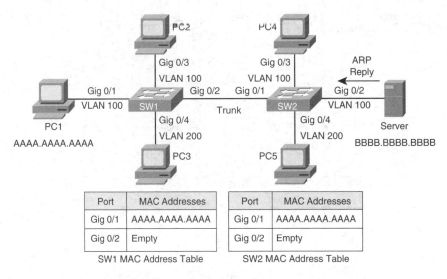

Figure 4-4   *ARP Reply Sent from the Server*

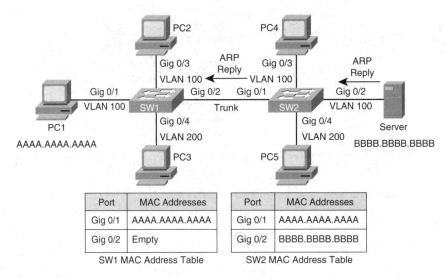

Figure 4-5   *Switch SW2 Forwarding the ARP Reply*

After receiving the server's ARP reply, PC1 now knows the MAC address of the server.
Therefore, PC1 can now send a properly constructed Telnet segment destined for the
server, as depicted in Figure 4-7.

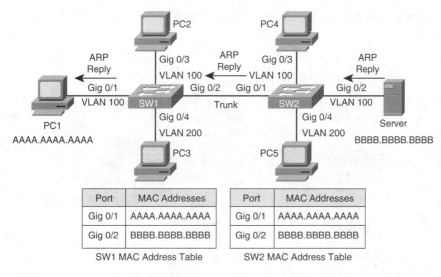

Figure 4-6   *Switch SW1 Forwarding the ARP Reply*

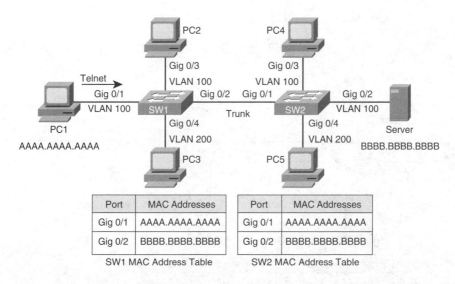

Figure 4-7   *PC1 Sending a Telnet Segment*

Switch SW1 has the server's MAC address of BBBB.BBBB.BBBB in its MAC address table. Therefore, when switch SW1 receives the Telnet segment from PC1, that segment is forwarded out of the Gig 0/2 port of switch SW1, as seen in Figure 4-8.

Similar to the behavior of switch SW1, switch SW2 forwards the Telnet segment out its Gig 0/2 port. This forwarding, shown in Figure 4-9, is possible because switch SW2 has an entry for the segment's destination MAC address of BBBB.BBBB.BBBB in its MAC address table.

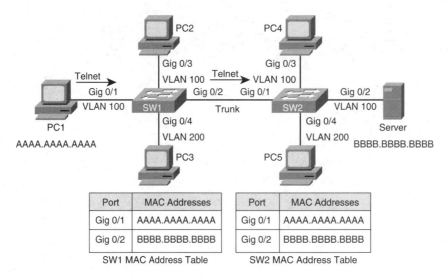

Figure 4-8 *Switch SW1 Forwarding the Telnet Segment*

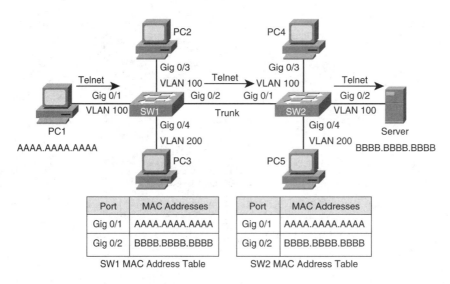

Figure 4-9 *Switch SW2 Forwarding the Telnet Segment*

Finally, the server responds to PC1, and a bidirectional Telnet session is established between the PC and the server, as illustrated in Figure 4-10. Because PC1 learned the MAC address of the server as a result of its earlier ARP request and stored that result in its local ARP cache, the transmission of subsequent Telnet segments does not require additional ARP requests. If unused for a period of time, however, entries in a PC's ARP cache can time out.

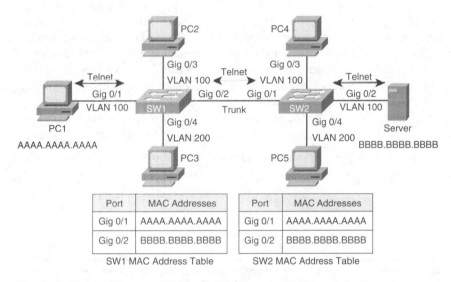

Port	MAC Addresses
Gig 0/1	AAAA.AAAA.AAAA
Gig 0/2	BBBB.BBBB.BBBB

SW1 MAC Address Table

Port	MAC Addresses
Gig 0/1	AAAA.AAAA.AAAA
Gig 0/2	BBBB.BBBB.BBBB

SW2 MAC Address Table

Figure 4-10 *Bidirectional Telnet Session Between PC1 and the Server*

When troubleshooting an issue involving Layer 2 switch communication, a thorough understanding of the preceding steps can help you identify potential problems. If you were troubleshooting an issue similar to the previous example, where a PC is attempting to communicate with a server on a common VLAN, you might consider possibilities such as the following:

■ **Hardware issues:** Potential hardware problems include the cabling interconnecting devices and the devices themselves. For example, one switch port might be faulty. You could eliminate that possibility by moving a cable to a known good switch port.

Key Topic

■ **VLAN configuration:** For traffic to move from one VLAN to another, that traffic must be routed. Therefore, you might want to confirm that the PC and server in such a scenario are connected to ports in a common VLAN.

■ **Trunk configuration:** Switches are often interconnected via an Ethernet trunk (for example, an IEEE 802.1Q trunk). A trunk has the unique capability to carry traffic for multiple VLANs over a single link. When troubleshooting an issue like the one in the preceding scenario, you might want to confirm that the trunk is configured identically on each switch. For example, each switch should be using the same trunking encapsulation (for example, 802.1Q or ISL). Also, if you are using an 802.1Q trunk, each switch should have a common native VLAN (that is, the VLAN on an 802.1Q trunk, which does not add tag bytes to the frames in that VLAN). One other possibility is that traffic for one or more VLANs has been excluded on a trunk.

Layer 2 Troubleshooting Techniques

After you understand how a frame should flow through a Layer 2 portion of the network (that is, through Layer 2 switches), you can begin to troubleshoot a communications issue by following the path of a frame. For example, you can examine the first switch along the path of a frame. If that switch has not learned the MAC address of the sender, you might need to check hardware and software (for example, the configuration and cabling of a PC) upstream from the switch. Perhaps the first-hop switch did learn the MAC address of the sender, but that MAC address was learned on an inappropriate VLAN. This result could prompt you to check the VLAN configuration of the switch. Alternatively, the switch might have learned the sender's MAC address but not on the port that connects to the sender. This unusual symptom suggests you have a duplicate MAC address.

As a reference, Table 4-2 provides a collection of Cisco Catalyst switch commands that can assist you in troubleshooting basic Layer 2 switch-related issues.

Table 4-2   *Cisco Catalyst Switch Troubleshooting Commands*

Command	Description
clear mac address-table dynamic	Clears dynamically learned MAC addresses from a switch's MAC address table; this can help a troubleshooter determine if a previously learned MAC address is relearned
	NOTE: On some versions of Cisco IOS running on Cisco Catalyst switches, the clear mac address-table command contains a hyphen between mac and address (that is, clear mac-address-table).
show mac address-table	Displays MAC addresses learned by a switch along with each associated port and VLAN of the MAC address
	NOTE: On some versions of Cisco IOS running on Cisco Catalyst switches, the show mac address-table command contains a hyphen between mac and address (that is, show mac-address-table).
show vlan	Shows to which VLANs the ports of a switch belong
show interfaces trunk	Displays which VLANs are permitted on the trunk ports of a switch and which switch ports are configured as trunks
show interfaces switchport	Displays summary information for the ports on a switch, including VLAN and trunk configuration information

Table 4-2 *Cisco Catalyst Switch Troubleshooting Commands* (*Continued*)

Command	Description
traceroute mac source_MAC_address destination_MAC_address	Uses Cisco Discovery Protocol (CDP) information to produce a list of switches to be transited for traffic traveling from a specified source MAC address to a specified destination MAC address

Examples 4-1, 4-2, and 4-3 provide sample output from a few of the commands described in Table 4-2.

Example 4-1   show mac address-table *Command Output*

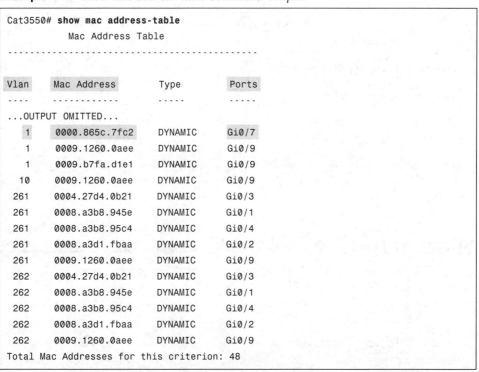

Key
Topic

```
Cat3550# show mac address-table
          Mac Address Table
-------------------------------------------


Vlan    Mac Address       Type        Ports
----    -----------       -----       -----
...OUTPUT OMITTED...
   1    0000.865c.7fc2    DYNAMIC     Gi0/7
   1    0009.1260.0aee    DYNAMIC     Gi0/9
   1    0009.b7fa.d1e1    DYNAMIC     Gi0/9
  10    0009.1260.0aee    DYNAMIC     Gi0/9
 261    0004.27d4.0b21    DYNAMIC     Gi0/3
 261    0008.a3b8.945e    DYNAMIC     Gi0/1
 261    0008.a3b8.95c4    DYNAMIC     Gi0/4
 261    0008.a3d1.fbaa    DYNAMIC     Gi0/2
 261    0009.1260.0aee    DYNAMIC     Gi0/9
 262    0004.27d4.0b21    DYNAMIC     Gi0/3
 262    0008.a3b8.945e    DYNAMIC     Gi0/1
 262    0008.a3b8.95c4    DYNAMIC     Gi0/4
 262    0008.a3d1.fbaa    DYNAMIC     Gi0/2
 262    0009.1260.0aee    DYNAMIC     Gi0/9
Total Mac Addresses for this criterion: 48
```

Example 4-2   show vlan *Command Output*

Key
Topic

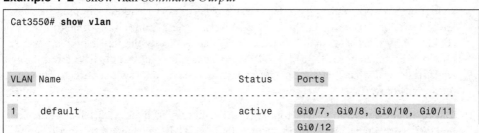

```
Cat3550# show vlan


VLAN Name                            Status    Ports
-----------------------------------------------------------------
1    default                         active    Gi0/7, Gi0/8, Gi0/10, Gi0/11
                                               Gi0/12
```

```
10    VLAN0010                      active
20    SPAN                          active
261   VLAN0261                      active    Gi0/1, Gi0/2, Gi0/3, Gi0/4
                                              Gi0/5, Gi0/6
262   VLAN0262                      active    Gi0/1, Gi0/2, Gi0/3, Gi0/4
...OUTPUT OMITTED...
```

Example 4-3   show interfaces trunk *Command Output*

```
Cat3550# show interfaces trunk


Port          Mode            Encapsulation   Status        Native vlan
Gi0/9         desirable       n-isl           trunking      1


Port          Vlans allowed on trunk
Gi0/9            1-4094


Port                Vlans allowed and active in management domain
Gi0/9               1,10,20,261-262


Port                Vlans in spanning tree forwarding state and not pruned
Gi0/9               1,10,20,261-262
```

Spanning Tree Protocol Troubleshooting

Administrators of corporate telephone networks often boast about their telephone system (that is, a PBX system) having the *five nines* of availability. If a system has five nines of availability, it is available 99.999 percent of the time, which translates to about five minutes of downtime per year.

Traditionally, corporate data networks struggled to compete with corporate voice networks in terms of availability. Today, however, many networks that traditionally carried only data now carry voice, video, and data. Therefore, availability becomes an even more important design consideration.

To improve network availability at Layer 2, many networks have redundant links between Layer 2 switches. However, unlike Layer 3 packets, Layer 2 frames lack a time-to-live (TTL) field. As a result, a Layer 2 frame can circulate endlessly through a looped Layer 2 topology. Fortunately, IEEE 802.1D STP allows a network to physically have Layer 2 loops while strategically blocking data from flowing over one or more switch ports to prevent the looping of traffic.

This section reviews how an STP topology is dynamically formed. Additionally, this section discusses commands useful in troubleshooting STP issues. Finally, the section concludes with a discussion of troubleshooting EtherChannel technology, which can bond multiple physical connections into a single logical connection.

Reviewing STP Operation

STP prevents Layer 2 loops from occurring in a network, because such an occurrence could result in a broadcast storm or a corruption of a switch's MAC address table. Switches in an STP topology are classified as one of the following:

- **Root bridge:** The root bridge is a switch elected to act as a reference point for a spanning tree. The switch with the lowest bridge ID (BID) is elected as the root bridge. The BID is made up of a priority value and a MAC address.

- **Nonroot bridge:** All other switches in the STP topology are considered nonroot bridges.

Figure 4-11 illustrates the root bridge election in a network. Notice that because both bridge priorities are 32768, the switch with the lowest MAC address (that is, SW1) is elected as the root bridge.

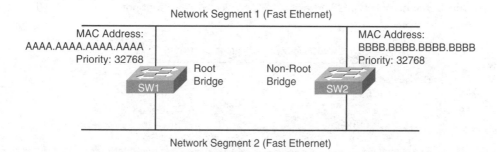

Figure 4-11 *Root Bridge Election*

Ports that interconnect switches in an STP topology are categorized as one of the port types described in Table 4-3 and illustrated in Figure 4-12.

Table 4-3 *STP Port Types*

Port Type	Description
Root port	Every nonroot bridge has a single root port, which is the port on that switch that is closest to the root bridge, in terms of cost.
Designated port	Every network segment has a single designated port, which is the port on that segment that is closest to the root bridge, in terms of cost. Therefore, all ports on a root bridge are designated ports.
Nondesignated port	Nondesignated ports block traffic to create a loop-free topology.

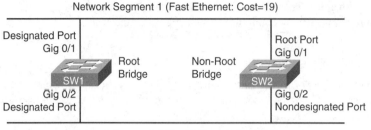

Figure 4-12 *STP Port Types*

Notice the root port for switch SW2 is selected based on the lowest port ID, because the costs of both links are equal. Specifically, each link has a cost of 19, because both links are Fast Ethernet links.

Figure 4-13 shows a similar topology to Figure 4-12. In this figure, however, the top link is running at a speed of 10 Mbps, whereas the bottom link is running at a speed of 100 Mbps. Because switch SW2 seeks to get back to the root bridge (that is, switch SW1) with the least cost, port Gig 0/2 on switch SW2 is selected as the root port.

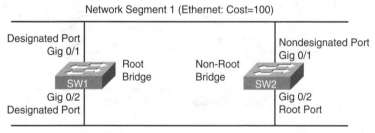

Figure 4-13 *STP with Different Port Costs*

Specifically, port Gig 0/1 has a cost of 100, and Gig 0/2 has a cost of 19. Table 4-4 shows the port costs for various link speeds.

Table 4-4 *Port Costs*

Link Speed	STP Port Cost
10 Mbps (Ethernet)	100
100 Mbps (Fast Ethernet)	19
1 Gbps (Gigabit Ethernet)	4
10 Gbps (Ten Gig Ethernet)	2

Nondesignated ports do not forward traffic during normal operation but do receive bridge protocol data units (BPDUs). BPDU packets contain information on ports, addresses, priorities, and costs and ensure that the data ends up where it was intended to go. BPDU messages are exchanged across bridges to detect loops in a network topology. The loops are then removed by shutting down selected bridge interfaces and placing redundant switch ports in a backup, or blocked, state. If a link in the topology goes down, the nondesignated port detects the link failure and determines whether it needs to transition to the forwarding state.

If a nondesignated port does need to transition to the forwarding state, it does not do so immediately. Rather, it transitions through the following states:

1. **Blocking:** The port remains in the blocking state for 20 seconds by default. During this time the nondesignated port evaluates BPDUs in an attempt to determine its role in the spanning tree.

2. **Listening:** The port moves from the blocking state to the listening state and remains in this state for 15 seconds by default. During this time, the port sources BPDUs, which inform adjacent switches of the port's intent to forward data.

3. **Learning:** The port moves from the listening state to the learning state and remains in this state for 15 seconds by default. During this time, the port begins to add entries to its MAC address table.

4. **Forwarding:** The port moves from the learning state to the forwarding state and begins to forward frames.

Collecting Information About an STP Topology

Some Layer 2 topologies dynamically form a spanning tree using default port costs and bridge priorities. Other Layer 2 topologies have been configured with nondefault port costs or bridge priorities. For example, a network administrator might want to influence a particular switch to become a root bridge to ensure optimal pathing through a Layer 2 topology. The administrator can reduce the bridge priority on the switch he wants to become the root bridge, thus influencing that switch to assume the role of root bridge.

When troubleshooting an STP topology, one of the first tasks is to learn which switch is acting as the root bridge, in addition to learning the port roles on the various switches in the topology. Not only is this information important in understanding how frames are currently flowing through the topology, but comparing the current STP state of a topology to a baseline state can provide clues as to the underlying cause of an issue.

The **show spanning-tree** [**vlan** *vlan_id*] command can display information about the STP state of a switch. Consider Example 4-4, which shows the output from the **show spanning-tree vlan 1** command. The VLAN is specified because Cisco Catalyst switches, by default, use per-VLAN spanning tree (PVST). PVST allows a switch to run a separate STP instance for each VLAN. The output in Example 4-4 shows that switch SW2 is not the root bridge for the spanning tree of VLAN1, because the MAC address of the root bridge is different from the MAC address of switch SW2. The Gig 0/9 port of switch SW2 is the root port of the switch, whereas port Gig 0/10 is a nondesignated port. (That is, it is a blocking port.) Note that the port cost of Gig 0/9 is 19, whereas the port cost of Gig 0/10 is 100.

Example 4-4 show spanning-tree vlan *Command Output*

```
SW2# show spanning-tree vlan 1



VLAN0001
  Spanning tree enabled protocol ieee
  Root ID    Priority    32768
             Address     0009.122e.4181
             Cost        19
             Port        9 (GigabitEthernet0/9)
             Hello Time   2 sec  Max Age 20 sec  Forward Delay 15 sec

  Bridge ID  Priority    32769  (priority 32768 sys-id-ext 1)
             Address     000d.28e4.7c80
             Hello Time   2 sec  Max Age 20 sec  Forward Delay 15 sec
             Aging Time 300


Interface           Role Sts Cost      Prio.Nbr Type
------------------- ---- --- --------- -------- ----------------------------
Gi0/9               Root FWD 19        128.9    P2p
Gi0/10              Altn BLK 100       128.10   Shr
```

The **show spanning-tree interface** *interface_id* **detail** command shows information contained in BPDUs. Also, as shown in Example 4-5, this command displays the number of BPDUs sent and received.

Example 4-5 show spanning-tree interface *Command Output*

```
SW2# show spanning-tree interface gig 0/9 detail
 Port 9 (GigabitEthernet0/9) of VLAN0001 is root forwarding
   Port path cost 19, Port priority 128, Port Identifier 128.9.
   Designated root has priority 32768, address 0009.122e.4181
   Designated bridge has priority 32768, address 0009.122e.4181
   Designated port id is 128.303, designated path cost 0
   Timers: message age 2, forward delay 0, hold 0
   Number of transitions to forwarding state: 1
   Link type is point-to-point by default
   BPDU: sent 1, received 1245
```

STP Troubleshooting Issues

If STP fails to operate correctly, Layer 2 frames can endlessly circulate through a network. This behavior can lead to a couple of major issues: MAC address table corruption and broadcast storms.

Corruption of a Switch's MAC Address Table

The MAC address table of a switch can dynamically learn what MAC addresses are available off of its ports; however, in the event of an STP failure, the MAC address table of a switch can become corrupted. To illustrate, consider Figure 4-14. PC1 is transmitting traffic to PC2. When the frame sent from PC1 is transmitted on segment A, the frame is seen on the Gig 0/1 ports of switches SW1 and SW2, causing both switches to add an entry to their MAC address tables associating a MAC address of AAAA.AAAA.AAAA with port Gig 0/1. Because STP is not functioning, both switches then forward the frame out segment B. As a result, PC2 receives two copies of the frame. Also, switch SW1 sees the frame forwarded out the Gig 0/2 port of switch SW2. Because the frame has a source MAC address of AAAA.AAAA.AAAA, switch SW1 incorrectly updates its MAC address table indicating that a MAC address of AAAA.AAAA.AAAA resides off port Gig 0/2. Similarly, switch SW2 sees the frame forwarded onto segment B by switch SW1 on its Gig 0/2 port. Therefore, switch SW2 also incorrectly updates its MAC address table.

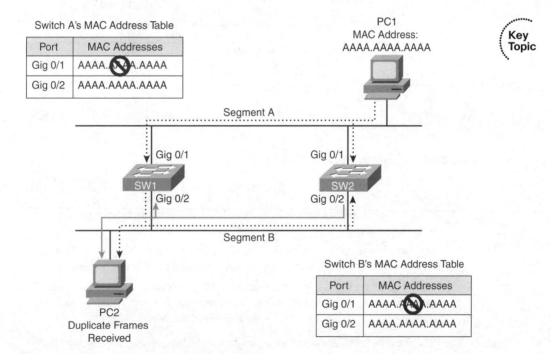

Figure 4-14 *MAC Address Table Corruption*

Broadcast Storms

As previously mentioned, when a switch receives a broadcast frame (that is, a frame destined for a MAC address of FFFF.FFFF.FFFF), the switch floods the frame out all switch ports except the port on which the frame was received. Because a Layer 2 frame does not have a TTL field, a broadcast frame endlessly circulates through the Layer 2 topology, consuming resources on both switches and attached devices (for example, user PCs).

Figure 4-15 illustrates how a broadcast storm can form in a Layer 2 topology when STP is not functioning correctly.

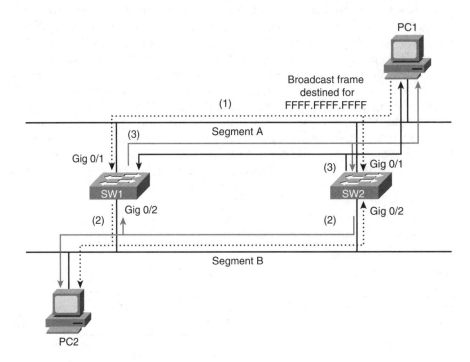

Figure 4-15   *Broadcast Storm*

1. PC1 sends a broadcast frame onto Segment A, and the frame enters each switch on port Gig 0/1.

2. Both switches flood a copy of the broadcast frame out of their Gig 0/2 ports (that is, onto Segment B), causing PC2 to receive two copies of the broadcast frame.

3. Both switches receive a copy of the broadcast frame on their Gig 0/2 ports (that is, from Segment B) and flood the frame out of their Gig 0/1 ports (that is, onto Segment A), causing PC1 to receive two copies of the broadcast frame.

This behavior continues, as the broadcast frame copies continue to loop through the network. The performance of PC1 and PC2 is impacted, because they also continue to receive copies of the broadcast frame.

Troubleshooting EtherChannel

An exception to STP operation can be made if two switches are interconnected via multiple physical links and those links are configured as an *EtherChannel*. An EtherChannel logically combines the bandwidth of multiple physical interfaces into a logical connection between switches, as illustrated in Figure 4-16. Specifically, Figure 4-16 shows four Gigabit Ethernet links logically bonded into a single EtherChannel link.

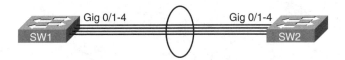

Figure 4-16 *EtherChannel*

When multiple ports are combined into a logical EtherChannel, STP treats the logical bundle as a single port for STP calculation purposes. Following are common troubleshooting targets to consider when troubleshooting an EtherChannel issue:

■ **Mismatched port configurations:** The configurations of all ports making up an EtherChannel, on both switches, should be identical. For example, all ports should have the same speed, duplex, trunk mode, and native VLAN configurations.

■ **Mismatched EtherChannel configuration:** Both switches forming the EtherChannel should be configured for the same EtherChannel negotiation protocol. The options are Link Aggregation Control Protocol (LACP) and Port Aggregation Protocol (PAgP).

■ **Inappropriate EtherChannel distribution algorithm:** EtherChannel determines which physical link to use to transmit frames based on a hash calculation. The hashing approach selected should distribute the load fairly evenly across all physical links. For example, a hash calculation might be based only on the destination MAC address of a frame. If the frames are destined for only a few different MAC addresses, the load distribution could be uneven.

Trouble Ticket: STP

This trouble ticket is the first of a series of trouble tickets presented throughout the remainder of the book. All the trouble tickets are based on the same basic network topology, although addressing and links might vary for some trouble tickets.

All trouble tickets begin with a problem report and a network topology diagram. Some of the trouble tickets provide you with baseline data, and all the trouble tickets offer output from appropriate verification commands (for example, **show** or **debug** commands) that you can examine.

After you hypothesize the underlying cause of the network issue and formulate a solution, you can check the *Suggested Solution* comments to confirm your hypothesis. Realize, however, that some trouble tickets might be resolvable by more than one method. Therefore, your solution might be different from the suggested solution.

Trouble Ticket #1

You receive the following trouble ticket:

> Users on network 192.168.1.0/24 are experiencing latency or no connectivity when attempting to reach network 10.1.2.0/24.

This trouble ticket references the topology shown in Figure 4-17.

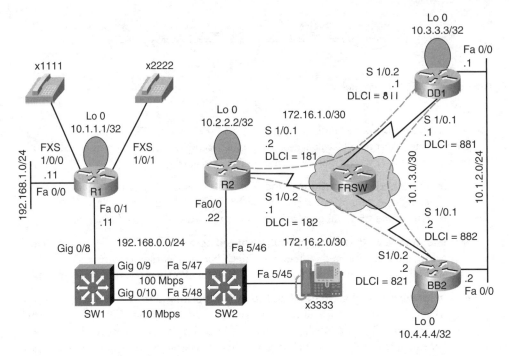

Figure 4-17   *Topology for Trouble Ticket #1*

As you follow the path of the traffic from network 192.168.1.0/24 to 10.1.2.0/24, you notice high port utilization levels on switches SW1 and SW2. Therefore, you decide to investigate these switches further.

You have previously issued **show** commands on these switches as part of your baseline collection process. A selection of the **show** command output is presented in Examples 4-6 and 4-7.

Example 4-6   *Baseline* show *Output from Switch SW1*

```
SW1# show spanning-tree vlan 1

VLAN0001
  Spanning tree enabled protocol ieee
  Root ID    Priority    32768
             Address     0009.122e.4181
             Cost        19
             Port        9 (GigabitEthernet0/9)
             Hello Time  2 sec  Max Age 20 sec  Forward Delay 15 sec
  Bridge ID  Priority    32769  (priority 32768 sys-id-ext 1)
             Address     000d.28e4.7c80
             Hello Time  2 sec  Max Age 20 sec  Forward Delay 15 sec
             Aging Time 300
```

```
Interface          Role Sts Cost      Prio.Nbr Type
------------------- ------------------ ------------------------------------------
Gi0/8              Desg FWD 19        128.8    P2p
Gi0/9              Root FWD 19        128.9    P2p
Gi0/10             Altn BLK 100       128.10   Shr

SW1# show spanning-tree summary
Switch is in pvst mode
Root bridge for: none
Extended system ID              is enabled
Portfast Default                is disabled
PortFast BPDU Guard Default     is disabled
Portfast BPDU Filter Default    is disabled
Loopguard Default               is disabled
EtherChannel misconfig guard    is enabled
UplinkFast                      is disabled
BackboneFast                    is disabled
Configured Pathcost method used is short


Name             Blocking Listening Learning Forwarding STP Active
---------------- -------------------------------------------------------------
VLAN0001                1        0        0          2         3
---------------- -------------------------------------------------------------
1 vlan                  1        0        0          2         3
SW1# show spanning-tree interface gig 0/10 detail
 Port 10 (GigabitEthernet0/10) of VLAN0001 is alternate blocking
   Port path cost 100, Port priority 128, Port Identifier 128.10.
   Designated root has priority 32768, address 0009.122e.4181
   Designated bridge has priority 32768, address 0009.122e.4181
   Designated port id is 128.304, designated path cost 0
   Timers: message age 1, forward delay 0, hold 0
   Number of transitions to forwarding state: 0
   Link type is shared by default
   BPDU: sent 1, received 276
```

Example 4-7   *Baseline* show *Output from Switch SW2*

```
SW2# show spanning-tree vlan 1

VLAN0001
  Spanning tree enabled protocol ieee
  Root ID    Priority    32768
             Address     0009.122e.4181
```

```
                      This bridge is the root
                      Hello Time   2 sec  Max Age 20 sec  Forward Delay 15 sec

       Bridge ID  Priority    32768
                  Address     0009.122e.4181
                  Hello Time   2 sec  Max Age 20 sec  Forward Delay 15 sec
                  Aging Time 300


Interface         Role Sts Cost      Prio.Nbr Type
----------------- ---- --- --------- -------- --------------------------------

Fa5/46            Desg FWD 19        128.302  Shr
Fa5/47            Desg FWD 19        128.303  P2p
Fa5/48            Desg FWD 100       128.304  Shr
```

When you connect to the console of switch SW1, you receive the console messages displayed in Example 4-8.

Example 4-8   *Console Messages on Switch SW1*

```
SW1#
00:15:45: %SW_MATM-4-MACFLAP_NOTIF: Host 0009.b7fa.d1e1 in vlan 1 is flapping
  between port Gi0/8 and port Gi0/9
SW1#
00:16:35: %SW_MATM-4-MACFLAP_NOTIF: Host 0009.b7fa.d1e1 in vlan 1 is flapping
  between port Gi0/8 and port Gi0/9
SW1#
00:16:37: %SW_MATM-4-MACFLAP_NOTIF: Host c001.0e8c.0000 in vlan 1 is flapping
  between port Gi0/9 and port Gi0/10
SW1#
00:16:41: %SW_MATM-4-MACFLAP_NOTIF: Host 0009.b7fa.d1e1 in vlan 1 is flapping
  between port Gi0/8 and port Gi0/9
```

You also issue the **show spanning-tree vlan 1** command on switches SW1 and SW2, as shown in Examples 4-9 and 4-10.

Example 4-9   show spanning-tree vlan 1 *Command Output on Switch SW1*

```
SW1# show spanning-tree vlan 1

Spanning tree instance(s) for vlan 1 does not exist.
```

Example 4-10 show spanning-tree vlan 1 *Command Output on Switch SW2*

```
SW2# show spanning-tree vlan 1

Spanning tree instance(s) for vlan 1 does not exist.
```

Take a moment to look through the baseline information, the topology, and the **show** command output. Then hypothesize the underlying cause for the connectivity issue reported in the trouble ticket. Finally, on a separate sheet of paper, write out a proposed action plan for resolving the reported issue.

Suggested Solution

The **%SW_MATM-4-MACFLAP_NOTIF** console message appearing on switch SW1 indicates that the port of a MAC address in the MAC address table of switch SW1 is flapping between a couple of ports. This is the MAC address table corruption issue discussed previously. The underlying cause of such an issue was STP not functioning correctly.

This suspicion is confirmed from the output in the **show spanning-tree vlan 1** command, issued on switches SW1 and SW2, which indicates that there is no STP instance for VLAN 1 on either switch. Therefore, as a solution, STP could be enabled for VLAN 1 on both switches, which is depicted in Examples 4-11 and 4-12.

Example 4-11 *Enabling STP for VLAN 1 on Switch SW1*

```
SW1# conf term
Enter configuration commands, one per line.   End with CNTL/Z.
SW1(config)# spanning-tree vlan 1
SW1(config)# end
```

Example 4-12 *Enabling STP for VLAN 1 on Switch SW2*

```
SW2# conf term
Enter configuration commands, one per line.   End with CNTL/Z.
SW2(config)# spanning-tree vlan 1
SW2(config)# end
```

After giving STP sufficient time to converge, after the enabling of STP for VLAN 1, the **show spanning-tree vlan 1** is once again issued on switches SW1 and SW2, as illustrated in Examples 4-13 and 4-14. The output in these examples confirms that STP is now functioning correctly.

Example 4-13 *Checking the STP Status for VLAN 1 on Switch SW1*

```
SW1# show spanning-tree vlan 1
...OUTPUT OMITTED...
```

```
Interface         Role Sts Cost      Prio.Nbr Type
----------------------------------------------------------------------
Gi0/8             Desg FWD 19        128.8    P2p
Gi0/9             Root FWD 19        128.9    P2p
Gi0/10            Altn BLK 100       128.10   Shr
```

Example 4-14   *Checking the STP Status for VLAN 1 on Switch SW2*

```
SW2# show spanning-tree vlan 1
...OUTPUT OMITTED...
Interface         Role Sts Cost      Prio.Nbr Type
----------------------------------------------------------------------
Fa5/46            Desg FWD 19        128.302  Shr
Fa5/47            Desg FWD 19        128.303  P2p
Fa5/48            Desg FWD 100       128.304  Shr
```

Exam Preparation Tasks

Review All the Key Topics

Review the most important topics from inside the chapter, noted with the Key Topics icon in the outer margin of the page. Table 4-5 lists these key topics and the page numbers where each is found.

Key Topic

Table 4-5   *Key Topics for Chapter 4*

Key Topic Element	Description	Page Number
List	Possible reasons for a Layer 2 issue	87
Table 4-2	Cisco Catalyst switch troubleshooting commands	88
Example 4-1	The **show mac address-table** command	89
Example 4-2	The **show vlan** command	89
Example 4-3	The **show interfaces trunk** command	90
List	STP bridge types	91
Table 4-3	STP port types	91
Table 4-4	STP port costs	92
List	STP forwarding states	93
Example 4-4	The **show spanning-tree vlan** command	94
Figure 4-14	MAC address table corruption	95
Figure 4-15	Broadcast storm	96
List	Common EtherChannel issues	97

Complete Tables and Lists from Memory

Print a copy of Appendix B, "Memory Tables" (found on the CD), or at least the section for this chapter, and complete the tables and lists from memory. Appendix C, "Memory Tables Answer Key," also on the CD, includes completed tables and lists to check your work.

Define Key Terms

Define the following key terms from this chapter, and check your answers in the Glossary:

Media Access Control (MAC) address, virtual LAN (VLAN), Address Resolution Protocol (ARP), trunk, Spanning Tree Protocol (STP), root bridge, root port, designated port, non-designated port, blocking, listening, learning, forwarding, EtherChannel

Command Reference to Check Your Memory

This section includes the most important EXEC commands covered in this chapter. To determine how well you have memorized the commands as a side effect of your other studies, cover the left side of the table with a piece of paper; read the descriptions on the right side; and see whether you remember the command.

Table 4-6 *Chapter 4 EXEC Command Reference*

Command	Description
clear mac address-table dynamic	Clears dynamically learned MAC addresses from the MAC address table of a switch; this can allow a troubleshooter to determine whether a previously learned MAC address is relearned
	NOTE: On some versions of Cisco IOS running on Cisco Catalyst switches, the **clear mac address-table** command contains a hyphen between **mac** and **address** (that is, **clear mac-address-table**).
show vlan	Shows to which VLANs the ports of a switch belong
show interfaces trunk	Displays what VLANs are permitted on the trunk ports of a switch and what switch ports are configured as trunks
show interfaces switchport	Displays summary information for the ports on a switch, including VLAN and trunk configuration information
traceroute mac source_MAC address destination_MAC_address	Uses CDP information to produce a list of switches to be transited for traffic traveling from a specified source MAC address to a specified destination MAC address
show spanning-tree [vlan vlan_id]	Displays information about the STP state of a switch
show spanning-tree interface interface_id detail	Shows information contained in BPDUs, in addition to the number of BPDUs sent and received

This chapter covers the following subjects:

Resolving InterVLAN Routing Issues: This section begins by contrasting Layer 3 switches and routers. Troubleshooting procedures are also compared for these platforms. Lastly, this section discusses two approaches for routing packets using Layer 3 switches: routed ports and Switched Virtual Interfaces (SVIs).

Router Redundancy Troubleshooting: This section discusses three approaches to providing first-hop router redundancy. Options include: Hot Standby Routing Protocol (HSRP), Virtual Router Redundancy Protocol (VRRP), and Gateway Load Balancing Protocol (GLBP). Troubleshooting strategies are discussed for HSRP with suggestions on how to modify those strategies for troubleshooting VRRP and GLBP.

Cisco Catalyst Switch Performance Tuning: This section examines the architecture of a Cisco Catalyst switch and points out different architectural components that could become troubleshooting targets. Also, you are presented with a series of **show** commands used to gather information about different aspects of a switch's performance.

Trouble Ticket: HSRP: This section presents you with a trouble ticket and an associated topology. You are also given **show** and **debug** command output (baseline output and output collected after a reported issue occurred). Based on the information provided, you hypothesize an underlying cause for the reported issue and develop a solution. You can then compare your solution with a suggested solution.

CHAPTER 5

Advanced Cisco Catalyst Switch Troubleshooting

This chapter builds on Chapter 4, "Basic Cisco Catalyst Switch Troubleshooting," by continuing to focus on troubleshooting Cisco Catalyst Switch platforms. Although the term *switch* might conjure up the image of a Layer 2 device, many modern switches can also route. Specifically, many switches can make forwarding decisions based on Layer 3 information (for example, IP address information). Therefore, this chapter starts by discussing a couple of ways to make a Layer 3 (or multilayer) switch perform routing.

Next, because many Layer 3 switches reside in a wiring closet, these switches might very well act as the default gateway for endpoints (for example, user PCs). Rather than having this switch (or perhaps a router at the distribution layer) become a single point of failure for endpoints relying on the IP address maintained by that switch (or router), you can take advantage of a first-hop redundancy protocol. A first-hop redundancy protocol allows clients to continue to reach their default gateway's IP address, even if the Layer 3 switch or router that had been servicing that IP address becomes available. This chapter contrasts three first-hop redundancy protocols and discusses the troubleshooting of first-hop redundancy.

Often a trouble reported by a user comes in some variation of, "The network is slow." Although such a description is less than insightful, troubleshooters are likely to encounter network performance issues resulting in a poor user experience. This chapter focuses on troubleshooting performance problems that originate from a Cisco Catalyst switch.

Finally, this chapter presents another trouble ticket. This trouble ticket describes a first-hop redundancy protocol not operating as expected. Given a collection of **show** and **debug** output, you are challenged to determine the underlying cause of the issue and formulate a solution.

"Do I Know This Already?" Quiz

The "Do I Know This Already?" quiz helps you determine your level of knowledge of this chapter's topics before you begin. Table 5-1 details the major topics discussed in this chapter and their corresponding quiz questions.

Table 5-1 *"Do I Know This Already?" Section-to-Question Mapping*

Foundation Topics Section	Questions
Resolving InterVLAN Routing Issues	1–3

continues

Table 5-1   *"Do I Know This Already?" Section-to-Question Mapping   (Continued)*

Foundation Topics Section	Questions
Router Redundancy Troubleshooting	4–7
Cisco Catalyst Switch Performance Troubleshooting	8 10

1. What are two differences between Layer 3 switches and routers? (Choose two.)

   a. Layer 3 switches do not maintain a routing table.

   b. Layer 3 switches usually forward traffic faster than routers.

   c. Layer 3 switches support more interface types than routers.

   d. Layer 3 switches usually support fewer features than routers.

2. What type of special memory is used by Layer 3 switches, and not routers, that supports very rapid route lookups?

   a. NBAR

   b. TCAM

   c. NetFlow

   d. MIB

3. What type of interface can be created on a Layer 3 switch to support routing between VLANs on that switch?

   a. BVI

   b. VPI

   c. SVI

   d. VCI

4. What is the default priority for an HSRP interface?

   a. 0

   b. 100

   c. 256

   d. 1000

5. What is the name for the router in a VRRP virtual router group that is actively forwarding traffic on behalf of the virtual router group?

   a. virtual forwarder

   b. active virtual gateway

   c. virtual router master

   d. active virtual forwarder

6. Which of the following statements is true concerning GLBP?

    a. GLBP is an industrial-standard first-hop redundancy protocol.

    b. GLBP allows multiple routers to simultaneously forward traffic for the group of GLBP routers.

    c. The active virtual forwarder in a GLBP group is responsible for responding to ARP requests with different MAC addresses.

    d. A GLBP group has multiple active virtual gateways.

7. Which of the following are a Cisco proprietary first-hop router redundancy protocols? (Choose two.)

    a. HSRP

    b. VRRP

    c. GLBP

    d. DSCP

8. What are two components of a switch's control plane? (Choose two.)

    a. Backplane

    b. Memory

    c. CPU

    d. Forwarding logic

9. Which three of the following are situations when a switch's TCAM would punt a packet to the switch's CPU? (Choose the three best answers.)

    a. OSPF sends a multicast routing update.

    b. An administrator Telnets to a switch.

    c. An ACL is applied to a switch port.

    d. A switch's TCAM has reached capacity.

10. The output of a **show processes cpu** command on a switch displays the following in the first line of the output:

```
CPU utilization for five seconds: 10%/7%; one minute: 12%; five minutes: 6%
```

Based on the output, what percent of the switch's CPU is being consumed with interrupts?

    a. 10 percent

    b. 7 percent

    c. 12 percent

    d. 6 percent

Foundation Topics

Resolving InterVLAN Routing Issues

As mentioned in Chapter 4, "Basic Cisco Catalyst Switch Troubleshooting," for traffic to pass from one VLAN to another VLAN, that traffic has to be routed. Several years ago, one popular approach to performing interVLAN routing with a Layer 2 switch was to create a *router on a stick* topology, where a Layer 2 switch is interconnected with a router via a trunk connection, as seen in Figure 5-1.

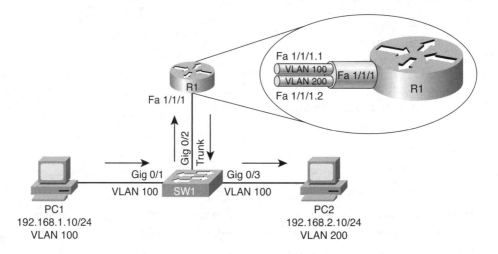

Figure 5-1   *Router on a Stick*

In Figure 5-1, router R1's Fast Ethernet 1/1/1 interface has two subinterfaces, one for each VLAN. Router R1 can route between VLANs 100 and 200, while simultaneously receiving and transmitting traffic over the trunk connection to the switch.

More recently, many switches have risen above their humble Layer 2 beginnings and started to route traffic. Some literature refers to these switches that can route as *Layer 3 switches*. Other sources might call such switches *multilayer switches*, because of the capability of a switch to make forwarding decisions based on information from multiple layers of the OSI model.

This section refers to these switches as Layer 3 switches because the focus is on the capability of the switches to route traffic based on Layer 3 information (that is, IP address information). Specifically, this section discusses troubleshooting Layer 3 switch issues and contrasts troubleshooting a Layer 3 switch versus a router.

Contrasting Layer 3 Switches with Routers

Because a Layer 3 switch performs many of the same functions as a router, it is important for a troubleshooter to distinguish between commonalities and differences in these two platforms.

Table 5-2 lists the characteristics that Layer 3 switches and routers have in common, as well as those characteristics that differ.

Table 5-2 *Layer 3 Switch and Router Characteristics: Compare and Contrast*

Layer 3 Switch/Router Shared Characteristics	Layer 3 Switch/Router Differentiating Characteristics
Both can build and maintain a routing table using both statically configured routes and dynamic routing protocols.	Routers usually support a wider selection of interface types (for example, non-Ethernet interfaces).
Both can make packet forwarding decisions based on Layer 3 information (for example, IP addresses).	Switches leverage application-specific integrated circuits (ASIC) to approach wire speed throughput. Therefore, most Layer 3 switches can forward traffic faster than their router counterparts.
	A Cisco IOS version running on routers typically supports more features than a Cisco IOS version running on a Layer 3 switch, because many switches lack the specialized hardware required to run many of the features available on a router.

Control Plane and Data Plane Troubleshooting

Many router and Layer 3 switch operations can be categorized as control plane or data plane operations. For example, routing protocols operate in a router's control plane, whereas the actual forwarding of data is handled by a router's data plane.

Fortunately, the processes involved in troubleshooting control plane operations are identical on both Layer 3 switch and router platforms. For example, the same command-line interface (CLI) commands could be used to troubleshoot an Open Shortest Path First (OSPF) issue on both types of platforms.

Data plane troubleshooting, however, can vary between Layer 3 switches and routers. For example, if you were troubleshooting data throughput issues, the commands you issued might vary between types of platforms, because Layer 3 switches and routers have fundamental differences in the way traffic is forwarded through the device.

First, consider how a router uses Cisco Express Forwarding (CEF) to efficiently forward traffic through a router. CEF creates a couple of tables that reside at the data plane. These are the *forwarding information base* (FIB) and the *adjacency table*. These tables are constructed from information collected from the router's control plane (for example, the control plane's IP routing table and Address Resolution Protocol [ARP] cache). When troubleshooting a router, you might check control plane operations with commands such as **show ip route**. However, if the observed traffic behavior seems to contradict information shown in the output of control plane verification commands, you might want to examine information contained in the router's CEF Forwarding Information Base (FIB) and adjacency tables. You can use the commands presented in Table 5-3 to view information contained in a router's FIB and adjacency table.

Table 5-3   *Router Data Plan Verification Commands*

Command	Description
show ip cef	Displays the router's Layer 3 forwarding information, in addition to multicast, broadcast, and local IP addresses.
show adjacency	Verifies that a valid adjacency exists for a connected host.

Example 5-1 and Example 5-2 provide sample output from the **show ip cef** and **show adjacency** commands, respectively.

Example 5-1   show ip cef *Command Output*

```
R4# show ip cef
Prefix               Next Hop          Interface
0.0.0.0/0            10.3.3.1          FastEthernet0/0
0.0.0.0/32           receive
10.1.1.0/24          10.3.3.1          FastEthernet0/0
10.1.1.2/32          10.3.3.1          FastEthernet0/0
10.3.3.0/24          attached          FastEthernet0/0
10.3.3.0/32          receive
10.3.3.1/32          10.3.3.1          FastEthernet0/0
10.3.3.2/32          receive
10.3.3.255/32        receive
10.4.4.0/24          10.3.3.1          FastEthernet0/0
10.5.5.0/24          10.3.3.1          FastEthernet0/0
10.7.7.0/24          10.3.3.1          FastEthernet0/0
10.7.7.2/32          10.3.3.1          FastEthernet0/0
10.8.8.0/24          attached          FastEthernet0/1
10.8.8.0/32          receive
10.8.8.1/32          receive
10.8.8.4/32          10.8.8.4          FastEthernet0/1
10.8.8.5/32          10.8.8.5          FastEthernet0/1
10.8.8.6/32          10.8.8.6          FastEthernet0/1
10.8.8.7/32          10.8.8.7          FastEthernet0/1
10.8.8.255/32        receive
192.168.0.0/24       10.3.3.1          FastEthernet0/0
224.0.0.0/4          drop
224.0.0.0/24         receive
255.255.255.255/32   receive
```

Example 5-2   show adjacency *Command Output*

```
R4# show adjacency
Protocol  Interface              Address
IP        FastEthernet0/0        10.3.3.1(21)
IP        FastEthernet0/1        10.8.8.6(5)
IP        FastEthernet0/1        10.8.8.7(5)
IP        FastEthernet0/1        10.8.8.4(5)
IP        FastEthernet0/1        10.8.8.5(5)
```

Although many Layer 3 switches also leverage CEF to efficiently route packets, some Cisco Catalyst switches take the information contained in CEF's FIB and adjacency table and compile that information into Ternary Content Addressable Memory (TCAM). This special memory type uses a mathematical algorithm to very quickly look up forwarding information.

The specific way a switch's TCAM operates depends on the switch platform. However, from a troubleshooting perspective, you can examine information stored in a switch's TCAM using the **show platform** series of commands on Cisco Catalyst 3560, 3750, and 4500 switches. Similarly, TCAM information for a Cisco Catalyst 6500 switch can be viewed with the **show mls cef** series of commands.

Comparing Routed Switch Ports and Switched Virtual Interfaces

On a router, an interface often has an IP address, and that IP address might be acting as a default gateway to hosts residing off of that interface. However, if you have a Layer 3 switch with multiple ports belonging to a VLAN, where should the IP address be configured?

You can configure the IP address for a collection of ports belonging to a VLAN under a virtual VLAN interface. This virtual VLAN interface is called a *Switched Virtual Interface* (SVI). Figure 5-2 shows a topology using SVIs, and Example 5-3 shows the corresponding configuration. Notice that two SVIs are created: one for each VLAN (that is, VLAN 100 and VLAN 200). An IP address is assigned to an SVI by going into interface configuration mode for a VLAN. In this example, because both SVIs are local to the switch, the switch's routing table knows how to forward traffic between members of the two VLANs.

Example 5-3   *SVI Configuration*

Key
Topic

```
Cat3550# show run
...OUTPUT OMITTED...
!
interface GigabitEthernet0/7
 switchport access vlan 100
 switchport mode access
!
interface GigabitEthernet0/8
 switchport access vlan 100
 switchport mode access
```

```
!
interface GigabitEthernet0/9
 switchport access vlan 200
 switchport mode access
!
interface GigabitEthernet0/10
 switchport access vlan 200
 switchport mode access
!
...OUTPUT OMITTED...
!
interface Vlan100
 ip address 192.168.1.1 255.255.255.0
!
interface Vlan200
 ip address 192.168.2.1 255.255.255.0
```

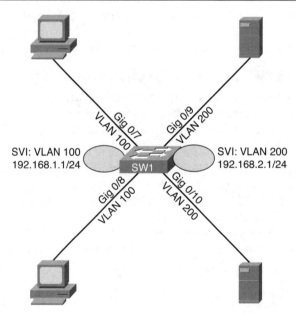

Figure 5-2 *SVI Used for Routing*

Although SVIs can route between VLANs configured on a switch, a Layer 3 switch can be
configured to act more as a router (for example, in an environment where you are replacing
a router with a Layer 3 switch) by using *routed ports* on the switch. Because the ports on
many Cisco Catalyst switches default to operating as switch ports, you can issue the **no
switchport** command in interface configuration mode to convert a switch port to a routed
port. Figure 5-3 and Example 5-4 illustrate a Layer 3 switch with its Gigabit Ethernet 0/9
and 0/10 ports configured as routed ports.

Figure 5-3   *Routed Ports on a Layer 3 Switch*

Example 5-4   *Configuration for Routed Ports on a Layer 3 Switch*

```
Cat3550# show run
...OUTPUT OMITTED...
!
interface GigabitEthernet0/9
 no switchport
 ip address 192.168.1.2 255.255.255.0
!
interface GigabitEthernet0/10
 no switchport
 ip address 192.168.2.2 255.255.255.0
!
...OUTPUT OMITTED...
```

When troubleshooting Layer 3 switching issues, keep the following distinctions in mind between SVIs and routed ports:

■ A routed port is considered to be in the down state if it is not operational at both Layer 1 and Layer 2.

■ An SVI is considered to be in a down state only when none of the ports in the corresponding VLAN are active.

■ A routed port does not run switch port protocols such as Spanning Tree Protocol (STP) or Dynamic Trunking Protocol (DTP).

Router Redundancy Troubleshooting

Many devices, such as PCs, are configured with a *default gateway*. The default gateway parameter identifies the IP address of a next-hop router. As a result, if that router were to become unavailable, devices that relied on the default gateway's IP address would be unable to send traffic off their local subnet.

Fortunately, Cisco offers technologies that provide next-hop gateway redundancy. These technologies include HSRP, VRRP, and GLBP.

This section reviews the operation of these three *first-hop redundancy protocols* and provides a collection of Cisco IOS commands that can be used to troubleshoot an issue with one of these three protocols.

Note that although this section discusses *router* redundancy, keep in mind that the term *router* is referencing a device making forwarding decisions based on Layer 3 information.

Therefore, in your environment, a Layer 3 switch might be used in place of a router to support HSRP, VRRP, or GLBP.

HSRP

Hot Standby Router Protocol (HSRP) uses virtual IP and MAC addresses. One router, known as the *active router*, services requests destined for the virtual IP and MAC addresses. Another router, known as the *standby router*, can service such requests in the event the active router becomes unavailable. Figure 5-4 illustrates a basic HSRP topology.

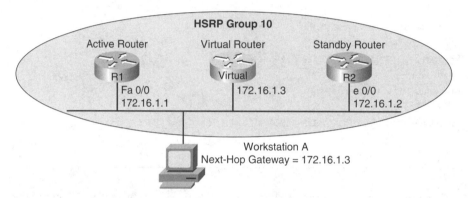

Figure 5-4   *Basic HSRP Operation*

Examples 5-5 and 5-6 show the HSRP configuration for routers R1 and R2.

Example 5-5   *HSRP Configuration on Router R1*

```
R1# show run
...OUTPUT OMITTED...
interface FastEthernet0/0
 ip address 172.16.1.1 255.255.255.0
 standby 10 ip 172.16.1.3
 standby 10 priority 150
 standby 10 preempt
...OUTPUT OMITTED...
```

Example 5-6   *HSRP Configuration on Router R2*

```
R2# show run
...OUTPUT OMITTED...
interface Ethernet0/0
 ip address 172.16.1.2 255.255.255.0
 standby 10 ip 172.16.1.3
...OUTPUT OMITTED...
```

Notice that both routers R1 and R2 have been configured with the same virtual IP address of 172.16.1.3 for an HSRP group of 10. Router R1 is configured to be the active router with the **standby 10 priority 150** command. Router R2 has a default HSRP priority of 100 for group 10, and with HSRP, higher priority values are more preferable. Also, notice that router R1 is configured with the **standby 10 preempt** command, which means that if router R1 loses its active status, perhaps because it is powered off, it will regain its active status when it again becomes available.

Converging After a Router Failure

By default, HSRP sends hello messages every three seconds. Also, if the standby router does not hear a hello message within ten seconds by default, the standby router considers the active router to be down. The standby router then assumes the active role.

Although this ten-second convergence time applies for a router becoming unavailable for a reason such as a power outage or a link failure, convergence happens more rapidly if an interface is administratively shut down. Specifically, an active router sends a *resign* message if its active HSRP interface is shut down.

Also, consider the addition of another router to the network segment whose HSRP priority for group 10 is higher than 150. If it were configured for preemption, the newly added router would send a *coup* message, to inform the active router that the newly added router was going to take on the active role. If, however, the newly added router were not configured for preemption, the currently active router would remain the active router.

HSRP Verification and Troubleshooting

When verifying an HSRP configuration or troubleshooting an HSRP issue, you should begin by determining the following information about the HSRP group under inspection:

■ Which router is the active router

■ Which routers, if any, are configured with the preempt option

■ What is the virtual IP address

■ What is the virtual MAC address

The **show standby brief** command can be used to show a router's HSRP interface, HSRP group number, and preemption configuration. Additionally, this command identifies the router that is currently the active router, the router that is currently the standby router, and the virtual IP address for the HSRP group. Examples 5-7 and 5-8 show the output from the **show standby brief** command issued on routers R1 and R2, where router R1 is currently the active router.

Example 5-7   show standby brief *Command Output on Router R1*

```
R1# show standby brief
                     P indicates configured to preempt.
                     |
Interface   Grp Prio P State   Active     Standby       Virtual IP
Fa0/0        10  150 P Active   local      172.16.1.2    172.16.1.3
```

Example 5-8 show standby brief *Command Output on Router R2*

```
R2# show standby brief
                     P indicates configured to preempt.
                     |
 Interface   Grp Prio P State     Active        Standby       Virtual IP
 Et0/0        10  100    Standby   172.16.1.1    local         172.16.1.3
```

In addition to an interface's HSRP group number, the interface's state, and the HSRP group's virtual IP address, the **show standby** *interface_id* command also displays the HSRP group's virtual MAC address. Issuing this command on router R1, as shown in Example 5-9, shows that the virtual MAC address for HSRP group 10 is **0000.0c07.ac0a**.

Example 5-9 show standby fa 0/0 *Command Output on Router R1*

```
R1# show standby fa 0/0
FastEthernet0/0 - Group 10
  State is Active
    1 state change, last state change 01:20:00
  Virtual IP address is 172.16.1.3
  Active virtual MAC address is 0000.0c07.ac0a
    Local virtual MAC address is 0000.0c07.ac0a (v1 default)
  Hello time 3 sec, hold time 10 sec
    Next hello sent in 1.044 secs
  Preemption enabled
  Active router is local
  Standby router is 172.16.1.2, priority 100 (expires in 8.321 sec)
  Priority 150 (configured 150)
  IP redundancy name is "hsrp-Fa0/0-10" (default)
```

The default virtual MAC address for an HSRP group, as seen in Figure 5-5, is based on the HSRP group number. Specifically, the virtual MAC address for an HSRP group begins with a vendor code of **0000.0c**, followed with a well-known HSRP code of **07.ac**. The last two hexadecimal digits are the hexadecimal representation of the HSRP group number. For example, an HSRP group of 10 yields a default virtual MAC address of **0000.0c07.ac0a**, because **10** in decimal equates to **0a** in hexadecimal.

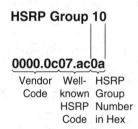

Figure 5-5 *HSRP Virtual MAC Address*

Once you know the current HSRP configuration, you might then check to see if a host on the HSRP virtual IP address' subnet can ping the virtual IP address. Based on the topology previously shown in Figure 5-4, Example 5-10 shows a successful ping from Workstation A.

Example 5-10   *Ping Test from Workstation A to the HSRP Virtual IP Address*

```
C:\>ping 172.16.1.3

Pinging 172.16.1.3 with 32 bytes of data:

Reply from 172.16.1.3: bytes=32 time=2ms TTL=255
Reply from 172.16.1.3: bytes=32 time=1ms TTL=255
Reply from 172.16.1.3: bytes=32 time=1ms TTL=255
Reply from 172.16.1.3: bytes=32 time=1ms TTL=255

Ping statistics for 172.16.1.3:
    Packets: Sent = 4, Received = 4, Lost = 0 (0% loss),
Approximate round trip times in milli-seconds:
    Minimum = 1ms, Maximum = 2ms, Average = 1ms
```

A client could also be used to verify the appropriate virtual MAC address learned by the client corresponding to the virtual MAC address reported by one of the HSRP routers. Example 5-11 shows Workstation A's ARP cache entry for the HSRP virtual IP address of 172.16.1.3. Notice in the output that the MAC address learned via ARP does match the HSRP virtual MAC address reported by one of the HSRP routers.

Example 5-11   *Workstation A's ARP Cache*

```
C:\>arp -a

Interface: 172.16.1.4 --- 0x4
  Internet Address      Physical Address      Type
  172.16.1.3            00-00-0c-07-ac-0a     dynamic
```

You can use the **debug standby terse** command to view important HSRP changes, such as a state change. Example 5-12 shows this **debug** output on router R2 because router R1's Fast Ethernet 0/0 interface is shut down. Notice that router R2's state changes from Standby to Active.

Example 5-12   **debug standby terse** *Command Output on Router R2: Changing HSRP to Active*

```
R2#
*Mar  1 01:25:45.930: HSRP: Et0/0 Grp 10 Standby: c/Active timer expired
  (172.16.1.1)
```

```
*Mar  1 01:25:45.930: HSRP: Et0/0 Grp 10 Active router is local, was 172.16.1.1
*Mar  1 01:25:45.930: HSRP: Et0/0 Grp 10 Standby router is unknown, was local
*Mar  1 01:25:45.930: HSRP: Et0/0 Grp 10 Standby -> Active
*Mar  1 01:25:45.930: %HSRP-6-STATECHANGE: Ethernet0/0 Grp 10 state Standby ->
  Active
*Mar  1 01:25:45.930: HSRP: Et0/0 Grp 10 Redundancy "hsrp-Et0/0-10" state Standby
  -> Active
*Mar  1 01:25:48.935: HSRP: Et0/0 Grp 10 Redundancy group hsrp-Et0/0-10 state
  Active -> Active
*Mar  1 01:25:51.936: HSRP: Et0/0 Grp 10 Redundancy group hsrp-Et0/0-10 state
  Active -> Active
```

When router R1's Fast Ethernet 0/0 interface is administratively brought up, router R1 reassumes its previous role as the active HSRP router for HSRP group 10, because router R1 is configured with the preempt option. The output shown in Example 5-13 demonstrates how router R2 receives a coup message, letting router R2 know that router R1 is taking back its active role.

Example 5-13 debug standby terse *Command Output on Router R2: Changing HSRP to Standby*

```
R2#
*Mar  1 01:27:57.979: HSRP: Et0/0 Grp 10 Coup   in  172.16.1.1 Active  pri 150
  vIP 172.16.1.3
*Mar  1 01:27:57.979: HSRP: Et0/0 Grp 10 Active: j/Coup rcvd from higher pri
  router (150/172.16.1.1)
*Mar  1 01:27:57.979: HSRP: Et0/0 Grp 10 Active router is 172.16.1.1, was local
*Mar  1 01:27:57.979: HSRP: Et0/0 Grp 10 Active -> Speak
*Mar  1 01:27:57.979: %HSRP-6-STATECHANGE: Ethernet0/0 Grp 10 state Active -> Speak
*Mar  1 01:27:57.979: HSRP: Et0/0 Grp 10 Redundancy "hsrp-Et0/0-10" state Active
  -> Speak
*Mar  1 01:28:07.979: HSRP: Et0/0 Grp 10 Speak: d/Standby timer expired (unknown)
*Mar  1 01:28:07.979: HSRP: Et0/0 Grp 10 Standby router is local
*Mar  1 01:28:07.979: HSRP: Et0/0 Grp 10 Speak -> Standby
*Mar  1 01:28:07.979: HSRP: Et0/0 Grp 10 Redundancy "hsrp-Et0/0-10" state Speak
  -> Standby
```

VRRP

Virtual Router Redundancy Protocol (VRRP), similar to HSRP, allows a collection of routers to service traffic destined for a single IP address. Unlike HSRP, the IP address serviced by a VRRP group does not have to be a virtual IP address. The IP address can be the address of a physical interface on the *virtual router master*, which is the router responsible for forwarding traffic destined for the VRRP group's IP address. A VRRP group can have multiple routers acting as *virtual router backups*, as shown in Figure 5-6, any of which could take over in the event of the virtual router master becoming unavailable.

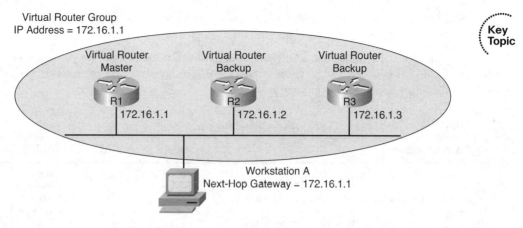

Figure 5-6 *Basic VRRP Operation*

GLBP

Gateway Load Balancing Protocol (GLBP) can load balance traffic destined for a next-hop gateway across a collection of routers, known as a *GLBP group*. Specifically, when a client sends an Address Resolution Protocol (ARP) request, in an attempt to determine the MAC address corresponding to a known IP address, GLBP can respond with the MAC address of one member of the GLBP group. The next such request would receive a response containing the MAC address of a different member of the GLBP group, as depicted in Figure 5-7. Specifically, GLBP has one *active virtual gateway* (AVG), which is responsible for replying to ARP requests from hosts. However, multiple routers acting as *active virtual forwarders* (AVFs) can forward traffic.

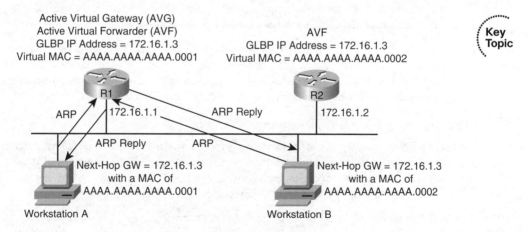

Figure 5-7 *Basic GLBP Operation*

Troubleshooting VRRP and GLBP

Because VRRP and GLBP perform a similar function to HSRP, you can use a similar troubleshooting philosophy. Much like HSRP's **show standby brief** command, similar information can be gleaned for VRRP operation with the **show vrrp brief** command and for GLBP operation with the **show glbp brief** command.

Although HSRP, VRRP, and GLBP have commonalities, it is important for you as a troubleshooter to understand the differences. Table 5-4 compares several characteristics of these first-hop router redundancy protocols.

Table 5-4   *Comparing HSRP, VRRP, and GLBP*

Characteristic	HSRP	VRRP	GLBP
Cisco proprietary	Yes	No	Yes
Interface IP address can act as virtual IP address	No	Yes	No
More than one router in a group can simultaneously forward traffic for that group	No	No	Yes
Hello timer default value	3 seconds	1 second	3 seconds

Cisco Catalyst Switch Performance Troubleshooting

Switch performance issues can be tricky to troubleshoot, because the problem reported is often subjective. For example, if a user reports that the network is running "slow," the user's perception might mean that the network is slow compared to what he expects. However, network performance might very well be operating at a level that is hampering productivity and at a level that is indeed below its normal level of operation. At that point, as part of the troubleshooting process, you need to determine what network component is responsible for the poor performance. Rather than a switch or a router, the user's client, server, or application could be the cause of the performance issue.

If you do determine that the network performance is not meeting technical expectations (as opposed to user expectations), you should isolate the source of the problem and diagnose the problem on that device. This section assumes that you have isolated the device causing the performance issue, and that device is a Cisco Catalyst switch.

Cisco Catalyst Switch Troubleshooting Targets

Cisco offers a variety of Catalyst switch platforms, with different port densities, different levels of performance, and different hardware. Therefore, troubleshooting one of these switches can be platform dependent. Many similarities do exist, however. For example, all Cisco Catalyst switches include the following hardware components:

- **Ports:** A switch's ports physically connect the switch to other network devices. These ports (also known as *interfaces*) allow a switch to receive and transmit traffic.

- **Forwarding logic:** A switch contains hardware that makes forwarding decisions. This hardware rewrites a frame's headers.

- **Backplane:** A switch's backplane physically interconnects a switch's ports. Therefore, depending on the specific switch architecture, frames flowing through a switch enter via a port (that is, the ingress port), flow across the switch's backplane, and are forwarded out of another port (that is, an egress port).

- **Control plane:** A switch's CPU and memory reside in a control plane. This control plane is responsible for running the switch's operating system.

Figure 5-8 depicts these switch hardware components. Notice that the control plane does not directly participate in frame forwarding. However, the forwarding logic contained in the forwarding hardware comes from the control plane. Therefore, there is an indirect relationship between frame forwarding and the control plane. As a result, a continuous load on the control plane could, over time, impact the rate at which the switch forwards frames. Also, if the forwarding hardware is operating at maximum capacity, the control plane begins to provide the forwarding logic. So, although the control plane does not architecturally appear to impact switch performance, it should be considered when troubleshooting.

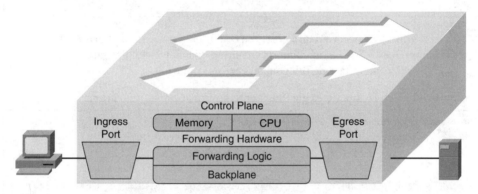

Figure 5-8   *Cisco Catalyst Switch Hardware Components*

The following are two common troubleshooting targets to consider when diagnosing a suspected switch issue:

- Port errors
- Mismatched duplex settings

The sections that follow evaluate these target areas in greater detail.

Port Errors

When troubleshooting a suspected Cisco Catalyst switch issue, a good first step is to check port statistics. For example, examining port statistics can let a troubleshooter know if an excessive number of frames are being dropped. If a TCP application is running slow, the reason might be that TCP flows are going into *TCP slow start*, which causes the window size, and therefore the bandwidth efficiency, of TCP flows to be reduced. A common reason that a TCP flow enters slow start is packet drops. Similarly, packet drops for a UDP flow used for voice or video could result in noticeable quality degradation, because dropped UDP segments are not retransmitted.

Although dropped frames are most often attributed to network congestion, another possibility is that the cabling could be bad. To check port statistics, a troubleshooter could leverage a **show interfaces** command. Consider Example 5-14, which shows the output of the **show interfaces gig 0/9 counters** command on a Cisco Catalyst 3550 switch. Notice that this output shows the number of inbound and outbound frames seen on the specified port.

Example 5-14   show interfaces gig 0/9 counters *Command Output*

```
SW1# show interfaces gig 0/9 counters

Port              InOctets    InUcastPkts    InMcastPkts    InBcastPkts
Gi0/9             31265148          20003           3179              1


Port             OutOctets   OutUcastPkts   OutMcastPkts   OutBcastPkts
Gi0/9             18744149           9126             96              6
```

To view errors that occurred on a port, you could add the keyword of **errors** after the **show interfaces** *interface_id* **counters** command. Example 5-15 illustrates sample output from the **show interfaces gig 0/9 counters errors** command.

Example 5-15   show interfaces gig 0/9 counters errors *Command Output*

```
SW1# show interfaces gig 0/9 counters errors
Port           Align-Err      FCS-Err     Xmit-Err     Rcv-Err  UnderSize
Gi0/9                  0            0            0           0          0


Port         Single-Col  Multi-Col   Late-Col Excess-Col Carri-Sen     Runts     Giants
Gi0/9              5603          0       5373          0          0         0          0
```

Table 5-5 provides a reference for the specific errors that might show up in the output of the **show interfaces** *interface_id* **counters errors** command.

Table 5-5   *Errors in the* **show interfaces interface_id counters errors** *Command*

Error Counter	Description
Align-Err	An alignment error occurs when frames do not end with an even number of octets, while simultaneously having a bad Cyclic Redundancy Check (CRC). An alignment error normally suggests a Layer 1 issue, such as cabling or port (either switch port or NIC port) issues.
FCS-Err	A Frame Check Sequence (FCS) error occurs when a frame has an invalid checksum, although the frame has no framing errors. Like the Align-Err error, an FCS-Err often points to a Layer 1 issue.

continues

Table 5-5 *Errors in the* **show interfaces interface_id counters errors** *Command*   *(Continued)*

Error Counter	Description
Xmit-Err	A transmit error (that is, Xmit-Err) occurs when a port's transmit buffer overflows. A speed mismatch between inbound and outbound links often results in a transmit error.
Rcv-Err	A receive error (that is, Rcv-Err) occurs when a port's receive buffer overflows. Congestion on a switch's backplane could cause the receive buffer on a port to fill to capacity, as frames await access to the switch's backplane. However, most likely, a Rcv-Err is indicating a duplex mismatch.
UnderSize	An undersize frame is a frame with a valid checksum but a size less than 64 bytes. This issue suggests that a connected host is sourcing invalid frame sizes.
Single-Col	A Single-Col error occurs when a single collisions occurs before a port successfully transmits a frame. High bandwidth utilization on an attached link or a duplex mismatch are common reasons for a Single-Col error.
Multi-Col	A Multi-Col error occurs when more than one collision occurs before a port successfully transmits a frame. Similar to the Single-Col error, high bandwidth utilization on an attached link or a duplex mismatch are common reasons for a Multi-Col error.
Late-Col	A late collision is a collision that is not detected until well after the frame has begun to be forwarded. While a Late-Col error could indicate that the connected cable is too long, this is an extremely common error seen in mismatched duplex conditions.
Excess-Col	The Excess-Col error occurs when a frame experienced sixteen successive collisions, after which the frame was dropped. This error could result from high bandwidth utilization, a duplex mismatch, or too many devices on a segment.
Carri-Sen	The Carri-Sen counter is incremented when a port wants to send data on a half-duplex link. This is normal and expected on a half-duplex port, because the port is checking the wire, to make sure no traffic is present, prior to sending a frame. This operation is the carrier sense procedure described by the Carrier Sense Multiple Access with Collision Detect (CSMA/CD) operation used on half-duplex connections. Full-duplex connections, however, do not use CSMA/CD.
Runts	A runt is a frame that is less than 64 bytes in size and has a bad CRC. A runt could result from a duplex mismatch or a Layer 1 issue.
Giants	A giant is a frame size greater than 1518 bytes (assuming the frame is not a jumbo frame) that has a bad FCS. Typically, a giant is caused by a problem with the NIC in an attached host.

Mismatched Duplex Settings

As seen in Table 5-5, duplex mismatches can cause a wide variety of port errors. Keep in mind that almost all network devices, other than shared media hubs, can run in full-duplex mode. Therefore, if you have no hubs in your network, all devices should be running in full-duplex mode.

A new recommendation from Cisco is that switch ports be configured to autonegotiate both speed and duplex. Two justifications for this recommendation are as follows:

■   If a connected device only supported half-duplex, it would be better for a switch port to negotiate down to half-duplex and run properly than being forced to run full-duplex which would result in multiple errors.

■   The automatic medium-dependent interface crossover (auto-MDIX) feature can automatically detect if a port needs a crossover or a straight-through cable to interconnect with an attached device and adjust the port to work regardless of which cable type is connected. You can enable this feature in interface configuration mode with the **mdix auto** command on some models of Cisco Catalyst switches. However, the auto-MDIX feature requires that the port autonegotiate both speed and duplex.

In a mismatched duplex configuration, a switch port at one end of a connection is configured for full-duplex, whereas a switch port at the other end of a connection is configured for half-duplex. Among the different errors previously listed in Table 5-5, two of the biggest indicators of a duplex mismatch are a high Rcv-Err counter or a high Late-Col counter. Specifically, a high Rcv-Err counter is common to find on the full-duplex end of a connection with a mismatched duplex, while a high Late-Col counter is common on the half-duplex end of the connection.

To illustrate, examine Examples 5-16 and 5-17, which display output based on the topology depicted in Figure 5-9. Example 5-16 shows the half-duplex end of a connection, and Example 5-17 shows the full-duplex end of a connection.

Figure 5-9   *Topology with Duplex Mismatch*

Example 5-16   *Output from the* **show interfaces gig 0/9 counters errors** *and the* **show interfaces gig 0/9 | include duplex** *Commands on a Half-Duplex Port*

```
SW1# show interfaces gig 0/9 counters errors

Port          Align-Err     FCS-Err    Xmit-Err     Rcv-Err UnderSize
Gi0/9                 0           0           0           0         0


Port        Single-Col Multi-Col  Late-Col Excess-Col Carri-Sen   Runts    Giants
Gi0/9             5603         0      5373          0         0        0         0
```

```
SW1# show interfaces gig 0/9 | include duplex
  Half-duplex, 100Mb/s, link type is auto, media type is 10/100/1000BaseTX
SW1# show interfaces gig 0/9 counters errors
```

Example 5-17   *Output from the* **show interfaces fa 5/47 counters errors** *and the* **show interfaces fa 5/47 | include duplex** *Commands on a Full-Duplex Port*

```
SW2# show interfaces fa 5/47 counters errors


Port          Align-Err      FCS-Err   Xmit-Err    Rcv-Err UnderSize OutDiscards
Fa5/47               0         5248          0       5603        27           0


Port        Single-Col Multi-Col  Late-Col Excess-Col Carri-Sen      Runts     Giants
Fa5/47               0         0         0          0         0        227          0


Port        SQETest-Err Deferred-Tx IntMacTx-Err IntMacRx-Err Symbol-Err
Fa5/47               0           0            0            0          0

SW2# show interfaces fa 5/47 | include duplex
  Full-duplex, 100Mb/s
SW1# show interfaces gig 0/9 counters errors
```

In your troubleshooting, even if you only have access to one of the switches, if you suspect a duplex mismatch, you could change the duplex settings on the switch over which you do have control. Then, you could clear the interface counters to see if the errors continue to increment. You could also perform the same activity (for example, performing a file transfer) the user was performing when he noticed the performance issue. By comparing the current performance to the performance experienced by the user, you might be able to conclude that the problem has been resolved by correcting a mismatched duplex configuration.

TCAM Troubleshooting

As previously mentioned, the two primary components of forwarding hardware are forwarding logic and backplane. A switch's backplane, however, is rarely the cause of a switch performance issue, because most Cisco Catalyst switches have high-capacity backplanes. However, it is conceivable that in a modular switch chassis, the backplane will not have the throughput to support a fully populated modular chassis, where each card in the chassis supports the highest combination of port densities and port speeds.

The architecture of some switches allows groups of switch ports to be handled by separated hardware. Therefore, you might experience a performance gain by simply moving a cable from one switch port to another. However, to strategically take advantage of this design characteristic, you must be very familiar with the architecture of the switch with which you are working.

A multilayer switch's forwarding logic can impact switch performance. Recall that a switch's forwarding logic is compiled into a special type of memory called ternary content addressable memory (TCAM), as illustrated in Figure 5-10. TCAM works with a switch's CEF feature to provide extremely fast forwarding decisions. However, if a switch's TCAM is unable, for whatever reason, to forward traffic, that traffic is forwarded by the switch's CPU, which has a limited forwarding capability.

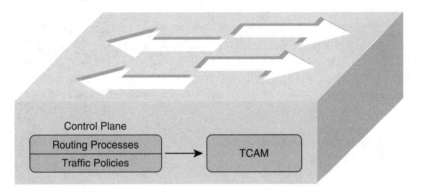

Figure 5-10   *Populating the TCAM*

The process of the TCAM sending packets to a switch's CPU is called *punting*. Consider a few reasons why a packet might be punted from a TCAM to its CPU:

- Routing protocols, in addition to other control plane protocols such as STP, that send multicast or broadcast traffic will have that traffic sent to the CPU.

- Someone connecting to a switch administratively (for example, establishing a Telnet session with the switch) will have their packets sent to the CPU.

- Packets using a feature not supported in hardware (for example, packets traveling over a GRE tunnel) are sent to the CPU.

- If a switch's TCAM has reached capacity, additional packets will be punted to the CPU. A TCAM might reach capacity if it has too many installed routes or configured access control lists.

From the events listed, the event most likely to cause a switch performance issue is a TCAM filling to capacity. Therefore, when troubleshooting switch performance, you might want to investigate the state of the switch's TCAM. Please be sure to check documentation for your switch model, because TCAM verification commands can vary between platforms.

As an example, the Cisco Catalyst 3550 Series switch supports a collection of **show tcam** commands, whereas Cisco Catalyst 3560 and 3750 Series switches support a series of **show platform tcam** commands. Consider the output from the **show tcam inacl 1 statistics** command issued on a Cisco Catalyst 3550 switch, as shown in Example 5-18. The number **1** indicates TCAM number one, because the Cisco Catalyst 3550 has three TCAMs. The **inacl** refers to access control lists applied in the ingress direction. Notice that fourteen masks are allocated, while 402 are available. Similarly, seventeen entries are currently allocated, and 3311 are available. Therefore, you could conclude from this output that TCAM number one is not approaching capacity.

Example 5-18   show tcam inacl 1 statistics *Command Output on a Cisco Catalyst 3550 Series Switch*

```
Cat3550# show tcam inacl 1 statistics
Ingress ACL TCAM#1: Number of active labels: 3
Ingress ACL TCAM#1: Number of masks    allocated:   14, available:   402
Ingress ACL TCAM#1: Number of entries allocated:    17, available: 3311
```

On some switch models (for example, a Cisco Catalyst 3750 platform), you can use the **show platform ip unicast counts** command to see if a TCAM allocation has failed. Similarly, you can use the **show controllers cpu-interface** command to display a count of packets being forwarded to a switch's CPU.

On most switch platforms, TCAMs cannot be upgraded. Therefore, if you conclude that a switch's TCAM is the source of the performance problems being reported, you could either use a switch with higher-capacity TCAMs or reduce the number of entries in a switch's TCAM. For example, you could try to optimize your access control lists or leverage route summarization to reduce the number of route entries maintained by a switch's TCAM. Also, some switches (for example, Cisco Catalyst 3560 or 3750 Series switches) enable you to change the amount of TCAM memory allocated to different switch features. For example, if your switch ports were configured as routing ports, you could reduce the amount of TCAM space used for storing MAC addresses, and instead use that TCAM space for Layer 3 processes.

High CPU Utilization Level Troubleshooting

The load on a switch's CPU is often low, even under high utilization, thanks to the TCAM. Because the TCAM maintains a switch's forwarding logic, the CPU is rarely tasked to forward traffic. The **show processes cpu** command that you earlier learned for use on a router can also be used on a Cisco Catalyst switch to display CPU utilization levels, as demonstrated in Example 5-19.

Example 5-19   show processes cpu *Command Output on a Cisco Catalyst 3550 Series Switch*

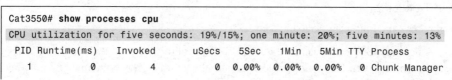

```
Cat3550# show processes cpu
CPU utilization for five seconds: 19%/15%; one minute: 20%; five minutes: 13%
  PID Runtime(ms)    Invoked      uSecs    5Sec    1Min   5Min TTY Process
    1          0          4          0    0.00%   0.00%  0.00%   0 Chunk Manager
```

```
    2             0          610          0   0.00%   0.00%   0.00%    0 Load Meter
    3           128            5      25600   0.00%   0.00%   0.00%    0 crypto sw pk pro
    4          2100          315       6666   0.00%   0.05%   0.05%    0 Check heaps
...OUTPUT OMITTED...
```

Notice in the output in Example 5-19 that the switch is reporting a 19 percent CPU load, with 15 percent of the CPU load used for interrupt processing. The difference between these two numbers is 4, suggesting that 4 percent of the CPU load is consumed with control plane processing.

Although such load utilization values might not be unusual for a router, these values might be of concern for a switch. Specifically, a typical CPU load percentage dedicated to interrupt processing is no more than five percent. A value as high as ten percent is considered acceptable. However, the output given in Example 5-19 shows a fifteen percent utilization. Such a high level implies that the switch's CPU is actively involved in forwarding packets that should normally be handled by the switch's TCAM. Of course, this value might only be of major concern if it varies from baseline information. Therefore, your troubleshooting efforts benefit from having good baseline information.

Periodic spikes in processor utilization are also not a major cause for concern if such spikes can be explained. Consider the following reasons that might cause a switch's CPU utilization to spike:

- The CPU processing routing updates

- Issuing a **debug** command (or other processor-intensive commands)

- Simple Network Management Protocol (SNMP) being used to poll network devices

If you determine that a switch's high CPU load is primarily the result of interrupts, you should examine the switch's packet switching patterns and check the TCAM utilization. If, however, the high CPU utilization is primarily the result of processes, you should investigate those specific processes.

A high CPU utilization on a switch might be a result of STP. Recall that an STP failure could lead to a broadcast storm, where Layer 2 broadcast frames endlessly circulate through a network. Therefore, when troubleshooting a performance issue, realize that a switch's high CPU utilization might be a symptom of another issue.

Trouble Ticket: HSRP

This trouble ticket focuses on HSRP. HSRP was one of three first-hop redundancy protocols discussed in this chapter's "Router Redundancy Troubleshooting" section.

Trouble Ticket #2

You receive the following trouble ticket:

A new network technician configured HSRP on routers BB1 and BB2, where BB1 was the active router. The configuration was initially working; however, now BB2 is acting as the active router, even though BB1 seems to be operational.

This trouble ticket references the topology shown in Figure 5-11.

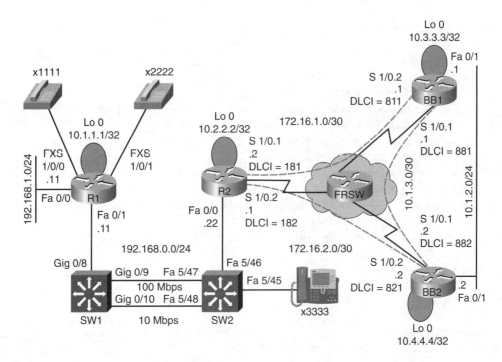

Figure 5-11 *Trouble Ticket #2 Topology*

As you investigate this issue, you examine baseline data collected after HSRP was initially configured. Examples 5-20 and 5-21 provide **show** and **debug** command output collected when HSRP was working properly. Notice that router BB1 was acting as the active HSRP router, whereas router BB2 was acting as the standby HSRP router.

Example 5-20 *Baseline Output for Router BB1*

```
BB1# show standby brief
                         P indicates configured to preempt.
                         |
Interface   Grp Prio P State    Active    Standby      Virtual IP
Fa0/1        1   150    Active    local     172.16.1.3     172.16.1.4

BB1# debug standby
HSRP debugging is on
*Mar  1 01:14:21.487: HSRP: Fa0/1 Grp 1 Hello  in  172.16.1.3 Standby pri 100 vIP
    172.16.1.4
*Mar  1 01:14:23.371: HSRP: Fa0/1 Grp 1 Hello  out 172.16.1.1 Active  pri 150 vIP
    172.16.1.4
```

```
BB1# u all
All possible debugging has been turned off

BB1# show standby fa 0/1 1
FastEthernet0/1 - Group 1
  State is Active
    10 state changes, last state change 00:12:40
  Virtual IP address is 172.16.1.4
  Active virtual MAC address is 0000.0c07.ac01
    Local virtual MAC address is 0000.0c07.ac01 (v1 default)
  Hello time 3 sec, hold time 10 sec
    Next hello sent in 1.536 secs
  Preemption disabled
  Active router is local
  Standby router is 172.16.1.3, priority 100 (expires in 9.684 sec)
  Priority 150 (configured 150)
  IP redundancy name is "hsrp-Fa0/1-1" (default)

BB1# show run
...OUTPUT OMITTED...
hostname BB1
!
interface Loopback0
 ip address 10.3.3.3 255.255.255.255
!
interface FastEthernet0/0
 ip address 10.1.2.1 255.255.255.0
!
interface FastEthernet0/1
 ip address 172.16.1.1 255.255.255.0
 standby 1 ip 172.16.1.4
 standby 1 priority 150
!
router ospf 1
 network 0.0.0.0 255.255.255.255 area 0
```

Example 5-21 *Baseline Output for Router BB2*

```
BB2# show standby brief
                      P indicates configured to preempt.
                    |
```

```
Interface   Grp Prio P State     Active          Standby         Virtual IP
Fa0/1         1  100    Standby   172.16.1.1      local           172.16.1.4


BB2# show run
...OUTPUT OMITTED...
hostname BB2
!
interface Loopback0
 ip address 10.4.4.4 255.255.255.255
!
interface FastEthernet0/0
 ip address 10.1.2.2 255.255.255.0
!
interface FastEthernet0/1
 ip address 172.16.1.3 255.255.255.0
 standby 1 ip 172.16.1.4
!
router ospf 1
 network 0.0.0.0 255.255.255.255 area 0
```

As part of testing the initial configuration, a ping was sent to the virtual IP address of
172.16.1.4 from router R2 in order to confirm that HSRP was servicing requests for that IP
address. Example 5-22 shows the output from the **ping** command.

Example 5-22   *PINGing the Virtual IP Address from Router R2*

```
R2# ping 172.16.1.4
Type escape sequence to abort.
Sending 5, 100-byte ICMP Echos to 172.16.1.4, timeout is 2 seconds:
!!!!!
```

As you begin to gather information about the reported problem, you reissue the **show
standby brief** command on routers BB1 and BB2. As seen in Examples 5-23 and 5-24,
router BB1 is administratively up with an HSRP priority of 150, whereas router BB2 is administratively up with a priority of 100.

Example 5-23   *Examining the HSRP State of Router BB1's FastEthernet 0/1 Interface*

```
BB1# show standby brief
                     P indicates configured to preempt.
                     |
Interface   Grp Prio P State     Active          Standby         Virtual IP
Fa0/1         1  150    Standby   172.16.1.3      local           172.16.1.4
```

Example 5-24   *Examining the HSRP State of Router BB2's FastEthernet 0/1 Interface*

```
BB2# show standby brief
                          P indicates configured to preempt.
                          |
 Interface    Grp Prio P State    Active         Standby        Virtual IP
 Fa0/1        1   100    Active    local          172.16.1.1     172.16.1.4
```

Take a moment to look through the baseline information, the topology, and the **show** command output. Then, hypothesize the underlying cause, explaining why router BB2 is currently the active HSRP router, even thought router BB1 has a higher priority. Finally, on a separate sheet of paper, write out a proposed action plan for resolving the reported issue.

Suggested Solution

Upon examination of BB1's output, it becomes clear that the preempt feature is not enabled for the Fast Ethernet 0/1 interface on BB1. The absence of the preempt feature explains the reported symptom. Specifically, if BB1 had at one point been the active HSRP router for HSRP group 1, and either router BB1 or its Fast Ethernet 0/1 interface became unavailable, BB2 would have become the active router. Then, if BB1 or its Fast Ethernet 0/1 interface once again became available, BB1 would assume a standby HSRP role, because BB1's FastEthernet 0/1 interface was not configured for the preempt feature.

To resolve this configuration issue, the preempt feature is added to BB1's Fast Ethernet 0/1 interface, as shown in Example 5-25. After enabling the preempt feature, notice that router BB1 regains its active HSRP role.

Example 5-25   *Enabling the Preempt Feature on Router BB1's FastEthernet 0/1 Interface*

```
BB1# conf term
Enter configuration commands, one per line.  End with CNTL/Z.
BB1(config)#int fa 0/1
BB1(config-if)#standby 1 preempt
BB1(config-if)#end
BB1#
*Mar  1 01:17:39.607: %HSRP-5-STATECHANGE: FastEthernet0/1 Grp 1 state Standby ->
  Active

BB1#show standby brief
                          P indicates configured to preempt.
                          |
 Interface    Grp Prio P State    Active         Standby        Virtual IP
 Fa0/1        1   150  P Active    local          172.16.1.3     172.16.1.4
```

Exam Preparation Tasks

Review All Key Topics

Review the most important topics from inside the chapter, noted with the Key Topics icon in the outer margin of the page. Table 5-6 lists these key topics and the page numbers where each is found.

Key
Topic

Table 5-6 *Key Topics for Chapter 5*

Key Topic Element	Description	Page Number
Table 5-2	Similarities and differences between routers and Layer 3 switches	111
Table 5-3	Router data plane verification commands	112
Example 5-3	SVI configuration	113
List	Differences between SVIs and routed ports	115
Examples 5-5 and 5-6	HSRP configuration	116
Figure 5-6	Basic VRRP Operation	121
Figure 5-7	Basic GLBP Operation	121
Table 5-4	Comparing HSRP, VRRP, and GLBP	122
List	Cisco Catalyst hardware components	122
Table 5-5	Errors in the **show interfaces** *interface_id* **counters errors** command	124
List	Reasons why a packet might be punted from a TCAM to its CPU	128
Example 5-19	Output from the **show processes cpu** command on a Cisco Catalyst 3550 Series switch	129

Complete Tables and Lists from Memory

Print a copy of Appendix B, "Memory Tables," (found on the CD) or at least the section for this chapter, and complete the tables and lists from memory. Appendix C, "Memory Tables Answer Key," also on the CD, includes completed tables and lists to check your work.

Define Key Terms

Define the following key terms from this chapter, and check your answers in the Glossary:

Layer 3 switch, switched virtual interface (SVI), Hot Standby Router Protocol (HSRP), Virtual Router Redundancy Protocol (VRRP), Global Load Balancing Protocol (GLBP), control plane, backplane, Ternary Content Addressable Memory (TCAM)

Command Reference to Check Your Memory

This section includes the most important configuration and EXEC commands covered in this chapter. To determine how well you have memorized the commands as a side effect of your other studies, cover the left side of Tables 5-7 and 5-8 with a piece of paper, read the descriptions on the right side, and see whether you remember the command.

Table 5-7 *Chapter 5 Configuration Command Reference*

Command	Description
standby *group ip virtual-ip-address*	Interface configuration mode command, used to specify the virtual IP address to be serviced by an HSRP group.
standby group **priority** priority	Interface configuration mode command, used to configure an interface's HSRP priority (which defaults to 100).
standby group **preempt**	Interface configuration mode command, which causes a previously active HSRP router to regain its active status if it becomes available.
mdix auto	Interface configuration mode command for a switch that allows the switch port to automatically detect and adjust to the connected cable type (that is, either straight-through or cross-over).

Table 5-8 *Chapter 5 EXEC Command Reference*

Command	Description
show standby *interface-id group*	Displays the HSRP configuration applied to a specified interface in a specified HSRP group.
show standby brief	Provides a summary view of a router's HSRP configuration.
debug standby	Shows HSRP state changes and information about sent and received HSRP packets.
show vrrp brief	Provides a summary view of a router's VRRP configuration.
show glbp brief	Provides a summary view of a router's GLBP configuration.
show ip cef	Displays the router's Layer 3 forwarding information, in addition to multicast, broadcast, and local IP addresses.
show adjacency	Verifies that a valid adjacency exists for a connected host.
show tcam inacl *tcam_number* statistics	A Cisco Catalyst 3550 Series switch command that displays the amount of TCAM memory allocated and used for inbound access control lists.
show platform ip unicast counts	A Cisco Catalyst 3750 Series switch command that can be used to see if a TCAM allocation has failed.
show controllers cpu-interface	A Cisco Catalyst 3750 Series switch command that can be used to display a count of packets being forwarded to a switch's CPU.

This chapter covers the following subjects:

Layer 3 Troubleshooting: This section begins by reviewing basic routing concepts. For example, you examine the changes to a frame's header as that frame's data is routed from one network to another. You see how Layer 2 information can be learned and stored in a router. Cisco Express Forwarding (CEF) is also discussed. Finally, this section presents a collection of **show** commands, useful for troubleshooting IP routing.

EIGRP Troubleshooting: This section begins by generically reviewing how an IP routing protocol's data structures interact with a router's IP routing table. Then, EIGRP's data structures are considered, followed by a review of basic EIGRP operation. Finally, this section provides a collection of **show** and **debug** commands useful for troubleshooting various EIGRP operations.

Trouble Ticket: EIGRP: This section presents you with a trouble ticket and an associated topology. You are also given **show** command output. Based on the information provided, you hypothesize an underlying cause for the reported issue and develop a solution. You can then compare your solution with a suggested solution.

CHAPTER 6

Introduction to Troubleshooting Routing Protocols

Enterprise networks (that is, networks containing multiple subnets) depend on routing technologies to move traffic from one subnet to another. Routers, or Layer 3 switches discussed in Chapter 5, "Advanced Cisco Catalyst Switch Troubleshooting," can be configured to route packets using statically configured route entries or using dynamically configured routing protocols. Also, routers can learn about the existence of networks by examining the networks directly connected to the routers' interfaces.

Routing packets is considered to be a Layer 3 process; however, Layer 2 information (for example, MAC address information) is also required to route packets. An understanding of this basic routing process is critical to troubleshooting issues with various routing protocols. Therefore, this chapter begins with a discussion of fundamental routing concepts. Then, a specific routing protocol (that is, Enhanced Interior Gateway Routing Protocol [EIGRP]) is discussed. You also learn techniques for troubleshooting an EIGRP-based network.

Finally, this chapter presents you with a trouble ticket. This trouble ticket describes an EIGRP issue. Given a collection of **show** command output, you are challenged to determine the underlying cause of the issue and formulate a solution.

"Do I Know This Already?" Quiz

The "Do I Know This Already?" quiz helps you to determine your level of knowledge of this chapter's topics before you begin. Table 6-1 details the major topics discussed in this chapter and their corresponding quiz questions.

Table 6-1 *"Do I Know This Already?" Section-to-Question Mapping*

Foundation Topics Section	Questions
Layer 3 Troubleshooting	1–2
EIGRP Troubleshooting	3–6

1. A router is attempting to route a packet over an Ethernet network from a PC with an IP address of 10.1.1.2 to a server with an IP address of 172.16.1.2. If you examined a frame exiting the PC destined for the server, what would be the two MAC addresses found in the frame's header? (Choose two.)

    a. The PC's MAC address

    b. The server's MAC address

    c. The router's MAC address

    d. A broadcast MAC address

2. Identify two data structures maintained by CEF. (Choose two.)

    a. IP routing table

    b. Router ARP cache

    c. FIB

    d. Adjacency table

3. A router is running two routing protocols: EIGRP and RIPv2. Each routing protocol knows of a route for network 10.1.2.0/24. What determines which route will be injected into the router's IP routing table?

    a. The metric of each route

    b. The advertised distance of each routing protocol

    c. The administrative distance of each routing protocol

    d. The feasible distance of each routing protocol

4. Identify three EIGRP data structures. (Choose three.)

    a. EIGRP topology table

    b. EIGRP adjacency table

    c. EIGRP neighbor table

    d. EIGRP interface table

5. Which two distances does EIGRP consider when selecting the best route for a particular network?

    a. Advertised distance

    b. Successor distance

    c. Topological distance

    d. Feasible distance

6. Which command would you use to display all routes known to a router's EIGRP routing process?

    a. show ip eigrp interfaces

    b. show ip eigrp neighbors

    c. show ip eigrp topology

    d. show ip route eigrp

Foundation Topics

Layer 3 Troubleshooting

When troubleshooting connectivity issues for an IP-based network, the network layer (that is, Layer 3) of the OSI reference model is often an appropriate place to begin your troubleshooting efforts. For example, if you are experiencing connectivity issues between two hosts on a network, you could check Layer 3 by pinging between the hosts. If the pings are successful, you can conclude that the issue resides at upper layers of the OSI reference model (that is, Layers 4–7). However, if the pings fail, you can focus your troubleshooting efforts on Layers 1–3. This section discusses fundamental routing concepts and provides you with a collection of Cisco IOS Software commands that could prove to be useful when troubleshooting routing issues.

Basic Routing Processes

To review basic routing processes, consider Figure 6-1. In this topology, PC1 needs to send traffic to Server1. Notice that these hosts are on different networks. So, the question becomes, how does a packet from a source IP address of 192.168.1.2 get routed to a destination IP address of 192.168.3.2?

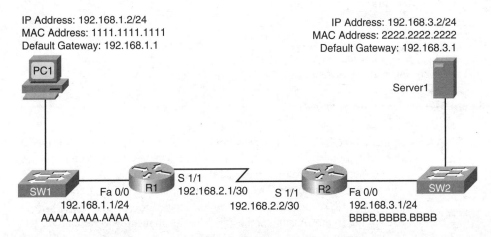

Figure 6-1 *Basic Routing Topology*

Consider the following walkthrough of this process, step-by-step:

Step 1.   PC1 compares its IP address and subnet mask of 192.168.1.2/24 with the destination IP address and subnet mask of 192.168.3.2/24. PC1 concludes that the destination IP address resides on a remote subnet. Therefore, PC1 needs to send the packet to its default gateway, which could have been manually configured on PC1 or dynamically learned via DHCP. In this example, PC1 has a default gateway of 192.168.1.1 (that is, router R1). In order to construct a

Key Topic

properly constructed Layer 2 frame, however, PC1 also needs the MAC address of its default gateway. PC1 ARPs for router R1's MAC address. Once PC1 receives an ARP Reply from router R1, PC1 adds router R1's MAC address to its ARP cache. PC1 now sends its data in a frame destined for Server1, as shown in Figure 6-2.

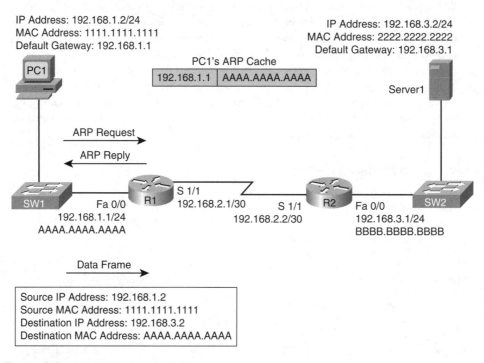

Figure 6-2   *Basic Routing: Step #1*

Step 2.   Router R1 receives the frame sent from PC1 and interrogates the IP header. An IP header contains a Time-to-Live (TTL) field, which is decremented once for each router hop. Therefore, router R1 decrements the packet's TTL field. If the value in the TTL field is reduced to zero, the router discards the frame and sends a *time exceeded* Internet Control Message Protocol (ICMP) message back to the source. Assuming the TTL is not decremented to zero, router R1 checks its routing table to determine the best path to reach network 192.168.3.0/24. In this example, router R1's routing table has an entry stating that network 192.168.3.0/24 is accessible via interface Serial 1/1. Note that ARPs are not required for serial interfaces, because these interface types do not have MAC addresses. Router R1, therefore, forwards the frame out of its Serial 1/1 interface, as depicted in Figure 6-3.

Step 3.   When router R2 receives the frame, it decrements the TTL in the IP header, just as router R1 did. Again, assuming the TTL did not get decremented to zero, router R2 interrogates the IP header to determine the destination network. In this case, the destination network of 192.168.3.0/24 is directly attached to router R2's Fast Ethernet 0/0 interface. Similar to how PC1 sent out an ARP Request to determine the MAC address of its default gateway, router R2 sends an ARP Request to determine the MAC address of Server1. Once an ARP Reply is received from Server1, router R2 forwards the frame out of its Fast Ethernet 0/0 interface to Server1, as illustrated in Figure 6-4.

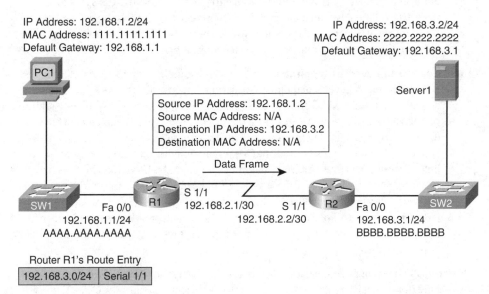

Figure 6-3   *Basic Routing: Step #2*

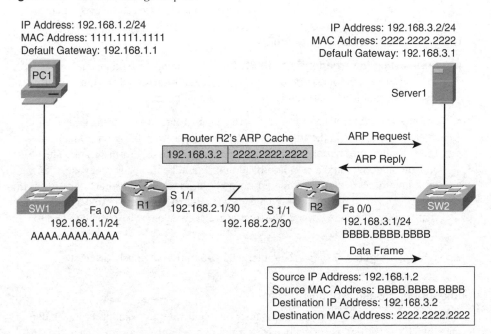

Figure 6-4   *Basic Routing: Step #3*

The previous steps identified two router data structures:

- **IP routing table:** When a router needed to route an IP packet, it consulted its IP routing table to find the best match. The best match is the route that has the *longest prefix*. Specifically, a route entry with the longest prefix is the most specific network. For example, imagine that a router has an entry for network 10.0.0.0/8 and for network 10.1.1.0/24. Also, imagine that the router is seeking the best match for a destination address of 10.1.1.1/24. The router would select the 10.1.1.0/24 route entry as the best entry, because that route entry has the longest prefix.

- **Layer 3 to Layer 2 mapping:** In the previous example, router R2's ARP cache contained Layer 3 to Layer 2 mapping information. Specifically, the ARP cache had a mapping that said a MAC address of 2222.2222.2222 corresponded to an IP address of 192.168.3.2. While an ARP cache is the Layer 3 to Layer 2 mapping data structure used for Ethernet-based networks, similar data structures are used for Frame Relay and Asynchronous Transfer mode (ATM) point-to-multipoint links. For point-to-point links, however, an egress interface might be shown in the IP routing table, as opposed to a next-hop IP address. For these types of links (for example, point-to-point Frame Relay or ATM Permanent Virtual Circuits [PVC], High-level Data Link Control [HDLC], or Point-to-Point Protocol [PPP] links), the information required to construct an outgoing frame can be gleaned from the egress interface, thus not requiring a next-hop IP address.

Continually querying a router's routing table and its Layer 3 to Layer 2 mapping data structure (for example, an ARP cache) is less than efficient. Fortunately, Cisco Express Forwarding (CEF), as introduced in Chapter 5, makes lookups much more efficient. CEF gleans its information from the router's IP routing table and Layer 3 to Layer 2 mapping tables. Then, CEF's data structures can be referenced when forwarding packets. The two primary CEF data structures are as follows:

- **Forwarding Information Base (FIB):** The FIB contains Layer 3 information, similar to the information found in an IP routing table. Additionally, a FIB contains information about multicast routes and directly connected hosts.

- **Adjacency table:** When a router is performing a route lookup using CEF, the FIB references an entry in the adjacency table. The adjacency table entry contains the frame header information required by the router to properly form a frame. Therefore, an egress interface and a next-hop IP address would be in an adjacency entry for a multipoint interface, whereas a point-to-point interface would require only egress interface information. Note that if a host is *adjacent* to a router, the router can reach that host over a single Layer 2 hop (that is, traffic would not have to be routed to reach an adjacency).

As a reference, Figure 6-5 shows the router data structures previously discussed.

Troubleshooting Basic Routing

When troubleshooting some routing issues, you might want to examine a router's IP routing table. If the traffic's observed behavior is not conforming to information in the IP routing table, however, recall that the IP routing table is maintained by a router's control plane. CEF, however, operates in the data plane. Therefore, you might also want to view CEF information, because CEF's data structures (that is, the FIB and the adjacency table) contain all the information required to make packet forwarding decisions. For your reference, Table 6-2 contains a collection of commands useful for verifying both IP routing table information (that is, control plane information) and CEF information (that is, data plane information).

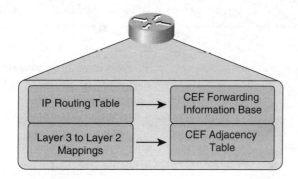

Figure 6-5 *A Router's Data Structures*

Table 6-2 *Troubleshooting Layer 3 Forwarding Information*

Key
Topic

show ip route *ip-address*	Displays a router's best route to the specified IP address.
show ip route *network subnet-mask*	Displays a router's best route to the specified network, if the specific route (with a matching subnet mask length) is found in the router's IP routing table.
show ip route *network subnet-mask* **longer-prefixes**	Displays all routes in a router's IP routing table that are encompassed by the specified network address and subnet mask. (NOTE: This command is often useful when troubleshooting route summarization issues.)
show ip cef *ip-address*	Displays information (for example, next-hop IP address and egress interface) required to forward a packet, similar to the output of the **show ip route** *ip-address* command. (NOTE: The output of this command comes from CEF. Therefore, routing protocol information is not presented in the output.)
show ip cef *network subnet-mask*	Displays information from a router's FIB showing the information needed to route a packet to the specified network with the specified subnet mask.

continues

Table 6-2   *Troubleshooting Layer 3 Forwarding Information*   (*Continued*)

Command	Description
show ip cef exact-route *source-ip-address destination-ip-address*	Displays the adjacency that will be used to forward a packet from the specified source IP address to the specified destination IP address. (NOTE: This command is useful if the router is load balancing across multiple adjacencies, and you want to see which adjacency will be used for a certain combination of source and destination IP addresses.)

Example 6-1 provides sample output from the **show ip route** *ip-address* command. The output shows that the next-hop IP address to reach an IP address of 192.168.1.11 is 192.168.0.11, which is accessible via interface Fast Ethernet 0/0. Because this information is coming from the control plane, it includes information about the routing protocol, which is OSPF in this case.

Example 6-1   show ip route ip-address *Command Output*

```
R2# show ip route 192.168.1.11
Routing entry for 192.168.1.0/24
  Known via "ospf 1", distance 110, metric 11, type intra area
  Last update from 192.168.0.11 on FastEthernet0/0, 00:06:45 ago
  Routing Descriptor Blocks:
  * 192.168.0.11, from 10.1.1.1, 00:06:45 ago, via FastEthernet0/0
      Route metric is 11, traffic share count is 1
```

Example 6-2 provides sample output from the **show ip route** *network subnet-mask* command. The output indicates that network 192.168.1.0/24 is accessible out of interface Fast Ethernet 0/0, with a next-hop IP address of 192.168.0.11.

Example 6-2   show ip route network subnet_mask *Command Output*

```
R2# show ip route 192.168.1.0 255.255.255.0
Routing entry for 192.168.1.0/24
  Known via "ospf 1", distance 110, metric 11, type intra area
  Last update from 192.168.0.11 on FastEthernet0/0, 00:06:57 ago
  Routing Descriptor Blocks:
  * 192.168.0.11, from 10.1.1.1, 00:06:57 ago, via FastEthernet0/0
      Route metric is 11, traffic share count is 1
```

Example 6-3 provides sample output from the **show ip route** *network subnet-mask* [longer-prefixes] command, with and without the **longer-prefixes** option. Notice that the router responds that the subnet 172.16.0.0 255.255.0.0 is not in the IP routing table. However, after adding the **longer-prefixes** option, two routes are displayed, because these routes are subnets of the 172.16.0.0/16 network.

Example 6-3   show ip route network subnet-mask [longer-prefixes] *Command Output*

```
R2# show ip route 172.16.0.0 255.255.0.0
% Subnet not in table
R2# show ip route 172.16.0.0 255.255.0.0 longer-prefixes
Codes: C - connected, S - static, R - RIP, M - mobile, B - BGP
       D - EIGRP, EX - EIGRP external, O - OSPF, IA - OSPF inter area
       N1 - OSPF NSSA external type 1, N2 - OSPF NSSA external type 2
       E1 - OSPF external type 1, E2 - OSPF external type 2
       i - IS-IS, su - IS-IS summary, L1 - IS-IS level-1, L2 - IS-IS level-2
       ia - IS-IS inter area, * - candidate default, U - per-user static route
       o - ODR, P - periodic downloaded static route

Gateway of last resort is not set

     172.16.0.0/30 is subnetted, 2 subnets
C       172.16.1.0 is directly connected, Serial1/0.1
C       172.16.2.0 is directly connected, Serial1/0.2
```

Example 6-4 provides sample output from the **show ip cef** *ip-address* command. The output indicates that, according to CEF, an IP address of 192.168.1.11 is accessible out of interface Fast Ethernet 0/0, with a next-hop IP address of 192.168.0.11.

Example 6-4   show ip cef ip-address *Command Output*

```
R2# show ip cef 192.168.1.11
192.168.1.0/24, version 42, epoch 0, cached adjacency 192.168.0.11
0 packets, 0 bytes
  via 192.168.0.11, FastEthernet0/0, 0 dependencies
    next hop 192.168.0.11, FastEthernet0/0
    valid cached adjacency
```

Example 6-5 provides sample output from the **show ip cef** *network subnet_mask* command. The output indicates that network 192.168.1.0/24 is accessible off of interface Fast Ethernet 0/0, with a next-hop IP address of 192.168.0.11.

Example 6-5   show ip cef network subnet-mask *Command Output*

```
R2# show ip cef 192.168.1.0 255.255.255.0
192.168.1.0/24, version 42, epoch 0, cached adjacency 192.168.0.11
0 packets, 0 bytes
  via 192.168.0.11, FastEthernet0/0, 0 dependencies
    next hop 192.168.0.11, FastEthernet0/0
    valid cached adjacency
```

Example 6-6 provides sample output from the **show ip cef exact-route** *source-ip-address destination-ip-address* command. The output indicates that a packet sourced from an IP address of 10.2.2.2 and destined for an IP address of 192.168.1.11 will be sent out of interface Fast Ethernet 0/0 to a next-hop IP address of 192.168.0.11.

Example 6-6   show ip cef exact-route source-ip-address destination-ip-address
Command Output

```
R2# show ip cef exact-route 10.2.2.2 192.168.1.11
10.2.2.2          -> 192.168.1.11   : FastEthernet0/0 (next hop 192.168.0.11)
```

For a multipoint interface (for example, a point-to-multipoint Frame Relay/ATM PVC or an Ethernet interface), after a router knows the next-hop address for a packet, it needs appropriate Layer 2 information (for example, next-hop MAC address, Data Link Connection Identifier [DLCI], or Virtual Path Identifier/Virtual Circuit Identifier [VPI/VCI]) to properly construct a frame (or a cell, in the case of ATM). Table 6-3 outlines some useful commands for viewing a router's Layer 3 to Layer 2 mapping information.

Table 6-3   *Troubleshooting Layer 3 to Layer 2 Mapping Information*

Command	Description
show ip arp	Displays a router's ARP cache, containing IP address to MAC address mappings. (NOTE: By default, a router's ARP cache stores information for four hours. Therefore, you might need to execute a **clear ip arp** command to allow a router to relearn information after you make a topology change.)
show frame-relay map	Displays Frame Relay DLCIs associated with different next-hop IP addresses.
show adjacency detail	Displays the frame headers in a router's CEF adjacency table used to encapsulate a frame being sent to an adjacency.

Example 6-7 provides sample output from the **show ip arp** command. The output shows the learned or configured MAC addresses along with their associated IP addresses.

Example 6-7   show ip arp *Command Output*

```
R2# show ip arp
Protocol  Address            Age (min)   Hardware Addr   Type    Interface
Internet  192.168.0.11               0   0009.b7fa.d1e1  ARPA    FastEthernet0/0
Internet  192.168.0.22               -   c001.0f70.0000  ARPA    FastEthernet0/0
```

Example 6-8 provides sample output from the **show ip frame-relay map** command. The output shows the Frame Relay subinterfaces that correspond to DLCIs (that is, Frame Relay PVC identifiers) known to the router. Notice that these subinterfaces are point-to-point subinterfaces, meaning that next-hop IP address information is not required to properly construct a frame.

Example 6-8   show frame-relay map *Command Output*

```
R2# show frame-relay map
Serial1/0.2 (up): point-to-point dlci, dlci 182(0xB6,0x2C60), broadcast
          status defined, active
Serial1/0.1 (up): point-to-point dlci, dlci 181(0xB5,0x2C50), broadcast
          status defined, active
```

Example 6-9 provides sample output from the **show adjacency detail** command. The output shows the CEF information used to construct frame headers for the various router interfaces and subinterfaces.

Example 6-9   show adjacency detail *Command Output*

```
R2# show adjacency detail
Protocol Interface              Address
IP       Serial1/0.1           point2point(25)
                               0 packets, 0 bytes
                               2C510800
                               CEF    expires: 00:02:18
                                      refresh: 00:00:19
                               Epoch: 0
IP       Serial1/0.2           point2point(25)
                               0 packets, 0 bytes
                               2C610800
                               CEF    expires: 00:02:18
                                      refresh: 00:00:19
                               Epoch: 0
IP       FastEthernet0/0       192.168.0.11(9)
                               0 packets, 0 bytes
                               0009B7FAD1E1C0010F7000000800
                               ARP          04:02:59
                               Epoch: 0
```

EIGRP Troubleshooting

The Cisco proprietary Enhanced Interior Gateway Routing Protocol (EIGRP) is considered to be a balanced hybrid routing protocol (or an advanced distance-vector routing protocol). Specifically, EIGRP advertises routes to directly attached neighbors, like a distance-vector routing protocol, while using a series of tables, similar to a link-state routing protocol.

EIGRP also offers the benefit of fast convergence after a link failure. Load balancing is supported over both equal-cost paths (a default behavior) and unequal-cost paths (through the *variance* feature).

This section discusses strategies for troubleshooting an EIGRP-based network. Before considering the specifics of EIGRP troubleshooting, however, this section takes a more generic look at how the data structures of various IP routing protocols interact with a router's IP routing table.

Data Structures of IP Routing Protocols

As traffic is routed through a network, the routers encountered along the way from the source to the destination need consistency in how they route traffic. For example, if one router selected the best path based on hop count, and another router selected the best path based on a link's bandwidth, a routing loop could conceivably occur. Fortunately, having a common routing protocol configured on all routers within a topology helps ensure consistency in routing decisions.

That is not to say that a topology could not have more than one routing protocol. You could strategically redistribute routes between routing protocols. Also, you could use static routes in conjunction with dynamic routing protocols. However, you must take care in environments with redundant links and multiple routing protocols to avoid potential routing loops.

To better troubleshoot specific dynamic routing protocols, consider, generically, how dynamic routing protocols' data structures interact with a router's IP routing table.

Figure 6-6 shows the interaction between the data structures of an IP routing protocol and a router's IP routing table. Realize, however, that not all routing protocols maintain their own data structures. For example, Routing Information Protocol (RIP) is a routing protocol that works directly with an IP routing table in a router, rather than maintaining a separate data structure.

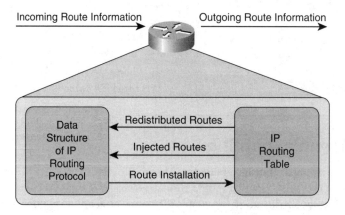

Figure 6-6   *Interaction between IP Routing Protocol Data Structures and IP Routing Tables*

As a router receives route information from a neighboring router, that information is stored in the data structures of the IP routing protocol (if the IP routing protocol uses data structures). A data structure might also be populated by the local router. For example, a router might be configured for route redistribution where route information is redistributed by a routing information source (for example, a dynamic routing protocol, a static route, or a connected route). Also, the router might be configured to have specific inter-faces participate in an IP routing protocol.

The data structure analyzes all the information it receives to select the best route to certain networks. This best route is determined by looking for the route with the best metric. The data structure of an IP routing protocol will then inject that best route into the router's IP routing table, if that same route information has not already been learned by a more believable routing source. Specifically, different routing protocols have different *administrative distances*. An administrative distance of a routing protocol can be thought of as the *believability* of that routing protocol. As an example, RIP has an administrative distance of 120, whereas OSPF has an administrative distance of 110. Therefore, if both RIP and OSPF had knowledge of a route to a specific network, the OSPF route would be injected into the router's IP routing table because OSPF has a more believable administrative distance. Therefore, the best route selected by an IP routing protocol's data structure is only a *candidate* to be injected into the router's IP routing table. As a reminder, the following is a list of the administrative distances. The lower the administrative distance, the more preferred the route.

Connected interface	0
Static route	1
Enhanced Interior Gateway Routing Protocol (EIGRP) summary route	5
External Border Gateway Protocol (BGP)	20
Internal EIGRP	90
IGRP	100
OSPF	110
Intermediate System-to-Intermediate System (IS-IS)	115
Routing Information Protocol (RIP)	120
Exterior Gateway Protocol (EGP)	140
On Demand Routing (ODR)	160
External EIGRP	170
Internal BGP	200
Unknown*	255

If an IP routing protocol's data structure identifies more than one route to a destination network, multiple routes might be injected into a router's IP routing table if those multiple routes have an equal metric. In some cases, however, a routing protocol (for example, EIGRP) might support load balancing across unequal-cost paths. In such an instance, multiple routes might be injected into a router's IP routing table, even though those routes have different metrics.

Depending on the IP routing protocol in use, a router will periodically advertise all of its routes, or updates to its routing information, to its neighbors. Also be aware that some routing protocols need to establish a relationship with a neighboring router before exchanging route information with that neighbor. This relationship is called an *adjacency* or a *neighborship*.

Data Structures of EIGRP

Now that you have reviewed, from a generic perspective, how an IP routing protocol's data structure interacts with a router's IP routing table, consider the specific data structures used by EIGRP, as described in Table 6-4.

Table 6-4   *EIGRP Data Structures*

Data Structure	Description
EIGRP interface table	All of a router's interfaces that have been configured to participate in an EIGRP routing process are listed in this table. However, if an interface has been configured as a passive interface (that is, an interface that does not send routing information), that interface does not appear in this table.
EIGRP neighbor table	This table lists a router's EIGRP neighbors (that is, neighboring routers from whom an EIGRP Hello message has been received). A neighbor is removed from this table if the neighbor has not been heard from for a period of time defined as the *hold-time*. Also, if an interface, from which a neighbor is known, is removed from the EIGRP interface table because it goes down, the neighbor is removed from this table unless there is a multiple link and one of the interfaces is still up. In that case, the second interface will still provide the neighborship.
EIGRP topology table	This table contains routes learned by a router's EIGRP routing process. The best route for a network in this table becomes a candidate to be injected into the router's IP routing table. If multiple routes in this table have an equal metric, or if EIGRP's variance feature is configured, more than one route might become candidates for injection into the IP routing table, but only to a maximum of 4 by default.

EIGRP Operation

Like most high-end routing protocols, EIGRP supports variable-length subnet masking (VLSM), and advertisements are sent via multicast (that is, to an address of 224.0.0.10). By default, EIGRP automatically performs route summarization. This could be an issue for a topology containing discontiguous subnets of the same major classful network. To turn off automatic summarization, you can issue the **no auto-summary** command in router configuration mode for an EIGRP autonomous system.

EIGRP also supports load balancing across unequal-cost cost paths using the *variance* feature. By default, the variance value for an EIGRP routing process defaults to a variance of one, meaning the load balancing will only occur over equal-cost paths. You can, however, issue the **variance** *multiplier* command in router configuration mode to specify a range of metrics over which load balancing will occur. For example, imagine that a route had a metric of 200000, and you configured the **variance 2** command for the EIGRP routing process. This would cause load balancing to occur over routes with a metric in the range of 200000 through 400000 (2 * 200000). As you can see, a route could have a metric as high as 400000 (that is, the variance multiplier multiplied by the best metric) and still be used.

Upon learning of a neighbor, due to the receipt of an EIGRP Hello packet, an EIGRP router will perform a full exchange of routing information with the newly established neighbor. Once the neighborship has been formed, however, only updated route information will be exchanged with that neighbor.

Routing information learned from EIGRP neighbors is inserted into the EIGRP topology table. The best route for a specific network in the IP EIGRP topology table becomes a candidate to be injected into the router's IP routing table. If that route is indeed injected into the IP routing table, that route becomes known as the *successor* route. This is the route that is then advertised to neighboring routers.

The following parameters are used to determine the best route:

- **Advertised Distance (AD):** The distance from a neighbor to the destination network

- **Feasible Distance (FD):** The AD plus the metric to reach the neighbor advertising the AD

EIGRP's metric is calculated with the following formula:

EIGRP metric = [K1 * bandwidth + ((K2 * bandwidth) / (256 − load)) + K3 * delay] * [K5 / (reliability + K4)]

By default, the K values are as follows:

- K1 = 1

- K2 = 0

- K3 = 1

- K4 = 0

- K5 = 0

As a result of these default K values, EIGRP's default metric can be calculated as

default EIGRP metric = bandwidth + delay

where:

- **bandwidth** = 10,000,000 / minimum bandwidth in kbps * 256

- **delay** = sum of delays of all interfaces in path in tens of milliseconds * 256

EIGRP Troubleshooting Commands

With an understanding of EIGRP's data structures, and an understanding of how data structures play a role in populating a router's IP routing table, you can now strategically use Cisco IOS **show** and **debug** commands to collect information about specific steps in the routing process. Table 6-5 shows a collection of such commands, along with their description, and the step of the routing process or EIGRP data structure each command can be used to investigate.

Table 6-5 *EIGRP Troubleshooting Commands*

Command	Routing Component or Data Structure	Description
show ip eigrp interfaces	EIGRP interface table	This command displays all of a router's interfaces configured to participate in an EIGRP routing process (with the exception of passive interfaces).
show ip eigrp neighbors	EIGRP neighbor table	This command shows a router's EIGRP neighbors.
show ip eigrp topology	EIGRP topology table	This command displays routes known to a router's EIGRP routing process. These routes are contained in the EIGRP topology table.
show ip route eigrp	IP routing table	This command shows routes known to a router's IP routing table that were injected by the router's EIGRP routing process.
debug ip routing	IP routing table	This command displays updates that occur in a router's IP routing table. Therefore, this command is not specific to EIGRP.
debug eigrp packets	Exchanging EIGRP information with neighbors	This command can be used to display all EIGRP packets exchanged with a router's EIGRP neighbors. However, the focus of the command can be narrowed to only display specific EIGRP packet types (for example, EIGRP Hello packets).
debug ip eigrp	Exchanging EIGRP information with neighbors	This command shows information contained in EIGRP packets and reveals how an EIGRP routing process responds to that information.

Example 6-10 provides sample output from the **show ip eigrp interfaces** command. Although three interfaces are configured to participate in EIGRP autonomous system 100, only two of those interfaces have a peer, because the other interface is a loopback interface.

Example 6-10 show ip eigrp interfaces *Command Output*

```
R2# show ip eigrp interfaces
IP-EIGRP interfaces for process 100
```

Interface	Peers	Xmit Queue Un/Reliable	Mean SRTT	Pacing Time Un/Reliable	Multicast Flow Timer	Pending Routes
Lo0	0	0/0	0	0/1	0	0
Se1/0.1	1	0/0	880	0/15	4155	0
Fa0/0	1	0/0	193	0/2	828	0

Example 6-11 provides sample output from the **show ip eigrp neighbors** command. In the output, notice that two neighbors are known to this router. Also notice that the output shows off of which interface each neighbor resides.

Example 6-11   show ip eigrp neighbors *Command Output*

```
R2# show ip eigrp neighbors
IP-EIGRP neighbors for process 100
H   Address          Interface      Hold Uptime    SRTT  RTO    Q    Seq
                                     (sec)          (ms)         Cnt  Num
1   192.168.0.11     Fa0/0          12 00:01:34    193   1158   0    3
0   172.16.1.1       Se1/0.1        12 00:01:39    880   5000   0    23
```

Example 6-12 provides sample output from the **show ip eigrp topology** command. The output displays the routes known to the EIGRP topology table. Also, notice that the output contains the feasible distance (FD) for each route. Recall that the FD is the advertised distance (AD) from a neighbor, plus the metric required to reach that neighbor. Finally, notice that the state of each route is *passive*. This is the desired state. A route that stays in the *active* state, however, could indicate a problem. A state of active means that the router is actively searching for a route. If a route remains in this state, the resulting condition is an EIGRP *stuck-in-active* (SIA) error.

Example 6-12   show ip eigrp topology *Command Output*

```
R2# show ip eigrp topology
IP-EIGRP Topology Table for AS(100)/ID(10.2.2.2)

Codes: P - Passive, A - Active, U - Update, Q - Query, R - Reply,
       r - reply Status, s - sia Status

P 10.1.3.0/30, 1 successors, FD is 2681856
        via 172.16.1.1 (2681856/2169856), Serial1/0.1
P 10.2.2.2/32, 1 successors, FD is 128256
        via Connected, Loopback0
P 10.3.3.3/32, 1 successors, FD is 2297856
        via 172.16.1.1 (2297856/128256), Serial1/0.1
P 10.1.2.0/24, 1 successors, FD is 2195456
        via 172.16.1.1 (2195456/281600), Serial1/0.1
P 10.0.0.0/8, 1 successors, FD is 128256
        via Summary (128256/0), Null0
```

```
P 10.1.1.1/32, 1 successors, FD is 409600
        via 192.168.0.11 (409600/128256), FastEthernet0/0
P 10.4.4.4/32, 1 successors, FD is 2323456
        via 172.16.1.1 (2323456/409600), Serial1/0.1
P 192.168.0.0/24, 1 successors, FD is 281600
        via Connected, FastEthernet0/0
P 192.168.1.0/24, 1 successors, FD is 284160
        via 192.168.0.11 (284160/28160), FastEthernet0/0
P 172.16.0.0/16, 1 successors, FD is 2169856
        via Summary (2169856/0), Null0
P 172.16.1.0/30, 1 successors, FD is 2169856
        via Connected, Serial1/0.1
```

Example 6-13 provides sample output from the **show ip route eigrp** command. The output of this command only shows entries in the IP routing table that were learned via EIGRP.

Example 6-13   show ip route eigrp *Command Output*

```
R2# show ip route eigrp
      172.16.0.0/16 is variably subnetted, 3 subnets, 2 masks
D        172.16.0.0/16 is a summary, 00:01:36, Null0
      10.0.0.0/8 is variably subnetted, 7 subnets, 4 masks
D        10.1.3.0/30 [90/2681856] via 172.16.1.1, 00:01:36, Serial1/0.1
D        10.3.3.3/32 [90/2297856] via 172.16.1.1, 00:01:36, Serial1/0.1
D        10.1.2.0/24 [90/2195456] via 172.16.1.1, 00:01:36, Serial1/0.1
D        10.0.0.0/8 is a summary, 00:01:36, Null0
D        10.1.1.1/32 [90/409600] via 192.168.0.11, 00:01:36, FastEthernet0/0
D        10.4.4.4/32 [90/2323456] via 172.16.1.1, 00:01:36, Serial1/0.1
D     192.168.1.0/24 [90/284160] via 192.168.0.11, 00:01:36, FastEthernet0/0
```

Example 6-14 provides sample output from the **debug ip routing** command. The output shown reflects a loopback interface on a neighboring router being administratively shut down and then brought back up. Specifically, the loopback interface has an IP address of 10.1.1.1, and it is reachable via an EIGRP neighbor with an IP address of 192.168.0.11.

Example 6-14   debug ip routing *Command Output*

```
R2# debug ip routing
IP routing debugging is on
*Mar  1 00:20:11.215: RT: delete route to 10.1.1.1 via 192.168.0.11, eigrp metric
  [90/409600]
*Mar  1 00:20:11.219: RT: SET_LAST_RDB for 10.1.1.1/32
  OLD rdb: via 192.168.0.11, FastEthernet0/0
```

```
*Mar  1 00:20:11.227: RT: no routes to 10.1.1.1
*Mar  1 00:20:11.227: RT: NET-RED 10.1.1.1/32
*Mar  1 00:20:11.231: RT: delete subnet route to 10.1.1.1/32
*Mar  1 00:20:11.235: RT: NET-RED 10.1.1.1/32
*Mar  1 00:20:17.723: RT: SET_LAST_RDB for 10.1.1.1/32
  NEW rdb: via 192.168.0.11
*Mar  1 00:20:17.723: RT: add 10.1.1.1/32 via 192.168.0.11, eigrp metric
  [90/409600]
*Mar  1 00:20:17.723: RT: NET-RED 10.1.1.1/32
```

Example 6-15 provides sample output from the **debug eigrp packets** command. This command can produce a large volume of output by default. However, you can specify specific EIGRP packet types you want to see in the output.

Example 6-15   debug eigrp packets *Command Output*

```
R2# debug eigrp packets
EIGRP Packets debugging is on
    (UPDATE, REQUEST, QUERY, REPLY, HELLO, IPXSAP, PROBE, ACK, STUB, SIAQUERY,
SIAREPLY)
*Mar  1 00:20:48.151: EIGRP: Received HELLO on FastEthernet0/0 nbr 192.168.0.11
*Mar  1 00:20:48.155:    AS 100, Flags 0x0, Seq 0/0 idbQ 0/0 iidbQ un/rely 0/0
  peerQ un/rely 0/0
*Mar  1 00:20:48.187: EIGRP: Sending HELLO on FastEthernet0/0
*Mar  1 00:20:48.191:    AS 100, Flags 0x0, Seq 0/0 idbQ 0/0 iidbQ un/rely 0/0
...OUTPUT OMITTED...
*Mar  1 00:20:59.091: EIGRP: Received QUERY on FastEthernet0/0 nbr 192.168.0.11
*Mar  1 00:20:59.095:    AS 100, Flags 0x0, Seq 6/0 idbQ 0/0 iidbQ un/rely 0/0
  peerQ un/rely 0/0
...OUTPUT OMITTED...
*Mar  1 00:20:59.287: EIGRP: Received REPLY on Serial1/0.1 nbr 172.16.1.1
*Mar  1 00:20:59.291:    AS 100, Flags 0x0, Seq 25/16 idbQ 0/0 iidbQ un/rely 0/0
  peerQ un/rely 0/0
*Mar  1 00:20:59.295: EIGRP: Enqueueing ACK on Serial1/0.1 nbr 172.16.1.1
...OUTPUT OMITTED...
*Mar  1 00:21:06.915: EIGRP: Sending UPDATE on FastEthernet0/0
*Mar  1 00:21:06.915:    AS 100, Flags 0x0, Seq 19/0 idbQ 0/0 iidbQ un/rely 0/0
  serno 17-17
*Mar  1 00:21:06.919: EIGRP: Enqueueing UPDATE on Serial1/0.1 iidbQ un/rely 0/1
  serno 17-17
*Mar  1 00:21:06.923: EIGRP: Enqueueing UPDATE on Serial1/0.1 nbr 172.16.1.1 iidbQ
  un/rely 0/0 peerQ un/rely 0/0 serno 17-17
```

Example 6-16 provides sample output from the **debug ip eigrp** command. This command provides real-time tracking of EIGRP messages, much like the **debug eigrp packets** command. However, the **debug ip eigrp** command focuses more on showing what the EIGRP routing process is doing in response to the messages, as illustrated in the highlighted text.

Example 6-16 *debug ip eigrp Command Output*

```
R2# debug ip eigrp
IP-EIGRP Route Events debugging is on
*Mar  1 00:21:30.123: IP-EIGRP(Default-IP-Routing-Table:100): Processing incoming
  QUERY packet
*Mar  1 00:21:30.127: IP-EIGRP(Default-IP-Routing-Table:100): Int 10.1.1.1/32 M
  4294967295 - 0 4294967295 SM 4294967295 - 0 4294967295
*Mar  1 00:21:30.147: IP-EIGRP(Default-IP-Routing-Table:100): 10.1.1.1/32 - don't
  advertise out Serial1/0.1
*Mar  1 00:21:30.155: IP-EIGRP(Default-IP-Routing-Table:100): Int 10.1.1.1/32
  metric 4294967295 - 0 4294967295
*Mar  1 00:21:30.335: IP-EIGRP(Default-IP-Routing-Table:100): Processing incoming
  REPLY packet
*Mar  1 00:21:30.339: IP-EIGRP(Default-IP-Routing-Table:100): Int 10.1.1.1/32 M
  4294967295 - 0 4294967295 SM 4294967295 - 0 4294967295
*Mar  1 00:21:30.343: IP-EIGRP(Default-IP-Routing-Table:100): 10.1.1.1/32 routing
  table not updated thru 192.168.0.11
*Mar  1 00:21:30.903: IP-EIGRP(Default-IP-Routing-Table:100): 10.1.1.1/32 - not in
  IP routing table
*Mar  1 00:21:30.907: IP-EIGRP(Default-IP-Routing-Table:100): Int 10.1.1.1/32
  metric 4294967295 - 0 4294967295
*Mar  1 00:21:36.739: IP-EIGRP(Default-IP-Routing-Table:100): Processing incoming
  UPDATE packet
*Mar  1 00:21:36.739: IP-EIGRP(Default-IP-Routing-Table:100): Int 10.1.1.1/32 M
  409600 - 256000 153600 SM 128256 - 256 128000
*Mar  1 00:21:36.743: IP-EIGRP(Default-IP-Routing-Table:100): route installed for
  10.1.1.1 ()
*Mar  1 00:21:36.775: IP-EIGRP(Default-IP-Routing-Table:100): Int 10.1.1.1/32
  metric 409600 - 256000 153600
*Mar  1 00:21:36.779: IP-EIGRP(Default-IP-Routing-Table:100): 10.1.1.1/32 - don't
  advertise out Serial1/0.1
```

Trouble Ticket: EIGRP

This trouble ticket focuses on EIGRP. You are presented with baseline data, a trouble ticket, and information collected while investigating the reported issue. You are then challenged to identify the issue and create an action plan to resolve that issue.

Trouble Ticket #3

You receive the following trouble ticket:

> EIGRP has just been configured as the routing protocol for the network. After configuring EIGRP on all routers and instructing all router interfaces to participate in EIGRP, router R2 does not appear to be load balancing across its links to BB1 and BB2 when sending traffic to network 10.1.2.0/24.

This trouble ticket references the topology shown in Figure 6-7.

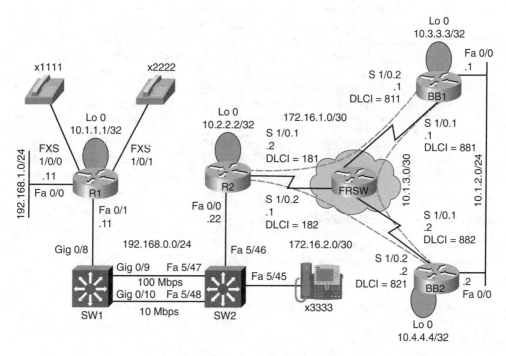

Figure 6-7 *Trouble Ticket #3 Topology*

As you investigate this issue, you examine baseline data collected after EIGRP was initially configured. Example 6-17 confirms that router R2's IP routing table contains only a single path to get to the backbone network of 10.1.2.0/24.

Example 6-17 *Baseline IP Routing Table on Router R2*

```
R2# show ip route
Codes: C - connected, S - static, R - RIP, M - mobile, B - BGP
       D - EIGRP, EX - EIGRP external, O - OSPF, IA - OSPF inter area
       N1 - OSPF NSSA external type 1, N2 - OSPF NSSA external type 2
       E1 - OSPF external type 1, E2 - OSPF external type 2
       i - IS-IS, su - IS-IS summary, L1 - IS-IS level-1, L2 - IS-IS level-2
       ia - IS-IS inter area, * - candidate default, U - per-user static route
       o - ODR, P - periodic downloaded static route

Gateway of last resort is not set

     172.16.0.0/30 is subnetted, 2 subnets
C       172.16.1.0 is directly connected, Serial1/0.1
C       172.16.2.0 is directly connected, Serial1/0.2
     10.0.0.0/8 is variably subnetted, 6 subnets, 3 masks
```

```
C        10.2.2.2/32 is directly connected, Loopback0
D        10.1.3.0/30 [90/3072000] via 172.16.2.2, 00:00:34, Serial1/0.2
D        10.3.3.3/32 [90/2713600] via 172.16.2.2, 00:00:34, Serial1/0.2
D        10.1.2.0/24 [90/2585600] via 172.16.2.2, 00:00:34, Serial1/0.2
D        10.1.1.1/32 [90/409600] via 192.168.0.11, 00:00:46, FastEthernet0/0
D        10.4.4.4/32 [90/2688000] via 172.16.2.2, 00:00:34, Serial1/0.2
C    192.168.0.0/24 is directly connected, FastEthernet0/0
D    192.168.1.0/24 [90/284160] via 192.168.0.11, 00:18:33, FastEthernet0/0
```

You then view the EIGRP topology table on router R2 to see if EIGRP has learned more than one route to reach the 10.1.2.0/24 network. The output, shown in Example 6-18, indicates that the EIGRP topology table knows two routes that could be used to reach the 10.1.2.0/24 network.

Example 6-18   *EIGRP Topology Table on Router R2*

Key Topic

```
R2# show ip eigrp topology
IP-EIGRP Topology Table for AS(1)/ID(10.2.2.2)


Codes: P - Passive, A - Active, U - Update, Q - Query, R - Reply,
       r - reply Status, s - sia Status

P 10.1.3.0/30, 1 successors, FD is 3072000
        via 172.16.2.2 (3072000/2169856), Serial1/0.2
        via 172.16.1.1 (4437248/2169856), Serial1/0.1
P 10.2.2.2/32, 1 successors, FD is 128256
        via Connected, Loopback0
P 10.1.2.0/24, 1 successors, FD is 2585600
        via 172.16.2.2 (2585600/281600), Serial1/0.2
        via 172.16.1.1 (3950848/281600), Serial1/0.1
P 10.3.3.3/32, 1 successors, FD is 2713600
        via 172.16.2.2 (2713600/409600), Serial1/0.2
        via 172.16.1.1 (4053248/128256), Serial1/0.1
P 10.1.1.1/32, 1 successors, FD is 409600
        via 192.168.0.11 (409600/128256), FastEthernet0/0
P 10.4.4.4/32, 1 successors, FD is 2688000
        via 172.16.2.2 (2688000/128256), Serial1/0.2
        via 172.16.1.1 (4078848/409600), Serial1/0.1
P 192.168.0.0/24, 1 successors, FD is 281600
        via Connected, FastEthernet0/0
P 192.168.1.0/24, 1 successors, FD is 284160
        via 192.168.0.11 (284160/28160), FastEthernet0/0
P 172.16.1.0/30, 1 successors, FD is 3925248
        via Connected, Serial1/0.1
P 172.16.2.0/30, 1 successors, FD is 2560000
        via Connected, Serial1/0.2
```

Finally, you examine the EIGRP configuration on router R1, as presented in Example 6-19.

Example 6-19 *EIGRP Configuration on Router R2*

```
R2# show run | begin router
router eigrp 1
 network 10.2.2.2 0.0.0.0
 network 172.16.1.0 0.0.0.3
 network 172.16.2.0 0.0.0.3
 network 192.168.0.0
 auto-summary
```

Take a moment to look through the **show** command output and the topology. Then, hypothesize the underlying cause, explaining why router R2's IP routing table only shows one route to network 10.1.2.0/24, even though the EIGRP topology table knows of two routes to that network. Finally, on a separate sheet of paper, write out a proposed action plan for resolving the reported issue.

Suggested Solution

Upon examination of router R2's EIGRP topology table (as previously shown in Example 6-18), it becomes clear that the reason router R2 is only injecting one of the 10.1.2.0/24 routes into the IP routing table, is that the feasible distances of the two routes are different. By default, EIGRP load balances over routes with equal-cost metrics (that is, equal feasible distances); however, the two routes present in the EIGRP topology table have different metrics.

Examine the two metrics (that is, 2585600 and 3950848), and notice that the metrics differ by less than a factor of two. Specifically, if you took the smallest metric of 2585600 and multiplied it by two, the result would be 5171200, which is greater than the largest metric of 3950848.

Because the metrics for the two routes vary by less than a factor of two, EIGRP's variance feature could be configured to specify a variance of two, as shown in Example 6-20. Specifically, this configuration tells EIGRP on router R2 to not only inject the best EIGRP route into the IP routing table, but rather inject the route with the best metric in addition to any route whose metric is within a factor of two of the best metric (that is, in the range 2585600–5171200). This allows the route with a metric of 3950848 to also be injected into the IP routing table.

Example 6-20 *Enabling the Variance Feature on Router R2*

Key
Topic

```
R2# conf term
Enter configuration commands, one per line.  End with CNTL/Z.
R2(config)# router eigrp 1
R2(config-router)# variance 2
```

To confirm that router R2 can now load balance across routers BB1 and BB2 to reach the 10.1.2.0/24 network, examine the output of the **show ip route** command seen in

Example 6-21. This output confirms that router R2 can now load balance over two unequal-cost paths to reach the 10.1.2.0/24 network.

Example 6-21   *Examining Router R2's IP Routing Table After Enabling the Variance Feature*

```
R2# show ip route
Codes: C - connected, S - static, R - RIP, M - mobile, B - BGP
       D - EIGRP, EX - EIGRP external, O - OSPF, IA - OSPF inter area
       N1 - OSPF NSSA external type 1, N2 - OSPF NSSA external type 2
       E1 - OSPF external type 1, E2 - OSPF external type 2
       i - IS-IS, su - IS-IS summary, L1 - IS-IS level-1, L2 - IS-IS level-2
       ia - IS-IS inter area, * - candidate default, U - per-user static route
       o - ODR, P - periodic downloaded static route

Gateway of last resort is not set

     172.16.0.0/30 is subnetted, 2 subnets
C       172.16.1.0 is directly connected, Serial1/0.1
C       172.16.2.0 is directly connected, Serial1/0.2
     10.0.0.0/8 is variably subnetted, 6 subnets, 3 masks
C       10.2.2.2/32 is directly connected, Loopback0
D       10.1.3.0/30 [90/3072000] via 172.16.2.2, 00:00:03, Serial1/0.2
                    [90/4437248] via 172.16.1.1, 00:00:03, Serial1/0.1
D       10.3.3.3/32 [90/2713600] via 172.16.2.2, 00:00:03, Serial1/0.2
                    [90/4053248] via 172.16.1.1, 00:00:03, Serial1/0.1
D       10.1.2.0/24 [90/2585600] via 172.16.2.2, 00:00:03, Serial1/0.2
                    [90/3950848] via 172.16.1.1, 00:00:03, Serial1/0.1
D       10.1.1.1/32 [90/409600] via 192.168.0.11, 00:00:03, FastEthernet0/0
D       10.4.4.4/32 [90/2688000] via 172.16.2.2, 00:00:03, Serial1/0.2
                    [90/4078848] via 172.16.1.1, 00:00:03, Serial1/0.1
C    192.168.0.0/24 is directly connected, FastEthernet0/0
D    192.168.1.0/24 [90/284160] via 192.168.0.11, 00:00:04, FastEthernet0/0
```

Exam Preparation Tasks

Review All Key Topics

Review the most important topics from inside the chapter, noted with the Key Topics icon in the outer margin of the page. Table 6-6 lists these key topics and the page numbers where each is found.

Key Topic

Table 6-6 *Key Topics for Chapter 6*

Key Topic Element	Description	Page Number
List	Steps to route traffic from one subnet to another	141
List	Router data structures	144
List	CEF data structures	144
Table 6-2	Troubleshooting Layer 3 forwarding information	145
Table 6-3	Troubleshooting Layer 3 to Layer 2 mapping information	148
Table 6-4	EIGRP data structures	152
Table 6-5	EIGRP troubleshooting commands	154
Example 6-18	Viewing an EIGRP topology table	160
Example 6-20	Enabling the EIGRP variance feature	161

Complete Tables and Lists from Memory

Print a copy of Appendix B, "Memory Tables," (found on the CD) or at least the section for this chapter, and complete the tables and lists from memory. Appendix C, "Memory Tables Answer Key," also on the CD, includes completed tables and lists to check your work.

Define Key Terms

Define the following key terms from this chapter, and check your answers in the Glossary:

Forwarding Information Base (FIB), adjacency table, Data Link Connection Identifier (DLCI), Virtual Path Identifier/Virtual Circuit Identifier (VPI/VCI), administrative distance, EIGRP interface table, EIGRP neighbor table, EIGRP topology table, variance

Command Reference to Check Your Memory

This section includes the most important configuration and EXEC commands covered in this chapter. To determine how well you have memorized the commands as a side effect of your other studies, cover the left side of the table with a piece of paper, read the descriptions on the right side, and see whether you remember the command.

Table 6-7   *Chapter 6 Configuration Command Reference*

Command	Description
router eigrp *autonomous-system-number*	Global configuration mode command that starts the EIGRP routing process. (NOTE: All routers that exchange EIGRP routing information must use the same autonomous system number.)
network *network* [**wildcard-mask**]	Router configuration mode command that specifies a connected network whose interface will participate in the EIGRP routing process.
no auto-summary	Router configuration mode command that disables automatic network summarization.
variance *multiplier*	Router configuration mode command that determines the metric values over which EIGRP will load-balance traffic.

Table 6-8   *Chapter 6 EXEC Command Reference*

Command	Description
show ip route *IP_address*	Displays a router's best route to the specified IP address.
show ip route *network subnet_mask*	Displays a router's best route to the specified network, if the specific route (with a matching subnet mask length) is found in the router's IP routing table.
show ip route *network subnet_mask* **longer-prefixes**	Displays all routes in a router's IP routing table that are encompassed by the specified network address and subnet mask. (NOTE: This command is often useful when troubleshooting route summarization issues.)
show ip cef *ip-address*	Displays information (for example, next-hop IP address and egress interface) required to forward a packet, similar to the output of the **show ip route** *IP_address* command. (NOTE: The output of this command comes from CEF. Therefore, routing protocol information is not presented in the output.)
show ip cef *network subnet_mask*	Displays information from a router's FIB showing the information needed to route a packet to the specified network with the specified subnet mask.
show ip cef exact-route *source- ip-address destination-ip-address*	Displays the adjacency that will be used to forward a packet from the specified source IP address to the specified destination IP address. (NOTE: This command is useful if the router is load balancing across multiple adjacencies, and you want to see which adjacency will be used for a certain combination of source and destination IP addresses.)

Table 6-8 *Chapter 6 EXEC Command Reference* *(Continued)*

Command	Description
show ip arp	Displays a router's ARP cache, containing IP address to MAC address mappings. (NOTE: By default, a router's ARP cache stores information for four hours. Therefore, you might need to execute a **clear ip arp** command to allow a router to re-learn information after you make a topology change.)
show frame-relay map	Displays Frame Relay DLCIs associated with different next-hop IP addresses.
show adjacency detail	Displays the frame headers in a router's CEF adjacency table used to encapsulate a frame being sent to an adjacency.
show ip eigrp interfaces	Displays all of a router's interfaces configured to participate in an EIGRP routing process (with the exception of passive interfaces).
show ip eigrp neighbors	Shows a router's EIGRP neighbors.
show ip eigrp topology	Displays routes known to a router's EIGRP routing process. (NOTE: These routes are contained in the EIGRP topology table.)
show ip route eigrp	Displays routes known to a router's IP routing table that were injected by the router's EIGRP routing process.
debug ip routing	Displays updates that occur in a router's IP routing table. (NOTE: This is command is not specific to EIGRP.)
debug eigrp packets	Displays all EIGRP packets exchanged with a router's EIGRP neighbors. (NOTE: The focus of the command can be narrowed to only display specific EIGRP packet types, such as EIGRP Hello packets.)
debug ip eigrp	Displays information contained in EIGRP packets and reveals how an EIGRP routing process responds to that information.

This chapter covers the following subjects:

OSPF Troubleshooting: This section begins by introducing you to OSPF routing structures, followed by a review of OSPF operation. Finally, you are presented with a collection of **show** and **debug** commands useful for troubleshooting OSPF operations.

Trouble Ticket: OSPF: This section presents you with a trouble ticket and an associated topology. You are also given **show** command output. Based on the information provided, you hypothesize an underlying cause for the reported issues and develop solutions. You can then compare your solutions with the suggested solutions.

Route Redistribution Troubleshooting: This section introduces the concept of route redistribution and discusses how a route from one routing process can be injected into a different routing process. Common route redistribution troubleshooting targets are identified, along with strategies for troubleshooting a route redistribution issue.

Trouble Ticket: Route Redistribution with EIGRP and OSPF: This section presents you with a trouble ticket and an associated topology. You are also given **show** command output. Based on the information provided, you hypothesize an underlying cause for the reported issue and develop a solution. You can then compare your solution with a suggested solution.

CHAPTER 7

OSPF and Route Redistribution Troubleshooting

This chapter reviews the characteristics of Open Shortest Path First (OSPF), including OSPF data structures, router types, link-state advertisement (LSA) types, and network types. You also see how an OSPF adjacency is formed. Then you are presented with a collection of commands useful for troubleshooting OSPF networks.

This chapter contains two trouble tickets, the first of which addresses OSPF. Presented with a trouble ticket, a topology, and a collection of **show** command output, you are challenged to resolve the issue (or possibly multiple issues) in an OSPF-based network.

Next, you review the concept of route redistribution, where routes learned via one routing process can be injected into another routing process. Troubleshooting strategies for route redistribution are then presented.

Finally, this chapter challenges you with another trouble ticket. This final trouble ticket focuses on route redistribution.

"Do I Know This Already?" Quiz

The "Do I Know This Already?" quiz helps you determine your level of knowledge of this chapter's topics before you begin. Table 7-1 details the major topics discussed in this chapter and their corresponding quiz questions.

Table 7-1 *"Do I Know This Already?" Section-to-Question Mapping*

Foundation Topics Section	Questions
OSPF Troubleshooting	1–6
Route Redistribution Troubleshooting	7–8

1. Which OSPF data structure contains topological information for all areas in which an OSPF router is participating?

    a. OSPF Routing Information Base

    b. OSPF link-state database

    c. OSPF interface table

    d. OSPF neighbor table

2. What OSPF LSA type is sourced by all OSPF routers?

    a. Type 1

    b. Type 2

    c. Type 3

    d. Type 4

    e. Type 5

3. What type of OSPF router has at least one of its connected networks participating in OSPF area 0?

    a. Internal

    b. ABR

    c. Backbone

    d. ASBR

4. What is the default OSPF network type on LAN interfaces?

    a. Point-to-point

    b. Nonbroadcast

    c. Point-to-multipoint

    d. Broadcast

5. What OSPF adjacency state occurs when two OSPF routers have received Hello messages from each other, and each router saw its own OSPF router ID in the Hello message it received?

    a. Exchange

    b. ExStart

    c. 2-Way

    d. Loading

6. What command displays the LSA headers in a router's OSPF link-state database?

    a. show ip ospf neighbor

    b. show ip ospf database

    c. show ip ospf statistics

    d. show ip ospf interface

7. When performing route redistribution, the destination routing protocol needs a metric to assign to routes being redistributed into that routing protocol. What is this metric called?

    a. External metric

    b. Internal metric

    c. Seed metric

    d. Source metric

8. Which of the following commands would you use to enable the Cisco IOS IP route profiling feature?

    a.   Router(config)#**ip route profile**

    b.   Router(config-if)#**ip route profile**

    c.   Router(config)#**route profiling ip**

    d.   Router(config-if)#**route profiling ip**

Foundation Topics

OSPF Troubleshooting

Chapter 6, "Introduction to Troubleshooting Routing Protocols," began with a discussion on troubleshooting routing protocols from a generic perspective. Chapter 6 also reviewed router and Cisco Express Forwarding (CEF) data structures, as well as Enhanced Interior Gateway Routing Protocol (EIGRP), including EIGRP data structures. Finally, the chapter concluded with coverage of a collection of commands for gathering information from EIGRP data structures.

This section addresses the OSPF routing protocol in a similar fashion to the Chapter 6 treatment of EIGRP. Specifically, this section examines OSPF data structures, reviews OSPF operation, and presents you with commands useful for collecting information from the OSPF data structures.

OSPF is a nonproprietary link-state protocol. Like EIGRP, OSPF offers fast convergence and is a popular enterprise routing protocol.

OSPF Data Structures

Whereas EIGRP has three major data structures (that is, EIGRP interface table, EIGRP neighbor table, and EIGRP topology table), OSPF uses four data structures, as described in Table 7-2.

Table 7-2 *OSPF Data Structures*

Data Structure	Description
OSPF interface table	All the router interfaces that have been configured to participate in an OSPF routing process are listed in this table.
OSPF neighbor table	OSPF neighbors learned via Hello packets are present in this table. A neighbor is removed from this table if Hellos have not been heard from the neighbor within the dead time interval. Additionally, a neighbor is removed from this table if the interface associated with the neighbor goes down.
OSPF link-state database	This data structure contains topology information for all areas in which a router participates, in addition to information about how to route traffic to networks residing in other areas or autonomous systems.
OSPF Routing Information Base	The OSPF Routing Information Base (RIB) stores the results of the OSPF shortest path first (SPF) calculations.

Of the data structures listed in Table 7-2, the OSPF link-state database contains the most comprehensive collection of information. Therefore, the OSPF link-state database is valuable to view for OSPF troubleshooting.

An OSPF link-state database stored in an OSPF router contains comprehensive information about the topology within a specific OSPF area. Note that if a router is participating in more than one OSPF area, the router contains more than one OSPF link-state database (one for each area). Because an OSPF link-state database contains the topology of an OSPF area, all routers participating in that OSPF area should have identical OSPF link-state databases.

In addition to networks residing in OSPF areas, an OSPF router can store information about routes redistributed into OSPF in an OSPF link-state database. Information about these redistributed routes is stored in an area separate from the area-specific OSPF link-state databases.

OSPF Operation

Because OSPF is a link-state protocol, it receives LSAs from adjacent OSPF routers. The Dijkstra SPF algorithm takes the information contained in the LSAs to determine the shortest path to any destination within an area of the network.

Although multiple routers can participate in a single OSPF area, larger OSPF networks are often divided into multiple areas. In a multiarea OSPF network, a backbone area (numbered *area 0*) must exist, and all other areas must connect to area 0. If an area is not physically adjacent to area 0, a *virtual link* can be configured to logically connect the nonadjacent area with area 0.

OSPF Metric

OSPF uses a metric of *cost*, which is a function of bandwidth. Cost can be calculated as follows:

cost = 100,000,000 / bandwidth (in bps)

Designated Router

A multiaccess network can have multiple routers residing on a common network segment. Rather than having all routers form a full mesh of adjacencies with one another, a *designated router* (DR) can be elected, and all other routers on the segment can form an adjacency with the DR, as illustrated in Figure 7-1.

A DR is elected based on router priority, with larger priority values being more preferable. If routers have equal priorities, the DR is elected based on the highest OSPF router ID. An OSPF router ID is determined by the IP address of the loopback interface of the router or by the highest IP address on an active interface, or it can be statically defined if the router is not configured with a loopback interface.

A backup designated router (BDR) is also elected. Routers on the multiaccess network also form adjacencies if the DR becomes unavailable.

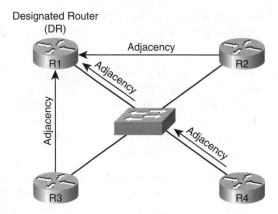

Figure 7-1   *Designated Router Adjacencies*

OSPF Router Types

When an OSPF network grows beyond a single area, you need to be aware of the role played by each OSPF router in a topology. Specifically, four OSPF router types exist:

■ **Internal router:** All the networks directly connected to an internal router belong to the same OSPF area. Therefore, an internal router has a single link-state database.

■ **Area border router (ABR):** An ABR connects to more than one OSPF area and therefore maintains multiple link-state databases (one for each connected area). A primary responsibility of an ABR is to exchange topological information between the backbone area and other connected areas.

■ **Backbone router:** A backbone router has at least one of its connected networks participating in OSPF area 0 (that is, the backbone area). If all the connected networks are participating in the backbone area, the router is also considered to be an internal router. However, if a backbone router has one or more connected networks participating in another area, the backbone router is also considered to be an ABR.

■ **Autonomous system boundary router (ASBR):** An ASBR has at least one connected route participating in an OSPF area and at least one connected route participating in a different autonomous system. The primary role of an ASBR is to exchange information between an OSPF autonomous system and one or more external autonomous systems.

As an example, Figure 7-2 illustrates these various OSPF router types.

Table 7-3 lists the OSPF router type or types for each OSPF router in the topology (that is, routers R1, R2, R3, and R4).

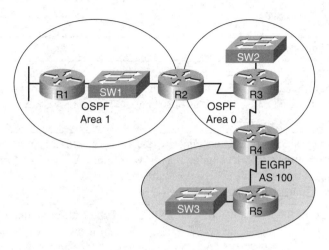

Figure 7-2 *OSPF Router Types*

Table 7-3 *OSPF Router Types in Figure 7-2*

Router	OSPF Router Type(s)
R1	Internal (because all the connected routes of the router belong to the same OSPF area)
R2	ABR (because the connected routes of the router belong to more than one OSPF area)
	Backbone (because the router has at least one connected route participating in OSPF area 0)
R3	Internal (because all the connected routes of the router belong to the same OSPF area)
	Backbone (because the router has at least one connected route participating in OSPF area 0)
R4	Backbone (because the router has at least one connected route participating in OSPF area 0)
	ASBR (because the router has at least one connected route participating in an OSPF area and one connected route participating in a different autonomous system)

OSPF LSA Types

As previously mentioned, an OSPF router receives LSAs from adjacent OSPF neighbors. However, OSPF uses multiple LSA types. Table 7-4 lists the common LSA types you might encounter when troubleshooting a Cisco-based OSPF network.

Table 7-4   *LSA Types*

Key
Topic

LSA Type	Description
1	All OSPF routers source Type 1 LSAs. These advertisements list information about directly connected subnets, the OSPF connection types of a router, and the known OSPF adjacencies of a router. A Type 1 LSA is not sent out of its local area.
2	The designated router on a multiaccess network sends a Type 2 LSA for that network if the network contains at least two routers. A Type 2 LSA contains a listing of routers connected to the multiaccess network and, like a Type 1 LSA, is constrained to its local area.
3	A Type 3 LSA is sourced by an ABR. Each Type 3 LSA sent into an area contains information about a network reachable in a different area. Note that network information is exchanged only between the backbone area and a nonbackbone area, as opposed to being exchanged between two nonbackbone areas.
4	Similar to a Type 3 LSA, a Type 4 LSA is sourced by an ABR. However, instead of containing information about OSPF networks, a Type 4 LSA contains information stating how to reach an ASBR.
5	A Type 5 LSA is sourced by an ASBR and contains information about networks reachable outside the ospf domain. A Type 5 LSA is sent to all OSPF areas, except for stub areas. Note: The ABR for a stub area sends default route information into the stub area, rather than the network-specific Type 5 LSAs.
7	A Type 7 LSA is sourced from a router within a not-so-stubby-area (NSSA). Whereas a stub area does not connect to an external autonomous system, an NSSA can. Those external routes are announced by an ABR of the NSSA using Type 7 LSAs. Like a stub area, however, external routes known to another OSPF area are not forwarded into an NSSA.

To illustrate how the database of an OSPF router is populated with these various LSA types, once again consider Figure 7-2. Table 7-5 shows the number of each LSA type present in the OSPF routers of the topology. Note that the topology has no Type 7 LSAs because it does not contain NSSAs.

Table 7-5 *OSPF LSA Types in Figure 7-2*

Router	Type 1 LSAs	Type 2 LSAs	Type 3 LSAs	Type 4 LSAs	Type 5 LSAs
R1	2 (because two routers are in area 1)	1 (because only one of the multiaccess networks of area 1 contains at least two routers)	3 (because the area 1 database contains the three networks in area 0)	1 (because the topology contains only one ASBR)	2 (because the EIGRP AS contains two networks that are external to the OSPF AS)
R2	5 (because area 1 has two routers and area 0 has three routers)	1 (because area 1 contains only one multiaccess network containing at least two routers, while area 0 contains zero multiaccess networks with at least two routers)	5 (because the area 1 database contains the three networks in area 0, and the area 0 database contains the two networks in area 1)	1 (because the topology contains only one ASBR)	2 (because the EIGRP AS contains two networks that are external to the OSPF AS)
R3	3 (because area 0 has three routers)	0 (because area 0 does not contain any multiaccess networks with at least two routers)	2 (because the area 0 database contains the two networks in area 1)	1 (because the topology contains only one ASBR)	2 (because the EIGRP AS contains two networks that are external to the OSPF AS)
R4	3 (because area 0 has three routers)	0 (because area 0 does not contain multiaccess networks with at least two routers)	2 (because the area 0 database contains the two networks in area 1)	1 (because the topology contains only one ASBR)	2 (because the EIGRP AS contains two networks that are external to the OSPF AS)

OSPF Network Types

OSPF can support multiple network types. For example, a multiaccess network such as Ethernet is considered to be an OSPF *broadcast* network. Table 7-6 shows a listing of supported OSPF network types and characteristics of each.

Table 7-6 *OSPF Network Types and Characteristics*

	Broadcast	Nonbroadcast	Point-to-Point	Point-to-Multipoint
Characteristics	Default OSPF network type on LAN interfaces	Default OSPF network type on Frame Relay serial interfaces	Default OSPF network type on non-Frame Relay serial interfaces	Can be configured on any interface
	Neighbors automatically discovered	Neighbors statically configured	Routers at each end of a link form adjacencies	Neighbors automatically determined
	All routers on same subnet	All routers on same subnet	Each point-to-point link on a separate subnet	All routers on same subnet
	Has a designated router	Has a designated router	Does not have a designated router	Does not have a designated router

Forming an OSPF Adjacency

Although two OSPF routers can form an adjacency (that is, become neighbors) through the exchange of Hello packets, the following parameters in the Hello packets must match:

- **Hello timer:** This timer defaults to 10 seconds for broadcast and point-to-point network types. The default is 30 seconds for nonbroadcast and point-to-multipoint network types.

- **Dead timer:** This timer defaults to 40 seconds for broadcast and point-to-point network types. The default is 120 seconds for nonbroadcast and point-to-multipoint network types.

- **Area number:** Both ends of a link must be in the same OSPF area.

- **Area type:** In addition to a normal OSPF area type, an area type could be either stub or NSSA.

- **Subnet:** Note that this common subnet is not verified on point-to-point OSPF networks.

- **Authentication information:** If one OSPF interface is configured for authentication, the OSPF interface at the other end of the link should be configured with matching authentication information (for example, authentication type and password).

Adjacencies are not established upon the immediate receipt of Hello messages. Rather, an adjacency transitions through multiple states, as described in Table 7-7.

Table 7-7 *Adjacency States*

State	Description
Down	This state indicates that no Hellos have been received from a neighbor.
Attempt	This state occurs after a router sends a unicast Hello (as opposed to a multicast Hello) to a configured neighbor and has not yet received a Hello from that neighbor.
Init	This state occurs on a router that has received a Hello message from its neighbor; however, the OSPF router ID of the receiving router was not contained in the Hello message. If a router remains in this state for a long period, something is probably preventing that router from correctly receiving Hello packets from the neighboring router.
2-Way	This state occurs when two OSPF routers have received Hello messages from each other, and each router saw its own OSPF router ID in the Hello message it received. The 2-Way state could be a final state for a multiaccess network if the network has already elected a designated router and a backup designated router.
ExStart	This state occurs when the designated and nondesignated routers of a multiaccess network begin to exchange information with other routers in the multiaccess network. If a router remains in this state for a long period, a maximum transmission unit (MTU) mismatch could exist between the neighboring routers, or a duplicate OSPF router ID might exist.
Exchange	This state occurs when the two routers forming an adjacency send one another database descriptor (DBD) packets containing information about a router's link-state database. Each router compares the DBD packets received from the other router to identify missing entries in its own link-state database. Like the ExStart state, if a router remains in the Exchange state for a long period, the issue could be an MTU mismatch or a duplicate OSPF router ID.
Loading	Based on the missing link-state database entries identified in the Exchange state, the Loading state occurs when each neighboring router requests the other router to send those missing entries. If a router remains in this state for a long period, a packet might have been corrupted, or a router might have a memory corruption issue. Alternatively, it is possible that such a condition could result from the neighboring routers having an MTU mismatch.
Full	This state indicates that the neighboring OSPF routers have successfully exchanged their link-state information with one another, and an adjacency has been formed.

Tracking OSPF Advertisements Through a Network

When troubleshooting an OSPF issue, tracking the path of OSPF advertisements can be valuable in determining why certain entries are in a router's RIB.

As an example, notice network 192.168.1.0/24 in the topology provided in Figure 7-3, and consider how this network is entered into the RIB of the other OSPF routers.

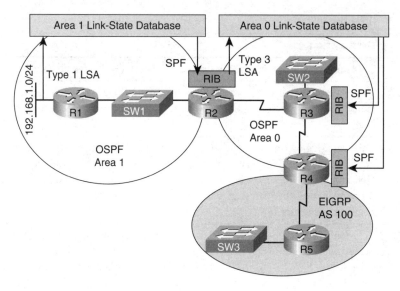

Figure 7-3   *Tracking an OSPF Advertisement*

The following steps describe how network 192.168.1.0/24, which is directly connected to router R1, is learned by the RIB of routers R2, R3, and R4.

Step 1.   Router R1 creates an LSA for the 192.168.1.0/24 network in the area 1 link-state database.

Step 2.   Router R2, which also has a copy of the area 1 link-state database, runs the SPF algorithm to determine the best path through area 1 to reach the 192.168.1.0/24 network. The result is stored in router R2's RIB.

Step 3.   Router R2 informs area 0 routers about this network by injecting a Type 3 LSA into the link-state database of area 0. This LSA includes the cost to reach the 192.168.1.0/24 network, from the perspective of router R2.

Step 4.   Each of the other area 0 routers (that is, routers R3 and R4) run the SPF algorithm to determine the cost to reach router R2. This cost is then added to the cost router R2 advertised in its Type 3 LSA, and the result is stored in the RIB for routers R3 and R4.

OSPF Troubleshooting Commands

With an understanding of OSPF's data structures and an understanding of OSPF's router types, network types, LSA types, and adjacency states, you can now strategically use Cisco IOS **show** and **debug** commands to collect information about specific steps in the routing process. Table 7-8 shows a collection of such commands, along with their descriptions, and the step of the routing process or OSPF data structure each command can be used to investigate.

Table 7-8 *OSPF Troubleshooting Commands*

Key
Topic

Command	Routing Component or Data Structure	Description
show ip ospf interface [brief]	OSPF interface table	This command displays all of a router's interfaces configured to participate in an OSPF routing process. The **brief** option provides a more concise view of OSPF interface information.
show ip ospf neighbor	OSPF neighbor table	This command displays the state of OSPF neighbors learned off a router's active OSPF interfaces.
show ip ospf database	OSPF link-state database	This command displays the LSA headers contained in a router's OSPF link-state database.
show ip ospf statistics	OSPF RIB	This command provides information about how frequently a router is executing the SPF algorithm. Additionally, this command shows when the SPF algorithm last ran.
debug ip ospf monitor	OSPF RIB	This command provides real-time updates showing when a router's SPF algorithm is scheduled to run.
debug ip routing	IP routing table	This command displays updates that occur in a router's IP routing table. Therefore, this command is not specific to OSPF.
show ip route ospf	IP routing table	This command shows routes known to a router's IP routing table that were learned via OSPF.
debug ip ospf packet	Exchanging OSPF information with neighbors	This command shows the transmission and reception of OSPF packets in real time. This command is useful for monitoring Hello messages.
debug ip ospf adj	Exchanging OSPF information with neighbors	This command provides real-time updates about the formation of an OSPF adjacency.

continues

Table 7-8 *OSPF Troubleshooting Commands* *(Continued)*

Command	Routing Component or Data Structure	Description
debug ip ospf events	Exchanging OSPF information with neighbors	This command shows real-time information about OSPF events, including the transmission and reception of Hello messages and LSAs. This command might be useful on a router that appears to be ignoring Hello messages received from a neighboring router.
show ip ospf virtual-links	OSPF interface table	This command provides information about the status of OSPF virtual links that are required for areas not physically adjacent to the backbone area (that is, area 0).

Example 7-1 provides sample output from the **show ip ospf interface brief** command. Notice that the output shows summary information about all the router interfaces participating in an OSPF routing process, including the OSPF process ID (PID), the OSPF area, and the network associated with each interface. Additionally, the output contains the OSPF metric of cost, information about the state of an interface, and the number of neighbors that an interface has.

Example 7-1   show ip ospf interface brief *Command Output*

```
R2# show ip ospf interface brief
Interface    PID   Area         IP Address/Mask    Cost   State   Nbrs F/C
Lo0          1     0            10.2.2.2/32        1      LOOP    0/0
Se1/0.2      1     0            172.16.2.1/30      64     P2P     1/1
Se1/0.1      1     0            172.16.1.2/30      64     P2P     1/1
Fa0/0        1     0            192.168.0.22/24    10     DR      1/1
```

Example 7-2 provides sample output from the **show ip ospf neighbor** command. A neighbor's OSPF router ID is shown. For a multiaccess segment (FastEthernet 0/0 in this example), the neighbor's priority, used for designated router election, is shown. The remaining dead time for a neighbor is displayed. Finally, the output contains information about each neighbor's interface (and the IP address of that interface) through which the neighbor is reachable.

Example 7-2   show ip ospf neighbor *Command Output*

```
R2# show ip ospf neighbor
Neighbor ID     Pri    State          Dead Time    Address          Interface
10.4.4.4         0     FULL/   -      00:00:38     172.16.2.2       Serial1/0.2
10.3.3.3         0     FULL/   -      00:00:38     172.16.1.1       Serial1/0.1
10.1.1.1         1     FULL/BDR       00:00:36     192.168.0.11     FastEthernet0/0
```

Example 7-3 provides sample output from the **show ip ospf database** command. The database of the router has been populated with various LSAs, as previously discussed. The *Router Link States* in the database come from Type 1 LSAs, whereas the *Net Link States* come from Type 2 LSAs.

Example 7-3   show ip ospf database *Command Output*

```
R2# show ip ospf database
              OSPF Router with ID (10.2.2.2) (Process ID 1)
          Router Link States (Area 0)
Link ID          ADV Router       Age        Seq#         Checksum   Link count
10.1.1.1         10.1.1.1         969        0x8000000C   0x0092ED   3
10.2.2.2         10.2.2.2         968        0x80000013   0x00FD7D   6
10.3.3.3         10.3.3.3         1598       0x80000007   0x00DAEA   6
10.4.4.4         10.4.4.4         1597       0x80000007   0x0009B1   6
          Net Link States (Area 0)


Link ID          ADV Router       Age        Seq#         Checksum
10.1.2.2         10.4.4.4         1622       0x80000001   0x00CE1D
192.168.0.22     10.2.2.2         968        0x8000000B   0x008AF8
```

Example 7-4 provides sample output from the **show ip ospf statistics** command. Notice that the primary focus of the command is on the SPF algorithm. For example, you can see from the output how many times the SPF algorithm has been executed for a particular OSPF area.

Example 7-4   show ip ospf statistics *Command Output*

```
R2# show ip ospf statistics
              OSPF Router with ID (10.2.2.2) (Process ID 1)
  Area 0: SPF algorithm executed 23 times
  Summary OSPF SPF statistic
  SPF calculation time
Delta T     Intra    D-Intra    Summ    D-Summ    Ext    D-Ext    Total    Reason
00:21:00    12       0          0       0         0      0        16       R, N,
00:20:50    16       0          0       0         0      0        20       R,
00:19:40    12       4          0       0         0      0        20       R, N,
00:19:30    12       0          0       0         0      0        16       R, N,
00:19:20    16       0          0       0         4      0        24       R,
```

00:18:09	12	4	0	0	0	0	16	R, N,
00:17:59	12	0	0	0	0	0	16	R, N,
00:17:49	16	0	0	0	0	0	20	N,
00:16:37	4	4	0	0	0	0	8	R, N,
00:16:27	16	0	0	0	0	0	20	R, N,

```
   RIB manipulation time during SPF (in msec):
Delta T    RIB Update    RIB Delete
00:21:00   3             0
00:20:52   4             0
00:19:42   0             3
00:19:32   3             0
00:19:22   7             0
00:18:10   3             0
00:18:00   7             0
00:17:50   0             0
00:16:39   0             0
00:16:29   0             0
```

Example 7-5 provides sample output from the **debug ip ospf monitor** command. This command provides real-time information about when the SPF algorithm is scheduled to run and when it actually does run.

Example 7-5   debug ip ospf monitor *Command Output*

```
R2# debug ip ospf monitor
OSPF spf monitoring debugging is on
*Mar  1 00:29:11.923: OSPF: Schedule SPF in area 0
       Change in LS ID 10.1.1.1, LSA type R, , spf-type Full
*Mar  1 00:29:11.927: OSPF: reset throttling to 5000ms
*Mar  1 00:29:11.927: OSPF: schedule SPF: spf_time 00:29:11.928 wait_interval 5000ms
*Mar  1 00:29:16.927: OSPF: Begin SPF at 1756.928ms, process time 1132ms
*Mar  1 00:29:16.927:        spf_time 00:29:11.928, wait_interval 5000ms
*Mar  1 00:29:16.947: OSPF: wait_interval 10000ms next wait_interval 10000ms
*Mar  1 00:29:16.947: OSPF: End SPF at 1756.948ms, Total elapsed time 20ms
*Mar  1 00:29:16.951:        Schedule time 00:29:16.948, Next wait_interval 10000ms
*Mar  1 00:29:16.955:        Intra: 12ms, Inter: 0ms, External: 0ms
*Mar  1 00:29:16.955:        R: 4, N: 2, Stubs: 10
*Mar  1 00:29:16.955:        SN: 0, SA: 0, X5: 0, X7: 0
*Mar  1 00:29:16.955:        SPF suspends: 0 intra, 0 total
*Mar  1 00:29:26.175: OSPF: Schedule SPF in area 0
       Change in LS ID 10.1.1.1, LSA type R, , spf-type Full
*Mar  1 00:29:26.947: OSPF: Begin SPF at 1766.948ms, process time 1160ms
*Mar  1 00:29:26.947:        spf_time 00:29:16.948, wait_interval 10000ms
*Mar  1 00:29:26.971: OSPF: wait_interval 10000ms next wait_interval 10000ms
*Mar  1 00:29:26.975: OSPF: End SPF at 1766.972ms, Total elapsed time 28ms
*Mar  1 00:29:26.975:        Schedule time 00:29:26.972, Next wait_interval 10000ms
```

```
*Mar  1 00:29:26.975:     Intra: 16ms, Inter: 0ms, External: 0ms
*Mar  1 00:29:26.975:     R: 4, N: 2, Stubs: 11
*Mar  1 00:29:26.975:     SN: 0, SA: 0, X5: 0, X7: 0
*Mar  1 00:29:26.975:     SPF suspends: 0 intra, 0 total
```

Example 7-6 provides sample output from the **debug ip routing** command. The output reflects a loopback interface (with an IP address of 10.1.1.1) on a neighboring router being administratively shut down and brought back up.

Example 7-6   debug ip routing *Command Output*

```
R2# debug ip routing
IP routing debugging is on
*Mar  1 00:29:58.163: RT: del 10.1.1.1/32 via 192.168.0.11, ospf metric [110/11]
*Mar  1 00:29:58.163: RT: delete subnet route to 10.1.1.1/32
*Mar  1 00:29:58.163: RT: NET-RED 10.1.1.1/32
*Mar  1 00:30:08.175: RT: SET_LAST_RDB for 10.1.1.1/32
  NEW rdb: via 192.168.0.11
*Mar  1 00:30:08.179: RT: add 10.1.1.1/32 via 192.168.0.11, ospf metric [110/11]
*Mar  1 00:30:08.183: RT: NET-RED 10.1.1.1/32
```

Example 7-7 provides sample output from the **show ip route ospf** command. This command produces a subset of the output from the **show ip route** command, showing only those route entries learned via OSPF.

Example 7-7   show ip route ospf *Command Output*

```
R2# show ip route ospf
     10.0.0.0/8 is variably subnetted, 6 subnets, 3 masks
O        10.1.3.0/30 [110/128] via 172.16.2.2, 00:00:20, Serial1/0.2
                     [110/128] via 172.16.1.1, 00:00:20, Serial1/0.1
O        10.3.3.3/32 [110/65] via 172.16.1.1, 00:00:20, Serial1/0.1
O        10.1.2.0/24 [110/74] via 172.16.2.2, 00:00:20, Serial1/0.2
                     [110/74] via 172.16.1.1, 00:00:20, Serial1/0.1
O        10.1.1.1/32 [110/11] via 192.168.0.11, 00:00:20, FastEthernet0/0
O        10.4.4.4/32 [110/65] via 172.16.2.2, 00:00:20, Serial1/0.2
```

Example 7-8 provides sample output from the **debug ip ospf packet** command. The output confirms OSPF packets are being received from specific neighbors and over what interfaces those OSPF packets are being received. For example, the output indicates that an OSPF neighbor with a router ID of 10.1.1.1 sent an OSPF packet, and that packet came into this router on FastEthernet 0/0.

Example 7-8   debug ip ospf packet *Command Output*

```
R2# debug ip ospf packet
OSPF packet debugging is on
*Mar  1 00:30:42.995: OSPF: rcv. v:2 t:1 l:48 rid:10.1.1.1
       aid:0.0.0.0 chk:5422 aut:0 auk: from FastEthernet0/0
*Mar  1 00:30:45.039: OSPF: rcv. v:2 t:4 l:76 rid:10.1.1.1
       aid:0.0.0.0 chk:E9B4 aut:0 auk: from FastEthernet0/0
*Mar  1 00:30:45.179: OSPF: rcv. v:2 t:1 l:48 rid:10.3.3.3
       aid:0.0.0.0 chk:D294 aut:0 auk: from Serial1/0.1
*Mar  1 00:30:45.363: OSPF: rcv. v:2 t:1 l:48 rid:10.4.4.4
       aid:0.0.0.0 chk:D192 aut:0 auk: from Serial1/0.2
*Mar  1 00:30:47.727: OSPF: rcv. v:2 t:5 l:44 rid:10.3.3.3
       aid:0.0.0.0 chk:2EF0 aut:0 auk: from Serial1/0.1
```

Example 7-9 provides sample output from the **debug ip adj** command. This command shows real-time details as a router establishes an adjacency with an OSPF neighbor, including the states through which the adjacency transitions.

Example 7-9   debug ip ospf adj *Command Output*

```
R2# debug ip ospf adj
OSPF adjacency events debugging is on
*Mar  1 00:31:44.719: OSPF: Rcv LS UPD from 10.3.3.3 on Serial1/0.1 length 100
  LSA count 1
*Mar  1 00:31:57.475: OSPF: Cannot see ourself in hello from 10.4.4.4 on
  Serial1/0.2, state INIT
*Mar  1 00:31:57.807: OSPF: 2 Way Communication to 10.4.4.4 on Serial1/0.2,
  state 2WAY
*Mar  1 00:31:57.811: OSPF: Send DBD to 10.4.4.4 on Serial1/0.2 seq 0x7FD opt
  0x52 flag 0x7 len 32
*Mar  1 00:31:57.815: OSPF: Rcv DBD from 10.4.4.4 on Serial1/0.2 seq 0xDF9 opt
  0x52 flag 0x7 len 32  mtu 1500 state EXSTART
*Mar  1 00:31:57.819: OSPF: NBR Negotiation Done. We are the SLAVE
*Mar  1 00:31:57.819: OSPF: Send DBD to 10.4.4.4 on Serial1/0.2 seq 0xDF9 opt
  0x52 flag 0x2 len 152
*Mar  1 00:31:57.983: OSPF: Build router LSA for area 0, router ID 10.2.2.2, seq
  0x80000014
*Mar  1 00:31:58.191: OSPF: Rcv DBD from 10.4.4.4 on Serial1/0.2 seq 0xDFA opt
  0x52 flag 0x3 len 152  mtu 1500 state EXCHANGE
*Mar  1 00:31:58.195: OSPF: Send DBD to 10.4.4.4 on Serial1/0.2 seq 0xDFA opt
  0x52 flag 0x0 len 32
*Mar  1 00:31:58.199: OSPF: Rcv LS UPD from 10.3.3.3 on Serial1/0.1 length 112
  LSA count 1
*Mar  1 00:31:58.455: OSPF: Rcv DBD from 10.4.4.4 on Serial1/0.2 seq 0xDFB opt
  0x52 flag 0x1 len 32  mtu 1500 state EXCHANGE
*Mar  1 00:31:58.459: OSPF: Exchange Done with 10.4.4.4 on Serial1/0.2
*Mar  1 00:31:58.463: OSPF: Synchronized with 10.4.4.4 on Serial1/0.2, state FULL
*Mar  1 00:31:58.463: %OSPF-5-ADJCHG: Process 1, Nbr 10.4.4.4 on Serial1/0.2 from
  LOADING to FULL, Loading Done
```

Example 7-10 provides sample output from the **debug ip ospf events** command. This command produces real-time information about OSPF events, including the transmission and reception of OSPF Hello messages and LSAs.

Example 7-10   debug ip ospf events *Command Output*

```
R2# debug ip ospf events
OSPF events debugging is on
*Mar  1 00:32:23.007: OSPF: Rcv hello from 10.1.1.1 area 0 from FastEthernet0/0
  192.168.0.11
*Mar  1 00:32:23.011: OSPF: End of hello processing
*Mar  1 00:32:25.195: OSPF: Rcv hello from 10.3.3.3 area 0 from Serial1/0.1
  172.16.1.1
*Mar  1 00:32:25.199: OSPF: End of hello processing
*Mar  1 00:32:27.507: OSPF: Rcv hello from 10.4.4.4 area 0 from Serial1/0.2
  172.16.2.2
*Mar  1 00:32:27.511: OSPF: End of hello processing
*Mar  1 00:32:28.595: OSPF: Send hello to 224.0.0.5 area 0 on Serial1/0.1 from
  172.16.1.2
*Mar  1 00:32:28.687: OSPF: Send hello to 224.0.0.5 area 0 on Serial1/0.2 from
  172.16.2.1
*Mar  1 00:32:29.163: OSPF: Send hello to 224.0.0.5 area 0 on FastEthernet0/0
  from 192.168.0.22
*Mar  1 00:32:32.139: OSPF: Rcv LS UPD from 10.3.3.3 on Serial1/0.1 length 100
  LSA count 1
*Mar  1 00:32:33.007: OSPF: Rcv hello from 10.1.1.1 area 0 from FastEthernet0/0
  192.168.0.11
*Mar  1 00:32:33.011: OSPF: End of hello processing
*Mar  1 00:32:35.087: OSPF: Rcv hello from 10.3.3.3 area 0 from Serial1/0.1
  172.16.1.1
*Mar  1 00:32:35.091: OSPF: End of hello processing
```

Example 7-11 provides sample output from the **show ip ospf virtual-links** command. The output indicates that the other end of the virtual link has an OSPF router ID of 10.2.2.2. Also, notice that the transit area (that is, the area between the discontiguous area and area 0) is area 1.

Example 7-11   show ip ospf virtual-links *Command Output*

```
R1# show ip ospf virtual-links
Virtual Link OSPF_VL5 to router 10.2.2.2 is up
  Run as demand circuit
  DoNotAge LSA allowed.
  Transit area 1, via interface FastEthernet0/1, Cost of using 1
  Transmit Delay is 1 sec, State POINT_TO_POINT,
  Timer intervals configured, Hello 10, Dead 40, Wait 40, Retransmit 5
    Hello due in 00:00:00
    Adjacency State FULL (Hello suppressed)
    Index 1/2, retransmission queue length 0, number of retransmission 0
```

```
First 0x0(0)/0x0(0) Next 0x0(0)/0x0(0)
Last retransmission scan length is 0, maximum is 0
Last retransmission scan time is 0 msec, maximum is 0 msec
```

Trouble Ticket: OSPF

This trouble ticket focuses on OSPF. You are presented with baseline data, a trouble ticket, and information collected while investigating the reported issue. You are then challenged to identify the issue (or issues) and create an action plan to resolve that issue(s).

Trouble Ticket #4

You receive the following trouble ticket:

> For vendor interoperability reasons, a company changed its routing protocol from EIGRP to OSPF. The network was divided into areas, and all interfaces were instructed to participate in OSPF. The configuration was initially working. However, now none of the routers have full reachability to all the subnets.

This trouble ticket references the topology shown in Figure 7-4.

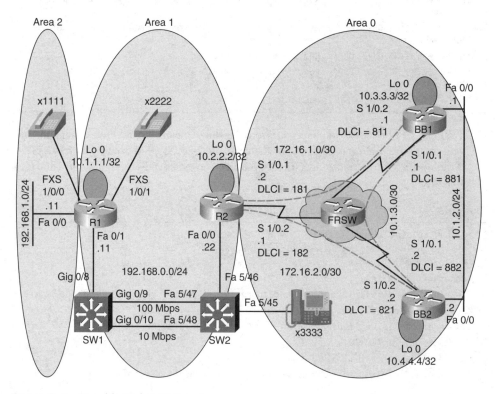

Figure 7-4 *Trouble Ticket #4 Topology*

As you investigate this issue, you examine baseline data collected after OSPF was initially configured. Example 7-12 shows baseline data collected from router R1, when the network was fully operational. Notice that router R1 is configured with a virtual link because it does not physically touch area 0.

Example 7-12   *Baseline Configuration Data from Router R1*

```
R1# show run | begin router
router ospf 1
 area 1 virtual-link 10.2.2.2
 network 10.1.1.1 0.0.0.0 area 1
 network 192.168.0.0 0.0.0.255 area 1
 network 192.168.1.0 0.0.0.255 area 2

R1# show ip ospf neighbor

Neighbor ID     Pri    State       Dead Time    Address        Interface
10.2.2.2        0      FULL/ -     -            192.168.0.22   OSPF_VL2
10.2.2.2        1      FULL/DR     00:00:38     192.168.0.22   FastEthernet0/1

R1# show ip route
Codes: C - connected, S - static, R - RIP, M - mobile, B - BGP
       D - EIGRP, EX - EIGRP external, O - OSPF, IA - OSPF inter area
       N1 - OSPF NSSA external type 1, N2 - OSPF NSSA external type 2
       E1 - OSPF external type 1, E2 - OSPF external type 2
       i - IS-IS, su - IS-IS summary, L1 - IS-IS level-1, L2 - IS-IS level-2
       ia - IS-IS inter area, * - candidate default, U - per-user static route
       o - ODR, P - periodic downloaded static route

Gateway of last resort is not set

     172.16.0.0/30 is subnetted, 2 subnets
O       172.16.1.0 [110/134] via 192.168.0.22, 01:34:44, FastEthernet0/1
O       172.16.2.0 [110/81] via 192.168.0.22, 01:34:44, FastEthernet0/1
     10.0.0.0/8 is variably subnetted, 6 subnets, 3 masks
O       10.2.2.2/32 [110/2] via 192.168.0.22, 02:24:31, FastEthernet0/1
O       10.1.3.0/30 [110/145] via 192.168.0.22, 01:34:44, FastEthernet0/1
O       10.3.3.3/32 [110/92] via 192.168.0.22, 01:34:44, FastEthernet0/1
O       10.1.2.0/24 [110/91] via 192.168.0.22, 01:34:45, FastEthernet0/1
C       10.1.1.1/32 is directly connected, Loopback0
O       10.4.4.4/32 [110/82] via 192.168.0.22, 01:34:45, FastEthernet0/1
C    192.168.0.0/24 is directly connected, FastEthernet0/1
C    192.168.1.0/24 is directly connected, FastEthernet0/0
R1# show ip ospf
```

```
Routing Process "ospf 1" with ID 10.1.1.1
Supports only single TOS(TOS0) routes
Supports opaque LSA
Supports Link-local Signaling (LLS)
Supports area transit capability It is an area border router
Initial SPF schedule delay 5000 mcooo
Minimum hold time between two consecutive SPFs 10000 msecs
Maximum wait time between two consecutive SPFs 10000 msecs
 Incremental-SPF disabled
 Minimum LSA interval 5 secs

Minimum LSA arrival 1000 msecs
 LSA group pacing timer 240 secs
 Interface flood pacing timer 33 msecs
 Retransmission pacing timer 66 msecs
 Number of external LSA 0. Checksum Sum 0x000000
 Number of opaque AS LSA 0. Checksum Sum 0x000000
 Number of DCbitless external and opaque AS LSA 0
 Number of DoNotAge external and opaque AS LSA 0
 Number of areas in this router is 3. 3 normal 0 stub 0 nssa
 Number of areas transit capable is 1
 External flood list length 0
    Area BACKBONE(0)
Number of interfaces in this area is 1
    Area has no authentication
    SPF algorithm last executed 01:35:17.308 ago
    SPF algorithm executed 9 times
    Area ranges are
    Number of LSA 12. Checksum Sum 0x063B08
    Number of opaque link LSA 0. Checksum Sum 0x000000
    Number of DCbitless LSA 0
    Number of indication LSA 0
    Number of DoNotAge LSA 7
    Flood list length 0
    Area 1
Number of interfaces in this area is 2 (1 loopback)
    This area has transit capability: Virtual Link Endpoint
    Area has no authentication
    SPF algorithm last executed 02:25:04.377 ago
    SPF algorithm executed 22 times
    Area ranges are
```

```
      Number of LSA 10. Checksum Sum 0x059726
      Number of opaque link LSA 0. Checksum Sum 0x000000
      Number of DCbitless LSA 0
      Number of indication LSA 0
      Number of DoNotAge LSA 0
      Flood list length 0
     Area 2
     Number of interfaces in this area is 1
      Number of indication LSA 0
      Number of DoNotAge LSA 0
      Flood list length 0
      Area has no authentication
      SPF algorithm last executed 02:25:15.880 ago
      SPF algorithm executed 9 times
      Area ranges are
      Number of LSA 10. Checksum Sum 0x05F97B
      Number of opaque link LSA 0. Checksum Sum 0x000000
      Number of DCbitless LSA 0
R1# show ip ospf interface fa0/1
FastEthernet0/1 is up, line protocol is up
  Internet Address 192.168.0.11/24, Area 1
  Process ID 1, Router ID 10.1.1.1, Network Type BROADCAST, Cost: 1
  Transmit Delay is 1 sec, State BDR, Priority 1
  Designated Router (ID) 10.2.2.2, Interface address 192.168.0.22
  Backup Designated router (ID) 10.1.1.1, Interface address 192.168.0.11
  Timer intervals configured, Hello 10, Dead 40, Wait 40, Retransmit 5
    oob-resync timeout 40
    Hello due in 00:00:00
  Supports Link-local Signaling (LLS)
  Index 2/2, flood queue length 0
  Next 0x0(0)/0x0(0)
  Last flood scan length is 1, maximum is 1
  Last flood scan time is 0 msec, maximum is 4 msec
  Neighbor Count is 1, Adjacent neighbor count is 1
    Adjacent with neighbor 10.2.2.2  (Designated Router)
  Suppress hello for 0 neighbor(s)
```

Example 7-13 shows baseline configuration data collected from router R2.

Example 7-13   *Baseline Configuration Data from Router R2*

```
R2# show run | begin router
router ospf 1
 area 1 virtual-link 10.1.1.1
 network 10.2.2.2 0.0.0.0 area 1
 network 172.16.1.0 0.0.0.3 area 0
 network 172.16.2.0 0.0.0.3 area 0
 network 192.168.0.0 0.0.0.255 area 1


R2# show ip ospf neighbor


Neighbor ID     Pri    State        Dead Time    Address        Interface
10.4.4.4        0      FULL/  -     00:00:34     172.16.2.2     Serial1/0.2
10.3.3.3        0      FULL/  -     00:00:37     172.16.1.1     Serial1/0.1
10.1.1.1        0      FULL/  -        -         192.168.0.11   OSPF_VL0
10.1.1.1        1      FULL/BDR     00:00:39     192.168.0.11   FastEthernet0/0


R2# show ip route
Codes: C - connected, S - static, R - RIP, M - mobile, B – BGP
       D - EIGRP, EX - EIGRP external, O - OSPF, IA - OSPF inter area
       N1 - OSPF NSSA external type 1, N2 - OSPF NSSA external type 2
       E1 - OSPF external type 1, E2 - OSPF external type 2
       i - IS-IS, su - IS-IS summary, L1 - IS-IS level-1, L2 - IS-IS level-2
       ia - IS-IS inter area, * - candidate default, U - per-user static route
       o - ODR, P - periodic downloaded static route
Gateway of last resort is not set


     172.16.0.0/30 is subnetted, 2 subnets
C        172.16.1.0 is directly connected, Serial1/0.1
C        172.16.2.0 is directly connected, Serial1/0.2
     10.0.0.0/8 is variably subnetted, 6 subnets, 3 masks
C        10.2.2.2/32 is directly connected, Loopback0
O        10.1.3.0/30 [110/144] via 172.16.2.2, 01:34:50, Serial1/0.2
O        10.3.3.3/32 [110/91] via 172.16.2.2, 01:34:50, Serial1/0.2
O        10.1.2.0/24 [110/90] via 172.16.2.2, 01:34:50, Serial1/0.2
O        10.1.1.1/32 [110/11] via 192.168.0.11, 02:24:36, FastEthernet0/0
O        10.4.4.4/32 [110/81] via 172.16.2.2, 01:34:50, Serial1/0.2
C    192.168.0.0/24 is directly connected, FastEthernet0/0
O IA 192.168.1.0/24 [110/11] via 192.168.0.11, 01:34:50, FastEthernet0/0


R2# show run | begin router
router ospf 1
 area 1 virtual-link 10.1.1.1
 network 10.2.2.2 0.0.0.0 area 1
```

```
 network 172.16.1.0 0.0.0.3 area 0
 network 172.16.2.0 0.0.0.3 area 0
 network 192.168.0.0 0.0.0.255 area 1
```

Example 7-14 shows baseline configuration data collected from router BB1.

Example 7-14 *Baseline Configuration Data from Router BB1*

```
BB1# show run | begin router
router ospf 1
 network 0.0.0.0 255.255.255.255 area 0

BB1# show ip ospf neighbor

Neighbor ID     Pri    State        Dead Time    Address      Interface
10.4.4.4        1      FULL/DR      00:00:38     10.1.2.2     FastEthernet0/
0
10.2.2.2        0      FULL/        00:00:39     172.16.1.2   Serial1/0.2
10.4.4.4        0      FULL/   -    00:00:38     10.1.3.2     Serial1/0.1

BB1# show ip route
Codes: C - connected, S - static, R - RIP, M - mobile, B - BGP
       D - EIGRP, EX - EIGRP external, O - OSPF, IA - OSPF inter area
       N1 - OSPF NSSA external type 1, N2 - OSPF NSSA external type 2
       E1 - OSPF external type 1, E2 - OSPF external type 2
       i - IS-IS, su - IS-IS summary, L1 - IS-IS level-1, L2 - IS-IS level-2
       ia - IS-IS inter area, * - candidate default, U - per-user static route
       o - ODR, P - periodic downloaded static route
Gateway of last resort is not set

     172.16.0.0/30 is subnetted, 2 subnets
C       172.16.1.0 is directly connected, Serial1/0.2
O       172.16.2.0 [110/90] via 10.1.2.2, 01:35:01, FastEthernet0/0
     10.0.0.0/8 is variably subnetted, 6 subnets, 3 masks
O IA    10.2.2.2/32 [110/91] via 10.1.2.2, 01:35:01, FastEthernet0/0
C       10.1.3.0/30 is directly connected, Serial1/0.1
C       10.3.3.3/32 is directly connected, Loopback0
C       10.1.2.0/24 is directly connected, FastEthernet0/0
O IA    10.1.1.1/32 [110/101] via 10.1.2.2, 01:35:01, FastEthernet0/0
O       10.4.4.4/32 [110/11] via 10.1.2.2, 01:35:01, FastEthernet0/0
O IA 192.168.0.0/24 [110/100] via 10.1.2.2, 01:35:01, FastEthernet0/0
O IA 192.168.1.0/24 [110/101] via 10.1.2.2, 01:35:01, FastEthernet0/0
```

Example 7-15 shows baseline configuration data collected from router BB2.

Example 7-15   *Baseline Configuration Data from Router BB2*

```
BB2# show run | begin router
router ospf 1
 network 0.0.0.0 255.255.255.255 area 0


BB2# show ip ospf neighbor
10.2.2.2           0    FULL/ -          00:00:32    172.16.2.1      Serial1/0.2
10.3.3.3           0    FULL/ -          00:00:39    10.1.3.1        Serial1/0.1
10.3.3.3           1    FULL/BDR         00:00:35    10.1.2.1
FastEthernet0/0
Neighbor ID     Pri   State            Dead Time   Address         Interface
BB2# show ip route
Codes: C - connected, S - static, R - RIP, M - mobile, B - BGP
       D - EIGRP, EX - EIGRP external, O - OSPF, IA - OSPF inter area
       N1 - OSPF NSSA external type 1, N2 - OSPF NSSA external type 2
       E1 - OSPF external type 1, E2 - OSPF external type 2
       i - IS-IS, su - IS-IS summary, L1 - IS-IS level-1, L2 - IS-IS level-2
       ia - IS-IS inter area, * - candidate default, U - per-user static route
       o - ODR, P - periodic downloaded static route


Gateway of last resort is not set


     172.16.0.0/30 is subnetted, 2 subnets
O IA 192.168.1.0/24 [110/101] via 10.1.2.2, 01:35:01, FastEthernet0/0
O       172.16.1.0 [110/143] via 10.1.2.1, 01:35:06, FastEthernet0/0
C       172.16.2.0 is directly connected, Serial1/0.2
     10.0.0.0/8 is variably subnetted, 6 subnets, 3 masks
O IA    10.2.2.2/32 [110/81] via 172.16.2.1, 01:35:06, Serial1/0.2
C       10.1.3.0/30 is directly connected, Serial1/0.1
O       10.3.3.3/32 [110/11] via 10.1.2.1, 01:35:06, FastEthernet0/0
C       10.1.2.0/24 is directly connected, FastEthernet0/0
O IA    10.1.1.1/32 [110/91] via 172.16.2.1, 01:35:06, Serial1/0.2
C       10.4.4.4/32 is directly connected, Loopback0
O IA 192.168.0.0/24 [110/90] via 172.16.2.1, 01:35:06, Serial1/0.2
O IA 192.168.1.0/24 [110/91] via 172.16.2.1, 01:35:06, Serial1/0.2
```

Now that you have seen the baseline data, the following examples present you with data collected after the trouble ticket was issued. Example 7-16 shows information collected from router R1. Notice that router R1's routing table can no longer see the Loopback 0 IP address of router BB2 (that is, 10.4.4.4/32). Also, notice that the virtual link between area 2 and area 0 is down.

Example 7-16 *Information Gathered from Router R1 After the Trouble Ticket Was Issued*

```
R1# show ip route
Codes: C - connected, S - static, R - RIP, M - mobile, B - BGP
       D - EIGRP, EX - EIGRP external, O - OSPF, IA - OSPF inter area
       N1 - OSPF NSSA external type 1, N2 - OSPF NSSA external type 2
       E1 - OSPF external type 1, E2 - OSPF external type 2
       i - IS-IS, su - IS-IS summary, L1 - IS-IS level-1, L2 - IS-IS level-2
       ia - IS-IS inter area, * - candidate default, U - per-user static route
       o - ODR, P - periodic downloaded static route


Gateway of last resort is not set

     172.16.0.0/30 is subnetted, 2 subnets
O IA    172.16.1.0 [110/134] via 192.168.0.22, 00:00:31, FastEthernet0/1
O IA    172.16.2.0 [110/81] via 192.168.0.22, 00:00:31, FastEthernet0/1
     10.0.0.0/8 is variably subnetted, 5 subnets, 3 masks
O       10.2.2.2/32 [110/2] via 192.168.0.22, 00:00:51, FastEthernet0/1
O IA    10.1.3.0/30 [110/198] via 192.168.0.22, 00:00:31, FastEthernet0/1
O IA    10.3.3.3/32 [110/135] via 192.168.0.22, 00:00:31, FastEthernet0/1
O IA    10.1.2.0/24 [110/144] via 192.168.0.22, 00:00:32, FastEthernet0/1
C       10.1.1.1/32 is directly connected, Loopback0
C    192.168.0.0/24 is directly connected, FastEthernet0/1
C    192.168.1.0/24 is directly connected, FastEthernet0/0
R1# show run | begin router
router ospf 1
 log-adjacency-changes
 area 2 virtual-link 10.2.2.2
 network 10.1.1.1 0.0.0.0 area 1
 network 192.168.0.0 0.0.0.255 area 1
 network 192.168.1.0 0.0.0.255 area 2
R1# show ip ospf virtual-links
Virtual Link OSPF_VL4 to router 10.2.2.2 is down
  Run as demand circuit
  DoNotAge LSA allowed.
  Transit area 2, Cost of using 65535
  Transmit Delay is 1 sec, State DOWN,
  Timer intervals configured, Hello 10, Dead 40, Wait 40, Retransmit 5
```

Example 7-17 shows the IP routing table on router R2 after the trouble ticket was issued. Notice that the routing table of router R1 can no longer see the Loopback 0 IP address of router BB2 (that is, 10.4.4.4/32). Also, notice that network 192.168.1.0/24, connected to router R1's Fast Ethernet 0/0 interface, is not present in router R2's IP routing table.

Example 7-17 *Router R2's IP Routing Table After the Trouble Ticket Was Issued*

```
R2# show ip route
Codes: C - connected, S - static, R - RIP, M - mobile, B - BGP
       D - EIGRP, EX - EIGRP external, O - OSPF, IA - OSPF inter area
       N1 - OSPF NSSA external type 1, N2 - OSPF NSSA external type 2
       E1 - OSPF external type 1, E2 - OSPF external type 2
       i - IS-IS, su - IS-IS summary, L1 - IS-IS level-1, L2 - IS-IS level-2
       ia - IS-IS inter area, * - candidate default, U - per-user static route
       o - ODR, P - periodic downloaded static route

Gateway of last resort is not set

     172.16.0.0/30 is subnetted, 2 subnets
C       172.16.1.0 is directly connected, Serial1/0.1
C       172.16.2.0 is directly connected, Serial1/0.2
     10.0.0.0/8 is variably subnetted, 5 subnets, 3 masks
C       10.2.2.2/32 is directly connected, Loopback0
O       10.1.3.0/30 [110/197] via 172.16.1.1, 00:00:53, Serial1/0.1
O       10.3.3.3/32 [110/134] via 172.16.1.1, 00:00:53, Serial1/0.1
O       10.1.2.0/24 [110/143] via 172.16.1.1, 00:00:53, Serial1/0.1
O       10.1.1.1/32 [110/11] via 192.168.0.11, 00:00:53, FastEthernet0/0
C    192.168.0.0/24 is directly connected, FastEthernet0/0
```

Before moving forward to investigate the remainder of the network, do you already see an issue that needs to be resolved? The fact that router R2 cannot see network 192.168.1.0/24 off of router R1 is independent of any configuration on routers BB1 or BB2. So, take a few moments to review the information collected thus far, and hypothesize the issue that is preventing router R2 from seeing network 192.168.1.0/24. On a separate sheet of paper, write your solution to the issue you identified.

Issue #1: Suggested Solution

The virtual link configuration on router R1 was incorrect. Specifically, the transit area in the **area** *number* **virtual-link** *router-id* command was configured as area 2. However, the transit area should have been area 1. Example 7-18 shows the commands used to correct this misconfiguration.

Example 7-18 *Correcting the Virtual Link Configuration Router of R1*

```
R1# conf term
Enter configuration commands, one per line.  End with CNTL/Z.
R1(config)#router ospf 1
R1(config-router)#no area 2 virtual-link 10.2.2.2
R1(config-router)#area 1 virtual-link 10.2.2.2
```

After you correct the virtual link configuration on router R1, network 192.168.1.0/24 is present in router R2's IP routing table, as illustrated in Example 7-19. Notice, however, that the Loopback 0 IP address of router BB2 (that is, 10.4.4.4/32) is still not visible in router R2's IP routing table.

Example 7-19 *Router R2's IP Routing Table After Correcting the Virtual Link Configuration*

```
R2# show ip route
Codes: C - connected, S - static, R - RIP, M - mobile, B - BGP
       D - EIGRP, EX - EIGRP external, O - OSPF, IA - OSPF inter area
       N1 - OSPF NSSA external type 1, N2 - OSPF NSSA external type 2
       E1 - OSPF external type 1, E2 - OSPF external type 2
       i - IS-IS, su - IS-IS summary, L1 - IS-IS level-1, L2 - IS-IS level 2
       ia - IS-IS inter area, * - candidate default, U - per-user static route
       o - ODR, P - periodic downloaded static route
Gateway of last resort is not set
     172.16.0.0/30 is subnetted, 2 subnets
C       172.16.1.0 is directly connected, Serial1/0.1
C       172.16.2.0 is directly connected, Serial1/0.2
     10.0.0.0/8 is variably subnetted, 5 subnets, 3 masks
C       10.2.2.2/32 is directly connected, Loopback0
O       10.1.3.0/30 [110/197] via 172.16.1.1, 00:00:18, Serial1/0.1
O       10.3.3.3/32 [110/134] via 172.16.1.1, 00:00:18, Serial1/0.1
O       10.1.2.0/24 [110/143] via 172.16.1.1, 00:00:18, Serial1/0.1
O       10.1.1.1/32 [110/11] via 192.168.0.11, 00:00:18, FastEthernet0/0
C     192.168.0.0/24 is directly connected, FastEthernet0/0
O IA 192.168.1.0/24 [110/11] via 192.168.0.11, 00:00:18, FastEthernet0/0
```

With one issue now resolved, continue to collect information on router R2. Example 7-20 indicates that router R2 has not formed an adjacency with router BB2, which has an OSPF router ID of 10.4.4.4.

Example 7-20 *OSPF Neighbors of Router R2*

```
R2# show ip ospf neighbor
Neighbor ID     Pri    State      Dead Time   Address        Interface
10.3.3.3         0     FULL/  -   00:00:37    172.16.1.1     Serial1/0.1
10.1.1.1         0     FULL/  -      -        192.168.0.11   OSPF_VL1
10.1.1.1         1     FULL/DR    00:00:39    192.168.0.11   FastEthernet0/0
Example 7-20 shows the OSPF configuration of router R2.


R2# show run | begin router
router ospf 2
 log-adjacency-changes
 area 1 virtual-link 10.1.1.1
 network 10.2.2.2 0.0.0.0 area 1
```

```
network 172.16.1.0 0.0.0.3 area 0
network 172.16.2.0 0.0.0.3 area 0
network 192.168.0.0 0.0.0.255 area 1
```

Even though router R2 has not formed an adjacency with router BB2, Example 7-21 shows the output of a **ping** command, verifying that router R2 can reach router BB2.

Example 7-21   *Pinging Router BB2 from Router R2*

```
R2# ping 172.16.2.2
Type escape sequence to abort.
Sending 5, 100-byte ICMP Echos to 172.16.2.2, timeout is 2 seconds:
!!!!!
Success rate is 100 percent (5/5), round-trip min/avg/max = 52/92/144 ms
```

The topology diagram indicates that router R2 connects with router BB2 via subinterface Serial 1/0.2. Therefore, the **show interface s1/0.2** command is issued on router R2. The output provided in Example 7-22 states that the subinterface is up and functional.

Example 7-22   *Serial 1/0.2 Subinterface of Router R2*

```
R2# show interface s1/0.2
Serial1/0.2 is up, line protocol is up
  Hardware is M4T
  Internet address is 172.16.2.1/30
  MTU 1500 bytes, BW 1250 Kbit, DLY 20000 usec,
     reliability 255/255, txload 1/255, rxload 1/255
  Encapsulation FRAME-RELAY
  Last clearing of "show interface" counters never
```

Example 7-23 confirms that router BB2 is adjacent at Layer 2 with router R2.

Example 7-23   *CDP Neighbors of Router R2*

```
R2# show cdp neighbor
Capability Codes: R - Router, T - Trans Bridge, B - Source Route Bridge
                  S - Switch, H - Host, I - IGMP, r - Repeater

Device ID      Local Intrfce    Holdtme    Capability  Platform  Port ID
BB1            Ser 1/0.1        152        R S I       2691      Ser 1/0.2
BB2            Ser 1/0.2        143        R S I       2691      Ser 1/0.2
R1             Fas 0/0          144        R S I       2611XM    Fas 0/1
```

The output of Example 7-24 shows the OSPF status of router R2's Serial 1/0.2 subinterface.

Example 7-24   *OSPF Status of Router R2 on Subinterface Serial 1/0.2*

```
R2# show ip ospf interface s1/0.2
Supports Link-local Signaling (LLS)
Index 3/4, flood queue length 0
Next 0x0(0)/0x0(0)
Last flood scan length is 1, maximum is 4
Last flood scan time is 0 msec, maximum is 4 msec
Neighbor Count is 0, Adjacent neighbor count is 0
Suppress hello for 0 neighbor(s)
```

Now that data has been collected for router R2, the troubleshooting focus moves to router BB1. Notice that BB1 also lacks a route to router BB2's Loopback 0 IP address of 10.4.4.4/32. Also, even though router BB1 has two direct connections to router BB2, router BB1 has not formed an OSPF adjacency with router BB2. Notice that router BB2 is router BB1's Cisco Discovery Protocol (CDP) neighbor, both on interface FastEthernet 0/0 and on subinterface Serial 1/0.1.

Example 7-25   *Data Collected from Router BB1 After the Trouble Ticket*

```
BB1# show ip route
Codes: C - connected, S - static, R - RIP, M - mobile, B - BGP
       D - EIGRP, EX - EIGRP external, O - OSPF, IA - OSPF inter area
       N1 - OSPF NSSA external type 1, N2 - OSPF NSSA external type 2
       E1 - OSPF external type 1, E2 - OSPF external type 2
       i - IS-IS, su - IS-IS summary, L1 - IS-IS level-1, L2 - IS-IS level-2
       ia - IS-IS inter area, * - candidate default, U - per-user static route
       o - ODR, P - periodic downloaded static route
Gateway of last resort is not set
     172.16.0.0/30 is subnetted, 2 subnets
C       172.16.1.0 is directly connected, Serial1/0.2
O       172.16.2.0 [110/213] via 172.16.1.2, 00:01:02, Serial1/0.2
     10.0.0.0/8 is variably subnetted, 5 subnets, 3 masks
O IA    10.2.2.2/32 [110/134] via 172.16.1.2, 00:01:02, Serial1/0.2
C       10.1.3.0/30 is directly connected, Serial1/0.1
C       10.3.3.3/32 is directly connected, Loopback0
C       10.1.2.0/24 is directly connected, FastEthernet0/0
O IA    10.1.1.1/32 [110/144] via 172.16.1.2, 00:01:02, Serial1/0.2
O IA 192.168.0.0/24 [110/143] via 172.16.1.2, 00:01:02, Serial1/0.2
BB1# show ip ospf neighbor

Neighbor ID     Pri    State        Dead Time   Address      Interface
10.2.2.2        0      FULL/  -     00:00:30    172.16.1.2   Serial1/0.2

BB1# show run | begin router
router ospf 1
```

```
 log-adjacency-changes
 network 0.0.0.0 255.255.255.255 area 0


BB1# show cdp neigh
Capability Codes: R - Router, T - Trans Bridge, B - Source Route Bridge
                  S - Switch, H - Host, I - IGMP, r - Repeater


Device ID        Local Intrfce    Holdtme    Capability  Platform  Port ID
BB2              Ser 1/0.1        148        R S I       2691      Ser 1/0.1
BB2              Fas 0/0          148        R S I       2691      Fas 0/0
R2               Ser 1/0.2        130        R S I       2691      Ser 1/0.1
BB1# show run

...OUTPUT OMITTED...
interface FastEthernet0/0
 ip address 10.1.2.1 255.255.255.0
 ip ospf network non-broadcast
 duplex auto
speed auto
!
interface Serial1/0
 no ip address
 encapsulation frame-relay
!
interface Serial1/0.1 point-to-point
 ip address 10.1.3.1 255.255.255.252
 ip ospf hello-interval 60
 ip ospf dead-interval 200
 frame-relay interface-dlci 881
!
interface Serial1/0.2 point-to-point
 bandwidth 750
 ip address 172.16.1.1 255.255.255.252
 frame-relay interface-dlci 811
...OUTPUT OMITTED...
```

The data collection continues on router BB2. Example 7-26 provides output from several **show** commands. Notice that router BB2 has not learned networks via OSPF.

Based on the preceding **show** command output from routers R2, BB1, and BB2, hypothesize what you consider to be the issue or issues still impacting the network. Then, on a separate sheet of paper, write how you would solve the identified issue or issues.

Example 7-26 *Data Collected from Router BB2 After the Trouble Ticket*

```
BB2# show ip route
Codes: C - connected, S - static, R - RIP, M - mobile, B - BGP
       D - EIGRP, EX - EIGRP external, O - OSPF, IA - OSPF inter area
       N1 - OSPF NSSA external type 1, N2 - OSPF NSSA external type 2
       E1 - OSPF external type 1, E2 - OSPF external type 2
       i - IS-IS, su - IS-IS summary, L1 - IS-IS level-1, L2 - IS-IS level-2
       ia - IS-IS inter area, * - candidate default, U - per-user static route
       o - ODR, P - periodic downloaded static route
Gateway of last resort is not set


     172.16.0.0/30 is subnetted, 1 subnets
C       172.16.2.0 is directly connected, Serial1/0.2
     10.0.0.0/8 is variably subnetted, 3 subnets, 3 masks
C       10.1.3.0/30 is directly connected, Serial1/0.1
C       10.1.2.0/24 is directly connected, FastEthernet0/0
C       10.4.4.4/32 is directly connected, Loopback0


BB2# show run | begin router
router ospf 1
 log-adjacency-changes
 network 0.0.0.0 255.255.255.255 area 0


BB2# show ip ospf interface s1/0.1
Serial1/0.1 is up, line protocol is up
  Internet Address 10.1.3.2/30, Area 0
  Process ID 1, Router ID 10.4.4.4, Network Type POINT_TO_POINT, Cost: 64
  Transmit Delay is 1 sec, State POINT_TO_POINT,
  Timer intervals configured, Hello 10, Dead 40, Wait 40, Retransmit 5
    oob-resync timeout 40
    Hello due in 00:00:09
  Supports Link-local Signaling (LLS)
  Index 2/2, flood queue length 0
  Next 0x0(0)/0x0(0)
  Last flood scan length is 1, maximum is 3
  Last flood scan time is 0 msec, maximum is 4 msec
  Neighbor Count is 0, Adjacent neighbor count is 0
  Suppress hello for 0 neighbor(s)


BB2# show ip ospf interface s1/0.2
Serial1/0.2 is up, line protocol is up
  Internet Address 172.16.2.2/30, Area 0
  Process ID 1, Router ID 10.4.4.4, Network Type NON_BROADCAST, Cost: 80
  Transmit Delay is 1 sec, State DR, Priority 1
  Designated Router (ID) 10.4.4.4, Interface address 172.16.2.2
```

```
    No backup designated router on this network
    Timer intervals configured, Hello 30, Dead 120, Wait 120, Retransmit 5
      oob-resync timeout 120
      Hello due in 00:00:09
    Supports Link-local Signaling (LLS)
    Index 3/3, flood queue length 0
    Next 0x0(0)/0x0(0)
    Last flood scan length is 1, maximum is 1
    Last flood scan time is 0 msec, maximum is 4 msec
    Neighbor Count is 0, Adjacent neighbor count is 0
    Suppress hello for 0 neighbor(s)
!
interface FastEthernet0/0
 ip address 10.1.2.2 255.255.255.0
!
interface Serial1/0
 no ip address
 encapsulation frame-relay
!
interface Serial1/0.1 point-to-point
 ip address 10.1.3.2 255.255.255.252
 frame-relay interface-dlci 882
!
interface Serial1/0.2 point-to-point
 bandwidth 1250
 ip address 172.16.2.2 255.255.255.252
 ip ospf network non-broadcast
 frame-relay interface-dlci 821
!
...OUTPUT OMITTED...
```

Issue #2: Suggested Solution

Subinterface Serial 1/0.1 on router BB1 had nondefault Hello and Dead timers, which did not match the timers at the far end of the Frame Relay link. Example 7-27 illustrates how these nondefault values were reset.

Example 7-27   *Correcting the Nondefault Timer Configuration of Router BB1*

```
BB1# conf term
Enter configuration commands, one per line.  End with CNTL/Z.
BB1(config)#int s1/0.1
BB1(config-subif)#no ip ospf hello-interval 60
BB1(config-subif)#no ip ospf dead-interval 200
```

Issue #3: Suggested Solution

Interface FastEthernet 0/0 on router BB1 was configured with an incorrect OSPF network type of nonbroadcast. Example 7-28 demonstrates how this OSPF interface was reset to its default OSPF network type (that is, the broadcast OSPF network type).

Example 7-28   *Correcting the Incorrect OSPF Network Type Configuration of Router BB1*

```
BB1# conf term
Enter configuration commands, one per line.  End with CNTL/Z.
BB1(config)#int fa 0/0
BB1(config-if)#no ip ospf network non-broadcast
```

Issue #4: Suggested Solution

Similar to the incorrect OSPF network type on router BB1's FastEthernet 0/0 interface, the Serial 1/0.2 subinterface on router BB2 was configured incorrectly. A point-to-point Frame Relay subinterface defaults to an OSPF network type of point-to-point; however, Serial 1/0.2 had been configured as an OSPF network type of nonbroadcast. Example 7-29 reviews how this nondefault OSPF network type configuration was removed.

Example 7-29   *Correcting Router BB2's Incorrect OSPF Network Type Configuration*

```
BB2# conf term
Enter configuration commands, one per line.  End with CNTL/Z.
BB2(config)#int s1/0.2
BB2(config-subif)#no ip ospf network non-broadcast
```

After all of the previous misconfigurations are corrected, all routers in the topology once again have full reachability throughout the network. Examples 7-30, 7-31, 7-32, and 7-33 show output from the **show ip route** and **show ip ospf neighbor** commands issued on all routers, confirming the full reachability of each router.

Example 7-30   *Confirming the Full Reachability of Router R1*

```
R1# show ip route
Codes: C - connected, S - static, R - RIP, M - mobile, B - BGP
       D - EIGRP, EX - EIGRP external, O - OSPF, IA - OSPF inter area
       N1 - OSPF NSSA external type 1, N2 - OSPF NSSA external type 2
       E1 - OSPF external type 1, E2 - OSPF external type 2
       i - IS-IS, su - IS-IS summary, L1 - IS-IS level-1, L2 - IS-IS level-2
       ia - IS-IS inter area, * - candidate default, U - per-user static route
       o - ODR, P - periodic downloaded static route

Gateway of last resort is not set

     172.16.0.0/30 is subnetted, 2 subnets
O       172.16.1.0 [110/134] via 192.168.0.22, 00:00:03, FastEthernet0/1
O       172.16.2.0 [110/81] via 192.168.0.22, 00:00:03, FastEthernet0/1
```

```
        10.0.0.0/8 is variably subnetted, 6 subnets, 3 masks
O        10.2.2.2/32 [110/2] via 192.168.0.22, 00:08:18, FastEthernet0/1
O        10.1.3.0/30 [110/145] via 192.168.0.22, 00:00:03, FastEthernet0/1
O        10.3.3.3/32 [110/92] via 192.168.0.22, 00:00:03, FastEthernet0/1
O        10.1.2.0/24 [110/91] via 192.168.0.22, 00:00:04, FastEthernet0/1
C        10.1.1.1/32 is directly connected, Loopback0
O        10.4.4.4/32 [110/82] via 192.168.0.22, 00:00:04, FastEthernet0/1
C     192.168.0.0/24 is directly connected, FastEthernet0/1
C     192.168.1.0/24 is directly connected, FastEthernet0/0


R1# show ip ospf neighbor


Neighbor ID     Pri    State       Dead Time    Address         Interface
10.2.2.2        0      FULL/  -      -           192.168.0.22    OSPF_VL5
10.2.2.2        1      FULL/BDR    00:00:34      192.168.0.22    FastEthernet0/1
```

Example 7-31   *Confirming the Full Reachability of Router R2*

```
R2# show ip route
Codes: C - connected, S - static, R - RIP, M - mobile, B - BGP
       D - EIGRP, EX - EIGRP external, O - OSPF, IA - OSPF inter area
       N1 - OSPF NSSA external type 1, N2 - OSPF NSSA external type 2
       E1 - OSPF external type 1, E2 - OSPF external type 2
       i - IS-IS, su - IS-IS summary, L1 - IS-IS level-1, L2 - IS-IS level-2
       ia - IS-IS inter area, * - candidate default, U - per-user static route
       o - ODR, P - periodic downloaded static route


Gateway of last resort is not set


     172.16.0.0/30 is subnetted, 2 subnets
C        172.16.1.0 is directly connected, Serial1/0.1
C        172.16.2.0 is directly connected, Serial1/0.2
     10.0.0.0/8 is variably subnetted, 6 subnets, 3 masks
C        10.2.2.2/32 is directly connected, Loopback0
O        10.1.3.0/30 [110/144] via 172.16.2.2, 00:00:15, Serial1/0.2
O        10.3.3.3/32 [110/91] via 172.16.2.2, 00:00:15, Serial1/0.2
O        10.1.2.0/24 [110/90] via 172.16.2.2, 00:00:15, Serial1/0.2
O        10.1.1.1/32 [110/11] via 192.168.0.11, 00:08:29, FastEthernet0/0
O        10.4.4.4/32 [110/81] via 172.16.2.2, 00:00:15, Serial1/0.2
C     192.168.0.0/24 is directly connected, FastEthernet0/0
O IA  192.168.1.0/24 [110/11] via 192.168.0.11, 00:00:15, FastEthernet0/0


R2# show ip ospf neighbor
```

```
Neighbor ID     Pri   State        Dead Time   Address        Interface
10.4.4.4        0     FULL/ -      00:00:33    172.16.2.2     Serial1/0.2
10.3.3.3        0     FULL/ -      00:00:38    172.16.1.1     Serial1/0.1
10.1.1.1        0     FULL/ -      -           192.168.0.11   OSPF_VL1
10.1.1.1        1     FULL/DR      00:00:30    192.168.0.11   FastEthernet0/0
```

Example 7-32 *Confirming the Full Reachability of Router BB1*

```
BB1# show ip route
Codes: C - connected, S - static, R - RIP, M - mobile, B - BGP
       D - EIGRP, EX - EIGRP external, O - OSPF, IA - OSPF inter area
       N1 - OSPF NSSA external type 1, N2 - OSPF NSSA external type 2
       E1 - OSPF external type 1, E2 - OSPF external type 2
       i - IS-IS, su - IS-IS summary, L1 - IS-IS level-1, L2 - IS-IS level-2
       ia - IS-IS inter area, * - candidate default, U - per-user static route
       o - ODR, P - periodic downloaded static route

Gateway of last resort is not set

     172.16.0.0/30 is subnetted, 2 subnets
C       172.16.1.0 is directly connected, Serial1/0.2
O       172.16.2.0 [110/90] via 10.1.2.2, 00:00:29, FastEthernet0/0
     10.0.0.0/8 is variably subnetted, 6 subnets, 3 masks
O IA    10.2.2.2/32 [110/91] via 10.1.2.2, 00:00:29, FastEthernet0/0
C       10.1.3.0/30 is directly connected, Serial1/0.1
C       10.3.3.3/32 is directly connected, Loopback0
C       10.1.2.0/24 is directly connected, FastEthernet0/0
O IA    10.1.1.1/32 [110/101] via 10.1.2.2, 00:00:29, FastEthernet0/0
O       10.4.4.4/32 [110/11] via 10.1.2.2, 00:00:29, FastEthernet0/0
O IA 192.168.0.0/24 [110/100] via 10.1.2.2, 00:00:29, FastEthernet0/0
O IA 192.168.1.0/24 [110/101] via 10.1.2.2, 00:00:29, FastEthernet0/0
BB1# show ip ospf neighbor

Neighbor ID     Pri   State        Dead Time   Address        Interface
10.4.4.4        1     FULL/DR      00:00:34    10.1.2.2       FastEthernet0/
10.2.2.2        0     FULL/ -      00:00:39    172.16.1.2     Serial1/0.2
10.4.4.4        0     FULL/ -      00:00:33    10.1.3.2       Serial1/0.1
```

Example 7-33 *Confirming the Full Reachability of Router BB2*

```
BB2# show ip route
Codes: C - connected, S - static, R - RIP, M - mobile, B - BGP
       D - EIGRP, EX - EIGRP external, O - OSPF, IA - OSPF inter area
       N1 - OSPF NSSA external type 1, N2 - OSPF NSSA external type 2
       E1 - OSPF external type 1, E2 - OSPF external type 2
       i - IS-IS, su - IS-IS summary, L1 - IS-IS level-1, L2 - IS-IS level-2
       ia - IS-IS inter area, * - candidate default, U - per-user static route
       o - ODR, P - periodic downloaded static route

Gateway of last resort is not set

     172.16.0.0/30 is subnetted, 2 subnets
O       172.16.1.0 [110/143] via 10.1.2.1, 00:00:42, FastEthernet0/0
C       172.16.2.0 is directly connected, Serial1/0.2
     10.0.0.0/8 is variably subnetted, 6 subnets, 3 masks
O IA    10.2.2.2/32 [110/81] via 172.16.2.1, 00:00:42, Serial1/0.2
C       10.1.3.0/30 is directly connected, Serial1/0.1
O       10.3.3.3/32 [110/11] via 10.1.2.1, 00:00:42, FastEthernet0/0
C       10.1.2.0/24 is directly connected, FastEthernet0/0
O IA    10.1.1.1/32 [110/91] via 172.16.2.1, 00:00:42, Serial1/0.2
C       10.4.4.4/32 is directly connected, Loopback0
O IA 192.168.0.0/24 [110/90] via 172.16.2.1, 00:00:42, Serial1/0.2
O IA 192.168.1.0/24 [110/91] via 172.16.2.1, 00:00:42, Serial1/0.2


BB2# show ip ospf neighbor

Neighbor ID     Pri   State          Dead Time   Address       Interface
10.2.2.2         0    FULL/  -       00:00:38    172.16.2.1    Serial1/0.2
10.3.3.3         0    FULL/  -       00:00:29    10.1.3.1      Serial1/0.1
10.3.3.3         1    FULL/BDR       00:00:34    10.1.2.1      FastEthernet0/0
```

Route Redistribution Troubleshooting

Route redistribution allows routes learned via one method (for example, statically configured, locally connected, or learned via a routing protocol) to be injected into a different routing protocol. If two routing protocols are mutually redistributed, the routes learned via each routing protocol are injected into the other routing protocol.

A network might benefit from route redistribution in the following scenarios:

■ Transitioning to a more advanced routing protocol

■ Merger of companies

■ Different areas of administrative control

Route Redistribution Overview

A router that sits at the boundary of the routing domains to be redistributed is known as a *boundary router*, as illustrated in Figure 7-5. A boundary router can redistribute static routes, connected routes, or routes learned via one routing protocol into another routing protocol.

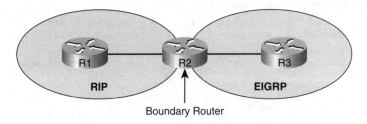

Figure 7-5 *Boundary Router*

Different routing protocols use different types of metrics, as illustrated in Figure 7-6. Therefore, when a route is injected into a routing protocol, a metric used by the destination routing protocol needs to be associated with the route being injected.

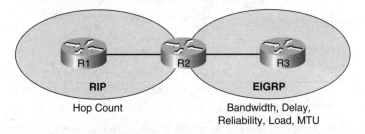

Figure 7-6 *Differing Metric Parameters Between Routing Protocols*

The metric assigned to a route being injected into another routing process is called a *seed metric*. The seed metric is needed to communicate relative levels of reachability between dissimilar routing protocols. A seed metric can be defined in one of three ways:

■ The **default-metric** command

■ The **metric** parameter in the **redistribute** command

■ A route map configuration

If a seed metric is not specified, a default seed metric is used. Keep in mind, however, that RIP and EIGRP have a default metric that is considered unreachable. Therefore, if you do not configure a nondefault seed metric when redistributing routes into RIP or EIGRP, the redistributed route will not be reachable.

Some routing protocols (for example, EIGRP, OSPF, and Intermediate System-to-Intermediate System [IS-IS]) can tag routes as either *internal* (that is, routes locally configured or connected) or *external* (that is, routes learned by another routing process) and give priority to internal routes versus external routes. The capability to distinguish between internal and external routes can help prevent a potential routing loop, where two routing protocols continually redistribute a route into one another.

As described in Chapter 6, a routing protocol can send routes into and learn routes from a router's IP routing table, as depicted in Figure 7-7.

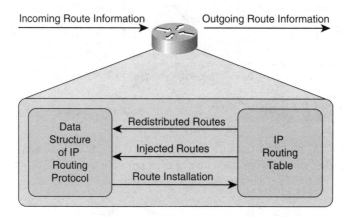

Figure 7-7   *Routing Data Structures*

If a router is running two routing protocols, however, the routing protocols do not exchange routes directly between themselves. Rather, only routes in a router's IP routing table can be redistributed, as seen in Figure 7-8.

Two prerequisites must be met for the routes of one IP routing protocol to be redistributed into another IP routing protocol:

■   A route needs to be installed in a router's IP routing table.

■   The destination IP routing protocol needs a reachable metric to assign to the redistributed routes.

Route Redistribution Troubleshooting Targets

Effective troubleshooting of route redistribution requires knowledge of verification and troubleshooting commands for each routing protocol. Table 7-9 identifies troubleshooting targets to investigate when working to resolve a route redistribution issue.

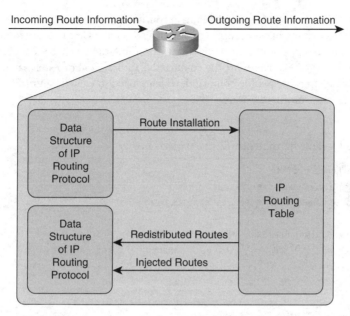

Figure 7-8 *Route Redistribution Between Two IP Routing Protocols*

Table 7-9 *Troubleshooting Targets for Route Redistribution*

Key
Topic

Troubleshooting Target	Troubleshooting Recommendation
Source routing protocol	Verify that a route to be redistributed from a routing protocol has been learned by that routing protocol. Therefore, you can issue appropriate **show** commands for the data structures of the source routing protocol to ensure that the source routing protocol has learned the route in question.
Route selection	Because a route must be in a router's IP routing table to be redistributed, you should ensure that the routes of the source routing protocol are indeed being injected into the router's IP routing table.
Redistribution configuration	If a route has been injected into a router's IP routing table from a source routing protocol but not redistributed into the destination routing protocol, you should check the redistribution configuration. This involves checking the metric applied to routes as they are redistributed into the destination routing protocol, checking for any route filtering that might be preventing redistribution, and checking the redistribution syntax to confirm the correct routing process ID or autonomous system number is specified.
Destination routing protocol	If a route has been successfully redistributed into a destination routing protocol but the route has not been successfully learned by neighboring routers, you should investigate the destination routing protocol. You could use traditional methods of troubleshooting a destination routing protocol; however, keep in mind that the redistributed route might be marked as an external route. Therefore, check the characteristics of the destination routing protocol to determine if it treats external routes differently from internal ones.

Although the previously discussed **debug ip routing** command can provide insight into routing loops that might be occurring, you can also use the Cisco IOS IP route profiling feature to troubleshoot route instability. Route profiling can be enabled in global configuration mode with the **ip route profile** command. Example 7-34 provides sample output from the **show ip route profile** command, which is used to view the information collected from the IP route profiling feature.

Example 7-34   show ip route profile *Command Output*

```
R4# show ip route profile
IP routing table change statistics:
Frequency of changes in a 5 second sampling interval
-------------------------------------------------------------
```

Change/ interval	Fwd-path change	Prefix add	Nexthop change	Pathcount change	Prefix refresh
0	38	38	41	41	41
1	3	3	0	0	0
2	0	0	0	0	0
3	0	0	0	0	0
4	0	0	0	0	0
5	0	0	0	0	0
10	0	0	0	0	0
15	0	0	0	0	0
20	0	0	0	0	0
25	0	0	0	0	0
30	0	1	0	1	0
55	0	0	0	0	0
80	0	0	0	0	0
105	0	0	0	0	0
130	0	0	0	0	0
155	0	0	0	0	0
280	0	0	0	0	0
405	0	0	0	0	0
530	0	0	0	0	0
655	0	0	0	0	0
780	0	0	0	0	0
1405	0	0	0	0	0
2030	0	0	0	0	0
2655	0	0	0	0	0
3280	0	0	0	0	0
3905	0	0	0	0	0
7030	0	0	0	0	0
10155	0	0	0	0	0
13280	0	0	0	0	0
Overflow	0	0	0	0	0

Key Topic

The IP route profiling feature measures the number and type of IP routing table updates every 5 seconds. The left column in the output of the **show ip route profile** command represents the number of changes that occurred during a 5-second interval. As an example, consider the row in the output that has a 30 in the left column. The number 1 under the Prefix Add column indicates that during one 5-second interval, 30–54 prefixes were added to the IP routing table. The range of 30–54 was determined by examining the output. Notice that the next value in the Change/ Interval column after 30 is 55. Therefore, a number appearing in the 30 row indicates during how many 5-second timing intervals a particular IP routing update occurred 30–54 times.

Ideally, only numbers in the first row (that is, the 0 row) should change in a stable network. If numbers in other rows change, a routing loop might be occurring.

Trouble Ticket: Route Redistribution with EIGRP and OSPF

This trouble ticket focuses on redistribution of EIGRP and OSPF. You are presented with baseline data, a trouble ticket, a topology, and information collected while investigating the reported issue. You are then challenged to identify the issue and create an action plan to resolve it.

Because different IP routing protocols might exhibit different characteristics when performing route redistribution, you should research the syntax used for your specific protocols. As a reference for this trouble ticket, Table 7-10 provides a collection of commands that might be useful in troubleshooting EIGRP or OSPF route redistribution.

Table 7-10 *Route Redistribution Verification and Troubleshooting Syntax for EIGRP and OSPF*

Command	Description
router ospf *process-id*	Global configuration mode command that enables an OSPF process on a router
redistribute eigrp *autonomous-system-number* [subnets]	Router configuration mode command that redistributes routes, including subnets (if the optional **subnets** parameter is specified), from a specified EIGRP autonomous system into OSPF

continues

Table 7-10   *Route Redistribution Verification and Troubleshooting Syntax for EIGRP and OSPF   (Continued)*

default-metric *metric*	Router configuration mode command that specifies the metric used for routes redistributed into OSPF
router eigrp *autonomous-system-number*	Global configuration mode command that enables an EIGRP routing process on a router
redistribute ospf *process-id*	Router configuration mode command that redistributes routes from a specified OSPF process ID into EIGRP
default-metric *bandwidth delay reliability load mtu*	Router configuration mode command that specifies the parameters used to calculate the seed metric for routes being redistributed into EIGRP, using the following EIGRP metric parameters: *bandwidth* (in kbps) *delay* (in tens of microseconds) *reliability* (maximum of 255) *load* (minimum of 1) *mtu* (in bytes)

Trouble Ticket #5

You receive the following trouble ticket:

Company A has acquired company B. Company A's network (that is, routers R1 and R2) uses EIGRP, whereas Company B's network (that is, routers BB1 and BB2) uses OSPF. Router R2 was configured as a boundary router, and router R2's configuration specifies that EIGRP and OSPF are mutually redistributed. The configuration was originally functional. However, routers R1, BB1, and BB2 do not currently see all the subnets present in the network.

This trouble ticket references the topology shown in Figure 7-9.

You begin your troubleshooting efforts by analyzing baseline information collected when the configuration was working properly. Examples 7-35, 7-36, 7-37, and 7-38 provide output from the **show ip route** command on each router.

Example 7-35   *Baseline Output for Router R1*

```
R1# show ip route
Codes: C - connected, S - static, R - RIP, M - mobile, B - BGP
       D - EIGRP, EX - EIGRP external, O - OSPF, IA - OSPF inter area
       N1 - OSPF NSSA external type 1, N2 - OSPF NSSA external type 2
       E1 - OSPF external type 1, E2 - OSPF external type 2
       i - IS-IS, su - IS-IS summary, L1 - IS-IS level-1, L2 - IS-IS level-2
       ia - IS-IS inter area, * - candidate default, U - per-user static route
```

```
        o - ODR, P - periodic downloaded static route

Gateway of last resort is not set


     172.16.0.0/30 is subnetted, 2 subnets
D EX    172.16.1.0 [170/1734656] via 192.168.0.22, 00:04:39, FastEthernet0/1
D EX    172.16.2.0 [170/1734656] via 192.168.0.22, 00:04:39, FastEthernet0/1
     10.0.0.0/8 is variably subnetted, 6 subnets, 3 masks
D       10.2.2.2/32 [90/156160] via 192.168.0.22, 00:04:39, FastEthernet0/1
D EX    10.1.3.0/30 [170/1734656] via 192.168.0.22, 00:04:39, FastEthernet0/1
D EX    10.3.3.3/32 [170/1734656] via 192.168.0.22, 00:04:39, FastEthernet0/1
D EX    10.1.2.0/24 [170/1734656] via 192.168.0.22, 00:04:40, FastEthernet0/1
C       10.1.1.1/32 is directly connected, Loopback0
D EX    10.4.4.4/32 [170/1734656] via 192.168.0.22, 00:04:40, FastEthernet0/1
C    192.168.0.0/24 is directly connected, FastEthernet0/1
C    192.168.1.0/24 is directly connected, FastEthernet0/0
```

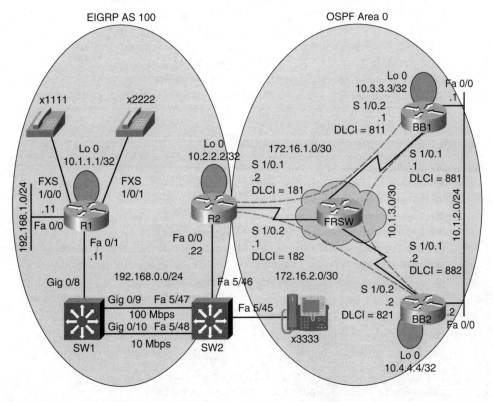

Figure 7-9   *Trouble Ticket #5: Topology*

Example 7-36   *Baseline Output for Router R2*

```
R2# show ip route
Codes: C - connected, S - static, R - RIP, M - mobile, B - BGP
       D - EIGRP, EX - EIGRP external, O - OSPF, IA - OSPF inter area
       N1 - OSPF NSSA external type 1, N2 - OSPF NSSA external type 2
       E1 - OSPF external type 1, E2 - OSPF external type 2
       i - IS-IS, su - IS-IS summary, L1 - IS-IS level-1, L2 - IS-IS level-2
       ia - IS-IS inter area, * - candidate default, U - per-user static route
       o - ODR, P - periodic downloaded static route

Gateway of last resort is not set

     172.16.0.0/30 is subnetted, 2 subnets
C       172.16.1.0 is directly connected, Serial1/0.1
C       172.16.2.0 is directly connected, Serial1/0.2
     10.0.0.0/8 is variably subnetted, 6 subnets, 3 masks
C       10.2.2.2/32 is directly connected, Loopback0
O       10.1.3.0/30 [110/144] via 172.16.2.2, 00:07:12, Serial1/0.2
O       10.3.3.3/32 [110/91] via 172.16.2.2, 00:07:12, Serial1/0.2
O       10.1.2.0/24 [110/90] via 172.16.2.2, 00:07:12, Serial1/0.2
D       10.1.1.1/32 [90/409600] via 192.168.0.11, 00:04:46, FastEthernet0/0
O       10.4.4.4/32 [110/81] via 172.16.2.2, 00:07:12, Serial1/0.2
C    192.168.0.0/24 is directly connected, FastEthernet0/0
D    192.168.1.0/24 [90/284160] via 192.168.0.11, 00:04:46, FastEthernet0/0
```

Example 7-37   *Baseline Output for Router BB1*

```
BB1# show ip route
Codes: C - connected, S - static, R - RIP, M - mobile, B - BGP
       D - EIGRP, EX - EIGRP external, O - OSPF, IA - OSPF inter area
       N1 - OSPF NSSA external type 1, N2 - OSPF NSSA external type 2
       E1 - OSPF external type 1, E2 - OSPF external type 2
       i - IS-IS, su - IS-IS summary, L1 - IS-IS level-1, L2 - IS-IS level-2
       ia - IS-IS inter area, * - candidate default, U - per-user static route
       o - ODR, P - periodic downloaded static route

Gateway of last resort is not set

     172.16.0.0/30 is subnetted, 2 subnets
C       172.16.1.0 is directly connected, Serial1/0.2
O       172.16.2.0 [110/90] via 10.1.2.2, 00:07:08, FastEthernet0/0
     10.0.0.0/8 is variably subnetted, 6 subnets, 3 masks
O E2    10.2.2.2/32 [110/64] via 10.1.2.2, 00:07:08, FastEthernet0/0
C       10.1.3.0/30 is directly connected, Serial1/0.1
C       10.3.3.3/32 is directly connected, Loopback0
```

```
C        10.1.2.0/24 is directly connected, FastEthernet0/0
O E2     10.1.1.1/32 [110/64] via 10.1.2.2, 00:04:49, FastEthernet0/0
O        10.4.4.4/32 [110/11] via 10.1.2.2, 00:07:08, FastEthernet0/0
O E2 192.168.0.0/24 [110/64] via 10.1.2.2, 00:07:08, FastEthernet0/0
O E2 192.168.1.0/24 [110/64] via 10.1.2.2, 00:04:49, FastEthernet0/0
```

Example 7-38 *Baseline Output for Router BB2*

```
BB2# show ip route
Codes: C - connected, S - static, R - RIP, M - mobile, B - BGP
       D - EIGRP, EX - EIGRP external, O - OSPF, IA - OSPF inter area
       N1 - OSPF NSSA external type 1, N2 - OSPF NSSA external type 2
       E1 - OSPF external type 1, E2 - OSPF external type 2
       i - IS-IS, su - IS-IS summary, L1 - IS-IS level-1, L2 - IS-IS level-2
       ia - IS-IS inter area, * - candidate default, U - per-user static route
       o - ODR, P - periodic downloaded static route

Gateway of last resort is not set

     172.16.0.0/30 is subnetted, 2 subnets
O        172.16.1.0 [110/143] via 10.1.2.1, 00:08:48, FastEthernet0/0
C        172.16.2.0 is directly connected, Serial1/0.2
     10.0.0.0/8 is variably subnetted, 6 subnets, 3 masks
O E2     10.2.2.2/32 [110/64] via 172.16.2.1, 00:08:48, Serial1/0.2
C        10.1.3.0/30 is directly connected, Serial1/0.1
O        10.3.3.3/32 [110/11] via 10.1.2.1, 00:08:48, FastEthernet0/0
C        10.1.2.0/24 is directly connected, FastEthernet0/0
O E2     10.1.1.1/32 [110/64] via 172.16.2.1, 00:06:30, Serial1/0.2
C        10.4.4.4/32 is directly connected, Loopback0
O E2 192.168.0.0/24 [110/64] via 172.16.2.1, 00:08:48, Serial1/0.2
O E2 192.168.1.0/24 [110/64] via 172.16.2.1, 00:06:30, Serial1/0.2
```

Router R2, acting as a boundary router, had previously been configured for mutual route redistribution. Example 7-39 illustrates this route redistribution configuration.

Example 7-39 *Mutual Route Redistribution on Router R2*

```
R2# show run | begin router
router eigrp 100
 redistribute ospf 1 metric 1500 100 255 1 1500
 network 10.2.2.2 0.0.0.0
 network 192.168.0.0
 no auto-summary
!
```

```
router ospf 1
 redistribute eigrp 100 metric 64 subnets
 network 172.16.1.0 0.0.0.3 area 0
 network 172.16.2.0 0.0.0.3 area 0
```

To begin the troubleshooting process, you issue the **show ip route** command on all routers to determine exactly what routes are missing from the IP routing table of each router.

Router R1's IP routing table lacks all OSPF-learned routes, as shown in Example 7-40.

Example 7-40   *Router R1's IP Routing Table*

```
R1# show ip route
Codes: C - connected, S - static, R - RIP, M - mobile, B - BGP
       D - EIGRP, EX - EIGRP external, O - OSPF, IA - OSPF inter area
       N1 - OSPF NSSA external type 1, N2 - OSPF NSSA external type 2
       E1 - OSPF external type 1, E2 - OSPF external type 2
       i - IS-IS, su - IS-IS summary, L1 - IS-IS level-1, L2 - IS-IS level-2
       ia - IS-IS inter area, * - candidate default, U - per-user static route
       o - ODR, P - periodic downloaded static route

Gateway of last resort is not set

      10.0.0.0/32 is subnetted, 2 subnets
D        10.2.2.2 [90/156160] via 192.168.0.22, 00:09:44, FastEthernet0/1
C        10.1.1.1 is directly connected, Loopback0
C     192.168.0.0/24 is directly connected, FastEthernet0/1
C     192.168.1.0/24 is directly connected, FastEthernet0/0
```

Router R1, which is acting as the boundary router, is actively participating in both the EIGRP and OSPF routing processes. Therefore, all routes are visible in the IP routing table of router R2, as shown in Example 7-41.

Example 7-41   *IP Routing Table of Router R2*

```
R2# show ip route
Codes: C - connected, S - static, R - RIP, M - mobile, B - BGP
       D - EIGRP, EX - EIGRP external, O - OSPF, IA - OSPF inter area
       N1 - OSPF NSSA external type 1, N2 - OSPF NSSA external type 2
       E1 - OSPF external type 1, E2 - OSPF external type 2
       i - IS-IS, su - IS-IS summary, L1 - IS-IS level-1, L2 - IS-IS level-2
       ia - IS-IS inter area, * - candidate default, U - per-user static route
       o - ODR, P - periodic downloaded static route
```

```
Gateway of last resort is not set

     172.16.0.0/30 is subnetted, 2 subnets
C       172.16.1.0 is directly connected, Serial1/0.1
C       172.16.2.0 is directly connected, Serial1/0.2
     10.0.0.0/8 is variably subnetted, 6 subnets, 3 masks
C       10.2.2.2/32 is directly connected, Loopback0
O       10.1.3.0/30 [110/144] via 172.16.2.2, 00:07:12, Serial1/0.2
O       10.3.3.3/32 [110/91] via 172.16.2.2, 00:07:12, Serial1/0.2
O       10.1.2.0/24 [110/90] via 172.16.2.2, 00:07:12, Serial1/0.2
D       10.1.1.1/32 [90/409600] via 192.168.0.11, 00:04:46, FastEthernet0/0
O       10.4.4.4/32 [110/81] via 172.16.2.2, 00:07:12, Serial1/0.2
C    192.168.0.0/24 is directly connected, FastEthernet0/0
D    192.168.1.0/24 [90/284160] via 192.168.0.11, 00:04:46, FastEthernet0/0
```

Router BB1, which is running OSPF, has some routes that originated in EIGRP. However, the 10.1.1.1/32 and the 10.2.2.2/32 networks, which are the IP addresses of the Loopback 0 interfaces on routers R1 and R2, are missing from the IP routing table of router BB1, as illustrated in Example 7-42.

Example 7-42 *IP Routing Table of Router BB1*

```
BB1# show ip route
Codes: C - connected, S - static, R - RIP, M - mobile, B - BGP
       D - EIGRP, EX - EIGRP external, O - OSPF, IA - OSPF inter area
       N1 - OSPF NSSA external type 1, N2 - OSPF NSSA external type 2
       E1 - OSPF external type 1, E2 - OSPF external type 2
       i - IS-IS, su - IS-IS summary, L1 - IS-IS level-1, L2 - IS-IS level-2
       ia - IS-IS inter area, * - candidate default, U - per-user static route
       o - ODR, P - periodic downloaded static route

Gateway of last resort is not set

     172.16.0.0/30 is subnetted, 2 subnets
C       172.16.1.0 is directly connected, Serial1/0.2
O       172.16.2.0 [110/90] via 10.1.2.2, 00:13:00, FastEthernet0/0
     10.0.0.0/8 is variably subnetted, 4 subnets, 3 masks
C       10.1.3.0/30 is directly connected, Serial1/0.1
C       10.3.3.3/32 is directly connected, Loopback0
C       10.1.2.0/24 is directly connected, FastEthernet0/0
O       10.4.4.4/32 [110/11] via 10.1.2.2, 00:13:00, FastEthernet0/0
O E2 192.168.0.0/24 [110/64] via 10.1.2.2, 00:01:14, FastEthernet0/0
O E2 192.168.1.0/24 [110/64] via 10.1.2.2, 00:01:14, FastEthernet0/0
```

The IP routing table of router BB2, as depicted in Example 7-43, is similar to the IP routing table of router BB1.

Example 7-43   *IP Routing Table of Router BB2*

```
BB2# show ip route
Codes: C - connected, S - static, R - RIP, M - mobile, B - BGP
       D - EIGRP, EX - EIGRP external, O - OSPF, IA - OSPF inter area
       N1 - OSPF NSSA external type 1, N2 - OSPF NSSA external type 2
       E1 - OSPF external type 1, E2 - OSPF external type 2
       i - IS-IS, su - IS-IS summary, L1 - IS-IS level-1, L2 - IS-IS level-2
       ia - IS-IS inter area, * - candidate default, U - per-user static route
       o - ODR, P - periodic downloaded static route

Gateway of last resort is not set

     172.16.0.0/30 is subnetted, 2 subnets
O       172.16.1.0 [110/143] via 10.1.2.1, 00:13:39, FastEthernet0/0
C       172.16.2.0 is directly connected, Serial1/0.2
     10.0.0.0/8 is variably subnetted, 4 subnets, 3 masks
C       10.1.3.0/30 is directly connected, Serial1/0.1
O       10.3.3.3/32 [110/11] via 10.1.2.1, 00:13:39, FastEthernet0/0
C       10.1.2.0/24 is directly connected, FastEthernet0/0
C       10.4.4.4/32 is directly connected, Loopback0
O E2 192.168.0.0/24 [110/64] via 172.16.2.1, 00:01:53, Serial1/0.2
O E2 192.168.1.0/24 [110/64] via 172.16.2.1, 00:01:53, Serial1/0.2
```

Because router R2 is acting as the boundary router, you examine its redistribution configuration, as shown in 7-44.

Example 7-44   *Redistribution Configuration on Router R2*

```
R2# show run | begin router
router eigrp 100
 redistribute ospf 1
 network 10.2.2.2 0.0.0.0
 network 192.168.0.0
 no auto-summary
!
router ospf 1
 log-adjacency-changes
 redistribute eigrp 100 metric 64
 network 172.16.1.0 0.0.0.3 area 0
 network 172.16.2.0 0.0.0.3 area 0
```

Take a moment to look through the baseline configuration information, the topology, the **show** command output collected after the issue was reported, and the syntax reference presented in Table 7-10. Then hypothesize the underlying cause or causes of the reported issue, explaining why routers R1, BB1, and BB2 do not see all the networks in the topology, even though mutual redistribution does appear to be configured on router R2.

Suggested Solution

After examining the redistribution configuration on router R2, you might have noticed the following issues:

- The EIGRP routing process on router R2 lacked a default metric, which would be assigned to routes being redistributed into the EIGRP routing process. Example 7-45 shows the commands used to correct this misconfiguration.

Example 7-45   *Adding a Default Metric for Router R2's EIGRP Routing Process*

```
R2# conf term
Enter configuration commands, one per line.  End with CNTL/Z.
R2(config)#router eigrp 100
R2(config-router)#default-metric 1500 100 255 1 1500
R2(config-router)#end
```

- The OSPF routing process lacked the **subnets** parameter at the end of the **redistribute** command. The **subnets** parameter is required to allow nonclassful networks to be redistributed into OSPF. Example 7-46 illustrates how this configuration can be corrected.

Example 7-46   *Redistributing Subnets into Router R2's OSPF Routing Process*

```
R2# conf term
Enter configuration commands, one per line.  End with CNTL/Z.
R2(config)#router ospf 1
R2(config-router)#no redistribute eigrp 100 metric 64
R2(config-router)#redistribute eigrp 100 metric 64 subnets
R2(config-router)#end
```

After making the suggested corrections, all routers in the topology have IP routing tables that contain all advertised networks. Examples 7-47, 7-48, 7-49, and 7-50 illustrate the IP routing tables of these routers.

Example 7-47   *IP Routing Table of Router R1*

```
R1# show ip route
Codes: C - connected, S - static, R - RIP, M - mobile, B - BGP
       D - EIGRP, EX - EIGRP external, O - OSPF, IA - OSPF inter area
       N1 - OSPF NSSA external type 1, N2 - OSPF NSSA external type 2
```

```
          E1 - OSPF external type 1, E2 - OSPF external type 2
          i - IS-IS, su - IS-IS summary, L1 - IS-IS level-1, L2 - IS-IS level-2
          ia - IS-IS inter area, * - candidate default, U - per-user static route
          o - ODR, P - periodic downloaded static route


Gateway of last resort is not set


     172.16.0.0/30 is subnetted, 2 subnets
D EX    172.16.1.0 [170/1734656] via 192.168.0.22, 00:04:39, FastEthernet0/1
D EX    172.16.2.0 [170/1734656] via 192.168.0.22, 00:04:39, FastEthernet0/1
     10.0.0.0/8 is variably subnetted, 6 subnets, 3 masks
D       10.2.2.2/32 [90/156160] via 192.168.0.22, 00:18:05, FastEthernet0/1
D EX    10.1.3.0/30 [170/1734656] via 192.168.0.22, 00:04:39, FastEthernet0/1
D EX    10.3.3.3/32 [170/1734656] via 192.168.0.22, 00:04:39, FastEthernet0/1
D EX    10.1.2.0/24 [170/1734656] via 192.168.0.22, 00:04:40, FastEthernet0/1
C       10.1.1.1/32 is directly connected, Loopback0
D EX    10.4.4.4/32 [170/1734656] via 192.168.0.22, 00:04:40, FastEthernet0/1
C     192.168.0.0/24 is directly connected, FastEthernet0/1
C     192.168.1.0/24 is directly connected, FastEthernet0/0
```

Example 7-48   *IP Routing Table of Router R2*

```
R2# show ip route
Codes: C - connected, S - static, R - RIP, M - mobile, B - BGP
       D - EIGRP, EX - EIGRP external, O - OSPF, IA - OSPF inter area
       N1 - OSPF NSSA external type 1, N2 - OSPF NSSA external type 2
       E1 - OSPF external type 1, E2 - OSPF external type 2
       i - IS-IS, su - IS-IS summary, L1 - IS-IS level-1, L2 - IS-IS level-2
       ia - IS-IS inter area, * - candidate default, U - per-user static route
       o - ODR, P - periodic downloaded static route


Gateway of last resort is not set


     172.16.0.0/30 is subnetted, 2 subnets
C       172.16.1.0 is directly connected, Serial1/0.1
C       172.16.2.0 is directly connected, Serial1/0.2
     10.0.0.0/8 is variably subnetted, 6 subnets, 3 masks
C       10.2.2.2/32 is directly connected, Loopback0
O       10.1.3.0/30 [110/144] via 172.16.2.2, 00:21:04, Serial1/0.2
O       10.3.3.3/32 [110/91] via 172.16.2.2, 00:21:04, Serial1/0.2
O       10.1.2.0/24 [110/90] via 172.16.2.2, 00:21:04, Serial1/0.2
D       10.1.1.1/32 [90/409600] via 192.168.0.11, 00:18:38, FastEthernet0/0
O       10.4.4.4/32 [110/81] via 172.16.2.2, 00:21:04, Serial1/0.2
C     192.168.0.0/24 is directly connected, FastEthernet0/0
D     192.168.1.0/24 [90/284160] via 192.168.0.11, 00:18:38, FastEthernet0/0
```

Example 7-49 *IP Routing Table of Router BB1*

```
BB1# show ip route
Codes: C - connected, S - static, R - RIP, M - mobile, B - BGP
       D - EIGRP, EX - EIGRP external, O - OSPF, IA - OSPF inter area
       N1 - OSPF NSSA external type 1, N2 - OSPF NSSA external type 2
       E1 - OSPF external type 1, E2 - OSPF external type 2
       i - IS-IS, su - IS-IS summary, L1 - IS-IS level-1, L2 - IS-IS level-2
       ia - IS-IS inter area, * - candidate default, U - per-user static route
       o - ODR, P - periodic downloaded static route

Gateway of last resort is not set


     172.16.0.0/30 is subnetted, 2 subnets
C       172.16.1.0 is directly connected, Serial1/0.2
O       172.16.2.0 [110/90] via 10.1.2.2, 00:21:08, FastEthernet0/0
     10.0.0.0/8 is variably subnetted, 6 subnets, 3 masks
O E2    10.2.2.2/32 [110/64] via 10.1.2.2, 00:04:44, FastEthernet0/0
C       10.1.3.0/30 is directly connected, Serial1/0.1
C       10.3.3.3/32 is directly connected, Loopback0
C       10.1.2.0/24 is directly connected, FastEthernet0/0
O E2    10.1.1.1/32 [110/64] via 10.1.2.2, 00:04:44, FastEthernet0/0
O       10.4.4.4/32 [110/11] via 10.1.2.2, 00:21:08, FastEthernet0/0
O E2 192.168.0.0/24 [110/64] via 10.1.2.2, 00:04:44, FastEthernet0/0
O E2 192.168.1.0/24 [110/64] via 10.1.2.2, 00:04:44, FastEthernet0/0
```

Example 7-50 *IP Routing Table of Router BB2*

```
BB2# show ip route
Codes: C - connected, S - static, R - RIP, M - mobile, B - BGP
       D - EIGRP, EX - EIGRP external, O - OSPF, IA - OSPF inter area
       N1 - OSPF NSSA external type 1, N2 - OSPF NSSA external type 2
       E1 - OSPF external type 1, E2 - OSPF external type 2
       i - IS-IS, su - IS-IS summary, L1 - IS-IS level-1, L2 - IS-IS level-2
       ia - IS-IS inter area, * - candidate default, U - per-user static route
       o - ODR, P - periodic downloaded static route

Gateway of last resort is not set


     172.16.0.0/30 is subnetted, 2 subnets
O       172.16.1.0 [110/143] via 10.1.2.1, 00:21:13, FastEthernet0/0
C       172.16.2.0 is directly connected, Serial1/0.2
     10.0.0.0/8 is variably subnetted, 6 subnets, 3 masks
O E2    10.2.2.2/32 [110/64] via 172.16.2.1, 00:04:50, Serial1/0.2
C       10.1.3.0/30 is directly connected, Serial1/0.1
O       10.3.3.3/32 [110/11] via 10.1.2.1, 00:21:13, FastEthernet0/0
```

```
C          10.1.2.0/24 is directly connected, FastEthernet0/0
O E2    10.1.1.1/32 [110/64] via 172.16.2.1, 00:04:50, Serial1/0.2
C          10.4.4.4/32 is directly connected, Loopback0
O E2 192.168.0.0/24 [110/64] via 172.16.2.1, 00:04:50, Serial1/0.2
O E2 192.168.1.0/24 [110/64] via 172.16.2.1, 00:04:50, Serial1/0.2
```

Exam Preparation Tasks

Review All the Key Topics

Review the most important topics from inside the chapter, noted with the Key Topics icon in the outer margin of the page. Table 7-11 lists these key topics and the page numbers where each is found.

Key Topic

Table 7-11 *Key Topics for Chapter 7*

Key Topic Element	Description	Page Number
Table 7-2	OSPF data structures	170
List	OSPF router types	172
Table 7-3	OSPF router types in Figure 7-2	173
Table 7-4	LSA types	174
Table 7-5	OSPF LSA types in Figure 7-2	175
Table 7-6	OSPF Network Types and Characteristics	176
List	OSPF Hello packet parameters that must match for an adjacency to form	176
Table 7-7	Adjacency states	177
Table 7-8	OSPF troubleshooting commands	179
List	Reasons a network might benefit from route redistribution	205
List	Ways to define a seed metric	205
List	Prerequisites for IP route redistribution	206
Table 7-9	Troubleshooting targets for route redistribution	207
Example 7-34	Output from the **show ip route** profile command	208
Table 7-10	Route redistribution verification and troubleshooting syntax	209

Complete Tables and Lists from Memory

Print a copy of Appendix B, "Memory Tables" (found on the CD), or at least the section for this chapter, and complete the tables and lists from memory. Appendix C, "Memory Tables Answer Key," also on the CD, includes completed tables and lists to check your work.

Define Key Terms

Define the following key terms from this chapter, and check your answers in the Glossary:

OSPF interface table, OSPF neighbor table, OSPF link-state database, OSPF Routing Information Base (RIB), link-state advertisement (LSA), Dijkstra shortest path first (SPF) algorithm, virtual link, OSPF internal router, OSPF area border router (ABR), OSPF backbone router, OSPF Autonomous System Boundary Router (ASBR), route redistribution, boundary router

Command Reference to Check Your Memory

This section includes the most important configuration and EXEC commands covered in this chapter. To determine how well you have memorized the commands as a side effect of your other studies, cover the left side of the table with a piece of paper; read the descriptions on the right side; and see whether you remember the command.

Table 7-12 *Chapter 7 Configuration Command Reference*

Command	Description
ip route profile	Global configuration mode command that enables the Cisco IOS IP route profiling feature, which collects information regarding the frequency of IP routing table updates
router ospf *process-id*	Global configuration mode command that enables an OSPF process on a router
redistribute eigrp *autonomous-system-number* [**subnets**]	Router configuration mode command that redistributes routes, including subnets (if the optional **subnets** parameter is specified), from a specified EIGRP autonomous system into OSPF
default-metric *metric*	Router configuration mode command that specifies the metric used for routes redistributed into OSPF
router eigrp *autonomous-system-number*	Global configuration mode command that enables an EIGRP routing process on a router
redistribute ospf *process-id*	Router configuration mode command that redistributes routes from a specified OSPF process ID into EIGRP
default-metric *bandwidth delay reliability load mtu*	Router configuration mode command that specifies the parameters used to calculate the seed metric for routes being redistributed into EIGRP, using the following EIGRP metric parameters: *bandwidth* (in kbps) *delay* (in tens of microseconds) *reliability* (maximum of 255) *load* (minimum of 1) *mtu* (in bytes)

Table 7-13   *Chapter 7 EXEC Command Reference*

Command	Description
show ip ospf interface [brief]	Displays all of a router's interfaces configured to participate in an OSPF routing process (Note: The **brief** option provides a more concise view of OSPF interface information.)
show ip ospf neighbor	Displays the state of OSPF neighbors learned off of the active OSPF interfaces of a router
show ip ospf database	Displays the LSA headers contained in the OSPF link-state database of a router
show ip ospf statistics	Provides information about how frequently a router is executing the SFP algorithm. (Note: This command also shows when the SPF algorithm last ran.)
debug ip ospf monitor	Provides real-time updates showing when the SPF algorithm of a router is scheduled to run
debug ip routing	Displays updates that occur in an IP routing table (Note: This command is not specific to OSPF.)
show ip route ospf	Shows routes known to a router's IP routing table that were learned via OSPF
debug ip ospf packet	Shows the transmission and reception of OSPF packets in real time (Note: This command is useful for monitoring Hello messages.)
debug ip ospf adj	Provides real-time updates about the formation of an OSPF adjacency
debug ip ospf events	Shows real-time information about OSPF events, including the transmission and reception of Hello messages and LSAs (Note: This command might be useful on a router that appears to be ignoring Hello messages received from a neighboring router.)
show ip ospf virtual-links	Provides information about the status of OSPF virtual links, which are required for areas not physically adjacent to the backbone area (that is, area 0)
show ip route profile	Displays information collected by the Cisco IOS IP route profiling feature, which shows the frequency of IP routing table updates

This chapter covers the following subjects:

BGP Troubleshooting Issues: This section begins by introducing you to the Border Gateway Protocol (BGP) data structures, followed by a review of BGP operation. Finally, you are presented with a collection of **show** and **debug** commands useful for troubleshooting BGP operations.

Trouble Ticket: BGP: This section presents you with a trouble ticket and an associated topology. You are also given **show** command output. Based on the information provided, you hypothesize an underlying cause for the reported issue and develop a solution. You can then compare your solutions with those that have been suggested.

Router Performance Issues: This section discusses how to troubleshoot performance issues on a router, focusing on CPU utilization, packet switching modes, and memory utilization.

CHAPTER 8

Troubleshooting BGP and Router Performance Issues

This chapter begins by discussing Border Gateway Protocol (BGP). You will see how to use BGP between autonomous systems. Additionally, you will be equipped with a collection of **show** and **debug** commands, which can prove useful when troubleshooting a BGP issue.

To reinforce the theory of BGP troubleshooting, you are presented with a trouble ticket. The trouble ticket deals with a suboptimal path selection that BGP makes. You are then challenged to determine the cause of this path selection and reconfigure BGP to select a more appropriate path.

At that point, you will have covered troubleshooting approaches for multiple IP routing protocols (that is, Enhanced Interior Gateway Routing Protocol [EIGRP], Open Shortest Path First [OSPF], and BGP). Finally in this chapter, you review from a more generic perspective the troubleshooting of router performance issues. These issues can stem from a lack of available router memory, a lack of available buffers, or perhaps the packet switching mode of the router.

"Do I Know This Already?" Quiz

The "Do I Know This Already?" quiz helps you determine your level of knowledge of this chapter's topics before you begin. Table 8-1 details the major topics discussed in this chapter and their corresponding quiz questions.

Table 8-1 *"Do I Know This Already?" Section-to-Question Mapping*

Foundation Topics Section	Questions
BGP Troubleshooting Issues	1–2
Router Performance Issues	3–5

   1. Identify two BGP data structures. (Choose the two best answers.)

   a. BGP table

   b. link-state database

   c. interface table

   d. neighbor table

2. Which command displays the network prefixes present in the BGP table?

    a. show ip bgp neighbors

    b. show ip bgp

    c. show ip route bgp

    d. show ip bgp summary

3. Which router process is in charge of handling interface state changes?

    a. TCP Timer process

    b. IP Background process

    c. Net Background process

    d. ARP Input process

4. Which of the following is the least efficient (that is, the most CPU intensive) of a router's packet switching modes?

    a. Fast switching

    b. CEF

    c. Optimum switching

    d. Process switching

5. Identify two common reasons a router displays a MALLOCFAIL error. (Choose the two best answers.)

    a. Cisco IOS bug

    b. Security issue

    c. QoS issue

    d. BGP filtering

Foundation Topics

BGP Troubleshooting Issues

Chapter 6, "Introduction to Troubleshooting Routing Protocols," and Chapter 7, "OSPF and Route Redistribution Troubleshooting," focused on interior gateway protocols (IGP). An IGP is used within an autonomous system (AS), where an *autonomous system* is defined as a network under a single administrative control. This chapter, however, focuses on an exterior gateway protocol (EGP)—specifically BGP.

An EGP, like BGP, is a routing protocol typically used between autonomous systems. For example, if your enterprise network connects to more than one Internet service provider (ISP), you might be running BGP between your network (that is, your AS) and each ISP (each of which is a separate AS).

This section examines BGP data structures, reviews BGP operation, and presents commands useful for collecting information from the BGP data structures.

BGP Data Structures

Figure 8-1 reviews how the data structures of an IP routing protocol interact with an IP routing table.

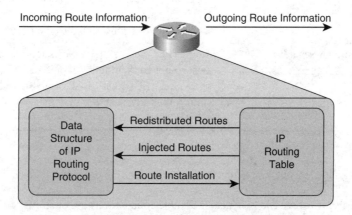

Figure 8-1   *Data Structure and IP Routing Table Interaction*

Table 8-2 describes how BGP operates within this framework.

Table 8-2 *Interaction Between the Data Structures of a BGP and an IP Routing Table*

Component of Routing Process	Description
Incoming Route Information	A BGP router receives BGP updates from a BGP neighbor. Unlike OSPF and EIGRP neighbors, BGP neighbors do not need to be directly connected. Rather, BGP neighbors can be multiple hops away from one another. Therefore, BGP neighbors are often referred to as *peers*.
Data Structure of IP Routing Protocol	BGP maintains two data structures: the neighbor table and the BGP table. The neighbor table contains status information about BGP neighbors, whereas the BGP table contains network prefixes learned from BGP neighbors.
Injecting and Redistributing Routes	Routes can be inserted in the BGP table by advertisements received from BGP neighbors or by locally injected routes. For a route to be locally injected (either through a manual configuration or through a redistribution configuration), it must be present in the IP routing table.
Route Installation	Similar to OSPF and EIGRP, BGP might have more than one route to a network prefix in its BGP table. BGP then selects what it considers to be the best route to that network prefix; that best route becomes a candidate to be inserted into the IP routing table.
Outgoing Route Information	Routes in a router's BGP table that are considered the best routes to their network prefixes are advertised to the router's BGP peers. BGP offers several features to limit routes advertised to BGP peers or received from BGP peers.

Figure 8-2 illustrates BGP's two data structures, which are described in the list that follows.

- **Neighbor table:** The BGP neighbor table contains a listing of all BGP neighbors configured for a router, including each neighbor's IP address, AS number, the state of the neighborship, and several other statistics.

- **BGP table:** The BGP table, sometimes referred to as the BGP Routing Information Base (RIB), contains routes learned from BGP peers and routes locally injected into the BGP table of a router.

Unlike OSPF and EIGRP, BGP does not consider a link's bandwidth when making a routing decision. Instead, BGP uses the following criteria when deciding how to forward a packet. The criteria are listed in the order in which BGP prioritizes each criterion.

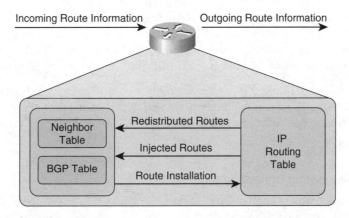

Figure 8-2   *BGP Data Structures*

1. BGP prefers the path with the highest weight. Note that the BGP **weight** parameter is a Cisco-specific parameter.

2. BGP prefers the path with the highest local preference value.

3. BGP prefers the path originated by BGP on the local router.

4. BGP prefers the path with the shortest autonomous system.

5. BGP prefers the path with the lowest origin type. (**NOTE:** IGP < EGP < INCOMPLETE.)

6. BGP prefers the path with the lowest multi-exit discriminator (MED).

7. BGP prefers eBGP paths over iBGP paths.

8. BGP prefers the path with the lowest IGP metric to the BGP next-hop.

9. BGP prefers the path that points to a BGP router with the lowest BGP router ID.

A BGP router always learns its neighbors through manual configuration of those neighbors as opposed to dynamically learning about neighbors. This manual configuration requirement makes sense when you consider that BGP neighbors do not have to be physically adjacent. When a BGP neighbor is statically configured, the AS number of the neighbor is specified.

A BGP router attempts to establish a session with its configured neighbors using TCP port 179. After a session has been established, BGP OPEN messages are exchanged to communicate each neighbor's BGP characteristics.

The following are reasons why the peering of two BGP routers might fail:

■   The AS numbers must match between the AS number in messages received from a neighbor and the AS number a router has configured for that neighbor. If the AS numbers fail to match, the session is reset.

■   TCP establishes a BGP session. Therefore, a lack of IP connectivity between two BGP routers prevents a peering relationship from forming between those routers.

- A BGP router might have multiple active IP addresses configured across its various interfaces. A router might send a BGP message from one of its IP addresses that does not match the IP address configured for that router on its peer. If the peer does not recognize the source IP address of the BGP message, the peering relationship fails.

After initially establishing a peering relationship, two BGP peers exchange information in their BGP tables. Incremental updates are sent thereafter. If a network prefix is removed from the BGP table of a router, that router sends a WITHDRAW message to appropriate peers.

BGP Troubleshooting Commands

With an understanding of BGP's data structures and path selection criteria, you can now strategically use Cisco IOS **show** and **debug** commands to collect information about specific steps in the BGP routing process. Table 8-3 shows a collection of such commands, along with their descriptions, and the step of the routing process or BGP data structure that each command can be used to investigate.

Key
Topic

Table 8-3   *BGP Troubleshooting Commands*

Command	Routing Component or Data Structure	Description
show ip bgp summary	Neighbor table	This command displays a router's BGP router ID, AS number, information about the BGP's memory usage, and summary information about BGP neighbors.
show ip bgp neighbors	Neighbor table	This command displays the detailed information about all the BGP neighbors of a router.
show ip bgp	BGP table	This command displays the network prefixes present in the BGP table.
debug ip routing	IP routing table	This command displays updates that occur in a router's IP routing table. Therefore, this command is not specific to BGP.
show ip route bgp	IP routing table	This command shows routes known to a router's IP routing table that were learned via BGP.
debug ip bgp	Exchanging BGP information with neighbors	Although this command does not show the contents of BGP updates, the output does provide real-time information about BGP events, such as the establishment of a peering relationship.

Table 8-3   *BGP Troubleshooting Commands*   *(Continued)*

Command	Routing Component or Data Structure	Description
debug ip bgp updates	Exchanging BGP information with neighbors	This command shows real-time information about BGP updates sent and received by a BGP router.

Example 8-1 provides sample output from the **show ip bgp summary** command. Notice that the output shows that the BGP router ID is 10.2.2.2, and the router is in AS 65001. You can also determine how much memory is being used by the BGP network entries and see summary information about the BGP neighbors of this router.

Example 8-1   show ip bgp summary *Command Output*

```
R2#show ip bgp summary
 BGP router identifier 10.2.2.2, local AS number 65001
BGP table version is 11, main routing table version 11
 10 network entries using 1170 bytes of memory
14 path entries using 728 bytes of memory
6/5 BGP path/bestpath attribute entries using 744 bytes of memory
2 BGP AS-PATH entries using 48 bytes of memory
0 BGP route-map cache entries using 0 bytes of memory
0 BGP filter-list cache entries using 0 bytes of memory
BGP using 2690 total bytes of memory
BGP activity 10/0 prefixes, 14/0 paths, scan interval 60 secs

Neighbor        V    AS  MsgRcvd MsgSent  TblVer  InQ OutQ  Up/Down  State/PfxRcd
172.16.1.1      4  65002      11      15      11    0    0  00:07:45             4
172.16.2.2      4  65003       8      12      11    0    0  00:03:19             4
```

Example 8-2 provides sample output from the **show ip bgp neighbors** command. The output from this command provides detailed information about each neighbor. The truncated output shown here is for a neighbor with a BGP router ID of 10.3.3.3. Among the large number of statistics shown is information about the BGP session with this neighbor. For example, you can see that the BGP state of the session is Established, and the two TCP ports being used for the session are 52907 and 179.

Example 8-2   show ip bgp neighbors *Command Output*

```
R2#show ip bgp neighbors
BGP neighbor is 172.16.1.1,  remote AS 65002, external link
  BGP version 4, remote router ID 10.3.3.3
  BGP state = Established, up for 00:10:05
  Last read 00:00:04, last write 00:00:05, hold time is 180, keepalive interval
```

```
is 60 seconds
  Neighbor capabilities:
    Route refresh: advertised and received(old & new)
    Address family IPv4 Unicast: advertised and received
  Message statistics:
    InQ depth is 0
    OutQ depth is 0
                          Sent          Rcvd
    Opens:                 1             1
    Notifications:         0             0
    Updates:               5             2
    Keepalives:            12            12
    Route Refresh:         0             0
    Total:                 18            15
  Default minimum time between advertisement runs is 30 seconds


 For address family: IPv4 Unicast
  BGP table version 11, neighbor version 11/0
 Output queue size : 0
  Index 1, Offset 0, Mask 0x2
  1 update-group member
                          Sent          Rcvd
    Prefix activity:      ----          ----
      Prefixes Current:    10            5 (Consumes 260 bytes)
      Prefixes Total:      10            5
      Implicit Withdraw:   0             0
      Explicit Withdraw:   0             0
      Used as bestpath:    n/a           3
      Used as multipath:   n/a           0

                          Outbound      Inbound
    Local Policy Denied Prefixes:  --------    --------
      Total:               0             0
    Number of NLRIs in the update sent: max 3, min 1


    Connections established 1; dropped 0
    Last reset never
Connection state is ESTAB, I/O status: 1, unread input bytes: 0
Connection is ECN Disabled, Minimum incoming TTL 0, Outgoing TTL 1
Local host: 172.16.1.2, Local port: 52907
Foreign host: 172.16.1.1, Foreign port: 179
Enqueued packets for retransmit: 0, input: 0  mis-ordered: 0 (0 bytes)
```

```
Event Timers (current time is 0x1268DC):
Timer          Starts   Wakeups        Next
Retrans            16         0         0x0
TimeWait            0         0         0x0
AckHold            14        12         0x0
SendWnd             0         0         0x0
KeepAlive           0         0         0x0
GiveUp              0         0         0x0
PmtuAger            0         0         0x0
DeadWait            0         0         0x0

iss:   43311306  snduna:   43311857  sndnxt:   43311857   sndwnd:  15834
irs: 2939679566  rcvnxt: 2939679955  rcvwnd:      15996 delrcvwnd:    388

SRTT: 279 ms, RTTO: 504 ms, RTV: 225 ms, KRTT: 0 ms
minRTT: 48 ms, maxRTT: 488 ms, ACK hold: 200 ms
Flags: active open, nagle
IP Precedence value : 6

Datagrams (max data segment is 1460 bytes):
Rcvd: 18 (out of order: 0), with data: 14, total data bytes: 388
Sent: 29 (retransmit: 0, fastretransmit: 0, partialack: 0, Second Congestion: 0),
with data: 15, total data bytes: 550
...OUTPUT OMITTED...
```

Example 8-3 provides sample output from the **show ip bgp** command. The output from this command shows the network prefixes present in the BGP table, along with information such as the next-hop IP addresses to reach those networks. Notice that some network prefixes are reachable via more than one path. For example, the 10.1.2.0/24 network is reachable via a next-hop IP address of 172.16.2.2 or 172.16.1.1. The **>** sign indicates which path BGP has selected as the best path. In this case, the path BGP selected as the best path has a next-hop IP address of 172.16.1.1.

Example 8-3   show ip bgp *Command Output*

```
R2#show ip bgp
BGP table version is 11, local router ID is 10.2.2.2
Status codes: s suppressed, d damped, h history, * valid, > best, i - internal,
              r RIB-failure, S Stale
Origin codes: i - IGP, e - EGP, ? - incomplete

   Network          Next Hop         Metric LocPrf Weight Path
*> 10.1.1.1/32      192.168.0.11         11         32768 ?
*  10.1.2.0/24      172.16.2.2            0             0 65003 i
*>                  172.16.1.1            0             0 65002 i
*  10.1.3.0/30      172.16.2.2            0             0 65003 i
```

```
*>                      172.16.1.1           0             0 65002 i
*> 10.2.2.2/32          0.0.0.0              0         32768 ?
*  10.3.3.3/32          172.16.2.2                         0 65003 65002 i
*>                      172.16.1.1           0             0 65002 i
*  10.4.4.4/32          172.16.1.1                         0 65002 65003 i
*>                      172.16.2.2           0             0 65003 i
*  172.16.1.0/30        172.16.1.1           0             0 65002 i
*>                      0.0.0.0              0         32768 i
*  172.16.2.0/30        172.16.2.2           0             0 65003 i
*>                      0.0.0.0              0         32768 i
*> 192.168.0.0          0.0.0.0              0         32768 ?
*> 192.168.1.0          192.168.0.11        11         32768 ?
```

Example 8-4 provides sample output from the **debug ip routing** command. The output from this command shows updates to a router's IP routing table. In this example, the Loopback 0 interface (with an IP address of 10.3.3.3) of a neighboring router was administratively shut down and then administratively brought back up. As the 10.3.3.3/32 network became unavailable and then once again became available, you can see that the 10.3.3.3/32 route was deleted and then added to this router's IP routing table. Notice that this output is not specific to BGP. Therefore, you can use the **debug ip routing** command with routing processes other than BGP.

Example 8-4   debug ip routing *Command Output*

```
R2#debug ip routing
IP routing debugging is on
*Mar  1 00:20:55.707: RT: 10.3.3.3/32 gateway changed from 172.16.1.1 to
172.16.2.2
*Mar  1 00:20:55.711: RT: NET-RED 10.3.3.3/32
*Mar  1 00:20:55.735: RT: del 10.3.3.3/32 via 172.16.2.2, bgp metric [20/0]
*Mar  1 00:20:55.739: RT: delete subnet route to 10.3.3.3/32
*Mar  1 00:20:55.743: RT: NET-RED 10.3.3.3/32
*Mar  1 00:21:25.815: RT: SET_LAST_RDB for 10.3.3.3/32
  NEW rdb: via 172.16.1.1

*Mar  1 00:21:25.819: RT: add 10.3.3.3/32 via 172.16.1.1, bgp metric [20/0]
*Mar  1 00:21:25.823: RT: NET-RED 10.3.3.3/32
```

Example 8-5 provides sample output from the **show ip route bgp** command. This command displays a subset of a router's IP routing table. Specifically, only routes in the IP routing table which have been learned via BGP are displayed.

Example 8-5   show ip route bgp *Command Output*

```
R2#show ip route bgp
      10.0.0.0/8 is variably subnetted, 6 subnets, 3 masks
 B       10.1.3.0/30 [20/0] via 172.16.1.1, 00:11:26
```

```
B       10.3.3.3/32 [20/0] via 172.16.1.1, 00:00:34
B       10.1.2.0/24 [20/0] via 172.16.1.1, 00:11:26
B       10.4.4.4/32 [20/0] via 172.16.2.2, 00:07:35
```

Example 8-6 provides sample output from the **debug ip bgp** command. The output of this command does not show the contents of BGP updates; however, this command can be useful in watching real-time state changes for BGP peering relationships. In this example, you can see a peering session being closed for the neighbor with an IP address of 172.16.1.1.

Example 8-6   debug ip bgp *Command Output*

```
R2#debug ip bgp
BGP debugging is on for address family: IPv4 Unicast
*Mar  1 00:23:26.535: BGP: 172.16.1.1 remote close, state CLOSEWAIT
*Mar  1 00:23:26.535: BGP: 172.16.1.1 -reset the session
*Mar  1 00:23:26.543: BGPNSF state: 172.16.1.1 went from nsf_not_active to
  nsf_not_active
*Mar  1 00:23:26.547: BGP: 172.16.1.1 went from Established to Idle
*Mar  1 00:23:26.547: %BGP-5-ADJCHANGE: neighbor 172.16.1.1 Down Peer closed the
  session
*Mar  1 00:23:26.547: BGP: 172.16.1.1 closing
*Mar  1 00:23:26.651: BGP: 172.16.1.1 went from Idle to Active
*Mar  1 00:23:26.663: BGP: 172.16.1.1 open active delayed 30162ms (35000ms max,
  28% jitter)
```

Example 8-7 provides sample output from the **debug ip bgp updates** command. This command produces more detailed output than the **debug ip bgp** command. Specifically, you can see the content of BGP updates. In this example, you see a route of 10.3.3.3/32 being added to a router's IP routing table.

Example 8-7   debug ip bgp updates *Command Output*

```
R2#debug ip bgp updates
BGP updates debugging is on for address family: IPv4 Unicast
*Mar  1 00:24:27.455: BGP(0): 172.16.1.1 NEXT_HOP part 1 net 10.3.3.3/32, next
  172.16.1.1
*Mar  1 00:24:27.455: BGP(0): 172.16.1.1 send UPDATE (format) 10.3.3.3/32, next
  172.16.1.1, metric 0, path 65002
*Mar  1 00:24:27.507: BGP(0): 172.16.1.1 rcv UPDATE about 10.3.3.3/32 — withdrawn
*Mar  1 00:24:27.515: BGP(0): Revise route installing 1 of 1 routes for
  10.3.3.3/32 -> 172.16.2.2(main) to main IP table
*Mar  1 00:24:27.519: BGP(0): updgrp 1 - 172.16.1.1 updates replicated for
  neighbors: 172.16.2.2
*Mar  1 00:24:27.523: BGP(0): 172.16.1.1 send UPDATE (format) 10.3.3.3/32, next
  172.16.1.2, metric 0, path 65003 65002
```

```
*Mar  1 00:24:27.547: BGP(0): 172.16.2.2 rcvd UPDATE w/ attr: nexthop 172.16.2.2,
  origin i, path 65003 65002
*Mar  1 00:24:27.551: BGP(0): 172.16.2.2 rcvd 10.3.3.3/32...duplicate ignored
*Mar  1 00:24:27.555: BGP(0): updgrp 1 - 172.16.1.1 updates replicated for
  neighbors: 172.16.2.2
*Mar  1 00:24:27.675: BGP(0): 172.16.2.2 rcv UPDATE w/ attr: nexthop 172.16.2.2,
  origin i, originator 0.0.0.0, path 65003 65001 65002, community , extended
  community
*Mar  1 00:24:27.683: BGP(0): 172.16.2.2 rcv UPDATE about 10.3.3.3/32 — DENIED
  due to: AS-PATH contains our own AS;
...OUTPUT OMITTED...
```

Trouble Ticket: BGP

This trouble ticket focuses on BGP. You are presented with baseline data, a trouble ticket, and information collected while investigating the reported issue. You are then challenged to identify the underlying issue and create an action plan to resolve that issue.

Trouble Ticket #6

You receive the following trouble ticket:

> Company A (that is, routers R1 and R2) has connections to two service providers (that is, BB1 and BB2). Router R2 is running BGP and is peering with routers BB1 and BB2. The bandwidth between routers R2 and BB2 is greater than the bandwidth between routers R2 and BB1. Therefore, company A wants to use the R2-to-BB2 link as the primary link to the backbone network (that is, a default route). However, company A noticed that the R2-to-BB1 link is being used.

This trouble ticket references the topology shown in Figure 8-3.

You begin by examining the baseline data collected after company A was dual-homed to its two ISPs. Example 8-8 shows the output from the **show ip route** command on router R1. Notice that router R1 has a default route in its IP routing table. This default route was learned via OSPF from router R2.

Example 8-8   *Baseline Output for Router R1*

```
R1#show ip route
Codes: C - connected, S - static, R - RIP, M - mobile, B - BGP
       D - EIGRP, EX - EIGRP external, O - OSPF, IA - OSPF inter area
       N1 - OSPF NSSA external type 1, N2 - OSPF NSSA external type 2
       E1 - OSPF external type 1, E2 - OSPF external type 2
       i - IS-IS, su - IS-IS summary, L1 - IS-IS level-1, L2 - IS-IS level-2
       ia - IS-IS inter area, * - candidate default, U - per-user static route
       o - ODR, P - periodic downloaded static route
```

```
Gateway of last resort is 192.168.0.22 to network 0.0.0.0


     10.0.0.0/32 is subnetted, 2 subnets
O        10.2.2.2 [110/2] via 192.168.0.22, 00:05:33, FastEthernet0/1
C        10.1.1.1 is directly connected, Loopback0
C     192.168.0.0/24 is directly connected, FastEthernet0/1
C     192.168.1.0/24 is directly connected, FastEthernet0/0
O*E2 0.0.0.0/0 [110/1] via 192.168.0.22, 00:05:33, FastEthernet0/1
```

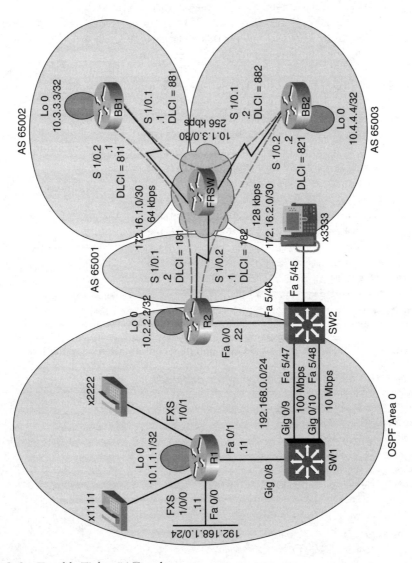

Figure 8-3   *Trouble Ticket #6 Topology*

Router R2 was configured for both OSPF and BGP, with the BGP-learned default route being injected into OSPF, and with OSPF-learned routes being redistributed into BGP. Example 8-9 shows the initial IP routing table for router R2. Notice that the next-hop router for the default route is 172.16.1.1 (that is, router BB1).

Example 8-9   *Baseline IP Routing Table on Router R2*

```
R2#show ip route
Codes: C - connected, S - static, R - RIP, M - mobile, B - BGP
       D - EIGRP, EX - EIGRP external, O - OSPF, IA - OSPF inter area
       N1 - OSPF NSSA external type 1, N2 - OSPF NSSA external type 2
       E1 - OSPF external type 1, E2 - OSPF external type 2
       i - IS-IS, su - IS-IS summary, L1 - IS-IS level-1, L2 - IS-IS level-2
       ia - IS-IS inter area, * - candidate default, U - per-user static route
       o - ODR, P - periodic downloaded static route

Gateway of last resort is 172.16.1.1 to network 0.0.0.0

     172.16.0.0/30 is subnetted, 2 subnets
C       172.16.1.0 is directly connected, Serial1/0.1
C       172.16.2.0 is directly connected, Serial1/0.2
     10.0.0.0/8 is variably subnetted, 6 subnets, 3 masks
C       10.2.2.2/32 is directly connected, Loopback0
B       10.1.3.0/30 [20/0] via 172.16.1.1, 00:01:40
B       10.3.3.3/32 [20/0] via 172.16.1.1, 00:01:40
B       10.1.2.0/24 [20/0] via 172.16.1.1, 00:01:40
O       10.1.1.1/32 [110/11] via 192.168.0.11, 00:08:17, FastEthernet0/0
B       10.4.4.4/32 [20/0] via 172.16.2.2, 00:01:40
C    192.168.0.0/24 is directly connected, FastEthernet0/0
O    192.168.1.0/24 [110/11] via 192.168.0.11, 00:08:17, FastEthernet0/0
B*   0.0.0.0/0 [20/0] via 172.16.1.1, 00:01:40
```

Example 8-10 illustrates the initial OSPF and BGP configuration on router R2.

Example 8-10   *Initial Router Configuration on Router R2*

```
R2#show run | begin router
router ospf 1
 log-adjacency-changes
 network 10.2.2.2 0.0.0.0 area 0
 network 192.168.0.0 0.0.0.255 area 0
 default-information originate
!
router bgp 65001
 no synchronization
 bgp log-neighbor-changes
 network 172.16.1.0 mask 255.255.255.252
```

```
network 172.16.2.0 mask 255.255.255.252
redistribute ospf 1
neighbor 172.16.1.1 remote-as 65002
neighbor 172.16.2.2 remote-as 65003
no auto-summary
```

Example 8-11 shows the output of the **show ip bgp summary** command on router R2, which confirms that router R2 resides in BGP AS 65001. The output also confirms BGP adjacencies have been formed with routers BB1 and BB2.

Example 8-11   *BGP Configuration Summary on Router R2*

```
R2#show ip bgp summary
BGP router identifier 10.2.2.2, local AS number 65001
BGP table version is 18, main routing table version 18
11 network entries using 1287 bytes of memory
20 path entries using 1040 bytes of memory
8/5 BGP path/bestpath attribute entries using 992 bytes of memory
4 BGP AS-PATH entries using 96 bytes of memory
0 BGP route-map cache entries using 0 bytes of memory
0 BGP filter-list cache entries using 0 bytes of memory
BGP using 3415 total bytes of memory
BGP activity 38/27 prefixes, 75/55 paths, scan interval 60 secs

Neighbor        V    AS MsgRcvd MsgSent   TblVer  InQ OutQ Up/Down  State/PfxRcd
172.16.1.1      4 65002     102      97       18    0    0 00:02:47        7
172.16.2.2      4 65003     100      97       18    0    0 00:02:47        7
```

Router BB1 is configured for BGP and is sourcing a default route advertisement. Example 8-12 shows the IP routing table of router BB1.

Example 8-12   *Initial IP Routing Table on Router BB1*

```
BB1#show ip route
Codes: C - connected, S - static, R - RIP, M - mobile, B - BGP
       D - EIGRP, EX - EIGRP external, O - OSPF, IA - OSPF inter area
       N1 - OSPF NSSA external type 1, N2 - OSPF NSSA external type 2
       E1 - OSPF external type 1, E2 - OSPF external type 2
       i - IS-IS, su - IS-IS summary, L1 - IS-IS level-1, L2 - IS-IS level-2
       ia - IS-IS inter area, * - candidate default, U - per-user static route
       o - ODR, P - periodic downloaded static route

Gateway of last resort is 0.0.0.0 to network 0.0.0.0

     172.16.0.0/30 is subnetted, 2 subnets
```

```
C          172.16.1.0 is directly connected, Serial1/0.2
B          172.16.2.0 [20/0] via 10.1.3.2, 00:03:01
        10.0.0.0/8 is variably subnetted, 6 subnets, 3 masks
B          10.2.2.2/32 [20/0] via 172.16.1.2, 00:01:59
C          10.1.3.0/30 is directly connected, Serial1/0.1
C          10.3.3.3/32 is directly connected, Loopback0
C          10.1.2.0/24 is directly connected, FastEthernet0/0
B          10.1.1.1/32 [20/11] via 172.16.1.2, 00:01:59
B          10.4.4.4/32 [20/0] via 10.1.3.2, 00:40:10
B       192.168.0.0/24 [20/0] via 172.16.1.2, 00:01:59
B       192.168.1.0/24 [20/11] via 172.16.1.2, 00:01:59
S*      0.0.0.0/0 is directly connected, Null0
```

Router BB2's IP routing table, as shown in Example 8-13, is similar to router BB1's IP routing table. Notice that router BB2 is also sourcing a default route and is advertising it via BGP to router R2. Therefore, router R2 has two paths to reach a default route in its BGP table.

Example 8-13 *Initial IP Routing Table on Router BB2*

```
BB2#show ip route
Codes: C - connected, S - static, R - RIP, M - mobile, B - BGP
       D - EIGRP, EX - EIGRP external, O - OSPF, IA - OSPF inter area
       N1 - OSPF NSSA external type 1, N2 - OSPF NSSA external type 2
       E1 - OSPF external type 1, E2 - OSPF external type 2
       i - IS-IS, su - IS-IS summary, L1 - IS-IS level-1, L2 - IS-IS level-2
       ia - IS-IS inter area, * - candidate default, U - per-user static route
       o - ODR, P - periodic downloaded static route

Gateway of last resort is 0.0.0.0 to network 0.0.0.0

        172.16.0.0/30 is subnetted, 2 subnets
B          172.16.1.0 [20/0] via 10.1.3.1, 00:03:11
C          172.16.2.0 is directly connected, Serial1/0.2
        10.0.0.0/8 is variably subnetted, 6 subnets, 3 masks
B          10.2.2.2/32 [20/0] via 172.16.2.1, 00:02:09
C          10.1.3.0/30 is directly connected, Serial1/0.1
B          10.3.3.3/32 [20/0] via 10.1.3.1, 00:40:10
C          10.1.2.0/24 is directly connected, FastEthernet0/0
B          10.1.1.1/32 [20/11] via 172.16.2.1, 00:02:09
C          10.4.4.4/32 is directly connected, Loopback0
B       192.168.0.0/24 [20/0] via 172.16.2.1, 00:02:09
B       192.168.1.0/24 [20/11] via 172.16.2.1, 00:02:09
S*      0.0.0.0/0 is directly connected, Null0
```

As shown earlier, in Example 8-9, router R2 preferred the 64-kbps link to router BB1 to reach a default route, as opposed to the 128-kbps link to router BB2. Therefore, the outbound routing from router R2 is suboptimal.

Also, the inbound routing, coming into the enterprise via router R2, is suboptimal. To illustrate this point, consider Example 8-14, which shows the BGP table on router BB1. Notice that router BB1 prefers a next-hop router of router R2 to reach the 10.1.1.1/32 network, which resides inside the enterprise network (that is, the network comprised of routers R1 and R2). Using a next-hop router of R2 would force traffic over the 64-kbps link rather than sending traffic from router BB1 over the 256-kbps link to router BB2, and then over the 128-kbps link to router R2, and finally across the FastEthernet connection to router R1.

Example 8-14 *BGP Forwarding Table on Router BB1*

```
BB1#show ip bgp
BGP table version is 130, local router ID is 10.3.3.3
Status codes: s suppressed, d damped, h history, * valid, > best, i - internal,
              r RIB-failure, S Stale
Origin codes: i - IGP, e - EGP, ? - incomplete

   Network          Next Hop            Metric LocPrf Weight Path
*  0.0.0.0          10.1.3.2                 0             0 65003 i
*>                  0.0.0.0                  0         32768 i
*  10.1.1.1/32      10.1.3.2                               0 65003 65001 ?
*>                  172.16.1.2              11             0 65001 ?
*  10.1.2.0/24      10.1.3.2                 0             0 65003 i
*>                  0.0.0.0                  0         32768 i
*  10.1.3.0/30      10.1.3.2                 0             0 65003 i
*>                  0.0.0.0                  0         32768 i
*  10.2.2.2/32      10.1.3.2                               0 65003 65001 ?
*>                  172.16.1.2               0             0 65001 ?
*> 10.3.3.3/32      0.0.0.0                  0         32768 i
*  10.4.4.4/32      172.16.1.2                             0 65001 65003 i
*>                  10.1.3.2                 0             0 65003 i
*  172.16.1.0/30    172.16.1.2               0             0 65001 i
*>                  0.0.0.0                  0         32768 i
*  172.16.2.0/30    172.16.1.2               0             0 65001 i
*>                  10.1.3.2                 0             0 65003 i
*  192.168.0.0      10.1.3.2                               0 65003 65001 ?
*>                  172.16.1.2               0             0 65001 ?
*  192.168.1.0      10.1.3.2                               0 65003 65001 ?
*>                  172.16.1.2              11             0 65001 ?
```

As you formulate your solution to correct the inbound and outbound path selection issues, you should limit your configuration to router R2. The reason for this limitation is that routers BB1 and BB2 are acting as ISP routers. In a real-world environment, the administrator of an enterprise network would probably not have privileges to configure the ISP routers.

BGP has multiple attributes that can be manipulated to influence path selection. The suggested solution, however, focuses on how the BGP local preference attribute can influence the outbound path selection and how the BGP ASPATH attribute can influence the inbound path selection. You can configure route maps to set these BGP attributes. If you choose to base your solution on local preference and ASPATH attributes, Table 8-4 provides a syntax reference that might be helpful.

Key Topic

Table 8-4   *Configuring ASPATH and Local Preference BGP Attributes*

Command	Description
Router(config)# **route-map** *tag* [**permit** | **deny**] [*seq-num*]	Creates a route map
Router(config-route-map)# **set local-preference** *local-preference*	Sets the local preference BGP attribute for routes matched by a route map
Router(config-route-map)# **set as-path prepend** *autonomous-system-number-1* [*...autonomous-system-number-n*]	Defines an autonomous system path to prepend to an autonomous system path known by the BGP forwarding table
Router(config)# **router bgp** *as-number*	Enables a BGP process for a specific autonomous system
Router(config-router)# **neighbor** *ip-address* **route-map** *route-map-name* [**in** | **out**]	Applies a specified route map to routes received from or advertised to a specified BGP neighbor

Take a moment to look through the provided **show** command output. Then, on a separate sheet of paper, create a plan for correcting the suboptimal path selection.

Suggested Solution

Local preference values can be applied to routes coming into a router. This can cause that router to make its outbound routing decisions based on those local preference values. Higher local preference values are preferred over lower local preference values.

An AS path (that is, a listing of the autonomous systems that must be transited to reach a specific destination network) advertised to a neighbor can influence the BGP path selection of that neighbor. Specifically, BGP can make routing decisions based on the smallest number of autonomous systems that must be crossed to reach a destination network. Using a route map, you can prepend one or more additional instances of your local AS to the ASPATH advertised to a router's neighbor, thereby making that path appear less attractive to your neighbor.

Therefore, the suggested solution configures local preference values for routes advertised into router R2 from routers BB1 and BB2 to prefer routes being advertised via router BB2. Example 8-15 shows this configuration, which influences outbound path selection.

Example 8-15 *Local Preference Configuration on Router R2*

```
R2(config)#route-map LOCALPREF-BB1
R2(config-route-map)#set local-preference 100
R2(config-route-map)#exit
R2(config)#route-map LOCALPREF-BB2
R2(config-route-map)#set local-preference 200
R2(config-route-map)#exit
R2(config)#router bgp 65001
R2(config-router)#neighbor 172.16.1.1 route-map LOCALPREF-BB1 in
R2(config-router)#neighbor 172.16.2.2 route-map LOCALPREF-BB2 in
R2(config-router)#exit
```

To influence inbound path selection, this suggested solution configured a route map to prepend two additional instances of AS 65001 to routes being advertised via BGP from router R2 to router BB1. Example 8-16 shows this configuration, which causes router BB1 to use router BB2 as a next-hop router when sending traffic into the enterprise network. It does this because the path via router BB2 appears to be fewer AS hops away from the enterprise networks.

Example 8-16 *ASPATH Configuration on Router R2*

```
R2(config)#route-map ASPATH 10
R2(config-route-map)#set as-path prepend 65001 65001
R2(config-route-map)#exit
R2(config)#router bgp 65001
R2(config-router)#neighbor 172.16.1.1 route-map ASPATH out
R2(config-router)#end
```

Example 8-17 confirms that router R2 now prefers router BB2 (that is, a next-hop IP address of 172.16.2.2) to reach the default network.

Example 8-17 *Preferred Path of Router R2 to Backbone Networks*

```
R2#show ip bgp
BGP table version is 16, local router ID is 10.2.2.2
Status codes: s suppressed, d damped, h history, * valid, > best, i - internal,
              r RIB-failure, S Stale
Origin codes: i - IGP, e - EGP, ? - incomplete

   Network          Next Hop          Metric LocPrf Weight Path
*  0.0.0.0          172.16.1.1             0    100      0 65002 i
*>                  172.16.2.2             0    200      0 65003 i
*> 10.1.1.1/32      192.168.0.11          11           32768 ?
```

```
*    10.1.2.0/24         172.16.1.1                    0   100      0 65002 i
*>                       172.16.2.2                    0   200      0 65003 i
*    10.1.3.0/30         172.16.1.1                    0   100      0 65002 i
*>                       172.16.2.2                    0   200      0 65003 i
*>   10.2.2.2/32         0.0.0.0                       0        32768 ?
*    10.3.3.3/32         172.16.1.1                    0   100      0 65002 i
*>                       172.16.2.2                        200      0 65003 65002 i
*    10.4.4.4/32         172.16.1.1                        100      0 65002 65003 i
*>                       172.16.2.2                    0   200      0 65003 i
*>   172.16.1.0/30       0.0.0.0                       0        32768 i
*                        172.16.1.1                    0   100      0 65002 i
*                        172.16.2.2                        200      0 65003 65002 i
*>   172.16.2.0/30       0.0.0.0                       0        32768 i
*                        172.16.1.1                        100      0 65002 65003 i
*                        172.16.2.2                    0   200      0 65003 i
*>   192.168.0.0         0.0.0.0                       0        32768 ?
*>   192.168.1.0         192.168.0.11                 11        32768 ?
```

Example 8-18 confirms that router BB1 will not prefer to send traffic to the enterprise network (that is, to routers R1 and R2) via router R2, but rather via router BB2. Notice from the output that more AS hops appear to be required to reach enterprise networks via router R2 (that is, 172.16.1.2) compared to router BB2 (that is, 10.1.3.2). Therefore, router BB1 prefers to send traffic into the enterprise network via router BB2, as opposed to router R2.

Example 8-18   *Preferred Path of Router BB1 to Enterprise Networks*

```
BB1#show ip bgp
BGP table version is 142, local router ID is 10.3.3.3
Status codes: s suppressed, d damped, h history, * valid, > best, i - internal,
              r RIB-failure, S Stale
Origin codes: i - IGP, e - EGP, ? - incomplete

    Network          Next Hop         Metric LocPrf Weight Path
*   0.0.0.0          172.16.1.2                       0 65001 65001 65001 65003 i
*                    10.1.3.2              0           0 65003 i
*>                   0.0.0.0               0       32768 i
*>  10.1.1.1/32      10.1.3.2                          0 65003 65001 ?
*                    172.16.1.2          11            0 65001 65001 65001 ?
*   10.1.2.0/24      172.16.1.2                        0 65001 65001 65001 65003 i
*                    10.1.3.2              0           0 65003 i
*>                   0.0.0.0               0       32768 i
*   10.1.3.0/30      172.16.1.2                        0 65001 65001 65001 65003 i
*                    10.1.3.2              0           0 65003 i
*>                   0.0.0.0               0       32768 i
```

```
*> 10.2.2.2/32      10.1.3.2                      0 65003 65001 ?
*                   172.16.1.2        0           0 65001 65001 65001 ?
*> 10.3.3.3/32      0.0.0.0           0       32768 i
*  10.4.4.4/32      172.16.1.2                    0 65001 65001 65001 65003 i
*>                  10.1.3.2          0           0 65003 i
*  172.16.1.0/30    172.16.1.2        0           0 65001 65001 65001 i
*>                  0.0.0.0           0       32768 i
*  172.16.2.0/30    172.16.1.2        0           0 65001 65001 65001 i
*>                  10.1.3.2          0           0 65003 i
*> 192.168.0.0      10.1.3.2                      0 65003 65001 ?
*                   172.16.1.2        0           0 65001 65001 65001 ?
*> 192.168.1.0      10.1.3.2                      0 65003 65001 ?
*                   172.16.1.2       11           0 65001 65001 65001 ?
```

Router Performance Issues

Chapter 5, "Advanced Cisco Catalyst Switch Troubleshooting," discussed how performance issues on a Cisco Catalyst switch can be the source of network problems. Similarly, a router performance issue can impact user data flowing through the network.

Also, as an administrator you might notice sluggish response to Telnet sessions you attempt to establish with a router or longer-than-normal ping response times. Such symptoms might indicate a router performance issue.

This section investigates three potential router issues, each of which might result in poor router performance. These three issues are

Key Topic

- Excessive CPU utilization

- The packet switching mode of a router

- Excessive memory utilization

Excessive CPU Utilization

A router's processor (that is, CPU) utilization escalating to a high level but only remaining at that high level for a brief time could represent normal behavior. However, if a router's CPU utilization continually remains at a high level, network performance issues might result. Aside from latency that users and administrators can experience, a router whose CPU is overtaxed might not send routing protocol messages to neighboring routers in a timely fashion. As a result, routing protocol adjacencies can fail, resulting in some networks becoming unreachable.

Processes That Commonly Cause Excessive CPU Utilization

One reason that the CPU of a router might be overloaded is that the router is running a process that is taking up an unusually high percentage of its CPU resources. Following are four such processes that can result in excessive CPU utilization.

Key
Topic

■   **ARP Input process:** The ARP Input process is in charge of sending Address Resolution Protocol (ARP) requests. This process can consume an inordinate percentage of CPU resources if the router has to send numerous ARP requests.

One configuration that can cause such a high number of ARP requests is having a default route configured that points to a broadcast network. For example, perhaps a router had the **ip route 0.0.0.0 0.0.0.0 fa 0/1** command entered in global configuration mode. Such a configuration can cause an ARP to be sent to all IP addresses available off of that broadcast interface that are not reachable via a better route. From a security perspective, numerous ARP requests can result from an attacker performing a ping sweep of a subnet.

■   **Net Background process:** An interface has a certain number of buffers available to store packets. These buffers are sometimes referred to as the queue of an interface. If an interface needs to store a packet in a buffer but all the interface buffers are in use, the interface can pull from a main pool of buffers that the router maintains. The process that allows an interface to allocate one of these globally available buffers is Net Background. If the *throttles*, *ignored*, and *overrun* parameters are incrementing on an interface, the underlying cause might be the Net Background process consuming too many CPU resources.

■   **IP Background process:** The IP Background process handles an interface changing its state. A state change might be an interface going from an Up state to a Down state, or vice versa. Another example of state change is an interface's IP address changing. Therefore, anything that can cause repeated state changes, such as bad cabling, might result in the IP Background process consuming a high percentage of CPU resources.

■   **TCP Timer process:** The TCP Timer process runs for each TCP router connection. Therefore, many connections can result in a high CPU utilization by the TCP Timer process.

Cisco IOS Commands Used for Troubleshooting High Processor Utilization

Table 8-5 offers a collection of **show** commands that can be valuable when troubleshooting high CPU utilization on a router.

Table 8-5   *Commands for Troubleshooting High CPU Utilization*

Key
Topic

Command	Description
show arp	Displays the ARP cache for a router. If several entries are in the Incomplete state, you might suspect a malicious scan (for example, a ping sweep) of a subnet.
show interface *interface-id*	Displays a collection of interface statistics. If the throttles, over-runs, or ignore counters continually increment, you might suspect that the Net Background process is attempting to allocate buffer space for an interface from the main buffer pool of the router.
show tcp statistics	Provides information about the number of TCP segments a router sends and receives, including the number of connections initiated, accepted, established, and closed. A high number of connections can explain why the TCP Timer process might be consuming excessive CPU resources.
show processes cpu	Displays average CPU utilization over 5-second, 1-minute, and 5-minute intervals, in addition to listing all the router processes and the percentage of CPU resources consumed by each of those processes.
show processes cpu history	Displays a graphical view of CPU utilization over the past 60 seconds, 1 hour, and 3 days. This graphical view can indicate if an observed high CPU utilization is a temporary spike in utilization or if the high CPU utilization is an ongoing condition.

Example 8-19 shows sample output from the **show arp** command. In the output, only a single instance exists of an Incomplete ARP entry. However, a high number of such entries can suggest the scanning of network resources, which might indicate malicious reconnaissance traffic.

Example 8-19   show arp *Command Output*

```
R2#show arp
Protocol  Address          Age (min)  Hardware Addr   Type    Interface
Internet  10.3.3.2             61      0009.b7fa.d1e0  ARPA    Ethernet0/0
Internet  10.3.3.1              -      00d0.06fe.9ea0  ARPA    Ethernet0/0
Internet  192.168.1.50         0       Incomplete      ARPA
```

Example 8-20 shows sample output from the **show interface** *interface-id* command. Note the throttles, overrun, and ignored counters. If these counters continue to increment, the Net Background process might be consuming excessive CPU resources while it allocates buffers from the main buffer pool of the router.

Example 8-20   show interface interface-id *Command Output*

```
R2#show interface e0/0
Ethernet0/0 is up, line protocol is up
  Hardware is AmdP2, address is 00d0.06fe.9ea0 (bia 00d0.06fe.9ea0)
  Internet address is 10.3.3.1/24
  MTU 1500 bytes, BW 10000 Kbit, DLY 1000 usec,
      reliability 255/255, txload 1/255, rxload 1/255
  Encapsulation ARPA, loopback not set
  Keepalive set (10 sec)
  ARP type: ARPA, ARP Timeout 04:00:00
  Last input 00:00:02, output 00:00:02, output hang never
  Last clearing of "show interface" counters never
  Input queue: 0/75/0/0 (size/max/drops/flushes); Total output drops: 0
  Queueing strategy: fifo
  Output queue: 0/40 (size/max)
  5 minute input rate 0 bits/sec, 1 packets/sec
  5 minute output rate 0 bits/sec, 0 packets/sec
      2156 packets input, 164787 bytes, 0 no buffer
      Received 861 broadcasts, 0 runts, 0 giants, 0 throttles
      0 input errors, 0 CRC, 0 frame, 0 overrun, 0 ignored
      0 input packets with dribble condition detected
      2155 packets output, 212080 bytes, 0 underruns
      0 output errors, 0 collisions, 7 interface resets
      0 babbles, 0 late collision, 0 deferred
      0 lost carrier, 0 no carrier
      0 output buffer failures, 0 output buffers swapped out
```

Example 8-21 shows sample output from the **show tcp statistics** command. If the output indicates numerous connections, the TCP Timer process might be consuming excessive CPU resources while simultaneously maintaining all those connections.

Example 8-21   show tcp statistics *Command Output*

```
R2#show tcp statistics
Rcvd: 689 Total, 0 no port
      0 checksum error, 0 bad offset, 0 too short
      474 packets (681 bytes) in sequence
      0 dup packets (0 bytes)
      0 partially dup packets (0 bytes)
      0 out-of-order packets (0 bytes)
      0 packets (0 bytes) with data after window
      0 packets after close
      0 window probe packets, 0 window update packets
      1 dup ack packets, 0 ack packets with unsend data
      479 ack packets (14205 bytes)
Sent: 570 Total, 0 urgent packets
```

```
      1 control packets (including 0 retransmitted)
      562 data packets (14206 bytes)
      0 data packets (0 bytes) retransmitted
      0 data packets (0 bytes) fastretransmitted
      7 ack only packets (7 delayed)
      0 window probe packets, 0 window update packets
  0 Connections initiated, 1 connections accepted, 1 connections established
  0 Connections closed (including 0 dropped, 0 embryonic dropped)
  0 Total rxmt timeout, 0 connections dropped in rxmt timeout
  0 Keepalive timeout, 0 keepalive probe, 0 Connections dropped in keepalive
```

Example 8-22 shows sample output from the **show processes cpu** command. The output in this example indicates a 34 percent CPU utilization in the past 5 seconds, with 13 percent of CPU resources being spent on interrupts. The output also shows the 1-minute CPU utilization average as 36 percent and the 5-minute average as 32 percent. Individual processes running on the router are also shown, along with their CPU utilization levels. Note the ARP Input, Net Background, TCP Timer, and IP Background processes referred to in this section.

Example 8-22   show processes cpu *Command Output*

```
R2#show processes cpu
CPU utilization for five seconds: 34%/13%; one minute: 36%; five minutes: 32%
PID Runtime(ms)    Invoked      uSecs   5Sec   1Min   5Min   TTY Process
...OUTPUT OMITTED...
  12          4         69         57   0.00%  0.00%  0.00%    0 ARP Input
  13          0          1          0   0.00%  0.00%  0.00%    0 HC Counter Timer
  14          0          5          0   0.00%  0.00%  0.00%    0 DDR Timers
  15         12          2       6000   0.00%  0.00%  0.00%    0 Entity MIB API
  16          4          2       2000   0.00%  0.00%  0.00%    0 ATM Idle Timer
  17          0          1          0   0.00%  0.00%  0.00%    0 SERIAL A'detect
  18          0       3892          0   0.00%  0.00%  0.00%    0 GraphIt
  19          0          2          0   0.00%  0.00%  0.00%    0 Dialer event
  20          0          1          0   0.00%  0.00%  0.00%    0 Critical Bkgnd
  21        132        418        315   0.00%  0.00%  0.00%    0 Net Background
  22          0         15          0   0.00%  0.00%  0.00%    0 Logger
...OUTPUT OMITTED...
  46          0        521          0   0.00%  0.00%  0.00%    0 SSS Test Client
  47         84        711        118   0.00%  0.00%  0.00%    0 TCP Timer
  48          4          3       1333   0.00%  0.00%  0.00%    0 TCP Protocols
  49          0          1          0   0.00%  0.00%  0.00%    0 Socket Timers
  50          0         15          0   0.00%  0.00%  0.00%    0 HTTP CORE
```

```
  51          12        5       2400   0.00%   0.00%   0.00%   0 PPP IP Route
  52           4        5        800   0.00%   0.00%   0.00%   0 PPP IPCP
  53         273      157       1738   0.00%   0.00%   0.00%   0 IP Background
  54           0       74          0   0.00%   0.00%   0.00%   0 IP RIB Update
...OUTPUT OMITTED...
```

Example 8-23 shows sample output from the **show processes cpu history** command. The graphical output produced by this command is useful in determining if a CPU spike is temporary or if it is an ongoing condition.

Example 8-23   show processes cpu history *Command Output*

```
R2#show processes cpu history


R2   01:06:21 AM Monday Mar 1 1993 UTC


      111113333311111      33333       1111122222     222222
100
 90
 80
 70
 60
 50
 40
 30
 20
 10
   0....5....1....1....2....2....3....3....4....4....5....5....
            0    5    0    5    0    5    0    5    0    5
             CPU% per second (last 60 seconds)


                  2
    2112411211332216331212211212212222221111111111111111111111111
100
 90
 80
 70
 60
 50
 40
 30                 *
 20                 *
 10                 #
```

```
       0....5....1....1....2....2....3....3....4....4....5....5....
              0    5    0    5    0    5    0    5    0    5
                  CPU% per minute (last 60 minutes)
                * = maximum CPU%    # = average CPU%


        8
        0
100
 90
 80 *
 70 *
 60 *
 50 *
 40 *
 30 *
 20 *
 10 *
       0....5....1....1....2....2....3....3....4....4....5....5....6....6....7.
              0    5    0    5    0    5    0    5    0    5    0    5    0
                  CPU% per hour (last 72 hours)
                * = maximum CPU%    # = average CPU%
```

Understanding Packet Switching Modes

In addition to the high CPU utilization issues previously discussed, a router's packet switching mode can impact router performance. Before discussing the most common switching modes, realize that the way a router handles packets (or is capable of handling packets) largely depends on the router's architecture. Therefore, for real-world troubleshooting, please consult the documentation for your router to determine how it implements packet switching.

In general, however, Cisco routers support the following three primary modes of packet switching:

- Process switching

- Fast switching

- Cisco Express Forwarding

Packet switching involves the router making a decision about how a packet should be forwarded and then forwarding that packet out of the appropriate router interface.

Operation of Process Switching

When a router routes a packet (that is, performs packet switching), the router removes the packet's Layer 2 header, examines the Layer 3 addressing, and decides how to forward the packet. The Layer 2 header is then rewritten (which involves changing the source and destination MAC addresses and computing a new cyclic redundancy check [CRC]), and the packet is forwarded out of the appropriate interface. With process switching, as illustrated in Figure 8-4, the router's CPU becomes directly involved with packet switching decisions. As a result, the performance of a router configured for process switching can suffer significantly.

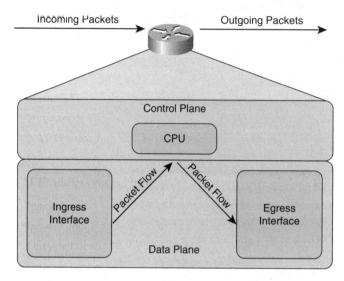

Figure 8-4 *Data Flow with Process Switching*

An interface can be configured for process switching by disabling fast switching on that interface. The interface configuration mode command used to disable fast switching is **no ip route-cache**.

Operation of Fast Switching

Fast switching uses a fast cache maintained in a router's data plane. The fast cache contains information about how traffic from different data flows should be forwarded. As seen in Figure 8-5, the first packet in a data flow is process-switched by a router's CPU. After the router determines how to forward the first frame of a data flow, that forwarding information is stored in the fast cache. Subsequent packets in that same data flow are forwarded based on information in the fast cache, as opposed to being process-switched. As a result, fast switching reduces a router's CPU utilization more than process switching does.

Fast switching can be configured in interface configuration mode with the command **ip route-cache**.

Operation of Cisco Express Forwarding

As described in Chapter 5, Cisco Express Forwarding (CEF) maintains two tables in the data plane. Specifically, the Forwarding Information Base (FIB) maintains Layer 3 forwarding information, whereas the Adjacency Table maintains Layer 2 information for next hops listed in the FIB.

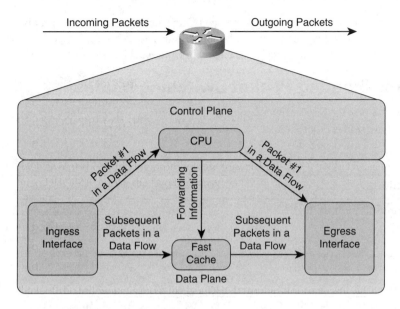

Figure 8-5 *Data Flow with Fast Switching*

Using these tables, populated from a router's IP routing table and ARP cache, CEF can efficiently make forwarding decisions. Unlike fast switching, CEF does not require the first packet of a data flow to be process-switched. Rather, an entire data flow can be forwarded at the data plane, as seen in Figure 8-6.

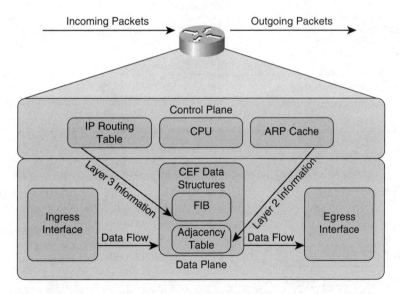

Figure 8-6 *Data Flow with Cisco Express Forwarding*

On many router platforms, CEF is enabled by default. If it is not, you can globally enable it with the **ip cef** command. Alternatively, you can enable CEF for a specific interface with the interface configuration mode command **ip route-cache cef**.

Troubleshooting Packet Switching Modes

Table 8-6 provides a selection of commands you can use when troubleshooting the packet switching modes of a router.

Key
Topic

Table 8-6   *Commands for Troubleshooting a Router's Packet Switching Modes*

Command	Description
show ip interface *interface_id*	Displays multiple interface statistics, including information about the packet switching mode of an interface.
show ip cache	Displays the contents of fast cache from a router if fast switching is enabled.
show processes cpu | include IP Input	Displays information about the IP input process on a router. The CPU utilization for this process might show a high value if the CPU of a router is actively engaged in process-switching traffic.
show ip cef	Displays the contents of a router FIB.
show ip cef adjacency *egress-interface-id next-hop-ip-address* detail	Displays destinations reachable via the combination of the specified egress interface and next-hop IP address.
show adjacency detail	Provides information contained in the adjacency table of a router, including protocol and timer information.
show cef not-cef-switched	Displays information about packets the router forwards using a packet switching mechanism other than CEF.

Example 8-24 shows sample output from the **show ip interface** *interface-id* command. The output indicates that fast switching is enabled on interface Fast Ethernet 0/0. The reference to flow switching being disabled refers to the Cisco IOS NetFlow feature, which you can use to collect traffic statistics. CEF switching is also enabled.

Example 8-24   show ip interface interface-id *Command Output*

```
R4#show ip interface fa 0/0
FastEthernet0/0 is up, line protocol is up
...OUTPUT OMITTED...
```

```
    ICMP mask replies are never sent
    IP fast switching is enabled
    IP fast switching on the same interface is disabled
    IP Flow switching is disabled
    IP CEF switching is enabled
    IP CEF Fast switching turbo vector
    IP multicast fast switching is enabled
    IP multicast distributed fast switching is disabled
    IP route-cache flags are Fast, CEF
...OUTPUT OMITTED...
```

Example 8-25 shows sample output from the **show ip cache** command. If fast switching is enabled and CEF is disabled, a router begins to populate its fast cache. This command shows the contents of a router's fast cache.

Example 8-25   show ip cache *Command Output*

```
R4#show ip cache
IP routing cache 3 entries, 588 bytes
    12 adds, 9 invalidates, 0 refcounts
Minimum invalidation interval 2 seconds, maximum interval 5 seconds,
    quiet interval 3 seconds, threshold 0 requests
Invalidation rate 0 in last second, 0 in last 3 seconds
Last full cache invalidation occurred 04:13:57 ago

Prefix/Length          Age        Interface       Next Hop
10.8.8.4/32            00:00:07   FastEthernet0/1  10.8.8.4
10.8.8.6/32            00:00:10   FastEthernet0/1  10.8.8.6
192.168.0.0/24         00:00:10   FastEthernet0/0  10.3.3.1
```

Example 8-26 shows sample output from the **show processes cpu | include ip input** command. In the output, the IP input process was using only 0.08 percent of its router's CPU capacity during the last 5-second interval. However, a high percentage value might indicate that a router was performing process switching, where the CPU was directly involved in packet switching.

Example 8-26   show processes cpu | include IP Input *Command Output*

```
R4#show processes cpu | include IP Input
   63      3178      7320      434  0.08%  0.06%  0.04%   0 IP Input
```

Example 8-27 shows sample output from the **show ip cef** command. The output contains the contents of the FIB for a router. Note that if a next-hop of the network prefix is set to *receive*, that network is local to the router, whereas *attached* indicates that the network is directly connected to the router.

Example 8-27 show ip cef *Command Output*

```
R4#show ip cef
Prefix                 Next Hop              Interface
0.0.0.0/0              drop                  Null0 (default route handler entry)
0.0.0.0/32             receive
10.1.1.0/24            10.3.3.1              FastEthernet0/0
10.1.1.2/32            10.3.3.1              FastEthernet0/0
10.3.3.0/24            attached              FastEthernet0/0
10.3.3.0/32            receive
10.3.3.1/32            10.3.3.1              FastEthernet0/0
10.3.3.2/32            receive
10.3.3.255/32          receive
10.4.4.0/24            10.3.3.1              FastEthernet0/0
10.5.5.0/24            10.3.3.1              FastEthernet0/0
10.7.7.0/24            10.3.3.1              FastEthernet0/0
10.7.7.2/32            10.3.3.1              FastEthernet0/0
10.8.8.0/24            attached              FastEthernet0/1
10.8.8.0/32            receive
10.8.8.1/32            receive
10.8.8.4/32            10.8.8.4              FastEthernet0/1
10.8.8.5/32            10.8.8.5              FastEthernet0/1
10.8.8.6/32            10.8.8.6              FastEthernet0/1
10.8.8.7/32            10.8.8.7              FastEthernet0/1
10.8.8.255/32          receive
192.168.0.0/24         10.3.3.1              FastEthernet0/0
224.0.0.0/4            drop
224.0.0.0/24           receive
255.255.255.255/32     receive
```

Example 8-28 shows sample output from the **show ip cef adjacency** *egress-interface-id next-hop-IP-address* **detail** command. This command shows the IP addresses that the router knows how to reach using the specified combination of next-hop IP address and egress interface. In this example, 10.8.8.6 is the IP address of a host and not a router. Therefore, no other IP addresses are known to have a next-hop IP address of 10.8.8.6 with an egress interface of Fast Ethernet 0/1.

Example 8-28 show ip cef adjacency egress-interface-id next-hop-IP-address detail *Command Output*

```
R4#show ip cef adjacency fa 0/1 10.8.8.6 detail
IP CEF with switching (Table Version 25), flags=0x0
  25 routes, 0 reresolve, 0 unresolved (0 old, 0 new), peak 0
  25 leaves, 21 nodes, 25640 bytes, 90 inserts, 65 invalidations
  0 load sharing elements, 0 bytes, 0 references
  universal per-destination load sharing algorithm, id 24360DB1
```

```
   5(2) CEF resets, 1 revisions of existing leaves
   Resolution Timer: Exponential (currently 1s, peak 1s)
   0 in-place/0 aborted modifications
   refcounts:  5702 leaf, 5632 node

   Table epoch: 0 (25 entries at this epoch)

Adjacency Table has 5 adjacencies
10.8.8.6/32, version 10, epoch 0, cached adjacency 10.8.8.6
0 packets, 0 bytes
  via 10.8.8.6, FastEthernet0/1, 0 dependencies
    next hop 10.8.8.6, FastEthernet0/1
    valid cached adjacency
```

Example 8-29 shows sample output from the **show adjacency detail** command. When you see a particular adjacency listed in the FIB, you can issue this command to confirm the router has information about how to reach that adjacency.

Example 8-29   show adjacency detail *Command Output*

```
R4#show adjacency detail
Protocol Interface              Address
IP        FastEthernet0/0       10.3.3.1(19)
                                  32 packets, 1920 bytes
                                  00D006FE9EA00009B7FAD1E00800
                                  ARP            03:53:01
                                  Epoch: 0
IP        FastEthernet0/1       10.8.8.6(5)
                                  4 packets, 264 bytes
                                  0008A3B895C40009B7FAD1E10800
                                  ARP            03:53:35
                                  Epoch: 0
...OUTPUT OMITTED...
```

Example 8-30 shows sample output from the **show cef not-cef-switched** command. Even though CEF is enabled, some traffic might still be switched through another packet-switching path, perhaps because a feature was enabled that required the processor of the router (identified as *RP* in the output) to handle specific traffic types. The **show cef not-cef-switched** command shows information about such traffic that was not CEF-switched.

Example 8-30   show cef not-cef-switched *Command Output*

```
R4#show cef not-cef-switched
CEF Packets passed on to next switching layer
Slot  No_adj No_encap Unsupp'ted Redirect  Receive  Options   Access    Frag
RP       0      0         0        0        6676       0         0         0
```

Now that you have reviewed the different packet-switching options for a router, you can better analyze how a router is forwarding specific traffic. Following is a list of troubleshooting steps you can follow if you suspect that network traffic is being impacted by a performance problem on one of the routers along the path from the source to the destination.

Step 1. Use the **traceroute** command to determine which router along the path is causing excessive delay.

Step 2. After you identify a router that is causing unusually high delay, use the **show processes cpu** command to see the CPU utilization of that router and identify any processes that might be consuming an unusually high percentage of the CPU.

Step 3. Use the **show ip route** *ip-address* command to verify that the router has a route to the destination IP address.

Step 4. Use the **show ip cef** command to determine whether all the router interfaces are configured to use CEF.

Step 5. Use the **show ip cef** *ip-address* **255.255.255.255** command to verify that CEF has an entry in its FIB that can reach the specified IP address. Part of the output from this command will be the next-hop adjacency to which traffic should be forwarded, along with the egress interface used to send traffic to that next-hop.

Step 6. Issue the **show adjacency** *interface-id* **detail** command to verify that CEF has an entry in its adjacency table for the egress interface identified in Step 5.

Step 7. With the **show ip arp** command, you can then confirm that the router knows the MAC address associated with the next-hop IP address shown in the output from Step 6.

Step 8. You can then connect to the next-hop device and verify that the MAC address identified in Step 7 is indeed correct.

You can repeat these steps on the next-hop device or on another router whose response time displayed in the output from Step 1 is suspect.

Excessive Memory Utilization

Much like a PC, router performance can suffer if it lacks sufficient available memory. For example, perhaps you install a version of Cisco IOS on a router, and that router does not have the minimum amount of memory required to support that specific Cisco IOS image. Even though the router might load the image and function, its performance might be sluggish.

Common Memory Troubleshooting Targets

Assuming a router *does* have the recommended amount of memory for its installed Cisco IOS image, consider the following as potential memory utilization issues:

■ **Memory leak:** When a router starts a process, that process can allocate a block of memory. When the process completes, the process should return its allocated memory to the router's pool of memory. If not all the allocated memory is returned to the router's main memory pool, a memory leak occurs. Such a condition usually results from a bug in the Cisco IOS version running on the router, requiring an upgrade of the router's Cisco IOS image.

Example 8-31 shows sample output from the **show memory allocating-process totals** command. This command can help identify memory leaks. The output shows information about memory availability on a router after the Cisco IOS image of the router has been decompressed and loaded.

Example 8-31   show memory allocating-process totals *Command Output*

```
R4#show memory allocating-process totals
                 Head     Total(b)     Used(b)     Free(b)     Lowest(b)
Largest(b)
Processor     83D27480    67463064    15347168    52115896    50311080    50127020
     I/O      7C21800      4057088     2383016     1674072     1674072     1674044


Allocator PC Summary for: Processor

    PC          Total    Count   Name
0x809D7A30     1749360     180   Process Stack
0x80A7F664      918024      10   Init
0x81CEF6A0      882576       4   pak subblock chunk
0x81C04D9C      595344      54   TCL Chunks
0x800902A4      490328       6   MallocLite
...OUTPUT OMITTED...
```

The *Head* column in the output refers to the address (in hexadecimal) of the memory allocation chain. The *Total* column is the total of used bytes and free bytes, which are individually shown in their own columns. The *Lowest* column shows the lowest amount of free memory (in bytes) that has been available since the router last booted. The *Largest* column indicates the largest block of available memory. Following this summary information, the output shows detailed memory allocation information for each process running on a router.

- **Memory allocation failure:** A memory allocation failure (which produces a MALLOCFAIL error message) occurs when a process attempts to allocate a block of memory and fails to do so. One common cause for a MALLOCFAIL error is a security issue. For example, a virus or a worm that has infested the network can result in a MALLOCFAIL error. Alternatively, a MALLOCFAIL error might be the result of a bug in the router's version of Cisco IOS. You can use the Cisco Bug Toolkit (available from http://www.cisco.com/cgi-bin/Support/Bugtool/launch_bugtool.pl) to research any such known issues with the version of Cisco IOS running on a router.

- **Buffer leak:** Similar to a memory leak, in which a process does not return all of its allocated memory to the router upon terminating, a buffer leak occurs when a process does not return a buffer to the router when the process has finished using the buffer. Consider the output of the **show interfaces** command seen in Example 8-32.

Example 8-32 *Identifying a Wedged Interface*

```
R4#show interfaces
...OUTPUT OMITTED...
  Input queue: 76/75/780/0 (size/max/drops/flushes); Total output drops: 0
  Queueing strategy: fifo
  Output queue: 0/40 (size/max)
...OUTPUT OMITTED...
```

Notice the numbers 76 and 75 highlighted in the output. These values indicate that an input queue of the interface has a capacity of 75 packets, and that queue currently has 76 packets. This is an oversubscription of the queue space. An interface in this condition is called a *wedged interface*. In such a condition, the router does not forward traffic coming into the wedged interface.

The **show buffers** command can also be helpful in diagnosing a buffer leak. To illustrate, consider the output of the **show buffers** command shown in Example 8-33.

Example 8-33 show buffers *Command Output*

```
R4#show buffers
Buffer elements:
      1118 in free list (500 max allowed)
      570 hits, 0 misses, 1119 created

Public buffer pools:
Small buffers, 104 bytes (total 71, permanent 50, peak 71 @ 00:21:43):
      53 in free list (20 min, 150 max allowed)
      317 hits, 7 misses, 0 trims, 21 created
      0 failures (0 no memory)
Middle buffers, 600 bytes (total 49, permanent 25, peak 49 @ 00:21:43):
      5 in free list (10 min, 150 max allowed)
      122 hits, 8 misses, 0 trims, 24 created
...OUTPUT OMITTED...
```

This output indicates that the router has 49 middle buffers, but only 5 of those 49 buffers are available. Such a result might indicate a process allocating buffers but failing to deallocate them. Like a memory leak, a buffer leak might require updating the Cisco IOS image of a router.

Excessive BGP Memory Use

Earlier in this chapter you learned about troubleshooting BGP. If a router is running BGP, be aware that BGP runs multiple processes and can consume significant amounts of router memory. The **show processes memory | include BGP** command, as shown in Example 8-34, can show you how much memory is being consumed by the various BGP processes of a router. If BGP is consuming a large percentage of your router memory, you might consider filtering out unneeded BGP routes, upgrading the memory on that router, or running BGP on a different platform that has more memory.

Example 8-34   show processes memory | include BGP *Command Output*

```
R1#show processes memory | include BGP
   77   0       16960        0       10068        0        0 BGP Router
  108   0           0        0        6892        0        0 BGP I/O
  112   0           0        0        9892        0        0 BGP Scanner
```

Depending on the router platform, your router might have multiple line cards with different amounts of memory available on each line card. The **show diag** command can help you isolate a specific line card that is running low on memory, perhaps because that line card is running BGP.

Exam Preparation Tasks

Review All the Key Topics

Key Topic

Review the most important topics from inside the chapter, noted with the Key Topics icon in the outer margin of the page. Table 8-7 lists these key topics and the page numbers where each is found.

Table 8-7   *Key Topics for Chapter 8*

Key Topic Element	Description	Page Number
Table 8-2	Interaction between BGP's data structures and a router's IP routing table	228
List	BGP data structures	228
Numbered List	BGP path selection criteria	229
List	Common reasons for failure of BGP peering	229
Table 8-3	BGP troubleshooting commands	230
Table 8-4	Configuring ASPATH and local preference BGP attributes	242
List	Reasons for poor router performance	245
List	Four processes that can cause excessive CPU utilization	246
Table 8-5	Commands for troubleshooting high CPU utilization	247
List	Packet-switching modes	251
Table 8-6	Commands for troubleshooting the packet-switching modes of a router	254
Steps	Steps for troubleshooting a router performance issue	258
List	Common memory utilization issues	258
Example 8-33	Sample output from the **show buffers** command	260

Complete Tables and Lists from Memory

Print a copy of Appendix B, "Memory Tables" (found on the CD), or at least the section for this chapter, and complete the tables and lists from memory. Appendix C, "Memory Tables Answer Key," also on the CD, includes completed tables and lists to check your work.

Define Key Terms

Define the following key terms from this chapter, and check your answers in the Glossary:

autonomous system (AS), BGP's neighbor table, BGP table, ASPATH, local preference, ARP Input process, Net Background process, IP Background process, TCP Timer process, process switching, fast switching, Cisco Express Forwarding (CEF), memory leak, memory allocation failure, buffer leak

Command Reference to Check Your Memory

This section includes the most important configuration and EXEC commands covered in this chapter. To determine how well you have memorized the commands as a side effect of your other studies, cover the left side of the table with a piece of paper; read the descriptions on the right side; and see whether you remember the command.

Table 8-8 *Chapter 8 Configuration Command Reference*

Command	Description
route-map *tag* [permit | deny] [*seq-num*]	Global configuration mode command that creates a route map
set local-preference *local-preference*	Route map configuration mode command that sets the local preference BGP attribute for routes matched by a route map
set as-path prepend *autonomous-system-number-1* [...*autonomous-system-number-n*]	Route map configuration mode command that defines an autonomous system path to prepend to an autonomous system path known by the BGP forwarding table
router bgp *as-number*	Global configuration mode command that enables a BGP process for a specific autonomous system
neighbor *ip-address* route-map *route-map-name* [in | out]	Router configuration mode command that applies a specified route map to routes received from or advertised to a specified BGP neighbor
[no] ip route-cache	Interface configuration mode utility used to enable fast switching (or disable fast switching with the **no** option)
ip cef	Global configuration mode command used to globally enable CEF
ip route-cache cef	Interface configuration mode command used to enable CEF for an interface

Table 8-9 *Chapter 8 EXEC Command Reference*

Command	Description
show ip bgp summary	Displays the router BGP router ID, AS number, information about the BGP memory usage, and summary information about BGP neighbors
show ip bgp neighbors	Displays detailed information about all the BGP neighbors of a router
show ip bgp	Displays the network prefixes present in the BGP table
debug ip routing	Displays updates that occur in the IP routing table
show ip route bgp	Shows routes known to a routing table that were learned via BGP
debug ip bgp	Provides real-time information about BGP events, such as the establishment of a peering relationship (Note: This command does not show the contents of BGP updates.)
debug ip bgp updates	Shows real-time information about BGP updates sent and received by a BGP router, including the contents of those BGP updates
show arp	Displays a router's ARP cache (Note: If a large number of the entries are in the Incomplete state, you might suspect a malicious scan [for example, a ping sweep] of a subnet.)
show interface *interface-id*	Shows a collection of interface statistics (Note: If the throttles, overruns, or ignore counters continually increment, you might suspect that the Net Background process is attempting to allocate buffer space for an interface from the router's main buffer pool.)
show tcp statistics	Provides information about the number of TCP segments a router sends and receives, including the number of connections initiated, accepted, established, and closed (Note: A high number of connections might explain why the TCP Timer process is consuming excessive CPU resources.)
show processes cpu	Displays average CPU utilization over 5-second, 1-minute, and 5-minute intervals, in addition to listing all of the router processes and the percentage of CPU resources consumed by each of those processes

Table 8-9   *Chapter 8 EXEC Command Reference*   *(Continued)*

Command	Description
show processes cpu history	Shows a graphical view of CPU utilization over the past 60 seconds, 1 hour, and 3 days (Note: This graphical view can indicate if an observed high CPU utilization is a temporary spike in utilization or if the high CPU utilization is an ongoing condition.)
show ip interface *interface-id*	Displays multiple interface statistics, including information about the packet switching mode of an interface
show ip cache	Shows the contents of the fast cache for a router if fast switching is enabled
show processes cpu | include IP Input	Displays information about the IP Input process on a router (Note: The CPU utilization for this process might show a high value if the CPU of a router is actively engaged in process-switching traffic.)
show ip cef	Shows the contents of the FIB for a router
show ip cef adjacency *egress-interface-id next-hop-ip-address* detail	Displays destinations reachable via the combination of the specified egress interface and next-hop IP address
show adjacency detail	Provides information contained in a router's adjacency table, including protocol and timer information
show cef not-cef-switched	Displays information about packets forwarded by the router using a packet-switching mechanism other than CEF
show memory allocating-process totals	Shows information about memory availability on a router after the router's Cisco IOS image has been decompressed and loaded (Note: This command can help identify memory leaks.)
show buffer	Shows how many buffers (of various types) are currently free (Note: This command can be helpful in diagnosing a buffer leak.)
show processes memory | include bgp	Shows how much memory is being consumed by the various BGP processes of a router
show diag	Shows the memory available on the line cards of a router

This chapter covers the following subjects:

Introduction to Cisco IOS Security: This section begins by reviewing various security measures that might be put in place on Cisco routers and switches to protect three different planes of network operation. These planes are: the management plane, the control plane, and the data plane. Once you review these security measures, this section considers how your troubleshooting efforts might be impacted by having various layers of security in place.

Security Troubleshooting Targets: This section describes the basic operation and troubleshooting tips for Cisco IOS firewalls and AAA services. Although complete configuration details for Cisco IOS firewalls and AAA is beyond the scope of the TSHOOT course, as a reference, this section does provide a couple of basic configuration examples with an explanation of the syntax used.

Trouble Ticket: Cisco IOS Security: This section presents you with a trouble ticket and an associated topology. You are also given **show** command output and a syntax reference. Based on the information provided, you hypothesize how to correct the reported issues. You can then compare your solutions with the suggested solutions.

CHAPTER 9

Security Troubleshooting

This chapter begins by reviewing various security solutions you might deploy on Cisco routers and switches. Some of these solutions are designed to protect the routers and switches themselves. Other solutions protect data flowing over the network and other network devices in the network.

Adding security to a network can complicate your efforts to troubleshoot a reported issue. So, this chapter provides suggestions for carrying out your troubleshooting efforts in a secured network.

Although some networks might have dedicated firewall appliances, a Cisco IOS router, running an appropriate feature set, can also act as a firewall. This chapter reviews the two types of Cisco IOS firewalls supported on many of today's router platforms, including a basic configuration example and troubleshooting tips.

In larger networks, a dedicated security server might be used to, for example, authenticate user logins on a router. Having a centralized server can make password and user updates much more efficient than having to manually apply such updates to each individual router in a topology. This centralized server is often referred to as a AAA server. This chapter discusses popular authentication, authorization, and accounting (AAA) protocols, along with techniques for troubleshooting issues that might arise in a AAA environment.

"Do I Know This Already?" Quiz

The "Do I Know This Already?" quiz helps you determine your level of knowledge of this chapter's topics before you begin. Table 9-1 details the major topics discussed in this chapter and their corresponding quiz questions.

Table 9-1 *"Do I Know This Already?" Section-to-Question Mapping*

Foundation Topics Section	Questions
Introduction to Cisco IOS Security	1–6
Security Troubleshooting Targets	7–8

1. What are the three planes of router and switch operation that should be secured? (Choose the three best answers.)

    a. Management plane

    b. Architectural plane

    c. Data plane

    d. Control plane

2. What command can you use to prevent an attacker from performing password recovery on some platforms?

    a. config-reg 0x2124

    b. service password-encryption

    c. no service password-recovery

    d. enable secret 5

3. What alternative to Telnet provides secure access to a router's command-line interface? (Choose the best answer.)

    a. TACACS+

    b. SSL

    c. HTTPS

    d. SSH

4. Identify two Cisco Catalyst switch features that can mitigate the introduction of a rogue switch into a network by an attacker, where the attacker attempts to make the newly added rogue switch become the root bridge for the topology. (Choose the two best answers.)

    a. Root Guard

    b. Backbone Fast

    c. Uplink Fast

    d. BPDU Guard

5. What Cisco IOS feature, available on some router platforms, can recognize the signature of well-known attacks, and prevent traffic from those attacks from entering the network?

    a. VPN

    b. IPS

    c. Cisco IOS firewall

    d. ACL

6. Which of the following steps should be performed first when troubleshooting a secured network environment? (Choose the best answer.)

   a. Disable the network security features to eliminate them as potential sources of the reported issue.

   b. Begin your troubleshooting at Layer 1, and work your way up to the levels where the security features reside.

   c. Determine whether the reported behavior is actually appropriate behavior, based on the network's security policy.

   d. Begin your troubleshooting at Layer 7, and work your way down to the levels where the security features reside.

7. What are two types of Cisco IOS firewalls? (Choose the two best answers.)

   a. MQC-Based Policy Firewall

   b. Classic Cisco IOS Firewall

   c. Zone-Based Policy Firewall

   d. Basic Cisco IOS Firewall

8. Which two of the following are true concerning TACACS+ but not true concerning RADIUS? (Choose the two best answers.)

   a. TCP-based

   b. Encrypts the entire packet

   c. Standards-based

   d. Offers robust accounting features

Foundation Topics

Introduction to Cisco IOS Security

As the number of security threats continues to grow and the level of required sophistication for an attacker continues to decline, strategically securing today's production networks is a necessity. Adding security features to a network, however, can make troubleshooting that network more difficult.

For example, in addition to troubleshooting basic Layer 2 and Layer 3 connectivity, you also need to check such things as firewall, intrusion prevention system (IPS), and virtual private network (VPN) configurations. Also, a network's security policy might limit what you as a troubleshooter are allowed to do while troubleshooting. For example, you might not be allowed to remove certain access control lists (ACL), even though removing them might simplify your troubleshooting efforts.

This section focuses on securing the different planes of operation on routers and switches. Following are these three planes of operation:

- **Management plane:** The management plane of operation is used to manage a router or a switch. This management involves, for example, accessing and configuring a device.

- **Control plane:** The control plane of operation encompasses protocols used between routers and switches. These protocols include, for example, routing protocols and Spanning Tree Protocol (STP).

- **Data plane:** The data plane is the plane of operation in charge of forwarding data through a router or switch.

The sections that follow also provide you with tips for troubleshooting network security issues.

Securing the Management Plane

When you connect to a router or a switch for management purposes (for example, to make a configuration change), you are accessing the management plane. As shown in Figure 9-1, the management plane can be accessed in several ways, and from a security perspective, each of these access methods should be secured.

Modes of Access

The methods of accessing the management plane illustrated in Figure 9-1 allow three primary modes of access, as described in the list that follows:

- **Command-line interface (CLI) access:** A router or switch's CLI can be accessed via a serial connection, known as a console connection. This connection enables an administrator to directly connect into the managed device. Although a console connection can be password protected, physical security is also a requirement. For example, if attackers gained physical access to a router or switch, they could connect to the console connection and perform a password recovery procedure, thus granting them access.

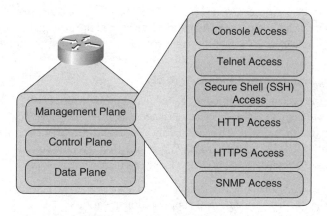

Figure 9-1 *Methods of Accessing the Management Plane*

To prevent a potentially malicious user from performing password recovery on a device, some platforms support the disabling of the password recovery service. The global configuration mode command to disable the password recovery service is **no service password-recovery.**

The ability to disable password recovery, however, does not provide complete protection from an attacker. For example, although attackers that gained physical access to a device would not be able to recover the password of the device, they could wipe out the configuration. Also, if they had gained sufficient information about the network, its protocols, and addressing schemes, they could conceivably recreate a working configuration. They could then add to that working configuration a backdoor for them to gain access to the device and potentially monitor, intercept, or alter traffic flowing through that device. Therefore, physical security remains a critical aspect of overall network security.

CLI access can also be gained over a network connection using protocols such as Telnet and Secure Shell (SSH). Telnet is not considered secure, because its packets are sent in clear text. Conversely, SSH encrypts its traffic, preventing an eavesdropper from interpreting any intercepted traffic.

■ **Web access:** Many network devices can be monitored and configured via a web-based interface (for example, the Cisco Configuration Professional [CCP] or Cisco Security Device Manager [SDM] applications). Although either HTTP or HTTPS can be used to access these web-based administrative interfaces, HTTPS is more secure. For example, if an attacker were to intercept HTTP traffic between an administrator's workstation and a managed router, the attacker might be able to interpret configurations being performed on the router. If HTTPS where used instead, an attacker would not be able to interpret any intercepted configuration information, because HTTPS encrypts its transmissions.

■   **SNMP access:** As discussed in Chapter 3, "The Maintenance and Troubleshooting Toolbox," Simple Network Management Protocol (SNMP) is commonly used to monitor network devices. Devices enabled to support SNMP can be configured to support read-only access or read-write access. SNMP versions 1 and 2c use community strings that must match between the monitoring device and the managed device. SNMP version 3, however, offers enhanced security through encryption and authentication.

Protecting Management Plane Access

Other than the previously mentioned requirement for physical security, network security can be used to limit access to a device's management plane over a network connection. For example, ACLs can be created to permit only specific protocols (such as SSH as opposed to Telnet and HTTPS as opposed to HTTP) coming from specific sources (for example, the IP addresses of administrators) to access a device's management plane.

Once a connection is made with the device to be managed, the connecting user should then be authenticated. Cisco devices support authentication via a single password, or via a username and password combination. If you choose to use usernames and passwords, those credentials could be locally configured on a device. However, for scalability, you might want to have those credentials stored centrally on a server (for example, a Remote Authentication Dial In User Service [RADIUS] or Terminal Access Controller Access-Control System Plus [TACACS+] server). By centrally locating a common user database accessible by multiple network devices, you eliminate the need to maintain a separate user database on each network device.

From a troubleshooting perspective, you should understand how to access a device. For example, a device might be accessible via SSH with username and password credentials. Also, you might need physical access to a device. If so, you should understand how you can be granted physical access of that secured device.

Securing the Control Plane

Control plane protocols include routing protocols (for example, Enhanced Interior Gateway Routing Protocol [EIGRP], Open Shortest Path First [OSPF], and Border Gateway Protocol [BGP]), STP, and Address Resolution Protocol (ARP). These protocols often create data structures that are used directly or indirectly for packet-forwarding decisions by a device. Therefore, such protocols should be secured. Additionally, the control plane itself should be protected from a denial-of-service (DoS) attack, where all of a control plane's resources are consumed by malicious traffic.

Securing Routing Protocols

Although routing protocols can differ in their implementation of authentication methods, most enterprise routing protocols support some sort of authentication. This authentication allows adjacent routers to authenticate one another, thereby preventing an attacker from inserting a rogue router into a network, in an attempt to influence routing decisions. Similar authentication methods are available for router redundancy protocols (that is, Hot Standby Routing Protocol [HSRP], Virtual Router Redundancy Protocol [VRRP], and Gateway Load Balancing Protocol [GLBP]).

Securing STP

Chapter 4, "Basic Cisco Catalyst Switch Troubleshooting," discussed how STP could be used to add redundancy to a network, while preventing problems which could stem from Layer 2 topological loops. STP achieves this loop-free topology by electing one switch as the *root bridge*. The network administrator can influence which switch becomes the root bridge through the manipulation of a switch's bridge priority, where the switch with the lowest bridge priority becomes the root bridge. Every other switch in the network designates a *root port*, which is the port on the switch that is closest to the root bridge, in terms of cost. The bridge priorities of switches are learned through the exchange of Bridge Protocol Data Units (BPDU). After the election of a root bridge, all the switch ports in the topology are either in the *blocking* state (where user data is not forwarded) or in the *forwarding* state (where user data is forwarded).

If the root bridge fails, the STP topology will reconverge by electing a new root bridge. If an attacker has access to two switch ports (each from a different switch), they might be able to introduce a rogue switch into the network. The rogue switch can then be configured with a lower bridge priority than the bridge priority of the root bridge. After the rogue switch announces its *superior BPDUs*, the STP topology reconverges, where all traffic traveling from one switch to another switch now passes through the rogue switch, thus allowing the attacker to capture that traffic.

As an example, consider the topology shown in Figure 9-2. Data traveling from PC1 to Server1 passes through SW2 and SW3 (the root bridge).

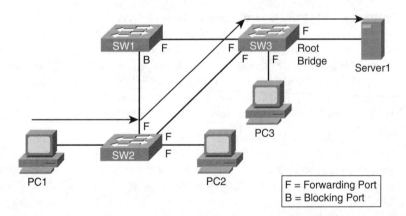

Figure 9-2 *Converged STP Topology*

Notice PC2 and PC3. If an attacker gains access to the switch ports of these two PCs, the attacker could introduce a rogue switch that advertised superior BPDUs, causing the rogue switch to be elected as the new root bridge. The new data path between PC1 and Server1, as illustrated in Figure 9-3, now passes through the attacker's rogue switch. The attacker can configure one of the switch ports as a Switch Port Analyzer (SPAN) port. A SPAN port can receive a copy of traffic crossing another port or VLAN. In this example, the attacker could use the SPAN port to send a copy of traffic crossing the switch to the attacker's PC.

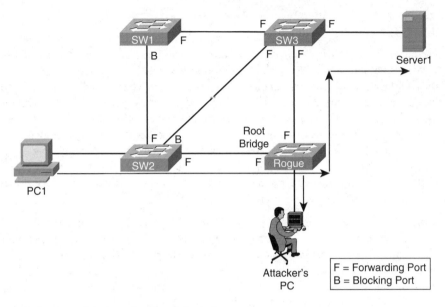

Figure 9-3   *Introduction of a Rogue Switch*

Consider two approaches for protecting a network from this type of STP attack:

Key
Topic

■ **Protecting with Root Guard:** The Root Guard feature can be enabled on all switch
    ports in the network off of which the root bridge should not appear (that is, every
    port that is not a *root port*, the port on each switch that is considered to be closest to
    the root bridge). If a port configured for Root Guard receives a superior BPDU, in-
    stead of believing the BPDU, the port goes into a *root-inconsistent* state. While a
    port is in the root-inconsistent state, no user data is sent across the port. However, af-
    ter the superior BPDUs stop, the port returns to the forwarding state.

■ **Protecting with BPDU Guard:** The BPDU Guard feature is enabled on ports con-
    figured with Cisco's PortFast feature. The PortFast feature is enabled on ports that
    connect out to end-user devices, such as PCs, and it reduces the amount of time re-
    quired for the port to go into the forwarding state after being connected. The logic of
    PortFast is that a port that connects to an end-user device does not have the poten-
    tial to create a topology loop. Therefore, the port can go active sooner by skipping
    STP's Listening and Learning states, which by default take 15 seconds each. Because
    these PortFast ports are connected to end-user devices, these ports should never re-
    ceive a BPDU. Therefore, if a port enabled for BPDU Guard receives a BPDU, the port
    is disabled.

Securing DHCP and ARP

On today's networks, most clients obtain their IP address information dynamically, using
Dynamic Host Configuration Protocol (DHCP), rather than having their IP address information statically configured. To dynamically obtain IP address information, a client (for

example, a PC) dynamically discovers a DHCP server via a broadcast and sends out a DHCP request; the DHCP server sees the request; and a DHCP response (including such information as an IP address, subnet mask, and default gateway) is sent to the requesting client.

However, if an attacker connects a rogue DHCP server to the network, the rogue DHCP server can respond to a client's DHCP discovery request. Even though both the rogue DHCP server and the actual DHCP server respond to the request, the rogue DHCP server's response will be used by the client if it reaches the client before the response from the actual DHCP server, as illustrated in Figure 9-4.

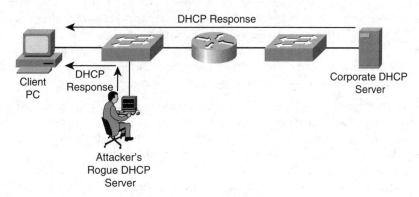

Figure 9-4   *DHCP Server Spoofing*

The DHCP response from an attacker's DHCP server might assign the attacker's IP address as the client's default gateway. As a result, the client sends traffic to the attacker's IP address. The attacker can then capture the traffic and then forward the traffic to an appropriate default gateway. From the client's perspective, everything is functioning correctly, so this type of DHCP server spoofing attack can go undetected for a long period of time.

The *DHCP snooping* feature on Cisco Catalyst switches can be used to combat a DHCP server spoofing attack. This option is off on most Catalyst switches by default. With this solution, Cisco Catalyst switch ports are configured in either the *trusted* or *untrusted* state. If a port is trusted, it is allowed to receive DHCP responses (for example, DHCPOFFER, DHCPACK, or DHCPNAK). Conversely, if a port is untrusted, it is not allowed to receive DHCP responses, and if a DHCP response does attempt to enter an untrusted port, the port is disabled. Fortunately, not every switch port needs to be configured to support DHCP snooping, because if a port is not explicitly configured as a trusted port, it is implicitly considered to be an untrusted port.

Another type of DHCP attack is more of a DoS attack against the DHCP server. Specifically, the attacker can repeatedly request IP address assignments from the DHCP server, thus depleting the pool of addresses available from the DHCP server. The attacker can accomplish this by making the DHCP requests appear to come from different MAC addresses. To mitigate such a DoS attack, you can use the previously mentioned DHCP snooping feature to limit the number of DHCP messages per second that are allowed on an interface, thus preventing a flood of spoofed DHCP requests.

The DHCP snooping feature dynamically builds a DHCP binding table, which contains the MAC addresses associated with specific IP addresses. This DHCP binding table can be used by the *Dynamic ARP Inspection* (DAI) feature to help prevent Address Resolution Protocol (ARP) spoofing attacks.

Recall the purpose of ARP requests. When a network device needs to determine the MAC address that corresponds to an IP address, the device can send out an ARP request. The target device replies to the requesting device with an ARP reply. The ARP reply contains the requested MAC address.

Attackers can attempt to launch an attack by sending gratuitous ARP (GARP) replies. These GARP messages can tell network devices that the attacker's MAC address corresponds to specific IP addresses. For example, the attacker might be able to convince a PC that the attacker's MAC address is the MAC address of the PC's default gateway. As a result, the PC starts sending traffic to the attacker. The attacker captures the traffic and then forwards the traffic on to the appropriate default gateway.

To illustrate, consider Figure 9-5. PC1 is configured with a default gateway of 192.168.0.1. However, the attacker sent GARP messages to PC1, telling PC1 that the MAC address corresponding to 192.168.0.1 is BBBB.BBBB.BBBB, which is the attacker's MAC address. Similarly, the attacker sent GARP messages to the default gateway, claiming that the MAC address corresponding to PC1's IP address of 192.168.0.2 was BBBB.BBBB.BBBB. This *ARP cache poisoning* causes PC1 and Router1 to exchange traffic via the attacker's PC. Therefore, this type of ARP spoofing attack is considered to be a *man-in-the-middle* attack.

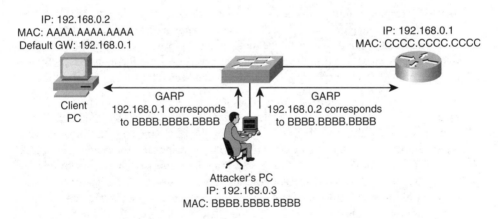

Figure 9-5   *ARP Spoofing*

Networks can be protected from ARP spoofing attacks using the DAI feature. DAI works similarly to DHCP snooping by using *trusted* and *untrusted* ports. ARP replies are allowed into the switch on trusted ports. However, if an ARP reply enters the switch on an untrusted port, the contents of the ARP reply are compared against the DHCP binding table to verify its accuracy. If the ARP reply is not consistent with the DHCP binding table, the ARP reply is dropped, and the port is disabled.

Securing Against a DoS Attack

Rather than intercepting or manipulating traffic, an attacker's goal might be to make a network device unusable. For example, an attacker might launch a DoS attack against a router's control plane.

To protect against flooding of a router's control plane, you could configure Cisco's control plane policing (CoPP) or control plane protection (CPP) feature. Although both features can limit specific traffic types entering the control plane, CPP offers finer control of the policing action.

Table 9-2 summarizes the previously discussed mitigations for control plane threats.

Table 9-2 *Mitigations for Control Plane Threats*

Target	Mitigations
Routing protocols	Authentication of routing protocols
STP	Root Guard
	BPDU Guard
DHCP and ARP	DHCP Snooping
	Dynamic ARP Inspection (DAI)
Control Plane Resources	Control Plane Policing (CoPP)
	Control Plane Protection (CPP)

Securing the Data Plane

Protecting the management and control planes focuses on protecting a network device (for example, a router or a switch). Protecting the data plane, however, focuses on protecting the actual data flowing through a network and protecting other devices (for example, hosts) on the network.

ACLs (or VLAN access maps on Cisco Catalyst switches) offer a fundamental approach to restricting traffic allowed on a network. For example, an ACL can permit or deny traffic based on source and destination IP address and port number information, in addition to time-of-day restrictions.

Although some networks have a firewall appliance, such as the Cisco Adaptive Security Appliance (ASA), a Cisco IOS router can also perform firewalling features, as shown in Figure 9-6. In the diagram, the Cisco IOS firewall allows Telnet traffic into the campus network from a host on the Internet, if the Telnet session originated from the campus network. If a user on the Internet attempted to establish a Telnet connection with a host inside the campus network, however, the Cisco IOS firewall would block the inbound Telnet traffic.

Similar to firewalling, intrusion prevention can be accomplished via a dedicated intrusion prevention system (IPS) appliance or through the Cisco IOS IPS feature. Figure 9-7 shows a Cisco IOS router configured with the IPS feature. The router is configured with a database of signatures that can recognize a collection of well-known attacks. Therefore, while non-malicious HTTP traffic is allowed to pass through the router, malicious traffic (for example, a SYN flood attack) is not permitted through the router.

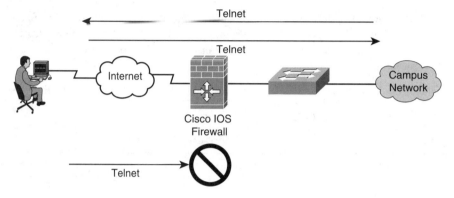

Figure 9-6   *Cisco IOS Firewall*

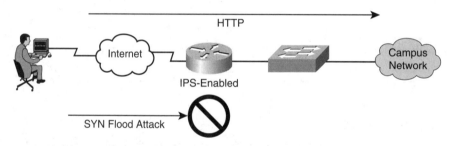

Figure 9-7   *Cisco IOS IPS Feature*

If unencrypted traffic flowing over an unprotected network is intercepted by an attacker, that attacker might be able to glean valuable information (for example, login credentials or account codes) from the intercepted traffic. This type of attack is known as a *man-in-the-middle attack*. Figure 9-8 illustrates an example of such an attack.

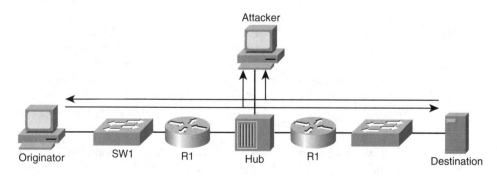

Figure 9-8   *Man-in-the-Middle Attack*

To prevent a man-in-the-middle attack, a secure virtual private network (VPN) tunnel can be constructed between the originator and destination, as illustrated in Figure 9-9. Because the traffic traveling over the logical VPN tunnel can be encrypted, a man-in-the-middle attacker would not be able to interpret any packets they intercepted. Although multiple VPN protocols exist, IPsec is one of the most popular approaches used to protect traffic flowing over a VPN tunnel.

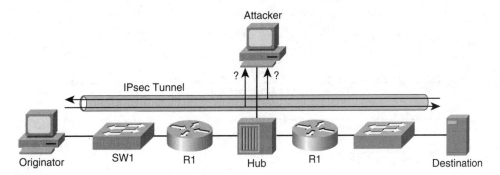

Figure 9-9   *Securing Traffic with a VPN*

As a few other examples of how a Cisco IOS router can protect network traffic and other network devices, consider the Unicast Reverse Path Forwarding (uRPF) feature. This feature allows a router to examine the source IP address of an incoming packet and, based on the router's IP routing table, determine how traffic would be routed back to that source address. If the router notices that the traffic came in on an interface that is different than the interface the router would use to send traffic back to that source IP address, the router can drop the traffic. The rationale for the router dropping this traffic is that this behavior could reflect an IP spoofing attack, where an attacker was impersonating a trusted IP address.

Routers can also play a role in granting users access to the network. For example, consider the IEEE 802.1X technology, as depicted in Figure 9-10.

An 802.1X network requires a client to authenticate before communicating on the network. Once the authentication occurs, a key is generated that is shared between the client and the device to which it attaches (for example, a wireless LAN controller or a Layer 2 switch). The key is then used to encrypt traffic coming from and being sent to the client. In the figure, you see the three primary components of an 802.1X network:

- **Supplicant:** The supplicant is the device that wants to gain access to the network.

- **Authenticator:** The authenticator forwards the supplicant's authentication request on to an authentication server. Once the authentication server has authenticated the supplicant, the authenticator receives a key that is used to communicate securely during a session with the supplicant.

- **Authentication Server:** The authentication server (for example, a RADIUS server) checks the supplicant's credentials. If the credentials are acceptable, the authentication server notifies the authenticator that the supplicant is allowed to communicate on the network. The authentication server also gives the authenticator a key that can be used to securely transmit data during the authenticator's session with the supplicant.

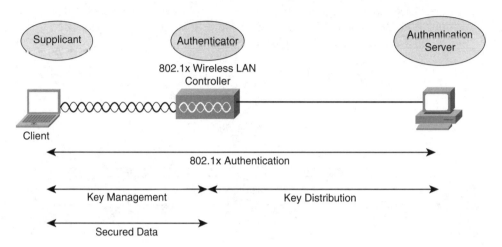

Figure 9-10   *Granting Network Access Using 802.1X*

An even more sophisticated approach to admission control is the Network Admission Control (NAC) feature. Beyond just checking credentials, NAC can check characteristics of the device seeking admission to the network. The client's operating system and version of anti-virus software are examples of these characteristics.

Troubleshooting Network Security Issues

Now that you have reviewed several security measures that networks might have in place to protect their management, control, and data planes, consider how these layers of security might impact your troubleshooting efforts. For example, troubleshooting is often concerned with establishing connectivity between two devices, whereas security features often strategically limit connectivity. Therefore, to effectively troubleshoot a network, you should clearly understand what security features are in place, in addition to the desired behavior of these features.

To begin your troubleshooting efforts in a secure network, you might first determine if the issue being reported is related to the network's security policy or if there is an underlying network problem.

If you determine that there is indeed a network problem, your troubleshooting steps might be limited to actions that conform to the network's security policy. For example, you might want to remove an IPsec configuration from a link between two offices. You should balance that action against the severity of the problem, the likelihood of a security incident occurring during the window of time the IPsec tunnel is deactivated, and the corporate security policy.

Security Troubleshooting Targets

Because adding security to a network can complicate your troubleshooting efforts, you should have an understanding of basic security configurations which you might encounter on a router. Therefore, this section addresses the basic configuration and troubleshooting of two of the more complex Cisco IOS security features: the Cisco IOS Firewall feature and the Authentication, Authorization, and Accounting (AAA) feature.

Configuring and Troubleshooting the Cisco IOS Firewall Feature

Table 9-3 summarizes the two categories of firewalls supported on Cisco IOS routers.

Table 9-3   *Types of Cisco IOS Firewalls*

Target	Mitigations
Classic Cisco IOS Firewall	This firewalling feature was previously known as Context-Based Access Control (CBAC). The Classic Cisco IOS Firewall inspects traffic flowing from a trusted network to an untrusted network, and returning flows from the untrusted network can be permitted into the trusted network. However, if someone attempted to initiate a session from the untrusted network into the trusted network, that session would be denied.
Zone-Based Policy Firewall	This firewalling feature allows various router interfaces to be assigned to a zone. Interzone policies can then be configured to dictate what traffic is permitted between these defined zones.

As an example of a basic Classic Cisco IOS Firewall configuration, consider Figure 9-11. In this example, the campus network is considered the trusted network, whereas the Internet is considered the untrusted network. The goal of the configuration is to allow a user on the trusted network to communicate with a web server on the Internet. Therefore, return traffic from the web server should be allowed back into the trusted network. However, web traffic (that is, HTTP traffic) should not be allowed into the trusted network from the untrusted network if the web traffic is not return traffic from an already established session.

Example 9-1 shows the configuration of the Classic Cisco IOS Firewall depicted.

Example 9-1   *Classic Cisco IOS Firewall Configuration on Router R4*

```
R4# show run
...OUTPUT OMITTED...
 inspect name WEB http
!
interface FastEthernet0/1
 ip address 10.8.8.1 255.255.255.0
 ip access-group 100 in
 ip inspect WEB out
```

```
!
...OUTPUT OMITTED...
!
access-list 100 deny ip any any
...OUTPUT OMITTED...
```

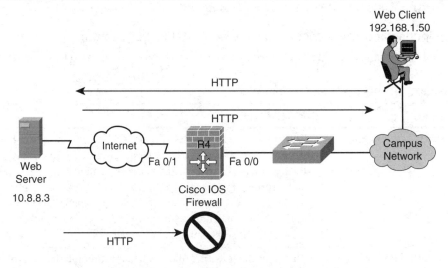

Figure 9-11 *Classic Cisco IOS Firewall Topology*

Notice that ACL 100 has been created to deny all IP traffic. This ACL has been applied in the inbound direction to interface Fast Ethernet 0/1. This blocks all IP traffic sourced from the untrusted network destined for the trusted network.

Also notice that an inspection rule named WEB has been created to inspect HTTP traffic, using the **inspect name WEB http** command. This inspection rule is then applied in the outbound direction to the Fast Ethernet 0/1 interface, using the **ip inspect WEB out** command.

When HTTP traffic leaves the trusted network destined for the untrusted network, via interface Fast Ethernet 0/1, the router inspects those HTTP traffic flows. As a result, when return HTTP comes back from the untrusted network, interface Fast Ethernet 0/1 allows that return traffic back into the router, even though an ACL has been applied to block all inbound IP traffic.

You can use the **show ip inspect session [detail] [all]** command to troubleshoot such a configuration. By itself, the **show ip inspect session** command shows current sessions being inspected by the Cisco IOS Firewall feature. The **detail** option provides additional details about the current sessions. The **all** option provides information about the way the router is performing its inspection.

Example 9-2 shows sample output from the **show ip inspect session** command. The output indicates that a trusted host with an IP address of 192.168.1.50 has opened two HTTP sessions with a host having an IP address of 10.8.8.3.

Example 9-2   show ip inspect session *Command Output*

```
R4#show ip inspect session
Established Sessions
 Session 84638E80 (192.168.1.50:1832)=>(10.8.8.3:80) http SIS_OPEN
 Session 84638BA8 (192.168.1.50:1830)=>(10.8.8.3:80) http SIS_OPEN
```

Example 9-3 provides sample output from the **show ip inspect session detail** command. The output shows the number of bytes sent by both the session initiator and the session responder. Also indicated in the output is that ACL 100 has been matched 116 times.

Example 9-3   show ip inspect session detail *Command Output*

```
R4#show ip inspect session detail
Established Sessions
 Session 84638E80 (192.168.1.50:1832)=>(10.8.8.3:80) http SIS_OPEN
  Created 00:01:54, Last heard 00:01:32
  Bytes sent (initiator:responder) [408:166394]
  In  SID 10.8.8.3[80:80]=>192.168.1.50[1832:1832] on ACL 100   (116 matches)
 Session 84638BA8 (192.168.1.50:1830)=>(10.8.8.3:80) http SIS_OPEN
  Created 00:02:52, Last heard 00:01:33
  Bytes sent (initiator:responder) [1262:333173]
  In  SID 10.8.8.3[80:80]=>192.168.1.50[1830:1830] on ACL 100   (253 matches)
```

Example 9-4 provides sample output from the **show ip inspect session all** command. This output contains information about the interface's inspection configuration.

Example 9-4   show ip inspect all *Command Output*

```
R4#show ip inspect all
Session audit trail is enabled
Session alert is enabled
one-minute (sampling period) thresholds are [unlimited : unlimited] connections
max-incomplete sessions thresholds are [unlimited : unlimited]
max-incomplete tcp connections per host is unlimited. Block-time 0 minute.
tcp synwait-time is 30 sec — tcp finwait-time is 5 sec
tcp idle-time is 3600 sec — udp idle-time is 30 sec
tcp reassembly queue length 16; timeout 5 sec; memory-limit 1024 kilo bytes
dns-timeout is 5 sec
Inspection Rule Configuration
 Inspection name WEB
     http alert is on audit-trail is on timeout 3600

Interface Configuration
 Interface FastEthernet0/1
  Inbound inspection rule is not set
  Outgoing inspection rule is WEB
```

```
      http alert is on audit-trail is on timeout 3600
    Inbound access list is 100
    Outgoing access list is not set


Established Sessions
  Session 84638E80 (192.168.1.50:1832)=>(10.8.8.3:80) http SIS_OPEN
  Session 84638BA8 (192.168.1.50:1830)=>(10.8.8.3:80) http SIS_OPEN
```

To see real-time updates about the sessions being monitored by a router, you can enter the **ip inspect audit-trail** global configuration mode command. This command causes syslog messages to be created whenever a router creates a new stateful inspection session. Example 9-5 shows sample syslog output (which is sent to a router's console by default) reflecting a new stateful inspection session. The syslog output shows that a new HTTP inspection session began, with an IP address of 192.168.1.50 acting as the initiator and an IP address of 10.8.8.3 acting as the responder. When 192.168.1.50 sends traffic to 10.8.8.3, it does so using TCP port 80 (that is, the default HTTP port). However, when 10.8.8.3 responds to 192.168.1.50, it does so using TCP port 1841.

Example 9-5 *Syslog Output Generated Due to the* **ip inspect audit-trail** *Command*

```
R4#
*Mar  3 12:46:32.465: %SYS-5-CONFIG_I: Configured from console by console
*Mar  3 12:47:10.115: %FW-6-SESS_AUDIT_TRAIL_START: Start http session: initiator
  (192.168.1.50:1841) — responder (10.8.8.3:80)
```

For even more detailed information, you could use the **debug ip inspect object-creation** command. As Example 9-6 demonstrates, the debug output can provide information such as the initiator's and responder's IP addresses, the ACL being used, and the Layer 4 protocol (for example, TCP or UDP) in use. Interestingly, the debug output references Context-Based Access Control (CBAC), the feature that has been renamed as Classic Cisco IOS Firewall.

Example 9-6 **debug ip inspect object-creation** *Command Output*

```
*Mar  3 14:17:55.794: CBAC* OBJ_CREATE: Pak 83A830FC sis 84638BA8 initiator_addr
  (192.168.1.50:1979) responder_addr (10.8.8.3:80)
initiator_alt_addr (192.168.1.50:1979) responder_alt_addr (10.8.8.3:80)
*Mar  3 14:17:55.798: CBAC OBJ-CREATE: sid 846524D4 acl 100 Prot: tcp
*Mar  3 14:17:55.798:  Src 10.8.8.3 Port [80:80]
*Mar  3 14:17:55.798:  Dst 192.168.1.50 Port [1979:1979]
*Mar  3 14:17:55.798: CBAC OBJ_CREATE: create host entry 84641108 addr 10.8.8.3
  bucket 9 (vrf 0:0) insp_cb 0x83EBD140
*Mar  3 14:17:56.251: CBAC* OBJ_CREATE: Pak 83A830FC sis 84638E80 initiator_addr
  (192.168.1.50:1980) responder_addr (10.8.8.3:80)
initiator_alt_addr (192.168.1.50:1980) responder_alt_addr (10.8.8.3:80)
*Mar  3 14:17:56.255: CBAC OBJ-CREATE: sid 84652528 acl 100 Prot: tcp
*Mar  3 14:17:56.255:  Src 10.8.8.3 Port [80:80]
```

```
*Mar  3 14:17:56.255:  Dst 192.168.1.50 Port [1980:1980]
*Mar  3 14:17:56.255: CBAC OBJ_CREATE: create host entry 84641108 addr 10.8.8.3
  bucket 9 (vrf 0:0) insp_cb 0x83EBD140
```

Configuring and Troubleshooting AAA

Enforcing router login security in larger networks can be challenging if you have to manage multiple user databases (for example, having a separate user database locally configured on each router of your network). Fortunately, with AAA services, you can have a single repository for user credentials. Then, when a network administrator attempts to log into, for example, a router, the credentials they supply can be authenticated against a centralized AAA database.

Another advantage of giving different network administrators their own login credentials, as opposed to an enable secret password used on all routers, is that users can quickly be added and deleted from the database without the need to touch each router. Not only can AAA services serve administrative logins connecting to a router, AAA services can also control connections passing through a router to, for example, resources inside a network.

Three services are offered by a AAA server, as follows:

■ **Authentication:** The authentication service can check user credentials to confirm they are who they claim to be.

■ **Authorization:** Once authenticated, the authorization service determines what that user is allowed to do.

■ **Accounting:** The accounting service can collect and store information about a user's login. This information can be used, for example, to keep an audit trail of what was performed on a network.

Figure 9-12 shows a AAA topology where only authentication is being performed. The user at an IP address of 192.168.1.50 is attempting to establish a Telnet session with a router at an IP address of 10.3.3.2. The router's configuration causes the router to prompt the user for username and password credentials and to check those credentials against a AAA server (a TACACS+ server in this example, as opposed to a RADIUS server). If the provided credentials match the database being referenced by the AAA server, the user is permitted to log in to the router.

The Cisco IOS implementation of AAA services includes multiple configuration options, and discussing a complete AAA configuration is beyond the scope of the TSHOOT course. However, Example 9-7 provides a basic configuration example. For more information on AAA configuration, please consult the Cisco IOS Security Configuration Guide available at the following URL: http://tinyurl.com/3ufo6j.

Example 9-7 *AAA Configuration for Authenticating Remote Logins*

```
R4#show run
...OUTPUT OMITTED...
aaa new-model
aaa authentication login ADMIN group tacacs+
```

```
!
tacacs-server host 192.168.0.40 key cisco
!
line vty 0 4
 password cisco
 login authentication ADMIN
!
...OUTPUT OMITTED...
```

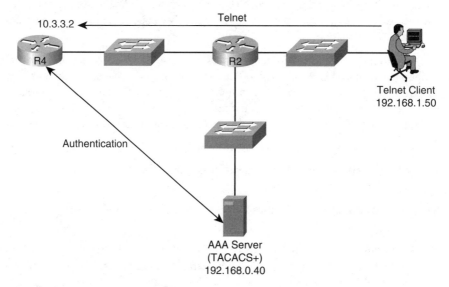

Figure 9-12 *AAA Sample Topology*

In the previous example, the **aaa new-model** command is used to enable AAA services on the router. The **aaa authentication login ADMIN group tacacs+** command defines a method list named **ADMIN**, which requires authentication via a TACACS+ server for logins. The TACACS+ server is defined as having an IP address of **192.168.0.40** with a shared secret key of **cisco**. The method list of **ADMIN** is then applied as the authentication method list for connections coming into the router over VTY lines 0 through 4. Therefore, when someone attempts to Telnet into this router, they are challenged to provide valid username and password credentials, which are then validated by the TACACS+ server.

From a troubleshooting perspective, you can view real-time information about authentication attempts using the **debug aaa authentication** command, as demonstrated in Example 9-8.

Example 9-8   debug aaa authentication *Command Output*

```
*Mar  3 14:39:39.435: AAA/BIND(0000000E): Bind i/f
*Mar  3 14:39:39.435: AAA/AUTHEN/LOGIN (0000000E): Pick method list 'ADMIN'
*Mar  3 14:39:59.211: AAA: parse name=tty66 idb type=-1 tty=-1
```

```
*Mar   3 14:39:59.211: AAA: name=tty66 flags=0x11 type=5 shelf=0 slot=0 adapter=0
  port=66 channel=0
*Mar   3 14:39:59.211: AAA/MEMORY: create_user (0x83C938B4) user='kevin'
  ruser='NULL' ds0=0 port='tty66' rem_addr='192.168.1.50' authen_type=ASCII
  service=ENABLE priv=15 initial_task_id='0', vrf= (id=0)
*Mar   3 14:39:59.211: AAA/AUTHEN/START (4286245615): port='tty66' list=''
  action=LOGIN service=ENABLE
*Mar   3 14:39:59.211: AAA/AUTHEN/START (4286245615): non-console enable - default
  to enable password
*Mar   3 14:39:59.215: AAA/AUTHEN/START (4286245615): Method=ENABLE
*Mar   3 14:39:59.215: AAA/AUTHEN(4286245615): Status=GETPASS
*Mar   3 14:40:00.710: AAA/AUTHEN/CONT (4286245615): continue_login
  (user='(undef)')
*Mar   3 14:40:00.710: AAA/AUTHEN(4286245615): Status=GETPASS
*Mar   3 14:40:00.710: AAA/AUTHEN/CONT (4286245615): Method=ENABLE
*Mar   3 14:40:00.770: AAA/AUTHEN(4286245615): Status=PASS
*Mar   3 14:40:00.770: AAA/MEMORY: free_user (0x83C938B4) user='NULL' ruser='NULL'
  port='tty66' rem_addr='192.168.1.50' authen_type=ASCII service=ENABLE priv=15
  vrf= (id=0)
```

From the preceding output, you can see that the **ADMIN** method list was used, that the username was **kevin**, and that the IP address of the client was **192.168.1.50**. To gather similar types of information for AAA's authorization and accounting features, you can use the **debug aaa authorization** and **debug aaa accounting** commands.

The two most popular AAA protocols used for communicating between a network device and a AAA server are TACACS+ and RADIUS. Table 9-4 contrasts these two protocols.

Table 9-4 *Contrasting the TACACS+ and RADIUS Protocols*

Key Topic

Characteristic	TACACS+	RADIUS
Transport Layer Protocol	TCP	UDP
Modularity	Provides separate services for authentication, authorization, and accounting	Combines authentication and authorization functions
Encryption	Encrypts entire packet	Only encrypts the password
Accounting Functionality	Offers basic accounting features	Offers robust accounting features
Standards-based	No (Cisco proprietary)	Yes

When troubleshooting a TACACS+ configuration, consider the following common error conditions:

- **The TACACS+ server is offline:** This condition might be indicated by the text "Connection refused by remote host" appearing in the output of the **debug aaa authentication** command.

- **The shared secret key configured on the AAA client doesn't match the key configured on the AAA server:** This condition might be indicated by the text "Invalid AUTHEN/START packet (check keys)" appearing in the output of the debug aaa authentication command.

- **An invalid username/password combination was provided by the AAA client:** This condition might be indicated by the text "Authentication failure" appearing in the output of the debug aaa authentication command.

When troubleshooting a RADIUS configuration, consider the following common error conditions:

- **The RADIUS server is offline:** This condition might be indicated by the text "No response from server" appearing in the output of the **debug radius** command.

- **The shared secret key configured on the AAA client doesn't match the key configured on the AAA server:** This condition might be indicated by the text "Reply for *id* fails decrypt" appearing in the output of the debug radius command.

- **A user is attempting to use a service for which they are not authorized:** This condition might be indicated by the text "No appropriate authorization type for user" appearing in the output of the debug radius command.

- **An invalid username/password combination was provided by the AAA client:** This condition might be indicated by the text "Received from id *id* IP_address:*port_number*. Access-Reject" appearing in the output of the debug radius command.

Although multiple TACACS+ and RADIUS servers are available on the market today, be aware of the Cisco product offering in this area—Cisco Secure ACS. Figure 9-13 shows the web-based console view of Cisco Secure ACS.

By clicking the Reports and Activity button, you can access a collection of valuable troubleshooting information. For example, you can retrieve reports about successful and unsuccessful authentication attempts.

Trouble Ticket: Cisco IOS Security

This trouble ticket focuses on Cisco IOS security. You are presented with a trouble ticket detailing three issues that need resolution. You are given sample **show** command output and are then challenged to identify resolutions for each issue described.

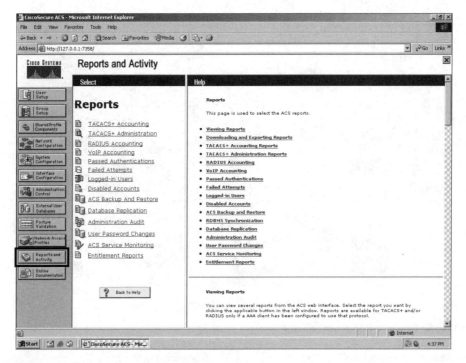

Figure 9-13 *Cisco Secure ACS Web-Based Console*

Trouble Ticket #7

You receive the following trouble ticket:

> A new administrator for Company A has forgotten the enable secret password assigned to router R1 and can no longer log in. Also, when this administrator connects to router R2 via Telnet, the connection is timed out after only one second. The administrator reports this short timeout does not give him sufficient time to correct the configuration. Also, the administrator configured an access list on router R2 to prevent anyone on the backbone (that is, connections coming in to router R2 via the Frame Relay network) from connecting to the Loopback 0 interfaces on routers R1 or R2 via Telnet. However, the access list does not seem to be working.

This trouble ticket references the topology shown in Figure 9-14.

Because a plethora of Cisco IOS security troubleshooting and configuration commands exist, this trouble ticket illustrates verification and configuration commands relevant to the issues described. Table 9-5 presents the syntax for these commands.

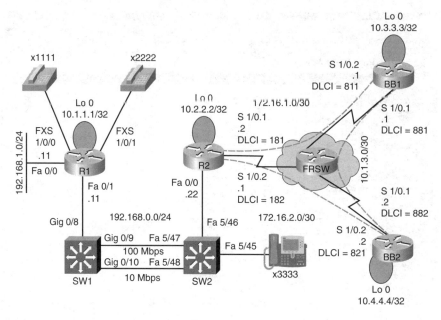

Figure 9-14   *Trouble Ticket #7 Topology*

Key Topic

Table 9-5   *Sampling of Cisco IOS Security Troubleshooting Syntax*

Command	Description
Router(config-line)# **exec-timeout** *minutes* [*seconds*]	Specifies how long the EXEC process running on a line waits for user input before timing out the connection (defaults to 10 minutes)
Router(config)# **access-list** *number* {**deny** | **permit**} *protocol source wildcard-mask destination wildcard-mask* [**eq** *port-number*] [**log**]	Creates an extended IP access list, where the access list number is in the range 100–199
rommon> confreg 0x2142	Configures a router in ROM Monitor configuration mode to ignore its startup configuration when it boots
rommon> **reset**	Causes a router in ROM Monitor configuration mode to reboot
Router(config)# **config-register 0x2102**	Configures a router to uses its startup configuration the next time the router boots
Router(config)# **enable secret** *password*	Configures a router's privileged mode password
Router# **show access-lists**	Displays access lists configured on a router
Router# **show logging**	Displays output collected from logged access list entries

The trouble ticket identified the following three issues:

1. A forgotten enable secret password.

2. An **exec-timeout** parameter set too low.

3. An ACL misconfiguration.

The sections that follow address each issue individually.

Issue #1: Forgotten Enable Secret Password

The first issue to be addressed by this trouble ticket is password recovery. The administrator reportedly forgot the enable secret password on to router R1, which is a Cisco 2611XM router.

On a separate sheet of paper, write out the steps you would go through to perform password recovery on this router. If you are not familiar with password recovery steps, you might need to research password recovery at Cisco.com.

Issue #1: Suggested Solution

To begin the password recovery process on router R1, the router was rebooted, and during the first few seconds of the router booting up, a **Break** was sent from the terminal emulator to the router. The **Break** caused the ROM Monitor prompt (that is, *rommon*) to appear on router R1's console.

The configuration register was set to 0x2142 with the command **confreg 0x2142**. Setting the configuration register to this value causes the router to ignore its startup configuration when the router boots. The router was then rebooted by issuing the **reset** command at the rommon prompt.

Because the router ignored the startup configuration, after the router booted, a prompt was presented, asking the administrator if he wanted to go through the setup dialog. A **no** was entered at this prompt. The **enable** command was entered to go into privileged configuration mode. From privileged mode, the startup configuration, stored in the router's NVRAM, was merged with the existing running configuration using the command **copy star run**. This command does not *replace* the running configuration with the startup configuration. Rather, these two configurations are *merged*. After this merger, all the physical interfaces were administratively shut down. Therefore, the **no shutdown** command was entered for interfaces Fast Ethernet 0/0 and Fast Ethernet 0/1.

The enable secret password was reset to **cisco** using the command **enable secret cisco**. Next, the configuration register was set back to its normal value of 0x2102 with the command **config-register 0x2102**. The running configuration was copied to the startup configuration with the command **copy run star**. The router was then rebooted with the **reload** command. After the router rebooted, the administrator could access the router's privileged mode using an enable secret password of **cisco**. Example 9-9 demonstrates this password recovery procedure.

Example 9-9   *Performing Password Recovery on Router R1*

```
System Bootstrap, Version 12.2(7r) [cmong 7r], RELEASE SOFTWARE (fc1)
Copyright (c) 2002 by cisco Systems, Inc.
C2600 platform with 131072 Kbytes of main memory
...BREAK SEQUENCE SENT...
monitor: oommand "boot" aborted due to user interrupt
rommon 1 > confreg 0x2142
You must reset or power cycle for new config to take effect
rommon 2 > reset
...OUTPUT OMITTED...
          ---- System Configuration Dialog ----
Would you like to enter the initial configuration dialog? [yes/no]: no
Press RETURN to get started!
...OUTPUT OMITTED...
Router>enable
Router#copy star run
Destination filename [running-config]?
...OUTPUT OMITTED...
R1(config)# enable secret cisco
R1(config)# config-register 0x2102
R1(config)# end
*Mar  3 12:43:26.016: %SYS-5-CONFIG_I: Configured from console by console
R1# copy run star
Destination filename [startup-config]?
Building configuration...
[OK]
R1# reload
Proceed with reload? [confirm]
...OUTPUT OMITTED...
Press RETURN to get started!
R1>
R1>enable
Password:cisco
R1#
```

Issue #2: An exec-timeout Parameter Set Too Low

The second issue addressed in this trouble ticket is recovering from a misconfiguration on router R2, which causes a Telnet session to timeout after only one second of inactivity. The challenge with such a misconfiguration is that when an administrator Telnets to the router to correct the configuration, he might be logged out if he pauses for as little as a single second.

Example 9-10 shows router R2's misconfiguration. Note the **exec-timeout 0 1** command. This command causes a user that connected via a VTY line to be timed out after only one second of inactivity.

Example 9-10 *Incorrect* **exec-timeout** *Configuration on Router R2*

```
R2#show run | begin line vty 0 4
line vty 0 4
 exec-timeout 0 1
 password cisco
 login
```

On a separate sheet of paper, write out how you would approach this seemingly paradoxical situation, where you have to log in to the router to correct the configuration, while you will be logged out of the router with only a single second's pause.

Issue #2: Suggested Solution

One fix to this issue is to continuously tap on the keyboard's down arrow with one hand, while using the other hand to enter the commands required to correct the **exec-timeout** misconfiguration. Example 9-11 shows the commands entered to set the **exec-timeout** parameter such that a Telnet session never times out. You could also attach to the console or aux port on the device and change these parameters for the telnet session.

Example 9-11 *Correcting an* **exec-timeout** *Misconfiguration*

```
R2#conf term
R2(config)#line vty 0 4
R2(config-line)#exec-timeout 0 0
```

Issue #3: ACL Misconfiguration

This trouble ticket's final troubleshooting issue was an ACL misconfiguration. The goal of the ACL on router R2 was to prevent Telnet traffic coming in from the backbone (that is, coming in over subinterfaces Serial 1/0.1 or Serial 1/0.2) destined for the loopback interface on router R1 or R2 (that is, IP addresses 10.1.1.1 or 10.2.2.2). Example 9-12 shows the ACL configuration on router R2.

Example 9-12 *Baseline ACL Configuration on Router R2*

```
R2#show run
...OUTPUT OMITTED...
interface s1/0.1
 ip access-group 100 out
!
interface s1/0.2
 ip access-group 100 out
!
access-list 100 deny tcp any host 10.1.1.1 eq telnet
access-list 100 deny tcp any host 10.2.2.2 eq telnet
access-list 100 permit ip any any
```

Based on the trouble ticket and the proceeding **show** command output, on a separate sheet of paper, formulate your strategy for resolving the reported issue.

Issue #3: Suggested Solution

Upon examination, the ACL (an extended IP ACL numbered 100) on router R2 appears to be configured correctly. However, ACL 100 was applied in the outbound direction on router R2's Frame Relay subinterfaces. ACL 100 should have been applied in the incoming direction on these subinterfaces. This suggested solution replaces the incorrect **ip access-group** commands, as shown in Example 9-13.

Example 9-13 *Correcting the Application of ACL 100 on Router R2*

```
R2#conf term
R2(config)#interface s1/0.1
R2(config-if)#no ip access-group 100 out
R2(config-if)#ip access-group 100 in
R2(config-if)#interface s1/0.2
R2(config-if)#no ip access-group 100 out
R2(config-if)#ip access-group 100 in
```

After making the previous update, Telnet connections destined for the Loopback interfaces on routers R1 and R2, coming into router R2 over its Frame Relay subinterfaces are now denied.

Exam Preparation Tasks

Review All Key Topics

Review the most important topics from inside the chapter, noted with the Key Topics icon in the outer margin of the page. Table 9-6 lists these key topics and the page numbers where each is found.

Key Topic

Table 9-6 *Key Topics for Chapter 9*

Key Topic Element	Description	Page Number
List	Three planes of operation	270
List	Three modes of router access	270
List	Ways to protect a network from an STP attack	274
Table 9-2	Mitigations for control plane threats	277
List	Three primary components of an 802.1X network	279
Table 9-3	Types of Cisco IOS firewalls	281
List	Three services offered by a AAA server	285
Table 9-4	Contrasting the TACACS+ and RADIUS protocols	287
List	Troubleshooting common TACACS+ issues	288
List	Troubleshooting common RADIUS issues	288
Table 9-5	Sampling of Cisco IOS security troubleshooting syntax	290

Complete the Tables and Lists from Memory

Print a copy of Appendix B, "Memory Tables," (found on the CD) or at least the section for this chapter, and complete the tables and lists from memory. Appendix C, "Memory Tables Answer Key," also on the CD, includes completed tables and lists to check your work.

Define Key Terms

Define the following key terms from this chapter, and check your answers in the Glossary:

intrusion prevention system (IPS), intrusion detection system (IDS), virtual private network (VPN), access control list (ACL), management plane, control plane, data plane, Root Guard, BPDU Guard, DHCP snooping, Dynamic ARP Inspection (DAI), Classic Cisco IOS Firewall, Zone-Based Policy Firewall, authentication, authorization, accounting

Command Reference to Check Your Memory

This section includes the most important configuration and EXEC commands covered in this chapter. To determine how well you have memorized the commands as a side effect of your other studies, cover the left side of the table with a piece of paper, read the descriptions on the right side, and see whether you remember the command.

Table 9-7 *Chapter 9 Configuration Command Reference*

Command	Description
ip inspect audit-trail	Global configuration mode command that causes a router to generate syslog messages whenever the router creates a new stateful inspection session.
aaa new-model	Global configuration mode command used to enable AAA services on a router.
aaa authentication login *method-list* **group tacacs+**	Global configuration mode command that defines a method list that requires authentication via a TACACS+ server for logins.
tacacs-server host *ip-address* **key** *key*	Global configuration mode command that specifies the IP address of a TACACS+ server for a AAA router to use, along with a key that must match a key configured on the specified TACACS+ server.
login authentication *method-list*	Line configuration mode command that specifies what AAA method list should be used for login authentication for a line (for example, a console line or a VTY line).
exec-timeout *minutes* [*seconds*]	Line configuration mode command that specifies how long the EXEC process running on a line waits for user input before timing out the connection (defaults to 10 minutes).
access-list number {**deny** | **permit**} *protocol source wildcard-mask destination wildcard-mask* [**eq** port-number] [**log**]	Global configuration mode command that creates an extended IP access list, where the access list number is in the range 100–199.
confreg 0x2142	ROM Monitor command that configures a router to ignore its startup configuration when it boots.
reset	ROM Monitor command that causes a router to reboot.

Table 9-7 *Chapter 9 Configuration Command Reference*   *(Continued)*

Command	Description
config-register 0x2102	Global configuration mode command that configures a router to use its startup configuration the next time the router boots.
enable secret *password*	Global configuration mode command that configures a router's privileged mode password.

Table 9-8 *Chapter 9 EXEC Command Reference*

Command	Description
show ip inspect session	Displays the IP addresses, port numbers, and protocol that make up an inspection session.
show ip inspect session detail	Displays information such as the number of bytes sent and received by both the inspection session initiator and responder.
show ip inspect session all	Displays information about an interface's inspection configuration.
debug ip inspect object-creation	Displays information such as the initiator's and responder's IP addresses, the ACL being used, and the Layer 4 protocol (for example, TCP or UDP) in use.
debug aaa authentication	Displays real-time information for authentication attempts on a router configured for AAA authentication.
debug aaa authorization	Displays real-time information for authorization requests on a router configured for AAA authorization.
debug aaa accounting	Displays real-time accounting information for a router configured for AAA accounting.
show access-lists	Displays access lists configured on a router.
show logging	Displays output collected from logged access list entries.

This chapter covers the following subjects:

NAT Troubleshooting: This section begins by reviewing the purpose and basic operation of Network Address Translation (NAT). As a reference, sample topologies are provided, along with their configurations. Common NAT troubleshooting targets are identified, and a syntax reference is provided to aid in troubleshooting NAT issues.

DHCP Troubleshooting: This section reviews basic Dynamic Host Configuration Protocol (DHCP) operation and various types of DHCP messages. You are given three configuration examples corresponding to the three roles a router can play in a DHCP environment: DHCP relay agent, DHCP client, and DHCP server. Common DHCP troubleshooting targets are reviewed, along with recommended DHCP troubleshooting practices. Finally, this section presents a collection of commands that might prove useful in troubleshooting a suspected DHCP issue.

Trouble Ticket: NAT: This section presents you with a trouble ticket and an associated topology. You are also given **show** and **debug** command output that confirms the reported issue. Then you are challenged to hypothesize how to correct the reported issue. At that point you can compare your solution against a suggested one.

CHAPTER 10

IP Services Troubleshooting

This chapter begins by reviewing a common IP service found at the boundary of many networks: NAT. The NAT service allows a company to use as many private IP addresses as they need for devices inside of their network and then translate those addresses into publicly routable IP addresses. This translation is possible even if the number of a company's private IP addresses is greater than the number of its allocated public IP addresses. Although NAT does a great job of IP address conservation by using private IP address space, adding NAT to a network does introduce potential troubleshooting concerns. Not every application coexists peacefully with NAT, and adding a NAT configuration to a router comes with the possibility that there will be one or more errors in that configuration. Therefore, this chapter discusses common NAT troubleshooting issues and provides a syntax guide for effectively troubleshooting those issues.

Another common IP service addressed in this chapter is DCHP. Realize that a router might be a DHCP client, where one (or more) of its interfaces obtains an IP address from an external DHCP server. Alternatively, a router can be configured to act as a DHCP server. A router can also serve as a DHCP relay agent, which allows DHCP client broadcast traffic (that is, broadcast traffic a DHCP client sends in an attempt to dynamically discover a DHCP server) to be forwarded through the router, even though a router typically blocks broadcast traffic. DHCP troubleshooting issues and tips are provided along with monitoring, troubleshooting, and configuration syntax for DHCP.

Finally, this chapter challenges you with a trouble ticket addressing NAT. You are guided through a data collection process that confirms a reported issue. Based on the information collected, you identify a probable cause for the issue and construct a plan to resolve the issue. A suggested solution is provided, which you can compare against your own solution.

"Do I Know This Already?" Quiz

The "Do I Know This Already?" quiz helps you determine your level of knowledge of this chapter's topics before you begin. Table 10-1 details the major topics discussed in this chapter and their corresponding quiz questions.

Table 10-1   *"Do I Know This Already?" Section-to-Question Mapping*

Foundation Topics Section	Questions
NAT Troubleshooting	1–5
DHCP Troubleshooting	6–9

1. What type of NAT uses a one-to-one mapping of private internal IP addresses to public external IP addresses?

    a. Static NAT

    b. Dynamic NAT

    c. NAT Overloading

    d. Overlapping NAT

2. What NAT IP address is a public IP address that references an inside device?

    a. Inside Local

    b. Inside Global

    c. Outside Local

    d. Outside Global

3. Which three of the following are potential NAT troubleshooting issues? (Choose the three best answers.)

    a. Using NAT over a VPN

    b. NAT being incompatible with the version of Cisco IOS used on a router

    c. NAT hiding true IP address information

    d. Applications that are not NAT compatible

4. Which two of the following interface operations occur after NAT performs its translation of a global address to an inside address, as traffic comes into an interface? (Choose the two best answers.)

    a. Decryption of IPsec traffic

    b. Output ACL applied

    c. Input ACL applied

    d. Cisco IOS Firewall inspection performed

5. Which command removes all dynamic entries from a router's NAT translation table?

    a. erase ip nat *

    b. clear ip nat translation *

    c. write erase ip nat *

    d. clear nat all

6. Identify the four DHCP messages that are exchanged between a DHCP client and server as the client is obtaining an IP address. (Choose the four best answers.)

    a. DHCPREQUEST

    b. DHCPDISCOVER

    c. DHCPOFFER

    d. DHCPRELEASE

    e. DHCPACK

7. Which two of the following protocols are forwarded by a DCHP relay agent, in addition to DHCP? (Choose the two best answers.)

    a. TFTP

    b. FTP

    c. DNS

    d. NTP

8. Which of the following is most likely a DHCP troubleshooting issue? (Choose the best answer.)

    a. A router not forwarding multicasts

    b. A router not forwarding broadcasts

    c. The DHCP server service not manually started

    d. Switches in the topology not configured to support IGMP snooping

9. Which of the following commands releases all current DHCP leases?

    a. erase ip dhcp binding *

    b. clear ip dhcp binding *

    c. clear ip dhcp mapping *

    d. delete ip dhcp binding *

Foundation Topics

NAT Troubleshooting

Some IP addresses are routable through the public Internet, whereas others are considered private and are intended for use within an organization. Because these private IP addresses might need to communicate outside of their local networks, NAT allows private IP addresses (as defined in RFC 1918) to be translated into Internet-routable IP addresses (that is, public IP addresses).

Types of NAT

Table 10-2 identifies four types of NAT.

Table 10-2 *Types of NAT*

Type of NAT	Description
Static NAT	A one-to-one mapping of private internal IP addresses to public external IP addresses
Dynamic NAT	A dynamic mapping of private internal IP addresses to a pool of public external IP addresses
NAT Overloading	Allows multiple private internal IP addresses to use a single public external IP address by keeping track of Layer 4 port numbers, which make each session unique (that is, Port Address Translation [PAT])
Overlapping NAT	Used when private internal IP addresses at one location overlap destination private internal IP addresses at another location

Sample NAT Topology

Consider Figure 10-1, which shows a basic NAT topology. Note that even though the IP addresses of 172.16.1.1 and 192.168.1.1 are actually private IP addresses, for the purpose of this discussion, assume they are publicly routable IP addresses. The reason for the use of these private IP addresses to represent public IP addresses is to avoid using an entity's registered IP address in the example.

In the topology, a client with a private IP address of 10.1.1.1 wants to communicate with a server on the public Internet. The IP address of the server is 192.168.1.1. Router R1 is configured for NAT. Router R1 takes packets coming from 10.1.1.1 destined for 192.168.1.1 and changes the source IP address in the packet headers to 172.16.1.1 (which is assumed to be a publicly routable IP address for the purposes of this discussion). When the server at IP address 192.168.1.1 receives traffic from the client, the return traffic of the server is sent to a destination address of 172.16.1.1. When router R1 receives traffic from the outside network destined for 172.16.1.1, the router translates the destination IP address to 10.1.1.1 and forwards the traffic to the inside network, where the client receives the traffic.

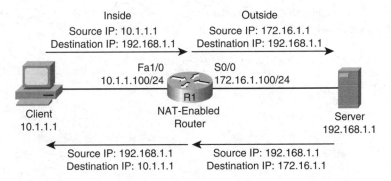

Figure 10-1 *Basic NAT Topology*

To effectively troubleshoot a NAT configuration, you should be familiar with the terminology describing the various IP addresses involved in a translation, as outlined in Table 10-3.

Table 10-3 *Names of NAT IP Addresses*

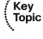

Advantage	Definition
Inside Local	A private IP address referencing an inside device
Inside Global	A public IP address referencing an inside device
Outside Local	A private IP address referencing an outside device
Outside Global	A public IP address referencing an outside device

As a memory aid, remember that *inside* always refers to an inside device, whereas *outside* always refers to an outside device. Also, think of the word *local* as being similar to the Spanish word *loco*, which means crazy. That is what a local address could be thought of. It is a crazy made-up address (that is, a private IP address not routable on the Internet). Finally, let the *g* in *global* remind you of the *g* in *good*, because a global address is a good (that is, routable on the Internet) IP address.

Based on these definitions, Table 10-4 categorizes the IP addresses previously shown in Figure 10-1.

Table 10-4 *Classifying the NAT IP Addresses in Figure 10-1*

Advantage	NAT IP Address Type
Inside Local	10.1.1.1
Inside Global	172.16.1.1
Outside Local	None
Outside Global	192.168.1.1

Again, refer to Figure 10-1. Example 10-1 shows how router R1 in that figure can be configured for dynamic NAT to support the translation shown.

Example 10-1 *Dynamic NAT Sample Configuration*

```
R1# show run
...OUTPUT OMITTED...
interface FastEthernet1/0
 ip address 10.1.1.100 255.255.255.0
 ip nat inside
!
interface Serial 0/0
 ip address 172.16.1.100 255.255.255.0
 ip nat outside
!
ip nat pool OUTSIDE_POOL 172.16.1.1 172.16.1.10 netmask 255.255.255.0
ip nat inside source list 1 pool OUTSIDE_POOL
!
access-list 1 permit 10.0.0.0 0.0.0.255
...OUTPUT OMITTED...
```

In the example, ACL 1 identifies the inside addresses (the 10.1.1.0/24 network in this example) to be translated. A pool of addresses named OUTSIDE_POOL is defined as IP addresses in the range 172.16.1.1 to 172.16.1.10. **The ip nat inside source list 1 pool OUTSIDE_POOL** command associates the internal range of addresses defined by ACL 1 with the range of outside addresses defined by the **OUTSIDE_POOL** pool. Finally, you need to indicate what router interface is acting as the inside interface and what interface is acting as the outside interface. Note that you can have multiple interfaces acting as inside or outside interfaces. The **ip nat inside** command is issued for interface Fast Ethernet 1/0, and the **ip nat outside** command is issued for Serial 0/0.

Potential NAT Troubleshooting Issues

From a troubleshooting perspective, adding NAT into a network introduces potential troubleshooting issues. Consider the following situations in which NAT might cause an issue for end users:

- **Using NAT over a VPN:** Some VPN protocols check the checksum of a packet to verify its integrity. The checksum calculated for a packet before NAT is different from a checksum calculated for that same packet after NAT (because performing NAT on a packet changes IP address information). Therefore, a VPN protocol (for example, IPsec) might reject such a packet because it appears to have been altered. Workarounds are available, including NAT Traversal, NAT Transparency, and IPsec over TCP/UDP.

- **NAT hiding true IP address information:** Because NAT translates an inside IP address to an outside IP address, tracing a data flow from end to end for troubleshooting purposes can be challenging. You can start troubleshooting by using the **show ip**

nat translation command to verify whether the translation does exist in the translation table.

■ **Applications that are not NAT compatible:** When some applications initialize, they randomly determine what ports are going to be used for communication, which might be incompatible with how NAT handles incoming traffic. Some Voice over IP (VoIP) protocols face such an issue, as they select the User Datagram Protocol (UDP) port numbers to be used for their Real-time Transport Protocol (RTP) media streams. Also, when setting up communication with a remote device, an application might include IP address information in the payload of a packet. If the remote device attempted to return traffic to the IP address embedded in that payload, that IP address might be unreachable because of the NAT translation. Therefore, you should avoid NAT for some applications; use NAT-aware applications, or configure NAT to work with NAT-unaware applications.

■ **Delays experienced due to NAT's processing:** Because NAT manipulates Layer 3 information of packets, the packets are subject to a bit more delay than they would otherwise experience. This delay might become more evident on routers performing numerous NAT translations.

Order of Operations for an Interface

Also critical for troubleshooting is an understanding of when NAT performs its translation in relation to other interface operations, such as evaluating an ACL. This order of operations depends on the direction of the traffic flow (that is, flowing from the inside network to the outside network or vice versa). Following is a listing of the order of interface operations for traffic flowing from the inside network into the outside network:

Key Topic

1. Decryption of IPsec traffic

2. Input ACL applied

3. Input policing applied

4. Input accounting applied

5. Policy-based routing (PBR)

6. Redirecting traffic to a web cache

7. NAT translating local to global addresses

8. Crypto map application

9. Output ACL applied

10. Cisco IOS Firewall inspection performed

11. TCP intercept feature applied

12. Encryption performed

Following is a listing of the order of interface operations for traffic flowing from the outside network into the inside network. Notice, for example, that an output ACL might need to reference a translated IP address for a packet as opposed to the original IP address of the packet.

1. Decryption of IPsec traffic

2. Input ACL applied

3. Input policing applied

4. Input accounting applied

5. NAT translating global to local addresses

6. Policy Based Routing (PBR)

7. Redirecting traffic to a web cache

8. Crypto map application

9. Output ACL applied

10. Cisco IOS Firewall inspection performed

11. TCP intercept feature applied

12. Encryption performed

Now that you have reviewed the basic operation of NAT, consider some of the most common causes for a NAT issue:

- An ACL referenced by a NAT configuration is incorrect.

- Inside and outside interfaces are not correctly assigned.

- Incorrect IP addresses (or address ranges) are referenced by a NAT configuration.

- Applications are not NAT aware.

- A routing loop occurs as a result of a NAT address translation.

NAT Troubleshooting Syntax

Table 10-5 provides a reference table of commands that could be useful in troubleshooting a NAT configuration.

Table 10-5 *NAT Troubleshooting Commands*

Command	Description
clear ip nat translation *	Removes all dynamic entries from a router's NAT translation table
show ip nat translations	Used to see all entries in a router's NAT translation table

Table 10-5 *NAT Troubleshooting Commands*   *(Continued)*

Command	Description
show ip nat statistics	Used to display NAT configuration and statistical information on a router, such as inside and outside interfaces, total translations, number of expired translations, inside address ACL, and outside address pool information
debug ip nat	Provides real-time information about NAT translations as they occur, including the IP address being translated and the IP identification number that can be used to match packets in the output with packets captured with a protocol analyzer
ip nat pool *pool-name start-ip end-ip* {netmask *subnet-mask* | prefix-length *prefix-length*}	Global configuration mode command that defines a pool of inside global addresses into which inside local addresses can be translated
ip nat inside source list *access-list* pool *pool-name* [overload]	Global configuration mode command that associates an ACL defining an inside local address space with the specified pool of inside global addresses (Note: The **overload** keyword enables PAT, which allows multiple inside addresses to share a common outside address.)
ip nat translation max-entries *number*	Global configuration mode command that specifies the maximum number of entries permitted in a router's NAT table
ip nat {inside | outside}	Interface configuration mode command that identifies an interface as an inside or outside NAT interface

Example 10-2 provides sample output from the **show ip nat translations** command and how to change this output with the **clear ip nat translation** * command. Initially, the **show ip nat translations** command shows three statically configured NAT translations and one dynamically learned translation (which is highlighted in the output). Then, after issuing the **clear ip nat translation** * command, the dynamically learned NAT entry is deleted from the IP NAT table, leaving the three statically configured NAT entries.

Example 10-2   show ip nat translations *and* clear ip nat translation * *Command Output*

```
R1# show ip nat translations
Pro Inside global      Inside local      Outside local       Outside global
--- 192.168.1.12       192.168.0.1       ---                 ---
--- 192.168.1.13       192.168.0.2       ---                 ---
tcp 192.168.1.27:23    192.168.0.27:23   192.168.1.50:1158   192.168.1.50:1158
--- 192.168.1.27       192.168.0.27      ---                 ---
```

```
R1# clear ip nat translation *
R1# show ip nat translations
Pro Inside global      Inside local      Outside local      Outside global
--- 192.168.1.12       192.168.0.1       ---                ---
--- 192.168.1.13       192.168.0.2       ---                ---
--- 192.168.1.27       192.168.0.27      ---                ---
```

Example 10-3 provides sample output from the **show ip nat statistics** command. The output shows which interfaces are acting as the inside and outside interfaces and the current number of static and dynamic translations.

Example 10-3   show ip nat statistics *Command Output*

```
R1#show ip nat statistics
Total active translations: 4 (3 static, 1 dynamic; 1 extended)
Outside interfaces:
  FastEthernet0/0
Inside interfaces:
  FastEthernet0/1
Hits: 10   Misses: 0
CEF Translated packets: 5, CEF Punted packets: 0
Expired translations: 0
Dynamic mappings:
Appl doors: 0
Normal doors: 0
Queued Packets: 0
```

Example 10-4 provides sample output from the **debug ip nat** command. The output shows that when a source IP address of 192.168.1.50 is attempting to communicate with a destination IP address of 192.168.1.27, the router translates the destination IP address into 192.168.0.27. Also, when a source IP address of 192.168.1.11 is attempting to communicate with a destination IP address of 192.168.1.50, the router translates the source IP address of 192.168.1.11 into an IP address of 192.168.1.27.

Example 10-4   debug ip nat *Command Output*

```
R1#debug ip nat
IP NAT debugging is on
*Mar  3 13:01:28.162: NAT*: s=192.168.1.50, d=192.168.1.27->192.168.0.27 [10202]
*Mar  3 13:01:28.162: NAT: s=192.168.1.11->192.168.1.27, d=192.168.1.50 [210]
*Mar  3 13:01:30.991: NAT*: s=192.168.1.50, d=192.168.1.27->192.168.0.27 [10370]
```

```
*Mar  3 13:01:30.991: NAT: s=192.168.1.11->192.168.1.27, d=192.168.1.50 [211]
*Mar  3 13:01:37.025: NAT*: s=192.168.1.50, d=192.168.1.27->192.168.0.27 [10540]
*Mar  3 13:01:37.029: NAT: s=192.168.1.11->192.168.1.27, d=192.168.1.50 [214]
```

DHCP Troubleshooting

DHCP serves as one of the most common methods of assigning IP address information to a network host. Specifically, DHCP allows a DHCP client to obtain an IP address, subnet mask, default gateway IP address, DNS server IP address, and other types of IP address information from a DHCP server.

If you have a cable modem or DSL connection in your home, your cable modem or DSL router might obtain its IP address from your service provider via DHCP. In many corporate networks, when a PC boots up, that PC receives its IP address configuration information from a corporate DHCP server.

Basic DHCP Operation

Figure 10-2 illustrates the exchange of messages that occur as a DHCP client obtains IP address information from a DHCP server.

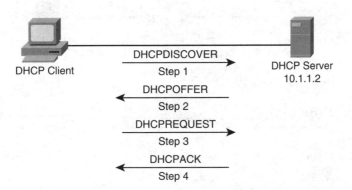

Figure 10-2 *Obtaining IP Address Information from a DHCP Server*

Step 1.   When a DHCP client initially boots, it has no IP address, default gateway, or other such configuration information. Therefore, the way a DHCP client initially communicates is by sending a broadcast message (that is, a DHCPDISCOVER message) to a destination address of 255.255.255.255 in an attempt to discover a DHCP server.

Step 2.   When a DHCP server receives a DHCPDISCOVER message, it can respond with a DHCPOFFER message. Because the DHCPDISCOVER message is sent as a broadcast, more than one DHCP server might respond to this discover request. However, the client typically selects the server that sent the first DHCPOFFER response it received.

Step 3.   The DHCP client communicates with this selected server by sending a DHCPREQUEST message asking the DHCP server to provide IP configuration parameters.

Step 4.   Finally, the DHCP server responds to the client with a DHCPACK message. This DHCPACK message contains a collection of IP configuration parameters.

Notice that in Step 1, the DHCPDISCOVER message was sent as a broadcast. By default, a broadcast cannot cross a router boundary. Therefore, if a client resides on a different network than the DHCP server, the next-hop router of the client should be configured as a DHCP relay agent. You can use the **ip helper-address** *ip-address* interface configuration mode command to configure a router interface to relay DHCP requests to either a unicast IP address or a directed broadcast address.

DHCP Configurations

To illustrate the configuration of DHCP, consider Figure 10-3 and Example 10-5. In the figure, the DHCP client belongs to the 172.16.1.0/24 network, whereas the DHCP server belongs to the 10.1.1.0/24 network. Router R1 is configured as a DHCP relay agent, using the syntax shown in Example 10-5.

Figure 10-3   *DHCP Relay Agent*

Key
Topic

Example 10-5   *DHCP Relay Agent Configuration*

```
R1# conf term
Enter configuration commands, one per line.   End with CNTL/Z.
R1(config)# service dhcp
R1(config)# interface fa 0/0
R1(config-if)# ip helper-address 10.1.1.2
```

In the configuration, notice the **service dhcp** command. This command enables the DHCP service on the router, which must be enabled for the DHCP relay agent feature to function. This command is typically not required, because the DHCP service is enabled by default; however, when troubleshooting a DHCP relay agent issue, you might want to confirm that the service is enabled. Also, the **ip helper-address 10.1.1.2** command specifies the IP address of the DHCP server, although the **ip helper-address 10.1.1.255** command could have been used instead. Specifically, 10.1.1.255 is the directed broadcast IP address for the 10.1.1.0/24 network. Although using a directed broadcast address might enable you to reach all DHCP servers on a particular subnet, Cisco recommends that you use a specific IP address as opposed to a directed broadcast. One reason for this recommendation is that a directed broadcast causes all hosts on the target subnet to examine the DHCPDISCOVER packet, even if those hosts are not DHCP servers. Yet another rationale for this recommendation is that some routers block directed broadcasts (because of a potential security risk).

When you configure a router to act as a DHCP relay agent, realize that it relays a few other broadcast types in addition to a DHCP message. Some other protocols that are forwarded by a DHCP relay agent include the following:

- TFTP
- Domain Name System (DNS)
- Internet Time Service (ITS)
- NetBIOS name server
- NetBIOS datagram server
- BootP
- TACACS

As a reference, Table 10-6 provides a comprehensive listing of DHCP message types you might encounter while troubleshooting a DHCP issue.

Table 10-6   *DHCP Message Types*

DHCP Message	Description
DHCPDISCOVER	A client sends this message in an attempt to locate a DHCP server. This message is sent to a broadcast IP address of 255.255.255.255 using UDP port 67.
DHCPOFFER	A DHCP server sends this message in response to a DHCPDISCOVER message using UDP port 68.
DHCPREQUEST	This message is a request for IP configuration parameters sent from a client to a specific DHCP server.
DHCPDECLINE	This message is sent from a client to a DHCP server to inform the server that an IP address is already in use on the network.
DHCPACK	A DHCP server sends this message to a client and includes IP configuration parameters.
DHCPNAK	A DHCP server sends this message to a client and informs the client that the DHCP server declines to provide the client with the requested IP configuration information.
DHCPRELEASE	A client sends this message to a DHCP server and informs the DHCP server that the client has released its DHCP lease, thus allowing the DHCP server to reassign the client IP address to another client.
DHCPINFORM	This message is sent from a client to a DHCP server and requests IP configuration parameters. Such a message might be sent from an access server requesting IP configuration information for a remote client attaching to the access server.

In addition to acting as a DHCP relay agent, a router might act as a DHCP client. Specifically, the interface of a router might obtain its IP address from a DHCP server. Also, a router can act as a DHCP server. The text that follows considers each scenario.

Figure 10-4 shows a router acting as a DHCP client, where the router's Fast Ethernet 0/0 interface obtains its IP address from a DHCP server. Example 10-6 provides the configuration for the router in the topology (that is, router R1). Notice the **dhcp** option used in the **ip address** command, instead of the usual IP address and subnet mask information.

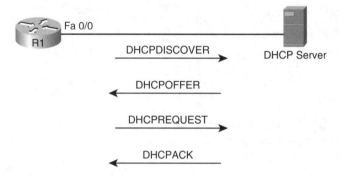

Figure 10-4   *Router Acting as a DHCP Client*

Example 10-6   *DHCP Client Configuration*

```
R1#conf term
R1(config)#int fa 0/0
R1(config-if)#ip address dhcp
```

Figure 10-5 shows a router acting as a DHCP server, and Example 10-7 shows the router configuration. The **ip dhcp excluded-address 10.8.8.1** command prevents DHCP from assigning the 10.8.8.1 IP address to a client. This exclusion occurs because this IP address is one of the interfaces of the router. The **ip dhcp pool POOL-A** command creates a DHCP pool named **POOL-A**. This pool can hand out IP addresses from the 10.8.8.0/24 network, with a default gateway of 10.8.8.1, a DNS server of 192.168.1.1, and a WINS server of 192.168.1.2.

Example 10-7   *DHCP Server Configuration*

```
R1#show run
...OUTPUT OMITTED...
ip dhcp excluded-address 10.8.8.1
!
ip dhcp pool POOL-A
   network 10.8.8.0 255.255.255.0
   default-router 10.8.8.1
   dns-server 192.168.1.1
   netbios-name-server 192.168.1.2
...OUTPUT OMITTED...
```

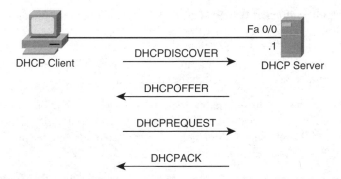

Figure 10-5 *Router Acting as a DHCP Server*

Potential DHCP Troubleshooting Issues

When troubleshooting what you suspect might be a DHCP issue, consider the following potential issues:

- **A router not forwarding broadcasts:** By default, a router does not forward broadcasts, including DHCPDISCOVER broadcast messages. Therefore, a router needs to be explicitly configured to act as a DHCP relay agent if the DHCP client and DHCP server are on different subnets.

- **DHCP pool out of IP addresses:** A DHCP pool contains a finite number of addresses. Once a DCHP pool becomes depleted, new DHCP requests are rejected.

- **Misconfiguration:** The configuration of a DHCP server might be incorrect. For example, the range of network addresses to be given out by a particular pool might be incorrect, or the exclusion of addresses statically assigned to routers or DNS servers might be incorrect.

- **Duplicate IP addresses:** A DHCP server might hand out an IP address to a client that is already statically assigned to another host on the network. These duplicate IP addresses can cause connectivity issues for both the DHCP client and the host that had been statically configured for the IP address.

- **Redundant services not communicating:** Some DHCP servers can coexist with other DHCP servers for redundancy. For this redundancy to function, these DHCP servers need to communicate with one another. If this interserver communication fails, the DHCP servers can hand out overlapping IP addresses to their clients.

- **The "pull" nature of DHCP:** When a DHCP client wants an IP address, it can request an IP address from a DHCP server. However, the DHCP server has no ability to initiate a change in the client IP address after the client obtains an IP address. In other words, the DHCP client pulls information from the DHCP server, but the DHCP server cannot push information to the DHCP client.

At this point in this section, you have reviewed basic DHCP operations and potential DHCP troubleshooting targets. When you begin your troubleshooting efforts, you might want to collect the following information to help you better isolate the underlying cause of the DHCP issue you are investigating.

- **The configuration of the DHCP server:** For example, confirm that the pools are correctly defined with appropriate network addresses, default gateways, and other relevant IP address information.

- **The configuration of the DHCP relay agent:** For example, determine if the target addresses a unicast IP address or a directed broadcast address.

- **Determine the size of a DHCP pool:** Because a pool in a DHCP server accommodates only a limited number of IP addresses, determine how many IP addresses (if any) are still available from a given DHCP pool.

DHCP Troubleshooting Syntax

Table 10-7 provides a collection of commands that can be useful in troubleshooting a DHCP issue.

Table 10-7   *DHCP Troubleshooting Commands*

Command	Description
show ip dhcp conflict	Identifies any IP address conflicts a router identifies, along with the method the router used to identify the conflicts (this is, via ping or gratuitous ARP)
show ip dhcp binding	Displays IP addresses that an IOS DHCP server assigns, their corresponding MAC addresses, and lease expirations
clear ip dhcp binding *	Releases all current DHCP leases
clear ip dhcp conflict *	Clears all currently identified DHCP conflicts
debug ip dhcp server events	Provides real-time information about DHCP address assignments and database updates
debug ip dhcp server packet	Displays real-time decodes of DHCP packets

Table 10-7 *DHCP Troubleshooting Commands*

Command	Description
ip helper-address *ip-address*	Interface configuration mode command that causes an interface to forward specific received UDP broadcasts to the destination IP address, which can be either a specific IP address or a directed broadcast address
ip dhcp excluded-address *beginning-ip-address* [*ending-ip-address*]	Specifies a range of IP addresses not to be assigned to DHCP clients
ip dhcp pool *pool-name*	Creates a DHCP pool
network *network-address subnet-mask*	Identifies a subnet to be used by a DHCP pool
default-router *ip-address*	Specifies the IP address of a default gateway to be given to a DHCP client
dns-server *ip-address*	Configures the IP address of a DNS server to be given to a DHCP client
netbios-name-server *ip-address*	Defines the IP address of a WINS server to be given to a DHCP client
lease {*days hours minutes* | *infinite*}	Determines the duration of a DHCP lease given to a DHCP client

Example 10-8 provides sample output from the **show ip dhcp conflict** command. The output indicates a duplicate 172.16.1.3 IP address on the network, which the router discovered via a ping. You can resolve this conflict by issuing the **clear ip dhcp conflict *** command.

Example 10-8   show ip dhcp conflict *Command Output*

```
R1#show ip dhcp conflict
IP address         Detection method   Detection time
172.16.1.3         Ping               Oct 15 2009 8:56 PM
```

Example 10-9 shows sample output from the **show ip dhcp binding** command. The output indicates that an IP address of 10.1.1.2 was assigned to a DHCP client with a MAC address of 3030.312e.3066.3163. You can release this DHCP lease with the **clear ip dhcp binding *** command.

Example 10-9   show ip dhcp binding *Command Output*

```
R1#show ip dhcp binding
Bindings from all pools not associated with VRF:
IP address Client-ID/         Lease expiration      Type       Hardware address/
User name
10.1.1.2   0063.6070.000f.2d03.Oct 03 2009 12:03 PM Automatic 3030.312e.3066.3163.
  0e30.3030.302d.4661.
```

Example 10-10 shows sample output from the **debug ip dhcp server events** command. The output shows updates to the DHCP database.

Example 10-10   debug ip dhcp server events *Command Output*

```
R1#debug ip dhcp server events
*Mar  1 00:06:47.427: DHCPD: Seeing if there is an internally specified pool class:
*Mar  1 00:06:47.431:    DHCPD: htype 1 chaddr c001.0f1c.0000
*Mar  1 00:06:47.431:    DHCPD: remote id 020a00000a01010101000000
*Mar  1 00:06:47.435:    DHCPD: circuit id 00000000
*Mar  1 00:06:49.415: DHCPD: Seeing if there is an internally specified pool class:
*Mar  1 00:06:49.419:    DHCPD: htype 1 chaddr c001.0f1c.0000
*Mar  1 00:06:49.419:    DHCPD: remote id 020a00000a01010101000000
*Mar  1 00:06:49.423:    DHCPD: circuit id 00000000
*Mar  1 00:06:52.603: DHCPD: no subnet configured for 192.168.1.238.
```

Example 10-11 shows sample output from the **debug ip dhcp server packet** command. The output shows a DHCPRELEASE message being received when a DHCP client with an IP address of 10.1.1.3 is shut down. You can also see the four-step process of a DHCP client obtaining an IP address of 10.1.1.4 with the following messages: DHCPDISCOVER, DHCPOFFER, DHCPREQUEST, and DHCPACK.

Example 10-11   debug ip dhcp server packet *Command Output*

```
R1#debug ip dhcp server packet
*Mar  1 00:07:39.867: DHCPD: DHCPRELEASE message received from client
  0063.6973.636f.2d63.3030.312e.3066.3163.2e30.3030.302d.4661.302f.30 (10.1.1.3).
*Mar  1 00:07:41.855: DHCPD: DHCPRELEASE message received from client
  0063.6973.636f.2d63.3030.312e.3066.3163.2e30.3030.302d.4661.302f.30 (10.1.1.3).
*Mar  1 00:07:41.859: DHCPD: Finding a relay for client
  0063.6973.636f.2d63.3030.312e.3066.3163.2e30.3030.302d.4661.302f.30 on interface
  FastEthernet0/1.
*Mar  1 00:07:54.775: DHCPD: DHCPDISCOVER received from client
  0063.6973.636f.2d63.3030.312e.3066.3163.2e30.3030.302d.4661.302f.30 on interface
  FastEthernet0/1.
*Mar  1 00:07:54.779: DHCPD: Allocate an address without class information
  (10.1.1.0)
*Mar  1 00:07:56.783: DHCPD: Sending DHCPOFFER to client
  0063.6973.636f.2d63.3030.312e.3066.3163.2e30.3030.302d.4661.302f.30 (10.1.1.4).
*Mar  1 00:07:56.787: DHCPD: broadcasting BOOTREPLY to client c001.0f1c.0000.
```

```
*Mar  1 00:07:56.879: DHCPD: DHCPREQUEST received from client
   0063.6973.636f.2d63.3030.312e.3066.3163.2e30.3030.302d.4661.302f.30.
*Mar  1 00:07:56.887: DHCPD: No default domain to append - abort update
*Mar  1 00:07:56.887: DHCPD: Sending DHCPACK to client
   0063.6973.636f.2d63.3030.312e.3066.3163.2e30.3030.302d.4661.302f.30 (10.1.1.4).
*Mar  1 00:07:56.891: DHCPD: broadcasting BOOTREPLY to client c001.0f1c.0000.
```

Trouble Ticket: NAT

This trouble ticket focuses on the previously discussed IP service of NAT. You are presented with a trouble ticket detailing an issue that needs resolution. You are given sample **show** and **debug** command output and are then challenged to identify a resolution for the issue described.

Trouble Ticket #8

You receive the following trouble ticket:

Company A is dual-homed out to the Internet (that is, routers BB1 and BB2, where each router represents a different ISP). Inside IP addresses in the 192.168.0.0/24 subnet should be translated into the IP address of interface Serial 1/0.1 on router R2, whereas inside IP addresses in the 192.168.1.0/24 subnet should be translated into the IP address of interface Serial 1/0.2 on router R2. Router R2's NAT translation table shows two active translations. The configuration, therefore, seems to be partially working. However, no additional NAT translations can be set up.

This trouble ticket references the topology shown in Figure 10-6.

Because router R2 is the one configured to perform NAT, the following **show** and **debug** command output collects information about the NAT configuration of router R2. Initially, notice the output of the **show ip nat translations** command issued on router R2, as shown in Example 10-12.

Example 10-12 show ip nat translations *Command Output on Router R2*

```
R2#show ip nat translations
Pro Inside global      Inside local       Outside local      Outside global
icmp 172.16.1.2:7      192.168.0.11:7     10.4.4.4:7         10.4.4.4:7
icmp 172.16.2.1:512    192.168.1.50:512   10.1.3.2:512       10.1.3.2:512
```

The **debug ip nat** command is issued next. The output provided in Example 10-13 shows NAT translations as they occur.

Example 10-13 debug ip nat *Command Output on Router R2*

```
R2#debug ip nat
IP NAT debugging is on
*Mar  1 00:34:16.651: NAT*: s=10.4.4.4, d=172.16.1.2->192.168.0.11 [4092]
*Mar  1 00:34:16.711: NAT*: s=192.168.0.11->172.16.1.2, d=10.4.4.4 [4093]
*Mar  1 00:34:16.843: NAT*: s=10.4.4.4, d=172.16.1.2->192.168.0.11 [4093]
```

```
*Mar  1 00:34:16.939: NAT*: s=192.168.0.11->172.16.1.2, d=10.4.4.4 [4094]
*Mar  1 00:34:16.963: NAT*: s=192.168.1.50->172.16.2.1, d=10.1.3.2 [13977]
*Mar  1 00:34:17.115: NAT*: s=10.4.4.4, d=172.16.1.2->192.168.0.11 [4094]
*Mar  1 00:34:17.163: NAT*: s=192.168.0.11->172.16.1.2, d=10.4.4.4 [4095]
*Mar  1 00:34:17.187: NAT*: s=10.1.3.2, d=172.16.2.1->192.168.1.50 [13977]
*Mar  1 00:34:17.315: NAT*: s=10.4.4.4, d=172.16.1.2->192.168.0.11 [4095]
```

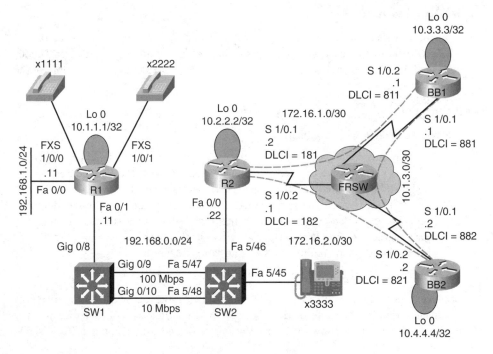

Figure 10-6   *Trouble Ticket #8 Topology*

The trouble ticket indicated that no more than two active translations can be supported at any time. To verify that symptom, Example 10-14 shows an attempt to send a ping from router R1. Notice that the ping response indicates that 10.4.4.4 is unreachable.

Example 10-14   *Attempting to Ping 10.4.4.4 from Router R1*

```
R1#ping 10.4.4.4

Type escape sequence to abort.
Sending 5, 100-byte ICMP Echos to 10.4.4.4, timeout is 2 seconds:
U.U.U
Success rate is 0 percent (0/5)
```

To determine whether the inability to ping 10.4.4.4 is a result of NAT or some other issue, the NAT translation table on router R2 is cleared with the **clear ip nat translation** * command. Then, with the NAT translation table of router R2 cleared, Example 10-15 shows the result of another ping from router R1 to 10.4.4.4. This time, the ping is successful.

Example 10-15   *Reattempting to Ping 10.4.4.4 from Router R1*

```
R1#ping 10.4.4.4

Type escape sequence to abort.
Sending 5, 100-byte ICMP Echos to 10.4.4.4, timeout is 2 seconds:
!!!!!
Success rate is 100 percent (5/5), round-trip min/avg/max = 72/137/240 ms
```

Example 10-16 shows the NAT translation table of router R2 after R1 performs a ping to 10.4.4.4.

Example 10-16   *NAT Translation Table of Router R2*

```
R2#show ip nat translations
Pro Inside global    Inside local     Outside local     Outside global
icmp 172.16.1.2:10   192.168.0.11:10   10.4.4.4:10        10.4.4.4:10
```

The output from the previous commands confirms that router R2 is capable of supporting only two simultaneous NAT translations. This symptom often indicates that a router's NAT pool (or pools in this case) is depleted, perhaps because the NAT configuration did not use the **overload** option in the **ip nat inside source** command. Recall that the **overload** option enables PAT, which allows multiple inside local IP addresses to share a common inside global IP address.

Example 10-17 shows the running configuration of router R2. Interestingly, both the **ip nat inside source** commands have the **overload** option, thus eliminating that as a potential cause for the reported issue.

Example 10-17   *Running Configuration of Router R2*

```
R2# show run
...OUTPUT OMITTED...
hostname R2
!
interface Loopback0
 ip address 10.2.2.2 255.255.255.255
!
interface FastEthernet0/0
 ip address 192.168.0.22 255.255.255.0
```

```
 ip nat inside
!
interface Serial1/0
 no ip address
 encapsulation frame-relay
!
interface Serial1/0.1 point-to-point
 ip address 172.16.1.2 255.255.255.252
 ip nat outside
 frame-relay interface-dlci 181
!
interface Serial1/0.2 point-to-point
 ip address 172.16.2.1 255.255.255.252
 ip nat outside
 ip virtual-reassembly
 frame-relay interface-dlci 182
!
router ospf 1
 network 0.0.0.0 255.255.255.255 area 0
!
ip nat translation max-entries 2
ip nat inside source list 1 interface Serial1/0.2 overload
ip nat inside source list 2 interface Serial1/0.1 overload
!
access-list 1 permit 192.168.1.0 0.0.0.255
access-list 2 permit 192.168.0.0 0.0.0.255
!
...OUTPUT OMITTED...
```

Based on the output of the previous **show** and **debug** commands, on a separate sheet of paper, write out what you believe to be the underlying issue and how you would resolve it.

Suggested Solution

In the running configuration of router R2, you might have noticed the **ip nat translation max-entries 2** command. This command limits the maximum number of NAT translations on router R2 to only two.

To resolve this issue, this configuration command is removed, as shown in Example 10-18.

Example 10-18   *Removing the ip nat translation max-entries 2 Command of Router R2*

```
R2#conf term
Enter configuration commands, one per line.  End with CNTL/Z.
R2(config)#no ip nat translation max-entries 2
R2(config)#end
```

To demonstrate that the removal of the **ip nat translation max-entries 2** command did indeed resolve the reported issue, three NAT translations were established across router R2, as confirmed in Example 10-19.

Example 10-19 *Confirming That Router R2 Supports Multiple NAT Translations*

```
R2#show ip nat translations
Pro Inside global       Inside local      Outside local       Outside global
icmp 172.16.1.2:12      192.168.0.11:12   10.4.4.4:12         10.4.4.4:12
icmp 172.16.2.1:13      192.168.1.11:13   10.3.3.3:13         10.3.3.3:13
icmp 172.16.2.1:512     192.168.1.50:512  10.1.3.2:512        10.1.3.2:512
```

Exam Preparation Tasks

Review All the Key Topics

Key Topic

Review the most important topics from inside the chapter, noted with the Key Topics icon in the outer margin of the page. Table 10-8 lists these key topics and the page numbers where each is found.

Table 10-8 *Key Topics for Chapter 10*

Key Topic Element	Description	Page Number
Table 10-2	Types of NAT	302
Table 10-3	Names of NAT IP addresses	303
Table 10-4	Classifying the NAT IP addresses in Figure 10-1	303
Example 10-1	Dynamic NAT sample configuration	304
List	Potential NAT troubleshooting issues	304
List	Order of operations for an interface	305
List	Common causes for a NAT issue	306
Table 10-5	Table 10-5 NAT troubleshooting commands	306
Steps	Obtaining an IP address from a DHCP server	309
Example 10-5	DHCP relay agent configuration	310
Table 10-6	DHCP message types	311
Example 10-6	DHCP client configuration	312
Example 10-7	DHCP server configuration	312
List	Potential DHCP troubleshooting issues	313
List	Information to collect when investigating a DHCP issue	314
Table 10-7	DHCP troubleshooting commands	314

Complete Tables and Lists from Memory

Print a copy of Appendix B, "Memory Tables" (found on the CD), or at least the section for this chapter, and complete the tables and lists from memory. Appendix C, "Memory Tables Answer Key," also on the CD, includes completed tables and lists to check your work.

Define Key Terms

Define the following key terms from this chapter, and check your answers in the Glossary:

Network Address Translation (NAT), static NAT, dynamic NAT, NAT overloading, overlapping NAT, Dynamic Host Configuration Protocol (DHCP)

Command Reference to Check Your Memory

This section includes the most important configuration and EXEC commands covered in this chapter. To determine how well you have memorized the commands as a side effect of your other studies, cover the left side of the table with a piece of paper; read the descriptions on the right side; and see whether you remember the command.

Table 10-9   *Chapter 10 Configuration Command Reference*

Command	Description
ip nat {inside | outside}	Interface configuration mode command that identifies an interface as an inside or outside NAT interface
ip nat pool *pool-name start-ip end-ip* {netmask *subnet-mask* | prefix-length *prefix-length*}	Global configuration mode command that defines a pool of inside global addresses into which inside local addresses can be translated
ip nat inside source list *access-list* pool *pool-name* [overload]	Global configuration mode command that associates an ACL defining an inside local address space with the specified pool of inside global addresses (Note: The overload keyword enables PAT, which allows multiple inside addresses to share a common outside address.)
ip nat translation max-entries *number*	Global configuration mode command that specifies the maximum number of entries permitted in the NAT table of a router
ip helper-address *ip-address*	Interface configuration mode command that causes an interface to forward specific received UDP broadcasts to the destination IP address, which can be either a specific IP address or a directed broadcast address
ip dhcp excluded-address *beginning-ip-add*ress [*ending-ip-address*]	Global configuration mode command that specifies a range of IP addresses not to be assigned to DHCP clients

continues

Table 10-9 *Chapter 10 Configuration Command Reference (Continued)*

Command	Description
ip dhcp pool *pool-name*	Global configuration mode command that creates a DHCP pool
network *network-address subnet-mask*	DHCP configuration mode command that identifies a subnet to be used by a DHCP pool
default-router *ip-address*	DHCP configuration mode command that specifies the IP address of a default gateway to be given to a DHCP client
dns-server *ip-address*	DHCP configuration mode command that configures the IP address of a DNS server to be given to a DHCP client
netbios-name-server *ip-address*	DHCP configuration mode command that defines the IP address of a WINS server to be given to a DHCP client
lease {*days hours minutes*	**infinite**}	DHCP configuration mode command that determines the duration of a DHCP lease given to a DHCP client
ip address *dhcp*	Interface configuration mode command that tells an interface to obtain its IP address via DHCP

Table 10-10 *Chapter 10 EXEC Command Reference*

Advantage	Limitation
clear ip nat translation *	Removes all dynamic entries from the NAT translation table of a router
show ip nat translations	Shows all entries in the NAT translation table of a router
show ip nat statistics	Displays NAT configuration and statistical information on a router, such as inside and outside interfaces, total translations, number of expired translations, inside address ACL, and outside address pool information
debug ip nat	Provides real-time information about NAT translations as they occur, including the IP address being translated and an IP identification number that can match packets in the output with packets captured with a protocol analyzer
show ip dhcp conflict	Displays any IP address conflicts that a router identifies, along with the method the router used to identify the conflicts (this is, via ping or gratuitous ARP)

Table 10-10   *Chapter 10 EXEC Command Reference   (Continued)*

Advantage	Limitation
show ip dhcp binding	Displays IP addresses assigned by an IOS DHCP server, their corresponding MAC addresses, and lease expirations
clear ip dhcp binding *	Releases all current DHCP leases
clear ip dhcp conflict *	Clears all currently identified DHCP conflicts
debug ip dhcp server events	Provides real-time information about DHCP address assignments and database updates
debug ip dhcp server packet	Displays real-time decodes of DHCP packets

This chapter covers the following subjects:

Voice Troubleshooting: This section introduces you to design and troubleshooting considerations that arise when adding voice traffic to a data network. Several protocols are involved when a Cisco IP Phone registers with its call agent to place and receive voice calls. This section reviews the function of these protocols along with recommendations for troubleshooting voice issues. One of the major troubleshooting targets for voice networks involves quality of service. Therefore, this section concludes by providing an overview of quality of service (QoS) configuration, verification, and troubleshooting commands.

Video Troubleshooting: This section considers video traffic in an IP network, including unique design and troubleshooting challenges. Also, unlike voice, video-based networks often rely on an infrastructure that supports IP multicasting. Because multicasting has not been addressed in any depth thus far in this book, this section serves as a primer to multicast technologies. Included in this primer are commands used to configure, monitor, and troubleshoot multicast networks. Finally, this section considers common video troubleshooting issues and recommends resolutions for those issues.

Trouble Tickets: Unified Communications: This section presents you with two trouble tickets focused on unified communications. You are presented with a topology used by both trouble tickets, in addition to a collection of **show** command output. For each trouble ticket, you are challenged to hypothesize how to correct the reported issue. You can also compare your solutions with suggested solutions.

CHAPTER 11

IP Communications Troubleshooting

Data networks, as the name suggests, were once relegated to being a transmission medium for data; however, network designers have seen the wisdom in combining voice, video, and data on the same network. This type of network, called a *converged network*, can be far more cost effective than maintaining separate networks for each of these media types. This chapter considers the troubleshooting of both voice and video networks.

This chapter begins by introducing voice networks, along with a discussion of how adding voice to a network impacts design decisions. You are also introduced to the roles played by a variety of protocols that allow a Cisco IP Phone to place and receive calls. Common troubleshooting issues for voice networks are addressed, one of which is quality of service.

Because voice traffic is latency-sensitive, the underlying network needs to be able to recognize voice traffic and treat it with high priority. Although a full discussion of quality of service technologies is well beyond the scope of the TSHOOT curriculum, this chapter does provide fundamental configuration, verification, and troubleshooting commands that can get you started in your configuration or troubleshooting of quality of service configurations.

Other than voice, another aspect of IP communications involves sending video over IP networks. For example, you might have an IP-based video conference system, or you might have a video server that sends out a video stream to multiple recipients. This chapter introduces you to some of the video solutions you might encounter, along with unique design and troubleshooting challenges that accompany video networks.

Interestingly, many video networks heavily rely on IP multicast technologies. Therefore, this chapter offers you a mini-course on multicasting, which discusses the theory, configuration, monitoring, and troubleshooting of multicasting.

This chapter concludes with two trouble tickets focused on unified communications. The first trouble ticket addresses an IP phone registration issue, whereas the second trouble ticket addresses a quality of service issue.

"Do I Know This Already?" Quiz

The "Do I Know This Already?" quiz helps you determine your level of knowledge of this chapter's topics before you begin. Table 11-1 details the major topics discussed in this chapter and their corresponding quiz questions.

Table 11-1 *"Do I Know This Already?" Section-to-Question Mapping*

Foundation Topics Section	Questions
Voice Troubleshooting	1–5
Video Troubleshooting	6–9

1. What IP telephony component provides translation between VoIP and non-VoIP networks?

   a. Gatekeeper

   b. Gateway

   c. Call agent

   d. MCU

2. What protocol does a Cisco Catalyst switch use to inform an attached Cisco IP Phone of the VLAN to which the phone belongs?

   a. NTP

   b. DHCP

   c. CDP

   d. TFTP

3. What DHCP option corresponds to the IP address of a TFTP server?

   a. Option 66

   b. Option 80

   c. Option 110

   d. Option 150

4. Which four of the following are common voice troubleshooting targets? (Choose the four best answers.)

   a. Security

   b. IP services

   c. Power

   d. NAT

   e. QoS

5. Identify three valid types of the Cisco AutoQoS feature. (Choose the three best answers.)

   a. AutoQoS Enterprise on a Cisco Catalyst switch

   b. AutoQoS VoIP on a Cisco Catalyst switch

   c. AutoQoS VoIP on a Cisco IOS router

   d. AutoQoS Enterprise on a Cisco IOS router

6. Which video conferencing product offers CD-quality audio and high definition video? (Choose the best answer.)

    a. Cisco Presence Server

    b. Cisco Unified Video Advantage

    c. Cisco TelePresence

    d. Cisco Video Advantage

7. What is the Cisco recommended maximum one-way delay for a video surveillance application?

    a. 150ms

    b. 200ms

    c. 214ms

    d. 500ms

8. What command could be used to display a router's IP multicast routing table?

    a. show ip mroute

    b. show multicast route

    c. show ip route multicast

    d. show mroute

9. Which four of the following are common video troubleshooting targets? (Choose the four best answers.)

    a. Bandwidth

    b. Pervasiveness of video applications

    c. NTP

    d. QoS

    e. Multicast

Foundation Topics

Voice Troubleshooting

Modern enterprise network designs need to support the transmission of voice traffic. This voice traffic can come from both analog phones (much like the phones typically found in homes) and IP phones, which are Ethernet devices that transmit voice IP packets. Because the analog phones cannot generate IP packets, they connect to analog gateways (such as Cisco routers), which convert the analog waveforms into IP packets.

The term *Voice over IP* (VoIP) is used to describe the transmission of voice over an IP network using voice-enabled routers. However, the term *IP telephony* refers to the use of IP phones and a call-processing server (for example, Cisco Unified Communications Manager). More recently, Cisco began using the term *Unified Communications*, which encompasses more than just voice. Unified communications includes a collection of applications and technologies that enhance user collaboration. This section, however, focuses on the IP telephony component of unified communications.

Overview of IP Telephony

An IP telephony network not only duplicates the features offered in traditional corporate Private Branch Exchange (PBX) systems, but IP telephony expands on those features. Figure 11-1 shows the basic components of an IP telephony network, which are described in greater detail in the list that follows:

- **IP phone:** An IP phone provides IP voice to the desktop.

Key
Topic

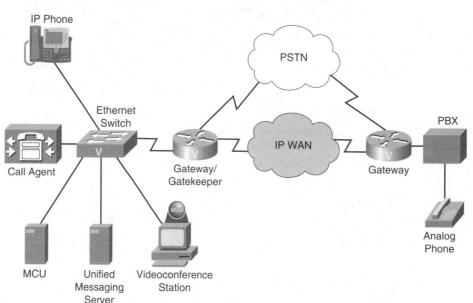

Figure 11-1   *IP Telephony Components*

- **Gatekeeper:** A gatekeeper provides call admission control (CAC), bandwidth control and management, and address translation features.

- **Gateway:** A gateway provides translation between VoIP and non-VoIP networks, such as the *Public Switched Telephone Network* (PSTN). A gateway also provides physical access for local analog and digital voice devices, such as telephones, fax machines, key sets, and PBXs.

- **Multipoint control unit (MCU):** An MCU mixes audio and/or video streams, thus allowing participants in multiple locations to attend the same conference.

- **Call agent:** A call agent provides call control for IP phones, Call Admission Control (CAC), bandwidth control and management, and address translation. Although a call agent could be server-based, Cisco also supports a router-based call agent, known as *Cisco Unified Communications Manager Express* (UCME).

- **Application server:** An application server provides services such as voice mail, unified messaging, and presence information (which can show the availability of another user).

- **Videoconference station:** A videoconference station provides access for end-user participation in videoconferencing. The videoconference station contains a video capture device for video input and a microphone for audio input. The user can view video streams and hear audio originating at a remote user station. Cisco targets its Cisco Unified Video Advantage product at desktop videoconferencing applications.

Design Considerations for Voice Networks

Successfully transmitting voice traffic over an IP network involves more than merely superimposing voice packets on an existing data network. Voice traffic needs to be treated in a special way, where it has higher priority than many other traffic types. Other design considerations include the availability of the voice network, securing the voice network, and a collection of other voice-related services. First, consider voice quality.

Quality of Service for Voice Traffic

Unlike much data traffic, voice traffic is highly latency-sensitive and drop-sensitive. Therefore, when a network experiences congestion due to a lack of bandwidth, the following symptoms can occur:

- **Delay:** *Delay* is the time required for a packet to travel from its source to its destination. You might have witnessed delay on the evening news, when the news anchor is talking via satellite with a foreign news correspondent. Due to the satellite delay, the conversation begins to feel unnatural.

Key Topic

- **Jitter:** *Jitter* is the uneven arrival of packets. For example, in a voice conversation, packet #1 arrives. Then, 20 minutes later, packet #2 arrives. After another 70 minutes, packet #3 arrives, and then packet #4 arrives 20 minutes behind packet #3. This variation in arrival times is not necessarily resulting in dropped packets. However, this jitter can make the conversation sound as if packets are being dropped.

- **Drops:** Packet drops occur when a link is congested and a buffer overflows. Some types of traffic, such as UDP traffic (for example, voice and video traffic), are not retransmitted if packets are dropped.

Fortunately, Cisco offers a collection of quality of service (QoS) features that can recognize high-priority traffic (for example, voice and video) and treat that special traffic in a special way. To effectively configure QoS in a network, you should consider how traffic is treated end-to-end through the network. This implies not only configuring QoS on WAN routers, but also configuring QoS on multiple switches and routers along the traffic's path.

For example, even a wiring closet switch could benefit from a QoS configuration. Cisco recommends marking traffic as close to the source as possible. However, you typically do not want end users setting their own priority markings. Therefore, you can use Cisco Catalyst switches to create a *trust boundary*, which is a point in the network that does not trust incoming markings. An exception to having a wiring closet switch acting as a trust boundary would be a Cisco IP Phone connected to the switch. Because a Cisco IP Phone performs priority marking for voice traffic, you can extend the trust boundary to the phone.

High Availability for Voice Traffic

PBX administrators often boast about their telephone system having the *five nines* of availability, meaning that their network is up 99.999 percent of the time. This uptime percentage equates to only five minutes of down time per year. Unfortunately, a common perception about data networks is that they are not nearly as reliable. As a result, many organizations are reluctant to replace their PBX and its track record of high availability with a voice system that relies on what is perceived to be a less reliable data network.

To combat this somewhat-deserved stigma, today's network designers must focus on the redundancy and reliability of their designs. Fortunately, by using data components (for example, routers and switches) with a high mean time between failures (MTBF) and including redundant links with fast converging protocols, today's networks can also approach the five nines of availability.

Securing Voice Traffic

Similar to data traffic, voice traffic needs to be protected as it flows across a network. Beyond protecting voice traffic with traditional precautions such as firewalling, protecting voice traffic from potential eavesdroppers might include the following:

- Separating voice and data traffic into different VLANs

- Encrypting and authenticating voice media packets

- Encrypting and authenticating voice signaling traffic

Other Services for Voice Traffic

In addition to QoS, availability, and security, introducing voice traffic into a data network brings with it several other design considerations:

- **In-Line Power:** A Cisco IP Phone requires -48 Volts of direct current (DC) to boot up and operate. This voltage can be provided by an external power brick, which connects into a wall power outlet and converts the wall outlet's 120 Volts of alternating current (AC) into the phone's required -48 VDC. Alternately, power can be provided by a Cisco Catalyst switch. Specifically, the switch can apply the required voltage across the same leads used for Ethernet (that is, pins 1, 2, 3, and 6 in an RJ-45 connector). One approach for in-line power (also known as *Power over Ethernet* [*PoE*]) is a Cisco-proprietary approach, which uses a Fast Link Pulse (FLP) to determine if a switch port is connected to a device needing power. An industry-standard approach to providing in-line power, however, is IEEE 802.3af. The 802.3af approach looks for a 25,000 Ohm resistance attached to a switch port. The presence of this resistance on a switch port indicates that the port should provide power to the attached device. From a design and troubleshooting perspective, you should confirm that a Cisco Catalyst switch and its attached Cisco IP Phones support the same type of in-line power.

- **DHCP:** Chapter 10, "IP Services Troubleshooting," introduced DHCP operation and how an end station could obtain IP address information via DHCP. Beyond IP address, subnet mask, DNS server, and default gateway information, a Cisco IP Phone can also obtain via DHCP the IP address (that is, DHCP option 150) or DNS name (that is, DHCP option 66) of a TFTP server.

- **TFTP:** A Cisco IP Phone communicates with a TFTP server to receive some or all of its configuration information, in addition to firmware updates. This TFTP server might be a Cisco Unified Communications Manager (UCM) server if that server is acting as a call-processing agent for the Cisco IP Phone. Alternately, a Cisco IOS router might be acting as the TFTP server, if that router is configured as a Cisco UCME call agent.

- **NTP:** Cisco IP Phones can also benefit from Network Time Protocol (NTP). Most models of Cisco IP Phones obtain their time information from their call agent. This time is then displayed on the phone. However, having accurate time information goes well beyond the convenience of having the local time displayed on a phone. For example, a call agent might be configured to permit or deny certain calls (for example, international calls) based on office hours.

- **CDP:** Cisco Discovery Protocol (CDP) is used by a Cisco Catalyst switch to inform an attached Cisco IP Phone of the phone's VLAN.

- **VLAN:** Many Cisco IP Phones include a PC port, which allows a PC to connect to the Cisco IP Phone for its Ethernet network connectivity. The Cisco IP Phone then connects to a Cisco Catalyst switch in a wiring closet. To keep the voice and data traffic separate, the Cisco IP Phone can place the phone's voice traffic and the PC's data traffic in different VLANs. Traffic from these two VLANs is sent to the Cisco Catalyst switch over a single IEEE 802.1Q trunk connection, as seen in Figure 11-2. The voice VLAN is often referred to as an *auxiliary* VLAN, and the data VLAN is the native VLAN (that is, an untagged VLAN) on the 802.1Q trunk. Even though this connection between a Cisco IP Phone and the Cisco Catalyst switch is a trunk connection, many Cisco Catalyst switches allow the switch port to be configured as a multi-VLAN access port, rather than a trunk port. Specifically, even though a single connection supporting more than one VLAN is typically referred to as a *trunk connection*, a multi-VLAN access port is an access port that can send and receive untagged traffic (that is, the native VLAN traffic) in addition to traffic from an auxiliary VLAN.

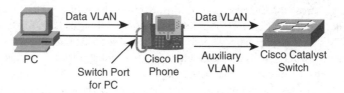

Figure 11-2   *IP Voice and Data VLAN Separation*

Cisco IP Phone Boot-Up Process

Understanding the steps involved in a Cisco IP Phone booting up can aid in troubleshooting a Cisco IP Phone that does not successfully register with its call agent. Recall that a call agent could be a Cisco UCM server or a Cisco UCME router. These call agents could also act as DHCP and TFTP servers.

As an example of a Cisco IP Phone's boot-up process, consider the steps illustrated in Figure 11-3. Assumptions for this example include the following:

■ The call agent is a UCME router.

■ The Cisco Catalyst switch and Cisco IP Phone both support the 802.3af PoE standard.

■ The UCME router is also acting as a DHCP server and TFTP server.

■ DNS services are not being used. Therefore, a Cisco IP Phone will obtain the IP address of the TFTP server via DHCP rather than the TFTP server's DNS name.

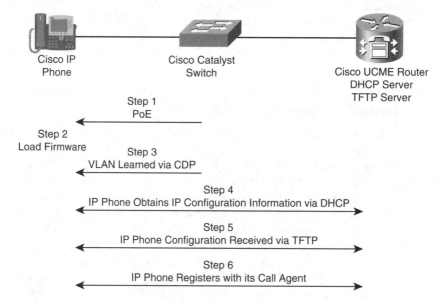

Figure 11-3   *Boot-Up Process for a Cisco IP Phone*

■ The Cisco IP Phone is using Skinny Client Control Protocol (SCCP) as its signaling protocol, as opposed to Session Initiation Protocol (SIP).

The following is the phone boot-up process:

Step 1.   The Cisco IP Phone receives power via PoE.

Step 2.   The Cisco IP Phone loads its firmware from its flash storage.

Step 3.   The Cisco Catalyst switch informs the Cisco IP Phone of the phone's VLAN.

Step 4.   The Cisco IP Phone requests and receives its IP configuration information (including DHCP option 150, which is the IP address of a TFTP server) via DHCP.

Step 5.   The Cisco IP Phone requests and receives a portion of its configuration information (including the IP address of the phone's call agent) from its TFTP server.

Step 6.   The Cisco IP Phone registers with its call agent and is now able to place and receive calls. Note that the protocol that carries voice calls between the two IP phones is *Real-time Transport Protocol* (RTP).

Common Voice Troubleshooting Issues

Because Cisco IP Phones rely on their underlying data network for communication, a troubleshooting issue on the data network could impact phone operation. Data networking troubleshooting targets should therefore be considered when troubleshooting a reported voice issue. Additionally, as a reference, Table 11-2 offers a collection of common voice troubleshooting targets and recommended solutions.

Table 11-2   *Common Voice Troubleshooting Targets*

Voice Troubleshooting Target	Recommended Solutions
IP Services	Check the configuration of the following IP services: CDP, DHCP, TFTP, NTP.
QoS	Check QoS configurations on routers and switches to confirm that voice traffic is being correctly classified, is being allocated a minimum amount of bandwidth, and is given priority treatment.
Security	Confirm voice and data VLAN separation. Additionally, check the encryption and authentication configurations for voice media and voice signaling traffic.
Power	In a modular Cisco Catalyst switch chassis (for example, a Cisco Catalyst 6500 chassis), the switch's power supply might not be sufficient to provide PoE to all attached Cisco IP Phones. Therefore, check the switch's power capacity and current utilization level.

Overview of Quality of Service

One of the biggest potential troubleshooting targets for voice traffic involves QoS. Although a comprehensive treatment of QoS is a study in itself and beyond the scope of the TSHOOT curriculum, this section introduces you to basic QoS configuration principles and commands used to monitor and troubleshoot a QoS configuration.

First, understand that QoS can classify traffic into different traffic classes. Cisco recommends that this classification be performed as close to the source as possible. When the traffic is classified, Cisco also recommends marking the traffic with a priority marking. One such marking is *Differentiated Services Code Point* (DSCP). A DSCP marking uses the six left-most bits in the Type of Service (ToS) byte in an IPv4 header. These six bits can be used to create as many as 64 different DSCP values (in the range 0–63). The Internet Engineering Task Force (IETF) selected a subset of these values and assigned names to those values. These names are called *Per-Hop Behaviors* (PHB), because these DSCP values can influence how traffic is treated at each hop (that is, router hop or switch hop) along the path from the traffic's source to its destination.

As an example, the DSCP numerical value of 46 also has the PHB name of *Expedited Forwarding* (EF). Cisco IOS accepts either DSCP numerical values or DSCP PHB names. A PHB of EF is the DSCP value that Cisco recommends you use to mark voice packets (specifically, voice payload traffic, not voice signaling traffic). Fortunately, a Cisco IP Phone, by default, marks voice frames leaving the phone with a PHB of EF. Therefore, if routers or switches in the topology are configured to classify traffic based on DSCP markings, they can easily recognize voice packets sourced from a Cisco IP Phone. If, however, you have analog phones in your network connected into voice gateways, realize that those voice packets are marked with a default DSCP value of zero (that is, a DSCP PHB of Default). Therefore, you might want to configure that voice gateway to mark those voice packets with a DSCP value of EF before transmitting those packets out of the router.

Once traffic has been classified and marked, routers and switches can examine those markings and make decisions based on those markings (for example, forwarding decisions or dropping decisions).

MQC

Cisco IOS offers a powerful three-step approach to QoS configuration, as illustrated in Figure 11-4. This approach is known as the *Modular Quality of Service Command Line Interface*, or *MQC* for short.

The following are the steps for the Modular Qos CLI:

Step 1.   The first step of MQC is to create class maps, which categorize traffic types. The following command enters you into class map configuration mode:

```
Router(config)#class-map [match-any | match-all] class-name
```

Step 2.   Once in class-map configuration mode, you can specify multiple match statements to match traffic, and all traffic meeting the criteria you specified with the **match** commands is categorized under the class map. If multiple match statements are specified, by default, all match statements must be met before a packet is classified by the class map. However, if you use the **match-any**

option, if any individual match condition is met, the packet is classified by the class map. After the class maps are defined, the first step of MQC is complete.

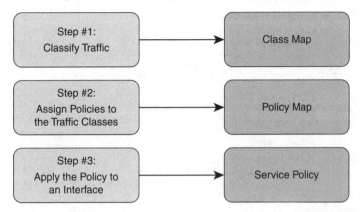

Figure 11-4 *Modular QoS CLI*

Step 3. The second step is to create a policy map that defines how the classified traffic is to be treated. To enter policy map configuration mode, issue the following command:

```
Router(config)#policy-map policy-name
```

Step 4. From policy map configuration mode, enter policy map class configuration mode, with the following command:

```
Router(config-pmap)#class class-name
```

Step 5. From policy map class configuration mode, you can assign QoS policies to traffic classified by each class map. You might also have a situation where a packet matches more than one class map. In that case, the first class map identified in the policy map is used. Up to 256 class maps can be associated with a single policy map.

Step 6. Finally, in the third step of MQC, the policy map is applied to an interface, Frame Relay map class, or ATM virtual circuit with the following command:

```
Router(config-if)#service-policy {input | output} policy-map-name
```

Example 11-1 provides an MQC sample configuration that classifies various types of e-mail traffic (for example, SMTP, IMAP, and POP3) into one class map. The KaZaa protocol, which is frequently used for music downloads, is placed in another class map. Voice over IP traffic is classified by yet another class map. Then, the policy map assigns bandwidth allocations or limitations to these traffic types.

Example 11-1 *MQC Sample Configuration*

Key
Topic

```
R1# conf term
R1(config)# class-map match-any EMAIL
R1(config-cmap)# match protocol pop3
R1(config-cmap)# match protocol imap
R1(config-cmap)# match protocol smtp
```

```
R1(config-cmap)# exit
R1(config)# class-map MUSIC
R1(config-cmap)# match protocol kazaa2
R1(config-cmap)# exit
R1(config)# class-map VOICE
R1(config-cmap)# match protocol rtp audio
R1(config-cmap)# exit
R1(config)# policy-map TSHOOT-EXAMPLE
R1(config-pmap)# class EMAIL
R1(config-pmap-c)# bandwidth 128
R1(config-pmap-c)# exit
R1(config-pmap)# class MUSIC
R1(config-pmap-c)# police 32000
R1(config-pmap-c)# exit
R1(config-pmap)# class VOICE
R1(config-pmap-c)# priority 256
R1(config-pmap-c)# exit
R1(config-pmap)# exit
R1(config)# interface serial 0/1
R1(config-if)# service-policy output TSHOOT-EXAMPLE
```

Notice that the policy map named **TSHOOT-EXAMPLE** makes at least 128 kbps of bandwidth available to e-mail traffic. However, KaZaa version 2 traffic has its bandwidth limited to 32 kbps. Voice packets not only have access to 256 kbps of bandwidth, but they receive priority treatment, meaning that they are sent first (that is, ahead of other traffic), up to a 256-kbps limit.

The next logical question is, "What happens to all the traffic that was not classified by one of the configured class maps?" Interestingly, Cisco created a class map named **class-default**, which categorizes any traffic not matched by one of the defined class maps.

Finally in the example, the policy map is applied in the outbound direction on the Serial 0/1 interface.

Table 11-3 provides a listing of verification and troubleshooting commands for MQC configurations.

Table 11-3   *MQC Verification Commands*

Command	Description
show class-map [*class-map-name*]	Used to view what a class map is matching.
show policy-map [*policy-map-name*]	Used to view the policy applied to the classes within a policy map.
show policy-map interface *interface-identifier* [**input** | **output**]	Used to view policy map statistics for packets crossing a specific interface.

Example 11-2 provides sample output from the **show class-map** command. The output shows each class map, including the default class map of **class-default**. You can also see how traffic is classified in each class. For example, the **EMAIL** class is using **match-any** logic, where a packet is classified in the class if it is POP3, IMAP, or SMTP.

Example 11-2 show class-map *Command Output*

```
R1# show class-map
 Class Map match-any class-default (id 0)
   Match any

 Class Map match-all MUSIC (id 2)
   Match protocol kazaa2

 Class Map match-any EMAIL (id 1)
   Match protocol pop3
   Match protocol imap
   Match protocol smtp

 Class Map match-all VOICE (id 3)
   Match protocol rtp audio
```

Example 11-3 provides sample output from the **show policy-map** command. The output shows how each class of traffic is to be treated. For example, the **EMAIL** class has access to at least 128 kbps of bandwidth if it requires that much and more if it needs it and more is available. The **MUSIC** class of traffic has a maximum bandwidth utilization limit of 32 kbps. If traffic exceeds that 32-kbps limit, that excess traffic is dropped. The **VOICE** class of traffic guarantees the voice traffic has access to as much as 256 kbps of bandwidth if that much is required. This traffic is configured to have priority treatment, meaning this traffic is sent ahead of other traffic types. However, traffic from this class is not allowed to exceed 256 kbps, to prevent protocol starvation of other traffic classes.

Example 11-3 show policy-map *Command Output*

```
R1# show policy-map
 Policy Map TSHOOT-EXAMPLE
   Class EMAIL
     Bandwidth 128 (kbps) Max Threshold 64 (packets)
   Class MUSIC
    police cir 32000 bc 1500
      conform-action transmit
      exceed-action drop
   Class VOICE
```

```
Strict Priority
Bandwidth 256 (kbps) Burst 6400 (Bytes)
```

Example 11-4 provides sample output from the **show policy-map interface** *interface-identifier* command. The output in this example is from interface Serial 0/1. The output shows how traffic is classified in each class and how the policy map is treating each traffic class. Additionally, the output shows packet and byte counts for traffic matching each class.

Example 11-4   show policy-map interface interface-identifier *Command Output*

```
R1# show policy-map interface serial0/1
 Serial0/1

  Service-policy output: TSHOOT-EXAMPLE

    Class-map: EMAIL (match-any)
      0 packets, 0 bytes
      5 minute offered rate 0 bps, drop rate 0 bps
      Match: protocol pop3
        0 packets, 0 bytes
        5 minute rate 0 bps
      Match: protocol imap
        0 packets, 0 bytes
        5 minute rate 0 bps
      Match: protocol smtp
        0 packets, 0 bytes
        5 minute rate 0 bps
      Queueing
        Output Queue: Conversation 265
        Bandwidth 128 (kbps) Max Threshold 64 (packets)
        (pkts matched/bytes matched) 0/0
        (depth/total drops/no-buffer drops) 0/0/0

    Class-map: MUSIC (match-all)
      0 packets, 0 bytes
      5 minute offered rate 0 bps, drop rate 0 bps
      Match: protocol kazaa2
      police:
          cir 32000 bps, bc 1500 bytes
        conformed 0 packets, 0 bytes; actions:
          transmit
        exceeded 0 packets, 0 bytes; actions:
          drop
        conformed 0 bps, exceed 0 bps
```

```
Class-map: VOICE (match-all)
  0 packets, 0 bytes
  5 minute offered rate 0 bps, drop rate 0 bps
  Match: protocol rtp audio
  Queueing
    Strict Priority
    Output Queue: Conversation 264
    Bandwidth 256 (kbps) Burst 6400 (Bytes)
    (pkts matched/bytes matched) 0/0
    (total drops/bytes drops) 0/0
Class-map: class-default (match-any)
  23 packets, 1715 bytes
  5 minute offered rate 0 bps, drop rate 0 bps
  Match: any
```

AutoQoS

Optimizing a QoS configuration for VoIP can be a daunting task. Fortunately, Cisco added a feature called *AutoQoS VoIP* to many of its router and switch platforms to generate router-based or switch-based QoS configurations designed to ensure voice quality.

A few years after introducing AutoQoS VoIP, Cisco introduced AutoQoS Enterprise, which can automatically generate a QoS configuration on a router that seeks to provide appropriate QoS parameters for all of an enterprise's traffic types (that is, not just voice traffic).

Table 11-4 summarizes the platform support for these two versions of AutoQoS.

Table 11-4 *AutoQoS Platform Support*

Key
Topic

AutoQoS Version	Platform Support
AutoQoS VoIP	Routers Catalyst Switches
AutoQoS Enterprise	Routers

First, consider the configuration of AutoQoS VoIP on a router. In interface configuration mode (or Frame Relay DLCI configuration mode), AutoQoS can be enabled with the following command:

```
Router(config-if)# auto qos voip [trust] [fr-atm]
```

The **trust** option indicates that Auto QoS should classify voice traffic based on DSCP markings, instead of using Network-Based Application Recognition (NBAR). The **fr-atm** option allows Frame Relay Discard Eligible (DE) markings to be converted into ATM Cell Loss Priority (CLP) markings, and vice versa.

Before enabling AutoQoS on a router interface, consider the following prerequisites:

- CEF must be enabled.

- A QoS policy must not be currently attached to the interface.

- The correct bandwidth should be configured on the interface.

- An IP address must be configured on an interface if its speed is equal to or less than 768 kbps.

Note that the interface's bandwidth determines which AutoQoS features are enabled. If an interface's bandwidth is equal to or less than 768 kbps, it is considered to be a low-speed interface. On a low-speed interface, AutoQoS might configure Multilink PPP (MLP), which requires an IP address on the physical interface. AutoQoS takes that IP address from the physical interface and uses it for a virtual multilink interface it creates.

To verify that AutoQoS is configured for a router interface, you can use the following command:

```
Router# show auto qos voip [interface interface-identifier]
```

This command displays global and interface (or optionally, only interface) configuration mode commands added by the AutoQoS VoIP feature.

Example 11-5 shows a sample of configuring and verifying AutoQoS VoIP on a router.

Example 11-5   *Configuring and Verifying AutoQoS VoIP on a Router*

```
R1# conf term
R1(config)# int s0/0
R1(config-if)# auto qos voip
R1(config-if)# end
R1# show auto qos
 !
  ip access-list extended AutoQoS-VoIP-RTCP
   permit udp any any range 16384 32767
 !
  ip access-list extended AutoQoS-VoIP-Control
   permit tcp any any eq 1720
   permit tcp any any range 11000 11999
   permit udp any any eq 2427
   permit tcp any any eq 2428
   permit tcp any any range 2000 2002
   permit udp any any eq 1719
   permit udp any any eq 5060
 !
  class-map match-any AutoQoS-VoIP-RTP-UnTrust
    match protocol rtp audio
    match access-group name AutoQoS-VoIP-RTCP
```

```
!
 class-map match-any AutoQoS-VoIP-Control-UnTrust
   match access-group name AutoQoS-VoIP-Control
!
 class-map match-any AutoQoS-VoIP-Remark
   match ip dscp ef
   match ip dscp cs3
     match ip dscp af31
!
   policy-map AutoQoS-Policy-UnTrust
    class AutoQoS-VoIP-RTP-UnTrust
     priority percent 70
     set dscp ef
    class AutoQoS-VoIP-Control-UnTrust
     bandwidth percent 5
     set dscp af31
    class AutoQoS-VoIP-Remark
     set dscp default
    class class-default
     fair-queue


   encapsulation ppp
   no fair-queue
   ppp multilink
   ppp multilink group 2001100114
!
 interface Multilink2001100114
   bandwidth 128
   ip address 10.1.1.1 255.255.255.0
   service-policy output AutoQoS-Policy-UnTrust
   ppp multilink
   ppp multilink fragment delay 10
   ppp multilink interleave
   ppp multilink group 2001100114
   ip rtp header-compression iphc-format
!
rmon event 33333 log trap AutoQoS description "AutoQoS SNMP traps for Voice
   Drops" owner AutoQoS
rmon alarm 33334 cbQosCMDropBitRate.1271.1273 30 absolute rising-threshold 1
   33333 falling-threshold 0 owner AutoQoS
```

Next, consider the configuration of AutoQoS VoIP on some models of Cisco Catalyst switches (for example, most new models of Cisco IOS-based Catalyst switches). To configure AutoQoS on these platforms, issue one of the following commands from interface configuration mode:

```
Switch(config-if)# auto qos voip trust
```

This command configures the interface to trust Class of Service (CoS) markings (that is, Layer 2 QoS priority markings on an Ethernet connection) for classifying VoIP traffic.

```
Switch(config-if)# auto qos voip cisco-phone
```

This command configures the interface to trust CoS markings only if those markings came from an attached Cisco IP Phone. CDP is used to detect an attached Cisco IP Phone.

Example 11-6 shows a sample of configuring and verifying AutoQoS VoIP on a switch.

Example 11-6   *Configuring and Verifying AutoQoS VoIP on a Switch*

```
Cat3550# conf term
Cat3550(config)# int gig 0/1
Cat3550(config-if)# auto qos voip cisco-phone
Cat3550(config-if)# end
Cat3550# show run
Building configuration...
...OUTPUT OMITTED...
mls qos map cos-dscp 0 8 16 24 32 46 48 56
mls qos
!
interface GigabitEthernet0/1
 mls qos trust device cisco-phone
 mls qos trust cos
auto qos voip cisco-phone
 wrr-queue bandwidth 10 20 70 1
 wrr-queue queue-limit 50 25 15 10
 wrr-queue cos-map 1 0 1
 wrr-queue cos-map 2 2 4
 wrr-queue cos-map 3 3 6 7
 wrr-queue cos-map 4 5
 priority-queue out
 spanning-tree portfast
...OUTPUT OMITTED...
```

Next, consider the configuration of AutoQoS Enterprise. This version of AutoQoS has the same collection of prerequisites shown earlier for AutoQoS VoIP. However, unlike Auto-QoS VoIP, AutoQoS Enterprise targets all known applications on an enterprise network. Fortunately, you do not have to specify the individual applications and protocols you want to support. AutoQoS Enterprise instead dynamically learns the applications and protocols seen on an interface. Cisco recommends that this learning process, called the *discovery phase*, be conducted for at least two or three days. During this time, a router can use existing DSCP values (that is, Layer 3 QoS markings) or NBAR to classify traffic seen on an interface. Traffic can be classified into as many as ten classes by AutoQoS Enterprise. The following interface configuration mode command is issued to begin the discovery phase of AutoQoS Enterprise:

```
Router(config-if)# auto discovery qos [trust]
```

The **trust** keyword instructs the router to classify traffic based on existing DSCP markings, as opposed to using NBAR.

After the discovery phase runs for at least two or three days, you can issue the **show auto discovery qos** command to see what traffic has been classified and what behavior is specified in the recommended policy.

After examining the output of the **show auto discovery qos** command, if you are satisfied with the proposed configuration, you can apply the configuration by issuing the **auto qos** command in interface configuration mode for the interface that performed the discovery phase.

Example 11-7 shows these commands being issued for the Fast Ethernet 0/0 interface on a router named R4. The output of the **show auto discovery qos** command shows the ten classes of traffic that could be populated by the AutoQoS Enterprise feature, as indicated by the highlighted output.

Example 11-7 *Configuring AutoQoS Enterprise*

```
R4# conf term
R4(config)# int fa0/0
R4(config-if)# auto discovery qos
R4(config-if)# end
R4# show auto discovery qos
FastEthernet0/0
 AutoQoS Discovery enabled for applications
 Discovery up time: 1 minutes, 7 seconds
AutoQoS Class information:
 Class Voice:
  Recommended Minimum Bandwidth: 5 Kbps/<1% (PeakRate)
  Detected applications and data:
  Application/       AverageRate        PeakRate           Total
  Protocol           (kbps/%)           (kbps/%)           (bytes)
  ------             ------             ----               ------
  rtp audio          1/<1               5/<1               10138
Class Interactive Video:
  No data found.
 Class Signaling:
  Recommended Minimum Bandwidth: 0 Kbps/0% (AverageRate)
  Detected applications and data:
  Application/       AverageRate        PeakRate           Total
  Protocol           (kbps/%)           (kbps/%)           (bytes)
  ------             ------             -----              ------
  skinny             0/0                0/0                2218
Class Streaming Video:
  No data found.
 Class Transactional:
   No data found.
```

```
Class Bulk:
  No data found.
Class Scavenger:
  No data found.
Class Management:
  No data found.
Class Routing:
  Recommended Minimum Bandwidth: 0 Kbps/0% (AverageRate)
  Detected applications and data:
  Application/      AverageRate       PeakRate          Total
  Protocol          (kbps/%)          (kbps/%)          (bytes)
  --------          --------          --------          --------
  eigrp             0/0               0/0               1110
  icmp              0/0               0/0               958
Class Best Effort:
  Current Bandwidth Estimation: 44 Kbps/<1% (AverageRate)
  Detected applications and data:
  Application/      AverageRate       PeakRate          Total
  Protocol          (kbps/%)          (kbps/%)          (bytes)
  --------          --------          --------          --------
  http              44/<1             121/1             372809
  unknowns          0/0               0/0               232


Suggested AutoQoS Policy for the current uptime:
 !
class-map match-any AutoQoS-Voice-Fa0/0
  match protocol rtp audio
 !
 policy-map AutoQoS-Policy-Fa0/0
  class AutoQoS-Voice-Fa0/0
   priority percent 1
   set dscp ef
  class class-default
   fair-queue
R4# conf term
R4(config)# int fa 0/0
R4(config-if)# auto qos
R4(config-if)# end
R4#
```

Video Troubleshooting

Like voice traffic, video traffic is latency-sensitive. Therefore, many of the same design and troubleshooting considerations for voice traffic (for example, QoS considerations) also apply to video traffic.

An additional consideration for video traffic, however, is multicasting. Specifically, a video server might send a single video stream to a multicast group. End-user devices wanting to receive the video stream can join the multicast group. Multicast configuration, however, needs to be added to routers and switches to support this type of transmission. With the addition of multicast configurations comes the potential of additional troubleshooting targets. This section describes the basic theory, configuration, and troubleshooting of a multicast network.

This section then concludes with a listing of potential video network troubleshooting targets.

Introduction to IP-Based Video

Figure 11-5 illustrates a sample IP-based video network.

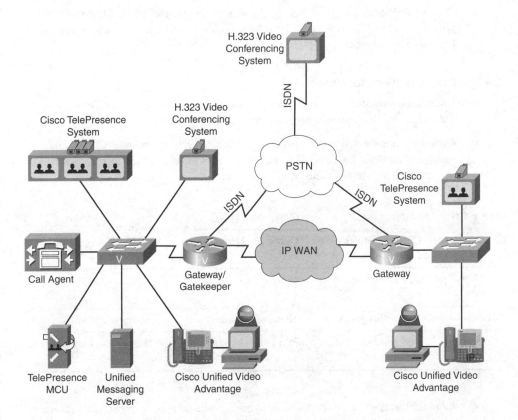

Figure 11-5 *IP-Based Video Network*

Many components in the figure are identical to components seen in a voice network. Three types of video solutions are shown, as follows:

- **H.323 Video Conferencing System:** Multiple third parties offer H.323 video conferencing systems, which can be used to set up a video conference over an IP or ISDN network.

- **Cisco Unified Video Advantage:** The Cisco Unified Video Advantage product uses a PC, a video camera, and a Cisco IP Phone as a video conferencing station. Specifically, the camera connects to a USB port on the PC. Software is loaded on the PC, and the PC is connected to the PC port on a Cisco IP Phone. Alternately, the Cisco IP Phone could be the software-based Cisco IP Communicator running on the PC. When a voice call is placed between two users running the Cisco Unified Video Advantage product, a video call can automatically be started, with the video appearing on each user's PC.

- **Cisco TelePresence:** The Cisco TelePresence solution uses CD-quality audio and High Definition (HD) video (that is, 1080p) displayed on large monitors to create life-like video conferences.

Design Considerations for Video

Due to the bandwidth-intensive and latency-sensitive nature of video, consider the following when designing or troubleshooting a video network:

- **QoS:** Like voice, video packets need to be allocated an appropriate amount of bandwidth and be treated with high priority. Table 11-5 shows the QoS metrics that Cisco recommends for various types of video applications.

Key
Topic

Table 11-5   *Recommended QoS Metrics for Video*

QoS Metric	Cisco Unified Video Advantage	Cisco TelePresence	Video Surveillance
One-Way Delay	200 ms maximum	150 ms maximum	500 ms maximum
Jitter	10 ms maximum	10 ms maximum	10 ms maximum
Packet Loss	0.05 percent maximum	0.05 percent maximum	0.5 percent maximum

- **Availability:** Also like voice, video networks should be built on an underlying data network with reliable components and redundancy, such that the availability of the video network can approach an uptime of 99.999 percent.

- **Security:** Just as an eavesdropper could capture unencrypted voice packets and interpret the information contained in those packets, unencrypted video packets could also be captured and interpreted. Therefore, appropriate security measures, such as encryption and authentication, should be in place in a video network.

- **Multicasting:** More common in a video environment rather than in a voice environment is the use of multicasting technologies. Multicasting allows a multicast server to send traffic (for example, a video stream) to a destination Class D IP address known as a *multicast group*. End stations wanting to receive the traffic sent to the multicast group can join the group, thus allowing the multicast server (for example, a video server) to send a single stream of traffic, which is received by multiple recipients wishing to receive the traffic.

Multicasting

QoS, availability, and security considerations were discussed in the previous section. However, this chapter has not yet addressed multicasting in detail. Therefore, this section introduces you to multicasting operation, configuration, and troubleshooting.

Introduction to Multicasting

Consider a video stream that needs to be sent to multiple recipients in a company. One approach is to unicast the traffic. The source server sends a copy of every packet to every receiver. Obviously, this approach has serious scalability limitations.

An alternate approach is to broadcast the video stream, so that the source server only has to send each packet once. However, everyone within a broadcast domain of the network receives the packet, in that scenario, even if they do not want it.

IP multicast technologies provide the best of both worlds. With IP multicast, the source server only sends one copy of each packet, and packets are only sent to intended recipients.

Specifically, receivers join a multicast group, denoted by a Class D IP address (that is, in the range 224.0.0.0 through 239.255.255.255). The source sends traffic to the Class D address, and through switch and router protocols, packets are forwarded only to intended stations. These multicast packets are sent via UDP (that is, best effort). When doing a multicast design, also be aware of the potential for duplicate packets being received and the potential for packets arriving out of order.

Figure 11-6 shows a simple multicast network, where a multicast server is sending traffic to a destination IP address of 224.1.1.1. Notice that there are three workstations in this network. However, only two of the three workstations joined the multicast group. Therefore, only the two multicast group members receive traffic from the multicast server.

Internet Group Management Protocol

The protocol used between clients (for example, PCs) and routers to let routers know which of their interfaces have multicast receivers attached is Internet Group Management Protocol (IGMP). As an example, Figure 11-7 shows a PC sending an IGMP Join message to a multicast-enabled router. The router receives this IGMP Join message on its Fast Ethernet 0/0 interface. Therefore, the router knows that when it receives traffic destined for a particular multicast group (as identified in the IGMP Join message), that traffic should be forwarded out its Fast Ethernet 0/0 interface.

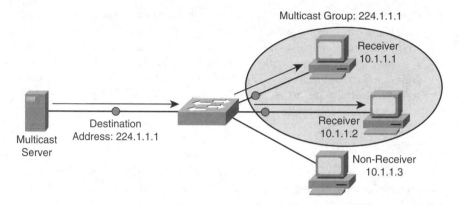

Figure 11-6 *Sample Multicast Topology*

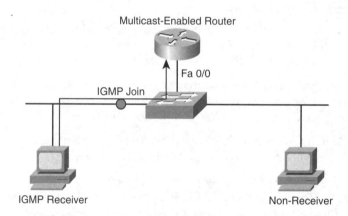

Figure 11-7 *Joining a Multicast Group*

There are three versions of IGMP. However, only two versions are in wide-scale deployment:

- **IGMP Version 1:** When a PC wants to join a multicast group, it sends an IGMP Report message to the router, letting the router know that it wants to receive traffic for a specific group. Every 60 seconds, by default, the router sends an IGMP Query message to determine if the PC still wants to belong to the group. There can be up to a three-minute delay before the time the router realizes that the receiver left the group. The destination address of this router query is 224.0.0.1, which addresses all IP multicast hosts.

- **IGMP Version 2:** IGMPv2 is similar to IGMP Version 1, except that IGMP Version 2 can send queries to a specific group, and a *Leave* message is supported. Specifically, a receiver can proactively send a Leave message when it no longer wants to participate in a multicast group, allowing the router to prune its interface earlier.

IGMP Version 1 and Version 2 hosts and routers do have some interoperability. When an IGMPv2 hosts sends an IGMPv2 report to an IGMPv1 router, the IGMP message type appears to be invalid, and it is ignored. Therefore, an IGMPv2 host must send IGMPv1 reports to an IGMPv1 router.

In an environment with an IGMPv2 router and a mixture of IGMPv1 and IGMPv2 receivers, the version 1 receivers respond normally to IGMPv1 or IGMPv2 queries. However, as illustrated in Figure 11-8, a version 2 router must ignore any leave message while IGMPv1 receivers are present because if the router processed the IGMPv2 leave message, it would send a group-specific query, which would not be correctly interpreted by an IGMPv1 receiver.

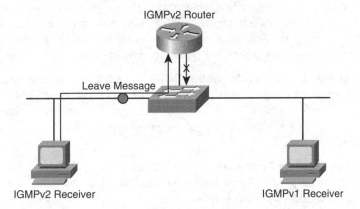

Figure 11-8   *Mixed IGMPv1 and IGMPv2 Topology*

As mentioned earlier, multicast routers can periodically send queries out of an interface to determine if any multicast receivers still exist off of that interface. However, there might be a situation where more than one multicast router exists on a broadcast media segment (for example, Ethernet). Therefore, one router must be designated as the *querier* for that segment. This IGMP designated *querier* is the router that has the lowest unicast IP address. To determine which router on a multi-access network is the querier, you can issue the following command:

```
Router# show ip igmp interface [interface-id]
```

The output from this command identifies the IP address of the IGMP querier. Additionally, the following command displays the IP multicast groups of which a router is aware:

```
Router# show ip igmp group
```

When a Layer 2 switch receives a multicast frame on an interface, by default, the switch floods the frame out all other interfaces. To prevent this behavior, the switch needs awareness of what interfaces are connected to receivers for specific multicast groups. *IGMP snooping* is a feature that can be enabled on many Cisco Catalyst switches, which allows a switch to autonomously determine which interfaces are connected to receivers for specific multicast groups by eavesdropping on the IGMP traffic being exchanged between clients and routers. To globally enable IGMP snooping on a Cisco Catalyst switch, issue the following command:

```
Switch(config)# ip igmp snooping
```

Once enabled globally, individual VLANs can be enabled or disabled for IGMP snooping with the following command:

```
Switch(config)# ip igmp snooping vlan vlan_id
```

Multicast Addressing

In a multicast network, the multicast source sends multicast packets with a Class D destination address. The 224.0.0.0 through 239.255.255.255 address range is the Class D address range, because the first four bits in the first octet of a Class D address are 1110. Some ranges of addresses in the Class D address space are dedicated for special purposes:

- **Reserved Link Local Addresses:** 224.0.0.0–224.0.0.255. These addresses are used, for example, by many network protocols. OSPF uses 224.0.0.5 and 224.0.0.6. RIPv2 uses 224.0.0.9, and EIGRP uses 224.0.0.10. Other well-known addresses in this range include 224.0.0.1, which addresses all multicast hosts, and 224.0.0.2, which addresses all multicast routers.

- **Globally Scoped Addresses:** 224.0.1.0–238.255.255.255. These addresses are used for general-purpose multicast applications, and they have the ability to extend beyond the local autonomous system.

- **Source-Specific Multicast (SSM) Addresses:** 232.0.0.0–232.255.255.255. These addresses are used in conjunction with IGMPv3, to allow multicast receivers to request not only membership in a group but also to request specific sources from which to receive traffic. Therefore, in an SSM environment, multiple sources with different content can all be sending to the same multicast group.

- **GLOP Addresses:** 233.0.0.0–233.255.255.255. These addresses provide a globally unique multicast address range, based on autonomous system numbers.

- **Limited Scope Addresses:** 239.0.0.0–239.255.255.255. These addresses are used for internal multicast applications (for example, traffic that doesn't leave an autonomous system), much like the 10.0.0.0/8 address space is a private IP address space.

In addition to Layer 3 addresses, multicast applications must also have Layer 2 addresses (that is, MAC addresses). Fortunately, these Layer 2 addresses can be constructed directly from the Layer 3 multicast addresses. A MAC address is a 48-bit address, and the first half (that is, 24 bits) of a multicast MAC address (in hex) is 01-00-5e. The 25th bit is always 0. The last 23 bits in the multicast MAC address come directly from the last 23 bits of the multicast IP address. Consider the following example:

Given a multicast IP address of 224.1.10.10, calculate the corresponding multicast MAC address.

Step 1.   First, convert the last three octets to binary:

```
0000.0001.0000.1010.0000.1010
```

Step 2. If the right-most bit isn't already 0, it should be changed to a 0, because the 25th bit of a multicast MAC address is always 0:

`0000.0001.0000.1010.0000.1010`

Step 3. Convert each nibble (that is, each 4-bit section) into its hexadecimal equivalent:

`01-0a-0a`

Step 4. Prepend 01-00-5e to the calculated address to produce the multicast MAC address:

`01-00-5e-01-0a-0a`

Distribution Trees

To combat the issue of receiving duplicate packets, Cisco routers perform a Reverse Path Forwarding (RPF) check to determine if a multicast packet is entering a router on the appropriate interface. An RPF check examines the source address of an incoming packet and checks it against the router's unicast routing table to see what interface should be used to get back to the source network. If the incoming multicast packet is using that interface, the RPF check passes, and the packet is forwarded. If the multicast packet is coming in on a different interface, the RPF check fails, and the packet is discarded, as shown in Figure 11-9.

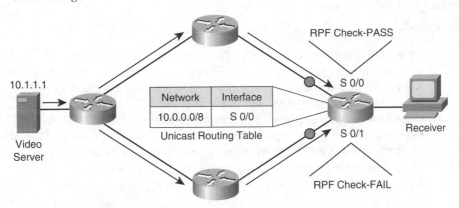

Figure 11-9 *RPF Check*

Only members of a multicast group receive packets destined for that group; however, the sender does not need to be a member of the group. Multicast traffic flows from a source to a destination over a *distribution tree*, which is a loop-free path. The two types of distribution trees are as follows:

■ **Source Distribution Tree:** A source distribution tree, as depicted in Figure 11-10, creates an optimal path between each source router and each last-hop router (that is, a router connected to a receiver), at the expense of increased memory usage. Source distributions trees place (S, G) states in a router's multicast routing table to indicate the address of the source (S) and the address of the group (G).

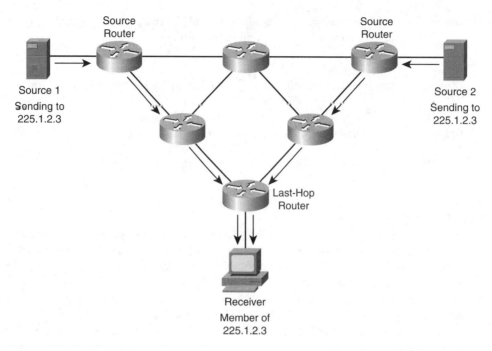

Figure 11-10   *Source Distribution Tree*

■   **Shared Distribution Tree:** A shared distribution tree, as seen in Figure 11-11, creates a tree from a central *rendezvous point* (RP) router to all last-hop routers, with
source distribution trees being created from all sources to the rendezvous point, at
the expense of increased delay. Shared distribution trees place (*, G) states in a
router's multicast routing table to indicate that any device could be the source (that is,
using the wildcard * character) for the group (G). This (*, G) state is created in routers
along the shared tree from the RP to the last-hop routers. Because each source for a
group does not require its own (S, G), the memory requirement is less for a shared
tree compared to a source tree.

PIM-DM Mechanics

Cisco routers can use the *Protocol Independent Multicast* (PIM) protocol to construct IP
multicast distribution trees. PIM's protocol independence means that it can run over any
IP network, regardless of the underlying unicast routing protocol (for example, OSPF or
EIGRP). The two varieties of PIM are *PIM Dense Mode* (PIM-DM) and *PIM Sparse
Mode* (PIM-SM). PIM-DM uses a source distribution tree, whereas PIM-SM uses a shared
distribution tree.

A router is enabled for multicast routing with the following global configuration mode
command:

```
Router(config)# ip multicast-routing
```

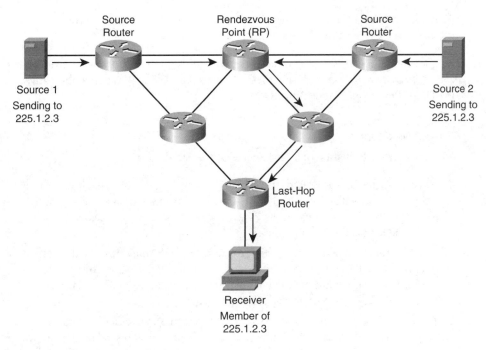

Figure 11-11 *Shared Distribution Tree*

Once IP multicast is globally enabled, individual interfaces need to be configured for PIM support. To configure an interface to participate in an IP multicast network, using PIM, issue the following interface configuration mode command:

```
Router(config-if)# ip pim {dense-mode | sparse-mode | sparse-dense-mode}
```

Cisco recommends sparse-dense-mode, which uses dense-mode to automatically learn the location of an RP, after which the interface runs in sparse-mode. First, consider the formation of a PIM Dense Mode distribution tree:

1. A multicast source comes up and begins flooding multicast traffic throughout the network.

2. If more than one router is forwarding over a common broadcast medium (for example, an Ethernet link), *Assert* messages are used to determine the PIM forwarder. The router with the better metric, or (by default) the highest IP address, wins the election.

3. Some routers might not have multicast receivers for the group whose traffic is currently being flooded. Those routers send a *Prune* message to their upstream router, requesting that their branch of the distribution tree be pruned off. However, if there is another router on the same broadcast medium as the router that sent the prune, and if that other router does have IP multicast receivers attached, the prune message is ignored. The reason that the prune message is ignored is because the router that is attached to IP multicast receivers sends a *Join Override* message.

4. If a receiver comes up on a router that was previously pruned from the tree, that router can rejoin the tree by sending a *Graft* message.

A major consideration for PIM-DM, however, is that this *flood-and-prune* behavior repeats every three minutes. Therefore, PIM-DM does not scale well. A better alternative to PIM-DM is PIM Sparse Mode (PIM-SM).

PIM-SM Mechanics

Next, consider the formation of a PIM Sparse Mode distribution tree:

1. A receiver sends an IGMP Report message to its router indicating that it wants to participate in a particular multicast group. The receiver's router (that is, the last-hop router) sends a *Join* message to the RP, creating (*, G) state along a shared tree between the RP and the last-hop router.

2. A source comes up and creates a source tree between its router (that is, the first-hop router) and the RP. (S, G) state is created in routers along this path. However, before the source tree is completely established, the source sends its multicast packets to the RP encapsulated inside of unicast *Register* messages.

3. After the RP receives the first multicast packet over the source tree, it sends a *Register Stop* message to the source, telling the source to stop sending the multicast traffic inside of Register messages. Two trees now exist: (1) a source tree from the first-hop router to the RP and (2) a shared tree from the RP to the last-hop router. However, this might not be the optimal path.

4. The last-hop router discovers from where the multicast traffic is arriving, and the last-hop router sends a *Join* message directly to the first-hop router to form an optimal path (that is, a source path tree) between the source and the receiver.

5. Because the last-hop router no longer needs multicast traffic from the RP, as it is receiving the multicast traffic directly from the first-hop router, it sends an (S, G) *RP-bit Prune* message to the RP, requesting the RP to stop sending multicast traffic.

6. With the shared tree to the last-hop router pruned, the RP no longer needs to receive multicast traffic from the first-hop router. So, the RP sends an *(S, G) Prune* message to the first-hop router. At this point, traffic flows in an optimal path from the first-hop router to the last-hop router. The process of cutting over from the path via the RP to the direct path is called *Shortest-Path Tree* (SPT) *Switchover*.

Comparing PIM-DM versus PIM-SM suggests that PIM-SM offers the benefits of PIM-DM (that is, optimal pathing) without PIM-DM's flood-and-prune behavior.

You can determine a distribution tree's topology by examining the multicast routing table of multicast routers in the topology. The **show ip mroute** command displays a router's multicast routing table, as demonstrated in Example 11-8.

Example 11-8   show ip mroute *Command Output*

```
Router# show ip mroute
IP Multicast Routing Table
Flags: D - Dense, S - Sparse, B - Bidir Group, s - SSM Group, C - Connected,
       L - Local, P - Pruned, R - RP-bit set, F - Register flag,
       T - SPT-bit set, J - Join SPT, M - MSDP created entry,
       X - Proxy Join Timer Running, A - Candidate for MSDP Advertisement,
       U - URD, I - Received Source Specific Host Report, Z - Multicast Tunnel,
       Y - Joined MDT-data group, y - Sending to MDT-data group
Timers: Uptime/Expires
Interface state: Interface, Next-Hop or VCD, State/Mode

(*, 224.0.100.4), 02:37:12, RP is 192.168.47.14, flags: S
  Incoming interface: Serial0, RPF neighbor 10.4.53.4
  Outgoing interface list:
    Ethernet1, Forward/Sparse, 02:37:12/0:03:42
    Ethernet2, Forward/Sparse, 02:52:12/0:01:23

(192.168.46.0/24, 224.0.100.4), 02:37:12, flags: RT
  Incoming interface: Ethernet1, RPF neighbor 10.4.53.4
  Outgoing interface list:
    Ethernet2, Forward/Sparse, 02:44:21/0:01:47
```

Notice the highlighted (*, G) and (S, G) entries. Other valuable information contained in the mroute table includes the incoming interface (IIF), which shows on which interface traffic is entering the router, and the outgoing interface list (OIL), which shows the router interfaces over which the multicast traffic is being forwarded.

Rendezvous Points

In a PIM-SM network, one or more routers need to be designated as a *rendezvous point* (RP). Non-RPs can be configured to point to a statically defined RP with the global configuration mode command **ip pim rp-address** *ip-address*. However, in larger topologies, Cisco recommends that RPs be automatically discovered. Cisco routers support two methods for automatically discovering an RP: Auto-RP and Bootstrap Router (BSR). Although Auto-RP is a Cisco approach, BSR is a standards-based approach to make the location of RPs known throughout a multicast network.

Common Video Troubleshooting Issues

As with voice networks, data networking troubleshooting targets should be considered when troubleshooting a reported video issue. Additionally, as a reference, Table 11-6 offers a collection of common video troubleshooting targets and recommended solutions.

Table 11-6   *Common Video Troubleshooting Targets*

Video Troubleshooting Target	Recommended Solutions
Bandwidth	Video streams can be bursty in nature and consume large quantities of bandwidth. Therefore, although sufficient bandwidth should be allocated for supported video applications, you should confirm that the video traffic is not consuming too much bandwidth (that is, an amount of bandwidth that would negatively impact other important traffic).
Pervasiveness of Video Applications	The volume of video traffic on a network might be somewhat unpredictable, because users might introduce their own video traffic on a network without the knowledge of network administrators. Therefore, your policy for network use should address the types of traffic a user is allowed to send and receive. Also, you might want to block video from portions of your network.
Security	In addition to protecting the content of your network's video streams, realize that security measures you have in place might be conflicting with your video applications. For example, if a video stream cannot be established, you might check your firewalls and router ACLs to confirm they are not blocking video media (that is, RTP) packets, video maintenance (for example, RTCP) packets, or video-signaling packets (for example, H.323).
QoS	Because video traffic is latency-sensitive, QoS mechanisms should be in place to ensure video packets are sent with priority treatment, and sufficient bandwidth should be allocated for your supported video applications.
Multicast	Because many video applications rely on multicast technologies to transmit a video stream to a multicast group, much of your video troubleshooting might be focused on multicast troubleshooting. For example, confirm that both routers and switches are properly configured with multicast protocols (for example, PIM-SM on a router and IGMP Snooping on a switch).

Trouble Tickets: Unified Communications

This section presents two trouble tickets based on Unified Communications issues. In the first trouble ticket (that is, Trouble Ticket #9), a Cisco IP Phone is failing to register with its Cisco Unified Communications Manager Express (UCME) router. Once that issue is resolved, the second trouble ticket (that is, Trouble Ticket #10) addresses poor voice quality on the network. In each of these trouble tickets, you are given sample **show** command output and are then challenged to identify a resolution for the issue described.

Trouble Ticket #9

You receive the following trouble ticket:

A Cisco IP Phone with directory number 3333 (connected to interface Fast Ethernet 5/45 on switch SW2) is unable to register with router R1, which is configured as a UCME call agent. This is a new installation and has never worked. Therefore, no baseline data is available.

This trouble ticket references the topology shown in Figure 11-12.

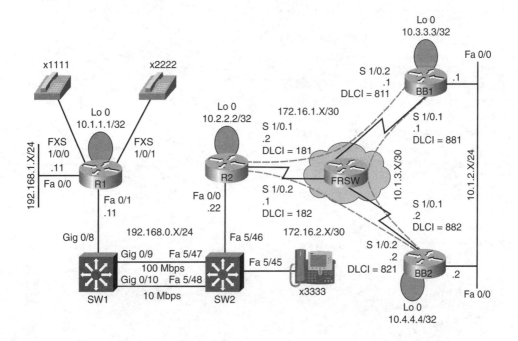

Figure 11-12 *Trouble Ticket #9—Topology*

Assume that you have already verified reachability between switch SW2 and router R1 and have decided to focus your efforts on the configuration of the Cisco Unified Communications Manager Express router (that is, router R1). Example 11-9 shows the running configuration for router R1.

Example 11-9   *Running Configuration of Router R1*

```
R1# show run
Building configuration...
...OUTPUT OMITTED...
hostname R1
!
ip cef
!
ip dhcp excluded-address 192.168.0.1 192.168.0.100
!
ip dhcp pool TSHOOT
   network 192.168.1.0 255.255.255.0
   option 150 ip 192.168.0.11
   default-router 192.168.0.11
!
interface Loopback0
 ip address 10.1.1.1 255.255.255.255
!
interface FastEthernet0/0
 ip address 192.168.1.11 255.255.255.0
!
interface FastEthernet0/1
 ip address 192.168.0.11 255.255.255.0
!
router ospf 1
network 0.0.0.0 255.255.255.255 area 0
!
voice-port 1/0/0
!
voice-port 1/0/1
!
dial-peer voice 1111 pots
 destination-pattern 1111
 port 1/0/0
!
dial-peer voice 2222 pots
 destination-pattern 2222
 port 1/0/1
!
telephony-service
 max-ephones 5
 max-dn 10
 ip source-address 192.168.0.11 port 2000
 create cnf-files version-stamp Jan 01 2002 00:00:00
 max-conferences 4 gain -6
```

```
!
ephone-dn  1
 number 1000
!
ephone  1
 mac-address 0008.A3D1.FBC4
 button  1:1
!
...OUTPUT OMITTED...
```

Assume you have confirmed that the MAC address configured for ephone 1 is correct. Although the TSHOOT curriculum does not cover the configuration of a UCME router, Table 11-7 offers a reference for some of the commands used in Example 11-9.

Table 11-7   *Sampling of Cisco UCME Configuration Commands*

Command	Description
telephony-service	Global configuration mode command that enters the configuration mode for setting up Cisco UCME parameters.
max-ephones *number*	Telephony service configuration mode command that specifies the maximum number of Ethernet phone directory numbers supported on the UCME system. (NOTE: The default is 0.)
max-dn *number*	Telephony service configuration mode command that specifies the maximum number of Ethernet phones supported on the UCME system. (NOTE: The default is 0.)
create cnf-files	Telephony service configuration mode command that creates .XML configuration files for configured ephones.
ephone-dn *tag*	Global configuration mode command that enters ephone-dn configuration mode for a locally significant ephone-dn tag.
number *directory-number*	Ephone-dn configuration mode command that specifies the directory number for an ephone-dn.
ephone *tag*	Global configuration mode command that enters ephone configuration mode for a locally significant ephone tag.

continues

Table 11-7 *Sampling of Cisco UCME Configuration Commands* *(Continued)*

Command	Description
mac-address *MAC-address*	Ephone configuration mode command that specifies the MAC address for an ephone. (NOTE: The MAC address is entered in the following format: xxxx.xxxx.xxxx.)
button *button-number:ephone-dn-tag*	Ephone configuration mode command that associates a previously configured ephone-dn with a button on the ephone.
ip source-address *ip-address*	Global configuration mode command that specifies the IP address on the UCME router used to send and receive Skinny Client Control Protocol (SCCP) messages when communicating with Cisco IP Phones.
dial-peer voice *tag* **pots**	Global configuration mode command that creates a Plain Old Telephone Service (POTS) dial peer.
destination-pattern *pattern*	Dial peer configuration mode command that specifies the pattern of a dial string to be matched. (NOTE: Wildcards can be used.)
port *port-identifier*	Dial peer configuration mode command that specifies a voice port that a POTS dial peer references.

In an attempt to determine why the ephone registration is failing, you issue a **debug ephone** command on router R1. However, no debug output is generated.

Therefore, you decide to look through the running configuration of router R1, as previously presented in Example 11-9. On a separate sheet of paper, identify any misconfiguration you find and how you would correct that misconfiguration.

Suggested Solution: Trouble Ticket #9

In the running configuration of router R1, you might have noticed that the DHCP pool named THSOOT specified a network address space of 192.168.1.0 255.255.255.0. However, if you examine the topology provided in Figure 11-12, you can see that the IP phone (with directory number 3333) should be assigned an IP address in the 192.168.0.0 255.255.255.0 address space.

Example 11-10 shows the correction of this misconfiguration. Notice that after the configuration is corrected, the ephone successfully registers.

Example 11-10 *Correcting the DHCP Pool Misconfiguration on Router R1*

```
R1# conf term
R1(config)# ip dhcp pool TSHOOT
R1(dhcp-config)# no network 192.168.1.0 255.255.255.0
R1(dhcp-config)# network 192.168.0.0 255.255.255.0
```

```
R1(dhcp-config)# end
R1#
*Mar  3 15:19:24.304: %IPPHONE-6-REG_ALARM: 22: Name=SEP0008A3D1FBC4 Load=7.1(2.0)
Last=Reset-Reset
*Mar  3 15:19:24.308: %IPPHONE-6-REGISTER: ephone-1:SEP0008A3D1FBC4
IP:192.168.0.101 Socket:1 DeviceType:Phone has registered.
```

Trouble Ticket #10

Now that router R1 has been properly configured as a UCME router, the IP Phone (that is, directory number 3333) and the analog phones (that is, directory numbers 1111 and 2222) can call one another. Although the voice quality between these phones is fine on the LAN, the following trouble ticket indicates quality issues when placing calls over the Frame Relay WAN connections:

> When placing calls across the Frame Relay WAN, users are complaining that the voice quality is poor for calls originating on an analog phone, whereas the voice quality is fine for calls originating on an IP phone.

This trouble ticket references the previous topology (that is, Figure 11-12). Because the trouble ticket implies a QoS issue, you decide to investigate the configuration of router R2 sitting at the WAN edge. Example 11-11 shows the output from a collection of **show** commands.

Example 11-11 *Verifying Configuration on Router R2*

```
R2# show class-map
 Class Map match-any class-default (id 0)
   Match any
 Class Map match-all VOICE (id 1)
   Match    dscp ef (46)
R2# show policy-map
  Policy Map TSHOOT
    Class VOICE
      Strict Priority
      Bandwidth 256 (kbps) Burst 1600 (Bytes)
    Class class-default
      Flow based Fair Queueing
      Bandwidth 0 (kbps) Max Threshold 64 (packets)
R2# show policy-map interface s1/0
 Serial1/0
  Service-policy output: TSHOOT
    Class-map: VOICE (match-all)
      0 packets, 0 bytes
      5 minute offered rate 0 bps, drop rate 0 bps
      Match:  dscp ef (46)
      Queueing
        Strict Priority
```

```
      Output Queue: Conversation 264
      Bandwidth 64 (kbps) Burst 1600 (Bytes)
      (pkts matched/bytes matched) 0/0
      (total drops/bytes drops) 0/0
  Class-map: class-default (match-any)
    8 packets, 1010 bytes
    5 minute offered rate 0 bps, drop rate 0 bps
    Match: any
    Queueing
      Flow Based Fair Queueing
      Maximum Number of Hashed Queues 256
      (total queued/total drops/no-buffer drops) 0/0/0
```

Router R2's configuration appears to be classifying voice traffic based on a packet's DSCP values. Specifically, if a packet is marked with a DSCP PHB value of EF (that is, Expedited Forwarding, which has a decimal equivalent of 46), that packet is classified into the **VOICE** class. Traffic in this class has access to as much as 256 kbps of bandwidth and is given priority treatment.

Also provided as a reference, Example 11-12 shows the configuration of router R1.

Example 11-12 *Verifying Configuration on Router R1*

```
R1# show run
...OUTPUT OMITTED...
hostname R1
!
ip cef
!
ip dhcp excluded-address 192.168.0.1 192.168.0.100
!
ip dhcp pool TSHOOT
   network 192.168.0.0 255.255.255.0
   option 150 ip 192.168.0.11
   default-router 192.168.0.11
interface Loopback0
 ip address 10.1.1.1 255.255.255.255
interface FastEthernet0/0
 ip address 192.168.1.11 255.255.255.0
!
interface FastEthernet0/1
 ip address 192.168.0.11 255.255.255.0
!
router ospf 1
 network 0.0.0.0 255.255.255.255 area 0
!
```

```
dial-peer voice 1111 pots
 destination-pattern 1111
 port 1/0/0
!
dial-peer voice 2222 pots
ip nat inside
destination-pattern 2222
 port 1/0/1
!
telephony-service
 max-ephones 5
 max-dn 10
 ip source-address 192.168.0.11 port 2000
 create cnf-files version-stamp Jan 01 2002 00:00:00
 max-conferences 4 gain -6
!
ephone-dn  1
 number 1000
!
ephone  1
 mac-address 0008.A3D1.FBC4
 button  1:1
```

Based on the **show** command output, hypothesize how you could resolve the reported
quality issue. You can then compare your recommended solution with the following suggested solution. Note that many possible solutions exist to solve this particular trouble
ticket.

Suggested Solution: Trouble Ticket #10

Because router R2 is giving priority treatment to traffic marked with a DSCP PHB value
of EF, you should ensure that all voice packets are being marked with that value. Cisco IP
Phones, by default, mark voice packets with an EF. However, by examining the configuration of router R1 (that is, the router to which the two analog phones are attached), there
does not seem to be any configuration that marks voice packets sourced from the analog
voice ports with any DSCP value.

Therefore, router R1 should be configured to mark voice traffic with a DSCP PHB of EF.
Although you could do this manually, using more than one approach, this suggested solution leverages the AutoQoS VoIP feature. By enabling AutoQoS VoIP on Router R1's Fast
Ethernet 0/1 interface, voice packets will be automatically recognized (based on their use
of RTP). Example 11-13 illustrates the application and verification of the AutoQoS VoIP
feature to router R1.

Example 11-13   *Applying and Verifying AutoQoS VoIP on Router R1*

```
R1#conf term
R1(config)#int fa 0/1
R1(config-if)#auto qos voip
R1(config-if)#end
R1#show run
...OUTPUT OMITTED...
hostname R1
!
ip cef
!
ip dhcp excluded-address 192.168.0.1 192.168.0.100
!
ip dhcp pool TSHOOT
   network 192.168.0.0 255.255.255.0
   option 150 ip 192.168.0.11
   default-router 192.168.0.11
!
class-map match-any AutoQoS-VoIP-Remark
 match ip dscp ef
 match ip dscp cs3
match ip dscp af31
class-map match-any AutoQoS-VoIP-Control-UnTrust
 match access-group name AutoQoS-VoIP-Control
class-map match-any AutoQoS-VoIP-RTP-UnTrust
 match protocol rtp audio
 match access-group name AutoQoS-VoIP-RTCP
!
policy-map AutoQoS-Policy-UnTrust
 class AutoQoS-VoIP-RTP-UnTrust
  priority percent 70
  set dscp ef
 class AutoQoS-VoIP-Control-UnTrust
  bandwidth percent 5
```

```
   set dscp af31
 class AutoQoS-VoIP-Remark
   set dscp default
 class class-default
   fair-queue
!
interface Loopback0
 ip address 10.1.1.1 255.255.255.255
!
interface FastEthernet0/0
 ip address 192.168.1.11 255.255.255.0
!
interface FastEthernet0/1
ip address 192.168.0.11 255.255.255.0
 auto qos voip
 service-policy output AutoQoS-Policy-UnTrust
!
router ospf 1
 network 0.0.0.0 255.255.255.255 area 0
!
ip access-list extended AutoQoS-VoIP-Control
 permit tcp any any eq 1720
 permit tcp any any range 11000 11999
 permit udp any any eq 2427
 permit tcp any any eq 2428
 permit tcp any any range 2000 2002
permit udp any any eq 1719
 permit udp any any eq 5060
ip access-list extended AutoQoS-VoIP-RTCP
permit udp any any range 16384 32767
!
rmon event 33333 log trap AutoQoS description "AutoQoS SNMP traps for Voice Drops"
owner AutoQoS
```

```
rmon alarm 33333 cbQosCMDropBitRate.1081.1083 30 absolute rising-threshold 1 33333
falling-threshold 0 owner AutoQoS
!
voice-port 1/0/0
!
voice-port 1/0/1
!
dial-peer voice 2222 pots
 destination-pattern 2222
 port 1/0/0
!
dial-peer voice 3333 pots
 destination-pattern 3333
port 1/0/1
!
telephony-service
 max-ephones 5
 max-dn 10
 ip source-address 192.168.0.11 port 2000
 create cnf-files version-stamp Jan 01 2002 00:00:00
 max-conferences 4 gain -6
!
ephone-dn  1
 number 1000
!
ephone  1
mac-address 0008.A3D1.FBC4
 button  1:1
...OUTPUT OMITTED...
```

The highlighted commands in this example indicate the commands automatically entered by the AutoQoS VoIP feature. After AutoQoS VoIP is applied, router R1 begins to mark RTP audio packets (that is, voice packets) with a DSCP PHB of EF. Then, when those voice packets reach router R2, router R2 is able to classify them into the **VOICE** class, which receives priority treatment in being sent out over the Frame Relay WAN links, thus resolving the reported issue.

Exam Preparation Tasks

Review All Key Topics

Review the most important topics from inside the chapter, noted with the Key Topics icon in the outer margin of the page. Table 11-8 lists these key topics and the page numbers where each is found.

Table 11-8 *Key Topics for Chapter 11*

Key Topic Element	Description	Page Number
List	IP telephony components	330
List	Symptoms of having a lack of bandwidth	331
List	Supporting services for voice traffic	332
Steps	Boot-up process for a Cisco IP Phone	335
Table 11-2	Common voice troubleshooting targets	335
List	MQC steps	336
Example 11-1	MQC sample configuration	337
Table 11-3	MQC verification commands	338
Table 11-4	AutoQoS platform support	341
List	AutoQoS configuration prerequisites	342
Table 11-5	Recommended QoS metrics for video	348
List	IGMP versions	350
Table 11-6	Common video troubleshooting targets	358

Complete Tables and Lists from Memory

Print a copy of Appendix B, "Memory Tables," (found on the CD) or at least the section for this chapter, and complete the tables and lists from memory. Appendix C, "Memory Tables Answer Key," also on the CD, includes completed tables and lists to check your work.

Define Key Terms

Define the following key terms from this chapter, and check your answers in the Glossary:

Voice over IP (VoIP), IP telephony, unified communications, IP phone, gatekeeper, gateway, multipoint control unit (MCU), call agent, application server, videoconference station, delay, jitter, drops, Differentiated Services Code Point (DSCP), Modular Quality of Service Command-Line Interface (MQC), AutoQoS VoIP, AutoQoS Enterprise, Cisco

Unified Video Advantage, Cisco TelePresence, multicasting, Internet Group Management Protocol (IGMP), Protocol Independent Multicast (PIM), rendezvous point (RP)

Command Reference to Check Your Memory

This section includes the most important configuration and EXEC commands covered in this chapter. To determine how well you have memorized the commands as a side effect of your other studies, cover the left side of the table with a piece of paper, read the descriptions on the right side, and see whether you remember the command.

Table 11-9   *Chapter 11 Configuration Command Reference*

Command	Description
class-map [match-any | match-all] *class-name*	Global configuration mode command that creates a class map and enters class map configuration mode.
policy-map *policy-name*	Global configuration mode command that creates a policy map and enters policy map configuration mode.
class *class-name*	Policy map configuration mode command that enters policy map class configuration mode.
service-policy {input | output} *policy-map-name*	Interface configuration mode command that applies a policy map in either the inbound or outbound direction.
auto qos voip [trust] [fr-atm]	Interface configuration mode command for a router that enables AutoQoS VoIP on an interface. (NOTE: The **trust** keyword indicates that traffic should be classified based on its DSCP value rather than being based on NBAR. The **fr-atm** keyword can cause a Frame Relay Discard Eligible (DE) bit to be translated into an ATM Cell Loss Priority (CLP) bit, and vice versa.)
auto qos voip trust	Interface configuration mode command for a switch that configures an interface to trust Class of Service (CoS) markings (that is, Layer 2 QoS priority markings on an Ethernet link) for classifying VoIP traffic.
auto qos voip cisco-phone	Interface configuration mode command for a switch that configures the interface to trust CoS markings only if those markings came from an attached Cisco IP Phone. (NOTE: CDP is used to detect an attached Cisco IP Phone.)
auto discovery qos [trust]	Interface configuration mode command on a router issued to begin the discovery phase on an interface for the Auto-QoS Enterprise feature. (NOTE: The **trust** keyword instructs the router to classify traffic based on existing DSCP markings, as opposed to using NBAR.)

Table 11-9   *Chapter 11 Configuration Command Reference   (Continued)*

Command	Description
auto qos	Interface configuration mode command on a router used to apply a policy map generated by AutoQoS Enterprise.
ip multicast-routing	Global configuration mode command used to enable IP multicast routing.
ip pim {dense-mode | sparse-mode | sparse-dense-mode}	Interface configuration mode command used to enable an interface to participate in a specified PIM mode.
ip pim rp-address *ip-address*	Global configuration mode command used to specify the IP address of a rendezvous point (RP) in a PIM Sparse Mode network.
ip igmp snooping	Global configuration mode command used on a Cisco Catalyst switch to globally enable IGMP snooping on the switch.
[no] ip igmp snooping vlan *vlan_id*	Global configuration mode command used on a Cisco Catalyst switch to enable (or disable, using the **no** option) IGMP snooping for a specific VLAN.

Table 11-10   *Chapter 11 EXEC Command Reference*

Command	Description
show class-map [*class-map-name*]	Used to view what a class map is matching.
show policy-map [*policy-map-name*]	Used to view the policy applied to the classes within a policy map.
show policy-map interface *interface-identifier* [**input** | **output**]	Used to view class map and policy map configuration and statistical information for packets crossing a specific interface.
show auto qos voip [**interface** *interface-identifier*]	Displays global and interface (or optionally, only interface) configuration mode commands added by the AutoQoS VoIP feature.
show auto discovery qos	Used to view how the AutoQoS Enterprise feature has classified traffic and the recommended policy generated by AutoQoS Enterprise.
show ip igmp interface [*interface-id*]	Can be used to identify the IP address of an IGMP querier.
show ip igmp group	Displays the IP multicast groups of which the router is aware.

This chapter covers the following subjects:

Reviewing IPv6: This section introduces the purpose and structure of IP version 6 (IPv6) addressing. You consider the various types of IPv6 addresses, routing protocols supporting IPv6, and basic syntax for enabling a router to route IPv6 traffic. A sample configuration is provided to illustrate the configuration of a router to support IPv6. Additionally, as an organization is migrating from IPv4 to IPv6, there might be portions of the network that are still running IPv4 with other portions of the network running IPv6. For IPv6 traffic to span an IPv4 portion of the network, one option is to create a tunnel spanning the IPv4 network. Then, IPv6 traffic can travel inside the tunnel to transit the IPv4 network. This section discusses the syntax and provides an example of tunneling IPv6 over an IPv4 tunnel.

OSPFv3 Troubleshooting: This section contrasts the characteristics of two versions of OSPF, specifically OSPFv2 and OSPFv3. OSPFv3 can support the routing of IPv6 networks, whereas OSPFv2 cannot. OSPFv3 configuration syntax is presented, along with a sample configuration. You are also provided with a collection of verification troubleshooting commands and a listing of common OSPFv3 issues.

Trouble Ticket: IPv6 and OSPF: This section presents you with a trouble ticket addressing a network experiencing OSPF adjacency issues. You are presented with a collection of **show** and **debug** command output and challenged to resolve a series of misconfigurations. Suggested solutions are also provided.

RIPng Troubleshooting: This section contrasts the characteristics of RIP next generation (RIPng) with RIPv2. You are given a set of RIPng configuration commands along with a sample configuration. From a troubleshooting perspective, you compare RIPng troubleshooting commands with those commands used to troubleshoot RIPv1 and RIPv2. Finally, this section identifies some of the more common RIPng troubleshooting issues you might encounter.

Trouble Ticket: IPv6 and RIPng: This section challenges you to resolve a couple of RIPng issues being observed in a network. Specifically, load balancing and default route advertisements are not behaving as expected. To assist in your troubleshooting efforts, you are armed with a collection of **show** and **debug** command output. Your proposed solutions can then be compared with suggested solutions.

CHAPTER 12

IPv6 Troubleshooting

With the global proliferation of IP-based networks, available IPv4 addresses are rapidly becoming extinct. Fortunately, IPv6 provides enough IP addresses for many generations to come. This section introduces IPv6's address structure and discusses some of its unique characteristics. As part of an IPv4 to IPv6 migration, you might also need to update the IP routing protocol in use, because the existing IP routing protocol might not be compatible with IPv6. This chapter identifies a collection of IP routing protocols capable of routing IPv6 traffic. Additionally, you see how to tunnel IPv6 traffic across an IPv4 network.

After reviewing the fundamentals of IPv6, this chapter focuses on troubleshooting OSPF version 3 (OSPFv3), a routing protocol compatible with IPv6 routes. Troubleshooting OSPFv3 bears many similarities with troubleshooting OSPFv2, as discussed in Chapter 7, "OSPF and Route Redistribution Troubleshooting." Although you can certainly leverage many of your OSPFv2 troubleshooting strategies with OSPFv3, you do need to understand the subtle distinctions. Therefore, this section introduces you to the commonalities and differences in these two OSPF versions. OSPFv3 configuration, verification, and troubleshooting are also discussed.

To help you practice your OSPFv3 troubleshooting skills, this chapter challenges you with a trouble ticket addressing OSPFv3 issues present in a given network topology. Output from **show** and **debug** commands is provided to help you identify the underlying issues. Based on this collected information, you identify why the observed behavior is occurring and propose solutions. You can compare your solutions with suggested solutions.

Like OSPFv3, RIPng also supports IPv6 routes. This chapter contrasts RIPng with its predecessor, RIPv2. Configuration and troubleshooting syntax references are provided, in addition to a sample configuration. You are also given a listing of common RIPng troubleshooting issues you might encounter.

Finally, a trouble ticket addressing RIPng is presented. As with the OSPFv3 trouble ticket, you are challenged to resolve the identified issues, equipped with a collection of **show** and **debug** command output. Suggested solutions are provided.

"Do I Know This Already?" Quiz

The "Do I Know This Already?" quiz helps you determine your level of knowledge of this chapter's topics before you begin. Table 12-1 details the major topics discussed in this chapter and their corresponding quiz questions.

Table 12-1   *"Do I Know This Already?" Section-to-Question Mapping*

Foundation Topics Section	Questions
Reviewing IPv6	1–5
OSPFv3 Troubleshooting	6–8
RIPng Troubleshooting	9–11

1. Identify three IPv6 address types. (Choose the three best answers.)

    a. Unicast

    b. Broadcast

    c. Multicast

    d. Anycast

2. How can the following IPv6 address be condensed?
    0AA0:0123:4040:0000:0000:0000:000A:100B

    a. AA0::123:404:A:100B

    b. AA::123:404:A:1B

    c. AA0:123:4040::A:100B

    d. 0AA0:0123:4040::0::000A:100B

3. Identify three approaches for routing IPv6. (Choose the three best answers.)

    a. OSPFv2

    b. RIPng

    c. Static routes

    d. EIGRP

4. What command is used to enable IPv6 routing on a router?

    a. Router(config)# **ipv6 unicast-routing**

    b. Router(config)# **ipv6 routing**

    c. Router(config)# **ip routing ipv6**

    d. Router(config)# **ip routing unicast-ipv6**

5. You want to tunnel IPv6 traffic across an IPv4 portion of a network. In interface con-figuration mode for the tunnel you are configuring, what IP address would you enter after the tunnel source command?

    a. The IPv6 address assigned to the local tunnel interface

    b. The IPv4 address assigned to the local interface on which the tunnel is built

    c. The IPv6 address assigned to the remote tunnel interface

    d. The IPv4 address assigned to the remote interface on which the tunnel is built

6. Identify two OSPFv3 characteristics that are not characteristics of OSPFv2. (Choose the two best answers.)

   a. Uses a hierarchical structure divided into areas

   b. Requires direct connectivity from the backbone area to all other areas

   c. Uses link-local addresses to identify neighbors

   d. Allows communication between two nodes connected to a common link, even though the two nodes might not share a common subnet

7. In what configuration mode is the following OSPFv3 command issued?

```
ipv6 ospf process-id area area-id
```

   a. Router configuration mode

   b. Route-map configuration mode

   c. Global configuration mode

   d. Interface configuration mode

8. What command lists the state of a router's adjacency with all configured OSPFv3 neighbors? (Choose the best answer.)

   a. show ipv6 ospf

   b. show ipv6 ospf neighbor

   c. show ipv6 ospf interface

   d. debug ipv6 ospf adj

9. RIPng sends routing updates to what multicast address?

   a. 224.0.0.9

   b. FF02::9

   c. FE80::

   d. 224.0.0.5

10. What interface configuration mode command instructs an interface to participate in a specified RIPng routing process? (Choose the best answer.)

   a. ipv6 rip *process-name* **default-information** {only | originate}

   b. ipv6 interface *process-name*

   c. ipv6 router rip *process-name*

   d. ipv6 rip *process-name* **enable**

11. Which of the following commands shows the contents of an IPv6 routing table?

   a. show ipv6 rip [*process-name*] [database | next-hops]

   b. show ipv6 route

   c. show ripng route

   d. show rip route ipv6

Foundation Topics

Reviewing IPv6

With the worldwide depletion of IP version 4 (IPv4) addresses, many organizations have migrated, are in the process of migrating, or are considering migrating their IPv4 addresses to IPv6 addresses. IPv6 dramatically increases the number of available IP addresses. In fact, IPv6 offers approximately $5 * 10^{28}$ IP addresses for each person on the planet.

Beyond the increased address space, IPv6 offers many other features:

Key Topic

- Simplified header.
    - IPv4 header: Uses 12 fields.
    - IPv6 header: Uses 5 fields.
- No broadcasts.
- No fragmentation (performs MTU discovery for each session).
- Can coexist with IPv4 during a transition.
    - Dual stack (running IPv4 and IPv6 simultaneously).
    - IPv6 over IPv4 (tunneling IPv6 over an IPv4 tunnel).

This section reviews IPv6 address types, the IPv6 address structure, and routing options for IPv6. Subsequent sections in this chapter address troubleshooting IPv6 routing protocols, specifically OSPFv3 and RIPng.

IPv6 Address Types

IPv6 has three types of addresses:

Key Topic

- Unicast
- Multicast
- Anycast

Unicast

With unicast, a single IPv6 address is applied to a single interface, as illustrated in Figure 12-1. The communication flow can be thought of as a one-to-one communication flow.

In Figure 12-1, a server (that is, AAAA::1) is sending traffic to a single client (that is, AAAA::2).

Multicast

With multicast, a single IPv6 address (that is, a multicast group) represents multiple devices on a network, as seen in Figure 12-2. The communication flow is one-to-many.

In Figure 12-2, a server (that is, AAAA::1) is sending traffic to a multicast group (that is, FF00::A). Two clients (that is, AAAA::2 and AAAA::3) have joined this group. Those clients receive the traffic from the server, whereas any client that did not join the group (for example, AAAA::4) does not receive the traffic.

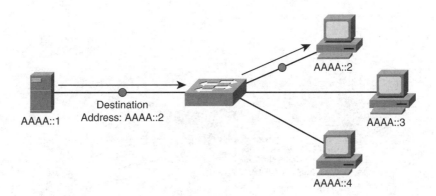

Figure 12-1   *IPv6 Unicast Example*

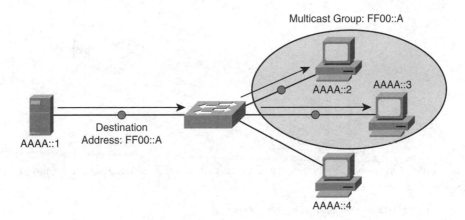

Figure 12-2   *IPv6 Multicast Example*

Anycast

With anycast, a single IPv6 address is assigned to multiple devices, as depicted in Figure 12-3. The communication flow is one-to-nearest (from the perspective of a router's routing table).

In Figure 12-3, a client with an IPv6 address of AAAA::1 wants to send traffic to a destination IPv6 address of AAAA::2. Notice that two servers (that is, Server A and Server B) have an IPv6 address of AAAA::2. In the figure, the traffic destined for AAAA::2 is sent to Server A, via router R2, because the network on which Server A resides appears to be closer than the network on which Server B resides, from the perspective of router R1's IPv6 routing table.

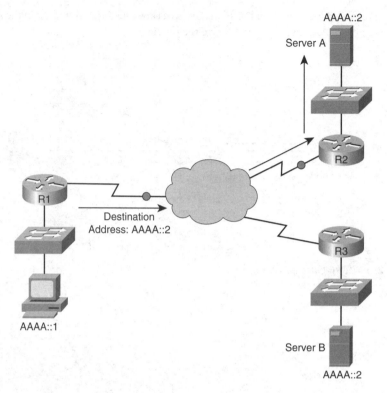

Figure 12-3 *IPv6 Anycast Example*

IPv6 Address Format

An IPv6 address has the following address format, where X equals a hexadecimal digit in the range of 0–F:

XXXX:XXXX:XXXX:XXXX:XXXX:XXXX:XXXX:XXXX

A hexadecimal digit is four bits in size (that is, four binary bits can represent sixteen values). Notice that an IPv6 address has eight fields, and each field contains four hexadecimal digits. The following formula reveals why an IPv6 address is a 128-bit address:

4 bits per digit * 4 digits per field * 8 fields = 128 bits in an IPv6 address

Because IPv6 addresses can be difficult to work with, due to their size, the following rules exist for abbreviating these addresses:

■ Leading zeros in a field can be omitted.

■ Contiguous fields containing all zeros can be represented with a double colon. (NOTE: This can only be done once for a single IPv6 address.)

As an example, consider the following IPv6 address:

ABCD:0123:4040:0000:0000:0000:000A:000B

Using the rules for abbreviation, the IPv6 address can be rewritten as

`ABCD:123:4040::A:B`

Also, the Extended Unique Identifier (EUI-64) format can be used to cause the router to automatically populate the low-order 64 bits of an IPv6 address based on an interface's MAC address.

IPv6 Routing Options

IPv6 maintains a separate routing table from IPv4. Following are methods of populating this IPv6 routing table:

- **Static routes:** Configured similar to IPv4 static routes.

- **RIP next generation (RIPng):** Has many of the same characteristics as RIPv2 (for example, a distance vector routing protocol with a 15 hop-count maximum).

- **OSPFv3:** Builds on OSPFv2 to add support for IPv6 network characteristics (for example, 128-bit network addresses and link-local addresses).

- **IS-IS for IPv6:** Similar to IS-IS for IPv4, with a few IPv6 extensions added (for example, new Type, Length, Value [TLV] attributes, and a new protocol ID).

- **Multiprotocol BGP:** Allows BGP to route protocols other than IPv4 (for example, IPv6).

- **EIGRP:** Configured on the interfaces with IPv6 addressing, similar to OSPFv3.

Configuring IPv6 Support

As a reference, Table 12-2 presents basic IPv6 configuration commands.

Table 12-2 *IPv6 Configuration Commands*

Command	Description
ipv6 cef	Global configuration mode command that configures Cisco Express Forwarding for IPv6.
ipv6 unicast-routing	Global configuration mode command that instructs a router to forward IPv6 traffic.
ipv6 address *ipv6-address/prefix-length* [eui-64]	Interface configuration mode command that assigns an IPv6 address to an interface. (NOTE: The **eui-64** option allows a router to complete the low-order 64 bits of an address, based on an interface's MAC address.)

Example 12-1 demonstrates how to enable a router to support IPv6 routing and how to assign IPv6 addresses to router interfaces.

Example 12-1   *IPv6 Configuration Example*

```
R1# show run
...OUTPUT OMITTED...
ipv6 unicast-routing
ipv6 cef
!
interface FastEthernet0/0
 ipv6 address B:B:B:B::2/64
!
interface FastEthernet0/1
 ipv6 address A:A:A:A::2/64
...OUTPUT OMITTED...
```

As Example 12-1 demonstrates, IPv6 unicast routing is enabled with the **ipv6 unicast-routing** command issued in global configuration mode. Cisco Express Forwarding support for IPv6 is then globally enabled using the **ipv6 cef** command. Finally, under interface configuration mode for both the Fast Ethernet 0/0 and 0/1 interfaces, IPv6 addresses are assigned with the **ipv6 address** *ipv6-address/prefix-length* command.

Tunneling IPv6 Through an IPv4 Tunnel

When an enterprise is migrating from an IPv4 to IPv6 environment, there might be times when IPv6 networks might be separated by one or more IPv4 networks. One option that allows these different address formats to peacefully coexist is to tunnel IPv6 traffic over an IPv4 tunnel.

Table 12-3 provides a command reference for setting up such a tunnel.

Table 12-3   *Commands Used to Tunnel IPv6 via IPv4*

Command	Description
interface tunnel *interface-id*	Global configuration mode command that creates a virtual IPv4 tunnel interface over which encapsulated IPv6 packets can flow.
tunnel source *ipv4-address*	Interface configuration mode command that identifies the IPv4 address of the local end of a tunnel.
tunnel destination *ipv4-address*	Interface configuration mode command that identifies the IPv4 address of the remote end of a tunnel.
tunnel mode ipv6ip	Interface configuration mode command that configures an interface to act as a manual IPv6 tunnel.
ipv6 address *ipv6-address/prefix-length*	Interface configuration mode command that specifies the IPv6 address assigned to a tunnel interface.

Table 12-3 *Commands Used to Tunnel IPv6 via IPv4*   (Continued)

Command	Description
ipv6 ospf *process-id* **area** *area-id*	Interface configuration mode command that allows the IPv6 address configured on a tunnel interface to participate in an OSPFv3 routing process.

Figure 12-4 depicts a topology tunneling IPv6 traffic over an IPv4 tunnel.

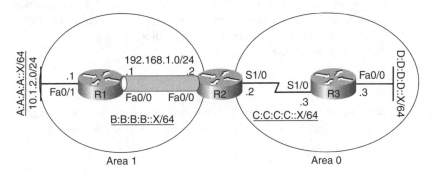

Figure 12-4 *IPv6 over IPv4 Tunnel*

Examples 12-2 and 12-3 show the configuration of the depicted IPv6 over IPv4 tunnel. Notice that each router specifies the source and destination IPv4 addresses of the tunnel, from the perspective of each router. The tunnel interface is then assigned an IPv6 address, told to participate in OSPF Area 1, and instructed to act as a manual IPv6 tunnel. The configuration and troubleshooting of OSPFv3, which is the version of OSPF that supports IPv6, is discussed in the next section.

Example 12-2 *Configuring IPv6 Parameters on Router R1's Tunnel Interface*

Key Topic

```
R1# show run
...OUTPUT OMITTED...
interface tunnel 1
 tunnel source 192.168.1.1
 tunnel destination 192.168.1.2
 ipv6 address b:b:b:b::1/64
 ipv6 ospf 1 area 1
 tunnel mode ipv6ip
```

Example 12-3 *Configuring IPv6 Parameters on Router R2's Tunnel Interface*

```
R2# show run
...OUTPUT OMITTED...
interface tunnel 1
 tunnel source 192.168.1.2
```

```
tunnel destination 192.168.1.1
ipv6 address b:b:b:b::2/64
ipv6 ospf 1 area 1
tunnel mode ipv6ip
```

OSPFv3 Troubleshooting

As mentioned in the previous section, not all routing protocols (or all versions of some routing protocols) are compatible with IPv6. For example, although OSPFv2 is incompatible with IPv6, OSPFv3 can be used on IPv6 networks. This section discusses OSPFv3's characteristics and configuration. Additionally, you will learn some common OSPFv3 troubleshooting issues and commands.

Characteristics of OSPFv3

OSPFv3 builds on OSPFv2. Therefore, when you are working with OSPFv3, you will notice many similarities with OSPFv2. Following are some of these similarities:

- Uses a hierarchical structure divided into areas.

- Requires direct connectivity from the backbone area to all other areas.

- Uses many of the same packet types (for example, Hello packets).

- Adjacencies formed with neighbors.

Beyond the characteristics OPSFv3 has in common with OSPFv2, several enhancements have been made to provide support for IPv6 networks. Following is a sampling of some of OSPFv3's enhancements:

Key Topic

- Routes over links rather than over networks.

- Uses IPv6 link-local addresses to identify neighbors.

- Can support multiple IPv6 subnets on a single link.

- Allows communication between two nodes connected to a common link, even though the two nodes might not share a common subnet.

- Supports multiple instances of OSPFv3 running over a common link.

- Does not require the use of ARP.

Configuring OSPFv3

The primary difference in configuring OSPFv3, as opposed to OSPFv2, is that you go into interface configuration mode to tell an interface to participate in an OSPF routing process. In OSPFv2, you would go into router configuration mode for an OSPF process and specify network addresses and wildcard masks. These addresses and masks determined which of a router's interface would participate in the OSPF routing process.

Table 12-4 provides basic OSPFv3 configuration commands.

Table 12-4   *OSPFv3 Configuration Commands*

Key
Topic

Command	Description
ipv6 ospf *process-id* **area** *area-id*	Interface configuration mode command that allows the IPv6 address configured on an interface to participate in an OSPFv3 routing process.
ipv6 router ospf *process-id*	Global configuration mode command that enables an OSPFv3 routing process on a router.
router-id *ipv4-address*	Router configuration mode command that specifies an IPv4 address to be used by OSPFv3 as a router's router ID.

Example 12-4 shows a sample OSPFv3 configuration on a router (that is, router R1), which is illustrated in Figure 12-5. Notice that an interface can simultaneously be configured with both IPv4 and IPv6 addresses. Also, notice the **ipv6 ospf 100 area 1** command issued in interface configuration mode for the Fast Ethernet 0/0 and 0/1 interfaces. This command causes both interfaces to participate in OSPFv3 routing process 100 as members of Area 1. The OSPFv3 process was started with the **ipv6 router ospf 100** command, and then in router configuration mode, an IPv4 address of 10.1.1.1 was specified as the address to use for the OSPF router ID.

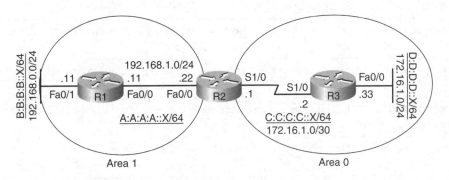

Figure 12-5   *OSPFv3 Sample Configuration Topology*

Example 12-4   *Sample OSPFv3 Configuration*

Key
Topic

```
R1# show run
...OUTPUT OMITTED...
interface FastEthernet0/0
 ip address 192.168.1.11 255.255.255.0
 ipv6 address A:A:A:A::11/64
 ipv6 ospf 100 area 1
!
interface FastEthernet0/1
 ip address 192.168.0.11 255.255.255.0
```

```
  ipv6 address B:B:B:B::11/64
  ipv6 ospf 100 area 1
 !
ipv6 router ospf 100
 router-id 10.1.1.1
...OUTPUT OMITTED...
```

Troubleshooting OSPFv3

When troubleshooting an OSPFv3 issue, you can draw on your knowledge of troubleshooting OSPFv2, because many of the same troubleshooting issues arise in both environments. In fact, you do not need to relearn a completely different set of syntax for troubleshooting OSPFv3. In many cases, you can simply replace the **ip** keyword in a **show** command with a keyword of **ipv6**. For example, when troubleshooting OSPFv2, you might issue the **show ip ospf interface** command to view an interface's OSPF parameters. In an OSPFv3 environment, you could simply replace **ip** with **ipv6**, and give the **show ipv6 ospf interface** command. Table 12-5 provides a command reference of commonly used commands for troubleshooting OSPFv3 issues.

Table 12-5   *OSPFv3 Troubleshooting Commands*

Command	Description
show ipv6 ospf	Displays OSPFv3 routing process, router ID, various timers, and information about each area on a router.
show ipv6 ospf interface	Shows IPv6 link local address, area ID, process ID, router ID, and cost.
show ipv6 ospf neighbor	Lists the state of a router's adjacency with all configured OSPFv3 neighbors.
debug ipv6 ospf adj	Displays information about OSPFv3 adjacencies.
debug ip ipv6 ospf hello	Shows OSPFv3 HELLO packet information.

Many of the same root causes for an OSPFv2 issue could also result in an OSPFv3 issue. As just a few examples, consider the following list of potential reasons an OSPFv3 adjacency might not be formed:

- Mismatched HELLO parameters
- Mismatched IP MTU setting
- Interface configured as passive
- Mismatched area type

Although OSPFv2 and OSPFv3 do have many common characteristics, understanding the subtle differences between these OSPF versions can be valuable in your troubleshooting efforts. A listing of major differences was provided earlier in this section. To reinforce these OSPFv3 troubleshooting concepts, the next section in this chapter presents an OSPFv3 trouble ticket.

Trouble Ticket: IPv6 and OSPF

This section presents a trouble ticket based on an IPv6 and OSPF configuration. You are given sample **show** command output and are challenged to identify a resolution for the issue described.

Trouble Ticket #11

You receive the following trouble ticket:

> Company A recently added IPv6 addressing to its existing IPv4 addressing. OSPFv3 is the protocol being used to route the IPv6 traffic.

> Although the configuration was originally functional, now several OSPFv3 adjacencies are not forming. Full IPv6 reachability throughout the topology needs to be established.

This trouble ticket references the topology shown in Figure 12-6.

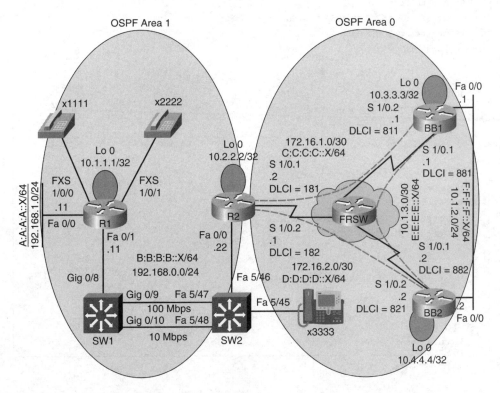

Figure 12-6 *Trouble Ticket #11 Topology*

Viewing Baseline Information

The routers in the topology were similarly configured for IPv6 and OSPFv3. The **show run** command was issued on router R2, the output of which is provided in Example 12-5. The configuration on the other routers in the topology was consistent with the configuration shown for router R2.

Example 12-5   *Working Configuration on Router R2*

```
R2# show run
Building configuration...

hostname R2
--- OUTPUT OMITTED ---
!
ipv6 unicast-routing
ipv6 cef

!
interface Loopback0
 ip address 10.2.2.2 255.255.255.255
!
interface FastEthernet0/0
 ip address 192.168.0.22 255.255.255.0
 ipv6 address B:B:B:B::22/64
 ipv6 ospf 1 area 1

!
interface Serial1/0.1 point-to-point
 ip address 172.16.1.2 255.255.255.252
 ipv6 address C:C:C:C::2/64
 ipv6 ospf 1 area 0

 frame-relay interface-dlci 181
!
interface Serial1/0.2 point-to-point
 ip address 172.16.2.1 255.255.255.252
 ipv6 address D:D:D:D::1/64
 ipv6 ospf 1 area 0

 frame-relay interface-dlci 182
!
!
--- OUTPUT OMITTED ---
ipv6 router ospf 1
```

Originally, all routers had full reachability throughout the topology, as verified in Examples 12-6, 12-7, 12-8, and 12-9.

Example 12-6   *Router R1's Initial IPv6 Routing Table*

```
R1# show ipv6 route
IPv6 Routing Table - 10 entries
Codes: C - Connected, L - Local, S - Static, R - RIP, B - BGP
       U - Per-user Static route
       I1 - ISIS L1, I2 - ISIS L2, IA - ISIS interarea, IS - ISIS summary
       O - OSPF intra, OI - OSPF inter, OE1 - OSPF ext 1, OE2 - OSPF ext 2
       ON1 - OSPF NSSA ext 1, ON2 - OSPF NSSA ext 2
C    A:A:A:A::/64 [0/0]
     via ::, FastEthernet0/0
L    A:A:A:A::11/128 [0/0]
     via ::, FastEthernet0/0
C    B:B:B:B::/64 [0/0]
     via ::, FastEthernet0/1
L    B:B:B:B::11/128 [0/0]
     via ::, FastEthernet0/1
OI   C:C:C:C::/64 [110/65]
     via FE80::C201:8FF:FE2C:0, FastEthernet0/1
OI   D:D:D:D::/64 [110/65]
     via FE80::C201:8FF:FE2C:0, FastEthernet0/1
OI   E:E:E:E::/64 [110/129]
     via FE80::C201:8FF:FE2C:0, FastEthernet0/1
OI   F:F:F:F::/64 [110/75]
     via FE80::C201:8FF:FE2C:0, FastEthernet0/1
L    FE80::/10 [0/0]
     via ::, Null0
L    FF00::/8 [0/0]
     via ::, Null0
```

Example 12-7   *Router R2's Initial IPv6 Routing Table*

```
R2# show ipv6 route
IPv6 Routing Table - 11 entries
Codes: C - Connected, L - Local, S - Static, R - RIP, B - BGP
       U - Per-user Static route
       I1 - ISIS L1, I2 - ISIS L2, IA - ISIS interarea, IS - ISIS summary
       O - OSPF intra, OI - OSPF inter, OE1 - OSPF ext 1, OE2 - OSPF ext 2
       ON1 - OSPF NSSA ext 1, ON2 - OSPF NSSA ext 2
O    A:A:A:A::/64 [110/11]
     via FE80::209:B7FF:FEFA:D1E1, FastEthernet0/0
C    B:B:B:B::/64 [0/0]
     via ::, FastEthernet0/0
L    B:B:B:B::22/128 [0/0]
```

```
        via ::, FastEthernet0/0
C    C:C:C:C::/64 [0/0]
        via ::, Serial1/0.1
L    C:C:C:C::2/128 [0/0]
        via ::, Serial1/0.1
C    D:D:D:D::/64 [0/0]
        via ::, Serial1/0.2
L    D:D:D:D::1/128 [0/0]
        via ::, Serial1/0.2
O    E:E:E:E::/64 [110/128]
        via FE80::C202:8FF:FE98:0, Serial1/0.1
        via FE80::C200:8FF:FE2C:0, Serial1/0.2
O    F:F:F:F::/64 [110/74]
        via FE80::C202:8FF:FE98:0, Serial1/0.1
        via FE80::C200:8FF:FE2C:0, Serial1/0.2
L    FE80::/10 [0/0]
        via ::, Null0
L    FF00::/8 [0/0]
        via ::, Null0
```

Example 12-8 *Router BB1's Initial IPv6 Routing Table*

```
BB1# show ipv6 route
IPv6 Routing Table - 11 entries
Codes: C - Connected, L - Local, S - Static, R - RIP, B - BGP
       U - Per-user Static route
       I1 - ISIS L1, I2 - ISIS L2, IA - ISIS interarea, IS - ISIS summary
       O - OSPF intra, OI - OSPF inter, OE1 - OSPF ext 1, OE2 - OSPF ext 2
       ON1 - OSPF NSSA ext 1, ON2 - OSPF NSSA ext 2
OI   A:A:A:A::/64 [110/75]
        via FE80::C201:8FF:FE2C:0, Serial1/0.2
OI   B:B:B:B::/64 [110/74]
        via FE80::C201:8FF:FE2C:0, Serial1/0.2
C    C:C:C:C::/64 [0/0]
        via ::, Serial1/0.2
L    C:C:C:C::1/128 [0/0]
        via ::, Serial1/0.2
O    D:D:D:D::/64 [110/74]
        via FE80::C200:8FF:FE2C:0, FastEthernet0/0
C    E:E:E:E::/64 [0/0]
        via ::, Serial1/0.1
L    E:E:E:E::1/128 [0/0]
        via ::, Serial1/0.1
C    F:F:F:F::/64 [0/0]
        via ::, FastEthernet0/0
```

```
L    F:F:F:F::1/128 [0/0]
        via ::, FastEthernet0/0
L    FE80::/10 [0/0]
        via ::, Null0
L    FF00::/8 [0/0]
        via ::, Null0
```

Example 12-9   *Router BB2's Initial IPv6 Routing Table*

```
BB2# show ipv6 route
IPv6 Routing Table - 11 entries
Codes: C - Connected, L - Local, S - Static, R - RIP, B - BGP
       U - Per-user Static route
       I1 - ISIS L1, I2 - ISIS L2, IA - ISIS interarea, IS - ISIS summary
       O - OSPF intra, OI - OSPF inter, OE1 - OSPF ext 1, OE2 - OSPF ext 2
       ON1 - OSPF NSSA ext 1, ON2 - OSPF NSSA ext 2
OI   A:A:A:A::/64 [110/75]
        via FE80::C201:8FF:FE2C:0, Serial1/0.2
OI   B:B:B:B::/64 [110/74]
        via FE80::C201:8FF:FE2C:0, Serial1/0.2
O    C:C:C:C::/64 [110/74]
        via FE80::C202:8FF:FE98:0, FastEthernet0/0
C    D:D:D:D::/64 [0/0]
        via ::, Serial1/0.2
L    D:D:D:D::2/128 [0/0]
        via ::, Serial1/0.2
C    E:E:E:E::/64 [0/0]
        via ::, Serial1/0.1
L    E:E:E:E::2/128 [0/0]
        via ::, Serial1/0.1
C    F:F:F:F::/64 [0/0]
        via ::, FastEthernet0/0
L    F:F:F:F::2/128 [0/0]
        via ::, FastEthernet0/0
L    FE80::/10 [0/0]
        via ::, Null0
L    FF00::/8 [0/0]
        via ::, Null0
```

Example 12-10 provides an additional sampling of baseline verification commands issued on router R2.

Example 12-10 *Additional Baseline Verification Commands on Router R2*

```
R2# show ipv6 ospf interface serial 1/0.2
Serial1/0.2 is up, line protocol is up
  Link Local Address FE80::C201:8FF:FE2C:0, Interface ID 14
  Area 0, Process ID 1, Instance ID 0, Router ID 10.2.2.2
  Network Type POINT_TO_POINT, Cost: 64
  Transmit Delay is 1 sec, State POINT_TO_POINT,
  Timer intervals configured, Hello 10, Dead 40, Wait 40, Retransmit 5
    Hello due in 00:00:04
  Index 1/2/3, flood queue length 0
  Next 0x0(0)/0x0(0)/0x0(0)
  Last flood scan length is 1, maximum is 2
  Last flood scan time is 0 msec, maximum is 0 msec
  Neighbor Count is 1, Adjacent neighbor count is 1
    Adjacent with neighbor 10.4.4.4
  Suppress hello for 0 neighbor(s)
R2# show ipv6 ospf
 Routing Process "ospfv3 1" with ID 10.2.2.2
 It is an area border router
 SPF schedule delay 5 secs, Hold time between two SPFs 10 secs
 Minimum LSA interval 5 secs. Minimum LSA arrival 1 secs
 LSA group pacing timer 240 secs
 Interface flood pacing timer 33 msecs
Retransmission pacing timer 66 msecs
Number of external LSA 0. Checksum Sum 0x000000
 Number of areas in this router is 2. 2 normal 0 stub 0 nssa
 Reference bandwidth unit is 100 mbps
    Area BACKBONE(0)
    Number of interfaces in this area is 2
    SPF algorithm executed 8 times
    Number of LSA 14. Checksum Sum 0x063F6C
    Number of DCbitless LSA 0
    Number of indication LSA 0
    Number of DoNotAge LSA 0
    Flood list length 0
    Area 1
    Number of interfaces in this area is 1
    SPF algorithm executed 5 times
    Number of LSA 11. Checksum Sum 0x0481E4
    Number of DCbitless LSA 0
    Number of indication LSA 0
    Number of DoNotAge LSA 0
```

```
     Flood list length 0
R2# show ipv6 ospf neighbor


Neighbor ID     Pri   State         Dead Time   Interface ID   Interface
10.4.4.4          1   FULL/  -      00:00:36    14             Serial1/0.2
10.3.3.3          1   FULL/  -      00:00:36    14             Serial1/0.1
10.1.1.1          1   FULL/BDR      00:00:39    4              FastEthernet0/0
```

Troubleshoot and Resolve the Identified OSPFv3 Adjacency Issue

The trouble ticket indicates that several adjacencies are not being formed. So, you decide to start your troubleshooting efforts on router R1 and check its adjacency with router R2, and then check the adjacencies between R2 and BB1 and BB2. Finally, you will check the adjacencies between BB1 and BB2.

Issue #1: Adjacency Between Routers R1 and R2

Example 12-11 shows the data collected from router R1.

Example 12-11 *Troubleshooting Data Collection on Router R1*

```
R1# show ipv6 ospf neighbor

R1# debug ipv6 ospf adj
OSPFv3 adjacency events debugging is on
R1# debug ipv6 ospf hello
OSPFv3 hello events debugging is on
R1# u all
All possible debugging has been turned off
R1# show run
...OUTPUT OMITTED...
hostname R1
!
ipv6 unicast-routing
ipv6 cef
!
interface Loopback0
 ip address 10.1.1.1 255.255.255.255
!
interface FastEthernet0/0
 ip address 192.168.1.11 255.255.255.0
ipv6 address A:A:A:A::11/64
 ipv6 ospf 100 area 1
!
interface FastEthernet0/1
 ip address 192.168.0.11 255.255.255.0
```

```
   ipv6 address B:B:B:B::11/64
   ipv6 ospf 100 area 1
!
ipv6 router ospf 100
...OUTPUT OMITTED...
R1# show ipv6 ospf interface fa 0/1
FastEthernet0/1 is up, line protocol is up
   Link Local Address FE80::209:B7FF:FEFA:D1E1, Interface ID 4
   Area 1, Process ID 100, Instance ID 0, Router ID 192.168.1.11
   Network Type BROADCAST, Cost: 1
   Transmit Delay is 1 sec, State DR, Priority 1
   Designated Router (ID) 192.168.1.11, local address FE80::209:B7FF:FEFA:D1E1
   No backup designated router on this network
   Timer intervals configured, Hello 10, Dead 40, Wait 40, Retransmit 5
     Hello due in 00:00:03
   Index 1/2/2, flood queue length 0
   Next 0x0(0)/0x0(0)/0x0(0)
   Last flood scan length is 1, maximum is 2
   Last flood scan time is 0 msec, maximum is 0 msec
   Neighbor Count is 0, Adjacent neighbor count is 0
   Suppress hello for 0 neighbor(s)
```

Notice that router R1 has not formed an adjacency with router R2. Therefore, as a first step in your troubleshooting efforts, you attempt to resolve the issue by preventing routers R1 and R2 from forming an adjacency. Example 12-12 shows the data collected from router R2.

Example 12-12   *Troubleshooting Data Collection on Router R2*

```
R2# show ipv6 ospf neighbor

R2# debug ipv6 ospf adj
  OSPFv3 adjacency events debugging is on
R2# u all
All possible debugging has been turned off
R2# show run
...OUTPUT OMITTED...
hostname R2
!
ipv6 unicast-routing
ipv6 cef
!
interface Loopback0
 ip address 10.2.2.2 255.255.255.255
```

```
!
interface FastEthernet0/0
ip address 192.168.0.22 255.255.255.0
 ipv6 address B:B:B:B::22/64
 ipv6 ospf hello-interval 60
 ipv6 ospf 1 area 1
!
interface Serial1/0
 no ip address
 encapsulation frame-relay
!
interface Serial1/0.1 point-to-point
 ip address 172.16.1.2 255.255.255.252
 ipv6 address C:C:C:C::2/64
ipv6 ospf 1 area 0
frame-relay interface-dlci 181
!
interface Serial1/0.2 point-to-point
 ip address 172.16.2.1 255.255.255.252
 ipv6 address D:D:D:D::1/64
 ipv6 ospf network point-to-multipoint
 ipv6 ospf 1 area 0
 frame-relay interface-dlci 182
!
ipv6 router ospf 1
 passive-interface default
...OUTPUT OMITTED...
```

Based on the output provided in Examples 12-11 and 12-12, hypothesize why routers R1 and R2 are not forming an adjacency. On a separate sheet of paper, write out your suggested solution to correct the issue.

Issue #1: Suggested Solution

Notice in Example 12-12 that router R2's HELLO timer on the Fast Ethernet 0/0 interface was set to a non-default value, whereas the other end of the link was still set to the default. Also, router R2 had its OSPFv3 process configured with the **passive-interface default** command, which prevented any of router R2's interfaces from forming OSPFv3 adjacencies. Example 12-13 shows the correction of these configuration issues on router R2.

Example 12-13 *Correcting Router R2's HELLO Timer and Passive-Interface Configuration*

```
R2# conf term
Enter configuration commands, one per line.  End with CNTL/Z.
R2(config)# int fa 0/0
R2(config-if)# no ipv6 ospf hello-interval 60
```

```
R2(config-if)# exit
R2(config)# ipv6 router ospf 1
R2(config-rtr)# no passive-interface default
```

Issue #2: Adjacency Between Routers R2 and BB2

After implementing the fix shown in Example 12-13, router R2 successfully forms OSPF adjacencies with routers R1 and BB1. However, an adjacency is not successfully formed with router BB2. Example 12-14 shows the output of the **show ipv6 ospf interface s1/0.2** command issued on router BB2. This command was issued to view the OSPFv3 configuration of router BB2's Serial 1/0.2 subinterface, which is the subinterface used to connect to router R2.

Example 12-14   *Viewing Router BB2's OSPFv3 Configuration on Subinterface Serial 1/0.2*

```
BB2# show ipv6 ospf interface s1/0.2
Serial1/0.2 is up, line protocol is up
Link Local Address FE80::C200:8FF:FE2C:0, Interface ID 14
Area 0, Process ID 1, Instance ID 0, Router ID 10.4.4.4
Network Type POINT_TO_POINT, Cost: 64
Transmit Delay is 1 sec, State POINT_TO_POINT,

R2# show ipv6 ospf neighbor

R2# debug ipv6 ospf adj
OSPFv3 adjacency events debugging is on

R2# u all
All possible debugging has been turned off

R2# show run
...OUTPUT OMITTED...
!
hostname R2
!
ipv6 unicast-routing
ipv6 cef
!
interface Loopback0
ip address 10.2.2.2 255.255.255.255
!
interface FastEthernet0/0
ip address 192.168.0.22 255.255.255.0
ipv6 address B:B:B:B::22/64
ipv6 ospf 1 area 1
!
interface Serial1/0
no ip address
```

```
encapsulation frame-relay
!
interface Serial1/0.1 point-to-point
ip address 172.16.1.2 255.255.255.252
ipv6 address C:C:C:C::2/64
ipv6 ospf 1 area 0
frame-relay interface-dlci 181
!
interface Serial1/0.2 point-to-point
ip address 172.16.2.1 255.255.255.252
ipv6 address D:D:D:D::1/64
ipv6 ospf network point-to-multipoint
ipv6 ospf 1 area 0
frame-relay interface-dlc1 182
!
...OUTPUT OMITTED...
```

Based on router R2's configuration (shown in Example 12-12) and the output shown in Example 12-14, determine why an OSPF adjacency is not being formed between routers R2 and BB2. Again, on a separate sheet of paper, write out your suggested solution.

Issue #2: Suggested Solution

Router R2's OSPF network type on subinterface Serial 1/0.2 was set to point-to-multipoint, while the other end of the link was the default network type of point-to-point. Example 12-15 shows the correction of router R2's misconfiguration.

Example 12-15 *Correcting Router R2's OSPF Network Type*

```
R2# conf term
Enter configuration commands, one per line.  End with CNTL/Z.
R2(config)# int s1/0.2
R2(config-subif)# no ipv6 ospf network point-to-multipoint
R2(config-subif)# exit
```

At this point in the troubleshooting process, routers R1 and R2 have formed adjacencies. Additionally, router R2 has formed adjacencies with routers BB1 and BB2. The output in Example 12-16 confirms the establishment of these adjacencies.

Example 12-16 *Confirming Router R2's OSPF Adjacencies*

```
R2# show ipv6 ospf neighbor

Neighbor ID     Pri    State        Dead Time    Interface ID    Interface
10.4.4.4          1    FULL/  -     00:00:36     14              Serial1/0.2
10.3.3.3          1    FULL/  -     00:00:36     14              Serial1/0.1
192.168.1.11      1    FULL/DR      00:00:39     4               FastEthernet0/0
```

Issue #3: Adjacency Between Routers BB1 and BB2

As seen in the output provided in Example 12-17, router BB1 has formed an adjacency with router BB2 over router BB1's Fast Ethernet 0/0 interface. However, an adjacency has not been successfully formed with router BB2 over router BB1's Serial 1/0.1 subinterface.

Example 12-17 *Determining Router BB1's Adjacencies*

```
BB1# show ipv6 ospf neigh

Neighbor ID      Pri    State           Dead Time    Interface ID    Interface
10.2.2.2          1     FULL/   -       00:00:37     13              Serial1/0.2
10.4.4.4          1     DOWN/   -          -         13              Serial1/0.1
10.4.4.4          1     FULL/DR         00:00:34     4               FastEthernet0/0
```

To investigate why an OSPF adjacency is not forming with router BB2 via router BB1's Serial 1/0.1 subinterface, the **debug ipv6 ospf adj** and **debug ipv6 ospf hello** commands were issued on router BB1, as seen in Example 12-18.

Example 12-18 *Debugging OSPFv3 Adjacency and Hello Events on Router BB1*

```
BB1# debug ipv6 ospf adj
  OSPFv3 adjacency events debugging is on
BB1# debug ipv6 ospf hello
  OSPFv3 hello events debugging is on
BB1#
*Mar  1 00:19:24.707: OSPFv3: Rcv DBD from 10.4.4.4 on Serial1/0.1 seq 0x1AEF opt
  0x0013 flag 0x7 len 28   mtu 1500 state EXSTART
*Mar  1 00:19:24.707: OSPFv3: Nbr 10.4.4.4 has larger interface MTU
*Mar  1 00:19:25.015: OSPFv3: Rcv hello from 10.2.2.2 area 0 from Serial1/0.2
  FE80::C201:8FF:FE2C:0 interface ID 13
*Mar  1 00:19:25.019: OSPFv3: End of hello processing
*Mar  1 00:19:28.583: OSPFv3: Send hello to FF02::5 area 0 on Serial1/0.2 from
  FE80::C202:8FF:FE98:0 interface ID 14
*Mar  1 00:19:28.647: OSPFv3: Rcv hello from 10.4.4.4 area 0 from Serial1/0.1
  FE80::C200:8FF:FE2C:0 interface ID 13
*Mar  1 00:19:28.651: OSPFv3: End of hello processing
*Mar  1 00:19:28.983: OSPFv3: Send hello to FF02::5 area 0 on FastEthernet0/0
  from FE80::C202:8FF:FE98:0 interface ID 4
*Mar  1 00:19:29.215: OSPFv3: Rcv hello from 10.4.4.4 area 0 from FastEthernet0/0
  FE80::C200:8FF:FE2C:0 interface ID 4
*Mar  1 00:19:29.219: OSPFv3: End of hello processing
BB1# u all
All possible debugging has been turned off
```

Because your troubleshooting on router BB1 is focused on BB1's Serial 1/0.1 subinterface, the **show ipv6 interface s1/0.1** command was issued, the output for which appears in Example 12-19.

Example 12-19   *Viewing the IPv6 Configuration on Router BB1's Serial 1/0.1 Subinterface*

```
BB1# show ipv6 interface s1/0.1
Serial1/0.1 is up, line protocol is up
  IPv6 is enabled, link-local address is FE80::C202:8FF:FE98:0
  Global unicast address(es):
    E:E:E:E::1, subnet is E:E:E:E::/64
  Joined group address(es):
    FF02::1
    FF02::2
    FF02::5
    FF02::1:FF00:1
    FF02::1:FF98:0
  MTU is 1400 bytes
  ICMP error messages limited to one every 100 milliseconds
  ICMP redirects are enabled
  ND DAD is enabled, number of DAD attempts: 1
  ND reachable time is 30000 milliseconds
  Hosts use stateless autoconfig for addresses.
```

Based on the output provided in Examples 12-18 and 12-19, determine why router BB1 is failing to form an OSPF adjacency with router BB2, via router BB1's Serial 1/0.1 subinterface. On a separate sheet of paper, write out your proposed solution to this issue.

Issue #3: Suggested Solution

The debug output seen in Example 12-18 indicates that router BB1's neighbor (that is, 10.4.4.4) reachable over subinterface Serial 1/0.1 has a larger MTU than router BB1's Serial 1/0.1 subinterface. The output in Example 12-19 indicates that router BB1's Serial 1/0.1 subinterface has an MTU of 1400 bytes. This is less than the default value of 1500 bytes. Example 12-20 shows how this MTU value was reset to its default value.

Example 12-20   *Correcting the MTU on Router BB1's Serial 1/0.1 Subinterface*

```
BB1# conf term
Enter configuration commands, one per line.  End with CNTL/Z.
BB1(config)# int s1/0.1
BB1(config-subif)# ipv6 mtu 1500
*Mar  1 00:20:00.019: %OSPFv3-5-ADJCHG: Process 1, Nbr 10.4.4.4 on Serial1/0.1
from LOADING to FULL, Loading Done
BB1(config-subif)# end
```

Notice, in Example 12-20, that an adjacency with router BB2 (that is, 10.4.4.4) was formed over router BB1's Serial 1/0.1 subinterface after setting the subinterface's MTU size to the default of 1500 bytes. Examples 12-21 and 12-22 further confirm that routers BB1 and BB2 have formed all appropriate adjacencies with their OSPF neighbors.

Example 12-21   *Router BB1's OSPF Adjacencies*

```
BB1# show ipv6 ospf neighbor
Neighbor ID     Pri   State          Dead Time    Interface ID   Interface
10.2.2.2          1   FULL/          00:00:37     13             Serial1/0.2
10.4.4.4          1   FULL/          00:00:30     13             Serial1/0.1
10.4.4.4          1   FULL/DR        00:00:31     4              FastEthernet0/0
```

Example 12-22   *Router BB2's OSPF Adjacencies*

```
BB2# show ipv6 ospf neighbor
Neighbor ID     Pri   State          Dead Time    Interface ID   Interface
10.2.2.2          1   FULL/          00:00:37     14             Serial1/0.2
10.3.3.3          1   FULL/          00:00:37     13             Serial1/0.1
10.3.3.3          1   FULL/BDR       00:00:31     4              FastEthernet0/0
```

To confirm that full reachability has been restored in the network, a series of **ping** commands were issued from router BB2, with one ping to each router in the topology. As seen in Example 12-23, all of the pings were successful.

Example 12-23   *Confirming Reachability to All Routers*

```
BB2# ping a:a:a:a::11

Type escape sequence to abort.
Sending 5, 100-byte ICMP Echos to A:A:A:A::11, timeout is 2 seconds:
!!!!!
Success rate is 100 percent (5/5), round-trip min/avg/max = 88/124/164 ms
BB2# ping b:b:b:b::22
Type escape sequence to abort.
Sending 5, 100-byte ICMP Echos to B:B:B:B::22, timeout is 2 seconds:
!!!!!
Success rate is 100 percent (5/5), round-trip min/avg/max = 44/83/164 ms
BB2# ping f:f:f:f::1
Type escape sequence to abort.
Sending 5, 100-byte ICMP Echos to F:F:F:F::1, timeout is 2 seconds:
!!!!!
```

```
Success rate is 100 percent (5/5), round-trip min/avg/max = 40/79/128 ms
BB2# ping e:e:e:e::2


Type escape sequence to abort.
Sending 5, 100-byte ICMP Echos to E:E:E:E::2, timeout is 2 seconds:
!!!!!
Success rate is 100 percent (5/5), round-trip min/avg/max = 0/0/0 ms
```

RIPng Troubleshooting

Just as OSPFv3 supports IPv6 routes while OSPFv2 does not, RIPng supports IPv6 routes, whereas RIP versions 1 and 2 do not. This section reviews RIPng theory, provides a collection of RIPng configuration commands, shows a sample configuration, offers a collection of helpful RIPng troubleshooting commands, and lists common RIPng troubleshooting issues.

Review RIPng Theory

RIPng is an enhancement to RIPv2; however, RIPng does have several characteristics similar to RIPv2, as follows:

- Distance-vector routing protocol

- Hop count metric

- Maximum hop count of fifteen

- Sends routing updates via multicast:
  - RIPv2: 224.0.0.9
  - RIPng: FF02::9

The following characteristics are enhancements of RIPng over RIPv2:

- Supports the routing of 128-bit IPv6 network addresses.

Key Topic

- Link-local addresses used for next-hop addresses.

- Next-hop addresses stored in Routing Information Base (RIB).

- Interfaces added to a RIP routing process in interface-configuration mode (as opposed to router configuration mode).

RIPng Configuration Commands

Similar to OSPFv3, RIPng uses interface configuration mode to tell an interface to participate in a RIP routing process. This is as opposed to RIPv1's and RIPv2's approach to using the **network** command in router configuration mode to configure an interface to participate in a RIP routing process.

Table 12-6 provides basic RIPng configuration commands.

Table 12-6   *RIPng Configuration Commands*

Command	Description
ipv6 rip *process-name* **enable**	Interface configuration mode command that instructs an interface to participate in the specified RIPng routing process.
ipv6 rip *process-name* **default-in-formation** {**only** | **originate**}	Interface configuration mode command that causes an interface to originate a default route advertisement (that is, an advertisement for network ::/0) and optionally suppress the advertisement of all other routes (using the **only** keyword).
ipv6 router rip *process-name*	Global configuration mode command that enters router configuration mode for the specified RIPng routing process.
maximum-paths *number*	Interface configuration mode command that specifies the number of equal-cost paths across which RIPng can load balance (defaults to 16 with a valid range of 1-64).

Example 12-24 shows a sample RIPng configuration on a router (that is, router R1), which is illustrated in Figure 12-7. Notice that an interface can simultaneously be configured with both IPv4 and IPv6 addresses. Also, notice the **ipv6 rip PROCESS1 enable** command issued in interface configuration mode. This command causes an interface to participate in the RIPng routing process named **PROCESS1**.

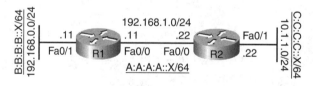

Figure 12-7   *RIPng Sample Configuration Topology*

Example 12-24 *Sample RIPng Configuration*

Key
Topic

```
R1# show run
...OUTPUT OMITTED...
hostname R1
!
ipv6 unicast-routing
ipv6 cef

!
interface FastEthernet0/0
 ip address 192.168.1.11 255.255.255.0
 ipv6 address A:A:A:A::11/64
 ipv6 rip PROCESS1 enable

!
interface FastEthernet0/1
 ip address 192.168.0.11 255.255.255.0
 ipv6 address B:B:B:B::11/64
 ipv6 rip PROCESS1 enable

!
ipv6 router rip PROCESS1
...OUTPUT OMITTED...
```

Troubleshooting RIPng

When troubleshooting a RIPng issue, you can take advantage of your RIPv1 and RIPv2 knowledge. Many commands used to troubleshoot RIPv1 and RIPv2 can be used for troubleshooting RIPng by simply replacing the **ip** keyword in a **show** command with a keyword of **ipv6**. For example, instead of using the RIPv2 **show ip rip database** command, you could use the **show ipv6 rip database** command in a network running RIPng. Table 12-7 provides a command reference of commonly used commands for troubleshooting RIPng issues.

Table 12-7 *RIPng Troubleshooting Commands*

Key
Topic

Command	Description
show ipv6 rip [*process-name*] [**database** | **next-hops**]	Displays information about the specified RIPng routing process, and optionally the contents of the RIPng database and a listing of next-hop addresses.
show ipv6 route	Shows the contents of the IPv6 routing table.
debug ipv6 rip	Provides real-time information about RIPng messages.

Following is a listing of common RIPng issues you might encounter:

- RIPng routes not appearing in the IPv6 routing table

- RIPng not performing appropriate load balancing

- Interface not sending RIPng updates

- Individual network advertisements not suppressed when sourcing a default route

Trouble Ticket: IPv6 and RIPng

This section presents a trouble ticket based on an IPv6 and RIPng configuration. You are given sample **show** command output and are challenged to identify a resolution for the issue described.

Trouble Ticket #12

You receive the following trouble ticket:

Company A (that is, routers R1 and R2) is dual-homed to two Internet service providers (ISPs). The ISP routers are BB1 and BB2. However, router R2 only sees a single path to reach a default route (rather than one path from each ISP) in its IPv6 routing table. Also, router R2 is seeing other ISP-advertised routes (specifically, E:E:E:E::/64 and F:F:F:F::/64) rather than just a default route in its IPv6 routing table. All routes that router R2 receives from the ISP routers, except a default route, should be suppressed (see Figure 12-8).

Viewing Baseline Information

All routers in the shown topology have been configured with IPv6 addressing on their physical interfaces and subinterfaces. Routers R1 and R2 are considered to be enterprise routers, whereas routers BB1 and BB2 are considered to be Internet service provider (ISP) routers, with whom the enterprise is dual homed.

The backbone ISP routers are configured to only send IPv6 default route advertisements (that is, advertisements for route ::/0) to the enterprise routers. Therefore, routers R1 and R2 do not have entries for the E:E:E:E::/64 and F:F:F:F::/64 networks. Router R1's configuration, which is representative of the basic IPv6 and RIPng configuration present on all the routers in the topology, is presented in Example 12-25.

Example 12-25 *Running Configuration on Router R1*

```
R1# show run
...OUTPUT OMITTED...
hostname R1
!
ipv6 unicast-routing
ipv6 cef
```

```
!
interface Loopback0
 ip address 10.1.1.1 255.255.255.255
!
interface FastEthernet0/0
 ip address 192.168.1.11 255.255.255.0
 ipv6 address A:A:A:A::11/64
 ipv6 rip PROCESS1 enable

!
interface FastEthernet0/1
 ip address 192.168.0.11 255.255.255.0
 ipv6 address B:B:B:B::11/64
 ipv6 rip PROCESS1 enable

!
ipv6 router rip PROCESS1

...OUTPUT OMITTED...
```

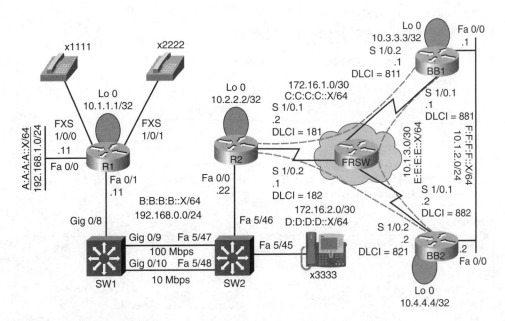

Figure 12-8 *Trouble Ticket #12 Topology*

Router R1's IPv6 routing table is shown in Example 12-26. Notice the absence of specific routes to the backbone IPv6 networks of E:E:E:E::/64 and F:F:F:F::/64. Instead, router R1 could reach these networks via the default route (that is, ::/0) in its routing table.

Example 12-26 *IPv6 Routing Table on Router R1*

```
R1# show ipv6 route
IPv6 Routing Table - 9 entries
Codes: C - Connected, L - Local, S - Static, R - RIP, B - BGP
       U - Per-user Static route
       I1 - ISIS L1, I2 - ISIS L2, IA - ISIS interarea, IS - ISIS summary
       O - OSPF intra, OI - OSPF inter, OE1 - OSPF ext 1, OE2 - OSPF ext 2
       ON1 - OSPF NSSA ext 1, ON2 - OSPF NSSA ext 2
R    ::/0 [120/3]
       via FE80::C201:EFF:FE64:0, FastEthernet0/1
C    A:A:A:A::/64 [0/0]
       via ::, FastEthernet0/0
L    A:A:A:A::11/128 [0/0]
       via ::, FastEthernet0/0
L    B:B:B:B::11/128 [0/0]
       via ::, FastEthernet0/1

R    C:C:C:C::/64 [120/2]
       via FE80::C201:EFF:FE64:0, FastEthernet0/1
R    D:D:D:D::/64 [120/2]
       via FE80::C201:EFF:FE64:0, FastEthernet0/1
L    FE80::/10 [0/0]
       via ::, Null0
L    FF00::/8 [0/0]
       via ::, Null0
```

Router R1's reachability to all IPv6 networks in the topology was confirmed by issuing a series of pings from R1, one to each IPv6 network in the topology. Example 12-27 shows the successful ping results.

Example 12-27 ping *Results for Router R1*

```
R1# ping a:a:a:a::11


Type escape sequence to abort.
Sending 5, 100-byte ICMP Echos to A:A:A:A::11, timeout is 2 seconds:
!!!!!
Success rate is 100 percent (5/5), round-trip min/avg/max = 1/1/1 ms
R1# ping b:b:b:b::22


Type escape sequence to abort.
```

```
Sending 5, 100-byte ICMP Echos to B:B:B:B::22, timeout is 2 seconds:
!!!!!
Success rate is 100 percent (5/5), round-trip min/avg/max = 20/54/88 ms
R1# ping c:c:c:c::1

Type escape sequence to abort.
Sending 5, 100-byte ICMP Echos to F:F:F:F::2, timeout is 2 seconds:
!!!!!
Success rate is 100 percent (5/5), round-trip min/avg/max = 64/145/337 ms
Type escape sequence to abort.
Sending 5, 100-byte ICMP Echos to C:C:C:C::1, timeout is 2 seconds:
!!!!!
Success rate is 100 percent (5/5), round-trip min/avg/max = 48/89/128 ms
R1# ping d:d:d:d::2

Type escape sequence to abort.
Sending 5, 100-byte ICMP Echos to D:D:D:D::2, timeout is 2 seconds:
!!!!!
Success rate is 100 percent (5/5), round-trip min/avg/max = 52/97/173 ms
R1# ping e:e:e:e::1

Type escape sequence to abort.
Sending 5, 100-byte ICMP Echos to E:E:E:E::1, timeout is 2 seconds:
!!!!!
Success rate is 100 percent (5/5), round-trip min/avg/max = 60/85/132 ms
R1# ping f:f:f:f::2
```

Router R2's routing table, provided in Example 12-28, shows that router R2 has two paths to reach the default network of ::/0: one path via router BB1 and one path via router BB2. These dual paths are made possible because RIPng (in addition to RIPv1 and RIPv2) can load balance across equal-cost paths. All versions of RIP use *hop count* as their metric.

Example 12-28 *IPv6 Routing Table on Router R2*

```
R2# show ipv6 route
IPv6 Routing Table - 10 entries
Codes: C - Connected, L - Local, S - Static, R - RIP, B - BGP
       U - Per-user Static route
       I1 - ISIS L1, I2 - ISIS L2, IA - ISIS interarea, IS - ISIS summary
       O - OSPF intra, OI - OSPF inter, OE1 - OSPF ext 1, OE2 - OSPF ext 2
```

```
              ON1 - OSPF NSSA ext 1, ON2 - OSPF NSSA ext 2
R    ::/0 [120/2]
        via FE80::C202:EFF:FEBC:0, Serial1/0.1
        via FE80::C200:EFF:FE64:0, Serial1/0.2
R    A:A:A:A::/64 [120/2]
        via FE80::200:B7FF:FEFA:D1C1, FastEthernet0/0
C    B:B:B:B::/64 [0/0]
       via ::, FastEthernet0/0
L    B:B:B:B::22/128 [0/0]
        via ::, FastEthernet0/0
C    C:C:C:C::/64 [0/0]

        via ::, Serial1/0.1
L    C:C:C:C::2/128 [0/0]
        via ::, Serial1/0.1
C    D:D:D:D::/64 [0/0]
        via ::, Serial1/0.2
L    D:D:D:D::1/128 [0/0]
        via ::, Serial1/0.2
L    FE80::/10 [0/0]
        via ::, Null0
L    FF00::/8 [0/0]
        via ::, Null0
```

Routers BB1 and BB2 both have listings for all of the topology's IPv6 networks in their IPv6 routing tables, as shown in Examples 12-29 and 12-30.

Example 12-29 *IPv6 Routing Table on Router BB1*

```
BB1# show ipv6 route
IPv6 Routing Table - 11 entries
Codes: C - Connected, L - Local, S - Static, R - RIP, B - BGP
       U - Per-user Static route
       I1 - ISIS L1, I2 - ISIS L2, IA - ISIS interarea, IS - ISIS summary
       O - OSPF intra, OI - OSPF inter, OE1 - OSPF ext 1, OE2 - OSPF ext 2
       ON1 - OSPF NSSA ext 1, ON2 - OSPF NSSA ext 2
R    A:A:A:A::/64 [120/3]
       via FE80::C201:EFF:FE64:0, Serial1/0.2
R    B:B:B:B::/64 [120/2]
       via FE80::C201:EFF:FE64:0, Serial1/0.2
C    C:C:C:C::/64 [0/0]
       via ::, Serial1/0.2
L    C:C:C:C::1/128 [0/0]
```

```
            via ::, Serial1/0.2
R    D:D:D:D::/64 [120/2]
            via FE80::C200:EFF:FE64:0, FastEthernet0/0
            via FE80::C200:EFF:FE64:0, Serial1/0.1
            via FE80::C201:EFF:FE64:0, Serial1/0.2
C    E:E:E:E::/64 [0/0]
            via ::, Serial1/0.1
L    E:E:E:E::1/128 [0/0]
            via ::, Serial1/0.1
C    F:F:F:F::/64 [0/0]
            via ::, FastEthernet0/0

L    F:F:F:F::1/128 [0/0]
            via ::, FastEthernet0/0
L    FE80::/10 [0/0]
            via ::, Null0
L    FF00::/8 [0/0]
            via ::, Null0
```

Example 12-30   *IPv6 Routing Table on Router BB2*

```
BB2# show ipv6 route
IPv6 Routing Table - 11 entries
Codes: C - Connected, L - Local, S - Static, R - RIP, B - BGP
       U - Per-user Static route
       I1 - ISIS L1, I2 - ISIS L2, IA - ISIS interarea, IS - ISIS summary
       O - OSPF intra, OI - OSPF inter, OE1 - OSPF ext 1, OE2 - OSPF ext 2
       ON1 - OSPF NSSA ext 1, ON2 - OSPF NSSA ext 2
R    A:A:A:A::/64 [120/3]
            via FE80::C201:EFF:FE64:0, Serial1/0.2
R    B:B:B:B::/64 [120/2]
            via FE80::C201:EFF:FE64:0, Serial1/0.2
R    C:C:C:C::/64 [120/2]
            via FE80::C201:EFF:FE64:0, Serial1/0.2
            via FE80::C202:EFF:FEBC:0, FastEthernet0/0
            via FE80::C202:EFF:FEBC:0, Serial1/0.1
C    D:D:D:D::/64 [0/0]
            via ::, Serial1/0.2
L    D:D:D:D::2/128 [0/0]
            via ::, Serial1/0.2
C    E:E:E:E::/64 [0/0]
            via ::, Serial1/0.1
L    E:E:E:E::2/128 [0/0]
            via ::, Serial1/0.1
C    F:F:F:F::/64 [0/0]
```

```
       via ::, FastEthernet0/0
L    F:F:F:F::2/128 [0/0]
       via ::, FastEthernet0/0
L    FE80::/10 [0/0]
       via ::, Null0
L    FF00::/8 [0/0]
     via ::, Null0
```

Notice that the IPv6 routing tables for routers BB1 and BB2 did not have a default route entry. The absence of the default route was because routers BB1 and BB2 were sourcing default route information to router R2, while suppressing more specific route information to router R2. Example 12-31 highlights the **ipv6 rip PROCESS1 default-information orig- inate** command used on router BB1 to create its default route advertisement. Router BB2 was configured with an identical command.

Example 12-31 *Advertising Default Route Information on Router BB1*

```
BB1# show run | begin Serial1/0.2
interface Serial1/0.2 point-to-point
 ip address 172.16.1.1 255.255.255.252
 ipv6 address C:C:C:C::1/64
 ipv6 rip PROCESS1 enable
 ipv6 rip PROCESS1 default-information only
 frame-relay interface-dlci 811
```

Troubleshoot and Resolve the Identified RIPng Issue

The **show ipv6 route** command was issued on router R2 to confirm that the IPv6 routing table included only a single path to reach the default network of ::/0. Example 12-32 pro- vides the output from this command, which also confirms the presence of the backbone routes E:E:E:E::/64 and F:F:F:F::/64 in the IPv6 routing table.

Example 12-32 *Confirmation of Troubleshooting Issues on Router R2*

```
R2# show ipv6 route
IPv6 Routing Table - 12 entries
Codes: C - Connected, L - Local, S - Static, R - RIP, B - BGP
       U - Per-user Static route
       I1 - ISIS L1, I2 - ISIS L2, IA - ISIS interarea, IS - ISIS summary
       O - OSPF intra, OI - OSPF inter, OE1 - OSPF ext 1, OE2 - OSPF ext 2
       ON1 - OSPF NSSA ext 1, ON2 - OSPF NSSA ext 2
R    ::/0 [120/2]
       via FE80::C200:EFF:FE64:0, Serial1/0.2
R    A:A:A:A::/64 [120/2]
       via FE80::209:B7FF:FEFA:D1E1, FastEthernet0/0
C    B:B:B:B::/64 [0/0]
```

```
            via ::, FastEthernet0/0
L    B:B:B:B::22/128 [0/0]
            via ::, FastEthernet0/0
C    C:C:C:C::/64 [0/0]
            via ::, Serial1/0.1
L    C:C:C:C::2/128 [0/0]
            via ::, Serial1/0.1
C    D:D:D:D::/64 [0/0]
            via ::, Serial1/0.2
L    D:D:D:D::1/128 [0/0]
            via ::, Serial1/0.2
R    E:E:E:E::/64 [120/2]
         via FE80::C200:EFF:FE64:0, Serial1/0.2
R    F:F:F:F::/64 [120/2]
         via FE80::C200:EFF:FE64:0, Serial1/0.2
L    FE80::/10 [0/0]
            via ::, Null0
L    FF00::/8 [0/0]
            via ::, Null0
```

The **show ipv6 rip database** command, as shown in Example 12-33, proves that router R2 received two default route advertisements; however, only one of those route advertisements was injected into the IPv6 routing table.

Example 12-33   *RIP Database on Router R2*

```
R2# show ipv6 rip database
RIP process "PROCESS1", local RIB
 A:A:A:A::/64, metric 2, installed
     FastEthernet0/0/FE80::209:B7FF:FEFA:D1E1, expires in 174 secs
 B:B:B:B::/64, metric 2
     FastEthernet0/0/FE80::209:B7FF:FEFA:D1E1, expires in 174 secs
D:D:D:D::/64, metric 2
     Serial1/0.2/FE80::C200:EFF:FE64:0, expires in 160 secs
E:E:E:E::/64, metric 2, installed
     Serial1/0.2/FE80::C200:EFF:FE64:0, expires in 160 secs
 F:F:F:F::/64, metric 2, installed
     Serial1/0.2/FE80::C200:EFF:FE64:0, expires in 160 secs
 ::/0, metric 2, installed
     Serial1/0.2/FE80::C200:EFF:FE64:0, expires in 160 secs
     Serial1/0.1/FE80::C202:EFF:FEBC:0, expires in 170 secs
```

Example 12-34 shows the running configuration on router R2.

Example 12-34   *Running Configuration on Router R2*

```
R2# show run
...OUTPUT OMITTED...
hostname R2
!
ipv6 unicast-routing
ipv6 cef
!
interface Loopback0
 ip address 10.2.2.2 255.255.255.255
!
interface FastEthernet0/0
 ip address 192.168.0.22 255.255.255.0
 ipv6 address B:B:B:B::22/64
 ipv6 rip PROCESS1 enable
!
interface Serial1/0
no ip address
 encapsulation frame-relay
 serial restart-delay 0
!
interface Serial1/0.1 point-to-point
 ip address 172.16.1.2 255.255.255.252
 ipv6 address C:C:C:C::2/64
 ipv6 rip PROCESS1 enable
 frame-relay interface-dlci 181
!
interface Serial1/0.2 point-to-point
 ip address 172.16.2.1 255.255.255.252
 ipv6 address D:D:D:D::1/64

ipv6 rip PROCESS1 enable
 frame-relay interface-dlci 182
!
ipv6 router rip PROCESS1
 maximum-paths 1
...OUTPUT OMITTED...
```

Issue #1: Router R2 Not Load Balancing Between Routers BB1 and BB2

The first issue you investigate is router R2 not load balancing between the ISP routers (that is, routers BB1 and BB2). Based on the **show** command output presented in Examples 12-32, 12-33, and 12-34, hypothesize why router R2's IPv6 routing table contains only a single entry for a default network (rather than having two entries, one for BB1 and one for BB2). On a separate sheet of paper, write out your proposed configuration change to resolve this issue.

Issue #1: Suggested Solution

A review of router R2's running configuration reveals the **maximum-paths 1** command in router configuration mode for the RIPng routing process. This command prevents two default route paths from appearing in router R2's IPv6 routing table. Example 12-35 shows how this command is removed from router R2's configuration in order to restore load balancing to a default route.

Example 12-35 *Restoring Load Balancing to a Default Route on Router R2*

```
R2# conf term
Enter configuration commands, one per line.  End with CNTL/Z.
R2(config)# ipv6 router rip PROCESS1
R2(config-rtr)# no maximum-paths 1
```

Issue #2: Backbone Routes Not Being Suppressed

The second issue you investigate is specific backbone routes (that is, E:E:E:E::/64 and F:F:F:F::/64) being advertized into Company A's enterprise network (that is, the network consisting of routers R1 and R2). The goal is to only advertise default route information into the enterprise network.

The **debug ipv6 rip** command was issued on router R2 to see if router BB2 was sending both default route information and specific route information. The output from this command, as presented in Example 12-36, confirms that router BB2 is not suppressing specific route information.

Example 12-36 *Debugging RIPng Traffic on Router R2*

```
R2# debug ipv6 rip
...OUTPUT OMITTED...
*Mar  1 00:33:30.747: RIPng: response received from FE80::C200:EFF:FE64:0 on
Serial1/0.2 for PROCESS1
*Mar  1 00:33:30.751:          src=FE80::C200:EFF:FE64:0 (Serial1/0.2)
*Mar  1 00:33:30.751:          dst=FF02::9
*Mar  1 00:33:30.755:          sport=521, dport=521, length=92
*Mar  1 00:33:30.755:          command=2, version=1, mbz=0, #rte=4
*Mar  1 00:33:30.755:          tag=0, metric=1, prefix=F:F:F:F::/64
*Mar  1 00:33:30.755:          tag=0, metric=1, prefix=E:E:E:E::/64
*Mar  1 00:33:30.755:          tag=0, metric=1, prefix=D:D:D:D::/64
*Mar  1 00:33:30.755:          tag=0, metric=1, prefix=::/0
...OUTPUT OMITTED...
```

Examples 12-37 and 12-38 show the RIPng configuration of the Serial 1/0.2 subinterface on routers BB1 and BB2. The Serial 1/0.2 subinterface on each router is the subinterface connecting to router R2.

Example 12-37   *Viewing the RIPng Configuration on Router BB1's Serial 1/0.2 Subinterface*

```
BB1# show run | begin Serial1/0.2
interface Serial1/0.2 point-to-point
 ip address 172.16.1.1 255.255.255.252
 ipv6 address C:C:C:C::1/64
 ipv6 rip PROCESS1 enable
 ipv6 rip PROCESS1 default-information only
 frame-relay interface-dlci 811
```

Example 12-38   *Viewing the RIPng Configuration on Router BB2's Serial 1/0.2 Subinterface*

```
BB2# show run | begin Serial1/0.2
interface Serial1/0.2 point-to-point
 ip address 172.16.2.2 255.255.255.252
 ipv6 address D:D:D:D::2/64
 ipv6 rip PROCESS1 enable
 ipv6 rip PROCESS1 default-information originate
 frame-relay interface-dlci 821
```

Based on the **debug** and **show** command output presented in Examples 12-36, 12-37, and 12-38, hypothesize why router R2 is receiving specific route information for networks E:E:E:E::/64 and F:F:F:F::/64. On a separate sheet of paper, write out your proposed configuration change to resolve this issue.

Issue #2: Suggested Solution

An inspection of router BB2's running configuration reveals the **ipv6 rip PROCESS1 default-information originate** command under subinterface configuration mode for Serial 1/0.2. The **originate** keyword in this command sources a default router advertisement, but it does not suppress the sending of more specific routes. Example 12-39 shows how this configuration was changed to use the **only** parameter. The **only** parameter causes the interface to only originate default route information, while suppressing more specific routes.

Example 12-39   *Suppressing Specific Route Information on Router BB2's Serial 1/0.2 Subinterface*

```
BB2# conf term
Enter configuration commands, one per line.  End with CNTL/Z.
BB2(config)# int s1/0.2
BB2(config-subif)# ipv6 rip PROCESS1 default-information only
```

After giving the E:E:E:E::/64 and F:F:F:F::/64 routes sufficient time to timeout of router R2's IPv6 routing table, the **show ipv6 route** was once again issued. The output, as shown in Example 12-40, confirms that the issues reported in the trouble ticket are resolved. Specifically, router R2 sees two paths across which it can load balance to reach a default route. Also, specific backbone routes (that is, E:E:E:E::/64 and F:F:F:F::/64) do not appear in router R2's IPv6 routing table.

Example 12-40   *Router R2's IPv6 Routing Table After Troubleshooting*

```
R2# show ipv6 route
IPv6 Routing Table - 10 entries
Codes: C - Connected, L - Local, S - Static, R - RIP, B - BGP
       U - Per-user Static route
       I1 - ISIS L1, I2 - ISIS L2, IA - ISIS interarea, IS - ISIS summary
       O - OSPF intra, OI - OSPF inter, OE1 - OSPF ext 1, OE2 - OSPF ext 2
       ON1 - OSPF NSSA ext 1, ON2 - OSPF NSSA ext 2
R   ::/0 [120/2]
      via FE80::C200:EFF:FE64:0, Serial1/0.2
      via FE80::C202:EFF:FEBC:0, Serial1/0.1
R   A:A:A:A::/64 [120/2]
      via FE80::209:B7FF:FEFA:D1E1, FastEthernet0/0
C   B:B:B:B::/64 [0/0]
      via ::, FastEthernet0/0
L   B:B:B:B::22/128 [0/0]
      via ::, FastEthernet0/0
C   C:C:C:C::/64 [0/0]
      via ::, Serial1/0.1
L   C:C:C:C::2/128 [0/0]
      via ::, Serial1/0.1
C   D:D:D:D::/64 [0/0]
      via ::, Serial1/0.2
L   D:D:D:D::1/128 [0/0]
      via ::, Serial1/0.2
L   FE80::/10 [0/0]
      via ::, Null0
L   FF00::/8 [0/0]
      via ::, Null0
```

Exam Preparation Tasks

Review All Key Topics

Review the most important topics from inside the chapter, noted with the Key Topics Icon in the outer margin of the page. Table 12-8 lists these key topics and the page numbers where each is found.

Table 12-8   *Key Topics for Chapter 12*

Key Topic Element	Description	Page Number
List	IPv6 features	376
List	Three types of IPv6 addresses	376
List	Rules for abbreviating IPv6 addresses	378
List	Methods of populating an IPv6 routing table	379
Table 12-2	IPv6 configuration commands	379
Example 12-1	IPv6 configuration example	380
Table 12-3	Commands used to tunnel IPv6 via IPv4	380
Example 12-2	IPv6 over IPv4 tunnel configuration example	381
List	OSPFv3 enhancements	382
Table 12-4	OSPFv3 configuration commands	383
Example 12-4	OSPFv3 sample configuration	383
Table 12-5	OSPFv3 troubleshooting commands	384
List	Reasons an OSPFv3 adjacency might not be formed	384
List	RIPng enhancements	399
Table 12-6	RIPng configuration commands	400
Example 12-24	RIPng sample configuration	401
Table 12-7	RIPng troubleshooting commands	401

Complete Tables and Lists from Memory

Print a copy of Appendix B, "Memory Tables," (found on the CD) or at least the section for this chapter, and complete the tables and lists from memory. Appendix C, "Memory Tables Answer Key," also on the CD, includes completed tables and lists to check your work.

Define Key Terms

Define the following key terms from this chapter, and check your answers in the Glossary:

IPv6 over IPv4 tunnel, IPv6 unicast, IPv6 multicast, IPv6 anycast, OSPFv3, RIP next generation (RIPng)

Command Reference to Check Your Memory

This section includes the most important configuration and EXEC commands covered in this chapter. To determine how well you have memorized the commands as a side effect of your other studies, cover the left side of the table with a piece of paper, read the descriptions on the right side, and see whether you remember the command.

Table 12-9   *Chapter 12 Configuration Command Reference*

Command	Description
ipv6 cef	Global configuration mode command that configures Cisco Express Forwarding for IPv6.
ipv6 unicast-routing	Global configuration mode command that instructs a router to forward IPv6 traffic.
ipv6 address *ipv6-address/prefix-length* [eui-64]	Interface configuration mode command that assigns an IPv6 address to an interface. (NOTE: The eui-64 option allows a router to complete the low-order 64 bits of an address, based on an interface's MAC address.)
service-policy {input	output} *policy-map-name*	Interface configuration mode command that applies a policy map in either the inbound or outbound direction.
interface tunnel *interface-id*	Global configuration mode command that creates a virtual IPv4 tunnel interface over which encapsulated IPv6 packets can flow.
tunnel source *ipv4-address*	Interface configuration mode command that identifies the IPv4 address of the local end of a tunnel.

continues

Table 12-9   *Chapter 12 Configuration Command Reference*   *(Continued)*

Command	Description
tunnel destination *ipv4-address*	Interface configuration mode command that identifies the IPv4 address of the remote end of a tunnel.
tunnel mode ipv6ip	Interface configuration mode command that configures an interface to act as a manual IPv6 tunnel.
ipv6 address *ipv6-address/prefix-length*	Interface configuration mode command that specifies the IPv6 address assigned to a tunnel interface.
ipv6 ospf *process-id* **area** *area-id*	Interface configuration mode command that allows the IPv6 address configured on an interface to participate in an OSPFv3 routing process.
ipv6 router ospf *process-id*	Global configuration mode command that enables an OSPFv3 routing process on a router.
router-id *ipv4-address*	Router configuration mode command that specifies an IPv4 address to be used by OSPFv3 as a router's router ID.
ipv6 rip *process-name* **enable**	Interface configuration mode command that instructs an interface to participate in the specified RIPng routing process.
ipv6 rip *process-name* **default-information {only | originate}**	Interface configuration mode command that causes an interface to originate a default route advertisement (that is, an advertisement for network ::/0) and optionally suppress the advertisement of all other routes (using the **only** keyword).
ipv6 router rip *process-name*	Global configuration mode command that enters router configuration mode for the specified RIPng routing process.
maximum-paths *number*	Interface configuration mode command that specifies the number of equal-cost paths across which RIPng can load balance (defaults to 16 with a valid range of 1–64).

Table 12-10   *Chapter 12 EXEC Command Reference*

Command	Description
show ipv6 ospf	Displays OSPFv3 routing process, router ID, various timers, and information about each area on a router.
show ipv6 ospf interface	Shows IPv6 link local address, area ID, process ID, router ID, and cost.
show ipv6 ospf neighbor	Lists the state of a router's adjacency with all configured OSPFv3 neighbors.
debug ipv6 ospf adj	Displays information about OSPFv3 adjacencies.
debug ip ipv6 ospf hello	Shows OSPFv3 HELLO packet information.
show ipv6 rip [*process-name*] [database | next-hops]	Displays information about the specified RIPng routing process, and optionally, the contents of the RIPng database and a listing of next-hop addresses.
show ipv6 route	Shows the contents of the IPv6 routing table.
debug ipv6 rip	Provides real-time information about RIPng messages.

This chapter covers the following subjects:

Application Network Services Troubleshooting: This section introduces you to the Cisco Application Network Services (ANS) architecture. Cisco ANS includes multiple pieces of dedicated equipment aimed at optimizing the performance of network-based applications (for example, improving the response time of a corporate web server for users at a remote office). Although this section introduces a collection of Cisco ANS components, the primary focus of this section is on Cisco IOS features that can improve application performance. Specifically, the Cisco IOS features addressed are NetFlow, IP service-level agreements (SLA), Network-Based Application Recognition (NBAR), and quality of service (QoS).

Wireless Troubleshooting Targets: This section begins by contrasting autonomous and split-MAC wireless network architectures. Next, this section highlights wired network issues that can impact wireless networks. These include power, VLAN, security, DHCP, and QoS issues.

CHAPTER 13

Advanced Services Troubleshooting

Large enterprise networks carry multiple types of application traffic for their users. However, an inherent characteristic of large enterprise networks is that these networks are typically geographically dispersed. Separating these sites over an IP WAN can impact the performance of network-based applications. Fortunately, Cisco offers a collection of ANS devices that can help optimize the performance of network-based applications. In addition to dedicated hardware, however, Cisco IOS Software offers a collection of features that can help collect baseline information for these applications and then help improve application performance (for example, response time).

Although this chapter introduces you to a collection of Cisco ANS devices, the primary focus on application optimization is on Cisco IOS features. These features include baselining features such as NetFlow, IP SLA, and NBAR, in addition to QoS features. Beyond reviewing the theory and configuration of these Cisco IOS features, this chapter highlights common troubleshooting issues you might encounter when working with these features.

Another advanced service present in many networks is wireless network technology. Although troubleshooting the many aspects of a wireless network is an in-depth study, this chapter places the troubleshooting focus on wired network configurations, which can impact wireless network clients. For example, a Cisco Catalyst switch on a wired network might have an incorrect Power over Ethernet (PoE) configuration, preventing a wireless access point (WAP) from receiving power. As another example, the security configuration on a router might include an access control list (ACL) that blocks Lightweight Access Point Protocol (LWAPP) traffic that should flow between a WAP and a wireless LAN controller (WLC).

The "Wireless Troubleshooting Targets" section of this chapter begins by reviewing the components that comprise both autonomous and split-MAC wireless networks. Then the focus shifts to power, VLAN, security, DHCP, and QoS issues on a wired network that might impact wireless clients.

"Do I Know This Already?" Quiz

The "Do I Know This Already?" quiz helps you determine your level of knowledge of this chapter's topics before you begin. Table 13-1 details the major topics discussed in this chapter and their corresponding quiz questions.

Table 13-1 *"Do I Know This Already?" Section-to-Question Mapping*

Foundation Topics Section	Questions
Application Network Services Troubleshooting	1–6
Wireless Troubleshooting Targets	7–10

1. Which of the following Cisco ANS components enhances web applications by measuring response time and managing application layer security? (Choose the best answer.)

   a. Cisco Application Velocity System (AVS)

   b. Cisco Global Site Selector (GSS)

   c. Cisco Content Switching Module (CSM)

   d. Cisco Application Control Engine (ACE)

2. What are the four basic processes involved in optimizing an application? (Choose the four best answers.)

   a. Deploy

   b. Monitor

   c. Expand

   d. Baseline

   e. Optimize

3. Which of the following is a common NetFlow troubleshooting issue? (Choose the best answer.)

   a. A virtual interface has not been configured.

   b. The interface configured for NetFlow has an incorrect **bandwidth** command configured.

   c. The NetFlow collector is on the same subnet as the router configured for NetFlow.

   d. The configuration of the NetFlow collector is incorrect.

4. What is IP SLA's default frequency for sending probes?

   a. 30 seconds

   b. 60 seconds

   c. 90 seconds

   d. 120 seconds

5. In what configuration mode is the **ip nbar protocol-discovery** command issued?

    a. Global configuration mode

    b. Policy-map-class configuration mode

    c. Interface configuration mode

    d. Router configuration mode

6. Which three of the following steps should be performed prior to configuring Auto-QoS on a router interface? (Select the three best answers.)

    a. Configure an IP address on the interface.

    b. Enable Cisco Express Forwarding on the router.

    c. Configure the **bandwidth** command on the interface.

    d. Enable RSVP on the interface.

7. What wireless network mode of operation is characterized by having the functions of a traditional wireless access point divided between a lightweight access point and a wireless LAN controller?

    a. Autonomous

    b. Split horizon

    c. Split-MAC

    d. Split tunneling

8. Which two ports does LWAPP traffic use? (Choose the two best answers.)

    a. TCP port 12222

    b. UDP port 12222

    c. TCP port 12223

    d. UDP port 12223

9. What command can you use to display the VLANs that are permitted on the trunk ports of a switch?

    a. show interfaces trunk

    b. show trunk interfaces

    c. show switchport trunk

    d. show trunk switchport

10. What interface configuration mode command can you enter in a Cisco Catalyst switch to instruct the interface to trust incoming DHCP markings?

    a. wrr-queue dscp

    b. wrr-queue bandwidth dscp

    c. mls qos trust dscp

    d. mls qos trust-device dscp

Foundation Topics

Application Network Services Troubleshooting

Cisco Application Network Services (ANS) is a collection of Cisco solutions that fall under the Cisco Service-Oriented Network Architecture (SONA) framework. ANS technologies can, for example, enhance the performance of applications within a data center, for users at a remote site, and for a teleworker, as illustrated in Figure 13-1.

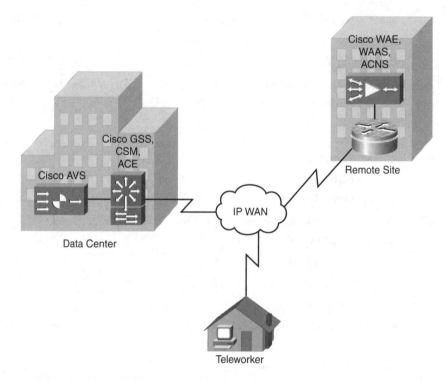

Figure 13-1 *ANS Sample Topology*

Table 13-2 describes some of the features offered by the ANS components seen in the topology.

Table 13-2 *ANS Network Components*

Component	Description
Cisco Application Velocity System (AVS)	Enhances web applications (for example, by measuring response time and by managing application layer security)
Cisco Global Site Selector (GSS)	Optimizes distributed data center environments

Table 13-2 *ANS Network Components*   (*Continued*)

Component	Description
Cisco Content Switching Module (CSM)	Performs load balancing across multiple devices (such as servers or firewalls)
Cisco Application Control Engine (ACE)	Performs intelligent load balancing and content switching to increase application availability
Cisco Wide Area Application Engine (WAAE)	Provides a platform on which users can run Cisco ACNS or Cisco WAAS software
Cisco Wide Area Application Software (WAAS)	Accelerates applications for remote office workers
Cisco Application and Content Networking System (ACNS)	Supports content distribution (for example, video streaming) to remote sites over an IP WAN

Keep in mind that the components presented are just a few examples of how application performance can be improved (or maintained) in a network. In addition to such specialized technologies, many Cisco IOS features can help ensure application performance. This section considers some of these Cisco IOS features and how they can be used to optimize application performance.

Application Optimization

The performance of network applications can be enhanced by gaining an understanding of the application traffic, followed by optimizing the network for those applications. After performing this optimization, you should again monitor the behavior of network traffic to determine what has changed as a result of your optimization. With your understanding of existing application traffic patterns, you can more efficiently deploy additional network applications.

This application optimization process can be summarized with the following four steps:

Step 1.   **Baseline:** The first step is to baseline the performance metrics of existing application traffic.

Step 2.   **Optimize:** After you understand the current behavior of the application traffic, you can optimize identified applications (for example, using QoS mechanisms).

Step 3.   **Monitor:** After implementing your optimization configuration, network traffic should again be monitored to determine how network traffic patterns are impacted by the new configuration.

Step 4.   **Deploy:** As a network evolves, new applications might be added, while existing applications might undergo multiple upgrades. Because the deployments of new applications or upgrades can affect the behavior of network applications, these steps should be repeated.

Not only do these steps help optimize network application performance, they can also aid in troubleshooting. For example, when troubleshooting an issue, you can compare data you collect against the baseline and monitoring data collected in the preceding steps. By identifying the difference in these data sets, you might be able to better determine the underlying cause for a troubleshooting issue.

NetFlow

The Cisco IOS NetFlow feature can be used when baselining network application performance. Recall from Chapter 3, "The Maintenance and Troubleshooting Toolbox," that NetFlow can distinguish between different traffic flows, where a *flow* is a series of packets, all of which share header information such as source and destination IP addresses, protocols numbers, port numbers, and Type of Service (TOS) field information. NetFlow can keep track of the number of packets and bytes observed in each flow. This information is stored in a *flow cache*. Also recall that the NetFlow feature can be used standalone on an individual router, or entries in the flow cache of a router can be exported to a *NetFlow collector* prior to the entries expiring. After the NetFlow collector has received flow information for a period of time, analysis software running on the NetFlow collector can produce reports detailing traffic statistics.

Figure 13-2 shows a sample NetFlow topology (originally presented in Chapter 3), where NetFlow is enabled on router R4, and a NetFlow collector is configured on a PC at IP address 192.168.1.50.

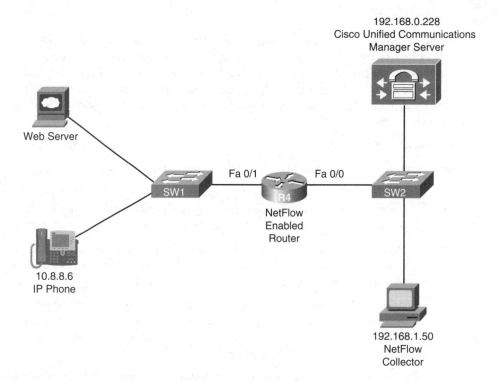

Figure 13-2 *NetFlow Sample Topology*

As a review, Example 13-1 shows the NetFlow configuration on router R4. The **ip flow ingress** command is issued for both the Fast Ethernet 0/0 and Fast Ethernet 0/1 interfaces, ensuring that all flows passing through the router, regardless of direction, can be monitored. Router R4 is configured to report its NetFlow information to a NetFlow collector at IP address 192.168.1.50. The **ip flow-export source lo 0** command indicates that all communication between router R4 and the NetFlow collector will be via interface Loopback 0. A NetFlow version of **5** was specified. Finally, the **ip flow-export destination 192.168.1.50 5000** command is issued to specify that the IP address of the NetFlow collector is **192.168.1.50**, and communication to the NetFlow collector should be done over UDP port **5000**. Because NetFlow does not have a standardized port number, please check the documentation of your NetFlow collector when selecting a port.

Example 13-1 *NetFlow Sample Configuration*

Key
Topic

```
R4# conf term
R4(config)# int fa 0/0
R4(config-if)# ip flow ingress
R4(config-if)# exit
R4(config)# int fa 0/1
R4(config-if)# ip flow ingress
R4(config-if)# exit
R4(config)# ip flow-export source lo 0
R4(config)# ip flow-export version 5
R4(config)# ip flow-export destination 192.168.1.50 5000
R4(config)# end
```

Although an external NetFlow collector is valuable for longer-term flow analysis, you can issue the **show ip cache flow** command at the command-line interface (CLI) prompt of a router to produce a summary of flow information, as demonstrated in Example 13-2. Again, you can use this information in collecting baseline information for network applications.

Example 13-2 *Viewing NetFlow Information*

Key
Topic

```
R4# show ip cache flow
...OUTPUT OMITTED...
Protocol      Total    Flows  Packets Bytes  Packets Active(Sec) Idle(Sec)
              Flows    /Sec   /Flow   /Pkt   /Sec    /Flow       /Flow
TCP-Telnet    12       0.0    50      40     0.1     15.7        14.2
TCP-WWW       12       0.0    40      785    0.1     7.1         6.2
TCP-other     536      0.1    1       55     0.2     0.3         10.5
UDP-TFTP      225      0.0    4       59     0.1     11.9        15.4
UDP-other     122      0.0    114     284    3.0     15.9        15.4
ICMP          41       0.0    13      91     0.1     49.9        15.6
IP-other      1        0.0    389     60     0.0     1797.1      3.4
Total:        949      0.2    18      255    3.8     9.4         12.5
```

SrcIf	SrcIPaddress	DstIf	DstIPaddress	Pr	SrcP	DstP	Pkts
Fa0/0	10.3.3.1	Null	224.0.0.10	58	0000	0000	62
Fa0/1	10.8.8.6	Fa0/0	192.168.0.228	06	C2DB	07D0	2
Fa0/0	192.168.0.228	Fa0/1	10.8.8.6	06	07D0	C2DB	1
Fa0/0	192.168.1.50	Fa0/1	10.8.8.6	11	6002	6BD2	9166
Fa0/1	10.8.8.6	Fa0/0	192.168.1.50	11	6BD2	6002	9166
Fa0/0	10.1.1.2	Local	10.3.3.2	06	38F2	0017	438

If NetFlow is not behaving as expected, consider the following list of common NetFlow troubleshooting targets that could be investigated:

Key Topic

■ No network connectivity exists between a NetFlow router and its configured NetFlow collector.

■ The router's NetFlow configuration is incorrect.

■ The NetFlow collector's configuration is incorrect.

■ An ACL or a firewall is blocking NetFlow traffic.

IP SLAs

You can use the Cisco IOS IP SLA feature to measure how the network treats traffic for specific applications. IP SLA accomplishes this by synthetically generating traffic bearing similar characteristics to application traffic (for example, identical port numbers and packet sizes). This traffic, called *probes*, is sent to a destination router. This destination router is configured to respond to the received probes with time-stamp information, which can then be used to calculate performance metrics for the traffic. Like NetFlow, IP SLAs can be used for baselining network application performance.

Key Topic

Following are the steps to configure the IP SLA feature:

Step 1.   Configure a router as an IP SLA responder.

Step 2.   Configure the type of IP SLA operation.

Step 3.   Determine the configuration options for the IP SLA operation.

Step 4.   Specify any thresholds (which could trigger other events when exceeded).

Step 5.   Specify when the IP SLA should run.

Step 6.   View the results (for example, via the Cisco IOS CLI or a Simple Network Management Protocol [SNMP]-based network management system [NMS]).

To illustrate a basic IP SLA configuration, consider the topology shown in Figure 13-3. In this topology, which is the basic topology used for all trouble tickets presented in this book, router R1 is configured as the source IP SLA router, whereas router BB2 is configured as the IP SLA responder.

Example 13-3 shows the configuration of the IP SLA responder (that is, router BB2). The **ip sla monitor responder** command is used to make router BB2 act as a responder. The

ip sla monitor responder type tcpConnect ipaddress 10.4.4.4 port 80 command tells router BB2 to specifically act as a responder for tcpConnect probes sent to a destination address of 10.4.4.4 (that is, the loopback interface of router BB2) with a destination port of 80 (that is, the HTTP port).

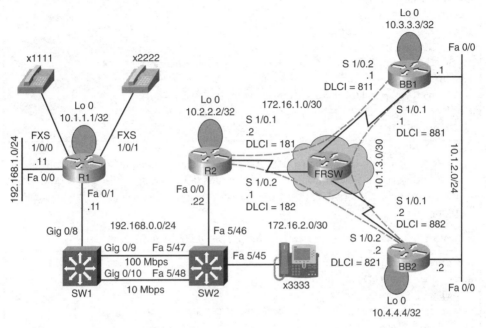

Figure 13-3 *IP SLA Sample Topology*

Example 13-3 *IP SLA Responder Configuration*

Key
Topic

```
BB2# show run
...OUTPUT OMITTED...
!
ip sla monitor responder
ip sla monitor responder type tcpConnect ipaddress 10.4.4.4 port 80
!
... OUTPUT OMITTED...
```

Example 13-4 shows the configuration of the IP SLA source (that is, router R1). Notice that a specific SLA monitoring instance (numbered **1**) is created with the command **ip sla monitor 1**. The **type** keyword specifies the type of SLA probes (that is, tcpConnect probes with a destination IP address of 10.4.4.4 and a destination port number of 80 and a source port number of 17406). The **tos 64** command causes the TOS byte in the IP headers of the probes to be marked with a 64 (that is, 01000000 in binary, which equates to an IP Precedence value of 2, because IP Precedence only considers the three leftmost bits in a TOS byte). You also have the option of using the **frequency** *seconds* to specify how often the probes are to be sent (the default value is 60 seconds). Finally, the **ip sla monitor**

schedule 1 life forever start-time now command indicates that the IP SLA monitor 1 instance should begin immediately and run forever.

Example 13-4   *IP SLA Source Configuration*

```
R1# show run
...OUTPUT OMITTED...
!
ip sla monitor 1
 type tcpConnect dest-ipaddr 10.4.4.4 dest-port 80 source-port 17406
 tos 64
ip sla monitor schedule 1 life forever start-time now
!
...OUTPUT OMITTED...
```

Next, you can view the collected IP SLA information, as demonstrated in Example 13-5. The output indicates that the latest round trip time (RTT) measured for a probe was 168 ms. Also, you can see that 13 of the probes were responded to successfully, while one probe failed.

Example 13-5   *Viewing Information Collected on the IP SLA Source*

```
R1# show ip sla monitor statistics
Round trip time (RTT)      Index 1
    Latest RTT: 168 ms
Latest operation start time: *16:10:52.453 UTC Sun Mar 3 2002
Latest operation return code: OK
Number of successes: 13
Number of failures: 1
Operation time to live: Forever
```

You can also view the information collected by the IP SLA responder, as shown in Example 13-6. The output indicates that this responder received 15 messages, of which there was a single error. You can also see the IP addresses of IP SLA sources to which this responder recently responded. In this example, there was a single IP SLA source of 192.168.0.11.

Example 13-6   *Viewing Information Collected on the IP SLA Responder*

```
BB2# show ip sla monitor responder
IP SLA Monitor Responder is: Enabled
Number of control message received: 15 Number of errors: 1
Recent sources:
     192.168.0.11 [00:38:01.807 UTC Fri Mar 1 2002]
     192.168.0.11 [00:37:01.783 UTC Fri Mar 1 2002]
     192.168.0.11 [00:36:01.791 UTC Fri Mar 1 2002]
     192.168.0.11 [00:35:01.791 UTC Fri Mar 1 2002]
     192.168.0.11 [00:34:01.779 UTC Fri Mar 1 2002]
```

```
Recent error sources:
    192.168.0.11 [00:24:01.807 UTC Fri Mar 1 2002]    RTT_FAIL

tcpConnect Responder:
  IP Address          Port
  10.4.4.4
```

- The source or destination IP addresses configured on the IP SLA source or responder is incorrect.

- The frequency of the probes is set for a value that is too long.

- The schedule is set to begin sending probes at some time in the future.

- The probes are being filtered by an ACL or a firewall.

Network-Based Application Recognition

Network-Based Application Recognition (NBAR) can classify various traffic types by examining information at Layers 3 through 7. Protocols that change port numbers (that is, stateful protocols) can also be tracked. Although Cisco IOS comes with multiple NBAR application signatures, there is a continuing need for additional signature recognition capabilities. For example, although your router might be able to recognize KaZaa traffic, it might not be able to recognize Bit Torrent traffic. Fortunately, you can install a Bit Torrent Packet Description Language Module (PDLM) into the router's flash. This PDLM can be referenced by the router's Cisco IOS configuration, thus allowing the router to recognize Bit Torrent traffic. PDLMs are available for download from the following URL:

http://www.cisco.com/cgi-bin/tablebuild.pl/pdlm

Note that this site, as shown in Figure 13-4, requires appropriate login credentials.

In addition to usefulness of NBAR in classifying traffic, it can function as a protocol discovery tool. Therefore, like NetFlow and IP SLA, NBAR can serve as a useful baselining tool.

The protocol discovery feature of NBAR can be enabled on an interface to determine the applications consuming the most bandwidth on that interface (that is, the *top talkers*).

To enable NBAR protocol discovery, enter the following command in interface configuration mode:

```
Router(config-if)# ip nbar protocol-discovery
```

After NBAR has collected traffic statistics for an interface, you can use the **show ip nbar protocol-discovery** command to view the statistics, as demonstrated in Example 13-7. This output indicates that the top five protocols seen on the Fast Ethernet 0/0 interface on router R4 are RTP, HTTP, SKINNY, TELNET, and EIGRP. The output shows packet count, byte count, average bit rate, and maximum bit rate statistics for each of these protocols.

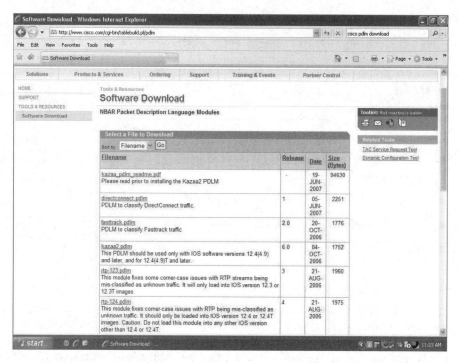

Figure 13-4   *PDLM Download Page*

Example 13-7   show ip nbar protocol-discovery *Command Output*

```
R4# show ip nbar protocol-discovery


FastEthernet0/0
                        Input                   Output
                        -----                   -----
    Protocol            Packet Count            Packet Count
                        Byte Count              Byte Count
                        5min Bit Rate (bps)     5min Bit Rate (bps)
                        5min Max Bit Rate (bps) 5min Max Bit Rate (bps)
    ------------------------------------------------------------------
    rtp                 922                     3923
                        65248                   290302
                        6000                    15000
                        9000                    15000
    http                171                     231
                        11506                   345647
                        0                       1000
                        3000                    13000
    skinny              34                      42
                        3080                    2508
```

```
                                0                        0
                                1000                     0
       telnet                   92                       0
                                5520                     0
                                0                        0
                                0                        0
       eigrp                    44                       21
                                3256                     1554
                                0                        0
                                0                        0
...OUTPUT OMITTED...
```

Recall that a router's NBAR signature recognition capability can be expanded by adding one or more PDLM files to a router's flash. You can reference these PDLM files using the following command:

```
Router(config)# ip nbar pdlm pdlm_file
```

Also, for applications that are recognized based on TCP or User Datagram Protocol (UDP) port numbers, you can modify the ports the NBAR uses with the following command:

```
Router(config)# ip nbar port-map protocol {tcp   udp} port_number [port_number]
```

The following is a listing of common NBAR troubleshooting issues you might encounter:

Key Topic

- **NBAR is not correctly recognizing applications:** This can occur if an application is using a nonstandard port. You can use the **show ip nbar port-map** *protocol* command to see what port(s) is associated with a specified application. For example, perhaps a web server is using TCP port 8080 instead of port 80. You can issue the **show ip nbar port-map http** command and see that NBAR is only recognizing TCP port 80 as HTTP traffic. You can then use the **ip nbar port-map http tcp 80 8080** command in global configuration mode to cause NBAR to recognize either TCP port 80 or 8080 as HTTP traffic.

- **NBAR does not support a specific application:** If a PDLM file exists for an application, you can download it from Cisco.com, copy it to the flash of a router, and reference it with the **ip nbar pdlm** *pdlm-file* command in global configuration mode.

- **NBAR degrades router performance:** Depending on the underlying router platform, the performance of a router might suffer as a result of NBAR's inspection of multiple flows. You can use the **show processes cpu** command to determine the CPU utilization of a router.

QoS

In addition to baselining the application traffic for a network, a component of the Cisco ANS framework is ensuring appropriate levels of service for network applications. One approach to achieving and maintaining appropriate service levels is the use of QoS.

Chapter 11, "IP Communications Troubleshooting," introduced QoS technologies and how many of these technologies could be configured using the three-step Modular QoS

CLI (MQC) process. Also discussed was the AutoQoS Enterprise feature, which can, using NBAR, dynamically discover network traffic patterns and generate a recommended QoS policy.

As a review, AutoQoS Enterprise is configured via a three-step process:

Key Topic

Step 1. Begin the AutoQoS Enterprise discovery phase with the **auto discovery qos** [**trust**] command in interface configuration mode.

Step 2. After the discovery phase runs for a period of time (at least two or three days based on the Cisco recommendation), view the collected information and recommended policy with the **show auto discovery qos** command.

Step 3. Apply the recommended policy using the **auto qos** command in interface configuration mode.

Originally presented in Chapter 11, Example 13-8 illustrates this three-step process. Notice that the AutoQoS Enterprise can recognize traffic in as many as ten different classes.

Key Topic

Example 13-8 *Configuring AutoQoS Enterprise*

```
R4# conf term
R4(config)# int fa0/0
R4(config-if)# auto discovery qos
R4(config-if)# end
R4# show auto discovery qos
FastEthernet0/0
 AutoQoS Discovery enabled for applications
 Discovery up time: 1 minutes, 7 seconds
 AutoQoS Class information:
 Class Voice:
  Recommended Minimum Bandwidth: 5 Kbps/<1% (PeakRate)
  Detected applications and data:
  Application/      AverageRate       PeakRate          Total
  Protocol          (kbps/%)          (kbps/%)          (bytes)
  ----------        -----------       --------          -----------
   rtp audio        1/<1              5/<1              10138
 Class Interactive Video:
  No data found.
 Class Signaling:
  Recommended Minimum Bandwidth: 0 Kbps/0% (AverageRate)
  Detected applications and data:
  Application/      AverageRate       PeakRate          Total
  Protocol          (kbps/%)          (kbps/%)          (bytes)
  ----------        -----------       --------          -----------
   skinny           0/0               0/0               2218
 Class Streaming Video:
  No data found.
 Class Transactional:
```

```
     No data found.
 Class Bulk:
   No data found.
 Class Scavenger:
   No data found.
 Class Management:
   No data found.
 Class Routing:
   Recommended Minimum Bandwidth: 0 Kbps/0% (AverageRate)
   Detected applications and data:
   Application/      AverageRate        PeakRate           Total
   Protocol          (kbps/%)           (kbps/%)           (bytes)
   -----------       -----------        --------           -----------
   eigrp             0/0                0/0                1110
   icmp              0/0                0/0                958
 Class Best Effort:
   Current Bandwidth Estimation: 44 Kbps/<1% (AverageRate)
   Detected applications and data:
   Application/      AverageRate        PeakRate           Total
   Protocol          (kbps/%)           (kbps/%)           (bytes)
   -----------       -----------        --------           -----------
   http              44/<1              121/1              372809
   unknowns          0/0                0/0                232


Suggested AutoQoS Policy for the current uptime:
 !
 class-map match-any AutoQoS-Voice-Fa0/0
  match protocol rtp audio
 !
 policy-map AutoQoS-Policy-Fa0/0
  class AutoQoS-Voice-Fa0/0
   priority percent 1
   set dscp ef
  class class-default
   fair-queue
R4# conf term
R4(config)# int fa 0/0
R4(config-if)# auto qos
R4(config-if)# end
R4#
```

Following is a listing of common reasons that AutoQoS (both AutoQoS VoIP and Auto-QoS Enterprise) might not function correctly on a router:

Key Topic

■ **Cisco Express Forwarding (CEF) is not enabled:** AutoQoS can use NBAR to recognize traffic types, and NBAR requires CEF to be enabled. You can enable CEF with the **ip cef** global configuration mode command.

■ **An interface's bandwidth is not correctly configured:** Cisco IOS assumes the bandwidth of a serial interface to be 1.544 Mbps (that is, the bandwidth of a T1 circuit). Because serial interfaces often run at different speeds, you should configure these interfaces with the **bandwidth** *bandwidth-in-kbps* command in interface configuration mode. Some routing protocols (for example, Enhanced Interior Gateway Routing Protocol [EIGRP] and Open Shortest Path First [OSPF]) can reference this bandwidth amount when calculating a route metric. In addition, AutoQoS can reference this bandwidth amount to determine which QoS mechanisms should be enabled on an interface. Therefore, if the bandwidth value of an interface is left at its default setting, AutoQoS might not optimally configure QoS on an interface.

■ **An interface has not been configured with an IP address:** One QoS mechanism that AutoQoS might configure is Multilink PPP (MLP), which is a link fragmentation and interleaving mechanism. Part of an MLP configuration involves the creation of a virtual multilink interface that needs to have an IP address assigned. AutoQoS takes the needed IP address from the physical interface being configured for AutoQoS. Therefore, an interface should be configured with an IP address prior to configuring the interface for AutoQoS.

■ **Only one side of a link has been configured:** AutoQoS is enabled on an interface. However, the interface in the router at the other end of the link needs a complementary configuration. For example, consider two routers interconnected via a serial link running at a link speed of 512 kbps. If you configured AutoQoS for the interface at one end of the link, that interface might be configured for QoS mechanisms that include MLP and RTP header compression (cRTP). However, these mechanisms will not function correctly until the interface at the other end of the link is similarly configured.

■ **The configuration created by AutoQoS has been modified:** AutoQoS configurations are based on QoS mechanisms available in Cisco IOS. Therefore, a configuration generated by AutoQoS can be customized. As a result, the underlying issue you are troubleshooting might be caused by the customization of AutoQoS' configuration.

Wireless Troubleshooting Targets

Troubleshooting wireless networks can require a variety of skill sets. For example, some troubleshooting scenarios might require an understanding of antenna theory and the radio frequency spectrum. Rather than focusing on such radio-specific troubleshooting targets, this section focuses on troubleshooting targets on a wired network that could impact a wireless network.

Specifically, after a review of the Cisco Unified Wireless Network operation, this section discusses such topics as how PoE, VLANs, security, DHCP, and QoS issues can result in issues for a wireless network.

Introducing the Cisco Unified Wireless Network

Wireless local-area networks (WLAN) offer network access via radio waves. Wireless clients (such as PCs or PDAs) access a *WAP* using half-duplex communication. The WAP allows a wireless client to communicate with the wired portion of a network.

Five primary components comprise the Cisco Unified Wireless Network architecture:

Key Topic

- **Wireless clients:** A wireless client device is typically an end-user device (such as a PC) that accesses a wireless network.

- **WAP:** WAPs offer network access for wireless clients.

- **Wireless network unification:** To offer wireless clients access to the resources of an organization, a wireless network needs to be integrated (that is, unified) with a wired LAN. This functionality is referred to as *network unification*.

- **Wireless network management:** Just as enterprise LANs benefit from network management solutions, a wireless LAN can use network management solutions to enhance security and reliability and offer assistance in WLAN deployments. An example of a wireless network management solution is the Cisco Wireless Control System (WCS).

- **Wireless Mobility:** Wireless mobility services include security threat detection, voice services, location services, and guest access.

Traditional WLANs use an access point in autonomous mode, where the access point is configured with a service set identifier (SSID), radio frequency (RF) channel, and RF power settings. However, having an autonomous access point tasked with all these responsibilities can limit scalability and hinder the addition of advanced wireless services.

Aside from autonomous mode, Cisco Unified Wireless Networks can alternatively operate in *split-MAC* mode. With split-MAC operation, an access point is considered a *lightweight access point*, which cannot function without a WLC.

Specifically, a WLAN client sending traffic to the wired LAN sends a packet to a lightweight access point, which encapsulates the packet using Lightweight Access Point Protocol (LWAPP). The encapsulated traffic is sent over an LWAPP tunnel to a WLC. LWAPP sends packets in a Layer 2 frame with an Ethertype of 0x88BB. LWAPP data traffic uses a UDP destination port of 12222, whereas LWAPP control traffic uses a UDP destination port of 12223.

A lightweight access point, as shown in Figure 13-5, performs functions such as beaconing, packet transmission, and frame queuing, whereas the WLC assumes roles such as authentication, key management, and resource reservation.

Chapter 9, "Security Troubleshooting," introduced 802.1X as a means of authenticating users attempting to gain access to a network. Wireless networks often leverage 802.1X technologies to authenticate wireless clients.

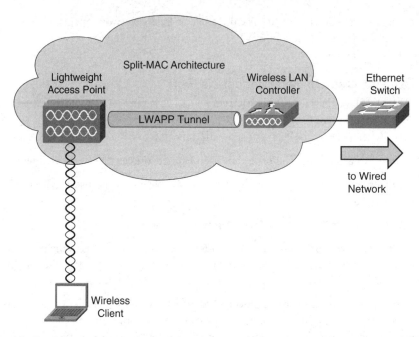

Figure 13-5   *Split-MAC Wireless Architecture*

Specifically, after a wireless client, such as a PC, associates with its access point, the access point only allows the client to communicate with the authentication server until the client successfully logs in and is authenticated, as illustrated in Figure 13-6. The WLC uses an Extensible Authentication Protocol (EAP) to communicate with the authentication server. Cisco Secure Access Control Server (ACS) can, for example, act as an authentication server.

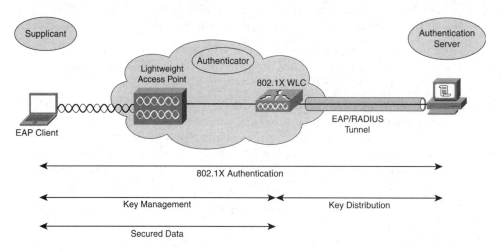

Figure 13-6   *Wireless Network Using 802.1X*

Supported EAP types include the following:

- **EAP-Transport Layer Security (EAP-TLS):** Wireless clients and authentication servers mutually authenticate using digital certificates.

- **EAP-Protected EAP (EAP-PEAP):** The authentication server (that is, a RADIUS server) is authenticated over a Transport Layer Security (TLS) tunnel using a digital certificate, whereas wireless clients are authenticated via Extensible Authentication Protocol—Generic Token Card (EAP-GTC) or Extensible Authentication Protocol—Microsoft Challenge Handshake Authentication Protocol version 2 (EAP-MSCHAPv2).

- **EAP Tunneled Transport Layer Security (EAP-TTLS):** The RADIUS server is authenticated over a TLS tunnel using the certificate of the server, and wireless clients authenticate using username and password credentials.

- **Cisco Lightweight Extensible Authentication Protocol (LEAP):** Cisco developed LEAP as an early and proprietary EAP method; however, LEAP's vulnerability to a dictionary attack represents a major LEAP weakness.

- **Cisco EAP-Flexible Authentication via Secure Tunneling (EAP-FAST):** Cisco proposed EAP-FAST to address weaknesses of LEAP.

Wireless network troubleshooters should also understand the following three WLAN controller components:

- **Ports:** A port on a WLAN controller physically connects the WLAN controller to the wired network (for example, to a Cisco Catalyst switch port).

- **Interfaces:** An interface of a WLAN controller logically maps to a VLAN on a wired network.

- **WLANs:** A WLAN can be configured with security features, QoS mechanisms, and other wireless network parameters. Also, a WLAN associates an SSID to a WLC interface.

Wired Network Issues Impacting Wireless Networks

Many issues that might be perceived as wireless problems result from underlying issues on the wired network. Examples of these issues include PoE, VLANs, security, DHCP, and QoS.

PoE

WAPs (in either an autonomous or split-MAC architecture) require power; however, these access points might need to be installed away from power outlets. For example, to provide appropriate coverage, an access point might be located in a drop ceiling. One option for providing power to such an access point is PoE (which was introduced in Chapter 11), where a Cisco Catalyst switch provides power to an attached device over the Ethernet leads in an unshielded twisted-pair (UTP) cable.

If the Cisco Catalyst switch is not appropriately configured to provide PoE, or if the switch has no additional power available, an attached WAP might fail to power on. In addition to verifying proper PoE configuration on the Cisco Catalyst switch, another troubleshooting aid is the Cisco Power Calculator, an online tool available at http://tools.cisco.com/cpc/launch.jsp. This tool can help determine the power capacity of a switch. Note that appropriate Cisco login credentials are required to access this tool.

VLANs

Traffic in a wireless network often belongs to its own VLAN; however, wireless users might experience connectivity issues if traffic from their wireless VLAN is not permitted over a trunk in the wired network. Therefore, trunk configurations on Cisco Catalyst switches might need to be inspected as part of troubleshooting wireless connectivity issues.

Chapter 4, "Basic Cisco Catalyst Switch Troubleshooting," introduced the troubleshooting of VLANs and trunks. As a review, Table 13-3 provides commands for gathering information about VLAN and trunk configuration information on a Cisco Catalyst switch.

Key Topic

Table 13-3　*VLAN and Trunk Troubleshooting Commands for a Cisco Catalyst Switch*

Command	Description
show vlan	Shows to which VLANs the ports of a switch belong
show interfaces trunk	Displays which VLANs are permitted on a switch's trunk ports, and which switch ports are configured as trunks
show interfaces switchport	Displays summary information for the ports on a switch, including VLAN and trunk configuration information

Security

Chapter 9 discussed how ACLs might inadvertently be configured to block traffic that should be permitted on a network. In the case of wireless networks configured in a split-MAC architecture, recall that UDP ports 12222 and 12223 (that is, the ports used by LWAPP) should be permitted between a WAP and a WLC. You can issue the **show access-lists** command to verify the access list configuration used on a router.

DHCP

Because an inherent characteristic of wireless networks is the mobility of wireless clients, those clients might need to roam from one subnet to another. In such an instance, a loss of wireless connectivity might result from a DHCP issue.

Chapter 10, "IP Services Troubleshooting," discussed troubleshooting DHCP; however, as a review, Table 13-4 offers a collection of **show**, **clear**, and **debug** commands useful in troubleshooting DHCP problems.

Table 13-4 *DHCP Troubleshooting Commands*

Command	Description
show ip dhcp conflict	Lists any IP address conflicts identified by a router, along with the method the router used to identify the conflicts (this is, via ping or gratuitous ARP)
show ip dhcp binding	Displays IP addresses assigned by an IOS DHCP server, their corresponding MAC addresses, and lease expirations
clear ip dhcp binding *	Releases all current DHCP leases
clear ip dhcp conflict *	Clears all currently identified DHCP conflicts
debug ip dhcp server events	Provides real-time information about DHCP address assignments and database updates
debug ip dhcp server packet	Displays real-time decodes of DHCP packets

QoS

Latency-sensitive traffic traveling over a wireless network (for example, Voice over Wireless LAN [VoWLAN]) might suffer from poor performance if QoS markings are not preserved as traffic crosses the boundary between the wireless and wired portions of a network.

You might want to review Chapter 11 for a more detailed discussion of QoS troubleshooting. The **mls qos trust dscp** interface configuration mode command, however, was not discussed in Chapter 11. You can issue this command on a Cisco Catalyst switch to cause an interface to trust incoming DSCP markings. To preserve priority markings on wireless traffic as it enters a wired network, you can issue this command on a Cisco Catalyst switch port that connects to a WLC.

Exam Preparation Tasks

Review All the Key Topics

Key Topic

Review the most important topics from inside the chapter, noted with the Key Topics icon in the outer margin of the page. Table 13-5 lists these key topics and the page numbers where each is found.

Table 13-5 *Key Topics for Chapter 13*

Key Topic Element	Description	Page Number
Table 13-2	ANS network components	422
Steps	Optimizing network applications	423
Example 13-1	NetFlow sample configuration	425
Example 13-2	Viewing NetFlow information	425
List	Common NetFlow troubleshooting issues	426
Steps	Configuring the IP SLA feature	426
Example 13-3	IP SLA responder configuration	427
Example 13-4	IP SLA source configuration	428
Example 13-5	Viewing information collected on the IP SLA source	428
Example 13-6	Viewing information collected on the IP SLA responder	428
List	Common IP SLA troubleshooting issues	429
List	Common NBAR troubleshooting issues	431
Steps	AutoQoS Enterprise configuration	432
Example 13-8	Configuring AutoQoS Enterprise	432
List	Common AutoQoS troubleshooting issues	434
List	Cisco Unified Wireless Network components	435
Table 13-3	VLAN and trunk troubleshooting commands for a Cisco Catalyst switch	438
Table 13-4	DHCP troubleshooting commands	439

Complete Tables and Lists from Memory

Print a copy of Appendix B, "Memory Tables" (found on the CD), or at least the section for this chapter, and complete the tables and lists from memory. Appendix C, "Memory Tables Answer Key," also on the CD, includes completed tables and lists to check your work.

Define Key Terms

Define the following key terms from this chapter, and check your answers in the Glossary:

Cisco Application Network Services (ANS), IP SLA, Network-Based Application Recognition (NBAR), Packet Description Language Module (PDLM), wireless client, wireless access point (WAP), wireless network unification, wireless network management, wireless mobility, autonomous mode, split-MAC mode, Lightweight Access Point Protocol (LWAPP), lightweight access point, wireless LAN controller (WLC), Extensible Authentication Protocol (EAP), Power over Ethernet (PoE)

Command Reference to Check Your Memory

This section includes the most important configuration and EXEC commands covered in this chapter. To determine how well you have memorized the commands as a side effect of your other studies, cover the left side of the table with a piece of paper; read the descriptions on the right side; and see whether you remember the command.

Table 13-6 *Chapter 13 Configuration Command Reference*

Command	Description
ip flow ingress	Interface configuration mode command used to enable NetFlow for that interface
ip flow-export source *interface-id*	Global configuration mode command used to specify the interface used to communicate with an external NetFlow collector
ip flow-export version {1 | 5 | 9}	Global configuration mode command used to specify the NetFlow version used by a device
ip flow-export destination *ip-address port*	Global configuration mode command used to specify the IP address and port number of an external NetFlow collector
ip sla monitor responder	Global configuration mode command that enables an IP SLA responder (Note: Some versions of Cisco IOS omit the **monitor** keyword in this command. Also note that this command is issued on the IP SLA responder router.)

continues

Table 13-6   *Chapter 13 Configuration Command Reference   (Continued)*

Command	Description
ip sla monitor responder type *type* **ipaddress** *ip-address* **port** *port*	Global configuration mode command that specifies the type of IP SLA probe to be received by the responder router, including the destination IP address and port number of the probe (Note: Some versions of Cisco IOS would instead use the **ip sla responder** *type* **ipaddress** *IP_address* **port** *port* command.)
ip sla monitor *entry*	Global configuration mode command that defines an IP SLA monitor entry and enters IP SLA configuration mode (Note: Some versions of Cisco IOS omit the **monitor** keyword in this command. Also note that this command is issued on the IP SLA source router.)
type tcpConnect dest-ipaddr *dest-ip-address* **dest-port** *dest-port* **source-port source-port**	IP SLA configuration mode command that defines that the type of IP SLA probe to be sent is a TCP Connect probe (Note: Some versions of Cisco IOS use the **tcp-connect** *dest-ip-address dest-port* **source-port** *source-port* command. Also note that this command is issued on the IP SLA source router.)
tos value	IP SLA TCP configuration mode command that specifies the decimal equivalent of the eight binary bits in the TOS byte of an IPv4 header (Note: This command is issued on the IP SLA source router.)
ip sla monitor schedule *entry* **life forever start-time now**	Global configuration mode command that immediately starts a specified IP SLA entry, which then runs forever (Note: Some versions of Cisco IOS omit the **monitor** keyword in this command.)
ip nbar protocol-discovery	Interface configuration mode command that enables NBAR protocol discovery on the interface
ip nbar pdlm *pdlm-file*	Global configuration mode command that adds the specified PDLM file to the NBAR protocol recognition capability of the router
ip nbar port-map *protocol* {**tcp** | **udp**} *port-number* [*port-number*]	Specifies one or more TCP or UDP ports used by NBAR to recognize the specified protocol
auto discovery qos [trust]	Interface configuration mode command issued on a router to begin the discovery phase on an interface for the AutoQoS Enterprise feature (Note: The **trust** keyword instructs the router to classify traffic based on existing DSCP markings, as opposed to using NBAR.)

Table 13-6 *Chapter 13 Configuration Command Reference*   *(Continued)*

Command	Description
auto qos	Interface configuration mode command on a router used to apply a policy map generated by AutoQoS Enterprise
mls qos trust dscp	Interface configuration mode command used on a switch to instruct an interface to trust Differentiated Services Code Point (DSCP) markings on packets entering the interface

This chapter covers the following subjects:

Remote Office Troubleshooting: This section identifies a collection of technologies that might become troubleshooting targets for a remote office network. The primary technologies that this section focuses on are virtual private network (VPN) technologies. Sample syntax is provided for a VPN using IP security (IPsec) and Generic Routing Encapsulation (GRE). Also, several useful **show** commands are provided as a troubleshooting reference.

Complex Network Troubleshooting: This section identifies how multiple network technologies map to the seven layers of the Open Systems Interconnection (OSI) reference model. Also, you are given a list of resources that a troubleshooter should have prior to troubleshooting a complex enterprise network. Finally, this section reviews key points from all trouble tickets previously presented.

CHAPTER 14

Large Enterprise Network Troubleshooting

Most large enterprise networks connect to one or more remote office locations, typically accessible via an IP WAN. The introduction of a remote location into a network can pose additional troubleshooting targets. As a couple of examples, consider quality of service (QoS) and security issues. The relatively limited bandwidth available on an IP WAN might create quality issues for latency-sensitive applications such as streaming voice or video. Also, because the IP WAN might span an untrusted network (for example, the Internet), security mechanisms should be in place to secure the traffic flowing between the headquarters and remote locations.

Although troubleshooting remote office network issues can involve several technologies (many of which have been discussed previously in this book), this chapter focuses on VPN technologies. Specifically, you will learn about the characteristics of site-to-site VPNs and remote-access VPNs, including common troubleshooting issues for those VPN types. You are also presented with a collection of commands useful in troubleshooting VPN-related issues.

Because troubleshooting a complex enterprise network requires understanding the operation of and the interaction between many networking technologies, this chapter reviews multiple network technologies discussed in previous chapters. Specifically, this chapter identifies at which layer(s) of the OSI model various networking technologies reside. Additionally, you are given a list of prerequisites a troubleshooter should have before troubleshooting a complex enterprise network. Finally, this chapter reviews each trouble ticket previously covered in this book. For each trouble ticket, this chapter reviews the reported symptoms, the Cisco IOS commands used to gather information, the identified issue, and the problem resolution.

"Do I Know This Already?" Quiz

The "Do I Know This Already?" quiz helps you determine your level of knowledge of this chapter's topics before you begin. Table 14-1 details the major topics discussed in this chapter and their corresponding quiz questions.

Table 14-1 *"Do I Know This Already?" Section-to-Question Mapping*

Foundation Topics Section	Questions
Remote Office Troubleshooting	1–4
Complex Network Troubleshooting	5–8

1. VPNs can generally be categorized as one of which two VPN types? (Choose the two best answers.)

   a. Centralized VPN

   b. Site-to-site VPN

   c. Remote-access VPN

   d. Distributed VPN

2. What VPN technology allows a VPN link between two remote offices to be dynamically created on an as-needed basis?

   a. ESP

   b. AH

   c. SHA-1

   d. DMVPN

3. Which of the following is generally true of a remote-access VPN but is generally not true of a site-to-site VPN? (Choose the best answer.)

   a. VPN client software needs to be installed on the remote-access VPN clients.

   b. IPsec is supported.

   c. User profiles are not supported.

   d. A router at the remote site terminates the VPN connection.

4. Which of the following commands displays IPsec security association settings? (Choose the best answer.)

   a. show crypto map

   b. show crypto engine connections active

   c. show ip protocols

   d. show crypto ipsec sa

5. If you are troubleshooting an EtherChannel issue, on which layer of the OSI model should you focus?

   a. Layer 1

   b. Layer 2

   c. Layer 3

   d. Layer 4

6. Which of the following symptoms are common results of a Spanning Tree Protocol issue? (Select the two best answers.)

   a. Routing protocols are not load balancing appropriately.

   b. A switch's MAC address table is corrupted.

   c. A switch's processor utilization is high.

   d. A switch's port experiences a security violation, resulting in the port entering the *errordisable* state.

7. Which of the following technologies can help provide default gateway redundancy for endpoints? (Choose the best answer.)

    a. NTP

    b. DHCP

    c. HSRP

    d. SRST

8. What feature can automatically deploy a QoS configuration on some router and switch platforms?

    a. AutoQoS

    b. NBAR

    c. CEF

    d. NetFlow

Foundation Topics

Remote Office Troubleshooting

Large enterprise networks often contain multiple remote offices connecting back to a network located at a corporate headquarters. Troubleshooting remote office network issues can require knowledge of a wide array of technologies, as illustrated in Figure 14-1.

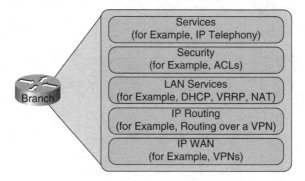

Figure 14-1   *Remote Office Troubleshooting Targets*

Each of the technology areas shown in the figure has previously been addressed in this book. Rather than reviewing each of these topics, this section primarily focuses on VPN issues that can impact remote office connectivity. For example, a VPN connection established through the Internet can be used as a backup to a private IP WAN connection, as shown in Figure 14-2.

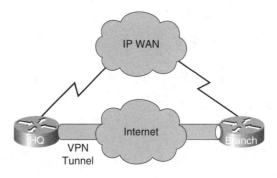

Figure 14-2   *Using a VPN Connection as a Backup Link*

VPN Types

As illustrated in Figure 14-3, most VPNs can be categorized as one of two types:

■ **Site-to-site VPNs:** A site-to-site VPN typically terminates in a router at the head-quarters and a router at the remote site. Such an arrangement does not require the clients at the remote site to have VPN client software installed.

■ **Remote-access VPNs:** A remote-access VPN requires VPN clients at the remote site to run VPN client software. Although this approach might require more administrative overhead to install client software on all clients, remote-access VPNs do offer more flexibility for mobile users. For example, clients can connect via their hotel's Internet connection using VPN client software on their laptop computer.

Each VPN type has unique design considerations.

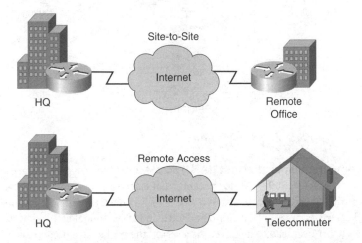

Figure 14-3 *Site-to-Site and Remote-Access VPNs*

Site-to-Site VPN Considerations

Figure 14-4 depicts a site-to-site VPN connection.

Following is a listing of potential issues that you should consider with site-to-site networks:

■ **Overlapping IP address spaces:** Notice that the Branch A and Headquarters locations have an overlapping IP address space (that is, 10.1.1.0/24). This overlap might prevent these two networks from communicating successfully. A fix for such an issue is to configure Network Address Translation (NAT) to support overlapping networks.

■ **Dynamic routing protocols:** Dynamic routing protocols (for example, Enhanced Interior Gateway Routing Protocol [EIGRP], Open Shortest Path First [OSPF], and Routing Information Protocol, version 2 [RIPv2]) typically send advertisements to a multicast address; however, IPsec tunnels transport only unicast IP packets. A Generic Routing Encapsulation (GRE) tunnel, however, can transport a variety of traffic types. Therefore, all IP traffic (including multicast and broadcast traffic) can initially be encapsulated within GRE packets, which are unicast IP packets. Those GRE packets can then be encapsulated inside IPsec packets to secure their transmission.

Key
Topic

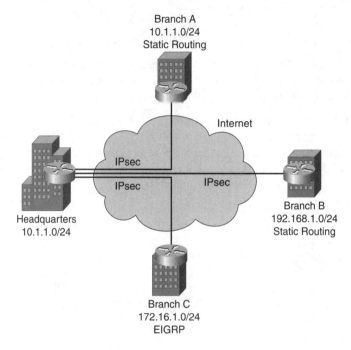

Figure 14-4   *Site-to-Site VPN Connection*

- **Maximum transmission unit (MTU) size:** Most Cisco router interfaces default to an MTU size of 1500 bytes for packets (that is, not including a Layer 2 header). However, when traffic is encapsulated inside a VPN tunnel, the tunnel header(s) add to the packet size. For example, a combined GRE and IPsec tunnel can add between 60 and 80 bytes of overhead to a packet. As a result, the packet size might exceed its MTU setting. When an interface attempts to transmit a packet that exceeds the MTU of the interface, the interface attempts to fragment the packet. If successful, each fragment receives its own header creating a new packet, which is of an acceptable size. However, fragmenting large packets can cause issues. First, the act of performing fragmentation increases the burden on a router processor. Additionally, some packets are marked with a Do Not Fragment (DF) bit, which can cause those packets to be dropped.

- **Misconfiguration:** The configuration of IPsec tunnels can be quite complex. As a result, a common troubleshooting issue for site-to-site VPNs is a misconfiguration of the VPN endpoints (for example, the routers at each side of the VPN tunnel).

- **Point-to-point nature of GRE tunnels:** Because GRE tunnels are point-to-point logical connections, suboptimal pathing might result. For example, consider Figure 14-5.

Imagine that Branch B wants to communicate with Branch C. The GRE tunnels are configured in a hub-and-spoke topology, where the Headquarters location is functioning as the hub. Therefore, traffic travels from Branch B to Headquarters and then from Headquarters to Branch C. Because traffic is not flowing directly from Branch B to Branch C, excessive delay and poor performance might result.

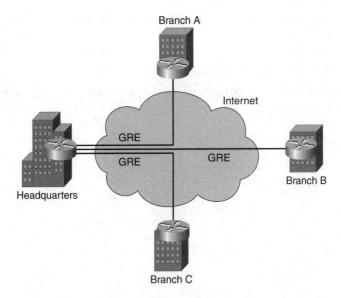

Figure 14-5 *Hub-and-Spoke GRE Tunnels*

Another option is to create a full mesh of VPN connections, as shown in Figure 14-6.

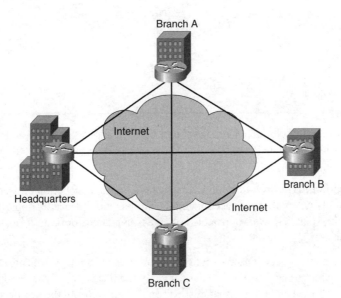

Figure 14-6 *Full Mesh of GRE Tunnels*

Full mesh networks, however, do not scale well. Specifically, the number of connections required to form a full mesh of connections between n sites equals $n(n-1)/2$. For example, if you had ten sites you wanted to interconnect in a full mesh topology, you would need to configure 45 (that is, $10(10-1)/2 = 45$) connections.

Rather than creating a full mesh of VPN connections between all sites in an enterprise network, you can alternatively use *Dynamic Multipoint VPN* (DMVPN) technology. DMVPM allows VPN connections to be dynamically created on an as-needed basis.

Figure 14-7 illustrates a DMVPN connection. In the figure, notice that when Branch B wants to communicate with Branch C, a dynamic VPN is formed between those two sites.

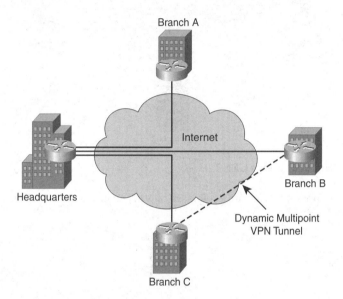

Figure 14-7   *DMVPN*

This DMVPN solution overcomes the performance issues of a hub-and-spoke topology, while simultaneously overcoming the scalability issues presented by a full mesh topology.

■ **Suboptimal routing:** Recall that a tunnel is a logical connection between two endpoints; however, that logical connection can span multiple router hops. If a portion of a tunnel spans a slow or unreliable link, the result can be poor performance for all tunnel traffic.

Another issue that can lead to suboptimal routing is *recursive routing*. For example, when configuring a GRE tunnel, you specify the IP address of the remote side of the tunnel. If the best route to that destination IP address (from the perspective of the IP routing table of the source router) is the source router's tunnel interface, the tunnel interface might experience flapping. Therefore, poor VPN performance can be linked to an inappropriate routing configuration on one or both of the VPN routers.

■ **Route processor overhead:** Depending on the security algorithms chosen to protect an IPsec tunnel, some router platforms might suffer from poor performance. Also, the number of VPN tunnels that can be terminated on a router depends on the underlying router platform. Table 14-2 contrasts the VPN tunnel capacity of various Integrated Services Router (ISR) platforms.

Table 14-2 *VPN Tunnel Capacity for Various ISR Platforms*

Router Platform	Maximum IPsec Speed and Number of Supported VPN Tunnels
Cisco 1841	95 Mbps IPsec VPN 800 tunnels
Cisco 2801	100 Mbps IPsec VPN 1500 tunnels
Cisco 2811	30 Mbps 1500 tunnels
Cisco 2821	140 Mbps 1500 tunnels
Cisco 2851	145 Mbps 1500 tunnels
Cisco 3825	175 Mbps 2000 tunnels
Cisco 3845	185 Mbps 2500 tunnels

Remote-Access VPN Considerations

Figure 14-8 depicts a remote-access VPN connection.

Following is a listing of potential troubleshooting issues that you should consider with remote-access networks:

- **Authentication:** Users connecting from their PC (running VPN client software) require user credentials (for example, username and password credentials) to gain access to a network. Therefore, one reason remote-access VPN users fail to establish a VPN tunnel is that they provide incorrect credentials. Alternatively, the users might provide correct credentials, but the authentication server might be configured incorrectly or might not be functioning.

- **User profiles:** Because users log into a remote-access VPN, different users can be assigned different policies through the use of user profiles. As a result, when remote-access VPN users are unable to connect to desired resources, the underlying issue might be their user profile.

- **MTU size:** Remote-access VPN clients have a similar issue with MTU sizes and fragmentation, as previously described for site-to-site VPNs. Fortunately, VPN client software often allows you to configure the MTU size of a tunnel.

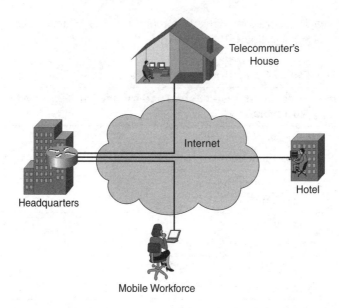

Figure 14-8   *Remote-Access VPN Connection*

■ **Misconfiguration:** VPN software running on a client machine often has multiple configuration options. As a result, a common issue for remote-access VPNs is the misconfiguration of the VPN client software.

■ **Client security software:** Security software running on a client machine might deny traffic required for VPN establishment. Therefore, firewall and anti-virus software running on a VPN client machine might result in the failure of a VPN connection.

Troubleshooting VPN Issues

VPNs involve multiple configuration elements. Therefore, as a troubleshooting aid, the following list provides a collection of questions to answer when troubleshooting a VPN issue:

■ How is IP addressing assigned? (For example, do overlapping IP address ranges exist?)

■ Is the VPN site-to-site or remote-access?

■ How are the MTU values configured on the router interfaces transited by the VPN?

■ What translations (if any) is NAT performing?

■ Are routing protocols routing traffic over a GRE tunnel or over a physical interface?

■ According to a router's IP routing table, is the best path to a tunnel destination's IP address the tunnel interface? (If so, a recursive routing issue might result.)

Table 14-3 lists a collection of Cisco IOS commands useful in troubleshooting VPN connections.

Table 14-3   *VPN Troubleshooting Commands*

Command	Description
show crypto ipsec sa	Displays IPsec security association settings
show crypto engine connections active	Displays configuration information for all active IPsec sessions
show crypto map	Displays the crypto map configuration of a router (for example, information about ACLs being referenced by the crypto map, the IP address of the IPsec peer, the security association lifetime, and the name of the crypto map transform set)
show ip route	Displays routes injected into a router's IP routing table, including next-hop IP address or exit interface information for IP routes
show ip protocols	Displays information about the active IP routing processes of a router
show interfaces tunnel *number*	Displays status and configuration information for a specified tunnel interface on a router

To illustrate the data collection process for a VPN using both IPsec and GRE technologies, consider Figure 14-9.

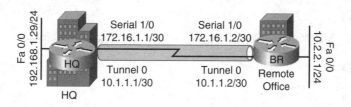

Figure 14-9   *IPsec and GRE Tunnel Topology*

Although the configuration of VPN tunnels is outside the scope of the TSHOOT curriculum, as a reference, Examples 14-1 and 14-2 illustrate the VPN configurations present on routers HQ and BR.

Example 14-1   *VPN Configuration on Router HQ*

```
HQ# show run
...OUTPUT OMITTED...
hostname HQ
!
crypto isakmp policy 1
```

```
  encr 3des
  authentication pre-share
  group 2
 !
crypto isakmp policy 2
  encr aes
  authentication pre-share
  group 2
crypto isakmp key cisco address 172.16.1.2
 !
crypto ipsec transform-set TSHOOT-TRANSFORM esp-aes esp-sha-hmac
 !
crypto map SDM_CMAP_1 1 ipsec-isakmp
  description Tunnel to172.16.1.2
  set peer 172.16.1.2
  set transform-set TSHOOT-TRANSFORM
  match address 100
 !
interface Tunnel0
  ip address 10.1.1.1 255.255.255.252
  ip mtu 1420
  tunnel source 172.16.1.1
  tunnel destination 172.16.1.2
  tunnel path-mtu-discovery
  crypto map SDM_CMAP_1
 !
interface FastEthernet0/0
  ip address 192.168.1.29 255.255.255.0
 !
interface Serial1/0
  ip address 172.16.1.1 255.255.255.0
  encapsulation ppp
  crypto map SDM_CMAP_1
 !
ip route 0.0.0.0 0.0.0.0 Tunnel0
ip route 10.1.1.0 255.255.255.0 172.16.1.2
ip route 172.16.1.2 255.255.255.255 Serial1/0
 !
 !
access-list 100 remark SDM_ACL Category=4
access-list 100 permit gre host 172.16.1.1 host 172.16.1.2
 !
...OUTPUT OMITTED...
```

Example 14-2   *VPN Configuration on Router BR*

```
BR# show run
...OUTPUT OMITTED...
hostname BR
!
crypto isakmp policy 1
 encr 3des
 authentication pre-share
 group 2
!
crypto isakmp policy 2
 encr aes
 authentication pre-share
 group 2
crypto isakmp key cisco address 172.16.1.1
!
crypto ipsec transform-set TSHOOT-TRANSFORM esp-aes esp-sha-hmac
!
crypto map SDM_CMAP_1 1 ipsec-isakmp
 set peer 172.16.1.1
 set transform-set TSHOOT-TRANSFORM
 match address SDM_1
!
interface Tunnel0
 ip address 10.1.1.2 255.255.255.252
 ip mtu 1420
 tunnel source 172.16.1.2
 tunnel destination 172.16.1.1
 tunnel path-mtu-discovery
 crypto map SDM_CMAP_1
!
interface FastEthernet0/0
 ip address 10.2.2.1 255.255.255.0
!
interface Serial1/0
 ip address 172.16.1.2 255.255.255.0
 encapsulation ppp
!
ip route 0.0.0.0 0.0.0.0 Tunnel0
ip route 10.1.1.0 255.255.255.0 172.16.1.1
ip route 172.16.1.1 255.255.255.255 Serial1/0
!
ip access-list extended SDM_1
 remark SDM_ACL Category=4
 permit gre host 172.16.1.2 host 172.16.1.1
...OUTPUT OMITTED...
```

Example 14-3 provides sample output from the **show crypto ipsec sa** command on router HQ. The output offers information about IPsec security association settings, including IP address information for the tunnel peers and information about the encryption and hashing algorithms being used to protect the tunnel traffic.

Example 14-3   show crypto ipsec sa *Command Output on Router HQ*

```
HQ# show crypto ipsec sa

interface: Serial1/0
    Crypto map tag: SDM_CMAP_1, local addr 172.16.1.1

    protected vrf: (none)
    local  ident (addr/mask/prot/port): (172.16.1.1/255.255.255.255/47/0)
    remote ident (addr/mask/prot/port): (172.16.1.2/255.255.255.255/47/0)
    current_peer 172.16.1.2 port 500
      PERMIT, flags={origin_is_acl,}
     #pkts encaps: 60, #pkts encrypt: 60, #pkts digest: 60
     #pkts decaps: 0, #pkts decrypt: 0, #pkts verify: 0
     #pkts compressed: 0, #pkts decompressed: 0
     #pkts not compressed: 0, #pkts compr. failed: 0
     #pkts not decompressed: 0, #pkts decompress failed: 0
     #send errors 4, #recv errors 0

      local crypto endpt.: 172.16.1.1, remote crypto endpt.: 172.16.1.2
      path mtu 1420, ip mtu 1420, ip mtu idb Tunnel0
      current outbound spi: 0x631F3197(1662988695)

      inbound esp sas:
       spi: 0x2441D1C7(608293319)
         transform: esp-aes esp-sha-hmac ,
         in use settings ={Tunnel, }
         conn id: 2002, flow_id: SW:2, crypto map: SDM_CMAP_1
         sa timing: remaining key lifetime (k/sec): (4451479/3185)
         IV size: 16 bytes
         replay detection support: Y
         Status: ACTIVE
```

```
      inbound ah sas:

      inbound pcp sas:

      outbound esp sas:
       spi: 0x631F3197(1662988695)
         transform: esp-aes esp-sha-hmac ,
         in use settings ={Tunnel, }
         conn id: 2001, flow_id: SW:1, crypto map: SDM_CMAP_1
         sa timing: remaining key lifetime (k/sec): (4451473/3183)
         IV size: 16 bytes
         replay detection support: Y
         Status: ACTIVE

      outbound ah sas:

      outbound pcp sas:

interface: Tunnel0
    Crypto map tag: SDM_CMAP_1, local addr 172.16.1.1

   protected vrf: (none)
   local  ident (addr/mask/prot/port): (172.16.1.1/255.255.255.255/47/0)
   remote ident (addr/mask/prot/port): (172.16.1.2/255.255.255.255/47/0)
   current_peer 172.16.1.2 port 500
     PERMIT, flags={origin_is_acl,}
    #pkts encaps: 60, #pkts encrypt: 60, #pkts digest: 60
    #pkts decaps: 0, #pkts decrypt: 0, #pkts verify: 0
    #pkts compressed: 0, #pkts decompressed: 0
    #pkts not compressed: 0, #pkts compr. failed: 0
    #pkts not decompressed: 0, #pkts decompress failed: 0
    #send errors 4, #recv errors 0

     local crypto endpt.: 172.16.1.1, remote crypto endpt.: 172.16.1.2
     path mtu 1420, ip mtu 1420, ip mtu idb Tunnel0
     current outbound spi: 0x631F3197(1662988695)

     inbound esp sas:
      spi: 0x2441D1C7(608293319)
         transform: esp-aes esp-sha-hmac ,
         in use settings ={Tunnel, }
         conn id: 2002, flow_id: SW:2, crypto map: SDM_CMAP_1
```

```
        sa timing: remaining key lifetime (k/sec): (4451479/3182)
        IV size: 16 bytes
        replay detection support: Y
        Status: ACTIVE


    inbound ah sas:


    inbound pcp sas:


    outbound esp sas:
      spi: 0x631F3197(1662988695)
        transform: esp-aes esp-sha-hmac ,
        in use settings ={Tunnel, }
        conn id: 2001, flow_id: SW:1, crypto map: SDM_CMAP_1
        sa timing: remaining key lifetime (k/sec): (4451473/3181)
        IV size: 16 bytes
        replay detection support: Y
        Status: ACTIVE


    outbound ah sas:


    outbound pcp sas:
```

Example 14-4 provides sample output from the **show crypto engine connections active**
command on router HQ. The output shows local interface and IP address information for
all active IPsec sessions. You can also see from the output the encryption and hashing algorithms being used.

Example 14-4   show crypto engine connections active *Command Output on Router HQ*

```
HQ# show crypto engine connections active
   ID Interface       IP-Address      State   Algorithm              Encrypt   Decrypt
    1 Serial1/0       172.16.1.1      set     HMAC_SHA+3DES_56_C          0         0
 2001 Serial1/0       172.16.1.1      set     AES+SHA                    28         0
 2002 Serial1/0       172.16.1.1      set     AES+SHA                     0         0
```

Example 14-5 provides sample output from the **show crypto map** command on router
HQ. The output includes such information as the peer IP address, the ACL used to classify
traffic to be sent over the tunnel, and the interfaces using a particular crypto map.

Example 14-5 show crypto map *Command Output on Router HQ*

```
HQ# show crypto map
Crypto Map "SDM_CMAP_1" 1 ipsec-isakmp
     Description: Tunnel to172.16.1.2
     Peer = 172.16.1.2
     Extended IP access list 100
          access-list 100 permit gre host 172.16.1.1 host 172.16.1.2
     Current peer: 172.16.1.2
     Security association lifetime: 4608000 kilobytes/3600 seconds
     PFS (Y/N): N
     Transform sets={
          TSHOOT-TRANSFORM,
     }
     Interfaces using crypto map SDM_CMAP_1:
          Serial1/0
          Tunnel0
```

Example 14-6 provides sample output from the **show ip route** command on router HQ. Notice that the route to the IP address of the tunnel destination is a physical interface and not a tunnel interface. This approach can help prevent the recursive routing issue previously discussed.

Example 14-6 show ip route *Command Output on Router HQ*

```
HQ# show ip route
Codes: C - connected, S - static, R - RIP, M - mobile, B - BGP
        D - EIGRP, EX - EIGRP external, O - OSPF, IA - OSPF inter area
        N1 - OSPF NSSA external type 1, N2 - OSPF NSSA external type 2
        E1 - OSPF external type 1, E2 - OSPF external type 2
        i - IS-IS, su - IS-IS summary, L1 - IS-IS level-1, L2 - IS-IS level-2
        ia - IS-IS inter area, * - candidate default, U - per-user static route
        o - ODR, P - periodic downloaded static route


Gateway of last resort is 0.0.0.0 to network 0.0.0.0

     172.16.0.0/16 is variably subnetted, 3 subnets, 2 masks
C        172.16.1.0/24 is directly connected, Serial1/0
C        172.16.2.0/24 is directly connected, FastEthernet0/1
C        172.16.1.2/32 is directly connected, Serial1/0
     10.0.0.0/8 is variably subnetted, 2 subnets, 2 masks
C        10.1.1.0/30 is directly connected, Tunnel0
S        10.1.1.0/24 [1/0] via 172.16.1.2
C     192.168.1.0/24 is directly connected, FastEthernet0/0
S*    0.0.0.0/0 is directly connected, Tunnel0
```

Example 14-7 provides sample output from the **show ip protocols** command on router HQ. The output normally displays information about routing protocols running on a router. However, in this example, the lack of any output indicates that no dynamic routing protocols are configured.

Example 14-7   show ip protocols *Command Output on Router HQ*

```
HQ# show ip protocols
```

Example 14-8 provides sample output from the **show interfaces tunnel 0** command on router HQ. From the output you can determine that the Tunnel 0 interface is operational at Layer 1 and Layer 2. You can also see the source and destination IP address of the tunnel and that the tunnel protocol in use is GRE.

Example 14-8   show interfaces tunnel 0 *Command Output on Router HQ*

```
HQ# show interfaces tunnel 0
Tunnel0 is up, line protocol is up
  Hardware is Tunnel
  Internet address is 10.1.1.1/30
  MTU 1514 bytes, BW 9 Kbit, DLY 500000 usec,
      reliability 255/255, txload 1/255, rxload 1/255
  Encapsulation TUNNEL, loopback not set
  Keepalive not set
  Tunnel source 172.16.1.1, destination 172.16.1.2
  Tunnel protocol/transport GRE/IP
    Key disabled, sequencing disabled
    Checksumming of packets disabled
  Tunnel TTL 255
  Fast tunneling enabled
  Path MTU Discovery, ager 10 mins, min MTU 92, MTU 0, expires never
  Tunnel transmit bandwidth 8000 (kbps)
  Tunnel receive bandwidth 8000 (kbps)
  Last input never, output 00:06:48, output hang never
  Last clearing of "show interface" counters never
  Input queue: 0/75/0/0 (size/max/drops/flushes); Total output drops: 4
  Queueing strategy: fifo
  Output queue: 0/0 (size/max)
  5 minute input rate 0 bits/sec, 0 packets/sec
  5 minute output rate 0 bits/sec, 0 packets/sec
     0 packets input, 0 bytes, 0 no buffer
     Received 0 broadcasts, 0 runts, 0 giants, 0 throttles
     0 input errors, 0 CRC, 0 frame, 0 overrun, 0 ignored, 0 abort
     60 packets output, 7216 bytes, 0 underruns
     0 output errors, 0 collisions, 0 interface resets
     0 output buffer failures, 0 output buffers swapped out
```

Complex Network Troubleshooting

Previous chapters in this book have addressed a wide array of networking technologies. Because many of these technologies can be found in the typical enterprise network, a successful troubleshooter of large enterprise networks needs a broad understanding of each of these technologies. In addition, a troubleshooter needs to understand how these technologies interoperate and impact one another. In some cases the troubleshooter might not have the depth of knowledge required in a specific technology. In such a situation, the troubleshooter should know how to obtain the required knowledge or identify who can provide the required expertise.

This section categorizes major networking troubleshooting areas based on the layers of the OSI model. Fundamental requirements for enterprise network troubleshooting are presented. Finally, this chapter reviews each of the trouble tickets presented in this book. Specifically, the symptoms of each trouble ticket are presented, along with the troubleshooting commands used and the suggested solution to the underlying issue or issues.

Troubleshooting Complex Networks

Complex enterprise networks are composed of multiple technologies that might reside at various layers of the OSI model. Knowing which technologies correspond to which OSI layers can help a troubleshooter better understand how issues with one technology can impact other technologies.

Table 14-4 identifies the OSI layer (or layers) that correspond to a variety of network technologies.

Table 14-4 *OSI Layers of Various Networking Technologies*

Key Topic

Technology	Layer 1	Layer 2	Layer 3	Layer 4	Layer 5	Layer 6	Layer 7
Security	X	X	X	X	X	X	X
Performance	X	X	X	X	X		
Packet Forwarding			X				
Routing Protocols			X				
Mapping Layer 2 QoS Markings to Layer 3		X	X				
Spanning Tree Protocol		X					
Frame Forwarding		X					
EtherChannel		X					
Physical Interfaces	X	X					
Cabling	X						

The following list identifies important prerequisites for troubleshooters to possess before they troubleshoot a complex enterprise network.

- A high-level understanding of multiple network technologies that might be encountered and access to specialized knowledge as needed

- An understanding of how network technologies impact one another

- An understanding of the architectural planes of a router (for example, the data plane and control plane) and the functions of each plane

- A familiarity with troubleshooting tools (for example, appropriate Cisco IOS commands and packet capture software)

- Previously collected baseline information, against which newly collected data can be compared

Case Study Review

Because troubleshooting large enterprise networks requires knowledge of multiple network technologies, this chapter concludes by reviewing each of the previously presented trouble tickets, highlighting the reported symptom(s), troubleshooting commands used to diagnose the issue, and presenting the underlying issue along with the implemented solution.

Trouble Ticket #1 Review

Trouble ticket #1 is presented in Chapter 4, "Basic Cisco Catalyst Switch Troubleshooting."

Symptom: Users were experiencing latency when attempting to reach a remote network.

Troubleshooting commands used:

- **show spanning-tree vlan** *vlan-id*

- **show spanning-tree summary**

- **show spanning-tree summaryinterface** *interface-id* **detail**

Issue: Spanning Tree Protocol (STP) was not configured on two switches, resulting in a Layer 2 topological loop that caused MAC address table corruption and a high CPU utilization on the Cisco Catalyst switches.

Resolution: STP was properly configured on the switches, eliminating the CPU utilization and MAC address table corruption issues.

Trouble Ticket #2 Review

Trouble ticket #2 is presented in Chapter 5, "Advanced Cisco Catalyst Switch Troubleshooting."

Symptom: Hot Standby Routing Protocol (HSRP) was not working properly. Specifically, an inappropriate router was the active HSRP router.

Troubleshooting commands used:

- **show standby brief**
- **debug standby**
- **ping ip-address**

Issue: The *preempt* feature was not enabled on the router that should be acting as the active HSRP router. Therefore, after that router rebooted, it did not regain its active status.

Resolution: The preempt feature was enabled on the router that should have been acting as the active HSRP router, resulting in that router regaining its active status.

Trouble Ticket #3 Review

Trouble ticket #3 is presented in Chapter 6, "Introduction to Troubleshooting Routing Protocols."

Symptom: A router configured for EIGRP was not load balancing appropriately.

Troubleshooting commands used:

- **show ip route**
- **show ip eigrp topology**
- **show run | begin router**

Issue: The paths across which the router should have load-balanced had different costs.

Resolution: EIGRP's *variance* feature was configured to enable load balancing across unequal cost paths.

Trouble Ticket #4 Review

Trouble ticket #4 is presented in Chapter 7, "OSPF and Route Redistribution Troubleshooting."

Symptom: Routers in a multiarea OSPF topology did not have full reachability to all networks.

Troubleshooting commands used:

- **show run | begin router**
- **show ip ospf neighbor**
- **show ip route**
- **show ip ospf**
- **show ip ospf interface** *interface-id*
- **show ip ospf virtual-links**

Issue #1: A virtual link configuration was incorrect. Specifically, the transit area (that is, the area between area 0 and the area that is not physically adjacent to area 0) configured in the **area** *number* **virtual-link** command was incorrect.

Resolution #1: The virtual link configuration was corrected by specifying the appropriate transit area in the **area** *number* **virtual-link** command.

Issue #2: One of the routers had nondefault Hello and Dead timers configured for a subinterface. These parameters did not match the parameters at the far end of the Frame Relay link, preventing an OSPF adjacency from forming over that link.

Resolution #2: The OSPF Hello and Dead timers were returned to their default settings, after which an OSPF adjacency formed between the routers at each end of the Frame Relay link.

Issues #3 and #4: Two of the routers had interfaces configured with incorrect OSPF network types.

Resolution #3 and #4: The interfaces with the incorrect OSPF network types were configured to use their default OSPF network types, after which OSPF adjacencies formed between the routers at each end of the links.

Trouble Ticket #5 Review

Trouble ticket #5 is presented in Chapter 7.

Symptom: Two companies merged, and they used different routing protocols (that is, OSPF and EIGRP). Route redistribution was not correctly performing mutual route redistribution between these two autonomous systems.

Troubleshooting commands used:

- **show ip route**
- **show run | begin router**

Issue #1: The EIGRP routing process configured on the router performing the redistribution lacked a default metric that would be assigned to routes being redistributed in the EIGRP routing process.

Resolution #1: The **default-metric 1500 100 255 1 1500** command was issued in router configuration mode for the EIGRP routing process. This made redistributed routes appear to have a bandwidth of 1500, a delay of 100, a reliability of 255, a load of 1, and an MTU of 1500.

Issue #2: The OSPF routing process configured on the router performing the redistribution lacked the **subnets** parameter at the end of the **redistribute** command. The **subnets** parameter is required to allow nonclassful networks to be redistributed into OSPF.

Resolution #2: The existing **redistribute** command in router configuration mode for the OSPF routing process was replaced with the **redistribute eigrp 100 metric 64 subnets** command, which instructed OSPF to redistribute routes from EIGRP AS 100 with a metric of 64 and to redistribute nonclassful networks (that is, subnets).

Trouble Ticket #6 Review

Trouble ticket #6 is presented in Chapter 8, "Troubleshooting BGP and Router Performance Issues."

Symptom: An enterprise is dual homed to the Internet using two service providers. The dual homing is configured using BGP. However, BGP selected the slower of the two links going out to the Internet.

Troubleshooting commands used:

- **show ip route**
- **show run | begin router**
- **show ip bgp summary**
- **show ip bgp**

Issue: The enterprise router was pointing to the service provider reachable over the slower link, because the router of that service provider had the lowest BGP router ID.

Resolution: The enterprise router was configured to assign local preference attributes to routes being advertised by the service provider routers. BGP prefers higher local preference values. Higher local preferences were applied to routes being advertised by the service provider reachable over the higher-speed link. Therefore, outbound traffic used the optimal path.

To influence inbound path selection (that is, traffic coming in from the Internet), the enterprise router was configured to prepend multiple instances of its AS on route advertisements sent over the slower-speed link. This caused the service provider routers to prefer the higher-speed link when sending traffic into the enterprise, because it appeared to require fewer AS hops.

Trouble Ticket #7 Review

Trouble ticket #7 is presented in Chapter 9, "Security Troubleshooting."

Symptom: The enable secret password for a router was forgotten. Also, a Telnet session to one of the routers in the topology timed out after only 1 second. Finally, an ACL was not preventing Telnet sessions as expected.

Troubleshooting command used:

- **show running-config**

Issue #1: The administrator forgot the enable secret password for a router. Therefore, the administrator was not able to access the privileged mode of the router.

Resolution #1: Password recovery was performed, which involved rebooting the router, entering ROMMON configuration mode, changing the configuration register to ignore the startup configuration, and rebooting the router. Privileged mode could then be entered, because the router booted up without a startup configuration. The startup configuration was copied to the running configuration, and the enable secret password was changed. Interfaces in the shutdown state were administratively brought up, and the configuration register was changed to use the startup configuration upon a reboot. Finally, the router was rebooted, and the router booted up using the startup configuration, which had the newly configured enable secret password.

Issue #2: The **exec-timeout** parameter for the VTY lines of a router was configured to **0 1**, which meant that a Telnet session would time out after only 1 second.

Resolution #2: The **exec-timeout** parameter for the VTY lines of the router was reconfigured to **0 0**, meaning that a Telnet session would never time out. However, the challenge was to perform this reconfiguration without timing out in the process. The solution was to repeatedly tap the down arrow on the keyboard (which did not enter characters in the CLI but still reset the idle timer of the VTY line) with one hand while typing the reconfiguration commands with the other hand.

Issue #3: An ACL was applied in the outbound direction on an interface, when it should have been applied in the inbound direction on the interface.

Resolution #3: The **ip access-group** command that applied the ACL in the incorrect direction was removed and replaced with an appropriate **ip access-group** command.

Trouble Ticket #8 Review

Trouble ticket #8 is presented in Chapter 10, "IP Services Troubleshooting."

Symptom: NAT was partially working on a router; however, only two NAT translations could simultaneously be set up. Additionally, NAT translations failed.

Troubleshooting commands used:

■ **show ip nat translations**

■ **debug ip nat**

■ **ping ip-address**

Issue: The **ip nat translation max-entries 2** command was preventing more than two simultaneous NAT translations.

Resolution: The **ip nat translation max-entries 2** command was removed, which allowed additional NAT translations to be created.

Trouble Ticket #9 Review

Trouble ticket #9 is presented in Chapter 11, "IP Communications Troubleshooting."

Symptom: A Cisco IP Phone was failing to register with a Cisco Unified Communications Manager Express (UCME) router.

Troubleshooting command used:

■ **show running-config**

Issue: The DHCP server configured on one of the routers in the topology was misconfigured. Specifically, the **network** command in DHCP configuration mode for the DHCP pool of the IP phones specified an incorrect IP address space.

Resolution: The incorrect **network** command in DHCP configuration mode was removed and replaced with a **network** command that specified the appropriate address space.

Trouble Ticket #10 Review

Trouble ticket #10 is presented in Chapter 11.

Symptom: Voice calls placed across a Frame Relay WAN link were suffering from poor voice quality if the call originated from an analog phone, whereas calls that originated from a Cisco IP Phone did not experience quality issues.

Troubleshooting commands used:

- **show class-map**
- **show running-config**

Issue: A Cisco IP Phone automatically marks voice packets with a DSCP value of Expedited Forwarding (EF). However, by default, calls originated from an analog phone are not marked with a DSCP value of EF.

Resolution: The AutoQoS VoIP feature was configured on a router, which caused voice traffic to be recognized (using NBAR) and marked with a DSCP value of EF.

Trouble Ticket #11 Review

Trouble ticket #11 is presented in Chapter 12, "IPv6 Troubleshooting."

Symptom: Routers in a topology were configured with IPv6 addressing, and OSPFv3 was chosen as the routing protocol. However, some of the OSPFv3 routers were not forming appropriate adjacencies.

Troubleshooting commands used:

- **show running-config**
- **show ipv6 route**
- **show ipv6 ospf interface** *interface-id*
- **show ipv6 ospf neighbor**

Issue #1: The HELLO timer on an interface on one of the routers was set to a nondefault value, whereas the other end of the link was configured for its default HELLO timer value. This prevented an adjacency from forming between these two routers.

Resolution #1: The router interface with a nondefault HELLO timer was configured to use the default HELLO timer value, after which an adjacency was formed between these two routers.

Issue #2: The OSPF network type on the subinterface of a router was set to point-to-multipoint, whereas the other end of the link was a default OSPF network type of point-to-point.

Resolution #2: The router subinterface with a nondefault OSPF network type was configured to use the default network type of point-to-point, after which an adjacency was formed between the routers at each end of the link.

Issue #3: Subinterfaces at opposite sides of a link had different MTU values. Specifically, one subinterface had a default MTU of 1500 bytes, whereas the other subinterface had a nondefault MTU of 1400 bytes.

Resolution #3: The subinterface with the nondefault MTU of 1400 bytes was reconfigured to have a default MTU of 1500 bytes, after which an adjacency formed between the routers at each end of the link.

Exam Preparation Tasks

Review All the Key Topics

Key
Topic

Review the most important topics from inside the chapter, noted with the Key Topics icon in the outer margin of the page. Table 14-5 lists these key topics and the page numbers where each is found.

Table 14-5   *Key Topics for Chapter 14*

Key Topic Element	Description	Page Number
List	Potential site-to-site network issues	449
List	Potential remote-access network issues	453
List	Questions to answer when troubleshooting a VPN issue	454
Table 14-3	VPN troubleshooting commands	455
Table 14-4	OSI layers of various networking technologies	463
List	Prerequisites for troubleshooting a complex enterprise network	464

Complete Tables and Lists from Memory

Print a copy of Appendix B, "Memory Tables" (found on the CD), or at least the section for this chapter, and complete the tables and lists from memory. Appendix C, "Memory Tables Answer Key," also on the CD, includes completed tables and lists to check your work.

Define Key Terms

Define the following key terms from this chapter, and check your answers in the Glossary:

virtual private network (VPN), site-to-site VPN, remote-access VPN, Generic Routing Encapsulation (GRE), IP security (IPsec), Dynamic Multipoint VPN (DMVPN)

Command Reference to Check Your Memory

This section includes the most important configuration and EXEC commands covered in this chapter. To determine how well you have memorized the commands as a side effect of your other studies, cover the left side of the table with a piece of paper; read the descriptions on the right side; and see whether you remember the command.

Table 14-6   *Chapter 14 EXEC Command Reference*

Command	Description
show crypto ipsec sa	Displays IPsec security association settings
show crypto engine connections active	Displays configuration information for all active IPsec sessions
show crypto map	Displays the crypto map configuration of a router (for example, information about ACLs being referenced by the crypto map, the IP address of the IPsec peer, the security association lifetime, and the name of the transform set of the crypto map)
show ip route	Displays routes injected into a router's IP routing table, including next-hop IP address or exit interface information for IP routes
show ip protocols	Displays information about a router's active IP routing processes
show interfaces tunnel *number*	Displays status and configuration information for a specified tunnel interface on a router

The first 14 chapters of this book cover the technologies, troubleshooting strategies, and commands required to be prepared to pass the 642-832 TSHOOT exam. Although these chapters supply detailed information, most people need more preparation than simply reading the first 14 chapters of this book. This chapter details a set of tools and a study plan to help you complete your preparation for the 642-832 TSHOOT exam.

This short chapter has two main sections, as follows:

- The first section lists information about the 642-832 TSHOOT exam and the exam preparation tools useful at this point in your study.

- The second section lists a suggested study plan now that you have completed all the earlier chapters in this book.

Note: This chapter makes reference to many of the chapters and appendixes included with this book, as well as tools available on the enclosed CD. Some of the appendixes, beginning with Appendix B, "Memory Tables," are included only on the CD that comes with this book. To access those, just insert the CD and make the appropriate selection from the opening interface.

CHAPTER 15

Final Preparation

Tools for Final Preparation

This section lists some information about the exam, available tools, and how to access those tools.

Information About the TSHOOT Exam

The TSHOOT exam number is 642-832. At the time of this writing, Cisco estimates that approximately ten percent of the TSHOOT exam will consist of multiple choice questions, with approximately ninety percent of exam questions being questions where you actively troubleshoot a trouble ticket.

Cisco has constructed questions on the TSHOOT exam in a way to combat brain dump sites on the Internet. For example, more than one troubleshooting scenario might have the same topology and challenge you with the same trouble ticket. However, the correct answer is dependent upon the underlying issue (for example, mismatched EIGRP AS numbers or auto summarization being turned on) that you need to discover. This approach prevents exam candidates from simply memorizing a response to a given trouble ticket.

Also, check the TSHOOT exam blueprint at Cisco.com in order to identify any topics or areas that you will not be tested on. Specifically, this book mirrors the topics covered in the TSHOOT course. However, at the time of this writing, not every topic covered in the TSHOOT course was on the TSHOOT exam blueprint (for examples, firewalls and multicast). Because Cisco can update this blueprint at any time, check the blueprint to ensure that you are studying relevant exam topics.

Exam Engine and Questions on the CD

The CD in the back of this book includes the Boson Exam Environment (BEE). The BEE is the exam-engine software that delivers and grades a set of free practice questions written by Cisco Press. The BEE supports multiple-choice questions, drag-and-drop questions, and many scenario-based questions that require the same level of analysis as the questions on the CCNP TSHOOT 642-832 exam. The installation process has two major steps. The first step is installing the BEE software—the CD in the back of this book has a recent copy of the BEE software, supplied by Boson Software (www.boson.com). The second step is activating and downloading the free practice questions. The practice questions written by Cisco Press for the CCNP TSHOOT 642-832 exam are not on the CD; instead, the practice questions must be downloaded from www.boson.com.

Note: The CD case in the back of this book includes the CD and a piece of paper. The paper contains the activation key for the practice questions associated with this book. *Do not lose this activation key.*

Install the Software from the CD

The following are the steps you should perform to install the software:

Step 1.   Insert the CD into your computer.

Step 2.   From the main menu, click the option to install the Boson Exam Environment (BEE). The software that automatically runs is the Cisco Press software needed to access and use all CD-based features, including the BEE, a PDF of this book, and the CD-only appendixes.

Step 3.   Respond to the prompt windows as you would with any typical software installation process.

The installation process might give you the option to register the software. This process requires you to establish a login at the www.boson.com website. You need this login to activate the exam; therefore, you should register when prompted.

Activate and Download the Practice Exam

After the Boson Exam Environment (BEE) is installed, activate the exam associated with this book.

Step 1.   Launch the BEE from the Start menu.

Step 2.   The first time you run the software, you should be asked to either log in or register an account. If you do not already have an account with Boson, select the option to register a new account. You must register to download and use the exam.

Step 3.   After you have registered or logged in, the software might prompt you to download the latest version of the software, which you should do. Note that this process updates the BEE, not the practice exam.

Step 4.   From the Boson Exam Environment main window, click the Exam Wizard button to activate and download the exam associated with this book.

Step 5.   From the Exam Wizard dialog box, select Activate a Purchased Exam and click the Next button. Although you did not purchase the exam directly, you purchased it indirectly when you bought the book.

Step 6.   In the EULA Agreement window, click Yes to accept the terms of the license agreement, and then click Next. If you do not accept the terms of the license agreement, you will be unable to install or use the software.

Step 7.   In the Activate Exam Wizard dialog box, enter the activation key from the paper inside the CD holder in the back of the book, and then click Next.

Step 8. Wait while the activation process downloads the practice questions. When the exam has been downloaded, the main BEE menu should list a new exam. If you do not see the exam, click the My Exams tab on the menu. You might also need to click the plus sign icon (+) to expand the menu and see the exam.

At this point, the software and practice questions are ready to use.

Activating Other Exams

You need to install the exam software and register only once. Then, for each new exam, you will need to complete only a few additional steps. For example, if you bought this book along with *CCENT/CCNA ICND1 Official Exam Certification Guide* or *CCNA ICND2 Official Exam Certification Guide*, you would need to perform the following steps:

Step 1. Launch the BEE (if it is not already open).

Step 2. Perform Steps 4 through 7 under the section "Activate and Download the Practice Exam," earlier in the chapter.

Step 3. Repeat Steps 1 and 2 for any exams in another Cisco Press book.

You can also purchase Boson ExSim-Max practice exams that are written and developed by Boson Software's subject-matter experts at www.boson.com. The ExSim-Max practice exams simulate the content on the actual certification exams, enabling you to gauge whether you are ready to pass the real exam. When you purchase an ExSim-Max practice exam, you receive an activation key. You can then activate and download the exam by performing Steps 1 and 2 above.

The Cisco CCNP Prep Center

Cisco provides a wide variety of CCNP preparation tools at a Cisco Systems website called CCNP Prep Center. CCNP Prep Center includes such resources as the following:

- Practice exam questions

- Quick learning modules

- CCNP discussion forums

- CCNP news and information

- CCNP TV

To use CCNP Prep Center, point your browser to http://www.cisco.com/go/prep-ccnp. Once there, you can explore its many features.

Study Plan

You could simply study using all the available tools, as mentioned earlier in this chapter; however, this section suggests a particular study plan, with a sequence of tasks that might work better than just randomly using the tools. Feel free to use the tools in any way and at any time to help you get fully prepared for the exam.

The suggested study plan separates the tasks into two categories:

- **Recall the Facts:** Perform recommended activities that help you remember all the necessary details from the first 14 chapters of the book.

- **Use the Exam Engine:** The exam engine on the CD can be used to study using a bank of unique questions available only with this book.

Recall the Facts

As with most exams, there are many facts, concepts, and definitions that must be recalled in order to do well on the test. This section suggests a couple of tasks that should help you remember the necessary information:

Step 1.   **Review and repeat, as needed, the activities in the "Exam Preparation Tasks" section at the end of each chapter.** Most of these activities help refine your knowledge of a topic while also helping you to memorize the facts.

Step 2.   **Using the Exam Engine, answer all the questions in the book database.** This question database includes all the questions printed in the beginning of each chapter. Although some of the questions might be familiar, repeating the questions will help improve your recall of the topics covered in the questions.

Use the Exam Engine

The exam engine includes two basic modes:

- **Study mode:** Study mode is most useful when you want to use the questions for a comprehensive review. In study mode, you can select options such as whether you want to randomize the order of the questions or the order of the answers, whether you want to automatically see answers to the questions, and many other options.

- **Simulation mode:** Simulation mode can either require or allow a set number of questions and a set time period. These timed exams not only enable you to study the TSHOOT exam topics, they also help you simulate the time pressure that can occur on the actual exam.

Choosing Study or Simulation Mode

Both study mode and simulation mode are useful for exam preparation. The following steps show how to move to the screen from which to select study or simulation mode:

Step 1.   Click the Choose Exam button, which should list the exam under the title ExSim for Cisco Press TSHOOT ECG.

Step 2.   Click the name of the exam once, which should highlight the exam name.

Step 3.   Click the Load Exam button.

The engine should display a window. Here you can choose Simulation Mode or Study Mode using the radio buttons.

Passing Scores for the TSHOOT Exam

When scoring your simulated exam using this book's exam engine, you should strive to get a score of 85 percent or better. However, the scoring on the book's exam engine does not match how Cisco scores the actual TSHOOT exam. Interestingly, Cisco does not publish many details about how they score their exams, with the result being that you cannot reasonably deduce which questions you missed or how many points are assigned to each question.

Cisco does publish some specific guidance about how they score the exam, whereas other details have been mentioned by Cisco personnel during public presentations about their exams. Some of the key facts about scoring are as follows:

- Cisco does give partial credit on simulation questions. So, complete as much of a simulation question as you can.

- Cisco might give more weight to some questions.

- The test does not adapt based on your answers to early questions in the test. For example, if you miss a BGP troubleshooting question, the test does not start giving you more BGP troubleshooting questions.

- Cisco scores range from 300 to 1000, with a passing grade usually (but not always) around 849.

- The 849 out of 1000 does not necessarily mean that you got 84.9% of the questions correct.

Answers to the "Do I Know This Already?" Quizzes

Chapter 1

1. A, C, and D
2. B and C
3. C
4. C
5. D
6. A
7. C and D
8. A, B, and D
9. A, C, and D
10. D
11. B
12. C
13. A
14. B

Chapter 2

1. B, C, and D
2. B
3. D
4. C
5. D
6. B
7. B and D
8. A
9. B
10. B and C
11. C and D
12. B
13. A, C, and D
14. A
15. A, C, and D
16. A and C

Chapter 3

1. B
2. C
3. A
4. A, B, and D
5. C
6. A and D
7. B

Chapter 4

1. A and D
2. A and C
3. A
4. A and C
5. B and D
6. B

Chapter 5

1. B and D
2. B
3. C
4. B
5. C
6. B
7. A and C
8. B and C
9. A, B, and D
10. B

Chapter 6

1. A and C
2. C and D
3. C
4. A, C, and D
5. A and D
6. C

Chapter 7

1. B
2. A
3. C
4. D
5. C
6. B
7. C
8. A

Chapter 8

1. A and D
2. B
3. B
4. D
5. A and B

Chapter 9

1. A, C, and D
2. C
3. D
4. A and D
5. B
6. C
7. B and C
8. A and B

Chapter 10

1. A
2. B
3. A, C, and D
4. B and D
5. B
6. A, B, C, and E
7. A and C
8. B
9. B

Chapter 11

1. B
2. C
3. D
4. A, B, C, and E
5. B, C, and D
6. C
7. D
8. A
9. A, B, D, and E

Chapter 12

1. A, C, and D
2. C
3. B, C, and D
4. A
5. B
6. C and D
7. D
8. B
9. B
10. D
11. B

Chapter 13

1. A
2. A, B, D, and E
3. D
4. B
5. C
6. A, B, and C
7. C
8. B and D
9. A
10. C

Chapter 14

1. B and C
2. D
3. A
4. D
5. B
6. B and C
7. C
8. A

access control list (ACL)   An ACL is a set of rules applied to a router that dictate what traffic is allowed or not allowed to enter or exit an interface.

accounting   The accounting service can collect and store information about a user login. This information can be used, for example, to keep an audit trail of what was performed on a network.

Address Resolution Protocol (ARP)   A network device that knows the IP address of a destination can send out an ARP request in an attempt to dynamically learn the MAC address of the destination device (or the MAC address of the next-hop gateway used to reach that device).

adjacency table   When a router is performing a route lookup using Cisco Express Forwarding (CEF), the Forwarding Information Base (FIB) references an entry in the adjacency table. The adjacency table entry contains the frame header information required by the router to properly form a frame. Therefore, an egress interface and a next-hop IP address would be in an adjacency entry for a multipoint interface, whereas a point-to-point interface would only require egress interface information.

administrative distance   An administrative distance is a measure of the believability of a routing protocol, with lower administrative distances being more believable. For example, Routing Information Protocol (RIP) has an administrative distance of 120, whereas Open Shortest Path First (OSPF) has an administrative distance of 110. Therefore, if a router ran both RIP and OSPF, and if both routing protocols knew of a route to reach a destination network, the router would install the OSPF-learned route into its IP routing table because of the preferable administrative distance of OSPF.

application server   An application server provides services such as voice mail, unified messaging, and presence information (which can show the availability of another user).

ARP Input process   The ARP Input process is in charge of sending ARP requests on a router.

ASPATH   ASPATH is a Border Gateway Protocol (BGP) attribute that contains a listing of the autonomous systems (AS) that must be transited to reach a specific destination network.

authentication   The authentication service can check user credentials to confirm that users are who they claim to be.

authorization   When authenticated, the authorization service determines what a user is allowed to do.

autonomous mode   Autonomous mode is a wireless network mode of operation in which an access point is configured with a service set identifier (SSID), radio frequency (RF) channel, and RF power settings. Having an autonomous access point tasked with all these responsibilities can limit scalability and hinder the addition of advanced wireless services.

autonomous system (AS)   An autonomous system is a network under a single administrative control.

AutoQoS Enterprise   AutoQoS Enterprise is a feature supported on some models of Cisco routers that learns current network traffic patterns and recommends a policy that could enforce the observed traffic behavior for as many as ten classes of traffic.

AutoQoS VoIP   AutoQoS VoIP is a Cisco IOS feature supported on some models of Cisco routers and switches that optimizes a router or switch port for voice quality.

backplane   The backplane of a switch physically interconnects a switch's ports. Therefore, depending on the specific switch architecture, frames flowing through a switch enter via a port (that is, an ingress port), flow across the switch's backplane, and are forwarded out of another port (that is, an egress port).

baseline   A baseline is a collection of network measurements taken when the network is functioning properly. Measurements taken during a troubleshooting scenario could be contrasted with baseline information.

BGP neighbor table   A BGP neighbor table contains a listing of all BGP neighbors configured for a router, including each neighbor's IP address, the autonomous system (AS) number, the state of the neighborship, and several other statistics.

BGP table   The BGP table, sometimes referred to as the BGP Routing Information Base (RIB), contains routes learned from Border Gateway Protocol (BGP) peers and routes locally injected into a router's BGP table.

blocking   Blocking is one of four Spanning Tree Protocol (STP) forwarding states for a port. A port remains in the blocking state for 20 seconds by default. During this time a nondesignated port evaluates bridge protocol data units (BPDUs) in an attempt to determine its role in a spanning tree.

bottom-up method   The bottom-up method of troubleshooting starts at the bottom (that is, Layer 1) of the OSI model and works its way up.

boundary router   A boundary router is a router that sits at the boundary of the routing domains to be redistributed.

BPDU Guard   The BPDU Guard feature is enabled on Cisco Catalyst switch ports configured with the Cisco PortFast feature. The PortFast feature is enabled on ports that connect to end-user devices, such as PCs, and reduces the time required for the port to transition into the forwarding state after being connected. The logic of PortFast is that a port connecting to an end-user device does not have the potential to create a topology loop. Therefore, the port can go active sooner by skipping the STP Listening and Learning states, which by default take 15 seconds each. Because PortFast ports are connected to end-user devices, these ports should never receive a bridge protocol data unit (BPDU). Therefore, if a port enabled for BPDU Guard receives a BPDU, the port is disabled.

buffer leak   A buffer leak occurs when a process does not return a buffer to the router when the process has finished using the buffer.

call agent   A call agent provides call control for IP phones, call admission control (CAC), bandwidth control and management, and address translation. Although a call agent can be server based, Cisco also supports a router-based call agent, known as Cisco Unified Communications Manager Express (UCME).

Cisco Application Network Services (ANS)   Cisco ANS is a collection of Cisco solutions that fall under the Cisco Service-Oriented Network Architecture (SONA) framework. ANS technologies can, for example, enhance the performance of applications within a data center, for users at a remote site, and for a teleworker.

Cisco Express Forwarding (CEF)   CEF maintains two tables in the data plane. Specifically, the Forwarding Information Base (FIB) maintains Layer 3 forwarding information, whereas the Adjacency Table maintains Layer 2 information for next-hops listed in the FIB. These sources of packet switching information can be used to efficiently make packet forwarding decisions.

Cisco Lifecycle Services   The Cisco Lifecycle Services maintenance model defines distinct phases in the life of a Cisco technology in a network. These phases are Prepare, Plan, Design, Implement, Operate, and Optimize. As a result, the Cisco Lifecycle Services model is often referred to as the PPDIOO model.

Cisco TelePresence   The Cisco TelePresence solution uses CD-quality audio and high-definition (HD) video (that is, 1080p) displayed on large monitors to create lifelike video conferences.

Cisco Unified Video Advantage   The Cisco Unified Video Advantage product uses a PC, a video camera, and a Cisco IP Phone as a video conferencing station. Specifically, a camera connects to a USB port on the PC. Software is loaded on the PC, and the PC is connected to the PC port on a Cisco IP Phone. Alternatively, the Cisco IP Phone could be the software-based Cisco IP Communicator product running on the PC. When a voice call is placed between two users running the Cisco Unified Video Advantage product, a video call can automatically be started, with video appearing on the PC of each user.

Classic Cisco IOS Firewall   The Classic Cisco IOS Firewall was previously known as Context-Based Access Control (CBAC). The Classic Cisco IOS Firewall inspects traffic flowing from a trusted network to an untrusted network. Returning flows from the untrusted network can be permitted into the trusted network. However, if someone attempts to initiate a session from the untrusted network into the trusted network, that session is denied by default.

comparing configurations   The comparing configurations method of troubleshooting compares a known good configuration with a current configuration. The difference in those configurations might give the troubleshooter insight into the underlying cause of a problem.

component swapping   The component swapping method of troubleshooting replaces individual network components (for example, a cable, switch, or router) in an attempt to isolate the cause of a problem.

control plane   The control plane of operation encompasses protocols used between routers and switches. These protocols include, for example, routing protocols and Spanning Tree Protocol (STP). Also, a router or switch's processor and memory reside in the control plane.

Data Link Connection Identifier (DLCI)   A DLCI is a locally significant identifier for a Frame Relay virtual circuit (VC).

data plane   The data plane is the plane of operation in charge of forwarding data through a router or switch.

delay   Delay is the time required for a packet to travel from its source to its destination.

designated port   Every network segment in a spanning tree has a single designated port, which is the port on that segment closest to the root bridge, in terms of cost. Therefore, all ports on a root bridge are designated ports.

DHCP snooping   The DHCP snooping feature on Cisco Catalyst switches can combat a DHCP server spoofing attack. With this solution, Cisco Catalyst switch ports are configured in either the trusted or untrusted state. If a port is trusted, it is allowed to receive DHCP responses (for example, DHCPOFFER, DHCPACK, or DHCPNAK). Conversely, if a port is untrusted, it is not allowed to receive DHCP responses, and if a DHCP response does attempt to enter an untrusted port, the port is disabled.

Differentiated Services Code Point (DSCP)   A DSCP marking uses the six leftmost bits in the Type of Service (TOS) byte in an IPv4 header. You can use these six bits to create as many as 64 different DSCP values (in the range 0–63). The Internet Engineering Task Force (IETF) selected a subset of these values and assigned names to those values. These names are called per-hop behaviors (PHBs) because these DSCP values can influence how traffic is treated at each hop (that is, each router hop or switch hop) along the path from the traffic source to its destination.

Dijkstra shortest path first (SPF) algorithm   Dijkstra's algorithm, which Open Shortest Path First (OSPF) uses, takes the information contained in the LSAs to determine the shortest path to any destination within an area of the network.

divide and conquer method   The divide and conquer method of troubleshooting begins in the middle (for example, Layer 3) of the OSI model and radiates out from that layer.

drops   Packet drops occur when a link is congested and a buffer overflows. Some types of traffic, such as UDP traffic (for example, voice traffic), are not retransmitted if packets are dropped.

Dynamic ARP Inspection (DAI)   The DAI feature can help prevent Address Resolution Protocol (ARP) spoofing attacks. DAI works similarly to DHCP snooping by using trusted and untrusted ports. ARP replies are allowed into the switch on trusted ports. However, if an ARP reply enters the switch on an untrusted port, the contents of the ARP reply are compared against the DHCP binding table to verify their accuracy. If the ARP reply is not consistent with the DHCP binding table, the ARP reply is dropped, and the port is disabled.

Dynamic Host Configuration Protocol (DHCP)   DHCP serves as one of the most common methods of assigning IP address information to a network host. Specifically, DHCP allows a client to obtain an IP address, subnet mask, default gateway IP address, Domain Name System (DNS) server IP address, and other types of information from a server.

Dynamic Multipoint VPN (DMVPN)   DMVPN is a technology that allows spoke sites, in a hub-and-spoke topology, to dynamically form a direct VPN tunnel between themselves, on an as-needed basis.

dynamic NAT   Dynamic NAT is a dynamic mapping of private internal IP addresses to a pool of public external IP addresses.

EIGRP interface table   All the router interfaces that have been configured to participate in an Enhanced Interior Gateway Routing Protocol (EIGRP) routing process are listed in this table. However, if an interface has been configured as passive (that is, an interface that does not send routing information), it does not appear in this table.

EIGRP neighbor table   This table lists the Enhanced Interior Gateway Routing Protocol (EIGRP) neighbors of a router (that is, neighboring routers from whom an EIGRP Hello message has been received). A neighbor is removed from this table if it has not been heard from for a period defined as the hold-time. Also, if an interface off of which a neighbor is known is removed from the EIGRP interface table because it goes down, the neighbor is removed from this table.

EIGRP topology table   This table contains routes learned by an Enhanced Interior Gateway Routing Protocol (EIGRP) routing process. The best route for a network in this table becomes a candidate to be injected into the router's IP routing table. If multiple routes in this table have an equal metric, or if EIGRP's variance feature is configured, more than one route might become a candidate for injection into the IP routing table.

Embedded Event Manager (EEM)   The EEM feature can create custom event definitions on a router and specify actions the router can take in response to these events.

EtherChannel   An EtherChannel logically combines the bandwidth of multiple physical interfaces into a logical connection between switches.

Extensible Authentication Protocol (EAP)   An EAP is an 802.1X protocol used to communicate between an 802.1X authenticator (for example, a wireless LAN controller) and an 802.1X authentication server (for example, a RADIUS server).

fast switching   Fast switching is a router packet switching mode that makes use of a Fast cache maintained in a router's data plane. The Fast cache contains information about how traffic from different data flows should be forwarded. The first packet in a data flow is process switched by a router's CPU. Once the router determines how to forward the first frame of a data flow, that forwarding information is then stored in the Fast cache. Subsequent packets in that same data flow are then forwarded based on information in the Fast cache, as opposed to being process switched. As a result, Fast switching reduces a router's CPU utilization, as compared to process switching.

FCAPS   FCAPS is a network management model defined by the ISO, where the acronym FCAPS stands for Fault management, Configuration management, Accounting management, Performance management, and Security management.

following the traffic path   Following the traffic path is a method of troubleshooting that checks components (for example, links and devices) over which traffic flows on its way from source to destination.

forwarding   Forwarding is one of four STP forwarding states for a port. A port moves from the learning state to the forwarding state and begins to forward frames.

Forwarding Information Base (FIB)   The FIB contains Layer 3 information, similar to the information found in an IP routing table. Additionally, an FIB contains information about multicast routes and directly connected hosts.

gatekeeper   A gatekeeper provides call admission control (CAC), bandwidth control and management, and address translation in an H.323 network.

gateway   A gateway provides translation between VoIP and non-VoIP networks, such as the Public Switched Telephone Network (PSTN). A gateway also provides physical access for local analog and digital voice devices, such as telephones, fax machines, key systems, and Private Branch Exchanges (PBX).

Gateway Load Balancing Protocol (GLBP)   GLBP can load-balance traffic destined for a next-hop gateway across a collection of routers, known as a GLBP group. Specifically, when a client sends an Address Resolution Protocol (ARP) request, in an attempt to determine the MAC address corresponding to a known IP address, GLBP can respond with the MAC address of one member of the GLBP group. The next such request would receive a response containing the MAC address of a different member of the GLBP group.

Generic Routing Encapsulation (GRE)   GRE is a tunnel encapsulation protocol that can encapsulate a variety of traffic, including unicast, multicast, and broadcast IP traffic, in addition to non-IP protocols such as Internetwork Packet Exchange (IPX) and AppleTalk. GRE, however, does not natively offer security for traffic traveling over the tunnel.

Hot Standby Routing Protocol (HSRP)   HSRP uses virtual IP and MAC addresses. One router, known as the active router, services requests destined for the virtual IP and MAC addresses. Another router, known as the standby router, can service such requests in the event the active router becomes unavailable.

input errors   The input errors value shown in the output of a **show interfaces** command indicates frames were not received correctly (for example, a cyclic redundancy check [CRC] error occurred), perhaps indicating a cabling problem or a duplex mismatch.

input queue drops   The input queue drops value shown in the output of a **show interfaces** command indicates that a router received information faster than the router could process it.

Internet Group Management Protocol (IGMP)   IGMP is a protocol used between clients (for example, PCs) and routers to let routers know which of their interfaces have multicast receivers attached.

interrupt driven task   An interrupt driven task is a network maintenance task that arises in response to a reported network issue.

intrusion detection system (IDS)   An IDS device receives a copy of traffic to be analyzed and can send an alert when it identifies traffic as malicious. Some IDS devices can dynamically configure a firewall or a router to block the malicious traffic.

intrusion prevention system (IPS)   An IPS device sits inline with the traffic that it analyzes and can drop traffic identified as malicious.

IP Background process   When an interface changes its state, the IP Background process handles that state change.

IP phone   An IP phone is an Ethernet device that provides IP voice to the desktop.

IP security (IPsec)   IPsec is a collection of VPN technologies that have the ability to secure traffic traveling over a virtual private network (VPN). IPsec by itself, however, supports only unicast IP traffic flowing over an IPsec tunnel.

IP SLA   The Cisco IOS IP SLA feature can measure how the network treats traffic for specific applications. IP SLA accomplishes this by synthetically generating traffic bearing similar characteristics (for example, port numbers and packet sizes). This traffic, called probes, is sent to a destination router configured to respond to the received probes with time-stamp information, which can then be used to calculate performance metrics for the traffic.

IP telephony   IP telephony refers to a telephony solution that uses IP phones and a call processing server (for example, Cisco Unified Communications Manager).

IPv6 anycast   An IPv6 anycast transmission can be thought of as a one-to-nearest communication flow, where a single IPv6 source address sends traffic to a single IPv6 destination address, and that single IPv6 destination address is assigned to multiple devices. The communication flow is one-to-nearest from the perspective of a router's IPv6 routing table.

IPv6 multicast   An IPv6 multicast transmission can be thought of as a one-to-many communication flow, where a single IPv6 source address sends traffic to an IPv6 multicast group. Devices needing to receive traffic destined for the multicast group can join the group.

IPv6 over IPv4 tunnel   An IPv6 over IPv4 tunnel allows IPv6 traffic to be transported over an IPv4 tunnel. Although the source and destination of the IP tunnel are defined as IPv4 addresses, IPv6 addresses can be assigned to the virtual tunnel interfaces, which allows the IPv6 traffic to be transmitted over the IPv4 tunnel.

IPv6 unicast   An IPv6 unicast transmission can be thought of as a one-to-one communication flow, where a single IPv6 source address sends traffic to a single IPv6 destination address.

IT Infrastructure Library (ITIL)   An ITIL defines a collection of best practice recommendations that work together to meet business goals.

jitter   Jitter is an uneven arrival of packets that can, for example, impact voice quality.

Layer 3 switch   A Layer 3 switch can act as a Layer 2 switch (that is, making forwarding decisions based on MAC addresses), or it can make forwarding decisions based on Layer 3 information (for example, IP address information).

learning   Learning is one of the four Spanning Tree Protocol (STP) states for a port. A port moves from the listening state to the learning state and remains in this state for 15 seconds by default. During this time, the port begins to add entries to its MAC address table.

lightweight access point   A lightweight access point is a wireless network device that performs functions such as beaconing, packet transmission, and frame queuing.

Lightweight Access Point Protocol (LWAPP)   LWAPP is a protocol used to communicate between a lightweight access point and a wireless LAN controller (WLC). LWAPP sends packets in a Layer 2 frame with an Ethertype of 0xBBBB. LWAPP data traffic uses a User Datagram Protocol (UDP) destination port of 12222, whereas LWAPP control traffic uses a UDP destination port of 12223.

link-state advertisement (LSA)   A link-state advertisement is a message sent and received by OSPF routers to educate routers about a network topology. Various LSA types exist.

listening   Listening is one of the four STP forwarding states for a port. A port moves from the blocking state to the listening state and remains in this state for 15 seconds by default. During this time, the port sources bridge protocol data units (BPDU), which inform adjacent switches of the port intent to forward data.

local preference   Local preference is a Border Gateway Protocol (BGP) attribute that can be applied to routes coming into a router. This might cause the router to make its outbound routing decisions based on those local preference values. Higher local preference values are preferred over lower local preference values.

management plane   The management plane of operation is used to manage a router or a switch. This management involves, for example, accessing and configuring a device.

Media Access Control (MAC) address   A MAC address is a 48-bit address assigned to various types of network hardware (for example, network interface cards in PCs). A Layer 2 switch can learn which MAC addresses reside on specific switch ports and make forwarding decisions based on that information.

memory allocation failure   A memory allocation failure (which produces a MALLOC-FAIL error message) occurs when a process attempts to allocate a block of memory and fails to do so.

memory leak   When a router starts a process, that process can allocate a block of memory. When the process completes, the process should return its allocated memory to the router's pool of memory. If not all the allocated memory is returned to the router's main memory pool, a memory leak occurs.

Modular Quality of Service Command-Line Interface (MQC)   MQC is a three-step process for configuring a variety of QoS mechanisms. These steps are (1) Create one or more class maps. (2) Create a policy map that specifies how traffic in the class maps is to be treated. (3) Apply the policy map (typically to an interface) in either the incoming or outgoing direction.

multicasting   Multicasting technology allows a multicast source (for example, a video server) to send a single stream of traffic to a Class D address, which represents a multicast group. Devices wishing to receive the stream can join the multicast group.

multipoint control unit (MCU)   An MCU mixes audio and/or video streams, thus allowing participants in multiple locations to attend the same conference.

NAT overloading   NAT overloading allows multiple private internal IP addresses to use a single public external IP address by keeping track of Layer 4 port numbers, which make each session unique (that is, Port Address Translation [PAT]).

Net Background process   An interface has a certain number of buffers available to store packets. These buffers are sometimes referred to as an interface's queue. If an interface needs to store a packet in a buffer but all the interface's buffers are in use, the interface can pull from a main pool of buffers that its router maintains. The process that allows an interface to allocate one of these globally available buffers is the Net Background process.

NetFlow   The NetFlow feature collects detailed information about traffic flows on routers and high-end switches. Collected information can optionally be sent to a NetFlow collector, which can produce reports about the traffic flows.

Network Address Translation (NAT)   NAT allows private IP addresses (as defined in RFC 1918) to be translated into Internet-routable IP addresses (that is, public IP addresses).

Network-Based Application Recognition (NBAR)   NBAR can classify various traffic types by examining information at Layers 3–7. Protocols that change port numbers (that is, stateful protocols) can also be tracked. You can expand the NBAR recognition capability by using Protocol Description Language Modules (PDLMs).

Network Management System (NMS)   A Network Management System (NMS) collects information from managed agents via Simple Network Management Protocol (SNMP).

nondesignated port   Nondesignated ports in a spanning tree block traffic to create a loop-free topology.

OSPF area border router (ABR)   An OSPF ABR connects to more than one OSPF area and therefore maintains multiple link-state databases (one for each connected area). A primary responsibility of an ABR is to exchange topological information between the backbone area and other connected areas.

OSPF autonomous system boundary router (ASBR)   An OSPF ASBR has at least one connected route participating in an OSPF area and at least one connected route participating in a different autonomous system. The primary role of an ASBR is to exchange information between an OSPF autonomous system and one or more external autonomous systems.

OSPF backbone router   An OSPF backbone router has at least one of its connected networks participating in OSPF area 0 (that is, the backbone area). If all the connected networks are participating in the backbone area, the router is also considered an internal router. Also, if a backbone router has one or more connected networks participating in another area, the backbone router is also considered an area border router (ABR).

OSPF interface table   All the router interfaces that have been configured to participate in an OSPF routing process are listed in the OSPF interface table.

OSPF internal router   All the networks directly connected to an OSPF internal router belong to the same OSPF area. Therefore, an OSPF internal router has a single link-state database.

OSPF link-state database   The OSPF link-state database is an OSPF data structure that contains topology information for all areas in which a router participates, in addition to information about how to route traffic to networks residing in other areas or autonomous systems.

OSPF neighbor table   OSPF neighbors learned via Hello packets are present in an OSPF neighbor table. A neighbor is removed from this table if Hellos have not been heard from the neighbor within the dead time interval. Additionally, a neighbor is removed from this table if the interface associated with the neighbor goes down.

OSPF Routing Information Base (RIB)   The OSPF RIB stores the results of OSPF's shortest path first (SPF) calculations.

OSPFv3   OSPFv3 is a version of the OSPF routing protocol that can support the routing of IPv6 traffic.

output errors   The output errors value shown in the output of a **show interfaces** command indicates frames were not transmitted correctly, perhaps due to a duplex mismatch.

output queue drops   The output queue drops value shown in the output of a **show interfaces** command indicates that a router received information faster than the information could be sent out of the outgoing interface (perhaps due to an input/output speed mismatch).

overlapping NAT   Overlapping NAT can allow communication between two subnets containing overlapping IP addresses.

Packet Description Language Module (PDLM)   A PDLM is a file (typically downloaded from the Cisco website and installed in a router's flash) that contains signature information for a specific protocol. A router's Cisco IOS configuration can be configured to reference a PDLM file to extend the Network-Based Application Recognition (NBAR) capability of the router.

Port Address Translation (PAT)   *See* NAT overloading.

Power over Ethernet (PoE)   PoE is a technology that allows an Ethernet switch (for example, a Cisco Catalyst switch) to provide power to an attached device (for example, an IP phone or a wireless access point) over the Ethernet leads in an unshielded twisted-pair (UTP) cable.

process switching   Process switching is a router packet switching mode in which the CPU of the router becomes directly involved with all packet-switching decisions.

Protocol Independent Multicast (PIM)   PIM is a multicast protocol used to construct IP multicast distribution trees. Protocol independence in PIM means that it can run over an IP network, regardless of the underlying unicast IP routing protocol (for example, Open Shortest Path First [OSPF] or Enhanced Interior Gateway Routing Protocol [EIGRP]). The two varieties of PIM are PIM Dense Mode (PIM-DM) and PIM Sparse Mode (PIM-SM). PIM-DM uses a source distribution tree, whereas PIM-SM uses a shared distribution tree.

remote-access VPN   A remote-access VPN requires virtual private network (VPN) clients at a remote site to run VPN client software. Although this approach might require more administrative overhead to install client software on all clients, remote-access VPNs do offer more flexibility for mobile users than site-to-site VPNs do. For example, clients can connect via the Internet connection at their hotel, using VPN client software on their laptop computer.

Remote Switch Port Analyzer (RSPAN)   The RSPAN feature of a Cisco Catalyst switch allows a port to receive a copy of traffic seen on a port or a VLAN on another switch.

rendezvous point (RP)   An RP is a centralized point in a PIM-SM multicast network. Clients wanting to receive a particular multicast stream initially receive the stream from the RP.

RIP next generation (RIPng)   RIPng is a version of the RIP routing protocol that can support the routing of IPv6 traffic.

root bridge   A root bridge is a switch that is elected as a reference point for a spanning tree.

Root Guard   The Root Guard feature can be enabled on all switch ports in a network off of which a root bridge should not appear. If a port configured for Root Guard receives a superior BPDU instead of believing the BPDU, the port goes into a root-inconsistent state. While a port is in the root-inconsistent state, no user data is sent across the port. However, after the superior BPDUs stop, the port returns to the forwarding state.

root port   Every nonroot bridge in a spanning tree has a single root port, which is the port on the switch that is closest to the root bridge, in terms of cost.

route redistribution   Route redistribution allows routes learned via one method (for example, statically configured, locally connected, or learned via a routing protocol) to be injected into a different routing protocol.

service-level agreement (SLA)   An SLA is an agreement between a service provider and the customer that specifies minimum service-level guarantees for various performance metrics. For example, an SLA might guarantee that 90 percent of the time, the customer will have 256 kbps of bandwidth available to the service provider cloud.

shoot from the hip   The shoot from the hip troubleshooting method occurs when a troubleshooter bypasses examined information and eliminates potential causes, based on the troubleshooter's experience and insight.

Simple Network Management Protocol (SNMP)   SNMP is the protocol used to communicate between an SNMP agent running on a network device and a network management station (NMS). SNMP allows an NMS to query a managed device. Also, if a managed device detects a defined event, the occurrence of that event can be reported to the NMS in the form of an SNMP trap.

site-to-site VPN   A site-to-site VPN typically terminates in a router at a headquarters and a router at the remote site. Such an arrangement does not require clients at the remote site to have VPN client software installed.

Spanning Tree Protocol (STP)   STP allows physically redundant links in a Layer 2 topology, while logically breaking any topological loops that could cause issues such as broadcast storms.

split-MAC mode   Split-MAC mode is a wireless network mode of operation whereby an access point is considered to be a lightweight access point, which cannot function without a wireless LAN controller (WLC). Specifically, a wireless LAN client sending traffic to the wired LAN sends a packet to a lightweight access point, which encapsulates the packet using the Lightweight Access Point Protocol (LWAPP). The encapsulated traffic is sent over an LWAPP tunnel to a WLC.

static NAT   Static NAT is one-to-one mapping of private internal IP addresses to public external IP addresses.

structured maintenance task   A structured maintenance task is a network maintenance task that is performed as part of a predefined plan.

Switched Port Analyzer (SPAN)   The SPAN feature of a Cisco Catalyst switch allows a port to receive a copy of traffic seen on another port or VLAN.

switched virtual interface (SVI)   You can configure the IP address for a collection of ports belonging to a VLAN under a virtual VLAN interface. This virtual VLAN interface is called a switched virtual interface (SVI).

TCP Timer process   The TCP Timer process runs for each of the TCP connections for a router. Therefore, a router with many simultaneous TCP connections could have a high CPU utilization due to the resources being consumed by the TCP Timer.

Telecommunications Management Network (TMN)   The TMN network management model is the Telecommunications Standardization Sector (ITU-T) variation of the FCAPS model. Specifically, TMN targets the management of telecommunications networks.

Ternary Content Addressable Memory (TCAM)   TCAM is a special type of memory that uses a mathematical algorithm to quickly look up forwarding information. The forwarding information in the TCAM comes from the routing processes and traffic policies residing in the control plane of the switch.

top-down method   The top-down method of troubleshooting starts at the top (that is, Layer 7) of the OSI model and works its way down.

trap   An SNMP trap is an event notification sent from a managed network device to a Network Management System (NMS).

trunk   A trunk is a type of link that can be used to interconnect switches. A trunk has the unique property of being able to carry traffic for multiple VLANs over a single connection.

unified communications   Unified communications is an IP communications framework that encompasses more than just voice. Unified communications includes a collection of applications and technologies that enhance user collaboration.

variance   Variance is an Enhanced Interior Gateway Routing Protocol (EIGRP) feature that supports load balancing over unequal-cost paths.

videoconference station   A videoconference station provides access for end-user participation in videoconferencing. The videoconference station contains a video capture device for video input and a microphone for audio input. A user can view video streams and hear the audio that originates at a remote user station. Cisco targets its Unified Video Advantage product at desktop videoconferencing applications.

virtual link   Non-backbone Open Shortest Path First (OSPF) areas (that is, areas other than area 0) must be adjacent to the backbone area. If, however, an OSPF area is not physically adjacent to area 0, a virtual link can be constructed to interconnect the discontiguous area to area 0. A virtual link spans a transit area, which is adjacent to area 0.

Virtual Path Identifier/Virtual Circuit Identifier (VPI/VCI)   A VPI/VCI is a pair of numbers identifying an ATM virtual circuit (VC).

virtual private network (VPN)   A VPN is a logical connection established through a network. That network can be an untrusted network. However, if the VPN is configured for appropriate security protocols, traffic can securely be sent over that untrusted network within the protection of the VPN tunnel

Virtual Router Redundancy Protocol (VRRP)   VRRP, similar to Hot Standby Routing Protocol (HSRP), allows a collection of routers to service traffic destined for a single IP address. Unlike HSRP, the IP address serviced by a VRRP group does not have to be a virtual IP address. The IP address can be the address of a physical interface on the virtual router master, which is the router responsible for forwarding traffic destined for the IP address of the VRRP group.

VLAN   A VLAN is analogous to a subnet, in that traffic needs to be routed to go from one VLAN to another. Ports on many Layer 2 switches can be logically grouped into different VLANs, thus creating multiple broadcast domains on a switch.

VoIP   VoIP is a technology that transmits voice over an IP network using voice-enabled routers.

wiki   A wiki (which is the Hawaiian word for fast) can act as a web-based collaborative documentation platform.

wireless access point   Wireless access points offer network access for wireless clients.

wireless client   A wireless client device is typically an end-user device (such as a laptop) that accesses a wireless network.

wireless LAN controller (WLC)   A WLC is a wireless network device that assumes roles such as authentication, key management, and resource reservation.

wireless mobility   Wireless mobility services include security threat detection, voice services, location services, and guest access.

wireless network management   Just as enterprise LANs benefit from network management solutions, a wireless LAN can use network management solutions to enhance security and reliability and offer assistance in WLAN deployments. An example of a wireless network management solution is the Cisco Wireless Control System (WCS).

wireless network unification   To offer wireless clients access to the resources of an organization, a wireless network needs to be integrated (that is, unified) with a wired LAN. This functionality is referred to as network unification.

Zone-Based Policy Firewall   The Zone-Based Policy Firewall feature allows various router interfaces to be assigned to a zone. Interzone policies can then be configured to dictate what traffic is permitted between these defined zones.

Index

S

![CISCO]

ciscopress.com: Your Cisco Certification and Networking Learning Resource

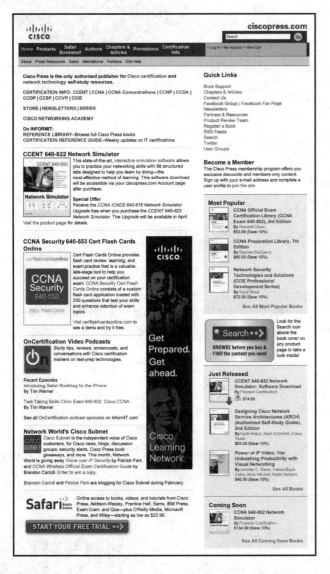

Subscribe to the monthly Cisco Press newsletter to be the first to learn about new releases and special promotions.

Visit **ciscopress.com/newsletters.**

While you are visiting, check out the offerings available at your finger tips.

–Free Podcasts from experts:
  · OnNetworking
  · OnCertification
  · OnSecurity

Podcasts

View them at **ciscopress.com/podcasts.**

–Read the latest author **articles** and **sample chapters** at **ciscopress.com/articles.**

–Bookmark the Certification Reference Guide available through our partner site at **informit.com/certguide.**

Connect with Cisco Press authors and editors via Facebook and Twitter, visit **informit.com/socialconnect.**

You've Studied, But Are You Ready?

Know you can pass.

The CD in this book includes a set of practice questions written by Cisco Press and delivered by the Boson Exam Environment (BEE). For practice exams written by Boson's team of leading subject-matter experts, get Boson's ExSim-Max.

Even if you read this book five times, can you really be sure you're ready to take the exam? With ExSim-Max practice exams, you can. ExSim-Max simulates the content and difficulty of the actual exam so accurately that if you can pass the ExSim-Max exam, you can pass the real exam, guaranteed*. Know you can pass with Boson.

Save time

Knowing the topics you need to focus on is important. That's why ExSim-Max provides a score report, which shows the topics that need additional attention. This allows you to go back and study exactly what you need to learn, pass our practice exam and know you are ready to take the real exam.

Be confident

Thinking you can pass is different than knowing you can. ExSim-Max simulates the complete exam experience, including topics covered, question types, question difficulty and time allowed, so you know what to expect. Most importantly, you'll know whether or not you are ready. Take the exam with confidence with ExSim-Max.

Pass the exam

If you can pass an ExSim-Max practice exam, you can pass the real exam. We are so sure of this that we guarantee it. That's right; you are guaranteed to pass the exam, or you get your money back with Boson's No Pass, No Pay guarantee*.

Get ExSim-Max and know you can pass.

*See website

As the original purchaser of this book, you are eligible for a special offer for ExSim-Max. Get your special offer at www.boson.com/ready.

boson.com

Try Safari Books Online FREE

Get online access to 5,000+ Books and Videos

FREE TRIAL—GET STARTED TODAY!
www.informit.com/safaritrial

> **Find trusted answers, fast**
> Only Safari lets you search across thousands of best-selling books from the top technology publishers, including Addison-Wesley Professional, Cisco Press, O'Reilly, Prentice Hall, Que, and Sams.

> **Master the latest tools and techniques**
> In addition to gaining access to an incredible inventory of technical books, Safari's extensive collection of video tutorials lets you learn from the leading video training experts.

WAIT, THERE'S MORE!

> **Keep your competitive edge**
> With Rough Cuts, get access to the developing manuscript and be among the first to learn the newest technologies.

> **Stay current with emerging technologies**
> Short Cuts and Quick Reference Sheets are short, concise, focused content created to get you up-to-speed quickly on new and cutting-edge technologies.

informIT.com

THE TRUSTED TECHNOLOGY LEARNING SOURCE

PEARSON

InformIT is a brand of Pearson and the online presence for the world's leading technology publishers. It's your source for reliable and qualified content and knowledge, providing access to the top brands, authors, and contributors from the tech community.

Addison-Wesley   **Cisco Press**   EXAM/**CRAM**   **IBM** Press.   QUE'   PRENTICE HALL   *SAMS*   Safari Books Online

---

LearnIT at InformIT

Looking for a book, eBook, or training video on a new technology? Seeking timely and relevant information and tutorials? Looking for expert opinions, advice, and tips? **InformIT has the solution.**

- Learn about new releases and special promotions by subscribing to a wide variety of newsletters.
  Visit **informit.com/newsletters**.

- Access FREE podcasts from experts at **informit.com/podcasts**.

- Read the latest author articles and sample chapters at **informit.com/articles**.

- Access thousands of books and videos in the Safari Books Online digital library at **safari.informit.com**.

- Get tips from expert blogs at **informit.com/blogs**.

Visit **informit.com/learn** to discover all the ways you can access the hottest technology content.

Are You Part of the IT Crowd?

Connect with Pearson authors and editors via RSS feeds, Facebook, Twitter, YouTube, and more! Visit **informit.com/socialconnect**.

informIT.com THE TRUSTED TECHNOLOGY LEARNING SOURCE   **PEARSON**

Addison-Wesley   **Cisco Press**   EXAM/**CRAM**   **IBM** Press.   QUE'   PRENTICE HALL   *SAMS*   Safari Books Online

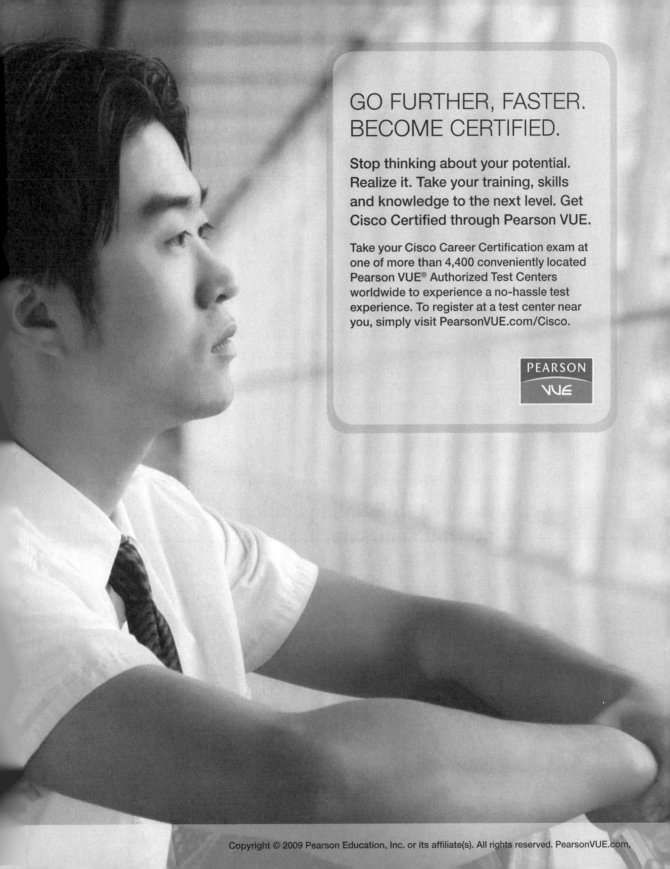

GO FURTHER, FASTER.
BECOME CERTIFIED.

Stop thinking about your potential.
Realize it. Take your training, skills
and knowledge to the next level. Get
Cisco Certified through Pearson VUE.

Take your Cisco Career Certification exam at
one of more than 4,400 conveniently located
Pearson VUE® Authorized Test Centers
worldwide to experience a no-hassle test
experience. To register at a test center near
you, simply visit PearsonVUE.com/Cisco.

PEARSON
VUE

Copyright © 2009 Pearson Education, Inc. or its affiliate(s). All rights reserved. PearsonVUE.com,

FREE Online Edition

Your purchase of **CCNP TSHOOT 642-832 Official Certification Guide** includes access to a free online edition for 45 days through the Safari Books Online subscription service. Nearly every Cisco Press book is available online through Safari Books Online, along with more than 5,000 other technical books and videos from publishers such as Addison-Wesley Professional, Exam Cram, IBM Press, O'Reilly, Prentice Hall, Que, and Sams.

SAFARI BOOKS ONLINE allows you to search for a specific answer, cut and paste code, download chapters, and stay current with emerging technologies.

Activate your FREE Online Edition at www.informit.com/safarifree

> **STEP 1:** Enter the coupon code: GKPUOXA.

> **STEP 2:** New Safari users, complete the brief registration form.
> Safari subscribers, just log in.

If you have difficulty registering on Safari or accessing the online edition, please e-mail customer-service@safaribooksonline.com

CCNP SWITCH 642-813
Official Certification Guide

David Hucaby, CCIE No. 4594

Cisco Press

800 East 96th Street

Indianapolis, IN 46240

CCNP SWITCH 642-813 Official Certification Guide

David Hucaby, CCIE No. 4594

Copyright© 2010 Pearson Education, Inc.

Published by
Cisco Press
800 East 96th Street
Indianapolis, IN 46240 USA

All rights reserved. No part of this book may be reproduced or transmitted in any form or by any means, electronic or mechanical, including photocopying, recording, or by any information storage and retrieval system, without written permission from the publisher, except for the inclusion of brief quotations in a review.

Printed in the United States of America

Sixth Printing: December 2011

Library of Congress Cataloging-in-Publication Data:

Hucaby, Dave.

  CCNP SWITCH 642-813 official certification guide / David Hucaby.

     p. cm.

  ISBN-13: 978-1-58720-243-8

  ISBN-10: 1-58720-243-3

  1. Virtual LANs—Examinations—Study guides. 2. Telecommunications engineers—Certification. 3. Cisco Systems, Inc.—Examinations—Study guides. I. Title.

  TK5103.8.H8327 2010

  004.6076—dc22

                                     2009050384

Warning and Disclaimer

This book is designed to provide information about the CCNP SWITCH Exam (Exam 642-813) for the CCNP Routing and Switching certification. Every effort has been made to make this book as complete and as accurate as possible, but no warranty or fitness is implied.

The information is provided on an "as is" basis. The authors, Cisco Press, and Cisco Systems, Inc. shall have neither liability nor responsibility to any person or entity with respect to any loss or damages arising from the information contained in this book or from the use of the discs or programs that may accompany it.

The opinions expressed in this book belong to the author and are not necessarily those of Cisco Systems, Inc.

Trademark Acknowledgments

All terms mentioned in this book that are known to be trademarks or service marks have been appropriately capitalized. Cisco Press or Cisco Systems, Inc., cannot attest to the accuracy of this information. Use of a term in this book should not be regarded as affecting the validity of any trademark or service mark.

Corporate and Government Sales

The publisher offers excellent discounts on this book when ordered in quantity for bulk purchases or special sales, which may include electronic versions and/or custom covers and content particular to your business, training goals, marketing focus, and branding interests. For more information, please contact: **U.S. Corporate and Government Sales**   1-800-382-3419   corpsales@pearsontechgroup.com

For sales outside the United States please contact: **International Sales**   international@pearsoned.com

Feedback Information

At Cisco Press, our goal is to create in-depth technical books of the highest quality and value. Each book is crafted with care and precision, undergoing rigorous development that involves the unique expertise of members from the professional technical community.

Readers' feedback is a natural continuation of this process. If you have any comments regarding how we could improve the quality of this book, or otherwise alter it to better suit your needs, you can contact us through email at feedback@ciscopress.com. Please make sure to include the book title and ISBN in your message.

We greatly appreciate your assistance.

Publisher: Paul Boger

Associate Publisher: Dave Dusthimer

Executive Editor: Brett Bartow

Managing Editor: Patrick Kanouse

Development Editor: Andrew Cupp

Senior Project Editor: Tonya Simpson

Editorial Assistant: Vanessa Evans

Book Designer: Louisa Adair

Composition: Mark Shirar

Indexer: Tim Wright

Business Operation Manager, Cisco Press: Anand Sundaram

Manager Global Certification: Erik Ullanderson

Copy Editor: Keith Cline

Technical Editors: Geoff Tagg and Sean Wilkins

Proofreader: Apostrophe Editing Services

About the Author

David Hucaby, CCIE No. 4594, is a lead network engineer for the University of Kentucky, where he works with healthcare networks based on the Cisco Catalyst, ASA, FWSM, and VPN product lines. David has a Bachelor of Science degree and Master of Science degree in electrical engineering from the University of Kentucky. He is the author of several Cisco Press titles, including *Cisco ASA, PIX, and FWSM Firewall Handbook*, Second Edition; *Cisco Firewall Video Mentor*; and *Cisco LAN Switching Video Mentor*.

David lives in Kentucky with his wife, Marci, and two daughters.

About the Technical Reviewers

Geoff Tagg runs a small U.K. networking company and has worked in the networking industry for nearly 30 years. Before that, he had 15 years of experience with systems programming and management on a wide variety of installations. Geoff has clients ranging from small local businesses to large multinationals and has combined implementation with training for most of his working life. Geoff's main specialties are routing, switching, and networked storage. He lives in Oxford, England, with his wife, Christine, and family, and is a visiting professor at nearby Oxford Brookes University.

Sean Wilkins is an accomplished networking consultant and has been in the field of IT since the mid-1990s, working with companies such as Cisco, Lucent, Verizon, and AT&T and several other private companies. Sean currently holds certifications with Cisco (CCNP/CCDP), Microsoft (MCSE), and CompTIA (A+ and Network+). He also has a Master of Science degree in information technology with a focus in network architecture and design, a Master's certificate in network security, a Bachelor of Science degree in computer networking, and an Associate of Applied Science degree in computer information systems. In addition to working as a consultant, Sean spends a lot of his time as a technical writer and editor for various companies.

Dedications

As always, this book is dedicated to the most important people in my life: my wife, Marci, and my two daughters, Lauren and Kara. Their love, encouragement, and support carry me along. I'm so grateful to God, who gives endurance and encouragement (Romans 15:5), and who has allowed me to work on projects like this.

Acknowledgments

It has been my great pleasure to work on another Cisco Press project. I enjoy the networking field very much, and technical writing even more. And more than that, I'm thankful for the joy and inner peace that Jesus Christ gives, making everything more abundant.

Technical writing may be hard work, but I'm finding that it's also quite fun because I'm working with very good friends. Brett Bartow, Drew Cupp, and Patrick Kanouse have given their usual expertise to this project, and they are appreciated.

I am very grateful for the insight, suggestions, and helpful comments that Geoff Tagg and Sean Wilkins contributed. Each one offered a different perspective, which helped make this a more well-rounded book and me a more educated author.

Contents at a Glance

On This Book's CD:

Contents

Command Syntax Conventions

The conventions used to present command syntax in this book are the same conventions used in the IOS Command Reference. The Command Reference describes these conventions as follows:

- **Boldface** indicates commands and keywords that are entered literally as shown. In actual configuration examples and output (not general command syntax), boldface indicates commands that are manually input by the user (such as a show command).

- *Italic* indicates arguments for which you supply actual values.

- Vertical bars (|) separate alternative, mutually exclusive elements.

- Square brackets ([ ]) indicate an optional element.

- Braces ({ }) indicate a required choice.

- Braces within brackets ([{ }]) indicate a required choice within an optional element.

Foreword

CCNP SWITCH 642-813 Official Certification Guide is an excellent self-study resource for the CCNP SWITCH exam. Passing this exam is a crucial step to attaining the valued CCNP Routing and Switching certification.

Gaining certification in Cisco technology is key to the continuing educational development of today's networking professional. Through certification programs, Cisco validates the skills and expertise required to effectively manage the modern enterprise network.

Cisco Press Certification Guides and preparation materials offer exceptional—and flexible—access to the knowledge and information required to stay current in your field of expertise or to gain new skills. Whether used as a supplement to more traditional training or as a primary source of learning, these materials offer users the information and knowledge validation required to gain new understanding and proficiencies.

Developed in conjunction with the Cisco certifications and training team, Cisco Press books are the only self-study books authorized by Cisco and offer students a series of exam practice tools and resource materials to help ensure that learners fully grasp the concepts and information presented.

Additional authorized Cisco instructor-led courses, e-learning, labs, and simulations are available exclusively from Cisco Learning Solutions Partners worldwide. To learn more, visit http://www.cisco.com/go/training.

I hope that you find these materials to be an enriching and useful part of your exam preparation.

Erik Ullanderson
Manager, Global Certifications
Learning@Cisco
January 2010

Introduction: Overview of Certification and How to Succeed

Professional certifications have been an important part of the computing industry for many years and will continue to become more important. Many reasons exist for these certifications, but the most popularly cited reason is that of credibility. All other considerations held equal, the certified employee/consultant/job candidate is considered more valuable than one who is not.

Objectives and Methods

The most important and somewhat obvious objective of this book is to help you pass the Cisco CCNP SWITCH exam (Exam 642-813). In fact, if the primary objective of this book were different, the book's title would be misleading; however, the methods used in this book to help you pass the SWITCH exam are designed to also make you much more knowledgeable about how to do your job. Although this book and the accompanying CD have many exam preparation tasks and example test questions, the method in which they are used is not to simply make you memorize as many questions and answers as you possibly can.

The methodology of this book helps you discover the exam topics about which you need more review, fully understand and remember exam topic details, and prove to yourself that you have retained your knowledge of those topics. So this book helps you pass not by memorization, but by helping you truly learn and understand the topics. The SWITCH exam is just one of the foundation topics in the CCNP Routing and Switching certification, and the knowledge contained within is vitally important to consider yourself a truly skilled routing and switching engineer or specialist. This book would do you a disservice if it did not attempt to help you learn the material. To that end, the book can help you pass the SWITCH exam by using the following methods:

- Covering all the exam topics and helping you discover which exam topics you have not mastered

- Providing explanations and information to fill in your knowledge gaps

- Supplying exam preparation tasks and example networks with diagrams and sample configurations that all enhance your ability to recall and deduce the answers to test questions

- Providing practice exercises on the exam topics and the testing process through test questions on the CD

Who Should Read This Book?

This book is not designed to be a general networking topics book, although it can be used for that purpose. This book is intended to tremendously increase your chances of passing the Cisco SWITCH exam. Although other objectives can be achieved from using this book, the book is written with one goal in mind: to help you pass the exam.

The SWITCH exam is primarily based on the content of the Cisco SWITCH course. You should have either taken the course, read through the SWITCH coursebook or this book, or have a couple of years of LAN switching experience.

Cisco Certifications and Exams

Cisco offers four levels of routing and switching certification, each with an increasing level of proficiency: Entry, Associate, Professional, and Expert. These are commonly known by their acronyms CCENT (Cisco Certified Entry Networking Technician), CCNA (Cisco Certified Network Associate), CCNP (Cisco Certified Network Professional), and CCIE (Cisco Certified Internetworking Expert). There are others, too, but this book focuses on the certifications for enterprise networks.

For the CCNP Routing and Switching certification, you must pass exams on a series of CCNP topics, including the SWITCH, ROUTE, and TSHOOT exams. For most exams, Cisco does not publish the scores needed for passing. You need to take the exam to find that out for yourself.

To see the most current requirements for the CCNP Routing and Switching certification, go to Cisco.com and click Training and Events. There you can find out other exam details such as exam topics and how to register for an exam.

The strategy you use to prepare for the SWITCH exam might be slightly different from strategies used by other readers, mainly based on the skills, knowledge, and experience you already have obtained. For instance, if you have attended the SWITCH course, you might take a different approach than someone who learned switching through on-the-job training. Regardless of the strategy you use or the background you have, this book is designed to help you get to the point where you can pass the exam with the least amount of time required.

How This Book Is Organized

Although this book can be read cover to cover, it is designed to be flexible and allow you to easily move between chapters and sections of chapters to cover only the material that you need more work with. The chapters can be covered in any order, although some chapters are related and build upon each other. If you do intend to read them all, the order in the book is an excellent sequence to use.

Each core chapter covers a subset of the topics on the CCNP SWITCH exam. The chapters are organized into parts, covering the following topics:

Part I: New CCNP Exam Approaches

- **Chapter 1, "The Planning Tasks of the CCNP Exams"**—This chapter explains the roles of a networking professional in the context of the Cisco Lifecycle Model, where network tasks form a cycle over time. The CCNP SWITCH exam covers real-world or practical skills that are necessary as a network is designed, planned, implemented, verified, and tuned.

Part II: Building a Campus Network

- **Chapter 2, "Switch Operation"**—This chapter covers Layer 2 and multilayer switch operation, how various content-addressable memory (CAM) and ternary content-addressable memory (TCAM) tables are used to make switching decisions, and how to monitor these tables to aid in troubleshooting.

- **Chapter 3, "Switch Port Configuration"**—This chapter covers basic Ethernet concepts, how to use scalable Ethernet, how to connect switch and devices together, and how to verify switch port operation to aid in troubleshooting.

- **Chapter 4, "VLANs and Trunks"**—This chapter covers basic VLAN concepts, how to transport multiple VLANs over single links, how to configure VLAN trunks, and how to verify VLAN and trunk operation.

- **Chapter 5, "VLAN Trunking Protocol"**—This chapter covers VLAN management using VTP, VTP configuration, traffic management through VTP pruning, and how to verify VTP operation.

- **Chapter 6, "Aggregating Switch Links"**—This chapter covers switch port aggregation with EtherChannel, EtherChannel negotiation protocols, EtherChannel configuration, and how to verify EtherChannel operation.

- **Chapter 7, "Traditional Spanning Tree Protocol"**—This chapter covers IEEE 802.1D Spanning Tree Protocol (STP) and gives an overview of the other STP types that might be running on a switch.

- **Chapter 8, "Spanning-Tree Configuration"**—This chapter covers the STP root bridge, how to customize the STP topology, how to tune STP convergence, redundant link convergence, and how to verify STP operation.

- **Chapter 9, "Protecting the Spanning Tree Protocol Topology"**—This chapter covers protecting the STP topology using Root Guard, BPDU Guard, and Loop Guard, and also how to use BPDU filtering and how to verify that these STP protection mechanisms are functioning properly.

- **Chapter 10, "Advanced Spanning Tree Protocol"**—This chapter covers Rapid Spanning Tree Protocol (RSTP) for Rapid PVST+ and Multiple Spanning Tree (MST) Protocol.

- **Chapter 11, "Multilayer Switching"**—This chapter covers interVLAN routing, multilayer switching with Cisco Express Forwarding (CEF), and how to verify that multilayer switching is functioning properly.

Part III: Designing Campus Networks

■ **Chapter 12, "Enterprise Campus Network Design"**—This chapter covers different campus network models, hierarchical network design, and how to design, size, and scale a campus network using a modular approach.

■ **Chapter 13, "Layer 3 High Availability"**—This chapter covers providing redundant router or gateway addresses on Catalyst switches and verifying that redundancy is functioning properly.

Part IV: Campus Network Services

■ **Chapter 14, "IP Telephony"**—This chapter covers how a Catalyst switch can provide power to operate a Cisco IP Phone, how voice traffic can be carried over the links between an IP Phone and a Catalyst switch, QoS for voice traffic, and how to verify that IP Telephony features are functioning properly.

■ **Chapter 15, "Integrating Wireless LANs"**—This chapter covers different approaches to integrating autonomous and lightweight wireless access points into a switched campus network.

Part V: Securing Switched Networks

■ **Chapter 16, "Securing Switch Access"**—This chapter covers switch authentication, authorization, and accounting (AAA); port security using MAC addresses; port-based security using IEEE 802.1x; DHCP snooping; and dynamic ARP inspection.

■ **Chapter 17, "Securing with VLANs"**—This chapter covers how to control traffic within a VLAN using access lists, implementing private VLANs, and monitoring traffic on switch ports for security reasons.

Part VI: Final Exam Preparation

■ **Chapter 18, "Final Preparation"**—This chapter explains how to use the practice exam CD to enhance your study, along with a basic study plan.

There is also an appendix that has answers to the "Do I Know This Already" quizzes and an appendix that tells you how to find any updates should there be changes to the exam.

Each chapter in the book uses several features to help you make the best use of your time in that chapter. The features are as follows:

■ **Assessment**—Each chapter begins with a "Do I Know This Already?" quiz that helps you determine the amount of time you need to spend studying each topic of the chapter. If you intend to read the entire chapter, you can save the quiz for later use. Questions are all multiple choice, to give a quick assessment of your knowledge.

■ **Foundation Topics**—This is the core section of each chapter that explains the protocols, concepts, and configuration for the topics in the chapter.

■ **Exam Preparation Tasks**—At the end of each chapter, this section collects key topics, references to memory table exercises to be completed as memorization practice, key terms to define, and a command reference that summarizes relevant commands presented in the chapter.

Finally, there is a CD-based practice exam. The companion CD contains a practice CCNP SWITCH exam containing a bank of test questions to reinforce your understanding of the book's concepts. This is the best tool for helping you prepare for the actual test-taking process.

The CD also contains the Memory Table exercises and answer keys that come up at the end of each chapter.

How to Use This Book for Study

Retention and recall are the two features of human memory most closely related to performance on tests. This exam-preparation guide focuses on increasing both retention and recall of the topics on the exam. The other human characteristic involved in successfully passing the exam is intelligence; this book does not address that issue!

This book is designed with features to help you increase retention and recall. It does this in the following ways:

- By providing succinct and complete methods of helping you decide what you recall easily and what you do not recall at all.

- By giving references to the exact passages in the book that review those concepts you most need to recall, so you can quickly be reminded about a fact or concept. Repeating information that connects to another concept helps retention, and describing the same concept in several ways throughout a chapter increases the number of connectors to the same pieces of information.

- Finally, accompanying this book is a CD that has exam-like questions. These are useful for you to practice taking the exam and to get accustomed to the time restrictions imposed during the exam.

When taking the "Do I Know This Already?" assessment quizzes in each chapter, make sure that you treat yourself and your knowledge fairly. If you come across a question that makes you guess at an answer, mark it wrong immediately. This forces you to read through the part of the chapter that relates to that question and forces you to learn it more thoroughly.

If you find that you do well on the assessment quizzes, it still might be wise to quickly skim through each chapter to find sections or topics that do not readily come to mind. Look for the Key Topics icons. Sometimes even reading through the detailed table of contents will reveal topics that are unfamiliar or unclear. If that happens to you, mark those chapters or topics and spend time working through those parts of the book.

Key Topic

CCNP SWITCH Exam Topics

Carefully consider the exam topics Cisco has posted on its website as you study, particularly for clues to how deeply you should know each topic. Beyond that, you cannot go wrong by developing a broader knowledge of the subject matter. You can do that by reading and studying the topics presented in this book. Remember that it is in your best interest to become proficient in each of the CCNP subjects. When it is time to use what you have learned, being well rounded counts more than being well tested.

Table I-1 shows the official exam topics for the SWITCH exam, as posted on Cisco.com. Note that Cisco has occasionally changed exam topics without changing the exam number, so do not be alarmed if small changes in the exam topics occur over time. When in doubt, go to Cisco.com and click Training and Events.

Table I-1—CCNP SWITCH Exam Topics

Exam Topic	Part of This Book Where Exam Topic Is Covered
Implement VLAN-based solution, given a network design and a set of requirements	
Determine network resources needed for implementing VLAN-based solution on a network. Create a VLAN-based implementation plan. Create a VLAN-based verification plan. Configure switch-to-switch connectivity for the VLAN-based solution. Configure loop prevention for the VLAN-based solution. Configure access ports for the VLAN-based solution. Verify the VLAN-based solution was implemented properly using **show** and **debug** commands. Document results of VLAN implementation and verification	Part II, "Building a Campus Network" Chapters 2–10
Implement a security extension of a Layer 2 solution, given a network design and a set of requirements	
Determine network resources needed for implementing a security solution. Create a implementation plan for the security solution. Create a verification plan for the security solution. Configure port security features. Configure general switch security features. Configure private VLANs. Configure VACL and PACL. Verify the security solution was implemented properly using **show** and **debug** commands. Document results of security implementation and verification.	Part V, "Securing Switched Networks" Chapters 16–17

Table I-1—CCNP SWITCH Exam Topics

Exam Topic	Part of This Book Where Exam Topic Is Covered
Implement switch-based Layer 3 services, given a network design and a set of requirements	
Determine network resources needed for implementing a switch-based Layer 3 solution. Create an implementation plan for the switch-based Layer 3 solution. Create a verification plan for the switch-based Layer 3 solution. Configure routing interfaces. Configure Layer 3 security. Verify the switch-based Layer 3 solution was implemented properly using **show** and **debug** commands. Document results of switch-based Layer 3 implementation and verification.	Part II, "Building a Campus Network" Chapter 11
Prepare infrastructure to support advanced services	
Implement a wireless extension of a Layer 2 solution. Implement a VoIP support solution. Implement video support solution.	Part IV, "Campus Network Services" Chapters 14–15
Implement high availability, given a network design and a set of requirements	
Determine network resources needed for implementing high availability on a network. Create a high availability implementation plan. Create a high availability verification plan. Implement first-hop redundancy protocols. Implement switch supervisor redundancy. Verify high-availability solution was implemented properly using **show** and **debug** commands. Document results of high-availability implementation and verification.	Part III, "Designing Campus Networks" Chapters 12–13

For More Information

If you have any comments about the book, you can submit those via the Ciscopress.com website. Just go to the website, select Contact Us, and type in your message. Cisco might make changes that affect the CCNP Routing and Switching certification from time to time. You should always check Cisco.com for the latest details. Also, you can look to http://www.ciscopress.com/title/ 1587202433, where we publish any information pertinent to how you might use this book differently in light of future changes from Cisco. For example, if Cisco decides to remove a major topic from the exam, it might post that on its website; Cisco Press will make an effort to list that information as well via an online updates appendix.

Part I: New CCNP Exam Approaches

This chapter illuminates some of the hands-on and practical skills that have become increasingly tested on the CCNP SWITCH exam. As you work through the chapter, notice how planning and design functions are integral to a network professional's job.

CHAPTER 1

The Planning Tasks of the CCNP Exams

Perspectives on CCNP Exam Topics Related to Planning

Cisco introduced the Cisco Certified Networking Professional (CCNP) certification back in 1998. Since then, Cisco has revised the exams and related courses on several occasions. Each major revision adjusted the scope of topics by expanding and adding some topics while shrinking or removing other topics. At the same time, the depth of coverage has changed over time, too, with the depth of coverage for each topic either becoming deeper or shallower.

The most current version of CCNP, corresponding with the 642-813 exam about which this book is written, narrows the breadth of topics included in CCNP compared to the previous version of CCNP. Cisco removed several sizable topics from CCNP, such as quality of service (QoS), wireless LANs (WLAN), and many security topics. In other words, the new CCNP squarely focuses on routing and switching.

Although the smaller number of CCNP topics might seem to make CCNP easier, two other factors compensate so that it is still a challenging, difficult, and therefore respected certification. First, the exams appear to require a higher level of mastery for most topics, making a clear distinction between the knowledge learned in CCNA and the advanced coverage in CCNP. Second, that mastery is more than just technical knowledge—it requires the ability to plan the implementation and verification of a network engineering project.

Many CCNP SWITCH exam topics list the word *plan*, collectively meaning that the CCNP candidate must approach problems in the same manner as a network engineer in a medium- to large-sized business. For example, you might find the following skills in such a workplace environment:

- The ability to analyze a network design document and extrapolate that design into the complete detailed implementation plan, including completed configurations for each router and switch

- The ability to analyze a design document and discover the missing items—questions that must be answered before a detailed implementation plan (including configurations) can be completed

- The ability to perform a peer review on another engineer's implementation plan, to discover weaknesses and omissions in the planned configurations, and to update the implementation plan

- The ability to build a verification plan that lists the specific **show** commands and command options that list key pieces of information—information that directly either confirms or denies whether each planned feature has been implemented correctly

- The ability to write a verification plan that can be understood and used by a less-experienced worker, allowing that worker to implement the change and to verify the changes worked, off-shift, when you are not on-site

- The ability to perform a peer review on another engineer's verification plan, to discover which key design features are not verified by that plan, and to discover inaccuracies in the plan

This chapter discusses the whole area of implementation and verification planning for the CCNP SWITCH exam, and it covers how you should prepare for these exam topics. By considering the ideas in this chapter first, you should have the right perspectives to know how to use the tools that help you add the planning skills and perspectives needed for the exam.

CCNP Switch Exam Topics That Do Not Require the CLI

Cisco lists a set of exam topics for each CCNP exam. These exam topics follow a general type of phrasing, typically starting with an action word that defines what action or skill you must do for the exam. (Unfortunately, this style seldom gives much insight into the breadth or depth of coverage of a given topic.)

For example, consider the basic topic of Layer 2 VLANs. Table 1-1 lists the topics or skills related to VLANs as found in the CCNP SWITCH exam blueprint.

Table 1-1   *CCNP SWITCH Exam Topics Related to VLAN*

Implement VLAN-based solution, given a network design and a set of requirements.
Determine network resources needed for implementing a VLAN-based solution on a network.
Create a VLAN-based implementation plan.
Create a VLAN-based verification plan.
Configure switch-to-switch connectivity for the VLAN-based solution.
Configure loop prevention for the VLAN-based solution.
Configure access ports for the VLAN-based solution.
Verify the VLAN-based solution was implemented properly using **show** and **debug** commands.
Document results of VLAN implementation and verification.

The four gray-highlighted exam topics focus on tasks that you can complete by using the commands available from the command-line interface (CLI). Specifically, you need to be able to create a VLAN, connect the VLAN from switch to switch, configure the Spanning Tree Protocol to prevent Layer 2 loops over the VLAN, and configure switch ports to use the VLAN where end users are connected. After those things are accomplished, you need to be able to use the CLI to verify that your configurations are correct working properly. The technical information you will need to study about configuring and using VLANs is presented in Chapter 4, "VLANs and Trunks."

Notice that the other nonshaded topics begin with words such as *determine*, *create*, and *document*. These represent the "bigger picture" skills necessary to plan and carry out a successful implementation. Although these topics may require knowledge of Catalyst IOS commands, these tasks do not require any hands-on activities from the CLI. Instead, when doing these tasks in real life, you would more likely be using a word processor rather than a terminal emulator.

Planning Exam Topics

After a first glance through the CCNP SWITCH exam topics (listed in the "Introduction"), you might think that the new CCNP certification has been changed significantly—and you therefore need to significantly change how you prepare for CCNP. However, by focusing on the following aspects of your study, you should be well prepared for the CCNP exams in general and the CCNP SWITCH exam in particular:

- As with any other Cisco career certification exam, understand the concepts and the configuration commands.

- As with any other Cisco career certification exam, master the verification tasks and troubleshooting (**show** and **debug**) commands.

- *Unlike* most other Cisco career certification exams, spend some time thinking about the concepts, configuration, and verification tasks as if you were writing or reviewing a network design document, a network project implementation plan, or a verification plan.

In this list, the first two tasks are what most people normally do when preparing for a Cisco exam. The third item represents the new type of preparation task, in which you simply think about the same concepts, commands, and features, but from a planning perspective.

Why is Cisco adding more career-oriented tasks into the CCNP exams? Because, over time, a networking professional may be called upon to deal with every aspect of a network. Tasks related to switch configuration tend to be snapshots in time, where some feature or function is needed right now. If a longer time period is examined, the same network professional must deal with many other networking aspects—such as planning for configuration commands, collaborating with other network professionals, and verifying work.

Cisco uses the prepare, plan, design, implement, operate, optimize (PPDIOO) network lifecycle approach to describe the life of a network over time. Figure 1-1 shows how the lifecycle is broken down into six phases, denoted by the letters in the PPDIOO acronym. Generally, after a network has gone from the prepare phase all the way through the operate phase, it is functional and begins supporting business activities. Some time later, some new features or new policies may need to be introduced, or the network might need to scale to support new growth. At that point, the organization needs to prepare for the new additions, and the lifecycle starts all over.

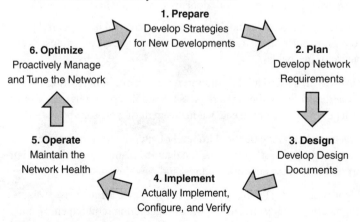

Figure 1-1   *The Cisco PPDIOO Network Lifecycle*

Relating the Exam Topics to a Typical Network Engineer's Job

The need to plan, and the need to document those plans, increases as the size of the organization increases. Even if only one person at a company cares about the router and switch infrastructure, that engineer probably does not want to be writing configurations at 2 a.m. Sunday morning when the change window begins. In addition, the company probably does not want to rely on one engineer's knowledge of its network, especially if that engineer becomes unavailable (for example, if the engineer leaves the company or takes any time off).

When the staff grows to three or four people, particularly when some of those people work different shifts, the need to document the design, implementation, and verification/operational procedures becomes more important. That team of people probably needs to agree on a common vision or design, and it needs to be based on collaboration and teamwork, with some oversight from peers.

For perspective, this section examines a medium- to large-sized company, along with some of the planning tasks done in the real world—the same kinds of tasks listed as part of the CCNP SWITCH exam topics.

A Fictitious Company and Networking Staff

Think about a company (perhaps the one where you already work) and its structure or organization. If the company is small or based in one location, the network might be rather small and have a modest number of users. The company might have a server room or a small data center.

If the company is large, it might be spread over many geographic locations, with many different campuses and remote sites. The data center might be located in one large space, or it may be distributed across several redundant locations. The company might have an enterprisewide IP telephony deployment, video over IP, network security devices, a growing teleworker community, multiple Internet connections, and several network connections to partner companies.

Regardless of the size of the company, the IT needs are basically the same. Consider the various roles in the network and the type of work done by the people in those roles:

- Help desk personnel may perform diagnosis of network health, taking a general problem statement from a customer down to a specific issue (for example, that a user's device is not responsive or reachable).

- Operations staff may be the second level of support for problems, both reacting to calls from the help desk and monitoring the network proactively. The operations staff also often implements changes on behalf of the engineering team during off-shift hours.

- The network engineering team may be the third level of support for problems, but they typically focus on project work, including the detailed planning for new configurations to support new sites, new network features, and new sites in the network.

- The network designers may actually log in to the network devices much less than the operations and engineering teams, instead focusing on gathering requirements from internal and external customers, translating those requirements into a network design, and even doing proof-of-concept testing—but leaving the details of how to deploy the design for all required sites to the network engineering team.

Of course, the number of individuals in each of these roles varies across different organizations. In a small organization, maybe only a single network designer and single network engineer are required, with perhaps two or three people as network operations specialists—not enough for 24×7 coverage with a specialist, but close. The help desk position may simply require most people to have the same networking skill set, depending on the size of the shop. On the other end of the scale, in the largest companies, the staff might consist of several departments of network engineers.

In any event, someone has to perform each of the functions to properly support the organization. Your job as a network professional or network engineer is to work independently, while providing plans, documentation, and verification to other IT professionals.

The Design Step

Next, consider the basic work flow when a new network project happens, new sites are added, or any noticeable change occurs. The network designer first develops the requirements and creates a plan. That plan typically lists the following:

- Project requirements
- Sites affected
- Sample configurations
- Traffic analysis
- Results from proof-of-concept testing
- Dependencies and assumptions
- Business requirements, financials, management commitments

Many other items might also be included.

The network designer often uses a peer review process to refine and confirm the design. The designer cannot simply work in a vacuum, define the design, and then toss the design document to network engineering to be deployed. In smaller shops, a peer review may simply be two or three people standing around a dry erase board discussing the project. In larger shops, the design peer review probably requires a thorough written document be distributed before the meeting, with attendance from network engineering, operations, and the help desk, and with formal sign-off required.

Implementation Planning Step

The next step in the life of the project occurs when a network engineer takes the approved design document from the design team and begins planning the implementation of the project. To do this task, the network engineer must interpret the example and general cases described in the design document, and develop a very specific implementation plan that lists all significant tasks and actions by each group and on each device. The design document, for instance, may show example cases of typical branch offices, a typical district (medium sized) site, and so on. The network engineer must then determine what must be done on every device to implement the project and must document those details in an implementation plan.

For example, a company might plan to deploy IP telephony across a campus network. The design document might list the following basic requirements:

■ Specific switch models with Power over Ethernet (PoE) at each remote office

■ The convention of placing all phones at a site in one VLAN/subnet, and all PCs in a second VLAN/subnet

■ VLAN trunking between the access layer switches and the distribution switches

■ A particular Catalyst IOS software version and feature set

■ High availability features designed to provide maximum uptime for telephone calls

■ QoS policies that give voice traffic premium treatment over other types of traffic

After a thorough review of the design, the network engineer then develops an implementation plan that includes items such as the following:

■ A list of all campus locations, with notations of which require a switch hardware upgrade (for PoE support) and which do not

■ Total numbers of switches to be ordered, prices, and delivery schedules

■ A table that lists the specific VLANs and subnet numbers used at each location for the phone and PC VLANs and subnets

■ The IP address ranges from each subnet that needs to be added to the DHCP servers configurations for dynamic address assignment

■ A list of the switches that require a Catalyst IOS software upgrade

■ Annotated sample configurations for typical access layer switches, including VLAN trunking, high availability, and QoS configuration commands

The preceding list represents the types of items that would be documented in the implementation plan for this project. The list is certainly not exhaustive but represents a smattering of what might end up in such a plan.

The implementation plan probably has many informal reviews as the network engineer works through the plan. In addition, larger shops often conduct a peer review when the plan is more fully developed, with network designers, operations, and fellow network engineers typically included in the review.

Verification Planning Step

The design step tells us "this is what we want to accomplish," whereas the implementation planning step tells us "this is exactly what we will do, and when, to accomplish this design." The verification plan explains how to verify or confirm that the implementation plan actually worked.

The verification plan is used with the actual implementation of the changes in the network. More often that not, the operations staff follows the implementation plan, or more specific instructions for each individual change window, taking the appropriate actions. The engineer who implements the changes then uses the verification plan to determine whether the changes met the requirements.

The most important part of the verification plan, at least as far as the CCNP exam is concerned, is to identify the commands that confirm a correct and functioning implementation. For example, suppose IP telephony is being implemented. The following list describes some of the actions that might be listed in the verification plan:

- After copy/pasting or entering the configuration changes in a switch, use the **show interfaces status** command to confirm connected devices and their speed and duplex modes.

- Use the **show cdp neighbor** command to verify active Cisco IP Phone identities.

- Use the **show mac-address-table dynamic interface** command to verify the MAC addresses of Cisco IP Phones and connected PCs.

- Observe the IP Phone display to confirm that the phone has obtained an IP address and has downloaded its firmware.

- Make test calls from IP Phones.

The important part of the verification plan lists the specific commands to be used (and at what point in the implementation process) and what output is expected. In practice, this plan should also include output samples, spelling out what should be seen when correct and what output would alert the operations staff that the change did not work correctly.

Documenting Implementation Results

After a set of changes is attempted or implemented during a change window, some documentation must be changed based on the results. Any deviation from the implementation plan should also be recorded for future reference.

Summary of the Role of Network Engineers

The CCNP certification focuses on skills required to do the job of a network engineer as generally described in this chapter. By interpreting the CCNP SWITCH exam topics, a CCNP network engineer

- *Does not* create the design document

- *Does* participate in design peer reviews, finding oversights, asking further questions that impact the eventual implementation, and confirming the portions of the design that appear complete and valid

- *Does* plan and document the specific configurations for each device, documenting those configurations in the implementation plan so that others can add the configuration to various devices

- *Does* participate in peer reviews of the implementation plans written by fellow network engineers, finding omissions, caveats, and problems.

- *Does* create the verification plan that others use to verify that the changes worked as planned when implemented off-shift

- *Does* perform peer reviews of other engineers' verification plans

- *Does* verify that the changes worked as planned when implemented

Now that you know a bit more about the role of a network engineer, the following section brings the discussion back to the best ways to prepare for the CCNP SWITCH exam.

How to Prepare for the Planning Topics on the Exam

Can you create a networking implementation plan for each technology area on a CCNP exam? Can you create a verification plan for those same technologies? According to the CCNP exam blueprint, these skills are now tested on the CCNP exams. These tasks normally involve large amounts of time devoted to project planning and documentation—things that are not practical during a timed Cisco exam.

Even though the exam might not ask you to literally create a plan, you do need the skills to perform those same tasks. The new CCNP SWITCH course doesn't have much content directly related to planning, other than some common-sense advice. In the past, the CCNP exams were limited to the scope of the corresponding course. With the new exams, such as 642-813, this isn't necessarily the case.

To come up with an implementation plan, you must begin with some goals or objectives. These are generally based on the following things:

■   Business requirements—What does the business need out of the network? What policies must be met?

■   Business constraints—How much will the planned solution (hardware and labor) cost?

■   Technical requirements—Which switch features should be leveraged? How should the switch configurations be carried out? What limitations are there?

As network professionals, we might or might not have a role in identifying these requirements, but we do have a role in carrying out the work. Usually, our work follows this sequence:

Step 1.   Plan the network architecture and every switch feature that will be used. This can be done as a detailed project plan or as something sketched on a napkin over lunch. The idea is to know what needs to be done beforehand.

Step 2.   Implement the plan with switches, cables, protocols, and features. The CCNP exams have traditionally focused on implementing things.

Step 3.   Verify that the implementation works and meets the objectives of the plan.

Now hold that up against the new 642-813 exam blueprint. There are several broad categories where you can find the words "implement" and "verify"—always with the words "create...a plan," as in the following examples:

Create a VLAN-based implementation plan

Create a VLAN-based verification plan

Create an implementation plan for the Security solution

Create a verification plan for the Security solution

Create an implementation plan for the Switch-based Layer 3 solution

Create a verification plan for the Switch-based Layer 3 solution

Create a High Availability implementation plan

Create a High Availability verification plan

So how would you "create a plan" on a Cisco exam? You might get multiple-choice questions that ask for a best approach to a problem. More likely, you might get one of those complex scenario questions. You know—the ones where you have to read a lengthy explanation in one window, squint at the network diagram in another window, and interact with some switches in some other windows, all on one small screen.

The key here is with the scenario description. It's nothing more than a huge word problem that lays out things like business requirements, business constraints, and a list of goals to reach. Even the network diagram becomes a part of the project definition. As you read through the scenario and look over the diagram, you have to **create an implementation plan** in your mind.

The scenarios don't give you a sequence of things to do; instead, they present a bunch of things to accomplish. You must figure out what specific features you'll need, what steps you'll need to configure for each feature, which switch you'll have to visit to type in configuration commands, and so on.

Even as you work through a scenario on the exam, you should spend time **creating a verification plan** so you can test and make sure each feature you have configured actually works as it should. Otherwise, whatever you typed into the switch emulators might not be correct and might not earn you valuable points.

Why did Cisco move toward such broad strokes on the exam blueprint? One possibility is to test your knowledge of the many Cisco IOS features and which ones can be used to accomplish something. For example, the exam blueprint covers the following types of plans:

- VLAN-based plans
- Security plans
- Switch-based Layer 3 plans
- High Availability plans

Those don't say much about specific switch features, commands, or protocols. Instead, you should think of each one as a big toolbox; you need to know which tools are in each toolbox so you can formulate a plan of attack on any given situation. As the old saying goes, not every problem needs a hammer.

Here is a sample scenario that should help you get a feel for this process. Suppose an exam question has a scenario text as follows, and a network diagram as shown in Figure 1-2:

> A company has a network as shown in the network diagram. Switches A and B form the core, while C and D act as distribution switches. Switches A through D are already configured with working links and routing protocols.
>
> Switch E is added into the access layer. It is connected to switches C and D by two uplinks each. Each pair of uplinks should be joined together as a single logical link using a standards-based approach.
>
> Switch E needs to support two distinct groups of users in the Accounting and Engineering departments, to be placed on VLAN 10 and 20, respectively. Each VLAN needs to have a highly available gateway address in the distribution layer, using the .1 address in the appropriate subnet. The network should be configured such that the Accounting users normally pass over the link between switches C and E, while Engineering users pass over the link between D and E.

Do not change the routing configuration on switches A, B, C, or D, other than to advertise the new Accounting and Engineering subnets. Make sure that all uplinks are functioning and that users in the Accounting and Engineering subnets can ping the 192.168.199.10 server located in the data center.

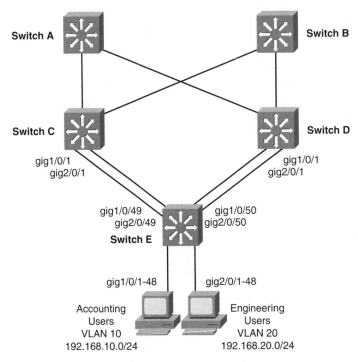

Figure 1-2 *Sample Exam Scenario Network Diagram*

Whew! That scenario covers plenty of ground, and it's really just one question on the exam! Notice that the scenario didn't really specify any switch features or protocols to be used. Instead, you have to put on your thinking cap and develop an implementation plan—fast! Remember that the exam clock is ticking. Your plan should include the following things:

- **Create VLANs**—VLAN 10 for Accounting and VLAN 20 for Engineering

- **VLAN extent**—The VLANs should exist on Switch E, where the users live, and also on C and D, where the gateways and routing protocols live.

- **EtherChannels**—Bundle one pair of uplinks between C and E and another pair between D and E. For a standards-based EtherChannel, use LACP.

- **Trunks**—VLANs 10 and 20 will need to be carried between Switches C and E and between D and E.

- **Layer 3 interfaces**—You'll need an interface vlan10 and an interface vlan20 to provide Layer 3 connectivity for the user subnets. Those will be configured on Switches C and D.

- **HSRP**—To get highly available gateways on both VLANs 10 and 20, you'll need to configure two different HSRP groups.

- **HSRP load balancing**—The two user groups need to normally pass over different uplinks. You'll need to tune the HSRP priorities so that the gateways are split across the two distribution switches.

- **Routing**—You will need to add the new subnets into the **network** commands for the preconfigured routing protocols on switches C and D.

The scenario also mentions some things to test and verify. Your mental verification plan can include things like the following:

Function to Verify	Example Commands	Verify on Switch
VLAN creation	**show vlan**	C, D, E
Working Ether-Channels toward Switches C and D	**show etherchannel summary**	C, D, E
VLAN trunking	**show interfaces** *type/num* **trunk**	C, D, E
Layer 3 interfaces	**show interfaces vlan10** **show interfaces vlan20** -OR- **show ip interface brief**	C, D
HSRP configuration and load balancing	**show standby brief**	C, D
Routing	**show ip route**	C, D
List	**ping 192.168.199.10 source vlan10** **ping 192.168.199.10 source vlan20**	C or D

To test whether the server is reachable from each user subnet, a regular, simple ping won't do. Instead, it's better to use extended pings so that the source address can be set to the Layer 3 interface that sits on each user subnet.

This book contains several tools to help you prepare for the planning topics and exam scenarios. At the end of each chapter, an "Exam Preparation Tasks" section presents a reminder of key topics covered in the chapter. The key topics can help you locate major features and functions that can be used to plan a switch configuration project.

After you have read through a chapter, you can continue to gain benefit from it by skimming for the Key Topic icons. Each chapter also presents the commands needed to configure a switch feature in the order in which they should be entered. Knowing this sequence of operation should help you understand the sequence of the implementation planning tasks.

Finally, each chapter ends with a command reference section in which configuration and verification commands are summarized in a table format. The left side of the table lists the task to be performed, while the right side shows the command syntax. Don't worry about memorizing the exact or complete command syntax, though. Instead, concentrate on the task and the basic command keywords.

Cisco Published SWITCH Exam Topics Covered in This Part

Implement a VLAN based solution, given a network design and a set of requirements:

- Determine network resources needed for implementing a VLAN-based solution on a network

- Create a VLAN-based implementation plan

- Create a VLAN-based verification plan

- Configure switch-to-switch connectivity for the VLAN-based solution

- Configure loop prevention for the VLAN-based solution

- Configure Access Ports for the VLAN-based solution

- Verify the VLAN-based solution was implemented properly using **show** and **debug** commands

- Document results of VLAN implementation and verification

Implement switch-based Layer 3 services, given a network design and a set of requirements:

- Determine network resources needed for implementing a switch-based Layer 3 solution

- Create an implementation plan for the switch-based Layer 3 solution

- Create a verification plan for the switch-based Layer 3 solution

- Configure routing interfaces

- Configure Layer 3 security

- Verify the switch-based Layer 3 solution was implemented properly using **show** and **debug** commands

- Document results of switch-based Layer 3 implementation and verification

(Always check Cisco.com for the latest posted exam topics.)

Part II: Building a Campus Network

This chapter covers the following topics that you need to master for the CCNP SWITCH exam:

Layer 2 Switch Operation—This section describes the functionality of a switch that forwards Ethernet frames.

Multilayer Switch Operation—This section describes the mechanisms that forward packets at OSI Layers 3 and 4.

Tables Used in Switching—This section explains how tables of information and computation are used to make switching decisions. Coverage focuses on the content-addressable memory table involved in Layer 2 forwarding, and the ternary content-addressable memory used in packet-handling decisions at Layers 2 through 4.

Monitoring Switching Tables—This section reviews the Catalyst commands that you can use to monitor the switching tables and memory. These commands can be useful when troubleshooting or tracing the sources of data or problems in a switched network.

CHAPTER 2

Switch Operation

To have a good understanding of the many features that you can configure on a Catalyst switch, you first should understand the fundamentals of the switching function.

This chapter serves as a primer, describing how an Ethernet switch works. It presents Layer 2 forwarding, along with the hardware functions that make forwarding possible. Multilayer switching is also explained. A considerable portion of the chapter deals with the memory architecture that performs switching at Layers 3 and 4 both flexibly and efficiently. This chapter also provides a brief overview of useful switching table management commands.

"Do I Know This Already?" Quiz

The "Do I Know This Already?" quiz allows you to assess whether you should read this entire chapter thoroughly or jump to the "Exam Preparation Tasks" section. If you are in doubt based on your answers to these questions or your own assessment of your knowledge of the topics, read the entire chapter. Table 2-1 outlines the major headings in this chapter and the "Do I Know This Already?" quiz questions that go with them. You can find the answers in Appendix A, "Answers to the 'Do I Know This Already?' Quizzes."

Table 2-1 *"Do I Know This Already?" Foundation Topics Section-to-Question Mapping*

Foundation Topics Section	Questions Covered in This Section
Layer 2 Switch Operation	1–5
Multilayer Switch Operation	6–9
Switching Tables	10–11
Troubleshooting Switching Tables	12

   1. Which of the following devices performs transparent bridging?

      a. Ethernet hub

      b. Layer 2 switch

      c. Layer 3 switch

      d. Router

2. When a PC is connected to a Layer 2 switch port, how far does the collision domain spread?

    a. No collision domain exists.

    b. One switch port.

    c. One VLAN.

    d. All ports on the switch.

3. What information is used to forward frames in a Layer 2 switch?

    a. Source MAC address

    b. Destination MAC address

    c. Source switch port

    d. IP addresses

4. What does a switch do if a MAC address cannot be found in the CAM table?

    a. The frame is forwarded to the default port.

    b. The switch generates an ARP request for the address.

    c. The switch floods the frame out all ports (except the receiving port).

    d. The switch drops the frame.

5. In the Catalyst 6500, frames can be filtered with access lists for security and QoS purposes. This filtering occurs according to which of the following?

    a. Before a CAM table lookup

    b. After a CAM table lookup

    c. Simultaneously with a CAM table lookup

    d. According to how the access lists are configured

6. Access list contents can be merged into which of the following?

    a. CAM table

    b. TCAM table

    c. FIB table

    d. ARP table

7. Multilayer switches using CEF are based on which of these techniques?

    a. Route caching

    b. Netflow switching

    c. Topology-based switching

    d. Demand-based switching

8. Which answer describes multilayer switching with CEF?

   a. The first packet is routed and then the flow is cached.

   b. The switch supervisor CPU forwards each packet.

   c. The switching hardware learns station addresses and builds a routing database.

   d. A single database of routing information is built for the switching hardware.

9. In a switch, frames are placed in which buffer after forwarding decisions are made?

   a. Ingress queues

   b. Egress queues

   c. CAM table

   d. TCAM

10. What size are the mask and pattern fields in a TCAM entry?

   a. 64 bits

   b. 128 bits

   c. 134 bits

   d. 168 bits

11. Access list rules are compiled as TCAM entries. When a packet is matched against an access list, in what order are the TCAM entries evaluated?

   a. Sequentially in the order of the original access list.

   b. Numerically by the access list number.

   c. Alphabetically by the access list name.

   d. All entries are evaluated in parallel.

12. Which Catalyst IOS command can you use to display the addresses in the CAM table?

   a. show cam

   b. show mac address-table

   c. show mac

   d. show cam address-table

Foundation Topics

Layer 2 Switch Operation

Consider a simple network that is built around many hosts that all share the same available bandwidth. This is known as a shared media network and was used in early legacy LANs made up of Ethernet hubs. The carrier sense multiple access collision detect (CSMA/CD) scheme determines when a device can transmit data on the shared LAN.

When more than one host tries to talk at one time, a collision occurs, and everyone must back off and wait to talk again. This forces every host to operate in half-duplex mode, by either talking *or* listening at any given time. In addition, when one host sends a frame, all connected hosts hear it. When one host generates a frame with errors, everyone hears that, too. This type of LAN is a *collision domain* because all device transmissions are susceptible to collisions.

An Ethernet switch operates at OSI Layer 2, making decisions about forwarding frames based on the destination MAC addresses found within the frames. This means that the Ethernet media is no longer shared among connected devices. Instead, at its most basic level, an Ethernet switch provides isolation between connected hosts in several ways:

- The collision domain's scope is severely limited. On each switch port, the collision domain consists of the switch port itself and the devices directly connected to that port—either a single host or, if a shared-media hub is connected, the set of hosts connected to the hub.

- Host connections can operate in full-duplex mode because there is no contention on the media. Hosts can talk *and* listen at the same time.

- Bandwidth is no longer shared. Instead, each switch port offers dedicated bandwidth across a switching fabric to another switch port. (These frame forwarding paths change dynamically.)

- Errors in frames are not propagated. Each frame received on a switch port is checked for errors. Good frames are regenerated when they are forwarded or transmitted. This is known as *store-and-forward* switching technology: Packets are received, stored for inspection, and then forwarded.

- You can limit broadcast traffic to a volume threshold.

- Other types of intelligent filtering or forwarding become possible.

Transparent Bridging

A Layer 2 switch is basically a multiport transparent bridge, where each switch port is its own Ethernet LAN segment, isolated from the others. Frame forwarding is based completely on the MAC addresses contained in each frame, such that the switch will not forward a frame unless it knows the destination's location. (When the switch does not know where the destination is, it makes some safe assumptions.) Figure 2-1 shows the progression from a two-port to a multiport transparent bridge, and then to a Layer 2 switch.

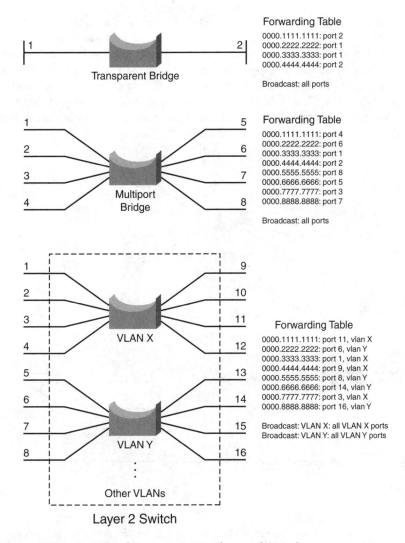

Figure 2-1   *A Comparison of Transparent Bridges and Switches*

The entire process of forwarding Ethernet frames then becomes figuring out what MAC addresses connect to which switch ports. A switch either must be told explicitly where hosts are located or must learn this information for itself. You can configure MAC address locations through a switch's command-line interface, but this quickly gets out of control when there are many stations on the network or when stations move around.

To dynamically learn about station locations, a switch listens to incoming frames and keeps a table of address information. As a frame is received on a switch port, the switch inspects the source MAC address. If that address is not in the address table already, the MAC address, switch port, and virtual LAN (VLAN) on which it arrived are recorded in the table. Learning the address locations of the incoming packets is easy and straightforward.

Incoming frames also include the destination MAC address. Again, the switch looks up this address in the address table, hoping to find the switch port and VLAN where the destination address is attached. If it is found, the frame can be forwarded out that switch port. If the address is not found in the table, the switch must take more drastic action— the frame is forwarded in a "best effort" fashion by *flooding* it out all switch ports assigned to the source VLAN. This is known as *unknown unicast flooding*, with the unicast destination location unknown. Figure 2-2 illustrates this process, using only a single VLAN for simplification.

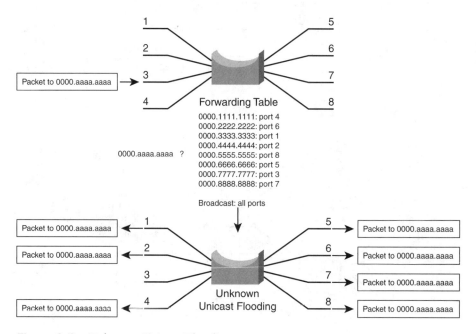

Figure 2-2   *Unknown Unicast Flooding*

A switch constantly listens to incoming frames on each of its ports, learning source MAC addresses. However, be aware that the learning process is allowed only when the Spanning Tree Protocol (STP) algorithm has decided that a port is stable for normal use. STP is concerned only with maintaining a loop-free network, where frames will not be forwarded recursively. If a loop formed, a flooded frame could follow the looped path, where it would be flooded again and again.

In a similar manner, frames containing a broadcast or multicast destination address also are flooded. These destination addresses are not unknown—the switch knows them well. They are destined for multiple locations, so they must be flooded by definition. In the case of multicast addresses, flooding is performed by default.

Follow That Frame!

You should have a basic understanding of the operations that a frame undergoes as it passes through a Layer 2 switch. This helps you get a firm grasp on how to configure the switch for complex functions. Figure 2-3 shows a typical Layer 2 Catalyst switch and the decision processes that take place to forward each frame.

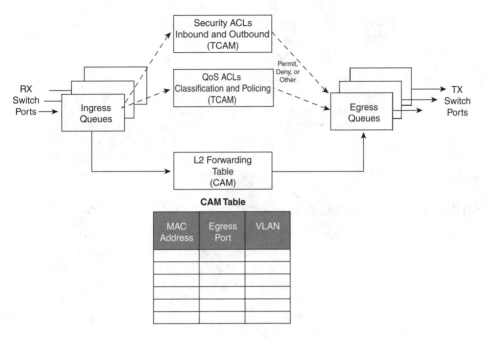

Figure 2-3   *Operations Within a Layer 2 Catalyst Switch*

When a frame arrives at a switch port, it is placed into one of the port's ingress queues. The queues each can contain frames to be forwarded, with each queue having a different priority or service level. The switch port then can be fine-tuned so that important frames get processed and forwarded before less-important frames. This can prevent time-critical data from being "lost in the shuffle" during a flurry of incoming traffic.

As the ingress queues are serviced and a frame is pulled off, the switch must figure out not only *where* to forward the frame, but also *whether* it should be forwarded and *how*. Three fundamental decisions must be made: one concerned with finding the egress switch port, and two concerned with forwarding policies. All these decisions are made *simultaneously* by independent portions of switching hardware and can be described as follows:

■ **L2 forwarding table**—The frame's destination MAC address is used as an index, or key, into the content-addressable memory (CAM), or address, table. If the address is found, the egress switch port and the appropriate VLAN ID are read from the table. (If the address is not found, the frame is marked for flooding so that it is forwarded out every switch port in the VLAN.)

■ **Security ACLs**—Access control lists (ACL) can be used to identify frames according to their MAC addresses, protocol types (for non-IP frames), IP addresses, protocols, and Layer 4 port numbers. The ternary content-addressable memory (TCAM) contains ACLs in a compiled form so that a decision can be made on whether to forward a frame in a single table lookup.

- **QoS ACLs**—Other ACLs can classify incoming frames according to quality of service (QoS) parameters, to police or control the rate of traffic flows, and to mark QoS parameters in outbound frames. The TCAM also is used to make these decisions in a single table lookup.

The CAM and TCAM tables are discussed in greater detail in the "Content-Addressable Memory" and "Ternary Content-Addressable Memory" sections, later in this chapter. After the CAM and TCAM table lookups have occurred, the frame is placed into the appropriate egress queue on the appropriate outbound switch port. The egress queue is determined by QoS values either contained in the frame or passed along with the frame. Like the ingress queues, the egress queues are serviced according to importance or time criticality; frames are sent out without being delayed by other outbound traffic.

Multilayer Switch Operation

Catalyst switches, such as the 3750 (with the appropriate Cisco IOS Software image), 4500, and 6500, can also forward frames based on Layers 3 and 4 information contained in packets. This is known as *multilayer switching (MLS)*. Naturally, Layer 2 switching is performed at the same time because even the higher-layer encapsulations still are contained in Ethernet frames.

Types of Multilayer Switching

Catalyst switches have supported two basic generations or types of MLS: route caching (first-generation MLS) and topology-based (second-generation MLS). This section presents an overview of both, although only the second generation is supported in the Cisco IOS Software–based switch families, such as the Catalyst 3750, 4500, and 6500. You should understand the two types and the differences between them:

- **Route caching**—The first generation of MLS, requiring a route processor (RP) and a switch engine (SE). The RP must process a traffic flow's first packet to determine the destination. The SE listens to the first packet and to the resulting destination, and sets up a "shortcut" entry in its MLS cache. The SE forwards subsequent packets in the same traffic flow based on shortcut entries in its cache.

  This type of MLS also is known by the names *Netflow LAN switching*, *flow-based* or *demand-based switching*, and "*route once, switch many*." Even if this isn't used to forward packets in Cisco IOS–based Catalyst switches, the technique generates traffic flow information and statistics.

Key Topic

- **Topology-based**—The second generation of MLS, utilizing specialized hardware. Layer 3 routing information builds and prepopulates a single database of the entire network topology. This database, an efficient table lookup in hardware, is consulted so that packets can be forwarded at high rates. The longest match found in the database is used as the correct Layer 3 destination. As the routing topology changes over time, the database contained in the hardware can be updated dynamically with no performance penalty.

This type of MLS is known as *Cisco Express Forwarding (CEF)*. A routing process running on the switch downloads the current routing table database into the *Forwarding Information Base (FIB)* area of hardware. CEF is discussed in greater detail in Chapter 11, "Multilayer Switching."

Follow That Packet!

The path that a Layer 3 packet follows through a multilayer switch is similar to that of a Layer 2 switch. Obviously, some means of making a Layer 3 forwarding decision must be added. Beyond that, several, sometimes unexpected, things can happen to packets as they are forwarded. Figure 2-4 shows a typical multilayer switch and the decision processes that must occur. Packets arriving on a switch port are placed in the appropriate ingress queue, just as in a Layer 2 switch.

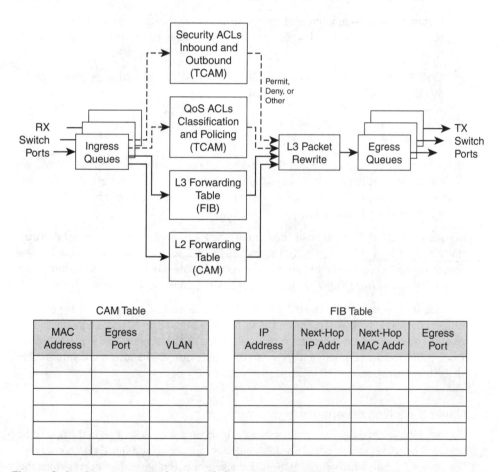

Figure 2-4 *Operations Within a Multilayer Catalyst Switch*

Each packet is pulled off an ingress queue and inspected for both Layer 2 and Layer 3 destination addresses. Now, the decision of *where* to forward the packet is based on two address tables, whereas the decision of *how* to forward the packet still is based on access list

results. As in Layer 2 switching, all these multilayer decisions are performed simultaneously in hardware:

- **L2 forwarding table**—The destination MAC address is used as an index to the
  CAM table. If the frame contains a Layer 3 packet to be forwarded, the destination
  MAC address is that of a Layer 3 port on the switch. In this case, the CAM table
  results are used only to decide that the frame should be processed at Layer 3.

- **L3 forwarding table**—The FIB table is consulted, using the destination IP address
  as an index. The longest match in the table is found (both address and mask), and the
  resulting next-hop Layer 3 address is obtained. The FIB also contains each next-hop
  entry's Layer 2 MAC address and the egress switch port (and VLAN ID) so that
  further table lookups are not necessary.

- **Security ACLs**—Inbound and outbound access lists are compiled into TCAM
  entries so that decisions of whether to forward a packet can be determined as a single
  table lookup.

- **QoS ACLs**—Packet classification, policing, and marking all can be performed as
  single table lookups in the QoS TCAM.

As with Layer 2 switching, the packet finally must be placed in the appropriate egress
queue on the appropriate egress switch port.

However, recall that during the multilayer switching process, the next-hop destination was
obtained from the FIB table, just as a router would do. The Layer 3 address identified the
next hop and found its Layer 2 address. Only the Layer 2 address would be used, so the
Layer 2 frames could be sent on.

The next-hop Layer 2 address must be put into the frame in place of the original destination address (the multilayer switch). The frame's Layer 2 source address also must become
that of the multilayer switch before it is sent on to the next hop. As any good router must
do, the Time-To-Live (TTL) value in the Layer 3 packet must be decremented by one.

Because the contents of the Layer 3 packet (the TTL value) have changed, the Layer 3
header checksum must be recalculated. And because both Layers 2 and 3 contents have
changed, the Layer 2 checksum must be recalculated. In other words, the entire Ethernet
frame must be rewritten before it goes into the egress queue. This also is accomplished efficiently in hardware.

Multilayer Switching Exceptions

To forward packets using the simultaneous decision processes described in the preceding
section, the packet must be "MLS-ready" and must require no additional decisions. For
example, CEF can directly forward most IP packets between hosts. This occurs when the
source and destination addresses (both MAC and IP) are known already and no other IP
parameters must be manipulated.

Other packets cannot be directly forwarded by CEF and must be handled in more detail.
This is done by a quick inspection during the forwarding decisions. If a packet meets cri-

teria such as the following, it is flagged for further processing and sent or "punted" to the switch CPU for *process switching*:

- ARP requests and replies

- IP packets requiring a response from a router (TTL has expired, MTU is exceeded, fragmentation is needed, and so on)

- IP broadcasts that will be relayed as unicast (DHCP requests, IP helper-address functions)

- Routing protocol updates

- Cisco Discovery Protocol packets

- IPX routing protocol and service advertisements

- Packets needing encryption

- Packets triggering Network Address Translation (NAT)

- Other non-IP and non-IPX protocol packets (AppleTalk, DECnet, and so on)

Tables Used in Switching

Catalyst switches maintain several types of tables to be used in the switching process. The tables are tailored for Layer 2 switching or MLS and are kept in very fast memory so that many fields within a frame or packet can be compared in parallel.

Content-Addressable Memory

All Catalyst switch models use a CAM table for Layer 2 switching. As frames arrive on switch ports, the source MAC addresses are learned and recorded in the CAM table. The port of arrival and the VLAN both are recorded in the table, along with a time stamp. If a MAC address learned on one switch port has moved to a different port, the MAC address and time stamp are recorded for the most recent arrival port. Then, the previous entry is deleted. If a MAC address is found already present in the table for the correct arrival port, only its time stamp is updated.

Switches generally have large CAM tables so that many addresses can be looked up for frame forwarding. However, there is not enough table space to hold every possible address on large networks. To manage the CAM table space, *stale entries* (addresses that have not been heard from for a period of time) are aged out. By default, idle CAM table entries are kept for 300 seconds before they are deleted. You can change the default setting using the following configuration command:

```
Switch(config)# mac address-table aging-time seconds
```

By default, MAC addresses are learned dynamically from incoming frames. You also can configure static CAM table entries that contain MAC addresses that might not be learned otherwise. To do this, use the following configuration command:

```
Switch(config)# mac address-table static mac-address vlan vlan-id interface type
    mod/num
```

Here, the MAC address (in dotted triplet hex format) is identified with the VLAN and the switch interface where it appears.

Note: You should be aware that there is a slight discrepancy in the CAM table command syntax. Until Catalyst IOS version 12.1(11)EA1, the syntax for CAM table commands used the keywords **mac-address-table**. In more recent Cisco IOS versions, the syntax has changed to use the keywords **mac address-table** (first hyphen omitted). The Catalyst 4500 and 6500 IOS Software are exceptions, however, and continue to use the **mac-address-table** keyword form. Many switch platforms support either syntax to ease the transition.

Exactly what happens when a host's MAC address is learned on one switch port, and then the host moves so that it appears on a different switch port? Ordinarily, the host's original CAM table entry would have to age out after 300 seconds, while its address was learned on the new port. To avoid having duplicate CAM table entries, a switch purges any existing entries for a MAC address that has just been learned on a different switch port. This is a safe assumption because MAC addresses are unique, and a single host should never be seen on more than one switch port unless problems exist in the network. If a switch notices that a MAC address is being learned on alternating switch ports, it generates an error message that flags the MAC address as "flapping" between interfaces.

Ternary Content-Addressable Memory

In traditional routing, ACLs can match, filter, or control specific traffic. Access lists are made up of one or more access control entities (ACE) or matching statements that are evaluated in sequential order. Evaluating an access list can take up additional time, adding to the latency of forwarding packets.

In multilayer switches, however, all the matching process that ACLs provide is implemented in hardware. TCAM allows a packet to be evaluated against an entire access list in a single table lookup. Most switches have multiple TCAMs so that both inbound and outbound security and QoS ACLs can be evaluated simultaneously, or entirely in parallel with a Layer 2 or Layer 3 forwarding decision.

The Catalyst IOS Software has two components that are part of the TCAM operation:

- **Feature Manager (FM)**—After an access list has been created or configured, the Feature Manager software compiles, or merges, the ACEs into entries in the TCAM table. The TCAM then can be consulted at full frame-forwarding speed.

- **Switching Database Manager (SDM)**—You can partition the TCAM on some Catalyst switches into areas for different functions. The SDM software configures or tunes the TCAM partitions, if needed. (The TCAM is fixed on Catalyst 4500 and 6500 platforms and cannot be repartitioned.)

TCAM Structure

The TCAM is an extension of the CAM table concept. Recall that a CAM table takes in an index or key value (usually a MAC address) and looks up the resulting value (usually a switch port or VLAN ID). Table lookup is fast and always based on an exact key match consisting of two input values: 0 and 1 bits.

TCAM also uses a table-lookup operation but is greatly enhanced to allow a more abstract operation. For example, binary values (0s and 1s) make up a key into the table, but a mask value also is used to decide which bits of the key are actually relevant. This effectively makes a key consisting of three input values: 0, 1, and X (don't care) bit values—a three-fold or *ternary* combination.

TCAM entries are composed of Value, Mask, and Result (VMR) combinations. Fields from frame or packet headers are fed into the TCAM, where they are matched against the value and mask pairs to yield a result. As a quick reference, these can be described as follows:

■ **Values** are always 134-bit quantities, consisting of source and destination addresses and other relevant protocol information—all patterns to be matched. The information concatenated to form the value depends on the type of access list, as shown in Table 2-2. Values in the TCAM come directly from any address, port, or other protocol information given in an ACE.

Table 2-2 *TCAM Value Pattern Components*

Access List Type	Value and Mask Components, 134 Bits Wide (Number of Bits)
Ethernet	Source MAC (48), destination MAC (48), Ethertype (16)
ICMP	Source IP (32), destination IP (32), protocol (16), ICMP code (8), ICMP type (4), IP type of service (ToS) (8)
Extended IP using TCP/UDP	Source IP (32), destination IP (32), protocol (16), IP ToS (8), source port (16), source operator (4), destination port (16), destination operator (4)
Other IP	Source IP (32), destination IP (32), protocol (16), IP ToS (8)
IGMP	Source IP (32), destination IP (32), protocol (16), IP ToS (8), IGMP message type (8)
IPX	Source IPX network (32), destination IPX network (32), destination node (48), IPX packet type (16)

■ **Masks** are also 134-bit quantities, in exactly the same format, or bit order, as the values. Masks select only the value bits of interest; a mask bit is set to exactly match a value bit or is not set for value bits that do not matter. The masks used in the TCAM stem from address or bit masks in ACEs.

■ **Results** are numeric values that represent what action to take after the TCAM lookup occurs. Whereas traditional access lists offer only a *permit* or *deny* result, TCAM lookups offer a number of possible results or actions. For example, the result can be a permit or deny decision, an index value to a QoS policer, a pointer to a next-hop routing table, and so on.

The TCAM always is organized by masks, where each unique mask has eight value patterns associated with it. For example, the Catalyst 6500 TCAM (one for security ACLs

Key
Topic

and one for QoS ACLs) holds up to 4096 masks and 32,768 value patterns. The trick is that each of the mask-value pairs is evaluated *simultaneously*, or in parallel, revealing the best or longest match in a single table lookup.

TCAM Example

Figure 2-5 shows how the TCAM is built and used. This is a simple example and might or might not be identical to the results that the Feature Manager produces because the ACEs might need to be optimized or rewritten to achieve certain TCAM algorithm requirements.

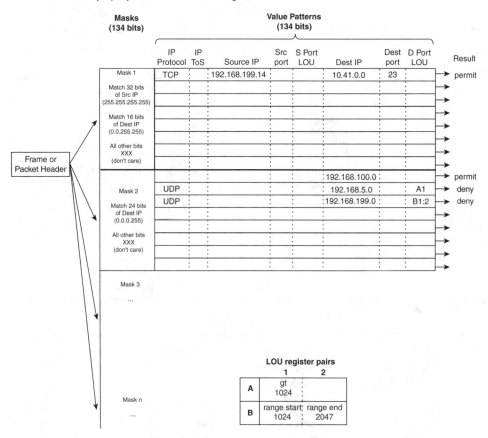

```
access-list 100 permit tcp host 192.168.199.14 10.41.0.0 0.0.255.255 eq telnet
access-list 100 permit ip any 192.168.100.0 0.0.0.255
access-list 100 deny udp any 192.168.5.0 0.0.0.255 gt 1024
access-list 100 deny udp any 192.168.199.0 0.0.0.255 range 1024 2047
```

Figure 2-5   *How an Access List Is Merged into TCAM*

The sample access list 100 (extended IP) is configured and merged into TCAM entries. First, the mask values must be identified in the access list. When an address value and a corresponding address mask are specified in an ACE, those mask bits must be set for matching. All other mask bits can remain in the "don't care" state. The access list contains only three unique masks: one that matches all 32 bits of the source IP address (found with an address mask of 0.0.0.0 or the keyword **host**), one that matches 16 bits of the destination address (found with an address mask of 0.0.255.255), and one that matches only 24 bits of the destination address (found with an address mask of 0.0.0.255). The keyword **any** in the ACEs means "match anything" or "don't care."

The unique masks are placed into the TCAM. Then, for each mask, all possible value patterns are identified. For example, a 32-bit source IP mask (Mask 1) can be found only in ACEs with a source IP address of 192.168.199.14 and a destination of 10.41.0.0. (The rest of Mask 1 is the destination address mask 0.0.255.255.) Those address values are placed into the first value pattern slot associated with Mask 1. Mask 2 has three value patterns: destination addresses 192.168.100.0, 192.168.5.0, and 192.168.199.0. Each of these is placed in the three pattern positions of Mask 2. This process continues until all ACEs have been merged.

When a mask's eighth pattern position has been filled, the next pattern with the same mask must be placed under a new mask. A bit of a balancing act occurs to try to fit all ACEs into the available mask and pattern entries without an overflow.

Port Operations in TCAM

You might have noticed that matching strictly based on values and masks covers only ACE statements that involve exact matches (either the **eq** port operation keyword or no Layer 4 port operations). For example, ACEs such as the following involve specific address values, address masks, and port numbers:

```
access-list test permit ip 192.168.254.0 0.0.0.255 any
access-list test permit tcp any host 192.168.199.10 eq www
```

What about ACEs that use port operators, where a comparison must be made? Consider the following:

```
access-list test permit udp any host 192.168.199.50 gt 1024
access-list test permit tcp any any range 2000 2002
```

A simple logical operation between a mask and a pattern cannot generate the desired result. The TCAM also provides a mechanism for performing a Layer 4 operation or comparison, also done during the single table lookup. If an ACE has a port operator, such as **gt**, **lt**, **neq**, or **range**, the Feature Manager software compiles the TCAM entry to include the use of the operator and the operand in a logical operation unit (LOU) register. Only a limited number of LOUs are available in the TCAM. If there are more ACEs with comparison operators than there are LOUs, the Feature Manager must break up the ACEs into multiple ACEs with only regular matching (using the **eq** operator).

In Figure 2-5, two ACEs require a Layer 4 operation:

- One that checks for UDP destination ports greater than 1024

- One that looks for the UDP destination port range 1024 to 2047

The Feature Manager checks all ACEs for Layer 4 operation and places these into LOU register pairs. These can be loaded with operations, independent of any other ACE parameters. The LOU contents can be reused if other ACEs need the same comparisons and values. After the LOUs are loaded, they are referenced in the TCAM entries that need them. This is shown by LOUs A1 and the B1:2 pair. A finite number (actually, a rather small number) of LOUs are available in the TCAM, so the Feature Manager software must use them carefully.

Monitoring Switching Tables

You can display or query the switching tables to verify the information that the switch has learned. As well, you might want to check the tables to find out on which switch port a specific MAC address has been learned.

CAM Table Operation

To view the contents of the CAM table, you can use the following form of the **show mac address-table** EXEC command:

```
Switch# show mac address-table dynamic [address mac-address | interface type
    mod/num | vlan vlan-id]
```

The entries that have been learned dynamically will be shown. You can add the **address** keyword to specify a single MAC address, or the **interface** or **vlan** keyword to see addresses that have been learned on a specific interface or VLAN.

For example, assume that you need to find the learned location of the host with MAC address 0050.8b11.54da. The **show mac address-table dynamic address 0050.8b11.54da** command might produce the output in Example 2-1.

Example 2-1 *Determining Host Location by MAC Address*

```
Switch# show mac address-table dynamic address 0050.8b11.54da
          Mac Address Table
-------------------------------------------------

Vlan     Mac Address       Type        Ports
----     -----------       ----        -----
  54     0050.8b11.54da    DYNAMIC     Fa1/0/1
Total Mac Addresses for this criterion: 1
Switch#
```

From this, you can see that the host somehow is connected to interface Fast Ethernet 1/0/1, on VLAN 54.

Tip: If your Catalyst IOS switch is not accepting commands of the form **mac address-table**, try adding a hyphen between the keywords. For example, the Catalyst 4500 and 6500 most likely will accept **show mac-address-table** instead.

Suppose that this same command produced no output, showing nothing about the interface and VLAN where the MAC address is found. What might that mean? Either the host has not sent a frame that the switch can use for learning its location, or something odd is going on. Perhaps the host is using two network interface cards (NIC) to load balance traffic; one NIC is only receiving traffic, whereas the other is only sending. Therefore, the switch never hears and learns the receiving-only NIC address.

To see all the MAC addresses that are currently found on interface GigabitEthernet1/0/29, you could use the **show mac address-table dynamic interface gig1/0/29** command. The output shown in Example 2-2 indicates that only one host has been learned on the interface. Perhaps only a single PC connects to that interface.

Example 2-2 *Determining Hosts Active on an Interface*

```
Switch# show mac address-table dynamic interface gigabitethernet1/0/29
          Mac Address Table
-------------------------------------------------

Vlan     Mac Address       Type        Ports
----     -----------       ----        -----
 537     0013.7297.3d4b    DYNAMIC     Gi1/0/29
Total Mac Addresses for this criterion: 1
Switch#
```

However, suppose the same command is used to check interface GigabitEthernet1/0/49. The output shown in Example 2-3 lists many MAC addresses—all found on a single interface. How can so many addresses be learned on one switch interface? This interface must lead to another switch or another part of the network where other devices are located.

Example 2-3 *Finding Many Hosts on an Interface*

```
Switch# show mac address-table dynamic interface gig1/0/49
          Mac Address Table
-------------------------------------------------

Vlan     Mac Address       Type        Ports
----     -----------       ----        -----
 580     0000.0c07.ac01    DYNAMIC     Gi1/0/49
 580     0007.0e0b.f918    DYNAMIC     Gi1/0/49
 580     000f.1f78.1094    DYNAMIC     Gi1/0/49
 580     0011.43ac.b083    DYNAMIC     Gi1/0/49
 580     0011.bb2d.3f6e    DYNAMIC     Gi1/0/49
 580     0014.6a86.1f1e    DYNAMIC     Gi1/0/49
 580     0014.6a86.1f3d    DYNAMIC     Gi1/0/49
 580     0014.6a86.1f3f    DYNAMIC     Gi1/0/49
 580     0014.6a86.1f47    DYNAMIC     Gi1/0/49
—More—
```

To see the CAM table's size, use the **show mac address-table count** command, as shown in Example 2-4. MAC address totals are shown for each active VLAN on the switch. This can give you a good idea of the size of the CAM table and how many hosts are using the network.

Example 2-4   *Checking the Size of the CAM Table*

```
Switch# show mac address-table count
Mac Entries for Vlan 1:
---------------------------
Dynamic Address Count  : 0
Static  Address Count  : 0
Total Mac Addresses    : 0

Mac Entries for Vlan 2:
---------------------------
Dynamic Address Count  : 89
Static  Address Count  : 0
Total Mac Addresses    : 89

Mac Entries for Vlan 580:
---------------------------
Dynamic Address Count  : 600
Static  Address Count  : 0
Total Mac Addresses    : 600

Total Mac Address Space Available: 4810
Switch#
```

CAM table entries can be cleared manually, if needed, by using the following EXEC command:

```
Switch# clear mac address-table dynamic [address mac-address | interface type
  mod/num | vlan vlan-id]
```

Tip: Frequently, you need to know where a user with a certain MAC address is connected. In a large network, discerning at which switch and switch port a MAC address can be found might be difficult. Start at the network's center, or core, and display the CAM table entry for the MAC address. Look at the switch port shown in the entry and find the neighboring switch connected to that port using CDP neighbor information. Then move to that switch and repeat the CAM table process. Keep moving from switch to switch until you reach the edge of the network where the MAC address connects.

TCAM Operation

The TCAM in a switch is more or less self-sufficient. Access lists are compiled or merged automatically into the TCAM, so there is nothing to configure. The only concept you need to be aware of is how the TCAM resources are being used.

TCAMs have a limited number of usable mask, value pattern, and LOU entries. If access lists grow to be large or many Layer 4 operations are needed, the TCAM tables and registers can overflow. If that happens while you are configuring an ACL, the switch will generate syslog messages that flag the TCAM overflow situation as it tries to compile the ACL into TCAM entries.

Exam Preparation Tasks

Review All Key Topics

Review the most important topics in the chapter, noted with the Key Topic icon in the outer margin of the page. Table 2-3 lists a reference of these key topics and the page numbers on which each is found.

Table 2-3   *Key Topics for Chapter 2*

Key Topic Element	Description	Page Number
Paragraph	Discusses collision domain	22
Paragraph	Discusses flooding and unknown unicast flooding	24
List	Describes topology-based switching	26
Paragraph	Discusses the CAM table	29
Paragraph	Explains TCAM operation	31

Define Key Terms

Define the following key terms from this chapter, and check your answers in the glossary:

collision domain, flooding, unknown unicast flooding, CEF, FIB, CAM, TCAM

Use Command Reference to Check Your Memory

This section includes the most important configuration and EXEC commands covered in this chapter. It might not be necessary to memorize the complete syntax of every command, but you should remember the basic keywords that are needed.

To test your memory of the CAM-related commands, cover the right side of Table 2-4 with a piece of paper, read the description on the left side, and then see how much of the command you can remember.

Remember that the CCNP exam focuses on practical or hands-on skills that are used by a networking professional. For the skills covered in this chapter, remember that the commands always involve the keywords **mac address-table**.

Table 2-4 *Commands Used to Monitor and Manipulate the CAM Table*

Function	Command
Find the location of a specific MAC address.	**show mac address-table dynamic address** *mac-address*
Display all MAC addresses learned on a specific interface.	**show mac address-table dynamic interface** *type number*
Display the current CAM table size.	**show mac address-table count**
Enter a static CAM table entry.	**mac address-table static** *mac-address* **vlan** *vlan-id* **interface** *type number*
Clear a CAM entry.	**clear mac address-table dynamic [address** *mac-address* **| interface** *type number* **| vlan** *vlan-id*]

This chapter covers the following topics that you need to master for the CCNP SWITCH exam:

Ethernet Concepts—This section discusses the concepts and technology behind various forms of Ethernet media.

Connecting Switches and Devices—This section discusses the physical cabling and connectivity used with Catalyst switches.

Switch Port Configuration—This section covers the configuration steps and commands needed to use Catalyst Ethernet, Fast Ethernet, and Gigabit and 10-Gigabit Ethernet switch ports in a network.

Switch Port Configuration

This chapter presents the various Ethernet network technologies used to establish switched connections within the campus network. You can connect a switch to an end device such as a PC or to another switch. The chapter also details the switch commands required for configuring and troubleshooting Ethernet LAN ports.

"Do I Know This Already?" Quiz

The "Do I Know This Already?" quiz allows you to assess whether you should read this entire chapter thoroughly or jump to the "Exam Preparation Tasks" section. If you are in doubt based on your answers to these questions or your own assessment of your knowledge of the topics, read the entire chapter. Table 3-1 outlines the major headings in this chapter and the "Do I Know This Already?" quiz questions that go with them. You can find the answers in Appendix A, "Answers to the 'Do I Know This Already?' Quizzes."

Table 3-1 *"Do I Know This Already?" Foundation Topics Section-to-Question Mapping*

Foundation Topics Section	Questions Covered in This Section
Ethernet Concepts	1–6
Connecting Switches and Devices	7–8
Switch Port Configuration	9–11

1. What does the IEEE 802.3 standard define?

    a. Spanning Tree Protocol

    b. Token Ring

    c. Ethernet

    d. Switched Ethernet

2. At what layer are traditional 10-Mbps Ethernet, Fast Ethernet, and Gigabit Ethernet the same?

    a. Layer 1

    b. Layer 2

    c. Layer 3

    d. Layer 4

3. At what layer are traditional 10-Mbps Ethernet, Fast Ethernet, and Gigabit Ethernet different?

    a. Layer 1

    b. Layer 2

    c. Layer 3

    d. Layer 4

4. What is the maximum cable distance for a Category 5 100BASE-TX connection?

    a. 100 feet

    b. 100 m

    c. 328 m

    d. 500 m

5. Ethernet autonegotiation determines which of the following?

    a. Spanning-tree mode

    b. Duplex mode

    c. Quality of service mode

    d. Error threshold

6. Which of the following cannot be automatically determined and set if the far end of a connection doesn't support autonegotiation?

    a. Link speed

    b. Link duplex mode

    c. Link media type

    d. MAC address

7. Which of these is not a standard type of gigabit interface converter (GBIC) or small form factor pluggable (SFP) module?

    a. 1000BASE-LX/LH

    b. 1000BASE-T

    c. 1000BASE-FX

    d. 1000BASE-ZX

8. What type of cable should you use to connect two switches back to back using their Fast Ethernet 10/100 ports?

    a. Rollover cable

    b. Transfer cable

    c. Crossover cable

    d. Straight-through cable

9. Assume that you have just entered the **configure terminal** command. To configure the speed of the first Fast Ethernet interface on Cisco Catalyst switch module number one to 100 Mbps, which one of these commands should you enter first?

   a. speed 100 mbps

   b. speed 100

   c. interface fastethernet 1/0/1

   d. interface fast ethernet 1/0/1

10. If a switch port is in the errdisable state, what is the first thing you should do?

    a. Reload the switch.

    b. Use the **clear errdisable port** command.

    c. Use the **shut** and **no shut** interface-configuration commands.

    d. Determine the cause of the problem.

11. Which of the following **show interface** output information can you use to diagnose a switch port problem?

    a. Port state.

    b. Port speed.

    c. Input errors.

    d. Collisions.

    e. All these answers are correct.

Foundation Topics

Ethernet Concepts

This section reviews the varieties of Ethernet and their application in a campus network. The bandwidth requirements for a network segment are determined by the types of applications in use, the traffic flows within the network, and the size of the user community served. Ethernet scales to support increasing bandwidths; the Ethernet medium should be chosen to match the need at each point in the campus network. As network bandwidth requirements grow, you can scale the links between access, distribution, and core layers to match the load.

Other network media technologies available include Fiber Distribution Data Interface (FDDI), Copper Distribution Data Interface (CDDI), Token Ring, and Asynchronous Transfer Mode (ATM). Although some networks still use these media, Ethernet has emerged as the most popular choice in installed networks. Ethernet is chosen because of its low cost, market availability, and scalability to higher bandwidths.

Ethernet (10 Mbps)

Ethernet is a LAN technology based on the Institute of Electrical and Electronics Engineers (IEEE) 802.3 standard. Ethernet (in contrast to Fast Ethernet and later versions) offers a bandwidth of 10 Mbps between end users. In its most basic form, Ethernet is a shared medium that becomes both a collision and a broadcast domain. As the number of users on the shared media increases, so does the probability that a user is trying to transmit data at any given time. When one user transmits at about the same time as another, a *collision* occurs. In other words, both users can't transmit data at the same time if they both are sharing the same network media.

Ethernet is based on the *carrier sense multiple access collision detect (CSMA/CD)* technology, which requires that transmitting stations back off for a random period of time when a collision occurs. If a station must wait its turn to transmit, it cannot transmit and receive at the same time. This is called *half-duplex* operation.

The more crowded an Ethernet segment becomes, the number of stations likely to be transmitting at a given time increases. Imagine standing in a crowded room trying to tell a story. Instead of attempting to talk over the crowd, you stop and politely wait while other people talk. The more people there are in the room, the more difficult talking becomes. Likewise, as an Ethernet segment becomes more crowded, it becomes more inefficient.

Key Topic

Ethernet switching addresses this problem by dynamically allocating a dedicated 10-Mbps bandwidth to each of its ports. The resulting increased network performance occurs by reducing the number of users connected to an Ethernet segment. In effect, collisions are less probable and the collision domain is reduced in size.

Although switched Ethernet's job is to offer fully dedicated bandwidth to each connected device, assuming that network performance will improve across the board when switching is introduced is a common mistake. For example, consider a workgroup of users connected by a shared-media Ethernet hub. These users regularly access an enterprise server located elsewhere in the campus network. To improve performance, the decision is made to replace the hub with an Ethernet switch so that all users get dedicated 10-Mbps connections. Because the switch offers dedicated bandwidth for connections between the end-user devices connected to its ports, any user-to-user traffic probably would see improved performance. However, the enterprise server still is located elsewhere in the network, and all the switched users still must share available bandwidth across the campus to reach it. As discussed earlier in the book, instead of throwing raw bandwidth at a problem, a design based on careful observation of traffic patterns and flows offers a better solution.

Because switched Ethernet can remove the possibility of collisions, stations do not have to listen to each other to take a turn transmitting on the wire. Instead, stations can operate in *full-duplex* mode—transmitting and receiving simultaneously. Full-duplex mode further increases network performance, with a net throughput of 10 Mbps in each direction, or 20 Mbps total throughput on each port.

Another consideration when dealing with 10-Mbps Ethernet is the physical cabling. Ethernet cabling involves the use of unshielded twisted-pair (UTP) wiring (10BASE-T Ethernet), usually restricted to an end-to-end distance of 100 meters (328 feet) between active devices. Keeping cable lengths as short as possible in the wiring closet also reduces noise and crosstalk when many cables are bundled together.

In a campus network environment, Ethernet can be found in the access layer, between end user devices and the access-layer switch. However, in modern networks, faster generations of Ethernet are usually used in the access layer. Ethernet typically is not used at either the distribution or the core layer due to its relatively low bandwidth capacity.

Note: Ethernet applications (10BASE2, 10BASE5, 10BASE-F, and so on) use other cabling technologies, although they are not discussed here. For the most part, 10BASE-T with UTP wiring is the most commonly used. A useful website for further reading about Ethernet technology is Charles Spurgeon's Ethernet Web Site, at www.ethermanage.com/ethernet/.

Fast Ethernet

Instead of requiring campuses to invest in a completely new technology to gain increased bandwidth, the networking industry developed a higher-speed Ethernet based on existing Ethernet standards. Fast Ethernet operates at 100 Mbps and is defined in the IEEE 802.3u standard. The Ethernet cabling schemes, CSMA/CD operation, and all upper-layer protocol operations are maintained with Fast Ethernet. The net result is the same data link Media Access Control (MAC) layer (OSI Layer 2) merged with a new physical layer (OSI Layer 1).

The campus network can use Fast Ethernet to link access- and distribution-layer switches, if no higher-speed links are available. These links can support the aggregate traffic from multiple Ethernet segments in the access layer. Fast Ethernet generally is used to connect end user workstations to the access-layer switch and to provide improved connectivity to enterprise servers.

Cabling for Fast Ethernet can involve either UTP or fiber. Table 3-2 lists the specifications for Fast Ethernet that define the media types and distances.

Table 3-2   *Cabling Specifications for Fast Ethernet*

Technology	Wiring Type	Pairs	Cable Length
100BASE-TX	EIA/TIA Category 5 UTP	2	100 m
100BASE-T2	EIA/TIA Category 3, 4, 5 UTP	2	100 m
100BASE-T4	EIA/TIA Category 3, 4, 5 UTP	4	100 m
100BASE-FX	Multimode fiber (MMF); 62.5-micron core, 125-micron outer cladding (62.5/125)	1	400 m half duplex or 2000 m full duplex
	Single-mode fiber (SMF)	1	10 km

Full-Duplex Fast Ethernet

As with traditional Ethernet, the natural progression to improve performance is to use full-duplex operation. Fast Ethernet can provide up to 100 Mbps in each direction on a switched connection, for 200 Mbps total throughput.

This maximum throughput is possible only when one device (a workstation, server, router, or another switch) is connected directly to a switch port. In addition, the devices at each end of the link must both support full-duplex operation, allowing each to transmit at will without having to detect and recover from collisions.

The Fast Ethernet specification also offers backward compatibility to support traditional 10-Mbps Ethernet. In the case of 100BASE-TX, switch ports often are called "10/100" ports, to denote the dual speed. To provide this support, the two devices at each end of a network connection automatically can negotiate link capabilities so that they both can operate at a maximum common level. This negotiation involves detecting and selecting the highest physical layer technology (available bandwidth) and half-duplex or full-duplex operation. To properly negotiate a connection, *both* ends should be configured for autonegotiation.

The link speed is determined by electrical signaling so that either end of a link can determine what speed the other end is trying to use. If both ends of the link are configured to autonegotiate, they will use the highest speed that is common to them.

A link's duplex mode, however, is negotiated through an exchange of information. This means that for one end to successfully autonegotiate the duplex mode, the other end also must be set to autonegotiate. Otherwise, one end never will see duplex information from the other end and won't be capable of determining the correct mode to use. If duplex autonegotiation fails, a switch port always falls back to its default setting: half-duplex.

Caution: Beware of a duplex mismatch when both ends of a link are not set for autonegotiation. During a mismatch, one end uses full duplex while the other end uses half duplex. The result is that the half-duplex station will detect a collision when both ends transmit; it will back off appropriately. The full-duplex station, however, will assume that it has the right to transmit at any time. It will not stop and wait for any reason. This can cause errors on the link and poor response times between the stations.

Autonegotiation uses the priorities shown in Table 3-3 for each mode of Ethernet to determine which technology to agree on. If both devices can support more than one technology, the technology with the highest priority is used. For example, if two devices can support both 10BASE-T and 100BASE-TX, both devices will use the higher-priority 100BASE-TX mode.

Table 3-3 *Autonegotiation Selection Priorities*

Priority	Ethernet Mode
7	100BASE-T2 (full duplex)
6	100BASE-TX (full duplex)
5	100BASE-T2 (half duplex)
4	100BASE-T4
3	100BASE-TX
2	10BASE-T (full duplex)
1	10BASE-T

To ensure proper configuration at both ends of a link, Cisco recommends that the appropriate values for transmission speed and duplex mode be configured manually on switch ports. This precludes any possibility that one end of the link will change its settings, resulting in an unusable connection. If you manually set the switch port, don't forget to manually set the device on the other end of the link accordingly. Otherwise, a speed or duplex mismatch between the two devices might occur.

Cisco provides one additional capability to Fast Ethernet, which allows several Fast Ethernet links to be bundled together for increased throughput. *Fast EtherChannel (FEC)* allows two to eight full-duplex Fast Ethernet links to act as a single physical link, for 400- to 1600-Mbps duplex bandwidth. This technology is described in greater detail in Chapter 6, "Aggregating Switch Links."

Gigabit Ethernet

You can scale Fast Ethernet by an additional order of magnitude with Gigabit Ethernet (which supports 1000 Mbps or 1 Gbps) using the same IEEE 802.3 Ethernet frame format as before. This scalability allows network designers and managers to leverage existing knowledge and technologies to install, migrate, manage, and maintain Gigabit Ethernet networks.

However, the physical layer has been modified to increase data-transmission speeds. Two technologies were merged to gain the benefits of each: the IEEE 802.3 Ethernet standard and the American National Standards Institute (ANSI) X3T11 FibreChannel. IEEE 802.3 provided the foundation of frame format, CSMA/CD, full duplex, and other Ethernet characteristics. FibreChannel provided a base of high-speed ASICs, optical components, and encoding/decoding and serialization mechanisms. The resulting protocol is termed IEEE 802.3z Gigabit Ethernet.

Gigabit Ethernet supports several cabling types, referred to as *1000BASE-X*. Table 3-4 lists the cabling specifications for each type.

Table 3-4   *Gigabit Ethernet Cabling and Distance Limitations*

GE Type	Wiring Type	Pairs	Cable Length
1000BASE-CX	Shielded twisted pair (STP)	1	25 m
1000BASE-T	EIA/TIA Category 5 UTP	4	100 m
1000BASE-SX	Multimode fiber (MMF) with 62.5-micron core; 850-nm laser	1	275 m
	MMF with 50-micron core; 850-nm laser	1	550 m
1000BASE-LX/LH	MMF with 62.5-micron core; 1300-nm laser	1	550 m
	MMF with 50-micron core; 1300-nm laser	1	550 m
	SMF with 9-micron core; 1300-nm laser	1	10 km
1000BASE-ZX	SMF with 9-micron core; 1550-nm laser	1	70 km
	SMF with 8-micron core; 1550-nm laser	1	100 km

In a campus network, you can use Gigabit Ethernet to connect individual devices to a switch or to connect two switches together.

The "Gigabit over copper" solution that the 1000BASE-T media provides is based on the IEEE 802.3ab standard. Most Gigabit Ethernet switch ports used between switches are fixed at 1000 Mbps. However, other switch ports can support a fallback to Fast or Legacy Ethernet speeds. Here, speed can be autonegotiated between end nodes to the highest common speed—10 Mbps, 100 Mbps, or 1000 Mbps. These ports are often called 10/100/1000 ports to denote the triple speed. Here, the autonegotiation supports the same priority scheme as Fast Ethernet, although 1000BASE-T full duplex becomes the highest priority, followed by 1000BASE-T half duplex. Gigabit Ethernet's port duplex mode always is set to full duplex on Cisco switches, so duplex autonegotiation is not possible.

Finally, Cisco has extended the concept of Fast EtherChannel to bundle several Gigabit Ethernet links to act as a single physical connection. With *Gigabit EtherChannel (GEC)*, two to eight full-duplex Gigabit Ethernet connections can be aggregated, for a single logical link of up to 16-Gbps throughput. Port aggregation and the EtherChannel technology are described further in Chapter 6.

Note: The 10-Gigabit Ethernet Alliance offers further reading about Gigabit Ethernet and its operation, migration, and standards. Refer to the "Archive White Papers" section on its website at http://www.10gea.org.

10-Gigabit Ethernet

Ethernet scales by orders of magnitude, beginning with 10 Mbps, progressing to 100 Mbps, and then to 1000 Mbps. To meet the demand for aggregating many Gigabit Ethernet links over a single connection, 10-Gigabit Ethernet was developed. Again, the Layer 2 characteristics of Ethernet have been preserved; the familiar 802.3 frame format and size, along with the MAC protocol, remain unchanged.

The 10-Gigabit Ethernet, also known as *10GbE*, and the IEEE 802.3ae standard differ from their predecessors only at the physical layer (PHY); 10GbE operates only at full duplex. The standard defines several different transceivers that can be used as Physical Media Dependent (PMD) interfaces. These are classified into the following:

- **LAN PHY**—Interconnects switches in a campus network, predominantly in the core layer

- **WAN PHY**—Interfaces with existing synchronous optical network (SONET) or synchronous digital hierarchy (SDH) networks typically found in metropolitan-area networks (MAN)

The PMD interfaces also have a common labeling scheme, much as Gigabit Ethernet does. Whereas Gigabit Ethernet uses 1000BASE-X to indicate the media type, 10-Gigabit Ethernet uses 10GBASE-X. Table 3-5 lists the different PMDs defined in the standard, along with the type of fiber and distance limitations. All the fiber-optic PMDs can be used as either a LAN or a WAN PHY, except for the 10GBASE-LX4, which is only a LAN PHY. Be aware that the long-wavelength PMDs carry a significantly greater expense than the others.

Table 3-5   *10-Gigabit Ethernet PMD Types and Characteristics*

PMD Type	Fiber Medium	Maximum Distance
10GBASE-SR/SW (850 nm serial)	MMF: 50 micron	66 m
	MMF: 50 micron (2GHz km modal bandwidth)	300 m
	MMF: 62.5 micron	33 m
10GBASE-LR/LW (1310 nm serial)	SMF: 9 micron	10 km
10GBASE-ER/EW (1550 nm serial)	SMF: 9 micron	40 km

continues

Table 3-5 *10-Gigabit Ethernet PMD Types and Characteristics (Continued)*

PMD Type	Fiber Medium	Maximum Distance
10GBASE-LX4/LW4 (1310 nm WWDM)	MMF: 50 micron	300 m
	MMF: 62.5 micron	300 m
	SMF: 9 micron	10 km
10GBASE-CX4	Copper: CX4 with Infiniband connectors	15 m

Transceiver types are denoted by a two-letter suffix. The first letter specifies the wavelength used: S = short, L = long, E = extra-long wavelength. The second letter specifies the PHY type: R = LAN PHY, W = WAN PHY. For LX4 and LW4, L refers to a long wavelength, X and W refer to the coding used, and 4 refers to the number of wavelengths transmitted. WWDM is wide-wavelength division multiplexing.

Cisco Catalyst switches supported 10-Gigabit Ethernet PMDs in the form of XENPAK, X2, and SFP+ transceivers. Generally, the X2 form factor is smaller than the XENPAK, and the SFP+ is smaller still, allowing more port density on a switch module.

For the most current switch compatibility listing, refer to the "Cisco 10-Gigabit Ethernet Transceiver Modules Compatibility Matrix" document at http://www.cisco.com/en/US/docs/interfaces_modules/transceiver_modules/compatibility/matrix/OL_6974.html.

Connecting Switches and Devices

Switch deployment in a network involves two steps: physical connectivity and switch configuration. This section describes the connections and cabling requirements for devices in a switched network.

Ethernet Port Cables and Connectors

Catalyst switches support a variety of network connections, including all forms of Ethernet. In addition, Catalyst switches support several types of cabling, including UTP and optical fiber.

Fast Ethernet (100BASE-FX) ports use two-strand multimode fiber (MMF) with MT-RJ or SC connectors to provide connectivity. The MT-RJ connectors are small and modular, each containing a pair of fiber-optic strands. The connector snaps into position, but you must press a tab to remove it. The SC connectors on the fiber cables are square in shape. These connectors snap in and out of the switch port connector as the connector is pushed in or pulled out. One fiber strand is used as a transmit path and the other as a receive path. The transmit fiber on one switch device should connect to the receive fiber on the other end.

All Catalyst switch families support 10/100 autosensing (using Fast Ethernet autonegotiation) and 10/100/1000 autosensing for Gigabit Ethernet. These ports use RJ-45 connectors on Category 5 UTP cabling to complete the connections. These ports can connect to other UTP-based Ethernet autosensing devices. UTP cabling is arranged so that RJ-45 pins 1,2 and 3,6 form two twisted pairs. These pairs connect straight through to the far end.

To connect two 10/100 switch ports back to back, as in an access-layer to distribution-layer link, you must use a Category 5 UTP crossover cable. In this case, RJ-45 pins 1,2 and 3,6 are still twisted pairs, but 1,2 on one end connects to 3,6 on the other end, and 3,6 on one end connects to 1,2 on the other end.

> **Note:**   Because UTP Ethernet connections use only pairs 1,2 and 3,6, some cable plant installers connect only these pairs and leave the remaining two pair positions empty. Although this move provides Ethernet connectivity, it is not good practice for future needs. Instead, all four RJ-45 connector pairs should be connected end to end. For example, a full four-pair UTP cable plant can be used for either Ethernet or Token Ring connectivity, without rewiring. (Token Ring UTP connections use pairs 3,6 and 4,5.)
> Also, to be compatible with the new IEEE 802.3ab standard for Gigabit Ethernet over copper (1000BASE-T), you must use all four pairs end to end.

Gigabit Ethernet Port Cables and Connectors

Gigabit Ethernet connections take a different approach by providing modular connectivity options. Catalyst switches with Gigabit Ethernet ports have standardized rectangular openings that can accept gigabit interface converter (GBIC) or small form factor pluggable (SFP) modules. The GBIC and SFP modules provide the media personality for the port so that various cable media can connect. In this way, the switch chassis is completely modular and requires no major change to accept a new media type. Instead, the appropriate module is hot-swappable and is plugged into the switch to support the new media. GBIC modules can use SC fiber-optic and RJ-45 UTP connectors. SFP modules can use LC and MT-RJ fiber-optic and RJ-45 UTP connectors. GBIC and SFP modules are available for the following Gigabit Ethernet media:

- **1000BASE-SX**—Short-wavelength connectivity using SC fiber connectors and MMF for distances up to 550 m (1804 feet).

- **1000BASE-LX/LH**—Long-wavelength/long-haul connectivity using SC fiber connectors and either MMF or single-mode fiber (SMF); MMF can be used for distances up to 550 m (1804 feet), and SMF can be used for distances up to 10 km (32,810 feet). MMF requires a special mode-conditioning cable for fiber distances less than 100 m (328 feet) or greater than 300 m (984 feet). This keeps the GBIC from overdriving the far-end receiver on a short cable and lessens the effect of differential mode delay on a long cable.

- **1000BASE-ZX**—Extended-distance connectivity using SC fiber connectors and SMF; works for distances up to 70 km, and even to 100 km when used with premium-grade SMF.

- **GigaStack**—Uses a proprietary connector with a high-data-rate copper cable with enhanced signal integrity and electromagnetic interference (EMI) performance; provides a GBIC-to-GBIC connection between stacking Catalyst switches or between any two Gigabit switch ports over a short distance. The connection is full duplex if only one of the two stacking connectors is used; if both connectors are used, they each become half duplex over a shared bus.

■   **1000BASE-T**—Sports an RJ-45 connector for four-pair UTP cabling; works for distances up to 100 m (328 feet).

> **Note:**   You must use a four-pair Category 5 (or greater) UTP crossover cable to connect two 1000BASE-T switch ports back to back. In this case, RJ-45 pins 1,2, 3,6, 4,5, and 7,8 are still twisted pairs on one end, connecting to pins 3,6, 1,2, 7,8, and 4,5 respectively on the other end.

> **Caution:**   The fiber-based modules always have the receive fiber on the left connector and the transmit fiber on the right connector, as you face the connectors. These modules could produce invisible laser radiation from the transmit connector. Therefore, always keep unused connectors covered with the rubber plugs, and don't ever look directly into the connectors.

Switch Port Configuration

You can configure the individual ports on a switch with various information and settings, as detailed in the following sections.

Selecting Ports to Configure

Before you can modify port settings, you must select one or more switch ports. Even though they have traditionally been called *ports*, Catalyst switches running the Cisco IOS Software refer to them as *interfaces*.

To select a single switch port, enter the following command in global configuration mode:

```
Switch(config)# interface type module/number
```

The port is identified by its Ethernet type (**fastethernet, gigabitethernet, tengigabitethernet,** or **vlan**), the physical module or "blade" where it is located, and the port number within the module. Some switches, such as the Catalyst 2950 and 3560, do not have multiple modules. For those models, ports have a module number of 0 (zero). As an example, the Fast Ethernet 0/14 interface is selected for configuration using the following command:

```
Switch(config)# interface fastethernet 0/14
```

The Catalyst 3750 is also a fixed-configuration switch, but it can be stacked with other switches in the 3750 family. Interfaces are referenced by module and port number, where the module number represents the switch position in the stack. For example, port 24 on the switch at position 2 in the stack would be referenced as Fast Ethernet 2/0/24.

Naturally, you can select and configure multiple interfaces in this fashion, one at a time. If you need to make many configuration changes for each interface in a 48-port switch or module, however, this can get very tedious. The Catalyst IOS Software also allows multiple interfaces to be selected in a single pass through the **interface range** configuration command. After you select the range, any interface configuration commands entered are applied to each of the interfaces in the range.

To select several arbitrary ports for a common configuration setting, you can identify them as a "range" entered as a list. All port numbers and the commas that separate them must be separated with spaces. Use the following command in global configuration mode:

```
Switch(config)# interface range type module/number [, type module/number ...]
```

For example, to select interfaces Fast Ethernet 1/0/3, 1/0/7, 1/0/9, and 1/0/48 for configuration, you could use this command:

```
Switch(config)# interface range fastethernet 1/0/3 , fastethernet 1/0/7 ,
  fastethernet 1/0/9 , fastethernet 1/0/48
```

You also can select a continuous range of ports, from a beginning interface to an ending interface. Enter the interface type and module, followed by the beginning and ending port number separated by a dash with spaces. Use this command in global configuration mode:

```
Switch(config)# interface range type module/first-number - last-number
```

For example, you could select all 48 Fast Ethernet interfaces on module 1 with the following command:

```
Switch(config)# interface range fastethernet 1/0/1 - 48
```

Finally, you sometimes need to make configuration changes to several groups or ranges of ports at the same time. You can define a macro that contains a list of interfaces or ranges of interfaces or both. Then, you can invoke the interface-range macro just before configuring the port settings. This applies the port settings to each interface that is identified by the macro. The steps for defining and applying this macro are as follows:

Step 1. Define the macro name and specify as many lists and ranges of interfaces as needed. The command syntax is open ended but follows the list and range syntax of the **interface range** commands defined previously:

```
Switch(config)# define interface-range macro-name type module/number
[,  type module/ number ...] [type module/first-number - last-number]
[...]
```

Step 2. Invoke the macro called *macro-name* just as you would with a regular interface, just before entering any interface-configuration commands:

```
Switch(config)# interface range macro macro-name
```

As an example, suppose that you need to configure Gigabit Ethernet 2/0/1, 2/0/3 through 2/0/5, 3/0/1, 3/0/10, and 3/0/32 through 3/0/48 with a set of identical interface configurations. You could use the following commands to define and apply a macro, respectively:

```
Switch(config)# define interface-range MyGroup gig 2/0/1 , gig 2/0/3 - 2/0/5 ,
  gig 3/0/1 , gig 3/0/10, gig 3/0/32 - 3/0/48
Switch(config)# interface range macro MyGroup
```

Remember to surround any commas and hyphens with spaces when you enter **interface range** commands.

Identifying Ports

You can add a text description to a switch port's configuration to help identify it. This description is meant as a comment field only, as a record of port use or other unique information. The port description is included when displaying the switch configuration and interface information.

To assign a comment or description to a port, enter the following command in interface configuration mode:

```
Switch(config-if)# description description-string
```

The description string can have embedded spaces between words, if needed. To remove a description, use the **no description** interface-configuration command.

As an example, interface Fast Ethernet 1/0/11 is labeled with "Printer in Bldg A, room 213":

```
Switch(config)# interface fast 1/0/11
Switch(config-if)# description Printer in Bldg A, room 213
```

Port Speed

You can assign a specific speed to switch ports through switch-configuration commands. Fast Ethernet 10/100 ports can be set to speeds of 10, 100, and Auto (the default) for autonegotiate mode. Gigabit Ethernet GBIC ports always are set to a speed of 1000, whereas 1000BASE-T ports can be set to speeds of 10, 100, 1000, and Auto (the default).

Note: If a 10/100 or a 10/100/1000 port is assigned a speed of Auto, both its speed and duplex mode will be negotiated.

To specify the port speed on a particular Ethernet port, use the following interface-configuration command:

```
Switch(config-if)# speed {10 | 100 | 1000 | auto}
```

Port Duplex Mode

You also can assign a specific link mode to Ethernet-based switch ports. Therefore, the port operates in half-duplex, full-duplex, or autonegotiated mode. Autonegotiation is allowed only on UTP Fast Ethernet and Gigabit Ethernet ports. In this mode, the port *participates* in a negotiation by attempting full-duplex operation first and then half-duplex operation if full duplex is not successful. The autonegotiation process repeats whenever the link status changes. Be sure to set both ends of a link to the same speed and duplex settings to eliminate any chance that the two ends will be mismatched.

Note: A 10-Mbps Ethernet link (fixed speed) defaults to half duplex, whereas a 100-Mbps Fast Ethernet (dual speed 10/100) link defaults to full duplex. Multispeed links default to autonegotiate the duplex mode.

To set the link mode on a switch port, enter the following command in interface configuration mode:

```
Switch(config-if)# duplex {auto | full | half}
```

For instance, you could use the commands in Example 3-1 to configure 10/100/1000 interfaces Gigabit Ethernet 3/1 for autonegotiation and 3/2 for 100-Mbps full duplex (no autonegotiation).

Example 3-1   *Configuring the Link Mode on a Switch Port*

```
Switch(config)# interface gig 3/1
Switch(config-if)# speed auto
Switch(config-if)# duplex auto
Switch(config-if)# interface gig 3/2
Switch(config-if)# speed 100
Switch(config-if)# duplex full
```

Managing Error Conditions on a Switch Port

A network-management application can be used to detect a serious error condition on a switch port. A switch can be polled periodically so that its port error counters can be examined to see whether an error condition has occurred. If so, an alert can be issued so that someone can take action to correct the problem.

Catalyst switches can detect error conditions automatically, without any further help. If a serious error occurs on a switch port, that port can be shut down automatically until someone manually enables the port again, or until a predetermined time has elapsed.

Detecting Error Conditions

By default, a Catalyst switch detects an error condition on every switch port for every possible cause. If an error condition is detected, the switch port is put into the errdisable state and is disabled. You can tune this behavior on a global basis so that only certain causes trigger any port being disabled. Use the following command in global configuration mode, where the **no** keyword is added to disable the specified cause:

Key Topic

```
Switch(config)# [no] errdisable detect cause [all | cause-name]
```

You can repeat this command to enable or disable more than one cause. One of the following triggers the errdisable state:

- **all**—Detects every possible cause

- **arp-inspection**—Detects errors with dynamic ARP inspection

- **bpduguard**—Detects when a spanning-tree bridge protocol data unit (BPDU) is received on a port configured for STP PortFast

- **channel-misconfig**—Detects an error with an EtherChannel bundle

- **dhcp-rate-limit**—Detects an error with DHCP snooping

- **dtp-flap**—Detects when trunking encapsulation is changing from one type to another

- **gbic-invalid**—Detects the presence of an invalid GBIC or SFP module

- **ilpower**—Detects an error with offering inline power

- **l2ptguard**—Detects an error with Layer 2 Protocol Tunneling

- **link-flap**—Detects when the port link state is "flapping" between the up and down states

- **loopback**—Detects when an interface has been looped back

- **pagp-flap**—Detects when an EtherChannel bundle's ports no longer have consistent configurations

- **psecure-violation**—Detects conditions that trigger port security configured on a port

- **rootguard**—Detects when an STP BPDU is received from the root bridge on an unexpected port

- **security-violation**—Detects errors related to port security

- **storm-control**—Detects when a storm control threshold has been exceeded on a port

- **udld**—Detects when a link is seen to be *unidirectional* (data passing in only one direction)

- **unicast-flood**—Detects conditions that trigger unicast flood blocking on a port

- **vmps**—Detects errors when assigning a port to a dynamic VLAN through VLAN membership policy server (VMPS)

Automatically Recover from Error Conditions

By default, ports put into the errdisable state must be re-enabled manually. This is done by issuing the **shutdown** command in interface configuration mode, followed by the **no shutdown** command. Before you re-enable a port from the errdisable condition, you always should determine the cause of the problem so that the errdisable condition doesn't occur again.

You can decide to have a switch automatically reenable an errdisabled port if it is more important to keep the link up until the problem can be resolved. To automatically reenable an errdisabled port, you first must specify the errdisable causes that can be reenabled. Use this command in global configuration mode, with a *cause-name* from the preceding list:

```
Switch(config)# errdisable recovery cause [all | cause-name]
```

If any errdisable causes are configured for automatic recovery, the errdisabled port stays down for 300 seconds, by default. To change the recovery timer, use the following command in global configuration mode:

```
Switch(config)# errdisable recovery interval seconds
```

You can set the interval from 30 to 86,400 seconds (24 hours).

As an example, you could use the following commands to configure all switch ports to be reenabled automatically in 1 hour after a port security violation has been detected:

```
Switch(config)# errdisable recovery cause psecurity-violation
Switch(config)# errdisable recovery interval 3600
```

Remember that the errdisable causes and automatic recovery are configured globally—the settings apply to all switch ports.

Enable and Use the Switch Port

If the port is not enabled or activated automatically, use the **no shutdown** interface-configuration command. To view a port's current speed and duplex state, use the **show interface** command. You can see a brief summary of all interface states with the **show interfaces status** command.

Troubleshooting Port Connectivity

Suppose that you are experiencing problems with a switch port. How would you troubleshoot it? The following sections cover a few common troubleshooting techniques.

Looking for the Port State

Use the **show interfaces** EXEC command to see complete information about the switch port. The port's current state is given in the first line of output, as in Example 3-2.

Key
Topic

Example 3-2 *Determining Port State Information*

```
Switch# show interfaces fastethernet 1/0/1
FastEthernet1/0/1 is up, line protocol is up
  Hardware is Fast Ethernet, address is 0009.b7ee.9801 (bia 0009.b7ee.9801)
  MTU 1500 bytes, BW 100000 Kbit, DLY 100 usec,
     reliability 255/255, txload 1/255, rxload 1/255
```

The first **up** tells the state of the port's physical or data link layer. If this is shown as **down**, the link is physically disconnected or a link cannot be detected. The second state, given as **line protocol is up**, shows the Layer 2 status. If the state is given as **errdisable**, the switch has detected a serious error condition on this port and has automatically disabled it.

To quickly see a list of states for all switch ports, use the **show interface status** EXEC command. Likewise, you can see a list of all ports in the errdisable state (and the cause) by using the **show interface status err-disabled** EXEC command.

Looking for Speed and Duplex Mismatches

Key
Topic

If a user notices slow response time or low throughput on a 10/100 or 10/100/1000 switch port, the problem could be a mismatch of the port speed or duplex mode between the switch and the host. This is particularly common when one end of the link is set to autonegotiate the link settings and the other end is not.

Use the **show interface** command for a specific interface and look for any error counts that are greater than 0. For example, in the following output in Example 3-3, the switch port is set to autonegotiate the speed and duplex mode. It has decided on 100 Mbps at half duplex. Notice that there are many *runts* (packets that were truncated before they were fully received) and input errors. These are symptoms that a setting mismatch exists between the two ends of the link.

Example 3-3 *Determining Link Speed and Duplex Mode*

```
Switch# show interfaces fastethernet 1/0/13
FastEthernet1/0/13 is up, line protocol is up
  Hardware is Fast Ethernet, address is 00d0.589c.3e8d (bia 00d0.589c.3e8d)
  MTU 1500 bytes, BW 10000 Kbit, DLY 1000 usec,
     reliability 255/255, txload 2/255, rxload 1/255
  Encapsulation ARPA, loopback not set
  Keepalive not set
  Auto-duplex (Half), Auto Speed (100), 100BASETX/FX  ARP type: ARPA, ARP
     Timeout 04:00:00
Last input never, output 00:00:01, output hang never
  Last clearing of "show interface" counters never
  Queueing strategy: fifo
  Output queue 0/40, 0 drops; input queue 0/75, 0 drops
  5 minute input rate 0 bits/sec, 0 packets/sec
  5 minute output rate 81000 bits/sec, 49 packets/sec
     500867 packets input, 89215950 bytes
     Received 12912 broadcasts, 374879 runts, 0 giants, 0 throttles
     374879 input errors, 0 CRC, 0 frame, 0 overrun, 0 ignored
     0 watchdog, 0 multicast
     0 input packets with dribble condition detected
     89672388 packets output, 2205443729 bytes, 0 underruns
     0 output errors, 0 collisions, 3 interface resets
     0 babbles, 0 late collision, 0 deferred
     0 lost carrier, 0 no carrier
     0 output buffer failures, 0 output buffers swapped out
```

Because this port is autonegotiating the link speed, it must have detected an electrical signal that indicated 100 Mbps in common with the host. However, the host most likely was configured for 100 Mbps at full duplex (not autonegotiating). The switch was incapable of exchanging duplex information, so it fell back to its default of half duplex. Again, always make sure both ends of a connection are set to the same speed and duplex.

Exam Preparation Tasks

Review All Key Topics

Review the most important topics in the chapter, noted with the Key Topic icon in the outer margin of the page. Table 3-6 lists a reference of these key topics and the page numbers on which each is found.

Key Topic

Table 3-6 *Key Topics for Chapter 3*

Key Topic Element	Description	Page Number
Paragraph	Describes the characteristics of Ethernet switching	44
Paragraph	Explains Ethernet autonegotiation	46
Paragraph	Discusses similarities and differences of Ethernet types	47
Paragraph	Describes 10-Gigabit Ethernet	49
Paragraph	Covers interface selection for configuration	52
Paragraph	Explains how to configure the port speed	54
Paragraph	Explains how to configure the port duplex mode	54
Paragraph	Explains how to configure port error detection	55
Paragraph	Explains how to verify the port state	57
Paragraph	Explains how to verify port speed and duplex mode	57

Define Key Terms

Define the following key terms from this chapter, and check your answers in the glossary:

CSMA/CD, duplex mode, autonegotiation, duplex mismatch, IEEE 802.3

Use Command Reference to Check Your Memory

This section includes the most important configuration and EXEC commands covered in this chapter. It might not be necessary to memorize the complete syntax of every command, but you should remember the basic keywords that are needed.

To test your memory of the port configuration commands, cover the right side of Table 3-7 with a piece of paper, read the description on the left side, and then see how much of the command you can remember.

Remember that the CCNP exam focuses on practical or hands-on skills that are used by a networking professional. Therefore, you should remember the commands needed to configure and test a switch interface.

Table 3-7 *Switch Port Configuration Commands*

Task	Command Syntax
Select a port.	interface *type module/number*
Select multiple ports.	interface range *type module/number* [, *type module/number ...*]
	or
	interface range *type module/first-number – last-number*
Define an interface macro.	define interface-range *macro-name type module/number* [, *type module/number ...*] [*type module/first-number – last-number*] [...]
	interface range macro *macro-name*
Identify port.	description *description-string*
Set port speed.	speed {10 | 100 | 1000 | auto}
Set port mode.	duplex {auto | full | half}
Detect port error conditions.	errdisable detect cause [all | *cause-name*]
Automatically recover from errdisable.	errdisable recovery cause [all | *cause-name*]
	errdisable recovery interval *seconds*
Manually recover from errdisable.	shutdown
	no shutdown

This chapter covers the following topics that you need to master for the CCNP SWITCH exam:

Virtual LANs—This section reviews VLANs, VLAN membership, and VLAN configuration on a Catalyst switch.

VLAN Trunks—This section covers transporting multiple VLANs over single links and VLAN trunking with Ethernet.

VLAN Trunk Configuration—This section outlines the Catalyst switch commands that configure VLAN trunks.

Troubleshooting VLANs and Trunks—This section provides commands to use when a VLAN or trunk is not operating properly.

CHAPTER 4

VLANs and Trunks

Switched campus networks can be broken up into distinct broadcast domains or virtual LANs (VLAN). A flat network topology, or a network with a single broadcast domain, can be simple to implement and manage. However, flat network topology is not scalable. Instead, the campus can be divided into segments using VLANs, while Layer 3 routing protocols manage interVLAN communication.

This chapter details the process of defining common workgroups within a group of switches. It covers switch configuration for VLANs, along with the method of identifying and transporting VLANs on various types of links.

"Do I Know This Already?" Quiz

The "Do I Know This Already?" quiz allows you to assess whether you should read this entire chapter thoroughly or jump to the "Exam Preparation Tasks" section. If you are in doubt based on your answers to these questions or your own assessment of your knowledge of the topics, read the entire chapter. Table 4-1 outlines the major headings in this chapter and the "Do I Know This Already?" quiz questions that go with them. You can find the answers in Appendix A, "Answers to the 'Do I Know This Already?' Quizzes."

Table 4-1 *"Do I Know This Already?" Foundation Topics Section-to-Question Mapping*

Foundation Topics Section	Questions Covered in This Section
Virtual LANs	1–4
VLAN Trunks	5–12
VLAN Trunk Configuration	
Troubleshooting VLANs and Trunks	13–14

1. A VLAN is which of the following?

    a. Collision domain

    b. Spanning-tree domain

    c. Broadcast domain

    d. VTP domain

2. Switches provide VLAN connectivity at which layer of the OSI model?

    a. Layer 1

    b. Layer 2

    c. Layer 3

    d. Layer 4

3. Which one of the following is needed to pass data between two PCs, each connected to a different VLAN?

    a. Layer 2 switch

    b. Layer 3 switch ✓

    c. Trunk ✗

    d. Tunnel

4. Which Catalyst IOS switch command is used to assign a port to a VLAN?

    a. access vlan *vlan-id*

    b. switchport access vlan *vlan-id* ✓

    c. vlan *vlan-id*

    d. set port vlan *vlan-id*

5. Which of the following is a standardized method of trunk encapsulation?

    a. 802.1d

    b. 802.1Q ✓

    c. 802.3z

    d. 802.1a

6. What is the Cisco proprietary method for trunk encapsulation?

    a. CDP

    b. EIGRP

    c. ISL ✓

    d. DSL

7. Which of these protocols dynamically negotiates trunking parameters?

    a. PAgP ✗

    b. STP

    c. CDP

    d. DTP ✓

8. How many different VLANs can an 802.1Q trunk support?

    a. 256

    b. 1024

    c. 4096 •

    d. 32,768

    e. 65,536

9. Which of the following incorrectly describes a native VLAN?

    a. Frames are untagged on an 802.1Q trunk.

    b. Frames are untagged on an ISL trunk.

    c. Frames can be interpreted by a nontrunking host.

    d. The native VLAN can be configured for each trunking port. ✕

10. If two switches each support all types of trunk encapsulation on a link between them, which one will be negotiated?

    a. ISL •

    b. 802.1Q

    c. DTP

    d. VTP

11. Which VLANs are allowed on a trunk link by default?

    a. None

    b. Only the native VLAN • ✗

    c. All active VLANs ✓

    d. Only negotiated VLANs

12. Which command configures a switch port to form a trunk without using negotiation?

    a. **switchport mode trunk** ✓

    b. **switchport mode trunk nonegotiate** • ✗

    c. **switchport mode dynamic auto**

    d. **switchport mode dynamic desirable**

13. Two hosts are connected to switch interfaces Fast Ethernet 0/1 and 0/33, but they cannot communicate with each other. Their IP addresses are in the 192.168.10.0/24 subnet, which is carried over VLAN 10. The **show vlan id 10** command generates the following output:

```
Switch# show vlan id 10
VLAN Name                           Status    Ports
-- ------------------- ----. ----------------
 -
   Users                            active    Fa0/1, Fa0/2, Fa0/3, Fa0/4,
                                              Fa0/5, Fa0/6, Fa0/7, Fa0/8,
                                              Fa0/9, Fa0/10, Fa0/11, Fa0/12,
```

```
Fa0/13, Fa0/14, Fa0/15, Fa0/16,
Fa0/17, Fa0/18, Fa0/19, Fa0/20,
Fa0/21, Fa0/22, Fa0/23, Fa0/25,
Fa0/26, Fa0/27, Fa0/28, Fa0/31,
Fa0/32, Fa0/34, Fa0/35, Fa0/36,
Fa0/37, Fa0/39, Fa0/40, Fa0/41,
Fa0/42, Fa0/43, Fa0/46
```

The hosts are known to be up and connected. Which of the following reasons might be causing the problem?

    a.   The two hosts are assigned to VLAN 1.

    b.   The two hosts are assigned to different VLANs.

    c.   Interface FastEthernet0/33 is a VLAN trunk.

    d.   The two hosts are using unregistered MAC addresses.

14. A trunk link between two switches did not come up as expected. The configuration on Switch A is as follows:

```
Switch A# show running-config interface gigabitethernet0/1
interface GigabitEthernet0/1
  switchport trunk encapsulation dot1q
  switchport trunk allowed vlan 1-10
  switchport mode dynamic auto
  no shutdown
```

The interface configuration on Switch B is as follows:

```
Switch B# show running-config interface gigabitethernet0/1
interface GigabitEthernet0/1
  switchport trunk encapsulation dot1q
  switchport mode dynamic auto
  switchport access vlan 5
  no shutdown
```

Which one of the following reasons is probably causing the problem?

    a.   The two switches don't have matching **switchport trunk allowed vlan** commands.

    b.   Neither switch has a native VLAN configured.

    c.   Both switches are configured in the dynamic auto mode.

    d.   Switch B is configured to use access VLAN 5.

Foundation Topics

Virtual LANs

Consider a network design that consists of Layer 2 devices only. For example, this design could be a single Ethernet segment, an Ethernet switch with many ports, or a network with several interconnected Ethernet switches. A full Layer 2–only switched network is referred to as a *flat network topology*. A flat network is a single broadcast domain, such that every connected device sees every broadcast packet that is transmitted. As the number of stations on the network increases, so does the number of broadcasts.

Because of the Layer 2 foundation, flat networks cannot contain redundant paths for load balancing or fault tolerance. The reason for this is explained in Chapters 7, "Traditional Spanning Tree Protocol," through 10, "Advanced Spanning Tree Protocol." To gain any advantage from additional paths to a destination, Layer 3 routing functions must be introduced.

A switched environment offers the technology to overcome flat network limitations. Switched networks can be subdivided into VLANs. By definition, a VLAN is a single broadcast domain. All devices connected to the VLAN receive broadcasts sent by any other VLAN members. However, devices connected to a different VLAN will not receive those same broadcasts. (Naturally, VLAN members also receive unicast packets directed toward them from other VLAN members.)

A VLAN consists of hosts defined as members, communicating as a *logical* network segment. In contrast, a physical segment consists of devices that must be connected to a physical cable segment. A VLAN can have connected members located anywhere in the campus network, as long as VLAN connectivity is provided among all members. Layer 2 switches are configured with a VLAN mapping and provide the logical connectivity among the VLAN members.

Figure 4-1 shows how a VLAN can provide logical connectivity between switch ports. Two workstations on the left Catalyst switch are assigned to VLAN 1, whereas a third workstation is assigned to VLAN 100. In this example, no communication can occur between VLAN 1 and VLAN 100. Both ends of the link between the Catalysts are assigned to VLAN 1. One workstation on the right Catalyst also is assigned to VLAN 1. Because there is end-to-end connectivity of VLAN 1, any of the workstations on VLAN 1 can communicate as if they were connected to a physical network segment.

VLAN Membership

When a VLAN is provided at an access-layer switch, an end user must have some means of gaining membership to it. Two membership methods exist on Cisco Catalyst switches:

- Static VLAN configuration

- Dynamic VLAN assignment

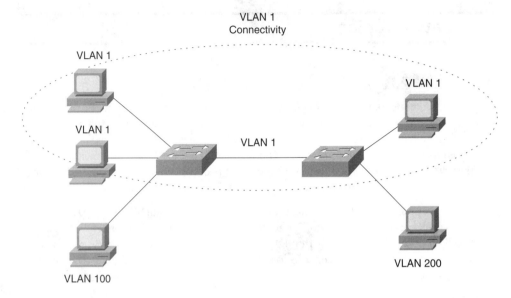

Figure 4-1   *VLAN Functionality*

Static VLANs

Static VLANs offer *port-based* membership, in which switch ports are assigned to specific VLANs. End-user devices become members in a VLAN based on the physical switch port to which they are connected. No handshaking or unique VLAN membership protocol is needed for the end devices; they automatically assume VLAN connectivity when they connect to a port. Normally, the end device is not even aware that the VLAN exists. The switch port and its VLAN simply are viewed and used as any other network segment, with other "locally attached" members on the wire.

Switch ports are assigned to VLANs by the manual intervention of the network administrator, hence the static nature. Each port receives a Port VLAN ID (PVID) that associates it with a VLAN number. The ports on a single switch can be assigned and grouped into many VLANs. Even though two devices are connected to the same switch, traffic will not pass between them if they are connected to ports on different VLANs. To perform this function, you could use either a Layer 3 device to route packets or an external Layer 2 device to bridge packets between the two VLANs.

The static port-to-VLAN membership normally is handled in hardware with application-specific integrated circuits (ASIC) in the switch. This membership provides good performance because all port mappings are done at the hardware level, with no complex table lookups needed.

Configuring Static VLANs

This section describes the switch commands needed to configure static VLANs. By default, all switch ports are assigned to VLAN 1, are set to be a VLAN type of Ethernet, and have a maximum transmission unit (MTU) size of 1500 bytes.

First, the VLAN must be created on the switch, if it does not already exist. Then, the VLAN must be assigned to specific switch ports. VLANs always are referenced by a VLAN number, which can range from 1 to 1005. VLANs 1 and 1002 through 1005 automatically are created and are set aside for special uses. For example, VLAN 1 is the default VLAN for every switch port. VLANs 1002 to 1005 are reserved for legacy functions related to Token Ring and FDDI switching.

Catalyst IOS switches also can support extended-range VLANs, in which the VLAN number can be 1 to 4094, for compatibility with the IEEE 802.1Q standard. The extended range is enabled only when the switch is configured for VTP transparent mode with the **vtp mode transparent** global configuration command. This is because of limitations with VTP Versions 1 and 2. VTP Version 3 does allow extended range VLANs to be used and advertised, but this version is not available in any IOS-based Catalyst switches at press time. (VTP is covered in Chapter 5, "VLAN Trunking Protocol.")

Tip: Although the extended range of VLAN numbers enables you to support more VLANs in your network, some limitations exist. For example, a switch normally maintains VLAN definitions in a special database file, separate from the switch configuration. The VLAN Trunking Protocol (VTP) uses the VLAN database so that VLAN definitions can be advertised and shared between switches over trunk links. When extended-range VLANs are created, they are not stored in the VLAN database file.

Why does this matter? As long as the switch remains in VTP transparent mode, the extended VLANs can be used. However, if the switch is later configured to participate in VTP as either a server or a client, you must manually delete the extended VLANs. For any switch ports that were assigned to the extended VLANs, you also must reconfigure them for VLAN membership within the normal VLAN range.

To configure static VLANs, begin by defining the VLAN with the following command in global configuration mode:

```
Switch(config)# vlan vlan-num
Switch(config-vlan)# name vlan-name
```

The VLAN numbered *vlan-num* is immediately created and stored in the database, along with a descriptive text string defined by *vlan-name* (up to 32 characters with no embedded spaces). The **name** command is optional; if it is not used, the default VLAN name is of the form **VLAN XXX**, where *XXX* represents the VLAN number. If you need to include spaces to separate words in the VLAN name, use underscore characters instead.

As an example, you can use the following commands to create VLANs 2 and 101:

```
Switch(config)# vlan 2
Switch(config-vlan)# name Engineering
Switch(config-vlan)# vlan 101
Switch(config-vlan)# name Marketing
```

To delete a VLAN from the switch configuration, you can use the **no vlan** *vlan-num* command.

Next, you should assign one or more switch ports to the VLAN. Use the following config-uration commands:

```
Switch(config)# interface type module/number
Switch(config-if)# switchport
Switch(config-if)# switchport mode access
Switch(config-if)# switchport access vlan vlan-num
```

The initial **switchport** command configures the port for Layer 2 operation. Switch ports on most Catalyst switch platforms default to Layer 2 operation. In that case, the **switch-port** command will already be present in the configuration and you won't have to enter it explicitly. Otherwise, the switch will reject any Layer 2 configuration command if the port is not already configured for Layer 2 operation.

The **switchport mode access** command forces the port to be assigned to only a single VLAN, providing VLAN connectivity to the access layer or end user. The port is given a static VLAN membership by the **switchport access vlan** command. Here, the logical VLAN is referenced by the *vlan-num* setting (1 to 1005 or 1 to 4094).

To verify VLAN configuration, use the **show vlan** command to output a list of all VLANs defined in the switch, along with the ports that are assigned to each VLAN. Example 4-1 shows some sample output from the **show vlan** command.

Example 4-1   *Verifying VLAN Configuration with the show vlan Command*

```
Switch#
show vlan
VLAN Name                             Status    Ports
---- -------------------------------- -------   --------------------------------
1    default                          active    Gi1/1, Gi1/2, Gi3/20, Gi4/20
2    Engineering                      active    Gi4/2, Gi4/3, Gi4/4, Gi4/5
                                                Gi4/6, Gi4/7, Gi4/8, Gi4/9
                                                Gi4/10, Gi4/11, Gi4/12
101  Marketing                        active    Gi2/5, Gi2/6, Gi2/7, Gi2/8
                                                Gi2/9, Gi2/10, Gi2/11, Gi2/12
                                                Gi2/13, Gi2/14, Gi2/15, Gi2/16
                                                Gi2/17, Gi2/18
```

Dynamic VLANs

Dynamic VLANs provide membership based on the MAC address of an end-user device. When a device is connected to a switch port, the switch must, in effect, query a database to establish VLAN membership. A network administrator also must assign the user's MAC address to a VLAN in the database of a VLAN Membership Policy Server (VMPS).

With Cisco switches, dynamic VLANs are created and managed using network-manage-ment tools such as CiscoWorks. Dynamic VLANs allow a great deal of flexibility and mo-bility for end users but require more administrative overhead.

Note: Dynamic VLANs are not covered in this text or in the SWITCH course or exam (at press time). For more information, refer to the "Configuring VMPS" section in a Catalyst

configuration guide such as http://www.cisco.com/en/US/docs/switches/lan/catalyst3560/
software/release/12.2_25_see/configuration/guide/swvlan.html#wp1212223.

Deploying VLANs

To implement VLANs, you must consider the number of VLANs you need and how best
to place them. As usual, the number of VLANs depends on traffic patterns, application
types, segmentation of common workgroups, and network-management requirements.

An important factor to consider is the relationship between VLANs and the IP addressing
schemes used. Cisco recommends a one-to-one correspondence between VLANs and IP
subnets. This recommendation means that if a subnet with a 24-bit mask (255.255.255.0) is
used for a VLAN, no more than 254 devices should be in the VLAN. In addition, you
should not allow VLANs to extend beyond the Layer 2 domain of the distribution switch.
In other words, the VLAN should not reach across a network's core and into another
switch block. The idea again is to keep broadcasts and unnecessary traffic movement out
of the core block.

VLANs can be scaled in the switch block by using two basic methods:

- End-to-end VLANs
- Local VLANs

End-to-End VLANs

End-to-end VLANs, also called *campuswide VLANs*, span the entire switch fabric of a
network. They are positioned to support maximum flexibility and mobility of end devices. Users can be assigned to VLANs regardless of their physical location. As a user
moves around the campus, that user's VLAN membership stays the same. This means that
each VLAN must be made available at the access layer in every switch block.

End-to-end VLANs should group users according to common requirements. All users in a
VLAN should have roughly the same traffic flow patterns, following the 80/20 rule. Recall
that this rule estimates that 80 percent of user traffic stays within the local workgroup,
whereas 20 percent is destined for a remote resource in the campus network. Although
only 20 percent of the traffic in a VLAN is expected to cross the network core, end-to-
end VLANs make it possible for 100 percent of the traffic within a single VLAN to cross
the core.

Because all VLANs must be available at each access-layer switch, VLAN trunking must be
used to carry all VLANs between the access- and distribution-layer switches.

Tip: End-to-end VLANs are not recommended in an enterprise network, unless there is a
good reason. In an end-to-end VLAN, broadcast traffic is carried over from one end of the
network to the other, creating the possibility for a broadcast storm or Layer 2 bridging
loop to spread across the whole extent of a VLAN. This can exhaust the bandwidth of dis-
tribution- and core-layer links, as well as switch CPU resources. Now the storm or loop has

disrupted users on the end-to-end VLAN, in addition to users on other VLANs that might be crossing the core.

When such a problem occurs, troubleshooting becomes more difficult. In other words, the risks of end-to-end VLANs outweigh the convenience and benefits.

Local VLANs

Because most enterprise networks have moved toward the 20/80 rule (where server and intranet/Internet resources are centralized), end-to-end VLANs have become cumbersome and difficult to maintain. The 20/80 rule reverses the traffic pattern of the end-to-end VLAN: Only 20 percent of traffic is local, whereas 80 percent is destined to a remote resource across the core layer. End users usually require access to central resources outside their VLAN. Users must cross into the network core more frequently. In this type of network, VLANs should be designed to contain user communities based on geographic boundaries, with little regard to the amount of traffic leaving the VLAN.

Local or geographic VLANs range in size from a single switch in a wiring closet to an entire building. Arranging VLANs in this fashion enables the Layer 3 function in the campus network to intelligently handle the interVLAN traffic loads, where traffic passes into the core. This scenario provides maximum availability by using multiple paths to destinations, maximum scalability by keeping the VLAN within a switch block, and maximum manageability.

VLAN Trunks

At the access layer, end-user devices connect to switch ports that provide simple connectivity to a single VLAN each. The attached devices are unaware of any VLAN structure and simply attach to what appears to be a normal physical network segment. Remember, sending information from an access link on one VLAN to another VLAN is not possible without the intervention of an additional device—either a Layer 3 router or an external Layer 2 bridge.

Note that a single switch port can support more than one IP subnet for the devices attached to it. For example, consider a shared Ethernet hub that is connected to a single Ethernet switch port. One user device on the hub might be configured for 192.168.1.1 255.255.255.0, whereas another is assigned 192.168.17.1 255.255.255.0. Although these subnets are discontiguous and unique, and both are communicating on one switch port, they cannot be considered separate VLANs. The switch port supports one VLAN, but multiple subnets can exist on that single VLAN.

A *trunk link*, however, can transport more than one VLAN through a single switch port. Trunk links are most beneficial when switches are connected to other switches or switches are connected to routers. A trunk link is not assigned to a specific VLAN. Instead, one, many, or all active VLANs can be transported between switches using a single physical trunk link.

Connecting two switches with separate physical links for each VLAN is possible. The top half of Figure 4-2 shows how two switches might be connected in this fashion.

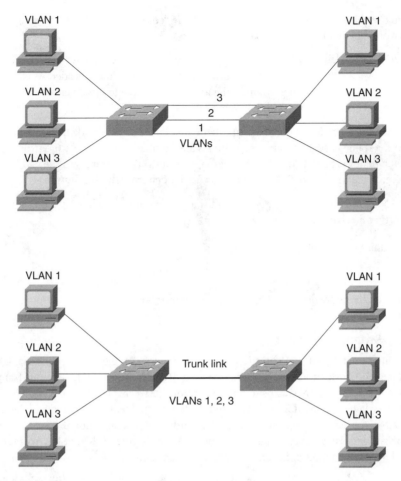

Figure 4-2 *Passing VLAN Traffic Using Single Links Versus Trunk Links*

As VLANs are added to a network, the number of links can grow quickly. A more efficient use of physical interfaces and cabling involves the use of trunking. The bottom half of the figure shows how one trunk link can replace many individual VLAN links.

Cisco supports trunking on both Fast Ethernet and Gigabit Ethernet switch links, and aggregated Fast and Gigabit EtherChannel links. To distinguish between traffic belonging to different VLANs on a trunk link, the switch must have a method of identifying each frame with the appropriate VLAN. The switches on *each end* of a trunk link both must have the same method for correlating frames with VLAN numbers. The next section covers several available identification methods.

VLAN Frame Identification (Tagging)

Because a trunk link can transport many VLANs, a switch must identify frames with their respective VLANs as they are sent and received over a trunk link. Frame identification, or *tagging*, assigns a unique user-defined ID to each frame transported on a trunk link.

Think of this ID as the VLAN number or VLAN "color," as if each VLAN were drawn on a network diagram in a unique color.

VLAN frame identification was developed for switched networks. As each frame is transmitted over a trunk link, a unique identifier is placed in the frame header. As each switch along the way receives these frames, the identifier is examined to determine to which VLAN the frames belong and then is removed.

If frames must be transported out another trunk link, the VLAN identifier is added back into the frame header. Otherwise, if frames are destined out an access (nontrunk) link, the switch removes the VLAN identifier before transmitting the frames to the end station. Therefore, all traces of VLAN association are hidden from the end station.

VLAN identification can be performed using two methods, each using a different frame identifier mechanism:

■   Inter-Switch Link (ISL) protocol

■   IEEE 802.1Q protocol

These methods are described in the sections that follow.

Inter-Switch Link Protocol

The Inter-Switch Link (ISL) protocol is a Cisco-proprietary method for preserving the source VLAN identification of frames passing over a trunk link. ISL performs frame identification in Layer 2 by encapsulating each frame between a header and a trailer. Any Cisco switch or router device configured for ISL can process and understand the ISL VLAN information. ISL primarily is used for Ethernet media, although Cisco has included provisions to carry Token Ring, FDDI, and ATM frames over Ethernet ISL. (A Frame-Type field in the ISL header indicates the source frame type.)

When a frame is destined out a trunk link to another switch or router, ISL adds a 26-byte header and a 4-byte trailer to the frame. The source VLAN is identified with a 15-bit VLAN ID field in the header. The trailer contains a cyclic redundancy check (CRC) value to ensure the data integrity of the new encapsulated frame. Figure 4-3 shows how Ethernet frames are encapsulated and forwarded out a trunk link. Because tagging information is added at the beginning and end of each frame, ISL sometimes is referred to as *double tagging*.

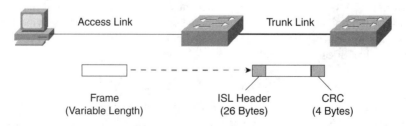

Figure 4-3   *ISL Frame Identification*

If a frame is destined for an access link, the ISL encapsulation (both header and trailer) is not rewritten into the frame before transmission. This removal preserves ISL information only for trunk links and devices that can understand the protocol.

Tip: The ISL method of VLAN identification or trunking encapsulation no longer is supported across all Cisco Catalyst switch platforms. Even so, you should still be familiar with it and know how it compares to the standards-based IEEE 802.1Q method.

IEEE 802.1Q Protocol

The IEEE 802.1Q protocol also can carry VLAN associations over trunk links. However, this frame-identification method is standardized, allowing VLAN trunks to exist and operate between equipment from multiple vendors.

In particular, the IEEE 802.1Q standard defines an architecture for VLAN use, services provided with VLANs, and protocols and algorithms used to provide VLAN services. You can find further information about the 802.1Q standard at http://grouper.ieee.org/groups/802/1/pages/802.1Q.html.

As with Cisco ISL, IEEE 802.1Q can be used for VLAN identification with Ethernet trunks. However, instead of encapsulating each frame with a VLAN ID header and trailer, 802.1Q embeds its tagging information within the Layer 2 frame. This method is referred to as *single tagging* or *internal tagging*.

802.1Q also introduces the concept of a *native VLAN* on a trunk. Frames belonging to this VLAN are *not* encapsulated with any tagging information. If an end station is connected to an 802.1Q trunk link, the end station can receive and understand only the native VLAN frames. This provides a simple way to offer full trunk encapsulation to the devices that can understand it, while giving normal-access stations some inherent connectivity over the trunk.

In an Ethernet frame, 802.1Q adds a 4-byte tag just after the source Address field, as shown in Figure 4-4.

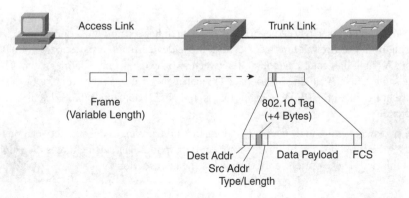

Figure 4-4   *IEEE 802.1Q Frame-Tagging Standard*

The first two bytes are used as a Tag Protocol Identifier (TPID) and always have a value of 0x8100 to signify an 802.1Q tag. The remaining two bytes are used as a Tag Control Information (TCI) field. The TCI information contains a three-bit Priority field, which is used to implement class-of-service (CoS) functions in the accompanying 802.1Q/802.1p prioritization standard. One bit of the TCI is a Canonical Format Indicator (CFI), flagging whether the MAC addresses are in Ethernet or Token Ring format. (This also is known as *canonical format*, or *little-endian* or *big-endian format*.)

The last 12 bits are used as a VLAN identifier (VID) to indicate the source VLAN for the frame. The VID can have values from 0 to 4095, but VLANs 0, 1, and 4095 are reserved.

Note that both ISL and 802.1Q tagging methods have one implication—they add to the length of an existing Ethernet frame. ISL adds a total of 30 bytes to each frame, whereas 802.1Q adds 4 bytes. Because Ethernet frames cannot exceed 1518 bytes, the additional VLAN tagging information can cause the frame to become too large. Frames that barely exceed the MTU size are called *baby giant frames*. Switches usually report these frames as Ethernet errors or oversize frames.

Note: Baby giant, or oversize, frames can exceed the frame size set in various standards. To properly handle and forward them anyway, Catalyst switches use proprietary hardware with the ISL encapsulation method. In the case of 802.1Q encapsulation, switches can comply with the IEEE 802.3ac standard, which extends the maximum frame length to 1522 bytes.

Dynamic Trunking Protocol

You can manually configure trunk links on Catalyst switches for either ISL or 802.1Q mode. In addition, Cisco has implemented a proprietary, point-to-point protocol called *Dynamic Trunking Protocol (DTP)* that negotiates a common trunking mode between two switches. The negotiation covers the encapsulation (ISL or 802.1Q) and whether the link becomes a trunk at all. This allows trunk links to be used without a great deal of manual configuration or administration. The use of DTP is explained in the next section.

Tip: You should disable DTP negotiation if a switch has a trunk link connected to a non-trunking router or firewall interface because those devices cannot participate in DTP negotiation. A trunk link can be negotiated between two switches only if both switches belong to the same VLAN Trunking Protocol (VTP) management domain or if one or both switches have not defined their VTP domain (that is, the NULL domain). VTP is discussed in Chapter 5.

If the two switches are in different VTP domains and trunking is desired between them, you must set the trunk links to on mode or nonegotiate mode. This setting forces the trunk to be established. These options are explained in the next section.

VLAN Trunk Configuration

By default, all switch ports in Layer 2 mode are nontrunking and operate as access links until some intervention changes the mode. Specifically, ports actively try to become trunks as long as the far end agrees. In that case, a common encapsulation is chosen, favoring ISL if both support it. The sections that follow demonstrate the commands necessary to configure VLAN trunks.

VLAN Trunk Configuration

Use the following commands to create a VLAN trunk link:

switchport no-negotiate (handwritten annotation)

Key Topic

```
Switch(config)# interface type mod/port
Switch(config-if)# switchport
Switch(config-if)# switchport trunk encapsulation {isl | dot1q | negotiate}
Switch(config-if)# switchport trunk native vlan vlan-id
Switch(config-if)# switchport trunk allowed vlan {vlan-list | all |
  {add | except | remove} vlan-list}
Switch(config-if)# switchport mode {trunk | dynamic {desirable | auto}}
```

A switch port must be in Layer 2 mode before it can support a trunk. To accomplish this, you use the **switchport** command with no other keywords. You then can configure the trunk encapsulation with the **switchport trunk encapsulation** command, as one of the following:

- **Isl**—VLANs are tagged by encapsulating each frame using the Cisco ISL protocol.

- **dot1q**—VLANs are tagged in each frame using the IEEE 802.1Q standard protocol. The only exception is the native VLAN, which is sent normally and is not tagged.

- **negotiate (the default)**—The encapsulation is negotiated to select either ISL or IEEE 802.1Q, whichever both ends of the trunk support. If both ends support both types, ISL is favored.

In the case of an IEEE 802.1Q trunk, you should configure the native VLAN with the **switchport trunk native vlan** command, identifying the untagged or native VLAN number as *vlan-id* (1 to 4094). By default, an 802.1Q trunk uses VLAN 1 as the native VLAN. In the case of an ISL trunk, using this command has no effect because ISL doesn't support an untagged VLAN.

The last command, **switchport trunk allowed vlan**, defines which VLANs can be trunked over the link. By default, a switch transports all active VLANs (1 to 4094) over a trunk link. An active VLAN is one that has been defined on the switch and has ports assigned to carry it.

There might be times when the trunk link should not carry all VLANs. For example, broadcasts are forwarded to every switch port on a VLAN—including the trunk link because it, too, is a member of the VLAN. If the VLAN does not extend past the far end of the trunk link, propagating broadcasts across the trunk makes no sense.

You can tailor the list of allowed VLANs on the trunk by using the **switchport trunk allowed vlan** command with one of the following:

- **vlan-list**—An explicit list of VLAN numbers, separated by commas or dashes.

- **all**—All active VLANs (1 to 4094) will be allowed.

- **add *vlan-list***—A list of VLAN numbers will be added to the already configured list; this is a shortcut to keep from typing a long list of numbers.

- **except *vlan-list***—All VLANs (1 to 4094) will be allowed, except for the VLAN numbers listed; this is a shortcut to keep from typing a long list of numbers.

- **remove *vlan-list***—A list of VLAN numbers will be removed from the already configured list; this is a shortcut to keep from typing a long list of numbers.

In the **switchport mode** command, you can set the trunking mode to any of the following:

- **trunk**—This setting places the port in permanent trunking mode. DTP is still operational, so if the far-end switch port is configured to trunk, dynamic desirable, or dynamic auto mode, trunking will be negotiated successfully.

  The trunk mode is usually used to establish an unconditional trunk. Therefore, the corresponding switch port at the other end of the trunk should be configured similarly. In this way, both switches always expect the trunk link to be operational without any negotiation. You also should manually configure the encapsulation mode to eliminate its negotiation.

- **dynamic desirable (the default)**—The port actively attempts to convert the link into trunking mode. In other words, it "asks" the far-end switch to bring up a trunk. If the far-end switch port is configured to trunk, dynamic desirable, or dynamic auto mode, trunking is negotiated successfully.

- **dynamic auto**—The port can be converted into a trunk link, but only if the far-end switch actively requests it. Therefore, if the far-end switch port is configured to trunk or dynamic desirable mode, trunking is negotiated. Because of the passive negotiation behavior, the link never becomes a trunk if both ends of the link are left to the dynamic auto default.

Tip: In all these modes, DTP frames are sent out every 30 seconds to keep neighboring switch ports informed of the link's mode. On critical trunk links in a network, manually configuring the trunking mode on both ends is best so that the link never can be negotiated to any other state.

If you decide to configure *both ends* of a trunk link as a fixed trunk (**switchport mode trunk**), you can disable DTP completely so that these frames are not exchanged. To do this, add the **switchport nonegotiate** command to the interface configuration. Be aware that after DTP frames are disabled, no future negotiation is possible until this configuration is reversed.

To view the trunking status on a switch port, use the **show interface** *type mod/port*
trunk command, as demonstrated in Example 4-2.

Example 4-2   *Determining Switch Port Trunking Status*

```
Switch# show interface gigabitethernet 2/1 trunk
Port        Mode          Encapsulation  Status       Native vlan
Gi2/1       on            802.1q         trunking     1


Port        Vlans allowed on trunk
Gi2/1       1-4094


Port        Vlans allowed and active in management domain
Gi2/1       1-2,526,539,998,1002-1005


Port        Vlans in spanning tree forwarding state and not pruned
Gi2/1       1-2,526,539,998,1002-1005
```

Trunk Configuration Example

As an example of trunk configuration, consider two switches, Switch D and Switch A,
which are distribution-layer and access-layer switches, respectively. The two switches are
connected by a link between their Gigabit Ethernet 2/1 interfaces. This link should be configured to be a trunk carrying only VLAN numbers 100 through 105, although more
VLANs exist and are used.

The trunk link should use 802.1Q encapsulation, with VLAN 100 as the native VLAN.
First, configure Switch-D to actively negotiate a trunk with the far-end switch. You could
use the following configuration commands on Switch-D:

```
Switch-D(config)# interface gigabitethernet 2/1
Switch-D(config-if)# switchport trunk encapsulation dot1q
Switch-D(config-if)# switchport trunk native vlan 100
Switch-D(config-if)# switchport trunk allowed vlan 100-105
Switch-D(config-if)# switchport mode dynamic desirable
```

At this point, you assume that Switch A is configured correctly, too. Now, you should try
to verify that the trunk is working as expected. On Switch D, you can view the trunk status with the following command:

```
Switch-D# show interface gigabitethernet 2/1 trunk
Port        Mode          Encapsulation  Status       Native vlan

Gi1/1       desirable     802.1q         not-trunking  100
Port        Vlans allowed on trunk
Gi1/1       100
Port        Vlans allowed and active in management domain
Gi1/1       100
Port        Vlans in spanning tree forwarding state and not pruned
Gi1/1       none
```

To your surprise, the trunk's status is not-trunking. Next, you should verify that the physical link is up:

```
Switch-D# show interface status
Port        Name              Status      Vlan      Duplex  Speed Type
Gi1/1                         notconnect  1            auto  1000 1000BaseCX
Gi1/2                         notconnect  1            auto  1000 1000BaseSX
Gi2/1                         connected   100          full  1000 1000BaseSX
```

What could be preventing the trunk from being established? If Switch D is in dynamic desirable negotiation mode, it is actively asking Switch A to bring up a trunk. Obviously, Switch A must not be in agreement. The desirable mode can negotiate a trunk with all other trunking modes, so Switch A's interface must not be configured for trunking. Instead, it is most likely configured as an access port (**switchport mode access**).

Switch A can be corrected by configuring its Gigabit Ethernet 2/1 interface to negotiate a trunk. Switch D is in dynamic desirable mode, so Switch A could use either trunk, dynamic desirable, or dynamic auto mode.

Now, suppose that you realize VLAN 103 should not be passed between these switches. You can use either of the following command sequences to manually prune VLAN 103 from the trunk:

```
Switch-D(config)# interface gigabitethernet 2/1
Switch-D(config-if)# switchport trunk allowed vlan 100-102,104-105
```

or

```
Switch-D(config-if)# switchport trunk allowed vlan remove 103
```

In the latter case, the previous range of 100 to 105 is kept in the configuration, and only 103 is automatically removed from the list.

When you manually prune VLANs from being allowed on a trunk, the same operation should be performed at both ends of the trunk link. Otherwise, one of the two switches still could flood broadcasts from that VLAN onto the trunk, using unnecessary bandwidth in only one direction.

For completeness, the configuration of Switch A at this point would look like the following:

```
Switch-A(config)# interface gigabitethernet 2/1
Switch-A(config-if)# switchport trunk encapsulation dot1q
Switch-A(config-if)# switchport trunk native vlan 100
Switch-A(config-if)# switchport trunk allowed vlan 100-105
Switch-A(config-if)# switchport trunk allowed vlan remove 103
Switch-A(config-if)# switchport mode dynamic desirable
```

Troubleshooting VLANs and Trunks

Remember that a VLAN is nothing more than a logical network segment that can be spread across many switches. If a PC in one location cannot communicate with a PC in another location, where both are assigned to the same IP subnet, make sure that both of their switch ports are configured for the same VLAN. If they are, examine the path between the two. Is the VLAN carried continuously along the path? If there are trunks along the way, is the VLAN being carried across the trunks?

To verify a VLAN's configuration on a switch, use the **show vlan id** *vlan-id* EXEC command, as demonstrated in Example 4-3. Make sure that the VLAN is shown to have an active status and that it has been assigned to the correct switch ports.

Key
Topic

Example 4-3   *Verifying Switch VLAN Configuration*

```
Switch# show vlan id 2
VLAN Name                             Status    Ports
---- -------------------------------- --------- --------
2    Engineering                      active    Gi2/1, Gi2/2, Gi2/3, Gi2/4
                                                Gi4/2, Gi4/3, Gi4/4, Gi4/5
                                                Gi4/6, Gi4/7, Gi4/8, Gi4/9
                                                Gi4/10, Gi4/11, Gi4/12


VLAN Type  SAID       MTU   Parent RingNo BridgeNo Stp  BrdgMode Trans1 Trans2
---- ----- ---------- ----- ------ ------ -------- ---- -------- ------ -------
2    enet  100002     1500  -      -      -        -    -        0      0


Primary Secondary Type              Ports
------- --------- ----------------- --------------------------------------------


Switch#
```

For a trunk, these parameters must be agreeable on both ends before the trunk can operate correctly:

■ Trunking mode (unconditional trunking, negotiated, or non-negotiated).

■ Trunk encapsulation (ISL, IEEE 802.1Q, or negotiated through DTP).

■ Native VLAN. You can bring up a trunk with different native VLANs on each end; however, both switches will log error messages about the mismatch, and the potential exists that traffic will not pass correctly between the two native VLANs.

■ The native VLAN mismatch is discovered through the exchange of CDP messages, not through examination of the trunk itself. Also, the native VLAN is configured independently of the trunk encapsulation, so it is possible to have a native VLAN mismatch even if the ports use ISL encapsulation. In this case, the mismatch is only cosmetic and won't cause a trunking problem.

■   Allowed VLANs. By default, a trunk allows all VLANs to be transported across it. If one end of the trunk is configured to disallow a VLAN, that VLAN will not be contiguous across the trunk.

To see a comparison of how a switch port is configured for trunking versus its active state, use the **show interface** *type mod/num* **switchport** command, as demonstrated in Example 4-4. Look for the administrative versus operational values, respectively, to see whether the trunk is working the way you configured it.

Notice that the port has been configured to negotiate a trunk through DTP (dynamic auto), but the port is operating in the static access (nontrunking) mode. This should tell you that both ends of the link probably are configured for the auto mode so that neither actively will request a trunk.

Example 4-4   *Comparing Switch Port Trunking Configuration and Active State*

```
Switch# show interface fastethernet 0/2 switchport
Name: Fa0/2
Switchport: Enabled
Administrative Mode: dynamic auto

Operational Mode: static access
Administrative Trunking Encapsulation: dot1q
Operational Trunking Encapsulation: native
Negotiation of Trunking: On
Access Mode VLAN: 1 (default)
Trunking Native Mode VLAN: 1 (default)
Administrative private-vlan host-association: none
Administrative private-vlan mapping: none
Operational private-vlan: none
Trunking VLANs Enabled: ALL
Pruning VLANs Enabled: 2-1001

Protected: false
Unknown unicast blocked: disabled
Unknown multicast blocked: disabled

Voice VLAN: none (Inactive)
Appliance trust: none
Switch#
```

For more concise information about a trunking port, you can use the **show interface** [*type mod/num*] **trunk** command, as demonstrated in Example 4-5.

Example 4-5   *Viewing Concise Information About a Trunking Port*

```
Switch# show interface fastethernet 0/2 trunk
Port       Mode         Encapsulation  Status       Native vlan
Fa0/2      auto         802.1q         not-trunking 1


Port       Vlans allowed on trunk
Fa0/2      1


Port       Vlans allowed and active in management domain
Fa0/2      1


Port       Vlans in spanning tree forwarding state and not pruned
Fa0/2      1
Switch#
```

Again, notice that the port is in the autonegotiation mode, but it is currently not-trunking. Because the port is not trunking, only the access VLAN (VLAN 1 in this example) is listed as allowed and active on the trunk.

To see whether and how DTP is being used on a switch, use the **show dtp** [**interface** *type mod/num*] command. Specifying an interface shows the DTP activity in greater detail.

Exam Preparation Tasks

Review All Key Topics

Review the most important topics in the chapter, noted with the Key Topic icon in the outer margin of the page. Table 4-2 lists a reference of these key topics and the page numbers on which each is found.

Table 4-2   *Key Topics for Chapter 4*

Key Topic Element	Description	Page Number
Paragraph	Explains VLAN characteristics	67
Paragraph	Discusses how to configure a VLAN	68
Paragraph	Discusses planning strategies for VLAN implementation	71
Paragraph	Explains the 802.1Q trunking protocol	75
Paragraph	Describes VLAN trunk link configuration	77
Paragraph	Discusses how to verify VLAN configuration	81
Paragraph	Explains how to verify that a trunk link is working properly	82

Define Key Terms

Define the following key terms from this chapter, and check your answers in the glossary:

VLAN, broadcast domain, VLAN number, end-to-end VLAN, local VLAN, 20/80 rule, VLAN trunk, ISL, 802.1Q, DTP, native VLAN

Use Command Reference to Check Your Memory

This section includes the most important configuration and EXEC commands covered in this chapter. It might not be necessary to memorize the complete syntax of every command, but you should remember the basic keywords that are needed .

To test your memory of the VLAN and trunk-related commands, cover the right side of Tables 4-3 and 4-4 with a piece of paper, read the description on the left side, and then see how much of the command you can remember.

Remember that the CCNP exam focuses on practical or hands-on skills that are used by a networking professional. For the skills covered in this chapter, notice that most of the commands involve the keyword **switchport**.

Table 4-3   *VLAN and Trunking Configuration Commands*

Task	Command Syntax
Create VLAN.	vlan *vlan-num* name *vlan-name*
Assign port to VLAN.	interface *type module/number* switchport mode access switchport access vlan *vlan-num*
Configure trunk.	interface *type mod/port* switchport trunk encapsulation {isl | dot1q | negotiate} switchport trunk native vlan *vlan-id* switchport trunk allowed vlan {*vlan-list* | all | {add | except | remove} *vlan-list*} switchport mode {trunk | dynamic {desirable | auto}}

Table 4-4   *VLAN and Trunking Troubleshooting Commands*

Task	Command Syntax
Verify VLAN configuration.	show vlan id *vlan-id*
Verify active trunk parameters.	show interface *type mod/num* trunk
Compare trunk configuration and active parameters.	show interface *type mod/num* switchport
Verify DTP operation.	show dtp [interface *type mod/num*]

This chapter covers the following topics that you need to master for the CCNP SWITCH exam:

VLAN Trunking Protocol—This section presents Cisco VLAN Trunking Protocol (VTP) for VLAN management in a campus network.

VTP Configuration—This section covers the Catalyst switch commands used to configure VTP.

VTP Pruning—This section details traffic management by pruning within VTP domains, along with the commands needed for configuration.

Troubleshooting VTP—This section gives a brief summary of things to consider and commands to use when VTP is not operating properly.

CHAPTER 5

VLAN Trunking Protocol

When VLANs are defined and used on switches throughout an enterprise or campus network, the administrative overhead can easily increase. Using the VLAN Trunking Protocol (VTP) makes VLAN administration more organized and manageable. This chapter covers VTP and its configuration.

A similar standards-based VLAN-management protocol for IEEE 802.1Q trunks is called *GARP VLAN Registration Protocol (GVRP)*. The GARP and GVRP protocols are defined in the IEEE 802.1D and 802.1Q (clause 11) standards, respectively. At press time, GVRP was not supported in any of the Cisco IOS Software–based Catalyst switches. Therefore, it is not covered in this text or in the SWITCH course.

"Do I Know This Already?" Quiz

The "Do I Know This Already?" quiz allows you to assess whether you should read this entire chapter thoroughly or jump to the "Exam Preparation Tasks" section. If you are in doubt based on your answers to these questions or your own assessment of your knowledge of the topics, read the entire chapter. Table 5-1 outlines the major headings in this chapter and the "Do I Know This Already?" quiz questions that go with them. You can find the answers in Appendix A, "Answers to the 'Do I Know This Already?' Quizzes."

Table 5-1 *"Do I Know This Already?" Foundation Topics Section-to-Question Mapping*

Foundation Topics Section	Questions Covered in This Section
VLAN Trunking Protocol	1–8
VTP Configuration	
VTP Pruning	9–10
Troubleshooting VTP	11–12

1. Which of the following is not a Catalyst switch VTP mode?

    a. Server

    b. Client

    c. Designated

    d. Transparent

2. A switch in VTP transparent mode can do which one of the following?

    a. Create a new VLAN

    b. Only listen to VTP advertisements

    c. Send its own VTP advertisements

    d. Cannot make VLAN configuration changes

3. Which one of the following is a valid VTP advertisement?

    a. Triggered update

    b. VLAN database

    c. Subset

    d. Domain

4. Which one of the following is needed for VTP communication?

    a. A Management VLAN

    b. A Trunk link

    c. An Access VLAN

    d. An IP address

5. Which one of the following VTP modes does not allow any manual VLAN configuration changes?

    a. Server

    b. Client

    c. Designated

    d. Transparent

6. Select all the parameters that decide whether to accept new VTP information:

    a. VTP priority

    b. VTP domain name

    c. Configuration revision number

    d. VTP server name

7. How many VTP management domains can a Catalyst switch participate in?

    a. 1

    b. 2

    c. Unlimited

    d. 4096

8. Which IOS command configures a Catalyst switch for VTP client mode?

    a. set vtp mode client

    b. vtp client

    c. vtp mode client

    d. vtp client mode

9. What is the purpose of VTP pruning?

    a. Limit the number of VLANs in a domain

    b. Stop unnecessary VTP advertisements

    c. Limit the extent of broadcast traffic

    d. Limit the size of the virtual tree

10. Which VLAN number is never eligible for VTP pruning?

    a. 0

    b. 1

    c. 1000

    d. 1001

11. Which of the following might present a VTP problem?

    a. Two or more VTP servers in a domain

    b. Two servers with the same configuration revision number

    c. A server in two domains

    d. A new server with a higher configuration revision number

12. If a VTP server is configured for VTP version 2, what else must happen for successful VTP communication in a domain?

    a. A VTP version 2 password must be set.

    b. All other switches in the domain must be version 2 capable.

    c. All other switches must be configured for VTP version 2.

    d. The VTP configuration revision number must be reset.

Foundation Topics

VLAN Trunking Protocol

As the previous chapter demonstrated, VLAN configuration and trunking on a switch or a small group of switches is fairly intuitive. Campus network environments, however, usually consist of many interconnected switches. Configuring and managing a large number of switches, VLANs, and VLAN trunks quickly can get out of control.

Cisco has developed a method to manage VLANs across the campus network. The VLAN Trunking Protocol (VTP) uses Layer 2 trunk frames to communicate VLAN information among a group of switches. VTP manages the addition, deletion, and renaming of VLANs across the network from a central point of control. Any switch participating in a VTP exchange is aware of and can use any VLAN that VTP manages.

VTP Domains

VTP is organized into *management domains,* or areas with common VLAN requirements. A switch can belong to only one VTP domain, in addition to sharing VLAN information with other switches in the domain. Switches in different VTP domains, however, do not share VTP information.

Switches in a VTP domain advertise several attributes to their domain neighbors. Each advertisement contains information about the VTP management domain, VTP revision number, known VLANs, and specific VLAN parameters. When a VLAN is added to a switch in a management domain, other switches are notified of the new VLAN through *VTP advertisements.* In this way, all switches in a domain can prepare to receive traffic on their trunk ports using the new VLAN.

VTP Modes

Key
Topic

To participate in a VTP management domain, each switch must be configured to operate in one of several modes. The VTP mode determines how the switch processes and advertises VTP information. You can use the following modes:

- **Server mode**—VTP servers have full control over VLAN creation and modification for their domains. All VTP information is advertised to other switches in the domain, while all received VTP information is synchronized with the other switches. By default, a switch is in VTP server mode. Note that each VTP domain must have at least one server so that VLANs can be created, modified, or deleted, and VLAN information can be propagated.

- **Client mode**—VTP clients do not allow the administrator to create, change, or delete any VLANs. Instead, they listen to VTP advertisements from other switches and modify their VLAN configurations accordingly. In effect, this is a passive listening mode. Received VTP information is forwarded out trunk links to neighboring switches in the domain, so the switch also acts as a VTP relay.

- **Transparent mode**—VTP transparent switches do not participate in VTP. While in transparent mode, a switch does not advertise its own VLAN configuration, and a switch does not synchronize its VLAN database with received advertisements. In VTP version 1, a transparent mode switch does not even relay VTP information it receives to other switches unless its VTP domain names and VTP version numbers match those of the other switches. In VTP version 2, transparent switches do forward received VTP advertisements out of their trunk ports, acting as VTP relays. This occurs regardless of the VTP domain name setting.

Tip: While a switch is in VTP transparent mode, it can create and delete VLANs that are local only to itself. These VLAN changes, however, are not propagated to any other switch.

VTP Advertisements

Each Cisco switch participating in VTP advertises VLANs (only VLANs 1 to 1005), revision numbers, and VLAN parameters on its trunk ports to notify other switches in the management domain. VTP advertisements are sent as multicast frames. The switch intercepts frames sent to the VTP multicast address and processes them with its supervisory processor. VTP frames are forwarded out trunk links as a special case.

Because all switches in a management domain learn of new VLAN configuration changes, a VLAN must be created and configured on only one VTP server switch in the domain.

By default, management domains are set to use nonsecure advertisements without a password. You can add a password to set the domain to secure mode. The same password must be configured on every switch in the domain so that all switches exchanging VTP information use identical encryption methods.

VTP switches use an index called the *VTP configuration revision number* to keep track of the most recent information. Every switch in a VTP domain stores the configuration revision number that it last heard from a VTP advertisement. The VTP advertisement process always starts with configuration revision number 0 (zero).

When subsequent changes are made on a VTP server, the revision number is incremented before the advertisements are sent. When listening switches (configured as members of the same VTP domain as the advertising switch) receive an advertisement with a greater revision number than is stored locally, the advertisement overwrites any stored VLAN information.

Because of this, it is very important to always force any newly added network switches to have revision number 0 before being attached to the network. Otherwise, a switch might have stored a revision number that is greater than the value currently in use in the domain.

The VTP revision number is stored in NVRAM and is not altered by a power cycle of the switch. Therefore, the revision number can be initialized to 0 only by using one of the following methods:

- Change the switch's VTP mode to transparent and then change the mode back to server.

- Change the switch's VTP domain to a bogus name (a nonexistent VTP domain), and then change the VTP domain back to the original name.

If the VTP revision number is not reset to 0, the switch might enter the network as a VTP server and have a pre-existing revision number (from a previous life) that is higher than in previous legitimate advertisements. The new switch's VTP information would be seen as more recent, so all other switches in the VTP domain would gladly accept its database of VLANs and overwrite their good VLAN database entries with null or deleted VLAN status information.

In other words, a new server switch might inadvertently cause every other working switch to flush all records of every VLAN in production. The VLANs would be deleted from the VTP database and from the switches, causing any switch port assigned to them to become inactive. This is referred to as a *VTP synchronization problem*. For critical portions of your network, you should consider using transparent VTP mode to prevent the synchronization problem from ever becoming an issue.

> **Tip:** It might seem intuitive that a switch acting as a VTP server could come online with a higher configuration revision number and wreak havoc on the whole domain. You should also be aware that this same thing can happen if a VTP client comes online with a higher revision, too!
>
> Even though it seems as if a client should strictly listen to advertisements from servers, a client can and does send out its own advertisements. When it first powers up, a client sends a summary advertisement from its own stored database. It realizes that it has a greater revision number if it receives an inferior advertisement from a server. Therefore, it sends out a subset advertisement with the greater revision number, which VTP servers will accept as more up-to-date information.

VTP advertisements can originate as requests from client mode switches that want to learn about the VTP database at boot. Advertisements also can originate from server mode switches as VLAN configuration changes occur.

VTP advertisements can occur in three forms:

- **Summary advertisements**—VTP domain servers send summary advertisements every 300 seconds and every time a VLAN database change occurs. The summary advertisement lists information about the management domain, including VTP version, domain name, configuration revision number, time stamp, MD5 encryption hash code, and the number of subset advertisements to follow. For VLAN configuration changes, summary advertisements are followed by one or more subset advertisements with more specific VLAN configuration data. Figure 5-1 shows the summary advertisement format.

- **Subset advertisements**—VTP domain servers send subset advertisements after a VLAN configuration change occurs. These advertisements list the specific changes that have been performed, such as creating or deleting a VLAN, suspending or activating a VLAN, changing the name of a VLAN, and changing a VLAN's maximum transmission unit (MTU). Subset advertisements can list the following VLAN parameters: status of the VLAN, VLAN type (such as Ethernet or Token Ring), MTU, length of the VLAN name, VLAN number, security association identifier (SAID) value, and

VLAN name. VLANs are listed individually in sequential subset advertisements. Figure 5-2 shows the VTP subset advertisement format.

Version (1 byte)	Type (Summary Adv) (1 byte)	Number of subset advertisements to follow (1 byte)	Domain name length (1 byte)
Management Domain Name (zero-padded to 32 bytes)			
Configuration Revision Number (4 bytes)			
Updater Identity (orginating IP address: 4 bytes)			
Update Time Stamp (12 bytes)			
MD5 Digest hash code (16 bytes)			

Figure 5-1 *VTP Summary Advertisement Format*

VTP Subset Advertisement

0	1	2	3
Version (1 byte)	Type (Subset Adv) (1 byte)	Subset sequence number (1 byte)	Domain name length (1 byte)
Management Domain Name (zero-padded to 32 bytes)			
Configuration Revision Number (4 bytes)			
VLAN Info Field 1 (see below)			
VLAN Info Field ...			
VLAN Info Field N			

VTP VLAN Info Field

0	1	2	3
Info Length	VLAN Status	VLAN Type	VLAN Name Length
VLAN ID		MTU Size	
802.10 SAID			
VLAN Name (padded with zeros to multiple of 4 bytes)			

Figure 5-2 *VTP Subset Advertisement and VLAN Info Field Formats*

■ **Advertisement requests from clients**—A VTP client can request any VLAN information it lacks. For example, a client switch might be reset and have its VLAN database cleared, and its VTP domain membership might be changed, or it might hear a VTP summary advertisement with a higher revision number than it currently has. After a client advertisement request, the VTP domain servers respond with summary and subset advertisements to bring it up to date. Figure 5-3 shows the advertisement request format.

0	1	2	3
Version (1 byte)	Type (Adv request) (1 byte)	Reserved (1 byte)	Domain name length (1 byte)
Management Domain Name (zero-padded to 32 bytes)			
Starting advertisement to request			

Figure 5-3 *VTP Advertisement Request Format*

Catalyst switches in server mode store VTP information separately from the switch configuration in NVRAM. VLAN and VTP data are saved in the vlan.dat file on the switch's flash memory file system. All VTP information, including the VTP configuration revision number, is retained even when the switch power is off. In this manner, a switch can recover the last known VLAN configuration from its VTP database after it reboots.

Tip: Remember that even in VTP client mode, a switch will store the last known VTP information—including the configuration revision number. Don't assume that a VTP client will start with a clean slate when it powers up.

VTP Configuration

By default, every switch operates in VTP server mode for the management domain NULL (a blank string), with no password or secure mode. If the switch hears a VTP summary advertisement on a trunk port from any other switch, it automatically learns the VTP domain name, VLANs, and the configuration revision number it hears. This makes it easy to bring up a new switch in an existing VTP domain. However, be aware that the new switch stays in VTP server mode, something that might not be desirable.

Tip: You should get into the habit of double-checking the VTP configuration of any switch before you add it into your network. Make sure that the VTP configuration revision number is set to 0. You can do this by isolating the switch from the network, powering it up, and using the **show vtp status** command, as demonstrated in the following output:

```
Switch# show vtp status
VTP Version                     : 2
Configuration Revision          : 0
Maximum VLANs supported locally : 1005
Number of existing VLANs        : 5
```

```
VTP Operating Mode               : Server
VTP Domain Name                  :
VTP Pruning Mode                 : Disabled
VTP V2 Mode                      : Disabled
VTP Traps Generation             : Disabled
MD5 digest                       : 0x57 0xCD 0x40 0x65 0x63 0x59 0x47 0xBD
Configuration last modified by 0.0.0.0 at 0-0-00 00:00:00
Switch#
```

Here, the switch has a configuration revision number of 0, and is in the default state of VTP server mode with an undefined VTP domain name. This switch would be safe to add to a network.

The following sections discuss the commands and considerations that you should use to configure a switch for VTP operation.

You should be aware that there are two supported ways to configure VLAN and VTP information in Catalyst IOS switches:

- Global configuration mode commands (for example, **vlan**, **vtp mode**, and **vtp domain**)

- VLAN database mode commands

The **vlan database** EXEC command still is supported in Catalyst IOS Software only for backward compatibility, but this is not covered in the SWITCH course or the exam.

Configuring a VTP Management Domain

Before a switch is added into a network, the VTP management domain should be identified. If this switch is the first one on the network, the management domain must be created. Otherwise, the switch might have to join an existing management domain with other existing switches.

Key
Topic

You can use the following global configuration command to assign a switch to a management domain, where the *domain-name* is a text string up to 32 characters long:

```
Switch(config)# vtp domain domain-name
```

Configuring the VTP Mode

Next, you need to choose the VTP mode for the new switch. The three VTP modes of operation and their guidelines for use are as follows:

- **Server mode**—Server mode can be used on any switch in a management domain, even if other server and client switches are in use. This mode provides some redundancy in case of a server failure in the domain. Each VTP management domain should have at least one server. The first server defined in a network also defines the management domain that will be used by future VTP servers and clients. Server mode is the default VTP mode and allows VLANs to be created and deleted.

Note: Multiple VTP servers can coexist in a domain. This usually is recommended for redundancy. The servers do not elect a primary or secondary server; they all simply function as servers. If one server is configured with a new VLAN or VTP parameter, it advertises the changes to the rest of the domain. All other servers synchronize their VTP databases to this advertisement, just as any VTP client would.

- **Client mode**—If other switches are in the management domain, you should configure a new switch for client mode operation. In this way, the switch is forced to learn any existing VTP information from a reliable existing server. After the switch has learned the current VTP information, you can reconfigure it for server mode if it will be used as a redundant server.

- **Transparent mode**—This mode is used if a switch will not share VLAN information with any other switch in the network. VLANs still can be created, deleted, and modified on the transparent switch. However, they are not advertised to other neighboring switches. VTP advertisements received by a transparent switch, however, are forwarded to other switches on trunk links.

Keeping switches in transparent mode can eliminate the chance for duplicate, overlapping VLANs in a large network with many network administrators. For example, two administrators might configure VLANs on switches in their respective areas but use the same VLAN identification or VLAN number. Even though the two VLANs have different meanings and purposes, they could overlap if both administrators advertised them using VTP servers.

Key Topic

You can configure the VTP mode with the following sequence of global configuration commands:

```
Switch(config)# vtp mode {server | client | transparent}
Switch(config)# vtp password password
```

If the domain is operating in secure mode, a password also can be defined. The password can be configured only on VTP servers and clients. The password itself is not sent; instead, an MD5 digest or hash code is computed and sent in VTP advertisements (servers) and is used to validate received advertisements (clients). The password is a string of 1 to 32 characters (case sensitive).

If secure VTP is implemented using passwords, begin by configuring a password on the VTP servers. The client switches retain the last-known VTP information but cannot process received advertisements until the same password is configured on them, too.

Table 5-2 shows a summary of the VTP modes. You can use this table for quick review as you study VTP operation.

Table 5-2 *Catalyst VTP Modes*

VTP Mode	Characteristics
Server	All VLAN and VTP configuration changes occur here. The server advertises settings and changes to all other servers and clients in a VTP domain. (This is the default mode for Catalyst switches.)
Client	Listens to all VTP advertisements from servers in a VTP domain. Advertisements are relayed out other trunk links. No VLAN or VTP configuration changes can be made on a client.
Transparent	VLAN configuration changes are made locally, independent of any VTP domain. VTP advertisements are not received but merely are relayed out other trunk links, if possible.

Configuring the VTP Version

Two versions of VTP are available for use in a management domain. Catalyst switches are capable of running either VTP version 1 or VTP version 2. Within a management domain, the two versions are not interoperable. Therefore, the same VTP version must be configured on every switch in a domain. VTP version 1 is the default protocol on a switch.

If a switch is capable of running VTP version 2, however, a switch can coexist with other version 1 switches, as long as its VTP version 2 is not enabled. This situation becomes important if you want to use version 2 in a domain. Then only one server mode switch needs to have VTP version 2 enabled. The new version number is propagated to all other version 2–capable switches in the domain, causing them all to automatically enable version 2 for use.

Key Topic

> **Tip:** A third version of VTP addresses some of the traditional shortcomings. For example, VTP version 3 supports extended VLAN numbers (1 to 4095) that are compatible with the IEEE 802.1Q trunking standard. At the time of this writing, VTPv3 is available only on Cisco Catalyst platforms running the CatOS (non-IOS) operating system. Therefore, only VTP versions 1 and 2 are covered on the SWITCH exam and in this text.

The two versions of VTP differ in the features they support. VTP version 2 offers the following additional features over Version 1:

■ **Version-dependent transparent mode**—In transparent mode, VTP version 1 matches the VTP version and domain name before forwarding the information to other switches using VTP. VTP version 2 in transparent mode forwards the VTP messages without checking the version number. Because only one domain is supported in a switch, the domain name doesn't have to be checked.

■ **Consistency checks**—VTP version 2 performs consistency checks on the VTP and VLAN parameters entered from the command-line interface (CLI) or by the Simple Network Management Protocol (SNMP). This checking helps prevent errors in such things as VLAN names and numbers from being propagated to other switches in the domain. However, no consistency checks are performed on VTP messages that are received on trunk links or on configuration and database data that is read from NVRAM.

- **Token Ring support**—VTP version 2 supports the use of Token Ring switching and Token Ring VLANs. (If Token Ring switching is being used, VTP version 2 must be enabled.)

- **Unrecognized Type-Length-Value (TLV) support**—VTP version 2 switches propagate received configuration change messages out other trunk links, even if the switch supervisor cannot parse or understand the message. For example, a VTP advertisement contains a Type field to denote what type of VTP message is being sent. VTP message type 1 is a summary advertisement, and message type 2 is a subset advertisement. An extension to VTP that utilizes other message types and other message length values could be in use. Instead of dropping the unrecognized VTP message, version 2 still propagates the information and keeps a copy in NVRAM.

The VTP version number is configured using the following global configuration command:

```
Switch(config)# vtp version {1 | 2}
```

By default, a switch uses VTP Version 1.

VTP Configuration Example

As an example, a switch is configured as the VTP server in a domain named MyCompany. The domain uses secure VTP with the password **bigsecret**. You can use the following configuration commands to accomplish this:

```
Switch(config)# vtp domain MyCompany
Switch(config)# vtp mode server
Switch(config)# vtp password bigsecret
```

VTP Status

The current VTP parameters for a management domain can be displayed using the **show vtp status** command. Example 5-1 demonstrates some sample output of this command from a switch acting as a VTP client in the VTP domain called CampusDomain.

Example 5-1   show vtp status *Reveals VTP Parameters for a Management Domain*

```
Switch# show vtp status
VTP Version                      : 2
Configuration Revision           : 89
Maximum VLANs supported locally  : 1005
Number of existing VLANs         : 74
VTP Operating Mode               : Client
VTP Domain Name                  : CampusDomain
VTP Pruning Mode                 : Enabled VTP V2 Mode : Disabled VTP
  Traps Generation               : Disabled
```

```
MD5 digest                      : 0x4B 0x07 0x75 0xEC 0xB1 0x3D 0x6F 0x1F
                                  Configuration
  last modified by 192.168.199.1 at 11-19-02 09:29:56
Switch#
```

VTP message and error counters also can be displayed with the **show vtp counters** command. You can use this command for basic VTP troubleshooting to see whether the switch is interacting with other VTP nodes in the domain. Example 5-2 demonstrates some sample output from the **show vtp counters** command.

Example 5-2   show vtp counters *Reveals VTP Message and Error Counters*

```
Switch# show vtp counters
VTP statistics:
Summary advertisements received     : 1
Subset advertisements received      : 2
Request advertisements received     : 1
Summary advertisements transmitted : 1630
Subset advertisements transmitted   : 0
Request advertisements transmitted : 4
Number of config revision errors    : 0
Number of config digest errors      : 0
Number of V1 summary errors         : 0

VTP pruning statistics:

Trunk             Join Transmitted Join Received   Summary advts received from
                                                   non-pruning-capable device
----------------- ---------------- --------------- -------------------------------
Gi0/1                 82352             82931        0
Switch#
```

VTP Pruning

Recall that, by definition, a switch must forward broadcast frames out all available ports in the broadcast domain because broadcasts are destined everywhere there is a listener. Unless forwarded by more intelligent means, multicast frames follow the same pattern.

In addition, frames destined for an address that the switch has not yet learned or has *forgotten* (the MAC address has aged out of the address table) must be forwarded out all ports in an attempt to find the destination. These frames are referred to as *unknown unicast.*

When forwarding frames out all ports in a broadcast domain or VLAN, trunk ports are included if they transport that VLAN. By default, a trunk link transports traffic from all VLANs, unless specific VLANs are removed from the trunk. Generally, in a network with several switches, trunk links are enabled between switches, and VTP is used to manage the propagation of VLAN information. This scenario causes the trunk links between switches to carry traffic from *all* VLANs, not just from the specific VLANs created.

Consider the network shown in Figure 5-4. When end user Host PC in VLAN 3 sends a broadcast, Catalyst switch C forwards the frame out all VLAN 3 ports, including the trunk link to Catalyst A. Catalyst A, in turn, forwards the broadcast on to Catalysts B and D over those trunk links. Catalysts B and D forward the broadcast out only their access links that have been configured for VLAN 3. If Catalysts B and D do not have any active users in VLAN 3, forwarding that broadcast frame to them would consume bandwidth on the trunk links and processor resources in both switches, only to have switches B and D discard the frames.

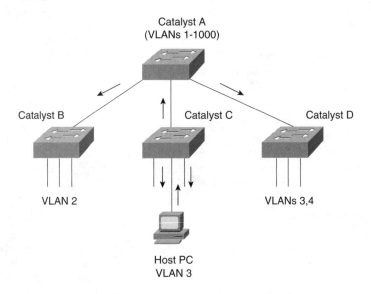

Figure 5-4 *Flooding in a Catalyst Switch Network*

Key Topic

VTP pruning makes more efficient use of trunk bandwidth by reducing unnecessary flooded traffic. Broadcast and unknown unicast frames on a VLAN are forwarded over a trunk link only if the switch on the receiving end of the trunk has ports in that VLAN.

VTP pruning occurs as an extension to VTP version 1, using an additional VTP message type. When a Catalyst switch has a port associated with a VLAN, the switch sends an advertisement to its neighbor switches that it has active ports on that VLAN. The neighbors keep this information, enabling them to decide whether flooded traffic from a VLAN should use a trunk port.

Figure 5-5 shows the network from Figure 5-4 with VTP pruning enabled. Because Catalyst B has not advertised its use of VLAN 3, Catalyst A will prune VLAN 3 from the trunk to B and will choose not to flood VLAN 3 traffic to Catalyst B over the trunk link. Catalyst D has advertised the need for VLAN 3, so traffic will be flooded to it.

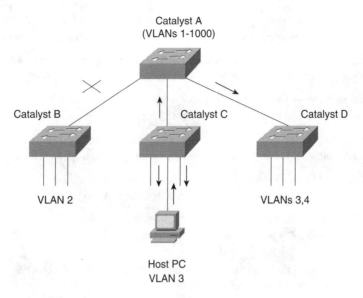

Figure 5-5   *Flooding in a Catalyst Switch Network Using VTP Pruning*

> **Tip:** Even when VTP pruning has determined that a VLAN is not needed on a trunk, an
> instance of the Spanning Tree Protocol (STP) will run for every VLAN that is allowed on
> the trunk link. To reduce the number of STP instances, you manually should "prune"
> unneeded VLANs from the trunk and allow only the needed ones. Use the **switchport
> trunk allowed vlan** command to identify the VLANs that should be added or removed
> from a trunk.

Enabling VTP Pruning

By default, VTP pruning is disabled on IOS-based switches. To enable pruning, use the following global configuration command:

```
Switch(config)# vtp pruning
```

If you use this command on a VTP server, it also advertises that pruning needs to be enabled for the entire management domain. All other switches listening to that advertisement
also will enable pruning.

When pruning is enabled, all general-purpose VLANs become eligible for pruning on all
trunk links, if needed. However, you can modify the default list of pruning eligibility with
the following interface-configuration command:

```
Switch(config)# interface type mod/num
Switch(config-if)# switchport trunk pruning vlan {{{add | except |  remove}
  vlan-list} | none}
```

By default, VLANs 2 through 1001 are eligible, or "enabled," for potential pruning on every trunk. Use one of the following keywords with the command to tailor the list:

■ *vlan-list*—An explicit list of eligible VLAN numbers (anything from 2 to 1001), separated by commas or by dashes.

■ **add** *vlan-list*—A list of VLAN numbers (anything from 2 to 1001) is added to the already configured list; this is a shortcut to keep from typing a long list of numbers.

■ **except** *vlan-list*—All VLANs are eligible except for the VLAN numbers listed (anything from 2 to 1001); this is a shortcut to keep from typing a long list of numbers.

■ **remove** *vlan-list*—A list of VLAN numbers (anything from 2 to 1001) is removed from the already configured list; this is a shortcut to keep from typing a long list of numbers.

■ **none**—No VLAN will be eligible for pruning.

Tip: Be aware that VTP pruning has no effect on switches in the VTP transparent mode. Instead, those switches must be configured manually to "prune" VLANs from trunk links. In this case, pruning is always configured on the upstream side of a trunk. (The downstream side switch doesn't have any ports that belong to the pruned VLAN, so there is no need to prune from that end.)

By default, VLANs 2 to 1001 are eligible for pruning. VLAN 1 has a special meaning because it sometimes is used for control traffic and is the default access VLAN on switch ports. Because of these historical reasons, VLAN 1 is never eligible for pruning. In addition, VLANs 1002 through 1005 are reserved for Token Ring and FDDI VLANs and are never eligible for pruning.

Troubleshooting VTP

If a switch does not seem to be receiving updated information from a VTP server, consider these possible causes:

■ The switch is configured for VTP transparent mode. In this mode, incoming VTP advertisements are not processed; they are relayed only to other switches in the domain.

■ If the switch is configured as a VTP client, there might not be another switch functioning as a VTP server. In this case, configure the local switch to become a VTP server itself.

■ The link toward the VTP server is not in trunking mode. VTP advertisements are sent only over trunks. Use the **show interface** *type mod/num* **switchport** to verify the operational mode as a trunk.

■ Make sure the VTP domain name is configured correctly to match that of the VTP server.

■ Make sure the VTP version is compatible with other switches in the VTP domain.

■ Make sure the VTP password matches others in the VTP domain. If the server doesn't use a password, make sure the password is disabled or cleared on the local switch.

Tip: Above all else, verify a switch's VTP configuration before connecting it to a production network. If the switch has been configured previously or used elsewhere, it might already be in VTP server mode and have a VTP configuration revision number that is higher than that of other switches in the production VTP domain. In that case, other switches will listen and learn from the new switch because it has a higher revision number and must know more recent information. This could cause the new switch to introduce bogus VLANs into the domain or, worse yet, to cause all other switches in the domain to delete all their active VLANs.

To prevent this from happening, reset the configuration revision number of every new switch before it is added to a production network.

Table 5-3 lists and describes the commands that are useful for verifying or troubleshooting VTP configuration.

Table 5-3 *VTP Configuration Troubleshooting Commands*

Function	Command Syntax
Displays current VTP parameters, including the last advertising server	**show vtp status**
Displays VTP advertisement and pruning statistics	**show vtp counters**
Displays defined VLANs	**show vlan brief**
Displays trunk status, including pruning eligibility	**show interface** *type mod/num* **switchport**
Displays VTP pruning state	**show interface** *type mod/num* **pruning**

Exam Preparation Tasks

Review All Key Topics

Review the most important topics in the chapter, noted with the Key Topic icon in the outer margin of the page. Table 5-4 lists a reference of these key topics and the page numbers on which each is found.

Table 5-4 *Key Topics for Chapter 5*

Key Topic Element	Description	Page Number
Paragraph	Describes VTP modes	90
Paragraph	Explains the VPN configuration revision number	91
Paragraph	Discusses the VTP synchronization problem and how to prevent it from occurring	92
Paragraph	Explains how to configure the VTP domain	95
Paragraph	Explains how to configure the VTP mode	96
Paragraph	Describes VTP version operation	97
Paragraph	Discusses how to verify VTP operation	98
Paragraph	Explains VTP pruning	100

Complete Tables and Lists from Memory

Print a copy of Appendix C, "Memory Tables," (found on the CD), or at least the section for this chapter, and complete the tables and lists from memory. Appendix D, "Memory Tables Answer Key," also on the CD, includes completed tables and lists to check your work.

Define Key Terms

Define the following key terms from this chapter, and check your answers in the glossary:

VTP, VTP domain, VTP configuration revision number, VTP synchronization problem, VTP pruning

Use Command Reference to Check Your Memory

This section includes the most important configuration and EXEC commands covered in this chapter. It might not be necessary to memorize the complete syntax of every command, but you should remember the basic keywords that are needed.

To test your memory of the VTP-related commands, cover the right side of Table 5-5 with a piece of paper, read the description on the left side, and then see how much of the command you can remember.

Remember that the CCNP exam focuses on practical or hands-on skills that are used by a networking professional. For the skills covered in this chapter, remember that the commands always involve the **vtp** keyword.

Table 5-5 *VTP Configuration Commands*

Task	Command Syntax
Define the VTP domain.	**vtp domain** *domain-name*
Set the VTP mode.	**vtp mode** {**server** | **client** | **transparent**}
Define an optional VTP password.	**vtp password** *password*
Configure VTP version.	**vtp version** {**1** | **2**}
Enable VTP pruning.	**vtp pruning**
Select VLANs eligible for pruning on a trunk interface.	**interface** *type mod/num* **switchport trunk pruning vlan** {**add** | **except** | **none** | **remove**} *vlan-list*

This chapter covers the following topics that you need to master for the CCNP SWITCH exam:

Switch Port Aggregation with EtherChannel—This section discusses the concept of aggregating, or "bundling," physical ports into a single logical link. Methods for load balancing traffic across the physical links also are covered.

EtherChannel Negotiation Protocols—This section discusses two protocols that dynamically negotiate and control EtherChannels: Port Aggregation Protocol (PAgP), a Cisco proprietary protocol, and Link Aggregation Control Protocol (LACP), a standards-based protocol.

EtherChannel Configuration—This section discusses the Catalyst switch commands needed to configure EtherChannel.

Troubleshooting an EtherChannel—This section gives a brief summary of things to consider and commands to use when an aggregated link is not operating properly.

CHAPTER 6

Aggregating Switch Links

In previous chapters, you learned about connecting switches and organizing users and devices into common workgroups. Using these principles, end users can be given effective access to resources both on and off the campus network. However, today's mission-critical applications and services demand networks that provide high availability and reliability.

This chapter presents technologies that you can use in a campus network to provide higher bandwidth and reliability between switches.

"Do I Know This Already?" Quiz

The "Do I Know This Already?" quiz allows you to assess whether you should read this entire chapter thoroughly or jump to the "Exam Preparation Tasks" section. If you are in doubt based on your answers to these questions or your own assessment of your knowledge of the topics, read the entire chapter. Table 6-1 outlines the major headings in this chapter and the "Do I Know This Already?" quiz questions that go with them. You can find the answers in Appendix A, "Answers to the 'Do I Know This Already?' Quizzes."

Table 6-1 *"Do I Know This Already?" Foundation Topics Section-to-Question Mapping*

Foundation Topics Section	Questions Covered in This Section
Switch Port Aggregation with EtherChannel	1–7
EtherChannel Negotiation Protocols	8–11
EtherChannel Configuration	11–12
Troubleshooting an EtherChannel	13

1. If Fast Ethernet ports are bundled into an EtherChannel, what is the maximum throughput supported on a Catalyst switch?

   a. 100 Mbps

   b. 200 Mbps

   c. 400 Mbps

   d. 800 Mbps

   e. 1600 Mbps

2. Which of these methods distributes traffic over an EtherChannel?

   a.   Round robin

   b.   Least-used link

   c.   A function of address

   d.   A function of packet size

3. What type of interface represents an EtherChannel as a whole?

   a.   Channel

   b.   Port

   c.   Port channel

   d.   Channel port

4. Which of the following is not a valid method for EtherChannel load balancing?

   a.   Source MAC address

   b.   Source and destination MAC addresses

   c.   Source IP address

   d.   IP precedence

   e.   UDP/TCP port

5. How can the EtherChannel load-balancing method be set?

   a.   Per switch port

   b.   Per EtherChannel

   c.   Globally per switch

   d.   Can't be configured

6. What logical operation is performed to calculate EtherChannel load balancing as a function of two addresses?

   a.   OR

   b.   AND

   c.   XOR

   d.   NOR

7. Which one of the following is a valid combination of ports for an EtherChannel?

   a.   Two access links (one VLAN 5, one VLAN 5)

   b.   Two access links (one VLAN 1, one VLAN 10)

   c.   Two trunk links (one VLANs 1 to 10, one VLANs 1, 11 to 20)

   d.   Two Fast Ethernet links (both full duplex, one 10 Mbps)

8. Which of these is a method for negotiating an EtherChannel?

   a. PAP

   b. CHAP

   c. LAPD

   d. LACP

9. Which of the following is a valid EtherChannel negotiation mode combination between two switches?

   a. PAgP auto, PAgP auto

   b. PAgP auto, PAgP desirable

   c. on, PAgP auto

   d. LACP passive, LACP passive

10. When is PAgP's "desirable silent" mode useful?

   a. When the switch should not send PAgP frames

   b. When the switch should not form an EtherChannel

   c. When the switch should not expect to receive PAgP frames

   d. When the switch is using LACP mode

11. Which of the following EtherChannel modes does not send or receive any negotiation frames?

   a. channel-group 1 mode passive

   b. channel-group 1 mode active

   c. channel-group 1 mode on

   d. channel-group 1 mode desirable

   e. channel-group 1 mode auto

12. Two computers are the only hosts sending IP data across an EtherChannel between two switches. Several different applications are being used between them. Which of these load-balancing methods would be more likely to use the most links in the EtherChannel?

   a. Source and destination MAC addresses.

   b. Source and destination IP addresses.

   c. Source and destination TCP/UDP ports.

   d. None of the other answers is correct.

13. Which command can be used to see the status of an EtherChannel's links?

   a. show channel link

   b. show etherchannel status

   c. show etherchannel summary

   d. show ether channel status

Foundation Topics

Switch Port Aggregation with EtherChannel

Key
Topic

As discussed in Chapter 3, "Switch Port Configuration," switches can use Ethernet, Fast Ethernet, Gigabit, or 10-Gigabit Ethernet ports to scale link speeds by a factor of ten. Cisco offers another method of scaling link bandwidth by aggregating, or *bundling*, parallel links, termed the *EtherChannel* technology. Two to eight links of either Fast Ethernet (FE), Gigabit Ethernet (GE), or 10-Gigabit Ethernet (10GE) are bundled as one logical link of *Fast EtherChannel (FEC), Gigabit EtherChannel (GEC),* or *10-Gigabit Etherchannel (10GEC)*, respectively. This bundle provides a full-duplex bandwidth of up to 1600 Mbps (eight links of Fast Ethernet), 16 Gbps (eight links of Gigabit Ethernet), or 160 Gbps (eight links of 10-Gigabit Ethernet).

This also provides an easy means to "grow," or expand, a link's capacity between two switches, without having to continually purchase hardware for the next magnitude of throughput. For example, a single Fast Ethernet link (200 Mbps throughput) can be incrementally expanded up to eight Fast Ethernet links (1600 Mbps) as a single Fast EtherChannel. If the traffic load grows beyond that, the growth process can begin again with a single Gigabit Ethernet link (2 Gbps throughput), which can be expanded up to eight Gigabit Ethernet links as a Gigabit EtherChannel (16 Gbps). The process repeats again by moving to a single 10-Gigabit Ethernet link, and so on.

Ordinarily, having multiple or parallel links between switches creates the possibility of bridging loops, an undesirable condition. EtherChannel avoids this situation by bundling parallel links into a single, logical link, which can act as either an access or a trunk link. Switches or devices on each end of the EtherChannel link must understand and use the EtherChannel technology for proper operation.

Although an EtherChannel link is seen as a single logical link, the link doesn't necessarily have an inherent total bandwidth equal to the sum of its component physical links. For example, suppose that an FEC link is made up of four full-duplex, 100-Mbps Fast Ethernet links. Although it is possible for the FEC link to carry a total throughput of 800 Mbps (if each link becomes fully loaded), the single resulting FEC bundle does not operate at this speed.

Instead, traffic is distributed across the individual links within the EtherChannel. Each of these links operates at its inherent speed (200 Mbps full duplex for FE) but carries only the frames placed on it by the EtherChannel hardware. If one link within the bundle is favored by the load-distribution algorithm, that link will carry a disproportionate amount of traffic. In other words, the load isn't always distributed equally among the individual links. The load-balancing process is explained further in the next section.

EtherChannel also provides redundancy with several bundled physical links. If one of the links within the bundle fails, traffic sent through that link automatically is moved to an adjacent link. Failover occurs in less than a few milliseconds and is transparent to the end user. As more links fail, more traffic is moved to further adjacent links. Likewise, as links are restored, the load automatically is redistributed among the active links.

Bundling Ports with EtherChannel

EtherChannel bundles can consist of up to eight physical ports of the same Ethernet media type and speed. Some configuration restrictions exist to ensure that only similarly configured links are bundled.

Generally, all bundled ports first must belong to the same VLAN. If used as a trunk, bundled ports must be in trunking mode, have the same native VLAN, and pass the same set of VLANs. Each of the ports should have the same speed and duplex settings before being bundled. Bundled ports also must be configured with identical spanning-tree settings.

Distributing Traffic in EtherChannel

Traffic in an EtherChannel is distributed across the individual bundled links in a deterministic fashion; however, the load is not necessarily balanced equally across all the links. Instead, frames are forwarded on a specific link as a result of a hashing algorithm. The algorithm can use source IP address, destination IP address, or a combination of source and destination IP addresses, source and destination MAC addresses, or TCP/UDP port numbers. The hash algorithm computes a binary pattern that selects a link number in the bundle to carry each frame.

If only one address or port number is hashed, a switch forwards each frame by using one or more low-order bits of the hash value as an index into the bundled links. If two addresses or port numbers are hashed, a switch performs an exclusive-OR (XOR) operation on one or more low-order bits of the addresses or TCP/UDP port numbers as an index into the bundled links.

For example, an EtherChannel consisting of two links bundled together requires a 1-bit index. If the index is 0, link 0 is selected; if the index is 1, link 1 is used. Either the lowest-order address bit or the XOR of the last bit of the addresses in the frame is used as the index. A four-link bundle uses a hash of the last 2 bits. Likewise, an eight-link bundle uses a hash of the last 3 bits. The hashing operation's outcome selects the EtherChannel's outbound link. Table 6-2 shows the results of an XOR on a two-link bundle, using the source and destination addresses.

Table 6-2 *Frame Distribution on a Two-Link EtherChannel*

Binary Address	Two-Link EtherChannel XOR and Link Number
Addr1: ... xxxxxxx0 Addr2: ... xxxxxxx0	... xxxxxxx0: Use link 0
Addr1: ... xxxxxxx0 Addr2: ... xxxxxxx1	... xxxxxxx1: Use link 1
Addr1: ... xxxxxxx1 Addr2: ... xxxxxxx0	... xxxxxxx1: Use link 1

continues

Table 6-2   *Frame Distribution on a Two-Link EtherChannel   (Continued)*

Binary Address	Two-Link EtherChannel XOR and Link Number
Addr1: ... xxxxxxx1	... xxxxxxx0: Use link 0
Addr2: ... xxxxxxx1	

The XOR operation is performed independently on each bit position in the address value. If the two address values have the same bit value, the XOR result is always 0. If the two address bits differ, the XOR result is always 1. In this way, frames can be distributed statistically among the links with the assumption that MAC or IP addresses themselves are distributed statistically throughout the network. In a four-link EtherChannel, the XOR is performed on the lower 2 bits of the address values, resulting in a 2-bit XOR value (each bit is computed separately) or a link number from 0 to 3.

As an example, consider a packet being sent from IP address 192.168.1.1 to 172.31.67.46. Because EtherChannels can be built from two to eight individual links, only the rightmost (least-significant) 3 bits are needed as a link index. From the source and destination addresses, these bits are 001 (1) and 110 (6), respectively. For a two-link EtherChannel, a 1-bit XOR is performed on the rightmost address bit: 1 XOR 0 = 1, causing Link 1 in the bundle to be used. A four-link EtherChannel produces a 2-bit XOR: 01 XOR 10 = 11, causing Link 3 in the bundle to be used. Finally, an eight-link EtherChannel requires a 3-bit XOR: 001 XOR 110 = 111, where Link 7 in the bundle is selected.

A conversation between two devices always is sent through the same EtherChannel link because the two endpoint addresses stay the same. However, when a device talks to several other devices, chances are that the destination addresses are distributed equally with 0s and 1s in the last bit (even and odd address values). This causes the frames to be distributed across the EtherChannel links.

Note that the load distribution is still proportional to the volume of traffic passing between pairs of hosts or link indexes. For example, suppose that there are two pairs of hosts talking across a two-link channel, and each pair of addresses results in a unique link index. Frames from one pair of hosts always travel over one link in the channel, whereas frames from the other pair travel over the other link. The links are both being used as a result of the hash algorithm, so the load is being distributed across every link in the channel.

However, if one pair of hosts has a much greater volume of traffic than the other pair, one link in the channel will be used much more than the other. This still can create a load imbalance. To remedy this condition, you should consider other methods of hashing algorithms for the channel. For example, a method that combines the source and destination addresses along with UDP or TCP port numbers in a single XOR operation can distribute traffic much differently. Then, packets are placed on links within the bundle based on the applications (port numbers) used within conversations between two hosts. The possible hashing methods are discussed in the following section.

Configuring EtherChannel Load Balancing

The hashing operation can be performed on either MAC or IP addresses and can be based solely on source or destination addresses, or both. Use the following command to configure frame distribution for all EtherChannel switch links:

```
Switch(config)# port-channel load-balance method
```

Notice that the load-balancing method is set with a global configuration command. You must set the method globally for the switch, not on a per-port basis. Table 6-3 lists the possible values for the *method* variable, along with the hashing operation and some sample supporting switch models.

Table 6-3   *Types of EtherChannel Load-Balancing Methods*

Key Topic

method Value	Hash Input	Hash Operation	Switch Model
src-ip	Source IP address	bits	All models
dst-ip	Destination IP address	bits	All models
src-dst-ip	Source and destination IP address	XOR	All models
src-mac	Source MAC address	bits	All models
dst-mac	Destination MAC address	bits	All models
src-dst-mac	Source and destination MAC	XOR	All models
src-port	Source port number	bits	6500, 4500
dst-port	Destination port number	bits	6500, 4500
src-dst-port	Source and destination port	XOR	6500, 4500

The default configuration is to use source XOR destination IP addresses, or the **src-dst-ip** method. The default for the Catalyst 2970 and 3560 is **src-mac** for Layer 2 switching. If Layer 3 switching is used on the EtherChannel, the **src-dst-ip** method will always be used, even though it is not configurable.

Normally, the default action should result in a statistical distribution of frames; however, you should determine whether the EtherChannel is imbalanced according to the traffic patterns present. For example, if a single server is receiving most of the traffic on an Ether-Channel, the server's address (the destination IP address) always will remain constant in the many conversations. This can cause one link to be overused if the destination IP address is used as a component of a load-balancing method. In the case of a four-link Ether-Channel, perhaps two of the four links are overused. Configuring the use of MAC addresses, or only the source IP addresses, might cause the distribution to be more balanced across all the bundled links.

Tip: To verify how effectively a configured load-balancing method is performing, you can use the **show etherchannel port-channel** command. Each link in the channel is displayed, along with a hex "Load" value. Although this information is not intuitive, you can use the hex values to get an idea of each link's traffic loads relative to the others.

In some applications, EtherChannel traffic might consist of protocols other than IP. For example, IPX or SNA frames might be switched along with IP. Non-IP protocols need to be distributed according to MAC addresses because IP addresses are not applicable. Here, the switch should be configured to use MAC addresses instead of the IP default.

Tip: A special case results when a router is connected to an EtherChannel. Recall that a router always uses its burned-in MAC address in Ethernet frames, even though it is forwarding packets to and from many different IP addresses. In other words, many end stations send frames to their local router address with the router's MAC address as the destination. This means that the destination MAC address is the same for all frames destined through the router.

Usually, this will not present a problem because the source MAC addresses are all different. When two routers are forwarding frames to each other, however, both source and destination MAC addresses remains constant, and only one link of the EtherChannel is used. If the MAC addresses remain constant, choose IP addresses instead. Beyond that, if most of the traffic is between the same two IP addresses, as in the case of two servers talking, choose IP port numbers to disperse the frames across different links.

You should choose the load-balancing method that provides the greatest distribution or variety when the channel links are indexed. Also consider the type of addressing that is being used on the network. If most of the traffic is IP, it might make sense to load balance according to IP addresses or TCP/UDP port numbers.

But if IP load balancing is being used, what happens to non-IP frames? If a frame can't meet the load-balancing criteria, the switch automatically falls back to the "next lowest" method. With Ethernet, MAC addresses must always be present, so the switch distributes those frames according to their MAC addresses.

A switch also provides some inherent protection against bridging loops with EtherChannels. When ports are bundled into an EtherChannel, no inbound (received) broadcasts and multicasts are sent back out over any of the remaining ports in the channel. Outbound broadcast and multicast frames are load-balanced like any other: The broadcast or multicast address becomes part of the hashing calculation to choose an outbound channel link.

EtherChannel Negotiation Protocols

EtherChannels can be negotiated between two switches to provide some dynamic link configuration. Two protocols are available to negotiate bundled links in Catalyst switches. The Port Aggregation Protocol (PAgP) is a Cisco-proprietary solution, and the Link

Aggregation Control Protocol (LACP) is standards based. Table 6-4 summarizes the negotiation protocols and their operation.

Table 6-4   *EtherChannel Negotiation Protocols*

Negotiation Mode		Negotiation Packets Sent?	Characteristics
PAgP	LACP		
On	On	No	All ports channeling
Auto	Passive	Yes	Waits to channel until asked
Desirable	Active	Yes	Actively asks to form a channel

(handwritten: (Passive) next to Auto row; (Active) / (D ctive) next to Desirable row)

Port Aggregation Protocol

To provide automatic EtherChannel configuration and negotiation between switches, Cisco developed the *Port Aggregation Protocol*. PAgP packets are exchanged between switches over EtherChannel-capable ports. Neighbors are identified and port group capabilities are learned and compared with local switch capabilities. Ports that have the same neighbor device ID and port group capability are bundled together as a bidirectional, point-to-point EtherChannel link.

(handwritten: P 2 P)

PAgP forms an EtherChannel only on ports that are configured for either identical static VLANs or trunking. PAgP also dynamically modifies parameters of the EtherChannel if one of the bundled ports is modified. For example, if the configured VLAN, speed, or duplex mode of a port in an established bundle is changed, PAgP reconfigures that parameter for all ports in the bundle.

PAgP can be configured in active mode (desirable), in which a switch actively asks a far-end switch to negotiate an EtherChannel, or in passive mode (auto, the default), in which a switch negotiates an EtherChannel only if the far end initiates it.

Link Aggregation Control Protocol

(handwritten: Neighbors i d ed / PGroup caps learned)

LACP is a standards-based alternative to PAgP, defined in IEEE 802.3ad (also known as IEEE 802.3 Clause 43, "Link Aggregation"). LACP packets are exchanged between switches over EtherChannel-capable ports. As with PAgP, neighbors are identified and port group capabilities are learned and compared with local switch capabilities. However, LACP also assigns roles to the EtherChannel's endpoints.

(handwritten: roles)

The switch with the lowest *system priority* (a 2-byte priority value followed by a 6-byte switch MAC address) is allowed to make decisions about what ports actively are participating in the EtherChannel at a given time.

Ports are selected and become active according to their *port priority* value (a 2-byte priority followed by a 2-byte port number), where a low value indicates a higher priority. A set of up to 16 potential links can be defined for each EtherChannel. Through LACP, a switch selects up to eight of these having the lowest port priorities as active EtherChannel links at any given time. The other links are placed in a standby state and will be enabled in the EtherChannel if one of the active links goes down.

Like PAgP, LACP can be configured in active mode (active), in which a switch actively asks a far-end switch to negotiate an EtherChannel, or in passive mode (passive), in which a switch negotiates an EtherChannel only if the far end initiates it.

EtherChannel Configuration

For each EtherChannel on a switch, you must choose the EtherChannel negotiation protocol and assign individual switch ports to the EtherChannel. Both PAgP- and LACP-negotiated EtherChannels are described in the following sections. You also can configure an EtherChannel to use the on mode, which unconditionally bundles the links. In this case, neither PAgP nor LACP packets are sent or received.

As ports are configured to be members of an EtherChannel, the switch automatically creates a logical port-channel interface. This interface represents the channel as a whole.

Configuring a PAgP EtherChannel

To configure switch ports for PAgP negotiation (the default), use the following commands:

```
Switch(config)# interface type mod/num
Switch(config-if)# channel-protocol pagp
Switch(config-if)# channel-group number mode {on | {{auto | desirable}
  [non-silent]}}
```

On all Cisco IOS–based Catalyst models, you can select between PAgP and LACP as a channel-negotiation protocol. Some older models, however, offer only PAgP, so the **channel-protocol** command is not available. Each interface that will be included in a single EtherChannel bundle must be configured and assigned to the same unique channel group *number* (1 to 64). Channel negotiation must be set to on (unconditionally channel, no PAgP negotiation), auto (passively listen and wait to be asked), or desirable (actively ask).

> **Note:** IOS-based Catalyst switches do not assign interfaces to predetermined channel groups by default. In fact, the interfaces are not assigned to channel groups until you configure them manually.
>
> This is different from Catalyst OS (CatOS) switches, such as the Catalyst 4000 (Supervisors I and II), 5000, and 6500 (hybrid mode). On those platforms, Ethernet line cards are broken up into default channel groups.

By default, PAgP operates in silent submode with the desirable and auto modes, and allows ports to be added to an EtherChannel even if the other end of the link is silent and never transmits PAgP packets. This might seem to go against the idea of PAgP, in which two endpoints are supposed to negotiate a channel. After all, how can two switches negotiate anything if no PAgP packets are received?

The key is in the phrase "*if* the other end is silent." The silent submode listens for any PAgP packets from the far end, looking to negotiate a channel. If none is received, silent submode assumes that a channel should be built anyway, so no more PAgP packets are expected from the far end.

This allows a switch to form an EtherChannel with a device such as a file server or a network analyzer that doesn't participate in PAgP. In the case of a network analyzer connected to the far end, you also might want to see the PAgP packets generated by the switch, as if you were using a normal PAgP EtherChannel.

If you expect a PAgP-capable switch to be on the far end, you should add the **non-silent** keyword to the desirable or auto mode. This requires each port to receive PAgP packets before adding them to a channel. If PAgP isn't heard on an active port, the port remains in the up state, but PAgP reports to the Spanning Tree Protocol (STP) that the port is down.

> **Tip:** In practice, you might notice a delay from the time the links in a channel group are connected until the time the channel is formed and data can pass over it. You will encounter this if both switches are using the default PAgP auto mode and silent submode. Each interface waits to be asked to form a channel, and each interface waits and listens before accepting silent channel partners. The silent submode amounts to approximately a 15-second delay.
>
> Even if the two interfaces are using PAgP auto mode, the link will still eventually come up, although not as a channel. You might notice that the total delay before data can pass over the link is actually approximately 45 or 50 seconds. The first 15 seconds are the result of PAgP silent mode waiting to hear inbound PAgP messages, and the final 30 seconds are the result of the STP moving through the listening and learning stages.

As an example of PAgP configuration, suppose that you want a switch to use an EtherChannel load-balancing hash of both source and destination port numbers. A Gigabit EtherChannel will be built from interfaces Gigabit Ethernet 3/1 through 3/4, with the switch actively negotiating a channel. The switch should not wait to listen for silent partners. You can use the following configuration commands to accomplish this:

```
Switch(config)# port-channel load-balance src-dst-port
Switch(config)# interface range gig 3/1 - 4
Switch(config-if)# channel-protocol pagp
Switch(config-if)# channel-group 1 mode desirable non-silent
```

Configuring a LACP EtherChannel

To configure switch ports for LACP negotiation, use the following commands:

```
Switch(config)# lacp system-priority priority
Switch(config)# interface type mod/num
Switch(config-if)# channel-protocol lacp
Switch(config-if)# channel-group number mode {on | passive | active}
Switch(config-if)# lacp port-priority priority
```

Key Topic

First, the switch should have its LACP system priority defined (1 to 65,535; default 32,768). If desired, one switch should be assigned a lower system priority than the other so that it can make decisions about the EtherChannel's makeup. Otherwise, both switches will have the same system priority (32,768), and the one with the lower MAC address will become the decision maker.

Each interface included in a single EtherChannel bundle must be assigned to the same unique channel group *number* (1 to 64). Channel negotiation must be set to on (unconditionally channel, no LACP negotiation), passive (passively listen and wait to be asked), or active (actively ask).

You can configure more interfaces in the channel group *number* than are allowed to be active in the channel. This prepares extra standby interfaces to replace failed active ones. Use the **lacp port-priority** command to configure a lower port priority (1 to 65,535; default 32,768) for any interfaces that must be active, and a higher priority for interfaces that might be held in the standby state. Otherwise, just use the default scenario, in which all ports default to 32,768 and the lower port numbers (in interface number order) are used to select the active ports.

As an example of LACP configuration, suppose that you want to configure a switch to negotiate a Gigabit EtherChannel using interfaces Gigabit Ethernet 2/1 through 2/4 and 3/1 through 3/4. Interfaces Gigabit Ethernet 2/5 through 2/8 and 3/5 through 3/8 are also available, so these can be used as standby links to replace failed links in the channel. This switch actively should negotiate the channel and should be the decision maker about the channel operation.

You can use the following configuration commands to accomplish this:

```
Switch(config)# lacp system-priority 100
Switch(config)# interface range gig 2/1 - 4 , gig 3/1 - 4
Switch(config-if)# channel-protocol lacp
Switch(config-if)# channel-group 1 mode active
Switch(config-if)# lacp port-priority 100
Switch(config-if)# exit
Switch(config)# interface range gig 2/5 - 8 , gig 3/5 - 8
Switch(config-if)# channel-protocol lacp
Switch(config-if)# channel-group 1 mode active
```

Notice that interfaces Gigabit Ethernet 2/5-8 and 3/5-8 have been left to their default port priorities of 32,768. This is higher than the others, which were configured for 100, so they will be held as standby interfaces.

Troubleshooting an EtherChannel

Key Topic

If you find that an EtherChannel is having problems, remember that the whole concept is based on consistent configurations on *both* ends of the channel. Here are some reminders about EtherChannel operation and interaction:

- EtherChannel on mode does not send or receive PAgP or LACP packets. Therefore, both ends should be set to on mode before the channel can form.

- EtherChannel desirable (PAgP) or active (LACP) mode attempts to ask the far end to bring up a channel. Therefore, the other end must be set to either desirable or auto mode.

- EtherChannel auto (PAgP) or passive (LACP) mode participates in the channel proto-col, but only if the far end asks for participation. Therefore, two switches in the auto or passive mode will not form an EtherChannel.

- PAgP desirable and auto modes default to the silent submode, in which no PAgP packets are expected from the far end. If ports are set to nonsilent submode, PAgP packets must be received before a channel will form.

First, verify the EtherChannel state with the **show etherchannel summary** command. Each port in the channel is shown, along with flags indicating the port's state, as shown in Example 6-1.

Example 6-1   show etherchannel summary *Command Output*

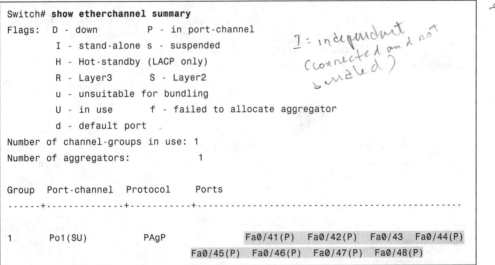

```
Switch# show etherchannel summary
Flags:  D - down         P - in port-channel
        I - stand-alone  s - suspended
        H - Hot-standby (LACP only)
        R - Layer3       S - Layer2
        u - unsuitable for bundling
        U - in use       f - failed to allocate aggregator
        d - default port
Number of channel-groups in use: 1
Number of aggregators:          1


Group  Port-channel  Protocol    Ports
------+-------------+-----------+--------------------------------------------------

1      Po1(SU)          PAgP        Fa0/41(P)  Fa0/42(P)  Fa0/43  Fa0/44(P)
                                    Fa0/45(P)  Fa0/46(P)  Fa0/47(P)  Fa0/48(P)
```

[handwritten annotation: I = independent (connected and not bundled)]

The status of the port channel shows the EtherChannel logical interface as a whole. This should show SU (Layer 2 channel, in use) if the channel is operational. You also can exam-ine the status of each port within the channel. Notice that most of the channel ports have flags (P), indicating that they are active in the port-channel. One port shows because it is physically not connected or down. If a port is connected but not bundled in the channel, it will have an independent, or (I), flag.

You can verify the channel negotiation mode with the **show etherchannel port** command, as shown in Example 6-2. The local switch is shown using desirable mode with PAgP (De-sirable-Sl is desirable silent mode). Notice that you also can see the far end's negotiation mode under the Partner Flags heading, as A, or auto mode.

Example 6-2   show etherchannel port *Command Output*

```
Switch# show etherchannel port
                  Channel-group listing:
                  ----------------------
```

```
Group: 1
----------
                     Ports in the group:
                     --------------------
Port: Fa0/41
-----------

Port state     = Up Mstr In-Bndl
Channel group = 1           Mode = Desirable-Sl      Gcchange = 0
Port-channel  = Po1         GC   = 0x00010001           Pseudo port-channel = Po1
Port index    = 0           Load = 0x00            Protocol =    PAgP

Flags:   S - Device is sending Slow hello.  C - Device is in Consistent state.
         A - Device is in Auto mode.        P - Device learns on physical port.
         d - PAgP is down.
Timers:  H - Hello timer is running.        Q - Quit timer is running.
         S - Switching timer is running.    I - Interface timer is running.

Local information:
                                   Hello   Partner  PAgP       Learning  Group
Port        Flags State   Timers   Interval Count   Priority   Method    Ifindex
Fa0/41      SC    U6/S7   H        30s      1       128        Any       55

Partner's information:

            Partner              Partner            Partner          Partner Group
Port        Name                 Device ID          Port      Age  Flags   Cap.

Fa0/41      FarEnd               00d0.5849.4100     3/1       19s  SAC     11

Age of the port in the current state: 00d:08h:05m:28s
```

Within a switch, an EtherChannel cannot form unless each of the component or member ports is configured consistently. Each must have the same switch mode (access or trunk), native VLAN, trunked VLANs, port speed, port duplex mode, and so on.

You can display a port's configuration by looking at the **show running-config interface** *type mod/ num* output. Also, the **show interface** *type mod/num* **etherchannel** shows all active EtherChannel parameters for a single port. If you configure a port inconsistently with others for an EtherChannel, you see error messages from the switch.

Some messages from the switch might look like errors but are part of the normal Ether-Channel process. For example, as a new port is configured as a member of an existing EtherChannel, you might see this message:

```
4d00h: %EC-5-L3DONTBNDL2: FastEthernet0/2 suspended: incompatible partner port
  with FastEthernet0/1
```

When the port first is added to the EtherChannel, it is incompatible because the STP runs on the channel and the new port. After STP takes the new port through its progression of states, the port is automatically added into the EtherChannel.

Other messages do indicate a port-compatibility error. In these cases, the cause of the error is shown. For example, the following message tells that Fast Ethernet0/3 has a different duplex mode than the other ports in the EtherChannel:

```
4d00h: %EC-5-CANNOT_BUNDLE2: FastEthernet0/3 is not compatible with
   FastEthernet0/1 and will be suspended (duplex of Fa0/3 is full, Fa0/1 is half)
```

Finally, you can verify the EtherChannel load-balancing or hashing algorithm with the **show etherchannel load-balance** command. Remember that the switches on either end of an EtherChannel can have different load-balancing methods. The only drawback to this is that the load balancing will be asymmetric in the two directions across the channel.

Table 6-5 lists the commands useful for verifying or troubleshooting EtherChannel operation.

Table 6-5   *EtherChannel Troubleshooting Commands*

Display Function	Command Syntax
Current EtherChannel status of each member port	show etherchannel summary show etherchannel port
Time stamps of EtherChannel changes	show etherchannel port-channel
Detailed status about each EtherChannel component	show etherchannel detail
Load-balancing hashing algorithm	show etherchannel load-balance
Load-balancing port index used by hashing algorithm	show etherchannel port-channel
EtherChannel neighbors on each port	show {pagp | lacp} neighbor
LACP system ID	show lacp sys-id

Exam Preparation Tasks

Review All Key Topics

Review the most important topics in the chapter, noted with the key topics icon in the outer margin of the page. Table 6-6 lists a reference of these key topics and the page numbers on which each is found.

Table 6-6 *Key Topics for Chapter 6*

Key Topic Element	Description	Page Number
Paragraph	Discusses aggregating links into EtherChannels	110
Paragraph	Explains how traffic is distributed in an EtherChannel	111
Table 6-3	Lists EtherChannel load-balancing methods	113
Paragraph	Describes the PAgP negotiation protocol	115
Paragraph	Describes the LACP negotiation protocol	115
Paragraph	Explains PAgP configuration	116
Paragraph	Explains LACP configuration	117
Paragraph	Discusses rules of thumb for proper EtherChannel operation	118

Complete Tables and Lists from Memory

Print a copy of Appendix C, "Memory Tables," (found on the CD), or at least the section for this chapter, and complete the tables and lists from memory. Appendix D, "Memory Tables Answer Key," also on the CD, includes completed tables and lists to check your work.

Define Key Terms

Define the following key terms from this chapter, and check your answers in the glossary:

EtherChannel, PAgP, LACP

Command Reference to Check Your Memory

This section includes the most important configuration and EXEC commands covered in this chapter. It might not be necessary to memorize the complete syntax of every command, but you should be able to remember the basic keywords that are needed.

To test your memory of the commands related to EtherChannels, cover the right side of Table 6-7 with a piece of paper, read the description on the left side, and then see how much of the command you can remember.

Remember that the CCNP exam focuses on practical or hands-on skills that are used by a networking professional. For the skills covered in this chapter, remember that an Ether-Channel is called a port-channel interface when you are configuring it. When you are displaying information about an EtherChannel, begin the commands with the **show etherchannel** keywords.

Table 6-7 *EtherChannel Configuration Commands*

Task	Command Syntax
Select a load-balancing method for the switch.	**port-channel load-balance** *method*
Use a PAgP mode on an interface.	**channel-protocol pagp**
	channel-group *number* **mode** {**on** | {{**auto** | **desirable**} [**non-silent**]}}
Assign the LACP system priority.	**lacp system-priority** *priority*
Use an LACP mode on an interface.	**channel-protocol lacp**
	channel-group *number* **mode** {**on** | **passive** | **active**}
	lacp port-priority *priority*

This chapter covers the following topics that you need to master for the CCNP SWITCH exam:

IEEE 802.1D Overview—This section discusses the original, or more traditional, Spanning Tree Protocol (STP). This protocol is the foundation for the default Catalyst STP and for all the enhancements that are described in Chapters 8, "Spanning-Tree Configuration," through 10, "Advanced Spanning Tree Protocol."

Types of STP—This section discusses other types of STP that might be running on a Catalyst switch—specifically, the Common Spanning Tree, Per-VLAN Spanning Tree (PVST), and PVST+.

CHAPTER 7

Traditional Spanning Tree Protocol

Previous chapters covered ways to connect two switches together with a VLAN trunk link. What if something happens to the trunk link? The two switches would be isolated from each other. A more robust network design would add redundant links between switches. Although this increases the network availability, it also opens up the possibility for conditions that would impair the network. In a Layer 2 switched network, preventing bridging loops from forming over redundant paths is important. Spanning Tree Protocol (STP) was designed to monitor and control the Layer 2 network so that a loop-free topology is maintained.

This chapter discusses the theory and operation of the STP. More specifically, the original, or traditional, STP is covered, as defined in IEEE 802.1D. Several chapters explain STP topics in this book. Here is a brief roadmap so that you can chart a course:

■ **Chapter 7, "Traditional Spanning Tree Protocol"**—Covers the theory of IEEE 802.1D

■ **Chapter 8, "Spanning-Tree Configuration"**—Covers the configuration commands needed for IEEE 802.1D

■ **Chapter 9, "Protecting the Spanning Tree Protocol Topology"**—Covers the features and commands to filter and protect a converged STP topology from conditions that could destabilize it

■ **Chapter 10, "Advanced Spanning Tree Protocol"**—Covers the newer 802.1w and 802.1s enhancements to STP, allowing more scalability and faster convergence

"Do I Know This Already?" Quiz

The "Do I Know This Already?" quiz allows you to assess whether you should read this entire chapter thoroughly or jump to the "Exam Preparation Tasks" section. If you are in doubt based on your answers to these questions or your own assessment of your knowledge of the topics, read the entire chapter. Table 7-1 outlines the major headings in this chapter and the "Do I Know This Already?" quiz questions that go with them. You can find the answers in Appendix A, "Answers to the 'Do I Know This Already?' Quizzes."

Table 7-1 *"Do I Know This Already?" Foundation Topics Section-to-Question Mapping*

Foundation Topics Section	Questions Covered in This Section
IEEE 802.1D Overview	1–10
Types of STP	11–12

1. How is a bridging loop best described?

    a. A loop formed between switches for redundancy

    b. A loop formed by the Spanning Tree Protocol

    c. A loop formed between switches where frames circulate endlessly

    d. The round-trip path a frame takes from source to destination

2. Which of these is one of the parameters used to elect a root bridge?

    a. Root path cost

    b. Path cost

    c. Bridge priority

    d. BPDU revision number

3. If all switches in a network are left at their default STP values, which one of the following is not true?

    a. The root bridge will be the switch with the lowest MAC address.

    b. The root bridge will be the switch with the highest MAC address.

    c. One or more switches will have a bridge priority of 32,768.

    d. A secondary root bridge will be present on the network.

4. Configuration BPDUs are originated by which of the following?

    a. All switches in the STP domain

    b. Only the root bridge switch

    c. Only the switch that detects a topology change

    d. Only the secondary root bridge when it takes over

5. Which of these is the single most important design decision to be made in a network running STP?

    a. Removing any redundant links

    b. Making sure all switches run the same version of IEEE 802.1D

    c. Root bridge placement

    d. Making sure all switches have redundant links

6. What happens to a port that is neither a root port nor a designated port?

    a. It is available for normal use.

    b. It can be used for load balancing.

    c. It is put into the Blocking state.

    d. It is disabled.

7. What is the maximum number of root ports that a Catalyst switch can have?

   a. 1

   b. 2

   c. Unlimited

   d. None

8. What mechanism is used to set STP timer values for all switches in a network?

   a. Configuring the timers on every switch in the network.

   b. Configuring the timers on the root bridge switch.

   c. Configuring the timers on both primary and secondary root bridge switches.

   d. The timers can't be adjusted.

9. MAC addresses can be placed into the CAM table, but no data can be sent or received if a switch port is in which of the following STP states?

   a. Blocking

   b. Forwarding

   c. Listening

   d. Learning

10. What is the default "hello" time for IEEE 802.1D?

   a. 1 second

   b. 2 seconds

   c. 30 seconds

   d. 60 seconds

11. Which of the following is the Spanning Tree Protocol defined in the IEEE 802.1Q standard?

   a. PVST

   b. CST

   c. EST

   d. MST

12. If a switch has 10 VLANs defined and active, how many instances of STP will run using PVST+ versus CST?

   a. 1 for PVST+, 1 for CST

   b. 1 for PVST+, 10 for CST

   c. 10 for PVST+, 1 for CST

   d. 10 for PVST+, 10 for CST

Foundation Topics

IEEE 802.1D Overview

A robust network design not only includes efficient transfer of packets or frames, but also considers how to recover quickly from faults in the network. In a Layer 3 environment, the routing protocols in use keep track of redundant paths to a destination network so that a secondary path can be used quickly if the primary path fails. Layer 3 routing allows many paths to a destination to remain up and active, and allows load sharing across multiple paths.

In a Layer 2 environment (switching or bridging), however, no routing protocols are used, and active redundant paths are neither allowed nor desirable. Instead, some form of bridging provides data transport between networks or switch ports. The Spanning Tree Protocol (STP) provides network link redundancy so that a Layer 2 switched network can recover from failures without intervention in a timely manner. The STP is defined in the IEEE 802.1D standard.

STP is discussed in relation to the problems it solves in the sections that follow.

Bridging Loops

Recall that a Layer 2 switch mimics the function of a transparent bridge. A transparent bridge must offer segmentation between two networks while remaining transparent to all the end devices connected to it. For the purpose of this discussion, consider a two-port Ethernet switch and its similarities to a two-port transparent bridge.

A transparent bridge (and the Ethernet switch) must operate as follows:

Key Topic

- The bridge has no initial knowledge of any end device's location; therefore, the bridge must "listen" to frames coming into each of its ports to figure out on which network each device resides. The bridge assumes that a device using the source MAC address is located behind the port that the frame arrives on. As the listening process continues, the bridge builds a table that correlates source MAC addresses with the bridge port numbers where they were detected.

- The bridge can constantly update its bridging table on detecting the presence of a new MAC address or on detecting a MAC address that has changed location from one Bridge Port to another. The bridge then can forward frames by looking at the destination MAC address, looking up that address in the bridge table, and sending the frame out the port where the destination device is known to be located.

- If a frame arrives with the broadcast address as the destination address, the bridge must forward, or flood, the frame out all available ports. However, the frame is not forwarded out the port that initially received the frame. In this way, broadcasts can reach all available Layer 2 networks. A bridge segments only collision domains—it does not segment broadcast domains.

- If a frame arrives with a destination address that is not found in the bridge table, the bridge cannot determine which port to forward the frame to for transmission. This type of frame is known as an *unknown unicast*. In this case, the bridge treats the frame as if it were a broadcast and floods it out all remaining ports. When a reply to that frame is overheard, the bridge can learn the location of the unknown station and can add it to the bridge table for future use.

■   Frames forwarded across the bridge cannot be modified by the bridge itself. Therefore, the bridging process is effectively *transparent*.

Bridging or switching in this fashion works well. Any frame forwarded, whether to a known or unknown destination, is forwarded out the appropriate port or ports so that it is likely to be received successfully at the end device. Figure 7-1 shows a simple two-port switch functioning as a bridge, forwarding frames between two end devices. However, this network design offers no additional links or paths for redundancy if the switch or one of its links fails. In that case, the networks on either side of the bridge would become isolated from each other.

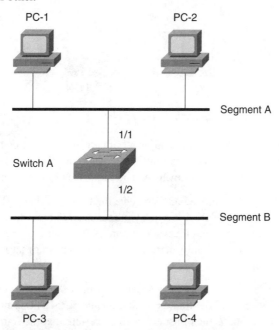

Figure 7-1   *Transparent Bridging with a Switch*

To add some redundancy, you can add a second switch between the two original network segments, as shown in Figure 7-2. Now, two switches offer the transparent bridging function in parallel. In theory, a single switch or a single link can fail without causing end-to-end connectivity to fail.

Consider what happens when PC-1 sends a frame to PC-4. For now, assume that both PC-1 and PC-4 are known to the switches and are in their address tables. PC-1 sends the frame onto network Segment A. Switch A and switch B both receive the frame on their 1/1 ports. Because PC-4 already is known to the switches, the frame is forwarded out ports 2/1 on each switch onto Segment B. The end result is that PC-4 receives two copies of the frame from PC-1. This is not ideal, but it is not disastrous, either.

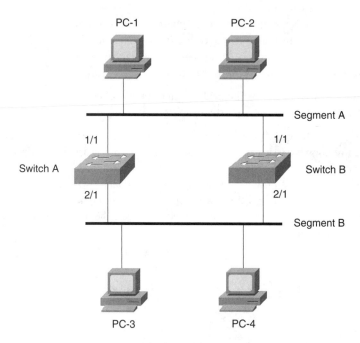

Figure 7-2   *Redundant Bridging with Two Switches*

Key Topic

Now, consider the same process of sending a frame from PC-1 to PC-4. This time, how-ever, neither switch knows anything about the location of PC-1 or PC-4. PC-1 sends the frame to PC-4 by placing it on Segment A. The sequence of events is as follows:

Step 1.   Both switch A and switch B receive the frame on their 1/1 ports. Because the MAC address of PC-1 has not yet been seen or recorded, each switch records PC-1's MAC address in its address table along with the receiving port num-ber, 1/1. From this information, both switches infer that PC-1 must reside on Segment A.

Step 2.   Because the location of PC-4 is unknown, both switches correctly decide that they must flood the frame out all available ports. This is an unknown unicast condition and is their best effort to make sure that the frame eventually reaches its destination.

Step 3.   Each switch floods or copies the frame to its 2/1 port on Segment B. PC-4, lo-cated on Segment B, receives the two frames destined for it. However, on Seg-ment B, switch A now hears the new frame forwarded by switch B, and switch B hears the new frame forwarded by switch A.

Step 4.   Switch A sees that the "new" frame is from PC-1 to PC-4. From the address table, the switch previously learned that PC-1 was on port 1/1, or Segment A. However, the source address of PC-1 has just been heard on port 2/1, or Seg-ment B. By definition, the switch must relearn the location of PC-1 with the most recent information, which it now incorrectly assumes to be Segment B. (Switch B follows the same procedure, based on the "new" frame from switch A.)

Step 5.   At this point, neither switch A nor switch B has learned the location of PC-4 because no frames have been received with PC-4 as the source address. Therefore, the new frame must be flooded out all available ports in an attempt to find PC-4. This frame then is sent out switch A's 1/1 port and onto Segment A, as well as switch B's 1/1 port and onto Segment A.

Step 6.   Now both switches relearn the location of PC-1 as Segment A and forward the "new" frames back onto Segment B; then the entire process repeats.

This process of forwarding a single frame around and around between two switches is known as a *bridging loop*. Neither switch is aware of the other, so each happily forwards the same frame back and forth between its segments. Also note that because two switches are involved in the loop, the original frame has been duplicated and now is sent around in two counter-rotating loops. What stops the frame from being forwarded in this fashion forever? Nothing! PC-4 begins receiving frames addressed to it as fast as the switches can forward them.

Notice how the learned location of PC-1 keeps changing as frames get looped. Even a simple unicast frame has caused a bridging loop to form, and each switch's bridge table is repeatedly corrupted with incorrect data.

What would happen if PC-1 sent a broadcast frame instead? The bridging loops (remember that two of them are produced by the two parallel switches) form exactly as before. The broadcast frames continue to circulate forever. Now, however, every end-user device located on both Segments A and B receives and processes every broadcast frame. This type of broadcast storm can easily saturate the network segments and bring every host on the segments to a halt.

The only way to end the bridging loop condition is to physically break the loop by disconnecting switch ports or shutting down a switch. Obviously, it would be better to *prevent* bridging loops than to be faced with finding and breaking them after they form.

Preventing Loops with Spanning Tree Protocol

Bridging loops form because parallel switches (or bridges) are unaware of each other. STP was developed to overcome the possibility of bridging loops so that redundant switches and switch paths could be used for their benefits. Basically, the protocol enables switches to become aware of each other so they can negotiate a loop-free path through the network.

Note: Because STP is involved in loop detection, many people refer to the catastrophic loops as "spanning-tree loops." This is technically incorrect because the Spanning Tree Protocol's entire function is to prevent bridging loops. The correct terminology for this condition is a *bridging loop*.

Loops are discovered before they are made available for use, and redundant links are effectively shut down to prevent the loops from forming. In the case of redundant links, switches can be made aware that a link shut down for loop prevention should be brought up quickly in case of a link failure. The section "Redundant Link Convergence" in Chapter 8 provides more information.

STP is communicated among all connected switches on a network. Each switch executes the spanning-tree algorithm based on information received from other neighboring switches. The algorithm chooses a reference point in the network and calculates all the redundant paths to that reference point. When redundant paths are found, the spanning-tree algorithm picks one path by which to forward frames and disables, or blocks, forwarding on the other redundant paths.

As its name implies, STP computes a tree structure that spans all switches in a subnet or network. Redundant paths are placed in a Blocking or Standby state to prevent frame forwarding. The switched network is then in a loop-free condition. However, if a forwarding port fails or becomes disconnected, the spanning-tree algorithm recomputes the spanning-tree topology so that the appropriate blocked links can be reactivated.

Spanning-Tree Communication: Bridge Protocol Data Units

STP operates as switches communicate with one another. Data messages are exchanged in the form of *bridge protocol data units* (BPDU). A switch sends a BPDU frame out a port, using the unique MAC address of the port itself as a source address. The switch is unaware of the other switches around it, so BPDU frames are sent with a destination address of the well-known STP multicast address 01-80-c2-00-00-00.

Two types of BPDU exist:

■   **Configuration BPDU**, used for spanning-tree computation

■   **Topology Change Notification (TCN) BPDU**, used to announce changes in the network topology

The Configuration BPDU message contains the fields shown in Table 7-2. The TCN BPDU is discussed in the "Topology Changes" section later in this chapter.

Table 7-2   *Configuration BPDU Message Content*

Field Description	Number of Bytes
Protocol ID (always 0)	2
Version (always 0)	1
Message Type (Configuration or TCN BPDU)	1
Flags	1
Root Bridge ID	8
Root Path Cost	4
Sender Bridge ID	8

Table 7-2   *Configuration BPDU Message Content   (Continued)*

Field Description	Number of Bytes
Port ID	2
Message Age (in 256ths of a second)	2
Maximum Age (in 256ths of a second)	2
Hello Time (in 256ths of a second)	2
Forward Delay (in 256ths of a second)	2

The exchange of BPDU messages works toward the goal of electing reference points as a foundation for a stable spanning-tree topology. Loops also can be identified and removed by placing specific redundant ports in a Blocking or Standby state. Notice that several key fields in the BPDU are related to bridge (or switch) identification, path costs, and timer values. These all work together so that the network of switches can converge on a common spanning-tree topology and select the same reference points within the network. These reference points are defined in the sections that follow.

By default, BPDUs are sent out all switch ports every 2 seconds so that current topology information is exchanged and loops are identified quickly.

Electing a Root Bridge

For all switches in a network to agree on a loop-free topology, a common frame of reference must exist to use as a guide. This reference point is called the *root bridge*. (The term *bridge* continues to be used even in a switched environment because STP was developed for use in bridges. Therefore, when you see *bridge*, think *switch*.)

Key
Topic

An election process among all connected switches chooses the root bridge. Each switch has a unique *bridge ID* that identifies it to other switches. The bridge ID is an 8-byte value consisting of the following fields:

- **Bridge Priority (2 bytes)**—The priority or weight of a switch in relation to all other switches. The Priority field can have a value of 0 to 65,535 and defaults to 32,768 (or 0x8000) on every Catalyst switch.

- **MAC Address (6 bytes)**—The MAC address used by a switch can come from the Supervisor module, the backplane, or a pool of 1,024 addresses that are assigned to every supervisor or backplane, depending on the switch model. In any event, this address is hard-coded and unique, and the user cannot change it.

When a switch first powers up, it has a narrow view of its surroundings and assumes that it is the root bridge itself. (This notion probably will change as other switches check in and enter the election process.) The election process then proceeds as follows: Every switch begins by sending out BPDUs with a root bridge ID equal to its own bridge ID and a sender bridge ID that is its own bridge ID. The sender bridge ID simply tells other switches who is the actual sender of the BPDU message. (After a root bridge is decided on, configuration BPDUs are sent only by the root bridge. All other bridges must forward or relay the BPDUs, adding their own sender bridge IDs to the message.)

Received BPDU messages are analyzed to see if a "better" root bridge is being announced. A root bridge is considered better if the root bridge ID value is *lower* than another. Again, think of the root bridge ID as being broken into Bridge Priority and MAC Address fields. If two bridge priority values are equal, the lower MAC address makes the bridge ID better. When a switch hears of a better root bridge, it replaces its own root bridge ID with the root bridge ID announced in the BPDU. The switch then is required to recommend or advertise the new root bridge ID in its own BPDU messages, although it still identifies itself as the sender bridge ID.

Sooner or later, the election converges and all switches agree on the notion that one of them is the root bridge. As might be expected, if a new switch with a lower bridge priority powers up, it begins advertising itself as the root bridge. Because the new switch does indeed have a lower bridge ID, all the switches soon reconsider and record it as the new root bridge. This also can happen if the new switch has a bridge priority equal to that of the existing root bridge but has a lower MAC address. root bridge election is an ongoing process, triggered by root bridge ID changes in the BPDUs every 2 seconds.

As an example, consider the small network shown in Figure 7-3. For simplicity, assume that each Catalyst switch has a MAC address of all 0s, with the last hex digit equal to the switch label.

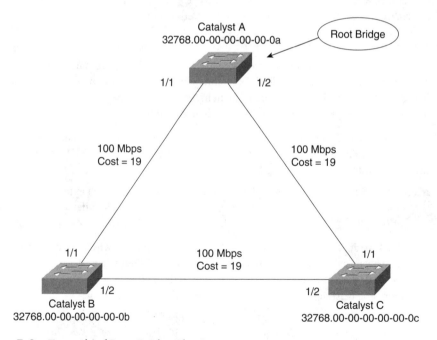

Figure 7-3   *Example of Root Bridge Election*

In this network, each switch has the default bridge priority of 32,768. The switches are interconnected with Fast Ethernet links. All three switches try to elect themselves as the root, but all of them have equal Bridge Priority values. The election outcome produces the root bridge, determined by the lowest MAC address—that of Catalyst A.

Electing Root Ports

Key Topic

Now that a reference point has been nominated and elected for the entire switched network, each nonroot switch must figure out where it is in relation to the root bridge. This action can be performed by selecting only one *root port* on each nonroot switch. The root port always points toward the current root bridge.

STP uses the concept of cost to determine many things. Selecting a root port involves evaluating the *root path cost*. This value is the cumulative cost of all the links leading to the root bridge. A particular switch link also has a cost associated with it, called the *path cost*. To understand the difference between these values, remember that only the root path cost is carried inside the BPDU. (Refer to Table 7-2.) As the root path cost travels along, other switches can modify its value to make it cumulative. The path cost, however, is not contained in the BPDU. It is known only to the local switch where the port (or "path" to a neighboring switch) resides.

Path costs are defined as a 1-byte value, with the default values shown in Table 7-3. Generally, the higher the bandwidth of a link, the lower the cost of transporting data across it. The original IEEE 802.1D standard defined path cost as 1000 Mbps divided by the link bandwidth in megabits per second. These values are shown in the center column of the table. Modern networks commonly use Gigabit Ethernet and OC-48 ATM, which are both either too close to or greater than the maximum scale of 1000 Mbps. The IEEE now uses a nonlinear scale for path cost, as shown in the right column of the table.

Tip: Be aware that there are two STP path cost scales, one that is little used with a linear scale and one commonly used that is nonlinear. If you decide to memorize some common path cost values, learn only the ones in the New STP Cost column of the table.

Table 7-3   *STP Path Cost*

Link Bandwidth	Old STP Cost	New STP Cost
4 Mbps	250	250
10 Mbps	100	100
16 Mbps	63	62
45 Mbps	22	39
100 Mbps	10	19
155 Mbps	6	14
622 Mbps	2	6
1 Gbps	1	4
10 Gbps	0	2

The root path cost value is determined in the following manner:

1. The root bridge sends out a BPDU with a root path cost value of 0 because its ports sit directly on the root bridge.

2. When the next-closest neighbor receives the BPDU, it adds the path cost of its own port where the BPDU arrived. (This is done as the BPDU is *received*.)

3. The neighbor sends out BPDUs with this new cumulative value as the root path cost.

4. The root path cost is incremented by the ingress port path cost as the BPDU is received at each switch down the line.

5. Notice the emphasis on incrementing the root path cost as BPDUs are *received*. When computing the spanning-tree algorithm manually, remember to compute a new root path cost as BPDUs *come in* to a switch port, not as they go out.

After incrementing the root path cost, a switch also records the value in its memory. When a BPDU is received on another port and the new root path cost is lower than the previously recorded value, this lower value becomes the new root path cost. In addition, the lower cost tells the switch that the path to the root bridge must be better using this port than it was on other ports. The switch has now determined which of its ports has the best path to the root: the root port.

Figure 7-4 shows the same network from Figure 7-3 in the process of root port selection.

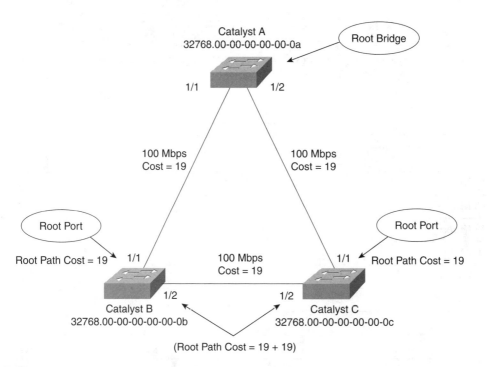

Figure 7-4   *Example of Root Port Selection*

The root bridge, Catalyst A, already has been elected. Therefore, every other switch in the network must choose one port that has the best path to the root bridge. Catalyst B selects its port 1/1, with a root path cost of 0 plus 19. Port 1/2 is not chosen because its root path cost is 0 (BPDU from Catalyst A) plus 19 (path cost of A–C link), plus 19 (path cost of C–B link), or a total of 38. Catalyst C makes an identical choice of port 1/1.

Electing Designated Ports

By now, you should begin to see the process unfolding: A starting or reference point has been identified, and each switch "connects" itself toward the reference point with the single link that has the best path. A tree structure is beginning to emerge, but links have only been identified at this point. All links still are connected and could be active, leaving bridging loops.

To remove the possibility of bridging loops, STP makes a final computation to identify one *designated port* on each network segment. Suppose that two or more switches have ports connected to a single common network segment. If a frame appears on that segment, all the bridges attempt to forward it to its destination. Recall that this behavior was the basis of a bridging loop and should be avoided.

Instead, only one of the links on a segment should forward traffic to and from that segment—the one that is selected as the designated port. Switches choose a designated port based on the lowest cumulative root path cost to the root bridge. For example, a switch always has an idea of its own root path cost, which it announces in its own BPDUs. If a neighboring switch on a shared LAN segment sends a BPDU announcing a lower root path cost, the neighbor must have the designated port. If a switch learns only of higher root path costs from other BPDUs received on a port, however, it then correctly assumes that its own receiving port is the designated port for the segment.

Notice that the entire STP determination process has served only to identify bridges and ports. All ports are still active, and bridging loops still might lurk in the network. STP has a set of progressive states that each port must go through, regardless of the type or identification. These states actively prevent loops from forming and are described in the next section.

In each determination process discussed so far, two or more links might have identical root path costs. This results in a tie condition, unless other factors are considered. All tie-breaking STP decisions are based on the following sequence of four conditions:

1. Lowest root bridge ID

2. Lowest root path cost to root bridge

3. Lowest sender bridge ID

4. Lowest sender port ID

Figure 7-5 demonstrates an example of designated port selection. This figure is identical to Figure 7-3 and Figure 7-4, with further spanning-tree development shown. The only changes are the choices of designated ports, although seeing all STP decisions shown on one network diagram is handy.

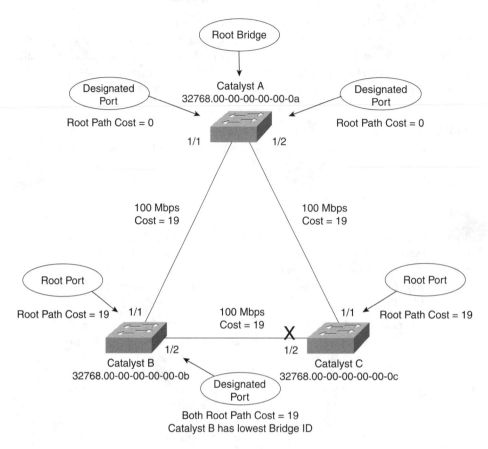

Figure 7-5   *Example of Designated Port Selection*

The three switches have chosen their designated ports (DP) for the following reasons:

■ **Catalyst A**—Because this switch is the root bridge, all its active ports are designated ports, by definition. At the root bridge, the root path cost of each port is 0.

■ **Catalyst B**—Catalyst A port 1/1 is the DP for the Segment A–B because it has the lowest root path cost (0). Catalyst B port 1/2 is the DP for segment B–C. The root path cost for each end of this segment is 19, determined from the incoming BPDU on port 1/1. Because the root path cost is equal on both ports of the segment, the DP must be chosen by the next criteria—the lowest sender bridge ID. When Catalyst B sends a BPDU to Catalyst C, it has the lowest MAC address in the bridge ID. Catalyst C also sends a BPDU to Catalyst B, but its sender bridge ID is higher. Therefore, Catalyst B port 1/2 is selected as the segment's DP.

■ **Catalyst C**—Catalyst A port 1/2 is the DP for Segment A–C because it has the lowest root path cost (0). Catalyst B port 1/2 is the DP for Segment B–C. Therefore, Catalyst C port 1/2 will be neither a root port nor a designated port. As discussed in the next section, any port that is not elected to either position enters the Blocking state. Where blocking occurs, bridging loops are broken.

STP States

To participate in STP, each port of a switch must progress through several states. A port begins its life in a Disabled state, moving through several passive states and, finally, into an active state if allowed to forward traffic. The STP port states are as follows:

Key Topic

- **Disabled**—Ports that are administratively shut down by the network administrator, or by the system because of a fault condition, are in the Disabled state. This state is special and is not part of the normal STP progression for a port.

- **Blocking**—After a port initializes, it begins in the Blocking state so that no bridging loops can form. In the Blocking state, a port cannot receive or transmit data and cannot add MAC addresses to its address table. Instead, a port is allowed to receive only BPDUs so that the switch can hear from other neighboring switches. In addition, ports that are put into standby mode to remove a bridging loop enter the Blocking state.

- **Listening**—A port is moved from Blocking to Listening if the switch thinks that the port can be selected as a root port or designated port. In other words, the port is on its way to begin forwarding traffic.

  In the Listening state, the port still cannot send or receive data frames. However, the port is allowed to receive and send BPDUs so that it can actively participate in the Spanning Tree topology process. Here, the port finally is allowed to become a root port or designated port because the switch can advertise the port by sending BPDUs to other switches. If the port loses its root port or designated port status, it returns to the Blocking state.

- **Learning**—After a period of time called the *Forward Delay* in the Listening state, the port is allowed to move into the Learning state. The port still sends and receives BPDUs as before. In addition, the switch now can learn new MAC addresses to add to its address table. This gives the port an extra period of silent participation and allows the switch to assemble at least some address information. The port cannot yet send any data frames, however.

- **Forwarding**—After another Forward Delay period of time in the Learning state, the port is allowed to move into the Forwarding state. The port now can send and receive data frames, collect MAC addresses in its address table, and send and receive BPDUs. The port is now a fully functioning switch port within the spanning-tree topology.

Remember that a switch port is allowed into the Forwarding state only if no redundant links (or loops) are detected and if the port has the best path to the root bridge as the root port or designated port.

Table 7-4 summarizes the STP port states and what can and cannot be done in those states.

Table 7-4 *STP States and Port Activity*

STP State	The Port Can...	The Port Cannot...	Duration
Disabled	N/A	Send or receive data	N/A
Blocking	Receive BPDUs	Send or receive data or learn MAC addresses	Indefinite if loop has been detected
Listening	Send and receive BPDUs	Send or receive data or learn MAC addresses	Forward Delay timer (15 seconds)
Learning	Send and receive BPDUs and learn MAC addresses	Send or receive data	Forward Delay timer (15 seconds)
Forwarding	Send and receive BPDUs, learn MAC addresses, and send and receive data		Indefinite as long as port is up and loop is not detected

Example 7-1 shows the output from a switch as one of its ports progresses through the STP port states.

Example 7-1 *Port Progressing Through the STP Port States*

```
*Mar 16 14:31:00 UTC: STP SW: Fa0/1 new disabled req for 1 vlans
Switch(config)# interface fastethernet 0/1
Switch(config-if)#no shutdown
Switch(config-if)#^-Z
*Mar 16 14:31:00 UTC: STP SW: Fa0/1 new blocking req for 1 vlans

Switch# show spanning interface fastethernet 0/1


Vlan            Port ID                     Designated                 Port ID
Name            Prio.Nbr      Cost Sts      Cost Bridge ID             Prio.Nbr
--------------- ------------- -------------- -------------------------- --------
VLAN0001        128.1          19 LIS          0 32769 000a.f40a.2980 128.1

*Mar 16 14:31:15 UTC: STP SW: Fa0/1 new learning req for 1 vlans

Switch# show spanning interface fastethernet 0/1
Vlan            Port ID                     Designated                 Port ID
Name            Prio.Nbr      Cost Sts      Cost Bridge ID             Prio.Nbr
--------------- ------------- -------------- -------------------------- --------
VLAN0001        128.1          19 LRN          0 32768 00d0.5849.4100  32.129

*Mar 16 14:31:30 UTC: STP SW: Fa0/1 new forwarding req for 1 vlans
```

```
Switch# show spanning interface fastethernet 0/1

Vlan                Port ID                      Designated              Port ID
Name                Prio.Nbr    Cost Sts    Cost Bridge ID              Prio.Nbr
----------------    -----------  ----------  --------------------------  --------

VLAN0001            128.1       19 FWD       0 32768 00d0.5849.4100   32.129
```

The example begins as the port is administratively disabled from the command line. When the port is enabled, successive **show spanning-tree interface** *type mod/port* commands display the port state as Listening, Learning, and then Forwarding. These are shown in the shaded text of the example. Notice also the time stamps and port states provided by the **debug spanning-tree switch state** command, which give a sense of the timing between port states. Because this port was eligible as a root port, the **show** command never could execute fast enough to show the port in the Blocking state.

You can manually work out a spanning-tree topology using a network diagram. Follow the basic steps listed in Table 7-5 to add information to the network diagram. By the time you reach step 5, your STP will have converged, just like the switches in a live network would do.

Table 7-5   *Manual STP Computation*

Task	Description
1. Identify path costs on links.	For each link between switches, write the path cost that each switch uses for the link.
2. Identify the root bridge.	Find the switch with the lowest bridge ID; mark it on the drawing.
3. Select root ports (1 per switch).	For each switch, find the one port that has the best path to the root bridge. This is the one with the lowest root path cost. Mark the port with an RP label.
4. Select designated ports (1 per segment).	For each link between switches, identify which end of the link will be the designated port. This is the one with the lowest root path cost; if equal on both ends, use STP tie-breakers. Mark the port with a DP label.
5. Identify the blocking ports.	Every switch port that is neither a root nor a designated port will be put into the Blocking state. Mark these with an *X*.

STP Timers

STP operates as switches send BPDUs to each other in an effort to form a loop-free topology. The BPDUs take a finite amount of time to travel from switch to switch. In addition, news of a topology change (such as a link or root bridge failure) can suffer from propagation delays as the announcement travels from one side of a network to the other. Because of the possibility of these delays, keeping the spanning-tree topology from settling out or converging until all switches have had time to receive accurate information is important.

STP uses three timers to make sure that a network converges properly before a bridging loop can form. The timers and their default values are as follows:

- **Hello Time**—The time interval between Configuration BPDUs sent by the root bridge. The Hello Time value configured in the root bridge switch determines the Hello Time for all nonroot switches because they just relay the Configuration BPDUs as they are received from the root. However, all switches have a locally configured Hello Time that is used to time TCN BPDUs when they are retransmitted. The IEEE 802.1D standard specifies a default Hello Time value of 2 seconds.

- **Forward Delay**—The time interval that a switch port spends in both the Listening and Learning states. The default value is 15 seconds.

- **Max (maximum) Age**—The time interval that a switch stores a BPDU before discarding it. While executing the STP, each switch port keeps a copy of the "best" BPDU that it has heard. If the switch port loses contact with the BPDU's source (no more BPDUs are received from it), the switch assumes that a topology change must have occurred after the Max Age time elapsed and so the BPDU is aged out. The default Max Age value is 20 seconds.

The STP timers can be configured or adjusted from the switch command line. However, the timer values never should be changed from the defaults without careful consideration. Then the values should be changed only on the root bridge switch. Recall that the timer values are advertised in fields within the BPDU. The root bridge ensures that the timer values propagate to all other switches.

Tip: The default STP timer values are based on some assumptions about the size of the network and the length of the Hello Time. A reference model of a network having a diameter of seven switches derives these values. The diameter is measured from the root bridge switch outward, including the root bridge.

In other words, if you draw the STP topology, the diameter is the number of switches connected in series from the root bridge out to the end of any branch in the tree. The Hello Time is based on the time it takes for a BPDU to travel from the root bridge to a point seven switches away. This computation uses a Hello Time of 2 seconds.

The network diameter can be configured on the root bridge switch to more accurately reflect the true size of the physical network. Making that value more accurate reduces the total STP convergence time during a topology change. Cisco also recommends that if changes need to be made, only the network diameter value should be modified on the root bridge switch. When the diameter is changed, the switch calculates new values for all three timers automatically.

Table 7-6 summarizes the STP timers, their functions, and their default values.

Table 7-6 *STP Timers*

Timer	Function	Default Value
Hello	Interval between configuration BPDUs.	2 seconds
Forward Delay	Time spent in Listening and Learning states before transitioning toward Forwarding state.	15 seconds
Max Age	Maximum length of time a BPDU can be stored without receiving an update. Timer expiration signals an indirect failure with designated or root bridge.	20 seconds

Topology Changes

To announce a change in the active network topology, switches send a TCN BPDU. Table 7-7 shows the format of these messages.

Table 7-7 *Topology Change Notification BPDU Message Content*

Field Description	# of Bytes
Protocol ID (always 0)	2
Version (always 0)	1
Message Type (Configuration or TCN BPDU)	1

A topology change occurs when a switch either moves a port into the Forwarding state or moves a port from the Forwarding or Learning states into the Blocking state. In other words, a port on an active switch comes up or goes down. The switch sends a TCN BPDU out its root port so that, ultimately, the root bridge receives news of the topology change. Notice that the TCN BPDU carries no data about the change but informs recipients only that a change has occurred. Also notice that the switch will not send TCN BPDUs if the port has been configured with PortFast enabled.

Key Topic

The switch continues sending TCN BPDUs every Hello Time interval until it gets an acknowledgment from its upstream neighbor. As the upstream neighbors receive the TCN BPDU, they propagate it on toward the root bridge and send their own acknowledgments. When the root bridge receives the TCN BPDU, it also sends out an acknowledgment. However, the root bridge sets the Topology Change flag in its Configuration BPDU, which is relayed to every other bridge in the network. This is done to signal the topology change and cause all other bridges to shorten their bridge table aging times from the default (300 seconds) to the Forward Delay value (default 15 seconds).

This condition causes the learned locations of MAC addresses to be flushed out much sooner than they normally would, easing the bridge table corruption that might occur because of the change in topology. However, any stations that are actively communicating during this time are kept in the bridge table. This condition lasts for the sum of the Forward Delay and the Max Age (default 15 + 20 seconds).

The theory behind topology changes is fairly straightforward, but it's often difficult to grasp how a working network behaves during a change. For example, suppose that you have a Layer 2 network (think of a single VLAN or a single instance of STP) that is stable and loop free. If a switch uplink suddenly failed or a new uplink was added, how would the various switches in the network react? Would users all over the network lose connectivity while the STP "recomputes" or reconverges?

Examples of different types of topology changes are presented in the following sections, along with the sequence of STP events. Each type has a different cause and a different effect. To provide continuity as the STP concepts are presented, the same network previously shown in Figures 7-3 through 7-5 is used in each of these examples.

Direct Topology Changes

A direct topology change is one that can be detected on a switch interface. For example, if a trunk link suddenly goes down, the switch on each end of the link can immediately detect a link failure. The absence of that link changes the bridging topology, so other switches should be notified.

Figure 7-6 shows a network that has converged into a stable STP topology. The VLAN is forwarding on all trunk links except port 1/2 on Catalyst C, where it is in the Blocking state.

This network has just suffered a link failure between Catalyst A and Catalyst C. The sequence of events unfolds as follows:

1. Catalyst C detects a link down on its port 1/1; Catalyst A detects a link down on its port 1/2.

2. Catalyst C removes the previous "best" BPDU it had received from the root over port 1/1. Port 1/1 is now down so that BPDU is no longer valid.

   Normally, Catalyst C would try to send a TCN message out its root port, to reach the root bridge. Here, the root port is broken, so that isn't possible. Without an advanced feature such as STP UplinkFast, Catalyst C isn't yet aware that another path exists to the root.

   Also, Catalyst A is aware of the link down condition on its own port 1/2. It normally would try to send a TCN message out its root port to reach the root bridge. Here, Catalyst A *is* the root, so that isn't really necessary.

3. The root bridge, Catalyst A, sends a Configuration BPDU with the TCN bit set out its port 1/1. This is received and relayed by each switch along the way, informing each one of the topology change.

4. Catalysts B and C receive the TCN message. The only reaction these switches take is to shorten their bridging table aging times to the Forward Delay time. At this point, they don't know how the topology has changed; they only know to force fairly recent bridging table entries to age out.

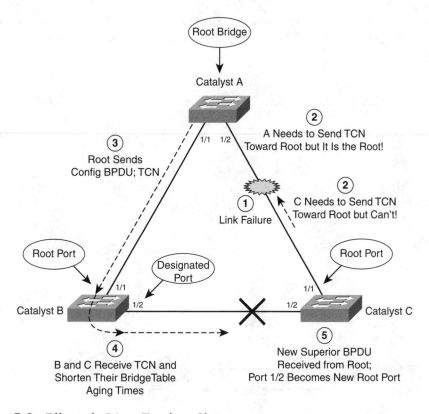

Figure 7-6 *Effects of a Direct Topology Change*

5. Catalyst C basically just sits and waits to hear from the root bridge again. The Config BPDU TCN message is received on port 1/2, which was previously in the Blocking state. This BPDU becomes the "best" one received from the root, so port 1/2 becomes the new root port.

Catalyst C now can progress port 1/2 from Blocking through the Listening, Learning, and Forwarding states.

As a result of a direct link failure, the topology has changed and STP has converged again. Notice that only Catalyst C has undergone any real effects from the failure. Switches A and B heard the news of the topology change but did not have to move any links through the STP states. In other words, the whole network did not go through a massive STP reconvergence.

The total time that users on Catalyst C lost connectivity was roughly the time that port 1/2 spent in the Listening and Learning states. With the default STP timers, this amounts to about two times the Forward Delay period (15 seconds), or 30 seconds total.

Indirect Topology Changes

Figure 7-7 shows the same network as Figure 7-6, but this time the link failure indirectly involves Catalysts A and C. The link status at each switch stays up, but something between them has failed or is filtering traffic. This could be another device, such as a service provider's switch, a firewall, and so on. As a result, no data (including BPDUs) can pass between those switches.

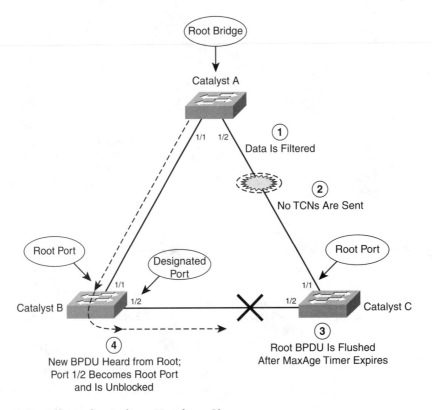

Figure 7-7 *Effects of an Indirect Topology Change*

STP can detect and recover from indirect failures, thanks to timer mechanisms. The sequence of events unfolds as follows:

1. Catalysts A and C both show a link up condition; data begins to be filtered elsewhere on the link.

2. No link failure is detected, so no TCN messages are sent.

3. Catalyst C already has stored the "best" BPDU it had received from the root over port 1/1. No further BPDUs are received from the root over that port. After the Max Age timer expires, no other BPDU is available to refresh the "best" entry, so it is flushed. Catalyst C now must wait to hear from the Root again on any of its ports.

4. The next Configuration BPDU from the root is heard on Catalyst C port 1/2. This BPDU becomes the new "best" entry, and port 1/2 becomes the root port. Now the port is progressed from Blocking through the Listening, Learning, and finally Forwarding states.

As a result of the indirect link failure, the topology doesn't change immediately. The absence of BPDUs from the root causes Catalyst C to take some action. Because this type of failure relies on STP timer activity, it generally takes longer to detect and mitigate.

In this example, the total time that users on Catalyst C lost connectivity was roughly the time until the Max Age timer expired (20 seconds), plus the time until the next Configuration BPDU was received (2 seconds) on port 1/2, plus the time that port 1/2 spent in the Listening (15 seconds) and Learning (15 seconds) states. In other words, 52 seconds elapse if the default timer values are used.

Insignificant Topology Changes

Figure 7-8 shows the same network topology as Figure 7-6 and Figure 7-7, with the addition of a user PC on access-layer switch Catalyst C. The user's switch port, 2/12, is just another link as far as the switch is concerned. If the link status goes up or down, the switch must view that as a topology change and inform the root bridge.

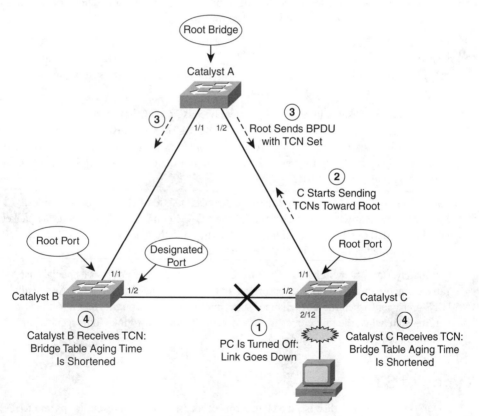

Figure 7-8 *Effects of an Insignificant Topology Change*

Obviously, user ports are expected to go up and down as the users reboot their machines, turn them on and off as they go to and from work, and so on. Regardless, TCN messages are sent by the switch, just as if a trunk link between switches had changed state.

To see what effect this has on the STP topology and the network, consider the following sequence of events:

1. The PC on Catalyst port 2/12 is turned off. The switch detects the link status going down.

2. Catalyst C begins sending TCN BPDUs toward the root, over its root port (1/1).

3. The root sends a TCN acknowledgment back to Catalyst C and then sends a Configuration BPDU with the TCN bit set to all downstream switches. This is done to inform every switch of a topology change somewhere in the network.

4. The TCN flag is received from the root, and both Catalysts B and C shorten their bridge table aging times. This causes recently idle entries to be flushed, leaving only the actively transmitting stations in the table. The aging time stays short for the duration of the Forward Delay and Max Age timers.

Notice that this type of topology change is mostly cosmetic. No actual topology change occurred because none of the switches had to change port states to reach the root bridge. Instead, powering off the PC caused all the switches to age out entries from their bridge or CAM tables much sooner than normal.

At first, this doesn't seem like a major problem because the PC link state affects only the "newness" of the CAM table contents. If CAM table entries are flushed as a result, they probably will be learned again. This becomes a problem when every user PC is considered. Now every time *any* PC in the network powers up or down, *every* switch in the network must age out CAM table entries.

Given enough PCs, the switches could be in a constant state of flushing bridge tables. Also remember that when a switch doesn't have a CAM entry for a destination, the packet must be flooded out all its ports. Flushed tables mean more unknown unicasts, which mean more broadcasts or flooded packets throughout the network.

Fortunately, Catalyst switches have a feature that can designate a port as a special case. You can enable the STP PortFast feature on a port with a single attached PC. As a result, TCNs aren't sent when the port changes state, and the port is brought right into the Forwarding state when the link comes up. The section "Redundant Link Convergence," in Chapter 8, covers PortFast in more detail.

Types of STP

So far, this chapter has discussed STP in terms of its operation to prevent loops and to recover from topology changes in a timely manner. STP was originally developed to operate in a bridged environment, basically supporting a single LAN (or one VLAN). Implementing STP into a switched environment has required additional consideration and modification to support multiple VLANs. Because of this, the IEEE and Cisco have approached

STP differently. This section reviews the three traditional types of STP that are encountered in switched networks and how they relate to one another. No specific configuration commands are associated with the various types of STP here. Instead, you need a basic understanding of how they interoperate in a network.

> **Note:**   The IEEE has produced additional standards for spanning-tree enhancements that greatly improve on its scalability and convergence aspects. These are covered in Chapter 10. When you have a firm understanding of the more traditional forms of STP presented in this chapter, you can grasp the enhanced versions much easier.

Common Spanning Tree

The IEEE 802.1Q standard specifies how VLANs are to be trunked between switches. It also specifies only a single instance of STP that encompasses all VLANs. This instance is referred to as the *Common Spanning Tree* (CST). All CST BPDUs are transmitted over trunk links using the native VLAN with untagged frames.

Having a single STP for many VLANs simplifies switch configuration and reduces switch CPU load during STP calculations. However, having only one STP instance can cause limitations, too. Redundant links between switches will be blocked with no capability for load balancing. Conditions also can occur that would cause CST to mistakenly enable forwarding on a link that does not carry a specific VLAN, whereas other links would be blocked.

Per-VLAN Spanning Tree

Cisco has a proprietary version of STP that offers more flexibility than the CST version. *Per-VLAN Spanning Tree* (PVST) operates a separate instance of STP for each individual VLAN. This allows the STP on each VLAN to be configured independently, offering better performance and tuning for specific conditions. Multiple spanning trees also make load balancing possible over redundant links when the links are assigned to different VLANs. One link might forward one set of VLANs, while another redundant link might forward a different set.

Because of its proprietary nature, PVST requires the use of Cisco Inter-Switch Link (ISL) trunking encapsulation between switches. In networks where PVST and CST coexist, interoperability problems occur. Each requires a different trunking method, so BPDUs are never exchanged between STP types.

Per-VLAN Spanning Tree Plus

Cisco has a second proprietary version of STP that allows devices to interoperate with both PVST and CST. *Per-VLAN Spanning Tree Plus* (PVST+) effectively supports three groups of STP operating in the same campus network:

- Catalyst switches running PVST

- Catalyst switches running PVST+

- Switches running CST over 802.1Q

Table 7-8 summarizes the three STP types and their basic functions.

Table 7-8 *Types of STP*

Type of STP	Function
CST	1 instance of STP, over the native VLAN; 802.1Q-based
PVST	1 instance of STP per VLAN; Cisco ISL-based
PVST+	Provides interoperability between CST and PVST; operates over both 802.1Q and ISL

To do this, PVST+ acts as a translator between groups of CST switches and groups of PVST switches. PVST+ can communicate directly with PVST by using ISL trunks. To communicate with CST, however, PVST+ exchanges BPDUs with CST as untagged frames over the native VLAN. BPDUs from other instances of STP (other VLANs) are propagated across the CST portions of the network by tunneling. PVST+ sends these BPDUs by using a unique multicast address so that the CST switches forward them on to downstream neighbors without interpreting them first. Eventually, the tunneled BPDUs reach other PVST+ switches where they are understood.

Exam Preparation Tasks

Review All Key Topics

Review the most important topics in the chapter, noted with the Key Topic icon in the outer margin of the page. Table 7-9 lists a reference of these key topics and the page numbers on which each is found.

Key
Topic

Table 7-9   *Key Topics for Chapter 7*

Key Topic Element	Description	Page Number
List	Describes transparent bridge operation	128
List	Explains a bridging loop	130
Paragraph	Discusses BPDUs	132
Paragraph	Discusses root bridge election	133
Paragraph	Explains root port selection and root path cost	135
Paragraph	Discusses designated port selection	137
List	Explains tie-breaking decision process	137
List	Discusses the sequence of STP port states	139
List	Explains the three STP timers and their uses	142
Paragraph	Explains STP topology changes	143
Paragraph	Describes the Common Spanning Tree	149
Paragraph	Describes Per-VLAN Spanning Tree	149

Complete Tables and Lists from Memory

Print a copy of Appendix C, "Memory Tables," (found on the CD), or at least the section for this chapter, and complete the tables and lists from memory. Appendix D, "Memory Tables Answer Key," also on the CD, includes completed tables and lists to check your work.

Define Key Terms

Define the following key terms from this chapter, and check your answers in the glossary:

transparent bridge, bridging loop, Spanning Tree Protocol (STP), BPDU, root bridge, root port, root path cost, designated port, Hello Time, Forward Delay, Max Age time, TCN, Common Spanning Tree (CST), PVST, PVST+

This chapter covers the following topics that you need to master for the CCNP SWITCH exam:

STP Root Bridge—This section discusses the importance of identifying a root bridge and suggestions for its placement in the network. This section also presents the root bridge configuration commands.

Spanning-Tree Customization—This section covers the configuration commands that enable you to alter the spanning-tree topology.

Tuning Spanning-Tree Convergence—This section discusses how to alter, or tune, the STP timers to achieve optimum convergence times in a network.

Redundant Link Convergence—This section describes the methods that cause a network to converge more quickly after a topology change.

Monitoring STP—This section offers a brief summary of the commands you can use to verify that an STP instance is working properly.

CHAPTER 8

Spanning-Tree Configuration

This chapter presents the design and configuration considerations necessary to implement the IEEE 802.1D Spanning Tree Protocol (STP) in a campus network. This chapter also discusses the commands needed to configure the STP features, previously described in Chapter 7, "Traditional Spanning Tree Protocol."

You can also tune STP or make it converge more efficiently in a given network. This chapter presents the theory and commands needed to accomplish this.

"Do I Know This Already?" Quiz

The "Do I Know This Already?" quiz allows you to assess whether you should read this entire chapter thoroughly or jump to the "Exam Preparation Tasks" section. If you are in doubt based on your answers to these questions or your own assessment of your knowledge of the topics, read the entire chapter. Table 8-1 outlines the major headings in this chapter and the "Do I Know This Already?" quiz questions that go with them. You can find the answers in Appendix A, "Answers to the 'Do I Know This Already?' Quizzes."

Table 8-1 *"Do I Know This Already?" Foundation Topics Section-to-Question Mapping*

Foundation Topics Section	Questions Covered in This Section
STP Root Bridge	1–5
Spanning-Tree Customization	6–7
Tuning Spanning-Tree Convergence	8–9
Redundant Link Convergence	10–12
Monitoring STP	13

1. Where should the root bridge be placed on a network?

    a. On the fastest switch

    b. Closest to the most users

    c. Closest to the center of the network

    d. On the least-used switch

2. Which of the following is a result of a poorly placed root bridge in a network?

   a. Bridging loops form.

   b. STP topology can't be resolved.

   c. STP topology can take unexpected paths.

   d. Root bridge election flapping occurs.

3. Which of these parameters should you change to make a switch become a root bridge?

   a. Switch MAC address

   b. Path cost

   c. Port priority

   d. Bridge priority

4. What is the default 802.1D STP bridge priority on a Catalyst switch?

   a. 0

   b. 1

   c. 32,768

   d. 65,535

5. Which of the following commands is most likely to make a switch become the root bridge for VLAN 5, assuming that all switches have the default STP parameters?

   a. spanning-tree root

   b. spanning-tree root vlan 5

   c. spanning-tree vlan 5 priority 100

   d. spanning-tree vlan 5 root

6. What is the default path cost of a Gigabit Ethernet switch port?

   a. 1

   b. 2

   c. 4

   d. 19

   e. 1000

7. What command can change the path cost of interface Gigabit Ethernet 3/1 to a value of 8?

   a. spanning-tree path-cost 8

   b. spanning-tree cost 8

   c. spanning-tree port-cost 8

   d. spanning-tree gig 3/1 cost 8

8. What happens if the root bridge switch and another switch are configured with different STP Hello timer values?

    a. Nothing—each sends hellos at different times.

    b. A bridging loop could form because the two switches are out of sync.

    c. The switch with the lower Hello timer becomes the root bridge.

    d. The other switch changes its Hello timer to match the root bridge

9. What network diameter value is the basis for the default STP timer calculations?

    a. 1

    b. 3

    c. 7

    d. 9

    e. 15

10. Where should the STP PortFast feature be used?

    a. An access-layer switch port connected to a PC

    b. An access-layer switch port connected to a hub

    c. A distribution-layer switch port connected to an access layer switch

    d. A core-layer switch port

11. Where should the STP UplinkFast feature be enabled?

    a. An access-layer switch.

    b. A distribution-layer switch.

    c. A core-layer switch.

    d. All these answers are correct.

12. If used, the STP BackboneFast feature should be enabled on which of these?

    a. All backbone- or core-layer switches

    b. All backbone- and distribution-layer switches

    c. All access-layer switches

    d. All switches in the network

13. Which one of the following commands can be used to verify the current root bridge in VLAN 10?

    a. show root vlan 10

    b. show root-bridge vlan 10

    c. show spanning-tree vlan 10 root

    d. show running-config

Foundation Topics

STP Root Bridge

Spanning Tree Protocol (STP) and its computations are predictable; however, other factors might subtly influence STP decisions, making the resulting tree structure neither expected nor ideal.

As the network administrator, you can make adjustments to the spanning-tree operation to control its behavior. The location of the root bridge should be determined as part of the design process. You can use redundant links for load balancing in parallel, if configured correctly. You can also configure STP to converge quickly and predictably if a major topology change occurs.

Tip: By default, STP is enabled for all active VLANs and on all ports of a switch. STP should remain enabled in a network to prevent bridging loops from forming. However, you might find that STP has been disabled in some way.

If an entire instance of STP has been disabled, you can reenable it with the following global configuration command:

```
Switch(config)# spanning-tree vlan vlan-id
```

If STP has been disabled for a specific VLAN on a specific port, you can reenable it with the following interface configuration command:

```
Switch (config-if)# spanning-tree vlan vlan-id
```

Root Bridge Placement

Although STP is wonderfully automatic with its default values and election processes, the resulting tree structure might perform quite differently than expected. The root bridge election is based on the idea that one switch is chosen as a common reference point, and all other switches choose ports that have the best-cost path to the root. The root bridge election is also based on the idea that the root bridge can become a central hub that interconnects other legs of the network. Therefore, the root bridge can be faced with heavy switching loads in its central location.

If the root bridge election is left to its default state, several things can occur to result in a poor choice. For example, the *slowest* switch (or bridge) could be elected as the root bridge. If heavy traffic loads are expected to pass through the root bridge, the slowest switch is not the ideal candidate. Recall that the only criteria for root bridge election is that the switch must have the lowest bridge ID (bridge priority and MAC address), which is not necessarily the best choice to ensure optimal performance. If the slowest switch has the same bridge priority as the others and has the lowest MAC address, the slowest switch will be chosen as the root.

A second factor to consider relates to redundancy. If all switches are left at their default states, only one root bridge is elected, with no clear choice for a backup. What happens if that switch fails? Another root bridge election occurs, but again, the choice might not be the ideal switch or the ideal location.

The final consideration is the location of the root bridge switch. As before, an election with default switch values could place the root bridge in an unexpected location in the network. More important, an inefficient spanning-tree structure could result, causing traffic from a large portion of the network to take a long and winding path just to pass through the root bridge.

Figure 8-1 shows a portion of a real-world hierarchical campus network.

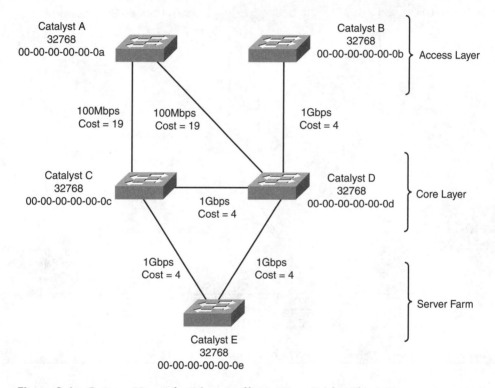

Figure 8-1   *Campus Network with an Inefficient Root Bridge Election*

Catalyst switches A and B are two access-layer devices; Catalysts C and D form the core layer, and Catalyst E connects a server farm into the network core. Notice that most of the switches use redundant links to other layers of the hierarchy. At the time of this example, however, many switches, such as Catalyst B, still have only a single connection into the core. These switches are slated for an "upgrade," in which a redundant link will be added to the other half of the core.

As you will see, Catalyst A will become the root bridge because of its low MAC address. All switches have been left to their default STP states—the bridge priority of each is 32,768 (or 32,768 plus the VLAN ID, if the extended system ID is enabled). Figure 8-2 shows the converged state of STP. For the purposes of this discussion, the root ports and designated ports are simply shown on the network diagram. As an exercise, you should work through the spanning-tree process yourself, based on the information shown in the figure. The more examples you can work out by hand, the better you will understand the entire spanning-tree process.

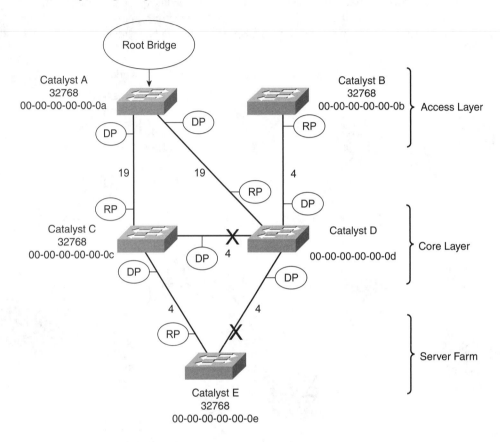

Figure 8-2 *Campus Network with STP Converged*

Notice that Catalyst A, one of the access-layer switches, has been elected the root bridge. Unfortunately, Catalyst A cannot take advantage of the 1-Gbps links, unlike the other switches. Also note the location of the X symbols over the ports that are neither root ports nor designated ports. These ports will enter the Blocking state, and no data packets will pass through them.

Finally, Figure 8-3 shows the same network with the blocking links removed. Now you can see the true structure of the final spanning tree.

Catalyst A, an access-layer switch, is the root bridge. Workstations on Catalyst A can reach servers on Catalyst E by crossing through the core layer (Catalyst C), as expected. However, notice what has happened to the other access-layer switch, Catalyst B. Workstations on this switch must cross into the core layer (Catalyst D), back into the access layer (Catalyst A), back through the core (Catalyst C), and finally to the server farm (Catalyst E).

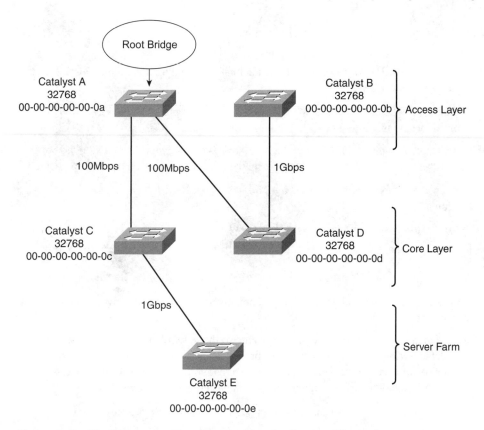

Figure 8-3   *Final Spanning-Tree Structure for the Campus Network*

This action is obviously inefficient. For one thing, Catalyst A is probably not a high-end switch because it is used in the access layer. However, the biggest issue is that other access-layer areas are forced to thread through the relatively slow uplinks on Catalyst A. This winding path will become a major bottleneck to the users.

Root Bridge Configuration

To prevent the surprises outlined in the previous section, you should *always* do two things:

Key Topic

■ Configure one switch as a root bridge in a determined fashion.

■ Configure another switch as a secondary root bridge, in case of a primary root bridge failure.

As the common reference point, the root bridge (and the secondary) should be placed near the center of the Layer 2 network. For example, a switch in the distribution layer would make a better root bridge choice than one in the access layer because more traffic is expected to pass through the distribution-layer devices. In a flat switched network (no Layer 3 devices), a switch near a server farm would be a more efficient root bridge than switches elsewhere. Most traffic will be destined to and from the server farm and will benefit from a predetermined, direct path.

Tip: A Catalyst switch can be configured to use one of the following formats for its STP bridge ID:

■   Traditional 802.1D bridge priority value (16 bits), followed by the unique switch MAC address for the VLAN

■   The 802.1t extended system ID (4-bit priority multiplier, plus a 12-bit VLAN ID), followed by a nonunique switch MAC address for the VLAN

If the switch can't support 1024 unique MAC addresses for its own use, the extended system ID is always enabled by default. Otherwise, the traditional method is enabled by default.

To begin using the extended system ID method, you can use the following global configuration command:

```
Switch(config)# spanning-tree extend system-id
```

Otherwise, you can use the traditional method by beginning the command with the **no** keyword.

You can configure a Catalyst switch to become the root bridge using one of two methods, which are configured as follows:

■   Manually setting the bridge priority value so that a switch is given a lower-than-default bridge ID value to win a root bridge election. You must know the bridge priorities of every other switch in a VLAN so that you can choose a value that is less than all the others. The command to accomplish this is as follows:

```
Switch(config)# spanning-tree vlan vlan-list priority bridge-priority
```

The *bridge-priority* value defaults to 32,768, but you can also assign a value of 0 to 65,535. If STP extended system ID is enabled, the default *bridge-priority* is 32,768 plus the VLAN number. In that case, the value can range from 0 to 61,440, but only as multiples of 4096. A lower bridge priority is preferable.

Remember that Catalyst switches run one instance of STP for each VLAN (PVST+), so the VLAN ID must always be given. You should designate an appropriate root bridge for each VLAN. For example, you could use the following command to set the bridge priority for VLAN 5 and VLANs 100 through 200 to 4096:

```
Switch(config)# spanning-tree vlan 5,100-200 priority 4096
```

■   Causing the would-be root bridge switch to choose its own priority, based on some assumptions about other switches in the network. You can accomplish this with the following command:

```
Switch(config)# spanning-tree vlan vlan-id root {primary | secondary}
  [diameter diameter]
```

This command is actually a macro on the Catalyst that executes several other commands. The result is a more direct and automatic way to force one switch to become the root bridge. Notice that the actual bridge priorities are not given in the command. Instead, the switch modifies its STP values according to the current values in use within the active network. *These values are modified only once, when the macro command is issued.* Use the **primary** keyword to make the switch attempt to become the primary root bridge. This command modifies the switch's bridge priority value to become less than the bridge priority of the current root bridge. If the current root priority is more than 24,576, the local switch sets its priority to 24,576. If the current root priority is less than that, the local switch sets its priority to 4096 less than the current root.

For the **secondary** root bridge, the root priority is set to an artificially low value of 28,672. There is no way to query or listen to the network to find another potential secondary root simply because there are no advertisements or elections of secondary root bridges. Instead, the fixed secondary priority is used under the assumption that it will be less than the default priorities (32,768) that might be used on switches elsewhere. You can also modify the network diameter by adding the **diameter** keyword to this command. This modification is discussed further in the "Tuning Spanning-Tree Convergence" section, later in the chapter.

As a final example, consider a switch that is currently using its default bridge priority for VLAN 100. In the extended system-id mode, the default priority is 32,768 plus 100 (the VLAN number). The output in Example 8-1 demonstrates this under the bridge ID information. The default priority is greater than the current root bridge priority of 4200, so the local switch cannot become the root.

Example 8-1   *Displaying the STP Bridge Priority Values*

```
Switch# show spanning-tree vlan 100
VLAN0100
  Spanning tree enabled protocol ieee
  Root  ID  Priority   4200

            Address       000b.5f65.1f80
            Cost          4
            Port          1 (GigabitEthernet0/1)
            Hello Time    2 sec  Max Age 20 sec  Forward Delay 15 sec


  Bridge  ID  Priority  32868  (priority  32768  sys-id-ext  100)

            Address       000c.8554.9a80
            Hello Time    2 sec  Max Age 20 sec  Forward Delay 15 sec
            Aging Time 300
[output omitted]
```

Now, the automatic method is used to attempt to make the switch become root for VLAN 100, using the command demonstrated in Example 8-2.

Example 8-2   *Using a Macro Command to Configure a Root Bridge*

```
Switch(config)# spanning-tree vlan 100 root primary
% Failed to make the bridge root for vlan 100
% It may be possible to make the bridge root by setting the priority
% for some (or all) of these instances to zero.
Switch(config)#
```

Why did this method fail? The current root bridge has a bridge priority of 4200. Because that priority is less than 24,576, the local switch will try to set its priority to 4096 less than the current root. Although the resulting priority would be 104, the local switch is using an extended system ID, which requires bridge priority values that are multiples of 4096. The only value that would work is 0, but the automatic method will not use it. Instead, the only other option is to manually configure the bridge priority to 0 with the following command:

```
Switch(config)# spanning-tree vlan 100 priority 0
```

Remember that on switches that use an extended system ID, the bridge priority is the configured priority (multiple of 4096) plus the VLAN number. Even though the priority was set to 0 with the previous command, the switch is actually using a value of 100—priority 0 plus VLAN number 100, as the output in Example 8-3 reveals.

Example 8-3 *Displaying Bridge Priorities with Extended System IDs*

```
Switch# show spanning-tree vlan 100
VLAN0100
  Spanning tree enabled protocol ieee
  Root  ID  Priority  100

              Address      000c.8554.9a80
              This bridge is the root

              Hello Time   2 sec  Max Age 20 sec  Forward Delay 15 sec


  Bridge  ID  Priority  100  (priority  0  sys-id-ext  100)

              Address      000c.8554.9a80
              Hello Time   2 sec  Max Age 20 sec  Forward Delay 15 sec
              Aging Time 300
[output omitted]
```

Note: The **spanning-tree vlan** *vlan-id* **root** command will not be shown in a Catalyst switch configuration because the command is actually a macro executing other switch commands. The actual commands and values produced by the macro will be shown, however. For example, the macro can potentially adjust the four STP values as follows:

```
Switch(config)# spanning-tree vlan 1 root primary
vlan 1 bridge priority set to 24576
vlan 1 bridge max aging time unchanged at 20
vlan 1 bridge hello time unchanged at 2
vlan 1 bridge forward delay unchanged at 15
```

Be aware that this macro doesn't guarantee that the switch will become the root and maintain that status. After the macro is used, it is entirely possible for another switch in the network to have its bridge priority configured to a lower value. The other switch would become the new root, displacing the switch that ran the macro.

On the root, it is usually good practice to directly modify the bridge priority to an artificially low value (even priority 1 or 0) with the **spanning-tree vlan** *vlan-id* **priority** *bridge-priority* command. This makes it more difficult for another switch in the network to win the root bridge election, unless it is manually configured with a priority that is even lower.

Spanning-Tree Customization

The most important decision you can make when designing your spanning-tree topology is the placement of the root bridge. Other decisions, such as the exact loop-free path structure, will occur automatically as a result of the spanning-tree algorithm (STA). Occasionally, the path might need additional tuning, but only under special circumstances and after careful consideration.

Recall the sequence of four criteria that STP uses to choose a path:

1. Lowest bridge ID

2. Lowest root path cost

3. Lowest sender bridge ID

4. Lowest sender port ID

The previous section discussed how to tune a switch's bridge ID to force it to become the root bridge in a network. You can also change the bridge priority on a switch to influence the value it uses in the sender bridge ID that it announced as it relays BPDUs to other neighboring switches.

Only the automatic STP computation has been discussed, using the default switch port costs to make specific path decisions. The following sections discuss ways you can influence the exact topology that results.

Tuning the Root Path Cost

The root path cost for each active port of a switch is determined by the cumulative cost as a BPDU travels along. As a switch *receives* a BPDU, the port cost of the receiving port is added to the root path cost in the BPDU. The port or port path cost is inversely proportional to the port's bandwidth. If desired, a port's cost can be modified from the default value.

Note: Before modifying a switch port's path cost, you should always calculate the root path costs of other alternative paths through the network. Changing one port's cost might influence STP to choose that port as a root port, but other paths still could be preferred. You also should calculate a port's existing path cost to determine what the new cost value should be. Careful calculation will ensure that the desired path indeed will be chosen.

Key
Topic

Use the following interface configuration command to set a switch port's path cost:

```
Switch (config-if)# spanning-tree [vlan vlan-id] cost cost
```

If the **vlan** parameter is given, the port cost is modified only for the specified VLAN. Otherwise, the cost is modified for the port as a whole (all active VLANs). The *cost* value can range from 1 to 65,535. There are standard or default values that correspond to port bandwidth, as shown in Table 8-2.

Table 8-2 *STP Port Cost*

Link Bandwidth	STP Cost
4 Mbps	250
10 Mbps	100
16 Mbps	62
45 Mbps	39
100 Mbps	19
155 Mbps	14
622 Mbps	6
1 Gbps	4
10 Gbps	2

For example, a Gigabit Ethernet interface has a default port cost of 4. You can use the following command to change the cost to 2, but only for VLAN 10:

```
Switch(config-if)# spanning-tree vlan 10 cost 2
```

You can see the port cost of an interface by using the following command:

```
Switch# show spanning-tree interface type mod/num [cost]
```

As an example, Gigabit Ethernet 0/1 is configured as a trunk port, carrying VLANs 1, 10, and 20. Example 8-4 shows the port cost for each of the VLANs.

Example 8-4 *Displaying STP Port Cost Values on an Interface*

```
Switch# show spanning-tree interface gigabitEthernet 0/1
Vlan            Role Sts Cost       Prio.Nbr Type
--------------- ---- --- ---------- -------- --------------------------
VLAN0001        Root FWD 4          128.1    P2p
VLAN0010        Desg FWD 2          128.1    P2p
VLAN0020        Root FWD 4          128.1    P2p
```

Tuning the Port ID

The fourth criteria of an STP decision is the port ID. The port ID value that a switch uses is actually a 16-bit quantity: 8 bits for the port priority and 8 bits for the port number. The port priority is a value from 0 to 255 and defaults to 128 for all ports. The port number can range from 0 to 255 and represents the port's actual physical mapping. Port numbers begin with 1 at port 0/1 and increment across each module. (The numbers might not be consecutive because each module is assigned a particular range of numbers.)

Tip: Port numbers are usually intuitive on a fixed configuration switch, such as a 48-port Catalyst 3560. The STP port number is simply the interface number, from 1 to 48.

However, it is not easy to find the STP port number in a switch with many modules and many ports. Notice how Gigabit Ethernet 3/16 is also known as port number 144 in the following example:

```
Switch# show spanning-tree interface gigabitEthernet 3/16
Vlan              Role Sts Cost        Prio.Nbr Type
----------------- ---- --- --------    -------- -------------------------
VLAN0010          Desg FWD 4           128.144  Edge P2p
VLAN0100          Desg FWD 4           128.144  Edge P2p
VLAN0200          Desg FWD 4           128.144  Edge P2p
Switch#
```

The entire port ID consists of the port priority followed by the port number. In the preceding example output, the port ID is 128.144. As a 16-bit quantity in hex, it is 8090. In addition, ports that are bundled into an EtherChannel or Port-channel interface always have a higher port ID than they would if they were not bundled.

Obviously, a switch port's port number is fixed because it is based only on its hardware location or index. The port ID, however, can be modified to influence an STP decision by using the port priority. You can configure the port priority with this interface-configuration command:

```
Switch(config-if)# spanning-tree [vlan vlan-list] port-priority port-priority
```

You can modify the port priority for one or more VLANs by using the **vlan** parameter. The VLAN numbers are given as *vlan-list*, a list of single values or ranges of values separated by commas. Otherwise, the port priority is set for the port as a whole (all active VLANs). The value of *port-priority* can range from 0 to 255 and defaults to 128. A lower port priority value indicates a more preferred path toward the root bridge.

As an example, you can use the following command sequence to change the port priority of Gigabit Ethernet 3/16 from 128 (the default) to 64 for VLANs 10 and 100:

```
Switch(config)# interface gigabitethernet 3/16
Switch(config-if)# spanning-tree vlan 10,100 port-priority 64
```

You can confirm the changes with the **show spanning-tree interface** command, as demonstrated in Example 8-5.

Example 8-5 *Confirming STP Port Priority Values After Configuration*

```
Switch# show spanning-tree interface gigabitEthernet 3/16
Vlan              Role Sts Cost     Prio.Nbr Type
----------------- ---- --- -------- -------- -------------------------------
VLAN0010          Desg FWD 4        64.144   Edge P2p
VLAN0100          Desg FWD 4        64.144   Edge P2p
VLAN0200          Desg FWD 4        128.144  Edge P2p
Switch#
```

Tuning Spanning-Tree Convergence

STP uses several timers, a sequence of states that ports must move through, and specific topology change conditions to prevent bridging loops from forming in a complex network. Each of these parameters or requirements is based on certain default values for a typical network size and function. For the majority of cases, the default STP operation is sufficient to keep the network loop free and enable users to communicate.

However, in certain situations, the default STP can cause network access to be delayed while timers expire and while preventing loops on links where loops are not possible. For example, when a single PC is connected to a switch port, a bridging loop is simply not possible. Another situation relates to the size of a Layer 2 switched network: The default STP timers are based on a benchmark network size.

In a network that is smaller, waiting until the default timer values expire might not make sense when they could be safely set to shorter values. In situations like this, you can safely make adjustments to the STP convergence process for more efficiency.

Modifying STP Timers

Recall that STP uses three timers to keep track of various port operation states and communication between bridges. The three STP timers can be adjusted by using the commands documented in the sections that follow. Remember that the timers need to be modified only on the root bridge because the root bridge propagates all three timer values throughout the network as fields in the configuration BPDU.

Manually Configuring STP Timers

Use one or more of the following global configuration commands to modify STP timers:

```
Switch(config)# spanning-tree [vlan vlan-id] hello-time seconds
Switch(config)# spanning-tree [vlan vlan-id] forward-time seconds
Switch(config)# spanning-tree [vlan vlan-id] max-age seconds
```

Notice that the timers can be changed for a single instance (VLAN) of STP on the switch by using the **vlan** *vlan-id* parameters. If you omit the **vlan** keyword, the timer values are configured for *all* instances (all VLANs) of STP on the switch.

The *Hello timer* triggers periodic "hello" (actually, the configuration BPDU) messages that are sent from the root to other bridges in the network. This timer also sets the interval in which a bridge expects to hear a hello relayed from its neighboring bridges. Configuration

BPDUs are sent every 2 seconds, by default. You can modify the Hello timer with the **hello-time** keyword, along with a value of 1 to 10 seconds, as in the following command:

```
Switch(config)# spanning-tree hello-time 1
```

The *Forward Delay timer* determines the amount of time a port stays in the Listening state before moving into the Learning state, and how long it stays in the Learning state before moving to the Forwarding state. You can modify the Forward Delay timer with the **forward-time** keyword. The default value is 15 seconds, but this can be set to a value of 4 to 30 seconds. This timer should be modified only under careful consideration because the value depends on the diameter of the network and the propagation of BPDUs across all switches. A value that is too low allows loops to form, possibly crippling a network.

The Max Age timer specifies a stored BPDU's lifetime that has been received from a neighboring switch with a designated port. Suppose that BPDUs are being received on a nondesignated switch port every 2 seconds, as expected. Then an indirect failure, or one that doesn't involve a physical link going down, occurs that prevents BPDUs from being sent. The receiving switch waits until the Max Age timer expires to listen for further BPDUs. If none is received, the nondesignated port moves into the Listening state, and the receiving switch generates configuration BPDUs. This port then becomes the designated port to restore connectivity on the segment.

To modify the Max Age timer, use the **max-age** keyword. The timer value defaults to 20 seconds but can be set from 6 to 40 seconds.

Automatically Configuring STP Timers

Modifying STP timers can be tricky, given the conservative nature of the default values and the calculations needed to derive proper STP operation. Timer values are basically dependent on the Hello Time and the switched network's diameter, in terms of switch hops. Catalyst switches offer a single command that can change the timer values in a more controlled fashion. As described earlier, the **spanning-tree vlan** *vlan-list* **root** macro command is a better tool to use than setting the timers with the individual commands. This global configuration command has the following syntax:

```
Switch(config)# spanning-tree vlan vlan-list root {primary | secondary} [diameter
   diameter [hello-time hello-time]]
```

Here, STP timers will be adjusted according to the formulas specified in the 802.1D standard by giving only the network's diameter (the maximum number of switches that traffic will traverse across a Layer 2 network) and an optional *hello-time*. If you do not specify a Hello Time, the default value of 2 seconds is assumed.

This command can be used only on a per-VLAN basis to modify the timers for a particular VLAN's spanning tree instance. The network diameter can be a value from one to seven switch hops. Because this command makes a switch become the root bridge, all the modified timer values resulting from this command will be propagated to other switches through the configuration BPDU.

As an example, suppose that a small network consists of three switches connected in a triangle fashion. The command output in Example 8-6 shows the current (default) STP timer values that are in use for VLAN 100.

Example 8-6 *Displaying the STP Timer Values in Use*

```
Switch# show spanning-tree vlan 100
VLAN0100
  Spanning tree enabled protocol ieee
  Root ID    Priority    100
             Address     000c.8554.9a80
             This bridge is the root
             Hello Time   2  sec  Max  Age  20  sec  Forward  Delay 15  sec


  Bridge ID  Priority    100    (priority 0 sys-id-ext 100)
             Address     000c.8554.9a80
             Hello Time   2 sec   Max Age 20 sec   Forward Delay 15 sec
             Aging Time 300
[output omitted]
```

The longest path that a packet can take through the sample network is three switches. This is considerably less than the reference diameter of seven that is used to calculate the default timer values. Therefore, you can safely assume that this network diameter is three, provided that no additional switches will be added to lengthen the longest path. Suppose that a Hello Time of 1 second is also desired, to shorten the time needed to detect a dead neighbor. The following command attempts to make the local switch become the root bridge and automatically adjusts the STP timers:

```
Switch(config)# spanning-tree vlan 100 root primary diameter 3 hello-time 1
```

You can confirm the new timer values with the **show spanning-tree vlan** *vlan-id* command, as demonstrated in Example 8-7.

Example 8-7 *Confirming STP Timer Configuration Changes*

```
Switch# show spanning-tree vlan 100
VLAN0100
  Spanning tree enabled protocol ieee
  Root ID    Priority    100
             Address     000c.8554.9a80
             This bridge is the root
             Hello Time   1  sec  Max  Age  7  sec  Forward  Delay  5  sec

  Bridge ID  Priority    100    (priority 0 sys-id-ext 100)
             Address     000c.8554.9a80
             Hello Time   1 sec   Max Age 7 sec   Forward Delay  5 sec
             Aging Time 300
```

Redundant Link Convergence

Some additional methods allow faster STP convergence if a link failure occurs:

- **PortFast**—Enables fast connectivity to be established on access-layer switch ports to workstations that are booting

- **UplinkFast**—Enables fast-uplink failover on an access-layer switch when dual uplinks are connected into the distribution layer

- **BackboneFast**—Enables fast convergence in the network backbone or core layer switches after a spanning-tree topology change occurs

Instead of modifying timer values, these methods work by controlling convergence on specifically located ports within the network hierarchy.

> **Tip:** The STP has been enhanced to allow almost instantaneous topology changes instead of having to rely on these Cisco-proprietary extensions. This enhancement is known as the Rapid Spanning Tree Protocol, or IEEE 802.1w, and is covered in Chapter 10, "Advanced Spanning Tree Protocol." You should become familiar with the topics in this chapter first because they provide the basis for the concepts in Chapter 10.

PortFast: Access-Layer Nodes

An end-user workstation is usually connected to a switch port in the access layer. If the workstation is powered off and then turned on, the switch will sense that the port link status has gone down and back up. The port will not be in a usable state until STP cycles from the Blocking state to the Forwarding state. With the default STP timers, this transition takes at least 30 seconds (15 seconds for Listening to Learning, and 15 seconds for Learning to Forwarding). Therefore, the workstation cannot transmit or receive any useful data until the Forwarding state finally is reached on the port.

> **Tip:** Port initialization delays of up to 50 seconds can be observed. As discussed, 30 of these seconds are due to the STP state transitions. If a switch port is running Port Aggregation Protocol (PAgP) to negotiate EtherChannel configuration, an additional 20-second delay can occur.

On switch ports that connect only to single workstations or specific devices, bridging loops never should be possible. The potential for a loop exists only if the workstation had additional connections back into the network and if it were bridging traffic itself. For example, this can happen on PCs that are running Windows XP when network bridging has been enabled. In most situations, this is not very likely to happen.

Catalyst switches offer the PortFast feature, which shortens the Listening and Learning states to a negligible amount of time. When a workstation link comes up, the switch immediately moves the PortFast port into the Forwarding state. Spanning-tree loop detection is still in operation, however, and the port moves into the Blocking state if a loop is ever detected on the port.

By default, PortFast is disabled on all switch ports. You can configure PortFast as a global default, affecting all switch ports with a single command. All ports that are configured for access mode (nontrunking) will have PortFast automatically enabled. You can use the following global configuration command to enable PortFast as the default:

```
Switch(config)# spanning-tree portfast default
```

You can also enable or disable the PortFast feature on specific switch ports by using the following interface configuration command:

```
Switch(config-if)# [no] spanning-tree portfast
```

Obviously, you should not enable PortFast on a switch port that is connected to a hub or another switch because bridging loops could form. One other benefit of PortFast is that Topology Change Notification (TCN) BPDUs are not sent when a switch port in PortFast mode goes up or down. This simplifies the TCN transmission on a large network when end-user workstations are coming up or shutting down.

Tip: You can also use a macro configuration command to force a switch port to support a single host. The following command enables STP PortFast, sets the port to access (nontrunking) mode, and disables PAgP to prevent the port from participating in an EtherChannel:

```
Switch(config)# interface type mod/num
Switch(config-if)# switchport host
switchport mode will be set to access
spanning-tree portfast will be enabled
channel group will be disabled
```

You can display the current PortFast status with the following command:

```
Switch# show spanning-tree interface type mod/num portfast
```

For example, the following output shows that port Fast Ethernet 0/1 supports only access VLAN 10 and has PortFast enabled:

```
Switch# show spanning-tree interface fastethernet 0/1 portfast
VLAN0010          enabled
Switch#
```

UplinkFast: Access-Layer Uplinks

Consider an access-layer switch that has redundant uplink connections to two distribution-layer switches. Normally, one uplink would be in the Forwarding state and the other would be in the Blocking state. If the primary uplink went down, up to 50 seconds could elapse before the redundant uplink could be used.

The UplinkFast feature on Catalyst switches enables leaf-node switches or switches at the ends of the spanning-tree branches to have a functioning root port while keeping *one or more* redundant or potential root ports in Blocking mode. When the primary root port uplink fails, another blocked uplink immediately can be brought up for use.

> **Tip:** Many Catalyst switches have two built-in, high-speed uplink ports (Gigabit Ethernet, for example). You might get the idea that UplinkFast can only toggle between two leaf-node uplink ports. This is entirely untrue. UplinkFast keeps a record of *all* parallel paths to the root bridge. All uplink ports but one are kept in the Blocking state. If the root port fails, the uplink with the next-lowest root path cost is unblocked and used without delay.

To enable the UplinkFast feature, use the following global configuration command:

```
Switch(config)# spanning-tree uplinkfast [max-update-rate pkts-per-second]
```

When UplinkFast is enabled, it is enabled for the entire switch and all VLANs. UplinkFast works by keeping track of possible paths to the root bridge. Therefore, the command *is not allowed on the root bridge switch*. UplinkFast also makes some modifications to the local switch to ensure that it does not become the root bridge and that the switch is not used as a transit switch to get to the root bridge. In other words, the goal is to keep UplinkFast limited to leaf-node switches that are farthest from the root.

First, the switch's bridge priority is raised to 49,152, making it unlikely that the switch will be elected to root bridge status. The port cost of all local switch ports is incremented by 3000, making the ports undesirable as paths to the root for any downstream switches.

The command also includes a **max-update-rate** parameter. When an uplink on a switch goes down, UplinkFast makes it easy for the local switch to update its bridging table of MAC addresses to point to the new uplink. However, UplinkFast also provides a mechanism for the local switch to notify other upstream switches that stations downstream (or within the access layer) can be reached over the newly activated uplink.

The switch accomplishes this by sending dummy multicast frames to destination 0100.0ccd.cdcd on behalf of the stations contained in its Content-Addressable Memory (CAM) table. The MAC addresses are used as the source addresses in the dummy frames, as if the stations actually had sent them. The idea is to quickly send the multicast frames over the new uplink, giving upstream hosts a chance to receive the frames and learn of the new path to those source addresses.

These multicast frames are sent out at a rate specified by the **max-update-rate** parameter in packets per second. This limits the amount of bandwidth used for the dummy multicasts if the CAM table is quite large. The default is 150 packets per second (pps), but the rate can range from 0 to 65,535 pps. If the value is 0, no dummy multicasts are sent.

> **Tip:** You can use the following command to display the current status of STP UplinkFast:
>
> ```
> Switch# show spanning-tree uplinkfast
> UplinkFast is enabled
> Station update rate set to 150 packets/sec.
> UplinkFast statistics
> Number of transitions via uplinkFast (all VLANs)          : 2
> Number of proxy multicast addresses transmitted (all VLANs)  : 52
> ```

```
Name                    Interface List
...................     ...............................
VLAN0001                Gi0/1(fwd)
VLAN0010                Gi0/1(fwd)
VLAN0100                Gi0/1(fwd)
Switch#
```

BackboneFast: Redundant Backbone Paths

In the network backbone, or core layer, a different method is used to shorten STP convergence. BackboneFast works by having a switch actively determine whether alternative
paths exist to the root bridge, in case the switch detects an *indirect link failure*. Indirect
link failures occur when a link that is not directly connected to a switch fails.

A switch detects an indirect link failure when it receives inferior BPDUs from its designated bridge on either its root port or a blocked port. (Inferior BPDUs are sent from a designated bridge that has lost its connection to the root bridge, making it announce itself as
the new root.)

Normally, a switch must wait for the Max Age timer to expire before responding to the inferior BPDUs. However, BackboneFast begins to determine whether other alternative
paths to the root bridge exist according to the following port types that received the inferior BPDU:

■ If the inferior BPDU arrives on a port in the Blocking state, the switch considers the
   root port and all other blocked ports to be alternative paths to the root bridge.

■ If the inferior BPDU arrives on the root port itself, the switch considers all blocked
   ports to be alternative paths to the root bridge.

■ If the inferior BPDU arrives on the root port and no ports are blocked, however, the
   switch assumes that it has lost connectivity with the root bridge. In this case, the
   switch assumes that it has become the root bridge, and BackboneFast allows it to do
   so before the Max Age timer expires.

Detecting alternative paths to the root bridge also involves an interactive process with
other bridges. If the local switch has blocked ports, BackboneFast begins to use the *Root
Link Query (RLQ)* protocol to see whether upstream switches have stable connections to
the root bridge.

First, RLQ Requests are sent out. If a switch receives an RLQ Request and either is the root
bridge or has lost connection to the root, it sends an RLQ Reply. Otherwise, the RLQ Request is propagated on to other switches until an RLQ Reply can be generated. On the local switch, if an RLQ Reply is received on its current root port, the path to the root bridge
is intact and stable. If it is received on a nonroot port, an alternative root path must be
chosen. The Max Age timer immediately is expired so that a new root port can be found.

BackboneFast is simple to configure and operates by short-circuiting the Max Age timer
when needed. Although this function shortens the time a switch waits to detect a root
path failure, ports still must go through full-length Forward Delay timer intervals during

the Listening and Learning states. Where PortFast and UplinkFast enable immediate transitions, BackboneFast can reduce the maximum convergence delay only from 50 to 30 seconds.

To configure BackboneFast, use the following global configuration command:

```
Switch(config)# spanning-tree backbonefast
```

When used, BackboneFast should be enabled on *all* switches in the network because BackboneFast requires the use of the RLQ Request and Reply mechanism to inform switches of Root Path stability. The RLQ protocol is active only when BackboneFast is enabled on a switch. By default, BackboneFast is disabled.

Tip: You can verify the current BackboneFast state with the following command:

```
Switch# show spanning-tree backbonefast
BackboneFast is enabled
Switch#
```

Monitoring STP

Because the STP running in a network uses several timers, costs, and dynamic calculations, predicting the current state is difficult. You can use a network diagram and work out the STP topology by hand, but any change on the network could produce an entirely different outcome. Then, figure in something like PVST+, in which you have one instance of STP running for each VLAN present. Obviously, simply viewing the STP status on the active network devices would be better.

You can display information about many aspects of the STP from a Catalyst switch command-line interface (CLI). Specifically, you need to find out the current root bridge and its location in the network. You also might want to see the bridge ID of the switch where you are connected, to see how it participates in STP. Use the information in Table 8-3 to determine what command is useful for what situation.

Table 8-3   *Commands for Displaying Spanning-Tree Information*

Task	Command Syntax
View all possible STP parameters for all VLANs. Port information is summarized.	Switch# **show spanning-tree**
View all possible STP information for all VLANs. Port information is very detailed.	Switch# **show spanning-tree detail**
View the total number of switch ports currently in each of the STP states.	Switch# **show spanning-tree** [vlan *vlan-id*] **summary**
Find the root bridge ID, the root port, and the root path cost.	Switch# **show spanning-tree** [vlan *vlan-id*] **root**
Show the bridge ID and STP timers for the local switch.	Switch# **show spanning-tree** [vlan *vlan-id*] **bridge**

continues

Table 8-3 *Commands for Displaying Spanning-Tree Information* *(Continued)*

Task	Command Syntax
Show the STP activity on a specific interface.	Switch# **show spanning-tree interface** *type port*
Show the STP UplinkFast status.	Switch# **show spanning-tree uplinkfast**
Show the STP BackboneFast status.	Switch# **show spanning-tree backbonefast**

Exam Preparation Tasks

Review All Key Topics

Review the most important topics in the chapter, noted with the Key Topic icon in the outer margin of the page. Table 8-4 lists a reference of these key topics and the page numbers on which each is found.

**Key
Topic**

Table 8-4 *Key Topics for Chapter 8*

Key Topic Element	Description	Page Number
Paragraph	Explains the pitfalls of a default root bridge election	156
Paragraph	Covers best practice for root bridge placement	159
Bullet	Discusses manual root bridge configuration	160
Bullet	Discusses automatic root bridge configuration	160
Paragraph	Explains how to configure the root path cost on an interface	164
Paragraph	Explains how STP timers can be adjusted on the root bridge	166
Paragraph	Explains the PortFast feature	169
Paragraph	Explains the UplinkFast feature	170
Paragraph	Explains the BackboneFast feature	172

Complete Tables and Lists from Memory

Print a copy of Appendix C, "Memory Tables," (found on the CD), or at least the section for this chapter, and complete the tables and lists from memory. Appendix D, "Memory Tables Answer Key," also on the CD, includes completed tables and lists to check your work.

Define Key Terms

Define the following key terms from this chapter, and check your answers in the glossary:

PortFast, UplinkFast, BackboneFast

Use Command Reference to Check Your Memory

This section includes the most important configuration and EXEC commands covered in this chapter. It might not be necessary to memorize the complete syntax of every command, but you should remember the basic keywords that are needed.

To test your memory of the STP configuration commands, cover the right side of Table 8-5 with a piece of paper, read the description on the left side, and then see how much of the command you can remember.

Remember that the CCNP exam focuses on practical or hands-on skills that are used by a networking professional. For the skills covered in this chapter, notice that the commands always begin with the keyword **spanning-tree**.

Table 8-5   *STP Configuration Commands*

Task	Command Syntax
Enable STP.	Switch(config)# **spanning-tree** *vlan-id*
Set bridge priority.	Switch(config)# **spanning-tree vlan** *vlan-id* **priority** *bridge-priority*
Set root bridge (macro).	Switch(config)# **spanning-tree vlan** *vlan-id* **root** {**primary** | **secondary**} [**diameter** *diameter*]
Set port cost.	Switch(config-if)# **spanning-tree** [**vlan** *vlan-id*] **cost** *cost*
Set port priority.	Switch(config-if)# **spanning-tree** [**vlan** *vlan-id*] **port-priority** *port-priority*
Set STP timers.	Switch(config)# **spanning-tree** [**vlan** *vlan-id*] **hello-time** *seconds*
	Switch(config)# **spanning-tree** [**vlan** *vlan-id*] **forward-time** *seconds*
	Switch(config)# **spanning-tree** [**vlan** *vlan-id*] **max-age** *seconds*
Set PortFast on an interface.	Switch(config-if)# **spanning-tree portfast**
Set UplinkFast on a switch.	Switch(config)# **spanning-tree uplinkfast** [**max-update-rate** *pkts-per-second*]
Set BackboneFast on a switch.	Switch(config)# **spanning-tree backbonefast**

This chapter covers the following topics that you need to master for the CCNP SWITCH exam:

Protecting Against Unexpected BPDUs—This section covers the Root Guard and BPDU Guard features, which protect against unexpected root candidates and unexpected BPDUs, respectively.

Protecting Against Sudden Loss of BPDUs—This section discusses the Loop Guard and UDLD features, which detect and protect against the loss of root bridge BPDUs and conditions causing unidirectional links, respectively.

Using BPDU Filtering to Disable STP on a Port—This section explains how to filter BPDUs on a switch port to prevent the port from participating in STP altogether. Bridging loops are neither detected nor prevented.

Troubleshooting STP Protection—This section summarizes the commands that diagnose or verify actions to protect the topology.

CHAPTER 9

Protecting the Spanning Tree Protocol Topology

Achieving and maintaining a loop-free Spanning Tree Protocol (STP) topology revolves around the simple process of sending and receiving bridge protocol data units (BPDU). Under normal conditions, with all switches playing fairly and according to the rules, a loop-free topology is determined dynamically.

This chapter discusses two basic conditions that can occur to disrupt the loop-free topology (even while STP is running):

On a port that has not been receiving BPDUs, BPDUs are not expected. When BPDUs suddenly appear for some reason, the STP topology can reconverge to give unexpected results.

On a port that normally receives BPDUs, BPDUs always are expected. When BPDUs suddenly disappear for some reason, a switch can make incorrect assumptions about the topology and unintentionally create loops.

"Do I Know This Already?" Quiz

The "Do I Know This Already?" quiz allows you to assess whether you should read this entire chapter thoroughly or jump to the "Exam Preparation Tasks" section. If you are in doubt based on your answers to these questions or your own assessment of your knowledge of the topics, read the entire chapter. Table 9-1 outlines the major headings in this chapter and the "Do I Know This Already?" quiz questions that go with them. You can find the answers in Appendix A, "Answers to the 'Do I Know This Already?' Quizzes."

Table 9-1 *"Do I Know This Already?" Foundation Topics Section-to-Question Mapping*

Foundation Topics Section	Questions Covered in This Section
Protecting Against Unexpected BPDUs	1–5
Protecting Against Sudden Loss of BPDUs	6–11
Using BPDU Filtering to Disable STP on a Port	12
Troubleshooting STP Protection	13

1. Why is it important to protect the placement of the root bridge?

    a. To keep two root bridges from becoming active

    b. To keep the STP topology stable

    c. So all hosts have the correct gateway

    d. So the root bridge can have complete knowledge of the STP topology

2. Which of the following features protects a switch port from accepting superior BPDUs?

    a. STP Loop Guard

    b. STP BPDU Guard

    c. STP Root Guard

    d. UDLD

3. Which of the following commands can you use to enable STP Root Guard on a switch port?

    a. spanning-tree root guard

    b. spanning-tree root-guard

    c. spanning-tree guard root

    d. spanning-tree rootguard enable

4. Where should the STP Root Guard feature be enabled on a switch?

    a. All ports

    b. Only ports where the root bridge should never appear

    c. Only ports where the root bridge should be located

    d. Only ports with PortFast enabled

5. Which of the following features protects a switch port from accepting BPDUs when PortFast is enabled?

    a. STP Loop Guard

    b. STP BPDU Guard

    c. STP Root Guard

    d. UDLD

6. To maintain a loop-free STP topology, which one of the following should a switch uplink be protected against?

    a. A sudden loss of BPDUs

    b. Too many BPDUs

    c. The wrong version of BPDUs

    d. BPDUs relayed from the root bridge

7. Which of the following commands can enable STP Loop Guard on a switch port?

    a. spanning-tree loop guard

    b. spanning-tree guard loop

    c. spanning-tree loop-guard

    d. spanning-tree loopguard enable

8. STP Loop Guard detects which of the following conditions?

    a. The sudden appearance of superior BPDUs

    b. The sudden lack of BPDUs

    c. The appearance of duplicate BPDUs

    d. The appearance of two root bridges

9. Which of the following features can actively test for the loss of the receive side of a link between switches?

    a. POST

    b. BPDU

    c. UDLD

    d. STP

10. UDLD must detect a unidirectional link before which of the following?

    a. The Max Age timer expires.

    b. STP moves the link to the Blocking state.

    c. STP moves the link to the Forwarding state.

    d. STP moves the link to the Listening state.

11. What must a switch do when it receives a UDLD message on a link?

    a. Relay the message on to other switches

    b. Send a UDLD acknowledgment

    c. Echo the message back across the link

    d. Drop the message

12. Which of the following features effectively disables spanning-tree operation on a switch port?

    a. STP PortFast

    b. STP BPDU filtering

    c. STP BPDU Guard

    d. STP Root Guard

13. To reset switch ports that have been put into the errdisable mode by UDLD, which one of the following commands should be used?

    a. clear errdisable udld

    b. udld reset

    c. no udld

    d. show udld errdisable

Foundation Topics

Protecting Against Unexpected BPDUs

A network running STP uses BPDUs to communicate between switches (bridges). Switches become aware of each other and of the topology that interconnects them. After a root bridge is elected, BPDUs are generated by the root and are relayed down through the spanning-tree topology. Eventually, all switches in the STP domain receive the root's BPDUs so that the network converges and a stable loop-free topology forms.

To maintain an efficient topology, the placement of the root bridge must be predictable. Hopefully, you configured one switch to become the root bridge and a second one to be the secondary root. What happens when a "foreign" or rogue switch is connected to the network, and that switch suddenly is capable of becoming the root bridge? Cisco added two STP features that help prevent the unexpected: Root Guard and BPDU Guard.

Root Guard

After an STP topology has converged and becomes loop free, switch ports are assigned the following roles:

- **Root port**—The one port on a switch that is closest (with the lowest root path cost) to the root bridge.

- **Designated port**—The port on a LAN segment that is closest to the root. This port relays, or transmits, BPDUs down the tree.

- **Blocking port**—Ports that are neither root nor designated ports.

- **Alternate port**—Ports that are candidate root ports (they are also close to the root bridge) but are in the Blocking state. These ports are identified for quick use by the STP UplinkFast feature.

- **Forwarding port**—Ports where no other STP activity is detected or expected. These are ports with normal end-user connections.

The root bridge always is expected to be seen on the root port and the alternative ports because these are "closest" (have the best-cost path) to it.

Suppose that another switch is introduced into the network with a bridge priority that is more desirable (lower) than that of the current root bridge. The new switch then would become the root bridge, and the STP topology might reconverge to a new shape. This is entirely permissible by the STP because the switch with the lowest bridge ID always wins the root election.

However, this is not always desirable for you, the network administrator, because the new STP topology might be something totally unacceptable. In addition, while the topology is reconverging, your production network might become unavailable.

The Root Guard feature was developed as a means to control where candidate root bridges can be connected and found on a network. Basically, a switch learns the current root

Key Topic

bridge's bridge ID. If another switch advertises a *superior BPDU*, or one with a better bridge ID, on a port where Root Guard is enabled, the local switch will not allow the new switch to become the root. As long as the superior BPDUs are being received on the port, the port will be kept in the *root-inconsistent* STP state. No data can be sent or received in that state, but the switch can listen to BPDUs received on the port to detect a new root advertising itself.

In essence, Root Guard designates that a port can only forward or relay BPDUs; the port can't be used to receive BPDUs. Root Guard prevents the port from ever becoming a root port where BPDUs normally would be received from the root bridge.

You can enable Root Guard only on a per-port basis. By default, it is disabled on all switch ports. To enable it, use the following interface configuration command:

```
Switch(config-if)# spanning-tree guard root
```

When the superior BPDUs no longer are received, the port is cycled through the normal STP states to return to normal use.

Use Root Guard on switch ports where you never expect to find the root bridge for a VLAN. In fact, Root Guard affects the entire port so that a root bridge never can be allowed on *any* VLAN on the port. When a superior BPDU is heard on the port, the entire port, in effect, becomes blocked.

Tip: You can display switch ports that Root Guard has put into the root-inconsistent state with the following command:

```
Switch# show spanning-tree inconsistentports
```

BPDU Guard

Recall that the traditional STP offers the PortFast feature, in which switch ports are allowed to immediately enter the Forwarding state as soon as the link comes up. Normally, PortFast provides quick network access to end-user devices, where bridging loops never are expected to form. Even while PortFast is enabled on a port, STP still is running and can detect a bridging loop. However, a loop can be detected only in a finite amount of time— the length of time required to move the port through the normal STP states.

Note: Remember that enabling PortFast on a port is not the same as disabling the STP on it.

By definition, if you enable PortFast, you do not expect to find anything that can cause a bridging loop—especially another switch or device that produces BPDUs. Suppose that a switch is connected by mistake to a port where PortFast is enabled. Now there is a potential for a bridging loop to form. An even greater consequence is that the potential now exists for the newly connected device to advertise itself and become the new root bridge.

The BPDU Guard feature was developed to further protect the integrity of switch ports that have PortFast enabled. If any BPDU (whether superior to the current root or not) is

Key
Topic

received on a port where BPDU Guard is enabled, that port immediately is put into the errdisable state. The port is shut down in an error condition and must be either manually re-enabled or automatically recovered through the errdisable timeout function.

By default, BPDU Guard is disabled on all switch ports. You can configure BPDU Guard as a global default, affecting all switch ports with a single command. All ports that have Port-Fast enabled also have BPDU Guard automatically enabled. You can use the following global configuration command to enable BPDU Guard as the default:

```
Switch(config)# spanning-tree portfast bpduguard default
```

You also can enable or disable BPDU Guard on a per-port basis, using the following inter-face configuration command:

```
Switch(config-if)# [no] spanning-tree bpduguard enable
```

When the BPDUs no longer are received, the port still remains in the errdisable state. See Chapter 3, "Switch Port Configuration," for more information about recovering from the errdisable state.

You should use BPDU Guard on all switch ports where STP PortFast is enabled. This pre-vents any possibility that a switch will be added to the port, either intentionally or by mis-take. An obvious application for BPDU Guard is on access-layer switch ports where users and end devices connect. BPDUs normally would not be expected there and would be de-tected if a switch or hub inadvertently were connected.

Naturally, BPDU Guard does not prevent a bridging loop from forming if an Ethernet hub is connected to the PortFast port. This is because a hub doesn't transmit BPDUs itself; it merely repeats Ethernet frames from its other ports. A loop could form if the hub became connected to two locations in the network, providing a path for frames to be looped with-out any STP activity.

You never should enable BPDU Guard on any switch uplink where the root bridge is lo-cated. If a switch has multiple uplinks, any of those ports could receive legitimate BPDUs from the root—even if they are in the Blocking state as a result of the UplinkFast feature. If BPDU Guard is enabled on an uplink port, BPDUs will be detected and the uplink will be put into the Errdisable state. This will preclude that uplink port from being used as an uplink into the network.

Protecting Against Sudden Loss of BPDUs

STP BPDUs are used as probes to learn about a network topology. When the switches par-ticipating in STP converge on a common and consistent loop-free topology, BPDUs still must be sent by the root bridge and must be relayed by every other switch in the STP do-main. The STP topology's integrity then depends on a continuous and regular flow of BP-DUs from the root.

What happens if a switch doesn't receive BPDUs in a timely manner or when it doesn't re-ceive any? The switch can view that condition as acceptable—perhaps an upstream switch or an upstream link is dead. In that case, the topology must have changed, so blocked ports eventually can be unblocked again.

However, if the absence of BPDUs is actually a mistake and BPDUs are not being received even though there is no topology change, bridging loops easily can form.

Cisco has added two STP features that help detect or prevent the unexpected loss of BPDUs:

- Loop Guard

- Unidirectional Link Detection (UDLD)

Loop Guard

Suppose that a switch port is receiving BPDUs and the switch port is in the Blocking state. The port makes up a redundant path; it is blocking because it is neither a root port nor a designated port. It will remain in the Blocking state as long as a steady flow of BPDUs is received.

If BPDUs are being sent over a link but the flow of BPDUs stops for some reason, the last-known BPDU is kept until the Max Age timer expires. Then that BPDU is flushed, and the switch thinks there is no longer a need to block the port. After all, if no BPDUs are received, there must not be another STP device connected there.

The switch then moves the port through the STP states until it begins to forward traffic— and forms a bridging loop. In its final state, the port becomes a designated port where it begins to relay or send BPDUs downstream, when it actually should be receiving BPDUs from upstream.

To prevent this situation, you can use the Loop Guard STP feature. When enabled, Loop Guard keeps track of the BPDU activity on nondesignated ports. While BPDUs are received, the port is allowed to behave normally. When BPDUs go missing, Loop Guard moves the port into the loop-inconsistent state. The port is effectively blocking at this point to prevent a loop from forming and to keep it in the nondesignated role.

Key Topic

When BPDUs are received on the port again, Loop Guard allows the port to move through the normal STP states and become active. In this fashion, Loop Guard automatically governs ports without the need for manual intervention.

By default, Loop Guard is disabled on all switch ports. You can enable Loop Guard as a global default, affecting all switch ports, with the following global configuration command:

```
Switch(config)# spanning-tree loopguard default
```

You also can enable or disable Loop Guard on a specific switch port by using the following interface-configuration command:

```
Switch(config-if)# [no] spanning-tree guard loop
```

Although Loop Guard is configured on a switch port, its corrective blocking action is taken on a per-VLAN basis. In other words, Loop Guard doesn't block the entire port; only the offending VLANs are blocked.

You can enable Loop Guard on all switch ports, regardless of their functions. The switch figures out which ports are nondesignated and monitors the BPDU activity to keep them nondesignated. Nondesignated ports are generally the alternative root ports and ports that normally are blocking.

UDLD

In a campus network, switches are connected by bidirectional links, where traffic can flow in two directions. Clearly, if a link has a physical layer problem, the two switches it connects detect a problem, and the link is shown as not connected.

What would happen if just one side of the link (receive or transmit) had an odd failure, such as malfunctioning transmit circuitry in a gigabit interface converter (GBIC) or small form factor pluggable (SFP) modules? In some cases, the two switches still might see a functional bidirectional link, although traffic actually would be delivered in only one direction. This is known as a *unidirectional link*.

A unidirectional link poses a potential danger to STP topologies because BPDUs will not be received on one end of the link. If that end of the link normally would be in the Blocking state, it will not be that way for long. A switch interprets the absence of BPDUs to mean that the port can be moved safely through the STP states so that traffic can be forwarded. However, if that is done on a unidirectional link, a bridging loop forms and the switch never realizes the mistake.

Key Topic

To prevent this situation, you can use the Cisco-proprietary Unidirectional Link Detection (UDLD) STP feature. When enabled, UDLD interactively monitors a port to see whether the link is truly bidirectional. A switch sends special Layer 2 UDLD frames identifying its switch port at regular intervals. UDLD expects the far-end switch to echo those frames back across the same link, with the far-end switch port's identification added.

If a UDLD frame is received in return and both neighboring ports are identified in the frame, the link must be bidirectional. However, if the echoed frames are not seen, the link must be unidirectional for some reason.

Naturally, an echo process such as this requires *both ends* of the link to be configured for UDLD. Otherwise, one end of the link will not echo the frames back to the originator. In addition, each switch at the end of a link sends its own UDLD messages independently, expecting echoes from the far end. This means that two echo processes are occurring on any given link.

UDLD messages are sent at regular intervals, as long as the link is active. You can configure the message interval UDLD uses. (The default is 15 seconds.) The objective behind UDLD is to detect a unidirectional link condition before STP has time to move a blocked port into the Forwarding state. To do this, the target time must be less than the Max Age timer plus two intervals of the Forward Delay timer, or 50 seconds. UDLD can detect a unidirectional link after about three times the UDLD message interval (45 seconds total, using the default).

UDLD has two modes of operation:

- **Normal mode**—When a unidirectional link condition is detected, the port is allowed to continue its operation. UDLD merely marks the port as having an undetermined state and generates a syslog message.

- **Aggressive mode**—When a unidirectional link condition is detected, the switch takes action to reestablish the link. UDLD messages are sent out once a second for 8 seconds. If none of those messages is echoed back, the port is placed in the Errdis-able state so that it cannot be used.

You configure UDLD on a per-port basis, although you can enable it globally for all fiber-optic switch ports (either native fiber or fiber-based GBIC or SFP modules). By default, UDLD is disabled on all switch ports. To enable it globally, use the following global con-figuration command:

```
Switch(config)# udld {enable | aggressive | message time seconds}
```

For normal mode, use the **enable** keyword; for aggressive mode, use the **aggressive** key-word. You can use the **message time** keywords to set the message interval to *seconds*, ranging from 7 to 90 seconds. (The default interval varies according to switch platform. For example, the Catalyst 3550 default is 7 seconds; the Catalyst 4500 and 6500 default is 15 seconds.)

You also can enable or disable UDLD on individual switch ports, if needed, using the fol-lowing interface configuration command:

```
Switch(config-if)# udld {enable | aggressive | disable}
```

Here, you can use the **disable** keyword to completely disable UDLD on a fiber-optic inter-face.

Note: The default UDLD message interval times differ among Catalyst switch platforms. Although two neighbors might have mismatched message time values, UDLD still works correctly. This is because each of the two neighbors simply echoes UDLD messages back as they are received, without knowledge of their neighbor's own time interval. The time interval is used only to decide when to send UDLD messages and as a basis for detecting a unidirectional link from the absence of echoed messages.

If you decide to change the default message time, make sure that UDLD still can detect a fault *before* STP decides to move a link to the Forwarding state.

You safely can enable UDLD on all switch ports. The switch globally enables UDLD only on ports that use fiber-optic media. Twisted-pair or copper media does not suffer from the physical layer conditions that allow a unidirectional link to form. However, you can enable UDLD on nonfiber links individually, if you want.

At this point, you might be wondering how UDLD can be enabled gracefully on the two end switches. Recall that in aggressive mode, UDLD disables the link if the neighbor does not reflect the messages back within a certain time period. If you are enabling UDLD on a production network, is there a chance that UDLD will disable working links before you can get the far end configured?

The answer is no. UDLD makes some intelligent assumptions when it is enabled on a link for the first time. First, UDLD has no record of any neighbor on the link. It starts sending out messages, hoping that a neighboring switch will hear them and echo them back. Obvi-ously, the device at the far end also must support UDLD so that the messages will be echoed back.

If the neighboring switch does not yet have UDLD enabled, no messages will be echoed. UDLD will keep trying (indefinitely) to detect a neighbor and will not disable the link. After the neighbor has UDLD configured also, both switches become aware of each other and the bidirectional state of the link through their UDLD message exchanges. From then on, if messages are not echoed, the link can accurately be labeled as unidirectional.

Finally, be aware that if UDLD detects a unidirectional condition on a link, it takes action on only that link. This becomes important in an EtherChannel: If one link within the channel becomes unidirectional, UDLD flags or disables only the offending link in the bundle, not the entire EtherChannel. UDLD sends and echoes its messages on each link within an EtherChannel channel independently.

Using BPDU Filtering to Disable STP on a Port

Ordinarily, STP operates on all switch ports in an effort to eliminate bridging loops before they can form. BPDUs are sent on all switch ports—even ports where PortFast has been enabled. BPDUs also can be received and processed if any are sent by neighboring switches.

You always should allow STP to run on a switch to prevent loops. However, in special cases when you need to prevent BPDUs from being sent or processed on one or more switch ports, you can use BPDU filtering to effectively disable STP on those ports.

By default, BPDU filtering is disabled on all switch ports. You can configure BPDU filtering as a global default, affecting all switch ports with the following global configuration command:

```
Switch(config)# spanning-tree portfast bpdufilter default
```

The **default** keyword indicates that BPDU filtering will be enabled automatically on all ports that have PortFast enabled. If PortFast is disabled on a port, then BPDU filtering will not be enabled there.

You also can enable or disable BPDU filtering on specific switch ports by using the following interface configuration command:

```
Switch(config-if)# spanning-tree bpdufilter {enable | disable}
```

Be very careful to enable BPDU filtering only under controlled circumstances in which you are absolutely sure that a switch port will have a single host connected and that a loop will be impossible. Enable BPDU filtering only if the connected device cannot allow BPDUs to be accepted or sent. Otherwise, you should permit STP to operate on the switch ports as a precaution.

Troubleshooting STP Protection

With several different types of STP protection features available, you might need to know which (if any) has been configured on a switch port. Table 9-2 lists and describes the EXEC commands useful for verifying the features presented in this chapter.

Table 9-2 *Commands for Verifying and Troubleshooting STP Protection Features*

Display Function	Command Syntax
List the ports that have been labeled in an inconsistent state.	Switch# **show spanning-tree inconsistentports**
Look for detailed reasons for inconsistencies.	Switch# **show spanning-tree interface** *type mod/num* [detail]
Display the global BPDU Guard, BPDU filter, and Loop Guard states.	Switch# **show spanning-tree summary**
Display the UDLD status on one or all ports.	Switch# **show udld** [*type mod/num*]
Reenable ports that UDLD aggressive mode has errdisabled.	Switch# **udld reset**

Exam Preparation Tasks

Review All Key Topics

Review the most important topics in the chapter, noted with the Key Topic icon in the outer margin of the page. Table 9-3 lists a reference of these key topics and the page numbers on which each is found.

Table 9-3   *Key Topics for Chapter 9*

Key Topic Element	Description	Page Number
Paragraph	Discusses the Root Guard feature	182
Paragraph	Discusses the BPDU Guard feature	183
Paragraph	Discusses the Loop Guard feature	185
Paragraph	Discusses the UDLD feature	186
Paragraph	Explains BPDU filtering	188

Complete Tables and Lists from Memory

Print a copy of Appendix C, "Memory Tables," (found on the CD), or at least the section for this chapter, and complete the tables and lists from memory. Appendix D, "Memory Tables Answer Key," also on the CD, includes completed tables and lists to check your work.

Define Key Terms

Define the following key terms from this chapter, and check your answers in the glossary:

Root Guard, superior BPDU, BPDU Guard, Loop Guard, UDLD, BPDU filtering

Use Command Reference to Check Your Memory

This section includes the most important configuration and EXEC commands covered in this chapter. It might not be necessary to memorize the complete syntax of every command, but you should remember the basic keywords that are needed.

With so many similar and mutually exclusive STP protection features available, you might have a hard time remembering which ones to use where. Use Figure 9-1 as a quick reference.

Figure 9-1 shows two backbone switches (Catalyst A and B), along with an access-layer switch (Catalyst C), with redundant uplinks. Users are connected to the access switch, where PortFast is in use. An additional access switch (Catalyst D) has an uplink to access-layer switch C. All switch-to-switch links are fiber-based Gigabit Ethernet. Obviously, a root bridge never should appear out of Catalyst D.

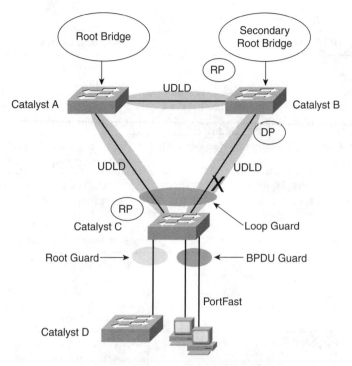

Root guard: Apply to ports where root is never expected.

BPDU guard: Apply to all user ports where PortFast is enabled.

Loop guard: Apply to nondesignated ports but okay to apply to all ports.

UDLD: Apply to all fiber-optic links between switches (must be enabled on both ends).

Permissible combinations on a switch port:
     Loop guard and UDLD
     Root guard and UDLD

Not permissible on a switch port:
     Root guard and Loop guard
     Root guard and BPDU guard

Figure 9-1   *Guidelines for Applying STP Protection Features in a Network*

To test your memory of the STP protection feature commands, cover the rightmost columns of Tables 9-4 and 9-5 with a piece of paper, read the description on the left side, then see how much of the command you can remember.

Remember that the CCNP exam focuses on practical or hands-on skills that are used by a networking professional.

Table 9-4 *STP Protection Configuration Commands*

Task	Global Command Syntax	Interface Command Syntax
Enable Root Guard	—	Switch(config-if)# **spanning-tree guard root**
Enable BPDU Guard	Switch(config)# **spanning-tree portfast bpduguard default**	Switch(config-if)# **spanning-tree bpduguard enable**
Enable Loop Guard	Switch(config)# **spanning-tree loopguard default**	Switch(config-if)# **spanning-tree guard loop**
Enable UDLD	Switch(config)# **udld {enable | aggressive | message time seconds}**	Switch(config-if)# **udld {enable | aggressive | disable}**
Enable BPDU filtering	Switch(config)# **spanning-tree bpdufilter default**	Switch(config-if)# **spanning-tree bpdufilter enable**

Table 9-5 *STP Protection Activity Commands*

Task	Command Syntax
Look for ports that have been put in an inconsistent state	Switch# **show spanning-tree inconsistentports**
Display the global BPDU Guard, BPDU filter, and Loop Guard states	Switch# **show spanning-tree summary**
Show UDLD status	Switch# **show udld** [*type mod/num*]
Reenable all ports that UDLD has errdisabled	Switch# **udld reset**

This chapter covers the following topics that you need to master for the CCNP SWITCH exam:

Rapid Spanning Tree Protocol—This section discusses the enhancements that allow switches to run STP efficiently, offering fast convergence.

Multiple Spanning Tree Protocol—This section discusses the latest IEEE standard that supports a reduced number of STP instances for a campus network while using RSTP for efficient operation.

CHAPTER 10

Advanced Spanning Tree Protocol

Familiarity with the IEEE 802.1D STP standard is essential because that protocol is used universally to maintain loop-free bridged and switched networks. However, it now is considered a legacy protocol, offering topology change and convergence times that are not as acceptable as they once were.

This chapter discusses the many STP enhancements that are available in new standards. Rapid STP (RSTP) is presented first because it provides the foundation for efficient STP activity. RSTP can be coupled with either per-VLAN STP (PVST+) or Multiple STP modes. This allows a Layer 2 campus network to undergo change quickly and efficiently, with little downtime for today's applications.

This chapter also covers Multiple STP (MST or MSTP). MST allows VLANs to be individually mapped into arbitrary STP instances while RSTP operates in the background. You can use MST to greatly simplify the Layer 2 topologies and STP operations when many VLANs (and many instances of STP) are present in a network.

"Do I Know This Already?" Quiz

The "Do I Know This Already?" quiz allows you to assess whether you should read this entire chapter thoroughly or jump to the "Exam Preparation Tasks" section. If you are in doubt based on your answers to these questions or your own assessment of your knowledge of the topics, read the entire chapter. Table 10-1 outlines the major headings in this chapter and the "Do I Know This Already?" quiz questions that go with them. You can find the answers in Appendix A, "Answers to the 'Do I Know This Already?' Quizzes."

Table 10-1 *"Do I Know This Already?" Foundation Topics Section-to-Question Mapping*

Foundation Topics Section	Questions Covered in This Section
Rapid Spanning Tree Protocol	1–8
Multiple Spanning Tree Protocol	9–12

1. Which one of the following commands enables the use of RSTP?

    a. spanning-tree mode rapid-pvst

    b. no spanning-tree mode pvst

    c. spanning-tree rstp

    d. spanning-tree mode rstp

    e. None. RSTP is enabled by default.

2. On which standard is RSTP based?

    a. 802.1Q

    b. 802.1D

    c. 802.1w

    d. 802.1s

3. Which of the following is not a port state in RSTP?

    a. Listening

    b. Learning

    c. Discarding

    d. Forwarding

4. When a switch running RSTP receives an 802.1D BPDU, what happens?

    a. The BPDU is discarded or dropped.

    b. An ICMP message is returned.

    c. The switch begins to use 802.1D rules on that port.

    d. The switch disables RSTP.

5. When does an RSTP switch consider a neighbor to be down?

    a. After three BPDUs are missed

    b. After six BPDUs are missed

    c. After the Max Age timer expires

    d. After the Forward timer expires

6. Which process is used during RSTP convergence?

    a. BPDU propagation

    b. Synchronization

    c. Forward timer expiration

    d. BPDU

7. What causes RSTP to view a port as a point-to-point port?

   a. Port speed

   b. Port media

   c. Port duplex

   d. Port priority

8. Which of the following events triggers a topology change with RSTP on a nonedge port?

   a. A port comes up or goes down.

   b. A port comes up.

   c. A port goes down.

   d. A port moves to the Forwarding state.

9. Which of the following is *not* a characteristic of MST?

   a. A reduced number of STP instances

   b. Fast STP convergence

   c. Eliminated need for CST

   d. Interoperability with PVST+

10. Which of the following standards defines the MST protocol?

   a. 802.1Q

   b. 802.1D

   c. 802.1w

   d. 802.1s

11. How many instances of STP are supported in the Cisco implementation of MST?

   a. 1

   b. 16

   c. 256

   d. 4096

12. What switch command can be used to change from PVST+ to MST?

   a. spanning-tree mst enable

   b. no spanning-tree pvst+

   c. spanning-tree mode mst

   d. spanning-tree mst

Foundation Topics

Rapid Spanning Tree Protocol

The IEEE 802.1D Spanning Tree Protocol was designed to keep a switched or bridged network loop free, with adjustments made to the network topology dynamically. A topology change typically takes 30 seconds, with a port moving from the Blocking state to the Forwarding state after two intervals of the Forward Delay timer. As technology has improved, 30 seconds has become an unbearable length of time to wait for a production network to fail over or "heal" itself during a problem.

The IEEE 802.1w standard was developed to use 802.1D's principal concepts and make the resulting convergence much faster. This is also known as the Rapid Spanning Tree Protocol (RSTP), which defines how switches must interact with each other to keep the network topology loop free in a very efficient manner.

As with 802.1D, RSTP's basic functionality can be applied as a single instance or multiple instances. This can be done by using RSTP as the underlying mechanism for the Cisco-proprietary Per-VLAN Spanning Tree Protocol (PVST+). The resulting combination is called *Rapid PVST+* (RPVST+). RSTP also is used as part of the IEEE 802.1s Multiple Spanning Tree (MST) operation. RSTP operates consistently in each, but replicating RSTP as multiple instances requires different approaches.

RSTP Port Behavior

In 802.1D, each switch port is assigned a role and a state at any given time. Depending on the port's proximity to the Root Bridge, it takes on one of the following roles:

■ Root port

■ Designated port

■ Blocking port (neither root nor designated)

The Cisco-proprietary UplinkFast feature also reserved a hidden alternate port role for ports that offered parallel paths to the root but were in the Blocking state.

Recall that each switch port also is assigned one of five possible states:

■ Disabled

■ Blocking

■ Listening

■ Learning

■ Forwarding

Only the Forwarding state allows data to be sent and received. A port's state is somewhat tied to its role. For example, a blocking port cannot be a root port or a designated port.

RSTP achieves its rapid nature by letting each switch interact with its neighbors through each port. This interaction is performed based on a port's role, not strictly on the BPDUs that are relayed from the root bridge. After the role is determined, each port can be given a state that determines what it does with incoming data.

The root bridge in a network using RSTP is elected just as with 802.1D—by the lowest Bridge ID. After all switches agree on the identity of the root, the following port roles are determined:

- **Root port**—The one switch port on each switch that has the best root path cost to the root. This is identical to 802.1D. (By definition, the root bridge has no root ports.)

- **Designated port**—The switch port on a network segment that has the best root path cost to the root.

- **Alternate port**—A port that has an alternative path to the root, different from the path the root port takes. This path is less desirable than that of the root port. (An example of this is an access-layer switch with two uplink ports; one becomes the root port, and the other is an alternate port.)

- **Backup port**—A port that provides a redundant (but less desirable) connection to a segment where another switch port already connects. If that common segment is lost, the switch might or might not have a path back to the root.

RSTP defines port states only according to what the port does with incoming frames. (Naturally, if incoming frames are ignored or dropped, so are outgoing frames.) Any port role can have any of these port states:

- **Discarding**—Incoming frames simply are dropped; no MAC addresses are learned. (This state combines the 802.1D Disabled, Blocking, and Listening states because all three did not effectively forward anything. The Listening state is not needed because RSTP quickly can negotiate a state change without listening for BPDUs first.)

- **Learning**—Incoming frames are dropped, but MAC addresses are learned.

- **Forwarding**—Incoming frames are forwarded according to MAC addresses that have been (and are being) learned.

BPDUs in RSTP

In 802.1D, BPDUs basically originate from the root bridge and are relayed by all switches down through the tree. Because of this propagation of BPDUs, 802.1D convergence must wait for steady-state conditions before proceeding.

RSTP uses the 802.1D BPDU format for backward compatibility. However, some previously unused bits in the Message Type field are used. The sending switch port identifies itself by its RSTP role and state. The BPDU version also is set to 2 to distinguish RSTP BPDUs from 802.1D BPDUs. In addition, RSTP uses an interactive process so that two neighboring switches can negotiate state changes. Some BPDU bits are used to flag messages during this negotiation.

BPDUs are sent out every switch port at Hello Time intervals, regardless of whether BPDUs are received from the root. In this way, any switch anywhere in the network can play an active role in maintaining the topology. Switches also can expect to receive regular BP-DUs from their neighbors. When three BPDUs are missed in a row, that neighbor is presumed to be down, and all information related to the port leading to the neighbor immediately is aged out. This means that a switch can detect a neighbor failure in three Hello intervals (default 6 seconds), versus the Max Age timer interval (default 20 seconds) for 802.1D.

Because RSTP distinguishes its BPDUs from 802.1D BPDUs, it can coexist with switches still using 802.1D. Each port attempts to operate according to the STP BPDU that is received. For example, when an 802.1D BPDU (version 0) is received on a port, that port begins to operate according to the 802.1D rules.

However, each port has a measure that locks the protocol in use, in case BPDUs from both 802.1D and RSTP are received within a short time frame. This can occur if the switches in a network are being migrated from one STP type to another. Instead of flapping or toggling the STP type during a migration, the switch holds the protocol type for the duration of a migration delay timer. After this timer expires, the port is free to change protocols if needed.

RSTP Convergence

The convergence of STP in a network is the process that takes all switches from a state of independence (each thinks it must be the STP root) to one of uniformity, in which each switch has a place in a loop-free tree topology. You can think of convergence as a two-stage process:

1. One common root bridge must be "elected," and all switches must know about it.

2. The state of every switch port in the STP domain must be brought from a Blocking state to the appropriate state to prevent loops.

Convergence generally takes time because messages are propagated from switch to switch. The traditional 802.1D STP also requires the expiration of several timers before switch ports can safely be allowed to forward data.

RSTP takes a different approach when a switch needs to decide how to participate in the tree topology. When a switch first joins the topology (perhaps it was just powered up) or has detected a failure in the existing topology, RSTP requires it to base its forwarding decisions on the type of port.

Port Types

Every switch port can be considered one of the following types:

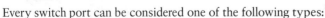

- **Edge port**—A port at the "edge" of the network, where only a single host connects. Traditionally, this has been identified by enabling the STP PortFast feature. RSTP keeps the PortFast concept for familiarity. By definition, the port cannot form a loop as it connects to one host, so it can be placed immediately in the Forwarding state. However, if a BPDU ever is received on an edge port, the port immediately loses its edge port status.

- **Root port**—The port that has the best cost to the root of the STP instance. Only one root port can be selected and active at any time, although alternative paths to the root can exist through other ports. If alternative paths are detected, those ports are identified as alternative root ports and immediately can be placed in the Forwarding state when the existing root port fails.

- **Point-to-point port**—Any port that connects to another switch and becomes a designated port. A quick handshake with the neighboring switch, rather than a timer expiration, decides the port state. BPDUs are exchanged back and forth in the form of a proposal and an agreement. One switch proposes that its port becomes a designated port; if the other switch agrees, it replies with an agreement message.

Point-to-point ports automatically are determined by the duplex mode in use. Full-duplex ports are considered point to point because only two switches can be present on the link. STP convergence can occur quickly over a point-to-point link through RSTP handshake messages.

Half-duplex ports, on the other hand, are considered to be on a shared medium with possibly more than two switches present. They are not point-to-point ports. STP convergence on a half-duplex port must occur between several directly connected switches. Therefore, the traditional 802.1D style convergence must be used. This results in a slower response because the shared-medium ports must go through the fixed Listening and Learning state time periods.

It's easy to see how two switches quickly can converge to a common idea of which one is the root and which one will have the designated port after just a single exchange of BPDUs. What about a larger network, where 802.1D BPDUs normally would have to be relayed from switch to switch?

RSTP handles the complete STP convergence of the network as a propagation of handshakes over point-to-point links. When a switch needs to make an STP decision, a handshake is made with the nearest neighbor. When that is successful, the handshake sequence is moved to the next switch and the next, as an ever-expanding wave moving toward the network's edges.

During each handshake sequence, a switch must take measures to completely ensure that it will not introduce a bridging loop before moving the handshake outward. This is done through a synchronization process.

Synchronization

To participate in RSTP convergence, a switch must decide the state of each of its ports. Nonedge ports begin in the Discarding state. After BPDUs are exchanged between the switch and its neighbor, the Root Bridge can be identified. If a port receives a superior BPDU from a neighbor, that port becomes the root port.

For each nonedge port, the switch exchanges a proposal-agreement handshake to decide the state of each end of the link. Each switch assumes that its port should become the designated port for the segment, and a proposal message (a configuration BPDU) is sent to the neighbor suggesting this.

When a switch receives a proposal message on a port, the following sequence of events occurs. Figure 10-1 shows the sequence, based on the center Catalyst switch:

1. If the proposal's sender has a superior BPDU, the local switch realizes that the sender should be the designated switch (having the designated port) and that its own port must become the new root port.

2. Before the switch agrees to anything, it must synchronize itself with the topology.

3. All nonedge ports immediately are moved into the Discarding (blocking) state so that no bridging loops can form.

4. An agreement message (a configuration BPDU) is sent back to the sender, indicating that the switch is in agreement with the new designated port choice. This also tells the sender that the switch is in the process of synchronizing itself.

5. The root port immediately is moved to the Forwarding state. The sender's port also immediately can begin forwarding.

6. For each nonedge port that is currently in the Discarding state, a proposal message is sent to the respective neighbor.

7. An agreement message is expected and received from a neighbor on a nonedge port.

8. The nonedge port immediately is moved to the Forwarding state.

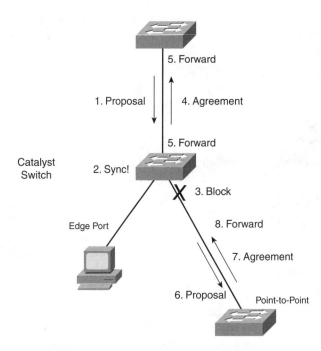

Figure 10-1 *Sequence of Events During RSTP Convergence*

Notice that the RSTP convergence begins with a switch sending a proposal message. The recipient of the proposal must synchronize itself by effectively isolating itself from the rest of the topology. All nonedge ports are blocked until a proposal message can be sent, causing the nearest neighbors to synchronize themselves. This creates a moving "wave" of synchronizing switches, which quickly can decide to start forwarding on their links only if their neighbors agree. Figure 10-2 shows how the synchronization wave travels through a network at three successive time intervals. Isolating the switches along the traveling wave inherently prevents bridging loops.

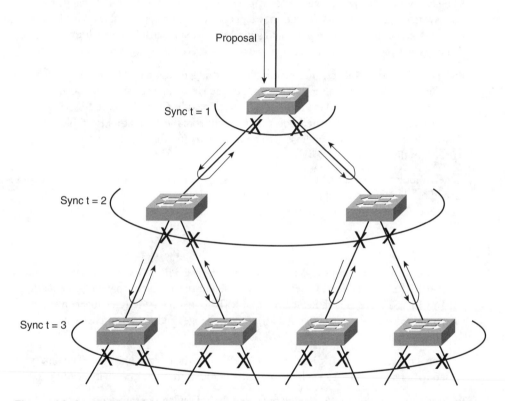

Figure 10-2   *RSTP Synchronization Traveling Through a Network*

The entire convergence process happens quickly, at the speed of BPDU transmission, without the use of any timers. However, a designated port that sends a proposal message might not receive an agreement message reply. Suppose that the neighboring switch does not understand RSTP or has a problem replying. The sending switch then must become overly cautious and must begin playing by the 802.1D rules—the port must be moved through the legacy Listening and Learning states (using the Forward Delay timer) before moving to the Forwarding state.

Topology Changes and RSTP

Recall that when an 802.1D switch detects a port state change (either up or down), it signals the root bridge by sending Topology Change Notification (TCN) BPDUs. The root bridge, in turn, must signal the topology change by sending out a TCN message that is re-layed to all switches in the STP domain.

RSTP detects a topology change only when a nonedge port transitions to the Forwarding state. This might seem odd because a link failure is not used as a trigger. RSTP uses all its rapid convergence mechanisms to prevent bridging loops from forming. Therefore, topology changes are detected only so that bridging tables can be updated and corrected as hosts appear first on a failed port and then on a different functioning port.

When a topology change is detected, a switch must propagate news of the change to other switches in the network so that they can correct their bridging tables, too. This process is similar to the convergence and synchronization mechanism; topology change (TC) messages propagate through the network in an ever-expanding wave.

BPDUs, with their TC bit set, are sent out all the nonedge designated ports. This is done until the TC timer expires, after two intervals of the Hello time. This notifies neighboring switches of the new link and the topology change. In addition, all MAC addresses associated with the nonedge designated ports are flushed from the content-addressable memory (CAM) table. This forces the addresses to be relearned after the change, in case hosts now appear on a different link.

All neighboring switches that receive the TC messages also must flush the MAC addresses learned on all ports except the one that received the TC message. Those switches then must send TC messages out their nonedge designated ports, and so on.

RSTP Configuration

By default, a switch operates in Per-VLAN Spanning Tree Plus (PVST+) mode using traditional 802.1D STP. Therefore, RSTP cannot be used until a different spanning-tree mode (MST or RPVST+) is enabled. Remember that RSTP is just the underlying mechanism that a spanning-tree mode can use to detect topology changes and converge a network into a loop-free topology.

The only configuration changes related to RSTP affect the port or link type. The link type is used to determine how a switch negotiates topology information with its neighbors.

To configure a port as an RSTP edge port, use the following interface configuration command:

```
Switch(config-if)# spanning-tree portfast
```

You already should be familiar with this command from the 802.1D STP configuration. After PortFast is enabled, the port is considered to have only one host and is positioned at the edge of the network.

By default, RSTP automatically decides that a port is a point-to-point link if it is operating in full-duplex mode. Ports connecting to other switches are usually full duplex because there are only two switches on the link. However, you can override the automatic determination, if needed. For example, a port connecting to one other switch might be operating at half duplex, for some reason. To force the port to act as a point-to-point link, use the following interface configuration command:

```
Switch(config-if)# spanning-tree link-type point-to-point
```

Rapid Per-VLAN Spanning Tree Protocol

Chapter 7, "Traditional Spanning Tree Protocol," describes PVST+ as the default STP mode on Catalyst switches. In PVST+, one spanning tree instance is created and used for each active VLAN that is defined on the switch. Each STP instance behaves according to the traditional 802.1D STP rules.

You can improve the efficiency of each STP instance by configuring a switch to begin using RSTP instead. This means that each VLAN will have its own independent instance of RSTP running on the switch. This mode is known as *Rapid PVST+* (RPVST+).

You need only one configuration step to change the STP mode and begin using RPVST+. You can use the following global configuration command to accomplish this:

Key Topic

```
Switch(config)# spanning-tree mode rapid-pvst
```

Be careful when you use this command on a production network because any STP process that is currently running must be restarted. This can cause functioning links to move through the traditional STP states, preventing data from flowing for a short time.

Tip: To revert back to the default PVST+ mode, using traditional 802.1D STP, you can use the following command:

```
Switch(config)# spanning-tree mode pvst
```

After you enable the RPVST+ mode, the switch must begin supporting both RSTP and 802.1D STP neighbors. The switch can detect the neighbor's STP type by the BPDU version that is received. You can see the neighbor type in the output of the **show spanning-tree vlan** *vlan-id* command, as demonstrated in Example 10-1.

Example 10-1 *Detecting a Neighboring Switch's STP Type*

```
Switch# show spanning-tree vlan 171
VLAN0171
  Spanning tree enabled protocol rstp

  Root ID    Priority    4267
             Address     00d0.0457.38aa
             Cost        3

             Port        833 (Port-channel1)
             Hello Time   2 sec  Max Age 20 sec  Forward Delay 15 sec

  Bridge ID  Priority    32939  (priority 32768 sys-id-ext 171)
             Address     0007.0d55.a800
```

```
              Hello Time   2 sec  Max Age 20 sec  Forward Delay 15 sec
              Aging Time 300


Interface          Role Sts Cost      Prio.Nbr Type
---------------    ---- ---- --------- -------- -------------------------------
Gi7/8              Desg FWD 4          128.392  P2p
Gi9/6              Altn BLK 4          128.518  P2p Peer(STP)
Po1                Root FWD 3          128.833  P2p
Po2                Desg FWD 3          128.834  P2p
Po3                Desg FWD 3          128.835  P2p
Switch#
```

The output in Example 10-1 shows information about the RSTP instance for VLAN 171. The first shaded line confirms that the local switch indeed is running RSTP. (The only other way to confirm the STP mode is to locate the **spanning-tree mode** command in the running configuration.)

In addition, this output displays all the active ports participating in the VLAN 171 instance of RSTP, along with their port types. The string **P2p** denotes a point-to-point RSTP port type in which a full-duplex link connects two neighboring switches that both are running RSTP. If you see **P2p Peer(STP)**, the port is a point-to-point type but the neighboring device is running traditional 802.1D STP.

Multiple Spanning Tree Protocol

Chapter 7 covered two "flavors" of spanning-tree implementations—IEEE 802.1Q and PVST+—both based on the 802.1D STP. These also represent the two extremes of STP operation in a network:

- **802.1Q**—Only a single instance of STP is used for all VLANs. If there are 500 VLANs, only 1 instance of STP will be running. This is called the Common Spanning Tree (CST) and operates over the trunk's native VLAN.

- **PVST+**—One instance of STP is used for each active VLAN in the network. If there are 500 VLANs, 500 independent instances of STP will be running.

In most networks, each switch has a redundant path to another switch. For example, an access-layer switch usually has two uplinks, each connecting to a different distribution- or core-layer switch. If 802.1Q's CST is used, only one STP instance will run. This means that there is only one loop-free topology at any given time and that only one of the two uplinks in the access-layer switch will be forwarding. The other uplink always will be blocking.

Obviously, arranging the network so that both uplinks can be used simultaneously would be best. One uplink should carry one set of VLANs, whereas the other should carry a different set as a type of load balancing.

PVST+ seems more attractive to meet that goal because it allows different VLANs to have different topologies so that each uplink can be forwarding. But think of the consequences: As the number of VLANs increases, so does the number of independent STP instances.

Each instance uses some amount of the switch CPU and memory resources. The more instances that are in use, the fewer CPU resources will be available for switching.

Beyond that, what is the real benefit of having 500 STP topologies for 500 VLANs, when only a small number of possible topologies exist for a switch with two uplinks? Figure 10-3 shows a typical network with an access-layer switch connecting to a pair of core switches. Two VLANs are in use, with the root bridges configured to support load balancing across the two uplinks. The right portion of the figure shows every possible topology for VLANs A and B. Notice that because the access-layer switch has only two uplinks, only two topologies actually matter—one in which the left uplink forwards, and one in which the right uplink forwards.

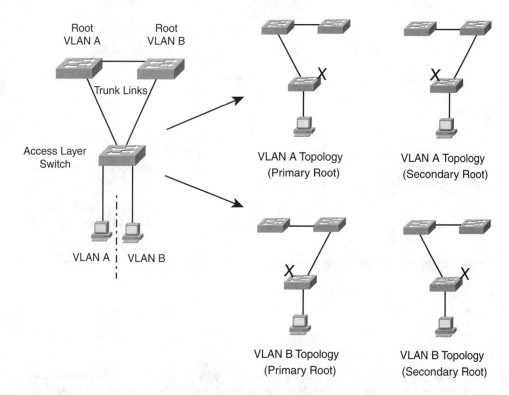

Figure 10-3 *Possible STP Topologies for Two VLANs*

Notice also that the number of useful topologies is independent of the number of VLANs. If 10 or 100 VLANs were used in the figure, there would still be only two possible outcomes at the access-layer switch. Therefore, running 10 or 100 instances of STP when only a couple would suffice is rather wasteful.

The Multiple Spanning Tree Protocol was developed to address the lack of and surplus of STP instances. As a result, the network administrator can configure exactly the number of

STP instances that makes sense for the enterprise network, no matter how many VLANs are in use. MST is defined in the IEEE 802.1s standard.

MST Overview

MST is built on the concept of mapping one or more VLANs to a single STP instance. Multiple instances of STP can be used (hence the name MST), with each instance supporting a different group of VLANs.

For the network shown in Figure 10-3, only two MST instances would be needed. Each could be tuned to result in a different topology so that Instance 1 would forward on the left uplink, whereas Instance 2 would forward on the right uplink. Therefore, VLAN A would be mapped to Instance 1, and VLAN B would be mapped to Instance 2.

To implement MST in a network, you need to determine the following:

■ The number of STP instances needed to support the desired topologies

■ Whether to map a set of VLANs to each instance

MST Regions

Key Topic

MST is different from 802.1Q and PVST+, although it can interoperate with them. If a switch is configured to use MST, it somehow must figure out which of its neighbors are using which type of STP. This is done by configuring switches into common MST regions, where every switch in a region runs MST with compatible parameters.

In most networks, a single MST region is sufficient, although you can configure more than one region. Within the region, all switches must run the instance of MST that is defined by the following attributes:

■ MST configuration name (32 characters)

■ MST configuration revision number (0 to 65535)

■ MST instance-to-VLAN mapping table (4096 entries)

If two switches have the same set of attributes, they belong to the same MST region. If not, they belong to two independent regions.

MST BPDUs contain configuration attributes so that switches receiving BPDUs can compare them against their local MST configurations. If the attributes match, the STP instances within MST can be shared as part of the same region. If not, a switch is seen to be at the MST region boundary, where one region meets another or one region meets traditional 802.1D STP.

Note: The entire MST instance-to-VLAN mapping table is not sent in the BPDUs because the instance mappings must be configured on each switch. Instead, a digest, or a hash code computed from the table contents, is sent. As the contents of the table change, the digest value will be different. Therefore, a switch quickly can compare a received digest to its own to see if the advertised table is the same.

Spanning-Tree Instances Within MST

MST was designed to interoperate with all other forms of STP. Therefore, it also must support STP instances from each. This is where MST can get confusing. Think of the entire enterprise network as having a single CST topology so that one instance of STP represents any and all VLANs and MST regions present. The CST maintains a common loop-free topology while integrating all forms of STP that might be in use.

To do this, CST must regard each MST region as a single "black box" bridge because it has no idea what is inside the region, nor does it care. CST maintains a loop-free topology only with the links that connect the regions to each other and to standalone switches running 802.1Q CST.

IST Instances

Something other than CST must work out a loop-free topology inside each MST region. Within a single MST region, an Internal Spanning Tree (IST) instance runs to work out a loop-free topology between the links where CST meets the region boundary and all switches inside the region. Think of the IST instance as a locally significant CST, bounded by the edges of the region.

Key Topic

The IST presents the entire region as a single virtual bridge to the CST outside. BPDUs are exchanged at the region boundary only over the native VLAN of trunks, as if a single CST were in operation. And, indeed, it is.

Figure 10-4 shows the basic concept behind the IST instance. The network at the left has an MST region, where several switches are running compatible MST configurations. Another switch is outside the region because it is running only the CST from 802.1Q.

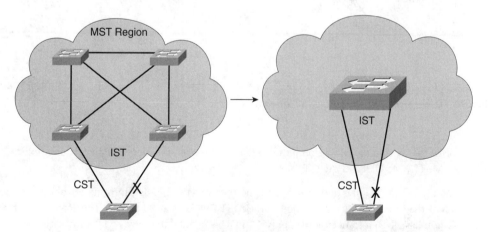

Figure 10-4 *Concepts Behind the IST Instance*

The same network is shown at the right, where the IST has produced a loop-free topology for the network inside the region. The IST makes the internal network look like a single bridge (the "big switch" in the cloud) that can interface with the CST running outside the region.

MST Instances

Recall that the whole idea behind MST is the capability to map multiple VLANs to a smaller number of STP instances. Inside a region, the actual MST instances (MSTI) exist alongside the IST. Cisco supports a maximum of 16 MSTIs in each region. The IST always exists as MSTI number 0, leaving MSTIs 1 through 15 available for use.

Figure 10-5 shows how different MSTIs can exist within a single MST region. The left portion of the figure is identical to that of Figure 10-4. In this network, two MST instances, MSTI 1 and MSTI 2, are configured with different VLANs mapped to each. Their topologies follow the same structure as the network on the left side of the figure, but each has converged differently.

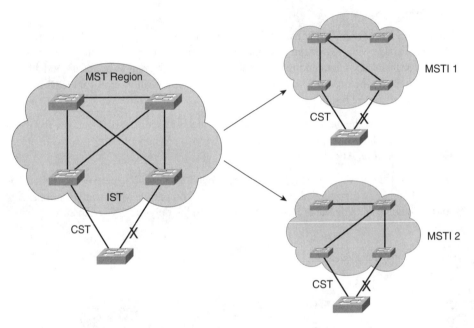

Figure 10-5   *Concepts Behind MST Instances*

Notice that within the MST cloud, there are now three independent STP instances coexisting: MSTI1, MSTI 2, and the IST.

Only the IST (MSTI 0) is allowed to send and receive MST BPDUs. Information about each of the other MSTIs is appended to the MST BPDU as an M-record. Therefore, even if a region has all 16 instances active, only 1 BPDU is needed to convey STP information about them all.

Each of the MSTIs is significant only within a region, even if an adjacent region has the same MSTIs in use. In other words, the MSTIs combine with the IST only at the region boundary to form a subtree of the CST. That means only IST BPDUs are sent into and out of a region.

What if an MST region connects with a switch running traditional PVST+? MST can detect this situation by listening to the received BPDUs. If BPDUs are heard from more than one VLAN (the CST), PVST+ must be in use. When the MST region sends a BPDU toward the PVST+ switch, the IST BPDUs are replicated into all the VLANs on the PVST+ switch trunk.

> **Tip:** Keep in mind that the IST instance is active on *every* port on a switch. Even if a port does not carry VLANs that have been mapped to the IST, IST must be running on the port. Also, by default, all VLANs are mapped to the IST instance. You must explicitly map them to other instances, if needed.

MST Configuration

You must manually configure the MST configuration attributes on each switch in a region. There is currently no method to propagate this information from one switch to another, as is done with a protocol such as VLAN Trunking Protocol (VTP). To define the MST region, use the following configuration commands in the order shown:

Key
Topic

Step 1.   Enable MST on the switch:

    Switch(config)# spanning-tree mode mst

Step 2.   Enter the MST configuration mode:

    Switch(config)# spanning-tree mst configuration

Step 3.   Assign a region configuration name (up to 32 characters):

    Switch(config-mst)# name name

Step 4.   Assign a region configuration revision number (0 to 65,535):

    Switch(config-mst)# revision version

The configuration revision number gives you a means of tracking changes to the MST region configuration. Each time you make changes to the configuration, you should increase the number by one. Remember that the region configuration (including the revision number) must match on all switches in the region. Therefore, you also need to update the revision numbers on the other switches to match.

Step 5.   Map VLANs to an MST instance:

    Switch(config-mst)# instance instance-id vlan vlan-list

The *instance-id* (0 to 15) carries topology information for the VLANs listed in *vlan-list*. The list can contain one or more VLANs separated by commas. You also can add a range of VLANs to the list by separating numbers with a hyphen. VLAN numbers can range from 1 to 4,094. (Remember that, by default, all VLANs are mapped to instance 0, the IST.)

Step 6.   Show the pending changes you have made:

    Switch(config-mst)# show pending

Step 7.   Exit the MST configuration mode; commit the changes to the active MST region configuration:

```
Switch(config-mst)# exit
```

After MST is enabled and configured, PVST+ operation stops and the switch changes to RSTP operation. A switch cannot run both MST and PVST+ at the same time.

You also can tune the parameters that MST uses when it interacts with CST or traditional 802.1D. The parameters and timers are identical to those discussed in Chapter 8, "Spanning-Tree Configuration." In fact, the commands are very similar except for the addition of the **mst** keyword and the *instance-id*. Instead of tuning STP for a VLAN instance, you use an MST instance.

Table 10-2 summarizes the commands as a quick reference. Notice that the timer configurations are applied to MST as a whole, not to a specific MST instance. This is because all instance timers are defined through the IST instance and BPDUs.

Table 10-2   *MST Configuration Commands*

Task	Command Syntax
Set root bridge (macro).	Switch(config)# **spanning-tree mst** *instance-id* **root {primary | secondary} [diameter** *diameter*]
Set bridge priority.	Switch(config)# **spanning-tree mst** *instance-id* **priority** *bridge-priority*
Set port cost.	Switch(config)# **spanning-tree mst** *instance-id* **cost** *cost*
Set port priority.	Switch(config)# **spanning-tree mst** *instance-id* **port-priority** *port-priority*
Set STP timers.	Switch(config)# **spanning-tree mst hello-time** *seconds*
	Switch(config)# **spanning-tree mst forward-time** *seconds*
	Switch(config)# **spanning-tree mst max-age** *seconds*

Exam Preparation Tasks

Review All Key Topics

Review the most important topics in the chapter, noted with the Key Topic icon in the outer margin of the page. Table 10-3 lists a reference of these key topics and the page numbers on which each is found.

Table 10-3 *Key Topics for Chapter 10*

Key Topic Element	Description	Page Number
Paragraph	Describes RSTP root bridge election and port states	199
Paragraph	Describes RSTP port states	199
Paragraph	Discusses RSTP compatibility with 802.1D STP	200
Paragraph	Describes RSTP port types	200
Paragraph	Explains the RSTP synchronization process	201
Paragraph	Discusses how RSTP detects topology changes	204
Paragraph	Explains how to configure an RSTP edge port	204
Paragraph	Explains how to enable the RPVST+ mode, using RSTP	205
Paragraph	Discusses how MST is organized into regions	208
Paragraph	Describes the IST instance	209
Paragraph	Describes MST instances	210
List	Explains how to configure MST	211

Complete Tables and Lists from Memory

Print a copy of Appendix C, "Memory Tables," (found on the CD), or at least the section for this chapter, and complete the tables and lists from memory. Appendix D, "Memory Tables Answer Key," also on the CD, includes completed tables and lists to check your work.

Define Key Terms

Define the following key terms from this chapter, and check your answers in the glossary:

RSTP, RPVST+, alternate port, backup port, discarding state, edge port, point-to-point port, synchronization, MST, MST region, IST instance, MST instance (MSTI)

Use Command Reference to Check Your Memory

This section includes the most important configuration and EXEC commands covered in this chapter. It might not be necessary to memorize the complete syntax of every command, but you should remember the basic keywords that are needed.

To test your memory of the Rapid STP and MST commands, cover the right side of Tables 10-4 and 10-5 with a piece of paper, read the description on the left side, and then see how much of the command you can remember.

Table 10-4 *RSTP Configuration Commands*

Task	Command Syntax
Define an edge port.	Switch(config-if)# **spanning-tree portfast**
Override a port type.	Switch(config-if)# **spanning-tree link-type point-to-point**

Table 10-5 *MST Region Configuration Commands*

Task	Command Syntax
Enable MST on a switch.	Switch(config)# **spanning-tree mode mst**
Enter MST configuration mode.	Switch(config)# **spanning-tree mst configuration**
Name the MST region.	Switch(config-mst)# **name** *name*
Set the configuration revision number.	Switch(config-mst)# **revision** *version*

This chapter covers the following topics that you need to master for the CCNP SWITCH exam:

InterVLAN Routing—This section discusses how you can use a routing function with a switch to forward packets between VLANs.

Multilayer Switching with CEF—This section discusses Cisco Express Forwarding (CEF) and how it is implemented on Catalyst switches. CEF forwards or routes packets in hardware at a high throughput.

Verifying Multilayer Switching—This section provides a brief summary of the commands that can verify the configuration and operation of interVLAN routing, CEF, and fallback bridging.

Using DHCP with a Multilayer Switch—This section covers the basic configuration needed to make a switch act as a DHCP server or as a DHCP relay so that hosts can request addresses and learn their local default gateway addresses.

CHAPTER 11

Multilayer Switching

Chapter 2, "Switch Operation," presents a functional overview of how multilayer switching (MLS) is performed at Layers 3 and 4. The actual MLS process can take two forms: interVLAN routing and Cisco Express Forwarding (CEF). This chapter expands on multilayer switch operation by discussing both of these topics in greater detail.

"Do I Know This Already?" Quiz

The "Do I Know This Already?" quiz allows you to assess whether you should read this entire chapter thoroughly or jump to the "Exam Preparation Tasks" section. If you are in doubt based on your answers to these questions or your own assessment of your knowledge of the topics, read the entire chapter. Table 11-1 outlines the major headings in this chapter and the "Do I Know This Already?" quiz questions that go with them. You can find the answers in Appendix A, "Answers to the 'Do I Know This Already?' Quizzes."

Table 11-1 *"Do I Know This Already?" Section-to-Question Mapping*

Foundation Topics Section	Questions Covered in This Section
InterVLAN Routing	1–5
Multilayer Switching with CEF	6–10
Verifying Multilayer Switching	11
Using DHCP with a Multilayer Switch	12

1. Which of the following arrangements can be considered interVLAN routing?

    a. One switch, two VLANs, one connection to a router.

    b. One switch, two VLANs, two connections to a router.

    c. Two switches, two VLANs, two connections to a router.

    d. All of these answers are correct.

2. How many interfaces are needed in a "router on a stick" implementation for interVLAN routing among four VLANs?

    a. 1

    b. 2

    c. 4

    d. Cannot be determined

3. Which of the following commands configures a switch port for Layer 2 operation?

    a. switchport

    b. no switchport

    c. ip address 192.168.199.1 255.255.255.0

    d. no ip address

4. Which of the following commands configures a switch port for Layer 3 operation?

    a. switchport

    b. no switchport

    c. ip address 192.168.199.1 255.255.255.0

    d. no ip address

5. Which one of the following interfaces is an SVI?

    a. interface fastethernet 0/1

    b. interface gigabit 0/1

    c. interface vlan 1

    d. interface svi 1

6. What information must be learned before CEF can forward packets?

    a. The source and destination of the first packet in a traffic flow

    b. The MAC addresses of both the source and destination

    c. The contents of the routing table

    d. The outbound port of the first packet in a flow

7. Which of the following best defines an adjacency?

    a. Two switches connected by a common link.

    b. Two contiguous routes in the FIB.

    c. Two multilayer switches connected by a common link.

    d. The MAC address of a host is known.

8. Assume that CEF is active on a switch. What happens to a packet that arrives needing fragmentation?

    a. The packet is switched by CEF and kept intact.

    b. The packet is fragmented by CEF.

    c. The packet is dropped.

    d. The packet is sent to the Layer 3 engine.

9. Suppose that a host sends a packet to a destination IP address and that the CEF-based switch does not yet have a valid MAC address for the destination. How is the ARP entry (MAC address) of the next-hop destination in the FIB obtained?

   a. The sending host must send an ARP request for it.

   b. The Layer 3 forwarding engine (CEF hardware) must send an ARP request for it.

   c. CEF must wait until the Layer 3 engine sends an ARP request for it.

   d. All packets to the destination are dropped.

10. During a packet rewrite, what happens to the source MAC address?

   a. There is no change.

   b. It is changed to the destination MAC address.

   c. It is changed to the MAC address of the outbound Layer 3 switch interface.

   d. It is changed to the MAC address of the next-hop destination.

11. What command can you use to view the CEF FIB table contents?

   a. show fib

   b. show ip cef fib

   c. show ip cef

   d. show fib-table

12. Which one of the following answers represents configuration commands needed to implement a DHCP relay function?

   a.
   ```
   interface vlan 5
   ip address 10.1.1.1 255.255.255.0
   ip helper-address 10.1.1.10
   ```

   b.
   ```
   interface vlan 5
   ip address 10.1.1.1 255.255.255.0
   ip dhcp-relay
   ```

   c.
   ```
   ip dhcp pool staff
   network 10.1.1.0 255.255.255.0
   default-router 10.1.1.1
   exit
   ```

   d.
   ```
   hostname Switch
   ip helper-address 10.1.1.10
   ```

Foundation Topics

InterVLAN Routing

Recall that a Layer 2 network is defined as a broadcast domain. A Layer 2 network can also exist as a VLAN inside one or more switches. VLANs essentially are isolated from each other so that packets in one VLAN cannot cross into another VLAN.

To transport packets between VLANs, you must use a Layer 3 device. Traditionally, this has been a router's function. The router must have a physical or logical connection to each VLAN so that it can forward packets between them. This is known as *interVLAN routing*.

InterVLAN routing can be performed by an external router that connects to each of the VLANs on a switch. Separate physical connections can be used, or the router can access each of the VLANs through a single trunk link. Part A of Figure 11-1 illustrates this concept. The external router also can connect to the switch through a single trunk link, carrying all the necessary VLANs, as illustrated in Part B of Figure 11-1. Part B illustrates what commonly is referred to as a "router on a stick" or a "one-armed router" because the router needs only a single interface to do its job.

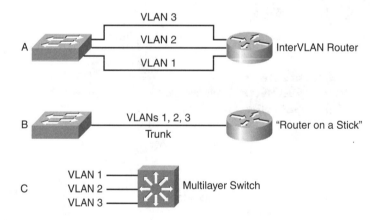

Figure 11-1 *Examples of InterVLAN Routing Connections*

Finally, Part C of Figure 11-1 shows how the routing and switching functions can be combined into one device: a multilayer switch. No external router is needed.

Types of Interfaces

Multilayer switches can perform both Layer 2 switching and interVLAN routing, as appropriate. Layer 2 switching occurs between interfaces that are assigned to Layer 2 VLANs or Layer 2 trunks. Layer 3 switching can occur between any type of interface, as long as the interface can have a Layer 3 address assigned to it.

As with a router, a multilayer switch can assign a Layer 3 address to a physical interface. It also can assign a Layer 3 address to a logical interface that represents an entire VLAN. This is known as a *switched virtual interface (SVI)*. Keep in mind that the Layer 3 address you configure becomes the default gateway for any hosts that are connected to the interface or VLAN. The hosts will use the Layer 3 interface to communicate outside of their local broadcast domains.

Configuring InterVLAN Routing

InterVLAN routing first requires that routing be enabled for the Layer 3 protocol. In the case of IP, you would enable IP routing. In addition, you must configure static routes or a dynamic routing protocol. These topics are covered fully in the CCNP ROUTE course. By default, every switch port on most Catalyst switch platforms is a Layer 2 interface, whereas every switch port on a Catalyst 6500 is a Layer 3 interface. If an interface needs to operate in a different mode, you must explicitly configure it.

An interface is either in Layer 2 or Layer 3 mode, depending on the use of the **switchport** interface configuration command. You can display a port's current mode with the following command:

```
Switch# show interface type mod/num switchport
```

If the **Switchport:** line in the command output is shown as enabled, the port is in Layer 2 mode. If this line is shown as disabled, as in the following example, the port is in Layer 3 mode:

```
Switch# show interface gigabitethernet 0/1 switchport
Name: Gi0/1
Switchport: Disabled
Switch#
```

Tip: Whenever you see the word *switchport*, think Layer 2. So if switchport is disabled, it must be Layer 3.

Figure 11-2 shows how the different types of interface modes can be used within a single switch.

Layer 2 Port Configuration

If an interface is in Layer 3 mode and you need to reconfigure it for Layer 2 functionality instead, use the following command sequence:

```
Switch(config)# interface type mod/num
Switch(config-if)# switchport
```

The **switchport** command puts the port in Layer 2 mode. Then you can use other **switchport** command keywords to configure trunking, access VLANs, and so on. As displayed in Figure 11-2, several Layer 2 ports exist, each assigned to a specific VLAN. A Layer 2 port also can act as a trunk, transporting multiple Layer 2 VLANs.

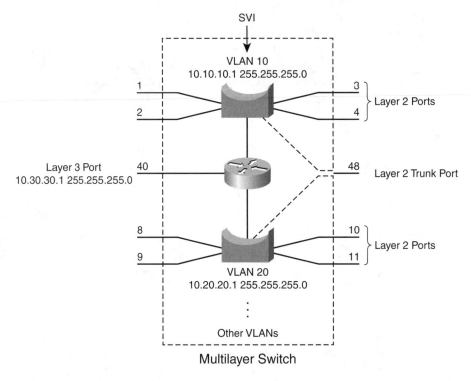

Figure 11-2   *Catalyst Switch with Various Types of Ports*

Layer 3 Port Configuration

Key Topic

Physical switch ports also can operate as Layer 3 interfaces, where a Layer 3 network address is assigned and routing can occur, as shown previously in Figure 11-2. For Layer 3 functionality, you must explicitly configure switch ports with the following command sequence:

```
Switch(config)# interface type mod/num
Switch(config-if)# no switchport
Switch(config-if)# ip address ip-address mask [secondary]
```

The **no switchport** command takes the port out of Layer 2 operation. You then can assign a network address to the port, as you would to a router interface.

Note: Keep in mind that a Layer 3 port assigns a network address to one specific physical interface. If several interfaces are bundled as an EtherChannel, the EtherChannel can also become a Layer 3 port. In that case, the network address is assigned to the port-channel interface—not to the individual physical links within the channel.

SVI Port Configuration

On a multilayer switch, you also can enable Layer 3 functionality for an entire VLAN on the switch. This allows a network address to be assigned to a logical interface—that of the VLAN itself. This is useful when the switch has many ports assigned to a common VLAN, and routing is needed in and out of that VLAN.

In Figure 11-2, you can see how an IP address is applied to the switched virtual interface called VLAN 10. Notice that the SVI itself has no physical connection to the outside world; to reach the outside, VLAN 10 must extend through a Layer 2 port or trunk to the outside.

The logical Layer 3 interface is known as an *SVI*. However, when it is configured, it uses the much more intuitive interface name **vlan** *vlan-id*, as if the VLAN itself is a physical interface. First, define or identify the VLAN interface; then assign any Layer 3 functionality to it with the following configuration commands:

```
Switch(config)# interface vlan vlan-id
Switch(config-if)# ip address ip-address mask [secondary]
```

The VLAN must be defined and active on the switch before the SVI can be used. Make sure that the new VLAN interface also is enabled with the **no shutdown** interface configuration command.

Note: The VLAN and the SVI are configured separately, even though they interoperate. Creating or configuring the SVI doesn't create or configure the VLAN; you still must define each one independently.

As an example, the following commands show how VLAN 100 is created and then defined as a Layer 3 SVI:

```
Switch(config)# vlan 100
Switch(config-vlan)# name Example_VLAN
Switch(config-vlan)# exit
Switch(config)# interface vlan 100
Switch(config-if)# ip address 192.168.100.1 255.255.255.0
Switch(config-if)# no shutdown
```

Multilayer Switching with CEF

Catalyst switches can use several methods to forward packets based on Layer 3 and Layer 4 information. The current generation of Catalyst multilayer switches uses the efficient Cisco Express Forwarding (CEF) method. This section describes the evolution of multilayer switching and discusses CEF in detail. Although CEF is easy to configure and use, the underlying switching mechanisms are more involved and should be understood.

Traditional MLS Overview

Multilayer switching began as a dual effort between a route processor (RP) and a switching engine (SE). The basic idea is to "route once and switch many." The RP receives the first packet of a new traffic flow between two hosts, as usual. A routing decision is made, and the packet is forwarded toward the destination.

To participate in multilayer switching, the SE must know the identity of each RP. The SE then can listen in to the first packet going to the router and also going away from the router. If the SE can switch the packet in both directions, it can learn a "shortcut path" so that subsequent packets of the same flow can be switched directly to the destination port without passing through the RP.

This technique also is known as *NetFlow switching* or *route cache switching*. Traditionally, NetFlow switching was performed on Cisco hardware, such as the Catalyst 6000 Supervisor 1/1a and Multilayer Switch Feature Card (MSFC), Catalyst 5500 with a Route Switch Module (RSM), Route Switch Feature Card (RSFC), or external router. Basically, the hardware consisted of an independent RP component and a NetFlow-capable SE component.

CEF Overview

NetFlow switching has given way to a more efficient form of multilayer switching: Cisco Express Forwarding. Cisco developed CEF for its line of routers, offering high-performance packet forwarding through the use of dynamic lookup tables.

CEF also has been carried over to the Catalyst switching platforms. The following platforms all perform CEF in hardware:

- Catalyst 6500 Supervisor 720 (with an integrated MSFC3)

- Catalyst 6500 Supervisor 2/MSFC2 combination

- Catalyst 4500 Supervisor III, IV, V, and 6-E

- Fixed-configuration switches, such as the Catalyst 3750, 3560, 3550, and 2950

CEF runs by default, taking advantage of the specialized hardware.

A CEF-based multilayer switch consists of two basic functional blocks, as shown in Figure 11-3: The Layer 3 engine is involved in building routing information that the Layer 3 forwarding engine can use to switch packets in hardware.

Forwarding Information Base

The Layer 3 engine (essentially a router) maintains routing information, whether from static routes or dynamic routing protocols. Basically, the routing table is reformatted into an ordered list with the most specific route first, for each IP destination subnet in the table. The new format is called a Forwarding Information Base (FIB) and contains routing or forwarding information that the network prefix can reference.

In other words, a route to 10.1.0.0/16 might be contained in the FIB along with routes to 10.1.1.0/24 and 10.1.1.128/25, if those exist. Notice that these examples are increasingly more specific subnets, as designated by the longer subnet masks. In the FIB, these would be ordered with the most specific, or longest match, first, followed by less specific subnets. When the switch receives a packet, it easily can examine the destination address and find the longest-match destination route entry in the FIB.

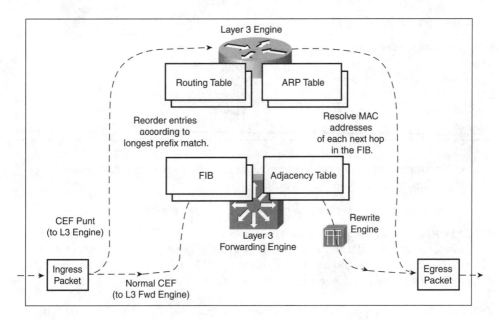

Figure 11-3 *Packet Flow Through a CEF-Based Multilayer Switch*

The FIB also contains the next-hop address for each entry. When a longest-match entry is found in the FIB, the Layer 3 next-hop address is found, too.

You might be surprised to know that the FIB also contains host route (subnet mask 255.255.255.255) entries. These normally are not found in the routing table unless they are advertised or manually configured. Host routes are maintained in the FIB for the most efficient routing lookup to directly connected or adjacent hosts.

As with a routing table, the FIB is dynamic in nature. When the Layer 3 engine sees a change in the routing topology, it sends an update to the FIB. Anytime the routing table receives a change to a route prefix or the next-hop address, the FIB receives the same change. Also, if a next-hop address is changed or aged out of the Address Resolution Protocol (ARP) table, the FIB must reflect the same change.

You can display FIB table entries related to a specific interface or VLAN with the following form of the **show ip cef** command:

```
Switch# show ip cef [type mod/num | vlan vlan-id] [detail]
```

The FIB entries corresponding to the VLAN 101 switched virtual interface might be shown as demonstrated in Example 11-1.

Example 11-1   *Displaying FIB Table Entries for a Specified VLAN*

```
Switch# show ip cef vlan 101
Prefix               Next Hop              Interface
10.1.1.0/24          attached              Vlan101
10.1.1.2/32          10.1.1.2              Vlan101
10.1.1.3/32          10.1.1.3              Vlan101
Switch#
```

You also can view FIB entries by specifying an IP prefix address and mask, using the following form of the **show ip cef** command:

```
Switch# show ip cef [prefix-ip prefix-mask] [longer-prefixes] [detail]
```

The output in Example 11-2 displays any subnet within 10.1.0.0/16 that is known by the switch, regardless of the prefix or mask length. Normally, only an exact match of the IP prefix and mask will be displayed if it exists in the CEF table. To see other longer match entries, you can add the **longer-prefixes** keyword.

Example 11-2   *Displaying FIB Table Entries for a Specified IP Prefix Address/Mask*

```
Switch# show ip cef 10.1.0.0 255.255.0.0 longer-prefixes
Prefix               Next Hop              Interface
10.1.1.0/24          attached              Vlan101
10.1.1.2/32          10.1.1.2              Vlan101
10.1.1.3/32          10.1.1.3              Vlan101
10.1.2.0/24          attached              Vlan102
10.1.3.0/26          192.168.1.2           Vlan99
                     192.168.1.3           Vlan99
10.1.3.64/26         192.168.1.2           Vlan99
                     192.168.1.3           Vlan99
10.1.3.128/26        192.168.1.4           Vlan99
                     192.168.1.3           Vlan99
[output omitted]
Switch#
```

Notice that the first three entries are the same ones listed in Example 11-1. Other subnets also are displayed, along with their next-hop router addresses and switch interfaces.

You can add the **detail** keyword to see more information about each FIB table entry for CEF, as demonstrated in Example 11-3.

Example 11-3   *Displaying Detailed CEF Entry Information*

```
Switch# show ip cef 10.1.3.0 255.255.255.192 detail
10.1.3.0/26, version 270, epoch 0, per-destination sharing
0 packets, 0 bytes
  via 192.168.1.2, Vlan99, 0 dependencies
```

```
    traffic share 1
    next hop 192.168.1.2, Vlan99
    valid adjacency
via 192.168.1.3, Vlan99, 0 dependencies
    traffic share 1
    next hop 192.168.1.3, Vlan99
    valid adjacency
0 packets, 0 bytes switched through the prefix
tmstats: external 0 packets, 0 bytes
            internal 0 packets, 0 bytes
Switch#
```

The version number describes the number of times the CEF entry has been updated since the table was generated. The epoch number denotes the number of times the CEF table has been flushed and regenerated as a whole. The 10.1.3.0/26 subnet has two next-hop router addresses, so the local switch is using per-destination load sharing between the two routers.

After the FIB is built, packets can be forwarded along the bottom dashed path in Figure 11-3. This follows the hardware switching process, in which no "expensive" or time-consuming operations are needed. At times, however, a packet cannot be switched in hardware, according to the FIB. Packets then are marked as "CEF punt" and immediately are sent to the Layer 3 engine for further processing, as shown in the top dashed path in Figure 11-3. Some of the conditions that can cause this are as follows:

■ An entry cannot be located in the FIB.

■ The FIB table is full.

■ The IP Time-To-Live (TTL) has expired.

■ The maximum transmission unit (MTU) is exceeded, and the packet must be fragmented.

■ An Internet Control Message Protocol (ICMP) redirect is involved.

■ The encapsulation type is not supported.

■ Packets are tunneled, requiring a compression or encryption operation.

■ An access list with the **log** option is triggered.

■ A Network Address Translation (NAT) operation must be performed (except on the Catalyst 6500 Supervisor 720, which can handle NAT in hardware).

CEF operations can be handled on a single hardware platform, such as the Catalyst 3560 and 3750 switches. The FIB is generated and contained centrally in the switch. CEF also can be optimized through the use of specialized forwarding hardware, using the following techniques:

■ **Accelerated CEF (aCEF)**—CEF is distributed across multiple Layer 3 forwarding engines, typically located on Catalyst 6500 line cards. These engines do not have the capability to store and use the entire FIB, so only a portion of the FIB is downloaded to them at any time. This functions as an FIB "cache," containing entries that are likely to be used again. If FIB entries are not found in the cache, requests are sent to the Layer 3 engine for more FIB information. The net result is that CEF is accelerated on the line cards, but not necessarily at a sustained wire-speed rate.

- **Distributed CEF (dCEF)**—CEF can be distributed completely among multiple Layer 3 forwarding engines for even greater performance. Because the FIB is self-contained for complete Layer 3 forwarding, it can be replicated across any number of independent Layer 3 forwarding engines. The Catalyst 6500 has line cards that support dCEF, each with its own FIB table and forwarding engine. A central Layer 3 engine (the MSFC3, for example) maintains the routing table and generates the FIB, which is then dynamically downloaded in full to each of the line cards.

Adjacency Table

A router normally maintains a routing table containing Layer 3 network and next-hop information, and an ARP table containing Layer 3 to Layer 2 address mapping. These tables are kept independently.

Recall that the FIB keeps the Layer 3 next-hop address for each entry. To streamline packet forwarding even more, the FIB has corresponding Layer 2 information for every next-hop entry. This portion of the FIB is called the *adjacency table*, consisting of the MAC addresses of nodes that can be reached in a single Layer 2 hop.

You can display the adjacency table's contents with the following command:

```
Switch# show adjacency [type mod/num | vlan vlan-id] [summary | detail]
```

As an example, the total number of adjacencies known on each physical or VLAN interface can be displayed with the **show adjacency summary** command, as demonstrated in Example 11-4.

Example 11-4   *Displaying the Total Number of Known Adjacencies*

```
Switch# show adjacency summary
Adjacency Table has 106 adjacencies
  Table epoch: 0 (106 entries at this epoch)
  Interface                 Adjacency Count
  Vlan99                    21
  Vlan101                   3
  Vlan102                   1
  Vlan103                   47
  Vlan104                   7
  Vlan105                   27
Switch#
```

Adjacencies are kept for each next-hop router and each host that is connected directly to the local switch. You can see more detailed information about the adjacencies by using the **detail** keyword, as demonstrated in Example 11-5.

Example 11-5 *Displaying Detailed Information About Adjacencies*

```
Switch# show adjacency vlan 99 detail
Protocol Interface            Address
IP       Vlan99               192.168.1.2(5)
                                0 packets, 0 bytes
                                000A5E45B145000E387D51000800
                                ARP          01:52:50
                                Epoch: 0
IP       Vlan99               192.168.1.3(5)
                                1 packets, 104 bytes
                                000CF1C909A0000E387D51000800
                                ARP          04:02:11
                              Epoch: 0
```

Notice that the adjacency entries include both the IP address (Layer 3) and the MAC address (Layer 2) of the directly attached host. The MAC address could be shown as the first six octets of the long string of hex digits (as shaded in the previous output) or on a line by itself. The remainder of the string of hex digits contains the MAC address of the Layer 3 engine's interface (six octets, corresponding to the Vlan99 interface in the example) and the EtherType value (two octets, where 0800 denotes IP).

The adjacency table information is built from the ARP table. Example 11-5 shows adjacency with the age of its ARP entry. As a next-hop address receives a valid ARP entry, the adjacency table is updated. If an ARP entry does not exist, the FIB entry is marked as "CEF glean." This means that the Layer 3 forwarding engine can't forward the packet in hardware because of the missing Layer 2 next-hop address. The packet is sent to the Layer 3 engine so that it can generate an ARP request and receive an ARP reply. This is known as the *CEF glean* state, in which the Layer 3 engine must glean the next-hop destination's MAC address.

The glean state can be demonstrated in several ways, as demonstrated in Example 11-6.

Example 11-6 *Displaying Adjacencies in the CEF Glean State*

```
Switch# show ip cef adjacency glean
Prefix                Next Hop          Interface
10.1.1.2/32           attached          Vlan101
127.0.0.0/8           attached          EOBC0/0
[output omitted]
Switch# show ip arp 10.1.1.2
Switch# show ip cef 10.1.1.2 255.255.255.255 detail
10.1.1.2/32, version 688, epoch 0, attached, connected
0 packets, 0 bytes
  via Vlan101, 0 dependencies
    valid glean adjacency
Switch#
```

Notice that the FIB entry for directly connected host 10.1.1.2/32 is present but listed in the glean state. The **show ip arp** command shows that there is no valid ARP entry for the IP address.

During the time that an FIB entry is in the CEF glean state waiting for the ARP resolution, subsequent packets to that host are immediately dropped so that the input queues do not fill and the Layer 3 engine does not become too busy worrying about the need for duplicate ARP requests. This is called *ARP throttling* or *throttling adjacency*. If an ARP reply is not received in 2 seconds, the throttling is released so that another ARP request can be triggered. Otherwise, after an ARP reply is received, the throttling is released, the FIB entry can be completed, and packets can be forwarded completely in hardware.

The adjacency table also can contain other types of entries so that packets can be handled efficiently. For example, you might see the following adjacency types listed:

- **Null adjacency**—Used to switch packets destined for the null interface. The null interface always is defined on a router or switch; it represents a logical interface that silently absorbs packets without actually forwarding them.

- **Drop adjacency**—Used to switch packets that can't be forwarded normally. In effect, these packets are dropped without being forwarded. Packets can be dropped because of an encapsulation failure, an unresolved address, an unsupported protocol, no valid route present, no valid adjacency, or a checksum error. You can gauge drop adjacency activity with the following command:

```
Switch# show cef drop
CEF Drop Statistics
Slot   Encap_fail  Unresolved Unsupported    No_route    No_adj  ChkSum_Err
RP      8799327             1       45827     5089667        32           0
Switch#
```

- **Discard adjacency**—Used when packets must be discarded because of an access list or other policy action.

- **Punt adjacency**—Used when packets must be sent to the Layer 3 engine for further processing. You can gauge the CEF punt activity by looking at the various punt adjacency reasons listed by the **show cef not-cef-switched** command:

```
Switch# show cef not-cef-switched
CEF Packets passed on to next switching layer
Slot   No_adj   No_encap  Unsupp'ted  Redirect   Receive  Options  Access  Frag
RP    3579706          0           0         0  41258564        0       0     0
Switch#
```

The reasons shown are as follows:

- **No_adj**—An incomplete adjacency

- **No_encap**—An incomplete ARP resolution

- **Unsupp'ted**—Unsupported packet features

- **Redirect**—ICMP redirect

- **Receive**—Layer 3 engine interfaces; includes packets destined for IP addresses that are assigned to interfaces on the Layer 3 engine, IP network addresses, and IP broadcast addresses

- **Options**—IP options present

- **Access**—Access list evaluation failure

- **Frag**—Fragmentation failure

Packet Rewrite

When a multilayer switch finds valid entries in the FIB and adjacency tables, a packet is almost ready to be forwarded. One step remains: The packet header information must be rewritten. Keep in mind that multilayer switching occurs as quick table lookups to find the next-hop address and the outbound switch port. The packet is untouched and still has the original destination MAC address of the switch itself. The IP header also must be adjusted, as if a traditional router had done the forwarding.

The switch has an additional functional block that performs a packet rewrite in real time. The packet rewrite engine (shown in Figure 11-3) makes the following changes to the packet just before forwarding:

Key Topic

- **Layer 2 destination address**—Changed to the next-hop device's MAC address

- **Layer 2 source address**—Changed to the outbound Layer 3 switch interface's MAC address

- **Layer 3 IP TTL**—Decremented by one because one router hop has just occurred

- **Layer 3 IP checksum**—Recalculated to include changes to the IP header

- **Layer 2 frame checksum**—Recalculated to include changes to the Layer 2 and Layer 3 headers

A traditional router normally would make the same changes to each packet. The multilayer switch must act as if a traditional router were being used, making identical changes. However, the multilayer switch can do this very efficiently with dedicated packet-rewrite hardware and address information obtained from table lookups.

Configuring CEF

CEF is enabled on all CEF-capable Catalyst switches by default. In fact, the Catalyst 6500 (with a Supervisor 720 and its integrated MSFC3, or a Supervisor 2 and MSFC2 combination) runs CEF inherently, so CEF never can be disabled.

Tip: Switches such as the Catalyst 3750 and 4500 run CEF by default, but you can disable CEF on a per-interface basis. You can use the **no ip route-cache cef** and **no ip cef** interface configuration commands to disable CEF on the Catalyst 3750 and 4500, respectively.

You should always keep CEF enabled whenever possible, except when you need to disable it for debugging purposes.

Verifying Multilayer Switching

The multilayer switching topics presented in this chapter are not difficult to configure; however, you might need to verify how a switch is forwarding packets. In particular, the following sections discuss the commands that you can use to verify the operation of inter-VLAN routing and CEF.

Verifying InterVLAN Routing

To verify the configuration of a Layer 2 port, you can use the following EXEC command:

```
Switch# show interface type mod/num switchport
```

The output from this command displays the access VLAN or the trunking mode and native VLAN. The administrative modes reflect what has been configured for the port, whereas the operational modes show the port's active status.

You can use this same command to verify the configuration of a Layer 3 or routed port. In this case, you should see the switchport (Layer 2) mode disabled, as in Example 11-7.

Example 11-7 *Verifying Configuration of a Layer 3 Switch Port*

```
Switch# show interface fastethernet 0/16 switchport
Name: Fa0/16
Switchport: Disabled
Switch#
```

To verify the configuration of an SVI, you can use the following EXEC command:

```
Switch# show interface vlan vlan-id
```

The VLAN interface should be up, with the line protocol also up. If this is not true, either the interface is disabled with the **shutdown** command or the VLAN itself has not been defined on the switch. Use the **show vlan** command to see a list of configured VLANs.

Example 11-8 shows the output produced from the **show vlan** command. Notice that each defined VLAN is shown, along with the switch ports that are assigned to it.

Example 11-8 *Displaying a List of Configured VLANs*

```
Switch# show vlan


VLAN Name                             Status     Ports
---- -------------------------------- ---------- -------------------------------
1    default                          active     Fa0/5,  Fa0/6,  Fa0/7,  Fa0/8
                                                 Fa0/9, Fa0/10, Fa0/11, Fa0/12
```

```
                                                    Fa0/13, Fa0/14, Fa0/15, Fa0/17
                                                    Fa0/18, Fa0/19, Fa0/20, Fa0/21
                                                    Fa0/22, Fa0/23, Fa0/24, Fa0/25
                                                    Fa0/26, Fa0/27, Fa0/28, Fa0/29
                                                    Fa0/30, Fa0/32, Fa0/33, Fa0/34
                                                    Fa0/36, Fa0/37, Fa0/38, Fa0/39
                                                    Fa0/41, Fa0/42, Fa0/43, Fa0/44
                                                    Fa0/45, Fa0/46, Fa0/47, Gi0/1
                                                    Gi0/2
2     VLAN0002                        active        Fa0/40
5     VLAN0005                        active
10    VLAN0010                        active
11    VLAN0011                        active        Fa0/31
12    VLAN0012                        active
99    VLAN0099                        active        Fa0/35
Switch#
```

You also can display the IP-related information about a switch interface with the **show ip interface** command, as demonstrated in Example 11-9.

Example 11-9 *Displaying IP-Related Information About a Switch Interface*

```
Switch# show ip interface vlan 101
Vlan101 is up, line protocol is up
  Internet address is 10.1.1.1/24
  Broadcast address is 255.255.255.255
  Address determined by setup command
  MTU is 1500 bytes
  Helper address is not set
  Directed broadcast forwarding is disabled
  Outgoing access list is not set
  Inbound  access list is not set
  Proxy ARP is enabled
  Local Proxy ARP is disabled
  Security level is default
  Split horizon is enabled
  ICMP redirects are always sent
  ICMP unreachables are always sent
  ICMP mask replies are never sent
  IP fast switching is enabled
  IP fast switching on the same interface is disabled
  IP Flow switching is disabled
  IP CEF switching is enabled
  IP Feature Fast switching turbo vector
  IP Feature CEF switching turbo vector
  IP multicast fast switching is enabled
```

```
     IP multicast distributed fast switching is disabled
     IP route-cache flags are Fast, Distributed, CEF
     Router Discovery is disabled
     IP output packet accounting is disabled
     IP access violation accounting is disabled
     TCP/IP header compression is disabled
     RTP/IP header compression is disabled
     Probe proxy name replies are disabled
     Policy routing is disabled
     Network address translation is disabled
     WCCP Redirect outbound is disabled
     WCCP Redirect inbound is disabled
     WCCP Redirect exclude is disabled
     BGP Policy Mapping is disabled
     Sampled Netflow is disabled
     IP multicast multilayer switching is disabled
Switch#
```

You can use the **show ip interface brief** command to see a summary listing of the Layer 3 interfaces involved in routing IP traffic, as demonstrated in Example 11-10.

Example 11-10 *Displaying a Summary Listing of Interfaces Routing IP Traffic*

```
Switch# show ip interface brief
Interface               IP-Address       OK? Method Status
Protocol
Vlan1                   unassigned       YES NVRAM  administratively down  down
Vlan54                  10.3.1.6         YES manual up                     up
Vlan101                 10.1.1.1         YES manual up                     up
GigabitEthernet1/1      10.1.5.1         YES manual up                     up
[output omitted]
Switch#
```

Verifying CEF

CEF operation depends on the correct routing information being generated and down-loaded to the Layer 3 forwarding engine hardware. This information is contained in the FIB and is maintained dynamically. To view the entire FIB, use the following EXEC command:

```
Switch# show ip cef
```

Example 11-11 shows sample output from this command.

Example 11-11 *Displaying the FIB Contents for a Switch*

```
Switch# show ip cef
Prefix              Next Hop          Interface
0.0.0.0/32          receive
```

```
192.168.199.0/24      attached             Vlan1
192.168.199.0/32      receive
192.168.199.1/32      receive
192.168.199.2/32      192.168.199.2        Vlan1
192.168.199.255/32    receive
Switch#
```

On this switch, only VLAN 1 has been configured with the IP address 192.168.199.1 255.255.255.0. Notice several things about the FIB for such a small configuration:

- **0.0.0.0/32**—An FIB entry has been reserved for the default route. No next hop is defined, so the entry is marked "receive" so that packets will be sent to the Layer 3 engine for further processing.

- **192.168.199.0/24**—The subnet assigned to the VLAN 1 interface is given its own entry. This is marked "attached" because it is connected directly to an SVI, VLAN 1.

- **192.168.199.0/32**—An FIB entry has been reserved for the exact network address. This is used to contain an adjacency for packets sent to the network address, if the network is not directly connected. In this case, there is no adjacency, and the entry is marked "receive."

- **192.168.199.1/32**—An entry has been reserved for the VLAN 1 SVI's IP address. Notice that this is a host route (/32). Packets destined for the VLAN 1 interface must be dealt with internally, so the entry is marked "receive."

- **192.168.199.2/32**—This is an entry for a neighboring multilayer switch, found on the VLAN 1 interface. The next-hop field has been filled in with the same IP address, denoting that an adjacency is available.

- **192.168.199.255/32**—An FIB entry has been reserved for the 192.168.199.0 subnet's broadcast address. The route processor (Layer 3 engine) handles all directed broadcasts, so the entry is marked "receive."

To see complete FIB table information for a specific interface, use the following EXEC command:

```
Switch# show ip cef type mod/num [detail]
```

Using DHCP with a Multilayer Switch

When a switch is configured with a Layer 3 address on an interface, it becomes the router or default gateway that connected hosts will use to send traffic to and from their local VLAN or subnet. How do those hosts know to use the Layer 3 interface as their default gateway? As well, how do those hosts know what IP address to use for their own identities?

Hosts can be manually configured to use a static IP address, subnet mask, default gateway address, and so on. That might be appropriate for some devices, such as servers, which would need stable and reserved addresses. For the majority of end user devices, static address assignment can become a huge administrative chore.

Instead, the Dynamic Host Configuration Protocol (DHCP) is usually leveraged to provide a means for dynamic address assignment to any host that can use the protocol. DHCP is defined in RFC 2131 and is built around a client/server model—hosts requesting IP addresses use a DHCP client, whereas address assignment is handled by a DHCP server.

Suppose a host connects to the network, but doesn't yet have an IP address. It needs to request an address via DHCP. How can it send a packet to a DHCP server without having a valid IP address to use as a source address? The answer lies in the DHCP negotiation, which plays out in the following four steps:

1. **The client sends a "DHCP Discover" message as a broadcast**—Even without a valid source address, the client can send to the broadcast address to find any DHCP server that might be listening. The client's MAC address is included in the broadcast message.

2. **A DHCP server replies with a "DHCP Offer" message**—The offer contains an offer for the use of an IP address, subnet mask, default gateway, and some parameters for using the IP address.

   The server also includes its own IP address to identify who is making the offer. (There could be multiple addresses offered, if more than one DHCP server received the broadcast DHCP Discover message.) Because the client doesn't yet have a valid IP address, the server must broadcast the offer so the client can receive it.

3. **The client sends a "DHCP Request" message**—When it is satisfied with a DHCP offer, the client formally requests use of the offered address. A record of the offer is included so that only the server that sent the offer will set aside the requested IP address. Again, the request is sent as a broadcast because the client hasn't officially started using a valid address.

4. **The DHCP server replies with a "DHCP ACK" message**—The IP address and all parameters for its use are returned to the client as formal approval to begin using the address. The ACK message is sent as a broadcast.

Because DHCP is a dynamic mechanism, IP addresses are offered on a leased basis. Before the offered lease time expires, the client must try to renew its address; otherwise, that address may be offered up to a different client.

Notice that DHCP is designed to work within a broadcast domain. Most of the messages in a DHCP exchange are sent as broadcasts. On this basis, the DHCP server would need to be located in the same broadcast domain as the client. In this scenario, you might have a dedicated DHCP server connected to the network and located in the same VLAN as the client. You can also configure a multilayer switch to operate as a DHCP server if you have configured a Layer 3 address on the switch interface or SVI where the client is located.

This design would require one DHCP server for each broadcast domain or VLAN on the network—something that isn't always practical at all! You can get around this requirement by configuring a multilayer switch to relay the DHCP negotiation across VLAN boundaries.

The following sections explain how to configure a DHCP server on a multilayer switch within a VLAN and how to configure DHCP relay between VLANs.

Configuring an IOS DHCP Server

After you have configured a Layer 3 address on a switch interface, you can configure a DHCP server that runs natively on the switch itself. The switch will intercept DHCP broadcast packets from client machines within a VLAN. Use the following command sequence to configure a DHCP server:

```
Switch(config)# ip dhcp excluded-address start-ip end-ip
Switch(config)# ip dhcp pool pool-name
Switch(config-dhcp)# network ip-address subnet-mask
Switch(config-dhcp)# default-router ip-address [ip-address2] [ip-address3] ...
Switch(config-dhcp)# lease {infinite | {days [hours [minutes]]}}
Switch(config-dhcp)# exit
```

If there are addresses within the IP subnet that should be reserved and not offered to clients, use the **ip dhcp excluded-address** command. You can define a range of addresses or a single address to be excluded.

The **ip dhcp pool** command uses a text string *pool-name* to define the pool or scope of addresses that will be offered. The **network** command identifies the IP subnet and subnet mask of the address range. The subnet should be identical to the one configured on the Layer 3 interface. In fact, the switch uses the **network** command to bind its DHCP server to the matching Layer 3 interface. By definition, the network and broadcast addresses for the subnet won't be offered to any client. The **default-router** command identifies the default router address that will be offered to clients. Generally, the default router should be the IP address of the corresponding Layer 3 interface on the switch.

Finally, you can set the IP address lease duration with the **lease** command. By default, leases are offered with a 1 day limit.

You can monitor the DHCP server address leases with the **show ip dhcp binding** command.

Tip: Many more commands are available for configuring the DHCP server. For the CCNP SWITCH exam, try to keep things simple and know the basic structure of DHCP pool configuration, as previously shown.

Configuring a DHCP Relay

If a DHCP server is centrally located in the network, you can configure the multilayer switch to relay DHCP messages between clients and the server, even if they are located on different VLANs or subnets.

First, configure a Layer 3 interface that joins the same VLAN as the client machines. This interface can be the default gateway for the clients and can act as a DHCP relay. Next, use the **ip helper-address** command to identify the IP address of the actual DHCP server, as in the following example:

```
Switch(config)# interface vlan5
Switch(config-if)# ip address 192.168.1.1 255.255.255.0
Switch(config-if)# ip helper-address 192.168.199.4
Switch(config-if)# exit
```

As a DHCP relay, the switch will intercept the broadcast DHCP messages from the client and will forward them on to the server address as unicast messages. The switch keeps track of the subnet where the client messages arrived so that it can relay the DHCP server responses back appropriately.

You can configure more than one helper address by repeating the **ip helper-address** command with different addresses. In this case, the switch will relay each DHCP request from a client to each of the helper addresses simultaneously. If more than one server replies, each reply will be relayed back to the client and the client will have to choose one acceptable response.

Exam Preparation Tasks

Review All Key Topics

Review the most important topics in the chapter, noted with the Key Topic icon in the outer margin of the page. Table 11-2 lists a reference of these key topics and the page numbers on which each is found.

Key Topic

Table 11-2 *Key Topics for Chapter 11*

Key Topic Element	Description	Page Number
Paragraph	Describes InterVLAN routing	220
Paragraph	Describes SVIs	221
Paragraph	Explains Layer 2 interface mode configuration	221
Paragraph	Explains Layer 3 interface mode configuration	222
Paragraph	Explains how to configure an SVI	223
Paragraph	Discusses the FIB and its contents	224
Paragraph	Explains the CEF Adjacency table	228
List	Explains which IP packet fields are changed during the packet rewrite process	231
List	Explains DHCP address negotiation	236
Paragraph	Discusses how to configure a DHCP relay	237

Complete Tables and Lists from Memory

Print a copy of Appendix C, "Memory Tables," (found on the CD), or at least the section for this chapter, and complete the tables and lists from memory. Appendix D, "Memory Tables Answer Key," also on the CD, includes completed tables and lists to check your work.

Define Key Terms

Define the following key terms from this chapter, and check your answers in the glossary:

interVLAN routing, SVI, FIB, adjacency table, packet rewrite, DHCP, DHCP relay

Use Command Reference to Check Your Memory

This section includes the most important configuration and EXEC commands covered in this chapter. It might not be necessary to memorize the complete syntax of every command, but you should be able to remember the basic keywords that are needed.

To test your memory of the interVLAN routing and CEF configuration and verification commands, use a piece of paper to cover the right side of Tables 11-3 through 11-5, respectively. Read the description on the left side, and then see how much of the command you can remember. Remember that the CCNP exam focuses on practical or hands-on skills that are used by a networking professional.

Table 11-3   *InterVLAN Routing Configuration Commands*

Task	Command Syntax
Put a port into Layer 2 mode.	Switch(config-if)# **switchport**
Put a port into Layer 3 mode.	Switch(config-if)# **no switchport**
Define an SVI.	Switch(config)# **interface vlan** *vlan-id*

Table 11-4   *Multilayer Switching Verification Commands*

Task	Command Syntax
Show a Layer 2 port status.	Switch# **show interface** *type mod/num* **switchport**
Show a Layer 3 port status.	Switch# **show interface** *type mod/num*
Show an SVI status.	Switch# **show interface vlan** *vlan-id*
View the FIB contents.	Switch# **show ip cef**
View FIB information for an interface.	Switch# **show ip cef** [*type mod/num* | **vlan** *vlan-id*] [**detail**]
View FIB information for an IP prefix.	Switch# **show ip cef** [*prefix-ip prefix-mask*] [**longer-prefixes**] [**detail**]
View FIB adjacency information.	Switch# **show adjacency** [*type mod/num* | **vlan** *vlan-id*] [**summary** | **detail**]
View counters for packets not switched by CEF.	Switch# **show cef not-cef-switched**

Table 11-5 *DHCP-Related Commands*

Task	Command Syntax
Exclude addresses from a DHCP server scope.	Switch(config-if)# **ip dhcp excluded-address** *start-ip end-ip*
Define a DHCP server scope.	Switch(config-if)# **ip dhcp pool** *pool-name*
Identify the IP subnet for the server scope.	Switch(config-dhcp)# **network** *ip-address subnet mask*
Identify the default router used in the server scope.	Switch(config-dhcp)# **default-router** *ip-address* [*ip-address2*] [*ip-address3*] ...
Define the DHCP server lease time.	Switch(config-dhcp)# **lease** {**infinite**	{*days* [*hours* [*minutes*]]}}
Enable DHCP relay on a Layer 3 interface.	Switch(config-if)# **ip helper-address** *ip-address*

Cisco Published SWITCH Exam Topics Covered in This Part

Implement high availability, given a network design and a set of requirements:

- Determine network resources needed for implementing high availability on a network

- Create a high-availability implementation plan

- Create a high-availability verification plan

- Implement first-hop redundancy protocols

- Implement switch supervisor redundancy

- Verify high-availability solution was implemented properly using show and debug commands

- Document results of high-availability implementation and verification

(Always check Cisco.com for the latest posted exam topics.)

Part III: Designing Campus Networks

This chapter covers the following topics that you need to master for the CCNP SWITCH exam:

Hierarchical Network Design—This section details a three-layer, hierarchical structure of campus network designs.

Modular Network Design—This section covers the process of designing a campus network, based on breaking it into functional modules. You also learn how to size and scale the modules in a design.

CHAPTER 12

Enterprise Campus Network Design

This chapter presents a logical design process that you can use to build a new switched campus network or to modify and improve an existing network. Networks can be designed in layers using a set of building blocks that can organize and streamline even a large, complex campus network. These building blocks then can be placed using several campus design models to provide maximum efficiency, functionality, and scalability.

"Do I Know This Already?" Quiz

The "Do I Know This Already?" quiz allows you to assess whether you should read this entire chapter thoroughly or jump to the "Exam Preparation Tasks" section. If you are in doubt based on your answers to these questions or your own assessment of your knowledge of the topics, read the entire chapter. Table 12-1 outlines the major headings in this chapter and the "Do I Know This Already?" quiz questions that go with them. You can find the answers in Appendix A, "Answers to the 'Do I Know This Already?' Quizzes."

Table 12-1 *"Do I Know This Already?" Foundation Topics Section-to-Question Mapping*

Foundation Topics Section	Questions Covered in This Section
Hierarchical Network Design	1–10
Modular Network Design	11–17

1. Where does a collision domain exist in a switched network?

   a. On a single switch port

   b. Across all switch ports

   c. On a single VLAN

   d. Across all VLANs

2. Where does a broadcast domain exist in a switched network?

   a. On a single switch port

   b. Across all switch ports

   c. On a single VLAN

   d. Across all VLANs

3. What is a VLAN primarily used for?

    a.   To segment a collision domain

    b.   To segment a broadcast domain

    c.   To segment an autonomous system

    d.   To segment a spanning-tree domain

4. How many layers are recommended in the hierarchical campus network design model?

    a.   1

    b.   2

    c.   3

    d.   4

    e.   7

5. What is the purpose of breaking a campus network into a hierarchical design?

    a.   To facilitate documentation

    b.   To follow political or organizational policies

    c.   To make the network predictable and scalable

    d.   To make the network more redundant and secure

6. End-user PCs should be connected into which of the following hierarchical layers?

    a.   Distribution layer

    b.   Common layer

    c.   Access layer

    d.   Core layer

7. In which OSI layer should devices in the distribution layer typically operate?

    a.   Layer 1

    b.   Layer 2

    c.   Layer 3

    d.   Layer 4

8. A hierarchical network's distribution layer aggregates which of the following?

    a.   Core switches

    b.   Broadcast domains

    c.   Routing updates

    d.   Access-layer switches

9. In the core layer of a hierarchical network, which of the following are aggregated?

   a. Routing tables

   b. Packet filters

   c. Distribution switches

   d. Access-layer switches

10. In a properly designed hierarchical network, a broadcast from one PC is confined to what?

    a. One access-layer switch port

    b. One access-layer switch

    c. One switch block

    d. The entire campus network

11. Which one or more of the following are the components of a typical switch block?

    a. Access-layer switches

    b. Distribution-layer switches

    c. Core-layer switches

    d. E-commerce servers

    e. Service provider switches

12. What are two types of core, or backbone, designs?

    a. Collapsed core

    b. Loop-free core

    c. Dual core

    d. Layered core

13. What is the maximum number of access-layer switches that can connect into a single distribution-layer switch?

    a. 1

    b. 2

    c. Limited only by the number of ports on the access-layer switch

    d. Limited only by the number of ports on the distribution-layer switch

    e. Unlimited

14. A switch block should be sized according to which two of the following parameters?

    a. The number of access-layer users

    b. A maximum of 250 access-layer users

    c. A study of the traffic patterns and flows

    d. The amount of rack space available

    e. The number of servers accessed by users

15. What evidence can be seen when a switch block is too large? (Choose all that apply.)

    a. IP address space is exhausted.

    b. You run out of access-layer switch ports.

    c. Broadcast traffic becomes excessive.

    d. Traffic is throttled at the distribution-layer switches.

    e. Network congestion occurs.

16. How many distribution switches should be built into each switch block?

    a. 1

    b. 2

    c. 4

    d. 8

17. What are the most important aspects to consider when designing the core layer in a large network? (Choose all that apply.)

    a. Low cost

    b. Switches that can efficiently forward traffic, even when every uplink is at 100 percent capacity

    c. High port density of high-speed ports

    d. A low number of Layer 3 routing peers

Foundation Topics

Hierarchical Network Design

A campus network is an enterprise network consisting of many LANs in one or more buildings, all connected and all usually in the same geographic area. A company typically owns the entire campus network and the physical wiring. Campus networks commonly consist of wired Ethernet LANs running at speeds of up to 10 Gbps and shared wireless LANs.

An understanding of traffic flow is a vital part of the campus network design. You might be able to leverage high-speed LAN technologies and "throw bandwidth" at a network to improve traffic movement. However, the emphasis should be on providing an overall design that is tuned to known, studied, or predicted traffic flows. The network traffic then can be effectively moved and managed, and you can scale the campus network to support future needs.

As a starting point, consider the simple network shown in Figure 12-1. A collection of PCs, printers, and servers are all connected to the same network segment and use the 192.168.1.0 subnet. All devices on this network segment must share the available bandwidth, and all are members of the same broadcast and collision domains.

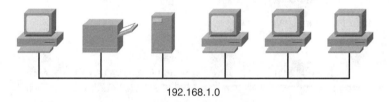

192.168.1.0

Figure 12-1 *Simple Shared Ethernet Network*

A network segment with six hosts might not seem crowded. Suppose the segment contains hundreds of hosts instead. Now the network might not perform very well. Through network segmentation, you can reduce the number of stations on a segment, which will help prevent collisions and broadcasts from reducing any one network segment's performance. By reducing the number of stations, the probability of a collision decreases because fewer stations can be transmitting at a given time. For broadcast containment, the idea is to provide a barrier at the edge of a LAN segment so that broadcasts cannot pass outward or be forwarded.

You can provide segmentation at Layer 3 by using either a router or a multilayer switch, as shown in Figure 12-2. The simple network of Figure 12-1 now has two segments or VLANs interconnected by Switch A, a multilayer switch. A Layer 3 device cannot propagate a collision condition from one segment to another, and it will not forward broadcasts between segments.

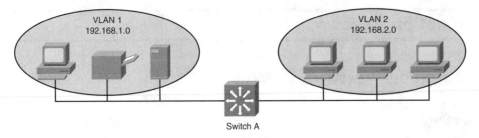

Figure 12-2 *Example of Network Segmentation*

The network might continue to grow as more users and devices are added to it. Switch A has a limited number of ports, so it cannot directly connect to every device. Instead, the network segments can be grown by adding a new switch to each, as shown in Figure 12-3.

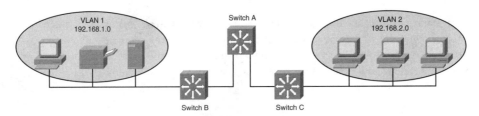

Figure 12-3 *Expanding a Segmented Network*

Switch B aggregates traffic to and from VLAN 1, while Switch C aggregates VLAN 2. As the network continues to grow, more VLANs can be added to support additional applications or user communities. As an example, Figure 12-4 shows how Voice over IP (VoIP) has been implemented by placing IP Phones into two new VLANs (10 and 20). The same two aggregating switches can easily support the new VLANs.

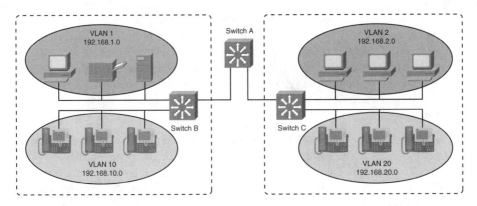

Figure 12-4 *Network Growth Through New VLANs*

Predictable Network Model

Ideally, you should design a network with a predictable behavior in mind to offer low maintenance and high availability. For example, a campus network needs to recover from failures and topology changes quickly and in a predetermined manner. You should scale the network to easily support future expansions and upgrades. With a wide variety of multiprotocol and multicast traffic, the network should be capable of efficiently connecting users with the resources they need, regardless of location.

In other words, design the network around traffic flows rather than a particular type of traffic. Ideally, the network should be arranged so that all end users are located at a consistent distance from the resources they need to use. If one user at one corner of the network passes through two switches to reach an email server, any other user at any other location in the network should also require two switch hops for email service.

Cisco has refined a hierarchical approach to network design that enables network designers to organize the network into distinct layers of devices. The resulting network is efficient, intelligent, scalable, and easily managed.

Key Topic

Figure 12-4 can be redrawn to emphasize the hierarchy that is emerging. In Figure 12-5, two layers become apparent: the access layer, where switches are placed closest to the end users; and the distribution layer, where access layer switches are aggregated.

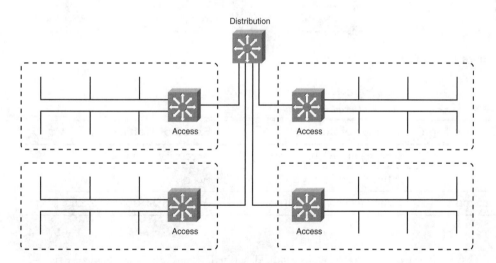

Figure 12-5   *Two-Layer Network Hierarchy Emerges*

As the network continues to grow, with more buildings, more floors, and larger groups of users, the number of access switches increases. As a result, the number of distribution switches increases. Now things have scaled to the point where the distribution switches need to be aggregated. This is done by adding a third layer to the hierarchy, the *core layer*, as shown in Figure 12-6.

Traffic flows in a campus network can be classified as three types, based on where the network service or resource is located in relation to the end user. Table 12-2 lists these types, along with the extent of the campus network that is crossed going from any user to the service.

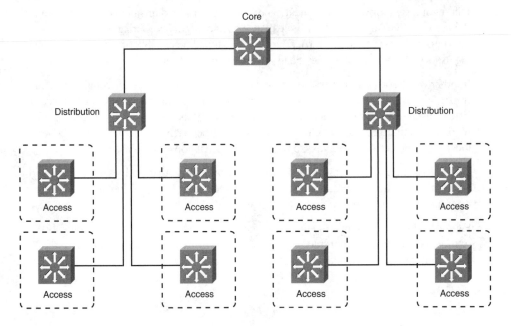

Figure 12-6   *Core Layer Emerges*

Table 12-2   *Types of Network Services*

Service Type	Location of Service	Extent of Traffic Flow
Local	Same segment/VLAN as user	Access layer only
Remote	Different segment/VLAN as user	Access to distribution layers
Enterprise	Central to all campus users	Access to distribution to core layers

Notice how easily the traffic paths can be described. Regardless of where the user is located, the traffic path always begins at the access layer and progresses into the distribution and perhaps into the core layers. Even a path between two users at opposite ends of the network becomes a consistent and predictable access > distribution > core > distribution > access layer.

Each layer has attributes that provide both physical and logical network functions at the appropriate point in the campus network. Understanding each layer and its functions or limitations is important to properly apply the layer in the design process.

Access Layer

The access layer is present where the end users are connected to the network. Access switches usually provide Layer 2 (VLAN) connectivity between users. Devices in this layer, sometimes called building access switches, should have the following capabilities:

- Low cost per switch port

- High port density

- Scalable uplinks to higher layers

- User access functions such as VLAN membership, traffic and protocol filtering, and quality of service (QoS)

- Resiliency through multiple uplinks

Distribution Layer

The distribution layer provides interconnection between the campus network's access and core layers. Devices in this layer, sometimes called building distribution switches, should have the following capabilities:

- Aggregation of multiple access-layer devices

- High Layer 3 throughput for packet handling

- Security and policy-based connectivity functions through access lists or packet filters

- QoS features

- Scalable and resilient high-speed links to the core and access layers

In the distribution layer, uplinks from all access-layer devices are aggregated, or come together. The distribution-layer switches must be capable of processing the total volume of traffic from all the connected devices. These switches should have a high port density of high-speed links to support the collection of access-layer switches.

VLANs and broadcast domains converge at the distribution layer, requiring routing, filtering, and security. The switches at this layer also must be capable of performing multilayer switching with high throughput.

Notice that the distribution layer usually is a Layer 3 boundary, where routing meets the VLANs of the access layer.

Core Layer

A campus network's core layer provides connectivity of all distribution-layer devices. The core, sometimes referred to as the backbone, must be capable of switching traffic as efficiently as possible. Core devices, sometimes called campus backbone switches, should have the following attributes:

- Very high throughput at Layer 3

- No costly or unnecessary packet manipulations (access lists, packet filtering)

■   Redundancy and resilience for high availability

■   Advanced QoS functions

Devices in a campus network's core layer or backbone should be optimized for high-performance switching. Because the core layer must handle large amounts of campuswide data, the core layer should be designed with simplicity and efficiency in mind.

Although campus network design is presented as a three-layer approach (access, distribution, and core layers), the hierarchy can be collapsed or simplified in certain cases. For example, small or medium-size campus networks might not have the size, multilayer switching, or volume requirements that would require the functions of all three layers. Here, you could combine the distribution and core layers for simplicity and cost savings. When the distribution and core layers are combined into a single layer of switches, a *collapsed core* network results.

Modular Network Design

Designing a new network that has a hierarchy with three layers is fairly straightforward. You can also migrate an existing network into a hierarchical design. The resulting network is organized, efficient, and predictable. However, a simple hierarchical design does not address other best practices like redundancy, in the case where a switch or a link fails, or scalability, when large additions to the network need to be added.

Consider the hierarchical network shown in the left portion of Figure 12-7. Each layer of the network is connected to the adjacent layer by single links. If a link fails, a significant portion of the network will become isolated. In addition, the access layer switches are aggregated into a single distribution layer switch. If that switch fails, all the users will become isolated.

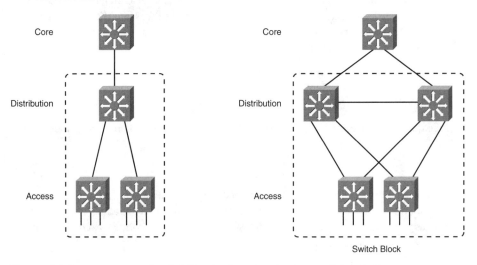

Figure 12-7   *Improving Availability in the Distribution and Access Layers*

To mitigate a potential distribution switch failure, you can add a second, redundant distribution switch. To mitigate a potential link failure, you can add redundant links from each access layer switch to each distribution switch. These improvements are shown in the right portion of Figure 12-7.

One weakness is still present in the redundant design of Figure 12-7: The core layer has only one switch. If that core switch fails, users in the access layer will still be able to communicate. However, they will not be able to reach other areas of the network, such as a data center, the Internet, and so on. To mitigate the effects of a core switch failure, you can add a second, redundant core switch, as shown in Figure 12-8. Now redundant links should be added between each distribution layer switch and each core layer switch.

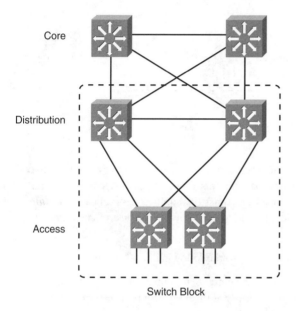

Figure 12-8 *Fully Redundant Hierarchical Network Design*

When the redundant switches and redundant links are added into the design, network growth can become confusing. For example, suppose many more access layer switches need to be added to the network of Figure 12-8 because several departments of users have moved into the building. Or perhaps they have moved into an adjacent building. Should the new access layer switches be dual-connected into the same two distribution switches? Should new distribution switches be added, too? If so, should each of the distribution switches be connected to every other distribution *and* every other core switch, creating a fully meshed network?

Figure 12-9 shows one possible network design that might result. There are so many interconnecting links between switches that it becomes a "brain-buster" exercise to figure out where VLANs are trunked, what the spanning-tree topologies look like, which links should have Layer 3 connectivity, and so on. Users might have connectivity through this network, but it might not be clear how they are actually working or what has gone wrong if they are not working. This network looks more like a spider web than an organized, streamlined design.

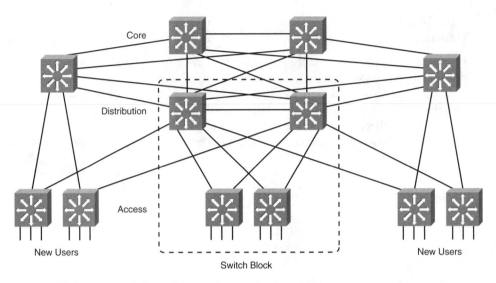

Figure 12-9   *Network Growth in a Disorganized Fashion*

To maintain organization, simplicity, and predictability, you can design a campus network in a logical manner, using a modular approach. In this approach, each layer of the hierarchical network model can be broken into basic functional units. These units, or *modules*, can then be sized appropriately and connected, while allowing for future scalability and expansion.

You can divide enterprise campus networks into the following basic elements:

■   **Switch block**—A group of access-layer switches, together with their distribution switches. The dashed rectangle in Figures 12-4 through 12-9 represents a switch block.

■   **Core block**—The campus network's backbone.

Other related elements can exist. Although these elements do not contribute to the campus network's overall function, they can be designed separately and added to the network design. For example, a data center can have its own access and distribution layer switches, forming a switch block that connects into the core layer. In fact, if the data center is very large, it might have its own core switches, too, which connect into the normal campus core.

Switch Block

Recall how a campus network is divided into access, distribution, and core layers. The switch block contains switching devices from the access and distribution layers. All switch blocks then connect into the core block, providing end-to-end connectivity across the campus.

Switch blocks contain a balanced mix of Layer 2 and Layer 3 functionality, as might be present in the access and distribution layers. Layer 2 switches located in wiring closets (access layer) connect end users to the campus network. With one end user per switch port, each user receives dedicated bandwidth access.

Upstream, each access-layer switch connects to devices in the distribution layer. Here, Layer 2 functionality transports data among all connected access switches at a central connection point. Layer 3 functionality also can be provided in the form of routing and other networking services (security, QoS, and so on). Therefore, a distribution-layer device should be a multilayer switch.

The distribution layer also shields the switch block from certain failures or conditions in other parts of the network. For example, broadcasts are not propagated from the switch block into the core and other switch blocks. Therefore, the Spanning Tree Protocol (STP) is confined to each switch block, where a VLAN is bounded, keeping the spanning-tree domain well defined and controlled.

Access-layer switches can support VLANs by assigning individual ports to specific VLAN numbers. In this way, stations connected to the ports configured for the same VLAN can share the same Layer 3 subnet. However, be aware that a single VLAN can support multiple subnets. Because the switch ports are configured for a VLAN number only (and not a network address), any station connected to a port can present any subnet address range. The VLAN functions as traditional network media and allows any network address to connect.

In this network design model, you should not extend VLANs beyond distribution switches. The distribution layer always should be the boundary of VLANs, subnets, and broadcasts. Although Layer 2 switches can extend VLANs to other switches and other layers of the hierarchy, this activity is discouraged. VLAN traffic should not traverse the network core.

Sizing a Switch Block

Containing access- and distribution-layer devices, the switch block is simple in concept. You should consider several factors, however, to determine an appropriate size for the switch block. The range of available switch devices makes the switch block size very flexible. At the access layer, switch selection usually is based on port density or the number of connected users.

The distribution layer must be sized according to the number of access-layer switches that are collapsed or brought into a distribution device. Consider the following factors:

- Traffic types and patterns

- Amount of Layer 3 switching capacity at the distribution layer

- Number of users connected to the access-layer switches

- Geographic boundaries of subnets or VLANs

- Size of spanning-tree domains

Designing a switch block based solely on the number of users or stations contained within the block is usually inaccurate. Usually, no more than 2000 users should be placed within a single switch block. Although this is useful for initially estimating a switch block's size, this idea doesn't take into account the many dynamic processes that occur on a functioning network.

Instead, switch block size should be based primarily on the following:

■   Traffic types and behavior

■   Size and number of common workgroups

Because of the dynamic nature of networks, you can size a switch block too large to handle the load that is placed on it. Also, the number of users and applications on a network tends to grow over time. A provision to break up or downsize a switch block is necessary. Again, base these decisions on the actual traffic flows and patterns present in the switch block. You can estimate, model, or measure these parameters with network-analysis applications and tools.

Note: The actual network-analysis process is beyond the scope of this book. Traffic estimation, modeling, and measurement are complex procedures, each requiring its own dedicated analysis tool.

Generally, a switch block is too large if the following conditions are observed:

■   The routers (multilayer switches) at the distribution layer become traffic bottlenecks. This congestion could be because of the volume of interVLAN traffic, intensive CPU processing, or switching times required by policy or security functions (access lists, queuing, and so on).

■   Broadcast or multicast traffic slows the switches in the switch block. Broadcast and multicast traffic must be replicated and forwarded out many ports. This process requires some overhead in the multilayer switch, which can become too great if significant traffic volumes are present.

Access switches can have one or more redundant links to distribution-layer devices. This situation provides a fault-tolerant environment in which access layer connectivity is preserved on a secondary link if the primary link fails. Because Layer 3 devices are used in the distribution layer, traffic can be load-balanced across both redundant links using redundant gateways.

Generally, you should provide two distribution switches in each switch block for redundancy, with each access-layer switch connecting to the two distribution switches. Then, each Layer 3 distribution switch can load-balance traffic over its redundant links into the core layer (also Layer 3 switches) using routing protocols.

Figure 12-10 shows a typical switch block design. At Layer 3, the two distribution switches can use one of several redundant gateway protocols to provide an active IP gateway and a standby gateway at all times. These protocols are discussed in Chapter 13, "Layer 3 High Availability."

Switch Block Redundancy

A switch block consists of two distribution switches that aggregate one or more access layer switches. Each access layer switch should have a pair of uplinks—one connecting to each distribution switch. The physical cabling is easy to draw, but the logical connectivity is not always obvious. For example, the left portion of Figure 12-11 shows a switch block that has a single VLAN that spans multiple access switches. You might find this where there are several separate physical switch chassis in an access layer room, or where two nearby communications rooms share a common VLAN. Notice how the single VLAN spans across every switch (both access and distribution) and across every link connecting the switches. This is necessary for the VLAN to be present on both access switches and to have redundant uplinks for high availability.

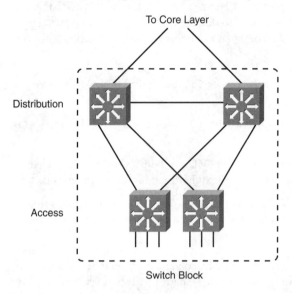

Figure 12-10 *Typical Switch Block Design*

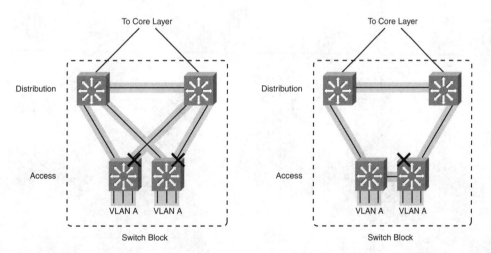

Figure 12-11 *Switch Block Redundancy Considerations*

Although this design works, it is not optimal and comes with the following consequences:

■   The switch block becomes fully dependent on spanning-tree convergence to keep the connections loop free. RSTP should be used on all the switches to improve the convergence time.

- The link between the two distribution switches must be a Layer 2 link. The access VLAN must extend across this link so that users on either access switch can reach the Layer 3 gateway.

Some people prefer to simplify the redundant connections by daisy chaining access layer switches, as shown in the rightmost portion of Figure 12-11. Each access switch has a single uplink to one of the distribution switches, so that the daisy chain of access switches has two redundant links as a whole. This design is not optimal, either; its consequences are as follows:

- The switch block depends on STP convergence; Rapid STP (RSTP) should be used whenever possible.

- The link between the two distribution switches must be a Layer 2 link that carries the access VLAN.

- The access layer switches must be connected by Layer 2 links along the daisy chain. Without these links, the access switches will not have a redundant path upward.

- When a link between two access switches fails, the users can become isolated from the Layer 3 gateway in the distribution layer. This can create strange behavior from the user's perspective.

Key Topic

As a best practice, all Layer 2 connectivity should be contained within the access layer. The distribution layer should have only Layer 3 links. Figure 12-12 shows two of the most common and best practice designs.

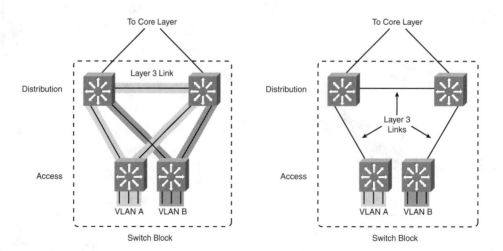

Figure 12-12 *Best Practice Designs for Switch Block Redundancy*

In the leftmost portion of Figure 12-12, VLANs do not span across switches at all. Each VLAN is contained within a single access-layer switch, switch chassis, or stacked switch, and extends across Layer 2 uplinks from each access-layer switch to each distribution switch. This best practice design offers the following attributes:

- No dependence on STP convergence; each VLAN extends to the distributions switches, but no further. Therefore, the STP topology is always converged.

- A Layer 3 link is needed between the distribution switches to carry routing updates.

It is also possible to keep Layer 2 VLANs limited to the access-layer switches. This design is shown in the rightmost portion of Figure 12-12 and is possible only if the access switches are Layer 3-capable. This best practice design offers the following attributes:

- No dependence on STP convergence; each VLAN extends to the distributions switches, but no further. Therefore, the STP topology is always converged.

- Layer 3 links between the access and distribution switches carry routing updates. Network stability is offered through the fast convergence of the routing protocol.

Core Block

A core block is required to connect two or more switch blocks in a campus network. Because all traffic passing to and from all switch blocks, data center blocks, and the enterprise edge block must cross the core block, the core must be as efficient and resilient as possible. The core is the campus network's basic foundation and carries much more traffic than any other block.

Recall that both the distribution and core layers provide Layer 3 functionality. The links between distribution and core layer switches can be Layer 3 routed interfaces. You can also use Layer 2 links that carry a small VLAN bounded by the two switches. In the latter case, a Layer 3 SVI is used to provide routing within each small VLAN.

The links between layers also should be designed to carry at least the amount of traffic load handled by the distribution switches. The links between core switches in the same core subnet should be of sufficient size to carry the aggregate amount of traffic coming into the core switch. Consider the average link utilization, but allow for future growth. An Ethernet core allows simple and scalable upgrades of magnitude; consider the progression from Ethernet to Fast Ethernet to Fast EtherChannel to Gigabit Ethernet to Gigabit Ether-Channel, and so on.

Two basic core block designs are presented in the following sections, each designed around a campus network's size:

- Collapsed core

- Dual core

Collapsed Core

A *collapsed core block* is one in which the hierarchy's core layer is collapsed into the distribution layer. Here, both distribution and core functions are provided within the same switch devices. This situation usually is found in smaller campus networks, where a separate core layer (and additional cost or performance) is not warranted.

Key Topic

Figure 12-13 shows the basic collapsed core design. Although the distribution- and core-layer functions are performed in the same device, keeping these functions distinct and properly designed is important. Note also that the collapsed core is not an independent building block but is integrated into the distribution layer of the individual standalone switch blocks.

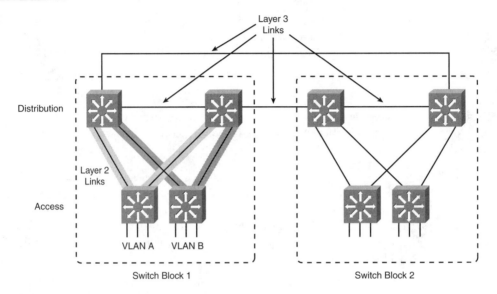

Figure 12-13   *Collapsed Core Design*

In the collapsed core design, each access-layer switch has a redundant link to each distribution- and core-layer switch. All Layer 3 subnets present in the access layer terminate at the distribution switches' Layer 3 ports, as in the basic switch block design. The distribution and core switches connect to each other by one or more links, completing a path to use during a redundancy failover.

Connectivity between the distribution and core switches is accomplished using Layer 3 links (Layer 3 switch interfaces, with no inherent VLANs). The Layer 3 switches route traffic to and from each other directly. Figure 2-3 shows the extent of two VLANs. Notice that VLAN A and VLAN B each extend only from the access-layer switches, where their respective users are located, down to the distribution layer over the Layer 2 uplinks. The VLANs terminate there because the distribution layer uses Layer 3 switching. This is good because it limits the broadcast domains, removes the possibility of Layer 2 bridging loops, and provides fast failover if one uplink fails.

At Layer 3, redundancy is provided through a redundant gateway protocol for IP (covered in Chapter 13). In some of the protocols, the two distribution switches provide a common default gateway address to the access-layer switches, but only one is active at any time. In other protocols, the two switches can both be active, load balancing traffic. If a distribution and core switch failure occurs, connectivity to the core is maintained because the redundant Layer 3 switch is always available.

Dual Core

A *dual core* connects two or more switch blocks in a redundant fashion. Although the collapsed core can connect two switch blocks with some redundancy, the core is not scalable when more switch blocks are added. Figure 12-14 illustrates the dual core. Notice that this core appears as an independent module and is not merged into any other block or layer.

Key Topic

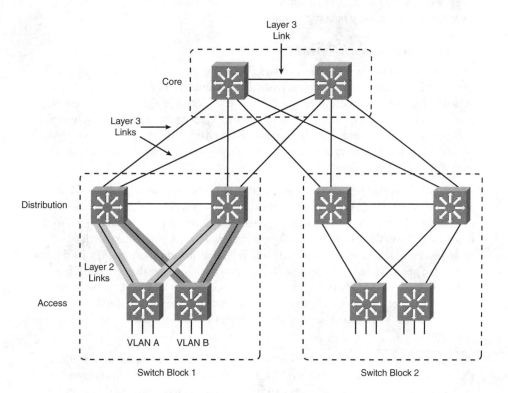

Figure 12-14 *Dual Core Design*

In the past, the dual core usually was built with Layer 2 switches to provide the simplest and most efficient throughput. Layer 3 switching was provided in the distribution layer. Multilayer switches now have become cost-effective and offer high switching performance. Building a dual core with multilayer switches is both possible and recommended. The dual core uses two identical switches to provide redundancy. Redundant links connect each switch block's distribution-layer portion to each of the dual core switches. The two core switches connect by a common link. In a Layer 2 core, the switches cannot be linked to avoid any bridging loops. A Layer 3 core uses routing rather than bridging, so bridging loops are not an issue.

In the dual core, each distribution switch has two equal-cost paths to the core, allowing the available bandwidth of both paths to be used simultaneously. Both paths remain active because the distribution and core layers use Layer 3 devices that can manage equal-cost paths in routing tables. The routing protocol in use determines the availability or loss of a neighboring Layer 3 device. If one switch fails, the routing protocol reroutes traffic using an alternative path through the remaining redundant switch.

Notice again in Figure 12-12 the extent of the access VLANs. Although Layer 3 devices have been added into a separate core layer, VLANs A and B still extend only from the Layer 2 access-layer switches down to the distribution layer. Although the distribution-layer switches use Layer 3 switch interfaces to provide Layer 3 functionality to the access layer, these links actually pass traffic only at Layer 2.

Core Size in a Campus Network

The dual core is made up of redundant switches and is bounded and isolated by Layer 3 devices. Routing protocols determine paths and maintain the core's operation. As with any network, you must pay some attention to the overall design of the routers and routing protocols in the network. Because routing protocols propagate updates throughout the network, network topologies might be undergoing change. The network's size (the number of routers) then affects routing protocol performance as updates are exchanged and network convergence takes place.

Although the network shown previously in Figure 12-14 might look small, with only two switch blocks of two Layer 3 switches (route processors within the distribution-layer switches) each, large campus networks can have many switch blocks connected into the core block. If you think of each multilayer switch as a router, you will recall that each route processor must communicate with and keep information about each of its directly connected peers. Most routing protocols have practical limits on the number of peer routers that can be directly connected on a point-to-point or multiaccess link. In a network with a large number of switch blocks, the number of connected routers can grow quite large. Should you be concerned about a core switch peering with too many distribution switches?

No, because the actual number of directly connected peers is quite small, regardless of the campus network size. Access-layer VLANs terminate at the distribution-layer switches. The only peering routers at that boundary are pairs of distribution switches, each providing routing redundancy for each of the access-layer VLAN subnets. At the distribution and core boundary, each distribution switch connects to only two core switches over Layer 3 switch interfaces. Therefore, only pairs of router peers are formed.

When multilayer switches are used in the distribution and core layers, the routing protocols running in both layers regard each pair of redundant links between layers as equal-cost paths. Traffic is routed across both links in a load-sharing fashion, utilizing the bandwidth of both.

One final core-layer design point is to scale the core switches to match the incoming load. At a minimum, each core switch must handle switching each of its incoming distribution links at 100 percent capacity.

Exam Preparation Tasks

Review All Key Topics

Review the most important topics in the chapter, noted with the Key Topic icon in the outer margin of the page. Table 12-3 lists a reference of these key topics and the page numbers on which each is found.

Key Topic

Table 12-3 *Key Topics for Chapter 12*

Key Topic Element	Description	Page Number
Paragraph	Describes the Cisco hierarchical network design principles	251
Paragraph	Describes the access layer	253
Paragraph	Describes the distribution layer	253
Paragraph	Describes the core layer	253
Paragraph	Explains modular network design using switch blocks	256
Paragraph	Discusses the pitfalls of letting VLANs span access layer switches	258
Paragraph	Discusses two best practice designs for switch block redundancy	260
Paragraph	Explains a collapsed core design	261
Paragraph	Discusses a dual core design	263

Complete Tables and Lists from Memory

Print a copy of Appendix C, "Memory Tables," (found on the CD), or at least the section for this chapter, and complete the tables and lists from memory. Appendix D, "Memory Tables Answer Key," also on the CD, includes completed tables and lists to check your work.

Define Key Terms

Define the following key terms from this chapter, and check your answers in the glossary:

hierarchical network design, access layer, distribution layer, core layer, switch block, collapsed core, dual core

This chapter covers the following topics that you need to master for the CCNP SWITCH exam:

Router Redundancy in Multilayer Switching—This section discusses three protocols that are available on Catalyst switches to provide redundant router or gateway addresses. The protocols include Hot Standby Routing Protocol (HSRP), Virtual Router Redundancy Protocol (VRRP), and Gateway Load Balancing Protocol (GLBP).

Supervisor and Route Processor Redundancy—This section covers the methods that can be used on some Catalyst switch platforms to operate an active-standby pair of hardware modules in one chassis. The redundancy modes include route processor redundancy (RPR), RPR+, stateful switchover (SSO), and nonstop forwarding (NSF).

CHAPTER 13

Layer 3 High Availability

A multilayer switch can provide routing functions for devices on a network, as described in Chapter 11, "Multilayer Switching." If that switch happens to fail, clients have no way of having their traffic forwarded; their gateway has gone away.

Other multilayer switches can be added into the network to provide redundancy in the form of redundant router or gateway addresses. This chapter describes the protocols that can be used for redundant router addresses, load balancing across multiple routers, and load balancing into a server farm.

This chapter also describes the features that support redundancy in hardware. Within a single multilayer switch chassis, two supervisor modules with integrated route processors can be used to provide hardware redundancy. If an entire supervisor module fails, the other module can pick up the pieces and continue operating the switch.

"Do I Know This Already?" Quiz

The "Do I Know This Already?" quiz allows you to assess whether you should read this entire chapter thoroughly or jump to the "Exam Preparation Tasks" section. If you are in doubt based on your answers to these questions or your own assessment of your knowledge of the topics, read the entire chapter. Table 13-1 outlines the major headings in this chapter and the "Do I Know This Already?" quiz questions that go with them. You can find the answers in Appendix A, "Answers to the 'Do I Know This Already?' Quizzes."

Table 13-1 *"Do I Know This Already?" Foundation Topics Section-to-Question Mapping*

Foundation Topics Section	Questions Covered in This Section
Router Redundancy in Multilayer Switching	1–10
Supervisor and Route Processor Redundancy	11–12

1. Which one of the following do multilayer switches share when running HSRP?

   a. Routing tables

   b. ARP cache

   c. CAM table

   d. IP address

2. What HSRP group uses the MAC address 0000.0c07.ac11?

    a. Group 0

    b. Group 7

    c. Group 11

    d. Group 17

3. Two routers are configured for an HSRP group. One router uses the default HSRP priority. What priority should be assigned to the other router to make it more likely to be the active router?

    a. 1

    b. 100

    c. 200

    d. 500

4. How many routers are in the Standby state in an HSRP group?

    a. 0

    b. 1

    c. 2

    d. All but the active router

5. A multilayer switch is configured as follows:

```
interface fastethernet 1/1
no switchport
ip address 192.168.199.3 255.255.255.0
standby 1 ip 192.168.199.2
```

Which IP address should a client PC use as its default gateway?

    a. 192.168.199.1

    b. 192.168.199.2

    c. 192.168.199.3

    d. Any of these

6. Which one of the following is based on an IETF RFC standard?

    a. HSRP

    b. VRRP

    c. GLBP

    d. STP

7. What VRRP group uses the virtual MAC address 0000.5e00.01ff?

   a. Group 0

   b. Group 1

   c. Group 255

   d. Group 94

8. Which one of the following protocols is the best choice for load balancing redundant gateways?

   a. HSRP

   b. VRRP

   c. GLBP

   d. GVRP

9. Which one of the following GLBP functions answers ARP requests?

   a. AVF

   b. VARP

   c. AVG

   d. MVR

10. By default, which of the following virtual MAC addresses will be sent to the next client that looks for the GLBP virtual gateway?

    a. The GLBP interface's MAC address

    b. The next virtual MAC address in the sequence

    c. The virtual MAC address of the least-used router

    d. 0000.0c07.ac00

11. Which one of these features is used to reduce the amount of time needed to rebuild the routing information after a supervisor module failure?

    a. NFS

    b. NSF

    c. RPR+

    d. SSO

12. Which one of the following features provides the fastest failover for supervisor or route processor redundancy?

    a. SSL

    b. SSO

    c. RPR+

    d. RPR

Foundation Topics

Router Redundancy in Multilayer Switching

Multilayer switches can act as IP gateways for connected hosts by providing gateway addresses at VLAN SVIs and Layer 3 physical interfaces. These switches can also participate in routing protocols, just as traditional routers do.

For high availability, multilayer switches should offer a means of preventing one switch (gateway) failure from isolating an entire VLAN. This chapter discusses several approaches to providing router redundancy, including the following:

■   Hot Standby Router Protocol (HSRP)

■   Virtual Router Redundancy Protocol (VRRP)

■   Gateway Load Balancing Protocol (GLBP)

These are also commonly called first-hop redundancy protocols (FHRP) because the first router hop is given high availability.

Packet-Forwarding Review

When a host must communicate with a device on its local subnet, it can generate an Address Resolution Protocol (ARP) request, wait for the ARP reply, and exchange packets directly. However, if the far end is located on a different subnet, the host must rely on an intermediate system (a router, for example) to relay packets to and from that subnet.

A host identifies its nearest router, also known as the *default gateway* or *next hop*, by its IP address. If the host understands something about routing, it recognizes that all packets destined off-net must be sent to the gateway's MAC address rather than the far end's MAC address. Therefore, the host first sends an ARP request to find the gateway's MAC address. Then packets can be relayed to the gateway directly without having to look for ARP entries for individual destinations.

If the host is not so savvy about routing, it might still generate ARP requests for every off-net destination, hoping that someone will answer. Obviously, the off-net destinations cannot answer because they never receive the ARP request broadcasts; these requests are not forwarded across subnets. Instead, you can configure the gateway to provide a proxy ARP function so that it will reply to ARP requests with its own MAC address, as if the destination itself had responded.

Now the issue of gateway availability becomes important. If the gateway router for a subnet or VLAN goes down, packets have no way of being forwarded off the local subnet. Several protocols are available that allow multiple routing devices to share a common gateway address so that if one goes down, another automatically can pick up the active gateway role. The sections that follow describe these protocols.

Hot Standby Router Protocol

HSRP is a Cisco-proprietary protocol developed to allow several routers (or multilayer switches) to appear as a single gateway IP address. RFC 2281 describes this protocol in more detail.

Basically, each of the routers that provides redundancy for a given gateway address is assigned to a common HSRP group. One router is elected as the primary, or *active,* HSRP router; another is elected as the *standby* HSRP router; and all the others remain in the *listen* HSRP state. The routers exchange HSRP hello messages at regular intervals so that they can remain aware of each other's existence and that of the active router.

Note: HSRP sends its hello messages to the multicast destination 224.0.0.2 ("all routers") using UDP port 1985.

An HSRP group can be assigned an arbitrary group number, from 0 to 255. If you configure HSRP groups on several VLAN interfaces, it can be handy to make the group number the same as the VLAN number. However, most Catalyst switches support only up to 16 unique HSRP group numbers. If you have more than 16 VLANs, you will quickly run out of group numbers. An alternative is to make the group number the same (that is, 1) for every VLAN interface. This is perfectly valid because the HSRP groups are locally significant only on an interface. In other words, HSRP Group 1 on interface VLAN 10 is unique and independent from HSRP Group 1 on interface VLAN 11.

HSRP Router Election

HSRP election is based on a priority value (0 to 255) that is configured on each router in the group. By default, the priority is 100. The router with the highest priority value (255 is highest) becomes the active router for the group. If all router priorities are equal or set to the default value, the router with the highest IP address on the HSRP interface becomes the active router. To set the priority, use the following interface configuration command:

```
Switch(config-if)# standby group priority priority
```

For example, suppose that one switch is left at its default priority of 100, while the local switch is intended to win the active role election. You can use the following command to set the HSRP priority to 200:

```
Switch(config-if)# standby 1 priority 200
```

When HSRP is configured on an interface, the router progresses through a series of states before becoming active. This forces a router to listen for others in a group and see where it fits into the pecking order. Devices participating in HSRP must progress their interfaces through the following state sequence:

1. Disabled

2. Init

3. Listen

4. Speak

5. Standby

6. Active

Only the standby (the one with the second-highest priority) router monitors the hello messages from the active router. By default, hellos are sent every 3 seconds. If hellos are missed for the duration of the holdtime timer (default 10 seconds, or three times the hello timer), the active router is presumed to be down. The standby router is then clear to assume the active role.

At that point, if other routers are sitting in the Listen state, the next-highest priority router is allowed to become the new standby router.

If you need to change the timer values, use the following interface configuration command. If you decide to change the timers on a router, you should change them identically on all routers in the HSRP group.

```
Switch(config-if)# standby group timers [msec] hello [msec] holdtime
```

The hello and holdtime values can be given in seconds or in milliseconds, if the **msec** keyword precedes a value. The hello time can range from 1 to 254 seconds or from 15 to 999 milliseconds. The holdtime always should be at least three times the hello timer and can range from 1 to 255 seconds or 50 to 3000 milliseconds.

As an example, the following command can be used to set the hello time at 100 milliseconds and the holdtime to 300 milliseconds:

```
Switch(config-if)# standby 1 timers msec 100 msec 300
```

Note: Be aware that decreasing the HSRP hello time allows a router failure to be detected more quickly. At the same time, HSRP hellos will be sent more often, increasing the amount of traffic on the interface.

Normally, after the active router fails and the standby becomes active, the original active router cannot immediately become active when it is restored. In other words, if a router is not already active, it cannot become active again until the current active router fails—even if its priority is higher than that of the active router. An interesting case arises when routers are just being powered up or added to a network. The first router to bring up its interface becomes the HSRP active router, even if it has the lowest priority of all.

You can configure a router to preempt or immediately take over the active role if its priority is the highest *at any time*. Use the following interface configuration command to allow preemption:

```
Switch(config-if)# standby group preempt [delay [minimum seconds] [reload
  seconds]]
```

By default, the local router immediately can preempt another router that has the active role. To delay the preemption, use the **delay** keyword followed by one or both of the following parameters:

- Add the **minimum** keyword to force the router to wait for *seconds* (0 to 3600 seconds) before attempting to overthrow an active router with a lower priority. This delay time begins as soon as the router is capable of assuming the active role, such as after an interface comes up or after HSRP is configured.

- Add the **reload** keyword to force the router to wait for *seconds* (0 to 3600 seconds) after it has been reloaded or restarted. This is handy if there are routing protocols that need time to converge. The local router should not become the active gateway before its routing table is fully populated; otherwise, it might not be capable of routing traffic properly.

- HSRP also can use an authentication method to prevent unexpected devices from spoofing or participating in HSRP. All routers in the same standby group must have an identical authentication method and key. You can use either plain-text or MD5 authentication, as described in the following sections.

Plain-Text HSRP Authentication

HSRP messages are sent with a plain-text key string (up to eight characters) as a simple method to authenticate HSRP peers. If the key string in a message matches the key configured on an HSRP peer, the message is accepted.

When keys are sent in the clear, they can be easily intercepted and used to impersonate legitimate peers. Plain-text authentication is intended only to prevent peers with a default configuration from participating in HSRP. Cisco devices use cisco as the default key string.

You can configure a plain-text authentication key for an HSRP group with the following interface configuration command:

```
Switch(config-if)# standby group authentication string
```

MD5 Authentication

A Message Digest 5 (MD5) hash is computed on a portion of each HSRP message and a secret key known only to legitimate HSRP group peers. The MD5 hash value is sent along with HSRP messages. As a message is received, the peer recomputes the hash of the expected message contents and its own secret key; if the hash values are identical, the message is accepted.

MD5 authentication is more secure than plain-text authentication because the hash value contained in the HSRP messages is extremely difficult (if not impossible) to reverse. The hash value itself is not used as a key; instead, the hash is used to validate the message contents.

You can configure MD5 authentication by associating a key string with an interface, using the following interface configuration command:

```
Switch(config-if)# standby group authentication md5 key-string [0 | 7] string
```

By default, the key *string* (up to 64 characters) is given as plain text. This is the same as specifying the **0** keyword. After the key string is entered, it is shown as an encrypted value in the switch configuration. You also can copy and paste an encrypted key string value into this command by preceding the string with the **7** keyword.

Alternatively, you can define an MD5 key string as a key on a key chain. This method is more flexible, enabling you to define more than one key on the switch. Any of the keys then can be associated with HSRP on any interface. If a key needs to be changed, you simply add a new key to the key chain and retire (delete) an old key.

First define the key chain globally with the **key chain** command; then add one key at a time with the **key** and **key-string** commands. The *key-number* index is arbitrary, but keys are tried in sequential order. Finally, associate the key chain with HSRP on an interface by referencing its *chain-name*. You can use the following commands to configure HSRP MD5 authentication:

```
Switch(config)# key chain chain-name
Switch(config-keychain)# key key-number
Switch(config-keychain-key)# key-string [0 | 7] string
Switch(config)# interface type mod/num
Switch(config-if)# standby group authentication md5 key-chain chain-name
```

Tip: HSRP MD5 authentication was introduced into some Catalyst switch platforms with Cisco IOS Software Release 12.2(25)S. At the time of this writing, this feature is available only on the Catalyst 3560 and 3750.

Conceding the Election

Consider an active router in an HSRP group: A group of clients sends packets to it for forwarding, and it has one or more links to the rest of the world. If one of those links fails, the router remains active. If all of those links fail, the router still remains active. But sooner or later, the path to the rest of the world is either crippled or removed, and packets from the clients no longer can be forwarded.

HSRP has a mechanism for detecting link failures and swaying the election, giving another router an opportunity to take over the active role. When a specific interface is tracked, HSRP reduces the router's priority by a configurable amount as soon as the interface goes down. If more than one interface is tracked, the priority is reduced even more with each failed interface. The priority is incremented by the same amount as interfaces come back up.

This is particularly useful when a switch has several paths out of a VLAN or subnet; as more interfaces fail and remove the possible paths, other HSRP peers should appear to be more desirable and take over the active role. To configure interface tracking, use the following interface configuration command:

```
Switch(config-if)# standby group track type mod/num [decrementvalue]
```

By default, the *decrementvalue* for an interface is 10. Keep in mind that interface tracking does not involve the state of the HSRP interface itself. Instead, the state of other specific interfaces affects the usefulness of the local router as a gateway. You also should be aware that the only way another router can take over the active role after interface tracking reduces the priority is if the following two conditions are met:

■ Another router now has a higher HSRP priority.

■ That same router is using **preempt** in its HSRP configuration.

Without preemption, the active role cannot be given to any other router.

HSRP Gateway Addressing

Each router in an HSRP group has its own unique IP address assigned to an interface. This address is used for all routing protocol and management traffic initiated by or destined to the router. In addition, each router has a common gateway IP address, the virtual router address, which is kept alive by HSRP. This address also is referred to as the *HSRP address* or the *standby address*. Clients can point to that virtual router address as their default gateway, knowing that a router always keeps that address active. Keep in mind that the actual interface address and the virtual (standby) address must be configured to be in the same IP subnet.

You can assign the HSRP address with the following interface command:

```
Switch(config-if)# standby group ip ip-address [secondary]
```

When HSRP is used an interface that has secondary IP addresses, you can add the **secondary** keyword so that HSRP can provide a redundant secondary gateway address.

Naturally, each router keeps a unique MAC address for its interface. This MAC address is always associated with the unique IP address configured on the interface. For the virtual router address, HSRP defines a special MAC address of the form 0000.0c07.ac*xx*, where *xx* represents the HSRP group number as a two-digit hex value. For example, HSRP Group 1 appears as 0000.0c07.ac01, HSRP Group 16 appears as 0000.0c07.ac10, and so on.

Figure 13-1 shows a simple network in which two multilayer switches use HSRP Group 1 to provide the redundant gateway address 192.168.1.1. CatalystA is the active router, with priority 200, and answers the ARP request for the gateway address. Because CatalystB is in the Standby state, it never is used for traffic sent to 192.168.1.1. Instead, only CatalystA performs the gateway routing function, and only its uplink to the access layer is utilized.

Example 13-1 shows the configuration commands you can use on CatalystA. CatalystB would be configured similarly, except that its HSRP priority would use the default value of 100.

Example 13-1 *Configuring an HSRP Group on a Switch*

```
CatalystA(config)# interface vlan 50
CatalystA(config-if)# ip address 192.168.1.10 255.255.255.0
CatalystA(config-if)# standby 1 priority 200
CatalystA(config-if)# standby 1 preempt
CatalystA(config-if)# standby 1 ip 192.168.1.1
```

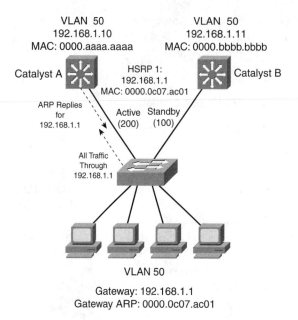

Figure 13-1   *Typical HSRP Scenario with One HSRP Group*

Load Balancing with HSRP

Consider a network in which HSRP is used on two distribution switches to provide a redundant gateway address for access-layer users. Only one of the two becomes the active HSRP router; the other remains in standby. All the users send their traffic to the active router over the uplink to the active router. The standby router and its uplink essentially sit idle until a router failure occurs.

Load balancing traffic across two uplinks to two HSRP routers with a single HSRP group is not possible. Then how is it possible to load balance with HSRP? The trick is to use two HSRP groups:

■   One group assigns an active router to one switch.

■   The other group assigns another active router to the other switch.

In this way, two different virtual router or gateway addresses can be used simultaneously. The rest of the trick is to make each switch function as the standby router for its partner's HSRP group. In other words, each router is active for one group and standby for the other group. The clients or end users also must have their default gateway addresses configured as one of the two virtual HSRP group addresses.

Figure 13-2 presents this scenario. Now, CatalystA is not only the active router for HSRP Group 1 (192.168.1.1), but it is also the standby router for HSRP Group 2 (192.168.1.2). CatalystB is configured similarly, but with its roles reversed. The remaining step is to configure half of the client PCs with the HSRP Group 1 virtual router address and the other half with the Group 2 address. This makes load balancing possible and effective. Each half of the hosts uses one switch as its gateway over one uplink.

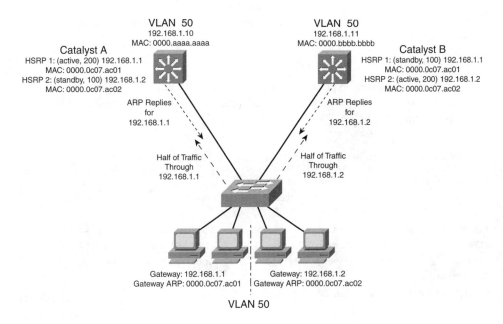

Figure 13-2 *Load Balancing with Two HSRP Groups*

Example 13-2 shows the configuration commands you can use for the scenario shown in Figure 13-2.

Example 13-2 *Configuring Load Balancing Between HSRP Groups*

```
CatalystA(config)# interface vlan 50
CatalystA(config-if)# ip address 192.168.1.10 255.255.255.0
CatalystA(config-if)# standby 1 priority 200
CatalystA(config-if)# standby 1 preempt
CatalystA(config-if)# standby 1 ip 192.168.1.1
CatalystA(config-if)# standby 1 authentication MyKey
CatalystA(config-if)# standby 2 priority 100
CatalystA(config-if)# standby 2 ip 192.168.1.2
CatalystA(config-if)# standby 2 authentication MyKey
CatalystB(config)# interface vlan 50
CatalystB(config-if)# ip address 192.168.1.11 255.255.255.0
CatalystB(config-if)# standby 1 priority 100
CatalystB(config-if)# standby 1 ip 192.168.1.1
CatalystB(config-if)# standby 1 authentication MyKey
CatalystB(config-if)# standby 2 priority 200
CatalystB(config-if)# standby 2 preempt
CatalystB(config-if)# standby 2 ip 192.168.1.2
CatalystB(config-if)# standby 2 authentication MyKey
```

You can use the following command to display information about the status of one or more HSRP groups and interfaces:

```
Router# show standby [brief] [vlan vlan-id | type mod/num]
```

Based on the configuration in Example 13-2, the output in Example 13-3 shows that the CatalystA switch is the active router for HSRP group 1 and the standby router for HSRP group 2 on interface VLAN 50.

Example 13-3   *Displaying the HSRP Router Role of a Switch: CatalystA*

```
CatalystA# show standby vlan 50 brief
                       P indicates configured to preempt.
                       |
Interface   Grp Prio P State    Active addr      Standby addr    Group addr
Vl50         1   200 P Active   local                192.168.1.11    192.168.1.1
Vl50         2   100   Standby  192.168.1.11    local           192.168.1.2
CatalystA#
CatalystA# show standby vlan 50
Vlan50 - Group 1

  Local state is Active, priority 200, may preempt
  Hellotime 3 sec, holdtime 10 sec
  Next hello sent in 2.248
  Virtual IP address is 192.168.1.1 configured
  Active router is local
  Standby router is 192.168.1.11 expires in 9.860
  Virtual mac address is 0000.0c07.ac01
  Authentication text "MyKey"
  2 state changes, last state change 00:11:58
  IP redundancy name is "hsrp-Vl50-1" (default)
Vlan50 - Group 2
  Local state is Standby, priority 100
  Hellotime 3 sec, holdtime 10 sec
  Next hello sent in 1.302
  Virtual IP address is 192.168.1.2 configured
  Active router is 192.168.1.11, priority 200 expires in 7.812
  Standby router is local
  Authentication text "MyKey"
  4 state changes, last state change 00:10:04
  IP redundancy name is "hsrp-Vl50-2" (default)
CatalystA#
```

The output from CatalystB in Example 13-4 shows that it has inverted roles from CatalystA for HSRP Groups 1 and 2.

Example 13-4   *Displaying the HSRP Router Role of a Switch: CatalystB*

```
CatalystB# show standby vlan 50 brief
                        P indicates configured to preempt.
                        |
Interface   Grp  Prio P State   Active addr    Standby addr    Group addr
Vl50        1    100    Standby 192.168.1.10   local           192.168.1.1
Vl50        2    200  P Active  local          192.168.1.10    192.168.1.2
CatalystB#
CatalystB# show standby vlan 50
Vlan50 - Group 1

  Local state is Standby, priority 100
  Hellotime 3 sec, holdtime 10 sec
  Next hello sent in 0.980
  Virtual IP address is 192.168.1.1 configured
  Active router is 192.168.1.10, priority 200 expires in 8.128
  Standby router is local
  Authentication text "MyKey"
  1 state changes, last state change 00:01:12
  IP redundancy name is "hsrp-Vl50-1" (default)
Vlan50 - Group 2
  Local state is Active, priority 200, may preempt
  Hellotime 3 sec, holdtime 10 sec
  Next hello sent in 2.888
  Virtual IP address is 192.168.1.2 configured
  Active router is local
  Standby router is 192.168.1.10 expires in 8.500
  Virtual mac address is 0000.0c07.ac02
  Authentication text "MyKey"
  1 state changes, last state change 00:01:16
CatalystB#
```

Virtual Router Redundancy Protocol

The Virtual Router Redundancy Protocol (VRRP) is a standards-based alternative to HSRP, defined in IETF standard RFC 2338. VRRP is so similar to HSRP that you need to learn only slightly different terminology and a couple of slight functional differences. When you understand HSRP operation and configuration, you will also understand VRRP. This section is brief, highlighting only the differences between HSRP and VRRP.

VRRP provides one redundant gateway address from a group of routers. The active router is called the *master router*, whereas all others are in the *backup state*. The master router is the one with the highest router priority in the VRRP group.

Key
Topic

VRRP group numbers range from 0 to 255; router priorities range from 1 to 254. (254 is the highest, 100 is the default.)

The virtual router MAC address is of the form 0000.5e00.01*xx*, where *xx* is a two-digit hex VRRP group number.

VRRP advertisements are sent at 1-second intervals. Backup routers optionally can learn the advertisement interval from the master router.

By default, all VRRP routers are configured to preempt the current master router if their priorities are greater.

Note: VRRP sends its advertisements to the multicast destination address 224.0.0.18 (VRRP), using IP protocol 112. VRRP was introduced in Cisco IOS Software Release 12.0(18)ST for routers. At press time, VRRP is available only for the Catalyst 4500 (Cisco IOS Release 12.2[31]SG), Catalyst 6500 Supervisor 2 (Cisco IOS Software Release 12.2[9]ZA or later) and Catalyst 6500 Supervisor 720 (Cisco IOS Software Release 12.2[17a]SX4 or later).

To configure VRRP, use the interface configuration commands documented in Table 13-2.

Table 13-2   *VRRP Configuration Commands*

Task	Command Syntax
Assign a VRRP router priority (default 100).	**vrrp** *group* **priority** *level*
Alter the advertisement timer (default 1 second).	**vrrp** *group* **timers advertise** [*msec*] *interval*
Learn the advertisement interval from the master router.	**vrrp** *group* **timers learn**
Disable preempting (default is to preempt).	**no vrrp** *group* **preempt**
Change the preempt delay (default 0 seconds).	**vrrp** *group* **preempt** [**delay** *seconds*]
Use authentication for advertisements.	**vrrp** *group* **authentication** *string*
Assign a virtual IP address.	**vrrp** *group* **ip** *ip-address* [**secondary**]
Track an object.	**vrrp** *group* **track** *object-number* [**decrement** *priority*]

As an example, the load-balancing scenario shown in Figure 13-2 is implemented using VRRP. You would use the configuration commands in Example 13-5 on the two Catalyst switches.

Example 13-5   *Configuring Load Balancing with VRRP*

```
CatalystA(config)# interface vlan 50
CatalystA(config-if)# ip address 192.168.1.10 255.255.255.0
CatalystA(config-if)# vrrp 1 priority 200
CatalystA(config-if)# vrrp 1 ip 192.168.1.1
```

```
CatalystA(config-if)# vrrp 2 priority 100
CatalystA(config-if)# no vrrp 2 preempt
CatalystA(config-if)# vrrp 2 ip 192.168.1.2
CatalystB(config)# interface vlan 50
CatalystB(config-if)# ip address 192.168.1.11 255.255.255.0
CatalystB(config-if)# vrrp 1 priority 100
CatalystB(config-if)# no vrrp 1 preempt
CatalystB(config-if)# vrrp 1 ip 192.168.1.1
CatalystB(config-if)# vrrp 2 priority 200
CatalystB(config-if)# vrrp 2 ip 192.168.1.2
```

You can use the following command to display information about VRRP status on one or more interfaces:

```
Switch# show vrrp [brief]
```

Example 13-6 shows this command executed on both CatalystA and CatalystB, with the output showing the alternating roles for the two VRRP groups configured in Example 13-5.

Example 13-6   *Displaying Switch Roles for VRRP Load Balancing*

```
CatalystA# show vrrp brief
Interface       Grp Pri Time  Own Pre State   Master addr    Group addr
Vlan50            1   200 3218      Y  Master  192.168.1.10   192.168.1.1
Vlan50            2   100 3609         Backup  192.168.1.11   192.168.1.2
CatalystA#
CatalystB# show vrrp brief
Interface       Grp Pri Time  Own Pre State   Master addr    Group addr
Vlan50            1   100 3609         Backup  192.168.1.10   192.168.1.1
Vlan50            2   200 3218      Y  Master  192.168.1.11   192.168.1.2
CatalystB#
```

Table 13-3 compares the detailed VRRP status between the CatalystA and CatalystB switches.

Table 13-3   *Verifying VRRP Status for Multiple VRRP Groups*

CatalystA	CatalystB
CatalystA# **show vrrp**	CatalystB# **show vrrp**
Vlan50 - Group 1	Vlan50 - Group 1
State is Master	State is Backup
Virtual IP address is 192.168.1.1	Virtual IP address is 192.168.1.1
Virtual MAC address is 0000.5e00.0101	Virtual MAC address is 0000.5e00.0101
Advertisement interval is 1.000 sec	Advertisement interval is 1.000 sec
Preemption is enabled	Preemption is disabled
min delay is 0.000 sec	Priority is 100
Priority is 200	Authentication is enabled
Authentication is enabled	Master Router is 192.168.1.10, priority
Master Router is 192.168.1.10 (local),	is 200
priority is 200	Master Advertisement interval is 1.000
Master Advertisement interval is 1.000	sec
sec	Master Down interval is 3.609 sec
Master Down interval is 3.218 sec	(expires in 2.833 sec)
Vlan50 - Group 2	Vlan50 - Group 2
State is Backup	State is Master
Virtual IP address is 192.168.1.2	Virtual IP address is 192.168.1.2
Virtual MAC address is 0000.5e00.0102	Virtual MAC address is 0000.5e00.0102
Advertisement interval is 1.000 sec	Advertisement interval is 1.000 sec
Preemption is disabled	Preemption is enabled
Priority is 100	min delay is 0.000 sec
Authentication is enabled	Priority is 200
Master Router is 192.168.1.11, priority	Authentication is enabled
is 200	Master Router is 192.168.1.11 (local),
Master Advertisement interval is 1.000	priority is 200
sec	Master Advertisement interval is 1.000
Master Down interval is 3.609 sec	sec
(expires in 2.977 sec)	Master Down interval is 3.218 sec
CatalystA#	CatalystB#

Gateway Load Balancing Protocol

You should now know how both HSRP and VRRP can effectively provide a redundant gateway (virtual router) address. You can accomplish load balancing by configuring only multiple HSRP/VRRP groups to have multiple virtual router addresses. More manual configuration is needed so that the client machines are divided among the virtual routers. Each group of clients must point to the appropriate virtual router. This makes load balancing somewhat labor-intensive, having a more or less fixed, or static, behavior.

The Gateway Load Balancing Protocol (GLBP) is a Cisco-proprietary protocol designed to overcome the limitations of existing redundant router protocols. Some of the concepts are the same as with HSRP/VRRP, but the terminology is different, and the behavior is much more dynamic and robust.

Note: GLBP was introduced in Cisco IOS Software Release 12.2(14)S for routers. At the
time of this writing, GLBP is available only for the Catalyst 6500 Supervisor 2 with IOS
Release 12.2(14)SY4 or later and Supervisor 720 with IOS Release 12.2(17a)SX4 switch platforms.

To provide a virtual router, multiple switches (routers) are assigned to a common GLBP
group. Instead of having just one active router performing forwarding for the virtual router
address, *all* routers in the group can participate and offer load balancing by forwarding a
portion of the overall traffic.

The advantage is that none of the clients has to be pointed toward a specific gateway address; they can all have the same default gateway set to the virtual router IP address. The
load balancing is provided completely through the use of virtual router MAC addresses in
ARP replies returned to the clients. As a client sends an ARP request looking for the virtual router address, GLBP sends back an ARP reply with the virtual MAC address of a selected router in the group. The result is that all clients use the same gateway address but
have differing MAC addresses for it.

Active Virtual Gateway

The trick behind this load balancing lies in the GLBP group. One router is elected the
active virtual gateway (AVG). This router has the highest priority value, or the highest IP
address in the group, if there is no highest priority. The AVG answers all ARP requests for
the virtual router address. Which MAC address it returns depends on which load-balancing algorithm it is configured to use. In any event, the virtual MAC address supported by
one of the routers in the group is returned.

Key
Topic

The AVG also assigns the necessary virtual MAC addresses to each of the routers participating in the GLBP group. Up to four virtual MAC addresses can be used in any group.
Each of these routers is referred to as an *active virtual forwarder* (AVF), forwarding traffic received on its virtual MAC address. Other routers in the group serve as backup or secondary virtual forwarders, in case the AVF fails. The AVG also assigns secondary roles.

Assign the GLBP priority to a router with the following interface configuration command:

```
Switch(config-if)# glbp group priority level
```

GLBP group numbers range from 0 to 1023. The router priority can be 1 to 255 (255 is the
highest priority), defaulting to 100.

As with HSRP, another router cannot take over an active role until the current active router
fails. GLBP does allow a router to preempt and become the AVG if it has a higher priority
than the current AVG. Use the following command to enable preempting and to set a time
delay before preempting begins:

```
Switch(config-if)# glbp group preempt [delay minimum seconds]
```

Routers participating in GLBP must monitor each other's presence so that another router
can assume the role of a failed router. To do this, the AVG sends periodic hello messages

to each of the other GLBP peers. In addition, it expects to receive hello messages from each of them.

Hello messages are sent at *hellotime* intervals, with a default of 3 seconds. If hellos are not received from a peer within a *holdtime*, defaulting to 10 seconds, that peer is presumed to have failed. You can adjust the GLBP timers with the following interface configuration command:

```
Switch(config-if)# glbp group timers [msec] hellotime [msec] holdtime
```

The timer values normally are given in seconds, unless they are preceded by the **msec** keyword, to indicate milliseconds. The *hellotime* can range from 1 to 60 seconds or from 50 to 60,000 milliseconds. The *holdtime* must be greater than the *hellotime* and can go up to 180 seconds or 180,000 milliseconds. You always should make the *holdtime* at least three times greater than the *hellotime* to give some tolerance to missed or delayed hellos from a functional peer.

Tip: Although you can use the previous command to configure the GLBP timers on each peer router, it is not necessary. Instead, just configure the timers on the router you have identified as the AVG. The AVG will advertise the timer values it is using, and every other peer will learn those values if they have not already been explicitly set.

Active Virtual Forwarder

Each router participating in the GLBP group can become an AVF, if the AVG assigns it that role, along with a virtual MAC address. The virtual MAC addresses always have the form 0007.b4xx.xxyy. The 16-bit value denoted by xx.xx represents six zero bits followed by a 10-bit GLBP group number. The 8-bit yy value is the virtual forwarder number.

By default, GLBP uses the periodic hello messages to detect AVF failures, too. Each router within a GLBP group must send hellos to every other GLBP peer. Hellos also are expected from every other peer. For example, if hellos from the AVF are not received by the AVG before its holdtime timer expires, the AVG assumes that the current AVF has failed. The AVG then assigns the AVF role to another router.

Naturally, the router that is given the new AVF role might already be an AVF for a different virtual MAC address. Although a router can masquerade as two different virtual MAC addresses to support the two AVF functions, it does not make much sense to continue doing that for a long period of time. The AVG maintains two timers that help resolve this condition.

The *redirect* timer is used to determine when the AVG will stop using the old virtual MAC address in ARP replies. The AVF corresponding to the old address continues to act as a gateway for any clients that try to use it.

When the *timeout* timer expires, the old MAC address and the virtual forwarder using it are flushed from all the GLBP peers. The AVG assumes that the previously failed AVF will not return to service, so the resources assigned to it must be reclaimed. At this point, clients still using the old MAC address in their ARP caches must refresh the entry to obtain the new virtual MAC address.

The *redirect* timer defaults to 600 seconds (10 minutes) and can range from 0 to 3600 seconds (1 hour). The *timeout* timer defaults to 14,400 seconds (4 hours) and can range from 700 to 64,800 seconds (18 hours). You can adjust these timers with the following interface configuration command:

```
Switch(config-if)# glbp group timers redirect redirect timeout
```

GLBP also can use a weighting function to determine which router becomes the AVF for a virtual MAC address in a group. Each router begins with a maximum weight value (1 to 254). As specific interfaces go down, the weight is decreased by a configured amount. GLBP uses thresholds to determine when a router can and cannot be the AVF. If the weight falls below the lower threshold, the router must give up its AVF role. When the weight rises above the upper threshold, the router can resume its AVF role.

By default, a router receives a maximum weight of 100. If you want to make a dynamic weighting adjustment, GLBP must know which interfaces to track and how to adjust the weight. You first must define an interface as a tracked object with the following global configuration command:

```
Switch(config)# track object-number interface type mod/num {line-protocol | ip
    routing}
```

The *object-number* is an arbitrary index (1 to 500) that is used for weight adjustment. The condition that triggers an adjustment can be **line-protocol** (the interface line protocol is up) or **ip routing**. (IP routing is enabled, the interface has an IP address, and the interface is up.)

Next, you must define the weighting thresholds for the interface with the following interface configuration command:

```
Switch(config-if)# glbp group weighting maximum [lower lower] [upper upper]
```

The maximum weight can range from 1 to 254 (default 100). The upper (default *maximum*) and lower (default 1) thresholds define when the router can and cannot be the AVF, respectively.

Finally, you must configure GLBP to know which objects to track so that the weighting can be adjusted with the following interface configuration command:

```
Switch(config-if)# glbp group weighting track object-number [decrement value]
```

When the tracked object fails, the weighting is decremented by *value* (1 to 254, default 10).

Likewise, a router that might serve as an AVF cannot preempt another when it has a higher weight value.

GLBP Load Balancing

The AVG establishes load balancing by handing out virtual router MAC addresses to clients in a deterministic fashion. Naturally, the AVG first must inform the AVFs in the group of the virtual MAC address that each should use. Up to four virtual MAC addresses, assigned in sequential order, can be used in a group.

You can use one of the following load-balancing methods in a GLBP group:

Key Topic

■ **Round robin**—Each new ARP request for the virtual router address receives the next available virtual MAC address in reply. Traffic load is distributed evenly across all routers participating as AVFs in the group, assuming that each of the clients sends and receives the same amount of traffic. This is the default method used by GLBP.

■ **Weighted**—The GLBP group interface's weighting value determines the proportion of traffic that should be sent to that AVF. A higher weighting results in more frequent ARP replies containing the virtual MAC address of that router. If interface tracking is not configured, the maximum weighting value configured is used to set the relative proportions among AVFs.

■ **Host dependent**—Each client that generates an ARP request for the virtual router address always receives the same virtual MAC address in reply. This method is used if the clients have a need for a consistent gateway MAC address. (Otherwise, a client could receive replies with different MAC addresses for the router over time, depending on the load-balancing method in use.)

On the AVG router (or its successors), use the following interface configuration command to define the method:

```
Switch(config-if)# glbp group load-balancing [round-robin | weighted | host-
    dependent]
```

Enabling GLBP

To enable GLBP, you must assign a virtual IP address to the group by using the following interface configuration command:

```
Switch(config-if)# glbp group ip [ip-address [secondary]]
```

If the *ip-address* is not given in the command, it is learned from another router in the group. However, if this router is to be the AVG, you must explicitly configure the IP address; otherwise, no other router knows what the value should be.

Figure 13-3 shows a typical network in which three multilayer switches are participating in a common GLBP group. CatalystA is elected the AVG, so it coordinates the entire GLBP process. The AVG answers all ARP requests for the virtual router 192.168.1.1. It has identified itself, CatalystB, and CatalystC as AVFs for the group.

In this figure, round-robin load balancing is being used. Each of the client PCs sends an ARP request to look for the virtual router address (192.168.1.1) in turn, from left to right. Each time the AVG replies, the next sequential virtual MAC address is sent back to a client. After the fourth PC sends a request, all three virtual MAC addresses (and AVF routers) have been used, so the AVG cycles back to the first virtual MAC address.

Notice that only one GLBP group has been configured, and all clients know of only one gateway IP address: 192.168.1.1. However, all uplinks are being used, and all routers are proportionately forwarding traffic.

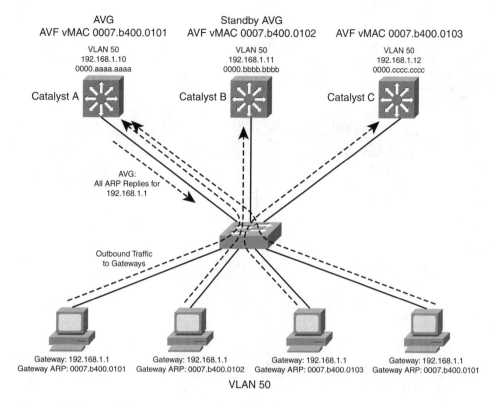

Figure 13-3 *Multilayer Switches in a GLBP Group*

Redundancy is also inherent in the GLBP group: CatalystA is the AVG, but the next-highest priority router can take over if the AVG fails. All routers have been given an AVF role for a unique virtual MAC address in the group. If one AVF fails, some clients remember the last-known virtual MAC address that was handed out. Therefore, another of the routers also takes over the AVF role for the failed router, causing the virtual MAC address to remain alive at all times.

Figure 13-4 shows how these redundancy features react when the current active AVG fails. Before its failure, CatalystA was the AVG because of its higher GLBP priority. After it failed, CatalystB became the AVG, answering ARP requests with the appropriate virtual MAC address for gateway 192.168.1.1. CatalystA also had been acting as an AVF, participating in the gateway load balancing. CatalystB also picks up this responsibility, using its virtual MAC address 0007.b400.0102 along with the one CatalystA had been using, 0007.b400.0101. Therefore, any hosts that know the gateway by any of its virtual MAC addresses still can reach a live gateway or AVF.

You can implement the scenario shown in Figures 13-3 and 13-4 with the configuration commands in Example 13-7 for CatalystA, CatalystB, and CatalystC, respectively.

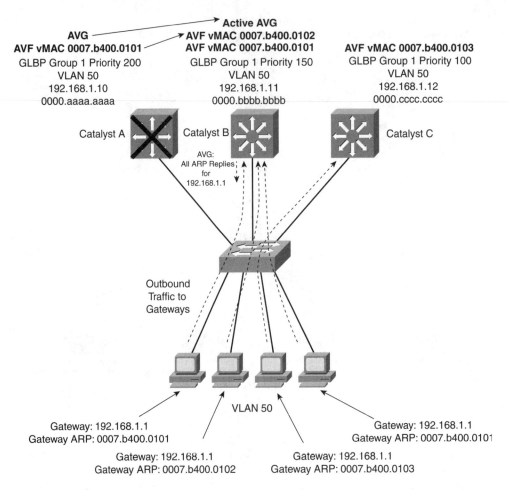

Figure 13-4 *How GLBP Reacts to a Component Failure*

Example 13-7 *Configuring GLBP Load Balancing*

```
CatalystA(config)# interface vlan 50
CatalystA(config-if)# ip address 192.168.1.10 255.255.255.0
CatalystA(config-if)# glbp 1 priority 200
CatalystA(config-if)# glbp 1 preempt
CatalystA(config-if)# glbp 1 ip 192.168.1.1
CatalystB(config)# interface vlan 50
CatalystB(config-if)# ip address 192.168.1.11 255.255.255.0
CatalystB(config-if)# glbp 1 priority 150
CatalystB(config-if)# glbp 1 preempt
CatalystB(config-if)# glbp 1 ip 192.168.1.1
CatalystC(config)# interface vlan 50
CatalystC(config-if)# ip address 192.168.1.12 255.255.255.0
CatalystC(config-if)# glbp 1 priority 100
CatalystC(config-if)# glbp 1 ip 192.168.1.1
```

You can verify GLBP operation with the **show glbp [brief]** command, as demonstrated in Example 13-8. With the **brief** keyword, the GLBP roles are summarized showing the interface, GLBP group number (Grp), virtual forwarder number (Fwd), GLBP priority (Pri), state, and addresses.

Example 13-8   *Verifying GLBP Operation*

```
CatalystA# show glbp brief
Interface   Grp  Fwd  Pri  State     Address          Active router     Standby router
V150        1    -    200  Active    192.168.1.1      local             192.168.1.11
V150        1    1    7    Active    0007.b400.0101   local             -
V150        1    2    7    Listen    0007.b400.0102   192.168.1.11      -
V150        1    3    7    Listen    0007.b400.0103   192.168.1.12      -
CatalystA#
```

```
CatalystB# show glbp brief
Interface   Grp  Fwd  Pri  State     Address          Active router     Standby router
V150        1    -    150  Standby   192.168.1.1      192.168.1.10      local
V150        1    1    7    Listen    0007.b400.0101   192.168.1.10      -
V150        1    2    7    Active    0007.b400.0102   local             -
V150        1    3    7    Listen    0007.b400.0103   192.168.1.12      -
CatalystB#
```

```
CatalystC# show glbp brief
Interface   Grp  Fwd  Pri  State     Address          Active router     Standby router


V150        1    -    100  Listen    192.168.1.1      192.168.1.10      192.168.1.11
V150        1    1    7    Listen    0007.b400.0101   192.168.1.10      -
V150        1    2    7    Listen    0007.b400.0102   192.168.1.11      -
V150        1    3    7    Active    0007.b400.0103   local             -
CatalystC#
```

Notice that CatalystA is shown to be the AVG because it has a dash in the Fwd column and is in the Active state. It also is acting as AVF for virtual forwarder number 1. Because the GLBP group has three routers, there are three virtual forwarders and virtual MAC addresses. CatalystA is in the Listen state for forwarders number 2 and 3, waiting to be given an active role in case one of those AVFs fails.

CatalystB is shown to have the Standby role, waiting to take over in case the AVG fails. It is the AVF for virtual forwarder number 2.

Finally, CatalystC has the lowest GLBP priority, so it stays in the Listen state, waiting for the active or standby AVG to fail. It is also the AVF for virtual forwarder number 3.

You also can display more detailed information about the GLBP configuration and status by omitting the **brief** keyword. Example 13-9 shows this output on the AVG router.

Because this is the AVG, the virtual forwarder roles it has assigned to each of the routers in the GLBP group also are shown.

Example 13-9 *Displaying Detailed GLBP Configuration and Status Information*

```
CatalystA# show glbp
Vlan50 - Group 1
  State is Active
    7 state changes, last state change 03:28:05
  Virtual IP address is 192.168.1.1
  Hello time 3 sec, hold time 10 sec
    Next hello sent in 1.672 secs
  Redirect time 600 sec, forwarder time-out 14400 sec
  Preemption enabled, min delay 0 sec
  Active is local
  Standby is 192.168.1.11, priority 150 (expires in 9.632 sec)
  Priority 200 (configured)
  Weighting 100 (default 100), thresholds: lower 1, upper 100
  Load balancing: round-robin
  There are 3 forwarders (1 active)
  Forwarder 1
    State is Active
      3 state changes, last state change 03:27:37
    MAC address is 0007.b400.0101 (default)
    Owner ID is 00d0.0229.b80a
    Redirection enabled
    Preemption enabled, min delay 30 sec
    Active is local, weighting 100
  Forwarder 2
    State is Listen
    MAC address is 0007.b400.0102 (learnt)
    Owner ID is 0007.b372.dc4a
    Redirection enabled, 598.308 sec remaining (maximum 600 sec)
    Time to live: 14398.308 sec (maximum 14400 sec)
    Preemption enabled, min delay 30 sec
    Active is 192.168.1.11 (primary), weighting 100 (expires in 8.308 sec)
  Forwarder 3
    State is Listen
    MAC address is 0007.b400.0103 (learnt)
    Owner ID is 00d0.ff8a.2c0a
    Redirection enabled, 599.892 sec remaining (maximum 600 sec)
    Time to live: 14399.892 sec (maximum 14400 sec)
    Preemption enabled, min delay 30 sec
    Active is 192.168.1.12 (primary), weighting 100 (expires in 9.892 sec)
CatalystA#
```

Verifying Gateway Redundancy

To verify the operation of the features discussed in this chapter, you can use the commands listed in Table 13-4. In particular, look for the active, standby, or backup routers in use.

Table 13-4   *Gateway Redundancy Verification Commands*

Task	Command Syntax
HSRP and VRRP	
Display HSRP status.	**show standby brief**
Display HSRP on an interface.	**show standby** *type mod/num*
Display VRRP status.	**show vrrp brief all**
Display VRRP on an interface.	**show vrrp interface** *type mod/num*
GLBP	
Display status of a GLBP group.	**show glbp** [*group*] [brief]

Supervisor and Route Processor Redundancy

The router or gateway redundancy protocols, such as HSRP, VRRP, and GLBP, can provide high availability only for the default gateway addresses. If one of the redundant gateway routers fails, another can pick up the pieces and appear to be the same gateway address.

But what happens to the devices that are connected directly to the router that fails? If the switching or routing engine fails, packets probably will not get routed and interfaces will go down. Some Cisco switches have the capability to provide redundancy for the supervisor engine itself. This is accomplished by having redundant hardware in place within a switch chassis, ready to take over during a failure.

You also should consider switch power as a vital part of achieving high availability. For example, if a switch has a single power supply and a single power cord, the whole switch will fail if the power supply fails or if the power cord is accidentally unplugged. Some switch platforms can have multiple power supplies; if one power supply fails, another immediately takes over the load.

Redundant Switch Supervisors

Modular switch platforms such as the Catalyst 4500R and 6500 can accept two supervisor modules installed in a single chassis. The first supervisor module to successfully boot becomes the active supervisor for the chassis. The other supervisor remains in a standby role, waiting for the active supervisor to fail.

The active supervisor always is allowed to boot up and become fully initialized and operational. All switching functions are provided by the active supervisor. The standby supervisor, however, is allowed to boot up and initialize only to a certain level. When the active module fails, the standby module can proceed to initialize any remaining functions and take over the active role.

Redundant supervisor modules can be configured in several modes. The redundancy mode affects how the two supervisors handshake and synchronize information. In addition, the mode limits the standby supervisor's state of readiness. The more ready the standby module is allowed to become, the less initialization and failover time will be required.

You can use the following redundancy modes on Catalyst switches:

Key Topic

- **Route processor redundancy (RPR)**—The redundant supervisor is only partially booted and initialized. When the active module fails, the standby module must reload every other module in the switch and then initialize all the supervisor functions.

- **Route processor redundancy plus (RPR+)**—The redundant supervisor is booted, allowing the supervisor and route engine to initialize. No Layer 2 or Layer 3 functions are started, however. When the active module fails, the standby module finishes initializing without reloading other switch modules. This allows switch ports to retain their state.

- **Stateful switchover (SSO)**—The redundant supervisor is fully booted and initialized. Both the startup and running configuration contents are synchronized between the supervisor modules. Layer 2 information is maintained on both supervisors so that hardware switching can continue during a failover. The state of the switch interfaces is also maintained on both supervisors so that links don't flap during a failover.

Tip: Sometimes the redundancy mode terminology can be confusing. In addition to the RPR, RPR+, and SSO terms, you might see single-router mode (SRM) and dual-router mode (DRM).

SRM simply means that two route processors (integrated into the supervisors) are being used, but only one of them is active at any time. In DRM, two route processors are active at all times. HSRP usually is used to provide redundancy in DRM.

Although RPR and RPR+ have only one active supervisor, the route processor portion is not initialized on the standby unit. Therefore, SRM is not compatible with RPR or RPR+.

SRM is inherent with SSO, which brings up the standby route processor. You usually will find the two redundancy terms together, as "SRM with SSO."

Configuring the Redundancy Mode

Table 13-5 details the redundancy modes you can configure on supported switch platforms.

Table 13-5 *Redundancy Modes, Platform Support, and Failover Time*

Redundancy Mode	Supported Platforms	Failover Time
RPR	Catalyst 6500 Supervisors 2 and 720, Catalyst 4500R Supervisors IV and V	Good (> 2 minutes)

continues

Table 13-5   *Redundancy Modes, Platform Support, and Failover Time (Continued)*

Redundancy Mode	Supported Platforms	Failover Time
RPR+	Catalyst 6500 Supervisors 2 and 720	Better (> 30 seconds)
SSO	Catalyst 6500 Supervisor 720, Catalyst 4500R Supervisors IV and V	Best (> 1 second)

Figure 13-5 shows how the supervisor redundancy modes compare with respect to the functions they perform. The shaded functions are performed as the standby supervisor initializes and then waits for the active supervisor to fail. When a failure is detected, the remaining functions must be performed in sequence before the standby supervisor can become fully active. Notice how the redundancy modes get progressively more initialized and ready to become active.

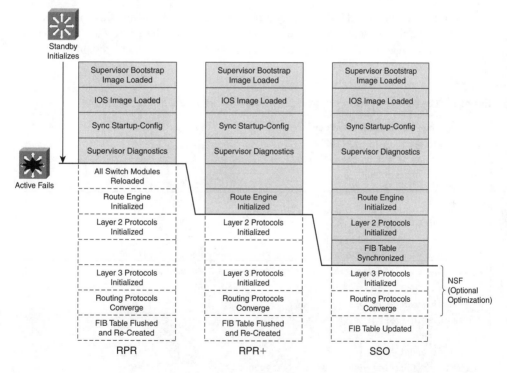

Figure 13-5   *Standby Supervisor Readiness as a Function of Redundancy Mode*

You can configure the supervisor redundancy mode by entering the redundancy configuration mode with the following command:

```
Router(config)# redundancy
```

Next, select the redundancy mode with one of the following commands:

```
Router(config-red)# mode {rpr | rpr-plus | sso}
```

If you are configuring redundancy for the first time on the switch, you must enter the previous commands on both supervisor modules. When the redundancy mode is enabled, you will make all configuration changes on the active supervisor only. The running configuration is synchronized automatically from the active to the standby module.

Tip: If you configure RPR+ with the **rpr-plus** keyword, the supervisor attempts to bring up RPR+ with its peer module. The IOS images must be of exactly the same release before RPR+ will work. If the images differ, the supervisor automatically falls back to RPR mode instead.

You can verify the redundancy mode and state of the supervisor modules by using the following command:

```
Router# show redundancy states
```

The output in Example 13-10 shows that the switch is using RPR+ and that the second supervisor module (denoted by unit ID 2 and "my state") holds the active role. The other supervisor module is in the standby state and is HOT, meaning that it has initialized as far as the redundancy mode will allow.

Example 13-10 *Verifying Supervisor Module Redundancy Mode and State*

```
Router# show redundancy states
       my state = 13 -ACTIVE
     peer state = 8   -STANDBY HOT
           Mode = Duplex
           Unit = Secondary

        Unit ID = 2

Redundancy Mode (Operational) = Route Processor Redundancy Plus
Redundancy Mode (Configured)  = Route Processor Redundancy Plus
     Split Mode = Disabled
   Manual Swact = Enabled
 Communications = Up

   client count = 11
client_notification_TMR = 30000 milliseconds
         keep_alive TMR = 9000 milliseconds
       keep_alive count = 1
   keep_alive threshold = 18
          RF debug mask = 0x0
Router#
```

Configuring Supervisor Synchronization

By default, the active supervisor synchronizes its startup configuration and configuration register values with the standby supervisor. You also can specify other information that should be synchronized.

First, use the following commands to enter the main-cpu configuration mode:

```
Router(config)# redundancy
Router(config-red)# main-cpu
```

Then use the following command to specify the information that will be synchronized:

```
Router(config-r-mc)# auto-sync {startup-config | config-register | bootvar}
```

You can repeat the command if you need to use more than one of the keywords. To return to the default, use the **auto-sync standard** command.

Nonstop Forwarding

You can enable another redundancy feature along with SSO on the Catalyst 4500R and 6500 (Supervisor 720 only). Nonstop Forwarding (NSF) is an interactive method that focuses on quickly rebuilding the Routing Information Base (RIB) table after a supervisor switchover. The RIB is used to generate the FIB table for CEF, which is downloaded to any switch modules or hardware that can perform CEF.

Instead of waiting on any configured Layer 3 routing protocols to converge and rebuild the FIB, a router can use NSF to get assistance from other NSF-aware neighbors. The neighbors then can provide routing information to the standby supervisor, allowing the routing tables to be assembled quickly. In a nutshell, the Cisco-proprietary NSF functions must be built in to the routing protocols on both the router that will need assistance and the router that will provide assistance.

NSF is supported by the Border Gateway Protocol (BGP), Enhanced Interior Gateway Routing Protocol (EIGRP), Open Shortest path First (OSPF), and Intermediate System-to-Intermediate System (IS-IS) routing protocols. NSF is available on the Catalyst 6500 Supervisor 720 (with the integrated MSFC3) and on the Catalyst 4500R Supervisor III, IV, and V running IOS Software Release 12.2(20)EWA or later.

To configure NSF, you must add the commands in Table 13-6 to any routing protocol configuration on the switch.

Table 13-6 *Configuring NSF (by Routing Protocol)*

Routing Protocol	Configuration Commands
BGP	Router(config)# **router bgp** *as-number*
	Router(config-router)# **bgp graceful-restart**
EIGRP	Router(config)# **router eigrp** *as-number*
	Router(config-router)# **nsf**

continues

Table 13-6 *Configuring NSF (by Routing Protocol) (Continued)*

Routing Protocol	Configuration Commands
OSPF	Router(config)# **router ospf** *process-id*
	Router(config-router)# **nsf**
IS-IS	Router(config)# **router isis** [*tag*]
	Router(config-router)# **nsf** [**cisco** | **ietf**]
	Router(config-router)# **nsf interval** [*minutes*]
	Router(config-router)# **nsf t3** {**manual** [*seconds*] | **adjacency**}
	Router(config-router)# **nsf interface wait** *seconds*

Exam Preparation Tasks

Review All Key Topics

Review the most important topics in the chapter, noted with the Key Topic icon in the outer margin of the page. Table 13-7 lists a reference of these key topics and the page numbers on which each is found.

Table 13-7 *Key Topics for Chapter 13*

Key Topic Element	Description	Page Number
Paragraph	Explains HSRP active and standby routers	271
Paragraph	Describes the virtual MAC address used by HSRP	275
Paragraph	Discusses VRRP master and backup routers and the virtual MAC address	279
Paragraph	Describes the GLBP active virtual gateway and active virtual forwarder roles	283
List	Describes the methods GLBP uses for load balancing traffic within a GLBP group	286
List	Describes Catalyst supervisor redundancy modes	292
Paragraph	Describes nonstop forwarding	295

Define Key Terms

Define the following key terms from this chapter, and check your answers in the glossary:

HSRP active router, HSRP standby router, VRRP master router, VRRP backup router, active virtual gateway (AVG), active virtual forwarder (AVF), Route Processor Redundancy (RPR), Route Processor Redundancy Plus (RPR+), Stateful Switchover (SSO), nonstop forwarding (NSF)

Use Command Reference to Check Your Memory

This section includes the most important configuration and EXEC commands covered in this chapter. It might not be necessary to memorize the complete syntax of every command, but you should remember the basic keywords that are needed.

To test your memory of the Layer 3 high-availability commands, cover the right side of Tables 13-8 through 13-10 with a piece of paper, read the description on the left side, and then see how much of the command you can remember.

Table 13-8 *HSRP Configuration Commands*

Task	Command Syntax
Set the HSRP priority.	**standby** *group* **priority** *priority*
Set the HSRP timers.	**standby** *group* **timers** *hello holdtime*
Allow router preemption.	**standby** *group* **preempt** [**delay** *seconds*]
Use group authentication.	**standby** *group* **authentication** *string*
Adjust priority by tracking an interface.	**standby** *group* **track** *type mod/num decrement-value*
Assign the virtual router address.	**standby** *group* **ip** *ip-address* [**secondary**]

Table 13-10 *GLBP Configuration Commands*

Task	Command Syntax
Assign a GLBP priority.	**glbp** *group* **priority** *level*
Allow GLBP preemption.	**glbp** *group* **preempt** [**delay minimum** *seconds*]
Define an object to be tracked.	**track** *object-number* **interface** *type mod/num* {**line-protocol** | **ip routing**}
Define the weighting thresholds.	**glbp** *group* **weighting** *maximum* [**lower** *lower*] [**upper** *upper*]
Track an object.	**glbp** *group* **weighting track** *object-number* [**decrement** *value*]
Choose the load-balancing method.	**glbp** *group* **load-balancing** [**round-robin** | **weighted** | **host-dependent**]
Assign a virtual router address.	**glbp** *group* **ip** [*ip-address* [**secondary**]]

Table 13-9   *VRRP Configuration Commands*

Task	Command Syntax
Assign a VRRP router priority (default 100).	**vrrp** *group* **priority** *level*
Alter the advertisement timer (default 1 second).	**vrrp** *group* **timers advertise** [**msec**] *interval*
Learn the advertisement interval from the master router.	**vrrp** *group* **timers learn**
Disable preempting (default is to preempt).	**no vrrp** *group* **preempt**
Change the preempt delay (default 0 seconds).	**vrrp** *group* **preempt** [**delay** *seconds*]
Use authentication for advertisements.	**vrrp** *group* **authentication** *string*
Assign a virtual IP address.	**vrrp** *group* **ip** *ip-address* [**secondary**]

Remember that the CCNP exam focuses on practical or hands-on skills that are used by a networking professional.

Cisco Published SWITCH Exam Topics Covered in This Part

Prepare infrastructure to support advanced services:

- Implement a wireless extension of a Layer 2 solution

- Implement a VoIP support solution

- Implement video support solution

(Always check Cisco.com for the latest posted exam topics.)

Part IV: Campus Network Services

This chapter covers the following topics that you need to master for the CCNP SWITCH exam:

Power over Ethernet (PoE)—This section discusses how a Catalyst switch can provide power to operate devices such as Cisco IP Phones.

Voice VLANs—This section explains how voice traffic can be carried over the links between an IP Phone and a Catalyst switch.

Voice QoS—This section provides an overview of the mechanisms that provide premium quality of service (QoS) for voice traffic.

CHAPTER 14

IP Telephony

In addition to carrying regular data, switched campus networks can carry packets that are related to telephone calls. Voice over IP (VoIP), otherwise known as *IP telephony* (IPT), uses IP Phones that are connected to switched Ethernet ports.

To properly and effectively carry the traffic for a successful phone call, a combination of many switching features must be used. For example, the Catalyst switches can provide power to IP Phones, form trunk links with IP Phones, and provide the proper level of QoS for voice packet delivery. This chapter covers all these topics as related to the Cisco IP Phone.

"Do I Know This Already?" Quiz

The "Do I Know This Already?" quiz allows you to assess whether you should read this entire chapter thoroughly or jump to the "Exam Preparation Tasks" section. If you are in doubt based on your answers to these questions or your own assessment of your knowledge of the topics, read the entire chapter. Table 14-1 outlines the major headings in this chapter and the "Do I Know This Already?" quiz questions that go with them. You can find the answers in Appendix A, "Answers to the 'Do I Know This Already?' Quizzes."

Table 14-1 *"Do I Know This Already?" Foundation Topics Section-to-Question Mapping*

Foundation Topics Section	Questions Covered in This Section
Power over Ethernet (PoE)	1–2
Voice VLANs	3–8
Voice QoS	9–12

1. For a Catalyst switch to offer Power over Ethernet to a device, what must occur?

   a. Nothing; power always is enabled on a port.

   b. The switch must detect that the device needs inline power.

   c. The device must send a CDP message asking for power.

   d. The switch is configured to turn on power to the port.

2. Which one of these commands can enable Power over Ethernet to a switch interface?

    a. inline power enable

    b. inline power on

    c. power inline on

    d. power inline auto

3. What does a Cisco IP Phone contain to allow it to pass both voice and data packets?

    a. An internal Ethernet hub

    b. An internal two-port switch

    c. An internal three-port switch

    d. An internal four-port switch

4. How can voice traffic be kept separate from any other data traffic through an IP Phone?

    a. Voice and data travel over separate links.

    b. A special-case 802.1Q trunk is used to connect to the switch.

    c. Voice and data can't be separated; they must intermingle on the link.

    d. Voice and data packets both are encapsulated over an ISL trunk.

5. What command configures an IP Phone to use VLAN 9 for voice traffic?

    a. switchport voice vlan 9

    b. switchport voice-vlan 9

    c. switchport voice 9

    d. switchport voip 9

6. What is the default voice VLAN condition for a switch port?

    a. switchport voice vlan 1

    b. switchport voice vlan dot1p

    c. switchport voice vlan untagged

    d. switchport voice vlan none

7. If the following interface configuration commands have been used, what VLAN numbers will the voice and PC data be carried over, respectively?

```
interface gigabitethernet1/0/1
    switchport access vlan 10
    switchport trunk native vlan 20
    switchport voice vlan 50
    switchport mode access
```

    a. VLAN 50, VLAN 20

    b. VLAN 50, VLAN 1

    c. VLAN 1, VLAN 50

    d. VLAN 20, VLAN 50

    e. VLAN 50, VLAN 10

8. What command can verify the voice VLAN used by a Cisco IP Phone?

    a. show cdp neighbor

    b. show interface switchport

    c. show vlan

    d. show trunk

9. When a PC is connected to the PC switch port on an IP Phone, how is QoS trust handled?

    a. The IP Phone always trusts the class of service (CoS) information coming from the PC.

    b. The IP Phone never trusts the PC and always overwrites the CoS bits.

    c. QoS trust for the PC data is handled at the Catalyst switch port, not the IP Phone.

    d. The Catalyst switch instructs the IP Phone how to trust the PC QoS information.

10. An IP Phone should mark all incoming traffic from an attached PC to have CoS 1. Complete the following switch command to make that happen:

```
switchport priority extend _____
```

    a. untrusted

    b. 1

    c. cos 1

    d. overwrite 1

11. What command can verify the Power over Ethernet status of each switch port?

    a. show inline power

    b. show power inline

    c. show interface

    d. show running-config

12. Which DSCP codepoint name usually is used for time-critical packets containing voice data?

    a. 7

    b. Critical

    c. AF

    d. EF

Foundation Topics

Power over Ethernet

A Cisco IP Phone is like any other node on the network—it must have power to operate. Power can come from two sources:

- An external AC adapter

- Power over Ethernet (DC) over the network data cable

The external AC adapter plugs into a normal AC wall outlet and provides 48V DC to the phone. These adapters, commonly called *wall warts*, are handy if no other power source is available. However, if a power failure occurs to the room or outlet where the adapter is located, the IP Phone will fail.

A more elegant solution is available as *inline power* or *Power over Ethernet* (PoE). Here, the same 48V DC supply is provided to an IP Phone over the same unshielded twisted-pair cable that is used for Ethernet connectivity. The DC power's source is the Catalyst switch itself. No other power source is needed, unless an AC adapter is required as a redundant source.

PoE has the benefit that it can be managed, monitored, and offered only to an IP Phone. In fact, this capability is not limited to Cisco IP Phones—any device that can request and use inline power in a compatible manner can be used. Otherwise, if a nonpowered device such as a normal PC is plugged into the same switch port, the switch will not offer power to it.

In a best practice design, the Catalyst switch should be connected to an uninterruptible power supply (UPS) so that it continues to receive and offer power even if the regular AC source fails. This allows an IP Phone or other powered device to be available for use even across a power failure.

How PoE Works

A Catalyst switch can offer power over its Ethernet ports only if it is designed to do so. It must have one or more power supplies that are rated for the additional load that will be offered to the connected devices. PoE is available on many platforms, including the Catalyst 3750, Catalyst 4500, and Catalyst 6500.

Two methods provide PoE to connected devices:

- **Cisco Inline Power (ILP)**—A Cisco-proprietary method developed before the IEEE 802.3af standard

- **IEEE 802.3af**—A standards-based method that offers vendor interoperability (see http://standards.ieee.org/getieee802/download/802.3af-2003.pdf)

Detecting a Powered Device

The switch always keeps the power disabled when a switch port is down. However, the switch must continually try to detect whether a powered device is connected to a port. If it is, the switch must begin providing power so that the device can initialize and become operational. Only then will the Ethernet link be established.

Because there are two PoE methods, a Catalyst switch tries both to detect a powered device. For IEEE 802.3af, the switch begins by supplying a small voltage across the transmit and receive pairs of the copper twisted-pair connection. It then can measure the resistance across the pairs to detect whether current is being drawn by the device. If 25K ohm resistance is measured, a powered device is indeed present.

The switch also can apply several predetermined voltages to test for corresponding resistance values. These values are applied by the powered device to indicate which of the five IEEE 802.3af power classes it belongs to. Knowing this, the switch can begin allocating the appropriate maximum power needed by the device. Table 14-2 defines the power classes.

Table 14-2 *IEEE 802.3af Power Classes*

Power Class	Maximum Power Offered at 48V DC	Notes
0	15.4 W	Default class
1	4.0 W	Optional class
2	7.0 W	Optional class
3	15.4 W	Optional class
4	Up to 50 W	Optional class (802.3at)

The default class 0 is used if either the switch or the powered device does not support or doesn't attempt the optional power class discovery. While class 4 was reserved under IEEE 802.3af, it is available under IEEE 802.3at, also called PoE Plus, as up to 50 W per connected device. Some Cisco Catalyst switches, such as the Catalyst 3750-E series, also offer up to 20 W of "enhanced PoE" power.

Cisco inline power device discovery takes a totally different approach than IEEE 802.3af. Instead of offering voltage and checking resistance, the switch sends out a 340 kHz test tone on the transmit pair of the twisted-pair Ethernet cable. A tone is transmitted instead of DC power because the switch first must detect an inline power-capable device before offering it power. Otherwise, other types of devices (normal PCs, for example) could be damaged.

A powered device such as a Cisco IP Phone loops the transmit and receives pairs of its Ethernet connection while it is powered off. When it is connected to an inline power switch port, the switch can "hear" its test tone looped back. Then it safely assumes that a known powered device is present, and power can be applied to it.

Supplying Power to a Device

A switch first offers a default power allocation to the powered device. On a Catalyst 3750-24-PWR, for example, an IP Phone first receives 15.4 W (0.32 amps at 48 V DC).

Power can be supplied in two ways:

■   For Cisco ILP, inline power is provided over data pairs 2 and 3 (RJ-45 pins 1,2 and 3,6) at 48 V DC.

■   For IEEE 802.3af, power can be supplied in the same fashion (pins 1,2 and 3,6) or over pairs 1 and 4 (RJ-45 pins 4,5 and 7,8).

Now the device has a chance to power up and bring up its Ethernet link, too. The power budget offered to the device can be changed from the default to a more appropriate value. This can help prevent the switch from wasting its total power budget on devices that use far less power than the per-port default. With IEEE 802.3af, the power budget can be changed by detecting the device's power class.

For Cisco ILP, the switch can attempt a Cisco Discovery Protocol (CDP) message exchange with the device. If CDP information is returned, the switch can discover the device type (Cisco IP Phone, for example) and the device's actual power requirements. The switch then can reduce the inline power to the amount requested by the device.

To see this in operation, look at Example 14-1. Here, the power was reduced from 15,000 mW to 6300 mW. This output was produced by the **debug ilpower controller** and **debug cdp packets** commands.

Example 14-1   *Displaying Inline Power Adjustment*

```
00:58:46: ILP uses AC Disconnect(Fa1/0/47): state= ILP_DETECTING_S, event=
  PHY_CSCO_DETECTED_EV
00:58:46: %ILPOWER-7-DETECT: Interface Fa1/0/47: Power Device detected: Cisco PD
00:58:46: Ilpower PD device 1 class 2 from interface (Fa1/0/47)
00:58:46: ilpower new power from pd discovery Fa1/0/47, power_status ok
00:58:46: Ilpower interface (Fa1/0/47) power status change, allocated power 15400
00:58:46: ILP Power apply to ( Fa1/0/47 ) Okay
00:58:46: ILP Start PHY Cisco IP phone detection ( Fa1/0/47 ) Okay
00:58:46: %ILPOWER-5-POWER_GRANTED: Interface Fa1/0/47: Power granted
00:58:46: ILP uses AC Disconnect(Fa1/0/47): state= ILP_CSCO_PD_DETECTED_S, event=
  IEEE_PWR_GOOD_EV
00:58:48: ILP State_Machine ( Fa1/0/47 ): State= ILP_PWR_GOOD_USE_IEEE_DISC_S,
  Event= PHY_LINK_UP_EV
00:58:48: ILP uses AC Disconnect(Fa1/0/47): state= ILP_PWR_GOOD_USE_IEEE_DISC_S,
  event= PHY_LINK_UP_EV
00:58:50: %LINK-3-UPDOWN: Interface FastEthernet1/0/47, changed state to up
00:58:50: CDP-AD: Interface FastEthernet1/0/47 coming up
00:58:50: ilpower_powerman_power_available_tlv: about sending patlv on Fa1/0/47
00:58:50:     req id 0, man id 1, pwr avail 15400, pwr man -1
00:58:50: CDP-PA: version 2 packet sent out on FastEthernet1/0/47
00:58:51: %LINEPROTO-5-UPDOWN: Line protocol on Interface FastEthernet1/0/47,
  changed state to up
00:58:54: CDP-PA: Packet received from SIP0012435D594D on interface
  FastEthernet1/0/47
00:58:54: **Entry NOT found in cache**
```

```
00:58:54: Interface(Fa1/0/47) - processing old tlv from cdp, request 6300,
  current
allocated 15400
00:58:54: Interface (Fa1/0/47) efficiency is 100
00:58:54: ilpower_powerman_power_available_tlv: about sending patlv on Fa1/0/47
00:58:54:    req id 0, man id 1, pwr avail 6300, pwr man -1
00:58:54: CDP-PA: version 2 packet sent out on FastEthernet1/0/47
```

Configuring PoE

PoE or inline power configuration is simple. Each switch port can automatically detect the presence of an inline power-capable device before applying power, or the feature can be disabled to ensure that the port can never detect or offer inline power. By default, every switch port attempts to discover an inline-powered device. To change this behavior, use the following interface-configuration commands:

```
Switch(config)# interface type mod/num
Switch(config-if)# power inline {auto [max milli-watts] | static [max
  milli-watts] | never}
```

By default, every switch interface is configured for auto mode, where the device and power budget automatically is discovered. In addition, the default power budget is 15.4 W. You can change the maximum power offered as **max** *milli-watts* (4000 to 15400).

You can configure a **static** power budget for a switch port if you have a device that cannot interact with either of the powered device-discovery methods. Again, you can set the maximum power offered to the device with **max** *milli-watts*. Otherwise, the default value of 15.4 W is used.

If you want to disable PoE on a switch port, use the **never** keyword. Power never will be offered and powered devices never will be detected on that port.

Verifying PoE

You can verify the power status for a switch port with the following EXEC command:

```
Switch# show power inline [type mod/num]
```

Example 14-2 provides some sample output from this command. If the class is shown as n/a, Cisco ILP has been used to supply power. Otherwise, the IEEE 802.3af power class (0 through 4) is shown.

Example 14-2 *Displaying PoE Status for Switch Ports*

```
Switch# show power inline
Module   Available   Used     Remaining
         (Watts)     (Watts)  (Watts)
------   ---------   -------- ----------
1            370.0      39.0      331.0
Interface Admin   Oper      Power    Device              Class Max
                            (Watts)
```

```
.........  ......  ..........  .......  ....................  ......  ....
Fa1/0/1    auto    on          6.5      AIR-AP1231G-A-K9      n/a     15.4
Fa1/0/2    auto    on          6.3      IP Phone 7940         n/a     15.4
Fa1/0/3    auto    on          6.3      IP Phone 7960         n/a     15.4
Fa1/0/4    auto    on          15.4     Ieee PD               0       15.4
Fa1/0/5    auto    on          4.5      Ieee PD               1       15.4
Fa1/0/6    static  on          15.4     n/a                   n/a     15.4
Fa1/0/7    auto    off         0.0      n/a                   n/a     15.4
[output omitted]
```

Tip: As you plan and implement PoE for IP Phones and wireless access points, be aware of the switch power budget—the total amount of power that a switch can offer end devices. In Example 14-2, the switch has 370 W total available. When power is offered to the connected devices, the switch has no more than 331 W remaining for other powered devices.

Voice VLANs

A Cisco IP Phone provides a data connection for a user's PC, in addition to its own voice data stream. This allows a single Ethernet drop to be installed per user. The IP Phone also can control some aspects of how the packets (both voice and user data) are presented to the switch.

Most Cisco IP Phone models contain a three-port switch, connecting to the upstream switch, the user's PC, and the internal VoIP data stream, as illustrated in Figure 14-1. The voice and user PC ports always function as access-mode switch ports. The port that connects to the upstream switch, however, can operate as an 802.1Q trunk or as an access-mode (single VLAN) port.

The link mode between the IP Phone and the switch is negotiated; you can configure the switch to instruct the phone to use a special-case 802.1Q trunk or a single VLAN access link. With a trunk, the voice traffic can be isolated from other user data, providing security and QoS capabilities.

As an access link, both voice and data must be combined over the single VLAN. This simplifies other aspects of the switch configuration because a separate voice VLAN is not needed, but it could compromise the voice quality, depending on the PC application mix and traffic load.

Voice VLAN Configuration

Key Topic

Although you can configure the IP Phone uplink as a trunk or nontrunk, the real consideration pertains to how the voice traffic will be encapsulated. The voice packets must be carried over a unique voice VLAN (known as the *voice VLAN ID* or *VVID*) or over the regular data VLAN (known as the *native VLAN* or the *port VLAN ID*, *PVID*). The QoS information from the voice packets also must be carried.

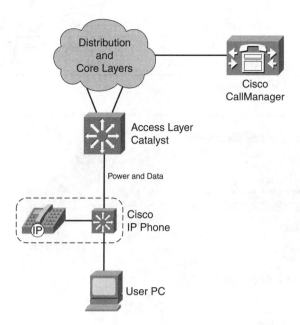

Figure 14-1   *Basic Connections to a Cisco IP Phone*

To configure the IP Phone uplink, just configure the switch port where it connects. The switch instructs the phone to follow the mode that is selected. In addition, the switch port does not need any special trunking configuration commands if a trunk is wanted. If an 802.1Q trunk is needed, a special-case trunk automatically is negotiated by the Dynamic Trunking Protocol (DTP) and CDP.

Use the following interface configuration command to select the voice VLAN mode that will be used:

```
Switch(config-if)# switchport voice vlan {vlan-id | dot1p | untagged | none}
```

Figure 14-2 shows the four different voice VLAN configurations. Pay particular attention to the link between the IP Phone and the switch.

Table 14-3 documents the four different voice VLAN configurations.

Table 14-3   *Trunking Modes with a Cisco IP Phone*

Keyword	Representation in Figure 14-2	Native VLAN (Untagged)	Voice VLAN	Voice QoS (CoS Bits)
vlan-id	A	PC data	VLAN *vlan-id*	802.1p
dot1p	B	PC data	VLAN 0	802.1p
untagged	C	PC data/voice	—	—

continues

Table 14-3   *Trunking Modes with a Cisco IP Phone (Continued)*

Keyword	Representation in Figure 14-2	Native VLAN (Untagged)	Voice VLAN	Voice QoS (CoS Bits)
none (default)	D	PC data/voice	—	—

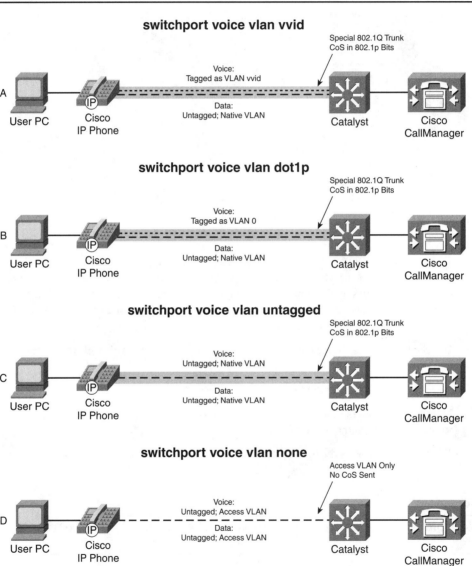

Figure 14-2   *Trunking Modes for Voice VLANs with a Cisco IP Phone*

The default condition for every switch port is **none**, where a trunk is not used. All modes except for **none** use the special-case 802.1Q trunk. The only difference between the **dot1p** and **untagged** modes is the encapsulation of voice traffic. The **dot1p** mode puts the voice packets on VLAN 0, which requires a VLAN ID (not the native VLAN) but doesn't require a unique voice VLAN to be created. The **untagged** mode puts voice packets in the native VLAN, requiring neither a VLAN ID nor a unique voice VLAN.

The most versatile mode uses the *vlan-id*, as shown in case A in Figure 14-2. Here, voice and user data are carried over separate VLANs. VoIP packets in the voice VLAN also carry the CoS bits in the 802.1p trunk encapsulation field.

Be aware that the special-case 802.1Q trunk automatically is enabled through a CDP information exchange between the switch and the IP Phone. The trunk contains only two VLANs—a voice VLAN (tagged VVID) and the data VLAN. The switch port's access VLAN is used as the data VLAN that carries packets to and from a PC that is connected to the phone's PC port.

If an IP Phone is removed and a PC is connected to the same switch port, the PC still will be capable of operating because the data VLAN still will appear as the access VLAN— even though the special trunk no longer is enabled.

Verifying Voice VLAN Operation

You can verify the switch port mode (access or trunk) and the voice VLAN by using the **show interface switchport** command. As demonstrated in Example 14-3, the port is in access mode and uses access VLAN 10 and voice VLAN 110.

Example 14-3   *Verifying Switch Port Mode and Voice VLAN*

```
Switch# show interfaces fastEthernet 1/0/1 switchport
Name: Fa1/0/1
Switchport: Enabled
Administrative Mode: dynamic auto
Operational Mode: static access
Administrative Trunking Encapsulation: negotiate
Operational Trunking Encapsulation: native
Negotiation of Trunking: On
Access Mode VLAN: 10 (VLAN0010)
Trunking Native Mode VLAN: 1 (default)
Administrative Native VLAN tagging: enabled
Voice VLAN: 110 (VoIP)
Administrative private-vlan host-association: none
Administrative private-vlan mapping: none
Administrative private-vlan trunk native VLAN: none
Administrative private-vlan trunk Native VLAN tagging: enabled
Administrative private-vlan trunk encapsulation: dot1q
Administrative private-vlan trunk normal VLANs: none
Administrative private-vlan trunk private VLANs: none
Operational private-vlan: none
```

```
Trunking VLANs Enabled: ALL
Pruning VLANs Enabled: 2-1001
Capture Mode Disabled
Capture VLANs Allowed: ALL
Protected: false
Unknown unicast blocked: disabled
Unknown multicast blocked: disabled
Appliance trust: none
Switch#
```

When the IP Phone trunk is active, it is not shown in the trunking mode from any Cisco IOS Software **show** command. However, you can verify the VLANs being carried over the trunk link by looking at the Spanning Tree Protocol (STP) activity. STP runs with two instances—one for the voice VLAN and one for the data VLAN, which can be seen with the **show spanning-tree interface** command.

For example, suppose that a switch port is configured with access VLAN 10, voice VLAN 110, and native VLAN 99. Example 14-4 shows the switch port configuration and STP information when the switch port is in access mode.

Example 14-4   *IP Phone Trunk Configuration and STP Information*

```
Switch# show running-config interface fastethernet 1/0/1
interface FastEthernet1/0/1
 switchport trunk native vlan 99
 switchport access vlan 10
 switchport voice vlan 110
Switch# show spanning-tree interface fastethernet 1/0/1
Vlan              Role Sts Cost     Prio.Nbr Type
---------------   ---- --- -------- -------- --------------------------
VLAN0010          Desg FWD 19       128.51   P2p
VLAN0110          Desg FWD 19       128.51   P2p
Switch#
```

The access VLAN (10) is being used as the data VLAN from the IP Phone.

Voice QoS

On a quiet, underutilized network, a switch generally can forward packets as soon as they are received. However, if a network is congested, packets cannot always be delivered in a timely manner. Traditionally, network congestion has been handled by increasing link bandwidths and switching hardware performance. This does little to address how one type of traffic can be preferred or delivered ahead of another.

Quality of service (QoS) is the overall method used in a network to protect and prioritize time-critical or important traffic. The most important aspect of transporting voice traffic across a switched campus network is maintaining the proper QoS level. Voice packets must be delivered in the most timely fashion possible, with little jitter, little loss, and little delay.

Remember, a user expects to receive a dial tone, a call to go through, and a good-quality audio connection with the far end when an IP Phone is used. Above that, any call that is made could be an emergency 911 call. It is then very important that QoS be implemented properly.

QoS Overview

The majority of this book has discussed how Layer 2 and Layer 3 Catalyst switches forward packets from one switch port to another. On the surface, it might seem that there is only one way to forward packets—just look up the next packet's destination in a content-addressable memory (CAM) or Cisco Express Forwarding (CEF) table and send it on its way. But that addresses only *whether* the packet can be forwarded, not *how* it can be forwarded.

Different types of applications have different requirements for how their data should be sent end to end. For example, it might be acceptable to wait a short time for a web page to be displayed after a user requests it. That same user probably cannot tolerate the same delays in receiving packets that belong to a streaming video presentation or an audio telephone call. Any loss or delay in packet delivery could ruin the purpose of the application.

Three basic things can happen to packets as they are sent from one host to another across a network:

■ **Delay**—As a packet is sent from one network device to another, its delivery is delayed by some amount of time. This can be caused by the time required to send the packet serially across a wire, the time required for a router or switch to perform table lookups or make decisions, the time required for the data to travel over a geographically long path, and so on. The total delay from start to finish is called the *latency*. This is seen most easily as the time from when a user presses a key until the time the character is echoed and displayed in a terminal session.

■ **Jitter**—Some applications involve the delivery of a stream of related data. As these packets are delivered, variations can occur in the amount of delay so that they do not all arrive at predictable times. The variation in delay is called *jitter*. Audio streams are particularly susceptible to jitter; if the audio data is not played back at a constant rate, the resulting speech or music sounds choppy.

■ **Loss**—In extreme cases, packets that enter a congested or error-prone part of the network are simply dropped without delivery. Some amount of packet loss is acceptable and recoverable by applications that use a reliable, connection-oriented protocol such as TCP. Other application protocols are not as tolerant, and dropped packets mean data is missing.

To address and alleviate these conditions, a network can employ three basic types of QoS:

■ Best-effort delivery

■ Integrated services model

■ Differentiated services model

Keep in mind that QoS works toward making policies or promises to improve packet delivery from a sender to a receiver. The same QoS policies should be used on *every* network device that connects the sender to the receiver. QoS must be implemented end to end before it can be totally effective.

Best-Effort Delivery

A network that just forwards packets in the order they were received has no real QoS. Switches and routers then make their "best effort" to deliver packets as quickly as possible, with no regard for the type of traffic or the need for priority service.

To get an idea of how QoS operates in a network, consider a fire truck or an ambulance trying to quickly work its way through a crowded city. The lights are flashing and the siren is sounding to signal that this is a "priority" vehicle needing to get through ahead of everyone else. The priority vehicle does not need to obey normal traffic rules.

However, the best effort scenario says that the fire truck must stay within the normal flow of traffic. At an intersection, it must wait in the line or queue of traffic like any other vehicle—even if its lights and siren are on. It might arrive on time or too late to help, depending on the conditions along the road.

Integrated Services Model

One approach to QoS is the integrated services (IntServ) model. The basic idea is to prearrange a path for priority data along the complete path, from source to destination. Beginning with RFC 1633, the Resource Reservation Protocol (RSVP) was developed as the mechanism for scheduling and reserving adequate path bandwidth for an application.

The source application itself is involved by requesting QoS parameters through RSVP. Each network device along the way must check to see whether it can support the request. When a complete path meeting the minimum requirements is made, the source is signaled with a confirmation. Then the source application can begin using the path.

Applying the fire truck example to the IntServ model, a fire truck would radio ahead to the nearest intersection before it left the firehouse. Police stationed at each intersection would contact each other in turn to announce that the fire truck was coming and to assess the traffic conditions. The police might reserve a special lane so that the fire truck could move at full speed toward the destination, regardless of what other traffic might be present.

Differentiated Services Model

As you might imagine, the IntServ model does not scale very well when many sources are trying to compete with each other to reserve end-to-end bandwidth. Another approach is the differentiated services (DiffServ) model, which permits each network device to handle packets on an individual basis. Each router or switch can be configured with QoS policies to follow, and forwarding decisions are made accordingly.

DiffServ requires no advance reservations; QoS is handled dynamically, in a distributed fashion. In other words, whereas IntServ applies QoS on a per-flow basis, DiffServ applies it on a per-hop basis to a whole group of similar flows. DiffServ also bases its QoS decisions on information contained in each packet header.

Continuing with the emergency vehicle analogy, here police are stationed at every intersection, as before. However, none of them knows a fire truck is coming until they see the lights or hear the siren. At each intersection, a decision is made as to how to handle the approaching fire truck. Other traffic can be held back, if needed, so that the fire truck can go right through.

Giving premium service to voice traffic focuses almost entirely on the DiffServ model. QoS is a complex and intricate topic in itself. The CCNP SWITCH course and exam cover only the theory behind DiffServ QoS, along with the features and commands that address voice QoS specifically.

DiffServ QoS

DiffServ is a per-hop behavior, with each router or switch inspecting each packet's header to decide how to go about forwarding that packet. All the information needed for this decision is carried along with each packet in the header. The packet itself cannot affect how it will be handled. Instead, it merely presents some flags, classifications, or markings that can be used to make a forwarding decision based on QoS policies that are configured into each switch or router along the path.

Layer 2 QoS Classification

Layer 2 frames themselves have no mechanism to indicate the priority or importance of their contents. One frame looks just as important as another. Therefore, a Layer 2 switch can forward frames only according to a best-effort delivery.

When frames are carried from switch to switch, however, an opportunity for classification occurs. Recall that a trunk is used to carry frames from multiple VLANs between switches. The trunk does this by encapsulating the frames and adding a tag indicating the source VLAN number. The encapsulation also includes a field that can mark the class of service (CoS) of each frame. This can be used at switch boundaries to make some QoS decisions. After a trunk is unencapsulated at the far-end switch, the CoS information is removed and lost.

The two trunk encapsulations handle CoS differently:

- **IEEE 802.1Q**—Each frame is tagged with a 12-bit VLAN ID and a User field. The User field contains three 802.1p priority bits that indicate the frame CoS, a unitless value ranging from 0 (lowest-priority delivery) to 7 (highest-priority delivery). Frames from the native VLAN are not tagged (no VLAN ID or User field), so they receive a default CoS that is configured on the receiving switch.

- **Inter-Switch Link (ISL)**—Each frame is tagged with a 15-bit VLAN ID. In addition, next to the frame Type field is a 4-bit User field. The lower 3 bits of the User field are used as a CoS value. Although ISL is not standards-based, Catalyst switches make CoS seamless by copying the 802.1p CoS bits from an 802.1Q trunk into the User CoS bits of an ISL trunk. This allows CoS information to propagate along trunks of differing encapsulations.

Layer 3 QoS Classification with DSCP

From the beginning, IP packets have always had a type of service (ToS) byte that can be used to mark packets. This byte is divided into a 3-bit IP Precedence value and a 4-bit ToS value. This offers a rather limited mechanism for QoS because only the 3 bits of IP Precedence are used to describe the per-hop QoS behavior.

The DiffServ model keeps the existing IP ToS byte but uses it in a more scalable fashion. This byte also is referred to as the Differentiated Services (DS) field, with a different format, as shown in Figure 14-3. The 6-bit DS value is known as the differentiated service codepoint (DSCP) and is the one value that is examined by any DiffServ network device.

ToS Byte:	P2	P1	P0	T3	T2	T1	T0	Zero
DS Byte:	DS5	DS4	DS3	DS2	DS1	DS0	ECN1	ECN0
	(Class Selector)			(Drop Precedence)				

Figure 14-3 *ToS and DSCP Byte Formats*

Do not be confused by the dual QoS terminology—the ToS and DS bytes are the same, occupying the same location in the IP header. Only the names are different, along with the way the value is interpreted. In fact, the DSCP bits have been arranged to be backward compatible with the IP precedence bits so that a non-DiffServ device still can interpret some QoS information.

The DSCP value is divided into a 3-bit class selector and a 3-bit Drop Precedence value. Table 14-4 shows how the IP precedence, DSCP per-hop behavior, and DSCP codepoint names and numbers relate.

Table 14-4 *Mapping of IP Precedence and DSCP Fields*

IP Precedence (3 Bits)			DSCP (6 Bits)				
Name	Value	Bits	Per-Hop Behavior	Class Selector	Drop Precedence	Codepoint Name	DSCP Bits (Decimal)
Routine	0	000	Default			Default	000 000 (0)
Priority	1	001	AF	1	1: Low	AF11	001 010 (10)
					2: Medium	AF12	001 100 (12)
					3: High	AF13	001 110 (14)
Immediate	2	010	AF	2	1: Low	AF21	010 010 (18)
					2: Medium	AF22	010 100 (20)
					3: High	AF23	010 110 (22)

Table 14-4 *Mapping of IP Precedence and DSCP Fields*

IP Precedence (3 Bits)			DSCP (6 Bits)				
Name	Value	Bits	Per-Hop Behavior	Class Selector	Drop Pre-cedence	Code-point Name	DSCP Bits (Decimal)
Flash	3	011	AF	3	1: Low	AF31	011 010 (26)
					2: Medium	AF32	011 100 (28)
					3: High	AF33	011 110 (30)
Flash Override	4	100	AF	4	1: Low	AF41	100 010 (34)
					2: Medium	AF42	100 100 (36)
					3: High	AF43	100 110 (38)
Critical	5	101	EF			EF	101 110 (46)*
Internet-work Control	6	110					(48–55)
Network Control	7	111					(56–63)

*IP precedence value 5 (DSCP EF) corresponds to the range of DSCP bits 101000 through 101111, or 40–47. However, only the value 101110 or 46 is commonly used and is given the EF designation.

The three class selector bits (DS5 through DS3) coarsely classify packets into one of eight classes:

■ Class 0, the default class, offers only best-effort forwarding.

Key Topic

■ Classes 1 through 4 are called assured forwarding (AF) service levels. Higher AF class numbers indicate the presence of higher-priority traffic.

Packets in the AF classes can be dropped, if necessary, with the lower-class numbers the most likely to be dropped. For example, packets with AF Class 4 will be delivered in preference to packets with AF Class 3.

■ Class 5 is known as expedited forwarding (EF), with those packets given premium service. EF is the least likely to be dropped, so it always is reserved for time-critical data such as voice traffic.

■ Classes 6 and 7 are called internetwork control and network control, respectively, and are set aside for network control traffic. Usually, routers and switches use these classes for things such as the Spanning Tree Protocol and routing protocols. This ensures timely delivery of the packets that keep the network stable and operational.

Each class represented in the DSCP also has three levels of drop precedence, contained in bits DS2 through DS0 (DS0 is always zero):

- Low (1)

- Medium (2)

- High (3)

Within a class, packets marked with a higher drop precedence have the potential for being dropped before those with a lower value. In other words, a lower drop precedence value gives better service. This gives finer granularity to the decision of what packets to drop when necessary.

Tip: The DSCP value can be given as a codepoint name, with the class selector providing the two letters and a number followed by the drop precedence number. For example, class AF Level 2 with drop precedence 1 (low) is written as AF21. The DSCP commonly is given as a decimal value. For AF21, the decimal value is 18. The relationship is confusing, and Table 14-2 should be a handy aid.

You should try to remember a few codepoint names and numbers. Some common values are EF (46) and most of the classes with low drop precedences: AF41 (34), AF31 (26), AF21 (18), and AF11 (10). Naturally, the default DSCP has no name (0).

Implementing QoS for Voice

To manipulate packets according to QoS policies, a switch somehow must identify which level of service each packet should receive. This process is known as *classification*. Each packet is classified according to the type of traffic (UDP or TCP port number, for example), according to parameters matched by an access list or something more complex, such as by stateful inspection of a traffic flow.

Recall that IP packets carry a ToS or DSCP value within their headers as they travel around a network. Frames on a trunk also can have CoS values associated with them. A switch then can decide whether to trust the ToS, DSCP, or CoS values already assigned to inbound packets. If it trusts any of these values, the values are carried over and used to make QoS decisions inside the switch.

If the QoS values are not trusted, they can be reassigned or overruled. This way, a switch can set the values to something known and trusted, and something that falls within the QoS policies that must be met. This prevents nonpriority users in the network from falsely setting the ToS or DSCP values of their packets to inflated levels so that they receive priority service.

Every switch must decide whether to trust incoming QoS values. Generally, an organization should be able to trust QoS parameters anywhere inside its own network. At the boundary with another organization or service provider, QoS typically should not be trusted. It is also prudent to trust only QoS values that have been assigned by the network devices themselves. Therefore, the QoS values produced by the end users should not be trusted until the network can verify or override them.

The perimeter formed by switches that do not trust incoming QoS is called the *trust boundary*. Usually, the trust boundary exists at the farthest reaches of the enterprise network (access-layer switches and WAN or ISP demarcation points). When the trust boundary has been identified and the switches there are configured with untrusted ports, everything else inside the perimeter can be configured to blindly trust incoming QoS values.

Key
Topic

> **Tip:** Every switch and router within a network must be configured with the appropriate QoS features and policies so that a trust boundary is completely formed. The SWITCH exam limits QoS coverage to basic QoS configuration using the Auto-QoS feature. You can find more information about advanced QoS topics in the Implementing Cisco Quality of Service (QoS) course

Figure 14-4 shows a simple network in which the trust boundary is defined at the edges, where the network connects to end users and public networks. On Catalyst A, port Gigabit Ethernet2/1 is configured to consider inbound data as untrusted. Catalyst B's port Fast Ethernet0/2 connects to a PC that also is untrusted. The Cisco IP Phone on Catalyst B port Fast Ethernet0/1 is a special case because it supports its own voice traffic and an end user's PC. Therefore, the trust boundary cannot be clearly defined on that switch port.

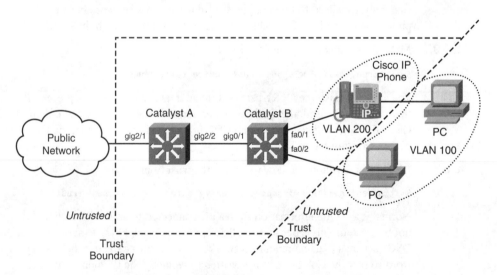

Figure 14-4 *QoS Trust Boundary Example*

Configuring a Trust Boundary

When a Cisco IP Phone is connected to a switch port, think of the phone as another switch (which it is). If you install the phone as a part of your network, you probably can trust the QoS information relayed by the phone.

However, remember that the phone also has two sources of data:

■ **The VoIP packets native to the phone—** The phone can control precisely what QoS information is included in the voice packets because it produces those packets.

■ **The user PC data switch port—** Packets from the PC data port are generated elsewhere, so the QoS information cannot necessarily be trusted to be correct or fair.

A switch instructs an attached IP Phone through CDP messages on how it should extend QoS trust to its own user data switch port. To configure the trust extension, use the following configuration steps:

Step 1.   Enable QoS on the switch:

```
Switch(config)# mls qos
```

By default, QoS is disabled globally on a switch and all QoS information is allowed to pass from one switch port to another. When you enable QoS, all switch ports are configured as untrusted, by default.

Step 2.   Define the QoS parameter that will be trusted:

```
Switch(config)# interface type mod/num
Switch(config-if)# mls qos trust {cos | ip-precedence | dscp}
```

You can choose to trust the CoS, IP precedence, or DSCP values of incoming packets on the switch port. Only one of these parameters can be selected. Generally, for Cisco IP Phones, you should use the **cos** keyword because the phone can control the CoS values on its two-VLAN trunk with the switch.

Step 3.   Make the trust conditional:

```
Switch(config-if)# mls qos trust device cisco-phone
```

You also can make the QoS trust conditional if a Cisco IP Phone is present. If this command is used, the QoS parameter defined in Step 2 is trusted only if a Cisco IP Phone is detected through CDP. If a phone is not detected, the QoS parameter is not trusted.

Step 4.   Instruct the IP Phone on how to extend the trust boundary:

```
Switch(config-if)# switchport priority extend {cos value | trust}
```

Normally, the QoS information from a PC connected to an IP Phone should not be trusted. This is because the PC's applications might try to spoof CoS or DSCP settings to gain premium network service. In this case, use the **cos** keyword so that the CoS bits are overwritten to *value* by the IP Phone as packets are forwarded to the switch. If CoS values from the PC cannot be trusted, they should be overwritten to a value of 0.

In some cases, the PC might be running trusted applications that are allowed to request specific QoS or levels of service. Here, the IP Phone can extend complete QoS trust to the PC, allowing the CoS bits to be forwarded through the phone unmodified. This is done with the **trust** keyword.

By default, a switch instructs an attached IP Phone to consider the PC port as untrusted. The phone will overwrite the CoS values to 0.

What about switch ports that don't connect to end-user or phone devices? Switch uplinks always should be considered as trusted ports—as long as they connect to other trusted devices that are within the QoS boundary. QoS parameters are trusted or overwritten at the network edge, as packets enter the trusted domain. After that, every switch inside the trusted boundary can implicitly trust and use the QoS parameters in any packet passing through.

You can configure a switch uplink port to be trusted with the following commands:

```
Switch(config)# interface type mod/num
Switch(config-if)# mls qos trust cos
```

Here, the trust is not conditional. The switch will trust only the CoS values that are found in the incoming packets.

Tip: A Cisco switch also has a CoS-to-DSCP map that is used to convert inbound CoS values to DSCP values. The CoS information is useful only on trunk interfaces because it can be carried within the trunk encapsulation. CoS must be converted to DSCP or IP precedence, which can be carried along in the IP packet headers on any type of connection.

Switches use a default CoS-to-DSCP mapping, which can be configured or changed. However, this is beyond the scope of the CCNP SWITCH course and exam.

Using Auto-QoS to Simplify a Configuration

You can also configure Cisco switches to support a variety of other QoS mechanisms and parameters. The list of features and configuration commands can be overwhelming, and the actual configuration can be quite complex. This is one reason why the bulk of QoS topics are no longer covered on the SWITCH exam.

Courses and testing aside, you will sometimes need to configure some advanced QoS features on a switch. To reduce the complexity, Cisco introduced the Auto-QoS feature on most switch platforms. By entering only a couple of configuration commands, you can enable the switch to automatically configure a variety of QoS parameters.

Auto-QoS is actually handled by a macro command, which in turn enters many other configuration commands as if they were entered from the command-line interface. Because of this, Auto-QoS is best used on a switch that still has the default QoS configuration. Otherwise, any existing QoS commands could be overwritten or could interfere with the commands produced by the Auto-QoS macro.

Tip: The Auto-QoS feature is designed to automatically configure many more advanced QoS parameters in specific applications. For example, Auto-QoS can be used on switch interfaces where Cisco IP Phones are connected. Auto-QoS is not meant to be used on all switches in a network. Therefore, you should consider using it in access layer switches and not necessarily the network core.

The configuration commands resulting from Auto-QoS were developed from rigorous testing and Cisco best practices. Auto-QoS handles the following types of QoS configuration:

■   Enabling QoS

■   CoS-to-DSCP mapping for QoS marking

■   Ingress and egress queue tuning

■   Strict priority queues for egress voice traffic

■   Establishing an interface QoS trust boundary

Use the following steps to configure Auto-QoS:

Step 1.   Select an interface at the QoS boundary:

```
Switch(config)# interface type mod/num
```

Step 2.   Enable Auto-QoS with the appropriate trust:

```
Switch(config-if)# auto qos voip {cisco-phone | cisco-softphone | trust}
```

If the switch port is connected to a Cisco IP Phone, you should use the **cisco-phone** keyword. After that has been enabled, the switch will trust the class of service information presented by the phone, if a phone is detected by CDP. If no phone is connected, the port is considered untrusted.

If a PC running the Cisco SoftPhone application is connected, choose the **cisco-softphone** keyword. Packets that are received with DSCP values of 24, 26, or 46 will be trusted; packets with any other value will have their DSCP values set to 0.

On a switch port acting as an uplink to another switch or router, you should use the **trust** keyword. All packets received on that port will be trusted, and the QoS information will be left intact.

Tip: If you have already configured Auto-QoS on an interface by using the **cisco-phone**, **cisco-softphone**, or **trust** keyword, you won't be allowed to use the **auto qos voip** command again on the same interface. Instead, first remove any existing Auto-QoS by entering the **no auto qos voip** command. Then use the **auto qos voip** command with the desired keyword to enable Auto-QoS.

Remember that the **auto qos voip** command is actually a macro that executes many other configuration commands for you. The **auto qos voip** command will appear in the switch configuration, along with the other commands it enters. You won't see the additional commands until you show the running configuration. However, using the **debug auto qos** EXEC command displays the additional commands in the resulting debug messages. (Do not forget to disable the debugging with **no debug auto qos** when you finish with it.)

Example 14-5 shows what Auto-QoS is doing behind the scenes. By entering one interface configuration command, you can effectively configure many QoS parameters—even if you do not understand their functions. The commands are shown here as a demonstration; the CCNP SWITCH course and exam do not cover their meaning or use.

Interface Fast Ethernet 0/37 normally has a Cisco IP Phone connected to it. Therefore, the **auto qos voip cisco-phone** command is used. Notice that among the many **mls qos** and **wrr-queue** QoS-related commands are two shaded commands that enable trust for CoS values coming from a Cisco phone. Interface Gigabit Ethernet 0/1 is an uplink to another trusted switch, so the **auto qos voip trust** command is used on it. The shaded **mls qos trust cos** command causes the CoS information to be implicitly trusted.

Example 14-5   *Auto-QoS Commands Revealed*

```
Switch# debug auto qos
AutoQoS debugging is on

Switch# config term
Enter configuration commands, one per line.  End with CNTL/Z.

Switch(config)# interface fastethernet 0/37
Switch(config-if)# auto qos voip cisco-phone
Switch(config-if)#

*Sep  7 04:14:41.618 EDT: mls qos map cos-dscp 0 8 16 26 32 46 48 56
*Sep  7 04:14:41.622 EDT: mls qos min-reserve 5 170
*Sep  7 04:14:41.622 EDT: mls qos min-reserve 6 85
*Sep  7 04:14:41.622 EDT: mls qos min-reserve 7 51
*Sep  7 04:14:41.626 EDT: mls qos min-reserve 8 34
*Sep  7 04:14:41.626 EDT: mls qos
*Sep  7 04:14:42.598 EDT: interface FastEthernet0/37
*Sep  7 04:14:42.598 EDT:    mls qos trust device cisco-phone
*Sep  7 04:14:42.602 EDT:    mls qos trust cos
*Sep  7 04:14:42.606 EDT:    wrr-queue bandwidth 10 20 70 1
*Sep  7 04:14:42.610 EDT:    wrr-queue min-reserve 1 5
*Sep  7 04:14:42.618 EDT:    wrr-queue min-reserve 2 6
*Sep  7 04:14:42.626 EDT:    wrr-queue min-reserve 3 7
*Sep  7 04:14:42.634 EDT:    wrr-queue min-reserve 4 8
*Sep  7 04:14:42.642 EDT:    no wrr-queue cos-map
*Sep  7 04:14:42.646 EDT:    wrr-queue cos-map 1   0 1
*Sep  7 04:14:42.650 EDT:    wrr-queue cos-map 2   2 4
*Sep  7 04:14:42.654 EDT:    wrr-queue cos-map 3   3 6 7
*Sep  7 04:14:42.658 EDT:    wrr-queue cos-map 4   5
*Sep  7 04:14:42.662 EDT:    priority-queue out

Switch(config-if)# interface gigabitethernet 0/1
Switch(config-if)# auto qos voip trust
Switch(config-if)#
*Sep  7 15:05:50.943 EDT: interface GigabitEthernet0/1
```

```
*Sep  7 15:05:50.947 EDT:   mls qos trust cos
*Sep  7 15:05:50.951 EDT:   wrr-queue bandwidth 10 20 70 1
*Sep  7 15:05:50.955 EDT:   wrr-queue queue-limit 50 25 15 10
*Sep  7 15:05:50.959 EDT:   no wrr-queue cos-map
*Sep  7 15:05:50.963 EDT:   wrr-queue cos-map 1   0 1
*Sep  7 15:05:50.967 EDT:   wrr-queue cos-map 2   2 4
*Sep  7 15:05:50.971 EDT:   wrr-queue cos-map 3   3 6 7
*Sep  7 15:05:50.975 EDT:   wrr-queue cos-map 4   5
*Sep  7 15:05:50.979 EDT:   priority-queue out
```

Verifying Voice QoS

A switch port can be configured with a QoS trust state with the connected device. If that device is an IP Phone, the switch can instruct the phone on whether to extend QoS trust to an attached PC.

To verify how QoS trust has been extended to the IP Phone itself, use the following EXEC command:

Switch# **show mls qos interface** *type mod/num*

Key
Topic

If the port is trusted, all traffic forwarded by the IP Phone is accepted with the QoS information left intact. If the port is not trusted, even the voice packets can have their QoS information overwritten by the switch. Example 14-6 demonstrates some sample output from the **show mls qos interface** command, where the switch port is trusting CoS information from the attached IP Phone.

Example 14-6   *Verifying QoS Trust to the IP Phone*

```
Switch# show mls qos interface fastethernet 0/1
FastEthernet0/1
trust state: trust cos
trust mode: trust cos
trust enabled flag: ena
COS override: dis
default COS: 0
DSCP Mutation Map: Default DSCP Mutation Map
Trust device: none
```

Next, you can verify how the IP Phone has been instructed to treat incoming QoS information from its attached PC or other device. This is shown in the **trust device:** line in Example 14-6, where the device is the IP Phone's device. You also can use the following EXEC command:

Switch# **show interface** *type mod/num* **switchport**

Here, the device trust is called *appliance trust*, as shown in Example 14-7.

Example 14-7   *Alternative Method for Verifying QoS Trust to an IP Phone*

```
Switch# show interface fastethernet 0/1 switchport
Name: Fa0/1
Switchport: Enabled
[output deleted...]
Voice VLAN: 2 (VLAN0002)
Appliance trust: none
```

Again, the IP Phone's device is not being trusted. If the switch port were configured with the **switchport priority extend trust** command, the appliance trust would show *trusted*. Example 14-8 shows the configuration commands that have been added to a switch interface where a Cisco IP Phone is connected.

Example 14-8   *Switch Port Configuration Commands to Support a Cisco IP Phone*

```
Switch# show running-config interface fastethernet 0/47
Building configuration...
Current configuration : 219 bytes
!
interface FastEthernet0/47
 switchport access vlan 10
 switchport trunk encapsulation dot1q
 switchport mode access
switchport voice vlan 100
 mls qos trust device cisco-phone
 mls qos trust cos
 no mdix auto
end
Switch#
```

If the IP Phone is not connected to the switch port, it is not detected and the trust parameter is not enabled, as Example 14-9 demonstrates.

Example 14-9   *Displaying IP Phone Connection and Trust Status*

```
Switch# show mls qos interface fastethernet 0/1
FastEthernet0/1
trust state: not trusted
trust mode: trust cos
trust enabled flag: dis
COS override: dis
default COS: 0
DSCP Mutation Map: Default DSCP Mutation Map
Trust device: cisco-phone
Switch#
```

When a Cisco IP Phone is connected, power is applied and the phone is detected. Then the conditional QoS trust (CoS, in this case) is enabled, as demonstrated in Example 14-10.

Example 14-10   *Conditional Trust (CoS) Enabled on a Cisco IP Phone*

```
6d18h: %ILPOWER-7-DETECT: Interface Fa1/0/1: Power Device detected: Cisco PD
6d18h: %ILPOWER-5-POWER_GRANTED: Interface Fa1/0/1: Power granted
6d18h: %LINK-3-UPDOWN: Interface FastEthernet1/0/1, changed state to up
6d18h: %LINEPROTO-5-UPDOWN: Line protocol on Interface FastEthernet1/0/1, changed
   state to up
6d18h: %SWITCH_QOS_TB-5-TRUST_DEVICE_DETECTED: cisco-phone detected on port Fa1/
   0/1, port trust enabled.
Switch# show mls qos interface fastethernet 1/0/1
FastEthernet1/0/1
trust state: trust cos
trust mode: trust cos
trust enabled flag: ena
COS override: dis
default COS: 0
DSCP Mutation Map: Default DSCP Mutation Map
Trust device: cisco-phone
Switch#
```

If you have used Auto-QoS to configure an interface, you can use the **show auto qos** [**interface** *type mod/num*] command to view the configuration status as demonstrated in Example 14-11.

Example 14-11   *Verifying Auto-Qos Interface Configuration*

```
Switch# show auto qos interface fastethernet 0/37
FastEthernet0/37
auto qos voip cisco-phone
```

Exam Preparation Tasks

Review All Key Topics

Review the most important topics in the chapter, noted with the Key Topic icon in the outer margin of the page. Table 14-5 lists a reference of these key topics and the page numbers on which each is found.

Table 14-5 *Key Topics for Chapter 14*

Key Topic Element	Description	Page Number
Paragraph	Describes Power over Ethernet for Cisco IP Phones	306
Table	Lists IEEE 802.3af PoE device classes	307
Paragraph	Explains voice VLANs	310
List	Describes delay, jitter, and packet loss—things that can affect packet delivery.	315
Paragraph	Describes best-effort packet delivery	316
Paragraph	Describes the differentiated services QoS model	316
Paragraph	Explains CoS marking on a trunk link	317
List	Describes the DSCP class breakdown, including EF	319
Paragraph	Describes a QoS trust boundary	321
List	Explains how to configure QoS trust on a switch interface	322
List	Explains how to configure Auto-QoS on a switch interface	324
Paragraph	Describes how to verify QoS configuration on a switch interface	326

Complete Tables and Lists from Memory

Print a copy of Appendix C, "Memory Tables," (found on the CD), or at least the section for this chapter, and complete the tables and lists from memory. Appendix D, "Memory Tables Answer Key," also on the CD, includes completed tables and lists to check your work.

Define Key Terms

Define the following key terms from this chapter, and check your answers in the glossary:

Power over Ethernet (PoE), power class, voice VLAN, quality of service (QoS), delay, jitter, packet loss, best effort delivery, differentiated services (DiffServ) model, CoS marking, expedited forwarding (EF), trust boundary, Auto-QoS

Use Command Reference to Check Your Memory

This section includes the most important configuration and EXEC commands covered in this chapter. It might not be necessary to memorize the complete syntax of every command, but you should remember the basic keywords that are needed.

To test your memory of the telephony and voice configuration commands, cover the right side of Tables 14-6 and 14-7 with a piece of paper, read the description on the left side, and then see how much of the command you can remember.

Remember that the CCNP exam focuses on practical or hands-on skills that are used by a networking professional.

Table 14-6 *IP Telephony Configuration Commands*

Task	Command Syntax
Set power over Ethernet behavior.	Switch(config-if)# **power inline** {**auto**	**never**}
Enable QoS globally.	Switch(config)# **mls qos**
Define QoS parameter that will be trusted on an interface.	Switch(config-if)# **mls qos trust** {**cos**	**ip-precedence**	**dscp**}
Conditionally trust a Cisco IP Phone.	Switch(config-if)# **mls qos trust device cisco-phone**
Define the trunking on a port to a Cisco IP Phone.	Switch(config-if)# **switchport voice vlan** {*vlan-id*	**dot1p**	**untagged**	**none**}
Define the trust relationship of the IP Phone.	Switch(config-if)# **switchport priority extend** {**cos** *value*	**trust**}
Enable Auto-QoS on an interface.	Switch(config-if)# **auto qos voip** {**cisco-phone**	**cisco-softphone**	**trust**}

Table 14-7 *IP Telephony Verification Commands*

Task	Command Syntax
Display Power over Ethernet status.	Switch# **show power inline** [*type mod/num*]
Verify the voice VLAN	Switch# **show interface** *type mod/num* **switchport**
Display how QoS trust is extended to the phone.	Switch# **show mls qos interface** *type mod/num*
Verify Auto-QoS settings.	Switch# **show auto qos** [**interface** *type mod/num*]

This chapter covers the following topics that you need to master for the CCNP SWITCH exam:

Wireless LAN Basics—This section discusses wireless networks as they compare to wired Ethernet networks.

WLAN Building Blocks—This section covers wireless service sets in addition to wireless access points and their coverage areas.

WLAN Architecture—This section explores the design and operation of traditional WLANs and the Cisco Unified Wireless network architectures.

Roaming in a Cisco Unified Wireless Network—This section explains various roaming scenarios as a client moves between lightweight APs and controllers.

Configuring Switch Ports for WLAN Use—This section covers the tasks necessary to provide connectivity to WLAN components.

CHAPTER 15

Integrating Wireless LANs

Switched networks generally form the foundation of an enterprise network. Connectivity is offered from the core layer downward to reach end users located at the access layer. Traditionally, these end users have used wires to connect to the access layer.

Wireless networks allow the access layer to be extended to end users without wires. By designing and placing wireless LAN devices across an entire area of the network, end users can even become mobile and move around without losing their network connections.

This chapter presents an overview of the technologies used in wireless LANs. By becoming familiar with these topics, you can understand, design, and use wireless LAN devices to expand your switched network to reach wireless users.

"Do I Know This Already?" Quiz

The "Do I Know This Already?" quiz allows you to assess whether you should read this entire chapter thoroughly or jump to the "Exam Preparation Tasks" section. If you are in doubt based on your answers to these questions or your own assessment of your knowledge of the topics, read the entire chapter. Table 15-1 outlines the major headings in this chapter and the "Do I Know This Already?" quiz questions that go with them. You can find the answers in Appendix A, "Answers to the 'Do I Know This Already?' Quizzes."

Table 15-1 *"Do I Know This Already?" Foundation Topics Section-to-Question Mapping*

Foundation Topics Section	Questions Covered In This Section
Wireless LAN Basics	1–2
WLAN Building Blocks	3–4
WLAN Architecture	5–10
Roaming in a Cisco Unified Wireless Network	11–12
Configuring Switch Ports for WLAN Use	13–16

1. Which one of the following standard sets is used in wireless LANs?

    a. IEEE 802.1
    b. IEEE 802.3
    c. IEEE 802.5
    d. IEEE 802.11

2. Which one of the following methods is used to minimize collisions in a wireless LAN?

  a. CSMA/CD

  b. CSMA/CA

  c. LWAPP

  d. LACP

3. A wireless scenario is made up of five wireless clients and two APs connected by a switch. Which one of the following correctly describes the wireless network?

  a. BSS

  b. ESS

  c. IBSS

  d. CBS

4. If a wireless access point is connected to a switch by a trunk port, which one of the following is mapped to a VLAN?

  a. Channel

  b. Frequency

  c. BSS

  d. SSID

5. Which of the following terms represents a Cisco wireless access point that cannot operate independently?

  a. Autonomous AP

  b. Roaming AP

  c. Lightweight AP

  d. Dependent AP

6. Suppose that an autonomous AP is used to support wireless clients. Which one of the following answers lists the devices that traffic must take when passing from one wireless client to another?

  a. Through the AP only.

  b. Through the AP and its controller.

  c. Through the controller only.

  d. None of these answers is correct; traffic can go directly over the air.

7. Suppose that a lightweight AP is used to support wireless clients. Which one of the following answers lists the device path that traffic must take when passing from one wireless client to another?

  a. Through the AP only.

  b. Through the AP and its controller.

  c. Through the controller only.

  d. None of these answers is correct; traffic can go directly over the air.

8. A lightweight access point is said to have which one of the following architectures?

    a. Proxy MAC

    b. Tunnel MAC

    c. Split-MAC

    d. Fat MAC

9. How does a lightweight access point communicate with a wireless LAN controller?

    a. Through an IPsec tunnel

    b. Through an LWAPP or CAPWAP tunnel

    c. Through a GRE tunnel

    d. Directly over Layer 2

10. Which one of the following types of traffic is sent securely over an LWAPP tunnel?

    a. Control messages

    b. User data

    c. DHCP requests

    d. 802.11 beacons

11. Which one of the following must be consistent for a wireless client to roam between lightweight APs that are managed by the same WLC?

    a. SSID

    b. Mobility group

    c. VLAN ID

    d. AP management VLAN

12. Which one of the following must be consistent for a wireless client to roam between lightweight APs that are managed by two different WLCs?

    a. VLAN ID

    b. SSID

    c. AP management VLAN

    d. Mobility group

13. Which one of the following locations is appropriate for an LAP?

    a. Access-layer switch port

    b. Distribution-layer switch port

    c. Core-layer switch port

    d. Data center switch port

14. Which one of the following locations is appropriate for a WLC?

    a.   Access-layer switch port

    b.   Distribution-layer switch port

    c.   Core-layer switch port

    d.   Data center switch port

15. Which one of the following is the correct switch configuration for a port connected to an LAP?

    a.   switchport mode trunk

    b.   switchport mode lap

    c.   switchport mode access

    d.   switchport mode transparent

16. Suppose an LAP/WLC combination is used to provide connectivity from SSID "staff" to VLAN 17. Which one of the following is the correct extent for the VLAN?

    a.   VLAN 17 exists on the LAP only.

    b.   VLAN 17 extends from the LAP to the access switch only.

    c.   VLAN 17 extends from the LAP to the WLC.

    d.   VLAN 17 extends from the distribution switch to the WLC.

Foundation Topics

Wireless LAN Basics

This chapter presents wireless LAN (WLAN) operation from a practical viewpoint, building on the knowledge you've gained from the switched LAN topics. After all, this is a book (and exam) about switching technology, so you should know enough about wireless LANs to be able to integrate them into your switched network.

Comparing Wireless and Wired LANs

How exactly does a wireless LAN get integrated with a wired LAN? Where does switching fit into a wireless LAN? Before answering these questions, it might be helpful to see how the two technologies compare.

At the most basic level, switched networks involve wires, and wireless networks don't. That might seem silly, but it points out some major differences in the physical layer.

A traditional Ethernet network is defined by the IEEE 802.3 standards. Every Ethernet connection must operate under tightly controlled conditions, especially regarding the physical link itself. For example, the link status, link speed, and duplex mode must all operate like the standards describe. Wireless LANs have a similar arrangement but are defined by the IEEE 802.11 standards.

Wired Ethernet devices have to transmit and receive Ethernet frames according to the carrier sense multiple access/collision detect (CSMA/CD) method. On a shared Ethernet segment, where PCs communicate in half-duplex mode, each PC can freely "talk" first, and then listen for collisions with other devices that are also talking. The whole process of detecting collisions is based on having wired connections of a certain maximum length, with a certain maximum latency as a frame travels from one end of the segment to another before being detected at the far end.

Full-duplex or switched Ethernet links are not plagued with collisions or contention for the bandwidth. They do have to abide by the same specifications, though. For example, Ethernet frames must still be transmitted and received within an expected amount of time on a full-duplex link. This forces the maximum length of full-duplex, twisted-pair cabling to be the same as that of a half-duplex link.

Even though wireless LANs are also based on a set of stringent standards, the wireless medium itself is challenging to control. Generally speaking, when a PC attaches to a wired Ethernet network, it shares that network connection with a known number of other devices that are also connected. When the same PC uses a wireless network, it does so over the air. No wires or outlets exist at the access layer, as other end users are free to use the same air.

A wireless LAN then becomes a shared network, where a varying number of hosts contend for the use of the "air" at any time. Collisions are a fact of life in a wireless LAN because every wireless connection is in half-duplex mode.

Tip: IEEE 802.11 WLANs are always half duplex because transmitting and receiving stations use the same frequency. Only one station can transmit at any time; otherwise, collisions occur. To achieve full-duplex mode, all transmitting would have to occur on one frequency, and all receiving would occur over a different frequency—much like full-duplex Ethernet links work. Although this is certainly possible and practical, the 802.11 standards do not permit full-duplex operation.

Avoiding Collisions in a WLAN

When two or more wireless stations transmit at the same time, their signals become mixed. Receiving stations can see the result only as garbled data, noise, or errors.

No clear-cut way exists to determine whether a collision has occurred. Even the transmitting stations won't realize it because their receivers must be turned off while they are transmitting. As a basic feedback mechanism, whenever a wireless station transmits a frame, the receiving wireless station must send an acknowledgment back to confirm that the frame was received error-free.

Acknowledgment frames serve as a rudimentary collision detection tool; however, it does not work to prevent collisions from occurring in the first place.

The IEEE 802.11 standards use the CSMA/CA method. Notice that wired 802.3 networks detect collisions, whereas 802.11 networks try to avoid collisions.

Collision avoidance works by requiring all stations to listen before they transmit a frame. When a station has a frame that needs to be sent, one of the two following conditions occurs:

- **No other device is transmitting**—The station can transmit its frame immediately. The intended receiving station must send an acknowledgment frame to confirm that the original frame arrived intact and collision-free.

- **Another device is already transmitting a frame**—The station must wait until the frame in progress has completed; then it must wait a random amount of time before transmitting its own frame.

Wireless frames can vary in size. When a frame is transmitted, how can other stations know when the frame will be completed and the wireless medium is available for others to use? Obviously, stations could simply listen for silence, but doing so is not always efficient. Other stations can listen, too, and would likely decide to transmit at the same time. The 802.11 standards require all stations to wait a short amount of time, called the DCF interframe space (DIFS), before transmitting anything at all.

Transmitting stations can provide an estimate of the amount of time needed to send a frame by including a duration value within the 802.11 header. The duration contains the number of timeslots (typically in microseconds) needed for the size of frame being sent. Other wireless stations must look at the duration value and wait that length of time before considering their own transmissions.

Because every listening station receives and follows the same duration value found in a transmitted frame, every one of them might decide to transmit their own frames after the duration time has elapsed. This would result in a collision—the very condition that should be avoided.

In addition to the duration timer, every wireless station must also implement a random backoff timer. Before transmitting a frame, a station must select a random number of timeslots to wait. This number lies between zero and a maximum contention window value. The idea here is that stations ready to transmit will each wait a random amount of time, minimizing the number of stations that will try to transmit immediately.

This whole process is called the distributed coordination function (DCF) and is illustrated in Figure 15-1. Three wireless users have a frame to send at varying times. The following sequence of events occurs:

1. User A listens and determines that no other users are transmitting. User A transmits his frame and advertises the frame duration.

2. User B has a frame to transmit. He must wait until user A's frame is completed, and then wait until the DIFS period has expired.

3. B waits a random backoff time before attempting to transmit.

4. While user B is waiting, user C has a frame to transmit. He listens and detects that no one is transmitting. User C waits a random time, which is shorter than User B's random time.

5. User B transmits a frame and advertises the frame duration.

6. User C must now wait the duration of user B's frame plus the DIFS time before attempting to transmit again.

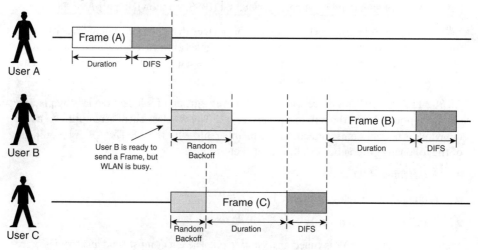

Figure 15-1 *Avoiding Collisions with the DCF Process*

Because the backoff timer is random, a chance still exists that two or more stations will choose the same value. Nothing else will prevent these stations from transmitting at the same time and causing a collision. This will simply be seen as an error over the wireless network; no acknowledgments will be returned, and the stations will have to reconsider sending their frames again.

Finally, what if a station waits until its random backoff timer expires and is ready to transmit, only to find that someone else is already transmitting? The waiting station must now wait the duration of the newly transmitted frame, followed by the DIFS time, and then the random backoff time.

WLAN Building Blocks

At the most basic level, a wireless medium has no inherent organization. For example, a PC with wireless capability can simply bring up its wireless adapter anywhere at any time. Naturally, there must be something else that can also send and receive over the wireless media before the PC can communicate.

Tip: In IEEE 802.11 terminology, any group of wireless devices is known as a service set. The devices must share a common service set identifier (SSID), which is a text string included in every frame sent. If the SSIDs match across the sender and receiver, the two devices can communicate.

The PC, as an end-user station, becomes a client of the wireless network. It must have a wireless network adapter and a supplicant, or software that interacts with the wireless protocols.

The 802.11 standards allow two or more wireless clients to communicate directly with each other, with no other means of network connectivity. This is known as an ad hoc wireless network, or an Independent basic service set (IBSS), as shown in part A of Figure 15-2.

No inherent control exists over the number of devices that can transmit and receive frames over a wireless medium. As well, many variables exist that can affect whether a wireless station can receive from or transmit to other stations. This makes providing reliable wireless access to all stations difficult.

An 802.11 BSS centralizes access and control over a group of wireless devices by placing an access point (AP) as the hub of the service set. Any wireless client attempting to use the wireless network must first arrange a membership with the AP. The AP can require any of the following criteria before allowing a client to join:

- A matching SSID

- A compatible wireless data rate

- Authentication credentials

Membership with the AP is called an *association*. The client must send an association request message, and the AP grants or denies the request by sending an association reply message. When associated, all communications to and from the client must pass through the AP, as shown in part B of Figure 15-2. Clients cannot communicate directly with each other as in an ad hoc network or IBSS.

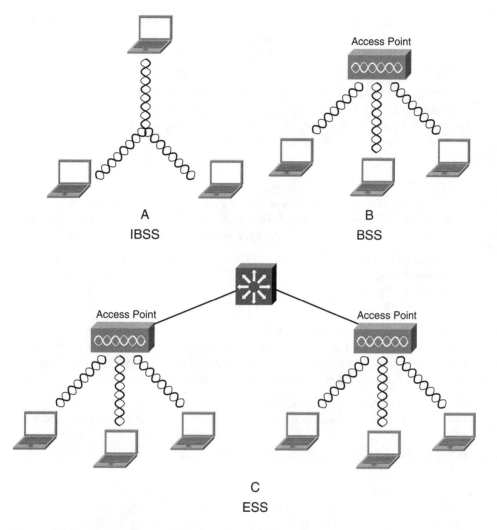

Figure 15-2 *Comparison of Wireless Service Sets*

Tip: Keep in mind that regardless of the association status, any PC is capable of listening to or receiving the frames that are sent over a wireless medium. Frames are freely available over the air to anyone who is within range to receive them.

A wireless AP is not a passive device like an Ethernet hub, however. An AP manages its wireless network, advertises its own existence so that clients can associate, and controls the communication process. For example, recall that every data frame sent successfully (without a collision) over a wireless medium must be acknowledged. The AP is responsible for sending the acknowledgment frames back to the sending stations.

Notice that a BSS involves a single AP and no explicit connection into a regular Ethernet network. In that setting, the AP and its associated clients make up a standalone network.

An AP can also uplink into an Ethernet network because it has both wireless and wired capabilities. If APs are placed at different geographic locations, they can all be interconnected by a switched infrastructure. This is called an 802.11 extended service set (ESS), as shown in part C of Figure 15-2.

In an ESS, a wireless client can associate with one AP while it is physically located near that AP. If the client later moves to a different location, it can associate with a different nearby AP. The 802.11 standards also define a method to allow the client to roam or to be passed from one AP to another as its location changes.

Access Point Operation

An AP's primary function is to bridge wireless data from the air to a normal wired network. An AP can accept "connections" from a number of wireless clients so that they become members of the LAN, as if the same clients were using wired connections.

An AP can also act as a bridge to form a single wireless link from one LAN to another over a long distance. In that case, an AP is needed on each end of the wireless link. AP-to-AP or line-of-sight links are commonly used for connectivity between buildings or between cities.

Cisco has developed an AP platform that can even bridge wireless LAN traffic from AP to AP in a daisy-chain fashion. This allows a large open outdoor area to be covered with a wireless LAN but without the use of network cabling. The APs form a mesh topology, much like an ESS where APs are interconnected by other wireless connections.

APs act as the central point of access (hence the AP name), controlling client access to the wireless LAN. Any client attempting to use the WLAN must first establish an association with an AP. The AP can allow open access so that any client can associate, or it can tighten control by requiring authentication credentials or other criteria before allowing associations.

The WLAN operation is tightly coupled to feedback from the far end of a wireless connection. For example, clients must handshake with an AP before they can associate and use the WLAN. At the most basic level, this assures a working two-way wireless connection because both client and AP must send and receive frames successfully. This process removes the possibility of one-way communication, where the client can hear the AP but the AP can't hear the client.

In addition, the AP can control many aspects of its WLAN by requiring conditions to be met before clients can associate. For example, the AP can require that clients support specific data rates, specific security measures, and specific credentials during client association.

You can think of an AP as a translational bridge, where frames from two dissimilar media are translated and then bridged at Layer 2. In simple terms, the AP is in charge of mapping a VLAN to an SSID. This is shown in the left portion of Figure 15-3, where VLAN 10 on the wired network is being extended to the AP over a switch port in access mode. The AP maps VLAN 10 to the wireless LAN using SSID Marketing. Users associated with the Marketing SSID will appear to be connected to VLAN 10.

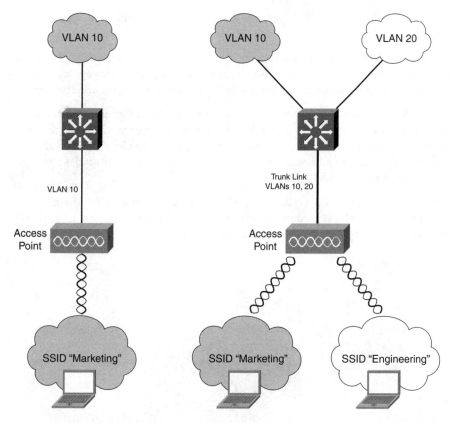

Figure 15-3   *Mapping VLANs to SSIDs*

This concept can be extended so that multiple VLANs are mapped to multiple SSIDs. To do this, the AP must be connected to the switch by a trunk link that carries the VLANs. In the right portion of Figure 15-3, VLAN 10 and VLAN 20 are both trunked to the AP. The AP uses the 802.1Q tag to map the VLAN numbers to SSIDs. For example, VLAN 10 is mapped to SSID Marketing, whereas VLAN 20 is mapped to SSID Engineering.

In effect, when an AP uses multiple SSIDs, it is trunking VLANs over the air to end users. The end users must use the appropriate SSID that has been mapped to their respective VLAN.

Wireless LAN Cells

An AP can provide WLAN connectivity to only the clients within its range. The signal range is roughly defined by the AP's antenna pattern. In an open-air setting, this might be a circular shape surrounding an omnidirectional antenna. At least the pattern will appear as a circle on a floor plan—keep in mind that the pattern is three-dimensional, also affecting floors above and below, in a multilevel building.

The AP's location must be carefully planned so that its range matches up with the coverage area that is needed. Even though you might design the AP's location according to a floor plan or an outdoor layout, the WLAN will operate under changing conditions.

Remember that although the AP's location will remain fixed, the wireless clients will change location quite frequently.

Roaming can make the AP's coverage turn out to be much different than you expect. After all, clients can move around and behind objects in a room, walls and doorways in a building, and so on. People will also be moving about, sometimes blocking the wireless signal.

The best approach to designing an AP's location and range or coverage area is to perform a site survey. A test AP is placed in a desirable spot while a test client moves about, taking live measurements of the signal strength and quality. The idea is to plot the AP's range using the actual environment into which it will be placed, with the actual obstacles that might interfere with the client's operation.

An AP's coverage area is called a cell. Clients within that cell can associate with the AP and use the wireless LAN. This concept is shown in Figure 15-4. One client is located outside the cell because it is beyond the AP's signal range.

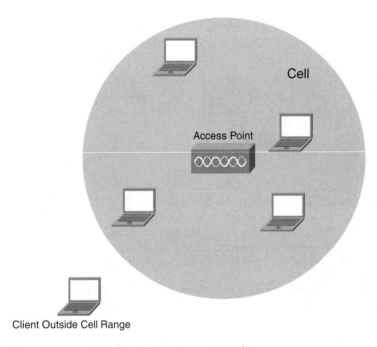

Client Outside Cell Range

Figure 15-4   *Wireless Clients in an AP Cell*

Suppose that a typical indoor AP cell has a radius of 100 feet covering several rooms or part of a hallway. Clients can move around within that cell area and use the WLAN from any location. However, that one cell is rather limiting because clients might need to operate in other surrounding rooms or on other floors without losing their connectivity.

To expand the overall WLAN coverage area, other cells can be placed in surrounding areas simply by distributing other APs throughout the area. The idea is to place the APs so that their cells cover every area where a client is likely to be located. In fact, their cell areas should overlap each other by a small percentage, as shown in Figure 15-5.

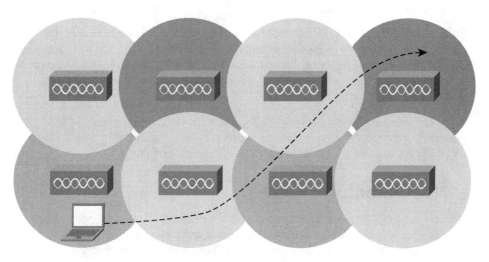

Figure 15-5   *AP Cells Arranged for Seamless Coverage*

> **Tip:** When AP cells overlap, adjacent APs cannot use identical frequencies. If two neighboring APs did use the same frequency, they would only interfere with each other. Instead, AP frequencies must be alternated or staggered across the whole coverage area.

When a client associates with one AP, it can freely move about. As the client moves from one AP's cell into another, the client's association is also passed from one AP to another. Moving from one AP to another is called *roaming*. This movement is also shown in Figure 15-5 as the laptop PC moves along a path that passes through several AP cells.

When a client moves from one AP to another, its association must be established with the new AP. As well, any data that the client was sending just prior to the roaming condition is also relayed from the old AP to the new AP. In this way, any client connects to the WLAN through only one AP at a time. This also minimizes the chance that any data being sent or received while roaming is lost.

If the client maintains its same IP address as it roams between APs, it undergoes *Layer 2 roaming*. If the client roams between APs located in different IP subnets, it undergoes *Layer 3 roaming*.

Key Topic

When you design a wireless LAN, you might be tempted to try to cover the most area possible with each AP. You could run each AP at its maximum transmit power to make the most of its range. Doing so would also reduce the number of APs necessary to cover an area, which would in turn reduce the overall cost. However, you should consider some other factors.

When an AP is configured to provide a large coverage area, it also opens the potential for overcrowding. Remember that an AP cell is essentially a half-duplex shared medium that all clients must share. As the number of clients goes up, the amount of available bandwidth and airtime goes down.

Instead, consider reducing the cell size (by reducing the transmit power) so that only clients in close proximity to the AP can associate and use bandwidth. The AP can also assist in controlling the number of clients that associate at any given time. This becomes important for time-critical or bandwidth-intensive traffic such as voice, video, and medical applications.

When cell sizes are reduced, they are often called *microcells*. This concept can be further extended for extremely controlled environments like stock exchanges. In those cases, the AP power and cell size are minimized, and the cells are called *picocells*.

WLAN Architecture

Wireless networks have traditionally consisted of individually configured and individually operating access points scattered about. Monitoring and maintaining such a diverse network has become too much of an administrative chore. The following sections explore the traditional architecture as well as the Cisco technologies used to provide a unified and centrally managed wireless network.

Traditional WLAN Architecture

Traditional WLAN architecture centers around the wireless access point. Each AP serves as the central hub of its own BSS, where clients located with the AP cell gain an association. The traffic to and from each client has to pass through the AP to reach any other part of the network.

Notice that even though an AP is centrally positioned to support its clients, it is quite isolated and self-sufficient. Each AP must be configured individually, although many APs might be configured with identical network policies. Each AP also operates independently—the AP handles its own use of radio frequency (RF) channels, clients associate with the AP directly, the AP enforces any security policies unassisted, and so on.

In a nutshell, each AP is standalone or autonomous within the larger network. Cisco calls this an *autonomous mode AP* to distinguish it from other architectures.

Because each AP is autonomous, managing security over the wireless network can be difficult. Each autonomous AP handles its own security policies, with no central point of entry between the wireless and wired networks. That means no convenient place exists for monitoring traffic for things like intrusion detection and prevention, quality of service, bandwidth policing, and so on.

Finally, managing the RF operation of many autonomous APs can be quite difficult. As the network administrator, you are in charge of selecting and configuring AP channels and detecting and resolving rogue APs that might be interfering. You must also manage things such as AP output power, ensuring the wireless coverage is sufficient, that it does not overlap too much, and that no coverage holes exist—even when an AP's radio fails.

Cisco has realized the autonomous AP shortcomings and has offered a more unified approach. You should understand some important concepts about WLANs that are based on autonomous APs so that you can compare the traditional architecture to the unified architecture, as it is presented in the next section.

First, consider the traffic patterns in an autonomous AP architecture. Figure 15-6 shows two wireless clients associated with an autonomous AP. All traffic to and from the clients must pass through the AP. Notice how traffic from Client A to some other part of the network passes through the AP, where it is bridged onto the switched network. Even traffic between two wireless clients cannot travel directly over the air—it must first pass through the AP and back out to the other client.

Key
Topic

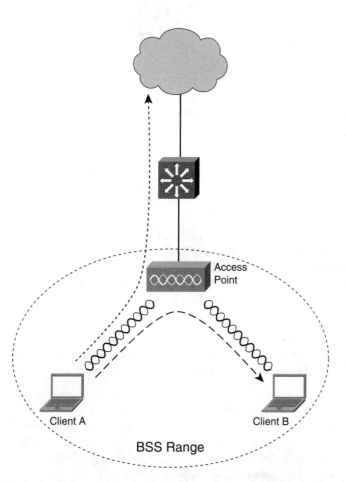

Figure 15-6 *Traffic Patterns Through an Autonomous AP*

Recall that an AP can support multiple SSIDs if multiple VLANs are extended to it over a trunk link. If you want to offer the same SSIDs from several autonomous APs, the VLANs must be extended to the APs in a contiguous fashion. This means that the switched network must carry the VLANs to each and every AP that needs them, as shown in Figure 15-7.

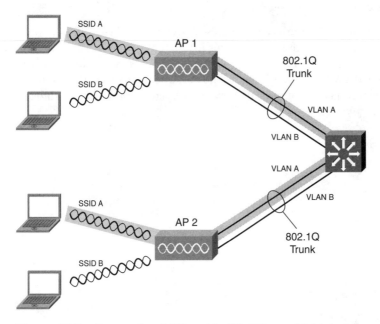

Figure 15-7 *Extent of an SSID and Its VLAN over Multiple Autonomous APs*

In the figure, SSID A and SSID B are offered on two APs. The two SSIDs correspond to VLAN A and VLAN B, respectively. The APs must be connected to a common switched network that extends VLANs A and B at Layer 2. This is done by carrying VLANs A and B over an 802.1Q trunk link to each AP.

Because SSIDs and their VLANs must be extended at Layer 2, you should consider how they are extended throughout the switched network. In Figure 15-7, SSID A and VLAN A have been shaded everywhere they appear. Naturally, they form a contiguous path that appears on both APs so that wireless clients can use SSID A in either location or while roaming between the two.

This concept becomes important when you think about extending SSIDs to many APs over a larger network. Perhaps you would like to offer an SSID on any AP served by your infrastructure so that wireless clients can roam anywhere in the area. To do that, the SSID and its VLAN would have to be extended everywhere that the user could possibly roam. This has the potential to look like an end-to-end or campuswide VLAN—something that goes against good network design practice, as presented in the early chapters of this book.

Cisco Unified Wireless Network Architecture

Cisco has collected a complete set of functions that are integral to wireless LANs and called them the Cisco Unified Wireless Network. This new architecture offers the following capabilities, which are centralized so that they affect wireless LAN devices located anywhere in the network:

■ WLAN security

■ WLAN deployment

■ WLAN management

■ WLAN control

To centralize these aspects of a WLAN, many of the functions found within autonomous APs have to be shifted toward some central location. The top portion of Figure 15-8 lists most of the activities performed by an autonomous AP. Notice that they have been grouped by real-time processes on the left and management processes on the right.

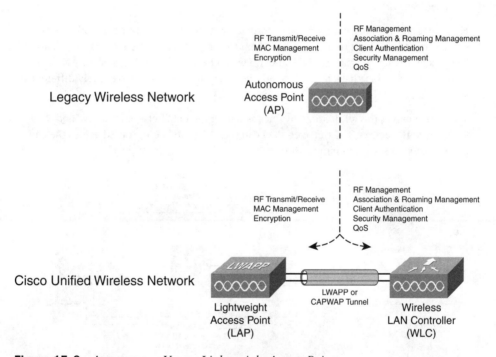

Figure 15-8   *Autonomous Versus Lightweight Access Points*

The real-time processes involve actually sending and receiving 802.11 frames, AP beacons, and probe messages. Data encryption is also handled in a real-time, per-packet basis. The AP must interact with wireless clients at the MAC layer. These functions must stay with the AP hardware, closest to the clients.

The management functions are not integral to handling frames over the RF channels but are things that should be centrally administered. Therefore, those functions are moved to a centrally located platform away from the AP.

In the Cisco unified wireless network, a lightweight access point (LAP) performs only the real-time 802.11 operation. The LAP gets its name because the code image and the local intelligence are stripped down, or lightweight, compared to the traditional autonomous AP.

The management functions are all performed on a wireless LAN controller (WLC), which is common to many LAPs. This is shown in the bottom portion of Figure 15-8. Notice that the LAP is left with duties in Layers 1 and 2, where frames are moved into and out of the RF domain. The LAP becomes totally dependent on the WLC for every other WLAN function, such as authenticating users, managing security policies, and even selecting RF channels and output power!

This division of labor is known as a *split-MAC architecture*, where the normal MAC operations are pulled apart into two distinct locations. This occurs for every LAP in the network—each one must bind itself to a WLC to boot up and support wireless clients. The WLC becomes the central hub that supports a number of LAPs scattered about in the switched network.

How does an LAP bind with a WLC to form a complete working access point? The two devices must bring up a tunnel between them to carry 802.11-related messages and also client data. Remember that the LAP and WLC can be located on the same VLAN or IP subnet, but they don't have to be. Instead, they can be located on two entirely different IP subnets in two entirely different locations.

The tunnel makes this all possible by encapsulating the data between the LAP and WLC within new IP packets. The tunneled data can then be switched or routed across the campus network, as shown in Figure 15-9.

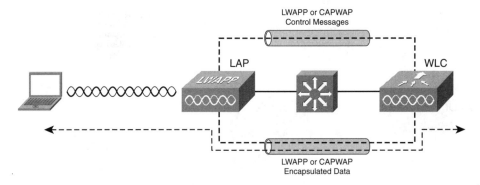

Figure 15-9   *Linking an LAP and WLC with LWAPP or CAPWAP*

The LAP and WLC pair uses either the Lightweight Access Point Protocol (LWAPP, developed by Cisco) or the Control and Provisioning Wireless Access Points protocol (CAPWAP, defined in RFC 4118) as the tunneling mechanism. Actually, these protocols consist of the two tunnels shown in Figure 15-9:

■   **Control messages**—Exchanges that are used to configure the LAP and manage its operation. The control messages are authenticated and encrypted so that the LAP is securely controlled by only the WLC.

■ **Data**—Packets to and from wireless clients associated with the LAP. The data is encapsulated within the LWAPP or CAPWAP protocol but is not encrypted or otherwise secured between the LAP and WLC.

Tip: Although Cisco developed LWAPP, it submitted the protocol as an IETF draft. The result is the CAPWAP standard in RFC 4118. LWAPP uses UDP destination ports 12222 and 12223 on the WLC end. Similarly, CAPWAP uses UDP ports 5246 and 5247.

Every LAP and WLC must also authenticate each other with digital certificates. An X.509 certificate is preinstalled in each device when it is purchased. By using certificates behind the scenes, every device is properly authenticated before becoming part of the Cisco Unified Wireless Network. This process helps ensure that no rogue LAP or WLC (or devices posing as an LAP or WLC) can be introduced into the network.

WLC Functions

When LWAPP or CAPWAP tunnels are built from a WLC to one or more LAPs, the WLC can begin offering a variety of additional functions. Think of all the puzzles and shortcomings that were discussed for the traditional WLAN architecture as you read over the following list of WLC activities:

■ **Dynamic channel assignment**—The WLC chooses and configures the RF channel used by each LAP based on other active access points in the area.

■ **Transmit power optimization**—The WLC sets the transmit power of each LAP based on the coverage area needed. Transmit power is also automatically adjusted periodically.

■ **Self-healing wireless coverage**—If an LAP radio dies, the coverage hole is "healed" by turning up the transmit power of surrounding LAPs automatically.

■ **Flexible client roaming**—Clients can roam at either Layer 2 or Layer 3 with very fast roaming times.

■ **Dynamic client load balancing**—If two or more LAPs are positioned to cover the same geographic area, the WLC can associate clients with the least used LAP. This distributes the client load across the LAPs.

■ **RF monitoring**—The WLC manages each LAP so that it scans channels to monitor the RF usage. By listening to a channel, the WLC can remotely gather information about RF interference, noise, signals from surrounding LAPs, and signals from rogue APs or ad-hoc clients.

■ **Security management**—The WLC can require wireless clients to obtain an IP address from a trusted DHCP server before allowing them to associate and access the WLAN.

Cisco WLCs are available in several platforms, differing mainly in the number of managed LAPs. Table 15-2 lists some WLC platforms.

Table 15-2   *Cisco WLC Platforms and Capabilities*

Model	Interface	Attribute
2100	8 10/100TX	Handles up to 6, 12, or 25 LAPs
4402	2 GigE	Handles up to 12, 25, or 50 LAPs
4404	4 GigE	Handles up to 100 LAPs
5500	8 GigE	Handles up to 12, 25, 50, 100, or 250 LAPs
WiSM	4 GigE bundled in an Ether-Channel for each controller	Catalyst 6500 module with two WLCs; handles up to 300 LAPs (150 per controller); up to 5 WiSMs in a single chassis
WLC module for ISR routers	Can be integrated in 2800 and 3800 routers	Handles up to 6, 8, 12, or 25 LAPs
Catalyst 3750G integrated WLC	N/A (integrated in 24-port 10/100/1000TX switch)	Handles up to 50 LAPs per switch, up to 200 LAPs per switch stack

You can also deploy several WLCs in a network to handle a large number of LAPs. In addition, multiple WLCs offer some redundancy so that LAPs can recover from a WLC failure.

Managing several WLCs can require a significant effort, due to the number of LAPs and clients to be managed and monitored. The Cisco Wireless Control System (WCS) is an optional server platform that can be used as a single GUI front-end to all the WLCs in a network. From the WCS, you can perform any WLAN management or configuration task, as well as RF planning and wireless user tracking.

The WCS uses building floor plans to display dynamic representations of wireless coverage. It can also be fed information about the building construction to improve its concept of RF signal propagation. Once this is done, the WCS can locate a wireless client to within a few meters by triangulating the client's signal as received by multiple LAPs.

The WCS can be teamed with the Cisco Wireless Location Appliance to track the location of thousands of wireless clients. You can even deploy active 802.11 RFID tags to track objects as they move around in the wireless coverage area. Tracking objects by their MAC addresses can be handy when you need to locate a rogue or malicious wireless client, or when you need to track corporate assets that tend to move around within a building or complex.

Lightweight AP Operation

The LAP is designed to be a "zero-touch" configuration. The LAP must find a WLC and obtain all of its configuration parameters, so you never have to actually configure it through its console port or over the network.

The following sequence of steps detail the bootstrap process that an LAP must complete before it becomes active:

Step 1.   The LAP obtains an IP address from a DHCP server.

Step 2.   The LAP learns the IP addresses of any available WLCs.

Step 3.   The LAP sends a join request to the first WLC in its list of addresses. If that one fails to answer, the next WLC is tried. When a WLC accepts the LAP, it sends a join reply back to the LAP, effectively binding the two devices.

Step 4.   The WLC compares the LAP's code image release to the code release stored locally. If they differ, the LAP downloads the code image stored on the WLC and reboots itself.

Step 5.   The WLC and LAP build a secure LWAPP or CAPWAP tunnel for management traffic and an LWAPP or CAPWAP tunnel (not secured) for wireless client data.

You should notice a couple of things from this list. In Step 2, the LAP can find the WLC IP addresses using any of these methods:

■   A DHCP server that adds option 43 to its reply containing a list of WLC addresses.

■   With the IP subnet broadcast option, the LAP broadcasts a join request message, hoping that a WLC is also connected to the local subnet or VLAN. This method works only if the LAP and WLC are Layer 2-adjacent.

An LAP is always joined or bound to one WLC at any time. However, the LAP can maintain a list of up to three WLCs (primary, secondary, and tertiary). As the LAP boots, it tries to contact each WLC address in sequential order. If it cannot find a responding WLC at all, the LAP tries an IP subnet broadcast to find any available WLC.

Suppose that the LAP has booted up and has successfully joined a WLC. If that WLC fails for some reason, the LAP will no longer be able to forward traffic or to maintain client associations. Therefore, when the LAP realizes its WLC is no longer responding, it reboots and begins the process of searching for live WLCs again. This means any client associations will be dropped while the LAP reboots and joins a different controller.

Tip: When an LAP is cut off from a WLC, client associations are normally dropped and no data can pass over the WLAN between clients. Cisco Hybrid Remote Edge Access Point (HREAP) is a special case for remote sites where the LAPs are separated from the WLC by a WAN link. With HREAP, the remote LAPs can keep operating even while the WAN link is down and their WLC is not available, much like an autonomous AP would do. This allows wireless users to keep communicating within the remote site until the link (and WLC) is restored.

Key
Topic

Traffic Patterns in a Cisco Unified Wireless Network

Because the LAPs connect to the wired network through logical LWAPP or CAPWAP tunnels, the traffic patterns into and out of the WLAN are different than traditional WLANs.

Consider the network shown in Figure 15-10. Two wireless clients are associated with the WLAN that is formed by the LAP and WLC combination. Traffic from Client A to a host somewhere on the network travels through the LAP, through the tunnel to the WLC, and then out onto the switched campus network.

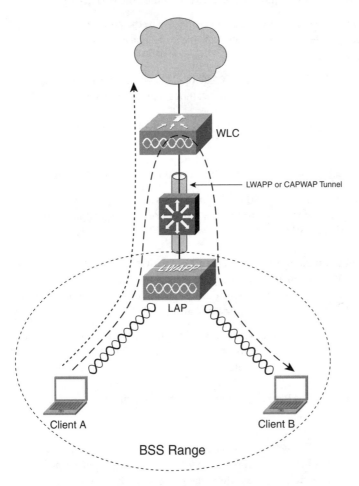

Figure 15-10   *Traffic Patterns Through an LAP*

Traffic between the two wireless clients, however, takes an interesting path. That traffic must go from Client A through the LAP, through the LWAPP or CAPWAP tunnel, into the WLC, back through the tunnel, through the LAP and on to Client B. This further illustrates what a vital role the WLC plays in the unified infrastructure.

Tip: Even though all traffic into and out of the WLAN must pass through the LWAPP or CAPWAP tunnel and the WLC, not all traffic operations are applied end-to-end across the tunnel.

For example, wireless encryption can still be used to secure data over the air, as with traditional WLANs. However, the encrypted data does not pass through the LWAPP or CAPWAP tunnel at all. Packets are encrypted as they leave the wireless client and unencrypted when they arrive on the LAP. The same is true for packet authentication, if it is used.

All the packet authentication and encryption functions remain within the LAP hardware and are not distributed to the WLC at all.

When autonomous APs are used in a network, the access VLANs serving the wireless clients must be extended or trunked all the way out to touch the APs. This is not true for LAPs.

First, consider the sample network shown in Figure 15-11. Two VLANs A and B are used to carry wireless client traffic that is associated to the respective SSIDs A and B. Notice that VLANs A and B exist on the trunk from switch SW2 to the WLC but go no further. Also notice that the WLC and the LAPs are connected by VLAN Z—something that is totally isolated from access VLANs A and B.

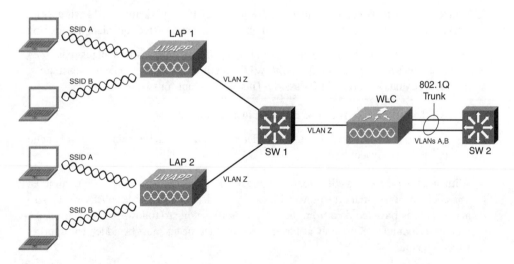

Figure 15-11 *Unified Wireless Network Supporting Multiple VLANs and SSIDs*

The access VLANs are actually carried over the LWAPP tunnel so that they logically touch the LAPs where the users reside. This is shown in Figure 15-12, where VLAN A is shaded as it extends to the two LAPs as SSID A.

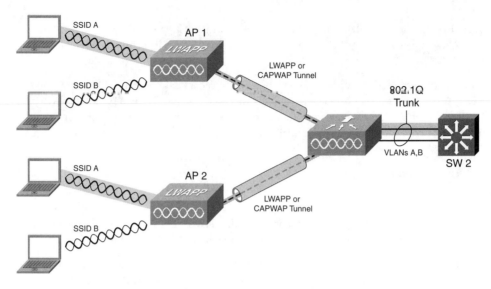

Figure 15-12   *VLAN A Extending over LWAPP/CAPWAP Tunnels*

Roaming in a Cisco Unified Wireless Network

Wireless clients must negotiate an association with LAPs, as with any 802.11 wireless network. However, the split-MAC architecture has an interesting effect on client associations.

Remember that the LAP handles mostly real-time wireless duties, so it will just pass the client's association requests on up to the WLC. In effect, the wireless clients negotiate their associations with the WLC directly. This is important for two reasons:

■   All client associations can be managed in a central location.

■   Client roaming becomes faster and easier; associations can be maintained or handed off at the controller level.

With autonomous APs, a client roams by moving its association from one AP to another. The client must negotiate the move with each AP independently, and the APs must also make sure any buffered data from the client is passed along to follow the association. Autonomous roaming occurs only at Layer 2; some other means must be added to support Layer 3 roaming.

With LAPs, a client still roams by moving its association. From the client's point of view, the association moves from AP to AP; actually it moves from WLC to WLC, according to the AP-WLC bindings.

Through the WLCs, LAPs can support both Layer 2 and Layer 3 roaming. Remember that the client's association is always contained within an LWAPP or CAPWAP tunnel. Moving to a new AP also moves the association into a new tunnel—the tunnel that connects the new AP to its WLC. The client's IP address can remain the same while roaming, no matter which tunnel the client passes through to reach the controllers.

The following sections discuss client roaming from the aspect of the WLC, where roaming and client associations are managed.

Intracontroller Roaming

In Figure 15-13, a wireless client has an active wireless association at location A. The association is with WLC1 through AP1. As you might expect, all traffic to and from the client passes through the LWAPP or CAPWAP tunnel between AP1 and WLC1.

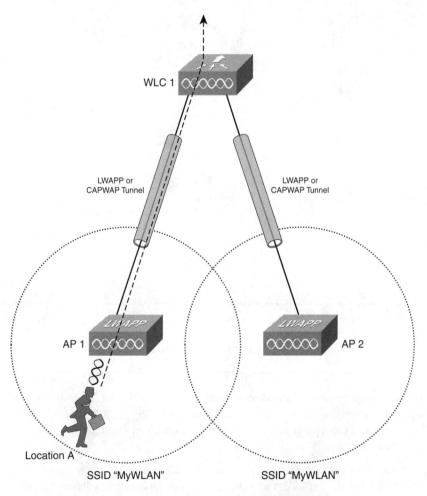

Figure 15-13 *Wireless Client in an LAP Cell Before Roaming*

The client begins moving in Figure 15-14 and roams into the area covered by AP2. For this example, notice two things: The cells provided by AP1 and AP2 both use the SSID My-WLAN, which enables the client to roam between them. In addition, both AP1 and AP2 are joined to a single controller, WC1.

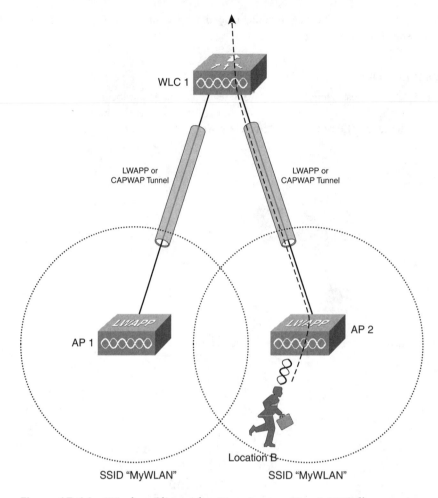

Figure 15-14   *Wireless Client After Roaming to a New LAP Cell*

In the figure, the client has moved its association to WLC1 through AP2. Although the AP has changed, the same controller is providing the association and the LWAPP or CAPWAP tunnel. This is known as an *intracontroller roam*, where the client's association stays within the same controller.

This type of roam is straightforward because controller WLC1 simply updates its tables to begin using the LWAPP or CAPWAP tunnel to AP2 to find the client. Any leftover data that was buffered from the old association is easily shifted over to the new association within the controller.

Intercontroller Roaming

In some cases, a client might roam from one controller to another. For example, a large wireless network might consist of too many LAPs to be supported by a single WLC. The

LAPs could also be distributed over several controllers for load balancing or redundancy purposes.

In Figure 15-15, a wireless client is using an association with WLC1 through AP1. This is similar to Figure 15-13, but now each of the adjacent LAP cells belongs to a different WLC. All the client's traffic passes through the tunnel from AP1 to WLC1.

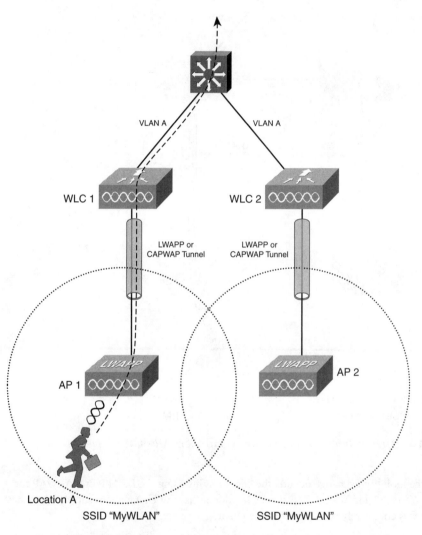

Figure 15-15   *Wireless Client Before Roaming to a Different Controller*

When the client moves into AP2's cell, the same SSID is found, and the client can move its association to WLC2. As long as the two controllers (WLC1 and WLC2) are located in the same IP subnet, they can easily hand off the client's association. This is done through a mobility message exchange where information about the client is transferred from one WLC to the other, as shown in Figure 15-16.

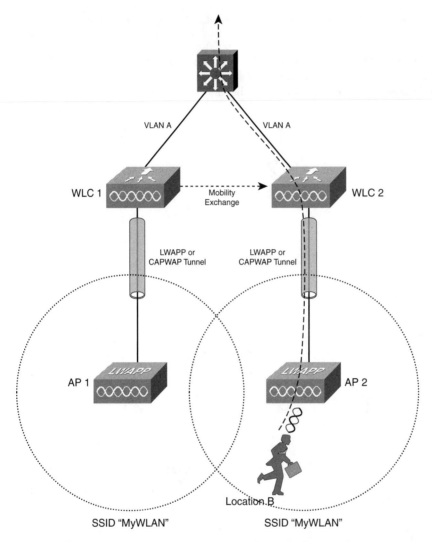

Figure 15-16   *After an Intercontroller Roam, Controllers Are on the Same Subnet*

When the mobility exchange occurs, the client begins using the LWAPP or CAPWAP tunnel between AP2 and WLC2. The client's IP address has not changed; in fact, the roaming process was completely transparent to the client.

Now consider the scenario shown in Figure 15-17. The two controllers WLC1 and WLC2 are located in different IP subnets, shown as VLAN A and VLAN B. The wireless client begins in AP1's cell with an association to WLC1. The client obtains an IP address within VLAN A because AP1 offers VLAN A on its SSID. All the client's traffic passes through the LWAPP or CAPWAP tunnel between AP1 and WLC1 and onto VLAN A.

When the client travels into the cell provided by AP2, something interesting happens. In Figure 15-18, the client moves its association over to WLC2, through AP2, which offers access to VLAN B. The client's IP address has remained constant, but WLC1 and WLC2 are not located on the same subnet or VLAN. Therefore, the client's IP address has moved into a foreign subnet.

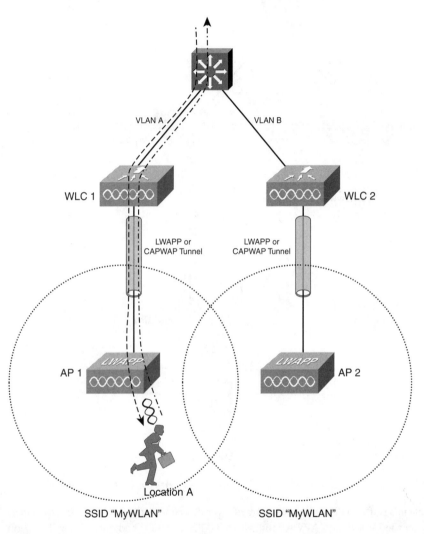

Figure 15-17   *Before an Intercontroller Roam, Controllers Are on Different Subnets*

The two controllers must begin working together to provide continuing service for the client, without requiring the client to obtain a new address. The two controllers bring up an Ether-IP tunnel between them for the specific purpose of carrying some of the client's traffic. The Ether-IP tunnel is simply a way that the controllers can encapsulate MAC-layer data inside an IP packet, using IP protocol 97. To move packets to and from the client, one controller encapsulates packets and sends them to the other controller. Packets received over the tunnel are unencapsulated by the other controller, where they reappear in their original form. (Ether-IP tunnels are defined in RFC 3378.)

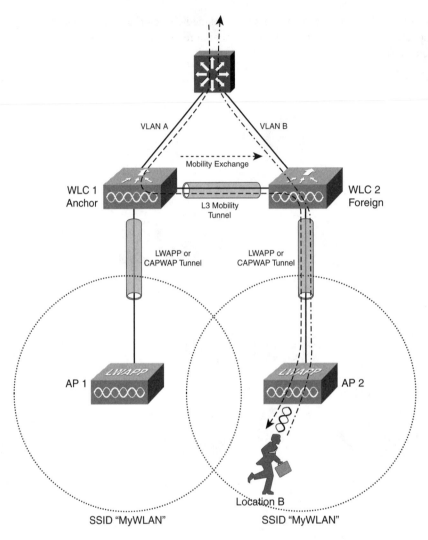

Figure 15-18 *After an Intercontroller Roam, Controllers Are on Different Subnets*

All the client's traffic will not be able to travel over the same path. Traffic leaving the client travels over the LWAPP or CAPWAP tunnel from AP2 to WLC2 and onto VLAN B, as you might expect. Even though the client has an IP address that is foreign to its new VLAN, it can still send packets onto the foreign VLAN.

Traffic coming toward the client takes a different path. In Figure 15-18, traffic enters the switch on VLAN A and is forwarded to WLC1. Why does it enter VLAN A and not VLAN B, where the client is now located? Remember that the client is still using an IP address it obtained on VLAN A, so it will continue to appear in VLAN A—no matter where it roams within the wireless network.

Traffic being sent to the client's destination address on VLAN A must be forwarded onto VLAN A. Therefore, WLC1 must accept that traffic and forward it onto the appropriate controller that has a current association with the client. WLC1 sends the traffic through the Ether-IP tunnel to WLC2, which in turn sends the traffic through the tunnel to AP2 and to the client.

Because the client originally joined the WLAN on WLC1, WLC1 will always refer to itself as the client's anchor point. Any controller that is serving the client from a different subnet is known as a foreign agent. As the client continues to roam, the anchor WLC will follow its movement by shifting the Ether-IP tunnel to connect with the client's foreign WLC.

Mobility Groups

For intercontroller roaming, a client must be able to roam from one LAP to another, where the LAPs are managed by different controllers. The controllers must be able to hand off a client's association information to each other during a roam.

To do this, the WLCs are configured into logical mobility groups. A client can roam to any LAP (and its associated WLC) as long as it stays within a mobility group.

A mobility group can have up to 24 WLCs of any type or platform. The number of LAPs contained in a mobility group can vary because the number of LAPs managed by any WLC can vary by platform.

Sometimes a wireless client might move across a mobility group boundary, where two adjacent LAPs are in two different mobility groups. In this case, the client can transfer its association into the new mobility group, but its IP address and all of its session information maintained in the WLCs will be dropped.

Configuring Switch Ports for WLAN Use

To implement a wireless LAN, both switches and access points must be configured. The CCNP SWITCH course and exam separate the configuration effort into two camps. The networking professional handles the design and configuration of the LAN switches to support the WLAN. The AP and WLC configuration is handled by a wireless LAN specialist. Therefore, the following sections cover only the configuration of switch ports where wireless devices are connected.

As you work through the remainder of this chapter, think about the steps you would need to execute to position and configure an AP and any WLC.

Configuring Support for Autonomous APs

Figure 15-19 shows a network scenario where one autonomous AP is connected into a campus network. Autonomous APs are normally positioned in the access layer of the network. Each SSID that is supported by the AP is mapped to a VLAN; when multiple SSIDs are offered, multiple VLANs must touch the AP. Therefore, you should configure the switch port connecting to the AP as a trunk link.

You can use the commands shown in Example 15-1 as a template to configure the switch port . In the scenario, interface Gigabit Ethernet 1/0/1 connects to the AP and acts as a trunk link, transporting VLANs 10, 20, and 30 to and from the AP. These VLANs correspond to the three SSIDs that are configured on the AP itself. You can optionally add the

spanning-tree portfast trunk command to shorten the time required for STP to bring the trunk link up into the forwarding state.

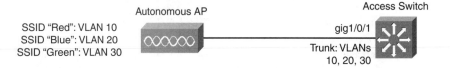

Figure 15-19 *Configuring a Switch to Support an Autonomous AP*

Example 15-1 *Switch Port Configuration for an Autonomous AP*

```
Switch(config)# interface gigabitethernet1/0/1
Switch(config-if)# switchport trunk encapsulation dot1q
Switch(config-if)# switchport trunk allowed vlan 10,20,30
Switch(config-if)# switchport mode trunk
Switch(config-if)# spanning-tree portfast trunk
```

Configuring Support for LAPs

Cisco LAPs are designed to be "zero-touch" devices, which can be installed and used with little or no manual intervention. The WLC can manage every aspect of LAP operation, including code image synchronization, so almost no information needs to be primed or pre-configured in the LAP itself.

Before you connect an LAP to a switch port, you should make sure that the port is properly configured. The LAP requires an access mode port—not a trunking port. The only VLAN needed at the LAP is one where the LAP can get an IP address and reach the WLC.

You can place the LAP on any VLAN that is convenient in a switch block. For example, the LAP can sit on the user access VLAN along with other end users in the area. Usually the best practice is to set aside a VLAN strictly for LAP management traffic. This VLAN contains one IP subnet reserved only for LAPs.

Any VLAN that is mapped to an SSID is transported over the LWAPP or CAPWAP tunnel from the LAP to the WLC. That means the LAP and WLC do not have to be connected with a Layer 2 VLAN or a trunk link at all.

Figure 15-20 shows a simple network scenario with an LAP and a WLC. The LAP should be located in the access layer, so it is connected to interface Gigabit Ethernet 1/0/10 on the access switch. The interface is configured for access mode using VLAN 100, which is set aside for LAP devices. The commands shown in Example 15-2 can be used as a template to configure the access switch port to connect to the LAP.

Example 15-2 *Switch Port Configuration for an LAP*

```
Switch(config)# vlan 100
Switch(config-vlan)# name ap-management
Switch(config-vlan)# exit
Switch(config)# interface gigabitethernet1/0/10
```

```
Switch(config-if)# switchport
Switch(config-if)# switchport access vlan 100
Switch(config-if)# switchport mode access
Switch(config-if)# spanning-tree portfast
Switch(config-if)# power inline auto
Switch(config-if)# exit
```

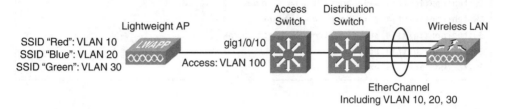

Figure 15-20 *Configuring a Switch to Support Cisco Unified Wireless Network Devices*

You can enable **spanning-tree portfast** on the access mode ports where LAPs connect. The LAP VLAN terminates on the LAPs and does not get extended any further. Therefore, no danger exists of that VLAN forming a loop somewhere in the wireless cloud.

When Power over Ethernet (PoE) is used to power an LAP from a switch interface, it is no different from using it to power a Cisco IP Phone. See Chapter 14, "IP Telephony," for PoE switch configuration information.

Configuring Support for WLCs

LAPs provide network access for wireless LAN users, whereas the WLCs aggregate WLAN traffic from the LAPs. Therefore, the WLCs should be located in the distribution layer of the campus network, as shown in Figure 15-20.

Cisco WLCs have a variety of interfaces that perform different functions. For the purposes of the CCNP SWITCH exam, you do not have to understand anything about those interfaces. Instead, you can assume that a wireless specialist will set the requirements for these interfaces and will work with you to come up with the appropriate switch configuration. Just be aware that the WLC needs direct connectivity to any VLANs that will be tunneled to the LAPs where the users are located.

The switch interfaces feeding a WLC should be configured as trunk links. Some WLCs need a single interface, others have several interfaces that should be bundled into a single EtherChannel. The WLC shown in Figure 15-20 has a four-interface Gigabit EtherChannel. The commands shown in Example 15-3 can be used as a template to configure the Ether-Channel and its associated physical interfaces. The member interfaces should always be configured as an unconditional EtherChannel, because the WLC cannot negotiate one with the switch.

Example 15-3 *Configuring Switch Ports for a WLC*

```
Switch(config)# interface range gigabitethernet1/0/41 - 44
Switch(config-if)# switchport
Switch(config-if)# channel-group 1 mode on
Switch(config-if)# exit
Switch(config)# interface port-channel 1
Switch(config-if)# switchport trunk encapsulation dot1q
Switch(config-if)# switchport trunk allowed vlan 10,20,30
Switch(config-if)# switchport mode trunk
Switch(config-if)# spanning-tree portfast trunk
Switch(config-if)# no shutdown
Switch(config-if)# exit
```

Exam Preparation Tasks

Review All Key Topics

Review the most important topics in the chapter, noted with the Key Topic icon in the outer margin of the page. Table 15-3 lists a reference of these key topics and the page numbers on which each is found.

Key
Topic

Table 15-3 *Key Topics for Chapter 15*

Key Topic Element	Description	Page Number
Paragraph	Explains the collision-avoidance mechanism	338
Tip	Defines an SSID as the common thread among WLAN clients that need to communicate with each other	340
Paragraph	Discusses how VLANs are mapped to SSIDs	343
Paragraph	Explains client roaming, Layer 2 roaming, and Layer 3 roaming	345
Paragraph	Discusses autonomous mode APs in traditional WLAN design	346
Paragraph	Explains how traffic between two WLAN clients must always pass through an AP	347
Paragraph	Discusses lightweight access points (LAP) and wireless LAN controllers (WLC)	350
Paragraph	Explains the split-MAC architecture	350
Paragraph	Explains the Lightweight Access Point Protocol (LWAPP) and Control and Provisioning Wireless Access Point tunnel protocols	350
Tip	Explains the HREAP functionality	353

Define Key Terms

Define the following key terms from this chapter, and check your answers in the glossary:

CSMA/CA, SSID, Layer 2 roaming, Layer 3 roaming, autonomous mode AP, lightweight access point (LAP), wireless LAN controller (WLC), split-MAC architecture, Lightweight Access Point Protocol (LWAPP), Control and Provisioning Wireless Access Point (CAP-WAP), Hybrid Remote Edge Access Point (HREAP)

Cisco Published SWITCH Exam Topics Covered in This Part

Implement a security extension of a Layer 2 solution, given a network design and a set of requirements:

- Determine network resources needed for implementing a security solution

- Create a implementation plan for the security solution

- Create a verification plan for the security solution

- Configure port security features

- Configure general switch security features

- Configure private VLANs

- Configure VACL and PACL

- Verify the security-based solution was implemented properly using show and debug commands

- Document results of security implementation and verification

(Always check Cisco.com for the latest posted exam topics.)

Part V: Securing Switched Networks

This chapter covers the following topics that you need to master for the CCNP SWITCH exam:

Port Security—This section explains how to configure switch ports to allow network access to only hosts with specific or learned MAC addresses.

Port-Based Authentication—This section discusses a method you can use to require user authentication before network access is offered to a client host.

Mitigating Spoofing Attacks—This section covers several types of attacks in which a malicious user generates spoofed information to become a man in the middle. When an attacker is wedged between other hosts and a router or gateway, for example, he can examine and exploit all traffic. DHCP snooping, IP Source Guard, and dynamic ARP inspection are three features that can be used to prevent these attacks.

Best Practices for Securing Switches—This section provides several guidelines for tightening control over Catalyst switches and the protocols they use for switch communication and maintenance.

CHAPTER 16

Securing Switch Access

Traditionally, users have been able to connect a PC to a switched network and gain immediate access to enterprise resources. As networks grow and as more confidential data and restricted resources become available, it is important to limit the access that users receive.

Catalyst switches have a variety of methods that can secure or control user access. Users can be authenticated as they connect to or through a switch and can be authorized to perform certain actions on a switch. User access can be recorded as switch accounting information. The physical switch port access also can be controlled based on the user's MAC address or authentication.

In addition, Catalyst switches can detect and prevent certain types of attacks. Several features can be used to validate information passing through a switch so that spoofed addresses can't be used to compromise hosts.

"Do I Know This Already?" Quiz

The "Do I Know This Already?" quiz allows you to assess whether you should read this entire chapter thoroughly or jump to the "Exam Preparation Tasks" section. If you are in doubt based on your answers to these questions or your own assessment of your knowledge of the topics, read the entire chapter. Table 16-1 outlines the major headings in this chapter and the "Do I Know This Already?" quiz questions that go with them. You can find the answers in Appendix A, "Answers to the 'Do I Know This Already?' Quizzes."

Table 16-1 *"Do I Know This Already?" Foundation Topics Section-to-Question Mapping*

Foundation Topics Section	Questions Covered in This Section
Port Security	1–4
Port-Based Authentication	5–9
Mitigating Spoofing Attacks	10–12
Best Practices for Securing Switches	13–14

1. Which switch feature can grant access through a port only if the host with MAC address 0005.0004.0003 is connected?

   a. SPAN

   b. MAC address ACL

   c. Port security

   d. Port-based authentication

2. Port security is being used to control access to a switch port. Which one of these commands will put the port into the errdisable state if an unauthorized station connects?

   a. switchport port-security violation protect

   b. switchport port-security violation restrict

   c. switchport port-security violation errdisable

   d. switchport port-security violation shutdown

3. If port security is left to its default configuration, how many different MAC addresses can be learned at one time on a switch port?

   a. 0

   b. 1

   c. 16

   d. 256

4. The following commands are configured on a Catalyst switch port. What happens when the host with MAC address 0001.0002.0003 tries to connect?

   ```
   switchport port-security
   switchport port-security maximum 3
   switchport port-security mac-address 0002.0002.0002
   switchport port-security violation shutdown
   ```

   a. The port shuts down.

   b. The host is allowed to connect.

   c. The host is denied a connection.

   d. The host can connect only when 0002.0002.0002 is not connected.

5. What protocol is used for port-based authentication?

   a. 802.1D

   b. 802.1Q

   c. 802.1x

   d. 802.1w

6. When 802.1x is used for a switch port, where must it be configured?

    a. Switch port and client PC

    b. Switch port only

    c. Client PC only

    d. Switch port and a RADIUS server

7. When port-based authentication is enabled globally, what is the default behavior for all switch ports?

    a. Authenticate users before enabling the port.

    b. Allow all connections without authentication.

    c. Do not allow any connections.

    d. There is no default behavior.

8. When port-based authentication is enabled, what method is available for a user to authenticate?

    a. Web browser

    b. Telnet session

    c. 802.1x client

    d. DHCP

9. The users in a department are using a variety of host platforms, some old and some new. All of them have been approved with a user ID in a RADIUS server database. Which one of these features should be used to restrict access to the switch ports in the building?

    a. AAA authentication

    b. AAA authorization

    c. Port security

    d. Port-based authentication

10. With DHCP snooping, an untrusted port filters out which one of the following?

    a. DHCP replies from legitimate DHCP servers

    b. DHCP replies from rogue DHCP servers

    c. DHCP requests from legitimate clients

    d. DHCP requests from rogue clients

11. Which two of the following methods does a switch use to detect spoofed addresses when IP Source Guard is enabled?

    a.   ARP entries

    b.   DHCP database

    c.   DHCP snooping database

    d.   Static IP source binding entries

    e.   Reverse path-forwarding entries

12. Which one of the following should be configured as a trusted port for dynamic ARP inspection?

    a.   The port where the ARP server is located.

    b.   The port where an end-user host is located.

    c.   The port where another switch is located.

    d.   None; all ports are untrusted.

13. Which two of the following methods should you use to secure inbound CLI sessions to a switch?

    a.   Disable all inbound CLI connections.

    b.   Use SSH only.

    c.   Use Telnet only.

    d.   Apply an access list to the vty lines.

14. Suppose you need to disable CDP advertisements on a switch port so that untrusted devices cannot learn anything about your switch. Which one of the following interface configuration commands should be used?

    a.   cdp disable

    b.   no cdp

    c.   no cdp enable

    d.   no cdp trust

Foundation Topics

Port Security

In some environments, a network must be secured by controlling what stations can gain access to the network itself. Where user workstations are stationary, their MAC addresses always can be expected to connect to the same access-layer switch ports. If stations are mobile, their MAC addresses can be learned dynamically or added to a list of addresses to expect on a switch port.

Catalyst switches offer the port security feature to control port access based on MAC addresses. To configure port security on an access-layer switch port, begin by enabling it on a per-interface basis with the following interface-configuration command:

```
Switch(config-if)# switchport port-security
```

Next, you must identify a set of allowed MAC addresses so that the port can grant them access. You can explicitly configure addresses or they can be learned dynamically from port traffic. On each interface that uses port security, specify the maximum number of MAC addresses that will be allowed access using the following interface configuration command:

```
Switch(config-if)# switchport port-security maximum max-addr
```

By default, port security will make sure that only one MAC address will be allowed access on each switch port. You can set the maximum number of addresses in the range of 1 to 1024.

Each interface using port security dynamically learns MAC addresses by default and expects those addresses to appear on that interface in the future. These are called *sticky MAC addresses*. MAC addresses are learned as hosts transmit frames on an interface. The interface learns up to the maximum number of addresses allowed. Learned addresses also can be aged out of the table if those hosts are silent for a period of time. By default, no aging occurs.

Key Topic

For example, to set the maximum number of MAC addresses that can be active on a switch port at any time to two, you could use the following command:

```
Switch(config-if)# switchport port-security maximum 2
```

You also can statically define one or more MAC addresses on an interface. Any of these addresses are allowed to access the network through the port. Use the following interface configuration command to define a static address:

```
Switch(config-if)# switchport port-security mac-address mac-addr
```

The MAC address is given in dotted-triplet format. If the number of static addresses configured is less than the maximum number of addresses secured on a port, the remaining addresses are learned dynamically. Be sure to set the maximum number appropriately.

As an example, you could use the following command to configure a static address entry on an interface, so that 0006.5b02.a841 will be expected:

```
Switch(config-if)# switchport port-security mac-address 0006.5b02.a841
```

Finally, you must define how each interface using port security should react if a MAC address is in violation by using the following interface-configuration command:

```
Switch(config-if)# switchport port-security violation {shutdown | restrict |
  protect}
```

A violation occurs if more than the maximum number of MAC addresses are learned or if an unknown (not statically defined) MAC address attempts to transmit on the port. The switch port takes one of the following configured actions when a violation is detected:

- **Shutdown**—The port immediately is put into the Errdisable state, which effectively shuts it down. It must be reenabled manually or through errdisable recovery to be used again.

- **Restrict**—The port is allowed to stay up, but all packets from violating MAC addresses are dropped. The switch keeps a running count of the number of violating packets and can send an SNMP trap and a syslog message as an alert of the violation.

- **Protect**—The port is allowed to stay up, as in the restrict mode. Although packets from violating addresses are dropped, no record of the violation is kept.

As an example of the restrict mode, a switch interface has received the following configuration commands:

```
interface GigabitEthernet0/11
 switchport access vlan 991
 switchport mode access
 switchport port-security
 switchport port-security violation restrict
 spanning-tree portfast
```

When the default maximum of one MAC address is exceeded on this interface, the condition is logged but the interface stays up. This is shown by the following syslog message:

```
Jun  3 17:18:41.888 EDT: %PORT_SECURITY-2-PSECURE_VIOLATION: Security violation
   occurred, caused by MAC address 0000.5e00.0101 on port GigabitEthernet0/11.
```

Tip: If an interface is undergoing the restrict or protect condition, you might need to clear the learned MAC addresses so that a specific host can use the switch port. You can clear a MAC address or the complete port cache with the following command:

```
Switch# clear port-security dynamic [address mac-addr | interface type mod/num]
```

In the shutdown mode, the port security action is much more drastic. When the maximum number of MAC addresses is exceeded, the following syslog messages indicate that the port has been shut down in the Errdisable state:

```
Jun  3 17:14:19.018 EDT: %PM-4-ERR_DISABLE: psecure-violation error detected on
   Gi0/11, putting Gi0/11 in err-disable state
Jun  3 17:14:19.022 EDT: %PORT_SECURITY-2-PSECURE_VIOLATION: Security violation
   occurred, caused by MAC address 0003.a089.efc5 on port GigabitEthernet0/11.
Jun  3 17:14:20.022 EDT: %LINEPROTO-5-UPDOWN: Line protocol on Interface Gigabit
   Ethernet0/11, changed state to down
Jun  3 17:14:21.023 EDT: %LINK-3-UPDOWN: Interface GigabitEthernet0/11, changed
   state   to down
```

You also can show the port status with the **show port-security interface** command, as demonstrated in Example 16-1.

Example 16-1 *Displaying Port Security Port Status*

```
Switch# show port-security interface gigabitethernet 0/11
Port Security               : Enabled
Port Status                 : Secure-shutdown

Violation Mode              : Shutdown
Aging Time                  : 0 mins
Aging Type                  : Absolute
SecureStatic Address Aging  : Disabled
Maximum MAC Addresses       : 1
Total MAC Addresses         : 0
Configured MAC Addresses    : 0
Sticky MAC Addresses        : 0
Last Source Address         : 0003.a089.efc5
Security Violation Count    : 1
Switch#
```

To see a quick summary of only ports in the Errdisable state, along with the reason for errdisable, you can use the **show interfaces status err-disabled** command, as demonstrated in Example 16-2.

Example 16-2 *Displaying Summary Information for Ports in the Errdisable State*

```
Switch# show interfaces status err-disabled
Port      Name            Status         Reason
Gi0/11    Test port       err-disabled psecure-violation
Switch#
TIP
When a port is moved to the errdisable state, you must either manually cycle it
or configure the switch to automatically re-enable ports after a prescribed delay.
To manually cycle a port and return it to service, use the following commands:
Switch(config)# interface type mod/num
Switch(config-if)# shutdown
Switch(config-if)# no shutdown
```

Finally, you can display a summary of the port-security status with the **show port-security** command, as demonstrated in Example 16-3.

Example 16-3 *Displaying Port Security Status Summary Information*

```
Switch# show port-security
Secure Port  MaxSecureAddr  CurrentAddr  SecurityViolation  Security Action
             (Count)        (Count)      (Count)
------------------------------------------------------------------------
    Gi0/11          5             1                0           Restrict
    Gi0/12          1             0                0           Shutdown
------------------------------------------------------------------------
Total Addresses in System (excluding one mac per port)     : 0
Max Addresses limit in System (excluding one mac per port) : 6176
Switch#
```

Port-Based Authentication

Catalyst switches can support port-based authentication, a combination of AAA authentication and port security. This feature is based on the IEEE 802.1x standard. When it is enabled, a switch port will not pass any traffic until a user has authenticated with the switch. If the authentication is successful, the user can use the port normally.

Key Topic

For port-based authentication, both the switch and the end user's PC must support the 802.1x standard, using the Extensible Authentication Protocol over LANs (EAPOL). The 802.1x standard is a cooperative effort between the client and the switch offering network service. If the client PC is configured to use 802.1x but the switch does not support it, the PC abandons the protocol and communicates normally. However, if the switch is configured for 802.1x but the PC does not support it, the switch port remains in the unauthorized state so that it will not forward any traffic to the client PC.

Note: 802.1x EAPOL is a Layer 2 protocol. At the point that a switch detects the presence of a device on a port, the port remains in the unauthorized state. Therefore, the client PC cannot communicate with anything other than the switch by using EAPOL. If the PC does not already have an IP address, it cannot request one. The PC also has no knowledge of the switch or its IP address, so any means other than a Layer 2 protocol is not possible. This is why the PC must also have an 802.1x-capable application or client software.

An 802.1x switch port begins in the unauthorized state so that no data other than the 802.1x protocol itself is allowed through the port. Either the client or the switch can initiate an 802.1x session. The authorized state of the port ends when the user logs out, causing the 802.1x client to inform the switch to revert back to the unauthorized state. The switch can also time out the user's authorized session. If this happens, the client must reauthenticate to continue using the switch port.

802.1x Configuration

Port-based authentication can be handled by one or more external Remote Authentication Dial-In User Service (RADIUS) servers. Although many Cisco switch platforms allow other authentication methods to be configured, only RADIUS is supported for 802.1x.

The actual RADIUS authentication method must be configured first, followed by 802.1x, as shown in the following steps:

Step 1. Enable AAA on the switch.

By default, AAA is disabled. You can enable AAA for port-based authentication by using the following global configuration command:

```
Switch(config)# aaa new-model
```

The **new-model** keyword refers to the use of method lists, by which authentication methods and sources can be grouped or organized. The new model is much more scalable than the "old model," in which the authentication source was explicitly configured.

Step 2. Define external RADIUS servers.

First, define each server along with its secret shared password. This string is known only to the switch and the server, and provides a key for encrypting the authentication session. Use the following global configuration command:

```
Switch(config)# radius-server host {hostname | ip-address} [key string]
```

This command can be repeated to define additional RADIUS servers.

Step 3. Define the authentication method for 802.1x.

Using the following command causes all RADIUS authentication servers that are defined on the switch to be used for 802.1x authentication:

```
Switch(config)# aaa authentication dot1x default group radius
```

Step 4. Enable 802.1x on the switch:

```
Switch(config)# dot1x system-auth-control
```

Step 5. Configure each switch port that will use 802.1x:

```
Switch(config)# interface type mod/num
Switch(config-if)# dot1x port-control {force-authorized | force-
  unauthorized | auto}
```

Here, the 802.1x state is one of the following:

force-authorized—The port is forced to always authorize any connected client. No authentication is necessary. This is the default state for all switch ports when 802.1x is enabled.

force-unauthorized—The port is forced to never authorize any connected client. As a result, the port cannot move to the authorized state to pass traffic to a connected client.

auto—The port uses an 802.1x exchange to move from the unauthorized to the authorized state, if successful. This requires an 802.1x-capable application on the client PC.

Tip: After 802.1x is globally enabled on a switch, all switch ports default to the **force-authorized** state. This means that any PC connected to a switch port can immediately start accessing the network. Ideally, you should explicitly configure each port to use the **auto** state so that connected PCs are forced to authenticate through the 802.1x exchange.

Step 6.   Allow multiple hosts on a switch port.

It might be obvious that port-based authentication is tailored to controlling access to a single host PC that is connected to a switch port. However, 802.1x also supports cases in which multiple hosts are attached to a single switch port through an Ethernet hub or another access-layer switch.

If the switch should expect to find multiple hosts present on the switch port, use the following interface configuration command:

```
Switch(config-if)# dot1x host-mode multi-host
```

Tip: You can use the **show dot1x all** command to verify the 802.1x operation on each switch port that is configured to use port-based authentication.

802.1x Port-Based Authentication Example

In Example 16-4, two RADIUS servers are located at 10.1.1.1 and 10.1.1.2. Switch ports Fast Ethernet 0/1 through 0/40 will use 802.1x for port-based authentication. When authenticated, the end users will be associated with VLAN 10.

Example 16-4   *Configuring 802.1x Port-Based Authentication*

```
Switch(config)# aaa new-model
Switch(config)# radius-server host 10.1.1.1 key BigSecret
Switch(config)# radius-server host 10.1.1.2 key AnotherBigSecret
Switch(config)# aaa authentication dot1x default group radius
Switch(config)# dot1x system-auth-control
Switch(config)# interface range FastEthernet0/1 - 40
Switch(config-if)# switchport access vlan 10
Switch(config-if)# switchport mode access
Switch(config-if)# dot1x port-control auto
```

Mitigating Spoofing Attacks

Malicious users sometimes can send spoofed information to trick switches or other hosts into using a rogue machine as a gateway. The attacker's goal is to become the man in the middle, with a naive user sending packets to the attacker as if it were a router. The attacker can glean information from the packets sent to it before it forwards them normally. This section describes three Cisco Catalyst features—DHCP snooping, IP Source Guard, and dynamic ARP inspection—that prevent certain types of spoofing attack.

DHCP Snooping

A DHCP server normally provides all the basic information a client PC needs to operate on a network. For example, the client might receive an IP address, a subnet mask, a default gateway address, DNS addresses, and so on.

Suppose that an attacker could bring up a rogue DHCP server on a machine in the same subnet as that same client PC. Now when the client broadcasts its DHCP request, the rogue server could send a carefully crafted DHCP reply with its own IP address substituted as the default gateway.

When the client receives the reply, it begins using the spoofed gateway address. Packets destined for addresses outside the local subnet then go to the attacker's machine first. The attacker can forward the packets to the correct destination, but in the meantime, it can examine every packet that it intercepts. In effect, this becomes a type of man-in-the-middle attack; the attacker is wedged into the path and the client doesn't realize it.

Cisco Catalyst switches can use the DHCP snooping feature to help mitigate this type of attack. When DHCP snooping is enabled, switch ports are categorized as trusted or untrusted. Legitimate DHCP servers can be found on trusted ports, whereas all other hosts sit behind untrusted ports.

A switch intercepts all DHCP requests coming from untrusted ports before flooding them throughout the VLAN. Any DHCP replies coming from an untrusted port are discarded because they must have come from a rogue DHCP server. In addition, the offending switch port automatically is shut down in the Errdisable state.

DHCP snooping also keeps track of the completed DHCP bindings as clients receive legitimate replies. This database contains the client MAC address, IP address offered, lease time, and so on.

You can configure DHCP snooping first by enabling it globally on a switch with the following configuration command:

```
Switch(config)# ip dhcp snooping
```

Next identify the VLANs where DHCP snooping should be implemented with the following command:

```
Switch(config)# ip dhcp snooping vlan vlan-id [vlan-id]
```

You can give a single VLAN number as *vlan-id* or a range of VLAN numbers by giving the start and end VLAN IDs of the range.

By default, all switch ports are assumed to be untrusted so that DHCP replies are not expected or permitted. Only trusted ports are allowed to send DHCP replies. Therefore, you should identify only the ports where known, trusted DHCP servers are located. You can do this with the following interface configuration command:

```
Switch(config)# interface type mod/num
Switch(config-if)# ip dhcp snooping trust
```

For untrusted ports, an unlimited rate of DHCP requests is accepted. If you want to rate-limit DHCP traffic on an untrusted port, use the following interface configuration command:

```
Switch(config)# interface type mod/num
Switch(config-if)# ip dhcp snooping limit rate rate
```

The *rate* can be 1 to 2048 DHCP packets per second.

You also can configure the switch to use DHCP option-82, the DHCP Relay Agent Information option, which is described in RFC 3046. When a DHCP request is intercepted on an untrusted port, the switch adds its own MAC address and the switch port identifier into the option-82 field of the request. The request then is forwarded normally so that it can reach a trusted DHCP server.

Adding option-82 provides more information about the actual client that generated the DHCP request. In addition, the DHCP reply (if any) echoes back the option-82 information. The switch intercepts the reply and compares the option-82 data to confirm that the request came from a valid port on itself. This feature is enabled by default. You can enable or disable option-82 globally with the following configuration command:

```
Switch(config)# [no] ip dhcp snooping information option
```

When DHCP snooping is configured, you can display its status with the following command:

```
Switch# show ip dhcp snooping [binding]
```

You can use the **binding** keyword to display all the known DHCP bindings that have been overheard. The switch maintains these in its own database. Otherwise, only the switch ports that are trusted or that have rate limiting applied are listed. All other ports are considered to be untrusted with an unlimited DHCP request rate.

As an example, interfaces Fast Ethernet 0/35 and 0/36 use access VLAN 104, are considered untrusted, and have DHCP rate limiting applied at three per second. A known DHCP server is located on the Gigabit Ethernet 0/1 uplink. Example 16-5 shows the configuration for this scenario.

Example 16-5 *DHCP Snooping Configuration*

```
Switch(config)# ip dhcp snooping
Switch(config)# ip dhcp snooping vlan 104
Switch(config)# interface range fastethernet 0/35 - 36
Switch(config-if)# ip dhcp snooping limit rate 3
Switch(config-if)# interface gigabitethernet 0/1
Switch(config-if)# ip dhcp snooping trust
```

Example 16-6 shows the resulting DHCP snooping status.

Example 16-6 *DHCP Snooping Status Display*

```
Switch# show ip dhcp snooping
Switch DHCP snooping is enabled
DHCP snooping is configured on following VLANs:
104
Insertion of option 82 is enabled
Interface                    Trusted      Rate limit (pps)
-----------------------      -------      ----------------
FastEthernet0/35             no           3
FastEthernet0/36             no           3
GigabitEthernet0/1           yes          unlimited
Switch#
```

IP Source Guard

Address spoofing is one type of attack that can be difficult to mitigate. Normally, a host is assigned an IP address and is expected to use that address in all the traffic it sends out. IP addresses are effectively used on the honor system, where hosts are trusted to behave themselves and use their own legitimate source addresses.

A rogue or compromised host PC doesn't necessarily play by those rules. It can use its legitimate address, or it can begin to use spoofed addresses—borrowed from other hosts or used at random. Spoofed addresses are often used to disguise the origin of denial-of-service attacks. If the source address doesn't really exist, no return traffic will find its way back to the originator.

Routers or Layer 3 devices can perform some simple tests to detect spoofed source addresses in packets passing through. For example, if the 10.10.0.0 network is known to exist on VLAN 10, packets entering from VLAN 20 should never have source addresses in that subnet.

However, it is difficult to detect spoofed addresses when they are used *inside* the VLAN or subnet where they should already exist. For example, within the 10.10.0.0 network on VLAN 10, as shown in Figure 16-1, a rogue host begins to send packets with a spoofed source address of 10.10.10.10. The 10.10.10.10 address is certainly within the 10.10.0.0/16 subnet, so it doesn't stand out as an obvious spoof. Therefore, the rogue host might be very successful in attacking other hosts in its own subnet or VLAN.

Cisco Catalyst switches can use the IP source guard feature to detect and suppress address spoofing attacks—even if they occur within the same subnet. A Layer 2 switch, and a Layer 2 port in turn, normally learns and stores MAC addresses. The switch must have a way to look up MAC addresses and find out what IP address are associated with them.

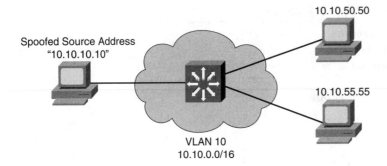

Figure 16-1 *Using a Spoofed Address Within a Subnet*

IP Source Guard does this by making use of the DHCP snooping database and static IP source binding entries. If DHCP snooping is configured and enabled, the switch learns the MAC and IP addresses of hosts that use DHCP. Packets arriving on a switch port can be tested for one of the following conditions:

■ The source IP address must be identical to the IP address learned by DHCP snooping or a static entry. A dynamic port ACL is used to filter traffic. The switch automatically creates this ACL, adds the learned source IP address to the ACL, and applies the ACL to the interface where the address is learned.

■ The source MAC address must be identical to the MAC address learned on the switch port and by DHCP snooping. Port security is used to filter traffic.

If the address is something other than the one learned or statically configured, the switch drops the packet.

To configure IP Source Guard, first configure and enable DHCP snooping, as presented in the previous section. If you want IP Source Guard to detect spoofed MAC addresses, you also need to configure and enable port security.

For the hosts that do not use DHCP, you can configure a static IP source binding with the following configuration command:

```
Switch(config)# ip source binding mac-address vlan vlan-id ip-address interface
   type mod/num
```

Here, the host's MAC address is bound to a specific VLAN and IP address, and is expected to be found on a specific switch interface.

Next, enable IP source guard on one or more switch interfaces with the following configuration commands:

```
Switch(config)# interface type mod/num
Switch(config-if)# ip verify source [port-security]
```

The **ip verify source** command inspects the source IP address only. You can add the **port-security** keyword to inspect the source MAC address, too.

To verify the IP source guard status, you can use the following EXEC command:

```
Switch# show ip verify source [interface type mod/num]
```

If you need to verify the information contained in the IP source binding database, either learned or statically configured, you can use the following EXEC command:

```
Switch# show ip source bindng [ip-address] [mac-address] [dhcp-snooping | static]
   [interface type mod/num] [vlan vlan-id]
```

Dynamic ARP Inspection

Hosts normally use the Address Resolution Protocol (ARP) to resolve an unknown MAC address when the IP address is known. If a MAC address is needed so that a packet can be forwarded at Layer 2, a host broadcasts an ARP request that contains the IP address of the target in question. If any other host is using that IP address, it responds with an ARP reply containing its MAC address.

The ARP process works well among trusted and well-behaved users. However, suppose that an attacker could send its own crafted ARP reply when it overhears an ARP request being broadcast. The reply could contain its own MAC address, causing the original re-quester to think that it is bound to the IP address in question. The requester would add the bogus ARP entry into its own ARP cache, only to begin forwarding packets to the spoofed MAC address.

In effect, this scheme places the attacker's machine right in the middle of an otherwise le-gitimate path. Packets will be sent to the attacker instead of another host or the default gateway. The attacker can intercept packets and (perhaps) forward them on only after ex-amining the packets' contents.

This attack is known as *ARP poisoning* or *ARP spoofing*, and it is considered to be a type of man-in-the-middle attack. The attacker wedges into the normal forwarding path, transparent to the end users. Cisco Catalyst switches can use the dynamic ARP inspection (DAI) feature to help mitigate this type of attack.

DAI works much like DHCP snooping. All switch ports are classified as trusted or un-trusted. The switch intercepts and inspects all ARP packets that arrive on an untrusted port; no inspection is done on trusted ports.

When an ARP reply is received on an untrusted port, the switch checks the MAC and IP addresses reported in the reply packet against known and trusted values. A switch can gather trusted ARP information from statically configured entries or from dynamic en-tries in the DHCP snooping database. In the latter case, DHCP snooping must be enabled in addition to DAI.

If an ARP reply contains invalid information or values that conflict with entries in the trusted database, it is dropped and a log message is generated. This action prevents invalid or spoofed ARP entries from being sent and added to other machines' ARP caches.

You can configure DAI by first enabling it on one or more client VLANs with the follow-ing configuration command:

```
Switch(config)# ip arp inspection vlan vlan-range
```

The VLAN range can be a single VLAN ID, a range of VLAN IDs separated by a hyphen, or a list of VLAN IDs separated by commas.

By default, all switch ports associated with the VLAN range are considered to be un-trusted. You should identify trusted ports as those that connect to other switches. In other words, the local switch will not inspect ARP packets arriving on trusted ports; it will as-sume that the neighboring switch also is performing DAI on all of its ports in that VLAN. Configure a trusted port with the following interface configuration command:

```
Switch(config)# interface type mod/num
Switch(config-if)# ip arp inspection trust
```

If you have hosts with statically configured IP address information, there will be no DHCP message exchange that can be inspected. Instead, you can configure an ARP access list that defines static MAC-IP address bindings that are permitted. Use the following config-uration commands to define the ARP access list and one or more static entries:

```
Switch(config)# arp access-list acl-name
Switch(config-acl)# permit ip host sender-ip mac host sender-mac [log]
[Repeat the previous command as needed]
Switch(config-acl)# exit
```

Now the ARP access list must be applied to DAI with the following configuration command:

```
Switch(config)# ip arp inspection filter arp-acl-name vlan vlan-range [static]
```

When ARP replies are intercepted, their contents are matched against the access list en-tries first. If no match is found, the DHCP snooping bindings database is checked next. You can give the **static** keyword to prevent the DHCP bindings database from being checked at all. In effect, this creates an implicit deny statement at the end of the ARP ac-cess list; if no match is found in the access list, the ARP reply is considered invalid.

Finally, you can specify further validations on the contents of ARP reply packets. By de-fault, only the MAC and IP addresses contained within the ARP reply are validated. This doesn't take the actual MAC addresses contained in the Ethernet header of the ARP reply.

To validate that an ARP reply packet is really coming from the address listed inside it, you can enable DAI validation with the following configuration command:

```
Switch(config)# ip arp inspection validate {[src-mac] [dst-mac] [ip]}
```

Be sure to specify at least one of the options:

- **src-mac**—Check the source MAC address in the Ethernet header against the sender MAC address in the ARP reply.

- **dst-mac**—Check the destination MAC address in the Ethernet header against the target MAC address in the ARP reply.

- **ip**—Check the sender's IP address in all ARP requests; check the sender's IP address against the target IP address in all ARP replies.

Example 16-7 demonstrates where DAI is enabled for all switch ports associated with VLAN 104 on an access-layer switch. The uplink to a distribution switch is considered to be trusted.

Example 16-7   *Configuring DAI to Validate ARP Replies*

```
Switch(config)# ip arp inspection vlan 104
Switch(config)# arp access-list StaticARP
Switch(config-acl)# permit ip host 192.168.1.10 mac host 0006.5b02.a841
Switch(config-acl)# exit
Switch(config)# ip arp inspection filter StaticARP vlan 104
Switch(config)# interface gigabitethernet 0/1
Switch(config-if)# ip arp inspection trust
```

You can display DAI status information with the **show ip arp inspection** command.

Best Practices for Securing Switches

Although you can configure and use many different features on Cisco Catalyst switches, you should be aware of some common weaknesses that can be exploited. In other words, do not become complacent and assume that everyone connected to your network will be good citizens and play by the rules. Think ahead and try to prevent as many things as possible that might be leveraged to assist an attacker.

This section presents a brief overview of many best-practice suggestions that can help secure your switched network:

- **Configure secure passwords**—Whenever possible, you should use the **enable secret** command to set the privileged-level password on a switch. This command uses a stronger encryption than the normal **enable password** command.

  You also should use external AAA servers to authenticate administrative users whenever possible. The usernames and passwords are maintained externally, so they are not stored or managed directly on the switch. In addition, having a centralized user management is much more scalable than configuring and changing user credentials on many individual switches and routers.

  Finally, you always should use the **service password-encryption** configuration command to automatically encrypt password strings that are stored in the switch configuration. Although the encryption is not excessively strong, it can prevent casual observers from seeing passwords in the clear.

- **Use system banners**—When users successfully access a switch, they should be aware of any specific access or acceptable use policies that are pertinent to your organization. You should configure system banners so that this type of information is displayed when users log in to a switch. The idea is to warn unauthorized users (if they gain access) that their activities could be grounds for prosecution—or that they are unwelcome, at the very least.

  You should use the **banner motd** command to define the text that is displayed to authenticated users. Try to avoid using other banner types that display information about your organization or the switch before users actually log in. Never divulge any extra information about your network that malicious users could use.

- **Secure the web interface**—Decide whether you will use the web interface to manage or monitor a switch. Some network professionals use the command line interface exclusively, so the web interface is not needed in a production environment. In this case, you should disable the web interface with the **no ip http server** global configuration command.

If you do decide to use the web interface, be sure to use the HTTPS interface, if it is supported on the switch platform. The standard HTTP web interface has some glaring weaknesses, mainly because none of the traffic is encrypted or protected. Enable the HTTPS interface with the **ip http secure server** global configuration command instead of the **ip http server** command.

In addition, try to limit the source addresses that can access the HTTPS interface. First, create an access list that permits only approved source addresses; then apply the access list to the HTTPS interface with the **ip http access-class** configuration command. As an example, the following configuration commands permit HTTPS connections that are sourced from the 10.100.50.0/24 network:

```
Switch(config)# ip http secure server
Switch(config)# access-list 1 permit 10.100.50.0 0.0.0.255
Switch(config)# ip http access-class 1
```

- **Secure the switch console**—In many environments, switches are locked away in wiring closets where physical security is used to keep people from connecting to the switch console. Even so, you always should configure authentication on any switch console. It is usually appropriate to use the same authentication configuration on the console as the virtual terminal (vty) lines.

- **Secure virtual terminal access**—You always should configure user authentication on *all* the vty lines on a switch. In addition, you should use access lists to limit the source IP addresses of potential administrative users who try to use Telnet or Secure Shell (SSH) to access a switch.

You can use a simple IP access list to permit inbound connections only from known source addresses, as in the following example:

```
Switch(config)# access-list 10 permit 192.168.199.10
Switch(config)# access-list 10 permit 192.168.201.100
Switch(config)# line vty 0 15
Switch(config-line)# access-class 10 in
```

Be sure you apply the access list to all the **line vty** entries in the switch configuration. Many times, the vty lines are separated into groups in the configuration. You can use the **show user all** command to see every possible line that can be used to access a switch.

- **Use SSH whenever possible**—Although Telnet access is easy to configure and use, Telnet is not secure. Every character you type in a Telnet session is sent to and echoed from a switch in the clear, with no encryption. Therefore, it is very easy to eavesdrop on Telnet sessions to overhear usernames and passwords.

Instead, you should use SSH whenever possible. SSH uses strong encryption to secure session data. Therefore, you need a strong-encryption IOS image running on a switch before SSH can be configured and used. You should use the highest SSH version that is available on a switch. The early SSHv1 and SSHv1.5 have some weaknesses, so you should choose SSHv2 whenever possible.

- **Secure SNMP access**—To prevent unauthorized users from making changes to a switch configuration, you should disable any read-write SNMP access. These are commands of the form **snmp-server community** *string* **RW**.

  Instead, you should have only read-only commands in the configuration. In addition, you should use access lists to limit the source addresses that have read-only access. Don't depend on the SNMP community strings for security because these are passed in the clear in SNMP packets.

- **Secure unused switch ports**—Every unused switch port should be disabled so that unexpected users can't connect and use them without your knowledge. You can do this with the **shutdown** interface configuration command.

  In addition, you should configure every user port as an access port with the **switchport mode access** interface configuration command. Otherwise, a malicious user might connect and attempt to negotiate trunking mode on a port. You also should consider associating every unused access port with a bogus or isolated VLAN. If an unexpected user does gain access to a port, he will have access only to a VLAN that is isolated from every other resource on your network.

Tip: You might consider using the **switchport host** interface configuration command as a quick way to force a port to support only a single PC. This command is actually a macro, as shown in the following example:

```
Switch(config)# interface fastethernet 1/0/1
Switch(config-if)# switchport host
switchport mode will be set to access
spanning-tree portfast will be enabled
channel group will be disabled
Switch(config-if)#
```

- **Secure STP operation**—A malicious user can inject STP bridge protocol data units (BPDU) into switch ports or VLANs, and can disrupt a stable, loop-free topology. You always should enable the BPDU guard feature so that access switch ports automatically are disabled if unexpected BPDUs are received.

- **Secure the use of CDP**—By default, CDP advertisements are sent on *every* switch port at 60-second intervals. Although CDP is a very handy tool for discovering neighboring Cisco devices, you shouldn't allow CDP to advertise unnecessary information about your switch to listening attackers.

  For example, the following information is sent in a CDP advertisement in the clear. An attacker might use the device ID to physically locate the switch, its IP address to target Telnet or SNMP attacks, or the native VLAN and switch port ID to attempt a VLAN hopping attack.

```
CDP - Cisco Discovery Protocol
  Version:              2
  Time to live:         180   seconds
  Checksum:             0xD0AE
  Device ID:            BldgA-Rm110
Version:                Cisco Internetwork Operating System Software .IOS
(tm) C3750 Software (C3750-I9-M), Version 12.2(20)SE4, RELEASE SOFTWARE
(fc1).Copyright  1986-2005 by cisco Systems, Inc..Compiled Sun 09-Jan-05
00:09 by antonino
  Platform:             cisco WS-C3750-48P
  IP Address:           192.168.100.85
  Port ID:              FastEthernet1/0/48
  Capabilities:         0x00000028  Switch   IGMP
  VTP Domain:           MyCompany
  Native VLAN:          101
  Duplex:     0x01      Full
```

CDP should be enabled only on switch ports that connect to other trusted Cisco devices. Do not forget that CDP must be enabled on access switch ports where Cisco IP Phones are connected. When the CDP messages reach the IP Phone, they won't be relayed on to a PC connected to the phone's data port. You can disable CDP on a port-by-port basis with the **no cdp enable** interface configuration command.

Exam Preparation Tasks

Review All Key Topics

Review the most important topics in the chapter, noted with the Key Topic icon in the outer margin of the page. Table 16-2 lists a reference of these key topics and the page numbers on which each is found.

Table 16-2 *Key Topics for Chapter 16*

Key Topic Element	Description	Page Number
Paragraph	Discusses port security and MAC address control using sticky MAC addresses	375
List	Explains the actions port security can take when the MAC address limits are violated	376
Paragraph	Discusses port-based authentication using IEEE 802.1x and EAPOL	378
Paragraph	Explains DHCP snooping	381
Paragraph	Describes ARP poisoning, ARP spoofing attacks, and dynamic ARP inspection	385

Complete Tables and Lists from Memory

Print a copy of Appendix C, "Memory Tables" (found on the CD), or at least the section for this chapter, and complete the tables and lists from memory. Appendix D, "Memory Tables Answer Key," also on the CD, includes completed tables and lists to check your work.

Define Key Terms

Define the following key terms from this chapter, and check your answers in the glossary:

sticky MAC address, IEEE 802.1x, DHCP snooping, ARP poisoning (also known as ARP spoofing), dynamic ARP inspection (DAI)

Use Command Reference to Check Your Memory

This section includes the most important configuration and EXEC commands covered in this chapter. It might not be necessary to memorize the complete syntax of every command, but you should remember the basic keywords that are needed.

To test your memory of the STP configuration commands, cover the right side of Tables 16-3 through 16-7 with a piece of paper, read the description on the left side, and then see how much of the command you can remember.

Table 16-3 *Port Security Configuration Commands*

Task	Command Syntax
Enable port security on an interface.	switchport port-security
Set the maximum number of learned addresses.	switchport port-security maximum *max-addr*
Define a static MAC address.	switchport port-security mac-address *mac-addr*
Define an action to take.	switchport port-security violation {shutdown | restrict | protect}

Table 16-4 *Port-Based Authentication Configuration Commands*

Task	Command Syntax
Define a method list for 802.1x.	aaa authentication dot1x default group radius
Globally enable 802.1x.	dot1x system-auth-control
Define the 802.1x behavior on a port.	dot1x port-control {force-authorized | force-unauthorized | auto}
Support more than one host on a port.	dot1x host-mode multi-host

Table 16-5 *DHCP Snooping Configuration Commands*

Task	Command Syntax
Globally enable DHCP snooping.	ip dhcp snooping
Define a trusted interface.	ip dhcp snooping trust
Limit the interface DHCP packet rate.	ip dhcp snooping limit rate *rate*

Table 16-6 *IP Source Guard Configuration Commands*

Task	Command Syntax
Define a static IP source binding entry.	ip source binding *mac-address* vlan *vlan-id ip-address* interface *type mod/num*
Enable IP source guard on an interface.	ip verify source [port-security]

Table 16-7 *Dynamic ARP Inspection Configuration Commands*

Task	Command Syntax
Enable DAI on a VLAN.	ip arp inspection vlan *vlan-range*
Define a trusted interface.	ip arp inspection trust
Define a static ARP inspection binding.	arp access-list *acl-name* permit ip host *sender-ip* mac host *sender-mac* [log]
Apply static ARP inspection bindings.	ip arp inspection filter *arp-acl-name* vlan *vlan-range* [static]
Validate addresses within ARP replies.	ip arp inspection validate {[src-mac] [dst-mac] [ip]}

This chapter covers the following topics that you need to master for the CCNP SWITCH exam:

VLAN Access Lists—This section discusses how traffic can be controlled within a VLAN. You can use VLAN access control lists (ACL) to filter packets even as they are bridged or switched.

Private VLANs—This section explains the mechanisms that you can use to provide isolation within a single VLAN. Private VLANs have a unidirectional nature; several of them can be isolated yet share a common subnet and gateway.

Securing VLAN Trunks—This section covers two types of attacks that can be leveraged against a VLAN trunk link. If a trunk link is extended to or accessible from an attacker, any VLAN carried over the trunk can be compromised in turn.

CHAPTER 17

Securing with VLANs

Traditionally, traffic has been filtered only at router boundaries, where packets naturally are inspected before being forwarded. This is true within Catalyst switches because access lists can be applied as a part of multilayer switching. Catalysts also can filter packets even if they stay within the same VLAN; VLAN access control lists, or VACLs, provide this capability.

Catalyst switches also have the capability to logically divide a single VLAN into multiple partitions. Each partition can be isolated from others, with all of them sharing a common IP subnet and a common gateway address. Private VLANs make it possible to offer up a single VLAN to many disparate customers or organizations without any interaction between them.

VLAN trunks are commonly used on links between switches to carry data from multiple VLANs. If the switches are all under the same administrative control, it is easy to become complacent about the security of the trunks. A few known attacks can be used to gain access to the VLANs that are carried over trunk links. Therefore, network administrators should be aware of the steps that can be taken to prevent any attacks.

"Do I Know This Already?" Quiz

The "Do I Know This Already?" quiz allows you to assess whether you should read this entire chapter thoroughly or jump to the "Exam Preparation Tasks" section. If you are in doubt based on your answers to these questions or your own assessment of your knowledge of the topics, read the entire chapter. Table 17-1 outlines the major headings in this chapter and the "Do I Know This Already?" quiz questions that go with them. You can find the answers in Appendix A, "Answers to the 'Do I Know This Already?' Quizzes."

Table 17-1 *"Do I Know This Already?" Foundation Topics Section-to-Question Mapping*

Foundation Topics Section	Questions Covered in This Section
VLAN Access Lists	1–4
Private VLANs	5–8
Securing VLAN Trunks	9–12

1. Which one of the following can filter packets even if they are not routed to another Layer 3 interface?

   a. IP extended access lists

   b. MAC address access lists

   c. VLAN access lists

   d. Port-based access lists

2. In what part of a Catalyst switch are VLAN ACLs implemented?

   a. NVRAM

   b. CAM

   c. RAM

   d. TCAM

3. Which one of the following commands can implement a VLAN ACL called test?

   a. access-list vlan test

   b. vacl test

   c. switchport vacl test

   d. vlan access-map test

4. After a VACL is configured, where is it applied?

   a. Globally on a VLAN

   b. On the VLAN interface

   c. In the VLAN configuration

   d. On all ports or interfaces mapped to a VLAN

5. Which of the following private VLANs is the most restrictive?

   a. Community VLAN

   b. Isolated VLAN

   c. Restricted VLAN

   d. Promiscuous VLAN

6. The vlan 100 command has just been entered. What is the next command needed to configure VLAN 100 as a secondary isolated VLAN?

   a. private-vlan isolated

   b. private-vlan isolated 100

   c. pvlan secondary isolated

   d. No further configuration necessary

7. What type of port configuration should you use for private VLAN interfaces that connect to a router?

   a. Host

   b. Gateway

   c. Promiscuous

   d. Transparent

8. Promiscuous ports must be _____ to primary and secondary VLANs, and host ports must be _____.

   a. Mapped, associated

   b. Mapped, mapped

   c. Associated, mapped

   d. Associated, associated

9. In a switch spoofing attack, an attacker makes use of which one of the following?

   a. The switch management IP address

   b. CDP message exchanges

   c. Spanning Tree Protocol

   d. DTP to negotiate a trunk

10. Which one of the following commands can be used to prevent a switch spoofing attack on an end-user port?

    a. switchport mode access

    b. switchport mode trunk

    c. no switchport spoof

    d. spanning-tree spoof-guard

11. Which one of the following represents the spoofed information an attacker sends in a VLAN hopping attack?

    a. 802.1Q tags

    b. DTP information

    c. VTP information

    d. 802.1x information

12. Which one of the following methods can be used to prevent a VLAN hopping attack?

    a. Use VTP throughout the network.

    b. Set the native VLAN to the user access VLAN.

    c. Prune the native VLAN off a trunk link.

    d. Avoid using EtherChannel link bundling.

Foundation Topics

VLAN Access Lists

Access lists can manage or control traffic as it passes through a switch. When normal access lists are configured on a Catalyst switch, they filter traffic through the use of the Ternary content-addressable memory (TCAM). Recall from Chapter 2, "Switch Operation," that access lists (also known as *router access lists*, or RACLs) are merged or compiled into the TCAM. Each ACL is applied to an interface according to the direction of traffic—inbound or outbound. Packets then can be filtered in hardware with no switching performance penalty. However, only packets that pass *between* VLANs can be filtered this way.

Packets that stay in the same VLAN do not cross a VLAN or interface boundary and do not necessarily have a direction in relation to an interface. These packets also might be non-IP, non-IPX, or completely bridged; therefore, they never pass through the multilayer switching mechanism. VLAN access lists (VACL) are filters that directly can affect how packets are handled *within* a VLAN.

VACLs are somewhat different from RACLs or traditional access control lists. Although they, too, are merged into the TCAM, they can permit, deny, or redirect packets as they are matched. VACLs also are configured in a route map fashion, with a series of matching conditions and actions to take.

VACL Configuration

VACLs are configured as a VLAN access map in much the same format as a route map. A VLAN access map consists of one or more statements, each having a common map name. First, you define the VACL with the following global configuration command:

```
Switch(config)# vlan access-map map-name [sequence-number]
```

Access map statements are evaluated in sequence according to the *sequence-number*. Each statement can contain one or more matching conditions, followed by an action.

Next, define the matching conditions that identify the traffic to be filtered. Matching is performed by access lists (IP, IPX, or MAC address ACLs), which you must configure independently. Configure a matching condition with one of the following access map configuration commands:

```
Switch(config-access-map)# match ip address {acl-number | acl-name}
Switch(config-access-map)# match ipx address {acl-number | acl-name}
Switch(config-access-map)# match mac address acl-name
```

You can repeat these commands to define several matching conditions; the first match encountered triggers an action to take. Define the action with the following access map configuration command:

```
Switch(config-access-map)# action {drop | forward [capture] | redirect type
  mod/num}
```

A VACL can either drop a matching packet, forward it, or redirect it to another interface. The TCAM performs the entire VACL match and action as packets are switched or bridged within a VLAN or routed into or out of a VLAN.

Finally, you must apply the VACL to a VLAN using the following global configuration command:

```
Switch(config)# vlan filter map-name vlan-list vlan-list
```

Notice that the VACL is applied globally to one or more VLANs listed and not to a VLAN interface (SVI). Recall that VLANs can be present in a switch as explicit interfaces or as inherent Layer 2 entities. The VLAN interface is the point where packets enter or leave a VLAN, so it does not make sense to apply a VACL there. Instead, the VACL needs to function *within* the VLAN itself, where there is no inbound or outbound direction.

For example, suppose that you need to filter traffic within VLAN 99 so that host 192.168.99.17 is not allowed to contact any other host on its local subnet. Access list local-17 is created to identify traffic between this host and anything else on its local subnet. Then a VLAN access map is defined: If the local-17 access list permits the IP address, the packet is dropped; otherwise, the packet is forwarded. Example 17-1 shows the commands necessary for this example.

Example 17-1   *Filtering Traffic Within the Local Subnet*

```
Switch(config)# ip access-list extended local-17
Switch(config-acl)# permit ip host 192.168.99.17 192.168.99.0  0.0.0.255
Switch(config-acl)# exit
Switch(config)# vlan access-map block-17 10
Switch(config-access-map)# match ip address local-17
Switch(config-access-map)# action drop
Switch(config-access-map)# vlan access-map block-17 20
Switch(config-access-map)# action forward
Switch(config-access-map)# exit
Switch(config)# vlan filter block-17 vlan-list 99
```

Private VLANs

Normally, traffic is allowed to move unrestricted within a VLAN. Packets sent from one host to another normally are heard only by the destination host because of the nature of Layer 2 switching.

However, if one host broadcasts a packet, all hosts on the VLAN must listen. You can use a VACL to filter packets between a source and destination in a VLAN if both connect to the local switch.

Sometimes it would be nice to have the capability to segment traffic within a single VLAN, without having to use multiple VLANs and a router. For example, in a single-VLAN server farm, all servers should be capable of communicating with the router or gateway, but the servers should not have to listen to each other's broadcast traffic. Taking this a step further, suppose that each server belongs to a separate organization. Now each server should be isolated from the others but still be capable of reaching the gateway to find clients not on the local network.

Another application is a service provider network. Here, the provider might want to use a single VLAN to connect to several customer networks. Each customer needs to be able to contact the provider's gateway on the VLAN. Clearly, the customer sites do not need to interact with each other.

Private VLANs (PVLAN) solve this problem on Catalyst switches. In a nutshell, a normal, or *primary*, VLAN can be logically associated with special unidirectional, or secondary, VLANs. Hosts associated with a secondary VLAN can communicate with ports on the primary VLAN (a router, for example), but not with another secondary VLAN. A secondary VLAN is configured as one of the following types:

- **Isolated**—Any switch ports associated with an isolated VLAN can reach the primary VLAN but not any other secondary VLAN. In addition, hosts associated with the same isolated VLAN cannot reach each other. They are, in effect, isolated from everything except the primary VLAN.

- **Community**—Any switch ports associated with a common community VLAN can communicate with each other and with the primary VLAN but not with any other secondary VLAN. This provides the basis for server farms and workgroups within an organization, while giving isolation between organizations.

All secondary VLANs must be associated with one primary VLAN to set up the unidirectional relationship. Private VLANs are configured using special cases of regular VLANs. However, the VLAN Trunking Protocol (VTP) does not pass any information about the private VLAN configuration. Therefore, private VLANs are only locally significant to a switch. Each of the private VLANs must be configured locally on each switch that interconnects them.

You must configure each physical switch port that uses a private VLAN with a VLAN association. You also must define the port with one of the following modes:

- **Promiscuous**—The switch port connects to a router, firewall, or other common gateway device. This port can communicate with anything else connected to the primary or any secondary VLAN. In other words, the port is in promiscuous mode, in which the rules of private VLANs are ignored.

- **Host**—The switch port connects to a regular host that resides on an isolated or community VLAN. The port communicates only with a promiscuous port or ports on the same community VLAN.

Figure 17-1 shows the basic private VLAN operation. Some host PCs connect to a secondary community VLAN. The two community VLANs associate with a primary VLAN, where the router connects. The router connects to a promiscuous port on the primary VLAN. A single host PC connects to a secondary isolated VLAN, so it can communicate only with the router's promiscuous port.

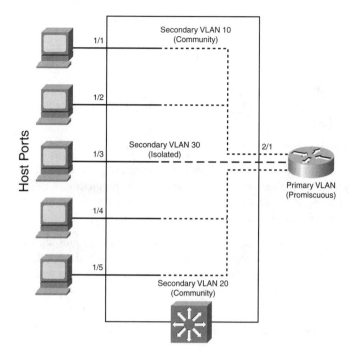

Figure 17-1   *Private VLAN Functionality Within a Switch*

Private VLAN Configuration

Defining a private VLAN involves several configuration steps. These steps are described in the sections that follow so that you can use them.

Configure the Private VLANs

To configure a private VLAN, begin by defining any secondary VLANs that are needed for isolation using the following configuration commands:

```
Switch(config)# vlan vlan-id
Switch(config-vlan)# private-vlan {isolated | community}
```

The secondary VLAN can be an isolated VLAN (no connectivity between isolated ports) or a community VLAN (connectivity between member ports).

Now define the primary VLAN that will provide the underlying private VLAN connectivity using the following configuration commands:

```
Switch(config)# vlan vlan-id
Switch(config-vlan)# private-vlan primary
Switch(config-vlan)# private-vlan association {secondary-vlan-list | add
  secondary-vlan-list | remove secondary-vlan-list}
```

Be sure to associate the primary VLAN with all its component secondary VLANs using the **association** keyword. If the primary VLAN already has been configured, you can add (**add**) or remove (**remove**) secondary VLAN associations individually.

These VLAN configuration commands set up only the mechanisms for unidirectional connectivity from the secondary VLANs to the primary VLAN. You also must associate the individual switch ports with their respective private VLANs.

Associate Ports with Private VLANs

First, define the function of the port that will participate on a private VLAN using the following configuration command:

```
Switch(config-if)# switchport mode private-vlan {host | promiscuous}
```

If the host connected to this port is a router, firewall, or common gateway for the VLAN, use the **promiscuous** keyword. This allows the host to reach all other promiscuous, isolated, or community ports associated with the primary VLAN. Otherwise, any isolated or community port must receive the **host** keyword.

For a nonpromiscuous port (using the **switchport mode private-vlan host** command), you must associate the switch port with the appropriate primary and secondary VLANs. Remember, only the private VLANs themselves have been configured until now. The switch port must know how to interact with the various VLANs using the following interface configuration command:

```
Switch(config-if)# switchport private-vlan host-association primary-vlan-id
    secondary-vlan-id
```

Note: When a switch port is associated with private VLANs, you do not have to configure a static access VLAN. Instead, the port takes on membership in the primary and secondary VLANs simultaneously. This does not mean that the port has a fully functional assignment to multiple VLANs. Instead, it takes on only the unidirectional behavior between the secondary and primary VLANs.

For a promiscuous port (using the **switchport mode private-vlan promiscuous** command), you must map the port to primary and secondary VLANs. Notice that promiscuous mode ports, or ports that can communicate with any other private VLAN device, are mapped, whereas other secondary VLAN ports are associated. One (promiscuous mode port) exhibits bidirectional behavior, whereas the other (secondary VLAN ports) exhibits unidirectional or logical behavior.

Use the following interface configuration command to map promiscuous mode ports to primary and secondary VLANs:

```
Switch(config-if)# switchport private-vlan mapping primary-vlan-id secondary-
    vlan-list | {add secondary-vlan-list} | {remove secondary-vlan-list}
```

As an example, assume that the switch in Figure 17-1 is configured as in Example 17-2. Host PCs on ports Fast Ethernet 1/1 and 1/2 are in community VLAN 10, hosts on ports Fast Ethernet 1/4 and 1/5 are in community VLAN 20, and the host on port Fast Ethernet 1/3 is in isolated VLAN 30. The router on port Fast Ethernet 2/1 is in promiscuous mode on primary VLAN 100. Each VLAN is assigned a role, and the primary VLAN is associated with its secondary VLANs. Then each interface is associated with a primary and secondary VLAN (if a host is attached) or mapped to the primary and secondary VLANs (if a promiscuous host is attached).

Example 17-2 *Configuring Ports with Private VLANs*

```
Switch(config)# vlan 10
Switch(config-vlan)# private-vlan community
Switch(config-vlan)# vlan 20
Switch(config-vlan)# private-vlan community
Switch(config-vlan)# vlan 30
Switch(config-vlan)# private-vlan isolated
Switch(config-vlan)# vlan 100
Switch(config-vlan)# private-vlan primary
Switch(config-vlan)# private-vlan association 10,20,30
Switch(config-vlan)# exit
Switch(config)# interface range fastethernet 1/1 - 1/2
Switch(config-if)# switchport mode private-vlan host
Switch(config-if)# switchport private-vlan host-association 100 10
Switch(config-if)# exit
Switch(config)# interface range fastethernet 1/4 - 1/5
Switch(config-if)# switchport mode private-vlan host
Switch(config-if)# switchport private-vlan host-association 100 20
Switch(config-if)# exit
Switch(config)# interface fastethernet 1/3
Switch(config-if)# switchport mode private-vlan host
Switch(config-if)# switchport private-vlan host-association 100 30
Switch(config-if)# exit
Switch(config)# interface fastethernet 2/1
Switch(config-if)# switchport mode private-vlan promiscuous
Switch(config-if)# switchport private-vlan mapping 100 10,20,30
```

Associate Secondary VLANs to a Primary VLAN SVI

On switched virtual interfaces, or VLAN interfaces configured with Layer 3 addresses, you must configure some additional private VLAN mapping. Consider a different example, where the SVI for the primary VLAN, VLAN 200, has an IP address and participates in routing traffic. Secondary VLANs 40 (an isolated VLAN) and 50 (a community VLAN) are associated at Layer 2 with primary VLAN 200 using the configuration in Example 17-3.

Example 17-3 *Associating Secondary VLANs to a Primary VLAN SVI*

```
Switch(config)# vlan 40
Switch(config-vlan)# private-vlan isolated
Switch(config-vlan)# vlan 50
Switch(config-vlan)# private-vlan community
Switch(config-vlan)# vlan 200
Switch(config-vlan)# private-vlan primary
Switch(config-vlan)# private-vlan association 40,50
```

```
Switch(config-vlan)# exit
Switch(config)# interface vlan 200
Switch(config-if)# ip address 192.168.199.1 255.255.255.0
```

Primary VLAN 200 can forward traffic at Layer 3, but the secondary VLAN associations with it are good at only Layer 2. To allow Layer 3 traffic switching coming from the secondary VLANs as well, you must add a private VLAN mapping to the primary VLAN (SVI) interface, using the following interface configuration command:

```
Switch(config-if)# private-vlan mapping {secondary-vlan-list | add secondary-
    vlan-list | remove secondary-vlan-list}
```

The primary VLAN SVI function is extended to the secondary VLANs instead of requiring SVIs for each of them. If some mapping already has been configured for the primary VLAN SVI, you can add (**add**) or remove (**remove**) secondary VLAN mappings individually.

For Example 17-3, you would map the private VLAN by adding the following commands:

```
Switch(config)# interface vlan 200
Switch(config-if)# private-vlan mapping 40,50
```

Securing VLAN Trunks

Because trunk links usually are bounded between two switches, you might think that they are more or less secure. Each end of the trunk is connected to a device that is under your control, VLANs carried over the trunk remain isolated, and so on.

Some attacks or exploits can be leveraged to gain access to a trunk or to the VLANs carried over a trunk. Therefore, you should become familiar with how the attacks work and what steps you can take to prevent them in the first place.

Switch Spoofing

Recall from Chapter 4, "VLANs and Trunks," that two switches can be connected by a common trunk link that can carry traffic from multiple VLANs. The trunk does not have to exist all the time. The switches dynamically can negotiate its use and its encapsulation mode by exchanging Dynamic Trunking Protocol (DTP) messages.

Although DTP can make switch administration easier, it also can expose switch ports to be compromised. Suppose that a switch port is left to its default configuration, in which the trunking mode is auto. Normally, the switch port would wait to be asked by another switch in the auto or on mode to become a trunk.

Now suppose that an end user's PC is connected to that port. A well-behaved end user would not use DTP at all, so the port would come up in access mode with a single-access VLAN. A malicious user, however, might exploit the use of DTP and attempt to negotiate a trunk with the switch port. This makes the PC appear to be another switch; in effect, the PC is spoofing a switch.

After the trunk is negotiated, the attacker has access to any VLAN that is permitted to pass over the trunk. If the switch port has been left to its default configuration, all VLANs configured on the switch are allowed onto the trunk. This scenario is shown in Figure 17-2. The attacker can receive any traffic being sent over the trunk on any VLAN. In addition, he can send traffic into any VLAN of his choice.

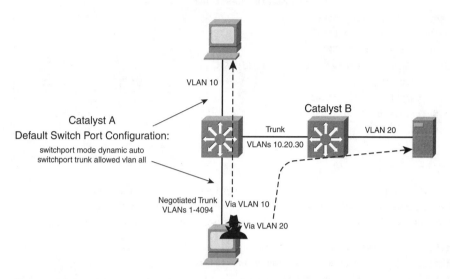

Figure 17-2 *An Example of Switch Spoofing to Gain Access to a Trunk*

To demonstrate this further, consider the output in Example 17-4, which shows the default access switch port configuration. Notice that trunking is possible because the port is set to dynamic auto mode, awaiting DTP negotiation from a connected device. If a trunk is negotiated, all VLANs are permitted to be carried over it.

Example 17-4 *Displaying the Default Switch Port Configuration*

```
Switch# show interfaces fastethernet 1/0/46 switchport
Name: Fa1/0/46
Switchport: Enabled
Administrative Mode: dynamic auto
Operational Mode: trunk
Administrative Trunking Encapsulation: negotiate
Negotiation of Trunking: On
Access Mode VLAN: 1 (default)
Trunking Native Mode VLAN: 1 (default)
Administrative Native VLAN tagging: enabled
Voice VLAN: none
Administrative private-vlan host-association: none
```

```
Administrative private-vlan mapping: none
Administrative private-vlan trunk native VLAN: none
Administrative private-vlan trunk Native VLAN tagging: enabled
Administrative private-vlan trunk encapsulation: dot1q
Administrative private-vlan trunk normal VLANs: none
Administrative private-vlan trunk private VLANs: none
Operational private-vlan: none
Trunking VLANs Enabled: ALL
Pruning VLANs Enabled: 2-1001
Capture Mode Disabled Capture VLANs Allowed: ALL
Protected: false
Unknown unicast blocked: disabled
Unknown multicast blocked: disabled
Appliance trust: none
Switch#
```

The solution to this situation is to configure *every* switch port to have an expected and controlled behavior. For example, instead of leaving an end-user switch port set to use DTP in auto mode, configure it to static access mode with the following commands:

```
Switch(config)# interface type mod/num
Switch(config-if)# switchport access vlan vlan-id
Switch(config-if)# switchport mode access
```

This way, an end user never will be able to send any type of spoofed traffic that will make the switch port begin trunking.

In addition, you might be wise to disable any unused switch ports to prevent someone from discovering a live port that might be exploited.

VLAN Hopping

When securing VLAN trunks, also consider the potential for an exploit called *VLAN hopping*. Here, an attacker positioned on one access VLAN can craft and send frames with spoofed 802.1Q tags so that the packet payloads ultimately appear on a totally different VLAN, all without the use of a router.

For this exploit to work, the following conditions must exist in the network configuration:

■ The attacker is connected to an access switch port.

■ The same switch must have an 802.1Q trunk.

■ The trunk must have the attacker's access VLAN as its native VLAN.

Figure 17-3 shows how VLAN hopping works. The attacker, situated on VLAN 10, sends frames that are doubly tagged as if an 802.1Q trunk were being used. Naturally, the attacker is not connected to a trunk; he is spoofing the trunk encapsulation to trick the switch into making the frames hop over to another VLAN.

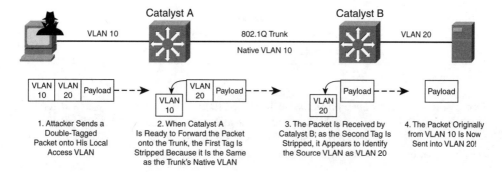

Figure 17-3 *VLAN Hopping Attack Process*

The regular frame—or malicious payload, in this case—is first given an 802.1Q tag with the VLAN ID of the target VLAN. Then a second bogus 802.1Q tag is added with the attacker's access VLAN ID.

When the local switch Catalyst A receives a doubly tagged frame, it decides to forward it out the trunk interface. Because the first (outermost) tag has the same VLAN ID as the trunk's native VLAN, that tag is removed as the frame is sent on the trunk. The switch believes that the native VLAN should be untagged, as it should. Now the second (innermost) tag is exposed on the trunk.

When Catalyst B receives the frame, it examines any 802.1Q tag it finds. The spoofed tag for VLAN 20 is found, so the tag is removed and the frame is forwarded onto VLAN 20. Now the attacker successfully has sent a frame on VLAN 10 and gotten the frame injected onto VLAN 20—all through Layer 2 switching.

Clearly, the key to this type of attack revolves around the use of untagged native VLANs. Therefore, to thwart VLAN hopping, you always should carefully configure trunk links with the following steps:

Step 1.   Set the native VLAN of a trunk to a bogus or unused VLAN ID.

Step 2.   Prune the native VLAN off both ends of the trunk.

For example, suppose that an 802.1Q trunk should carry only VLANs 10 and 20. You should set the native VLAN to an unused value, such as 800. Then you should remove VLAN 800 from the trunk so that it is confined to the trunk link itself. Example 17-5 demonstrates how to accomplish this.

Example 17-5   *Configuring the 802.1Q Trunk to Carry Only VLANs 10 and 20*

```
Switch(config)# vlan 800
Switch(config-vlan)# name bogus_native
Switch(config-vlan)# exit
Switch(config)# interface gigabitethernet 1/1
Switch(config-if)# switchport trunk encapsulation dot1q
```

```
Switch(config-if)# switchport trunk native vlan 800
Switch(config-if)# switchport trunk allowed vlan remove 800
Switch(config-if)# switchport mode trunk
```

Tip: Although maintenance protocols such as CDP, PAgP, and DTP normally are carried over the native VLAN of a trunk, they will not be affected if the native VLAN is pruned from the trunk. They still will be sent and received on the native VLAN as a special case even if the native VLAN ID is not in the list of allowed VLANs.

One alternative is to force all 802.1Q trunks to add tags to frames for the native VLAN, too. The double-tagged VLAN hopping attack won't work because the switch won't remove the first tag with the native VLAN ID (VLAN 10 in the example). Instead, that tag will remain on the spoofed frame as it enters the trunk. At the far end of the trunk, the same tag will be examined, and the frame will stay on the original access VLAN (VLAN 10).

To force a switch to tag the native VLAN on all its 802.1Q trunks, you can use the following command:

```
Switch(config)# vlan dot1q tag native
```

Exam Preparation Tasks

Review All Key Topics

Review the most important topics in the chapter, noted with the Key Topic icon in the outer margin of the page. Table 17-2 lists a reference of these key topics and the page numbers on which each is found.

Key Topic

Table 17-2 *Key Topics for Chapter 17*

Key Topic Element	Description	Page Number
Paragraph	Explains VLAN ACLs and how they are configured	398
Paragraph	Discusses private VLANs, primary and secondary VLANs, and isolated and community VLANs	400
List	Discusses promiscuous and host ports within a private VLAN	404
Paragraph	Explains the switch spoofing attack	
Paragraph	Explains the VLAN hopping attack	406
List	Explains the steps necessary to prevent a VLAN hopping attack	407

Complete Tables and Lists from Memory

Print a copy of Appendix C, "Memory Tables," (found on the CD), or at least the section for this chapter, and complete the tables and lists from memory. Appendix D, "Memory Tables Answer Key," also on the CD, includes completed tables and lists to check your work.

Define Key Terms

Define the following key terms from this chapter, and check your answers in the glossary:

VACL, private VLAN, primary VLAN, secondary VLAN, isolated VLAN, community VLAN, promiscuous port, host port, switch spoofing, VLAN hopping

Use Command Reference to Check Your Memory

This section includes the most important configuration and EXEC commands covered in this chapter. It might not be necessary to memorize the complete syntax of every command, but you should remember the basic keywords that are needed.

To test your memory of the VLAN ACL and private VLAN configuration, cover the right side of Tables 17-3 through 17-4 with a piece of paper, read the description on the left side, and then see how much of the command you can remember.

Table 17-3   *VLAN ACL Configuration Commands*

Task	Command Syntax
Define a VACL.	**vlan access-map** *map-name* [*sequence-number*]
Define a matching condition.	**match** {**ip address** {*acl-number* | *acl-name*}} | {**ipx address** {*acl-number* | *acl-name*} | {**mac address** *acl-name*}}
Define an action.	**action** {**drop** | **forward** [**capture**] | **redirect** *type mod/num*}
Apply the VACL to VLANs.	**vlan filter** *map-name* **vlan-list** *vlan-list*

Table 17-4   *Private VLAN Configuration Commands*

Task	Command Syntax
Define a secondary VLAN.	**vlan** *vlan-id* **private-vlan** {**isolated** | **community**}
Define a primary VLAN; associate it with secondary VLANs.	**vlan** *vlan-id* **private-vlan primary** **private-vlan association** {*secondary-vlan-list* | **add** *secondary-vlan-list* | **remove** *secondary-vlan-list*}
Associate ports with private VLANs.	**switchport mode private-vlan** {**host** | **promiscuous**}
Associate nonpromiscuous ports with private VLANs.	**switchport private-vlan host-association** *primary-vlan-id secondary-vlan-id*
Associate promiscuous ports with private VLANs.	**switchport private-vlan mapping** {*primary-vlan-id*} {*secondary-vlan-list*} | {**add** *secondary-vlan-list*} | {**remove** *secondary-vlan-list*}
Associate secondary VLANs with a primary VLAN Layer 3 SVI.	**private-vlan mapping** {*secondary-vlan-list* | **add** *secondary-vlan-list* | **remove** *secondary-vlan-list*}

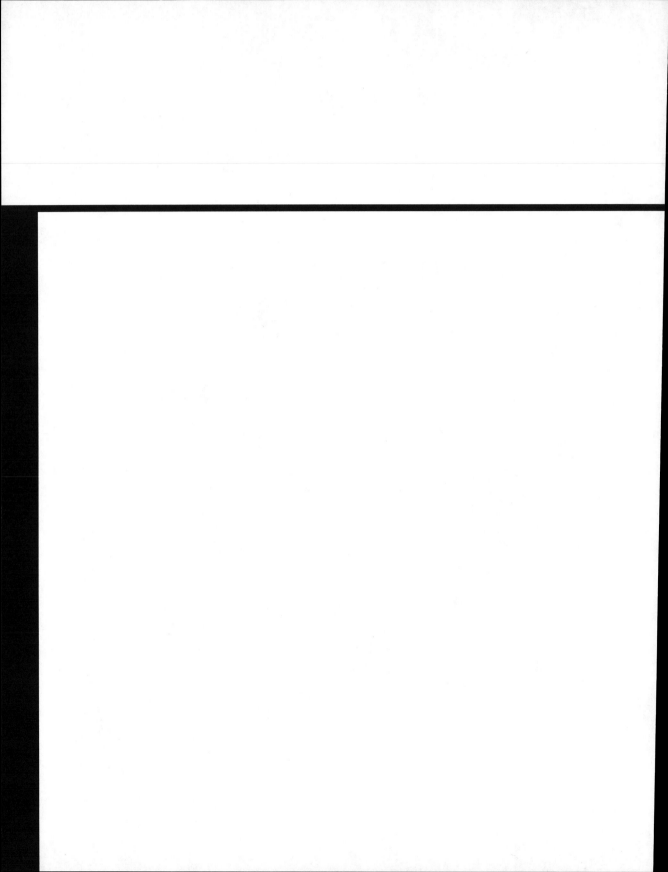

Part VI: Final Exam Preparation

Chapter 18:   **Final Preparation**

The first 17 chapters of this book cover the technologies, protocols, commands, and features required to be prepared to pass the CCNP SWITCH exam. Although these chapters supply the detailed information, most people need more preparation than just reading the first 17 chapters of this book. This chapter details a set of tools and a study plan to help you complete your preparation for the exam.

This short chapter has two main sections. The first section explains how to install the exam engine and practice exams from the CD that accompanies this book. The second section lists some suggestions for a study plan, now that you have completed all the earlier chapters in this book.

Note: Along with the exam engine and other features, Appendix C, "Memory Tables," and Appendix D, "Memory Tables Answer Key," are included only on the CD that comes with this book. To access those, just insert the CD and make the appropriate selection from the opening interface.

Final Preparation

Exam Engine and Questions on the CD

The CD in the back of this book includes the Boson Exam Environment (BEE). The BEE is the exam-engine software that delivers and grades a set of free practice questions written by Cisco Press. The BEE supports multiple-choice questions, drag-and-drop questions, and many scenario-based questions that require the same level of analysis as the questions on the CCNP SWITCH 642-813 exam. The installation process has two major steps. The first step is installing the BEE software—the CD in the back of this book has a recent copy of the BEE software, supplied by Boson Software (www.boson.com). The second step is activating and downloading the free practice questions. The practice questions written by Cisco Press for the CCNP SWITCH 642-813 exam are not on the CD; instead, the practice questions must be downloaded from www.boson.com.

Note: The CD case in the back of this book includes the CD and a piece of paper. The paper contains the activation key for the practice questions associated with this book. *Do not lose this activation key*.

Install the Exam Engine Software from the CD

The following are the steps you should perform to install the software:

Step 1. Insert the CD into your computer.

Step 2. From the main menu, click the option to install the Boson Exam Environment (BEE). The software that automatically runs is the Cisco Press software needed to access and use all CD-based features, including the BEE, a PDF of this book, and the CD-only appendixes.

Step 3. Respond to the prompt windows as you would with any typical software installation process.

The installation process might give you the option to register the software. This process requires you to establish a login at the www.boson.com website. You need this login to activate the exam; therefore, you should register when prompted.

Activate and Download the Practice Exam

After the Boson Exam Environment (BEE) is installed, activate the exam associated with this book.

Step 1.   Launch the BEE from the Start menu.

Step 2.   The first time you run the software, you should be asked to either log in or register an account. If you do not already have an account with Boson, select the option to register a new account. You must register to download and use the exam.)

Step 3.   After you have registered or logged in, the software might prompt you to download the latest version of the software, which you should do. Note that this process updates the BEE, not the practice exam.

Step 4.   From the Boson Exam Environment main window, click the Exam Wizard button to activate and download the exam associated with this book

Step 5.   From the Exam Wizard dialog box, select Activate a Purchased Exam and click the Next button. Although you did not purchase the exam directly, you purchased it indirectly when you bought the book.

Step 6.   In the EULA Agreement window, click Yes to accept the terms of the license agreement, and then click Next. If you do not accept the terms of the license agreement, you will be unable to install or use the software.

Step 7.   In the Activate Exam Wizard dialog box, enter the activation key from the paper inside the CD holder in the back of the book, and then click Next.

Step 8.   Wait while the activation process downloads the practice questions. When the exam has been downloaded, the main BEE menu should list a new exam. If you do not see the exam, click the My Exams tab on the menu. You might also need to click the plus sign icon (+) to expand the menu and see the exam.

At this point, the software and practice questions are ready to use.

Activating Other Exams

You need to install the exam software and register only once. Then, for each new exam, you will need to complete only a few additional steps. For example, if you bought this book along with another CCNP Official Certification Guide, you would need to perform the following steps:

Step 1.   Launch the BEE (if it is not already open).

Step 2.   Perform Steps 4 through 7 under the section "Activate and Download the Practice Exam," earlier in the chapter.

Step 3.   Repeat Steps 1 and 2 for any exams in other Cisco Press book.

You can also purchase Boson ExSim-Max practice exams that are written and developed by Boson Software's subject-matter experts at www.boson.com. The ExSim-Max practice exams simulate the content on the actual certification exams, enabling you to gauge whether you are ready to pass the real exam. When you purchase an ExSim-Max practice exam, you receive an activation key. You can then activate and download the exam by performing Steps 1 and 2 above.

Study Plan

With plenty of resources at your disposal, you should approach studying for the CCNP SWITCH exam with a plan. Consider the following ideas as you move from reading this book to preparing for the exam.

Recall the Facts

As with most exams, many facts, concepts, and definitions must be recalled to do well on the test. If you do not work with every Cisco LAN switching feature on a daily basis, you might have trouble remembering everything that might appear on the CCNP SWITCH exam.

You can refresh your memory and practice recalling information by reviewing the activities in the "Exam Preparation Tasks" section at the end of each chapter. These sections will help you study key topics, memorize the definitions of important LAN switching terms, and recall the basic command syntax of configuration and verification commands.

Practice Configurations

The latest revision to the CCNP exams includes an emphasis on practical knowledge. You need to be familiar with switch features and the order in which configuration steps should be implemented. You also need to know how to plan a LAN switching project and how to verify your results.

For the first time in the CCNP program, this means that hands-on experience is going to take you over the edge to confidently and accurately build or verify configurations (and pass the exam). If at all possible, you should try to gain access to some Cisco Catalyst switches and spend some time working with various features.

If you have access to a lab provided by your company, take advantage of it. You might also have some Cisco equipment in a personal lab at home. Otherwise, there are a number of sources for lab access, including online rack rentals from trusted Cisco Partners and the Cisco Partner E-Learning Connection (PEC), if you work for a partner. Nothing beats hands-on experience.

In addition, you can review the key topics in each chapter and follow the example configurations in this book. At the least, you will see the command syntax and the sequence the configuration commands should be entered.

Use the Exam Engine

The exam engine on the accompanying CD can also be used as a study tool, presenting a bank of unique exam-realistic questions available only with this book. The exam engine includes two basic modes:

- **Study mode**—This is most useful when you want to review material or practice recalling information, all without a time constraint. In study mode, you can customize how the questions will be presented, such as randomizing the order of the questions, randomizing the order of the answers, focusing on specific topics, automatically displaying answers as you go, and so on.

- **Simulation mode**—This mode simulates an actual CCNP SWITCH exam by using a set number of questions and a set time period. These timed exams allow you to study for the actual exam and to hone your time-management skills so that you can complete the full set of questions while under a time constraint.

The Cisco Learning Network

Cisco provides a wide variety of CCNP preparation tools at the Cisco Learning Network website, https://cisco.hosted.jivesoftware.com/index.jspa?ciscoHome=true. The Cisco Learning Network includes Quick Learning Modules, interviews about taking the CCNP exams, documents, discussions, blogs, and access to the CCNP Routing and Switching study group.

You can use the Cisco Learning Network without a registered login, but you can access many more resources by registering for an account or by using your Cisco.com user ID.

Part VII: Appendixes

Answers to the "Do I Know This Already?" Quizzes

Chapter 2

1. B

2. B

3. B

4. C

5. C

6. B

7. C

8. D

9. B

10. C

11. D

12. B

Chapter 3

1. C

2. B

3. A

4. B

5. B

6. B

7. C

8. C

9. C

10. D

11. E

Chapter 4

1. C

2. B

3. B

4. B

5. B

6. C

7. D

8. C

9. B

10. A

11. C

12. A

13. B and C

14. C

Chapter 5

1. C

2. A

3. C

4. B

5. B

6. B and C

7. A

8. C

9. C

10. B

11. D

12. B

Chapter 6

1. E
2. C
3. C
4. D
5. C
6. C
7. A
8. D
9. B
10. C
11. C
12. C
13. C

Chapter 7

1. C
2. C
3. B
4. B
5. C
6. C
7. A
8. B
9. D
10. B
11. B
12. C

Chapter 8

1. C

2. C

3. D

4. C

5. C

6. C

7. B

8. D

9. C

10. A

11. A

12. D

13. C

Chapter 9

1. B

2. C

3. C

4. B

5. B

6. A

7. B

8. B

9. C

10. C

11. C

12. B

13. B

Chapter 10

1. A
2. C
3. A
4. C
5. A
6. B
7. C
8. D
9. C
10. D
11. B
12. C

Chapter 11

1. D
2. A
3. A
4. B
5. C
6. C
7. C
8. D
9. C
10. C
11. C
12. A

Chapter 12

1. A

2. C

3. B

4. C

5. C

6. C

7. C

8. D

9. C

10. C

11. A and B

12. A and C

13. D

14. A and C

15. C, D, and E

16. B

17. B and C

Chapter 13

1. D

2. D

3. C

4. B

5. B

6. B

7. C

8. C

9. C

10. B

11. B

12. B

Chapter 14

1. B

2. D

3. C

4. B

5. A

6. D

7. E

8. B

9. D

10. C

11. B

12. D

Chapter 15

1. D

2. B

3. B

4. D

5. C

6. A

7. B

8. C

9. B

10. A

11. A

12. D

13. A

14. B

15. C

16. D

Chapter 16

1. C

2. D

3. B

4. B. The trick is in the maximum three keywords. This sets the maximum number of addresses that can be learned on a port. If only one static address is configured, two more addresses can be learned dynamically.

5. C

6. A

7. B

8. C

9. C. Because of the variety of user host platforms, port-based authentication (802.1x) cannot be used. The problem also states that the goal is to restrict access to physical switch ports, so AAA is of no benefit. Port security can do the job by restricting access according to the end users' MAC addresses.

10. B

11. C and D

12. C

13. B and D

14. C

Chapter 17

1. C
2. D
3. D
4. A
5. B
6. A
7. C
8. A
9. D
10. A
11. A
12. C

SWITCH Exam Updates: Version 1.1

> **Note:** Coverage of this topic should be integrated into your study of Chapter 11, "Multilayer Switching," right before the section "Multilayer Switching with CEF."

Controlling the Automatic State of an SVI

Because a Layer 3 SVI is bound to a Layer 2 VLAN on a switch, it normally follows the state of the VLAN on that switch automatically. If the switch has at least one Layer 2 interface that is up and active on the VLAN, the Layer 3 SVI will be brought up, too. If all the Layer 2 interfaces assigned to the VLAN are down, the Layer 3 interface will be brought down.

This is the default "autostate" behavior. The idea is to bring the Layer 3 interface down so that routing protocols will cease advertising a route to the IP subnet if no active switch interfaces exist on the VLAN where the subnet exists.

When the SVI autostate feature is enabled, a Layer 3 SVI can come up only if the following three conditions are met:

- The VLAN bound to the SVI exists and is active in the VLAN database on the switch

- The SVI is not administratively shut down

- At least one Layer 2 interface is assigned to the SVI's VLAN and is in the up state, with STP forwarding

As an example, a switch has VLAN 2 defined and assigned to a variety of Layer 2 interfaces, but none of the interfaces are up. A Layer 3 SVI called interface vlan2 is then defined. Watch what happens to interface vlan2 in the following console output:

```
Switch(config)#interface vlan2
Switch(config-if)#
*Apr 21 10:13:10.949: %LINK-3-UPDOWN: Interface Vlan2, changed state to up
Switch(config-if)#
Switch(config-if)#ip address 192.168.1.1 255.255.255.0
Switch(config-if)#^Z
Switch#
```

```
Switch# show ip interface brief
Interface          IP-Address      OK? Method Status                   Protocol
Vlan1              unassigned      YES manual administratively down     down
Vlan2              192.168.1.1     YES manual up                       down
FastEthernet1/0/1  unassigned      YES unset  down                     down
FastEthernet1/0/2  unassigned      YES unset  down                     down
```

Even before an IP address can be configured on the new SVI, the switch brings its status up but its line protocol stays down. In other words, the SVI now exists and is bound to VLAN 2, but it is unusable until at least one Layer 2 interface becomes active on VLAN 2.

In the following output, notice what happens as a PC is connected to interface FastEthernet1/0/1, which is assigned to VLAN 2:

```
Switch#
*Apr 21 10:21:31.925: %LINK-3-UPDOWN: Interface FastEthernet1/0/1, changed
  state to up
*Apr 21 10:21:32.009: %LINEPROTO-5-UPDOWN: Line protocol on Interface Vlan2,
  changed state to up
*Apr 21 10:21:32.932: %LINEPROTO-5-UPDOWN: Line protocol on Interface
  FastEthernet1/0/1, changed
state to up
Switch#
```

When the Layer 2 interface comes up, so does the line protocol of the SVI. When the PC is disconnected or powered down, the SVI is automatically taken down, as shown in the following output:

```
Switch#
*Apr 21 10:21:45.624: %LINEPROTO-5-UPDOWN: Line protocol on Interface
  FastEthernet1/0/1, changed state to
down
*Apr 21 10:21:45.624: %LINEPROTO-5-UPDOWN: Line protocol on Interface Vlan2,
  changed state to down
*Apr 21 10:21:46.622: %LINK-3-UPDOWN: Interface FastEthernet1/0/1, changed
  state to down
Switch#
```

You can override the default behavior by disabling autostate on a per-interface basis with the following command:

```
Switch(config-if)# switchport autostate exclude
```

When an interface is excluded, any influence that it might have had over the SVI state is removed. This command isn't normally used unless the interface is a special case, such as an interface where a network analyzer is connected. The analyzer would capture traffic without being an active participant in the VLAN that is assigned to the interface.

Note: Coverage of these topics should be integrated into your study of Chapter 13, "Layer 3 High Availability."

Monitoring the Network to Maximize Availability

You can (and should) design and implement a highly available network by leveraging many of the features presented in this book. For example, you can bring up redundant links between switches, redundant gateways between switches, and redundant route processors to provide as much "uptime" as possible for the end users and mission-critical applications. Once configured, these features are all automatic, requiring no further intervention.

But how will you know when some event occurs to trigger a high availability feature? Suppose a redundant link goes down for some reason. If you don't know about it and aren't able to fix it right away, then you no longer have redundant links to mitigate another future failure.

This section covers the following three important ways you can monitor the network to detect failures and gather information about switch activity:

- Syslog messages

- SNMP

- IP SLA

Syslog Messages

Catalyst switches can be configured to generate an audit trail of messages describing important events that have occurred. These system message logs (syslog) can then be collected and analyzed to determine what has happened, when it happened, and how severe the event was.

When system messages are generated, they always appear in a consistent format, as shown in Figure B-1. Each message contains the following fields:

- **Timestamp**—The date and time from the internal switch clock. By default, the amount of time that the switch has been up is used.

- **Facility Code**—A system identifier that categorizes the switch function or module that has generated the message; the facility code always begins with a percent sign.

- **Severity**—A number from 0 to 7 that indicates how important or severe the event is; a lower severity means the event is more critical.

- **Mnemonic**—A short text string that categorizes the event within the facility code.

- **Message Text**—A description of the event or condition that triggered the system message.

In Figure B-1, an event in the "System" or SYS facility has triggered the system message. The event is considered to be severity level 5. From the mnemonic CONFIG_I, you can infer that something happened with the switch configuration. Indeed, the text description says that the switch was configured by someone connected to the switch console port.

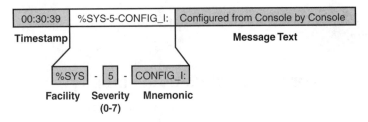

Figure B-1   *Catalyst Switch Syslog Message Format*

Generally, you should configure a switch to generate syslog messages that are occurring at or above a certain level of importance; otherwise, you might collect too much information from a switch that logs absolutely everything or too little information from a switch that logs almost nothing.

You can use the severity level to define that threshold. Figure B-2 shows each of the logging severity levels, along with a general list of the types of messages that are generated. Think of the severity levels as concentric circles. When you configure the severity level threshold on a switch, the switch will only generate logging messages that occur at that level or at any other level that is contained within it.

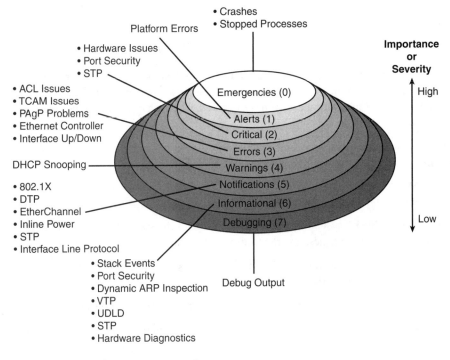

Figure B-2   *Syslog Severity Levels*

For example, if the syslog severity level is set to critical (severity level 2), the switch will generate messages in the Critical, Alerts, and Emergencies levels, but nothing else. Notice that the severity levels are numbered such that the most urgent events are reported at level 0 and the least urgent at level 7.

> **Tip:** You should try to have a good understanding of the severity level names and numbers, as well as their order, in case you need to identify them on the exam.
>
> Remember that the severity numbers are opposite of what you might perceive as the actual message importance. If the exam asks about an event that has a "high" or "greater" severity, that means the severity level number will be lower.

System messages can be sent to the switch console, collected in an internal memory buffer, and sent over the network to be collected by a syslog server. The configuration commands for each of these destinations are covered in the following sections.

Logging to the Switch Console

By default, system messages are sent to the switch console port at the Debugging level. You can change the console severity level with the following command:

```
Switch(config)# logging console severity
```

The *severity* parameter can be either a severity level keyword, such as **informational**, or the corresponding numeric value (0 to 7).

Remember that syslog information can be seen on the console only when you are connected to the console port. Even then, the console isn't a very efficient way to collect and view system messages because of its low throughput. If you are connected to a switch through a Telnet or SSH session, you can redirect the console messages to your remote access session by using the **terminal monitor** command.

Logging to the Internal Buffer

Every Catalyst switch has an internal memory buffer where syslog messages can be collected. The internal buffer is an efficient way to collect messages over time. As long as the switch is powered up, the logging buffer is available.

By default, the internal logging buffer is disabled. To enable it and begin sending system messages into the buffer, you can use the following command:

```
Switch(config)# logging buffered severity
```

The *severity* parameter can be either a severity level keyword, such as **informational**, or the corresponding numeric value (0 to 7).

The logging buffer has a finite size and operates in a circular fashion. If the buffer fills, the oldest messages roll off as new ones arrive. By default, the logging buffer is 4096 bytes or characters long, which is enough space to collect 50 lines of full-length text. If you depend on the logging buffer to keep a running history of logging messages, you might need to increase its size with the following command:

```
Switch(config)# logging buffered size
```

The buffer length is set to *size* (4096 to 2147483647) bytes. Be careful not to set the length too big because the switch reserves the logging buffer space from the memory it might need for other operations.

To review the internal logging buffer at any time, you can use the **show logging** command.

Logging to a Remote Syslog Server

Syslog servers provide the most robust method of logging message collection. Messages are sent from a switch to a syslog server over the network using UDP port 514. This means that a syslog server can be located anywhere, as long as it is reachable by the switch. A syslog server can collect logs from many different devices simultaneously and can archive the logging information for a long period of time.

To identify a syslog server and begin sending logging messages to it, you can use the following commands:

```
Switch(config)# logging host
Switch(config)# logging trap severity
```

The syslog server is located at hostname or IP address *host*. You can enter the **logging** *host* command more than once if you have more than one syslog server collecting logging information. The syslog server severity level can be either a severity level keyword, such as **informational**, or the corresponding numeric value (0 to 7).

Tip: Notice that each of the logging message destinations can have a unique severity level configured. For example, you might collect messages of severity level Debugging into the internal buffer, while collecting severity level Notifications to a syslog server.

Tip: By default, a switch will generate a system message every time it detects an interface going up or down. That sounds like a good thing, until you realize that the syslog server will be receiving news of every user powering their PC on and off each day. Each link state change will generate a message at the Errors (3) severity level, as well as a line protocol state change at Notifications (5) severity level. To prevent this from happening with Access layer interfaces where end users are connected, you can use the following interface configuration command:
```
Switch(config-if)# no logging event link-status
```

Adding Timestamps to Syslog Messages

If you are watching system messages appear in real time, it's obvious what time those events have occurred. However, if you need to review messages that have been collected and archived in the internal logging buffer or on a syslog server, message timestamps become really important.

By default, Catalyst switches add a simple "uptime" timestamp to logging messages. This is a cumulative counter that shows the hours, minutes, and seconds since the switch has been booted up. Suppose you find an important event in the logs and you want to know exactly when it occurred. With the uptime timestamp, you would have to backtrack and compute the time of the event based on how long the switch has been operating.

Even worse, as time goes on, the uptime timestamp becomes more coarse and difficult to interpret. In the following output, an interface went down 20 weeks and 2 days after the switch was booted. Someone made a configuration change 21 weeks and 3 days after the switch booted. At exactly what date and time did that occur? Who knows!

```
20w2d: %LINK-3-UPDOWN: Interface FastEthernet1/0/27, changed state to down
21w3d: %SYS-5-CONFIG_I: Configured from console by vty0 (172.25.15.246)
```

Instead, you can configure the switch to add accurate clock-like timestamps that are easily interpreted. Sometimes you also will need to correlate events in the logs of several network devices. In that case, it's important to synchronize the clocks (and timestamps) across all those devices.

Don't assume that a switch already has its internal clock set to the correct date and time. You can use the **show clock** command to find out, as in the following example:

```
Switch# show clock
*00:54:09.691 UTC Mon Mar 1 1993
Switch#
```

Here the clock has been set to its default value, and it's March 1, 1993! Clearly, that isn't useful at all.

You can use the following commands as a guideline to define the time zone and summer (daylight savings) time, and set the clock:

```
Switch(config)# clock timezone name offset-hours [offset-minutes]
Switch(config)# clock summer-time name date start-month date year hh:mm
  end-month day year hh:mm
[offset-minutes]
-OR-
Switch(config)# clock summer-time name recurring [start-week day month
  hh:mm end-week day month hh:mm [offset-minutes]
Switch(config)# exit
Switch# clock set hh:mm:ss
```

In the following example, the switch is configured for the Eastern time zone in the U.S. and the clock is set for 3:23pm. If no other parameters are given with the **clock summer-time recurring** command, U.S. daylight savings time is assumed.

```
Switch(config)# clock timezone EST -5
Switch(config)# clock summer-time EDT recurring
Switch(config)# exit
Switch# clock set 15:23:00
```

To synchronize the clocks across multiple switches in your network from common, trusted time sources, you should use the Network Time Protocol (NTP). As a simple ex-

ample, the following commands are used to enable NTP and use the NTP server at
192.43.244.18 (time.nist.gov) as an authoritative source:

```
Switch(config)# ntp server 192.43.244.18
```

After NTP is configured and enabled, you can use the **show ntp status** command to verify
that the switch clock is synchronized to the NTP server.

Finally, you can use the following command to begin using the switch clock as an accurate
timestamp for syslog messages:

```
Switch(config)# service timestamps log datetime [localtime] [show-timezone]
  [msec] [year]
```

Use the **localtime** keyword to use the local time zone configured on the switch; otherwise, UTC is assumed. Add the **show-timezone** keyword if you want the time zone name
added to the timestamps. Use the **msec** keyword to add milliseconds and the **year** keyword to add the year to the timestamps.

In the following example, the local time zone and milliseconds have been added into the
timestamps of the logging messages shown:

```
Switch(config)# service timestamps log datetime localtime show-timezone msec
Switch(config)# exit
Switch# show logging
*May  2 02:39:23.871 EDT: %DIAG-SP-6-DIAG_OK: Module 1: Passed Online Diagnostics
*May  2 02:39:27.827 EDT: %HSRP-5-STATECHANGE: Vlan62 Grp 1 state Standby -> Active
*May  2 02:41:40.431 EDT: %OIR-SP-6-INSCARD: Card inserted in slot 9, interfaces
  are now online
*May  3 08:24:13.944 EDT: %IP-4-DUPADDR: Duplicate address 10.1.2.1 on Vlan5,
  sourced by 0025.64eb.216f
*May 13 09:55:57.139 EDT: %SYS-5-CONFIG_I: Configured from console by herring on
  vty0 (10.1.1.7)
```

SNMP

The Simple Network Management Protocol (SNMP) enables a network device to share information about itself and its activities. A complete SNMP system consists of the following parts:

- **SNMP Manager**—A network management system that uses SNMP to poll and receive data from any number of network devices. The SNMP Manager usually is an
  application that runs in a central location.

- **SNMP Agent**—A process that runs on the network device being monitored. All
  types of data are gathered by the device itself and stored in a local database. The
  agent can then respond to SNMP polls and queries with information from the database, and it can send unsolicited alerts or "traps" to an SNMP Manager.

In the case of Catalyst switches in the network, each switch automatically collects data about itself, its resources, and each of its interfaces. This data is stored in a Management Information Base (MIB) database in memory and is updated in real time.

The MIB is organized in a structured, hierarchical fashion, forming a tree structure. In fact, the entire MIB is really a collection of variables that are stored in individual, more granular MIBs that form the branches of the tree. Each MIB is based on the Abstract Syntax Notation 1 (ASN.1) language. Each variable in the MIB is referenced by an object identifier (OID), which is a long string of concatenated indexes that follow the path from the root of the tree all the way to the variable's location.

Fortunately, only the SNMP manager and agent need to be concerned with interpreting the MIBs. As far as the SWITCH exam and course go, you should just be aware that the MIB structure exists and that it contains everything about a switch that can be monitored.

To see any of the MIB data, an SNMP manager must send an SNMP poll or query to the switch. The query contains the OID of the specific variable being requested so that the agent running on the switch knows what information to return. An SNMP manager can use the following mechanisms to communicate with an SNMP agent, all over UDP port 161:

- **Get Request**—The value of one specific MIB variable is needed.

- **Get Next Request**—The next or subsequent value following an initial Get Request is needed.

- **Get Bulk Request**—Whole tables or lists of values in a MIB variable are needed.

- **Set Request**—A specific MIB variable needs to be set to a value.

SNMP polls or requests are usually sent by the SNMP manager at periodic intervals. This makes real-time monitoring difficult because changing variables won't be noticed until the next poll cycle. However, SNMP agents can send unsolicited alerts to notify the SNMP manager of real-time events at any time. Alerts can be sent using the following mechanisms over UDP port 162:

- **SNMP Trap**—News of an event (interface state change, device failure, and so on) is sent without any acknowledgement that the trap has been received.

- **Inform Request**—News of an event is sent to an SNMP manager, and the manager is required to acknowledge receipt by echoing the request back to the agent.

As network management has evolved, SNMP has developed into three distinct versions. The original, SNMP version 1 (SNMPv1), is defined in RFC1157. It uses simple one-variable Get and Set requests, along with simple SNMP traps. SNMP managers can gain access to SNMP agents by matching a simple "community" text string. When a manager wants to read or write a MIB variable on a device, it sends the community string in the clear, as part of the request. The request is granted if that community string matches the agent's community string.

In theory, only managers and agents belonging to the same community should be able to communicate. In practice, any device has the potential to read or write variables to an agent's MIB database by sending the right community string, whether it's a legitimate SNMP manager or not. This creates a huge security hole in SNMPv1.

The second version of SNMP, SNMPv2C (RFC 1901), was developed to address some efficiency and security concerns. For example, SNMPv2c adds 64-bit variable counters, extending the useful range of values over the 32-bit counters used in SNMPv1. In addition, SNMPv2C offers the Bulk Request, making MIB data retrieval more efficient. It also offers Inform Requests, which make real-time alerts more reliable by requiring confirmation of receipt.

Despite the intentions of its developers, SNMPv2C does not address any security concerns over that of SNMPv1. SNMPv2C does offer 64-bit variable counters, which extend the capability to keep track of very large numbers, such as byte counters found on high-speed interfaces. With SNMPv2C, MIB variables can be obtained in a bulk form with a single request. In addition, event notifications sent from an SNMPv2C agent can be in the form of SNMP traps or inform requests. The latter form requires an acknowledgement from the SNMP manager that the inform message was received.

The third generation of SNMP, SNMPv3, is defined in RFCs 3410 through 3415. It addresses the security features that are lacking in the earlier versions. SNMPv3 can authenticate SNMP managers through usernames. When usernames are configured on the SNMP agent of a switch, they can be organized into SNMPv3 group names.

Each SNMPv3 group is defined with a security level that describes the extent to which the SNMP data will be protected. Data packets can be authenticated to preserve their integrity, encrypted to obscure their contents, or both. The following security levels are available. The naming scheme uses "auth" to represent packet authentication and "priv" to represent data privacy or encryption.

- **noAuthNoPriv**—SNMP packets are neither authenticated nor encrypted.

- **authNoPriv**—SNMP packets are authenticated but not encrypted.

- **authPriv**—SNMP packets are authenticated and encrypted.

As a best practice, you should use SNMPv3 to leverage its superior security features whenever possible. If you must use SNMPv1 for a device, you should configure the switch to limit SNMP access to a read-only role. Never permit read-write access because the simple community string authentication can be exploited to make unexpected changes to a switch configuration.

Catalyst switches offer one additional means of limiting SNMP access—an access list can be configured to permit only specific SNMP manager IP addresses. You should configure and apply an access list to your SNMP configurations whenever possible.

Because SNMP is a universal method for monitoring all sorts of network devices, it isn't unique to LAN switches. Therefore, you should understand the basics of how SNMP works, the differences between the different SNMP versions, and how you might apply SNMP to monitor a switched network. You can use Table B-1 as a memory aid for your exam study.

Table B-1 *Comparison of SNMP Versions and Their Features*

Version	Authentication	Data Protection	Unique Features
SNMPv1	Community string	None	32-bit counters
SNMPv2c	Community string	None	Added Bulk Request and Inform Request message types, 64-bit counters
SNMPv3	Username authentication	Hash-based MAC (SHA or MD5) DES, 3DES, AES (128, 192, 256-bit) encryption	Added user authentication, data integrity, and encryption

Configuring SNMPv1 and SNMPv2C

You should be familiar with the basic SNMP configuration. Fortunately, this involves just a few commands, as follows:

```
Switch(config)# access-list access-list-number permit ip-addr
Switch(config)# snmp-server community string [ro | rw] [access-list-number]
!
Switch(config)# snmp-server host host-address community-string [trap-type]
```

First, define a standard IP access list that permits only the IP addresses of your SNMP agent machines. Then apply that access list to the SNMPv1 community string with the **snmp-server community** command. Use the **ro** keyword to allow read-only access by the SNMP manager; otherwise, use the **rw** keyword to allow both read and write access.

Finally, use the **snmp-server host** command to identify the IP address of the SNMP manager where SNMP traps will be sent. By default, all types of traps are sent. You can use the **?** key in place of *trap-type* to see a list of the available trap types.

In Example B-1, the switch is configured to allow SNMP polling from network management stations at 192.168.3.99 and 192.168.100.4. The community string **MonitorIt** is used to authenticate the SNMP requests. All possible SNMP traps are sent to 192.168.3.99.

Example B-1 *Configuring SNMPv1 Access*

```
Switch(config)# access-list 10 permit 192.168.3.99
Switch(config)# access-list 10 permit 192.168.100.4
Switch(config)# snmp-server community MonitorIt ro 10
Switch(config)# snmp-server host 192.168.3.99 MonitorIt
```

Configuring SNMPv2C

Configuring SNMPv2C is similar to configuring SNMPv1. The only difference is with SNMP trap or inform configuration. You can use the following commands to configure basic SNMPv2C operation:

```
Switch(config)# access-list access-list-number permit ip-addr
Switch(config)# snmp-server community string [ro | rw] [access-list-number]
!
Switch(config)# snmp-server host host-address [informs] version 2c community-string
```

In the **snmp-server host** command, use the **version 2c** keywords to identify SNMPv2C operation. By default, regular SNMP traps are sent. To use inform requests instead, add the **informs** keyword.

Configuring SNMPv3

SNMPv3 configuration is a bit more involved than versions 1 or 2C, due mainly to the additional security features.

```
Switch(config)# access-list access-list-number permit ip-addr
!
Switch(config)# snmp-server group group-name v3 {noauth | auth | priv}
Switch(config)# snmp-server user user-name group-name v3 auth {md5 | sha}
  auth-password priv {des | 3des | aes {128 | 192 | 256} priv-password [access-
  list-number]
!
Switch(config)# snmp-server host host-address [informs] version 3 {noauth | auth |
  priv} user-name [trap-type]
```

First, use the **snmp-server group** command to define a *group-name* that will set the security level policies for SNMPv3 users. The security level is defined by the **noauth** (no packet authentication or encryption), **auth** (packets are authenticated but not encrypted), or **priv** (packets are both authenticated and encrypted) keyword. Only the security policy is defined in the group; no passwords or keys are required yet.

> **Tip:** The SNMPv3 **priv** keyword and packet encryption can be used only if the switch is running a cryptographic version of its Cisco IOS software image. The **auth** keyword and packet authentication can be used regardless.

Next, define a username that an SNMP manager will use to communicate with the switch. Use the **snmp-server user** command to define the *user-name* and associate it with the SNMPv3 *group-name*. The **v3** keyword configures the user to use SNMPv3.

The SNMPv3 user must also have some specifics added to its security policy. Use the **auth** keyword to define either MD5 or SHA as the packet authentication method, along with the *auth-password* text string that will be used in the hash computation. The **priv** keyword defines the encryption method (DES, 3DES, or AES 128/192/256-bit) and the *priv-password* text string that will be used in the encryption algorithm.

The same SNMPv3 username, authentication method and password, and encryption method and password must also be defined on the SNMP manager so it can successfully talk to the switch.

Finally, you can use the **snmp-server host** command to identify the SNMP manager that will receive either traps or informs. The switch can use SNMPv3 to send traps and informs, using the security parameters that are defined for the SNMPv3 *user-name*.

In Example B-2, a switch is configured for SNMPv3 operation. Access list 10 permits only stations at 192.168.3.99 and 192.168.100.4 with SNMP access. SNMPv3 access is defined for a group named NetOps using the **priv** (authentication and encryption) security level. One SNMPv3 user named mymonitor is defined; the network management station will use that username when it polls the switch for information. The username will require SHA packet authentication and AES-128 encryption, using the s3cr3tauth and s3cr3tpr1v passwords, respectively.

Finally, SNMPv3 informs will be used to send alerts to station 192.168.3.99 using the **priv** security level and username mymonitor.

Example B-2 *Configuring SNMPv3 Access*

```
Switch(config)# access-list 10 permit 192.168.3.99
Switch(config)# access-list 10 permit 192.168.100.4
Switch(config)# snmp-server group NetOps v3 priv
Switch(config)# snmp-server user mymonitor NetOps v3 auth sha s3cr3tauth priv aes
  128 s3cr3tpr1v 10
Switch(config)# snmp-server host 192.168.3.99 informs version 3 priv mymonitor
```

IP SLA

The Cisco IOS IP Service Level Agreement (IP SLA) feature can be used to gather realistic information about how specific types of traffic are being handled end-to-end across a network. To do this, an IP SLA device runs a preconfigured test and generates traffic that is destined for a far-end device. As the far end responds with packets that are received back at the source, IP SLA gathers data about what happened along the way.

IP SLA can be configured to perform a variety of tests. The simplest test involves ICMP echo packets that are sent toward a target address, as shown in Figure B-3. If the target answers with ICMP echo replies, IP SLA can then assess how well the source and destination were able to communicate. In this case, the echo failures (packet loss) and round trip transit (RTT) times are calculated, as shown in the following example:

```
Switch# show ip sla statistics aggregated
Round Trip Time (RTT) for        Index 1
Type of operation: icmp-echo
Start Time Index: 15:10:17.665 EDT Fri May 21 2010
RTT Values
        Number Of RTT: 24
        RTT Min/Avg/Max: 1/1/4 ms
Number of successes: 24
Number of failures: 0
```

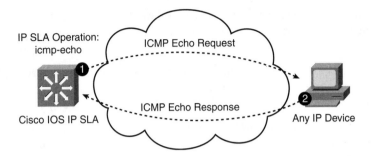

Figure B-3 *IP SLA ICMP Echo Test Operation*

For the ICMP echo test, IP SLA can use any live device at the far end—after all, most networked devices will reply when they are pinged. IP SLA also can test some network protocols, such as DNS, by sending requests to a server at the far end. Cisco IOS is needed only at the source of the IP SLA test because the far end is simply responding to ordinary request packets.

However, IP SLA is capable of running much more sophisticated tests. Table B-2 shows some sample test operations that are available with IP SLA.

Table B-2 *IP SLA Test Operations*

Test Type	Description	IP SLA Required on Target?
icmp-echo	ICMP Echo response time	No
path-echo	Hop-by-hop and end-to-end response times over path discovered from ICMP Echo	No
path-jitter	Hop-by-hop jitter over ICMP Echo path	Yes
dns	DNS query response time	No
dhcp	DHCP IP address request response time	No
ftp	FTP file retrieval response time	No
http	Web page retrieval response time	No
udp-echo	End-to-end response time of UDP echo	No
udp-jitter	Round trip delay, one-way delay, one-way jitter, one-way packet loss, and connectivity using UDP packets	Yes
tcp-connect	Response time to build a TCP connection with a host	No

To leverage its full capabilities, Cisco IOS IP SLA must be available on both the source and the target devices, as shown in Figure B-4. The source device handles the test scheduling and sets up each test over a special IP SLA control connection with the target device. The source generates the traffic involved in a test operation and analyzes the results as packets return from the target. The target end has a simpler role: respond to the incoming test packets. In fact, the target device is called an *IP SLA Responder*.

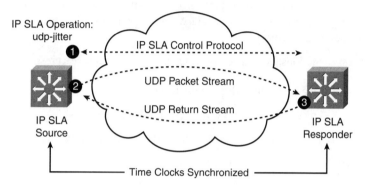

Figure B-4   *IP SLA UDP Jitter Test Operation*

The responder must also add timestamps to the packets it sends, to flag the time a test packet arrived and the time it left the responder. The idea is to account for any latency incurred while the responder is processing the test packets. For this to work accurately, both the source and responder must synchronize their clocks through NTP.

An IP SLA source device can schedule and keep track of multiple test operations. For example, an ICMP echo operation might run against target 10.1.1.1, while UDP jitter operations are running against targets 10.2.2.2, 10.3.3.3, and 10.4.4.4. Each test runs independently, at a configured frequency and duration.

Tip: To set up an IP SLA operation, the Cisco IP SLA source device begins by opening a control connection to the IP SLA responder over UDP port 1967. The source uses the control connection to inform the responder to begin listening on an additional port where the actual IP SLA test operation will take place.

What in the world does this have to do with LAN switching, and why would you want to run IP SLA on a Catalyst switch anyway? Here's a two-fold answer:

■ IP SLA will likely appear on your SWITCH exam

■ IP SLA is actually a useful tool in a switched campus network

To run live tests and take useful measurements without IP SLA, you would need to place some sort of probe devices at various locations in the network—all managed from a central system. With IP SLA, you don't need probes at all! Wherever you have a Catalyst switch, you already have an IP SLA "probe."

By leveraging IP SLA test operations, you can take advantage of some fancy features:

■ Generate SNMP traps when certain test thresholds are exceeded

■ Schedule further IP SLA tests automatically when test thresholds are crossed

■ Track an IP SLA test to trigger a next-hop gateway redundancy protocol, such as HSRP

■ Gather voice quality measurements from all over a network

Configuring IP SLA

You can use the following configuration steps to define and run an IP SLA test operation:

Step 1. Enable the IP SLA responder on the target switch.

```
Switch(config)# ip sla responder
```

By default, the IP SLA responder is disabled. If the IP SLA operation will involve jitter or time-critical measurements, the responder should be enabled on the target switch.

Step 2. Define a new IP SLA operation on the source switch.

```
Switch(config)# ip sla operation-number
```

The *operation-number* is an arbitrary index that can range from 1 to a very large number. This number uniquely identifies the test.

Step 3. Select the type of test operation to perform.

```
Switch(config-ip-sla)# test-type parameters...
```

The *test-type* keyword can be one of the following:

dhcp, dns, ethernet, ftp, http, icmp-echo, mpls, path-echo, path-jitter, slm, tcp-connect, udp-echo, or **udp-jitter**

The list of parameters following the *test-type* varies according to the test operation. As an example, consider the following **icmp-echo** operation syntax:

```
Switch(config-ip-sla)# icmp-echo destination-ip-addr [source-ip-addr]
```

The parameters are simple—a destination address to ping and an optional source address to use. If a switch has several Layer 3 interfaces, you can specify which one of their IP address to use as the source of the test packets.

As another example, the **udp-jitter** command is useful for testing time-critical traffic paths through a switched network. The command syntax is a little more complex, as follows:

```
Switch(config-ip-sla)# udp-jitter destination-ip-addr dest-udp-port
   [source-ip source-ip-addr] [source-port source-udp-port] [num-packets
   number-of-packets] [interval packet-interval]
```

In addition to the source and destination IP addresses, you can define the UDP port numbers that will be used for the packet stream. By default, 10 packets spaced at 20 milliseconds will be sent. You can override that by specifying the **num-packets** and **interval** keywords.

As an alternative, you can configure the **udp-jitter** operation to test Voice over IP (VoIP) call quality. To do this, the **udp-jitter** command must include the **codec** keyword and a codec definition. The IP SLA operation will then simulate a real-time stream of voice traffic using a specific codec. In this way, you can tailor the test to fit the type of calls that are actually being used in the network.

You can define the UDP jitter codec operation by using the following command syntax:

```
Switch(config-ip-sla)# udp-jitter destination-ip-addr dest-udp-port
   codec {g711alaw | g711ulaw | g729a}
```

There are other keywords and parameters you can add to the command, but those are beyond the scope of this book. By default, 1000 packets are sent, 20 milliseconds apart.

Step 4.   Schedule the test operation.

```
Switch(config)# ip sla schedule operation-number [life {forever |
   seconds}] [start-time {hh:mm[:ss] [month day | day month] | pending |
   now | after hh:mm:ss}] [ageout seconds] [recurring]
```

In a nutshell, the command tells the switch when to start the test, how long to let it run, and how long to keep the data that is collected.

Set the lifetime with the **life** keyword: **forever** means the operation will keep running forever, until you manually remove it. Otherwise, specify how many seconds it will run. By default, an IP SLA scheduled operation will run for 3600 seconds (one hour).

Set the start time with the **start-time** keyword. You can define the start time as a specific time or date, after a delay with the **after** keyword, or right now with the **now** keyword.

By default, the test statistics are collected and held in memory indefinitely. You can use the **ageout** keyword to specify how many seconds elapse before the data is aged out.

The **recurring** keyword can be used to schedule the test operation to run at the same time each day, as long as you have defined the starting time with *hh:mm:ss*, too.

Tip: Be aware that the IP SLA operation command syntax has changed along the way. In Cisco IOS releases 12.2(33) and later, the syntax is as shown in steps 2 through 4.

Prior to 12.2(33), the commands in steps 2 through 4 included additional keywords, as follows:

Step 2. `ip sla monitor` *operation-number*

Step 3. `type` *test-type*

Step 4. `ip sla monitor schedule` *operation-number*

It isn't clear which version of the IP SLA commands are used in the SWITCH exam; just be prepared to see the syntax in either form.

Using IP SLA

After you have configured an IP SLA operation, you can verify the configuration with the **show ip sla configuration** [*operation-number*] command. As an example, the following configuration commands are used to define IP SLA operation 100—an ICMP echo test that pings target 172.25.226.1 every 5 seconds.

```
Switch(config)# ip sla 100
Switch(config-ip-sla)# icmp-echo 172.25.226.1
Switch(config-ip-sla)# frequency 5
Switch(config-ip-sla)# exit
Switch(config)# ip sla schedule 100 life forever start-time now
```

Example B-3 shows the output of the **show ip sla configuration** command.

Example B-3 *Displaying the Current IP SLA Configuration*

```
Switch# show ip sla configuration
IP SLAs, Infrastructure Engine-II
Entry number: 100
Owner:
Tag:
Type of operation to perform: echo
Target address: 172.25.226.1
Source address: 0.0.0.0
Request size (ARR data portion): 28
Operation timeout (milliseconds): 5000
Type Of Service parameters: 0x0
Verify data: No
Vrf Name:
Schedule:
    Operation frequency (seconds): 5
    Next Scheduled Start Time: Start Time already passed
```

```
      Group Scheduled : FALSE
      Randomly Scheduled : FALSE
      Life (seconds): Forever
      Entry Ageout (seconds): never
      Recurring (Starting Everyday): FALSE
      Status of entry (SNMP RowStatus): Active
 Threshold (milliseconds): 5000
 Distribution Statistics:
      Number of statistic hours kept: 2
      Number of statistic distribution buckets kept: 1
      Statistic distribution interval (milliseconds): 20
 History Statistics:
      Number of history Lives kept: 0
      Number of history Buckets kept: 15
      History Filter Type: None
 Enhanced History:
```

You can use the **show ip sla statistics** [**aggregated**] [*operation-number*] command to display the IP SLA test analysis. By default, the most recent test results are shown. You can add the **aggregated** keyword to show a summary of the data gathered over the life of the operation. Example B-4 shows the statistics gathered for ICMP echo operation 100.

Example B-4 *Displaying IP SLA Statistics*

```
Switch# show ip sla statistics 100
Round Trip Time (RTT) for         Index 100
         Latest RTT: 1 ms
Latest operation start time: 15:52:00.834 EDT Fri May 28 2010
Latest operation return code: OK
Number of successes: 117
Number of failures: 0
Operation time to live: Forever


Switch# show ip sla statistics aggregated 100
Round Trip Time (RTT) for         Index 100
Type of operation: icmp-echo
Start Time Index: 15:43:55.842 EDT Fri May 28 2010
RTT Values
         Number Of RTT: 121
         RTT Min/Avg/Max: 1/1/4 ms
Number of successes: 121
Number of failures: 0
```

It isn't too difficult to configure an IP SLA operation manually and check the results every now and then. But does IP SLA have any greater use? Yes, you can also use an IP SLA operation to make some other switch features change behavior automatically, without any other intervention.

For example, HSRP can track the status of an IP SLA operation to automatically decrement the priority value when the target device stops answering ICMP echo packets. To do this, begin by using the track command to define a unique track *object number* index that will be bound to the IP SLA operation number.

```
Switch(config)# track object-number ip sla operation-number {state | reachability}
```

You can use the **state** keyword to track the return code or state of the IP SLA operation; the state is up if the IP SLA test was successful or down if it wasn't. The **reachability** keyword is slightly different—the result is up if the IP SLA operation is successful or has risen above a threshold; otherwise, the reachability is down.

Next, configure the HSRP standby group to use the tracked object to control the priority decrement value. As long as the tracked object (the IP SLA operation) is up or successful, the HSRP priority stays unchanged. If the tracked object is down, then the HSRP priority is decremented by *decrement-value* (default 10).

```
Switch(config-if)# standby group track object-number decrement decrement-value
```

In Example B-5, SwitchA and SwitchB are configured as an HSRP pair, sharing gateway address 192.168.1.1. SwitchA has a higher priority than SwitchB, so it is normally the active gateway. However, it is configured to ping an upstream router at 192.168.70.1 every five seconds; if that router doesn't respond, SwitchA will decrement its HSRP priority by 50, permitting SwitchB to take over.

Example B-5   *Tracking an IP SLA Operation in an HSRP Group*

```
Switch(config)# ip sla 10
Switch(config-ip-sla)# icmp-echo 192.168.70.1
Switch(config-ip-sla)# frequency 5
Switch(config-ip-sla)# exit
Switch(config)# ip sla schedule 10 life forever start-time now


Switch(config)# track 1 ip sla 10 reachability


Switch(config)# interface vlan10
Switch(config-if)# ip address 192.168.1.3 255.255.255.0
Switch(config-if)# standby 1 priority 200
Switch(config-if)# standby 1 track 1 decrement 50
Switch(config-if)# no shutdown
```

In some cases, you might need many IP SLA operations to take many measurements in a network. For example, you could use UDP jitter operations to measure voice call quality across many different parts of the network. Manually configuring and monitoring more than a few IP SLA operations can become overwhelming and impractical. Instead, you can leverage a network management application that can set up and monitor IP SLA tests automatically. To do this, the network management system needs SNMP read and write access to each switch that will use IP SLA. Tests are configured by writing to the IP SLA MIB, and results are gathered by reading the MIB.

GLOSSARY

20/80 rule   Network traffic pattern where 20 percent of traffic stays in a local area, while 80 percent travels to or from a remote resource.

802.1Q   A method of passing frames and their VLAN associations over a trunk link, based on the IEEE 802.1Q standard.

access layer   The layer of the network where end users are connected.

active virtual forwarder (AVF)   A GLBP router that takes on a virtual MAC address and forwards traffic received on that address.

active virtual gateway (AVG)   The GLBP router that answers all ARP requests for the virtual router address and assigns virtual MAC addresses to each router in the GLBP group.

adjacency table   A table used by CEF to collect the MAC addresses of nodes that can be reached in a single Layer 2 hop.

alternate port   In RSTP, a port other than the root port that has an alternative path to the root bridge.

ARP poisoning   Also known as ARP spoofing. An attack whereby an attacker sends specially crafted ARP replies so that its own MAC address appears as the gateway or some other targeted host. From that time on, unsuspecting clients unknowingly send traffic to the attacker.

Auto-QoS   An automated method to configure complex QoS parameters with a simple IOS macro command.

autonegotiation   A mechanism used by a device and a switch port to automatically negotiate the link speed and duplex mode.

autonomous mode AP   An access point that operates in a standalone mode, such that it is autonomous and can offer a functioning WLAN cell itself.

BackboneFast   An STP feature that can detect an indirect link failure and shorten the STP convergence time to 30 seconds by bypassing the Max Age timeout period.

backup port   In RSTP, a port that provides a redundant (but less desirable) connection to a segment where another switch port already connects.

best effort delivery Packets are forwarded in the order in which they are received, regardless of any policy or the packet contents.

BPDU Bridge protocol data unit; the data message exchanged by switches participating in the Spanning Tree Protocol.

BPDU filtering Prevents BPDUs from being sent or processed on a switch port.

BPDU Guard An STP feature that disables a switch port if any BPDU is received there.

bridging loop A condition where Ethernet frames are forwarded endlessly around a Layer 2 loop formed between switches.

broadcast domain The extent of a network where a single broadcast frame or packet will be seen.

CAM Content-addressable memory; the high-performance table used by a switch to correlate MAC addresses with the switch interfaces where they can be found.

CEF Cisco Express Forwarding; an efficient topology-based system for forwarding IP packets.

collapsed core A network design where the core and distribution layers are collapsed or combined into a single layer of switches.

collision domain The extent within a network that an Ethernet collision will be noticed or experienced.

Common Spanning Tree (CST) A single instance of STP defined in the IEEE 802.1Q standard.

community VLAN A type of secondary private VLAN; switch ports associated with a community VLAN can communicate with each other.

Control and Provisioning Wireless Access Point (CAPWAP) A standards-based tunneling protocol used to transport control messages and data packets between a WLC and an LAP. CAPWAP is defined in RFC 4118.

core layer The "backbone" layer of the network where all distribution layer switches are aggregated.

CoS marking A method of marking frames with a QoS value as they cross a trunk link between two switches.

CSMA/CA Carrier sense multiple access collision avoidance. The mechanism used in 802.11 WLANs by which clients attempt to avoid collisions.

CSMA/CD Carrier sense multiple access collision detect. A mechanism used on Ethernet networks to detect collisions and cause transmitting devices to back off for a random time.

delay The amount of time required for a packet to be forwarded across a network.

designated port One nonroot port selected on a network segment, such that only one switch forwards traffic to and from that segment.

DHCP   Dynamic Host Configuration Protocol; a protocol used to negotiate IP address assignment between a client and a server. The client and server must reside on the same VLAN.

DHCP relay   A multilayer switch that intercepts and relays DHCP negotiation messages between a client and a DHCP server, even if they exist on different VLANs.

DHCP snooping   A security feature that enables a switch to intercept all DHCP requests coming from untrusted switch ports before they are flooded to unsuspecting users.

differentiated services (DiffServ) model   Packet forwarding is handled according to local QoS policies on a per-device or per-hop basis.

discarding state   In RSTP, incoming frames are dropped and no MAC addresses are learned.

distribution layer   The layer of the network where access layer switches are aggregated and routing is performed.

DTP   Dynamic Trunking Protocol; a Cisco-proprietary method of negotiating a trunk link between two switches.

dual core   A network design that has a distinct core layer made up of a redundant pair of switches.

duplex mismatch   A condition where the devices on each end of a link use conflicting duplex modes.

duplex mode   The Ethernet mode that governs how devices can transmit over a connection—half-duplex mode forces only one device to transmit at a time, as all devices share the same media; full-duplex mode is used when only two devices share the media, such that both devices can transmit simultaneously.

Dynamic ARP Inspection (DAI)   A security feature that can mitigate ARP-based attacks. ARP replies received on untrusted switch ports are checked against known, good values contained in the DHCP snooping database.

edge port   In RSTP, a port at the "edge" of the network, where only a single host connects.

end-to-end VLAN   A single VLAN that spans the entire switched network, from one end to the other.

EtherChannel   A logical link made up of bundled or aggregated physical links.

expedited forwarding (EF)   The DSCP value used to mark time-critical packets for premium QoS handling. EF is usually reserved for voice bearer traffic.

FIB   Forwarding Information Base; a CEF database that contains the current routing table.

flooding   An Ethernet frame is replicated and sent out every available switch port.

forward delay   The time interval that a switch spends in the Listening and Learning states; default 15 seconds.

hello time   The time interval between configuration BPDUs sent by the root bridge; defaults to 2 seconds.

hierarchical network design   A campus network that is usually organized into an access layer, a distribution layer, and a core layer.

host port   A switch port mapped to a private VLAN such that a connected device can communicate with only a promiscuous port or ports within the same community VLAN.

HSRP active router   The router in an HSRP group that forwards traffic sent to the virtual gateway IP and MAC address.

HSRP standby router   A router in an HSRP group that waits until the active router fails before taking over that role.

Hybrid Remote Edge Access Point (HREAP)   A special mode where an LAP at a remote site can take on characteristics of a lightweight AP, as long as the LAP can reach the WLC, or an autonomous AP, when the WLC is unreachable.

IEEE 802.1x   The standard that defines port-based authentication between a network device and a client device.

IEEE 802.3   The standard upon which all generations of Ethernet (Ethernet, Fast Ethernet, Gigabit Ethernet, 10 Gigabit Ethernet) are based.

InterVLAN routing   The function performed by a Layer 3 device that connects and forwards packets between multiple VLANs.

ISL   Inter-Switch Link; a Cisco-proprietary method of tagging frames passing over a trunk link.

isolated VLAN   A type of secondary private VLAN; switch ports associated with an isolated VLAN are effectively isolated from each other.

IST instance   Internal spanning-tree instance; used by MST to represent an entire region as a single virtual bridge to a common spanning tree.

jitter   The variation in packet delivery delay times.

LACP   Link Aggregation Control Protocol; a standards-based method for negotiating EtherChannels automatically.

Layer 2 roaming   Movement of a WLAN client from one AP to another, while keeping its same IP address.

Layer 3 roaming   Movement of a WLAN client from one AP to another, where the APs are located across IP subnet boundaries.

lightweight access point (LAP)   An access point that runs a lightweight code image that performs real-time 802.11 operations. An LAP cannot offer a fully functioning WLAN cell by itself; instead, it must coexist with a wireless LAN controller.

Lightweight Access Point Protocol (LWAPP)   The tunneling protocol developed by Cisco that is used to transport control messages and data packets between a WLC and an LAP.

local VLAN   A single VLAN that is bounded by a small area of the network, situated locally with a group of member devices.

Loop Guard   An STP feature that disables a switch port if expected BPDUs suddenly go missing.

max age time   The time interval that a switch stores a BPDU before discarding it or aging it out; the default is 20 seconds.

MST   Multiple Spanning-Tree protocol, used to map one or more VLANs to a single STP instance, reducing the total number of STP instances.

MST instance (MSTI)   A single instance of STP running within an MST region; multiple VLANs can be mapped to the MST instance.

MST region   A group of switches running compatible MST configurations.

native VLAN   On an 802.1Q trunk link, frames associated with the native VLAN are not tagged at all.

Non-Stop Forwarding (NSF)   A redundancy method that quickly rebuilds routing information after a redundant Catalyst switch supervisor takes over.

packet loss   Packets are simply dropped without delivery for some reason.

packet rewrite   Just before forwarding a packet, a multilayer switch has to change several fields in the packet to reflect the Layer 3 forwarding operation.

PAgP   Port Aggregation Protocol; a Cisco-developed method for negotiating EtherChannels automatically.

point-to-point port   In the Cisco implementation of RSTP, a full-duplex port that connects to another switch and becomes a designated port.

PortFast   An STP feature used on a host port, where a single host is connected, that shortens the Listening and Learning states so that the host can gain quick access to the network.

power class   Categories of PoE devices based on the maximum amount of power required; power classes range from 0 to 4.

Power over Ethernet (PoE)   Electrical power supplied to a networked device over the network cabling itself.

primary VLAN   A normal Layer 2 VLAN used as the basis for a private VLAN when it is associated with one or more secondary VLANs.

private VLAN   A special purpose VLAN, designated as either primary or secondary, which can restrict or isolate traffic flow with other private VLANs.

promiscuous port   A switch port mapped to a private VLAN such that a connected device can communicate with any other switch port in the private VLAN.

PVST   Per-VLAN Spanning Tree; a Cisco-proprietary version of STP where one instance of STP runs on each VLAN present in a Layer 2 switch.

PVST+   Per-VLAN Spanning Tree Plus; a Cisco-proprietary version of PVST that enables PVST, PVST+, and CST to interoperate on a switch.

quality of service (QoS)   The overall method used in a network to protect and prioritize time-critical or important traffic.

root bridge   The single STP device that is elected as a common frame of reference for working out a loop-free topology.

Root Guard   An STP feature that controls where candidate root bridges can be found on a switch.

root path cost   The cumulative cost of all the links leading to the root bridge.

root port   Each switch selects one port that has the lowest root path cost leading toward the root bridge.

Route Processor Redundancy (RPR)   A redundancy mode where a redundant supervisor partially boots and waits to become active after the primary supervisor fails.

Route Processor Redundancy Plus (RPR+)   A redundancy mode where a redundant supervisor boots up and waits to begin Layer 2 or Layer 3 functions.

RPVST+   Also known as Rapid PVST+, where RSTP is used on a per-VLAN basis; in effect, RSTP replaces traditional 802.1D STP in the PVST+ operation.

RSTP   The Rapid Spanning-Tree Protocol, based on the IEEE 802.1w standard.

secondary VLAN   A unidirectional VLAN that can pass traffic to and from its associated primary VLAN, but not with any other secondary VLAN.

Spanning Tree Protocol (STP)   A protocol communicated between Layer 2 switches that attempts to detect a loop in the topology before it forms, thus preventing a bridging loop from occurring.

Split-MAC architecture   Normal Media Access Control (MAC) operations are divided into two distinct locations—the LAP and the WLC, such that the two form a completely functioning WLAN cell.

SSID   Service set identifier; a text string that identifies a service set, or a group of WLAN devices, that can communicate with each other.

stateful switchover (SSO)   A redundancy mode where a redundant supervisor fully boots and initializes, allowing configurations and Layer 2 tables to be synchronized between an active supervisor and a redundant one.

sticky MAC address   MAC addresses dynamically learned by the port security feature are remembered and expected to appear on the same switch ports.

superior BPDU A received BPDU that contains a better bridge ID than the current root bridge.

SVI Switched virtual interface; a logical interface used to assign a Layer 3 address to an entire VLAN.

switch block A network module or building block that contains a group of access layer switches, together with the pair of distribution switches that connect them.

switch spoofing A malicious host uses DTP to masquerade as a switch, with the goal of negotiating a trunk link and gaining access to additional VLANs.

synchronization In RSTP, the process by which two switches exchange a proposal-agreement handshake to make sure neither will introduce a bridging loop.

TCAM Ternary content-addressable memory; a switching table found in Catalyst switches that is used to evaluate packet forwarding decisions based on policies or access lists. TCAM evaluation is performed simultaneously with the Layer 2 or Layer 3 forwarding decisions.

TCN Topology Change Notification; a message sent out the root port of a switch when it detects a port moving into the Forwarding state or back into the Blocking state. The TCN is sent toward the root bridge, where it is reflected and propagated to every other switch in the Layer 2 network.

transparent bridge A network device that isolates two physical LANs but forwards Ethernet frames between them.

trust boundary A perimeter in a network, formed by switches and routers, where QoS decisions take place. QoS information found inside incoming traffic is evaluated at the trust boundary; either it is trusted or it is not trusted. In the latter case, the QoS information can be altered or overridden. All devices inside the trust boundary can assume that QoS information is correct and trusted, such that the QoS information already conforms to enterprise policies.

UDLD Unidirectional Link Detection; a feature that enables a switch to confirm that a link is operating bidirectionally. If not, the port can be disabled automatically.

unknown unicast flooding The action taken by a switch when the destination MAC address cannot be found; the frame is flooded or replicated out all switch ports except the receiving port.

UplinkFast An STP feature that enables access layer switches to unblock a redundant uplink when the primary root port fails.

VACL VLAN access control list; a filter that can control traffic passing within a VLAN.

VLAN Virtual LAN; a logical network existing on one or more Layer 2 switches, forming a single broadcast domain.

VLAN hopping A malicious host sends specially crafted frames that contain extra, spoofed 802.1Q trunking tags into an access port, while the packet payloads appear on a totally different VLAN.

VLAN number   A unique index number given to a VLAN on a switch, differentiating it from other VLANs on the switch.

VLAN trunk   A physical link that can carry traffic on more than one VLAN through logical tagging.

voice VLAN   The VLAN used between a Cisco IP Phone and a Catalyst switch to carry voice traffic.

VRRP backup router   A router in a VRRP group that waits until the master router fails before taking over that role.

VRRP master router   The router in a VRRP group that forwards traffic sent to the virtual gateway IP and MAC address.

VTP   VLAN Trunking Protocol; used to communicate VLAN configuration information among a group of switches.

VTP configuration revision number   An index that indicates the current version of VLAN information used in the VTP domain; a higher number is more preferable.

VTP domain   A logical grouping of switches that share a common set of VLAN requirements.

VTP pruning   VTP reduces unnecessary flooded traffic by pruning or removing VLANs from a trunk link, only when there are no active hosts associated with the VLANs.

VTP synchronization problem   An unexpected VTP advertisement with a higher configuration revision number is received, overriding valid information in a VTP domain.

wireless LAN controller (WLC)   A Cisco device that provides management functions to lightweight access points and aggregates all traffic to and from the LAPs.

Index

J

L

Q

R

W

You've Studied, But Are You Ready?

Know you can pass.

The CD in this book includes a set of practice questions written by Cisco Press and delivered by the Boson Exam Environment (BEE). For practice exams written by Boson's team of leading subject-matter experts, get Boson's ExSim-Max.

Even if you read this book five times, can you really be sure you're ready to take the exam? With ExSim-Max practice exams, you can. ExSim-Max simulates the content and difficulty of the actual exam so accurately that if you can pass the ExSim-Max exam, you can pass the real exam, guaranteed*. Know you can pass with Boson.

Save time

Knowing the topics you need to focus on is important. That's why ExSim-Max provides a score report, which shows the topics that need additional attention. This allows you to go back and study exactly what you need to learn, pass our practice exam and know you are ready to take the real exam.

Be confident

Thinking you can pass is different than knowing you can. ExSim-Max simulates the complete exam experience, including topics covered, question types, question difficulty and time allowed, so you know what to expect. Most importantly, you'll know whether or not you are ready. Take the exam with confidence with ExSim-Max.

Pass the exam

If you can pass an ExSim-Max practice exam, you can pass the real exam. We are so sure of this that we guarantee it. That's right; you are guaranteed to pass the exam, or you get your money back with Boson's No Pass, No Pay guarantee*.

Get ExSim-Max and know you can pass.

*See website

As the original purchaser of this book, you are eligible for a special offer for ExSim-Max. Get your special offer at www.boson.com/ready.

boson.com

CISCO

ciscopress.com: Your Cisco Certification and Networking Learning Resource

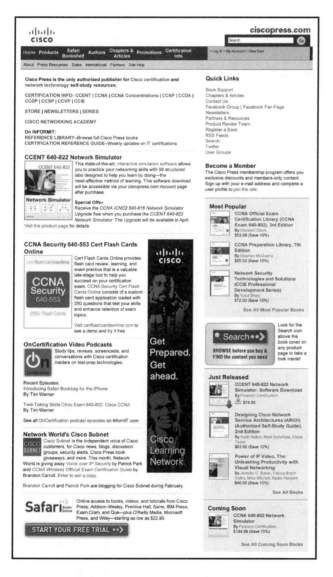

Subscribe to the monthly Cisco Press newsletter to be the first to learn about new releases and special promotions.

Visit **ciscopress.com/newsletters.**

While you are visiting, check out the offerings available at your finger tips.

–Free Podcasts from experts:
  · OnNetworking
  · OnCertification
  · OnSecurity

Podcasts

View them at **ciscopress.com/podcasts.**

–Read the latest author **articles** and **sample chapters** at **ciscopress.com/articles.**

–Bookmark the Certification Reference Guide available through our partner site at **informit.com/certguide.**

Connect with Cisco Press authors and editors via Facebook and Twitter, visit **informit.com/socialconnect.**

inform**IT**.com THE TRUSTED TECHNOLOGY LEARNING SOURCE

PEARSON

InformIT is a brand of Pearson and the online presence for the world's leading technology publishers. It's your source for reliable and qualified content and knowledge, providing access to the top brands, authors, and contributors from the tech community.

✦Addison-Wesley **Cisco Press** EXAM/**CRAM** **IBM Press.** **QUE** ‖ PRENTICE HALL **SAMS** | Safari

---

LearnIT at InformIT

Looking for a book, eBook, or training video on a new technology? Seeking timely and relevant information and tutorials? Looking for expert opinions, advice, and tips? **InformIT has the solution.**

- Learn about new releases and special promotions by subscribing to a wide variety of newsletters.
  Visit **informit.com/newsletters**.

- Access FREE podcasts from experts at **informit.com/podcasts**.

- Read the latest author articles and sample chapters at **informit.com/articles**.

- Access thousands of books and videos in the Safari Books Online digital library at **safari.informit.com**.

- Get tips from expert blogs at **informit.com/blogs**.

Visit **informit.com/learn** to discover all the ways you can access the hottest technology content.

Are You Part of the **IT** Crowd?

Connect with Pearson authors and editors via RSS feeds, Facebook, Twitter, YouTube, and more! Visit **informit.com/socialconnect**.

inform**IT**.com THE TRUSTED TECHNOLOGY LEARNING SOURCE **PEARSON**

✦Addison-Wesley **Cisco Press** EXAM/**CRAM** **IBM Press.** **QUE** ‖ PRENTICE HALL **SAMS** | Safari

Try Safari Books Online FREE
Get online access to 5,000+ Books and Videos

FREE TRIAL—GET STARTED TODAY!
www.informit.com/safaritrial

> **Find trusted answers, fast**
> Only Safari lets you search across thousands of best-selling books from the top
> technology publishers, including Addison-Wesley Professional, Cisco Press,
> O'Reilly, Prentice Hall, Que, and Sams.

> **Master the latest tools and techniques**
> In addition to gaining access to an incredible inventory of technical books,
> Safari's extensive collection of video tutorials lets you learn from the leading
> video training experts.

WAIT, THERE'S MORE!

> **Keep your competitive edge**
> With Rough Cuts, get access to the developing manuscript and be among the first
> to learn the newest technologies.

> **Stay current with emerging technologies**
> Short Cuts and Quick Reference Sheets are short, concise, focused content
> created to get you up-to-speed quickly on new and cutting-edge technologies.

FREE Online
Edition

Your purchase of **CCNP SWITCH 642-813 Official Certification Guide** includes access
to a free online edition for 45 days through the Safari Books Online subscription
service. Nearly every Cisco Press book is available online through Safari Books Online,
along with more than 5,000 other technical books and videos from publishers such as
Addison-Wesley Professional, Exam Cram, IBM Press, O'Reilly, Prentice Hall, Que,
and Sams.

SAFARI BOOKS ONLINE allows you to search for a specific answer, cut and paste
code, download chapters, and stay current with emerging technologies.

Activate your FREE Online Edition at
www.informit.com/safarifree

> **STEP 1:** Enter the coupon code: UZYFQGA.

> **STEP 2:** New Safari users, complete the brief registration form.
> Safari subscribers, just log in.

If you have difficulty registering on Safari or accessing the online edition,
please e-mail customer-service@safaribooksonline.com

CCNP ROUTE 642-902
Official Certification Guide

Wendell Odom, CCIE No. 1624

Cisco Press

800 East 96th Street

Indianapolis, IN 46240

CCNP ROUTE 642-902 Official Certification Guide

Wendell Odom

Copyright© 2010 Pearson Education, Inc.

Published by:
Cisco Press
800 East 96th Street
Indianapolis, IN 46240 USA

All rights reserved. No part of this book may be reproduced or transmitted in any form or by any means, electronic or mechanical, including photocopying, recording, or by any information storage and retrieval system, without written permission from the publisher, except for the inclusion of brief quotations in a review.

Printed in the United States of America

Fifth Printing   January 2012

Odom, Wendell.
  CCNP Route 642-902 official certification guide / Wendell Odom.
      p. cm.
  ISBN 978-1-58720-253-7 (hardback w/cd)
  1. Routers (Computer networks)--Examinations--Study guides. 2.
Routing protocols (Computer network protocols)--Examinations--Study
guides. 3. Internetworking (Telecommunication)--Examinations--Study
guides. 4. Telecommunications
engineers--Certification--Examinations--Study guides. I. Title.
  TK5105.543.O36 2010
  004.6'2--dc22
2009049908

ISBN-13: 978-1-58720-253-7

ISBN-10: 1-58720-253-0

Warning and Disclaimer

This book is designed to provide information about the Cisco ROUTE exam (642-902). Every effort has been made to make this book as complete and as accurate as possible, but no warranty or fitness is implied.

The information is provided on an "as is" basis. The authors, Cisco Press, and Cisco Systems, Inc. shall have neither liability nor responsibility to any person or entity with respect to any loss or damages arising from the information contained in this book or from the use of the discs or programs that may accompany it.

The opinions expressed in this book belong to the author and are not necessarily those of Cisco Systems, Inc.

Trademark Acknowledgments

All terms mentioned in this book that are known to be trademarks or service marks have been appropriately capitalized. Cisco Press or Cisco Systems, Inc., cannot attest to the accuracy of this information. Use of a term in this book should not be regarded as affecting the validity of any trademark or service mark.

Corporate and Government Sales

The publisher offers excellent discounts on this book when ordered in quantity for bulk purchases or special sales, which may include electronic versions and/or custom covers and content particular to your business, training goals, marketing focus, and branding interests. For more information, please contact: U.S. Corporate and Government Sales   1-800-382-3419   corpsales@pearsontechgroup.com

For sales outside the United States please contact: International Sales   international@pearsoned.com

Feedback Information

At Cisco Press, our goal is to create in-depth technical books of the highest quality and value. Each book is crafted with care and precision, undergoing rigorous development that involves the unique expertise of members from the professional technical community.

Readers' feedback is a natural continuation of this process. If you have any comments regarding how we could improve the quality of this book, or otherwise alter it to better suit your needs, you can contact us through email at feedback@ciscopress.com. Please make sure to include the book title and ISBN in your message.

We greatly appreciate your assistance.

Publisher: Paul Boger

Associate Publisher: Dave Dusthimer

Executive Editor: Brett Bartow

Managing Editor: Patrick Kanouse

Development Editor: Dayna Isley

Project Editor: Mandie Frank

Book Designer: Louisa Adair

Composition: Mark Shirar

Indexer: Ken Johnson

Business Operation Manager, Cisco Press: Anand Sundaram

Manager Global Certification: Erik Ullanderson

Technical Editors: Michelle Plumb, Jerold Swan, Rick Graziani

Copy Editor: Apostrophe Editing Services

Proofreader: Barbara Hacha

Editorial Assistant: Vanessa Evans

CISCO.

Americas Headquarters
Cisco Systems, Inc.
San Jose, CA

Asia Pacific Headquarters
Cisco Systems (USA) Pte. Ltd.
Singapore

Europe Headquarters
Cisco Systems International BV
Amsterdam, The Netherlands

Cisco has more than 200 offices worldwide. Addresses, phone numbers, and fax numbers are listed on the Cisco Website at www.cisco.com/go/offices.

CCDE, CCENT, Cisco Eos, Cisco HealthPresence, the Cisco logo, Cisco Lumin, Cisco Nexus, Cisco StadiumVision, Cisco TelePresence, Cisco WebEx, DCE, and Welcome to the Human Network are trademarks; Changing the Way We Work, Live, Play, and Learn and Cisco Store are service marks; and Access Registrar, Aironet, AsyncOS, Bringing the Meeting To You, Catalyst, CCDA, CCDP, CCIE, CCIP, CCNA, CCNP, CCSP, CCVP, Cisco, the Cisco Certified Internetwork Expert logo, Cisco IOS, Cisco Press, Cisco Systems, Cisco Systems Capital, the Cisco Systems logo, Cisco Unity, Collaboration Without Limitation, EtherFast, EtherSwitch, Event Center, Fast Step, Follow Me Browsing, FormShare, GigaDrive, HomeLink, Internet Quotient, IOS, iPhone, iQuick Study, IronPort, the IronPort logo, LightStream, Linksys, MediaTone, MeetingPlace, MeetingPlace Chime Sound, MGX, Networkers, Networking Academy, Network Registrar, PCNow, PIX, PowerPanels, ProConnect, ScriptShare, SenderBase, SMARTnet, Spectrum Expert, StackWise, The Fastest Way to Increase Your Internet Quotient, TransPath, WebEx, and the WebEx logo are registered trademarks of Cisco Systems, Inc. and/or its affiliates in the United States and certain other countries.

All other trademarks mentioned in this document or website are the property of their respective owners. The use of the word partner does not imply a partnership relationship between Cisco and any other company. (0812R)

About the Author

Wendell Odom, CCIE No. 1624, has been in the networking industry since 1981. He has worked as a network engineer, consultant, systems engineer, instructor, and course developer; he currently works writing and creating certification tools. He is author of all the previous editions of the *CCNA Exam Certification Guide* series from Cisco Press, as well as the *CCNP ROUTE 642-902 Official Certification Guide*, the *CCIE Routing and Switching Official Exam Certification Guide*, *Computer Networking First Step*, the *CCNA Video Mentor*, and he is the primary networking consultant for the *CCNA 640-802 Network Simulator*. He maintains lists of Cisco certification tools, suggestions, and links to his Cisco certification blog at www.certskills.com.

About the Technical Reviewers

Michelle Plumb is a full-time Cisco certified instructor for Skillsoft. Michelle has more than 19 years experience in the field as an IT professional and telephony specialist. She maintains a high level of Cisco and Microsoft certifications. Michelle has been a technical reviewer for numerous books related to the Cisco CCNP and CCVP course material track. Michelle currently lives in Scottsdale, Arizona, with her husband and two dogs.

Jerold Swan, CCIE No. 17783, CCSP, works as a senior network engineer for the Southern Ute Indian Tribe Growth Fund in southwest Colorado. Prior to that he was a Cisco instructor for Global Knowledge. He has also worked in IT in the service provider and higher education sectors. His areas of interest include routing protocols, security, and network monitoring. He is a graduate of Stanford University. His other interests include trail running, mountain biking, and volunteer search and rescue.

Rick Graziani teaches computer science and computer networking courses at Cabrillo College in Aptos, California. Rick has worked and taught in the computer networking and information technology field for almost 30 years. Prior to teaching Rick worked in IT for various companies including Santa Cruz Operation, Tandem Computers, and Lockheed Missiles and Space Corporation. He holds an M.A. degree in computer science and systems theory from California State University Monterey Bay. Rick also does consulting work for Cisco and other companies. When Rick is not working he is most likely surfing. Rick is an avid surfer who enjoys surfing at his favorite Santa Cruz breaks.

Dedications

For Jeffrey Lanier Odom. My favorite brother. Gentle soul. Lover of stupid jokes ("baby bigger," "tankety-tankety-tank," "supplies"…) Nice guy. Good friend. Miss you, bro. 10/7/1959—6/15/2009.

Acknowledgments

As usual, Brett Bartow, executive editor, deserves thanks for allowing me to be involved with this book. Brett continually keeps an eye on the horizon for the right projects for me, essentially completing a run of books from the basics, to CCENT, CCNA, now CCNP, and CCIE. My work life wouldn't be possible without Brett keeping me pointed in the right direction. Thanks, Brett!

Jay Swan and Michelle Plumb did a nice job for us with technical edits of the book. Jay was particularly helpful with both ends of the tech edit spectrum, noticing specific and easy-to-overlook errors, while keeping an eye out for the big picture of how the text in one section impacted other sections. Michelle's diligent work helped us uncover several specific issues and make this a better book. Thanks to you both for helping make this book much better!

Rick Graziani deserves thanks with this book for several reasons. First, Rick wrote the questions on the CD with this book, a task that can be laborious—but Rick did a great job and with a positive outlook. Additionally, Rick gave us an additional set of experienced and thoughtful technical editor eyes on the BGP chapters. And while he was working on the CD questions, Rick gladly went the extra mile to point out technical edits to the other book chapters as well. Rick's great attitude toward helping with the book was very impressive.

Dayna Isley worked as the development editor for this book. Dayna and I have worked very well together for a long time, and having such a trusted editor look over every word on this new book has helped quite a bit. Dayna's attention to detail helps keep me on the authoring straight-and-narrow, this time while navigating a sometimes fluid set of processes. Dayna, thanks for sifting through this process and making me look good on paper!

Patrick Kanouse, managing editor, led us through many new production tools (WriteRAP) and processes. Additionally, Patrick happily agreed to continue several additional production tasks at my request (translated: more work for him and his team), while allowing me to manage the entire illustration process for the first time on one of my books—none of which he had to do. Patrick, thanks for your great attitude and willingness to work with me on so many extras.

The folks on Patrick's production team probably had the biggest challenge with this book compared to my other books. Mandie Frank worked as project editor, guiding the book through the various back-end processes to complete the book. Mandie got to sift though all the changing processes, help figure out when we were doing which tasks, and keep us all on track. Thanks, Mandie! San Dee Phillips retired last year so she could work even more, coming back to do the copyedit work—thanks for jumping in again, San Dee! And for Mark Shirar, Ken Johnson, and Barbara Hacha, doing the composition, indexing, and proofreading, thanks so much for handling these details—I do see the difference with having professionals working on every step of the book creation process, and I do appreciate the results.

Thanks to Rich Bennett, good friend and part-time do-everything guy for my books and other projects. Thanks for doing all the Illustrator drawings and editing them all so many times!

The old expression "my better half" is lived out every day here at the Odom house in the person of my wife Kris. Many thanks to Kris, who listens when I need to talk through something in the book, and lets me go hide in the basement for a few weeks to meet the latest writing deadline. Thanks, doll!

Finally and foremost, many thanks to Jesus Christ, for demonstrating your love, and for helping me and my family learn better each day how to not be a clanging symbol, but instead to show others your love.

Contents at a Glance

Contents

Icons Used in This Book

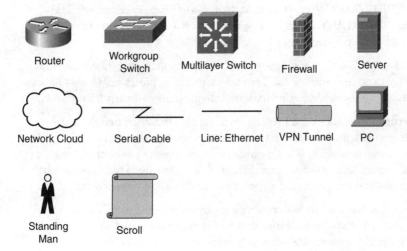

Router Workgroup Switch Multilayer Switch Firewall Server

Network Cloud Serial Cable Line: Ethernet VPN Tunnel PC

Standing Man Scroll

Command Syntax Conventions

The conventions used to present command syntax in this book are the same conventions used in the IOS Command Reference. The Command Reference describes these conventions as follows:

■ **Boldface** indicates commands and keywords that are entered literally as shown. In actual configuration examples and output (not general command syntax), boldface indicates commands that are manually input by the user (such as a **show** command).

■ *Italic* indicates arguments for which you supply actual values.

■ Vertical bars (|) separate alternative, mutually exclusive elements.

■ Square brackets ([ ]) indicate an optional element.

■ Braces ({ }) indicate a required choice.

■ Braces within brackets ([{ }]) indicate a required choice within an optional element.

Foreword

CCNP ROUTE 642-902 Official Certification Guide is an excellent self-study resource for the CCNP ROUTE exam. Passing this exam is a crucial step to attaining the valued CCNP Routing and Switching certification.

Gaining certification in Cisco technology is key to the continuing educational development of today's networking professional. Through certification programs, Cisco validates the skills and expertise required to effectively manage the modern enterprise network.

Cisco Press Certification Guides and preparation materials offer exceptional—and flexible—access to the knowledge and information required to stay current in your field of expertise or to gain new skills. Whether used as a supplement to more traditional training or as a primary source of learning, these materials offer users the information and knowledge validation required to gain new understanding and proficiencies.

Developed in conjunction with the Cisco certifications and training team, Cisco Press books are the only self-study books authorized by Cisco and offer students a series of exam practice tools and resource materials to help ensure that learners fully grasp the concepts and information presented.

Additional authorized Cisco instructor-led courses, e-learning, labs, and simulations are available exclusively from Cisco Learning Solutions Partners worldwide. To learn more, visit http://www.cisco.com/go/training.

I hope that you find these materials to be an enriching and useful part of your exam preparation.

Erik Ullanderson
Manager, Global Certifications
Learning@Cisco
January 2010

Introduction

This book focuses on one major goal: to help you prepare to pass the ROUTE exam (642-902). To help you prepare, this book achieves other useful goals as well: It explains a wide range of networking topics, shows how to configure those features on Cisco routers, and explains how to determine if the feature is working. As a result, you also can use this book as a general reference for IP routing and IP routing protocols. However, the motivation for this book, and the reason it sits within the Cisco Press Certification Guide series, is that its primary goal is to help you pass the ROUTE exam.

The rest of this introduction focuses on two topics: the ROUTE exam and a description of this book.

The CCNP ROUTE Exam

Cisco announced the ROUTE (642-902) exam in January 2010. The term ROUTE does not act as an acronym; instead, the name describes the content of the exam, which focuses on IP routing. Generally, the exam includes detailed coverage of the EIGRP, OSPF, and BGP IP routing protocols, IPv6, and a few other smaller topics related to IP routing.

Cisco first announced its initial Professional level certifications in 1998 with the CCNP Routing and Switching certification. CCNP Routing and Switching certification from its inception has included the same kinds of IP routing topics found in today's ROUTE exam, but the exam names changed over the years. The exam names have tracked the names of the associated Cisco authorized courses for the same topics: Advanced Cisco Router Configuration (ACRC) in the early days, Building Scalable Cisco Internetworks (BSCI) for much of the last 10 years, and now ROUTE, because the newly revised (in 2010) Cisco authorized course also goes by the name ROUTE.

Like its ancestors, the ROUTE exam is a part of the certification requirements for several Cisco certifications, as follows:

- Cisco Certified Networking Professional (CCNP)

- Cisco Certified Internetworking Professional (CCIP)

- Cisco Certified Design Professional (CCDP)

Each of these certifications emphasizes different perspectives on some similar topics. CCNP focuses on the skills needed by a network engineer working for an Enterprise–that is, a company that deploys networking gear for its own purposes. CCIP focuses on the skills required by network engineers deploying gear at a service provider, with the service provider then offering network services to customers. Finally, CCDP focuses more on design—but good design requires solid knowledge of the technology and configuration. So, although this book frequently refers to the most popular certification of these three—CCNP—the ROUTE exam does apply to several certifications.

Contents of the ROUTE Exam

Every student who ever takes an exam wants to know what's on the exam. As with all their exams, Cisco publishes a set of exam topics. These exam topics give general guidance as to what's on the exam.

You can find the exam topics at the Cisco website. The most memorable way to navigate is to go to www.cisco.com/go/ccnp, and look for the ROUTE exam. Also, you can go to the Cisco Learning Network website (www.cisco.com/go/learnnetspace)—a less memorable URL, but a great Cisco certification site. The Cisco Learning Network site hosts exam information, learning tools, and forums in which you can communicate with others and learn more about this and other Cisco exams.

Table I-1 lists the ROUTE exam topics, with a reference to the part of the book that covers the topic.

Table I-1 ROUTE Exam Topics

Book Part	Exam Topic
Implement an EIGRP based solution, given a network design and a set of requirements	
II	Determine network resources needed for implementing EIGRP on a network
II	Create an EIGRP implementation plan
II	Create an EIGRP verification plan
II	Configure EIGRP routing
II	Verify EIGRP solution was implemented properly using **show** and **debug** commands
II	Document results of EIGRP implementation and verification
Implement a multi-area OSPF Network, given a network design and a set of requirements	
III	Determine network resources needed for implementing OSPF on a network
III	Create an OSPF implementation plan
III	Create an OSPF verification plan
III	Configure OSPF routing
III	Verify OSPF solution was implemented properly using show and debug commands
III	Document results of OSPF implementation and verification plan
Implement an eBGP based solution, given a network design and a set of requirements	
V	Determine network resources needed for implementing eBGP on a network
V	Create an eBGP implementation plan
V	Create an eBGP verification plan
V	Configure eBGP routing
V	Verify eBGP solution was implemented properly using show and debug commands
V	Document results of eBGP implementation and verification plan

Table I-1 ROUTE Exam Topics

Book Part	Exam Topic
Implement an IPv6 based solution, given a network design and a set of requirements	
VI	Determine network resources needed for implementing IPv6 on a network
VI	Create an IPv6 implementation plan
VI	Create an IPv6 verification plan
VI	Configure IPv6 routing
VI	Configure IPv6 interoperation with IPv4
VI	Verify IPv6 solution was implemented properly using show and debug commands
VI	Document results of IPv6 implementation and verification plan
Implement an IPv4 or IPv6 based redistribution solution, given a network design and a set of requirements	
IV, VI	Create a redistribution implementation plan based upon the results of the redistribution analysis.
IV, VI	Create a redistribution verification plan
IV, VI	Configure a redistribution solution
IV, VI	Verify that a redistribution was implemented
IV, VI	Document results of a redistribution implementation and verification plan
IV, VI	Identify the differences between implementing an IPv4 and IPv6 redistribution solution
Implement Layer 3 Path Control Solution	
IV	Create a Layer 3 path control implementation plan based upon the results of the redistribution analysis.
IV	Create a Layer 3 path control verification plan
IV	Configure Layer 3 path control
IV	Verify that a Layer 3 path control was implemented
IV	Document results of a Layer 3 path control implementation and verification plan
Implement basic teleworker and branch services	
VII	Describe broadband technologies
VII	Configure basic broadband connections
VII	Describe basic VPN technologies
VII	Configure GRE
VII	Describe branch access technologies

How to Take the ROUTE Exam

As of the publication of this book, Cisco exclusively uses testing vendor Pearson Vue (www.vue.com) for delivery of all Cisco career certification exams. To register, go to www.vue.com, establish a login, and register for the 642-902 ROUTE exam. You also need to choose a testing center near to your home.

Who Should Take This Exam and Read This Book?

This book has one primary audience, with several secondary audiences. First, this book is intended for anyone wanting to prepare for the ROUTE 642-902 exam. The audience includes self-study readers—people who pass the test by studying 100 percent on their own. It includes Cisco Networking Academy students taking the CCNP curriculum, who use this book to round out their preparation as they get close to the end of the Academy curriculum.

The broader question about the audience may well be why you should take the ROUTE exam. First, the exam is required for the aforementioned CCNP, CCIP, and CCDP certifications from Cisco. These certifications exist at the midpoint of the Cisco certification hierarchy. These certifications have broader and deeper technology requirements as compared to the Cisco Certified Entry Network Technician (CCENT) and Cisco Certified Network Associate (CCNA) certifications.

The real question then about audience for this book—at least the intended audience—is whether you have motivation to get one of these Professional-level Cisco certifications. CCNP in particular happens to be a popular, well-respected certification. CCIP, although less popular in numbers, focuses on topics more important to service providers, so it gives you a good way to distinguish yourself from others looking for jobs at SP companies. CCDP has been a solid certification for a long time, particularly for engineers who spend a lot of time designing networks with customers, rather than troubleshooting.

Format of the CCNP ROUTE Exam

The ROUTE exam follows the same general format as the other Cisco exams. When you get to the testing center and check in, the proctor will give you some general instructions and then take you into a quiet room with a PC. When you're at the PC, you have a few things to do before the timer starts on your exam—for instance, you can take a sample quiz, just to get accustomed to the PC and to the testing engine. Anyone who has user-level skills in getting around a PC should have no problems with the testing environment.

When you start the exam, you will be asked a series of questions. You answer the question and then move on to the next question. *The exam engine does not let you go back and change your answer.* Yes, that's true—when you move on to the next question, that's it for the earlier question.

The exam questions can be in one of the following formats:

- Multiple choice (MC)
- Testlet
- Drag-and-drop (DND)
- Simulated lab (Sim)
- Simlet

The first three types of questions are relatively common in many testing environments. The multiple choice format simply requires that you point-and-click on a circle beside the correct answer(s). Cisco traditionally tells you how many answers you need to choose, and the testing software prevents you from choosing too many answers. Testlets are questions with one general scenario, with multiple MC questions about the overall scenario. Drag-and-drop questions require you to left-click and hold, move a button or icon to another area, and release the clicker to place the object somewhere else—typically into a list. So, for some questions, to get the question correct, you might need to put a list of five things into the proper order.

The last two types both use a network simulator to ask questions. Interestingly, the two types actually allow Cisco to assess two very different skills. First, Sim questions generally describe a problem, and your task is to configure one or more routers and switches to fix the problem. The exam then grades the question based on the configuration you changed or added. Interestingly, Sim questions are the only questions that Cisco (to date) has openly confirmed that partial credit is given.

The Simlet questions may well be the most difficult style of question on the exams. Simlet questions also use a network simulator, but instead of answering the question by changing the configuration, the question includes one or more MC questions. The questions require that you use the simulator to examine the current behavior of a network, interpreting the output of any **show** commands that you can remember to answer the question. Although Sim questions require you to troubleshoot problems related to a configuration, Simlets require you to both analyze working networks and networks with problems, correlating **show** command output with your knowledge of networking theory and configuration commands.

The Cisco Learning Network (learningnetwork.cisco.com) website has tools that let you experience the environment and see how each of these question types work. The environment should be the same as when you passed CCNA (a prerequisite for CCNP, CCIP, and CCDP).

CCNP ROUTE 642-902 Official Certification Guide

This section lists a general description of the contents of this book. The description includes an overview of each chapter, and a list of book features seen throughout the book.

Book Features and Exam Preparation Methods

This book uses several key methodologies to help you discover the exam topics on which you need more review, to help you fully understand and remember those details, and to help you prove to yourself that you have retained your knowledge of those topics. So, this book does not try to help you pass the exams only by memorization, but by truly learning and understanding the topics.

The book includes many features that provide different ways to study to be ready for the test. If you understand a topic when you read it, but do not study it any further, you probably will not be ready to pass the test with confidence. The book features included in this book give you tools that help you determine what you know, review what you know, better learn what you don't know, and be well prepared for the exam. These tools include

- **"Do I Know This Already?" Quizzes:** Each chapter begins with a quiz that helps you determine the amount of time you need to spend studying that chapter.

- **Foundation Topics:** These are the core sections of each chapter. They explain the protocols, concepts, and configuration for the topics in that chapter.

- **Exam Preparation Tasks:** The Exam Preparation Tasks section lists a series of study activities that should be done after reading the Foundation Topics section. Each chapter includes the activities that make the most sense for studying the topics in that chapter. The activities include

— **Planning Tables:** The ROUTE exam topics includes some perspectives on how an engineer plans for various tasks. The idea is that the CCNP-level engineer in particular takes the design from another engineer, plans the implementation, and plans the verification steps—handing off the actual tasks to engineers working during change-window hours. Because the engineer plans the tasks, but may not be at the keyboard when implementing a feature, that engineer must master the configuration and verification commands so that the planned commands work for the engineer making the changes off-shift. The planning tables at the end of the chapter give you the chance to take the details in the Foundation Topics core of the chapter and think about them as if you were writing the planning documents.

Key Topic

— **Key Topics Review:** The Key Topics icon is shown next to the most important items in the Foundation Topics section of the chapter. The Key Topics Review activity lists the Key Topics from the chapter, and page number. Although the contents of the entire chapter could be on the exam, you should definitely know the information listed in each key topic. Review these topics carefully.

— **Memory Tables:** To help you exercise your memory and memorize some lists of facts, many of the more important lists and tables from the chapter are included in a document on the CD. This document lists only partial information, allowing you to complete the table or list. CD-only Appendix D holds the incomplete tables, and Appendix E includes the completed tables from which you can check your work.

— **Definition of Key Terms:** Although the exams may be unlikely to ask a question such as "Define this term," the ROUTE exam requires that you learn and know a lot of networking terminology. This section lists the most important terms from the chapter, asking you to write a short definition and compare your answer to the glossary at the end of the book.

- **CD-based practice exam:** The companion CD contains an exam engine (from Boson software, www.boson.com), which includes 100 unique multiple-choice questions. Chapter 20 gives two suggestions on how to use these questions: either as study questions, or to simulate the ROUTE exam.

- **Companion website:** The website http://www.ciscopress.com/title/9781587202537 posts up-to-the-minute materials that further clarify complex exam topics. Check this site regularly for new and updated postings written by the author that provide further insight into the more troublesome topics on the exam.

Book Organization

This book contains 20 chapters, plus appendixes. The topics all focus in some way on IP routing and IP routing protocols, making the topics somewhat focused, but with deep coverage on those topics.

The book organizes the topics into seven major parts. Parts 1 and 7 include topics with less technical depth, and Parts 2 through 6 include the major technical topics in the book. The following list outlines the major part organization of this book:

Part I: "Perspectives on Network Planning": This part includes a single chapter:

- **Chapter 1: "Planning Tasks for the CCNP Exams":** This chapter discusses the CCNP ROUTE exam's perspectives on the planning process, including network design, implementation plans, and verification plans.

Part II: "EIGRP": This part starts with a CCNA-level EIGRP review and moves through EIGRP theory, configuration, authentication, route summarization, and more in the following chapters:

- **Chapter 2: "EIGRP Overview and Neighbor Relationships":** This chapter reviews CCNA-level EIGRP topics and then closely examines the concepts, configuration, and verification of EIGRP neighbor relationships.

- **Chapter 3: "EIGRP Topology, Routes, and Convergence":** This chapter examines the EIGRP topology database and the processes by which EIGRP processes this data to choose routes. It also examines the convergence process using feasible successors and with the Query process.

- **Chapter 4: "EIGRP Route Summarization and Filtering":** This chapter discusses the theory behind route summarization and route filtering. It also shows how to configure and verify both features for EIGRP.

Part III: "OSPF": Similar to Part II, this part starts with a CCNA-level OSPF review and moves through OSPF theory, configuration, authentication, metric tuning, default routing, route filtering, and route summarization, plus OSPF multiarea issues and different stubby area types, as follows:

- **Chapter 5: "OSPF Overview and Neighbor Relationships":** This chapter reviews CCNA-level OSPF topics and then closely examines the concepts, configuration, and verification of OSPF neighbor relationships.

- **Chapter 6: "OSPF Topology, Routes, and Convergence":** This chapter examines the OSPF topology database for routes internal to OSPF. The chapter also discusses how OSPF routers choose the best internal OSPF routes and how OSPF converges when a change occurs.

- **Chapter 7: "OSPF Route Summarization, Filtering, and Default Routing":** This chapter discusses the design, configuration, and verification of OSPF route summarization and route filtering. It also discusses default routes and how to manage the size of the OSPF database and IP routing tables by using stubby areas.

- **Chapter 8: "OSPF Miscellany":** This chapter discusses two additional OSPF topics: OSPF virtual links and OSPF issues when using NBMA networks (such as Frame Relay).

Part IV: "Path Control": The term path control refers to a wide variety of topics related to IP routing and IP routing protocols. This part examines the path control topics not specifically included in the other parts of the book:

- **Chapter 9: "Basic IGP Redistribution":** This chapter examines the concepts, configuration, and verification of IGP route redistribution. In particular, this chapter looks at the mechanics of redistribution without the use of route maps for any purpose.

- **Chapter 10: "Advanced IGP Redistribution":** This chapter essentially continues Chapter 9, in this case focusing on the more complex configuration and issues. In particular, this chapter shows how to manipulate and filter routes at the redistribution function by using route maps, and how to avoid routing loops and inefficient routes when multiple redistribution points exist.

- **Chapter 11: "Policy Routing and IP Service Level Agreement":** This chapter picks up two small path control topics that simply do not fit into any other broader chapter in this book: Policy Based Routing (PBR) and IP Service Level Agreement (IP SLA).

Part V: "BGP": This part assumes no prior knowledge of BGP. It first examines BGP design issues, to give perspective on why BGP works differently than its IGP cousins OSPF and EIGRP. This part examines basic BGP concepts, configuration, and verification, including the path control functions of influencing both inbound and outbound BGP routes:

- **Chapter 12: "Internet Connectivity and BGP":** This chapter introduces BGP. It begins with a review of Internet connectivity from a Layer 3 perspective. It then looks at the basics of how BGP works. It also examines some Internet access design issues, discussing the cases in which BGP can be helpful and the cases in which BGP has no practical use.

- **Chapter 13: "External BGP":** This chapter examines the configuration and verification of BGP between an Enterprise and its ISP(s).

- **Chapter 14: "Internal BGP and BGP Route Filtering":** This chapter examines the cases in which routers in the same ASN need to become BGP peers, creating an Internet BGP connection. It also discusses the need for BGP filtering and the mechanics of configuring BGP filtering.

- **Chapter 15: "BGP Path Control":** This chapter discusses the concept of the BGP

Best Path Algorithm to choose the best BGP routes and how to influence those choices. In particular, this chapter shows the basic configuration for BGP weight, Local Preference, AS_Path length, and Multi-Exit Discriminator (MED).

Part VI: "IPv6": This part assumes no prior knowledge of IPv6. The chapters in this part work through IPv6 addressing and IGP configuration (RIPng, EIGRP for IPv6, and OSPFv3). It also discusses route redistribution for IPv6 and IPv6/IPv4 coexistence mechanisms:

- **Chapter 16: "IP Version 6 Addressing":** This chapter begins with an overview of IP Version 6 (IPv6). It then dives into IPv6 addressing concepts, plus the related protocols, including address assignment options and neighbor discovery. The chapter shows how to configure and verify IPv6 addresses on Cisco routers.

- **Chapter 17: "IPv6 Routing Protocols and Redistribution":** This chapter introduces three IPv6 IGPs: RIP Next Generation (RIPng), EIGRP for IPv6, and OSPF Version 3 (OSPFv3). The chapter focuses on basic configuration and verification. It also discusses IPv6 redistribution in comparison with IPv4 IGP redistribution.

- **Chapter 18: "IPv4 and IPv6 Coexistence":** This chapter discusses the many options to use during the potentially long migration from a purely IPv4 network to a future purely IPv6 network.

Part VII: "Branch Office Networking": This short part includes one chapter that addresses a few small topics related to branch offices that connect to their Enterprise networks using the Internet:

- **Chapter 19: "Routing over Branch Internet Connections":** Branch office routers can be configured to use the Internet as a WAN connection path back to the rest of an Enterprise network. This chapter takes a wide look at the surprisingly large number of networking functions that must occur on a branch router in such cases. It also gives examples of configurations for IPsec and GRE tunnels, DHCP server, NAT, and DSL.

Part VIII: "Final Preparation": This short part includes one chapter as well. This chapter does not include any new technical topics:

- **Chapter 20: "Final Preparation":** This chapter suggests some study strategies for your final preparation before the ROUTE exam.

In addition to the core chapters of the book, the book has several appendixes as well. Some appendixes exist in the printed book, whereas others exist in softcopy form on the CD included with the book.

Printed Appendixes

Appendixes printed in the book include

- **Appendix A, "Answers to the "Do I Know This Already?" Quizzes":** Includes the answers to all the questions from Chapters 2 through 19.

- **Appendix B, "Conversion Tables":** Lists a decimal-to-binary conversion table, decimal values 0 through 255, along with the binary equivalents. It also lists a hex-to-decimal conversion table as well.

- **Appendix C, "CCNP ROUTE Exam Updates:** Version 1.0": Covers a variety of short topics that either clarify or expand upon topics covered earlier in the book. This appendix is updated from time to time, and posted at http://www.ciscopress.com/title/9781587202537, with the most recent version available at the time of printing included here as Appendix C. (The first page of the appendix includes instructions on how to check to see if a later version of Appendix C is available online.)

CD Appendixes

The appendixes included on the CD-ROM are

- **Appendix D, "Memory Tables":** This appendix holds the key tables and lists from each chapter with some of the content removed. You can print this appendix, and as a memory exercise, complete the tables and lists. The goal is to help you memorize facts that can be useful on the exams.

- **Appendix E, "Memory Tables Answer Key":** This appendix contains the answer key for the exercises in Appendix D.

- **Appendix F, "Completed Planning Practice Tables":** The end of Chapters 2 through 19 list planning tables that you can complete to help learn the content more deeply. If you use these tables, refer to this appendix for the suggested answers.

- **Glossary:** The glossary contains definitions for all the terms listed in the "Define Key Terms" section at the conclusion of Chapters 2 through 19.

For More Information

If you have any comments about the book, you can submit those via the www.ciscopress.com. Just go to the website, select Contact Us, and type in your message.

Cisco might make changes that affect the ROUTE exam from time to time. You should always check www.cisco.com/go/ccnp for the latest details.

This chapter covers the following subjects:

Perspectives on CCNP Exam Topics Related to Planning: This section outlines the goals of the CCNP certification.

How to Prepare for the Planning Topics on the Exams: This section explains what you should know generally about planning in order to be prepared for the exam.

Background Information on Implementation and Verification Plans: This short section discusses specific plans, and why there is no one specific plan used for the exam.

CHAPTER 1

Planning Tasks for the CCNP Exams

The predecessor exam to the ROUTE exam—the Building Scalable Cisco Internetworks (BSCI) exam—required mastery of the most typically used features of many routing and routing protocol technologies. The ROUTE exam requires that same mastery, but the ROUTE exam also includes many exam topics that use the words "plan" and "document." The predecessor BSCI exam did not include such wording in the exam topics, so presumably the new ROUTE exam adds this as a new requirement.

This opening chapter examines the meaning, purpose, and some perspectives on these planning and documentation tasks as they relate to preparing for and passing the ROUTE 642-902 exam.

Perspectives on CCNP Exam Topics Related to Planning

Cisco introduced the Cisco Certified Networking Professional (CCNP) certification in 1998. Since that time, Cisco has revised the exams and related courses on several occasions. Each major revision adjusted the scope of topics by expanding and adding some topics while shrinking or removing other topics. At the same time, the depth of coverage has changed over time as well, with the depth of coverage for each topic either becoming deeper or shallower.

The version of CCNP announced by Cisco in January 2010, including the 642-902 exam about which this book is written, narrows the breadth of topics included in CCNP compared to the previous version of CCNP. Cisco removed several sizable topics from CCNP—notably Quality of Service (QoS), Wireless LANs (WLANs), and many security topics. The new CCNP squarely focuses on routing and switching, but with a deeper troubleshooting requirement, with a new TSHOOT (642-832) exam. These changes also reflect that CCNP now requires only three exams instead of the four exams formerly required.

However, although the smaller number of CCNP topics may make CCNP easier, two other factors balance the CCNP so it is still a challenging, difficult, and respected certification. First, the exams appear to require a higher level of mastery for most topics. Second, that mastery is more than just technical knowledge; it requires the ability to plan the implementation and verification of a network engineering project.

Many CCNP ROUTE Exam Topics list the word "plan," collectively meaning that the CCNP candidate must approach problems in the same manner as a network engineer in a medium- to large-sized business. The skills related to these exam topics can be built as a side-effect of doing many network engineering jobs, for instance

■   The ability to analyze a network design document, extrapolate that design into the complete detailed implementation plan, including completed configurations for each router and switch.

■   The ability to analyze a design document and discover the missing items—questions that must be answered before a detailed implementation plan (including configurations) can be completed.

■   The ability to perform a peer review on another engineer's implementation plan, to discover weaknesses and omissions in the planned configurations, and to update the implementation plan.

■   The ability to build a verification plan that lists the specific **show** commands and command options that list key pieces of information—information that directly either confirms or denies whether each planned feature has been implemented correctly.

■   The ability to write a verification plan that can be understood and used by a less-experienced worker, allowing that worker to implement the change and to verify the changes worked, off-shift, when you are not on-site.

■   The ability to perform a peer review on another engineer's verification plan, to discover which key design features are not verified by that plan, and to discover inaccuracies in the plan.

This chapter discusses the whole area of implementation and verification planning for the CCNP ROUTE exam, including how you should prepare for these exam topics. By considering the ideas in this chapter first, you should have the right perspectives to know how to use the tools that help you add the planning skills and perspectives needed for the exam.

CCNP Route Exam Topics That Do Not Require the CLI

Cisco lists a set of Exam Topics for each Cisco exam. These Exam Topics follow a general type of phrasing, typically starting with an action word that defines what action or skill you must do for the exam. (Unfortunately, this style seldom gives much insight into the breadth or depth of coverage of a given topic.)

For example, consider the six Exam Topics for the CCNP ROUTE exam specifically related to EIGRP:

■   Determine network resources needed for implementing EIGRP on a network.

■   Create an EIGRP implementation plan.

■   Create an EIGRP verification plan.

■   Configure EIGRP routing.

■   Verify EIGRP solution was implemented properly using **show** and **debug** commands.

■   Document results of EIGRP implementation and verification.

The two gray-highlighted exam topics focus on the commands available from the CLI, specifically that you need to configure EIGRP, and to use both **show** and **debug** commands to verify (confirm) whether EIGRP is working correctly. The unhighlighted topics in the list require knowledge of the commands, but the tasks do not require any hands-on activities from the CLI. Instead, when doing these tasks in real life, you would more likely be using a word processor rather than a terminal emulator.

Besides this list of the EIGRP exam topics, the entire list of CCNP ROUTE Exam Topics includes many more items that use words like "document" and "plan." Of the roughly 40 CCNP ROUTE Exam Topics, approximately half of the exam topics refer to the various types of plans and documentation. In particular, the phase "Create a _____ verification plan" occurs six times in the CCNP ROUTE list of Exam Topics—one each for EIGRP, OSPF, eBGP, IPv6, redistribution, and Layer 3 path control.

Impressions on the Planning Exam Topics

After a first glance through the CCNP ROUTE Exam Topics, you might think that the new CCNP certification has been changed significantly—and you therefore need to significantly change how you prepare for CCNP. However, it turns out that by focusing on the following aspects of your study, you should be well prepared for the CCNP exams in general and the CCNP ROUTE exam in particular:

■   As with any other Cisco career certification exam, understand the concepts, configuration, and verification commands (**show** and **debug** commands).

■   As with any other Cisco career certification exam, master the configuration and verification tasks and commands.

■   Unlike most other Cisco career certification exams, spend some time thinking about the concepts, configuration, and verification tasks as if you were writing or reviewing a network design document, a network project implementation plan, or a verification plan.

In this list, the first two tasks are simply what most people normally do when preparing for a Cisco exam. The third item represents the new type of preparation task, in which you simply think about the same concepts, commands, and features, but from a planning perspective.

At this point in this brief first chapter, you can choose whether to keep reading the topics in order, or whether to skip to the section "How to Prepare for the Planning Topics on the Exam" later in this chapter. Those of you who have a pretty good idea of the planning tasks done by most IT shops can consider skipping ahead. For those of you with little or no experience in reading network design documents, building or using network implementation and verification plans, the next section can give you some useful perspectives before you dive into studying the technologies in CCNP ROUTE.

Relating the Exam Topics to a Typical Network Engineer's Job

The need to plan, and the need to document those plans, increases as the size of the organization increases. Even if only one person at a company cares about the router and switch infrastructure, that engineer probably does not want to be writing configurations at 2 a.m. Sunday morning when the change window begins. So, even in a small IT shop, some planning occurs when the engineer creates the configurations in a text editor before the weekend change window. When the staff grows to 3 to 4 people, particularly when some of those people work different shifts, the need to document the design, implementation, and verification/operational procedures becomes more important.

For perspective, this section examines a medium- to large-sized company, along with some of the planning tasks done in the real world—the same kinds of tasks listed as part of the CCNP Exam Topics.

A Fictitious Company and Networking Staff

Imagine if you will a medium to large company, one large enough to have several network engineers on staff. For the sake of discussion, this company has roughly 50,000 employees, with 1000 smallish remote sites, four large sites with at least 2000 employees on each large campus, and maybe a smattering of other sites with 500 or so employees. Of course, the company has a few data centers, has plans for a companywide IP telephony deployment, is adding video over IP, already has the usual security needs, and has a growing teleworker community, several network connections to partner companies, and Internet connections. Oh yeah, and there's always the growing need for smart buildings to reduce energy consumption, all hooked into the IP network.

With a company of this size, the job roles for this fictitious company includes IT customer support (Help Desk, manned 24x7), an operations team that covers most hours of the day, network engineering, and a design team.

Next, consider the various roles in the network and the type of work done by the people in those roles:

- Help desk personnel may perform diagnosis of network health, taking a general problem statement from a customer down to a specific issue, for example, that a user's device is not pingable.

- Operations staff may be the second level of support for problems, both reacting to calls from the Help Desk and monitoring the network proactively. The operations staff also often implements changes on behalf of the engineering team during off-shift hours.

- The network engineering team may be the third level of support for problems but typically focuses on project work, including the detailed planning for new configurations to support new sites, new network features, and new sites in the network.

- The network designers may actually log in to the network devices far less than the operations and engineering teams, instead focusing on gathering requirements from internal and external customers, translating those requirements into a network design, and even doing proof-of-concept testing—but leaving the details of how to deploy the design for all required sites to the network engineering team.

The number of individuals in each role varies in different organizations, of course. Maybe only a single network designer and single network engineer are required, with maybe 2 to 3 people as network operations specialists—not enough for 24x7 coverage with a specialist, but close. The Help Desk position may simply require most people to have the same fundamental networking skill set, depending on the size of the shop. On the other end of the scale, in the largest companies, the engineering staff might include several departments of network engineers.

The Design Step

Next, consider the basic workflow when a new network project happens, new sites are added, or any noticeable change occurs. The network designer begins the process by determining the requirements and creating a plan. That plan typically lists the following:

- The requirements for the project

- The sites affected

- Sample configurations

- Results from proof-of-concept testing

- Dependencies and assumptions

- Business requirements, financials, and management commitments

Many other items might be included as well.

After creating the design document, the network designer often uses a peer review process to refine and confirm the design. The designer cannot simply work in a vacuum, define the design, and then toss the design document to network engineering to be deployed. In smaller shops, a peer review may simply be 2 to 3 people standing around a dry erase board discussing the project. In larger shops, the design peer review probably requires a thorough written document be distributed before the meeting, with attendance from network engineering, operations, and the Help Desk, and with formal sign-off required.

Implementation Planning Step

The next step in the life of the project occurs when a network engineer takes the approved design document from the design team and begins planning the implementation of the project. To do this task, the network engineer must interpret the examples and general cases described in the design document and develop a very specific implementation plan that lists all significant tasks and actions by each group and on each device. The design document, for instance, may show example cases of typical branch offices—a typical one-router branch, a typical two-router larger branch, a typical district (medium-sized) site, and so on. The network engineer must then determine what must be done on every device to implement the project and document those details in an implementation plan.

For example, imagine this fictitious company plans to deploy IP telephony to the 1000 remote sites. The design document lists the following requirements:

■   Switches with Power over Ethernet (PoE) at each remote office (switch models listed in the design doc).

■   The convention of placing all phones at a site in one VLAN/subnet and all PCs in a second VLAN/subnet.

■   VLAN trunking between the switch and the 1 or 2 routers at each remote site.

■   A particular version and feature set of router IOS on the remote site routers to support Survivable Remote Site Telephony (SRST).

■   More aggressive tuning of EIGRP to improve convergence time, particularly by ensuring both routes from a remote site back into the network core are in the routing table at the same time.

The design document certainly contains more details than the preceding list, but the list gives you an idea of the starting point when the network engineer first work on his implementation plan by reviewing the design document.

After a thorough review of the design, the network engineer then develops an implementation plan that includes items like the following:

■   A list of all remote offices, with notations of which require a switch hardware upgrade (for PoE support) and which do not

■   Total numbers of switches to be ordered, prices, and delivery schedules

■   A table that lists the specific VLAN and subnet numbers used at each site for the phone VLAN/subnet and PC VLAN/subnet

■   The IP address ranges from each remote site subnet that needs to be added to the DHCP servers configurations for dynamic assignment

■   A list of the remote site routers that require a router hardware upgrade to support either trunking or the required IOS, including pricing and delivery schedules

■   A list of remote site routers that do not require a replacement router but do require a memory upgrade to support the needed IOS

■   Annotated sample configurations for typical sites, including VLAN trunking to the switch, SRST, and EIGRP convergence tuning

■   A reference to the location of the switch and router configuration for every device that will be configured as part of the project

The preceding list represents the types of items that would be documented in the implementation plan for this project. The list is certainly not exhaustive but represents a smattering of what might end up in such a plan.

The implementation plan probably has many informal reviews as the network engineer works through the plan. Additionally, larger shops often have a peer review after the plan is more fully developed, with network designers, operations, and fellow network engineers typically included in the review.

Verification Planning Step

The design step tells us "this is what we want to accomplish," whereas the implementation planning step tells us "this is exactly what we will do, and when, to accomplish this design." With that in mind, the verification plan tells whoever will actually perform the actions to implement a project how to answer this question:

"Did the actions we took per the implementation plan work?"

The verification plan is used with the actual implementation of the changes in the network. The larger the network, the less likely that the network engineer does any of the implementation work, instead planning the implementation. More often than not, the operations staff follows the implementation plan, or more specific instructions for each individual change window, taking the appropriate actions (copying in configurations, for instance). The engineer that implements the changes then uses the verification plan to determine if the changes met the requirements.

The most important part of the verification plan, at least for being ready to pass the CCNP exams, identifies what commands confirm whether each key design point was implemented correctly. For example, the section "Implementation Planning Step" earlier in this chapter briefly describes a project to deploy IP telephony to all remote sites. For that same project, the following list describes some of the actions listed in the verification plan:

- After copy/pasting a remote site's new router configuration, use the **show ip interface brief** command, confirm an up/up state on the two subinterfaces of Fa0/0, and confirm the IP addresses match the planning chart in IP address repository.

- For each remote site router, use the **show ip route** command to confirm two routes exist for each Data Center subnet. See "Data Center Subnet Reference" in the IP address repository.

- From the WAN edge routers, use the **show ip eigrp neighbors detail** command, and find neighbors listed as stub routers. For the routers configured in tonight's change window, compare this output to the Stub Router planning table in the implementation plan, and confirm that the correct remote site routers have been configured as EIGRP stubs.

Note: The "IP address repository" mentioned in the list does not exist in this chapter; it just represents the idea that an implementation plan would include some reference to the location of all subnet/address reference information.

The important part of the verification plan lists the specific commands used, at what point in the implementation process, and what output should be seen. In practice, this plan should also include samples of output, spelling out what should be seen when correct, and what output would tell the operations staff that the change did not work correctly.

Documenting the Results of the Implementation

Continuing the story of the typical but fictitious company, when a set of changes is attempted during a change window, some documentation must be changed based on the results. If a different final configuration is used, the implementation documents must be changed.

Note: This particular step is mentioned mainly because several CCNP ROUTE Exam Topics refer to the task of documenting the results of the implementation and verification.

Summary of the Role of Network Engineer

The CCNP certification focuses on skills required to do the job of network engineer as generally described in this chapter. For perspective, then, consider the following list, which compares and contrasts some of the expectations for CCNP network engineers by interpreting the CCNP ROUTE Exam Topics:

- Does not create the design document

- Does participate in design peer reviews, finding oversights, asking further questions that impact the eventual implementation, and confirming the portions of the design that appear complete and valid

- Does not deploy the configurations off-shift

- Does plan and document the specific configurations for each device, documenting those configurations in the implementation plan so that others can add the configuration to various devices

- Does participate in peer reviews of the implementation plans written by fellow network engineers, finding omissions, caveats, and problems

- Does not verify that the changes worked as planned when implemented off-shift

- Does create the verification plan that others use to verify that the changes worked as planned when implemented off-shift

- Does perform peer reviews of other engineers' verification plans

Now that you've had a chance to think generally about the role of the network engineer, the next section brings the discussion back around to the CCNP ROUTE exam, and how you should prepare for the exam.

How to Prepare for the Planning Topics on the Exams

Can you create a networking implementation plan for each technology area on the CCNP exams? Can you create a verification plan for those same technologies? According to the CCNP Exam Topics, these skills now fall into the scope of topics on the CCNP exams. However, Cisco can't reasonably ask you a question as open-ended as "Create an entire EIGRP implementation plan based on the following design document." Such a question would take too much time relative to the typical 1 minute 15 seconds or so average question time for a typical Cisco exam.

Even though the exam may not ask you to literally create a plan, you do need the skills to perform those same tasks. As with any other exam topic, expect the exam to ask questions that zero in on a small subset of the required skill.

To prepare for the planning-oriented topics, you do NOT need to learn any more facts about the technology or commands. The CCNP Exam Topics already cover the technology, particularly the configuration, verification, and troubleshooting of the listed technologies. For the planning-related Exam Topics, however, you do need to think about those technologies with a slightly different perspective. The question is whether you could, with only pencil, paper, and a word processor—but definitely without a router or switch CLI—do the following:

Step 1.   Read design goals extracted from a design document, develop a configuration that meets those goals, and discover missing information that needs to be gathered before you can complete the configuration.

Step 2.   Read an extract from the design and implementation plans to determine what is wrong or missing.

Step 3.   Read a configuration and design goal as stated in an implementation plan, and create the verification steps that would confirm whether the feature was working.

Step 4.   Analyze a portion of a verification plan, along with the stated configuration and design goals, and determine any problems or missing elements in the verification plan.

Figure 1-1 shows the same concepts, with numbers referencing the preceding steps.

After you have a solid understanding of the configuration and verification commands for a topic, to prepare for the planning-related Exam Topics, you simply need to take the time to think about those same topics, but from the perspective of the tasks shown in Figure 1-1. To that end, this book adds some tools to the end of each chapter. These tools should help organize your thinking and remind you to take some time to ponder the topics in a chapter from a design perspective.

The end of most chapters in this book include a new section titled "Planning Preparation" as part of the broader "Foundation Summary" review section. The "Planning Preparation" guides you through various aspects of the planning process, focused on the technologies included in that chapter. All the Planning Preparation tables list some information and give you the opportunity to complete the tables as an exercise. Appendix F, "Completed Planning Practice Tables," found on the CD included with this book, lists completed versions of the tables for reference. This section uses four different types of tables that mimic some of the planning and analysis tasks, as described under the next four headings.

Note: You may want to glance at the Planning Preparation tables at the end of Chapter 2, "EIGRP Overview and Neighbor Relationships," for perspective as you read through this chapter.

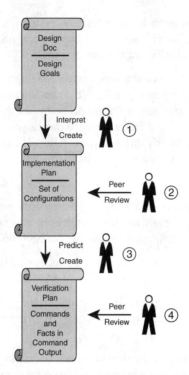

Figure 1-1   *Planning Tasks for the CCNP Candidate*

Planning Preparation: Design Review Table

When in a real design review, a network engineer must look at the requirements and decide what configuration options might be used. The Design Review table in the Planning Preparation section of most chapters lists design goals that you might see in a design document. Your job is to interpret each design goal, think about what features might be used to reach the goal, and then list those features.

This tool is designed to help you think about the broader view of a network that is typically seen in design documents.

Planning Preparation: Implementation Plan Peer Review Table

When you attend a real implementation plan peer review, you and other engineers can see the plan and immediately think of different questions. Those questions may be questions about the technology—some fact you used to know but forgot, some confusion about how a command would work given the specific design, or some question about the design goal that led to the listed configuration.

The Implementation Plan Peer Review table predicts some of the questions that might come to mind when performing a peer review. Your job with this table is to then answer the questions. Some questions may be basic, and really meant more for review, whereas others strive to force you to think about some of the subtleties of the topics in the chapter.

Create an Implementation Plan Table

The Implementation Plan table is a pure memory aid, but the task fits directly into the Exam Topics that read "Create a _____ implementation plan." This tool uses a table that simply lists the configuration topics from the chapter and asks that you write all related configuration commands from memory. Although you may not need to memorize every command and parameter for the exam, this exercise can help you mentally group commands together, which may aid in questions directed at building implementation plans.

Choose Commands for a Verification Plan Table

This final tool helps you think about verification commands by first thinking of the fact you need to discover and then choosing the command that lists the fact. Many resources—including Cisco documents, many Cisco authorized courses, and many books (mine included)—begin with the **show** commands and then explain the information displayed by the command. The reverse order of thinking is required to be prepared to create a verification plan. You must first decide what facts must be discovered to confirm a feature is working and then remember which commands supply that information.

This final planning preparation tool lists many of the key individual pieces of information that matter to the technologies included in that chapter. Your job is to list the commands that display the requested piece of information.

Background Information on Implementation and Verification Plans

The last major section of this chapter also discusses the topics of implementation and verification planning, but with a different twist. So far, this chapter has been focused on how you might prepare for CCNP exams. This section instead focuses on implementation and verification planning as an end to themselves.

No Single Plan Style

Upon reading the CCNP ROUTE Exam Topics, and seeing the references to "implementation plan" and "verification plan," you might be at least slightly curious to see examples of such plans. However, no such example implementation plan or verification plan exists in this book because no one specific type of plan matters to the exam. In fact, the Cisco authorized course for this exam, also called ROUTE, also does not offer a specific type or style of implementation or verification plan.

Several reasons exist as to why no one type of implementation or verification plan is suggested as the model for preparing for the exams, including the following:

- Every company does something different, from completely ad-hoc discussions around a white board to formal reviews and processes.

- Several standards exist for methodologies that include implementation and verification planning, but each uses different terminology, so a single suggested plan format would implicitly recommend one method or another.

- Creating a pseudo-standard example plan for the sake of CCNP was not actually necessary to assess the test-taker's planning skills.

Typical Elements in an Implementation Plan

Although no one style of plan matters, the types of items inside a plan have some interest for the exam. It is also useful to know a few terms regarding some of the formalized methods for implementation planning.

When an IT organization takes the time to require and review a written implementation plan for a project, those plans still vary in terms of depth and detail. The plan may include many details about the existing network, or it may rely on other documentation, ignoring those details in the implementation plan. The plan may list financials, particularly when hardware and software must be purchased, or it may leave those details out of the planning document, instead leaving those details for the management team to handle.

Just for perspective, Table 1-1 outlines some of the types of items you might see in a network implementation plan:

Table 1-1

The existing network:	Router and switch hardware IOS versions and feature sets RAM and flash in each device Existing configurations IP Subnet and Addressing Plan, Assignments, and Conventions
Management:	Personnel and roles, contact information Assumptions and dependencies Required management sign-offs New tools, reporting, status update process
New project details:	Design goals (reference to design doc possibly) Hardware upgrades Software upgrades Timelines to make changes Specific configurations for each device Migration issues (assuming a subset of sites are implemented in any one change window) Network diagrams, possibly for each interim step during a migration
Project completion:	Final sign-off requirements Definitions of success Submission of revised site documentation, operational procedures, and any other permanent documentation

Focus for Implementation Plans for CCNP

Although this sample includes typical elements, the three highlighted elements have some particular interest in the context of the CCNP exams. The Exam Topics do not state a general "Create a network project implementation plan," but rather focuses on a technology area. Specifically for CCNP ROUTE, the Exam Topics that mention an implementation plan specifically focus on EIGRP, OSPF, eBGP, redistribution, path control, and IPv6, respectively.

For the exam, the highlighted elements in the sample plan represent the most likely items to be within the scope of the Exam Topics. An EIGRP implementation plan in real life—say for a migration from RIP-2 to EIGRP—probably includes all the elements listed in the sample plan. However, because EIGRP is a Cisco IOS Software feature, the likely implementation plan topics relate to EIGRP configuration, verification, and issues about migrating from one design to another.

Structured Implementation Planning Methodologies

The Cisco authorized courses for the CCNP track mention a few structured methodologies that can be used to manage network projects. These methodologies include steps, terminology, and conventions that include the implementation planning, the actual implementation, and in some cases, specific items for verification planning. (In some cases, the verification plan is part of the implementation plan or change management process.) Table 1-2 lists these methodologies, and a few facts about each, for perspective.

Table 1-2 *Project Planning Methodologies*

Key Topic

Method	Owner	Comment
FCAPS	ISO	Fault, Configuration, Accounting, Performance, and Security: This standard focuses on network and systems management. Implementation planning falls into the change management category.
ITIL	Great Britain	Information Technology Infrastructure Library: A set of best practices for systems management that has been widely used in the IT industry. It is managed by the government of Great Britain. www.itil-official-site.com.
TMN	ITU-T	Telecommunications Management Network: Created by the ITU-T's Study Group 4, this ongoing effort defines system management practices from the ITU. Originally based on FCAPS. www.itu.int.
Cisco Lifecycle Services	Cisco	Quoting the Cisco website: "The Cisco Lifecycle Services approach defines the activities needed to help you successfully deploy and operate Cisco technologies and optimize their performance throughout the lifecycle of your network."
PPDIOO	Cisco	Prepare, Plan, Design, Implement, Operate, Optimize: The popular acronym for the steps defined by Cisco Lifestyle Services.

Typical Verification Plan Components

A typical verification plan is much smaller than the implementation plan. The verification plan often focuses on a specific change made on a specific day, or on a type a change made repeatedly at different sites over a longer migration period. The following list outlines the more common items in a verification plan:

■   The specific **show** and **debug** commands to be used

■   The specific facts in the output that must be confirmed

■   Explanations of why a particular command's output confirms that a feature is or is not working

■   Sample command output

■   Any data that should be gathered when the output is not correct

Conclusions

The various CCNP ROUTE Exam Topics that require planning and documentation do not require more technical knowledge, but they do require you to be more comfortable with the technical topics. The best way to become more comfortable is to have a job in which you use the features but that you can become very comfortable with the technology through study as well. For those of you with little experience with the technologies included in this book, please take the time to do the exercises in the "Planning Practice" sections near the end of each chapter—we believe such practice can help you prepare for the planning perspectives expected to be on the exams.

This chapter covers the following subjects:

EIGRP CCNA Review: This section reviews the EIGRP concepts, configuration, and verification commands assumed as prerequisites, specifically those details included in the CCNA Exam's coverage of EIGRP.

EIGRP Neighborships: This section discusses a variety of features that impact when a router attempts to form EIGRP neighbor relationships (neighborships), what must be true for those neighborships to work, and what might prevent those neighborships.

Neighborships over WANs: This short section examines the typical usage of EIGRP neighborships over various types of WAN technologies.

CHAPTER 2

EIGRP Overview and Neighbor Relationships

Enhanced Interior Gateway Routing Protocol (EIGRP) is configured with a few relatively simple commands. In fact, for most any size network, you could go to every router, configure the **router eigrp 1** command, followed by one or more **network** *net-id* subcommands (one for each classful network to which the router is connected), and EIGRP would likely work, and work very well, with no other configuration.

In spite of that apparent simplicity, here you sit beginning the first of three chapters of EIGRP coverage in this book. Many reasons exist for the amount of EIGRP material included here. First, EIGRP includes many optional configuration features that you need to both understand and master for the CCNP ROUTE exam. Many of these features require a solid understanding of EIGRP internals as well—a topic that can be conveniently ignored if you just do the minimal configuration, but something very important to planning, implementing, and optimizing a medium/large Enterprise network.

Another reason for the depth of EIGRP coverage in this book is due to a fundamental change in the philosophy of the CCNP exams, as compared with earlier CCNP exam versions. Cisco has increased the focus on planning for the implementation and verification of new network designs. The bar has been raised, and in a way that is consistent with typical engineering jobs. Not only do you need to understand all the EIGRP features, but you also need to be able to look at a set of design requirements, and from that decide which EIGRP configuration settings could be useful—and which are not useful. You also must be able to direct others as to what verification steps would tell them if the implementation worked or not, rather than just relying on typing a ? and looking around for that little piece of information you know exists somewhere.

Part II of this book contains three chapters. This chapter briefly reviews the basics of EIGRP, and delves into all topics related to how EIGRP routers form neighbor relationships. Chapter 3, "EIGRP Topology, Routes, and Convergence," then examines many topics related to how EIGRP chooses routes. Chapter 4, "EIGRP Route Summarization and Filtering," then moves on to examine route filtering and route summarization, which closes the discussion of specific EIGRP features.

This chapter in particular begins with the "EIGRP Basics" section, which is a review of the core prerequisite facts about EIGRP. Following the review, the chapter examines EIGRP neighbor relationships, including a variety of configuration commands that impact neighbor relationships, and the verification commands that you can use to confirm how well EIGRP neighbors work.

"Do I Know This Already?" Quiz

The "Do I Know This Already?" quiz allows you to assess if you should read the entire chapter. If you miss no more than one of these eight self-assessment questions, you might want to move ahead to the "Exam Preparation Tasks." Table 2-1 lists the major headings in this chapter and the "Do I Know This Already?" quiz questions covering the material in those headings so that you can assess your knowledge of these specific areas. The answers to the "Do I Know This Already?" quiz appear in Appendix A.

Table 2-1 *"Do I Know This Already?" Foundation Topics Section-to-Question Mapping*

Foundation Topics Section	Questions
EIGRP CCNA Review	1, 2
EIGRP Neighborships	3–7
Neighborships over WANs	8

1. A router has been configured with the commands **router eigrp 9** and **network 172.16.1.0 0.0.0.255**. No other EIGRP-related commands have been configured. The answers list the IP addresses that could be assigned to this router's Fa0/0 interface. Which answers list an IP address/prefix length that would cause the router to enable EIGRP on Fa0/0? (Choose two answers.)

    a. 172.16.0.1/23

    b. 172.16.1.1/26

    c. 172.16.1.1/24

    d. 172.16.0.255/23

    e. None of the other answers is correct.

2. Router R1 has working interfaces S0/0, S0/1, and S0/2, with IP address/prefix combinations of 10.10.10.1/24, 10.10.11.2/24, and 10.10.12.3/22. R1's configuration includes the commands **router eigrp 9** and **network 10.0.0.0**. The **show ip eigrp interfaces** command lists S0/0 and S0/1 in the command output, but not S0/2. Which answer gives a possible reason for the omission?

    a. R1 has EIGRP neighbors reachable via S0/0 and S0/1, but not via S0/2, so it is not included.

    b. S0/2 may currently be in a state other than up/up.

    c. The **network 10.0.0.0** command requires the use of mask 255.0.0.0 due to EIGRP being classful by default.

    d. S0/2 may be configured as a passive interface.

3. Routers R1 and R2 are EIGRP neighbors using their Fa0/0 interfaces, respectively. An engineer adds the **ip hello-interval eigrp 9 6** command to R1's Fa0/0 configuration. Which of the following is true regarding the results from this change?

    a. The **show ip eigrp neighbors** command on R1 lists the revised Hello timer.

    b. The **show ip eigrp interfaces** command on R1 lists the revised Hello timer.

    c. The R1-R2 neighborship fails due to Hello timer mismatch.

    d. The **show ip eigrp interfaces detail** command on R1 lists the revised Hello timer.

4. Routers R1 and R2, currently EIGRP neighbors over their Fa0/0 interfaces (respectively), both use EIGRP authentication. Tuesday at 8 p.m. the neighborship fails. Which of the following would *not* be useful when investigating whether authentication had anything to do with the failure?

    a. **debug eigrp packet**

    b. **show key chain**

    c. **show ip eigrp neighbor failure**

    d. **show clock**

5. Router R1 has been configured with the commands **router eigrp 9** and **network 172.16.2.0 0.0.0.255**, with no other current EIGRP configuration. R1's (working) Fa0/0 interface has been configured with IP address 172.16.2.2/26. R1 has found three EIGRP neighbors reachable via interface Fa0/0, including the router with IP address 172.16.2.20. When the engineer attempts to add the **neighbor 172.16.2.20 fa0/0** command in EIGRP configuration mode, which of the following occurs?

    a. Fa0/0 fails.

    b. The command is rejected.

    c. The existing three neighbors fail.

    d. The neighborship with 172.16.2.20 fails and then reestablishes.

    e. None of the other answers is correct.

6. Which of the following settings could prevent two potential EIGRP neighbors from becoming neighbors? (Choose two answers.)

    a. The interface used by one router to connect to the other router is passive in the EIGRP process.

    b. Duplicate EIGRP router IDs.

    c. Mismatched Hold Timers.

    d. IP addresses of 10.1.1.1/24 and 10.2.2.2/24, respectively.

7. An engineer has added the following configuration snippet to an implementation planning document. The configuration will be added to Router R1, whose Fa0/0 interface connects to a LAN to which Routers R2 and R3 also connect. R2 and R3 are already EIGRP neighbors with each other. Assuming the snippet shows all commands on R1 related to EIGRP authentication, which answer lists an appropriate comment to be made during the implementation plan peer review?

key chain fred
key 3
key-string whehew
interface fa0/0
ip authentication key-chain eigrp 9 fred

  a. The configuration is missing one authentication-related configuration command.

  b. The configuration is missing two authentication-related configuration commands.

  c. Authentication type 9 is not supported; type 5 should be used instead.

  d. The key numbers must begin with key 1, so change the **key 3** command to **key 1**.

8. A company has a Frame Relay WAN with one central-site router and 100 branch office routers. A partial mesh of PVCs exists: one PVC between the central site and each of the 100 branch routers. Which of the following could be true about the number of EIGRP neighborships?

  a. A partial mesh totaling 100: one between the central-site router and each of the 100 branches.

  b. A full mesh – (101 * 100) / 2 = 5050–One neighborship between each pair of routers.

  c. 101–One between each router (including the central site) and its nearby PE router.

  d. None of the answers is correct.

Foundation Topics

EIGRP CCNA Review

All the CCNP exams consider CCNA materials as prerequisites, so the Cisco Press CCNP Exam Certification Guide series of books also assumes the reader is already familiar with CCNA topics. However, the CCNP exams do test on features that overlap with CCNA. Additionally, most people forget some details along the way, so this section reviews the CCNA level topics as a brief refresher.

To that end, this section begins with a review of EIGRP configuration using only the **router eigrp** and **network** commands. Following that, the next section details the key fields used to verify that EIGRP is working. Finally, the last part of this introduction summarizes the basic EIGRP internals behind this initial simple example.

Configuration Review

Cisco IOS uses the **router eigrp** *asn* command, plus one or more **network** *net-id wild-card-mask* subcommands, to enable EIGRP on the router and on router interfaces. The rules for these commands are as follows:

Key
Topic

1. Neighboring routers' **router eigrp** *asn* commands must be configured with the same ASN parameter to become neighbors.

2. IOS enables only EIGRP on interfaces matched by an EIGRP **network** command. When enabled, the router does the following:
   a. Attempts to discover EIGRP neighbors on that interface by sending multicast EIGRP Hello messages
   b. Advertises to other neighbors about the subnet connected to the interface

3. If no wildcard-mask is configured on the EIGRP **network** command, the command's single parameter should be a classful network number (in other words, a class A, B, or C network number).

4. If no wildcard-mask is configured on the EIGRP **network** command, the command enables EIGRP on all of that router's interfaces directly connected to the configured classful network.

5. If the **network** command includes a wildcard-mask, the router performs access control list (ACL) logic when comparing the net-id configured in the **network** command with each interface's IP address, using the configured wildcard-mask as an ACL wild-card mask.

Example 2-1 shows a sample configuration for each router in Figure 2-1, with several variations in the **network** commands to make the details in the preceding list more obvious.

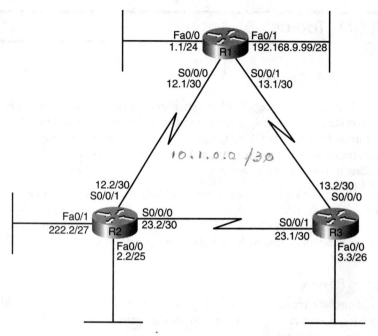

Note: All IP addresses begin with 10.1 unless otherwise noted.

Figure 2-1 *Three Router Internetwork*

Example 2-1 *EIGRP Configuration on Routers R1, R2, and R3*

```
! On Router R1: !!!!!!!!!!!!!!!!!!!!!!!!!!!!!!!!!!!!!!!!!!!!!!!!!
router eigrp 1
 network 10.0.0.0
 network 192.168.9.0
! On Router R2: !!!!!!!!!!!!!!!!!!!!!!!!!!!!!!!!!!!!!!!!!!!!!!!!!
router eigrp 1
 network 10.1.0.0 0.0.31.255
 network 10.1.2.2 0.0.0.0
! On Router R3: !!!!!!!!!!!!!!!!!!!!!!!!!!!!!!!!!!!!!!!!!!!!!!!!!
router eigrp 1
 network 10.1.0.0 0.0.255.255
```

First, note that all three routers use the **router eigrp 1** command, so all three routers' ASN values match.

Next, consider the two **network** commands on R1. The **network 10.0.0.0** command, without a *wildcard-mask* parameter, means that R1 matches all interface in class A network 10.0.0.0—which in this case means R1's Fa0/0, S0/0/0, and S0/0/1 interfaces. The **network 192.168.9.0** command, again without a wildcard, matches interface Fa0/1.

On R2, the **network 10.1.0.0 0.0.31.255** command requires a little more thought. The router uses the 0.0.31.255 value—the wildcard (WC) mask—just like an ACL WC mask.

IOS compares the 10.1.0.0 value with each interface IP address, but only for the bit positions for which the WC mask lists a binary 0. For example, 0.0.31.255 represents 19 binary 0s, followed by 13 binary 1s, so R2 would compare the first 19 bits of 10.1.0.0 with the first 19 bits of each interface's IP address. (Note that Appendix B lists a binary/decimal conversion table.)

Two features of the mechanics of the **network** command require a little extra attention. First, IOS may convert the *address* portion of the **network** *address wc-mask* command before putting the command into the running-config. Just as IOS does for the address/WC mask combinations for the **access-list** command, IOS inverts the WC mask and then performs a Boolean AND of the address and mask. For example, if you type the **network 10.1.1.1 0.0.255.255** command, IOS inverts the WC mask (to 255.255.0.0), ANDs this value with 10.1.1.1, resulting in 10.1.0.0. As a result, IOS stores the command **network 10.1.0.0 0.0.255.255**.

The second feature is that when you know for sure the values in the **network** command, you can easily find the range of interface addresses that match the address/WC mask combination in the **network** command. The low end of the range is the address as listed in the **network** command. To find the high end of the range, just add the address and WC mask together. For example, the **network 10.1.0.0 0.0.31.255** command has a range of 10.1.0.0 through 10.1.31.255. (Note that the math suggested in this paragraph does not work when the wildcard mask does not have a single string of consecutive binary 0s followed by a single string of consecutive binary 1s.)

Finally, on R3, the **network 10.1.0.0 0.0.255.255** command tells R3 to enable EIGRP on all interfaces whose IP addresses begin with 10.1, which includes all three interfaces on R3, as shown in Figure 2-1.

Taking a step back from the details, this config has enabled EIGRP, with ASN 1, on all three routers, and on all interfaces shown in Figure 2-1—except one interface. R2's Fa0/1 interface is not matched by any **network** commands on R2, so EIGRP is not enabled on that interface. The next section reviews the commands that can be used to confirm that EIGRP is enabled, the interfaces on which it is enabled, the neighbor relationships that have been formed, and which EIGRP routes have been advertised and learned.

Verification Review

Even before starting to configure the routers, an engineer first considers all requirements. Those requirements lead to a design, which in turn leads to a chosen set of configuration commands. Then, the verification process that follows must consider the design requirements. The goal of verification is to determine that the internetwork works as designed, not just that some EIGRP routes have been learned.

For the purposes of this section, assume that the only design goal for the internetwork in Figure 2-1 is that EIGRP be used so that all routers have routes to reach all subnets shown in the figure.

To verify such a simple design, an engineer should start by confirming on which interfaces EIGRP has been enabled on each router. The next step should be to determine if the EIGRP neighbor relationships that should occur are indeed up and working. Then, the

EIGRP topology table should be examined to confirm that there is at least one entry for each subnet or network in the design. Finally, the IP routes on each router should be examined, confirming that all routes are known. To that end, Table 2-2 summarizes five key **show** commands that provide the information to answer these questions:

Table 2-2 *Key EIGRP Verification Commands*

Command	Key Information
show ip eigrp interfaces	Lists the working interfaces on which EIGRP is enabled (based on the **network** commands); it omits passive interfaces.
show ip protocols	Lists the contents of the **network** configuration commands for each routing process, and a list of neighbor IP addresses.
show ip eigrp neighbors	Lists known neighbors; does not list neighbors for which some mismatched parameter is preventing a valid EIGRP neighbor relationship.
show ip eigrp topology	Lists all successor and feasible successor routes known to this router. It does not list all known topology details. (See Chapter 3 for more detail on successors and feasible successors.)
show ip route	Lists the contents of the IP routing table, listing EIGRP-learned routes with a code of D on the left side of the output.

Note: The table mentions some information that is covered later in this chapter (passive interfaces) or in other chapters (successor/feasible successors).

Example 2-2 shows samples of each command listed in Table 2-2. Note that the output highlights various samples of items that should be verified: the interfaces on which EIGRP is enabled, the known neighbors, the subnets in the topology table, and the EIGRP routes.

Example 2-2 *EIGRP Verification on Routers R1, R2, and R3*

```
! On Router R1: !!!!!!!!!!!!!!!!!!!!!!!!!!!!!!!!!!!!!!!!!!!!!!!
R1#show ip eigrp interfaces
IP-EIGRP interfaces for process 1


                        Xmit Queue   Mean  Pacing Time  Multicast   Pending
Interface        Peers  Un/Reliable  SRTT  Un/Reliable  Flow Timer  Routes
Fa0/0            0      0/0          0     0/1          0           0
Se0/0/0          1      0/0          25    0/15         123         0
Se0/0/1          1      0/0          23    0/15         111         0
Fa0/1            0      0/0          0     0/1          0           0
```

```
! On Router R2: !!!!!!!!!!!!!!!!!!!!!!!!!!!!!!!!!!!!!!!!!!!!!!
R2#show ip protocols
Routing Protocol is "eigrp 1"
  Outgoing update filter list for all interfaces is not set
  Incoming update filter list for all interfaces is not set
  Default networks flagged in outgoing updates
  Default networks accepted from incoming updates
  EIGRP metric weight K1=1, K2=0, K3=1, K4=0, K5=0
  EIGRP maximum hopcount 100
  EIGRP maximum metric variance 1
  Redistributing: eigrp 1
  EIGRP NSF-aware route hold timer is 240s
  Automatic network summarization is in effect
  Maximum path: 4
  Routing for Networks:
    10.1.2.2/32
    10.1.0.0/19
  Routing Information Sources:
    Gateway        Distance      Last Update
    10.1.12.1            90      00:19:36
    10.1.23.1            90      00:19:36
  Distance: internal 90 external 170
! On Router R3: !!!!!!!!!!!!!!!!!!!!!!!!!!!!!!!!!!!!!!!!!!!!!!
R3#show ip eigrp neighbors
IP-EIGRP neighbors for process 1
H   Address              Interface       Hold Uptime   SRTT   RTO   Q   Seq
                                         (sec)         (ms)         Cnt Num
1   10.1.23.2            Se0/0/1          11 00:19:53   31     200   0   6
0   10.1.13.1            Se0/0/0          10 00:19:53   32     200   0   6
! On Router R2: !!!!!!!!!!!!!!!!!!!!!!!!!!!!!!!!!!!!!!!!!!!!!!
R2#show ip eigrp topology
IP-EIGRP Topology Table for AS(1)/ID(10.1.222.2)

Codes: P - Passive, A - Active, U - Update, Q - Query, R - Reply,
       r - reply Status, s - sia Status

P 10.1.13.0/30, 2 successors, FD is 2681856
         via 10.1.23.1 (2681856/2169856), Serial0/0/0
         via 10.1.12.1 (2681856/2169856), Serial0/0/1
P 10.1.12.0/30, 1 successors, FD is 2169856
         via Connected, Serial0/0/1
P 10.1.3.0/26, 1 successors, FD is 2172416
         via 10.1.23.1 (2172416/28160), Serial0/0/0
P 10.1.2.0/25, 1 successors, FD is 28160
         via Connected, FastEthernet0/0
```

```
P  10.1.1.0/24, 1 successors, FD is 2172416
          via 10.1.12.1 (2172416/28160), Serial0/0/1
P  10.1.23.0/30, 1 successors, FD is 2169856
          via Connected, Serial0/0/0
P  192.168.9.0/24, 1 successors, FD is 2172416
          via 10.1.12.1 (2172416/28160), Serial0/0/1
! On Router R3: !!!!!!!!!!!!!!!!!!!!!!!!!!!!!!!!!!!!!!!!!!!
R3#show ip route
Codes: C - connected, S - static, R - RIP, M - mobile, B - BGP
       D - EIGRP, EX - EIGRP external, O - OSPF, IA - OSPF inter area
       N1 - OSPF NSSA external type 1, N2 - OSPF NSSA external type 2
       E1 - OSPF external type 1, E2 - OSPF external type 2
       i - IS-IS, su - IS-IS summary, L1 - IS-IS level-1, L2 - IS-IS level-2
       ia - IS-IS inter area, * - candidate default, U - per-user static route
       o - ODR, P - periodic downloaded static route

Gateway of last resort is not set

D    192.168.9.0/24 [90/2172416] via 10.1.13.1, 00:19:55, Serial0/0/0
     10.0.0.0/8 is variably subnetted, 6 subnets, 4 masks
C        10.1.13.0/30 is directly connected, Serial0/0/0
D        10.1.12.0/30 [90/2681856] via 10.1.23.2, 00:19:55, Serial0/0/1
                      [90/2681856] via 10.1.13.1, 00:19:55, Serial0/0/0
C        10.1.3.0/26 is directly connected, FastEthernet0/0
D        10.1.2.0/25 [90/2172416] via 10.1.23.2, 00:19:55, Serial0/0/1
D        10.1.1.0/24 [90/2172416] via 10.1.13.1, 00:19:55, Serial0/0/0
C        10.1.23.0/30 is directly connected, Serial0/0/1
```

To verify the interfaces on which EIGRP is enabled, both the **show ip eigrp interfaces** command (shown on R1), and the **show ip protocols** command (shown on R2) list the information. Later in this chapter, in the "Preventing Unwanted Neighbors Using Passive Interfaces" section, the discussion around the **passive-interface** EIGRP configuration subcommand shows an example of how one command lists passive EIGRP interfaces, and the other does not.

In this design, each router should form a neighbor relationship with the other two routers, in each case over a point-to-point serial link. The **show ip eigrp neighbors** command (on R3) confirms R3's neighbors.

Finally, one design goal was for all routers to have routes for all subnets/networks. You could move on to the **show ip route** command or first look for all prefixes in the **show ip eigrp topology** command. With relatively general requirements, just looking at the IP routing table is fine. The example highlights R3's topology data and IP route for subnet 10.1.1.0/24. Of more interest might be the fact that the **show ip route** command output on

R3 lists all subnet/network numbers except one: subnet 10.1.222.0/27. This subnet exists off R2's Fa0/1 interface, which is the interface on which EIGRP has not yet been enabled.

Internals Review

To complete the review of prerequisite CCNA-level EIGRP knowledge, this section looks at a few of the internals of EIGRP. Some of the facts listed here simply need to be memorized, whereas other topics will be discussed in more detail in the next several chapters.

EIGRP follows three general steps to add routes to the IP routing table, as follows:

Step 1.   **Neighbor discovery:** EIGRP routers send Hello messages to discover potential neighboring EIGRP routers and perform basic parameter checks to determine which routers should become neighbors.

Step 2.   **Topology Exchange:** Neighbors exchange full topology updates when the neighbor relationship comes up, and then only partial updates as needed based on changes to the network topology.

Step 3.   **Choosing Routes:** Each router analyzes their respective EIGRP topology tables, choosing the lowest-metric route to reach each subnet.

Because the majority of the rest of this chapter examines EIGRP neighborships, this review section skips any discussion of EIGRP neighbors, instead focusing on the second and third items in the preceding list.

Exchanging Topology Information

Each of these steps may cause a router to update one of three key tables used by EIGRP. First, the EIGRP neighbor table lists the neighboring routers. Second, the EIGRP topology table holds all the topology information learned from EIGRP neighbors. Finally, EIGRP chooses the best IP routes and places those into the IP routing table. (Table 2-2 earlier in this chapter lists the **show** commands that can be used to examine these tables.) EIGRP routers follow the process shown in Figure 2-2 to build the necessary information in these tables, with the end goal of populating the IP routing table.

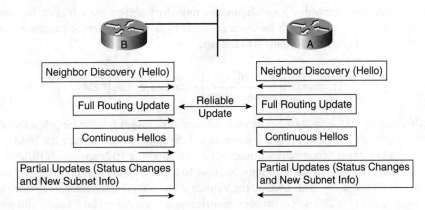

Figure 2-2   *EIGRP Discovery and Update Process*

EIGRP uses *Update messages* to send topology information to neighbors. These Update messages can be sent to multicast IP address 224.0.0.10 if the sending router needs to update multiple routers on the same subnet. Unlike OSPF, there is no concept of a designated router (DR) or backup designated router (BDR), but the use of multicast packets on LANs allows EIGRP to exchange routing information with all neighbors on the LAN efficiently.

The update messages are sent using the *Reliable Transport Protocol (RTP)*. The significance of RTP is that, like OSPF, EIGRP resends routing updates that are lost in transit. By using RTP to guarantee delivery of the EIGRP messages, EIGRP can better avoid loops.

Note: The acronym RTP also refers to a different protocol, Real-time Transport Protocol (RTP), which is used to transmit voice and video IP packets.

Neighbors use both full routing updates and partial updates as depicted in Figure 2-2. A full update means that a router sends information about all known routes, whereas a partial update includes only information about recently changed routes. Full updates occur when neighbors first come up. After that, the neighbors send only partial updates in reaction to changes to a route.

Calculating the Best Routes for the Routing Table

EIGRP topology information includes the subnet number and mask, along with the components of the EIGRP composite metric. Each router then calculates an integer metric for each route, using the individual values of the EIGRP metric components listed in the EIGRP topology database. By default, EIGRP only uses the bandwidth and delay settings when calculating the metric. Optionally, the calculation can also include interface load and interface reliability, although Cisco recommends against using either.

Note: Past documents and books often stated that EIGRP, and its predecessor IGRP, also could use MTU as a part of the metric, but MTU cannot be used and was never considered as part of the calculation. However, the MTU is listed in the EIGRP Update messages.

EIGRP calculates the metric for each possible route by inserting the values of the composite metric into a formula. If the choice is made to just use the default parameters of bandwidth and delay the formula is as follows:

$$\text{Metric} = \left(\left(\frac{10^7}{\text{least-bandwidth}} \right) + \text{cumulative-delay} \right) * 256$$

In this formula, the term *least-bandwidth* represents the lowest-bandwidth link in the route, using a unit of kilobits per second. For instance, if the slowest link in a route is a 10 Mbps Ethernet link, the first part of the formula is $10^7 / 10^4$, because 10 Mbps equals 10,000 Kbps, or 10^4 Kbps. You use 10^4 in the formula because 10 Mbps is equal to 10,000 kbps (10^4 kbps). The *cumulative-delay* value used by the formula is the sum of all the delay values for all links in the route, with a unit of "tens of microseconds." You can set both bandwidth and delay for each link, using the **bandwidth** and **delay** interface subcommands.

Table 2-3 summarizes some of the key facts about EIGRP.

Table 2-3   *EIGRP Feature Summary*

Feature	Description
Transport	IP, protocol type 88 (does not use UDP or TCP).
Metric	Based on constrained bandwidth and cumulative delay by default, and optionally load and reliability.
Hello interval	Interval at which a router sends EIGRP Hello messages on an interface.
Hold Timer	Timer used to determine when a neighboring router has failed, based on a router not receiving any EIGRP messages, including Hellos, in this timer period.
Update destination address	Normally sent to 224.0.0.10, with retransmissions being sent to each neighbor's unicast IP address. Can also be sent to the neighbor's unicast IP address.
Full or partial updates	Full updates are used when new neighbors are discovered; otherwise, partial updates are used.
Authentication	Supports MD5 authentication only.
VLSM/classless	EIGRP includes the mask with each route, also allowing it to support discontiguous networks and VLSM.
Route Tags	Allows EIGRP to tag routes as they are redistributed into EIGRP.
Next-hop field	Supports the advertisement of routes with a different next-hop router than the advertising router.
Manual route summarization	Allows route summarization at any point in the EIGRP network.
Automatic Summarization	EIGRP supports, and defaults to use, automatic route summarization at classful network boundaries.
Multiprotocol	Supports the advertisement of IPX and AppleTalk routes, and IP Version 6, which is discussed in Chapter 17 of this book.

This completes the CCNA-level EIGRP review. The rest of this chapter now examines EIGRP neighbor relationships.

EIGRP Neighborships

Like OSPF, EIGRP uses three major steps to achieve its goal of learning the best available loop-free routes:

Step 1.   Establish EIGRP neighbor relationships—*neighborships*—with other routers that share a common subnet.

Step 2.   Exchange EIGRP topology data with those neighbors.

Step 3.   Calculate the currently best IP route for each subnet, based on the known EIGRP topology data, and add those best routes to the IP routing table.

This three-step process hinges on the first step—the successful creation of neighbor relationships between EIGRP routers. The basic EIGRP configuration described earlier in this chapter, particularly the **network** command, most directly tells EIGRP on which interfaces to dynamically discover neighbors. After EIGRP neighborships have been formed with neighboring routers that are reachable through those interfaces, the final two steps occur without any additional direct configuration.

EIGRP dynamically discovers neighbors by sending EIGRP Hello messages on each EIGRP-enabled interface. When two routers hear EIGRP Hello messages from each other, they check the EIGRP parameters listed in those messages and decide whether the two routers should or should not become neighbors.

The rest of this section focuses on topics related to EIGRP neighborship, specifically:

■   Manipulating EIGRP Hello and Hold Timers

■   Controlling whether routers become neighbors by using either passive interfaces or statically defined neighbors

■   Authenticating EIGRP neighbors

■   Examining configuration settings that can prevent EIGRP neighborships

Manipulating EIGRP Hello and Hold Timers

The word *convergence* defines the overall process by which routers notice internetwork topology changes, communicate about those changes, and change their routing tables to contain only the best currently working routes. EIGRP converges very quickly even with all default settings.

One of the slower components of the EIGRP convergence process relates to the timers EIGRP neighbors use to recognize that the neighborship has failed. If the interface over which the neighbor is reachable fails, and IOS changes the interface state to anything other than "up/up", then a router immediately knows that the neighborship should fail. However, in some cases, the interface state may stay "up/up" during times when the link may not be usable. In such cases, EIGRP convergence relies on the Hold Timer to expire, which by default on LANs means a 15-second wait. (The default EIGRP hold time with interfaces/subinterfaces with a bandwidth of T1 or slower, with encapsulation of Frame Relay, is 180 seconds.)

The basic operation of these two timers is relatively simple. EIGRP uses the Hello messages in part as a confirmation that the link between the neighbors still works. If a router does not receive a Hello from a neighbor for one entire Hold time, that router considers the neighbor to have failed. For example, with a default LAN setting of Hello of 5, and Hold of 15, the local router sends Hellos every 5 seconds. The neighbor resets its downward-counting Hold Timer to 15 upon receiving a Hello from that neighbor. Under normal operation on a LAN, with defaults, the Hold Timer for a neighbor would vary from 15, down to 10, and then be reset to 15. However, if the Hellos were no longer received for 15 seconds, the neighborship would fail, driving convergence.

To optimize convergence, an engineer could simply reduce the Hello and Hold Timers, accepting insignificant additional overhead, in return for shorter convergence times. These settings can be made per interface/subinterface, and per EIGRP process.

Note: Although expected to be outside the scope of CCNP, EIGRP can also use the Bidirectional Forwarding Detection (BFD) feature that provides a means for subsecond detection of a failure in IP connectivity between two neighboring routers.

Configuring the Hello/Hold Timers

Most design engineers would normally choose Hello/Hold Timers that match on all router interfaces on a subnet. However, these settings do not have to match. More interestingly, by setting the Hello and Hold Timers to nondefault values, you can see some oddities with how EIGRP neighbors use these values.

For example, consider four WAN distribution routers, as shown in Figure 2-3. These routers may each have a number of Frame Relay PVCs to remote branches, or multiple MPLS VPN connections to branches. However, to communicate with each other and with data centers at the home office, these four routers connect via a core VLAN/subnet. Note that the design shows routers, rather than Layer 3 switches, but the concept applies the same in either case.

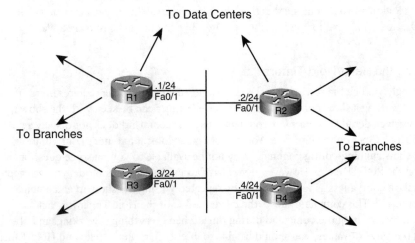

Figure 2-3   *Four WAN Distribution Routers on the Same VLAN/Subnet*

A design that hoped to speed EIGRP convergence might call for setting the Hello and Hold Timers to 2 and 6, respectively. (The Hold Timer does not have to be three times the Hello timer, but the 3:1 ratio is a reasonable guideline.) However, to make an important point about operation of the configuration commands, Example 2-3 sets only R1's Fa0/1 timers to the new values. Note that in this case, EIGRP has already been configured on all four routers, using ASN 9.

Example 2-3   *EIGRP Hello and Hold Timer Configuration—R1*

```
interface Fastethernet0/1
 ip hello-interval eigrp 9 2
 ip hold-time eigrp 9 6
```

A couple of interesting points can be made about the operation of these seemingly simple commands. First, these two settings can be made per interface/subinterface, but not per neighbor. In Figure 2-3, the Example 2-3 configuration then applies on R1 for all three neighbors reachable on interface Fa0/1.

The second interesting point about these commands is that one parameter (the Hello interval) tells R1 what to do, whereas the other (the Hold Timer) actually tells the neighboring routers what to do. As shown in Figure 2-4, **ip hello-interval eigrp 9 2** interface subcommand tells R1 to send Hellos every 2 seconds. However, the **ip hold-time eigrp 9 6** interface subcommand tells R1, again for the EIGRP process with ASN 9, to tell its neighbors to use a Hold Timer of 6 for their respective neighbor relationships with R1. In short, the EIGRP Hello message sent by R1 announces the Hold Timer that other routers should use in the neighbor relationship with R1. Figure 2-4 shows the same idea in graphical form.

Note: IOS does not prevent you from making the unfortunate configuration choice of setting the Hold timer to a value smaller than the Hello interval. In such a case, the neighborship repeatedly fails and recovers, flapping routes in and out of the routing table.

Verifying the Hello/Hold Timers

Interestingly, finding the settings for the Hello interval and Hold time requires more effort than simply using a **show** command. A router's Hello timer can be seen with the **show ip eigrp interface detail** *type number* command, but this command does not display a router's Hold Timer on the interface. You can of course look at a router's configuration, but the **show running-config** command may not be available to you on some question types on the ROUTE exam. However, if you have access to only user mode, you can typically make a good guess as to the settings by repeatedly using the **show ip eigrp neighbors** command. This command shows the current value of the Hold Timer for each neighbor. By repeating the command during times when everything is working, and observing the range of values, you should be able to infer each router's Hello and Hold Timer settings.

Example 2-4 shows examples of the command output on R1, R2, and R3. Note that the Hello and Hold Timer settings on R1 are all between 10—15 seconds, because the timers

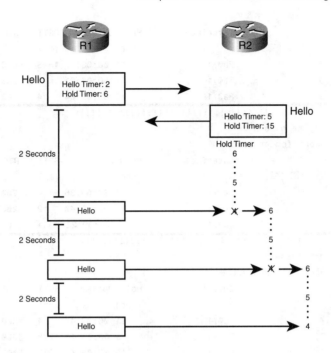

Figure 2-4 *R1 Announcing New Hello and Hold Timers*

on R2, R3, and R4 all still default to 5 and 15 seconds, respectively. R2's neighborship with R1 lists a Hold Timer of 4, which is within the expected range from 6 to 4 seconds remaining.

Example 2-4 *Demonstration that R2 and R3 Use R1's Configured Hold Timer*

```
! On Router R1: !!!!!!!!!!!!!!!!!!!!!!!!!!!!!!!!!!!!!!!!!!!!!
R1#show ip eigrp interfaces detail fa0/1
IP-EIGRP interfaces for process 9

                          Xmit Queue    Mean   Pacing Time   Multicast    Pending
Interface       Peers   Un/Reliable    SRTT   Un/Reliable   Flow Timer    Routes
Fa0/1             3         0/0         535       0/1           50           0
  Hello interval is 2 sec
  Next xmit serial <none>
  Un/reliable mcasts: 0/1  Un/reliable ucasts: 4/9
  Mcast exceptions: 1  CR packets: 1  ACKs suppressed: 1
  Retransmissions sent: 2  Out-of-sequence rcvd: 0
  Authentication mode is not set
  Use multicast


R1#show ip eigrp neighbors
IP-EIGRP neighbors for process 9
```

```
   H    Address                 Interface     Hold Uptime    SRTT    RTO   Q   Seq
                                              (sec)          (ms)          Cnt Num
   2    172.16.1.4              Fa0/1         11  00:03:17   1596    5000  0   7
   1    172.16.1.3              Fa0/1         11  00:05:21      1    200   0   5
   0    172.16.1.2              Fa0/1         13  00:09:04      4    200   0   2
   ! On Router R2: !!!!!!!!!!!!!!!!!!!!!!!!!!!!!!!!!!!!!!!!!!!!!!!
   R2#show ip eigrp neighbors
   IP-EIGRP neighbors for process 9
   H    Address                 Interface     Hold Uptime    SRTT    RTO   Q   Seq
                                              (sec)          (ms)          Cnt Num
   2    172.16.1.4              Fa0/1         11  00:03:36      4    200   0   6
   1    172.16.1.3              Fa0/1         11  00:05:40     12    200   0   4
   0    172.16.1.1              Fa0/1          4  00:09:22      1    200   0   2
   ! On Router R3: !!!!!!!!!!!!!!!!!!!!!!!!!!!!!!!!!!!!!!!!!!!!!!!
   R3#show ip eigrp neighbors
   IP-EIGRP neighbors for process 9
   H    Address                 Interface     Hold Uptime    SRTT    RTO   Q   Seq
                                              (sec)          (ms)          Cnt Num
   2    172.16.1.4              Fa0/1         11  00:03:40      4    200   0   5
   1    172.16.1.1              Fa0/1          5  00:05:44   1278    5000  0   4
   0    172.16.1.2              Fa0/1         13  00:05:44   1277    5000  0   4
```

Preventing Unwanted Neighbors Using Passive Interfaces

When an EIGRP **network** configuration subcommand matches an interface, EIGRP on that router does two things:

Step 1.   Attempts to find potential EIGRP neighbors by sending Hellos to the 224.0.0.10 multicast address

Step 2.   Advertises about the subnet connected to that interface

In some cases, however, no legitimate EIGRP neighbors may exist off an interface. For example, consider the small internetwork of Figure 2-5, with three routers, and with only one router connected to each LAN interface. Each router needs to advertise about the subnets connected to their various FastEthernet interfaces, but at the same time, there is no benefit to multicast EIGRP Hellos on those interfaces because only one router connects to each LAN.

The network designer may reasonably choose to limit EIGRP on those interfaces that have no legitimate EIGRP neighbors. However, the subnets connected to those same interfaces also typically need to be advertised by EIGRP. For example, subnet 10.1.1.0/24, off R1's Fa0/0 interface, still needs to be advertised by EIGRP, even though R1 should never find an EIGRP neighbor on that interface.

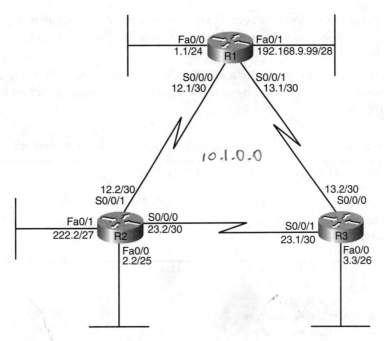

Note: All IP addresses begin with 10.1 unless otherwise noted.

Figure 2-5   *LAN Interfaces That Benefit from the Passive Interface Feature*

Given such a requirement—to advertise about the subnet, but disallow EIGRP neighborships on the interface—an engineer has two main configuration options to add to the implementation plan:

- Enable EIGRP on the interface using the EIGRP **network** command, but tell the
  router to not send any EIGRP messages on the interface by making the interface passive (using the **passive-interface** command).

- Do not enable EIGRP on the interface, and advertise about the connected route using
  route redistribution (and the **redistribute connected** configuration command).

The first option relies on the passive interface feature—a feature specifically created with
this design requirement in mind. When an interface is passive, EIGRP does not send any
EIGRP messages on the interface—multicasts or EIGRP unicasts—and the router ignores
any EIGRP messages received on the interface. However, EIGRP still advertises about the
connected subnets if matched with an EIGRP **network** command. As a result, the first option in the preceding list directly meets all design requirements. It has the added advantage
of being very secure in that no EIGRP neighborships are possible on the interface.

The second option—redistributing connected subnets—also works, but frankly it is the
less preferred option in this case. The passive interface option clearly meets the requirement, plus the redistribution process means that EIGRP advertises the connected route as

an external EIGRP route, which could cause problems in some cases with multiple redistribution points between routing domains (as discussed in Chapter 10, "Advanced IGP Redistribution").

The configuration of passive-interface itself is somewhat straightforward. To configure the **passive-interface** option, these three routers could be configured as follows in Example 2-5.

Example 2-5   *Configuration of* **passive-interface** *Commands on R1, R2, and R3*

```
! On Router R1: !!!!!!!!!!!!!!!!!!!!!!!!!!!!!!!!!!!!!!!!!!!!
router eigrp 1
 passive-interface fastethernet0/0
 passive-interface fastethernet0/1
 network 10.0.0.0
 network 192.168.9.0
! On Router R2: !!!!!!!!!!!!!!!!!!!!!!!!!!!!!!!!!!!!!!!!!!!!
router eigrp 1
 passive-interface default
 no passive-interface serial0/0/0
 no passive-interface serial0/0/1
 network 10.0.0.0
! On Router R3: !!!!!!!!!!!!!!!!!!!!!!!!!!!!!!!!!!!!!!!!!!!!
router eigrp 1
 passive-interface fastethernet0/0
 network 10.0.0.0
```

R1's configuration lists two **passive-interface** commands, one per LAN interface. As a result, R1 no longer sends EIGRP messages at all on these two interfaces, including the multicast EIGRP Hellos used to discover neighbors.

R2's configuration uses a slightly different option: the **passive-interface default** command. This command essentially changes the default for an interface from not being passive to instead being passive. Then, to make an interface not passive, you have to use a **no** version of the **passive-interface** command for those interfaces.

Two commands help to verify that the passive interface design is working properly. First, the **show ip eigrp interfaces** command omits passive interfaces, listing the nonpassive interfaces matched by a **network** command. Alternatively, the **show ip protocols** command explicitly lists all passive interfaces. Example 2-6 shows samples of both commands on R2.

Example 2-6 *Verifying the Results of* **passive-interface** *on R2*

```
R2#show ip eigrp interfaces
IP-EIGRP interfaces for process 1


                        Xmit Queue    Mean    Pacing Time   Multicast    Pending
Interface      Peers    Un/Reliable   SRTT    Un/Reliable   Flow Timer   Routes
Se0/0/0          1        0/0          32        0/15          159          0
Se0/0/1          1        0/0         1290       0/15         6443          0
R2#show ip protocols
Routing Protocol is "eigrp 1"
  Outgoing update filter list for all interfaces is not set
  Incoming update filter list for all interfaces is not set
  Default networks flagged in outgoing updates
  Default networks accepted from incoming updates
  EIGRP metric weight K1=1, K2=0, K3=1, K4=0, K5=0
  EIGRP maximum hopcount 100
  EIGRP maximum metric variance 1
  Redistributing: eigrp 1
  EIGRP NSF-aware route hold timer is 240s
  Automatic network summarization is in effect
  Maximum path: 4
  Routing for Networks:
    10.0.0.0
  Passive Interface(s):
    FastEthernet0/0
    FastEthernet0/1
  Routing Information Sources:
    Gateway         Distance      Last Update
    10.1.12.1            90       00:00:39
    10.1.23.1            90       00:00:39
  Distance: internal 90 external 170
```

Controlling Neighborships Using EIGRP Authentication

EIGRP authentication causes routers to authenticate every EIGRP message. To do so, the routers should use the same preshared key (PSK), generating an MD5 digest for each EIGRP message based on that shared PSK. If a router configured for EIGRP authentication receives an EIGRP message, and the message's MD5 digest does not pass the authentication checking based on the local copy of the key, the router silently discards the message. As a result, when authentication fails, two routers cannot become EIGRP neighbors, because they ignore the EIGRP Hello messages.

From a design perspective, EIGRP authentication helps prevent denial of service (DoS) attacks, but it does not provide any privacy. The EIGRP messages can be read by the device that physically receives the bits. Note that on LANs, the updates flow to the 224.0.0.10 multicast IP address, so any attacker could join the 224.0.0.10 multicast group and read the packets. However, authentication prevents attackers from forming neighborships with legitimate routers, preventing the advertisement of incorrect routing information.

Next, this section examines EIGRP authentication configuration generically, followed by a deeper look at the time-based authentication configuration settings, and finally showing an example of EIGRP authentication configuration.

EIGRP Authentication Configuration Checklist

The EIGRP authentication configuration process requires several commands, which are summarized as follows:

Step 1. Create an (authentication) key chain:

    a. Create the chain and give it a name with the **key chain** *name* global command (also puts the user into key chain config mode). The name does not have to match on the neighboring routers.

    b. Create one or more key numbers using the **key** *number* command in key chain configuration mode. The key numbers do have to match on the neighboring routers.

    c. Define the authentication key's value using the **key-string** *value* command in key configuration mode. The key strings must match on the neighboring routers.

    d. (Optional) Define the lifetime (time period) for both sending and accepting each key string.

Step 2. Enable EIGRP MD5 authentication on an interface, for a particular EIGRP ASN, using the **ip authentication mode eigrp** *asn* **md5** interface subcommand.

Step 3. Refer to the correct key chain to be used on an interface using the **ip authentication key-chain eigrp** *asn name-of-chain* interface subcommand.

The configuration at Step 1 is fairly detailed, but Steps 2 and 3 are relatively simple. Essentially, IOS configures the key values separately (Step 1) and then requires an interface subcommand to refer to the key values. To support the ability to have multiple keys, and even multiple sets of keys, the configuration includes the concept of a key chain and multiple keys on each key chain.

Key Chain Time-Based Logic

The key chain configuration concept, as outlined in Step 1, allows the engineer to migrate from one key value to another over time. Just like a real key chain that has multiple keys, the IOS key chain concept allows the configuration of multiple keys—each identified with a number. If no lifetime has been configured for a key, it is considered to be valid during all time frames. However, when a key has been defined with a lifetime, the key is valid only during the valid lifetime.

The existence of multiple keys in a key chain, and the existence of valid lifetimes for each key, can cause some confusion about when the keys are used. The rules can be summarized as follows:

■ **Sending EIGRP messages:** Use the lowest key number among all currently valid keys.

■ **Receiving EIGRP message:** Check the MD5 digest using ALL currently valid keys.

For example, consider the case shown in Figure 2-6. The figure represents the logic in a single router, Router R1, both when receiving and sending EIGRP messages on the right. The figure shows a key chain with four keys. All the keys have lifetimes configured. Key 1's lifetime has passed, making it invalid. Key 4's lifetime has yet to begin, making it invalid. However, keys 2 and 3 are both currently valid.

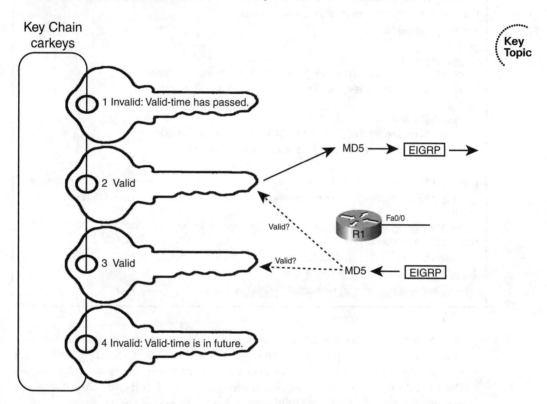

Figure 2-6   *EIGRP's Usage of Authentication Keys*

Figure 2-6 shows that the EIGRP message sent by Router R1 uses key 2, and key 2 only. Keys 1 and 4 are ignored because they are currently invalid; R1 then simply chooses the lowest-numbered key among the two valid keys. The figure also shows that R1 processes the received EIGRP message using both key 2 and key 3, because both are currently valid.

Note: Neighboring EIGRP routers that use authentication should be configured to use NTP to synchronize their time-of-day clocks. For quick tests in a lab, you can just set the time using the **clock set** exec command.

EIGRP Authentication Configuration and Verification Example

Example 2-7 shows a sample configuration, based on the network topology shown back in Figure 2-3 (the figure with four routers connected to a single LAN subnet). Key chain "carkeys" has two keys, each with different lifetimes, so that the router will use new keys automatically over time. The example shows the configuration on a single router, but similar configuration would be required on the other routers as well.

Example 2-7 *EIGRP Authentication Configuration on R1*

```
! Chain "carkeys" will be used on R1's Fa0/1 interface. R1 will use key "fred" for
! about a month, and then start using "wilma."
key chain carkeys
 key 1
  key-string fred
  accept-lifetime 08:00:00 Feb 11 2009 08:00:00 Mar 11 2009
  send-lifetime 08:00:00 Feb 11 2009 08:00:00 Mar 11 2009
 key 2
  key-string wilma
  accept-lifetime 08:00:00 Mar 11 2009 08:00:00 Apr 11 2009
  send-lifetime 08:00:00 Mar 11 2009 08:00:00 Apr 11 2009


! Next, R1's interface subcommands are shown. First, the key chain is referenced
! using the ip authentication key-chain command, and the ip authentication mode
eigrp
! command causes the router to use an MD5 digest of the key string.
interface FastEthernet0/1
 ip address 172.16.1.1 255.255.255.0
 ip authentication mode eigrp 9 md5
 ip authentication key-chain eigrp 9 carkeys
```

The best method to confirm the authentication worked is to verify that the neighbors remain up using the **show ip eigrp neighbors** command. However, if some neighbors do not remain active, and a problem exists, two commands in particular can be helpful: **show key chain** and **debug eigrp packet**. The first of these commands lists the key chain configuration and also lists which keys are valid right now—a key consideration when troubleshooting EIGRP authentication. The **debug** command lists a message regarding why neighboring routers have failed the authentication process.

Example 2-8 shows a sample output from each of these two commands. Note that in this case, again from Figure 2-3:

■ R1 and R2 have been configured to use MD5 authentication, but a typo exists in R2's key string.

■ R3 and R4 have not yet been configured for MD5 authentication.

Example 2-8 *EIGRP Authentication Verification on R1*

```
R1#show key chain
Key-chain carkeys:
    key 1 — text "fred"
```

```
           accept lifetime (08:00:00 UTC Feb 11 2009) - (08:00:00 UTC Mar 11 2009)
           send lifetime (08:00:00 UTC Feb 11 2009) - (08:00:00 UTC Mar 11 2009)
     key 2 — text "wilma"
           accept lifetime (08:00:00 UTC Mar 11 2009) - (08:00:00 UTC Apr 11 2009)
[valid now]
           send lifetime (08:00:00 UTC Mar 11 2009) - (08:00:00 UTC Apr 11 2009)
[valid now]
R1#debug eigrp packet
EIGRP Packets debugging is on
    (UPDATE, REQUEST, QUERY, REPLY, HELLO, IPXSAP, PROBE, ACK, STUB, SIAQUERY,
SIAREPLY)
R1#
Apr  1 08:09:01.951: EIGRP: Sending HELLO on FastEthernet0/1
Apr  1 08:09:01.951:    AS 9, Flags 0x0, Seq 0/0 idbQ 0/0 iidbQ un/rely 0/0
Apr  1 08:09:01.967: EIGRP: pkt key id = 2, authentication mismatch
Apr  1 08:09:01.967: EIGRP: FastEthernet0/1: ignored packet from 172.16.1.2,
opcode = 5 (invalid authentication)
Apr  1 08:09:02.287: EIGRP: FastEthernet0/1: ignored packet from 172.16.1.4,
opcode = 5 (missing authentication)
Apr  1 08:09:03.187: EIGRP: FastEthernet0/1: ignored packet from 172.16.1.3, opcode
= 5 (missing authentication)
```

In particular, note that the different highlighted phrasing in the debug output implies different problems. From 172.16.1.2 (R2), the message "invalid authentication" implies that the MD5 digest existed in the message, but was invalid. With the message "missing authentication," the meaning is that the message did not include an MD5 digest.

Also, when troubleshooting EIGRP authentication, keep the following in mind:

- Examine the configuration and the current time (**show clock**) on both routers.

- The key chain name on the two potential neighbors does not have to match.

- The key number and key string on the two potential neighbors must match.

- Check which keys are currently valid using the **show key chain** command.

- Both the **ip authentication mode eigrp** *asn* **md5** interface subcommand and the **ip authentication key-chain eigrp** *asn name-of-chain* interface subcommand must be configured on the interface; if one is omitted, authentication fails.

Controlling Neighborships with Static Configuration

EIGRP supports the ability to statically define neighbors instead of dynamically discovering neighbors.

Although seldom used, you can use this feature to reduce the overhead associated with EIGRP multicast messages. Frame Relay WANs in particular may benefit from the static neighbor definitions because to support multicasts and broadcasts over Frame Relay, a router must replicate the frame and send a copy over every PVC associated with the interface or subinterface. For example, if a multipoint subinterface has 10 PVCs associated

Key
Topic

with it, but only two of the remote routers used EIGRP, without static neighbors, all 10 routers would be sent a copy of the EIGRP multicast Hello packets. With static neighbor definitions for the two routers, EIGRP messages would be sent as unicasts to each of the two neighbors, with no EIGRP messages sent to the eight non-EIGRP routers, reducing overhead.

The configuration seems simple, but it has a few subtle caveats. This section examines the straightforward configuration first and then examines the caveats.

Configuring Static EIGRP Neighbors

To define a neighbor, both routers must configure the **neighbor** *ip-address outgoing-interface* EIGRP router subcommand. The IP address is the interface IP address of the neighboring router. Also, the configured IP address must be from the subnet connected to the interface listed in the **neighbor** command; otherwise, the command is rejected. Also, note that the EIGRP configuration still needs a **network** command that matches the interface referenced by the **neighbor** command.

For example, consider Figure 2-7, which adds a new router (R5) to the internetwork of Figure 2-3. R1 and R5 have a PVC connecting them, with IP addresses and subinterface numbers shown.

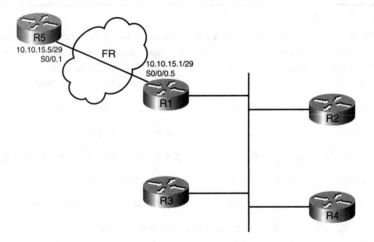

Figure 2-7   *Adding a Branch, with a Static EIGRP Neighbor*

Example 2-9 shows the configuration on both R1 and R5 to use static neighbor definitions. Of note, R1's **neighbor** command refers to R5's IP address on their common subnet (10.10.15.5), with R1's local interface (S0/0/0.5). R5 lists the reverse, with R1's 10.10.15.1 IP address, and R5's local S0/0.1 interface. Also note that both routers have a **network** command that references network 10.0.0.0, and both routers do advertise about subnet 10.10.15.0/29.

Example 2-9   *Static EIGRP Neighborship Between R1 and R5*

```
! New configuration on router R1
R1#show running-config
! lines omitted
router eigrp 9
 network 172.16.0.0
 network 10.0.0.0
 no auto-summary
 neighbor 10.10.15.5 Serial0/0/0.5
! R5's new config added to support the neighbor
R5#show running-config
! lines omitted
router eigrp 9
 network 10.0.0.0
 no auto-summary
 neighbor 10.10.15.1 Serial0/0.1
! Back to R1
R1#show ip eigrp neighbors detail
IP-EIGRP neighbors for process 9
H  Address               Interface      Hold Uptime   SRTT  RTO  Q   Seq
                                        (sec)         (ms)       Cnt Num
3  10.10.15.5            Se0/0/0.5       10 00:00:51   15  200  0   2
   Static neighbor
   Version 12.4/1.2, Retrans: 0, Retries: 0
2  172.16.1.2            Fa0/1           11 00:02:57    3  200  0   25
   Version 12.4/1.2, Retrans: 1, Retries: 0
1  172.16.1.3            Fa0/1           10 00:03:45    5  200  0   21
   Version 12.4/1.2, Retrans: 0, Retries: 0
0  172.16.1.4            Fa0/1           13 00:03:45    5  200  0   18
```

The **show ip eigrp neighbors** command does not identify a neighbor as static, but the **show ip eigrp neighbors detail** command does. Example 2-9 shows the more detailed output near the end, with the designation of 10.10.15.5 (R5) as a static neighbor.

Caveat When Using EIGRP Static Neighbors

IOS changes how it processes EIGRP packets on any interface referenced by an EIGRP **neighbor** command. Keeping in mind the design goal for this feature—to reduce multicasts—IOS disables all EIGRP multicast packet processing on an interface when an EIGRP **neighbor** command has been configured. For example, in Example 2-9, R1's S0/0/0.5 subinterface will not process EIGRP multicast packets any more as a result of R1's **neighbor 10.10.15.5 Serial0/0/0.5** EIGRP subcommand.

Because of the operation of the EIGRP **neighbor** command, if at least one EIGRP static neighbor is defined on an interface, no dynamic neighbors can be either discovered or continue to work if already discovered. For example, again in Figure 2-7 and Example 2-9, if R1 added a **neighbor 172.16.1.5 FastEthernet0/1** EIGRP subcommand, R1 would lose its current neighborships with Routers R2, R3, and R4.

Configuration Settings That Could Prevent Neighbor Relationships

Some of the configuration settings already mentioned in this chapter, when configured incorrectly, may prevent EIGRP neighborships. This section summarizes those settings, and introduces a few other configuration settings that can prevent neighbor relationships. The list of items that must match—and that do not have to match—can be a useful place to start troubleshooting neighbor initialization problems in real life, and to troubleshoot neighborship problems for Sim questions on the CCNP ROUTE exam.

Table 2-4 lists the neighbor requirements for both EIGRP and OSPF. (OSPF is included here just as a frame of reference for those more familiar with OSPF; this information will be repeated in Chapter 5, "OSPF Overview and Neighbor Relationships," which discusses OSPF neighborship requirements.) Following the table, the next few pages examine some of these settings for EIGRP.

Table 2-4   *Neighbor Requirements for EIGRP and OSPF*

Requirement	EIGRP	OSPF
The routers must be able to send/receive IP packets to one another.	Yes	Yes
Interfaces' primary IP addresses must be in same subnet.	Yes	Yes
Must not be passive on the connected interface.	Yes	Yes
Must use the same ASN (EIGRP) or process-ID (OSPF) on the **router** configuration command.	Yes	No
Hello interval/timer, plus either the Hold (EIGRP) or Dead (OSPF) timer, must match.	No	Yes
Must pass neighbor authentication (if configured).	Yes	Yes
Must be in same area.	N/A	Yes
IP MTU must match.	No	Yes
K-values (used in metric calculation) must match.	Yes	N/A
Router IDs must be unique.	No[1]	Yes

[1]Duplicate EIGRP RIDs do not prevent routers from becoming neighbors, but it can cause problems when adding external EIGRP routes to the routing table.

Going through Table 2-4 sequentially, the first two items (highlighted) relate to IP connectivity. Two routers must be able to send and receive IP packets with each other. Additionally, the primary IP address on the interfaces—in other words, the IP address configured *without* the secondary keyword on the **ip address** command—must be in the same subnet.

Note: It should not matter for CCNP ROUTE, but possibly for CCIE: EIGRP's rules about neighbor IP addresses being in the same subnet are less exact than OSPF. OSPF requires matching subnet numbers and masks. EIGRP just asks the question of whether the neighbor's IP address is in the range of addresses for the subnet as known to the local router. For example, two routers with addresses of 10.1.1.1/24 (range 10.1.1.1–10.1.1.254) and 10.1.1.2/30 (range 10.1.1.1–10.1.1.2) would actually allow EIGRP neighborship, because each router believes the neighbor's IP address to be in the same subnet as the local router.

The next four items in Table 2-4 (unhighlighted)—passive interfaces, matching the EIGRP ASN number, allowing mismatching Hello/Hold Timers, and authentication—have already been covered in this chapter, and do not require any further discussion.

The next two (highlighted) items in the table—matching the IP MTU and matching OSPF areas—do not prevent EIGRP neighborships. These topics, are requirements for OSPF neighborship and will be discussed in Chapter 5.

Finally, the last two items (unhighlighted) in the table (K-values and router-id) each require more than a cursory discussion for EIGRP and will be explained in the upcoming pages.

Configuring EIGRP Metric Components (K-values)

EIGRP calculates its integer metric, by default, using a formula that uses constraining bandwidth and cumulative delay. You can change the formula to use link reliability, link load, and even disable the use of bandwidth and/or delay. To change the formula, an engineer can configure five weighting constants, called *k-values*, which are represented in the metric calculation formula as constants k1, k2, k3, k4, and k5.

From a design perspective, Cisco strongly recommends against using link load and link reliability in the EIGRP metric calculation. Most shops that use EIGRP never touch the k-values at all. However, in labs, it can be useful to disable the use of bandwidth from the metric calculation, because that simplifies the metric math, and makes it easier to learn the concepts behind EIGRP.

The mechanics of setting these values (with the **metric weights** EIGRP subcommand) is covered in Chapter 3, in the "Metric Weights (K-values)" section. This command sets 5 variables (k1 through k5), each of which weights the metric calculation formula more or less heavily for various parts of the formula.

Mismatched k-value settings prevent two routers from becoming neighbors. Thankfully, determining if such a mismatch exists is easy. When a router receives an EIGRP Hello with mismatched K-values (as compared to itself), the router issues a log message stating that a k-value mismatch exists. You can also examine the values either by looking at running configuration, or look for the k-values listed in the output of the **show ip protocols** command, as shown in Example 2-10.

Example 2-10 *Mismatched K-values*

```
R2(config)#router eigrp 1
R2(config-router)#metric weights 0 1 0 1 1 0
R2(config-router)#end
Feb 23 18:48:21.599: %DUAL-5-NBRCHANGE: IP-EIGRP(0) 1: Neighbor 10.1.12.1
(Serial0/0/1) is down: metric changed
R2#
Feb 23 18:48:24.907: %DUAL-5-NBRCHANGE: IP-EIGRP(0) 1: Neighbor 10.1.12.1
(Serial0/0/1) is down: K-value mismatch
R2#show ip protocols
Routing Protocol is "eigrp 1"
  Outgoing update filter list for all interfaces is not set
  Incoming update filter list for all interfaces is not set
  Default networks flagged in outgoing updates
  Default networks accepted from incoming updates
  EIGRP metric weight K1=1, K2=0, K3=1, K4=1, K5=0

! lines omitted for brevity
```

EIGRP Router-ID

EIGRP uses a concept of a representing each router with a router ID (RID). The EIGRP RID is a 32-bit number, represented in dotted decimal. Each router determines its RID when the EIGRP process starts, using the same general rules as does OSPF for determining the OSPF RID, as follows:

Step 1. Use the configured value (using the **eigrp router-id** *a.b.c.d* EIGRP subcommand).

Step 2. Use the highest IPv4 address on an up/up loopback interface.

Step 3. Use the highest IPv4 address on an up/up non-loopback interface.

Although EIGRP does require each router to have an RID, the actual value is of little practical importance. The EIGRP **show** commands seldom list the RID value, and unlike for the OSPF RID, engineers do not need to know each router's EIGRP RID to interpret the EIGRP topology database. Additionally, although it is best to make EIGRP RIDs unique, duplicate RIDs do not prevent routers from becoming neighbors.

The only time the value of EIGRP RIDs matters is when injecting external routes into EIGRP. In that case, the routers injecting the external routes must have unique RIDs to avoid confusion.

Neighborship over WANs

EIGRP configuration and neighborship rules do not differ when comparing typical LAN and typical WAN technologies. However, some design and operational differences exist, particularly regarding which routers become neighbors with which other routers. This short section closes the EIGRP neighbor discussion with a brief look at Frame Relay, MPLS VPNs, and Metro Ethernet as implemented with Virtual Private LAN Service (VPLS).

Neighborship on Frame Relay

Frame Relay provides a Layer 2 WAN service. Each router connects to the service using a physical serial link, called a Frame Relay access link. The provider then creates logical connections, called *permanent virtual circuits (PVCs)*, which is a logical path between a pair of routers connected to the Frame Relay service. Any pair of routers that connect to the ends of a Frame Relay PVC can send Frame Relay frames to each other, IP packets, and they can become EIGRP neighbors. Figure 2-8 shows a typical case, with R1 as a central-site router, and R2, R3, and R4 acting as branch routers.

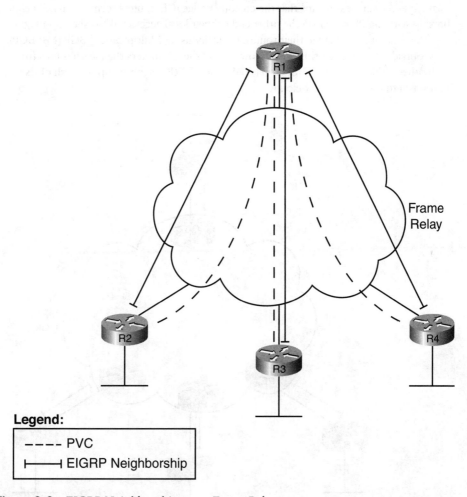

Figure 2-8 *EIGRP Neighborships over Frame Relay*

Figure 2-8 shows EIGRP neighborships, but note that all routers can learn all routes in the internetwork, even though not all routers become neighbors. The neighborships can only form when a PVC exists between the two routers.

Neighborship on MPLS VPN

Multiprotocol Label Switching (MPLS) Virtual Private Networks (VPNs) create a WAN service that has some similarities but many differences when compared to Frame Relay. The customer routers connect to the service, often times with serial links, but other times with Frame Relay PVCs or with Ethernet. The service itself is a Layer 3 service, forwarding IP packets through the cloud. As a result, no pre-defined PVCs need exist between the customer routers. Additionally, the service uses routers at the edge of the service provider cloud—generically called provider edge (PE) routers—and these routers are Layer 3 aware.

That Layer 3 awareness means that the customer edge (CE) routers form an EIGRP neighborship with the PE router on the other end of their local access link, as shown in Figure 2-9. The PE routers exchange their routes, typically using Multiprotocol BGP (MP-BGP), a topic outside the scope of this book. However, all the CE routers then learn routes from each other, although each CE router has only one EIGRP neighborship for each of its connections into the MPLS VPN cloud.

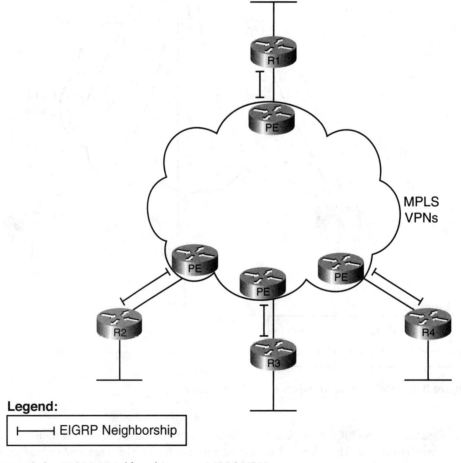

Figure 2-9   *EIGRP Neighborships over MPLS VPN*

Neighborship on Metro Ethernet

The term *Metropolitan Ethernet (MetroE)* represents a range of Layer 2 WAN services in which the CE device connects to the WAN service using some form of Ethernet. Because MetroE provides a Layer 2 Ethernet service, the service delivers an Ethernet frame sent by one customer router to one other customer router (for unicast frames), or to many other routers (for multicast or broadcast frames).

MetroE encompasses several underlying technologies to create the service. Of note for the purposes of this book are the Virtual Private Wire Service (VPWS) and the Virtual Private LAN Service (VPLS). Both technical specifications allow for connections using Ethernet links, with the service forwarding Ethernet frames. VPWS focuses on point-to-point topologies, whereas VPLS supports multipoint, approximating the concept of the entire WAN service acting like one large Ethernet switch. Because it is a Layer 2 service, MetroE does not have any Layer 3 awareness, and the customer routers (typically referenced as with the more general service provider term *customer premise equipment*, or CPE) see the MetroE service as a VLAN. Because the customer routers connect to the service as a VLAN, all the routers connected to the service can become EIGRP neighbors, as shown in Figure 2-10.

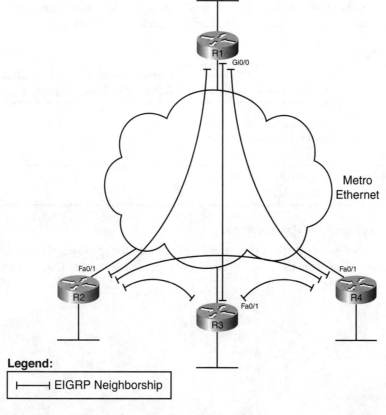

Figure 2-10   *EIGRP Neighborships over Metro Ethernet*

Exam Preparation Tasks

Planning Practice

The CCNP ROUTE exam expects test takers to be able to review design documents, create implementation plans, and create verification plans. This section provides some exercises that may help you to take a step back from the minute details of the topics in this chapter so that you can think about the same technical topics from the planning perspective.

For each planning practice table, simply complete the table. Note that any numbers in parentheses represent the number of options listed for each item in the solutions in Appendix F, "Completed Planning Practice Tables," which you can find on the CD-ROM accompanying this book.

Design Review Table

Table 2-5 lists several design goals related to this chapter. If these design goals were listed in a design document, and you had to take that document and develop an implementation plan, what implementation options come to mind? For any configuration items, a general description can be used, without concern about the specific parameters.

Table 2-5   *Design Review*

Design Goal	Possible Implementation Choices Covered in This Chapter
Improve EIGRP convergence.	
Implement EIGRP on each router so that neighborships are formed (2).	
Limit neighborship formation on interfaces matched with an EIGRP network command (3).	

Implementation Plan Peer Review Table

Table 2-6 shows a list of questions that others might ask, or that you might think about, during a peer review of another network engineer's implementation plan. Complete the table by answering the questions.

Table 2-6 *Notable Questions from This Chapter to Consider During an Implementation Plan Peer Review*

Question	Answer
What happens on a router interface on which an EIGRP **network** command matches the interface? (2)	
What configuration settings prevent EIGRP neighbor discovery on an EIGRP-enabled interface? (2)	
What configuration settings prevent any neighborships on an EIGRP-enabled interface?	
What settings do potential neighbors check before becoming EIGRP neighbors? (5)	
What settings that you might think would impact EIGRP neighbor relationships actually do not prevent neighborship? (3)	
What issues typically arise when the design calls for the use of EIGRP authentication key chains with lifetime settings? (2)	

Create an Implementation Plan Table

To practice skills useful when creating your own EIGRP implementation plan, list in Table 2-7 configuration commands related to the configuration of the following features. You may want to record your answers outside the book, and set a goal to complete this table (and others like it) from memory during your final reviews before taking the exam.

Table 2-7 *Implementation Plan Configuration Memory Drill*

Feature	Configuration Commands/Notes
Enabling EIGRP on interfaces	
Setting Hello and Hold Timers	
EIGRP authentication	
Passive interfaces	
Static EIGRP neighbors	
K-values	
EIGRP router ID	

Choose Commands for a Verification Plan Table

To practice skills useful when creating your own EIGRP verification plan, list in Table 2-8 all commands that supply the requested information. You may want to record your answers outside the book, and set a goal to complete this table (and others like it) from memory during your final reviews before taking the exam.

Table 2-8   *Verification Plan Memory Drill*

Information Needed	Command
Which routes have been added to the IP routing table by EIGRP?	
All routes in a router's routing table.	
The specific route for a single destination address or subnet.	
A list of all (both static and dynamically discovered) EIGRP neighbors.	
Notation of whether a neighbor was dynamically discovered or statically configured.	
Lists statistics regarding the numbers of EIGRP messages sent and received by a router.	
List interfaces on which EIGRP has been enabled (by virtue of the EIGRP **network** command).	
List the number of EIGRP peers known via a particular interface.	
The elapsed time since a neighborship was formed.	
The parameters of any EIGRP **network** commands.	
The configured Hello timer for an interface.	
The configured Hold Timer for an interface.	
The current actual Hold Timer for a neighbor.	
A router's EIGRP ASN.	
A list of EIGRP passive interfaces.	
A list of nonpassive EIGRP interfaces.	
The currently used EIGRP authentication key, when sending EIGRP packets.	
The currently used EIGRP authentication key, when receiving EIGRP packets.	
Lists EIGRP K-values.	
Lists traffic statistics about EIGRP.	
A router's EIGRP Router ID.	

Review All the Key Topics

Review the most important topics from inside the chapter, noted with the key topics icon in the outer margin of the page. Table 2-9 lists a reference of these key topics and the page numbers on which each is found.

Table 2-9 *Key Topics for Chapter 2*

Key Topic Element	Description	Page Number
List	Configuration step review for basic EIGRP configuration	23
Table 2-2	Key EIGRP verification commands	26
Table 2-3	Summary of EIGRP features and facts	31
List	Methods of disallowing EIGRP neighborships on an interface, while still advertising the connected subnet	37
Step list	Configuration checklist for EIGRP authentication	40
Figure 2-6	Conceptual view of which keys are used by EIGRP authentication based on timeframe	41
List	EIGRP authentication troubleshooting hints	43
Table 2-4	List of items that may impact the formation of EIGRP neighborships	46
List	Rules for choosing an EIGRP Router ID	48

Complete the Tables and Lists from Memory

Print a copy of Appendix D, "Memory Tables," (found on the CD), or at least the section for this chapter, and complete the tables and lists from memory. Appendix E, "Memory Tables Answer Key," also on the CD, includes completed tables and lists to check your work.

Define Key Terms

Define the following key terms from this chapter, and check your answers in the glossary.

K-value, neighborship, Hello interval, Hold Timer, passive interface

This chapter covers the following subjects:

Building the EIGRP Topology Table: This section discusses how a router seeds its local EIGRP topology table, and how neighboring EIGRP routers exchange topology information.

Building the IP Routing Table: This section explains how routers use EIGRP topology data to choose the best routes to add to their local routing tables.

Optimizing EIGRP Convergence: This section examines the items that have an impact on how fast EIGRP converges for a given route.

CHAPTER 3

EIGRP Topology, Routes, and Convergence

EIGRP, like OSPF, uses three major branches of logic, each of which populates a different table. EIGRP begins by forming neighbor relationships and listing those relationships in the EIGRP neighbor table (as described in Chapter 2, "EIGRP Overview and Neighbor Relationships"). EIGRP then exchanges topology information with these same neighbors, with newly learned information being added to the router's EIGRP topology table. Finally, each router processes the EIGRP topology table to choose the currently best IP routes, adding those IP routes to the IP routing table.

This chapter moves from the first major branch (neighborships, as covered in Chapter 2) to the second and third branches: EIGRP topology and EIGRP routes. To that end, the first major section of this chapter describes the protocol used by EIGRP to exchange the topology information and details exactly what information EIGRP puts in its messages between routers. The next major section shows how EIGRP examines the topology data to then choose the currently best route for each prefix. The final section of this chapter examines how to optimize the EIGRP convergence processes so that when the topology does change, the routers in the internetwork quickly converge to the then-best routes.

"Do I Know This Already?" Quiz

The "Do I Know This Already?" quiz allows you to assess if you should read the entire chapter. If you miss no more than one of these nine self-assessment questions, you might want to move ahead to the "Exam Preparation Tasks." Table 3-1 lists the major headings in this chapter and the "Do I Know This Already?" quiz questions covering the material in those headings, so you can assess your knowledge of these specific areas. The answers to the "Do I Know This Already?" quiz appear in Appendix A.

Table 3-1 *"Do I Know This Already?" Foundation Topics Section-to-Question Mapping*

Foundations Topics Section	Questions
Building the EIGRP Topology Table	1-3
Building the IP Routing Table	4–7
Optimizing EIGRP Convergence	8, 9

1. Which of the following are methods EIGRP uses to initially populate (seed) its EIGRP topology table, before learning topology data from neighbors? (Choose two.)

   a. By adding all subnets listed by the **show ip route connected** command

   b. By adding the subnets of working interfaces over which static neighbors have been defined

   c. By adding subnets redistributed on the local router from another routing source

   d. By adding all subnets listed by the **show ip route static** command

2. Which of the following are both advertised by EIGRP in the Update message and included in the formula for calculating the integer EIGRP metric? (Choose two.)

   a. Jitter

   b. Delay

   c. MTU

   d. Reliability

3. Router R1 uses S0/0 to connect via a T/1 to the Frame Relay service. Five PVCs terminate on the serial link. Three PVCs (101, 102, and 103) are configured on subinterface S0/0.1, and one each (104 and 105) are on S0/0.2 and S0/0.3. The configuration shows no configuration related to EIGRP WAN bandwidth control, and the **bandwidth** command is not configured at all. Which of the following is true about how IOS tries to limit EIGRP's use of bandwidth on S0/0?

   a. R1 limits EIGRP to around 250Kbps on DLCI 102.

   b. R1 limits EIGRP to around 250Kbps on DLCI 104.

   c. R1 limits EIGRP to around 150Kbps on every DLCI.

   d. R1 does not limit EIGRP because no WAN bandwidth control has been configured.

4. The output of **show ip eigrp topology** on Router R1 shows the following output, which is all the output related to subnet 10.11.1.0/24. How many feasible successor routes does R1 have for 10.11.1.0/24?

```
P 10.11.1.0/24, 2 successors, FD is 2172419
        via 10.1.1.2 (2172423/28167), Serial0/0/0.1
        via 10.1.1.6 (2172423/28167), Serial0/0/0.2
```

   a. 0

   b. 1

   c. 2

   d. 3

5. A network design shows that R1 has four different possible paths from itself to the Data Center subnets. Which of the following can influence which of those routes become feasible successor routes, assuming that you follow the Cisco recommended practice of not changing metric weights? (Choose two.)

   a. The configuration of EIGRP offset lists

   b. Current link loads

    c. Changing interface delay settings

    d. Configuration of variance

6. Router R1 is three router hops away from subnet 10.1.1.0/24. According to various **show interfaces** commands, all three links between R1 and 10.1.1.0/24 use the following settings: bandwidth: 1000, 500, 100000 and delay: 12000, 8000, 100. Which of the following answers correctly identifies a value that feeds into the EIGRP metric calculation? (Choose two correct answers.)

    a. Bandwidth of 101,500

    b. Bandwidth of about 34,000

    c. Bandwidth of 500

    d. Delay of 1200

    e. Delay of 2010

    f. Delay of 20100

7. Routers R1 and R2 are EIGRP neighbors. R1 has been configured with the **eigrp stub connected** command. Which of the following is true as a result? (Choose two correct answers.)

    a. R1 can learn EIGRP routes from R2, but R2 cannot learn EIGRP routes from R1.

    b. R1 can send IP packets to R2, but R2 cannot send IP packets to R1.

    c. R2 no longer learns EIGRP routes from R1 for routes not connected to R1.

    d. R1 no longer replies to R2's Query messages.

    e. R2 no longer sends to R1 Query messages.

8. A network design shows that R1 has four different possible paths from itself to the Data Center subnets. Which one of the following commands is most likely to show you all the possible next-hop IP addresses for these four possible routes?

    a. show ip eigrp topology

    b. show ip eigrp topology all-links

    c. show ip route eigrp

    d. show ip route eigrp all-links

    e. show ip eigrp topology all-learned

9. Router R1 lists 4 routes for subnet 10.1.1.0/24 in the output of the **show ip eigrp topology all-links** command. The **variance 100** command is configured, but no other related commands are configured. Which of the following rules are true regarding R1's decision of what routes to add to the IP routing table? Note that RD refers to reported distance and FD to feasible distance.

    a. Adds all routes for which the metric is <= 100 * the best metric among all routes

    b. Adds all routes because of the ridiculously high **variance** setting

    c. Adds all successor and feasible successor routes

    d. Adds all successor and feasible successor routes for which the metric is <= 100 * the best metric among all routes

Foundation Topics

Building the EIGRP Topology Table

The overall process of building the EIGRP topology table is relatively straightforward. EIGRP defines some basic topology information about each route for each unique prefix/length (subnet). This basic information includes the prefix, prefix length, metric information, and a few other details. EIGRP neighbors exchange topology information, with each router storing the learned topology information in their respective EIGRP topology table. EIGRP on a given router can then analyze the topology table, or topology database, and choose the best route for each unique prefix/length.

EIGRP uses much simpler topology data than does OSPF, which is a link state protocol that must describe the entire topology of a portion of a network with its topology database. EIGRP, essentially an advanced distance vector protocol, does not need to define nearly as much topology data, nor do EIGRP routers need to run the complex Shortest Path First (SPF) algorithm. This first major section examines the EIGRP topology database, how routers create and flood topology data, and some specific issues related to WAN links.

Seeding the EIGRP Topology Table

Before a router can send EIGRP topology information to a neighbor, that router must have some topology data in its topology table. Routers can, of course, learn about subnets and the associated topology data from neighboring routers. However to get the process started, each EIGRP router needs to add topology data for some prefixes, so it can then advertise these routes to its EIGRP neighbors. A router's EIGRP process adds subnets to its local topology table, without learning the topology data from an EIGRP neighbor, from two sources:

- Prefixes of connected subnets for interfaces on which EIGRP has been enabled on that router using the **network** command

- Prefixes learned by the redistribution of routes into EIGRP from other routing protocols or routing information sources

After a router adds such prefixes to its local EIGRP topology database, that router can then advertise the prefix information, along with other topology information associated with each prefix, to each working EIGRP neighbor. Each router adds any learned prefix information to their topology table, and then that router advertises the new information to other neighbors. Eventually, all routers in the EIGRP domain learn about all prefixes–unless some other feature, such as route summarization or route filtering, alters the flow of topology information.

The Content of EIGRP Update Message

EIGRP uses five basic protocol messages to do its work:

- Hello

- Update

- Query

- Reply

- ACK (acknowledgment)

EIGRP uses two messages as part of the topology data exchange process: Update and Ack. The Update message contains the topology information, whereas the ACK acknowledges receipt of the update packet.

The EIGRP Update message contains the following information:

- Prefix

- Prefix length

- Metric components: bandwidth, delay, reliability, and load

- Nonmetric items: MTU and hop count

Note: Many courses and books over the years have stated that MTU is part of the EIGRP metric. In practice, the MTU has never been part of the metric calculation, although it is included in the topology data for each prefix.

To examine this whole process in more detail, see Figure 3-1 and Figure 3-2. Figure 3-1 shows a portion of an Enterprise network that will be used in several examples in this chapter. Routers B1 and B2 represent typical branch office routers, each with two Frame Relay PVCs connected back to the main site. WAN1 and WAN2 are WAN distribution routers, each of which would normally have dozens or hundreds of PVCs.

The routers in Figure 3-1 have been configured and work. For EIGRP, all routers have been configured with as many defaults as possible, with the only configuration related to EIGRP being the **router eigrp 1** and **network 10.0.0.0** commands on each router.

Next, consider what Router B1 does for its connected route for subnet 10.11.1.0/24, which is located on B1's LAN. B1 matches its Fa0/0 interface IP address (10.11.1.1) due to its **network 10.0.0.0** configuration command. So as mentioned earlier, B1 seeds its own topology table with an entry for this prefix. This topology table entry also lists the interface bandwidth of the associated interface and delay of the associated interface. Using default settings for FastEthernet interfaces, B1 uses a bandwidth of 100,000 Kbps (the same as 100 Mbps) and a delay of 10, meaning 10 tens-of-microseconds. Router B1 also includes a default setting for the load (1) and reliability (255), even though the router, using the default K-value settings, will not use these values in its metric calculations. Finally, B1 adds to the topology database the MTU of the local interface and a hop count of zero because the subnet is connected.

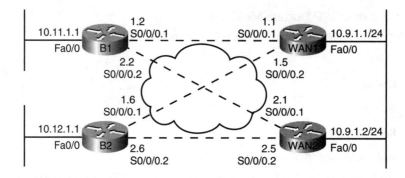

Note: All WAN IP addresses begin with 10.1.

Figure 3-1 *Typical WAN Distribution and Branch Office Design*

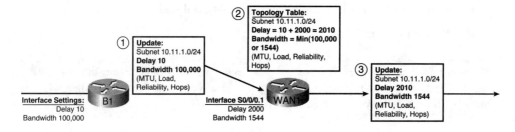

Figure 3-2 *Contents of EIGRP Update Messages*

Now that B1 has added some topology information to its EIGRP topology database, Figure 3-2 shows how B1 propagates the topology information to router WAN1 and beyond.

The steps in Figure 3-2 can be explained as follows:

Step 1.   B1 advertises the prefix (10.11.1.0/24) using an EIGRP Update message. The message includes the four metric components, plus MTU and hop count–essentially the information in B1's EIGRP topology table entry for this prefix.

Step 2.   WAN1 receives the Update message and adds the topology information for 10.11.1.0/24 to its own EIGRP topology table, with these changes:

a. WAN1 considers the interface on which it received the Update (S0/0/0.1) to be the outgoing interface of a potential route to reach 10.11.1.0/24.

b. WAN1 adds the delay of S0/0/0.1 (2000 tens-of-microseconds per Figure 3-2) to the delay listed in the Update message.

c. WAN1 compares the bandwidth of S0/0/0.1 (1544 Kbps per Figure 3-2) to the bandwidth listed in the Update message (100,000 Kbps) and chooses the lower value (1544) as the bandwidth for this route.

   d. WAN1 also updates load (highest value), reliability (lowest value), and MTU
   (lowest value) based on similar comparisons, and adds 1 to the hop count.

Step 3.   WAN1 then sends an Update to its neighbors, with the metric components
   listed in its own topology table.

This example provides a good backdrop to understand how EIGRP uses cumulative delay
and minimum bandwidth in its metric calculation. Note that at Step 2, router WAN1 adds
to the delay value but does not add the bandwidth. For bandwidth, WAN1 simply chooses
the lowest bandwidth, comparing the bandwidth of its own interface (S0/0/0.1) with the
bandwidth listed in the received EIGRP update.

Next, consider this logic on other routers—not shown in the figure—as WAN1 floods this
routing information throughout the Enterprise. WAN1 then sends this topology information to another neighbor, and that router sends the topology data to another, and so on. If
bandwidth of those links was 1544 or higher, the bandwidth setting used by those routers
would remain the same, because each router would see that the routing update's bandwidth (1544 Kbps) was lower than the link's bandwidth. However, each router would add
something to the delay.

As a final confirmation of the contents of this Update process, Example 3-1 shows the details of the EIGRP topology database for prefix 10.11.1.0/24 on both B1 and WAN1.

Example 3-1   *Topology Database Contents for 10.11.1.0/24, on B1 and WAN1*

```
! On Router B1: !!!!!!!!!!!!!!!!!!!!!!!!!!!!!!!!!!!!!!!!!!!!!!!!!
B1#show ip eigrp topology 10.11.1.0/24
IP-EIGRP (AS 1): Topology entry for 10.11.1.0/24
  State is Passive, Query origin flag is 1, 1 Successor(s), FD is 28160
  Routing Descriptor Blocks:
  0.0.0.0 (FastEthernet0/0), from Connected, Send flag is 0x0
      Composite metric is (28160/0), Route is Internal
      Vector metric:
        Minimum bandwidth is 100000 Kbit
        Total delay is 100 microseconds
        Reliability is 255/255
        Load is 1/255
        Minimum MTU is 1500
        Hop count is 0
! On Router WAN1: !!!!!!!!!!!!!!!!!!!!!!!!!!!!!!!!!!!!!!!!!!!!!!!!!!
WAN1#show ip eigrp topology 10.11.1.0/24
IP-EIGRP (AS 1): Topology entry for 10.11.1.0/24
  State is Passive, Query origin flag is 1, 1 Successor(s), FD is 2172416
  Routing Descriptor Blocks:
  10.1.1.2 (Serial0/0/0.1), from 10.1.1.2, Send flag is 0x0
      Composite metric is (2172416/28160), Route is Internal
      Vector metric:
        Minimum bandwidth is 1544 Kbit
        Total delay is 20100 microseconds
```

```
        Reliability is 255/255
        Load is 1/255
        Minimum MTU is 1500
        Hop count is 1
```

The highlighted portions of output match the details shown in Figure 3-2, but with one twist relating to the units on the delay setting. The IOS **delay** command, which lets you set the delay, along with the data stored in the EIGRP topology database, use a unit of tens-of-microsecond. However, the **show interfaces** and **show ip eigrp topology** commands list delay in a unit of microseconds. For example, WAN1's listing of "20100 microseconds" matches the "2010 tens-on-microseconds" shown in Figure 3-2.

The EIGRP Update Process

So far, this chapter has focused on the detailed information EIGRP exchanges with a neighbor about each prefix. This section takes a broader look at the process.

When EIGRP neighbors first become neighbors, they begin exchanging topology information using Update messages using these rules:

Key Topic

- When a neighbor first comes up, the routers exchange full updates, meaning the routers exchange all topology information.

- After all prefixes have been exchanged with a neighbor, the updates cease with that neighbor if no changes occur in the network. There is no periodic reflooding of topology data.

- If something changes–for example, one of the metric components change, links fail, links recover, new neighbors advertise additional topology information–the routers send partial updates about only the prefixes whose status or metric components have changed.

- If neighbors fail and then recover, or new neighbor adjacencies are formed, full updates occur over these adjacencies.

- EIGRP uses Split Horizon rules on most interfaces by default, which impacts exactly which topology data EIGRP sends during both full and partial updates.

Split Horizon, the last item in the list, needs a little more explanation. Split Horizon limits the prefixes that EIGRP advertises out an interface. Specifically, if the currently best route for a prefix lists a particular outgoing interface, Split Horizon means that EIGRP will not include that prefix in the Update sent out that same interface. For example, router WAN1 uses S0/0/0.1 as its outgoing interface for subnet 10.11.1.0/24, so WAN1 would not advertise prefix 10.11.1.0/24 in its Update messages sent out S0/0/0.1.

Note: Route summarization and route filtering, as explained in Chapter 4, "EIGRP Route Summarization and Filtering," also affect which subsets of the topology table are flooded.

To send the Updates, EIGRP uses the *Reliable Transport Protocol (RTP)* to send the EIGRP updates and confirm their receipt. On point-to-point topologies such as serial links, MPLS VPN, and Frame Relay when using point-to-point subinterfaces, the EIGRP Update and ACK messages use a simple process of acknowledging each Update with an ACK. On multiaccess data links, EIGRP typically sends Update messages to multicast address 224.0.0.10 and expects a unicast EIGRP ACK message from each neighbor in reply. RTP manages that process, setting timers so that the sender of an Update waits a reasonable time, but not too long, before deciding whether all neighbors received the Update or whether one or more neighbors did not reply with an ACK.

Although EIGRP relies on the RTP process, network engineers cannot manipulate how it works.

WAN Issues for EIGRP Topology Exchange

With all default settings, after you enable EIGRP on all the interfaces in an internetwork, the topology exchange process typically does not pose any problems. However, a few scenarios exist, particularly on Frame Relay, which can cause problems. This section summarizes two issues and shows the solution.

Split Horizon Default on Frame Relay Multipoint Subinterfaces

IOS support for Frame Relay allows the configuration of IP addresses on the physical serial interface, multipoint subinterfaces, and point-to-point subinterfaces. Additionally, IP packets can be forwarded over a PVC even when the routers on the opposite ends do not have to use the same interface or subinterface type. As a result, many small intricacies exist in the operation of IP and IP routing protocols over Frame Relay, particularly related to default settings on different interface types.

Frame Relay supports several reasonable configuration options using different interfaces and subinterfaces, each meeting different design goals. For instance, if the design includes a few centralized WAN distribution routers, with PVCs connecting each branch router to each distribution router, both distribution and branch routers might use point-to-point subinterface. Such a choice makes the Layer 3 topology simple, with all links acting like point-to-point links from a Layer 3 perspective. This choice also removes issues such as Split Horizon.

In some cases, a design might include a small set of routers that have a full mesh of PVCs connecting each. In this case, multipoint subinterfaces might be used, consuming a single subnet, reducing the consumption of the IP address space. This choice also reduces the number of subinterfaces.

Both options–using point-to-point subinterfaces or using multipoint subinterfaces–have legitimate reasons for being used. However, when using the multipoint subinterface option, a particular EIGRP issue can occur when the following are true:

■ Three or more routers, over Frame Relay, are configured as part of a single subnet.

■ The routers use multipoint interfaces.

■ Either permanently or for a time, a full mesh of PVCs between the routers does not exist.

For example, consider Router WAN1 shown earlier in Figure 3-1 and referenced again in Figure 3-3. In the earlier configurations, the WAN distribution routers and branch routers all used point-to-point subinterfaces and a single subnet per VC. To see the problem raised in this section, consider that same internetwork, but now the engineer has chosen to configure WAN1 to use a multipoint subinterface and a single subnet for WAN1, B1, and B2, as shown in Figure 3-3.

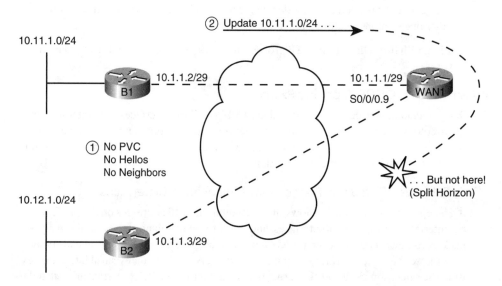

Figure 3-3 *Partial Mesh, Central Sites (WAN1) Uses Multipoint Subinterface*

The first issue to consider in this design is that B1 and B2 will not become EIGRP neighbors with each other, as noted with Step 1 in the figure. EIGRP routers must be reachable using Layer 2 frames before they can exchange EIGRP Hello messages and become EIGRP neighbors. In this case, there is no PVC between B1 and B2. B1 exchanges Hellos with WAN1, and become neighbors, as will B2 with WAN1. However, routers do not forward received EIGRP Hellos, so WAN1 will not receive a Hello from B1 and forward it to B2 or vice versa. In short, although in the same subnet (10.1.1.0/29), B1 and B2 will not become EIGRP neighbors.

The second problem occurs due to Split Horizon logic on Router WAN1, as noted with Step 2 in the figure. As shown with Step 2 in the figure, B1 could advertise its routes to WAN1, and WAN1 could advertise those routes to B2–and vice versa. However, with default settings, WAN1 will not advertise those routes due to its default setting of Split Horizon (a default interface subcommand setting of **ip split-horizon eigrp** *asn*.) As a result, WAN1 receives the Update from B1 on its S0/0/0.9 subinterface, but Split Horizon prevents WAN1 from advertising that topology data to B2 in Updates sent out interface S0/0/0.9, and vice versa.

The solution is somewhat simple–just configure the **no ip split-horizon eigrp** *asn* command on the multipoint subinterface on WAN1. The remote routers, B1 and B2 in this case, still do not become neighbors, but that does not cause a problem by itself. With Split Horizon disabled on WAN1, B1 and B2 learn routes to the other branch's subnets. Example 3-2 lists the complete configuration and the command to disable Split Horizon:

Note: Frame Relay configuration is considered a prerequisite because it is part of the CCNA exam and courses. Example 3-2 uses **frame-relay interface-dlci** commands and relies on Inverse ARP. However, if **frame-relay map** commands were used instead, disabling Inverse ARP, the EIGRP details discussed in this example would remain unchanged.

Example 3-2 *Frame Relay Multipoint Configuration on WAN1*

```
! On Router WAN1: !!!!!!!!!!!!!!!!!!!!!!!!!!!!!!!!!!!!!!!!!!!!!!!
interface Serial0/0/0
 no ip address
 encapsulation frame-relay

interface Serial0/0/0.9 multipoint
 ip address 10.1.1.1 255.255.255.248
 no ip split-horizon eigrp 1
 frame-relay interface-dlci 103
 frame-relay interface-dlci 104
!
router eigrp 1
 network 10.0.0.0
```

Note: The [no] **ip split-horizon** command controls Split Horizon behavior for RIP; the [no] **ip split-horizon eigrp** *asn* command controls Split Horizon behavior for EIGRP.

Displaying the EIGRP Split Horizon state of an interface is an unusually difficult piece of information to find without simply displaying the configuration. By default, IOS enables EIGRP Split Horizon. To find the setting for an interface, look for the presence or absence of the **no ip split-horizon eigrp** command on the configuration. Also, the **debug ip eigrp** command output displays messages stating when prefixes are not advertised out an interface due to split horizon.

EIGRP WAN Bandwidth Control

In a multiaccess WAN, one physical link passes traffic for multiple data link layer destinations. For example, a WAN distribution router connected to many branches using Frame Relay might literally terminate hundreds, or even thousands, of Frame Relay PVCs.

In a nonbroadcast multiaccess (NBMA) medium such as Frame Relay, when a router needs to send EIGRP updates, the Updates cannot be multicasted at Layer 2. So, the router must send a copy of the Update to each reachable neighbor. For a WAN distribution router with many Frame Relay PVCs, the sheer amount of traffic sent over the Frame Relay access link might overload the link.

The EIGRP WAN bandwidth control allows the engineer to protect a multiaccess Frame Relay interface from being overrun with too much EIGRP message traffic. By default, a router sends EIGRP messages out an interface but only up to 50 percent of the bandwidth defined on the interface with the **bandwidth** command. The engineer can adjust this percentage using the **ip bandwidth-percent eigrp** *asn percent* interface/subinterface subcommand. Regardless of the percentage, IOS then limits the rate of sending the EIGRP messages so that the rate is not exceeded. To accomplish this, IOS queues the EIGRP messages in memory, delaying them briefly.

The command to set the bandwidth percentage is simple, but there are a few caveats to keep in mind when trying to limit the bandwidth consumed by EIGRP:

- The IOS default for bandwidth on serial interfaces and subinterfaces is 1544 (Kbps).

- EIGRP limits the consumed bandwidth based on the percentage of interface/ subinterface bandwidth.

- This feature keys on the bandwidth of the interface or subinterface through which the neighbor is reachable, so don't set only the physical interface bandwidth and forget the subinterfaces.

- Recommendation: Set the bandwidth of point-to-point links to the speed of the Committed Information Rate (CIR) of the single PVC on the subinterface.

- General recommendation: Set the bandwidth of multipoint subinterfaces to around the total CIR for all VCs assigned to the subinterface.

- Note that for multipoint subinterfaces, IOS WAN bandwidth control first *divides the subinterface bandwidth by the number of configured PVCs* and then determines the EIGRP percentage based on that number.

For example, consider Figure 3-4, which shows a router with one multipoint subinterface and one point-to-point subinterface. With the configuration shown in Example 3-3, WAN1 uses the following bandwidth, at most, with each neighbor:

- B1, B2, and B3: 20 Kbps (20% of 300Kbps / 3 VCs)

- B4: 30 Kbps (30% of 100 Kbps)

Example 3-3 *Configuration of WAN1, One Multipoint, One Point-to-Point*

```
! On Router WAN1: !!!!!!!!!!!!!!!!!!!!!!!!!!!!!!!!!!!!!!!!!!!!!!!
interface Serial0/0/0.20 multipoint
 ip address 172.16.1.1 255.255.255.240
 frame-relay interface-dlci 201
 frame-relay interface-dlci 202
 frame-relay interface-dlci 203
```

```
    bandwidth 300
     ip bandwidth-percent eigrp 1 20
!
interface Serial0/0/0.21 point-to-point
 ip address 172.16.1.17 255.255.255.252
 frame-relay interface-dlci 221
    bandwidth 100
     ip bandwidth-percent eigrp 1 30
```

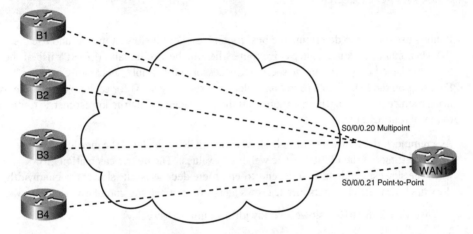

Figure 3-4 *WAN1, One Multipoint, One Point-to-Point*

Building the IP Routing Table

An EIGRP router builds IP routing table entries by processing the data in the topology table. Unlike OSPF, which uses a computationally complex SPF process, EIGRP uses a computationally simple process to determine which, if any, routes to add to the IP routing table for each unique prefix/length. This part of the chapter examines how EIGRP chooses the best route for each prefix/length and then examines several optional tools that can influence the choice of routes to add to the IP routing table.

Calculating the Metrics: Feasible Distance and Reported Distance

The EIGRP topology table entry, for a single prefix/length, lists one or more possible routes. Each possible route lists the various component metric values–bandwidth, delay, and so on. Additionally, for connected subnets, the database entry lists an outgoing interface. For routes not connected to the local router, in addition to an outgoing interface, the database entry also lists the IP address of the EIGRP neighbor that advertised the route.

EIGRP routers calculate an integer metric based on the metric components. Interestingly, an EIGRP router does this calculation both from its own perspective and from the perspective of the next-hop router of the route. The two calculated values are

Key Topic

■ **Feasible Distance (FD):** Integer metric for the route, from the local router's perspective, used by the local router to choose the best route for that prefix.

■ **Reported Distance (RD):** Integer metric for the route, from the neighboring router's perspective (the neighbor that told the local router about the route). Used by the local router when converging to new routes.

Note: Some texts use the term *Advertised Distance (AD)* instead of Reported Distance (RD) as used in this book. Be ready for either term on the CCNP ROUTE exam. However, this book uses RD exclusively.

Routers use the FD to determine the best route, based on the lowest metric, and use the RD when falling back to an alternative route when the best route fails. (EIGRP's use of the RD is explained in the upcoming section "Successor and Feasible Successor Concepts.") Focusing on the FD, when a router has calculated the integer FD for each possible route to reach a single prefix/length, that router can then consider adding the lowest-metric route to the IP routing table.

As a reminder, the following formula shows how EIGRP calculates the metric, assuming default settings of the EIGRP metric weights (K-values). The metric calculation grows when the slowest bandwidth in the end-to-end route decreases (the slower the bandwidth, the worse the metric), and its metric grows (gets worse) when the cumulative delay grows:

Metric = 256 * ((10^7 / slowest-bandwidth) + cumulative-delay)

An example certainly helps in this case. Figure 3-5 repeats some information about the topology exchange process between Routers B1 and WAN1 (refer to Figure 3-1), essentially showing the metric components as sent by B1 to WAN1 (Step 1) and the metric components from WAN1's perspective (Step 2).

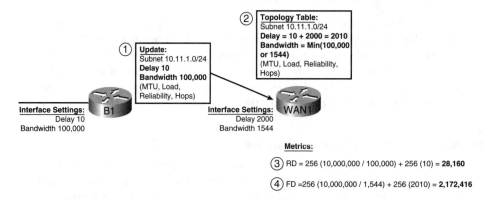

Figure 3-5   *Example Calculation of RD and FD on Router WAN1*

Steps 3 and 4 in Figure 3-5 show WAN1's calculation of the RD and FD for 10.11.1.0/24, respectively. Router WAN1 takes the metric components as received from B1, and plugs them into the formula, to calculate the RD, which is the same integer metric that Router

B1 would have calculated as its FD. Step 4 shows the same formula but with the metric components as listed at Step 2—after the adjustments made on WAN1. Step 4 shows WAN1's FD calculation, which is much larger due to the much lower constraining bandwidth plus the much larger cumulative delay.

WAN1 chooses its best route to reach 10.11.1.0/24 based on the lowest FD among all possible routes. Looking back to the much more detailed Figure 3-1, presumably a couple of other routes might have been possible, but WAN1 happens to choose the route shown in Figure 3-5 as its best route. As a result, WAN1's **show ip route** command lists the FD calculated in Figure 3-5 as the metric for this route, as shown in Example 3-4.

Example 3-4   *Router WAN1's EIGRP Topology and IP Route Information for 10.11.1.0/24*

```
! Below, note that WAN1's EIGRP topology table lists two possible next-hop
! routers: 10.1.1.2 (B1) and 10.9.1.2 (WAN2). The metric for each route,
! the first number in parenthesis, shows that the lower metric route is the one
! through 10.1.1.2 as next-hop. Also note that the metric components
! match Figure 3-5.
!
WAN1#show ip eigrp topo 10.11.1.0/24
IP-EIGRP (AS 1): Topology entry for 10.11.1.0/24
   State is Passive, Query origin flag is 1, 1 Successor(s), FD is 2172416
   Routing Descriptor Blocks:
   10.1.1.2 (Serial0/0/0.1), from 10.1.1.2, Send flag is 0x0
       Composite metric is (2172416/28160), Route is Internal
       Vector metric:
         Minimum bandwidth is 1544 Kbit
         Total delay is 20100 microseconds
         Reliability is 255/255
         Load is 1/255
         Minimum MTU is 1500
         Hop count is 1
   10.9.1.2 (FastEthernet0/0), from 10.9.1.2, Send flag is 0x0
       Composite metric is (2174976/2172416), Route is Internal
       Vector metric:
         Minimum bandwidth is 1544 Kbit
         Total delay is 20200 microseconds
         Reliability is 255/255
         Load is 1/255
         Minimum MTU is 1500
         Hop count is 2
!
! The next command not only lists the IP routing table entry for 10.11.1.0/24,
! it also lists the metric (FD), and components of the metric.
!
WAN1#show ip route 10.11.1.0
Routing entry for 10.11.1.0/24
```

```
       Known via "eigrp 1", distance 90, metric 2172416, type internal
       Redistributing via eigrp 1
       Last update from 10.1.1.2 on Serial0/0/0.1, 00:02:42 ago
       Routing Descriptor Blocks:
       * 10.1.1.2, from 10.1.1.2, 00:02:42 ago, via Serial0/0/0.1
           Route metric is 2172416, traffic share count is 1
           Total delay is 20100 microseconds, minimum bandwidth is 1544 Kbit
           Reliability 255/255, minimum MTU 1500 bytes
           Loading 1/255, Hops 1
    !
    ! Below, the route for 10.11.1.0/24 is again listed, with the metric (FD), and
    ! the same next-hop and outgoing interface information.
    !
    WAN1#show ip route eigrp
         10.0.0.0/8 is variably subnetted, 7 subnets, 2 masks
    D        10.11.1.0/24 [90/2172416] via 10.1.1.2, 00:10:40, Serial0/0/0.1
    D        10.12.1.0/24 [90/2172416] via 10.1.1.6, 00:10:40, Serial0/0/0.2
    D        10.1.2.0/30 [90/2172416] via 10.9.1.2, 00:10:40, FastEthernet0/0
    D        10.1.2.4/30 [90/2172416] via 10.9.1.2, 00:10:40, FastEthernet0/0
```

EIGRP Metric Tuning

EIGRP metrics can be changed using several methods: setting interface bandwidth, setting interface delay, changing the metric calculation formula by configuring k-values, and even by adding to the calculated metric using offset-lists. In practice, the most reasonable and commonly used methods are to set the interface delay and the interface bandwidth. This section examines all the methods, in part so you will know which useful tools exist, and in part to make you aware of some other design issues that then might impact the routes chosen by EIGRP.

Configuring Bandwidth and Delay

The **bandwidth** and **delay** interface subcommands set the bandwidth and delay associated with the interface. The commands themselves require little thought, other than keeping the units straight. The unit for the **bandwidth** command is Kilobits/second, and the **delay** command uses a unit of tens-of-microseconds.

If a design requires that you influence the choice of route by changing bandwidth or delay, setting the delay value is typically the better choice. IOS uses the bandwidth setting of an interface for many other reasons: calculating interface utilization, as the basis for several QoS parameters, and for SNMP statistics reporting. However, the delay setting has little influence on other IOS features besides EIGRP, so the better choice when influencing EIGRP metrics is to tune the delay.

Table 3-2 lists some of the common default values for both bandwidth and delay. As a reminder, **show** commands list the bandwidth in Kbps, which matches the **bandwidth** command, but lists the delay in microseconds, which does not match the tens-of-microseconds unit of the **delay** command.

Table 3-2 *Common Defaults for Bandwidth and Delay*

Interface Type	Bandwidth (Kbps)	Delay (Microseconds)
Serial	1544	20,000
GigE	1,000,000	10
FastE	100,000	100
Ethernet	10,000	1000

Note that on LAN interfaces that can run at different speeds, the bandwidth and delay settings default based on the current actual speed of the interface.

Choosing Bandwidth Settings on WAN Subinterfaces

Frame Relay and Metro Ethernet installations often use an access link with a particular physical sending rate–clock rate if you will–but with the contracted speed, over time, being more or less than the speed of the link. For example, with Frame Relay, the provider may supply a full T1 access link, so configuring **bandwidth 1544** for such an interface is reasonable. However, the subinterfaces have one or more PVCs associated with them, and those PVCs each have Committed Information Rates (CIR) that are typically less than the access link's clock speed. However, the cumulative CIRs for all PVC often exceeds the clock rate of the physical interface. Conversely, MetroE designs use Ethernet access links of 10 Mbps, 100 Mbps, or 1 Gbps actual link speed, but often the business contract limits the amount of traffic to some number below that link speed.

Choosing a useful interface **bandwidth** setting on the subinterfaces in a Frame Relay or MetroE design requires some thought, with most of the motivations for choosing one number or another being unrelated to EIGRP. For example, imagine the network shown in Figure 3-6. Router WAN1 has a single T1 (1.544 Mbps) access link. That interface has one multipoint subinterface, with three PVCs assigned to it. It also has nine other point-to-point subinterfaces, each with a single PVC assigned.

For the sake of discussion, the design in Figure 3-6 oversubscribes the T1 access link off Router WAN1 by a 2:1 factor. Assume all 12 PVCs have a CIR of 256 Kbps, making the total bandwidth for the 12 PVCs roughly 3 Mbps. The design choice to oversubscribe the access link may be reasonable given the statistical chance of all sites sending at the same time.

Now imagine that Router WAN1 has been configured with subinterfaces as shown in the figure:

- S0/0/0.20 - multipoint, 3 PVCs

- S0/0/0.21 through S0/0/0.29 – point-to-point, 1 PVC each

Next, consider the options for setting the **bandwidth** command's value on these 10 subinterfaces. The point-to-point subinterfaces could be set to match the CIR of each PVC (256 Kbps in this example). You could choose to set the bandwidth based on the CIR of all combined PVCs on the multipoint subinterface–in this case, setting **bandwidth 768** on multipoint subinterface s0/0/0.20. However, these bandwidths would total about 3 Mbps–twice the actual speed of WAN1's access link. Alternatively, you could set the various bandwidths so that the total matches the 1.5 Mbps of the access link. Or you could

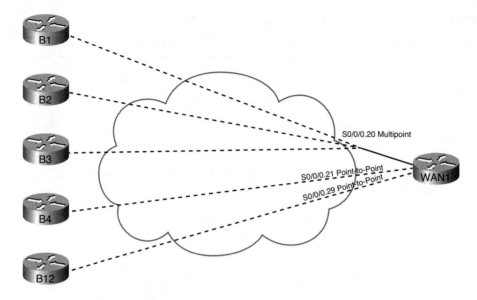

Figure 3-6   *One Multipoint and Nine Point-to-Point Subinterfaces*

split the difference, knowing that during times of low activity to most sites that the sites with active traffic get more than their CIR's worth of capacity anyway.

As mentioned earlier, these bandwidth settings impact much more than EIGRP. The settings impact interface statistics, both in **show** commands and in SNMP reporting. They impact QoS features to some extent as well. Given that the better option for setting EIGRP metrics is to set the interface delay, EIGRP metric tuning may not be the driving force behind the decision as to what bandwidth values to use. However, some installations may change these values over time while trying to find the right compromise numbers for features other than EIGRP. So, you need to be aware that changing those values may result in different EIGRP metrics and impact the choices of best routes.

Similar issues exist on the more modern Layer 2 WAN services like MetroE, particularly with the multipoint design of VPLS. Figure 3-7 shows a design that might exist after migrating the internetwork of Figure 3-6 to VPLS. Router WAN1 has been replaced by a Layer 3 switch, using a Gigabit interface to connect to the VPLS service. The remote sites might use the same routers as before, using a FastEthernet interface, or might be replaced with Layer 3 switch hardware as well.

Concentrating on the mechanics of what happens at the central site, WAN1 might use 802.1Q trunking. With 12 remote sites, WAN1 configures 12 VLAN interfaces, one per VLAN, with a different subnet used for the connection to each remote branch. Such a design, from a Layer 3 perspective, looks like the age-old Frame Relay design with a point-to-point link from the main site to each remote branch.

Additionally, the VPLS business contract might specify that WAN1 cannot send more than 200 Mbps of traffic into the VPLS cloud, with the excess being discarded by the VPLS service. To prevent unnecessary discards, the engineer likely configures a feature called *shaping*, which slows down the traffic leaving the Gi0/1 interface of WAN1 (regardless of VLAN). To meet the goal of 200 Mbps, WAN1 would send only part of the

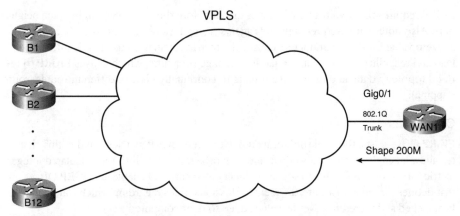

Figure 3-7 *VPLS Service–Issues in Choosing Bandwidth*

time–in this case averaging a sending rate of 1/5th of the time–so that the average rate is 1/5th of 1 Gbps, or 200 Mbps.

Of note with the shaping function, the shaping feature typically limits the cumulative traffic on the interface, not per VLAN (branch). As a result, if the only traffic waiting to be sent by WAN1 happens to be destined for branch B1, WAN1 sends 200 MBps of traffic to just branch B1.

Pulling the discussion back around to EIGRP, as with Frame Relay, other design and implementation needs may drive the decision to set or change the bandwidth on the associated interfaces. In this case, Layer 3 switch WAN1 probably has 12 VLAN interfaces. Each VLAN interface can be set with a bandwidth that influences EIGRP route choices. Should this setting be 1/12th of 1 Gbps, which is the speed at which the bits are actually sent? 1/12th of 200 Mbps, the shaping rate? Or knowing that a site might get most or all of that 200 Mbps for some short period of time, should the bandwidth be set somewhere in between? As with Frame Relay, there is no set answer; for the sake of EIGRP, be aware that changes to the bandwidth settings impact the EIGRP metrics.

Metric Weights (K-values)

Engineers can change the EIGRP metric calculation by configuring the weightings (also called k-values) applied to the EIGRP metric calculation. To configure new values, use the **metric weights** *tos k1 k2 k3 k4 k5* command in EIGRP configuration mode. To configure this command, configure any integer 0–255 inclusive for the five k-values. By default, k1 = k3 = 1, and the others default to 0. The **tos** parameter has only one valid value, 0, and can be otherwise ignored.

The full EIGRP metric formula is as follows. Note that some items reduce to 0 if the corresponding k-values are also set to 0. The listed formula is correct with default K-values. However, if K5 were set to 1 instead of the default of 0 the formula show would be incorrect. The last fraction, K5/(reliability+K4), would then be multiplied by the result from the rest of the formula.

$$256*\left[K1\left(\frac{10^7}{BW}\right) + \frac{K2\left(\frac{10^7}{BW}\right)}{(256 - \text{Load})} + K3(\text{delay}) + \frac{K5}{(\text{Reliability} + K4)}\right]$$

EIGRP requires that two routers' k-values match before those routers can become neighbors. Also note that Cisco recommends against using k-values k2, k4, and k5, because a nonzero value for these parameters causes the metric calculation to include interface load and reliability. The load and reliability change over time, which causes EIGRP to reflood topology data, and may cause routers to continually choose different routes (route flapping).

Offset Lists

EIGRP Offset Lists, the final tool for manipulating the EIGRP metrics listed in this chapter, allow an engineer to simply add a value–an offset, if you will-to the calculated integer metric for a given prefix. To do so, an engineer can create and enable an EIGRP Offset List that defines the value to add to the metric, plus some rules regarding which routes should be matched and therefore have the value added to their computed FD.

An Offset List can perform the following functions:

- Match prefixes/prefix lengths using an IP ACL, so that the offset is applied only to routes matched by the ACL with a permit clause

- Match the direction of the Update message, either sent (out) or received (in)

- Match the interface on which the Update is sent or received

- Set the integer metric added to the calculation for both the FD and RD calculations for the route

The configuration itself uses the following command in EIGRP configuration mode, in addition to any referenced IP ACLs:

offset-list {*access-list-number* ¦ *access-list-name*} {**in** ¦ **out**} **offset** [*interface-type interface-number*]

For example, consider again branch office Router B1 in Figure 3-1, with its connection to both WAN1 and WAN2 over a Frame Relay network. Formerly, WAN1 calculated a metric of 2,172,416 for its route, through B1, to subnet 10.11.1.0/24. (Refer to Figure 3-5 for the math behind WAN1's calculation of its route to 10.11.1.0/24.) Router B1 also calculated a value of 28,160 for the RD of that same direct route. Example 3-5 shows the addition of an offset on WAN1, for received updates from Router B1.

Example 3-5 *Inbound Offset of 3 on WAN1, for Updates Received on S0/0/0.1*

```
WAN1(config)#access-list 11 permit 10.11.1.0
WAN1(config)#router eigrp 1
WAN1(config-router)#offset-list 11 in 3 Serial0/0/0.1
WAN1(config-router)#end

Mar  2 11:34:36.667: %DUAL-5-NBRCHANGE: IP-EIGRP(0) 1: Neighbor 10.1.1.2
(Serial0/0/0.1) is resync: peer graceful-restart
WAN1#show ip eigrp topo 10.11.1.0/24
IP-EIGRP (AS 1): Topology entry for 10.11.1.0/24
  State is Passive, Query origin flag is 1, 1 Successor(s), FD is 2172416
```

```
     Routing Descriptor Blocks:
     10.1.1.2 (Serial0/0/0.1), from 10.1.1.2, Send flag is 0x0
         Composite metric is (2172419/28163), Route is Internal
         Vector metric:
           Minimum bandwidth is 1544 Kbit
           Total delay is 20100 microseconds
           Reliability is 255/255
           Load is 1/255
           Minimum MTU is 1500
           Hop count is 1
! output omitted for brevity
```

The configuration has two key elements: ACL 11 and the **offset-list** command. ACL 11
matches prefix 10.11.1.0, and that prefix only, with a permit clause. The **offset-list 11 in 3
s0/0/0.1** command tells Router WAN1 to examine all EIGRP Updates received on S0/0/0.1,
and if prefix 10.11.1.0 is found, add 3 to the computed FD and RD for that prefix.

The **show ip eigrp topology 10.11.1.0/24** command in Example 3-5 shows that the FD
and RD, highlighted in parentheses, are now each three larger as compared with the earlier
metrics.

Next, continuing this same example, Router B1 has now been configured to add an offset
(4) in its sent updates to all routers, but for prefix 10.11.1.0/24 only.

Example 3-6 *Outbound Offset of 4 on B1, for Updates Sent to All Neighbors, 10.11.1.0/24*

```
B1(config)#access-list 12 permit 10.11.1.0
B1(config)#router eigrp 1
B1(config-router)#offset-list 12 out 4
B1(config-router)#end
B1#
! Back to router WAN1
WAN1#show ip eigrp topology
IP-EIGRP Topology Table for AS(1)/ID(10.9.1.1)

Codes: P - Passive, A - Active, U - Update, Q - Query, R - Reply,
       r - reply Status, s - sia Status
```

```
P 10.11.1.0/24, 1 successors, FD is 2172419
        via 10.1.1.2 (2172423/28167), Serial0/0/0.1
! lines omitted for brevity
```

Note that the metrics, both FD and RD, are now four larger than in Example 3-5.

Optimizing EIGRP Convergence

The previous major section of this chapter focused on how EIGRP calculates metrics and how to change that metric calculation. However, that section discussed only one motivation for changing the metric: to make a router pick one route instead of another. This section, which focuses on optimizing the EIGRP convergence process, discusses another reason for choosing to manipulate the EIGRP metric calculations: faster convergence.

EIGRP converges very quickly, but EIGRP does not achieve the most optimal fast convergence times in all conditions. One design goal might be to tune EIGRP configuration settings so that EIGRP uses the faster convergence methods for as many routes as possible, and when not possible, that EIGRP converge as quickly as it can without introducing routing loops. As a result, routers might converge in some cases in a second instead of tens of seconds (from the point of a router realizing that a route has failed).

For those of you who have not thought about EIGRP convergence before now, you must first get a comfortable understanding of the concept of EIGRP Feasible Successors–the first topic in this section. Following that, the text examines the EIGRP query process. This section ends with EIGRP load balancing, which both allows spreading the load across multiple routes in addition to improving EIGRP convergence.

Fast Convergence to Feasible Successors

Earlier in this chapter, under the heading "Calculating the Metrics: Feasible Distance and Reported Distance," the text explains how a router, for each possible route, calculates two metric values. One value is the *feasible distance* (FD), which is the metric from that router's perspective. The other metic is the *reported distance* (RD), which is the integer metric from the perspective of the next-hop router.

EIGRP routers use the RD value when determining if a possible route can be considered to be a loop-free backup route called a *feasible successor*. This section explains the concepts and shows how to confirm the existence or nonexistence of such routes.

Successor and Feasible Successor Concepts

For each prefix/prefix length, when multiple possible routes exist, the router chooses the route with the smallest integer metric (smallest FD). EIGRP defines each such route as the *successor route* for that prefix, and EIGRP defines the next-hop router in such a route as the *successor*. EIGRP then creates an IP route for this prefix, with the successor as the next-hop router, and places that route into the IP routing table.

If more than one possible route exists for a given prefix/prefix length, the router examines these other (non-successor) routes and asks this question: Can any of these routes be used immediately if the currently best route fails, without causing a routing loop? EIGRP runs a simple algorithm to identify which routes could be used without causing a routing loop, and EIGRP keeps these loop-free backup routes in its topology table. Then, if the successor route (the best route) fails, EIGRP then immediately uses the best of these alternate loop-free routes for that prefix.

EIGRP calls these alternative, immediately usable, loop-free routes *feasible* successor routes, because they can feasibly be used as a new successor route when the current successor route fails. The next-hop router of such a route is called the *feasible successor*.

Note: In general conversation, the term *successor* may refer to the route or specifically to the next-hop router. Likewise, the term *feasible successor* may refer to the route, or the next-hop router, of an alternative route.

A router determines if a route is a feasible successor based on the *feasibility condition*, defined as follows:

> If a non-successor route's RD is less than the FD, the route is a feasible successor route.

Although technically correct, the preceding definition is much more understandable with an example as shown in Figure 3-8. The figure illustrates how EIGRP figures out which routes are feasible successors for Subnet 1.

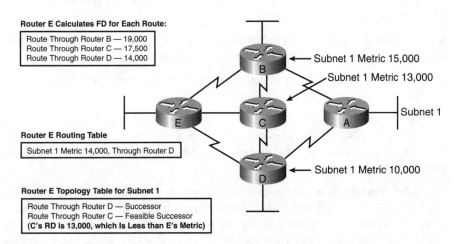

Figure 3-8   *Successors and Feasible Successors with EIGRP*

In Figure 3-8, Router E learns three routes to Subnet 1, from Routers B, C, and D. After calculating each route's metric, Router E finds that the route through Router D has the lowest metric. Router E adds this successor route for Subnet 1 to its routing table, as shown. The FD in this case for this successor route is 14,000.

EIGRP decides if a route can be a feasible successor if the reported distance for that route (the metric as calculated on that neighbor) is less than its own best computed metric (the FD). When that neighbor has a lower metric for its route to the subnet in question, that route is said to have met the *feasibility condition*.

For example, Router E computes a metric (FD) of 14,000 on its successor route (through Router D). Router C's computed metric–E's RD for this alternate router through Router C–is 13,000, which is lower than E's FD (14,000). As a result, E knows that C's best route for this subnet could not possible point toward router E, so Router E believes that its route, to Subnet 1, through Router C, would not cause a loop. As a result, Router E marks its topology table entry for the route through Router C as a feasible successor route.

Conversely, E's RD for the route through Router B, to Subnet 1, is 15,000, which is larger than Router E's FD of 14,000. So, this alternative route does not meet the feasibility condition, so Router E does not consider the route through Router B a feasible successor route.

If the route to Subnet 1 through Router D fails, Router E can immediately put the route through Router C into the routing table without fear of creating a loop. Convergence occurs almost instantly in this case. However, if both C and D fail, E would not have a feasible successor route, and would have to do additional work, as described later in the section "Converging by Going Active," before using the route through Router B.

By tuning EIGRP metrics, an engineer can create feasible successor routes in cases where none existed, improving convergence.

Verification of Feasible Successors

Determining which prefixes have both successor and feasible successor routes is somewhat simple if you keep the following in mind:

Key Topic

■ The **show ip eigrp topology** command does not list all known EIGRP routes, but instead lists only successor and feasible successor routes.

■ The **show ip eigrp topology all-links** command lists all possible routes, including those that are neither successor nor feasible successor routes.

For example, consider Figure 3-9, which again focuses on Router WAN1's route to Router B1's LAN subnet, 10.11.1.0/24. The configuration on all routers has reverted back to defaults for all settings that impact the metric: default bandwidth and delay, no offset lists, and all interfaces are up.

Figure 3-9 shows the three topologically possible routes to reach 10.11.1.0/24, labeled 1, 2, and 3. Route 1, direct to Router B1, is the current successor. Route 3, which goes to another branch router, back to the main site, and then to Router B1, is probably a route you would not want to use anyway. However, route 2, through WAN2, would be a reasonable back-up route.

If the PVC between WAN1 and B1 failed, WAN1 would converge to route 2 from the figure. However, with all default settings, route 2 is not an FS route, as demonstrated in Example 3-7.

Example 3-7   *Only a Successor Route on WAN1 for 10.11.1.0/24*

```
WAN1#show ip eigrp topology
IP-EIGRP Topology Table for AS(1)/ID(10.9.1.1)
```

```
Codes: P - Passive, A - Active, U - Update, Q - Query, R - Reply,
       r - reply Status, s - sia Status


P 10.11.1.0/24, 1 successors, FD is 2172416
       via 10.1.1.2 (2172416/28160), Serial0/0/0.1
! lines omitted for brevity; no other lines of output pertain to 10.11.1.0/24.


WAN1#show ip eigrp topology all-links
IP-EIGRP Topology Table for AS(1)/ID(10.9.1.1)


Codes: P - Passive, A - Active, U - Update, Q - Query, R - Reply,
       r - reply Status, s - sia Status


P 10.11.1.0/24, 1 successors, FD is 2172416, serno 45
       via 10.1.1.2 (2172416/28160), Serial0/0/0.1
       via 10.9.1.2 (2174976/2172416), FastEthernet0/0
! lines omitted for brevity; no other lines of output pertain to 10.11.1.0/24.
```

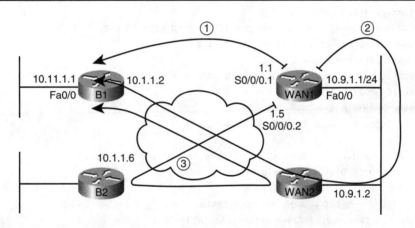

Note: All WAN IP addresses begin with 10.1

Figure 3-9 *Three Possible Routes from WAN1 to 10.11.1.0/24*

A quick comparison of the two commands show that the **show ip eigrp topology** command shows only one next-hop address (10.1.1.2), whereas the **show ip eigrp topology all-links** command shows two (10.1.1.2 and 10.9.1.2). The first command lists only successor and feasible successor routes, so in this case, only one such route for 10.11.1.0/24 exists—the successor route, direct to B1 (10.1.1.2).

The output of the **show ip eigrp topology all-links** command is particularly interesting in this case. It lists two possible next-hop routers: 10.1.1.2 (B1) and 10.9.1.2 (WAN2). It does not list the route through Router B2 (10.1.1.6) at all, because B2's current successor route for 10.11.1.0/24 is through WAN1. EIGRP Split Horizon rules tell B2 to not advertise 10.11.1.0/24 to WAN1.

Next, focus on the route labeled as option 2 in Figure 3-9, the route from WAN1, to WAN2, then to B1. Per the **show ip eigrp topology all-links** command, this route has an RD of 2,172,416–the second number in parenthesis as highlighted toward the end of Example 3-7. WAN1's successor route has a FD of that exact same value. So, this one possible alternate route for 10.11.1.0/24, through WAN2, does not meet the feasibility condition–but just barely. To be an FS route, the route's RD must be less than the FD, and in this example, the two are equal.

To meet the design requirement for quickest convergence, you could use any method to manipulate the metrics such that either WAN2's metric for 10.11.1.0 is lower, or WAN1's metric for its successor route is higher. Example 3-8 shows the results of simply adding back the offset-list on WAN1, as seen in Example 3-5, which increases WAN1's metric by 3.

Example 3-8   *Increasing WAN1's Metric for 10.11.1.0/24, Creating an FS Route*

```
WAN1#configure terminal
Enter configuration commands, one per line.  End with CNTL/Z.
WAN1(config)#access-list 11 permit 10.11.1.0
WAN1(config)#router eigrp 1
WAN1(config-router)#offset-list 11 in 3 s0/0/0.1
WAN1(config-router)#^Z
WAN1#show ip eigrp topology
IP-EIGRP Topology Table for AS(1)/ID(10.9.1.1)


Codes: P - Passive, A - Active, U - Update, Q - Query, R - Reply,
       r - reply Status, s - sia Status


P 10.11.1.0/24, 1 successors, FD is 2172419
        via 10.1.1.2 (2172419/28163), Serial0/0/0.1
        via 10.9.1.2 (2174976/2172416), FastEthernet0/0
! lines omitted for brevity; no other lines of output pertain to 10.11.1.0/24.
```

Note that now WAN1's successor route FD is 2,172,419, which is higher than WAN2's (10.9.1.2's) RD of 2,172,416. As a result, WAN1's route through WAN2 (10.9.1.2) now meets the feasibility condition. Also, the **show ip eigrp topology** command, which lists only successor and feasible successor routes, now lists this new feasible successor route. Also note that the output still states "1 successor," so this counter indeed counts successor routes and does not include FS routes.

When EIGRP on a router notices that a successor route has been lost, if a feasible successor exists in the EIGRP topology database, EIGRP places that feasible successor route into the routing table. The elapsed time from noticing that the route failed, until the route is replaced, is typically less than 1 second. (A Cisco Live conference presentation asserts this convergence approaches 200 milliseconds.) With well-tuned EIGRP Hold Timers and with feasible successor routes, convergence time can be held low.

Converging by Going Active

When EIGRP removes a successor route and no FS route exists, the router begins a process by which the router discovers if any loop-free alternative routes each reach that prefix. This process is called *going active* on a route. Routes for which the router has a successor route, and no failure has yet occurred, remain in a passive state. Routes for which the successor route fails, with no feasible successor routes, move to an active state, as follows:

■ Change the state, as listed in the **show ip eigrp topology** command, from passive (p) to active (a).

■ Send EIGRP *Query* messages to every neighbor except the neighbor in the failed route. The Query asks a neighbor whether that neighbor has a loop-free route for the listed prefix/length.

■ The neighbor considers itself to have a loop-free route if that neighbor is passive for that prefix/length. If so, the neighbor 1) sends an EIGRP Reply message, telling the original router that it does indeed have a loop-free route and 2) does not forward the Query.

■ If the neighbor itself is active on this route, that neighbor 1) floods EIGRP Query messages to its neighbors and 2) does not immediately send an EIGRP Reply back to the original router—instead waiting on replies to its own set of Query messages.

■ When a router has received Reply messages from all neighbors to which it sent any Query messages, that router can then send a Reply message to any of its neighbors as necessary.

■ When a router has received a Reply for all its Query messages, that router may safely use the best of the routes confirmed to be loop free.

Note: The EIGRP convergence process when going active on a route is sometimes also referenced by the name of the underlying algorithm, named Diffusing Update Algorithm (DUAL).

The process can and does work well in many cases, often converging to a new route in less than 10 seconds. However, in internetworks with many remote sites, with much redundancy, and with a large number of routers in a single end-to-end route, convergence when going active can be inefficient. For example, consider the internetwork in Figure 3-10. The figure shows five branch routers as an example, but the internetwork has 300 branch routers, each with a PVC connected to two WAN routers, WAN1 and WAN2. When Router WAN1 loses its route for the LAN subnet at branch B1, without an FS route, the Query process can get out of hand.

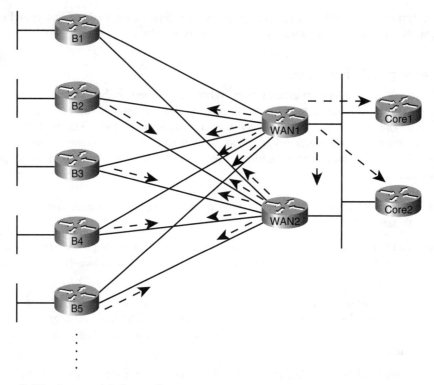

Figure 3-10   *Issues with Query Scope*

The arrowed lines show WAN1's Query messages and the reaction by several other routers to forward the Query messages. Although only 5 branch routers are shown, WAN1 would forward Query messages to 299 branch routers. WAN2 would do the same, assuming its route to B1's LAN also failed. These branch routers would then send Query messages back to the WAN routers. The network would converge, but more slowly than if an FS route existed.

> **Note:** EIGRP sends every Query and Reply message using RTP, so every message is acknowledged using an EIGRP ACK message.

By configuring EIGRP so that a router has FS routes for most routes, the whole Query process can be avoided. However, in some cases, creating FS routes for all routes on all routers is impossible, so engineers should take action to limit the scope of queries. The next two sections discuss two tools—stub routers and route summarization—that help reduce the work performed by the DUAL algorithm and the scope of Query messages.

The Impact of Stub Routers on Query Scope

Some routers, by design, should not be responsible for forwarding traffic between different sites. For example, consider the familiar internetwork shown throughout this chapter, most recently in Figure 3-10, and focus on the branch routers. If WAN2's LAN interface failed, and WAN1's PVC to B1 failed, then a route still exists from the core to branch B1's 10.11.1.0/24 subnet: WAN1–B2–WAN2–B1. (This is the same long route shown as route 3 in Figure 3-9.) However, this long route consumes the link bandwidth between the core and branch B2, and the traffic to/from B1 will be slower. Users at both branches will suffer, and these conditions may well be worse than just not using this long route.

Route filtering could be used to prevent WAN1 from learning such a route. However, using route filtering would require a lot of configuration on all the branch routers, with specifics for the subnets–and it would have to change over time. A better solution exists, which is to make the branch routers stub routers. EIGRP defines *stub routers* as follows:

A router that should not forward traffic between two remote EIGRP-learned subnets.

Key Topic

To accomplish this goal, the engineer configures the stub routers using the **eigrp stub** command. Stub routers do not advertise EIGRP-learned routes from one neighbor to other EIGRP neighbors. Additionally, and possibly more significantly, nonstub routers note which EIGRP neighbors are stub routers, and the nonstub routers do not send Query messages to the stub routers. This action greatly reduces the scope of Query messages when a route goes active, in addition to preventing the long, circuitous, and possibly harmful route.

The **eigrp stub** command has several options. When issued simply as **eigrp stub**, the router uses default parameters, which are the **connected** and **summary** options. (Note that IOS adds these two parameters onto the command as added to the running-config.) Table 3-3 lists the **eigrp stub** command options and explains some of the logic behind using them.

Table 3-3   *Parameters on the eigrp stub Command*

Key Topic

Option	This router is allowed to...
Connected	Advertise connected routes but only for interfaces matched with a **network** command.
Summary	Advertise auto-summarized or statically configured summary routes.
Static	Advertises static routes, assuming the **redistribute static** command is configured.
Redistributed	Advertises redistributed routes, assuming redistribution is configured.
Receive-only	Does not advertise any routes. This option cannot be used with any other option.

Note that stub routers still form neighborships, even in receive-only mode. The stub router simply performs less work and reduces the Query Scope because neighbors will not send these routers any Query messages.

For example, Example 3-9 shows the **eigrp stub connected** command on Router B2, with the results being noticable on WAN1 (**show ip eigrp neighbors detail**).

Example 3-9   *Evidence of Router B2 as an EIGRP Stub Router*

```
B2#configure terminal
B2(config)#router eigrp 1
B2(config-router)#eigrp stub connected
B2(config-router)#
Mar  2 21:21:52.361: %DUAL-5-NBRCHANGE: IP-EIGRP(0) 1: Neighbor 10.9.1.14
(FastEthernet0/0.12) is down: peer info changed
! A message like the above occurs for each neighbor.
```

```
WAN1#show ip eigrp neighbors detail
IP-EIGRP neighbors for process 1
H    Address                  Interface        Hold Uptime    SRTT    RTO   Q    Seq
                                               (sec)          (ms)        Cnt  Num
1    10.9.1.2                 Fa0/0             11 00:00:04     7    200   0    588
     Version 12.4/1.2, Retrans: 0, Retries: 0, Prefixes: 8
2    10.1.1.6                 Se0/0/0.2         13 00:21:23     1    200   0    408
     Version 12.4/1.2, Retrans: 2, Retries: 0, Prefixes: 2
     Stub Peer Advertising ( CONNECTED ) Routes
     Suppressing queries
0    10.9.1.6                 Fa0/0.4           12 00:21:28     1    200   0    175
     Version 12.2/1.2, Retrans: 3, Retries: 0, Prefixes: 6
```

The Impact of Summary Routes on Query Scope

In addition to EIGRP stub routers, route summarization also limits EIGRP Query scope and therefore improves convergence time. The reduction in Query scope occurs due to the following rule:

Key Topic

If a router receives an EIGRP Query for a prefix/prefix length, does not have an exactly matching (both prefix and prefix length) route, but does have a summary route that includes the prefix/prefix length, that router immediately sends an EIGRP Reply and does not flood the Query to its own neighbors.

For example, consider Figure 3-11. Multilayer Switches C1 and C2 sit in the core of the network shown in various other figures in this chapter, and both C1 and C2 run EIGRP. The IP subnetting design assigns all branch office LAN subnets from the range 10.11.0.0/16 and 10.12.0.0/16. As such, Routers WAN1 and WAN2 advertise summary routes for these ranges, rather than for individual subnets. So, under normal operation, ignoring the whole Query scope issue, C1 and C2 would never have routes for individual branch subnets like 10.11.1.0/24 but would have routes for 10.11.0.0/16 and 10.12.0.0/16.

The figure highlights three steps:

Step 1.   WAN1 and WAN2 advertise summary routes, so that C1, C2, and all other routers in the core have a route for 10.11.0.0/16 but not a route for 10.11.1.0/24.

Step 2.   Some time in the future, WAN1 loses its route for 10.11.1.0/24, so WAN1 sends a Query for 10.11.1.0/24 to C1 and C2.

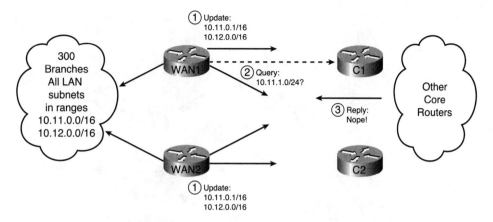

Figure 3-11   *Route Summaries Limiting Query Scope*

Step 3.   C1 and C2 send an EIGRP Reply immediately afterward, because both do not have a route for that specific prefix/length (10.11.1.0/24), but both do have a summary route (10.11.0.0/16) that includes that range of addresses.

Chapter 4, "EIGRP Route Summarization and Filtering," explains the configuration of EIGRP route summarization as an end to itself.

Stuck in Active

When a router notices a route failure and moves a route from passive to active state, that router sends Query messages to its neighbors. With a sufficiently large network, particularly when routers exist several router hops away, the number of Queries may not only be large, but there also may be a string of routers that all must wait on multiple Reply messages before they can, in turn, issue a Reply. For example, in Figure 3-12, Router R1 must wait on routers R11, R12, and R13 to send a Reply. R11 must wait on routers R21, R22, and R23. R21 must wait on three other routers, and so on—meaning that R1 may have to wait quite a while before getting a response.

Although the design shown in Figure 3-12 is admittedly contrived, the point is that a router may wait awhile before getting a Reply message in response to each Query message for an Active route. A router cannot use any alternative paths for that route until all such Reply messages have been received.

To deal with this potentially long time, IOS first sets a limit on how long it should take to receive all such replies. That timer, called the *active timer*, is set to 3 minutes by default. (The timer can be configured for an entire EIGRP process using the **timers active-time** *time* EIGRP subcommand, with a units of a number of minutes.) Routes for which a router does not receive a Reply within the active timer are considered to be Stuck-in-Active (SIA) routes.

IOS has two major branches of logic when reacting to SIA routes. Earlier versions of IOS took a rather drastic action, bringing down the uncooperative neighbors that had yet to send back an EIGRP Reply for that route. For example, in Figure 3-12, if R1 received Reply messages from R11 and R12, but not R13, and the active timer expired, R1 would bring

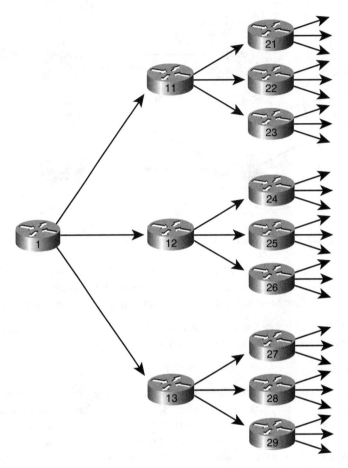

Figure 3-12 *Network Design That Causes Unreasonably Long Convergence*

down the neighborship with R13. The active route would be considered to have failed, and all routes known through the failed neighbor would also be considered to have failed–possibly generating more Query messages for other routes.

Later IOS versions (beginning in the 12.2 mainline) make an attempt to avoid failing the neighborship. At the halfway point through the Active timer–a seemingly long 90 seconds by default–a router sends an SIA-Query (Stuck-in-Active query) EIGRP message to each neighbor that has yet to send back a Reply. The purpose of the message is to either get an SIA-Reply back, meaning that the neighbor really is still waiting for replies to its own queries, or to get nothing in reply. In the first case, because the neighbor is alive and still working, there is no need to kill the neighborship. In the second case, the neighbor was not able to reply, so the action of failing the neighborship is reasonable.

Unequal Metric Route Load Sharing

Convergence to a feasible successor route should happen within a second after a router re-alizes the successor route has failed. Even in large well-designed networks, particularly with features like stub routers and route summarization in use, convergence can still happen in a reasonable amount of time even when going active. The next feature, load sharing, takes convergence to another level, giving instantaneous convergence, while reaching other goals as well.

IOS allows routing protocols to place multiple routes into the routing table for an individual prefix/length. IOS then balances traffic across those routes, by default balancing traffic on a per-destination IP address basis.

Load balancing, sometimes called load sharing, provides a primary benefit of making use of the available bandwidth, rather than using some links as simply backup links. For example, with the two-PVC designs repeatedly shown in this chapter (Figures 3-1, 3-9, and 3-10), without load sharing, a branch router would send traffic over one PVC, but not both. With load sharing, some traffic would flow over each PVC.

A useful secondary benefit–faster convergence–occurs when using load balancing. By placing multiple routes into the routing table for a single prefix, convergence happens essentially instantly. For example, if a branch router has two routes for each data center subnet—one using each PVC that connects the branch to the core—and one of the routes fails, the other route is already in the routing table. In this case, the router does not need to look for FS routes nor go active on the route. The router uses the usual EIGRP convergence tools only when all such routes are removed from the routing table.

The load balancing configuration requires two commands, one of which already defaults to a reasonable setting. First, you need to define the number of allowed routes for each prefix/prefix length using the **maximum-paths** *number* EIGRP subcommand. The default setting of 4 is often big enough, because most internetworks do not have enough redundancy to have more than four possible routes.

Note: The maximum number of paths varies based on IOS version and router platform. However, for the much older IOS versions, the maximum was 6 routes, with later versions typically supporting 16 or more.

The second part of the load balancing configuration overcomes a challenge introduced by EIGRP's metric calculation. The EIGRP integer metric calculation often results in 8-to-10-digit integer metrics, so the metrics of competing routes are seldom the exact same value. Calculating the exact same metric for different routes for the same prefix is statistically unlikely.

IOS includes the concept of EIGRP *variance* to overcome this problem. Variance lets you tell IOS that the EIGRP metrics can be close in value and still be considered worthy of being added to the routing table—and you can define how close.

The **variance** *multiplier* EIGRP router subcommand defines an integer between 1 and 128. The router then multiplies the variance times the successor route's FD–the metric of the best route to reach that subnet. Any FS routes whose metric is less than or equal to the product of the variance times the FD are considered to be equal routes and may be placed into the routing table, up to the number of routes defined by the **maximum-paths** command.

For example, consider the example as shown in Figure 3-13 and Table 3-4. In this exam-ple, to keep the focus on the concepts, the metrics are small easy-to-compare numbers, rather than the usual large EIGRP metrics. The example focuses on R4's three possible routes to reach Subnet 1. The figure shows the RD of each route next to Routers R1, R2, and R3, respectively.

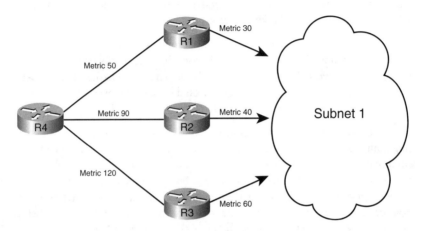

Figure 3-13 *Example of the Use of Variance*

Before considering the variance, note that in this case the route through R1 is the succes-sor route because it has the lowest metric. This also means that the FD is 50. The route through R2 is an FS route because its RD of 40 is less than the FD of 50. The route through R3 is not an FS route, because R3's RD of 60 is more than the FD of 50.

At a default variance setting of 1, the metrics must be exactly equal to be considered equal, so only the successor route is added to the routing table (the route through R1). With variance 2, the FD (50) is multiplied by the variance (2) for a product of 100. The route through R2, with FD 90, is less than 100, so R4 will add the route through R2 to the routing table as well. The router can then load balance traffic across these two routes. Table 3-4 summarizes these cases, plus one other, which is described after the table.

Table 3-4 *Example of Routes Chosen as Equal Due to Variance*

Next-hop	Metric	RD	Added to Routing Table at Variance 1?	Added to Routing Table at Variance 2?	Added to Routing Table at Variance 3?
R1	50	30	Yes	Yes	Yes
R2	90	40	No	Yes	Yes
R3	120	60	No	No	No

In the third case, with variance 3, the product of the FD (50) times 3 results equals 150. All three routes' calculated metrics (their FD values) are less than 150. However, the route through R3 is not an FS route, so it cannot be added to the routing table for fear of causing a routing loop. So, R4 adds only the routes through R1 and R2 to its IP routing table. (Note that the variance and maximum-paths settings can be verified by using the **show ip protocols** command.)

The following list summarizes the key points about variance:

■   The variance is multiplied by the current FD (the metric of the best route to reach the subnet).

■   Any FS routes whose calculated metric is less than or equal to the product of variance times FD are added to the IP routing table, assuming the **maximum-paths** setting allows more routes.

■   Routes that are neither successor nor feasible successor can never be added to the IP routing table, regardless of the variance setting.

When the routes have been added to the routing table, the router supports a couple of methods for how to load balance traffic across the routes. The router can balance the traffic proportionally with the metrics, meaning that lower metric routes send more packets. Also, the router can send all traffic over the lowest-metric route, with the other routes just being in the routing table for faster convergence in case the best route fails.

Exam Preparation Tasks

Planning Practice

The CCNP ROUTE exam expects test takers to review design documents, create implementation plans, and create verification plans. This section provides exercises that may help you to take a step back from the minute details of the topics in this chapter so that you can think about the same technical topics from the planning perspective.

For each planning practice table, simply complete the table. Note that any numbers in parentheses represent the number of options listed for each item in the solutions in Appendix F, "Completed Planning Practice Tables."

Design Review Table

Table 3-5 lists several design goals related to this chapter. If these design goals were listed in a design document, and you had to take that document and develop an implementation plan, what implementation options come to mind? For any configuration items, a general description can be used, without concern about the specific parameters.

Table 3-5   *Design Review*

Design Goal	Possible Implementation Choices Covered in This Chapter
Limit consumption of IP subnets in Frame Relay WAN design.	
In a relatively slow Frame Relay WAN, protect against consuming too much bandwidth with overhead EIGRP traffic.	
Plan to change bandwidth from 1X CIR to 2X CIR on all Frame Relay subinterfaces.	
Plan to set bandwidth to values other than actual interface speeds to manipulate EIGRP metrics.	
A goal of ensuring all remote routers' secondary EIGRP routes does not require Queries for convergence.	
What tools can we use to meet the design goal of fast convergence? (four items)	

Implementation Plan Peer Review Table

Table 3-6 shows a list of questions that others might ask, or that you might think about, during a peer review of another network engineer's implementation plan. Complete the table by answering the questions.

Table 3-6 *Notable Questions from This Chapter to Consider During an Implementation Plan Peer Review*

Question	Answer
A Frame Relay multipoint interface, with 20 PVCs attached, has a configuration for 10% of the bandwidth to be used for EIGRP. How much is allocated per PVC?	
Could any planned topologies have EIGRP Split Horizon issues?	
A configuration lists the **no ip split-horizon** command—when would that matter?	
The plan calls for setting all EIGRP K-values to 1. What negative effect could this have on routes in the IP routing table?	
The configuration uses offset lists. Will that impact the calculation of FD and/or RD?	
The plan lists a sample configuration migrating an interface from **delay 20** to **delay 200**. How much will the metric go up?	
The plan shows the use of the **variance 4** command. What must be configured to add other routes to a routing table? (two items)	

Create an Implementation Plan Table

To practice skills useful when creating your own EIGRP implementation plan, list in Table 3-7 configuration commands related to the configuration of the following features. You may want to record your answers outside the book and set a goal to complete this table (and others like it) from memory during your final reviews before taking the exam.

Table 3-7 *Implementation Plan Configuration Memory Drill*

Feature	Configuration Commands/Notes
Enabling EIGRP on interfaces	
Enabling or disabling Split Horizon for EIGRP	
Setting the Bandwidth consumed by EIGRP on an interface	
Setting an interface's logical bandwidth	
Setting an interface's logical delay	
K-values	
Configuring an EIGRP offset list that matches a prefix	
Configuring an EIGRP offset list that matches a prefix and prefix length	
Configuring unequal cost load balancing	
Configure an EIGRP stub router	

Choose Commands for a Verification Plan Table

To practice skills useful when creating your own EIGRP verification plan, list in Table 3-8 all commands that supply the requested information. You may want to record your answers outside the book, and set a goal to complete this table (and others like it) from memory during your final reviews before taking the exam.

Table 3-8   *Verification Plan Memory Drill*

Information Needed	Command
The composite metric values for all EIGRP prefixes.	
Display EIGRP Split Horizon settings.	
Calculate the maximum bandwidth EIGRP will consume on a physical or point-to-point subinterface.	
Calculate the maximum bandwidth EIGRP will consume per PVC on a multipoint Frame Relay subinterface.	
Display the increase in RD after implementing an EIGRP offset list.	
Display interface bandwidth and delay settings.	
Lists EIGRP K-values.	
Find the number of successor and feasible successor routes.	
Find all routes, including non-successors.	
Determine if the local router is a stub router.	
Determine if a neighboring router is a stub router.	
Find the current setting of variance and maximum-paths.	
Display messages each time EIGRP suppresses a prefix advertisement due to Split Horizon.	

Review all the Key Topics

Review the most important topics from the chapter, noted with the key topics icon in the outer margin of the page. Table 3-9 lists a reference of these key topics and the page numbers on which each is found.

Table 3-9 *Key Topics for Chapter 3*

Key Topic Element	Description	Page Number
List	Three sources for seeding a local router's EIGRP topology table	60
List	EIGRP message types (5)	61
List	Rules for EIGRP topology exchange	64
Definitions	Feasible Distance, Reported Distance	70
Definition	Feasibility Condition	79
Figure 3-8	Conceptual view of successors and feasible successors	79
List	Two commands to find all EIGRP routes versus all successor/feasible successor routes	80
List	EIGRP process of finding routes when going active	83
Definition	EIGRP stub router	85
Table 3-3	List of options on the **eigrp stub** command	85
Definition	Rule by which summary routes reduce Query scope	86
List	Rules for unequal-cost multipath	91

Complete the Tables and Lists from Memory

Print a copy of Appendix D, "Memory Tables," (found on the CD) or at least the section for this chapter, and complete the tables and lists from memory. Appendix E, "Memory Tables Answer Key," also on the CD, includes completed tables and lists to check your work.

Define Key Terms

Define the following key terms from this chapter, and check your answers in the glossary.

feasibility condition, feasible distance, feasible successor, full update, partial update, reported distance, advertised distance, successor, Split Horizon, bandwidth, delay, K-value, offset list, going active, DUAL, Query scope, EIGRP stub router, unequal-cost load balancing, variance

This chapter covers the following subjects:

Route Filtering: This section examines how to filter prefixes from being sent in EIGRP Updates or filter them from being processed when received in an EIGRP Update.

Route Summarization: This section discusses the concepts and configuration of EIGRP route summarization.

Default Routes: This section examines the benefits of using default routes, and the mechanics of two methods for configuring default routes with EIGRP.

EIGRP Route Summarization and Filtering

Engineers can choose to implement routing protocols such that all routers know routes to all prefixes in an internetwork. By allowing all routers to share all known prefixes, every router in an Enterprise has the potential ability to forward packets to all subnets in the Enterprise, assuming the internetwork is working correctly.

However, a reasonable network design may not need nor want the unfettered flow of routing information in an Enterprise. The design should consider the flow of data in the network, in particular, the fact that most data applications do not send packets directly between end user hosts. Most often, the packets go from one host to a server, and then the server communicates directly with the other end user host. So the design may require or desire that some routes are filtered so that routers in one part of the internetwork cannot forward packets to another part.

Additionally, the design may call for a general goal to reduce the size of the typical router's IP routing table. Although routers consume only a small amount of CPU to forward each packet, the amount of CPU required does increase slightly based on the number of routes. Additionally, a smaller routing table may be simpler and require less time when troubleshooting problems.

This chapter explains three categories of tools that you can use to limit the number of routes in the routing table: route filtering, route summarization, and default routes.

"Do I Know This Already?" Quiz

The "Do I Know This Already?" quiz allows you to assess if you should read the entire chapter. If you miss no more than one of these nine self-assessment questions, you might want to move ahead to the "Exam Preparation Tasks." Table 4-1 lists the major headings in this chapter and the "Do I Know This Already?" quiz questions covering the material in those headings so that you can assess your knowledge of these specific areas. The answers to the "Do I Know This Already?" quiz appear in Appendix A.

Table 4-1 *"Do I Know This Already?" Foundation Topics Section-to-Question Mapping*

Foundations Topics Section	Questions
Route Filtering	1–4
Route Summarization	5–7
Default Routes	8, 9

1. Router R1 has been configured for EIGRP. The configuration also includes an ACL with one line–**access-list 1 permit 10.10.32.0 0.0.15.255**–and the EIGRP configuration includes the **distribute-list 1 in** command. Which of the following routes could not be displayed in the output of the **show ip eigrp topology** command as a result? (Choose two answers.)

   a. 10.10.32.0/19

   b. 10.10.44.0/22

   c. 10.10.40.96/27

   d. 10.10.48.0/23

   e. 10.10.60.0/30

2. The command output that follows was gathered from router R1. If correctly referenced by an EIGRP distribution list that filters outbound Updates, which of the following statements is true about the filtering of various prefixes by this Prefix list? (Choose three answers.)

   ```
   R1#sh ip prefix-list
   ip prefix-list question: 3 entries
       seq 5 deny 10.1.2.0/24 ge 25 le 27
       seq 15 deny 10.2.0.0/16 ge 30 le 30
       seq 20 permit 0.0.0.0/0
   ```

   a. Prefix 10.1.2.0/24 will be filtered due to clause 5.

   b. Prefix 10.1.2.224/26 will be filtered due to clause 5.

   c. Prefix 10.2.2.4/30 will be filtered due to clause 15.

   d. Prefix 10.0.0.0/8 will be permitted.

   e. Prefix 0.0.0.0/0 will be permitted.

3. R1 has correctly configured EIGRP to filter routes using a route map named *question*. The configuration that follows shows the entire route map and related configuration. Which of the following is true regarding the filtering action on prefix 10.10.10.0/24 in this case?

   ```
   route-map question deny 10
    match ip address 1
   route-map question permit 20
    match ip address prefix-list fred
   !
   access-list 1 deny 10.10.10.0 0.0.0.255
   ip prefix-list fred permit 10.10.10.0/23 le 25
   ```

   a. It will be filtered due to the deny action in route map clause 10.

   b. It will be allowed because of the double negative (two deny references) in clause 10.

   c. It will be permitted due to matching clause 20's reference to prefix-list fred.

   d. It will be filtered due to matching the implied deny all route map clause at the end of the route map.

4. An engineer has typed four different single-line prefix lists in a word processor. The four answers show the four different single-line prefix lists. The engineer then does a copy/paste of the configuration into a router. Which of the lists could match a subnet whose prefix length is 27? (Choose two answers.)

    a.   ip prefix-list fred permit 10.0.0.0/24 ge 16 le 28

    b.   ip prefix-list barney permit 10.0.0.0/24 le 28

    c.   ip prefix-list wilma permit 10.0.0.0/24 ge 25

    d.   ip prefix-list betty permit 10.0.0.0/24 ge 28

5. An engineer plans to configure summary routes with the **ip summary-address eigrp** *asn prefix mask* command. Which of the following, when added to such a command, would create a summary that includes all four of the following subnets: 10.1.100.0/25, 10.1.101.96/27, 10.1.101.224/28, and 10.1.100.128/25?

    a.   10.1.0.0 255.255.192.0

    b.   10.1.64.0 255.255.192.0

    c.   10.1.100.0 255.255.255.0

    d.   10.1.98.0 255.255.252.0

6. R1 has 5 working interfaces, with EIGRP neighbors existing off each interface. R1 has routes for subnets 10.1.1.0/24, 10.1.2.0/24, and 10.1.3.0/24, with EIGRP integer metrics of roughly 1 million, 2 million, and 3 million, respectively. An engineer then adds the **ip summary-address eigrp 1 10.1.0.0 255.255.0.0** command to interface Fa0/0. Which of the following is true?

    a.   R1 loses and then reestablishes neighborships with all neighbors.

    b.   R1 no longer advertises 10.1.1.0/24 to neighbors connected to Fa0/0.

    c.   R1 advertises a 10.1.0.0/16 route out Fa0/0, with metric of around 3 million (largest metric of component subnets).

    d.   R1 advertises a 10.1.0.0/16 route out Fa0/0, with metric of around 2 million (median metric of component subnets).

7. In a lab, R1 connects to R2, which connects to R3. R1 and R2 each have several working interfaces, all assigned addresses in class A network 10.0.0.0. Router R3 has some working interfaces in class A network 10.0.0.0, and others in class B network 172.16.0.0. The engineer experiments with the **auto-summary** command on R2 and R3, enabling and disabling the command in various combinations. Which of the following combinations will result in R1 seeing a route for 172.16.0.0/16, instead of the individual subnets of class B network 172.16.0.0? (Choose two answers.)

    a.   **auto-summary** on R2 and **no auto-summary** on R3

    b.   **auto-summary** on R2 and **auto-summary** on R3

    c.   **no auto-summary** on R2 and **no auto-summary** on R3

    d.   **no auto-summary** on R2 and **auto-summary** on R3

8. Router R1 exists in an Enterprise that uses EIGRP as its routing protocol. The **show ip route** command output on router R1 lists the following phrase: "Gateway of last resort is 1.1.1.1 to network 2.0.0.0". Which of the following is most likely to have caused this output to occur on R1?

    a. R1 has been configured with an **ip default-network 2.0.0.0** command.

    b. R1 has been configured with an **ip route 0.0.0.0 0.0.0.0 1.1.1.1** command.

    c. R1 has been configured with an **ip route 2.0.0.0 255.0.0.0 1.1.1.1** command.

    d. Another router has been configured with an **ip default-network 2.0.0.0** command.

    e. Another router has been configured with an **ip route 2.0.0.0 255.0.0.0 1.1.1.1** command.

9. Enterprise Router R1 connects an Enterprise to the Internet. R1 needs to create and advertise a default route into the Enterprise using EIGRP. The engineer creating the implementation plan has chosen to base this default route on the **ip route** command, rather than using **ip default-network**. Which of the following is not a useful step with this style of default route configuration? (Choose two answers.)

    a. Create the default route on R1 using the **ip route 0.0.0.0 0.0.0.0** *outgoing-interface* command.

    b. Redistribute the statically configured default route.

    c. Disable auto-summary.

    d. Configure the **network 0.0.0.0** command.

    e. Ensure R1 has no manually configured summary routes using the **ip summary-address eigrp** command.

Foundation Topics

Route Filtering

Does a router in a branch office need to be able to forward packets to hosts in another branch office? Does a router in the sales division need to be able to forward packets to hosts in the manufacturing division? These questions are just a sampling of design questions for which route filtering can be part of the solution.

Route filtering allows the engineer to filter which routes are advertised in an EIGRP update. If routers in a branch do not need to learn routes about subnets in other branches, routers can filter that routing information. This filtering reduces the size of routing tables, saving memory, possibly improving routing performance, and makes the internetwork more secure by limiting the flow of packets.

EIGRP enables route filtering using the **distribute-list** router subcommand. The concept is relatively straightforward: The distribute list refers to either an access control list (ACL), prefix list, or route map. These three tools classify whether a route should be permitted to be sent/received in an EIGRP Update or be denied (filtered). The **distribute-list** command also specifies the direction–outbound updates or inbound updates–and optionally, the specific interface on which to filter updates.

For example, Figure 4-1 shows an expanded version of the internetwork used frequently in the previous two chapters. The figure adds several links between the WAN routers and some core Layer 3 switches. It also notes the address ranges for all data centers (10.16.0.0/16) and the range of addresses used for subnets in the manufacturing division (10.17.32.0/19).

The design engineer could make many choices about what routes to filter, for example:

■ Filter routes to WAN subnets so that the core and manufacturing do not learn those routes, because these subnets should not be the destination of any user traffic.

■ Filter manufacturing routes from being advertised to the branches, because the branches are in the sales division.

■ Filter routes for the subnets sitting between the Layer 3 switches in the core, preventing them from being advertised to either manufacturing or the sales branches, because no users in these divisions should be sending packets to these subnets.

The examples in this chapter focus on the second of these design options.

Filtering the subnets that exist between Layer 3 devices, as is suggested in the second and third items in the list, have both pros and cons. For example, the first design goal filters the WAN subnets, because no end users need to be able to send packets to those subnets. This meets the goal of having smaller routing tables. However, operations personnel may have a larger challenge when monitoring and troubleshooting, because when a **ping** or **traceroute** fails, they also need to figure out whether the command failed by design due to the purposefully filtered routes, or whether a problem has occurred.

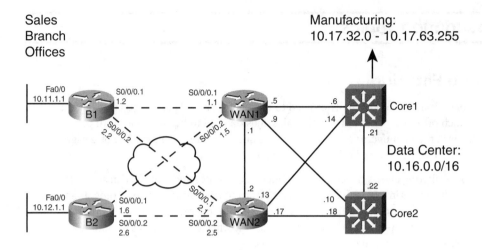

Sales
Branch
Offices

Manufacturing:
10.17.32.0 - 10.17.63.255

Data Center:
10.16.0.0/16

Note: All WAN IP addresses begin with 10.1.
          All LAN Core IP addresses begin with 10.9.1.

Figure 4-1   *Expanded Design with a Range of Addresses in Manufacturing*

This section next examines how to filter EIGRP routes using ACLs, prefix lists, and then route maps. All three of these tools will be used throughout this book, so this chapter lays the foundation for understanding these tools, in addition to showing how to use these tools when filtering EIGRP routes.

Filtering by Referencing ACLs

To filter EIGRP routes by matching them using ACLs, the ACL must match a route with a **permit** clause to then allow the route to be advertised, and match the route with a **deny** clause to filter the route. Before getting into how an ACL matches a route, first it is important to review what can be examined based on the configuration of an IP ACL.

EIGRP distribute lists support the use of standard IP ACLs. The syntax of both numbered and named standard ACLs allows a configuration of one dotted decimal number and its corresponding wildcard (WC) mask. When used for packet filtering, this number is compared to the source IP address of the packet. When referenced by the **distribute-list** command for the purpose of EIGRP route filtering, EIGRP compares the standard ACL source-address field to the subnet number (prefix) of each EIGRP route.

The best way to learn the specifics is to consider several examples. Figure 4-2 shows the specific size subnets being advertised from the manufacturing division into the core. The design calls for the WAN routers to filter these routes from being advertised toward the Sales division's branch offices.

Figure 4-2 shows the **distribute-list 2 out s0/0/0.1** command on Router WAN1 as one sample of the syntax. A command like this would need to be included in WAN1's configuration for each interface connected to a branch. ACL number 2 would then be configured

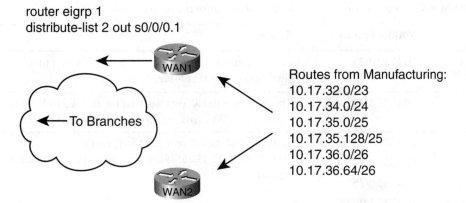

```
router eigrp 1
distribute-list 2 out s0/0/0.1
```

Figure 4-2 *Specific Manufacturing Routes to Be Filtered*

to match the manufacturing routes with a deny clause, and all other routes with a permit clause, filtering the routes.

If WAN1 has hundreds of serial subinterfaces for its WAN connections, then following the sample in the previous paragraph, WAN1 would have hundreds of **distribute-list 2 out serial** *number* commands, one per WAN interface/subinterface. Alternatively, the engineer could configure a single **distribute-list 2 out** command on Router WAN1, not specifying an interface. In this case, Router WAN1 would not advertise these routes to any neighbors, greatly reducing WAN1's configuration.

Given that this section represents the first use of ACLs in this book, at your option, take the time to try the following exercise as a review of ACLs. Consider the following **access-list** commands. Imagine that each command in this list is the first of two commands in a single access-list. The second and only other command is a command that permits all other routes—for example, **access-list 2 permit any**. Then, ask yourself—if used by a **distribute-list** on WAN1 to filter the manufacturing routes (as seen in Figure 4-2), and you want that ACL to filter only manufacturing routes, which of these 2-line ACLs meet the requirements?

```
access-list 3 deny 10.17.32.0
access-list 4 deny 10.17.32.0 0.0.0.255
access-list 5 deny 10.17.32.0 0.0.3.255
access-list 6 deny 10.16.0.0 0.1.255.255
```

To keep from giving away the answers, Table 4-2, which supplies the answers and explanation, is located on the next page.

Table 4-2 *Analysis of the Sample ACLs Used with the distribute-list Command*

ACL	Routes Filtered	Explanation
3	10.17.32.0/23	The ACL matches exactly prefix 10.17.32.0, so it matches a single manufacturing route.
4	10.17.32.0/23	The ACL matches all prefixes that begin with 10.17.32 because of the WC mask, again matching a single route.
5	10.17.32.0/23 10.17.34.0/24 10.17.35.0/25 10.17.35.128/25	The ACL matches all prefixes in the range 10.17.32.0–10.17.35.255, which includes four manufacturing routes.
6	All manufacturing and data center routes	The ACL matches all prefixes in the range 10.16.0.0–10.17.255.255, which includes the data center routes.

Note: To find the range of numbers matched by an ACL's address and wildcard mask values, use the address field as the low end of the range, and simply add the address and wildcard mask to find the high end of the range.

Example 4-1 shows the configuration on router WAN1 to filter the manufacturing routes, with distribute lists enabled on its two WAN subinterfaces. The ACL matches (with a deny action) all manufacturing routes, and matches all other routes with a permit clause.

Example 4-1 *WAN1's distribute-list to Filter Manufacturing Routes*

```
! On Router B1, before the filtering is applied:
B1#show ip route ¦ include 10.17
D       10.17.35.0/25 [90/2300416] via 10.1.1.1, 00:00:18, Serial0/0/0.1
D       10.17.34.0/24 [90/2300416] via 10.1.1.1, 00:00:18, Serial0/0/0.1
D       10.17.32.0/23 [90/2300416] via 10.1.1.1, 00:00:18, Serial0/0/0.1
D       10.17.36.0/26 [90/2300416] via 10.1.1.1, 00:00:18, Serial0/0/0.1
D       10.17.36.64/26 [90/2300416] via 10.1.1.1, 00:00:18, Serial0/0/0.1
D       10.17.35.128/25 [90/2300416] via 10.1.1.1, 00:00:18, Serial0/0/0.1
! On Router WAN1:


WAN1#configure terminal
Enter configuration commands, one per line.  End with CNTL/Z.
WAN1(config)#access-list 2 deny 10.17.32.0 0.0.31.255
WAN1(config)#access-list 2 permit any
WAN1(config)#router eigrp 1
WAN1(config-router)#distribute-list 2 out
WAN1(config-router)#^Z
WAN1#
```

```
! On Router B1, after the filtering is applied
B1#show ip route ¦ include 10.17
B1#
```

Note: The same configuration added to Router WAN1 was also added to Router WAN2; however, the commands were not repeated in Example 4-1.

The ACL in this case, ACL 2, matches all subnets with a value between 10.17.32.0–10.17.63.255, inclusive, based on the IP address value of 10.17.32.0 and WC mask of 0.0.31.255. By matching these routes with a **deny** clause, the ACL, used as a distribute list, filters the routes. The **access-list 2 permit any** command matches all other routes, allowing them to be advertised.

Filtering by Referencing IP Prefix Lists

The IOS IP **prefix-list** feature gives the network engineer another tool for matching routes when performing route filtering. IP prefix lists can examine both the prefix and the prefix length, and a range of prefixes or a range of prefix lengths. The command then sets either a deny or permit action for each matched prefix/length. To use the prefix-list, the configuration simply refers to the **prefix-list** with the same **distribute-list** command seen earlier.

Using IP prefix lists for route filtering has several advantages. First, IP prefix lists allow matching of the prefix length, whereas the ACLs used by the EIGRP **distribute-list** command cannot. (Some other route filtering configurations can match both the prefix and prefix length using extended ACLs.) Many people find IP prefix lists more intuitive for configuring route filtering. Finally, the internal processing of the IP prefix lists uses an internal tree structure that results in faster matching of routes as compared with ACLs.

This section begins by examining IP prefix lists as an end to itself, followed by an example of filtering EIGRP routes using a prefix list.

IP Prefix List Concepts

IP prefix lists provide mechanisms to match two components of an IP route:

■ The route prefix (the subnet number)

■ The prefix length (the subnet mask)

Each single IP prefix list has similar characteristics to a single ACL, with subtle similarities to both numbered and named ACLs. The IP prefix list consists of one or more global configuration commands (like numbered ACLs), with commands using the same name being in the same list (like named ACLs). As with named ACLs, each **ip prefix-list** command has a sequence number to allow later deletion of individual commands and insertion of commands into a particular sequence position. Each command has a **permit** or **deny** action— but because it is used only for matching routes, and not for packet filtering, the **permit** or **deny** keyword just implies whether a route is matched (**permit**) or not (**deny**).

The generic command syntax is as follows:

```
ip prefix-list list-name [seq seq-value] {deny ¦ permit prefix/
prefix-length} [ge ge-value] [le le-value]
```

The following statements summarize the logic:

Step 1.   The route's prefix must be within the range of addresses implied by the **prefix-list** command's *prefix/prefix-length* parameters.

Step 2.   The *route's prefix length* must match the *range of prefixes* implied by the **prefix-list** command's prefix-*length*, **ge**, and **le** parameters.

The matching of the prefix works much like the ACL matching logic. The configured prefix/prefix-length implies a range of IP addresses. For example, an **ip prefix-list barney deny 10.0.0.0/8**... implies any number whose first 8 bits (per the /8) match 10.0.0.0–in other words, all IPv4 addresses that begin with 10. Any route whose prefix is in this range–for example, 10.0.0.0, 10.1.1.0, and 10.5.255.128—would be considered to match this part of the logic.

However, IP prefix lists always examine the prefix length as well. To perform the logic of matching a route's prefix length, IOS considers the following parts of the **ip prefix-list** command:

■   The required *prefix-length* parameter

■   The optional *ge-value*, which stand for *greater-than-or-equal-to*

■   The optional *le-value*, which stand for *less-than-or-equal-to*

For a given **ip prefix-list** command, one of four configuration combinations affect the logic of matching prefix lengths, as listed in Table 4-3. The text following the table provides a more detailed explanation as compared with the summarized information in the table.

Table 4-3   *LE and GE Parameters on IP Prefix List, and the Implied Range of Prefix Lengths*

Prefix List Parameter	Range of Prefix Length
Neither	*conf-length must = route-length*
Both **ge** and **le**	*ge-value <= route-length <= le-value*
Only **le**	*conf-length <= route-length <= le-value*
Only **ge**	*ge-value <= route-length <= 32*

The first case in the table occurs when neither **ge** nor **le** is configured. In that case, an exact match of prefix-length must occur between the configured prefix length and a route's prefix length. For example, the command **ip prefix-list fred deny 10.0.0.0/8** matches route 10.0.0.0/8, but not 10.0.0.0/20.

The second case in the table occurs when both **ge** and **le** are configured. In that case, the route's prefix length must be between the configured **ge** and **le** values, inclusive. For instance, **ip prefix-list fred deny 10.0.0.0/8 ge 20 le 22** matches route 10.0.0.0/20, but not 10.0.0.0/8, because the prefix length must either be 20, 21, or 22.

The cases in which either **ge** or **le** is configured, but not both, requires a little more thought. A visual representation can help, as shown in Figure 4-3.

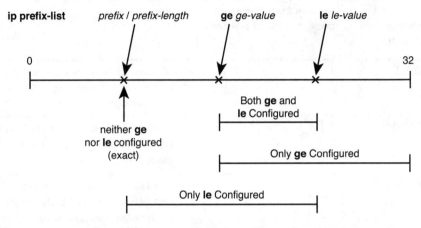

Figure 4-3   *Representation of Prefix Length Ranges for ip prefix-list Command*

In short, with only **ge** configured, the command matches prefix-length ranges from the *ge-value* up to 32 (the longest IPv4 prefix length), inclusive. With only **le** configured, the command matches prefix-length ranges between the *prefix-length* parameter and the *le-value*, inclusive.

Note: IOS requires that the configured prefix-length, ge-value, and le-value meet the following requirement: prefix-length <= ge-value <= le-value. Otherwise, IOS rejects the **ip prefix-list** command.

Samples of Prefix List Matching

Several examples can really help nail down prefix list logic. The following routes will be examined by a variety of prefix lists, with the routes numbered for easier reference:

1. 10.0.0.0/8
2. 10.128.0.0/9
3. 10.1.1.0/24
4. 10.1.2.0/24
5. 10.128.10.4/30
6. 10.128.10.8/30

Next, Table 4-4 shows the results of seven different one-line prefix lists applied to these six example routes. The table lists the matching parameters in the **prefix-list** commands, omitting the first part of the commands. The table explains which of the six routes would match the listed prefix list, and why.

Table 4-4   *Example Prefix Lists Applied to the List of Routes*

prefix-list Command Parameter	Routes Matched from previous list of prefixes	Result
10.0.0.0/8	1	Without **ge** or **le** configured, both the prefix (10.0.0.0) and length (8) must be an exact match.
10.128.0.0/9	2	Without **ge** or **le** configured, the prefix (10.128.0.0) and length (9) must be an exact match.
10.0.0.0/8 ge 9	2–6	The 10.0.0.0/8 means "all routes whose first octet is 10." The prefix length must be between 9 and 32, inclusive.
10.0.0.0/8 ge 24 le 24	3, 4	The 10.0.0.0/8 means "all routes whose first octet is 10," and the prefix range is 24 to 24—meaning only routes with prefix length 24.
10.0.0.0/8 le 28	1–4	The prefix length needs to be between 8 and 28, inclusive.
0.0.0.0/0	None	0.0.0.0/0 means "match all prefixes." However, because no le nor ge parameter is configured, the /0 also means that the prefix length must be 0. So, it would match all routes' prefixes, but none of their prefix lengths. Only a default route would match this prefix list.
0.0.0.0/0 le 32	All	The range implied by 0.0.0.0/0 is all IPv4 addresses. The **le 32** combined with prefix length 0 implies any prefix length between 0 and 32, inclusive. This is the syntax for "match all" prefix list logic.

Note: Pay particular attention to the match all logic of the final entry in the table.

Using IP Prefix Lists to Filter EIGRP Routes

After you master the logic behind IP prefix lists, using them with the **distribute-list** command requires minimal extra effort. For example, to refer to a prefix list name Fred, you could configure the **distribute-list prefix Fred...** command, instead of **distribute-list 2...** to refer to ACL 2. (Note that the prefix list names are case-sensitive.)

For example, using the internetwork of Figure 4-1 and Figure 4-2 again, consider the following revised design requirements for route filtering:

- Of the routes from manufacturing, filter only those routes that begin with 10.17.35 and 10.17.36.

- Of the routes for subnets on the WAN links, filter routes to prevent the core routers and branch routers from learning routes whose prefix length is /30.

Although the first of the preceding two requirements mainly exists to demonstrate the **ip prefix-list** command, the second goal may be more useful for real networks. Often, routes with a /30 prefix length are routes used between two routers, either on WAN links or over LANs between Layer 3-enabled devices. Users should not need to send packets to addresses in these subnets. So, the only need to have routes to these subnets is for network management (ping tests, for instance).

Example 4-2 shows the configuration on WAN1; the equivalent configuration has been added on WAN2 as well.

Example 4-2   *Filtering All Routes with a /30 Prefix Length*

```
! On Router WAN1: !!!!!!!!!!!!!!!!!!!!!!!!!!!!!!!!!!!!!!!!!!!!!!
WAN1#show running-config
! lines omitted for brevity
router eigrp 1
 network 10.0.0.0
 distribute-list prefix fred out
auto-summary
!
ip prefix-list fred seq 5 deny 10.17.35.0/24 ge 25 le 25
ip prefix-list fred seq 10 deny 10.17.36.0/24 ge 26 le 26
ip prefix-list fred seq 15 deny 0.0.0.0/0 ge 30 le 30
ip prefix-list fred seq 20 permit 0.0.0.0/0 le 32
! On Router B1:
B1#show ip route
Codes: C - connected, S - static, R - RIP, M - mobile, B - BGP
       D - EIGRP, EX - EIGRP external, O - OSPF, IA - OSPF inter area
       N1 - OSPF NSSA external type 1, N2 - OSPF NSSA external type 2
       E1 - OSPF external type 1, E2 - OSPF external type 2
       i - IS-IS, su - IS-IS summary, L1 - IS-IS level-1, L2 - IS-IS level-2
       ia - IS-IS inter area, * - candidate default, U - per-user static route
       o - ODR, P - periodic downloaded static route
```

```
Gateway of last resort is not set

      10.0.0.0/8 is variably subnetted, 7 subnets, 3 masks
C        10.11.1.0/24 is directly connected, FastEthernet0/0
D        10.12.1.0/24 [90/2684416] via 10.1.2.1, 00:06:15, Serial0/0/0.2
                       [90/2684416] via 10.1.1.1, 00:06:15, Serial0/0/0.1
C        10.1.2.0/30 is directly connected, Serial0/0/0.2
C        10.1.1.0/30 is directly connected, Serial0/0/0.1
D        10.16.1.0/24 [90/2172672] via 10.1.2.1, 00:00:32, Serial0/0/0.2
                       [90/2172672] via 10.1.1.1, 00:00:32, Serial0/0/0.1
D        10.17.34.0/24 [90/2300416] via 10.1.2.1, 00:06:15, Serial0/0/0.2
                        [90/2300416] via 10.1.1.1, 00:06:15, Serial0/0/0.1
D        10.17.32.0/23 [90/2300416] via 10.1.2.1, 00:06:15, Serial0/0/0.2
                        [90/2300416] via 10.1.1.1, 00:06:15, Serial0/0/0.1


B1#show ip route 10.17.32.0 255.255.248.0 longer-prefixes
! The legend is normally displayed; omitted here for brevity

      10.0.0.0/8 is variably subnetted, 7 subnets, 3 masks
D        10.17.34.0/24 [90/2300416] via 10.1.2.1, 00:04:12, Serial0/0/0.2
                        [90/2300416] via 10.1.1.1, 00:04:12, Serial0/0/0.1
D        10.17.32.0/23 [90/2300416] via 10.1.2.1, 00:04:12, Serial0/0/0.2
                        [90/2300416] via 10.1.1.1, 00:04:12, Serial0/0/0.1
```

The configuration on WAN1 includes a four-line prefix list. The first line (sequence number 5) matches 10.17.35.0/25 and 10.17.35.128/25, in part because it asks for a range of prefix lengths from 25 to 25–meaning an exact length of 25. Similarly, the second statement (sequence number 10) matches routes 10.17.36.0/26 and 10.17.36.64/26. The third statement (sequence number 15) uses wildcard logic (**0.0.0.0/0**) to match all prefixes, but only those with prefix length 30 (**ge 30 le 30**). The last command matches all prefixes, with prefix lengths from 0 to 32 (all prefix lengths).

The resulting IP routing table on branch Router B1 shows only a small number of routes. B1 has a route to the other example branch's subnet (10.12.1.0), and another in the range of addresses for the data centers (10.16.1.0/24). It has the two routes leaked from manufacturing. Note that the only two /30 routes known on B1 are two connected routes, so the **distribute-list** is filtering all the /30 routes.

Filtering by Using Route Maps

Route maps, the third EIGRP route filtering tool that can be referenced with the **distribute-list** command, provides programming logic similar to the If/Then/Else logic seen in programming languages. A single route map has one or more **route-map** commands in it, and routers process **route-map** commands in sequential order based on sequence numbers. Each **route-map** command has underlying matching parameters, configured with the aptly named **match** command. (To match all packets, the **route-map** clause simply omits the **match** command.)

Route maps can be used for many functions besides being used to filter routes for a single routing protocol like EIGRP. Route maps can be used to filter routes during the route redistribution process, and to set BGP Path Attributes (PAs) for the purpose of influencing the choice of the best routes in an internetwork.

When used for filtering EIGRP routes, route maps do provide a few additional features beyond what can be configured using ACLs and prefix lists. However, route maps can be tricky to understand and sometimes counterintuitive. This section begins with an examination of the concepts behind IOS route maps, followed by some examples of their use for filtering EIGRP routes.

Route Map Concepts

Route maps have many similarities when compared to ACLs and prefix lists. A single route map has several **route-map** commands, with the commands in the same route map all having the same text name. When referenced by the **distribute-list** command, IOS processes the commands in the route map sequentially, based on the sequence numbers in the commands. Like ACLs and prefix lists, IOS adds the sequence numbers automatically if omitted when configuring the **route-map** commands. And once a particular route has been matched and determined to be either filtered (deny) or allowed to pass (permit), even if more **route-map** commands exist later in the list, IOS stops processing the route-map for that route.

Each **route-map** command includes the name of the route map, an action (**permit** or **deny**), and possibly a sequence number (optional). After typing this command, the CLI user is in **route-map** configuration mode for that route-map clause. Any **match** commands configured in that mode apply to that single **route-map** command. For instance, Example 4-3 shows the configuration of a sample route map on router WAN1.

Example 4-3 *Pseudocode for Route Map Used as EIGRP Route Filter*

```
route-map sample-rm deny 8
 match (1st set of criteria)
route-map sample-rm permit 17
 match (2nd set of criteria)
route-map sample-rm deny 30
 match (3rd set of criteria)
route-map sample-rm permit 35
!
router eigrp 1
 distribute-list route-map sample-rm out
```

Example 4-3 shows pseudocode, ignoring the specifics of what is matched with the **match** commands. Focus on the actions in the **route-map** command (permit or deny), and the overall logic, as listed here:

- **Seq #8:** The action is **deny**, so discard or filter all routes matched by the **match** command (1st set of criteria).

- **Seq #17:** The action is **permit**, so allow through all routes matched by the **match** command (2ⁿᵈ set of criteria).

- **Seq #30:** The action is **deny**, so discard or filter all routes matched by the **match** command (3ʳᵈ set of criteria).

- **Seq #35:** The action is **permit**. The absence of a **match** command means "match all," so allow through all remaining routes.

The **match** command can reference an ACL or prefix list, but doing so does introduce the possibility of confusion. The confusing part is that the decision to filter a route or allow the route through is based on the **deny** or **permit** in the **route-map** command, and *not the deny or permit in the ACL or prefix list*. When referencing an ACL or prefix list from a route map, the ACL or prefix list simply matches all routes permitted by the ACL or prefix list. Routes that are denied by the ACL or prefix list simply do not match that **match** command's logic, making IOS then consider the next **route-map** command.

The following list summarizes the key points about route map logic when used for redistribution:

Key Topic

- **route-map** commands with the **permit** option either cause a route to be allowed through (if matched by the **match** command) or remain in the list of routes to be examined by the next **route-map** clause.

- **route-map** commands with the **deny** option either filter the route (if matched by the **match** command) or leave the route in the list of routes to be examined by the next **route-map** clause.

- If a clause's **match** commands refer to an ACL or prefix list, and the ACL or prefix list matches a route with the **deny** action, the route is not necessarily filtered. Instead, it just means that route does not match that particular **match** command and can then be considered by the next **route-map** clause.

- The **route-map** command includes an implied deny all clause at the end; to configure a permit all, use the **route-map** command, with a **permit** action, but without a **match** command.

Route maps have several more options on the **match command** as compared to what can be examined by ACLs and IP prefix lists. However, for the purposes of EIGRP route filtering, the items that may be matched do not provide significant help in filtering routes. However, when redistributing routes from other routing protocols, as is covered in Chapter 9, "Basic IGP Redistribution," and Chapter 10, "Advanced IGP Redistribution," some of the **match** command's other options can be very helpful.

Using Route Maps to Filter EIGRP Routes

The mechanics of the configuration works much like the other two filtering features. The **distribute-list** command refers to the feature that matches the packets, in this case a **route-map** command option. The **distribute-list** command again lists a direction (in or out), and optionally an interface.

Example 4-4 shows the configuration results in an excerpt from the **show running-config** command, along with the output of the **show route-map** command. The configuration implements the same logic as used in Example 4-2 earlier in this chapter, under the heading "Using IP Prefix Lists to Filter EIGRP Routes." The design criteria are the same as with that earlier example:

- Of the routes from manufacturing, filter only those routes that begin with 10.17.35 and 10.17.36.

- Filter WAN routers from advertising any /30 routes in the Layer 3 core.

Example 4-4 *Filtering All Routes with a /30 Prefix Length, Plus Some Routes from Manufacturing*

```
! On Router WAN2: !!!!!!!!!!!!!!!!!!!!!!!!!!!!!!!!!!!!!!!!!!!
WAN2#show running-config
! lines omitted for brevity
router eigrp 1
 network 10.0.0.0
 distribute-list route-map filter-man-slash30 out
 auto-summary
!
ip prefix-list manufacturing seq 5 permit 10.17.35.0/24 ge 25 le 25
ip prefix-list manufacturing seq 10 permit 10.17.36.0/24 ge 26 le 26
!
ip prefix-list slash30 seq 5 permit 0.0.0.0/0 ge 30 le 30
!
route-map filter-man-slash30 deny 8
 match ip address prefix-list manufacturing
!
route-map filter-man-slash30 deny 15
 match ip address prefix-list slash30
!
route-map filter-man-slash30 permit 23

! Notice - no match commands, so the above clause matches all remaining routes
!
! lines omitted for brevity
WAN2#show route-map
route-map filter-man-slash30, deny, sequence 8
  Match clauses:
    ip address prefix-lists: manufacturing
  Set clauses:
  Policy routing matches: 0 packets, 0 bytes
route-map filter-man-slash30, deny, sequence 15
  Match clauses:
    ip address prefix-lists: slash30
  Set clauses:
  Policy routing matches: 0 packets, 0 bytes
route-map filter-man-slash30, permit, sequence 23
```

```
Match clauses:
Set clauses:
Policy routing matches: 0 packets, 0 bytes
```

In particular, note that the first two **route-map** commands list a **deny** action, meaning that all routes matched in these two clauses will be filtered. The IP prefix lists referenced in the **match** commands, called **manufacturing** and **slash30**, respectively, each match (permit) the routes listed in one of the two design goals. Note that the logic of both prefix lists could have easily been configured into a single prefix list, reducing the length of the **route-map** command as well. Finally, note that the last **route-map** command has a **permit** action, with no **match** command, meaning that the default action is to allow the route to be advertised.

Also, it can be useful to take a moment and review Example 4-2 as a point of comparison for the use of the IP prefix lists in each case. In the **route-map** of Example 4-4, the prefix list needs to match the routes with a permit clause so that the route-map **deny** action causes the routes to be filtered. Earlier, Example 4-2 shows the same basic logic in the prefix list, but with an action of deny. The reasoning is that when the **distribute-list prefix-list...** command refers directly to an IP prefix list, IOS then filters routes denied by the prefix list.

Route Summarization

As mentioned in the introduction to this chapter, keeping routing tables small helps conserve memory and may improve the time required by a router to forward packets. Route filtering allows an engineer to reduce the size of the routing table, but with the side effect of limiting the destinations reachable by each router. That effect may or may not be acceptable, given the other design goals of a particular internetwork, and given the need to operate the network.

Route summarization allows an engineer to keep the routing tables more manageable, without limiting reachability. Instead of advertising routes for every subnet, a router advertises a single route that represents the same range of IP addresses as more than one subnet. Each router can forward packets to the same set of destinations, but the routing table is smaller. For example, instead of advertising routes 10.11.0.0/24, 10.11.1.0/24, 10.11.2.0/24, and so on–all subnets up through 10.11.255.0/24–a router could advertise a single route for 10.11.0.0/16, which includes the exact same range of addresses.

This section begins by examining some design issues related to route summarization. Then the text moves on to explain how to explicitly configure EIGRP summary routes, finishing with a discussion of automatically created summaries based on the **auto-summary** command and feature.

Route Summarization Design

Route summarization works best when the subnet planning process considers route summarization. To accommodate summarization, the engineer assigning subnets can assign larger address blocks to one part of the topology. The engineers working with that part of the internetwork can break the address blocks into individual subnets as needed. At the edge of that part of the network, the engineers can configure route summaries to be advertised to the other parts of the internetwork. In short, when possible, plan the route summaries before deploying the new parts of an internetwork, and then assign addresses to different parts of the internetwork within their assigned address blocks.

For example, consider Figure 4-4, which shows a variation on the same internetwork shown earlier in this chapter, with the address blocks planned before deployment.

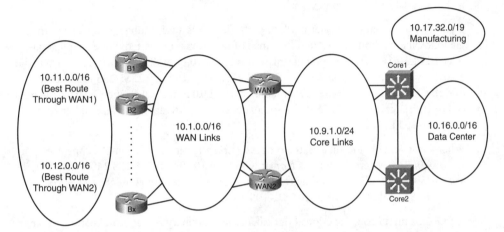

Figure 4-4   *Address Blocks Planned for Example Enterprise Internetwork*

Figure 4-4 shows the address blocks planned for various parts of the internetwork, as follows:

■ Assign branch subnets come from two consecutive ranges–10.11.0.0/16 and 10.12.0.0/16.

■ Assign WAN router-to-router subnets from the range 10.1.0.0/16.

■ Assign core LAN router-to-router subnets from the range 10.9.1.0/24.

■ Assign Data Center subnets from the range 10.16.0.0/16.

■ Give the manufacturing division, which has a separate IT staff, address block 10.17.32.0/19.

Inside each of the circles in Figure 4-4, the engineering staff can assign subnets as the need arises. As long as addresses are not taken from one range and used in another part of the internetwork, the routers at the boundary between the regions (circles) in Figure 4-4 can configure EIGRP route summarization to both create one large summary route and prevent the advertisement of the smaller individual routes.

Calculating Summary Routes

Note that the examples in this chapter generally use simpler examples of summary routes, using prefix lengths like /24 and /16 most often. However, for the exam, you need to be comfortable interpreting prefix/prefix length pairs, and subnet/mask pairs, whether they represent an actual subnet or a summary route.

The math to analyze a subnet/mask pair, or prefix/length pair, is identical to the math included as part of the CCNA certification. As such, this book does not attempt to explain those same concepts, other than this brief review of one useful shortcut when working with potential summary routes.

If you can trust that the subnet/mask or prefix/length is a valid subnet or summary, then the following method can tell you the range of numbers represented. For example, consider 10.11.0.0/16. Written in subnet/mask form, it is 10.11.0.0/255.255.0.0. Then, invert the mask by subtracting the mask from 255.255.255.255, yielding 0.0.255.255 in this case. Add this inverted mask to the subnet number (10.11.0.0 in this case), and you have the high end of the range (10.11.255.255). So, summary 10.11.0.0/16 represents all numbers from 10.11.0.0–10.11.255.255.

When using less obvious masks, the process works the same. For example, consider 10.10.16.0/20. Converting to mask format, you have 10.10.16.0/255.255.240.0. Inverting the mask gives you 0.0.15.255. Adding the inverted mask to the subnet number gives you 10.10.31.255, and a range of 10.10.16.0–10.10.31.255.

Before closing this short section about calculating summary routes, note that the process of adding the inveretd subnet mask assumes that the prefix/length or subnet/mask is a valid subnet number or valid summary route. If it is not, then you can still do the math, but neither the low end nor high end of the range is valid. For example, 10.10.16.0/19, similar to the previous example, is not actually a subnet number. 10.10.16.0 would be an IP address in subnet 10.10.0.0/19, with range of addresses 10.10.0.0–10.10.31.255.

Choosing Where to Summarize Routes

EIGRP supports route summarization at any router, unlike OSPF, which requires that summarization be performed only at area border routers (ABR) or autonomous system border routers (ASBR). EIGRP's flexibility helps when designing the internetwork, but it also poses some questions as to where to summarize EIGRP routes.

In some cases, the options are relatively obvious. For example, consider the 10.17.32.0/19 address block in manufacturing in Figure 4-4. The manufacturing division's router could summarize all its routes as a single 10.17.32.0/19 route when advertising to Core1. Alternately, Core1 could summarize all those same routes, advertising a summary for 10.17.32.0/19. In either case, packets from the rest of the internetwork shown in Figure 4-4 will flow toward Core1 and then to the Manufacturing division.

Next, consider the 10.16.0.0/16 address block in the Data Center. Because all these subnets reside to the right of Layer 3 switches Core1 and Core2, these two devices could summarize 10.16.0.0/16. However, these routes could also be summarized on WAN1/WAN2 for advertisement to the branches on the left. Summarizing on Core1/Core2 helps reduce the size of the routing tables on WAN1 and WAN2. However, the sheer number of subnets in a Data Center is typically small compared to the number of small remote sites, so the savings of routing table space may be small.

One advantage of summarizing 10.16.0.0/16 on WAN1/WAN2 instead of Core1/Core2 in this case is to avoid routing inefficiencies in the core of the internetwork. The later section "Suboptimal Forwarding with Summarization" discusses the concept with a different example.

Influencing the Choice of Best Route for Summary Routes

Often, engineers plan route summarization for the same address block on multiple routers. Such a design takes advantage of redundancy and can be used to perform basic load balancing of traffic across the various paths through the internetwork. Figure 4-5 shows one such example, with Routers WAN1 and WAN2 summarizing routes for the two address blocks located on the branch office LANs: 10.11.0.0/16 and 10.12.0.0/16.

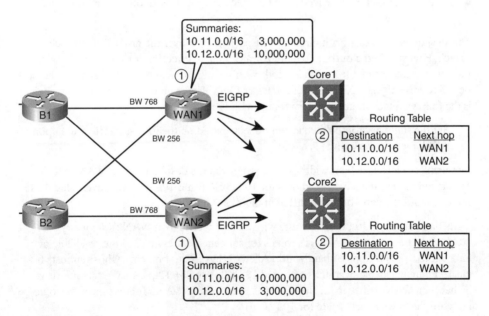

Figure 4-5   *Choosing Locations for Route Summarization*

The figure shows the advertisements of the summary routes. WAN1 and WAN2 both advertise the same summarizes: 10.11.0.0/16 for some branches and 10.12.0.0/16 for the others. Note that by advertising the WAN routes, instead of filtering, the operations staff might have an easier time monitoring and troubleshooting the internetwork, while still meeting the design goal of reducing the size of the routing table. (Also, note that Router WAN1 summarizes Manufacturing's routes of 10.17.32.0/19.)

In some cases, the network designer has no preference for which of the two or more routers should be used to reach hosts within the summary route range. For example, for most Data

Center designs, as shown earlier in Figure 4-4, the routes from the left of the figure toward the Data Center, through Core1 and Core2, would typically be considered equal.

However, in some cases, as in the design shown in Figure 4-5, the network designer wants to improve the metric of one of the summary routes for a single address block to make that route the preferred route. Using 10.11.0.0/16 as an example, consider this more detailed description of the design:

- Use two PVCs to each branch–one faster PVC with 768 Kbps CIR and one slower PVC (either 128 Kbps or 256 Kbps CIR).

- Roughly half the branches should have a faster PVC connecting to Router WAN1, and the other half of the branches should have a faster PVC connecting to Router WAN2.

- Assign user subnets from the range 10.11.0.0/16 for branches that use WAN1 as the primary WAN access point, and from 10.12.0.0/16 for the branches that use WAN2 as primary.

- Routing should be influenced such that packets flow in both directions over the faster WAN link, assuming that link is working.

This design requires that both directions of packets flow over the faster PVC to each branch. Focusing in the outbound (core-toward-branch) direction for now, by following the design, and setting the interface bandwidth settings to match the PVC speeds, the outbound routes will send packets over the faster PVCs. The main reason for the route choices is the following fact about summary routes with IOS:

> Set the summary route's metric components based on the lowest metric route upon which the summary route is based.

By setting the interface bandwidth settings to match the design, the two WAN routers should summarize and advertise routes for 10.11.0.0/16 and 10.12.0.0/16, advertising these routes toward the core–but with different metrics.

WAN1 advertises its 10.11.0.0/16 route with a lower metric than WAN2's summary for 10.11.0.0/16 because all of WAN1's routes for subnets that begin 10.11 are reachable over links set to use 768 Kbps of bandwidth. All WAN1's links to branches whose subnets begin 10.12 are reachable over links of speed 128 KBps or 256 Kbps, so WAN1's metric is higher than WAN2's metric for the 10.12.0.0/16 summary. WAN2 follows the same logic but with the lower metric route for 10.12.0.0/16.

As a result of the advertisements on WAN1 and WAN2, the core routers both have routing table entries that drive traffic meant for the faster-through-WAN1 branches to WAN1, and traffic for the faster-through-WAN2 branches to WAN2.

Suboptimal Forwarding with Summarization

The final concept to consider when summarizing routes is that the packets may take a longer path than if summarization is not used. The idea works a little like this story. Say you were travelling to Europe from the USA. You knew nothing of European geography, other than that you wanted to go to Paris. So, you look around and find hundreds of flights to Europe and just pick the cheapest one. When you get to Europe, you worry about how to get the rest of the way to Paris–be it a Taxi ride from the Paris airport, or whether it takes a day of train travel. Although you do eventually get to Paris, if you had chosen to know more about European geography before you left, you could have saved yourself some travel time in Europe.

Similarly, routers that learn a summary route do not know about the details of the subnets inside the summary. Instead, like the person who just picked the cheapest flight to Europe, the routers pick the lowest metric summary route for a prefix. That router forwards packets based on the summary route. Later, when these packets arrive at routers that do know all the subnets inside the summary, those routers can then use the best route–be it a short route or long route.

For example, Figure 4-6 shows the less efficient routing of packets to host 10.11.1.1, a host off Router B1, assuming that the route summarization shown in Figure 4-5 still exists. When WAN1's 768 Kbps CIR PVC to Router B1 fails, WAN1 does not change its route advertisement for its 10.11.0.0/16 summary route. When EIGRP advertises a summary route, the advertising router considers the summary route to be up and working unless all subordinate routes fail. Unless all of WAN1's specific routes in the 10.11.0.0/16 range failed, R1 would not notify routers on the right about any problem. So, when the example shown in Figure 4-6 begins, the 10.11.0.0/16 summary advertised by WAN1, as seen earlier in Figure 4-5, is still working, and both Core1 and Core2 use WAN1 as their next-hop router for their routes to 10.11.0.0/16.

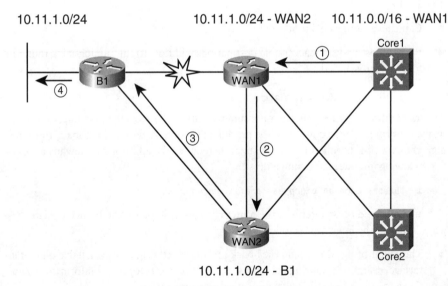

Figure 4-6 *Suboptimal Forwarding Path when Primary PVC Fails*

Following the steps in the figure:

Step 1.   Core 1 sends a packet to 10.11.1.1, using its route for 10.16.0.0/16, to WAN1.

Step 2.   WAN1, which has routes for all the subnets that begin 10.11, has a route for 10.11.1.0/24 with WAN2 as the next hop (because WAN1's link to B1 has failed).

Step 3.   WAN2 has a route for 10.11.1.0/24, with B1 as the next hop, so WAN2 forwards the packet.

Step 4.   B1 forwards the packet to host 10.11.1.1.

Route Summarization Benefits and Trade-Offs

The previous section showed details of a classic trade-off with route summarization: the benefits of the summary route versus the possibility of inefficient routing. For easier study, the benefits and trade-offs for route summarization are listed here:

Benefits:

■   Smaller routing tables, while all destinations still reachable.

■   Reduces Query scope: EIGRP Query stops at a router that has a summary route that includes the subnet listed in the Query but not the specific route listed in the Query.

■   EIGRP supports summarization at any location in the internetwork.

■   The summary has the metric of the best of the subnets being summarized.

Trade-offs:

■   Can cause suboptimal routing.

■   Packets destined for inaccessible destinations will flow to the summarizing router before being discarded.

Configuring EIGRP Route Summarization

The more difficult part of EIGRP route summarization relates to the planning, design, and analysis of trade-offs as covered in the preceding section. After you have made those design choices, configuring route summarization requires the addition of a few instances of the following interface subcommand:

```
ip summary-address eigrp asn prefix subnet-mask
```

When configured on an interface, the router changes its logic for the EIGRP Update messages sent out the interface, as follows:

■   The router brings down, and then back up, all EIGRP neighbors reachable on that interface, effectively causing neighbors to forget previous topology information, and listen to new information (when the neighborships recover).

■   When the neighborships recover, the router advertises the summary route, per the **ip summary-address** command, assuming the router has at least one route whose address range is inside the range of the summary route.

■   The router does *not* advertise the subordinate routes. (The term *subordinate route* refers to the routes whose address ranges are inside the range of addresses defined by the summary route.)

■   The router adds a route to its own routing table, for the summary prefix/prefix-length, with an outgoing interface of null0.

In Figure 4-7, WAN1 and WAN2 summarize the routes for the Data Center in the range 10.16.0.0/16, instead of sending individual routes for this range to the branch offices. Example 4-5 shows the results of summarization on both routers.

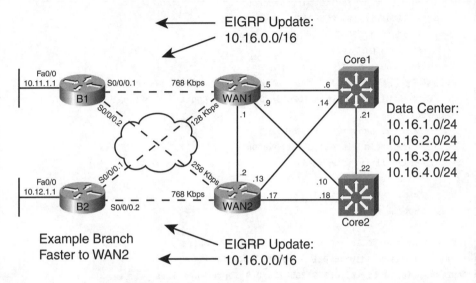

Figure 4-7   *Summary for 10.16.0.0/16 on WAN1, WAN2*

Example 4-5   *Summarizing Routes for Data Center (10.16.0.0/16) on WAN1/WAN2*

```
! On Router WAN2: !!!!!!!!!!!!!!!!!!!!!!!!!!!!!!!!!!!!!!!!!!!!!!!
WAN2#show running-config
! lines omitted for brevity
!
interface Serial0/0/0.1 point-to-point
 bandwidth 256
 ip address 10.1.2.1 255.255.255.252
 ip summary-address eigrp 1 10.16.0.0 255.255.0.0 5
 frame-relay interface-dlci 103
!
interface Serial0/0/0.2 point-to-point
 bandwidth 768
 ip address 10.1.2.5 255.255.255.252
 ip summary-address eigrp 1 10.16.0.0 255.255.0.0 5
 frame-relay interface-dlci 104
!
WAN2#show ip eigrp topology 10.16.0.0/16
IP-EIGRP (AS 1): Topology entry for 10.16.0.0/16
  State is Passive, Query origin flag is 1, 1 Successor(s), FD is 28416
```

```
    Routing Descriptor Blocks:
    0.0.0.0 (Null0), from 0.0.0.0, Send flag is 0x0
        Composite metric is (28416/0), Route is Internal
        Vector metric:
          Minimum bandwidth is 100000 Kbit
          Total delay is 110 microseconds
          Reliability is 255/255
          Load is 1/255
          Minimum MTU is 1500
          Hop count is 1
    10.1.2.2 (Serial0/0/0.1), from 10.1.2.2, Send flag is 0x0
        Composite metric is (11026688/3847936), Route is Internal
        Vector metric:
          Minimum bandwidth is 256 Kbit
          Total delay is 40110 microseconds
          Reliability is 255/255
          Load is 1/255
          Minimum MTU is 1500
          Hop count is 3


! Note that the following command lists only routes in the range
! of the summary - 10.16.0.0 - 10.16.255.255.
WAN2#show ip route 10.16.0.0 255.255.0.0 longer-prefixes
Codes: C - connected, S - static, R - RIP, M - mobile, B - BGP
       D - EIGRP, EX - EIGRP external, O - OSPF, IA - OSPF inter area
       N1 - OSPF NSSA external type 1, N2 - OSPF NSSA external type 2
       E1 - OSPF external type 1, E2 - OSPF external type 2
       i - IS-IS, su - IS-IS summary, L1 - IS-IS level-1, L2 - IS-IS level-2
       ia - IS-IS inter area, * - candidate default, U - per-user static route
       o - ODR, P - periodic downloaded static route


Gateway of last resort is not set


     10.0.0.0/8 is variably subnetted, 23 subnets, 6 masks
D        10.16.2.0/24 [90/156160] via 10.9.1.14, 00:19:06, FastEthernet0/0.12
D        10.16.3.0/24 [90/156160] via 10.9.1.14, 00:19:06, FastEthernet0/0.12
D        10.16.0.0/16 is a summary, 00:14:07, Null0
D        10.16.1.0/24 [90/28416] via 10.9.1.18, 00:19:06, FastEthernet0/1.16
                      [90/28416] via 10.9.1.14, 00:19:06, FastEthernet0/0.12
D        10.16.4.0/24 [90/156160] via 10.9.1.14, 00:19:06, FastEthernet0/0.12
WAN2#show ip route 10.16.0.0 255.255.0.0
Routing entry for 10.16.0.0/16
  Known via "eigrp 1", distance 5, metric 28416, type internal
  Redistributing via eigrp 1
```

```
Routing Descriptor Blocks:
* directly connected, via Null0
     Route metric is 28416, traffic share count is 1
     Total delay is 110 microseconds, minimum bandwidth is 100000 Kbit
     Reliability 255/255, minimum MTU 1500 bytes
     Loading 1/255, Hops 0
```

Example 4-5 shows the results only on Router WAN2, but WAN1 will be identically configured with the **ip summary-address** command. With only two branch office routers actually implemented in my lab, WAN2 needs only two **ip summary-address** commands: one for the subinterface connected to Router B1, and another for the subinterface connected to B2. With a full implementation, this same command would be needed on each subinterface connected to a branch router.

The example also shows how a router like WAN2 uses a summary route to null0. This route–10.16.0.0/16 with an outgoing interface of null0–causes the router (WAN2) to discard packets matched by this route. However, as you can see from the end of Example 4-5, WAN2 also has routes for all the known specific subnets. Pulling all these thoughts together, when the summarizing router receives a packet within the summary route's range

■   If the packet matches a more specific route than the summary route, the packet is forwarded based on that route.

■   When the packet does not match a more specific route, it matches the summary route and is discarded.

To ensure that the router adds this local summary route, the router uses the administrative distance (AD) setting of 5. The user may have typed the **ip summary-address eigrp 1 10.16.0.0 255.255.0.0** command, without the 5 at the end. Even so, IOS will add this default AD value as seen in Example 4-5. With an AD of 5, WAN2 will ignore any EIGRP-advertised summary routes for 10.16.0.0/16–for example, the summary created by neighbor WAN1—because EIGRP's default AD for internal routes is 90. In fact, the output of WAN2's **show ip eigrp topology 10.16.0.0/16** command lists two known routes for 10.16.0.0/16: one to null0 and the other to branch router WAN1 (outgoing interface S0/0/0.1). WAN2 uses the lower-AD route to null0, which prevents a routing loop. (Note that this summary route with outgoing interface null0 is often called a *discard route.*)

Next, consider the results on the branch routers. The following might be reasonable design requirements that should be verified on the branch routers:

■   Each branch router's route for 10.16.0.0/16 should use the primary (faster) PVC (see Figure 4-7).

■   Each branch router should be able to converge quickly to the other 10.16.0.0/16 summary route without using EIGRP Queries (in other words, there should be an FS route).

Example 4-6 confirms that both requirements are met.

Example 4-6   *Results of the 10.16.0.0/16 Summary on Routers B1, B2*

```
! Router B1 first !!!!!!!!!!!!!!!!!!!!!
B1#show ip route 10.16.0.0 255.255.0.0 longer-prefixes
! lines omitted for brevity


     10.0.0.0/8 is variably subnetted, 5 subnets, 3 masks
D       10.16.0.0/16 [90/3847936] via 10.1.1.1, 00:16:53, Serial0/0/0.1


B1#show ip eigrp topology
! lines omitted for brevity
P 10.16.0.0/16, 1 successors, FD is 3847936
        via 10.1.1.1 (3847936/28416), Serial0/0/0.1
        via 10.1.2.1 (10514688/28416), Serial0/0/0.2
! Router B2 Next !!!!!!!!!!!!!!!!!!!!!
B2#show ip route 10.16.0.0 255.255.0.0 longer-prefixes
! lines omitted for brevity


     10.0.0.0/8 is variably subnetted, 5 subnets, 3 masks
D       10.16.0.0/16 [90/3847936] via 10.1.2.5, 00:16:44, Serial0/0/0.2
```

First, on Router B1, the router has an IP route for 10.16.0.0/16, with outgoing interface S0/0/0.1. Per Figure 4-7, this subinterface indeed connects to the primary PVC. Per the **show ip eigrp topology** command, two possible routes for 10.16.0.0/16 are listed; this command only lists successor and feasible successor routes. Also, note that the FS route's RD (28,416) is less than the successor route's FD (3,847,936), which means the secondary route indeed meets the feasibility condition.

The reverse is true on Router B2. B2's best route for 10.16.0.0/16 uses its S0/0/0.2, which connects to B2's primary (faster) PVC through WAN2. Although not shown, it also lists its backup route over the slower PVC as a feasible successor.

The route summarization feature discussed in this section is sometimes referred to as *manual* route summarization to contrast it with the term *auto* summarization. EIGRP auto summarization is explained next.

Auto-summary

Automatic summarization, also called auto-summary, causes a router to automatically advertise a summary route under certain conditions, without the use of the **ip summary-address** command. When using auto-summary, if a router has interfaces in more than one Class A, B, or C network, then that router will advertise a single summary route for an entire Class A, B, or C network into the other classful network, rather than advertise routes for the individual subnets. The following is a more formal definition:

When a router has multiple working interfaces, and those interfaces use IP addresses in different classful networks, the router advertises a summary route for each classful network on interfaces attached to a different classful network.

The auto-summary feature first existed as a required feature of *classful routing protocols*. By definition, classful routing protocols (RIPv1 and IGRP) do not advertise subnet mask information. The omission of the subnet mask in routing updates causes several design problems–in particular, these protocols cannot support variable length subnet masks (VLSM), route summarization, or discontiguous network designs.

The newer IGPs–EIGRP, OSPF, and RIP-2–are classless routing protocols because they advertise the subnet mask and support VLSM. However, with auto-summary enabled, EIGRP acts like classful routing protocols in one specific way: they do not support discontiguous networks. To support discontiguous networks with EIGRP, simply disable auto-summary. The rest of this section further defines the terms and the problem, and shows the solution of disabling auto-summary.

To better understand discontiguous networks, consider this analogy. U.S. residents can appreciate the concept of a discontiguous network based on the common term *contiguous 48*, referring to the 48 U.S. states other than Alaska and Hawaii. To drive to Alaska from the contiguous 48 U.S. states, for example, you must drive through another country (Canada, for the geographically impaired), so Alaska is not contiguous with the 48 states. In other words, it is discontiguous.

More formally:

■ **Contiguous network:** A single classful network in which packets sent between every pair of subnets will pass only through subnets of that same classful network, without having to pass through subnets of any other classful network.

■ **Discontiguous network:** A single classful network in which packets sent between at least one pair of subnets must pass through subnets of a different classful network.

Figure 4-8 shows a classic example of a discontiguous network 10.0.0.0. Subnets of class A network 10.0.0.0 exist on the left and the right, with subnets of class B network 172.16.0.0 in the middle of the internetwork. Following the figure, the problem created by the auto-summary feature is described.

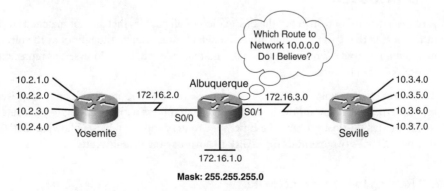

Figure 4-8   *Discontiguous Network 10.0.0.0*

The problem is that when EIGRP auto-summarizes routes at the boundary between classful networks, then routers in other classful networks cannot route packets to all the desti-

nations. For example, because both Yosemite and Seville use auto-summary, they both advertise a route for 10.0.0.0/8 to Albuquerque. Albuquerque may choose one of the two as
the better route–for example, it may choose the route to the left, through Yosemite. However, in that case, then Albuquerque cannot forward packets to the network 10.0.0.0 hosts
on the right. Even if Albuquerque decided to add both routes to its routing table, the load
sharing typically occurs per destination IP address, not per subnet. So, some packets
might be delivered to the correct host, and others not.

For EIGRP, two solutions exist. First, you could design the network to not use a discontiguous network. Alternatively, you can just disable auto-summary using the **no auto-summary** subcommand inside EIGRP configuration mode. This command affects the behavior
of the router on which it is configured only and tells that router to not advertise a summary route for the entire classful network. Instead, that router advertises all the subnets, as
if the auto-summary feature did not exist.

Note: The **auto-summary** and **no auto-summary** commands have no effect on routers
that connect to a single classful network.

For classful routing protocols, the only solution is to not use discontiguous classful
networks.

Note: Some confusion exists related to EIGRP's default for auto-summary. Some IOS
documentation claims that EIGRP defaults to use **no auto-summary** at later IOS releases,
including 12.4T, but experiments show the opposite. You can confirm the actual setting by
looking at the output of the **show ip protocols** command.

Default Routes

A router's default route matches the destination of all packets that are not matched by any
other route in the IP routing table. In fact, a default route can be thought of as the ultimate summary route–a route for the prefix that includes all IPv4 addresses, as represented
by prefix/length 0.0.0.0/0.

This section first examines the most common use of default routes inside an Enterprise: to
draw Internet traffic toward the Internet-connected routers without having to put routes
for all Internet destinations into the Enterprise routers' routing tables. Following that, this
section examines two methods for EIGRP to advertise the default route.

Default Routing to the Internet Router

Consider an Enterprise network and its connection to the Internet, as shown in Figure 4-9.
For now, the design shows a single Internet-facing router (I1). As is often the case, the entire Enterprise in this figure uses private IP addresses. In this case, all Enterprise subnets
are part of private class A network 10.0.0.0.

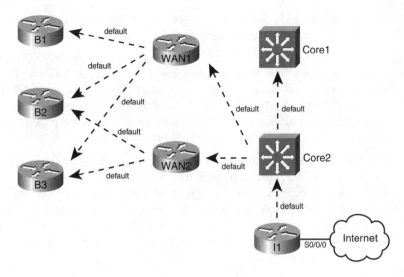

Figure 4-9   *Pulling Packets to the Internet Router (I1)*

From a design perspective, the entire Enterprise can use a default route to forward packets to the Internet. To accomplish this design, the Internet-facing router advertises a default route. All routers flood this default prefix throughout the EIGRP domain, building their own default routes.

When converged, all routers have a default route, plus the usual Enterprise routes. Packets destined for addresses inside the Enterprise use the same old routes, ignoring the default route. Packets destined outside the Enterprise use each router's respective default route because no other routes match the destination. Eventually, these packets arrive at Router I1. When I1 receives these packets, it can forward toward the Internet, either based on a default route or on routes learned using BGP.

Figure 4-9 shows a case with just one Internet-facing router, but with multiple, the same concepts can be used. The multiple Internet-facing routers can each advertise a default route, and each Enterprise router will think one of the available defaults is best–causing the packets to arrive at the nearest Internet access point.

Default Routing Configuration with EIGRP

This section examines the two main options for EIGRP to advertise default routes: to define a static default route and advertise it with EIGRP and to flag an existing route to be used also as a default route.

Advertising Static Default Routes with EIGRP

To cause the advertisement of the default routes shown in Figure 4-9, Router I1 can follow these steps:

Step 1.   Create a static route default route using the **ip route 0.0.0.0 0.0.0.0 S0/0/0** command.

Step 2.   Inject this route into the EIGRP topology database, either using the **network 0.0.0.0** command or by redistributing the static route.

First, examine the command listed for Step 1: **ip route 0.0.0.0 0.0.0.0 S0/0/0**. The prefix and mask together represent all IPv4 addresses. The reasoning is that if a mask of 255.255.0.0 means "the last two octets can be any value," and 255.0.0.0 means "the last three octets can be any value," then a subnet mask of 0.0.0.0 means that all four octets can be any value. The outgoing interface, S0/0/0 in this case, tells I1 to send packets for otherwise unknown destinations over the link to the Internet, as intended.

After Step 1, Router I1 has a route in its routing table, but EIGRP does not yet advertise the route. I1 could be configured to perform route redistribution for this static route. (Refer to Chapter 9 for more information on route redistribution.) The other option is to use the **network 0.0.0.0** EIGRP subcommand. Oddly enough, this is a special case in which IOS thinks "if my routing table has a default route in it, put a default route (0.0.0.0/0) into the EIGRP table." (If the route leaves the routing table, then the router will notify neighbors that the route has failed.)

Configuring a Default Network

The second option for creating a default route is to flag a route for a classful network–for a prefix that will be advertised into the EIGRP domain–as a route that can be used as a default route. Then each router can use the forwarding details in that route–the outgoing interface and next-hop router–as its default route.

Configuring this feature requires a couple of steps. The concepts require the most thought, with the configuration commands that follow being relatively simple:

Key Topic

Step 1.   On the router to which all traffic should be directed, identify a classful network that can be advertised into the EIGRP domain, and ensure that network is being advertised into EIGRP (typically using the EIGRP **network** command).

Step 2.   Configure that network as a default network using the global command **ip default-network** *network-number*.

Step 1 requires a class A, B, or C network, known in the routing table of the router that will generate the default route (Router I1 in Figure 4-9). Most often, that route is either created off a loopback interface for the purpose of making this process work, or an existing route on the Internet side of the router is used.

Figure 4-10 shows two examples. First, class C network 198.133.219.0/24 exists off I1's S0/0/0 interface, so I1 has a connected route for this class C network in its routing table. Alternatively, the engineer could configure a loopback interface, such as loopback 8, so that I1 would have a connected route for 192.31.7.0/24. In both cases, the routes would need to be advertised into EIGRP, by matching the address using the **network** command.

If the configuration stopped at Step 1, then the Enterprise routers simply know yet another route. By adding the **ip default-network** command to refer to one of these networks, EIGRP then flags this route as a candidate default route. As a result, each EIGRP router treats their route for this particular network also as if it were a default route.

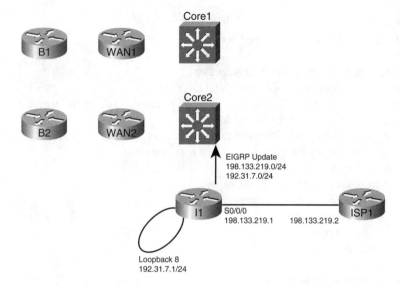

Figure 4-10 *Example Default Networks*

Example 4-7 shows an example of the configuration on Router I1, along with some of the **show** commands on Router I1.

Example 4-7 *Configuring a Default Network on Router I1*

```
I1#configure terminal
Enter configuration commands, one per line.  End with CNTL/Z.
I1(config)#interface loopback 8
I1(config-if)#ip address 192.31.7.1 255.255.255.0
I1(config-if)#router eigrp 1
I1(config-router)#network 192.31.7.0
I1(config-router)#exit
I1(config)#ip default-network 192.31.7.0
I1(config-router)#^Z


I1#show ip route
Codes: C - connected, S - static, R - RIP, M - mobile, B - BGP
       D - EIGRP, EX - EIGRP external, O - OSPF, IA - OSPF inter area
       N1 - OSPF NSSA external type 1, N2 - OSPF NSSA external type 2
       E1 - OSPF external type 1, E2 - OSPF external type 2
       i - IS-IS, su - IS-IS summary, L1 - IS-IS level-1, L2 - IS-IS level-2
       ia - IS-IS inter area, * - candidate default, U - per-user static route
       o - ODR, P - periodic downloaded static route

Gateway of last resort is not set

     10.0.0.0/8 is variably subnetted, 15 subnets, 3 masks
```

```
! lines omitted for brevity
C*   192.31.7.0/24 is directly connected, Loopback8

I1#show ip eigrp topology 192.31.7.0/24
IP-EIGRP (AS 1): Topology entry for 192.31.7.0/24
  State is Passive, Query origin flag is 1, 1 Successor(s), FD is 128256
  Routing Descriptor Blocks:
  0.0.0.0 (Loopback8), from Connected, Send flag is 0x0
      Composite metric is (128256/0), Route is Internal
      Vector metric:
        Minimum bandwidth is 10000000 Kbit
        Total delay is 5000 microseconds
        Reliability is 255/255
        Load is 1/255
        Minimum MTU is 1514
        Hop count is 0
      Exterior flag is set
```

The configuration has several results, as seen in the example:

■ A connected route for 192.31.7.0/24, a class C network

■ The advertisement of that network into EIGRP due to the **network 192.31.7.0** command

■ The setting of the exterior flag on the route

Because of the **ip default-network 192.31.7.0** command, the routing table lists the route as a candidate default route, as denoted by an asterisk.

Interestingly, the router with the **ip default-network** command configured — I1 in this case — does not use that route as a default route, as indicated by the highlighted phrase "Gateway of last resort not set." (*Gateway of last resort* refers to the next-hop router of a router's current default route.) Although I1 flags the route as a candidate default route, I1 itself does not use that route as its default, because I1 is actually the original advertiser of the default.

Moving on to another Enterprise router, in this case B1, you can see in Example 4-8 that not only does the remote router learn the candidate default route, but that the B1 uses this same information as B1's default route.

Example 4-8 *Gateway of Last Resort on Router B1*

```
B1#show ip route
Codes: C - connected, S - static, R - RIP, M - mobile, B - BGP
       D - EIGRP, EX - EIGRP external, O - OSPF, IA - OSPF inter area
       N1 - OSPF NSSA external type 1, N2 - OSPF NSSA external type 2
       E1 - OSPF external type 1, E2 - OSPF external type 2
       i - IS-IS, su - IS-IS summary, L1 - IS-IS level-1, L2 - IS-IS level-2
```

```
        ia - IS-IS inter area, * - candidate default, U - per-user static route
        o - ODR, P - periodic downloaded static route

Gateway of last resort is 10.1.1.1 to network 192.31.7.0


    10.0.0.0/8 is variably subnetted, 15 subnets, 3 masks
Lines omitted for brevity
D*    192.31.7.0/24 [90/2297856] via 10.1.1.1, 00:05:10, Serial0/0/0.1
```

In this case, B1 has indeed learned an EIGRP route for 192.31.7.0/24, a route flagged as exterior. Because this happens to be the only candidate default route learned by B1 at this point, it is the best default route. So, B1 sets its gateway of last resort to 10.1.1.1—the next-hop IP address of B1's route to 192.31.7.0/24. If B1 knew of multiple candidate default routes, it would have chosen the best route based on administrative distance and then metric, and used that route as the basis for the gateway of last resort.

Exam Preparation Tasks

Planning Practice

The CCNP ROUTE exam expects test takers to review design documents, create implementation plans, and create verification plans. This section provides some exercises that may help you to take a step back from the minute details of the topics in this chapter so that you can think about the same technical topics from the planning perspective.

For each planning practice table, simply complete the table. Note that any numbers in parentheses represent the number of options listed for each item in the solutions in Appendix F, "Completed Planning Practice Tables."

Design Review Table

Table 4-5 lists several design goals related to this chapter. If these design goals were listed in a design document, and you had to take that document and develop an implementation plan, what implementation options come to mind? For any configuration items, a general description can be used, without concern about the specific parameters.

Table 4-5 *Design Review*

Design Goal	Possible Implementation Choices Covered in This Chapter
Prevent the edge routers in sites for one division of the company from knowing routes for subnets in another division.	
The design shows the use of class B networks 172.16.0.0, 172.17.0.0, and 172.18.0.0 throughout the Enterprise, with a goal to reduce routing table sizes when possible. (3 options)	
R1 and R2 will advertise the same summary route; ensure that R1 is the preferred EIGRP path for that summary.	
Always ensure that the shortest path is taken with each route.	

Implementation Plan Peer Review Table

Table 4-6 shows a list of questions that others might ask, or that you might think about, during a peer review of another network engineer's implementation plan. Complete the table by answering the questions.

Table 4-6 *Notable Questions from This Chapter to Consider During an Implementation Plan Peer Review*

Question	Answer
The plan calls for filtering 10.10.10.0/26 and 10.10.12.0/26, but not 10.10.11.0/24. What tools can be used?	
A plan lists a configuration of an EIGRP distribution list, referring to route-map *one*. The route-maps clauses use only the deny option. However, it refers to prefix lists that use some deny and permit actions. Can any routes pass through the filter?	
A plan lists a configuration of an EIGRP distribution list, with a route-map with two clauses, each with a permit action. Both clauses refer to a different prefix list, each of which has some permit and deny actions. Characterize which routes will be filtered, and which will not, based on matching deny and permit clauses in each prefix list.	
The plan shows extensive use of class C private networks inside a large Enterprise. What effect might EIGRP auto-summary have?	
The plan shows a sample configuration of the **ip summary-address eigrp 1 10.10.0.0 255.255.252.0** command on Router R1. What routes should I see on R1? What will their administrative distance be?	

Create an Implementation Plan Table

To practice skills useful when creating your own EIGRP implementation plan, list in Table 4-7 configuration commands related to the configuration of the following features. You may want to record your answers outside the book and set a goal to complete this table (and others like it) from memory during your final reviews before taking the exam.

Table 4-7 *Implementation Plan Configuration Memory Drill*

Feature	Configuration Command/Notes
Filtering EIGRP routes using numbered ACLs	
Filtering EIGRP routes using prefix lists	
Enabling filtering EIGRP routes using route-maps	
Commands to create a route-map clause, and match based on a standard numbered ACL, a standard named ACL, and a prefix-list	
Configuring a summary route	
Enable/disable auto-summary	
Configure a default route using ip default-network	
Configure a default route using static routes	

Choose Commands for a Verification Plan Table

To practice skills that are useful when creating your own EIGRP verification plan, list in Table 4-8 all commands that supply the requested information. You may want to record your answers outside the book and set a goal to complete this table (and others like it) from memory during your final reviews before taking the exam.

Table 4-8 *Verification Plan Memory Drill*

Information Needed	Command
Display access lists.	
Display prefix lists.	
Display route maps.	
Verify whether a filter worked by displaying all known routes in a range of addresses.	
Display a summary IP route.	
On summarizing router, display EIGRP topology info on a summary route.	
On summarizing router, display IP routes for a summary route and it subordinate routes.	
On summarizing router, display the administrative distance of the null route.	
Display the current auto-summary setting.	
Determine if a prefix in the EIGRP topology table has been flagged as a candidate default route.	
Determine if an IP route has been flagged as a candidate default route.	
Display a router's preferred default route.	

Review all the Key Topics

Review the most important topics from this chapter, noted with the key topics icon in the outer margin of the page. Table 4-9 lists a reference of these key topics and the page numbers on which each is found.

Table 4-9   *Key Topics for Chapter 4*

Key Topic Element	Description	Page Number
List	Summary of matching logic for prefix lists	106
Table 4-3	Summary of comparisons of prefix length for IP prefix lists	106
List	Summary of matching logic for route maps	112
List	Benefits and negatives regarding the use of route summarization	120
List	A summary of what occurs when configuring an EIGRP summary route	120
Definition	auto-summary	124
List	Steps to advertise static default routes	127
List	Steps to configure a default network	128

Complete the Tables and Lists from Memory

Print a copy of Appendix D, "Memory Tables," (found on the CD), or at least the section for this chapter, and complete the tables and lists from memory. Appendix E, "Memory Tables Answer Key," also on the CD, includes completed tables and lists to check your work.

Define Key Terms

Define the following key terms from this chapter, and check your answers in the glossary.

Prefix list, route map, distribute list, address block, subordinate route, auto summary, default network, static default route, gateway of last resort

This chapter covers the following subjects:

OSPF Review: This section reviews the OSPF concepts, configuration, and verification commands assumed as prerequisites, specifically those details included in the CCNA Exam's coverage of OSPF.

OSPF Neighbors and Adjacencies on LANs: This section discusses a variety of features that impact when a router attempts to form OSPF neighbor relationships (neighborships), what must be true for those neighborships to work, and what might prevent those neighborships.

OSPF Neighbors and Adjacencies on WANs: This short section examines the typical usage of OSPF neighborships over various types of WAN technologies.

CHAPTER 5

OSPF Overview and Neighbor Relationships

Open Shortest Path First (OSPF) requires only a few relatively simple commands when using it in a small- to medium-sized internetwork. However, behind those commands resides a fairly complex routing protocol, with internals that can intimidate those new to OSPF. When compared to the less-complex EIGRP, OSPF requires more thought when planning and a few more configuration commands than does EIGRP. Additionally, the underlying complexity of OSPF makes operating and verifying an OSPF internetwork more challenging.

Part III of this book contains four chapters. This chapter briefly reviews the basics of OSPF and delves into all topics related to how OSPF routers form neighbor relationships. Chapter 6, "OSPF Topology, Routes, and Convergence," then examines how OSPF exchanges topology data, as stored in its Link State Database (LSDB), for internal OSPF routes. Chapter 6 also discusses how OSPF then chooses the best internal OSPF routes. Chapter 7, "OSPF Route Summarization, Filtering, and Default Routing," examines several tools that optimize the operation of OSPF, including route filtering, route summarization, and special OSPF area types. Finally, Chapter 8, "OSPF Virtual Links and Frame Relay Operations," discusses a few miscellaneous topics.

"Do I Know This Already?" Quiz

The "Do I Know This Already?" quiz allows you to assess if you should read the entire chapter. If you miss no more than one of these eight self-assessment questions, you might want to move ahead to the "Exam Preparation Tasks." Table 5-1 lists the major headings in this chapter and the "Do I Know This Already?" quiz questions covering the material in those headings so that you can assess your knowledge of these specific areas. The answers to the "Do I Know This Already?" quiz appear in Appendix A, "Answers to the 'Do I Know This Already?' Quiz."

Table 5-1 *"Do I Know This Already?" Foundation Topics Section-to-Question Mapping*

Foundations Topics Section	Question
OSPF Review	1–3
OSPF Neighbors and Adjacencies on LANs	4–7
OSPF Neighbors and Adjacencies on WANs	8

1. A router has been configured with the commands **router ospf 9, network 172.16.1.0 0.0.0.255 area 8**, and **network 172.16.0.0 0.0.255.255 area 9**, in that order. No other OSPF-related commands have been configured. The answers list the IP addresses that could be assigned to this router's Fa0/0 interface. Which answers list an IP address/prefix length that would cause the router to put Fa0/0 into area 9? (Choose two.)

    a. 172.16.0.1/23

    b. 172.16.1.1/26

    c. 172.16.1.1/24

    d. 172.16.0.255/23

    e. None of the other answers is correct.

2. Which of the following is true about an OSPF area border router (ABR)?

    a. The ABR must have multiple interfaces connected to the backbone area.

    b. An ABR is a router with two interfaces, each connected to a different non-backbone area.

    c. The only requirement to be considered an ABR is at least one interface connected to the backbone area.

    d. An ABR must have at least one interface in the backbone area plus at least one other interface in a nonbackbone area.

3. Which of the following can either directly or indirectly identify all the interfaces for which both 1) OSPF has been enabled and 2) OSPF is not passive? (Choose two.)

    a. show ip ospf database

    b. show ip ospf interface brief

    c. show ip protocols

    d. show ip route ospf

    e. show ip ospf neighbors

4. Router R1 directly connects to subnet 10.1.1.0/24 with its Fa0/0 interface. R1 can ping four other working OSPF routers in that subnet. R1 is neither the designated router (DR) nor backup DR (BDR). OSPF is working correctly on all five routers. Which of the following is true on R1? (Choose two.)

    a. The **show ip ospf neighbors** command lists two neighbors off Fa0/0.

    b. The **show ip ospf neighbors** command lists four neighbors off Fa0/0.

    c. The **show ip ospf neighbors** command lists two neighbors off Fa0/0 in the FULL state.

    d. The **show ip ospf neighbors** command lists two neighbors off Fa0/0 in the DISCO state.

5. Routers R1 and R2 are OSPF neighbors using their Fa0/0 interfaces, respectively, using default settings for all timers. An engineer adds the **ip ospf hello-interval 6** command to R1's Fa0/0 configuration. Which of the following is true regarding the results from this change? (Choose 2)

    a. The **show ip ospf neighbor** command on R1 lists the revised Hello timer.

    b. The **show ip ospf interface brief** command on R1 lists the revised Hello timer.

    c. The R1-R2 neighborship fails due to Hello timer mismatch.

    d. The **show ip ospf interface** command on R1 lists the revised Hello timer.

6. Routers R1 and R2, OSPF neighbors in area 0 over their Fa0/0 interfaces (respectively), currently both successfully use OSPF MD5 authentication. The OSPF configuration includes the **area 0 authentication** command under the **router ospf 1** command. Which of the following commands must have been configured on R1's Fa0/0 interface? (Choose two.)

    a. ip ospf authentication null

    b. ip ospf authentication message-digest

    c. ip ospf md5 whatever-it-is

    d. ip ospf message-digest-key 1 md5 whatever-it-is

    e. ip ospf md5 1 key whatever-it-is

7. Which of the following settings do not prevent two potential OSPF neighbors from becoming neighbors?

    a. The interface used to connect to that neighbor being passive in the OSPF process

    b. Duplicate OSPF router IDs

    c. Mismatched dead timers

    d. IP addresses of 10.1.1.1/24 and 10.2.2.2/24

    e. Mismatched OSPF process IDs

8. A company has a Frame Relay WAN with one central-site router and 100 branch office routers. A partial mesh of PVCs exists: one PVC between the central site and each of the 100 branch routers. All routers use point-to-point subinterfaces and one subnet per PVC. Which of the following is true about OSPF in this design?

    a. The central site router has 100 fully adjacent neighborships with the 100 branches.

    b. The central site router has neighborships with all branch routers, but fully adjacent neighbors with only two branches.

    c. The central site router has a neighborship with the Frame Relay switch.

    d. None of the other answers is correct.

Foundation Topics

OSPF Review

All the CCNP exams consider CCNA materials as prerequisites, so the Cisco Press CCNP Exam Certification Guide series of books also assumes the reader is already familiar with CCNA topics. However, the CCNP exams do include features that overlap with CCNA. Additionally, most people forget some details about CCNA topics along the way. This section is intended as a quick reminder of the basics from your earlier CCNA studies related to OSPF, with the addition of a few related details you may not have seen during your CCNA study.

Note that this section does not cover every detail of CCNA-level OSPF topics–the main goal is a quick refamiliarization. Following this review, throughout this and the next three chapters, the rest of the CCNA-level OSPF features, plus many new OSPF features, will be detailed.

To that end, this section begins with a review of OSPF terminology and link state theory, followed by a configuration and verification sample.

OSPF Link State Concepts

OPSF uses link state (LS) logic, which can be broken into three major branches. The first step, neighbor discovery, has the same overall goal as EIGRP's neighbor discovery process: to find the neighboring routers, and exchange enough information so that the two routers know whether they should exchange topology data. (Like EIGRP, OSPF keeps a list of neighbors in its neighbor table.)

The second step, topology database exchange, requires each OSPF router to cooperate by sending messages so that all routers learn topology information–information that is the equivalent of the kinds of information a human would draw and write in a diagram of the internetwork. Each router stores this topology information in its topology database, sometimes called its link state database (LSDB). The information communicated by OSPF routers and held in their LSDBs includes:

■   The existence of, and an identifier for, each router (router ID)

■   Each router interface, IP address, mask, and subnet

■   The list of routers reachable by each router on each interface

The third major step, route computation, means that each router independently analyzes the topology data to choose the best routes from their perspective. In particular, LS algorithms such as OSPF use a Shortest Path First (SPF) algorithm to analyze the data, choose the shortest (best) route for each reachable subnet, and add the correct next-hop/outgoing interface information for those routes to the IP routing table.

OSPF requires more planning than does EIGRP, particularly with regard to the necessity for a hierarchical design using OSPF areas. Each router interface exists in a single area, with some special routers, called area border routers (ABR), being the boundary between areas. Inside an area, routers exchange detailed topology information. However, the detailed topology information does not flow between areas. Instead, the ABRs advertise briefer information between areas, including information about subnets/masks, but the information advertised into one area does not include details about the topology of the other area. For perspective on the OSPF design issues, consider Figure 5-1, which shows a typical hierarchical design.

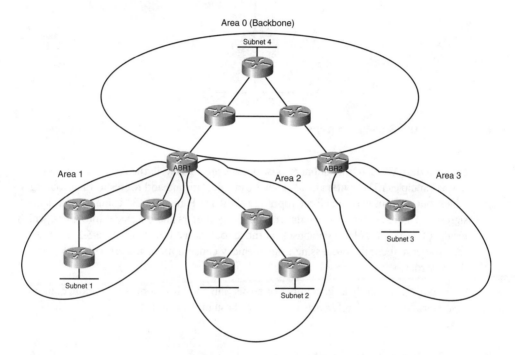

Figure 5-1   *Typical Hierarchical OSPF Design*

One area, called the backbone area, must connect to all other areas. Packets that need to pass between two nonbackbone areas must pass through (at least) one backbone router. The ABRs must keep a copy of the LSDB for each area to which they attach; for example, ABR1 has LSDBs for area 0, area 1, and area 2. However, the ABRs do not forward all the topology details between areas; instead, they simply advertise the subnets (prefix/length) between the areas.

Because of the sparse information advertised into one area about another area, topologically, routers inside one area know only about the subnets in another area. They do not know about the details of the topology in the other area; instead, from a topology perspective, it appears as if the subnets from another area connect to the ABR. Figure 5-2 shows the concept with the two routers in area 3 from Figure 5-1.

Figure 5-2 essentially shows the contents of area 3's LSDB in graphical form. Two routers exist, with a link between them, and one LAN subnet (Subnet 3) internal to the area. However, the other three sample subnets shown in Figure 5-1 (Subnets 1, 2, and 4) appear

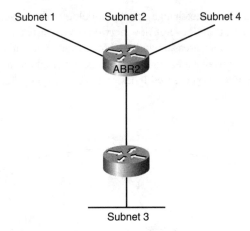

Figure 5-2 *Area 3 LSDB Concept*

connected to ABR2. (Other subnets exist outside area 3 as well; the figure just shows a few as examples.) The routers inside area 3 can calculate and add routes to their routing tables, but without needing all the topology shown in Figure 5-1. By using areas as a design as in Figure 5-1, network engineers can group routers and interfaces into areas, which results of smaller topology databases on those routers, as shown in Figure 5-2. As a result, each router reduces the processing time, memory consumption, and effort to calculate the best routes.

OSPF does have a fairly large number of terms. Table 5-2 lists some of the more common OSPF terms as an early reference as you read through the chapter.

Table 5-2 *Commonly Used OSPF Terms*

Term	Definition
Link state database	The data structure held by an OSPF router for the purpose of storing topology data.
Shortest Path First (SPF)	The name of the algorithm OSPF uses to analyze the LSDB. The analysis determines the best (lowest cost) route for each prefix/length.
Link State Update (LSU)	The name of the OSPF packet that holds the detailed topology information, specifically LSAs

Table 5-2   *Commonly Used OSPF Terms*

Term	Definition
Link State Advertisement (LSA)	The name of a class of OSPF data structures that hold topology information. LSAs are held in memory in the LSDB and communicated over the network in LSU messages.
Area	A contiguous grouping of routers and router interfaces. Routers in an area strive to learn all topology information about the area, but they do not learn topology information about areas to which they do not connect.
Area Border Router (ABR)	A router that has interfaces connected to at least two different OSPF areas, including the backbone area. ABRs hold topology data for each area, and calculate routes for each area, and advertise about those routes between areas.
Backbone router	Any router that has at least one interface connected to the backbone area.
Internal routers	A router that has interfaces connected to only one area, making the router completely internal to that one area.
Designated Router (DR)	On multiaccess data links like LANs, an OSPF router elected by the routers on that data link to perform special functions. These functions include the generation of LSAs representing the subnet, and playing a key role in the database exchange process.
Backup Designated Router (BDR)	A router on a multiaccess data link that monitors the DR and becomes prepared to take over for the DR, should the DR fail.

OSPF Configuration Review

Other than the configuration of the OSPF areas, the configuration of OSPF basics looks similar to a simple EIGRP configuration. IOS uses the **router ospf** *process-id* command, plus one or more **network** *net-id wildcard-mask* **area** *area-id* subcommands, to enable OSPF on the router and on router interfaces. The rules for these commands are as follows:

Key Topic

Step 1.   Neighboring routers' **router ospf** *process-id* commands do not have to be configured with the same *process-id* parameter to become neighbors.

Step 2.   IOS only enables OSPF on interfaces matched by an OSPF **network** command. When enabled, the router does the following:

   a. Attempts to discover OSPF neighbors on that interface by sending multicast OSPF Hello messages

   b. Includes the connected subnet in future topology database exchanges

Step 3.   To match an interface with the **network** command, IOS compares the *net-id* configured in the **network** command with each interface's IP address, while using the configured wildcard-mask as an ACL wildcard mask.

Step 4.   Regardless of the order in which the **network** commands are added to the configuration, IOS puts these commands into the configuration file with the most specific (most binary 0s) wildcard mask first. IOS lists the **network** commands in this sorted order in the configuration.

Step 5.   The first **network** command that matches an interface, per the order shown in the output of the **show running-config** command, determines the OSPF area number associated with the interface.

Example 5-1 shows a sample configuration for each router in Figure 5-3.

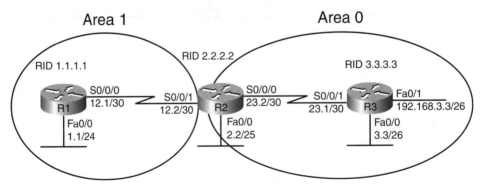

Note: All IP addresses begin with 10.1 unless otherwise noted.

Figure 5-3   *Three Router Internetwork with Two OSPF Areas*

Example 5-1   *OSPF Configuration on Routers R1, R2, and R3*

```
! On Router R1: !!!!!!!!!!!!!!!!!!!!!!!!!!!!!!!!!!!!!!!!!!!!!!!
interface loopback 1
 ip address 1.1.1.1 255.255.255.255
router ospf 1
 network 10.0.0.0 0.255.255.255 area 1
! On Router R2: !!!!!!!!!!!!!!!!!!!!!!!!!!!!!!!!!!!!!!!!!!!!!!!
interface loopback 1
 ip address 2.2.2.2 255.255.255.255

router ospf 2
 network 10.1.12.2 0.0.0.0 area 1
 network 10.1.0.0 0.0.255.255 area 0
! On Router R3: !!!!!!!!!!!!!!!!!!!!!!!!!!!!!!!!!!!!!!!!!!!!!!!
interface loopback 1
 ip address 3.3.3.3 255.255.255.255

router ospf 3
 network 10.1.0.0 0.0.255.255 area 0
 network 192.168.3.3 0.0.0.0 area 0
```

First, note that all three routers use a different process ID on their respective **router ospf** *process-id* commands; these mismatches do not prevent neighborship.

Next, consider the requirement that R1's S0/0/0 and R2's S0/0/1 must be in the same area. Typically, all routers on the same subnet need to be in the same area; the routers themselves are the boundary between areas. In this case, R1's **network 10.0.0.0 0.255.255.255 area 1** command matches all interfaces whose addresses begin with 10 in the first octet and assigns those interfaces (Fa0/0 and S0/0/0) to area 1. Similarly, R2's **network 10.1.12.2 0.0.0.0 area 1** command matches only one IP address–R2's S0/0/1 IP address–and places it in area 1. Looking further at R2's OSPF configuration, note that both **network** commands actually match the 10.1.12.2 S0/0/1 IP address: one with area 0, and one with area 1. However, R2 orders these two **network** commands with the most-specific wildcard mask first, placing the command with wildcard mask 0.0.0.0 first, and the one with wildcard 0.0.255.255 second. Then, R2 compares the commands to the interface IP addresses in order, so R2 places S0/0/1 into area 1. (Note that in real internetworks, choosing wildcard masks such that it is clear which **network** command should match each interface is the better choice.)

On R3, the **network 10.1.0.0 0.0.255.255 area 0** command matches interfaces Fa0/0 and S0/0/0, adding them to area 0. R3 then needs an additional **network** command to enable OSPF on R3's Fa0/1 interface with all three interfaces in area 0.

Finally, note that the addition of the loopback interfaces causes each router to choose an obvious OSPF router ID (RID). OSPF uses the same logic as does EIGRP to choose a router ID on each router, at the time the OSPF process is initialized, as follows, in the listed order of precedence:

Key Topic

1. Use the router ID defined in the **router-id** *x.x.x.x* OSPF router subcommand.

2. Use the highest IP address of any up loopback interface.

3. Use the highest IP address of any up non-loopback interface.

Note that for the second and third choices, the interface does not need to have OSPF enabled.

OSPF Verification Review

The verification process, whether it uses a formal verification plan or not, must have some knowledge of the intended design and function of the network. The design and implementation documents dictate what the network should do, and the verification plan should confirm whether the network is meeting those goals.

For the purposes of this OSPF review section, assume that the only design goal for the internetwork in Figure 5-3 is that OSPF be used so that all routers have routes to reach all subnets shown in the figure, within the constraints of the area design.

To verify such a simple design, an engineer should start by confirming on which interfaces OSPF has been enabled on each router. The next step should be to determine if the OSPF neighbor relationships that should occur are indeed up and working. Then, the OSPF topology table should be examined to confirm that non-ABRs have only topology information for their respective areas. Finally, the IP routes on each router should be examined, confirming that all routes are known. To that end, Table 5-3 summarizes five key **show** commands that provide the information to answer these questions:

Key Topic

Table 5-3 *Most Commonly Used OSPF show Commands*

Command	Key Information
show ip ospf interface brief	Lists the interfaces on which OSPF is enabled (based on the **network** commands); it omits passive interfaces.
show ip protocols	Lists the contents of the **network** configuration commands for each routing process, and a list of enabled but passive interfaces.
show ip ospf neighbors	Lists known neighbors, including neighbor state; does not list neighbors for which some mismatched parameter is preventing a valid OSPF neighbor relationship.
show ip ospf database	Lists all LSAs for all connected areas. (See Chapter 6 for more detail on the LSA types seen in the database.)
show ip route	Lists the contents of the IP routing table, listing OSPF-learned routes with a code of O on the left side of the output.

Example 5-2 shows samples of each command listed in Table 5-3. Note that the output highlights various samples of items that should be verified, including the interfaces on which OSPF is enabled, the known neighbors, the neighbors' state, the LSAs in the topology table, and the OSPF routes.

Example 5-2 *OSPF Verification on Routers R1, R2, and R3*

```
! On Router R2: !!!!!!!!!!!!!!!!!!!!!!!!!!!!!!!!!!!!!!!!!!!!!!
! Note that S0/0/1 is shown as in area 1, while the other 2 interfaces are all in
! Area 0.


R2#show ip ospf interface brief
Interface    PID   Area         IP Address/Mask    Cost   State  Nbrs F/C
Se0/0/0      2     0            10.1.23.2/30       64     P2P    1/1
Fa0/0        2     0            10.1.2.2/25        1      DR     0/0
Se0/0/1      2     1            10.1.12.2/30       64     P2P    1/1


! Next, note that R2 lists two "Routing Information Sources", 1.1.1.1 (R1) and
! 3.3.3.3 (R3). These routers, listed by RID, should mirror those listed
! in the output of the show ip ospf neighbors command that follows.

R2#show ip protocols
Routing Protocol is "ospf 2"
  Outgoing update filter list for all interfaces is not set
  Incoming update filter list for all interfaces is not set
  Router ID 2.2.2.2
  It is an area border router
  Number of areas in this router is 2. 2 normal 0 stub 0 nssa
  Maximum path: 4
  Routing for Networks:
    10.1.12.2 0.0.0.0 area 1
    10.1.0.0 0.0.255.255 area 0

 Reference bandwidth unit is 100 mbps
  Routing Information Sources:
    Gateway         Distance      Last Update
    3.3.3.3              110       00:01:08
    1.1.1.1              110       00:01:08
  Distance: (default is 110)


! Note that the Full state means that the database exchange process is
```

```
! fully completed between these two neighbors.
R2#show ip ospf neighbors

Neighbor ID    Pri   State          Dead Time   Address      Interface
3.3.3.3          0   FULL/  -       00:00:34    10.1.23.1    Serial0/0/0
1.1.1.1          0   FULL/  -       00:00:34    10.1.12.1    Serial0/0/1
```

```
! On Router R1: !!!!!!!!!!!!!!!!!!!!!!!!!!!!!!!!!!!!!!!!!!!!!!!
! Note that R1's LSDB includes a "Router Link State" for RID 1.1.1.1 (R1)
! and R2 (2.2.2.2), but not 3.3.3.3 (R3), because R3 is not attached  to area
1.


R1#show ip ospf database

                OSPF Router with ID (1.1.1.1) (Process ID 1)

                    Router Link States (Area 1)

Link ID        ADV Router     Age       Seq#          Checksum Link count
1.1.1.1        1.1.1.1        210       0x80000004    0x001533 3
2.2.2.2        2.2.2.2        195       0x80000002    0x0085DB 2


                    Summary Net Link States (Area 1)

Link ID        ADV Router     Age       Seq#          Checksum
10.1.2.0       2.2.2.2        190       0x80000001    0x00B5F0
10.1.3.0       2.2.2.2        190       0x80000001    0x00AE76
10.1.23.0      2.2.2.2        190       0x80000001    0x0031A4
192.168.3.0    2.2.2.2        191       0x80000001    0x008B3B


! Below, note that R1 has routes for all remote subnets, including R3's
! LAN subnets, even though R1 does not list R3 in its LSDB.


R1#show ip route ospf
      10.0.0.0/8 is variably subnetted, 5 subnets, 4 masks
O IA    10.1.3.0/26 [110/129] via 10.1.12.2, 00:04:13, Serial0/0/0
O IA    10.1.2.0/25 [110/65] via 10.1.12.2, 00:04:13, Serial0/0/0
O IA    10.1.23.0/30 [110/128] via 10.1.12.2, 00:04:13, Serial0/0/0
      192.168.3.0/26 is subnetted, 1 subnets
O IA    192.168.3.0 [110/129] via 10.1.12.2, 00:04:13, Serial0/0/0
```

OSPF Feature Summary

Table 5-4 summarizes some of the key facts about OSPF. The table includes some review items from the CCNA level OSPF topics, plus some topics that will be developed in chapters 5 through 8. The items that are not CCNA topics are included just for convenience when reviewing for final preparation before taking the exam.

Table 5-4 *OSPF Feature Summary*

Key
Topic

Feature	Description
Transport	IP, protocol type 89 (does not use UDP or TCP).
Metric	Based on cumulative cost of all outgoing interfaces in a route. The interface cost defaults to a function of interface bandwidth but can be set explicitly.
Hello interval	Interval at which a router sends OSPF Hello messages on an interface.
Dead interval	Timer used to determine when a neighboring router has failed, based on a router not receiving any OSPF messages, including Hellos, in this timer period.
Update destination address	Normally sent to 224.0.0.5 (All SPF Routers) and 224.0.0.6 (All Designated Routers).
Full or partial updates	Full updates are used when new neighbors are discovered; otherwise, partial updates are used.
Authentication	Supports MD5 and clear-text authentication.
VLSM/classless	OSPF includes the mask with each route, also allowing it to support discontiguous networks and VLSM.
Route Tags	Allows OSPF to tag routes as they are redistributed into OSPF.
Next-hop field	Supports the advertisement of routes with a different next-hop router than the advertising router.
Manual route summarization	Allows route summarization at ABR routers only.

This concludes the review of OSPF topics. The rest of this chapter focuses on OSPF topics related to the formation of OSPF neighbor relationships.

OSPF Neighbors and Adjacencies on LANs

With EIGRP, neighborship is relatively simple. If two EIGRP routers discover each other (using Hellos) and meet several requirements (like being in the same subnet), the two routers become neighbors. After becoming neighbors, the two EIGRP routers exchange topology information.

Comparing OSPF and EIGRP, OSPF neighborship is more complex. First, with EIGRP, two routers either become neighbors or they do not. With OSPF, even after all the neighbor parameter checks pass, two classes of neighborships exist: neighbors and fully adjacent neighbors. The OSPF neighbor discovery process has many pitfalls when the internetwork uses Frame Relay, with a class of issues that simply do not exist with EIGRP. Finally, OSPF uses an underlying Finite State Machine (FSM) with eight neighbor states used to describe the current state of each OSPF neighbor, adding another layer of complexity compared to EIGRP.

This section breaks down the OSPF neighbor relationship, the logic, and the OSPF configuration settings–anything that impacts OSPF neighborship on LAN interfaces. In particular, this section examines the following questions:

- On what interfaces will this router attempt to discover neighbors by sending multicast OSPF Hello messages?

- When a potential neighbor is discovered, do they meet all requirements to become neighbors at all?

This section examines these topics, in sequence.

Enabling OSPF Neighbor Discovery on LANs

OSPF sends multicast OSPF Hello messages on LAN interfaces, attempting to discover OSPF neighbors, when two requirements are met:

- OSPF has been enabled on the interface, either through the **network** router subcommand or the **ip ospf area** interface subcommand.

- The interface has not been made passive by the **passive-interface** router subcommand.

When both requirements are met, OSPF sends Hellos to the 224.0.0.5 multicast address, an address reserved for all OSPF-speaking routers. The Hello itself contains several parameters that must be checked, including the OSPF RID of the router sending the Hello, and the OSPF area that router has assigned to that LAN subnet.

Of the three configuration commands that might impact whether a router attempts to discover potential neighbors on an interface, one is commonly understood (**network**) and was already covered in this chapter's "OSPF Configuration Review" section. The second configuration command that impacts whether potential neighbors discover each other, **passive-interface**, works just like it does with EIGRP. In short, when a router configures an interface as passive to OSPF, OSPF quits sending OSPF Hellos, so the router will not discover neighbors. The router will still advertise about the interface's connected subnet if OSPF is enabled on the interface, but all other OSPF processing on the interface is stopped.

The third configuration command that impacts whether a router discovers potential neighbors using Hellos is the **ip ospf** *process-id* **area** *area-id* interface subcommand. This command acts as a replacement for the OSPF **network** command. Simply put, this command enables OSPF directly on the interface and assigns the area number.

To demonstrate the **ip ospf area** and **passive-interface** commands, Example 5-3 shows a revised configuration on Router R3 as seen originally back in Example 5-1. In this new example configuration, R3 has made two interfaces passive, because no other OSPF routers exist on its LAN subnets–making any attempt to discover OSPF neighbors have no benefit. Additionally, R3 has migrated its configuration away from the older **network** commands, instead using the **ip ospf area** interface subcommand.

Example 5-3 *Configuring passive-interface and ip ospf area*

```
Interface loopback 1
 Ip address 3.3.3.3 255.255.255.255

router ospf 3
 passive-interface FastEthernet0/0
 passive-interface FastEthernet0/1

interface FastEthernet0/0
 ip ospf 3 area 0
interface FastEthernet0/1
 ip ospf 3 area 0
interface Serial0/0/1
 ip ospf 3 area 0

R3#show ip protocols
Routing Protocol is "ospf 3"
  Outgoing update filter list for all interfaces is not set
  Incoming update filter list for all interfaces is not set
  Router ID 3.3.3.3
  Number of areas in this router is 1. 1 normal 0 stub 0 nssa
  Maximum path: 4
  Routing for Networks:
  Routing on Interfaces Configured Explicitly (Area 0):
    Serial0/0/1
    FastEthernet0/1
    FastEthernet0/0
  Reference bandwidth unit is 100 mbps
  Passive Interface(s):
    FastEthernet0/0
    FastEthernet0/1
  Routing Information Sources:
    Gateway         Distance      Last Update
  Distance: (default is 110)
```

Note that in the second half of Example 5-3 the **show ip protocols** command now lists the interfaces as matched with the **ip ospf area** commands, and it lists the passive interfaces. You can take the list of explicitly configured interfaces, remove the passive interfaces, and know which interfaces on which R3 will attempt to discover OSPF neighbors. Also, take a moment to compare this output with the same command's output in Example 5-2, with the earlier example listing the parameters of the configured **network** commands.

Settings That Must Match for OSPF Neighborship

After an OSPF router has discovered a potential neighbor by receiving a Hello from the other router, the local router considers the router that sent the Hello as a potential neighbor. The local router must examine the contents of the received Hello, plus a few other factors, compare those settings to its own, check for agreement, and only then may that other router be considered an OSPF neighbor.

For reference, the following list details the items seen in OSPF Hello messages. Note that some fields might not be present in a Hello, depending on the conditions in the network.

- OSPF Router ID
- Stub area flag
- Plus the following interface-specific settings:
  - Hello interval
  - Dead Interval
  - Subnet mask
  - List of neighbors reachable on the interface
  - Area ID
  - Router priority
  - Designated Router (DR) IP address
  - Backup DR (BDR) IP address
  - Authentication digest

Table 5-5 summarizes the items that two routers will compare when deciding whether they can become OSPF neighbors. For study purposes, the table also lists some items that one might think prevent OSPF neighborship but do not, with comparisons to EIGRP.

Table 5-5   *Neighbor Requirements for EIGRP and OSPF*

Requirement	OSPF	EIGRP
Interfaces' primary IP addresses must be in same subnet.	Yes	Yes
Must not be passive on the connected interface.	Yes	Yes
Must be in same area.	Yes	N/A
Hello interval/timer, plus either the Hold (EIGRP) or Dead (OSPF) timer, must match.	Yes	No
Router IDs must be unique.	Yes	No
IP MTU must match.	Yes[1]	No

Table 5-5 *Neighbor Requirements for EIGRP and OSPF*

Requirement	OSPF	EIGRP
Must pass neighbor authentication (if configured).	Yes	Yes
K-values (used in metric calculation) must match.	N/A	Yes
Must use the same ASN (EIGRP) or process-ID (OSPF) on the **router** configuration command.	No	Yes

[1]May allow the other router to be listed in the **show ip ospf neighbor** command, but the MTU mismatch will prevent proper operation of the topology exchange.

Note: Table 5-5 repeats most of the information listed in Chapter 2, Table 2-4, but in an order that focuses on OSPF issues.

The first few items in Table 5-5 require only a minor amount of discussion. First, OSPF checks the IP address (found as the source address of the Hello message) and mask (listed in the Hello message) of the potential neighbor, calculates the subnet number, and compares the subnet number and mask to its own interface IP address. Both the subnet number and mask must match. Additionally, the OSPF Hello messages include the area number on the subnet, as defined by that router. The receiving router compares the received Hello with its own configuration and rejects the potential neighbor if the area numbers do not match.

The next several headings inside this section examine the other three settings that can prevent OSPF neighborship: Hello and Dead intervals, OSPF Router ID, IP MTU, and authentication.

Optimizing Convergence Using Hello and Dead Timers

Using the same concept as EIGRP, but with different terminology, OSPF uses two timers to monitor the reachability of neighbors. With OSPF, the Hello interval defines how often the router sends a Hello on the interface. The Dead interval defines how long a router should wait, without hearing any Hello messages from that neighbor, before deciding that the neighbor failed. For example, with a default LAN interface setting of Hello of 10, and Dead of 40, the local router sends Hello messages every 10 seconds. The neighbor resets its downward-counting Hold timer to 40 upon receiving a Hello from that neighbor. Under normal operation on a LAN, with defaults, the Dead timer for a neighbor would vary from 40, down to 30, and then be reset to 40 upon receipt of the next Hello. However, if the Hello messages were no longer received for 40 seconds, the neighborship would fail, driving convergence.

To tune for faster convergence, you can configure OSPF to set a lower Hello and Dead timer. It speeds convergence in some cases; note that if the interface fails, OSPF will immediately realize that all neighbors reached through that interface have also failed and not wait on the Dead timer to count down to zero. For example, consider the internetwork in Figure 5-4. This internetwork has four routers connected to the same VLAN, with the interfaces, IP addresses, masks, and OSPF areas as shown.

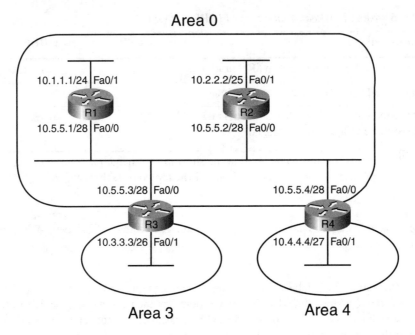

Figure 5-4 *Four OSPFs Routers on the Same Subnet, with Two OSPF Areas*

Example 5-4 verifies some of the facts about the routers in Figure 5-4, showing the changes to the Hello interval and the resulting failed neighborships. Each router has been assigned an obvious RID: 1.1.1.1 for R1, 2.2.2.2 for R2, and so on.

Example 5-4 *The Effect of Configuring a Different OSPF Hello Interval*

```
R4#show ip ospf neighbors
Neighbor ID     Pri   State          Dead Time   Address      Interface
1.1.1.1          1    2WAY/DROTHER   00:00:35    10.5.5.1     FastEthernet0/0
2.2.2.2          1    FULL/BDR       00:00:39    10.5.5.2     FastEthernet0/0
3.3.3.3          1    FULL/DR        00:00:38    10.5.5.3     FastEthernet0/0
R4#conf t
Enter configuration commands, one per line.  End with CNTL/Z.
R4(config)#interface fastethernet0/0
R4(config-if)#ip ospf hello-interval 9
R4(config-if)#^Z
*Apr 28 00:06:20.271: %SYS-5-CONFIG_I: Configured from console by console
R4#show ip ospf interface fa0/0
FastEthernet0/0 is up, line protocol is up
  Internet Address 10.5.5.4/28, Area 0
```

```
Process ID 4, Router ID 4.4.4.4, Network Type BROADCAST, Cost: 1
Enabled by interface config, including secondary ip addresses
Transmit Delay is 1 sec, State DROTHER, Priority 1
Designated Router (ID) 3.3.3.3, Interface address 10.5.5.3
Backup Designated router (ID) 2.2.2.2, Interface address 10.5.5.2
Timer intervals configured, Hello 9, Dead 36, Wait 36, Retransmit 5
  oob-resync timeout 40
  Hello due in 00:00:01
Supports Link-local Signaling (LLS)
Index 1/1, flood queue length 0
Next 0x0(0)/0x0(0)
Last flood scan length is 0, maximum is 3
Last flood scan time is 0 msec, maximum is 4 msec
Neighbor Count is 3, Adjacent neighbor count is 2
  Adjacent with neighbor 2.2.2.2  (Backup Designated Router)
  Adjacent with neighbor 3.3.3.3  (Designated Router)
Suppress hello for 0 neighbor(s)
R4#
*Apr 28 00:06:51.559: %OSPF-5-ADJCHG: Process 4, Nbr 1.1.1.1 on FastEthernet0/0
from 2WAY to DOWN, Neighbor Down: Dead timer expired
*Apr 28 00:06:57.183: %OSPF-5-ADJCHG: Process 4, Nbr 3.3.3.3 on FastEthernet0/0
from FULL to DOWN, Neighbor Down: Dead timer expired
*Apr 28 00:06:58.495: %OSPF-5-ADJCHG: Process 4, Nbr 2.2.2.2 on FastEthernet0/0
from FULL to DOWN, Neighbor Down: Dead timer expired
```

This example demonstrates several interesting facts. First, note that upon configuring the **ip ospf hello-interval 9** command under Fa0/0, the **show ip ospf interface fa0/0** command shows that not only did the Hello interval change, but the Dead timer was set to 4X the Hello interval, or 36. To directly set the Dead timer on the interface, use the **ip ospf dead-interval** *value* interface subcommand. Then, at the end of the example, note that all three of R4's neighbor relationships failed, because those routers now have mismatched Hello and Dead timers. However, the neighbor relationships failed only after the dead timers expired, as noted in the messages, and as confirmed by the timestamps on the messages.

Example 5-4 also shows the two normal, stable, and working neighbor states. Look to the heading "state" in the output of the **show ip ospf neighbors** command at the top of the example. The first word (before the /) lists the state or status of each neighbor. FULL refers to a fully adjacent neighbor, meaning the OSPF topology has been fully exchanged with that neighbor. The other state listed there, 2WAY, is a normal, stable, working state for neighbors with which topology data was not exchanged directly. As described in Chapter 6, in some cases OSPF routers exchange their topology information to one specific router on a LAN, called the designated router (DR), but they do not exchange their database directly with other routers. In the preceding example, taken from R4, R4 lists its relationship with R1 as 2WAY, which happens to be the status for a working neighbor that does not become fully adjacent.

Chapter 6's section "Exchange with a Designated Router" discusses the database exchange process when using a DR.

Note: OSPF has two methods to tune the Hello and Dead intervals to subsecond values. Like EIGRP, OSPF supports Bidirectional Forwarding Detection (BFD). Additionally, OSPF supports command **ip ospf dead-interval minimal hello-multiplier** *multiplier*, which sets the dead interval to one second, and the Hello interval to a fraction of a second based on the multiplier. For example, the command **ip ospf dead-interval minimal hello-multiplier 4** sets the dead interval to one second, with Hellos occurring four times (the multiple) per second, for an effective Hello interval of 1/4 seconds.

Using a Unique OSPF Router-ID

As mentioned earlier in the "OSPF CCNA Review" section, each OSPF router assigns itself a router ID, based on the same rules as EIGRP. In OSPF's case, that means a router first looks for the OSPF **router-id** *rid-value* OSPF subcommand; next, to the highest IP address of any up loopback interface; and finally, to the highest IP address of any up non-loopback interface.

An OSPF RID mismatch makes for unpredictable results because OSPF routers base their view of the topology on the topology database, and the database identifies routers based on their RIDs. By design, all OSPF RIDs in a domain should be unique; to avoid such issues, OSPF prevents neighborships between routers with duplicate RIDs.

The next example shows what happens when two routers discover each other as potential neighbors, but notice a duplicate RID. Using the same network as in Figure 5-4, each router has been assigned an obvious RID: 1.1.1.1 for R1, 2.2.2.2 for R2, and so on. Unfortunately, R4 has been mistakenly configured with RID 1.1.1.1, duplicating R1's RID. R4 is powered on after all three other routers have established neighbor relationships. Example 5-5 shows some of the results.

Example 5-5 *OSPF RID Mismatch – R1 and R4, R4 Connects after R1*

```
! On R1... the following output occurs AFTER R4 powers on. R1, RID 1.1.1.1,
! does not form a neighbor relationship with R4.

R1#show ip ospf neighbors

Neighbor ID     Pri   State      Dead Time   Address     Interface
2.2.2.2          1    FULL/BDR   00:00:35    10.5.5.2    FastEthernet0/0
3.3.3.3          1    FULL/DR    00:00:33    10.5.5.3    FastEthernet0/0
! On R3
! R3 does form a neighbor relationship, but does not learn routes from the
! R4. Note that R3 does not have a route for R4's 10.4.4.0/27 subnet.
```

```
R3#show ip ospf neighbors

Neighbor ID     Pri   State          Dead Time   Address     Interface
1.1.1.1           1   FULL/DROTHER   00:00:38    10.5.5.1    FastEthernet0/0
1.1.1.1           1   FULL/DROTHER   00:00:37    10.5.5.4    FastEthernet0/0
2.2.2.2           1   FULL/BDR       00:00:35    10.5.5.2    FastEthernet0/0
R3#show ip route ospf
     10.0.0.0/8 is variably subnetted, 4 subnets, 4 masks
O       10.2.2.0/25 [110/2] via 10.5.5.2, 00:06:56, FastEthernet0/0
O       10.1.1.0/24 [110/2] via 10.5.5.1, 00:01:34, FastEthernet0/0
```

As you can see from the output on R1, whose RID is duplicated with R4, the routers with duplicate RIDs do not form a neighbor relationship. Additionally, other routers, such as R3 as shown in the example, do form a neighbor relationship with the two routers, but the duplication confuses the topology flooding process. Because R3 formed its neighborship with R1 before R4, R3 does learn a route for R1's 10.1.1.0/24 subnet, but does not for R4's 10.4.4.0/27 subnet. However, with the same configuration, but a different sequence and timing of neighbors coming up, R3 might learn about 10.4.4.0/27 instead of 10.1.1.0/24.

Note: Note that the OSPF process will not start without an RID.

Using the Same IP MTU

The maximum transmission unit (MTU) of an interface tells IOS the largest IP packet that can be forwarded out the interface. This setting protects the packet from being discarded on data links whose Layer 2 features will not pass a frame over a certain size. For example, routers typically default to an IP MTU of 1500 bytes to accommodate Ethernet's rules about frames not exceeding 1526 bytes.

From a data plane perspective, when a router needs to forward a packet larger than the outgoing interface's MTU, the router either fragments the packet or discards it. If the IP header's don't fragment (DF) bit is set, the router discards the packet. If the DF bit is not set, the router can perform Layer 3 fragmentation on the packet, creating two (or more) IP packets with mostly identical IP headers, spreading the data that follows the original IP packet header out among the fragments. The fragments can then be forwarded, with the reassembly process being performed by the receiving host.

From a design perspective, the MTU used by all devices attached to the same data link ought to be the same value. However, routers have no dynamic mechanism to prevent the misconfiguration of MTU on neighboring routers.

When an MTU mismatch occurs between two OSPF neighbors, one router will attempt to become neighbors with the other router whose MTU differs. The other router will be listed in the list of neighbors (**show ip ospf neighbor**). However, the two routers will not exchange topology information, and the two routers will not calculate routes that use this neighbor as the next-hop router.

The IP MTU can be set on an interface using the **ip mtu** *value* interface subcommand and for all Layer 3 protocols with the **mtu** *value* interface subcommand. Example 5-6 shows an example, with R4 again configured so that it has problems.

Example 5-6 *Setting IP MTU and Failing the OSPF Database Exchange Process*

```
R4#configure terminal
Enter configuration commands, one per line.  End with CNTL/Z.
R4(config)#int fastethernet0/0
R4(config-if)#ip mtu 1498
R4(config-if)#^Z
R4#
R4#show ip interface fa0/0
FastEthernet0/0 is up, line protocol is up
  Internet address is 10.5.5.4/28
  Broadcast address is 255.255.255.255
  Address determined by non-volatile memory
  MTU is 1498 bytes
! lines omitted for brevity
R4#show ip ospf neighbors


Neighbor ID     Pri    State            Dead Time   Address         Interface
1.1.1.1           1    EXSTART/DROTHER  00:00:39    10.5.5.1        FastEthernet0/0
2.2.2.2           1    EXSTART/DROTHER  00:00:37    10.5.5.2        FastEthernet0/0
3.3.3.3           1    EXSTART/BDR      00:00:39    10.5.5.3        FastEthernet0/0


*Apr 28 12:36:00.231: %OSPF-5-ADJCHG: Process 4, Nbr 2.2.2.2 on FastEthernet0/0
from EXSTART to DOWN, Neighbor Down: Too many retransmissions
R4#show ip ospf neighbors


Neighbor ID     Pri    State            Dead Time   Address         Interface
1.1.1.1           1    INIT/DROTHER     00:00:39    10.5.5.1        FastEthernet0/0
2.2.2.2           1    DOWN/DROTHER         -       10.5.5.2        FastEthernet0/0
3.3.3.3           1    INIT/DROTHER     00:00:39    10.5.5.3        FastEthernet0/0
```

Note that you could argue that the mismatched MTU does not prevent routers from becoming neighbors, but it does prevent them from successfully exchanging topology data. When the mismatch occurs, a pair of routers tries to become neighbors, and they list each other in the output of **show ip ospf neighbors**, as seen in Example 5-6. However, the neighbor state (listed before the /, under heading "State") moves from EXSTART (which means the database exchange process is starting), but it fails as implied by the highlighted message in the example. Then, the state changes to DOWN, and later one router tries again, moving to INIT (initializing) state. So, the neighbor is listed in the output of **show ip ospf neighbors** command, but never succeeds at exchanging the topology data.

Chapter 6 discusses the database exchange process, making reference to neighbor states. Table 6-5, in Chapter 6's section "OSPF Message and Neighbor State Reference," summarizes the neighbor state values and their meaning.

OSPF Authentication

OSPF authentication causes routers to authenticate every OSPF message. To do so, the routers use the same preshared key value, generating an MD5 digest for each OSPF message and sending that digest as part of each OSPF message. If a router configured for OSPF authentication receives an OSPF message, and the received message's MD5 digest does not pass the authentication checking based on the local key value, the router silently discards the message. As a result, when authentication fails, two routers cannot become OSPF neighbors, because they ignore the inauthentic OSPF Hello messages.

OSPF authentication uses one of three types: type 0 (no authentication), type 1 (clear text), and type 2 (MD5), with MD5 being the only reasonable option in production networks. To configure to have no authentication, do nothing, because IOS defaults to not attempt OSPF authentication. However, for either of the other two OSPF authentication options, you need to follow two configuration steps, as follows:

Step 1. Authentication must be enabled, plus the authentication type must be selected, through one of two means:

    a. Enabling per interface using the **ip ospf authentication [message-digest]** interface subcommand

    b. Enabling on all interfaces in an area by changing the area-wide authentication setting using the **area** *area-no* **authentication [message-digest]** subcommand under router ospf

Step 2. The authentication keys must be configured per interface.

Key Topic

Table 5-6 lists the three OSPF authentication types, along with the *interface* commands to both enable authentication and to define the authentication keys. Note that the three authentication types can be seen in the messages generated by the **debug ip ospf adjacency** command.

Table 5-6 *OSPF Authentication Types*

Key Topic

Type	Meaning	Enabling Interface Subcommand	Authentication Key Configuration Interface Subcommand
0	None	**ip ospf authentication null**	—
1	Clear text	**ip ospf authentication**	**ip ospf authentication-key** *key-value*
2	MD5	**ip ospf authentication message-digest**	**ip ospf message-digest-key** *key-number* **md5** *key-value*

> **Note:** The maximum length of the key is 16 characters.

Although IOS defaults to use type 0 authentication (no authentication), you can override this default using the **area authentication** command in OSPF configuration mode. For example, on a router with 12 interfaces, you plan to use type 2 (MD5) authentication on all interfaces. Rather than add the **ip ospf authentication message-digest** command to all 12 interfaces, you could override the default that applies to all interface on that router, in a given area. Table 5-7 lists the commands to set the default values.

Table 5-7 *Effect of the* area authentication *Command on OSPF Interface Authentication Settings*

area authentication Command	Interfaces in That Area Default to Use...
default; no configuration required	Type 0
area *num* authentication	Type 1
area *num* authentication message-digest	Type 2

Note that if the area-wide default and the interface subcommand have both been configured, the interface setting takes precedence. For example, if the interface has been configured with the **ip ospf authentication** subcommand (type 1, clear text), and the **area authentication** command sets MD5 authentication, that particular interface uses clear text authentication.

Example 5-7 shows the authentication configuration on Router R3 from Figure 5-4. In this case, all four routers use MD5 authentication on their common subnet, with key number 1, and key value *really-a-secret*. R3 also configures simple password authentication on its Fa0/1 interface, just to demonstrate the various commands. Also for the purposes of demonstrating the commands, R3 overrides the default authentication, setting the default area 0 authentication to MD5.

Example 5-7 *OSPF Authentication Using Only Interface Subcommands*

```
! First, overriding the default in area 0 so that it uses MD5 authentication,
! meaning Fa0/0, in area 0, will use MD5.

R3#conf t
Enter configuration commands, one per line.  End with CNTL/Z.
R3(config)#router ospf 3
R3(config-router)# area 0 authentication message-digest
R3(config-router)#interface fastethernet0/0
R3(config-if)# ip ospf message-digest-key 1 md5 really-a-secret
!
```

```
! Next, two interface subcommands to enable simple password authentication
! on Fa0/1, which is in area 3.

R3(config-if)#interface fastethernet0/1
R3(config-if)#ip ospf authentication
R3(config-if)#ip ospf authentication-key secret
R3(config-if)# ctl-z
R3#
R3#show ip ospf interface fastethernet0/0
! Lines omitted for brevity - the last few lines list authentication information
  Message digest authentication enabled
    Youngest key id is 1


R3#show ip ospf interface fastethernet0/1
! Lines omitted for brevity - the last few lines list authentication information
  Simple password authentication enabled
```

Note that to verify whether OSPF authentication is enabled, and the authentication type, use the **show ip ospf interface** command, and look to the very end of the output, as shown at the end of Example 5-7. Note that these messages identify the configuration setting and do nothing to confirm whether authentication passed. To confirm whether it worked, look for the neighbor in the output of **show ip ospf neighbor**: A neighbor with whom authentication fails will not be listed. The reason is that the Hello will be rejected due to authentication, and the Hello contains several parameters that must be checked before a router will choose to become an OSPF neighbor with that router. You can also use the **debug ip ospf adj** command, whose output explicitly states that a mismatch exists with the authentication key.

Unlike EIGRP authentication, OSPF authentication does not allow the configuration of a key chain with time-based authentication keys. However, multiple keys can be configured on an interface, each with a different key number. To migrate to a new key, you would first configure a new key value on all routers in a subnet and then delete the configuration of the old keys.

To avoid having network failures during this cutover, OSPF actually sends and accepts messages that use all the currently configured authentication keys on the interface. For example, if the four routers in Figure 5-4 had been configured with key numbers 1 and 2, every OSPF message would be sent twice—once with each key.

This concludes the discussion of OSPF neighborships on LANs. The final brief section examines some issues with OSPF neighborship on WANs.

OSPF Neighbors and Adjacencies on WANs

To form OSPF neighbor relationships on WAN connections, OSPF still must meet the same requirements as on LANs. The area number must match with each neighbor; the IP subnet number and mask of each router must match; authentication must pass; and so on. In short, the items in Table 5-5 earlier in this chapter must be true.

However, the operation of OSPF on WAN links of various types requires some additional thought, particularly when developing an implementation and verification plan. In particular, depending on the WAN technology and configuration, the following additional questions may matter for proper OSPF operation over WAN connections:

■ Will the routers discover each other using multicast OSPF Hello messages, or do the neighbors require predefinition?

■ Will the routers try to elect a DR, and if so, which router should be allowed to be the DR?

■ With which other routers should each router become an OSPF neighbor?

The first two of these items depend in part on the setting of the OSPF *network type*, and the third question depends on the WAN service. This section first examines the concept of OSPF network types and then examines the use of OSPF over common WAN technologies included in the CCNP ROUTE exam.

OSPF Network Types

The OSPF network type–a per-interface setting–directs OSPF in regard to three important facts:

■ Whether the router can expect to discover neighbors using multicast Hello messages

■ Whether only two or more than two OSPF routers can exist in the subnet attached to the interface

■ Whether the router should attempt to elect an OSPF DR on that interface

For instance, LAN interfaces require a DR because of the default OSPF network type of *broadcast*. OSPF defines this interface network type to use multicast Hellos to dynamically discover neighbors, allows more than two routers to be in the same subnet, and to attempt to elect a DR. Conversely, point-to-point links and point-to-point WAN subinterfaces default to use a network type of *point-to-point*, meaning that only two OSPF routers can exist in the subnet, neighbors can be dynamically discovered through Hellos, and that the routers do not elect a DR.

Note: The discussion of the motivation for using OSPF DRs occurs in Chapter 6 section "Background of Designated Routers." For now, note that DRs become useful but are not always required, when a subnet supports more than two OSPF routers (for example, on a LAN subnet).

In production networks, the network type is often ignored, because there is no motivation to change this setting—you pick a combination that works, and most everyone ignores it. For the sake of CCNP ROUTE, you need to be aware of the setting and know a few of the caveats found in some Frame Relay configurations. To keep the discussion focused on the core topics, Chapters 6 and 7 avoid the Frame Relay configurations that require more consideration of the OSPF network type setting. Chapter 8's section "OSPF over Multipoint Frame Relay" discusses the OSPF network types in more depth.

Table 5-8 summarizes the OSPF network types and their meanings. Note that this per-interface or per-subinterface setting is configured with the **ip ospf network** *type* interface subcommand; the first column in the table lists the exact keyword according to this command. Note that the gray highlighted rows will be discussed in Chapter 8.

Table 5-8 *OSPF Network Types*

Key Topic

Interface Type	Uses DR/BDR?	Default Hello Interval	Dynamic Discovery of Neighbors?	More Than Two Routers Allowed in the Subnet?
Broadcast	Yes	10	Yes	Yes
Point-to-point[1]	No	10	Yes	No
Loopback	No	—	—	No
Nonbroadcast[2] (NBMA)	Yes	30	No	Yes
Point-to-multi-point	No	30	Yes	Yes
Point-to-multi-point nonbroad-cast	No	30	No	Yes

[1]Default on Frame Relay point-to-point subinterfaces.
[2]Default on Frame Relay physical and multipoint subinterfaces.

OSPF Neighborship over Point-to-Point Links

Point-to-point serial links can be a bit boring. You configure IP addresses on either end, configure the **clock rate** if using a back-to-back serial cable in a lab, and **no shutdown** the interfaces. When enabling OSPF on the interfaces, no extra effort is required compared to LANs—just enable OSPF on the interface, and rely on the default OSPF network type of *point-to-point*.

However, serial links can provide a convenient and uncluttered place to experiment with OSPF network types. As such, Figure 5-5 shows a small network with two routers, with

Example 5-8 that follows showing several examples of the OSPF network type. (This small network matches a portion of the network shown in Figure 5-1 earlier in this chapter.)

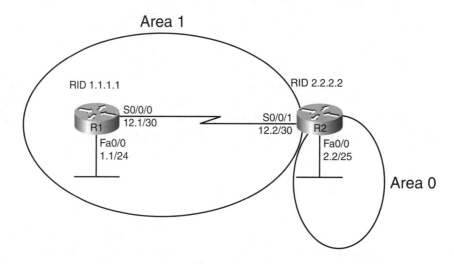

Note: All IP addresses begin with 10.1 unless otherwise noted.

Figure 5-5 *Simple Two Router Internetwork*

Example 5-8 demonstrates OSPF network types with all defaults on the HDLC link between R1 and R2.

Example 5-8 *OSPF Network Types, Default, on an HDLC Link*

```
R1#show run int s0/0/0
Building configuration...

Current configuration : 102 bytes
!
interface Serial0/0/0
 ip address 10.1.12.1 255.255.255.252
 no fair-queue
 clock rate 1536000
!
router ospf 1
 network 10.0.0.0 0.255.255.255 area 1
!
end

R1#show ip ospf interface s0/0/0
Serial0/0/0 is up, line protocol is up
  Internet Address 10.1.12.1/30, Area 1
```

```
   Process ID 1, Router ID 1.1.1.1, Network Type POINT_TO_POINT, Cost: 64
! lines omitted for brevity


R1#show ip ospf neighbor


Neighbor ID      Pri   State           Dead Time   Address     Interface
2.2.2.2            0   FULL/   -       00:00:31    10.1.12.2   Serial0/0/0
```

Example 5-8 begins listing R1's configuration on the serial link, mainly to make the point that the OSPF network type has not been explicitly configured. The **show ip ospf interface** command then lists the network type (point-to-point). Based on Table 5-8, this type should dynamically discover neighbors, and it does, with neighbor 2.2.2.2 (R2) being listed at the end of the example. In particular, note that under the state heading in the **show ip ospf neighbor** command output, after the /, only a dash is listed. This notation means that no attempt was made to elect a DR. If the network type had implied a DR should be elected, then some text would be listed after the /, for example, "/DR" meaning that the neighbor was the DR. (Refer back to the end of Example 5-4 for an example of the output of **show ip ospf neighbor** in which a DR has been elected.)

Example 5-9 shows an alternative where both routers change their OSPF network type on the serial link to nonbroadcast. This change is nonsensical in real designs and is only done for the purposes of showing the results: that the neighbors are not discovered dynamically, but once defined, a DR is elected.

Note: R2 has been preconfigured to match the configuration on R1 in Example 5-9, namely, the OSPF network type has been changed (**ip ospf network non-broadcast**), and R2 has been configured with a **neighbor 10.1.12.1** OSPF router subcommand.

Example 5-9 *Configuring OSPF Network Type Nonbroadcast on an HDLC Link*

```
R1#configure terminal
Enter configuration commands, one per line.  End with CNTL/Z.
R1(config)#interface s0/0/0
R1(config-if)#ip ospf network ?
  broadcast             Specify OSPF broadcast multi-access network
  non-broadcast         Specify OSPF NBMA network
  point-to-multipoint   Specify OSPF point-to-multipoint network
  point-to-point        Specify OSPF point-to-point network
R1(config-if)#ip ospf network non-broadcast
R1(config-if)#^Z


R1#show ip ospf neighbor


R1#configure terminal
Enter configuration commands, one per line.  End with CNTL/Z.
R1(config)#router ospf 1
```

```
R1(config-router)#neighbor 10.1.12.2
R1(config-router)#^Z
R1#


*Apr 28 20:10:15.755: %OSPF-5-ADJCHG: Process 1, Nbr 2.2.2.2 on Serial0/0/0 from
LOADING to FULL, Loading Done
R1#show ip ospf neighbor


Neighbor ID     Pri   State          Dead Time   Address       Interface
2.2.2.2          1    FULL/DR        00:01:58    10.1.12.2     Serial0/0/0
```

The example begins with R2 already configured, so the neighbor relationship has already failed. When the OSPF network type changes on R1's S0/0/0, the routers do not dynamically discover each other, based on the network type (nonbroadcast). However, by completing the configuration in the example by adding R1's **neighbor 10.1.12.2** command, the neighbor relationship is formed. Also, note that the final **show ip ospf neighbor** command lists a state of FULL, then a /, and then DR, meaning that a DR was indeed elected, as required by this OSPF network type.

Neighborship over Frame Relay Point-to-Point Subinterfaces

Frame Relay design allows several options for IP addressing and subnetting. One option treats each pair of routers on the ends of each PVC as a point-to-point topology, with one subnet assigned to each pair of routers. Another option treats more than two routers as a group, whether connected with a full mesh or partial mesh of PVCs, with a single subnet assigned to that group.

Many Frame Relay designs use the first option, treating each pair of routers on the ends of a PVC as a single subnet, as shown in Figure 5-6. In such cases, it makes sense to treat each PVC as a separate point-to-point connection, assigning a single subnet (at Layer 3) to each Layer 2 PVC.

With this design, if all the routers use point-to-point subinterfaces as shown in R1's configuration in the figure, you can ignore the OSPF network (interface) type, and OSPF works fine. IOS point-to-point subinterfaces unsurprisingly default to use OSPF network type point-to-point. The two routers discover each other using multicast OSPF Hellos, they do not bother to elect a DR, and everything works well.

Chapter 8 discusses alternative Frame Relay configurations.

Neighborship on MPLS VPN

Multiprotocol Label Switching (MPLS) virtual private networks (VPN) create a WAN service that has some similarities but many differences when compared to Frame Relay. The customer routers connect to the service, often times with serial links, but other times with Frame Relay PVCs or with Ethernet. The service itself is a Layer 3 service, forwarding IP packets through the cloud. As a result, no predefined PVCs need exist between the customer routers. Additionally, the service uses routers at the edge of the service provider cloud–generically called provider edge (PE) routers–and these routers are Layer 3-aware.

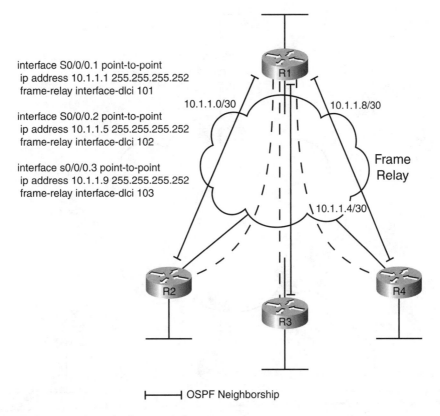

interface S0/0/0.1 point-to-point
ip address 10.1.1.1 255.255.255.252
frame-relay interface-dlci 101

10.1.1.0/30

interface S0/0/0.2 point-to-point
ip address 10.1.1.5 255.255.255.252
frame-relay interface-dlci 102

interface s0/0/0.3 point-to-point
ip address 10.1.1.9 255.255.255.252
frame-relay interface-dlci 103

10.1.1.8/30

Frame Relay

10.1.1.4/30

⊢———⊣ OSPF Neighborship

Figure 5-6 *Partial Meshed Frame Relay Network*

That Layer 3 awareness means that the customer edge (CE) routers form an OSPF neighborship with the PE router on the other end of their local access link, as shown in Figure 5-7. The PE routers exchange their routes, typically using Multiprotocol BGP (MP-BGP), a topic outside the scope of this book. So, unlike the design seen previously in Figure 5-6, the central site router will not have an OSPF neighborship with each branch office router but will have a neighborship with the MPLS VPN provider's PE router.

MPLS VPN does impact the data seen in the LSDB in the Enterprise routers and requires some different thinking in regard to area design. However, these details remain outside the scope of this book.

Neighborship on Metro Ethernet

In the like-named section "Neighborship on Metro Ethernet" in Chapter 2, that chapter explained the basic terminology with Metro Ethernet, including of VPWS, a point-to-point service, and VPLS, a multipoint service. In both cases, however, if the customer connects to the service using a router, the configuration typically uses VLAN trunking with subinterfaces off the FastEthernet or Gigabit Ethernet interface. If connecting with a Layer 3 switch, the configuration again often uses VLAN trunking, with the Layer 3 configuration being made on various VLAN interfaces inside the switch configuration.

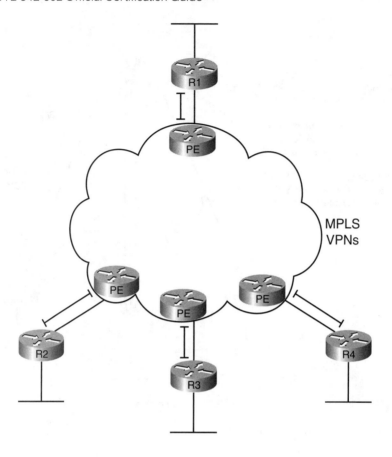

Figure 5-7   *OSPF Neighborships over MPLS VPN*

Because MetroE services provide Layer 2 connectivity, customer routers do not form OSPF neighborships with routers inside the service provider's network. Instead, the OSPF neighborships forms between customer routers, essentially as if the service were a large WAN. Figure 5-8 shows the basic idea, with four routers connected to the service.

Figure 5-8 shows four routers with any-to-any connectivity, typical of a VPWS service. However, from an OSPF design perspective, each pair of routers could communicate over a different VLAN, using a different Layer 3 subnet. Each Layer 3 subnet could be in a different area. Although (like MPLS VPN area design) beyond the scope of this book, these options give the network designer many options on how to define areas.

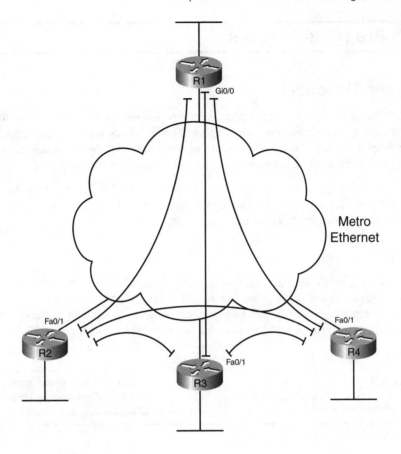

Figure 5-8   *OSPF Neighborships over Metro Ethernet*

Exam Preparation Tasks

Planning Practice

The CCNP ROUTE exam expects test takers to review design documents, create implementation plans, and create verification plans. This section provides some exercises that may help you to take a step back from the minute details of the topics in this chapter so that you can think about the same technical topics from the planning perspective.

For each planning practice table, simply complete the table. Note that any numbers in parentheses represent the number of options listed for each item in the solutions in Appendix F, "Completed Planning Practice Table."

Design Review Table

Table 5-9 lists several design goals related to this chapter. If these design goals were listed in a design document, and you had to take that document and develop an implementation plan, what implementation options come to mind? For any configuration items, a general description can be used, without concern about the specific parameters.

Table 5-9 *Design Review*

Design Goal	Possible Implementation Choices Covered in This Chapter
Improve OSPF convergence.	
Implement OSPF on each router so that neighborships are formed (2).	
Limit neighborship formation on OSPF-enabled interfaces (2).	
The design shows branch routers with WAN interfaces in area 0 and LAN interfaces in different areas for each branch. What LSDB information do you expect to see in the branch routers?	

Implementation Plan Peer Review Table

Table 5-10 shows a list of questions that others might ask, or that you might think about, during a peer review of another network engineer's implementation plan. Complete the table by answering the questions.

Table 5-10 *Notable Questions from This Chapter to Consider During an Implementation Plan Peer Review*

Question	Answers
What happens on a router interface on which an OSPF **network** command matches the interface? (2)	
What configuration settings prevent OSPF neighbor discovery on an OSPF-enabled interface?	
What settings do potential neighbors check before becoming OSPF neighbors? (7)	
What settings that you might think would impact OSPF neighbor relationships actually do not prevent neighborship?	
A design shows one main site and 100 branches, with OSPF, and MPLS VPNs. How many OSPF neighborships over the WAN do you expect to see on the central site router?	
A design shows one main site and 100 branches, with one Frame Relay PVC between the main site and each branch. How many OSPF neighborships over the WAN do you expect to see on the central site router?	
A design shows six routers connected to the same VLAN and subnet. How many OSPF fully adjacent neighborships over this subnet do you expect each router to have?	
A design shows one main site and 100 branches, each connected with a VPWS service. The configuration shows that the central site router uses a separate VLAN subinterface to connect to each branch, but the branch routers do not have a VLAN connecting to other branches. How many OSPF fully adjacent neighborships over the WAN do you expect to see on the central site router?	

Create an Implementation Plan Table

To practice skills useful when creating your own OSPF implementation plan, list in Table 5-11 configuration commands related to the configuration of the following features. You may want to record your answers outside the book and set a goal to complete this table (and others like it) from memory during your final reviews before taking the exam.

Table 5-11 *Implementation Plan Configuration Memory Drill*

Feature	Configuration Commands/Notes
Enabling OSPF on interfaces–traditional method	
Enabling OSPF on interfaces–using interface subcommands	
Setting Hello and Dead intervals	

Table 5-11   *Implementation Plan Configuration Memory Drill*

Feature	Configuration Commands/Notes
MD5 authentication, with no **router** subcommands	
MD5 authentication, with **router** subcommands	
Passive interfaces, with router subcommands	
OSPF router ID	

Choose Commands for a Verification Plan Table

To practice skills useful when creating your own OSPF verification plan, list in Table 5-12 all commands that supply the requested information. You may want to record your answers outside the book and set a goal to complete this table (and others like it) from memory during your final reviews before taking the exam.

Table 5-12   *Verification Plan Memory Drill*

Information Needed	Command
Which routes have been added to the IP routing table by OSPF	
All routes in a router's routing table	
The specific route for a single destination address or subnet	
A list of all (both static and dynamically discovered) OSPF neighbors	
List interfaces on which OSPF has been enabled	
List the number of OSPF neighbors and fully adjacent neighbors known via a particular interface	
The elapsed time since a neighborship was formed	
The configured Hello timer for an interface	
The configured Dead Interval timer for an interface	
The current actual dead timer for a neighbor	
A router's RID	
A list of OSPF passive interfaces	
The currently used OSPF authentication type	
The smallest-numbered OSPF authentication key number	
Lists traffic statistics about OSPF	

Note: Some of the entries in this table may not have been specifically mentioned in this chapter but are listed in this table for review and reference.

Review All the Key Topics

Review the most important topics from inside the chapter, noted with the key topics icon in the outer margin of the page. Table 5-13 lists a reference of these key topics and the page numbers on which each is found.

Key
Topic

Table 5-13 *Key Topics for Chapter 5*

Key Topic Element	Description	Page Number
Table 5-2	Common OSPF terminology	142
List	Base OSPF configuration steps	144
List	Rules for choosing the OSPF Router ID	146
Table 5-3	Five most commonly used OSPF **show** commands	146
Table 5-4	Summary table of OSPF features	149
List	Requirements before OSPF will attempt to dynamically discover neighbors	150
Table 5-5	Requirements for neighbor formation–OSPF and EIGRP	152
List	Rules for enabling OSPF authentication on an interface	159
Table 5-6	OSPF Authentication command summary	159
Table 5-7	Commands to set the default OSPF authentication type	160
Table 5-8	OSPF network types	163

Complete the Tables and Lists from Memory

Print a copy of Appendix D, "Memory Tables," (found on the CD), or at least the section for this chapter, and complete the tables and lists from memory. Appendix E, "Memory Tables Answer Key," also on the CD, includes completed tables and lists to check your work.

Define Key Terms

Define the following key terms from this chapter, and check your answers in the glossary:

Area, Area Border Router (ABR), Backbone router, Router ID, Hello Interval, Dead Interval, Fully adjacent, OSPF network type

This chapter covers the following subjects:

LSAs and the OSPF Link State Database: This section examines LSA Types 1, 2, and 3, and how they allow OSPF routers to model the topology and choose the best routes for each known subnet.

The Database Exchange Process: This section details how neighboring routers use OSPF messages to exchange their LSAs.

Choosing the Best Internal OSPF Routes: This section examines how OSPF routers calculate the cost for each possible route to each subnet.

CHAPTER 6

OSPF Topology, Routes, and Convergence

OSPF and EIGRP both use three major branches of logic, each of which populates a different table: the neighbor table, the topology table, and the IP routing table. This chapter examines topics related to the OSPF topology table–the contents, and the processes by which routers exchange this information–and how OSPF routers choose the best routes in the topology table to be added to the IP routing table.

In particular, this chapter begins by looking at the building blocks of OSPF topology, namely the OSPF link state advertisement (LSA). Following that, the chapter examines the process by which OSPF routers exchange LSAs with each other. Finally, the last major section of the chapter discusses how OSPF chooses the best route among many when running the Shortest Path First (SPF) algorithm.

Note that this chapter focuses on OSPF Version 2, the long-available version of OSPF that supports IPv4 routes. Chapter 17, "IPv6 Routing Protocols and Redistribution," discusses OSPF Version 3, which applies to IPv6.

"Do I Know This Already?" Quiz

The "Do I Know This Already?" quiz allows you to assess if you should read the entire chapter. If you miss no more than one of these nine self-assessment questions, you might want to move ahead to the "Exam Preparation Tasks." Table 6-1 lists the major headings in this chapter and the "Do I Know This Already?" quiz questions covering the material in those headings so that you can assess your knowledge of these specific areas. The answers to the "Do I Know This Already?" quiz appear in Appendix A.

Table 6-1 *"Do I Know This Already?" Foundation Topics Section-to-Question Mapping*

Foundations Topics Section	Questions
LSAs and the OSPF Link State Database	1–3
The Database Exchange Process	4, 5
Choosing the Best OSPF Routes	6–9

1. A network design shows area 1 with three internal routers, area 0 with four internal routers, and area 2 with five internal routers. Additionally, one ABR (ABR1) connects areas 0 and 1, plus a different ABR (ABR2) connects areas 0 and 2. How many Type 1 LSAs would be listed in ABR2's LSDB?

   a. 6

   b. 7

   c. 15

   d. 12

   e. None of the other answers is correct.

2. A network planning diagram shows a large internetwork with many routers. The configurations show that OSPF has been enabled on all interfaces, IP addresses correctly configured, and OSPF working. For which of the following cases would you expect a router to create and flood a Type 2 LSA?

   a. When OSPF is enabled on a LAN interface, and the router is the only router connected to the subnet.

   b. When OSPF is enabled on a point-to-point serial link, and that router has both the higher router ID and higher interface IP address on the link.

   c. When OSPF is enabled on a Frame Relay point-to-point subinterface, has the lower RID and lower subinterface IP address, and otherwise uses default OSPF configuration on the interface.

   d. When OSPF is enabled on a working LAN interface on a router, and the router has been elected BDR.

   e. None of the other answers is correct.

3. A verification plan shows a network diagram with branch office Routers B1 through B100, plus two ABRs, ABR1, and ABR2, all in area 100. The branches connect to the ABRs using Frame Relay point-to-point subinterfaces. The verification plan lists the output of the **show ip ospf database summary 10.100.0.0** command on a router B1, one of the branches. Which of the following is true regarding the output that could be listed for this command?

   a. The output lists nothing unless 10.100.0.0 has been configured as a summary route using the **area range** command.

   b. If 10.100.0.0 is a subnet in area 0, the output lists one Type 3 LSA, specifically the LSA with the lower metric when comparing ABR1's and ABR2's LSA for 10.100.0.0.

   c. If 10.100.0.0 is a subnet in area 0, the output lists two Type 3 LSAs, one each created by ABR1 and ABR2.

   d. None, because the Type 3 LSAs would exist only in the ABR's LSDBs.

4. Which of the following OSPF messages contains entire complete LSAs used during the database exchange process?

    a. LSR

    b. LSAck

    c. LSU

    d. DD

    e. Hello

5. Routers R1, R2, R3, and R4 connect to the same 10.10.10.0/24 LAN-based subnet. OSPF is fully working in the subnet. Later, R5, whose OSPF priority is higher than the other four routers, joins the subnet. Which of the following are true about the OSPF database exchange process over this subnet at this point? (Choose two.)

    a. R5 will send its DD, LSR, and LSU packets to the 224.0.0.5 all-DR-routers multicast address.

    b. R5 will send its DD, LSR, and LSU packets to the 224.0.0.6 all-DR-routers multicast address.

    c. The DR will inform R5 about LSAs by sending its DD, LSR, and LSU packets to the 224.0.0.6 all-SPF-routers multicast address.

    d. The DR will inform R5 about LSAs by sending its DD, LSR, and LSU packets to the 224.0.0.5 all-SPF-routers multicast address.

6. R1 is internal to area 1, and R2 is internal to area 2. Subnet 10.1.1.0/24 exists in area 2 as a connected subnet off R2. ABR ABR1 connects area 1 to backbone area 0, and ABR2 connects area 0 to area 2. Which of the following LSAs must R1 use when calculating R1's best route for 10.1.1.0/24?

    a. R2's Type 1 LSA

    b. Subnet 10.1.1.0/24's Type 2 LSA

    c. ABR1's Type 1 LSA in area 0

    d. Subnet 10.1.1.0/24's Type 3 LSA in Area 0

    e. Subnet 10.1.1.0/24's Type 3 LSA in Area 1

7. Which of the following LSA types describes topology information that, when changed, requires a router in the same area to perform an SPF calculation? (Choose two.)

    a. 1

    b. 2

    c. 3

    d. 4

    e. 5

    f. 7

8. The following output was taken from Router R3. A scan of R3's configuration shows that no **bandwidth** commands have been configured in this router. Which of the following answers lists configuration settings could be a part of a configuration that results in the following output? (Choose two.) Only two of the three interface's costs have been set directly.

```
R3#show ip ospf interface brief
Interface    PID   Area              IP Address/Mask     Cost   State  Nbrs F/C
Se0/0/0.2    3     34                10.10.23.3/29       647    P2P    1/1
Se0/0/0.1    3     34                10.10.13.3/29       1000   P2P    1/1
Fa0/0        3     34                10.10.34.3/24       20     BDR    1/1
```

  a. An **auto-cost reference-bandwidth 1000** command in router ospf mode
  b. An **auto-cost reference-bandwidth 2000** command in router ospf mode
  c. An **ip ospf cost 1000 interface S0/0/0.1** command in router ospf mode
  d. An **auto-cost reference-bandwidth 64700** command in router ospf mode

9. Which of the following LSA types describe information related to topology or subnets useful for calculating routes for subnets inside the OSPF domain? (Choose three.)

  a. 1
  b. 2
  c. 3
  d. 4
  e. 5
  f. 7

Foundation Topics

LSAs and the OSPF Link State Database

Every router that connects to a given OSPF area should learn the exact same topology data. Each router stores the data, composed of individual link state advertisements (LSA), in their own copy of the link state database (LSDB). Then, the router applies the Shortest Path First (SPF) algorithm to the LSDB to determine the best (lowest cost) route for each reachable subnet (prefix/length).

When a router uses SPF to analyze the LSDB, the SPF process has some similarities to how humans put a jigsaw puzzle together–but without a picture of what the puzzle looks like. Humans faced with such a challenge might first look for the obvious puzzle pieces, such as the corner and edge pieces, because they are easily recognized. You might then group puzzle pieces together if they have the same color or look for straight lines that might span multiple puzzle pieces. And of course, you would be looking at the shapes of the puzzle pieces to see which ones fit together.

Similarly, a router's SPF process must examine the individual LSAs and see how they fit together, based on their characteristics. To better appreciate the SPF process, the first section of this chapter examines the three LSA types OSPF uses to describe an Enterprise OSPF topology inside the OSPF domain. By understanding the types of LSAs, you can get a better understanding of what a router might look for to take the LSAs–the pieces of a network topology puzzle if you will–and build the equivalent of a network diagram.

For reference, Table 6-2 lists the various OSPF LSA types. Note that Chapter 9 explains three other LSA types, all used when redistributing routes into the OSPF domain.

Table 6-2 *OSPF LSA Types*

LSA Type	Common Name	Description
1	Router	Each router creates its own Type 1 LSA to represent itself for each area to which it connects. The LSDB for one area contains one Type 1 LSA per router per area, listing the RID and all interface IP addresses on that router that are in that area. Represents stub networks as well.
2	Network	One per transit network. Created by the DR on the subnet, and represents the subnet and the router interfaces connected to the subnet.
3	Net Summary	Created by ABRs to represent subnets listed in one area's type 1 and 2 LSAs when being advertised into another area. Defines the links (subnets) in the origin area, and cost, but no topology data.
4	ASBR Summary	Like a type 3 LSA, except it advertises a host route used to reach an ASBR.

Table 6-2 *OSPF LSA Types*

LSA Type	Common Name	Description
5	AS External	Created by ASBRs for external routes injected into OSPF.
6	Group Membership	Defined for MOSPF; not supported by Cisco IOS.
7	NSSA External	Created by ASBRs inside an NSSA area, instead of a type 5 LSA.
8	External Attributes	Not implemented in Cisco routers.
9–11	Opaque	Used as generic LSAs to allow for easy future extension of OSPF; for example, type 10 has been adapted for MPLS traffic engineering.

LSA Type 1: Router LSA

An LSA type 1, called a *router LSA*, identifies an OSPF router based on its OSPF router ID (RID). Each router creates a Type 1 LSA for itself and floods the LSA throughout the same area. To flood the LSA, the originating router sends the Type 1 LSA to its neighbors inside the same area, who in turn send it to their other neighbors inside the same area, until all routers in the area have a copy of the LSA.

Besides the RID of the router, this LSA also lists information about the attached links. In particular, the Type 1 LSA lists:

■   For each interface on which no DR has been elected, it lists the router's interface subnet number/mask and interface OSPF cost. (OSPF refers to these subnets as *stub networks*.)

■   For each interface on which a DR has been elected, it lists the IP address of the DR and a notation that the link attaches to a *transit network* (meaning a type 2 LSA exists for that network).

■   For each interface with no DR, but for which a neighbor is reachable, it lists the neighbor's RID.

As with all OSPF LSAs, OSPF identifies a Type 1 LSA using a 32-bit *link state identifier* (LSID). When creating its own Type 1 LSA, each router uses its own OSPF RID value as the LSID.

Internal routers each create a single Type 1 LSA for themselves, but ABRs create multiple Type 1 LSAs for themselves: one per area. The Type 1 LSA in one area will list only interfaces in that area and only neighbors in that area. However, the router still has only a single RID, so all its Type 1 LSAs for a single router list the same RID. The ABR then floods each of its Type 1 LSAs into the appropriate area.

To provide a better backdrop for the upcoming LSA discussions, Figure 6-1 shows a sample internetwork, which will be used in most of the examples in this chapter.

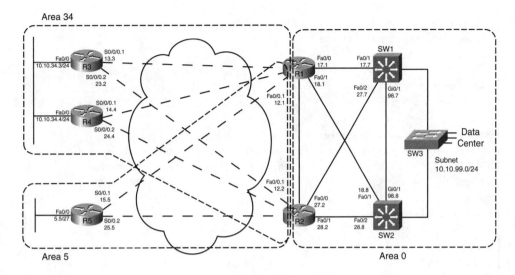

Figure 6-1   *Sample OSPF Multi-Area Design*

All routers that participate in an area, be they internal routers or ABRs, create and flood a Type 1 LSA inside the area. For example, in Figure 6-1, area 5 has one internal router (R5, RID 5.5.5.5), and two ABRs: R1 with RID 1.1.1.1 and R2 with RID 2.2.2.2. Each of these three routers create and flood their own Type 1 LSA inside area 5 so that all three routers know the same three Type 1 LSAs.

Next, to further understand the details inside a Type 1 LSA, first consider the OSPF configuration of R5 as an example. R5 has three IP-enabled interfaces: Fa0/0, S0/0.1, and S0/0.2. R5 uses point-to-point subinterfaces, so R5 should form neighbor relationships with both R1 and R2 with no extra configuration beyond enabling OSPF, in area 5, on all three interfaces. Example 6-1 shows this baseline configuration on R5.

Example 6-1   *R5 Configuration–IP Addresses and OSPF*

```
interface Fastethernet0/0
 ip address 10.10.5.5 255.255.255.224
 ip ospf 5 area 5
!
interface s0/0.1 point-to-point
 ip address 10.10.15.5 255.255.255.248
 frame-relay interface-dlci 101
 ip ospf 5 area 5
!
interface s0/0.2 point-to-point
```

```
 ip address 10.10.25.5 255.255.255.248
 frame-relay interface-dlci 102
 ip ospf 5 area 5
!
router ospf 5
 router-id 5.5.5.5
!
R5#show ip ospf interface brief
Interface    PID   Area            IP Address/Mask    Cost  State Nbrs F/C
se0/0.2       5     5              10.10.25.5/29       64    P2P   1/1
se0/0.1       5     5              10.10.15.5/29       64    P2P   1/1
fa0/0         5     5              10.10.5.5/27        1     DR    0/0
R5#show ip ospf neighbor


Neighbor ID    Pri   State         Dead Time   Address       Interface
2.2.2.2         0    FULL/  -      00:00:30    10.10.25.2    Serial0/0.2
1.1.1.1         0    FULL/  -      00:00:38    10.10.15.1    Serial0/0.1
```

R5's OSPF configuration enables OSPF, for process ID 5, placing three interfaces in area 5. As a result, R5's type 1 LSA will list at least these three interfaces as links, plus it will refer to the two working neighbors. Example 6-2 displays the contents of R5's area 5 LSDB, including the detailed information in R5's Type 1 LSA, including the following:

■ The LSID of R5's Type 1 LSA (5.5.5.5)

■ Three links that connect to a stub network, each listing the subnet/mask

■ Two links that state a connection to another router, one listing R1 (RID 1.1.1.1) and one listing R2 (RID 2.2.2.2)

Example 6-2 *R5 Configuration–IP Addresses and OSPF*

```
R5#show ip ospf database


            OSPF Router with ID (5.5.5.5) (Process ID 5)


                Router Link States (Area 5)


Link ID        ADV Router      Age       Seq#          Checksum Link count
1.1.1.1        1.1.1.1         835       0x80000002  0x006BDA 2
2.2.2.2        2.2.2.2         788       0x80000002  0x0082A6 2
5.5.5.5        5.5.5.5         787       0x80000004  0x0063C3 5


                Summary Net Link States (Area 5)
```

```
Link ID          ADV Router        Age        Seq#        Checksum
10.10.12.0       1.1.1.1           835        0x80000001  0x00F522
10.10.12.0       2.2.2.2           787        0x80000001  0x00D73C
! lines omitted for brevity

R5#show ip ospf database router 5.5.5.5

               OSPF Router with ID (5.5.5.5) (Process ID 5)

                 Router Link States (Area 5)

  LS age: 796
  Options: (No TOS-capability, DC)
  LS Type: Router Links
  Link State ID: 5.5.5.5
  Advertising Router: 5.5.5.5
  LS Seq Number: 80000004
  Checksum: 0x63C3
  Length: 84
  Number of Links: 5

    Link connected to: another Router (point-to-point)
     (Link ID) Neighboring Router ID: 2.2.2.2
     (Link Data) Router Interface address: 10.10.25.5
      Number of TOS metrics: 0
       TOS 0 Metrics: 64

    Link connected to: a Stub Network
     (Link ID) Network/subnet number: 10.10.25.0
     (Link Data) Network Mask: 255.255.255.248
      Number of TOS metrics: 0
       TOS 0 Metrics: 64

    Link connected to: another Router (point-to-point)
     (Link ID) Neighboring Router ID: 1.1.1.1
     (Link Data) Router Interface address: 10.10.15.5
      Number of TOS metrics: 0
       TOS 0 Metrics: 64

    Link connected to: a Stub Network
     (Link ID) Network/subnet number: 10.10.15.0
     (Link Data) Network Mask: 255.255.255.248
      Number of TOS metrics: 0
       TOS 0 Metrics: 64
```

```
Link connected to: a Stub Network
   (Link ID) Network/subnet number: 10.10.5.0
   (Link Data) Network Mask: 255.255.255.224
   Number of TOS metrics: 0
   TOS 0 Metrics: 1
```

The first command, **show ip ospf database**, displays a summary of the LSAs known to R5. The output mainly consists of a single line per LSA, listed by LSA ID. The three high-lighted lines of this command, in Example 6-2, highlight the RID of the three router (Type 1) LSAs, namely 1.1.1.1 (R1), 2.2.2.2 (R2), and 5.5.5.5 (R5).

The output of the **show ip ospf database router 5.5.5.5** command displays the detailed information in R5's router LSA. Looking at the highlighted portions, you see three stub networks–three interfaces on which no DR has been elected–and the associated subnet numbers. The LSA also lists the neighbor IDs of two neighbors (1.1.1.1 and 2.2.2.2) and the interfaces on which these neighbors can be reached.

Armed with the same kind of information in R1's and R2's Type 1 LSAs, a router has enough information to determine which routers connect, over which stub links, and then use the interface IP address configuration to figure out the interfaces that connect to the other routers. Figure 6-2 shows a diagram of area 5 that could be built just based on the detailed information held in the router LSAs for R1, R2, and R5.

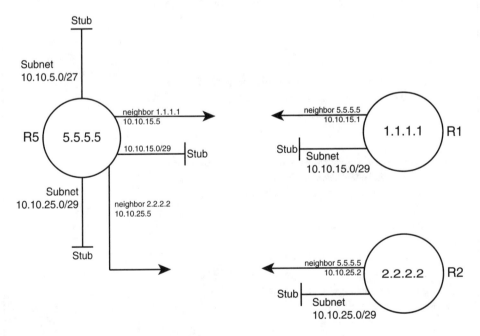

Figure 6-2   *Three Type 1 LSAs in Area 5*

Note that Figure 6-2 displays only information that could be learned from the Type 1 router LSAs inside area 5. Each Type 1 router LSA lists information about a router but only the details related to a specific area. As a result, Figure 6-2 shows R1's interface in area 5 but none of the interfaces in area 34 nor in area 0. To complete the explanation surrounding Figure 6-2, Example 6-3 lists R1's Type 1 router LSA for area 5.

Example 6-3 *R1's Type 1 LSA in Area 5*

```
R5#show ip ospf database router 1.1.1.1



            OSPF Router with ID (5.5.5.5) (Process ID 5)


                Router Link States (Area 5)


Routing Bit Set on this LSA
LS age: 1306
Options: (No TOS-capability, DC)
LS Type: Router Links
Link State ID: 1.1.1.1
Advertising Router: 1.1.1.1
LS Seq Number: 80000002
Checksum: 0x6BDA
Length: 48
Area Border Router
Number of Links: 2

  Link connected to: another Router (point-to-point)
   (Link ID) Neighboring Router ID: 5.5.5.5
   (Link Data) Router Interface address: 10.10.15.1
    Number of TOS metrics: 0
     TOS 0 Metrics: 64


  Link connected to: a Stub Network
   (Link ID) Network/subnet number: 10.10.15.0
   (Link Data) Network Mask: 255.255.255.248
    Number of TOS metrics: 0
     TOS 0 Metrics: 64
```

Note: Because the OSPF uses the RID for many purposes inside different LSAs—for instance, as the LSID of a type 1 LSA—Cisco recommends setting the RID to a stable, predictable value. To do this, use the OSPF **router-id** *value* OSPF subcommand, or define a loopback interface with an IP address, as discussed in Chapter 5's section "Using a Unique OSPF Router ID."

LSA Type 2: Network LSA

SPF requires that the LSDB model the topology with nodes (routers) and connections between nodes (links). In particular, each link must be between a pair of nodes. When a multiaccess data link exists—for instance, a LAN—OSPF must somehow model that LAN so that the topology represents nodes and links between only a pair of nodes. To do so, OSPF uses the concept of a Type 2 Network LSA.

OSPF routers actually choose whether to use a Type 2 LSA for a multiaccess network based on whether a designated router (DR) has or has not been elected on an interface. So, before discussing the details of the Type 2 network LSA, a few more facts about the concept of a DR need to be discussed.

Background on Designated Routers

As discussed in Chapter 5's section "OSPF Network Types," the OSPF network type assigned to a router interface tells that router whether to attempt to elect a DR on that interface. Then, when a router has heard a Hello from at least one other router, the routers elect a DR and BDR.

OSPF uses a DR in a particular subnet for two main purposes:

- To create and flood a Type 2 network LSA for that subnet

- To aid in the detailed process of database exchange over that subnet

Routers elect a DR, and a backup DR (BDR), based on information in the OSPF Hello. The Hello message lists each router's RID and a priority value. When no DR exists at the time, routers use the following election rules when neither a DR nor BDR yet exists:

- Choose the router with the highest priority (default 1, max 255, set with **ip ospf priority** *value* interface subcommand).

- If tied on priority, choose the router with highest RID.

- Choose a BDR, based on next-best priority, or if a tie, next-best (highest) RID.

Although the preceding describes the election when no DR currently exists, the rules differ a bit when a DR and BDR already exist. After a DR and BDR are elected, no election is held until either the DR or BDR fails. If the DR fails, the BDR becomes the DR—regardless of whether a higher priority router has joined the subnet—and a new election is held to choose a new BDR. If the BDR fails, a new election is held for BDR, and the DR remains unchanged.

On LANs, the choice of DR matters little from a design perspective, but does matter from an operational perspective. Throughout this chapter, note the cases in which output of **show** commands identify the DR and its role. Now, back to the topic of Type 2 LSAs.

> **Note:** On Frame Relay WAN links, the choice of DR may impact whether OSPF functions at all. This topic is covered in Chapter 8, "OSPF Virtual Links and Frame Relay Operations."

Type 2 Network LSA Concepts

OSPF uses the concept of a Type 2 LSA to model a multiaccess network–a network with more than two routers connected to the same subnet–while still conforming to the "a link connects only two nodes" rule for the topology. For example, consider the network in Figure 6-3 (also shown as Figure 5-4 in the previous chapter). As seen in Chapter 5, all four routers form neighbor relationships inside area 0, with the DR and BDR becoming fully adjacent with the other routers.

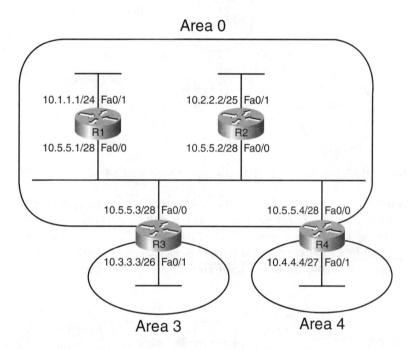

Figure 6-3   *Small Network, Four Routers, on a LAN*

OSPF cannot represent the idea of four routers connected via a single subnet by using a link connected to all four routers. Instead, OSPF defines the Type 2 network LSA, used as a *pseudonode*. Each router's Type 1 router LSA lists a connection to this pseudonode, often called a *transit network*, which is then modeled by a Type 2 network LSA. The Type 2 network LSA itself then lists references back to each Type 1 router LSA connected to it–four in this example, as shown in Figure 6-4.

The elected DR in a subnet creates the Type 2 LSA for that subnet. The DR identifies the LSA by assigning an LSID of the DR's interface IP address in that subnet. The type 2 LSA also lists the DR's RID as the router advertising the LSA.

Type 2 LSA show Commands

To see these concepts in the form of OSPF **show** commands, next consider area 34 back in Figure 6-1. This design shows that R3 and R4 connect to the same LAN, which means that

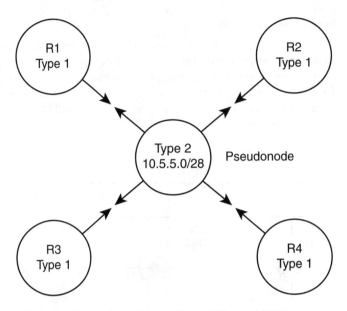

Figure 6-4   *OSPF Topology when Using a Type 2 Network LSA*

a DR will be elected. (OSPF elects a DR on LANs when at least two routers pass the neighbor requirements and can become neighbors.) If both R3 and R4 default to use priority 1, then R4 wins the election, due to its 4.4.4.4 RID (versus R3's 3.3.3.3). So, R4 creates the Type 2 LSA for that subnet and floods the LSA. Figure 6-5 depicts the area 34 topology, and Example 6-4 shows the related LSDB entries.

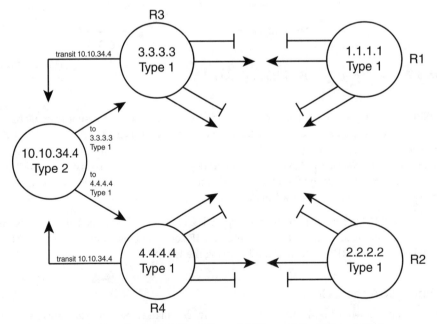

Figure 6-5   *Area 34 Topology with Four Type 1 LSAs and One Type 2 LSA*

Example 6-4   *Area 34 LSAs for R3, Network 10.10.34.0/24*

```
R3#show ip ospf database


                OSPF Router with ID (3.3.3.3) (Process ID 3)

                  Router Link States (Area 34)

Link ID          ADV Router       Age          Seq#       Checksum Link count
1.1.1.1          1.1.1.1          1061         0x80000002 0x00EA7A 4
2.2.2.2          2.2.2.2          1067         0x80000001 0x0061D2 4
3.3.3.3          3.3.3.3          1066         0x80000003 0x00E2E8 5
4.4.4.4          4.4.4.4          1067         0x80000003 0x007D3F 5

                   Net Link States (Area 34)


Link ID          ADV Router       Age          Seq#       Checksum
10.10.34.4       4.4.4.4          1104         0x80000001 0x00AB28

                  Summary Net Link States (Area 34)

Link ID          ADV Router       Age          Seq#       Checksum
10.10.5.0        1.1.1.1          1023         0x80000001 0x000BF2
10.10.5.0        2.2.2.2          1022         0x80000001 0x00EC0D
! lines omitted for brevity

R3#show ip ospf database router 4.4.4.4

                OSPF Router with ID (3.3.3.3) (Process ID 3)

                  Router Link States (Area 34)


  LS age: 1078
  Options: (No TOS-capability, DC)
  LS Type: Router Links
  Link State ID: 4.4.4.4
  Advertising Router: 4.4.4.4
  LS Seq Number: 80000003
  Checksum: 0x7D3F
  Length: 84
```

```
Number of Links: 5

  Link connected to: another Router (point-to-point)
   (Link ID) Neighboring Router ID: 2.2.2.2
   (Link Data) Router Interface address: 10.10.24.4
    Number of TOS metrics: 0
     TOS 0 Metrics: 64

  Link connected to: a Stub Network
   (Link ID) Network/subnet number: 10.10.24.0
   (Link Data) Network Mask: 255.255.255.248
    Number of TOS metrics: 0
     TOS 0 Metrics: 64

  Link connected to: another Router (point-to-point)
   (Link ID) Neighboring Router ID: 1.1.1.1
   (Link Data) Router Interface address: 10.10.14.4
    Number of TOS metrics: 0
     TOS 0 Metrics: 64

  Link connected to: a Stub Network
   (Link ID) Network/subnet number: 10.10.14.0
   (Link Data) Network Mask: 255.255.255.248
    Number of TOS metrics: 0
     TOS 0 Metrics: 64

  Link connected to: a Transit Network
   (Link ID) Designated Router address: 10.10.34.4
   (Link Data) Router Interface address: 10.10.34.4
    Number of TOS metrics: 0
     TOS 0 Metrics: 1

R3#show ip ospf database network 10.10.34.4

            OSPF Router with ID (3.3.3.3) (Process ID 3)


              Net Link States (Area 34)


  Routing Bit Set on this LSA
  LS age: 1161
  Options: (No TOS-capability, DC)
  LS Type: Network Links
  Link State ID: 10.10.34.4 (address of Designated Router)
  Advertising Router: 4.4.4.4
```

```
LS Seq Number: 80000001
Checksum: 0xAB28
Length: 32
Network Mask: /24
        Attached Router: 4.4.4.4
        Attached Router: 3.3.3.3
```

The **show ip ospf database** command lists a single line for each LSA. Note that the (high-lighted) heading for network LSAs lists one entry, with LSID 10.10.34.4, which is R4's Fa0/0 IP address. The LSID for Type 2 Network LSAs is the interface IP address of the DR that creates the LSA.

The **show ip ospf database router 4.4.4.4** command shows the new style of entry for the reference to a *Transit Network*, which again refers to a connection to a Type 2 LSA. The output lists a LSID of 10.10.34.4, which again is the LSID of the Type 2 LSA.

Finally, the **show ip ospf database network 10.10.34.4** command shows the details of the Type 2 LSA, based on its LSID of 10.10.34.4. Near the bottom, the output lists the attached routers, based on RID. The SPF process can then use the cross-referenced information, as shown in Figure 6-5, to determine which routers connect to this transit network (pseudonode). The SPF process has information in both the Type 1 LSAs that refer to the transit network link to a Type 2 LSA, and the Type 2 LSA has a list of RIDs of Type 1 LSAs that connect to the Type 2 LSA, making the process of modeling the network possible.

OSPF can model all the topology inside a single area using Type 1 and 2 LSAs. When a router uses its SPF process to build a model of the topology, it can then calculate the best (lowest cost) route for each subnet in the area. The next topic completes the LSA picture for internal OSPF routes by looking at Type 3 LSAs, which are used to model interarea routes.

LSA Type 3: Summary LSA

OSPF areas exist in part so that engineers can reduce the consumption of memory and compute resources in routers. Instead of having all routers, regardless of area, know all Type 1 and Type 2 LSAs inside an OSPF domain, ABRs do not forward Type 1 and Type 2 LSAs from one area into another area, and vice versa. This convention results in smaller per-area LSDBs, saving memory and reducing complexity for each run of the SPF algorithm, which saves CPU and improves convergence time.

However, even though ABRs do not flood Type 1 and Type 2 LSAs into other areas, routers still need to learn about subnets in other areas. OSPF advertises these interarea routes using the Type 3 summary LSA. ABRs generate a Type 3 LSA for each subnet in one area, and advertises each Type 3 LSA into the other areas.

For example, if subnet A exists in area 3, then the routers in area 3 learn of that subnet as part of Type 1 and Type 2 LSAs. However, an ABR connected to area 3 will not forward the Type 1 and Type 2 LSAs into other areas, instead creating a Type 3 LSA for each subnet (including subnet A). The routers inside the other areas can then calculate a route for the subnets (like subnet A) that exist inside another area.

Type 3 summary LSAs do not contain all the detailed topology information, so in comparison to Types 1 and 2, these LSAs summarize the information–hence the name *summary LSA*. Conceptually, a Type 3 LSA appears to be another subnet connected to the ABR that created and advertised the Type 3 LSA. The routers inside that area can calculate their best route to reach the ABR, which gives the router a good loop-free route to reach the subnet listed in a Type 3 LSA.

An example can certainly help in this case. First, consider the comparison shown in the top and bottom of Figure 6-6. The top depicts the topology shown back in Figure 6-1 if that design had used a single area. In that case, every router would have a copy of each Type 1 LSA (shown as a router name in the figure), and each Type 2 (abbreviated as T2 in the figure). The bottom of Figure 6-6 shows the area 5 topology, when holding to the three area design shown in Figure 6-1.

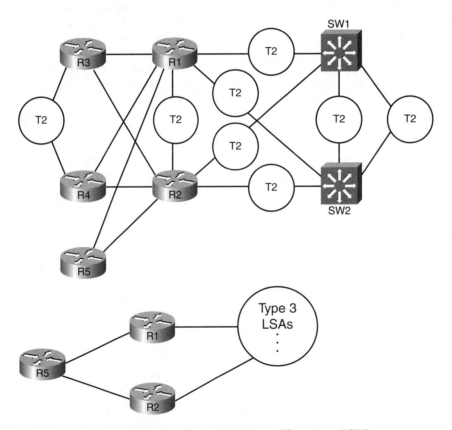

Figure 6-6   *Comparing a Single Area LSDB to a Three Area LSDB*

The ABR creates and floods each Type 3 LSA into the next area. The ABR assigns an LSID of the subnet number being advertised. It also adds its own RID to the LSA as well, so that routers know which ABR advertised the route. It also includes the subnet mask. The correlation between the advertising router's RID and the LSID (subnet number) allows the OSPF processes to create the part of the topology as shown with Type 3 LSAs at the bottom of Figure 6-6.

Example 6-5 focuses on the Type 3 LSAs in Area 34 of the network shown in Figure 6-1. Ten subnets exist outside area 34. As ABRs, both R1 and R2 create and flood a Type 3 LSA for each of these 10 subnets, resulting in 20 Type 3 LSAs listed in the output of the **show ip ospf database** command inside area 34. Then, the example focuses specifically on the Type 3 LSA for subnet 10.10.99.0/24.

Example 6-5   *Type 3 LSAs in Area 34*

```
R3#show ip ospf database



            OSPF Router with ID (3.3.3.3) (Process ID 3)

                Router Link States (Area 34)

Link ID         ADV Router      Age       Seq#        Checksum Link count
1.1.1.1         1.1.1.1         943       0x80000003  0x00E87B 4
2.2.2.2         2.2.2.2         991       0x80000002  0x005FD3 4
3.3.3.3         3.3.3.3         966       0x80000004  0x00E0E9 5
4.4.4.4         4.4.4.4         977       0x80000004  0x007B40 5


                Net Link States (Area 34)


Link ID         ADV Router      Age       Seq#        Checksum
10.10.34.4      4.4.4.4         977       0x80000002  0x00A929

                Summary Net Link States (Area 34)


Link ID         ADV Router      Age       Seq#        Checksum
10.10.5.0       1.1.1.1         943       0x80000002  0x0009F3
10.10.5.0       2.2.2.2         991       0x80000002  0x00EA0E
10.10.12.0      1.1.1.1         943       0x80000002  0x00F323
10.10.12.0      2.2.2.2         991       0x80000002  0x00D53D
10.10.15.0      1.1.1.1         943       0x80000002  0x0021BA
10.10.15.0      2.2.2.2         993       0x80000003  0x008313
10.10.17.0      1.1.1.1         946       0x80000002  0x00BC55
10.10.17.0      2.2.2.2         993       0x80000002  0x00A864
10.10.18.0      1.1.1.1         946       0x80000002  0x00B15F
10.10.18.0      2.2.2.2         994       0x80000002  0x009D6E
```

```
10.10.25.0      1.1.1.1        946        0x80000002 0x00355C
10.10.25.0      2.2.2.2        993        0x80000002 0x009439
10.10.27.0      1.1.1.1        946        0x80000002 0x0058AE
10.10.27.0      2.2.2.2        993        0x80000002 0x0030D3
10.10.28.0      1.1.1.1        947        0x80000002 0x004DB8
10.10.28.0      2.2.2.2        993        0x80000002 0x0025DD
10.10.98.0      1.1.1.1        946        0x80000002 0x004877
10.10.98.0      2.2.2.2        993        0x80000002 0x002A91
10.10.99.0      1.1.1.1        946        0x80000002 0x003D81
10.10.99.0      2.2.2.2        993        0x80000002 0x001F9B

R3#show ip ospf database summary 10.10.99.0


            OSPF Router with ID (3.3.3.3) (Process ID 3)


              Summary Net Link States (Area 34)


    Routing Bit Set on this LSA
    LS age: 1062
    Options: (No TOS-capability, DC, Upward)
    LS Type: Summary Links(Network)
    Link State ID: 10.10.99.0 (summary Network Number)
    Advertising Router: 1.1.1.1
    LS Seq Number: 80000002
    Checksum: 0x3D81
    Length: 28
    Network Mask: /24
          TOS: 0   Metric: 2


    Routing Bit Set on this LSA
    LS age: 1109
    Options: (No TOS-capability, DC, Upward)
    LS Type: Summary Links(Network)
    Link State ID: 10.10.99.0 (summary Network Number)
    Advertising Router: 2.2.2.2
    LS Seq Number: 80000002
    Checksum: 0x1F9B
    Length: 28
    Network Mask: /24
          TOS: 0   Metric: 2
```

Note: The Type 3 Summary LSA is not used for the purpose of route summarization. OSPF does support route summarization, and Type 3 LSAs may indeed advertise such a summary, but the Type 3 LSA does not inherently represent a summary route. The term *summary* reflects the idea that the information is sparse compared to the detail inside Type 1 and Type 2 LSAs.

The upcoming section "Calculating the Cost of Inter-area Routes" discusses how a router determines the available routes to reach subnets listed in a Type 3 LSA and how a router chooses which route is best.

Limiting the Number of LSAs

By default, Cisco IOS does not limit the number of LSAs a router can learn. However, it may be useful to protect a router from learning too many LSAs to protect router memory. Also, with a large number of LSAs, the router may be unable to process the LSDB with SPF well enough to converge in a reasonable amount of time.

The maximum number of LSAs learned from other routers can be limited by a router using the **max-lsa** *number* OSPF subcommand. When configured, if the router learns more than the configured number of LSAs from other routers (ignoring those created by the router itself), the router reacts. The first reaction is to issue log messages. The router ignores the event for a time period, after which the router repeats the warning message. This ignore-and-wait strategy can proceed through several iterations, ending when the router closes all neighborships, discards its LSDB, and then starts adding neighbors again. (The ignore time, and the number of times to ignore the event, can be configured with the **max-lsa** command.)

Summary of Internal LSA Types

OSPF uses Type 1, 2, and 3 LSAs to calculate the best routes for all routes inside the OSPF routing domain. Later, Chapter 9 explains Types 4, 5, and 7, which OSPF uses to calculate routes for external routes–routes redistributed into OSPF.

Table 6-3 summarizes some of the key points regarding OSPF Type 1, 2, and 3 LSAs. In particular for the ROUTE exam, the ability to sift through the output of various **show ip ospf database** commands can be important. Knowing what the OSPF LSID represents can help you interpret the output, and knowing the keywords used with the **show ip ospf database** *lsa-type lsid* commands can also be very useful. Table 6-3 summarizes these details.

Table 6-3 *Facts about LSA Types 1, 2, and 3*

Key Topic

LSA Type (Number)	LSA Type (Name)	This Type Represents	Display Using show ip ospf database keyword...	LSID Is Equal To	Created By
1	Router	A router	router	RID of router	Each router creates its own

Table 6-3 *Facts about LSA Types 1, 2, and 3*

LSA Type (Number)	LSA Type (Name)	This Type Represents	Display Using show ip ospf database *keyword...*	LSID Is Equal To	Created By
2	Network	A subnet in which a DR exists	**network**	DR's IP address in the subnet	The DR in that subnet
3	Summary	Subnet in another area	**summary**	Subnet number	An ABR

The Database Exchange Process

Every router in an area, when OSPF stabilizes after topology changes occur, should have an identical LSDB for that area. Internal routers (routers inside a single area) have only that area's LSAs, but an ABR's LSDB will contain LSAs for each area to which it connects. The ABR does, however, know which LSAs exist in each area.

OSPF routers flood both the LSAs they create, and the LSAs they learn from their neighbors, until all routers in the area have a copy of each of the most recent LSAs for that area. To manage and control this process, OSPF defines several messages, processes, and neighbor states that indicate the progress when flooding LSAs to each neighbor. This section begins by listing reference information for the OSPF messages and neighbor states. Next, the text describes the flooding process between two neighbors when a DR does not exist, followed by a description of the similar process used when a DR does exist. This section ends with a few items related to how the routers avoid looping the LSA advertisements and how they periodically reflood the information.

OSPF Message and Neighbor State Reference

For reference, Table 6-4 lists the OSPF message types that will be mentioned in the next few pages. Additionally, Table 6-5 lists the various neighbor states as well. Although useful for study, when you are first learning this topic, feel free to skip these tables for now.

Key Topic

Table 6-4 *OSPF Message Types and Functions*

Message Name/number	Description
Hello (1)	Used to discover neighbors, supply information used to confirm two routers should be allowed to become neighbors, to bring a neighbor relationship to a 2-way state, and to monitor a neighbor's responsiveness in case it fails
Database Description (DD or DBD) (2)	Used to exchange brief versions of each LSA, typically on initial topology exchange, so that a router knows a list of that neighbor's known LSAs

Table 6-4 *OSPF Message Types and Functions*

Message Name/number	Description
Link-State Request (LSR) (3)	A packet that lists the LSIDs of LSAs the sender of the LSR would like the receiver of the LSR to supply during database exchange
Link-State Update (LSU) (4)	A packet that contains fully detailed LSAs, typically sent in response to an LSR message
Link-State Acknowledgment (LSAck) (5)	Sent to confirm receipt of an LSU message

Table 6-5 *OSPF Neighbor State Reference*

Key Topic

State	Meaning
Down	No Hellos have been received from this neighbor for more than the dead interval.
Attempt	Used when the neighbor is defined with the **neighbor** command, after sending a Hello, but before receiving a Hello from that neighbor.
Init	A Hello has been received from the neighbor, but it did not have the local router's RID in it or lists parameters that do not pass the neighbor verification checks. This is a permanent state when Hello parameters do not match.
2Way	A Hello has been received from the neighbor, it has the router's RID in it, and all neighbor verification checks passed.
ExStart	Currently negotiating the DD sequence numbers and master/slave logic used for DD packets.
Exchange	Finished negotiating the DD process particulars, and currently exchanging DD packets.
Loading	All DD packets are exchanged, and the routers are currently sending LSR, LSU, and LSAck packets to exchange full LSAs.
Full	Neighbors are fully adjacent, meaning they believe that their LSDBs for that area are identical. Routing table (re)calculations can begin.

Exchange Without a Designated Router

As discussed in Chapter 5, the OSPF interface network type tells that router whether to attempt to elect a DR on that interface. The most common case for which routers do not elect a DR occur on point-to-point topologies, such as true point-to-point serial links and point-to-point subinterfaces. This section examines the database exchange process on such interfaces, in preparation for the slightly more complex process when using a DR on an OSPF broadcast network type, like a LAN.

Every OSPF neighborship begins by exchanging Hellos until the neighbors (hopefully) reach the 2-Way state. During these early stages, the routers discover each other by sending multicast Hellos and then check each other's parameters to make sure all items match (as listed in Chapter 5's Table 5-5). Figure 6-7 shows the details, with the various neighbor states listed on the outside of the figure and the messages listed in the middle.

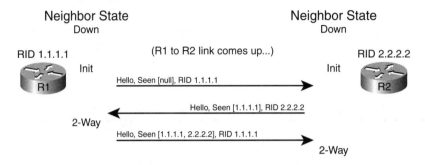

Figure 6-7 *Neighbor Initialization–Early Stages*

Figure 6-7 shows an example that begins with a failed neighborship, so the neighborship is in a down state. When a router tries to reestablish the neighborship, each router sends a multicast Hello and moves to an INIT state. After a router has both received a Hello and verified that all the required parameters agree, the router lists the other router's RID in the Hello as being seen, as shown in the bottom two Hello messages in the figure. When a router receives a Hello that lists its own RID as having been seen by the other router, the router can transition to 2-Way state.

When a router has reached the 2-Way state with a neighbor, as shown at the end of Figure 6-7, the router then decides whether it should exchange its LSDB entries. When no DR exists, the answer is always "yes." Each router next follows this general process:

Step 1. Discover the LSAs known to the neighbor but unknown to me.

Step 2. Discover the LSAs known by both routers, but the neighbor's LSA is more up to date.

Step 3. Ask the neighbor for a copy of all the LSAs identified in the first two steps.

Figure 6-8 details the messages and neighbor states used to exchange the LSAs between two neighbors.

Figure 6-8 shows many details. As with Figure 6-7, Figure 6-8 shows neighbor states on the outer edges of the flows (refer to Table 6-5 for reference). Routers display these neighbor states (in the **show ip ospf neighbor** command variants), so a particular state may be useful in determining how far two neighbors have gotten in the database exchange process. The more important neighbor states will be mentioned throughout the chapter.

The inner portions of Figure 6-8 represent the OSPF message flows, with Table 6-2 earlier in the chapter listing the messages for reference. The next several pages examine the process shown in Figure 6-8 in more detail.

Discovering a Description of the Neighbor's LSDB

After a router has decided to move forward from 2-Way state and exchange its LSDB with a neighbor, the routers use the sequence shown in Figure 6-8. The next step in that process

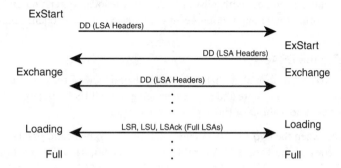

Figure 6-8   *Overview of the Database Exchange Process Between Two Neighbors*

requires both routers to tell each other the LSIDs of all their known LSAs in that area. The primary goal is for each neighbor to realize which LSAs it does not know, so it can then ask for those full LSAs to be sent. To learn the list of LSAs known by the neighbor, the neighboring routers follow these steps:

Step 1.   Multicast database description packets (abbreviated as both DD and DBD, depending on the reference) to 224.0.0.5, which is the all SPF routers multicast address.

Step 2.   When sending the first DD message, transition to the *ExStart* state until one router, the one with the higher RID, becomes master in a master/slave relationship.

Step 3.   After electing a master, transition the neighbor to the *Exchange* state.

Step 4.   Continue multicasting DD messages to each other until both routers have the same shared view of the LSIDs known collectively by both routers, in that area.

Note that the DD messages themselves do not list the entire LSAs, but rather LSA headers. These headers include the LSIDs of the LSAs and the LSA sequence number. The LS sequence number for an LSA begins at value 0x80000001 (hex) when initially created; the router creating the LSA increments the sequence number, and refloods the LSA, whenever the LSA changes. For example, if an interface moves from up to down state, that router changes its Type 1 LSA to list that interface state as down, increments the LSA sequence number, and refloods the LSA.

The master router for each exchange controls the flow of DD messages, with the slave responding to the master's DD messages. The master keeps sending DD messages until it lists all its known LSIDs in that area. The slave responds by placing LSA headers in its DD messages. Some of those LSA headers simply repeat what the slave heard from the master, for the purpose of acknowledging to the master that the slave learned that LSA header from the master. Additionally, the slave also includes the LSA headers for any LSAs that the master did not list.

This exchange of DD messages ends with each router knowing a list of LSAs that it does not have in its LSDB, but that the other router does have those LSAs. Additionally, each router also ends this process with a list of LSAs that the local router already knows, but for which the other router has a more recent copy (based on the sequence number).

Exchanging the LSAs

When the two neighbors realize that they have a shared view of the list of LSIDs, they transition to the Loading state and start exchanging the full LSAs–but only those that they do not yet know about or those that have changed.

For example, when the two routers in Figure 6-8 first become neighbors, neither router will have a copy of the Type 1 LSA for the other router. So, R1 will request that R2 send its LSA with LSID 2.2.2.2; R2 will send its Type 1 LSA; and R1 will acknowledge receipt. The mechanics work like this:

Step 1.   Transition the neighbor state to Loading.

Step 2.   For any missing LSAs, send a *Link State Request* (LSR) message, listing the LSID of the requested LSA.

Step 3.   Respond to any LSR messages with an *Link State Update* (LSU), listing one or more LSAs in each message.

Step 4.   Acknowledge receipt by either sending a *Link State Acknowledgment* (LSAck) message (called explicit acknowledgment), or by sending the same LSA that was received back to the other router in an LSU message (implicit acknowledgment).

Step 5.   When all LSAs have been sent, received, and acknowledged, transition the neighborship to the FULL state (fully adjacent).

Note: Because this section examines the case without a DR, all these messages flow as multicasts to 224.0.0.5, the all SPF routers multicast address, unless the neighbors have been defined with an OSPF **neighbor** command.

By the end of this process, both routers should have an identical LSDB for the area to which the link has been assigned. At that point, the two routers can run the SPF algorithm to choose the currently best routes for each subnet.

Exchange with a Designated Router

Database exchange with a DR differs slightly than database exchange when no DR exists. The majority of the process is similar, with the same messages, meanings, and neighbor states. The big difference is the overriding choice of with whom each router chooses to perform database exchange.

Non-DR routers do not exchange their databases directly with all neighbors on a subnet. Instead, they exchange their database with the DR. Then, the DR exchanges any new/changed LSAs with the rest of the OSPF routers in the subnet.

The concept actually follows along with the idea of a Type 2 LSA as seen earlier in Figure 6-4. Figure 6-9 represents four Type 1 LSAs, for four real routers on the same LAN, plus a single Type 2 LSA that represents the multiaccess subnet. The DR created the Type 2 LSA as part of its role in life.

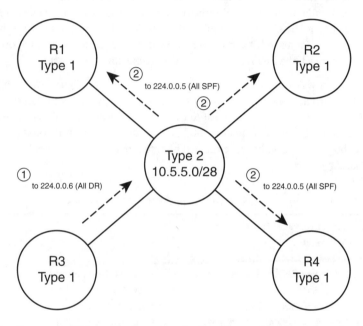

Figure 6-9 *Conceptual View–Exchanging the Database with a Pseudonode*

Figure 6-9 shows two conceptual steps for database exchange. The non-DR router (R3) first exchanges its database with the pseudonode, and then the type 2 pseudonode exchanges its database with the other routers. However, the pseudonode is a concept, not a router; to make the process depicted in Figure 6-9 work, the DR takes on the role of the Type 2 pseudonode. The messages differ slightly as well, as follows:

■ The non-DR performs database exchange with the same messages, as shown in Figure 6-9, but sends these messages to the 224.0.0.6 All-DR-routers multicast address.

Key Topic

■ The DR performs database exchange with the same messages but sends the messages to the 224.0.0.5 all-SPF-routers multicast address.

Consider these two conventions one at a time. First, the messages sent to 224.0.0.6 are processed by the DR and the BDR only. The DR actively participates, replying to the messages, with the BDR acting as a silent bystander. In effect, this allows the non-DR router to exchange their database directly with the DR and BDR, but with none of the other routers in the subnet.

Next, consider the multicast messages from the DR to the 224.0.0.5 all-SPF-router multi-cast address. All OSPF routers process these messages, so the rest of the routers—the DROthers to use the IOS term—also learn the newly exchanged LSAs. This process completes the second step shown in the conceptual Figure 6-9, where the DR, acting like the pseudonode, floods the LSAs to the other OSPF routers in the subnet.

The process occurs in the background and can be generally ignored. However, for operating an OSPF network, an important distinction must be made. With a DR in existence, a DROther router performs the database exchange process (as seen in Figure 6-9) with the DR/BDR only and not any other DROther routers in the subnet. For example, in Figure 6-9, R1 acts as DR, R2 acts as BDR, and R3/R4 act as DROther routers. Because the underlying process does not make R3 and R4 perform database exchange with each other, the routers do not reach the FULL neighbor state, remaining in 2-Way state.

Example 6-6 shows the resulting output for the LAN shown in Figure 6-9, with four routers. The output, taken from DROther R3, shows a 2-Way state with R4, the other DROther. It also shows on interface Fa0/0 that its own priority is 2. This output also shows a neighbor count (all neighbors) of 3 and an adjacent neighbor count (all fully adjacent neighbors) of 2, again because the neighborship between DROthers R3 and R4 is not a full adjacency.

Example 6-6   *Demonstrating OSPF FULL and 2-Way Adjacencies*

```
R3#show ip ospf interface fa0/0
FastEthernet0/0 is up, line protocol is up
  Internet Address 172.16.1.3/24, Area 0
  Process ID 75, Router ID 3.3.3.3, Network Type BROADCAST, Cost: 1
  Transmit Delay is 1 sec, State DROTHER, Priority 2
  Designated Router (ID) 1.1.1.1, Interface address 172.16.1.1
  Backup Designated router (ID) 2.2.2.2, Interface address 172.16.1.2
  Timer intervals configured, Hello 10, Dead 40, Wait 40, Retransmit 5
    oob-resync timeout 40
    Hello due in 00:00:02
  Supports Link-local Signaling (LLS)
  Cisco NSF helper support enabled
  IETF NSF helper support enabled
  Index 1/1, flood queue length 0
  Next 0x0(0)/0x0(0)
  Last flood scan length is 0, maximum is 4
  Last flood scan time is 0 msec, maximum is 0 msec
  Neighbor Count is 3, Adjacent neighbor count is 2
    Adjacent with neighbor 1.1.1.1  (Designated Router)
    Adjacent with neighbor 2.2.2.2  (Backup Designated Router)
  Suppress hello for 0 neighbor(s)
```

```
R3#show ip ospf neighbor fa0/0

Neighbor ID     Pri   State         Dead Time   Address      Interface
1.1.1.1          4    FULL/DR       00:00:37    172.16.1.1   FastEthernet0/0
2.2.2.2          3    FULL/BDR      00:00:37    172.16.1.2   FastEthernet0/0
44.44.44.44      1    2WAY/DROTHER  00:00:36    172.16.1.4   FastEthernet0/0
```

Flooding Throughout the Area

So far in this section, the database exchange process has focused on exchanging the database between neighbors. However, LSAs need to be flooded throughout an area. To do so, when a router learns new LSAs from one neighbor, that router then knows that its other neighbors in that same area may not know of that LSA. Similarly, when an LSA changes, for example, when an interface changes state, a router may learn the same old LSA but with a new sequence number, and again need to flood the changed LSA to other neighbors in that area.

Figure 6-10 shows a basic example of the process. In this case, R2, R3, and R4 have established neighbor relationships, with four LSAs in their LSDB in this area. R1 is again the new router added to the internetwork.

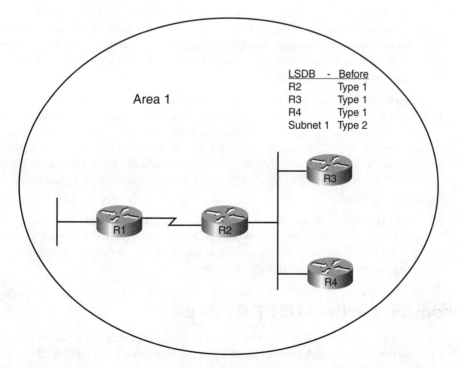

Figure 6-10   *Flooding Throughout an Area*

First, consider what happens as the new R1-R2 neighborship comes up and goes through database exchange. When R1 loads, and the link comes up, R1 and R2 reach a full state and have a shared view of the Area 1 LSDB. R2 has learned all R1's new LSAs (should only be R1's Type 1 router LSA), and R1 has learned all the area 1 LSAs known to R2, including the Type 1 LSAs for R3 and R4.

Next, think about the LSDBs of R3 and R4 at this point. The database exchange between R1-R2 did not inform R3 nor R4 about any of the new LSAs known by R1. So, R2, when it learns of R1's Type 1 LSA, sends DD packets to the DR on the R2/R3/R4 LAN. LSR/LSU packets follow, resulting in R3 and R4 learning about the new LSA for R1. If more routers existed in area 1, the flooding process would continue throughout the entire area, until all routers know of the best (highest sequence number) copy of each LSA.

The flooding process prevents the looping of LSAs as a side-effect of the database exchange process. Neighbors use DD messages to learn the LSA headers known by the neighbor, and then only request the LSAs known by the neighbor but not known by the local router. By requesting only unknown LSAs or new versions of old LSAs, routers prevent the LSAs advertisements from looping.

Periodic Flooding

Although OSPF does not send routing updates on a periodic interval, as do distance vector protocols, OSPF does reflood each LSA every 30 minutes based on each LSA's age variable. The router that creates the LSA sets this age to 0 (seconds). Each router then increments the age of its copy of each LSA over time. If 30 minutes pass with no changes to an LSA–meaning no other reason existed in that 30 minutes to cause a reflooding of the LSA–the owning router increments the sequence number, resets the timer to 0, and refloods the LSA.

Because the owning router increments the sequence number and resets the LSAge every 1800 seconds (30 minutes), the output of various **show ip ospf database** commands should also show an age of less than 1800 seconds. For example, referring back to Example 6-5, the Type 1 LSA for R1 (RID 1.1.1.1) shows an age of 943 seconds and a sequence number of 0x80000003. Over time the sequence number should increment once per every 30 minutes, with the LSAge cycle upward toward 1800 and then back to 0 when the LSA is reflooded.

Note also that when a router realizes it needs to flush an LSA from the LSDB for an area, it actually sets the age of the LSA to the MaxAge setting (3600) and refloods the LSA. All the other routers receive the LSA, see the age is already at the maximum, causing those routers to also remove the LSA from their LSDBs.

Choosing the Best OSPF Routes

All this effort to define LSA types, create areas, and fully flood the LSAs has one goal in mind: to allow all routers in that area to calculate the best, loop-free routes for all known subnets. Although the database exchange process may seem laborious, the process by which SPF calculates the best routes requires a little less thought, at least to the level required for the CCNP ROUTE exam. In fact, the choice of the best route for a given subnet, and calculated by a particular router, can be summarized as follows:

- Analyze the LSDB to find all possible routes to reach the subnet.

- For each possible route, add the OSPF interface cost for all outgoing interfaces in that route.

- Pick the route with the lowest total cost.

Key Topic

For humans, if you build a network diagram, note the OSPF cost for each interface (as shown with **show ip ospf interface**), you can easily add up the costs for each router's possible routes to each subnet and tell which route OSPF will choose. The routers must use a more complex SPF algorithm to derive a mathematical model of the topology based on the LSAs. This section examines both the simpler human view of metric calculation and folds in some of the basics of what SPF must do on a router to calculate the best routes. It also goes through the options for tuning the metric calculation to influence the choice of routes.

OSPF Metric Calculation for Internal OSPF Routes

The process of calculating the cost from a router to each subnet may be intuitive to most people. However, spending a few minutes considering the details is worthwhile, in part to link the concepts with the LSAs, and to be better prepared for questions on the ROUTE exam. This section breaks the discussion into three sections: intra-area routes, interarea routes, a short discussion about cases when both intra-area and interarea routes exist for the same subnet, and an explanation of SPF calculations.

Calculating the Cost of Intra-Area Routes

When a router analyzes the LSDB to calculate the best route to each subnet, it does the following:

Step 1.   Finds all subnets inside the area, based on the stub interfaces listed in the Type 1 LSAs and based on any Type 2 network LSAs

Step 2.   Runs SPF to find all possible paths through the area's topology, from itself to each subnet

Key Topic

Step 3.   Calculates the OSPF interface costs for all outgoing interfaces in each route, picking the lowest total cost route for each subnet as the best route

For example, Figure 6-11 shows the routers and links inside area 34, as a subset of the internetwork also shown in Figure 6-1. Figure 6-11 shows the interface numbers and OSPF costs.

Following the basic three-step process, at Step 1, R1 can determine that subnet 10.10.34.0/24 exists in area 34 because of the Type 2 LSA created by the DR in that subnet. For Step 2, R1 can then run SPF and determine four possible routes, two of which are clearly more reasonable to humans: R1-R3 and R1-R4. (The two other possible routes, R1-R3-R2-R4 and R1-R4-R2-R3, are possible and would be considered by OSPF but would clearly be higher cost.) For Step 3, R1 does the simple math of adding the costs of the outgoing interfaces in each route, as follows:

- R1-R3: Add R1's S0/0/0.3 cost (647) and R3's Fa0/0 cost (10), total 657

- R1-R4: Add R1's S0/0/0.4 cost (647) and R4's Fa0/0 cost (10), total 657

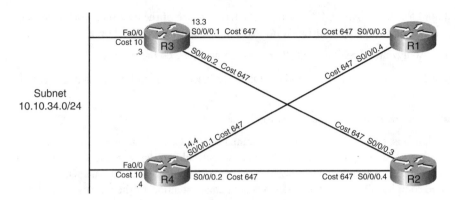

Figure 6-11   *Area 34 Portion of Figure 6-1*

The metrics tie, so with a default setting of **maximum-paths 4**, R1 adds both routes to its routing table. In particular, the routes list the metric of 657, and the next-hop IP address on the other end of the respectively links: 10.10.13.3 (R3's S0/0/0.1) and 10.10.14.4 (R4's S0/0/0.1).

Note that OSPF supports equal-cost load balancing, but it does not support unequal-cost load balancing. The **maximum-paths** OSPF subcommand can be set as low as 1, with the maximum being dependent on router platform and IOS version. Modern IOS versions typically support 16 or 32 concurrent routes to one destination (maximum).

Calculating the Cost of Interarea Routes

From a human perspective, the cost for interarea routes can be calculated just like for intra-area routes if we have the full network diagram, subnet numbers, and OSPF interface costs. To do so, just find all possible routes from a router to the destination subnet, add up the costs of the outgoing interfaces, and choose the router with the lowest total cost.

However, OSPF routers cannot do the equivalent for interarea routes, because routers internal to one area do not have topological data–LSA Types 1 and 2–for other areas. Instead, ABRs create and flood Type 3 summary LSAs into an area, listing the subnet number and mask, but not listing details about routers and links in the other areas. For example, Figure 6-12 shows both Areas 34 and 0 from Figure 6-1. Then consider how OSPF determines the lowest-cost route from router R3 for subnet 10.10.99.0/24, the Center subnet on the right.

R3 has a large number of possible routes to reach subnet 10.10.99.0/24. For example, just to get from R3 to R1, there are several possibilities: R3-R1, R3-R4-R1, and R3-R2-R1. From R1 the rest of the way to subnet 10.10.99.0/24, many more possibilities exist. The SPF algorithm has to calculate all possible routes inside an area to the ABR, so with more redundancy, SPF's run time goes up. And SPF has to consider all the options, whereas we humans can rule out some routes quickly because they appear to be somewhat ridiculous.

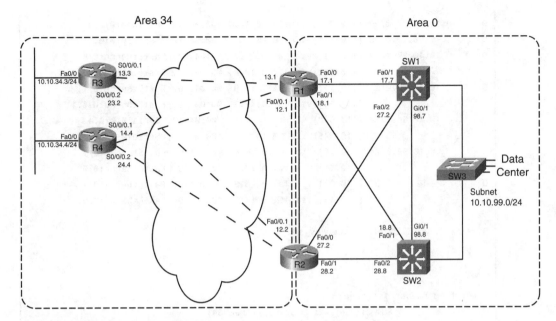

Figure 6-12   *Area 34 and Area 0 Portion of Figure 6-1*

Because of the area design, with R1 and R2 acting as ABRs, R3 does not process all the topology shown in Figure 6-12. Instead, R3 relies on the Type 3 Summary LSAs created by the ABRs, which have the following information:

■   The subnet number/mask represented by the LSA

■   The cost of the ABR's lowest-cost route to reach the subnet

■   The RID of the ABR

Example 6-7 begins to examine the information R3 will use to calculate its best route for subnet 10.10.99.0/24, on the right side of Figure 6-12. To see these details, Example 6-7 lists several commands taken from R1. It lists R1's best route (actually two that tie) for subnet 10.10.99.0/24, with cost 11. It also lists the Type 3 LSA R1 generated by R1 for 10.10.99.0/24, again listing cost 11, and listing the Type 3 LSA created by ABR R2 and flooded into area 34.

Example 6-7   *Route and Type 3 LSA on R1 for 10.10.99.0/24*

```
R1#show ip route ospf
      10.0.0.0/8 is variably subnetted, 15 subnets, 3 masks
O        10.10.5.0/27 [110/648] via 10.10.15.5, 00:04:19, Serial0/0/0.5
O        10.10.23.0/29 [110/711] via 10.10.13.3, 00:04:19, Serial0/0/0.3
```

```
O         10.10.24.0/29 [110/711] via 10.10.14.4, 00:04:19, Serial0/0.4
O         10.10.25.0/29 [110/711] via 10.10.15.5, 00:04:19, Serial0/0.5
O         10.10.27.0/24 [110/11] via 10.10.17.7, 00:04:19, FastEthernet0/0
                        [110/11] via 10.10.12.2, 00:04:19, FastEthernet0/0.1
O         10.10.28.0/24 [110/11] via 10.10.18.8, 00:04:19, FastEthernet0/1
                        [110/11] via 10.10.12.2, 00:04:19, FastEthernet0/0.1
O         10.10.34.0/24 [110/648] via 10.10.14.4, 00:04:19, Serial0/0.4
                        [110/648] via 10.10.13.3, 00:04:19, Serial0/0.3
O         10.10.98.0/24 [110/11] via 10.10.18.8, 00:04:19, FastEthernet0/1
                        [110/11] via 10.10.17.7, 00:04:19, FastEthernet0/0
O         10.10.99.0/24 [110/11] via 10.10.18.8, 00:04:19, FastEthernet0/1
                        [110/11] via 10.10.17.7, 00:04:19, FastEthernet0/0

R1#show ip ospf database summary 10.10.99.0

               OSPF Router with ID (1.1.1.1) (Process ID 1)

! omitting output for area 5...
               Summary Net Link States (Area 34)


  LS age: 216
  Options: (No TOS-capability, DC, Upward)
  LS Type: Summary Links(Network)
  Link State ID: 10.10.99.0 (summary Network Number)
  Advertising Router: 1.1.1.1

  LS Seq Number: 80000003
  Checksum: 0x951F
  Length: 28
  Network Mask: /24
        TOS: 0   Metric: 11




  LS age: 87
  Options: (No TOS-capability, DC, Upward)
  LS Type: Summary Links(Network)
  Link State ID: 10.10.99.0 (summary Network Number)
  Advertising Router: 2.2.2.2

  LS Seq Number: 80000002
  Checksum: 0x7938
  Length: 28
  Network Mask: /24
        TOS: 0   Metric: 11
```

Note: The examples use default bandwidth settings, but with all routers configured with the **auto-cost reference-bandwidth 1000** command. This command is explained in the upcoming section "Reference Bandwidth."

For routers in one area to calculate the cost of an interarea route, the process is simple when you realize that the Type 3 LSA lists the ABR's best cost to reach that interarea subnet. To calculate the cost:

Step 1.   Calculate the intra-area cost from that router to the ABR listed in the type 3 LSA.

Step 2.   Add the cost value listed in the Type 3 LSA. (This cost represents the cost from the ABR to the destination subnet.)

Key Topic

A router applies these two steps for each possible route to reach the ABR. Following the example of router R3 and subnet 10.10.99.0/24, Figure 6-13 shows the components of the calculation.

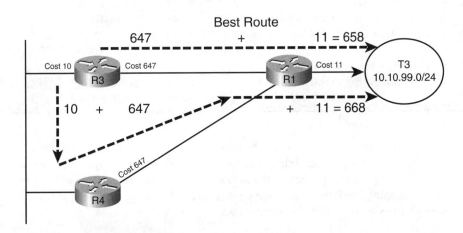

Figure 6-13   *R3's Calculation of Cost for 10.10.99.0/24*

Figure 6-13 shows the calculation of both routes, with intra-area cost to reach R1 either 647 or 657 in this case. For both routes, the cost listed in the Type 3 LSA sourced by R1, cost 11, is added.

When more than one ABR exists, as is the case as shown in Figure 6-12, each ABR should have created a Type 3 LSA for the subnet. In fact, the output in Example 6-7 showed the Type 3 LSA for 10.10.99.0/24 created by both R1 and another created by R2. For instance, in the internetwork used throughout this chapter, ABRs R1 and R2 would create a Type 3 LSA for 10.10.99.0/24. So, in this particular example, R3 would also have to calculate the best route to reach 10.10.99.0/24 through ABR R2. Then, R3 would choose the best route among all routes for 10.10.99.0/24.

Each router repeats this process for all known routes to reach the ABR, considering the Type 3 LSAs from each ABR. In this case, R3 ties on metrics for one route through R1 and one through R2, so R3 adds both routes to its routing table, as shown in Example 6-8.

Example 6-8   *Route and Type 3 LSA on R3 for 10.10.99.0/24*

```
R3#show ip route 10.10.99.0 255.255.255.0
Routing entry for 10.10.99.0/24
  Known via "ospf 3", distance 110, metric 658, type inter area
  Last update from 10.10.13.1 on Serial0/0/0.1, 00:08:06 ago
  Routing Descriptor Blocks:
  * 10.10.23.2, from 2.2.2.2, 00:08:06 ago, via Serial0/0/0.2
      Route metric is 658, traffic share count is 1
    10.10.13.1, from 1.1.1.1, 00:08:06 ago, via Serial0/0/0.1
      Route metric is 658, traffic share count is 1

R3#show ip route ospf
      10.0.0.0/8 is variably subnetted, 15 subnets, 3 masks
O IA    10.10.5.0/27 [110/1304] via 10.10.23.2, 00:07:57, Serial0/0/0.2
                     [110/1304] via 10.10.13.1, 00:07:57, Serial0/0/0.1
O IA    10.10.12.0/24 [110/657] via 10.10.23.2, 00:08:17, Serial0/0/0.2
                      [110/657] via 10.10.13.1, 00:08:17, Serial0/0/0.1
! lines omitted for brevity
O IA    10.10.99.0/24 [110/658] via 10.10.23.2, 00:08:17, Serial0/0/0.2
                      [110/658] via 10.10.13.1, 00:08:17, Serial0/0/0.1
```

Besides the information that matches the expected outgoing interfaces per the figures, the output also flags these routes as interarea routes. The first command lists "type inter area" explicitly, and the **show ip route ospf** command lists the same information with the code "O IA," meaning OSPF, interarea. Simply put, interarea routes are routes for which the subnet is known from a Type 3 summary LSA.

Special Rules Concerning Intra-area and Interarea Routes on ABRs

OSPF has a couple of rules concerning intra-area and interarea routes that take precedence over the simple comparison of the cost calculated for the various routes. The issue exists when more than one ABR connects to the same two areas. Many designs use two routers between the backbone and each nonbackbone area for redundancy, so this design occurs in many OSPF networks.

The issue relates to the fact that with two or more ABRs, the ABRs themselves, when calculating their own routing tables, can calculate both an intra-area route and interarea route for subnets in the backbone area. For example, consider the perspective of Router R1 from the last several examples, as depicted in Figure 6-14.

Conceptually, R1 could calculate both the intra-area route and interarea route to 10.10.99.0/24. However, the OSPF cost settings could be set so that the lower cost route

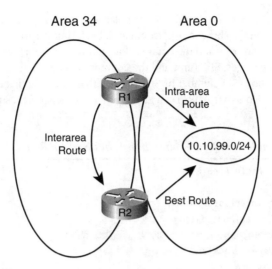

Figure 6-14   *R1's Choice: Intra-Area or Interarea Route to 10.10.99.0/24*

for R1 actually goes through area 34, to ABR R2, and then on through Area 0 to
10.10.99.0/24. However, two OSPF rules prevent such a choice by R1:

Step 1.   When choosing the best route, an intra-area route is always better than a competing interarea route, regardless of metric.

Step 2.   If an ABR learns a Type 3 LSA inside a nonbackbone area, the ABR ignores
that LSA when calculating its own routes.

Because of the first rule, R1 would never choose the interarea route if the intra-area
route were available. The second rule goes further, stating that R1 could never choose the
interarea route at all–R1 simply ignores that LSA for the purposes of choosing its own
best IP routes.

Metric and SPF Calculations

Before moving on to discuss how to influence route choices by changing the OSPF interface costs, first take a moment to consider the CPU-intensive SPF work done by a router.
SPF does the work to piece together topology information to find all possible routes to a
destination. As a result, SPF must execute when the intra-area topology changes, because
changes in topology impact the choice of best route. However, changes to Type 3 LSAs
do not drive a recalculation of the SPF algorithm, because the Type 3 LSAs do not actually describe the topology.

To take the analysis a little deeper, remember that an internal router, when finding the best
interarea route for a subnet, uses the intra-area topology to calculate the cost to reach the
ABR. When each route is identified, the internal router adds the intra-area cost to the
ABR, plus the corresponding Type 3 LSA's cost. A change to the Type 3 LSA–it fails,
comes back up, or the metric changes–does impact the choice of best route, so the
changed Type 3 LSA must be flooded. However, no matter the change, the change does
not affect the topology between a router and the ABR—and SPF focuses on processing
that topology data. So, only changes to Type 1 and 2 LSAs require an SPF calculation.

You can see the number of SPF runs, and the elapsed time since the last SPF run, using several variations on the **show ip ospf** command. Each time a Type 3 LSA changes and is flooded, SPF does not run, and the counter does not increment. However, each time a Type 1 or 2 LSA changes, SPF runs, and the counter increments. Example 6-9 highlights the counter that shows the number of SPF runs on that router, in that area, and the time since the last run. Note that ABRs list a group of messages per area, showing the number of runs per area.

Example 6-9 *Example with New Route Choices but No SPF Run*

```
R3#show ip ospf ¦ begin Area 34
   Area 34
       Number of interfaces in this area is 3
       Area has no authentication
       SPF algorithm last executed 00:41:02.812 ago
       SPF algorithm executed 15 times
       Area ranges are
       Number of LSA 25. Checksum Sum 0x0BAC6B
       Number of opaque link LSA 0. Checksum Sum 0x000000
       Number of DCbitless LSA 0
       Number of indication LSA 0
       Number of DoNotAge LSA 0
       Flood list length 0
```

Metric Tuning

Engineers have a couple of commands available that allow them to tune the values of the OSPF interface cost, thereby influencing the choice of best OSPF route. This section discusses the three methods: changing the reference bandwidth, setting the interface bandwidth, and setting the OSPF cost directly.

Changing the Reference Bandwidth

OSPF calculates the default OSPF cost for an interface based on the following formula:

$$\frac{Reference-bandwidth}{interface-bandwidth}$$

The reference-bandwidth, which you can set using the **auto-cost reference-bandwidth** *bandwidth* router subcommand, sets the numerator of the formula for that one router, with a unit of Mbps. This setting may be different on different routers, but Cisco recommends using the same setting on all routers in an OSPF routing domain.

For example, serial interfaces default to a bandwidth setting of 1544, meaning 1544 Kbps. The reference bandwidth defaults to 100, meaning 100 Mbps. After converting the reference bandwidth units to Kbps to match the bandwidth, the cost, calculated per the defaults, for serial links would be

$$\frac{100,000}{1544} = 64$$

Note: OSPF always rounds down when the calculation results in a fraction.

The primary motivation for changing the reference bandwidth is to accommodate good defaults for higher-speed links. With a default of 100 Mbps, the cost of FastEthernet interfaces calculates to cost 1. However, the minimum OSPF cost is 1, so Gigabit Ethernet and 10 Gigabit interfaces also then default to OSPF cost 1. By setting the OSPF reference bandwidth so that there is some difference in cost between the higher speed links, OSPF can then choose routes that use those higher speed interfaces.

Note: Although Cisco recommends that all routers use the same reference bandwidth, the setting is local to each router.

Note that in the examples earlier in this chapter, the bandwidth settings used default settings, but the **auto-cost reference-bandwidth 1000** command was used on each router to allow different costs for FastEthernet and Gigabit interfaces.

Setting Bandwidth

You can indirectly set the OSPF cost by configuring the **bandwidth** *speed* interface subcommand. In such cases, the formula shown in the previous section is used, just with the configured bandwidth value.

While on the topic of the interface bandwidth subcommand, a couple of seemingly trivial facts may matter to your choice of how to tune the OSPF cost. First, on serial links, the bandwidth defaults to 1544. On subinterfaces of those serial interfaces, the same bandwidth default is used.

On Ethernet interfaces, if not configured with the **bandwidth** command, the interface bandwidth matches the actual speed. For example, on an interface that supports autonegotiation for 10/100, the bandwidth is either 100,000 (kbps, or 100 Mbps) or 10,000 (Kbps, or 10 Mbps) depending on whether the link currently runs at 100 or 10 Mbps, respectively.

Configuring Cost Directly

The most controllable method to configure OSPF costs, but the most laborious, is to configure the interface cost directly. To do so, use the **ip ospf cost** *value* interface subcommand, substituting your chosen value as the last parameter.

Verifying OSPF Cost Settings

Several commands can be used to display the OSPF cost settings of various interfaces. Example 6-10 shows several, along with the configuration of all three methods for changing the OSPF cost. In this example, the following has been configured:

■ The reference bandwidth is set to 1000.

■ Interface S0/0/0.1 has its bandwidth set to 1000 Kbps.

■ Interface Fa0/0 has its cost set directly to 17.

Example 6-10   *R3 with OSPF Cost Values Set*

```
router ospf 3
 auto-cost reference-bandwidth 1000
interface S0/0/0.1
 bandwidth 1000
interface fa0/0
 ip ospf cost 17


R3#show ip ospf interface brief
Interface     PID   Area           IP Address/Mask     Cost   State  Nbrs F/C
Se0/0/0.2     3     34             10.10.23.3/29       647    P2P    1/1
Se0/0/0.1     3     34             10.10.13.3/29       1000   P2P    1/1
Fa0/0         3     34             10.10.34.3/24       17     BDR    1/1


R3#show ip ospf interface fa0/0
FastEthernet0/0 is up, line protocol is up
  Internet Address 10.10.34.3/24, Area 34
  Process ID 3, Router ID 3.3.3.3, Network Type BROADCAST, Cost: 17
  Enabled by interface config, including secondary ip addresses
  Transmit Delay is 1 sec, State BDR, Priority 1
  Designated Router (ID) 4.4.4.4, Interface address 10.10.34.4
  Backup Designated router (ID) 3.3.3.3, Interface address 10.10.34.3
! lines omitted for brevity
```

Exam Preparation Tasks

Planning Practice

The CCNP ROUTE exam expects test takers to review design documents, create implementation plans, and create verification plans. This section provides some exercises that may help you to take a step back from the minute details of the topics in this chapter so that you can think about the same technical topics from the planning perspective.

For each planning practice table, simply complete the table. Note that any numbers in parentheses represent the number of options listed for each item in the solutions in Appendix F, "Completed Planning Practice Tables."

Design Review Table

Table 6-6 lists several design goals related to this chapter. If these design goals were listed in a design document, and you had to take that document and develop an implementation plan, what implementation options come to mind? For any configuration items, a general description can be used, without concern about the specific parameters.

Table 6-6 *Design Review*

Design Goal	Possible Implementation Choices Covered in This Chapter
The design sets specific limits to the number of Type 1 and 2 LSAs in each area. Describe how to predict the number of each type of LSA.	
How could you tune OSPF metrics to favor 10 Gbps links over 1 Gbps and 1 Gig over 100 Mbps (2)?	
The design shows one physical path from ABR1 to core subnet 1 inside area 0, and one longer area 1 path to the same subnet. What can be done to ensure both paths can be used?	

Implementation Plan Peer Review Table

Table 6-7 shows a list of questions that others might ask, or that you might think about, during a peer review of another network engineer's implementation plan. Complete the table by answering the questions.

Table 6-7 *Notable Questions from This Chapter to Consider During an Implementation Plan Peer Review*

Question	Answers
What conditions must be true for a router to create/flood a Type 2 LSA? (2)	
The plan shows Frame Relay with all point-to-point subinterfaces. By default, will a DR/BDR be elected?	
The plan shows a reference bandwidth change planned for all routers with high speed links, but not all other routers. What is the impact? (2)	
The plan shows many different WAN links speeds but with the interface bandwidths not matching the actual speed. All OSPF cost changes are made explicitly with the **ip ospf cost** interface subcommand. Do the incorrect bandwidths cause any OSPF problems?	

Create an Implementation Plan Table

To practice skills useful when creating your own OSPF implementation plan, list in Table 6-8 configuration commands related to the configuration of the following features. You may want to record your answers outside the book and set a goal to complete this table (and others like it) from memory during your final reviews before taking the exam.

Table 6-8 *Implementation Plan Configuration Memory Drill*

Feature	Configuration Commands/Notes
Tune metrics by changing the formula for calculating OSPF cost based on interface bandwidth.	
Tune metrics by changing interface bandwidth.	
Change metrics by setting cost directly.	
Set the number of equal-cost OSPF routes allowed in a router's routing table.	
Influence the choice of DR on a LAN. (2)	

Choose Commands for a Verification Plan Table

To practice skills useful when creating your own OSPF verification plan, list in Table 6-9 all commands that supply the requested information. You may want to record your answers outside the book and set a goal to complete this table (and others like it) from memory during your final reviews before taking the exam.

Table 6-9   *Verification Plan Memory Drill*

Information Needed	Command(s)
Display a summary of the OSPF database.	
Display all Type 1 router LSAs known to a router.	
Display the details of a particular Type 1 router LSA.	
Display all Type 2 network LSAs known to a router.	
Display the details of a particular Type 2 router LSA.	
Display all Type 3 summary LSAs known to a router.	
Display the details of a particular Type 3 router LSA.	
Display a list of OSPF-enabled interfaces on a router.	
Determine on which interfaces a router has formed at least one OSPF neighborship.	
Determine the number of fully adjacent neighbors on an interface.	
Determine which transit networks connect to a Type 1 LSA.	
Determine the router that created and flooded a Type 3 LSA.	
Determine the router that created and flooded a Type 2 LSA.	
Determine the router that created and flooded a Type 1 LSA.	
Display the IP address of the current DR and BDR on a LAN.	
Display the OSPF interface cost (metric).	
Display all OSPF-learned routes.	
Display statistics about the number of SPF algorithm runs.	

Note: Some of the entries in this table may not have been specifically mentioned in this chapter but are listed in this table for review and reference.

Review All the Key Topics

Review the most important topics from inside the chapter, noted with the Key Topics icon in the outer margin of the page. Table 6-10 lists a reference of these key topics and the page numbers on which each is found.

Table 6-10   *Key Topics for Chapter 6*

Key Topic Element	Description	Page Number
Table 6-2	OSPF LSA types	179
List	Two main functions of a DR	186
Table 6-3	Facts about LSA Types 1, 2, and 3	195
Table 6-4	OSPF Message Types	196
Table 6-5	OSPF neighbor states	197
List	Key differences between database exchange with and without a DR	201
List	Three steps a router considers when choosing the best OSPF IP routes	205
List	Three steps to calculate OSPF costs for intra-area routes	205
List	Two steps for calculating OSPF costs for interarea routes	209

Complete the Tables and Lists from Memory

Print a copy of Appendix D, "Memory Tables," (found on the CD), or at least the section for this chapter, and complete the tables and lists from memory. Appendix E, "Memory Tables Answer Key," also on the CD, includes completed tables and lists to check your work.

Define Key Terms

Define the following key terms from this chapter, and check your answers in the glossary.

Link State Identifier (LSID), Designated Router (DR), Backup Designated Router (BDR), Internal Router, Area Border Router (ABR), All SPF Routers multicast, All DR multicast, Link State Advertisement, Database Description (DD) packet, Link State Request (LSR) packet, Link State Acknowledgement (LSA) packet, Link State Update (LSU) packet, Router LSA, Network LSA, Summary LSA, Type 1 LSA, Type 2 LSA, Type 3 LSA, Reference bandwidth, SPF calculation

This chapter covers the following subjects:

Route Filtering: This section introduces three separate methods of route filtering with OSPF and discusses the commands to configure two of these methods.

Route Summarization: This section examines how OSPF can summarize routes at ABRs and at ASBRs.

Default Routes and Stub Areas: This section examines the two main reasons an Enterprise might use default routes and then shows OSPF's solution to each need: flooding a domain-wide default route and using OSPF stub areas.

CHAPTER 7

OSPF Route Summarization, Filtering, and Default Routing

This chapter discusses several features that optimize OSPF operations: route filtering, route summarization, default routing, plus OSPF stub areas.

Of these topics, the chapter focuses most on route filtering and route summarization, both of which have the same reasoning and motivation as the same features in EIGRP, as discussed throughout Chapter 4, "EIGRP Route Summarization and Filtering." Route filtering can be used to purposefully prevent hosts in one part of an internetwork from sending packets to another part. It can also reduce the size of the topology table and IP routing table, reducing both OSPF memory and CPU consumption, plus make the packet forwarding process run slightly better. Route summarization can also reduce routing protocol and packet forwarding overhead, but with a potential negative effect of creating less-efficient paths through the internetwork.

Additionally, this chapter briefly covers default routing, again the same motivations as the equivalent EIGRP feature, as discussed in Chapter 4. Finally, an OSPF-unique feature, OSPF stub routers, can also be used to limit the amount of topology data in an area, again reducing overhead.

"Do I Know This Already?" Quiz

The "Do I Know This Already?" quiz allows you to assess if you should read the entire chapter. If you miss no more than one of these eight self-assessment questions, you might want to move ahead to the "Exam Preparation Tasks." Table 7-1 lists the major headings in this chapter and the "Do I Know This Already?" quiz questions covering the material in those headings so that you can assess your knowledge of these specific areas. The answers to the "Do I Know This Already?" quiz appear in Appendix A.

Table 7-1 *"Do I Know This Already?" Foundation Topics Section-to-Question Mapping*

Foundations Topics Section	Questions
Route Filtering	1–3
Route Summarization	4, 5
Default Routing and Stub Areas	6–8

1. Router B1, an internal router in area 1, displays the following output. The only two ABRs connected to area 1 are performing Type 3 LSA filtering. Which of the following answers is true based on the information in the output from B1?

```
B1# show ip route 10.1.0.0 255.255.0.0 longer-prefixes
! Legend lines omitted for brevity

        10.0.0.0/8 is variably subnetted, 17 subnets, 3 masks
O          10.1.2.0/24 [110/658] via 10.10.13.1, 00:00:32, Serial0/0/0.1
O IA       10.1.1.0/24 [110/658] via 10.10.23.2, 00:41:39, Serial0/0/0.2
O IA       10.1.3.0/24 [110/658] via 10.10.23.2, 00:41:39, Serial0/0/0.2
```

   a. A Type 3 LSA for 10.2.2.0/24 was filtered by both ABRs.

   b. A Type 3 LSA for 10.1.2.0/24 was not filtered by both ABRs.

   c. A Type 3 LSA for 10.1.3.0/24 was not filtered by at least one ABR.

   d. A Type 3 LSA for 10.1.1.0/24 was filtered by both ABRs.

2. The following command output was gathered from Router R1, an ABR between areas 0 (backbone) and area 1. In this internetwork, area 0 contains all the subnets of class A network 10.0.0.0. R1's OSPF process has a **distribute-list prefix question in** command configured. Assuming the subnets listed in the answers actually exist in area 0, which of the following occurs on router R1?

```
R1#sh ip prefix-list
ip prefix-list question: 3 entries
    seq 5 deny 10.1.2.0/24 ge 25 le 27
    seq 15 deny 10.2.0.0/16 ge 30 le 30
    seq 20 permit 0.0.0.0/0 le 32
```

   a. R1 will not create/flood a type 3 LSA for subnet 10.1.2.0/26 into area 1.

   b. R1 will not create/flood a Type 3 LSA for subnet 10.1.2.0/24 into area 1.

   c. R1 will not have an OSPF route for subnet 10.1.2.0/26 in its IP routing table.

   d. R1 will not have an OSPF route for subnet 10.1.2.0/24 in its IP routing table.

3. Use the same scenario as the previous question, with one change. Instead of the **distribute-list prefix question in** command configured on R1, R1's OSPF process has an **area 1 filter-list prefix question in** command configured. Again assuming that the subnets listed in the answers actually exist in area 0, which of the following occurs on router R1?

```
R1#sh ip prefix-list
ip prefix-list question: 3 entries
    seq 5 deny 10.1.2.0/24 ge 25 le 27
    seq 15 deny 10.2.0.0/16 ge 30 le 30
    seq 20 permit 0.0.0.0/0 le 32
```

   a. R1 will not create/flood a type 3 LSA for subnet 10.1.2.0/26 into area 1.

   b. R1 will not create/flood a Type 3 LSA for subnet 10.1.2.0/24 into area 1.

   c. R1 will not have an OSPF route for subnet 10.1.2.0/26 in its IP routing table.

   d. R1 will not have an OSPF route for subnet 10.1.2.0/24 in its IP routing table.

4. R1, an ABR between backbone area 0 and area 1, has intra-area routes in area 0 for 10.1.1.0/24, 10.1.2.0/24, and 10.1.3.0/24. These routes have metrics of 21, 22, and 23, respectively. An engineer then adds the **area 0 range 10.1.0.0 255.255.0.0** command under the OSPF process of R1. Which of the following is true? (Choose two.)

   a. R1 loses and then re-establishes neighborships with all neighbors.

   b. R1 no longer advertises 10.1.1.0/24 to neighbors into area 1.

   c. R1 advertises a 10.1.0.0/16 route into area 1 with a metric of 23 (largest metric).

   d. R1 advertises a 10.1.0.0/16 route into area 1 with metric of 21 (lowest metric).

5. The following output exists on Router R1, a router internal to area 1. What can you determine as true from the output of the **show ip ospf database summary** command?

```
Routing Bit Set on this LSA
LS age: 124
Options: (No TOS-capability, DC, Upward)
LS Type: Summary Links (Network)
Link State ID: 10.1.0.0 (summary Network Number)
Advertising Router: 1.1.1.1
LS Seq Number: 80000001
Checksum: 0x878F
Length: 28
Network Mask: /22
      TOS: 0  Metric: 11
```

   a. The LSA was created by an ABR due to an **area range** command.

   b. The LSA was created by an ASBR due to a **summary-address** command.

   c. If created by an **area range** command, the best metric for a subordinate subnet on that ABR must have been 11.

   d. None of the other answers is correct.

6. Router R1, an ASBR connected to the Internet and to backbone area 0, has been configured with a **default-information originate** command. Which of the following is true about the effects of this configuration command?

   a. R1 will always create and flood a default route into the OSPF domain.

   b. R1 will create and flood an LSA for prefix/length 0.0.0.0/0 into the OSPF domain if R1's IP routing table has a route to 0.0.0.0/0.

   c. R1 will set a flag on the LSA for the subnet between itself and one of the ISPs, noting this subnet as a default network, regardless of whether R1 has a default route.

   d. R1 will set a flag on the LSA for the subnet between itself and one of the ISPs, noting this subnet as a default network, but only if R1 has a route to 0.0.0.0/0.

7. Which of the following is true about routers internal to a totally NSSA area? (Choose two.)

   a. Routers cannot redistribute external routes into the area.

   b. Routers should have zero Type 3 LSAs in their LSDBs.

   c. Routers should have zero Type 5 LSAs in their LSDBs.

   d. Routers should learn default routes from the ABRs attached to the area.

8. ABR R1 has been configured with an **area 1 stub no-summary** command. Which stubby area type is area 1?

   a. Stub

   b. Totally stubby

   c. NSSA

   d. Totally NSSA

Foundation Topics

Route Filtering

OSPF supports several methods to filter routes. However, the OSPF's internal logic restricts most filtering, requiring that the filtering be done either on an ABR or ASBR. This same internal logic dictates what each type of filtering can do and what it cannot do. So, when thinking about OSPF route filtering, you need to go beyond the concept of matching IP prefix/length information and consider OSPF internals as well. This first major section begins with a discussion of the OSPF internals that impact OSPF route filtering, followed by information about two of OSPF's route filtering tools.

First, consider the difference in how OSPF chooses intra-area versus interarea routes. For intra-area routes, OSPF uses pure link state logic, with full topology information about the area, piecing together the topology map from the Type 1 and Type 2 LSAs. This logic relies on all routers inside the area having an identical copy of the LSDB for that area. With the full topology, the SPF algorithm can be run, finding all possible routes to each subnet.

For interarea routes, OSPF uses distance vector logic. The intra-area SPF calculation includes the calculation of the metric of the best route to reach each ABR in the area. To choose the best interarea route, a router uses distance vector logic of taking its known metric to reach the ABR and adds the metric for that subnet as advertised by the ABR. In particular, no additional SPF calculation is required to find all interarea routes for a given prefix/length, making this logic more like distance vector logic.

Keeping these thoughts in mind, next consider the concept of route filtering inside one area. First, OSPF routers do not advertise routes; instead, they advertise LSAs. Any filtering applied to OSPF messages would need to filter the transmission of LSAs. However, inside one area, all routers must know all LSAs, or the whole SPF concept fails, and routing loops could occur. As a result, OSPF cannot and does not allow the filtering of LSAs inside an area, specifically the Type 1 and Type 2 LSAs that describe the intra-area topology.

OSPF does allow some route filtering, however, taking advantage of the fact that OSPF uses distance vector logic with Type 3 LSAs (and the Type 5 LSAs used for external routes). Because of the underlying distance vector logic, an OSPF ABR can be configured to filter Type 3 LSAs, with no risk of creating routing loops. (The same applies for autonomous system border routers [ASBRs] filtering the Type 5 LSAs created for external routes.) As a result of these related concepts, IOS limits OSPF route filtering to the following:

- Filtering Type 3 LSAs on ABRs

- Filtering Type 5 LSAs on ASBRs

- Filtering the routes OSPF would normally add to the IP routing table on a single router

Of these, the second option occurs as an option of the route redistribution process as explained in Chapter 9, "Basic IGP Redistribution," so it will not be covered further in this chapter. The other two topics will be examined next.

Type 3 LSA Filtering

ABRs, by definition, connect to the backbone area and at least one other area. ABRs, as a fundamental part of their role as ABR, create and flood Type 3 Summary LSAs into one area to represent the subnets in the other areas connected to that ABR. Type 3 LSA filtering tells the ABR to filter the advertisement of these Type 3 LSAs.

For example, consider Figure 7-1, which shows a generalized design with two ABR routers. The figure focuses on three subnets in area 0 for which each ABR would normally create and flood a Type 3 Summary LSA into area 1. However, in this case, the engineer has made the following choices:

- On ABR1, filter subnet 3 from being advertised.

- On ABR2, filter both subnet 2 and 3 from being advertised.

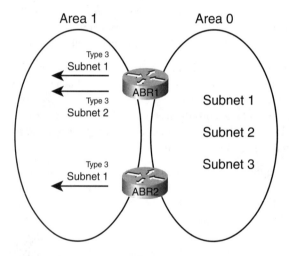

Figure 7-1   *Generic View of Type 3 LSA Filtering*

The goal of such a filtering plan could be to prevent all area 1 users from reaching subnet 3 and to allow access to subnet 2–but only through ABR1. If ABR1 were to fail, none of the area 1 routers could calculate a route for subnet 2 through ABR2, because ABR2 has not created and flooded a Type 3 LSA for that subnet. The goal for subnet 1 would be to allow each area 1 router to choose the best route through either ABR, while having a redundant route in case one route failed.

To configure type 3 LSA filtering, you use the **area** *number* **filter-list prefix** *name* **in | out** command under **router ospf**. The referenced **prefix-list** matches subnets, with subnets matched by a deny action being filtered, and subnets match with a permit action allowed through as normal. Then OSPF performs the filtering by not flooding the Type 3 LSAs into the appropriate areas. (See Chapter 4's section "IP Prefix List Concepts" for a review of IP prefix lists.)

The trickiest part of the configuration relates to the **in** and **out** parameters at the end of the **area filter-list** router subcommand. These parameters define the direction relative to the area listed in the command, as follows:

■   When **in** is configured, IOS filters prefixes being created and flooded *into the configured area.*

■   When **out** is configured, IOS filters prefixes coming *out of the configured area.*

The need for the **in** and **out** parameters makes more sense when you consider an ABR connected to at least three areas. Figure 7-2 shows just such a sample, with both the in and out directions represented.

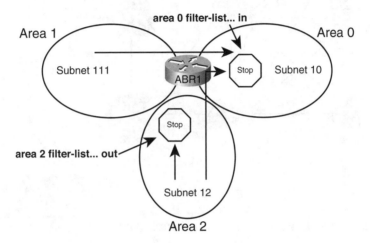

Figure 7-2   *Generic View of Type 3 LSA Filtering*

The **area 0 filter-list... in** command in the figure shows the ABR considers filtering routes from all other areas (area 1 and 2 in this case) when creating and flooding Type 3 LSAs into area 0. The **area 2 filter-list... out** command in the figure shows how the ABR only considers prefixes that exist in area 2. However, in this case, the ABR filters LSAs regardless of the area into which the Type 3 LSA would be advertised.

For example, consider the case of subnet 111, in area 1. Assume that all prefix lists happen to match subnet 111 so that subnet 111 should be filtered. The following list summarizes what happens on ABR1 regarding the potential advertisement of a Type 3 LSA for this subnet being flooded into areas 0 and 2.

■   ABR1 filters the subnet 111 LSA from being sent into area 0 due to the **area 0 filter-list... in** command.

■   ABR1 does not filter the subnet 111 LSA from being sent into area 2, because there is no **area 1 filter-list... out** command nor **area 2 filter-list... in** command.

As another example, Figure 7-3 shows an example internetwork with three candidate routes to be filtered by ABRs R1 and R2. ABRs R1 and R2 will play the roles of ABR1 and

ABR2 in Figure 7-1, with R1 filtering one of the three subnets, and R2 filtering two of the subnets. Note that R1 and R2 will each use different **in** and **out** keywords as well.

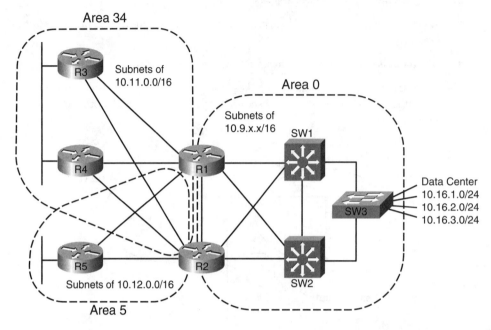

Figure 7-3   *Type 3 LSA Filtering Example*

Example 7-1 shows the configuration on both R1 and R2.

Example 7-1   *R1's and R2's distribute-list to Filter Manufacturing Routes*

```
! On Router R1:
ip prefix-list filter-into-area-34 seq 5 deny 10.16.3.0/24
ip prefix-list filter-into-area-34 seq 10 permit 0.0.0.0/0 le 32
!
router ospf 1
 area 34 filter-list prefix filter-into-area-34 in
```

```
! On Router R2:
ip prefix-list filter-out-of-area-0 seq 5 deny 10.16.2.0/23 ge 24 le 24
ip prefix-list filter-out-of-area-0 seq 10 permit 0.0.0.0/0 le 32
!
router ospf 2
 area 0 filter-list prefix filter-out-of-area-0 out
```

First, take a closer look at the specifics of the R1 configuration commands. The prefix list on R1 matches exactly route 10.16.3.0/24, with a **deny** action. The second prefix-list command matches all subnets, because the **0.0.0.0/0** parameter matches all subnet numbers, and the **le 32** parameter, combined with the original /0 prefix length, matches all prefix lengths from /0 to /32. The **area 34... in** command tells R1 to apply this filtering to all Type 3 LSAs that R1 creates and would otherwise flood into area 34. As a result, the area 34 LSDB will not contain a Type 3 LSA for 10.16.3.0/24, as injected by R1.

R2's configuration uses a slightly different prefix list. The filter examines all Type 3 LSAs for subnets in area 0. The first **prefix-list** command matches all prefixes in range 10.16.2.0–10.16.3.255 (per the **10.16.2.0/23** parameter) but specifically for a prefix length of exactly 24. This command matches two of the three data center subnets. The second **prefix-list** command matches all other subnets with the same match all logic seen earlier on R1, using a permit action. R2's **area 0... out** command tells R2 to filter the subnets that R2 learns in area 0 and for which R2 would normally create Type 3 LSAs to flood into all other areas. So, neither area 34 nor area 5 will learn these two filtered subnets (10.16.2.0/24 and 10.16.3.0/24) in Type 3 LSAs from R2.

The end result of this added configuration results in the following Type 3 LSAs for the three subnets shown on the right side of Figure 7-3:

■ Two Type 3 LSAs for 10.16.1.0/24 (created by R1 and R2, respectively)

■ One Type 3 LSA for 10.16.2.0/24 (created by R1)

■ None for 10.16.3.0/24

Example 7-2 confirms the contents of the LSDB in area 34, on Router R3.

Example 7-2   *Area 34 LSDB, as Seen on R3*

```
R3# show ip route 10.16.0.0 255.255.0.0 longer-prefixes
! Legend lines omitted for brevity

     10.0.0.0/8 is variably subnetted, 17 subnets, 3 masks
O IA    10.16.2.0/24 [110/658] via 10.10.13.1, 00:00:32, Serial0/0/0.1
O IA    10.16.1.0/24 [110/658] via 10.10.23.2, 00:41:39, Serial0/0/0.2
                     [110/658] via 10.10.13.1, 00:00:32, Serial0/0/0.1


R3#show ip ospf database | include 10.16
10.16.1.0        1.1.1.1            759         0x80000002 0x008988
10.16.1.0        2.2.2.2            745         0x80000002 0x006BA2
10.16.2.0        1.1.1.1            759         0x80000002 0x007E92
```

The first command in the example lists R3's routes for all subnets whose first two octets are 10.16. Note that R3 has no route to 10.16.3.0/24, because both R1 and R2 filtered the Type 3 LSA. R3 happens to have equal-cost routes for 10.16.1.0/24, which is possible because both R1 and R2 permitted the advertisement of the Type 3 LSA for that subnet. R3 has only one route for 10.16.2.0/24, through R1, because R2 filtered its Type 3 LSA for that prefix.

The second command in Example 7-2 lists all LSAs that include "10.16," which includes the two Type 3 LSAs for 10.16.1.0/24, and the single Type 3 LSA for 10.16.2.0/24.

Finally, note that although the configuration in Example 7-1 showed **area filter-list** com-mands with both **in** and **out** parameters for variety, the result of R2's **area filter-list... out** command is that R2 does not flood the filtered LSAs to either area 34 or area 5. If the de-sign goals specifically meant to filter only LSAs from being advertised from Area 0 into Area 34, the **area 34 filter-list... in** command should have been used on both routers.

Filtering OSPF Routes Added to the Routing Table

In some cases, an engineer may need to filter a route, but the area design does not work well compared to the filtering goals. For instance, if an area has 20 routers, and the engi-neer wants to filter the route so that five of the routers do not learn the route, Type 3 LSA filtering cannot be used. Type 3 LSA filtering can only filter the LSA from being flooded throughout the entire area.

The next feature discussed in this section, referenced as *filtering with distribute lists* (based on the configuration command it uses), allows individual routers to filter OSPF routes from getting into their respective IP routing tables. This type of filtering injects logic between the SPF algorithm on a router and that same router's IP routing table. This feature does not change the LSDB flooding process, does not change the LSAs added by ABRs or ASBRs, and does not change the SPF algorithm's choice of best route. However, when SPF chooses routes to add to the IP routing table, if a router has been configured with a **distribute-list in** OSPF router subcommand, enabling this feature, that router then filters the routes before adding them to that router's IP routing table. Figure 7-4 shows the general idea.

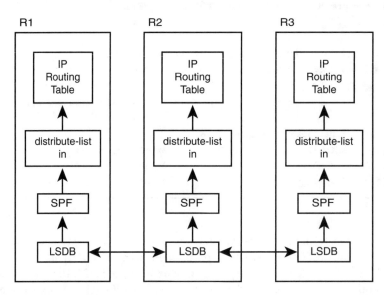

Figure 7-4   *OSPF Filtering with Distribute Lists*

In effect, you could prevent an OSPF route from being added to one or more routers' rout-ing tables, but without risking causing routing loops, because the intra-area LSDB topology remains intact. By filtering routes from being added to the IP routing table, you prevent the routers from forwarding packets to the filtered subnets, but presumably that's the intended goal of route filtering.

The mechanics of the **distribute-list** router subcommand has a few surprises, which are summarized in this list:

■ The command requires either an **in** or **out** direction. Only the **in** direction works for filtering routes as described in this section.

■ The command must refer to either a numbered ACL, named ACL, prefix list, or route map. Regardless, routes matched with a **permit** action are allowed into the routing table, and routes matched with a **deny** action are filtered.

■ Optionally, the command can include the **interface** *interface-name-and-number* parameters. The router compares these parameters to the route's outgoing interface.

Example 7-3 shows a sample configuration on Router R3 from Figure 7-3. In this case, all filtering listed in Examples 7-1 and 7-2 has been removed, so no routes or LSAs have been filtered. Then, the engineer adds the **distribute-list** command on R3 to filter the route for 10.16.1.0/24, based on prefix-list filter-1.

Example 7-3   *R3's distribute-list to Filter 10.16.1.0/24*

```
! On Router R3:
ip prefix-list filter-1 seq 5 deny 10.16.1.0/24
ip prefix-list filter-1 seq 10 permit 0.0.0.0/0 le 32
!
router ospf 3
 distribute-list prefix filter-1 in
!
R3#show ip route ospf | include 10.16.1
R3#
R3#show ip ospf database | include 10.16.1.0
10.16.1.0        1.1.1.1          1143       0x80000007 0x007F8D
10.16.1.0        2.2.2.2          1538       0x80000007 0x0061A7
```

Note that the configuration matches only prefix 10.16.1.0/24 with a deny clause and permits all other routes. As a result, OSPF on R3 does not add a route for subnet 10.16.1.0/24 to the IP routing table, as implied by the null output of the **show ip route ospf | include 10.16.1** command. The **show ip ospf database | include 10.16.1** command lists all LSAs that have 10.16.1 in the text output, showing the two Type 3 LSAs for the subnet.

Route Summarization

OSPF allows summarization at both ABRs and ASBRs but not on other OSPF routers. The main reason is again that the LSDB must be the same for all routers in a single area. So, if summarization is needed, the summary prefixes should be created at the edge of an area (ABR or ASBR) and flooded throughout that area. However, the idea of summarizing on a router internal to an area, hoping that some routers in the area use the summary route, and others in the same area do not, cannot be done with OSPF.

Good planning of route summaries can overcome the restriction of performing the summarization only on ABRs and ASBRs. A good OSPF area design includes consideration of future address summaries, and a good OSPF route summarization design considers the ABR locations. Although it is rare to design a large internetwork from scratch, an addressing plan that assigns all or most subnets in an area from one large address block does make address summarization easier.

OSPF summarization differs slightly on ABRs versus ASBRs. This section first examines route summarizations on ABRs and then ASBRs.

Manual Summarization at ABRs

The more difficult task with OSPF route summarization occurs when planning the design of IP address blocks and OSPF areas. When the IP addressing plan and OSPF design have been completed, if the subnet numbers inside an area happen to be from the same general range, and none of the subnets in that range exist in other OSPF areas, then a reasonable summary route can be created at the ABRs connected to that area. Without first having such a reasonable block of addresses, route summarization may not be a useful option.

After a range of subnets has been chosen for summarization, the parameters in the **area range** command must be planned. This command defines the parameters for the summary route, most notably the origin area from which the subnets exist, and the subnet number/mask that defines the summary route that should be advertised. The generic version of the command is listed next, followed by some notes about the various parameters:

```
area area-id range ip-address mask [cost cost]
```

- The configured area number refers to the area where the subnets exist; the summary will be advertised into all other areas connected to the ABR.

- The ABR compares the summary route's range of addresses with all intra-area OSPF routes, in the origin area, for which the ABR is creating Type 3 LSAs. If at least one subordinate subnet exists (subnets that sit inside the range), then the ABR advertises the summary route as a Type 3 LSA.

- The ABR does not advertise the subordinate subnet's Type 3 LSAs.

- The ABR assigns a metric for the summary route's Type 3 LSA, by default, to match the best metric among all subordinate subnets.

- The **area range** command can also explicitly set the cost of the summary.

- If no subordinate subnets exist, the ABR does not advertise the summary.

For example, Figure 7-3 (earlier in this chapter) lists three subnets on the right side of the figure, noted as Data Center subnets: 10.16.1.0/24, 10.16.2.0/24, and 10.16.3.0/24. ABR R1 could be configured to summarize these routes as 10.16.0.0/22, which includes all three subnets. (10.16.0.0/22 implies a range from 10.16.0.0–10.16.3.255.) The ABRs (R1 and R2) could be configured to advertise a summary route using the **area 0 range 10.16.0.0 255.255.252.0** router subcommand.

Behind the scenes, ABR route summarization causes the ABR to no longer advertise the subordinate routes' Type 3 LSAs, but to instead advertise one Type 3 LSA for the summary prefix. Figure 7-5 shows this concept on ABR R1, assuming the **area 0 range 10.16.0.0 255.255.252.0** router subcommand has been configured. The three Type 3 LSAs that would normally have been advertised are shown above the ABR, and the one Type 3 LSA for the summary route, which replaces the upper LSAs, is shown under the ABR.

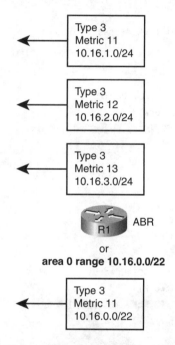

Figure 7-5   *OSPF Area Summarization–Consolidating Type 3 LSAs*

Example 7-4 shows some **show** command output related to this example. All route filtering in earlier examples has been removed, and both R1 and R2 have configured OSPF to summarize 10.16.0.0/22 with the **area 0 range 10.16.0.0 255.255.252.0** router OSPF subcommand. However, in R2's case, the **metric 12** parameter was used.

Example 7-4   *R1/R2/R3's Area Summarization on 10.16.0.0/16*

```
! On Router R1, before the summarization:
R1#sh ip route ospf | incl 10.16
O       10.16.2.0/24 [110/12] via 10.10.17.7, 00:00:24, FastEthernet0/0
O       10.16.3.0/24 [110/13] via 10.10.17.7, 00:00:24, FastEthernet0/0
O       10.16.1.0/24 [110/11] via 10.10.17.7, 00:00:34, FastEthernet0/0
```

```
! Next, configuring the summarization:
router ospf 1
 area 0 range 10.16.0.0 255.255.252.0
```

```
! Next, on R2, configuring the same summary
router ospf 2
 area 0 range 10.16.0.0 255.255.252.0 cost 12
```

```
! Next, from R3
R3#show ip ospf database summary 10.16.0.0

                OSPF Router with ID (3.3.3.3) (Process ID 3)

                    Summary Net Link States (Area 34)


    Routing Bit Set on this LSA
    LS age: 124
    Options: (No TOS-capability, DC, Upward)
    LS Type: Summary Links(Network)
    Link State ID: 10.16.0.0 (summary Network Number)
    Advertising Router: 1.1.1.1
    LS Seq Number: 80000001
    Checksum: 0x878F
    Length: 28
    Network Mask: /22
          TOS: 0  Metric: 11


    LS age: 103
    Options: (No TOS-capability, DC, Upward)
    LS Type: Summary Links(Network)
    Link State ID: 10.16.0.0 (summary Network Number)
    Advertising Router: 2.2.2.2
    LS Seq Number: 80000001
    Checksum: 0x739E
    Length: 28
    Network Mask: /22
          TOS: 0  Metric: 12


R3#show ip route 10.16.0.0 255.255.0.0 longer-prefixes
! legend omitted for brevity


     10.0.0.0/8 is variably subnetted, 16 subnets, 4 masks
O IA    10.16.0.0/22 [110/658] via 10.10.13.1, 00:03:46, Serial0/0/0.1
```

The example demonstrates the theory of what happens behind the scenes. R3 lists only two Type 3 LSAs related to the 10.16.1.0/24, 10.16.2.0/24, and 10.16.3.0/24 subnets: the Type 3 LSAs created by R1 and R2 for 10.16.0.0/22. However, the output does not denote that this LSA represents a summarized route–it simply looks like yet another Type 3 LSA.

(Any mention of the word "summary" in the output refers to the fact that Type 3 LSAs are called summary LSAs.) In this case, R3's path to reach both R1 and R2 ties, but the LSA for R1's 10.16.0.0/22 summary was injected with metric 11, based on the lowest metric subordinate route on R1, whereas R2's uses the explicitly configured metric 12. As a result, R3's best route for 10.16.0.0/22 uses R1, as shown in the route at the end of the example.

The first **show** command in the example shows R1's metrics for the three subordinate subnets, specifically metrics 11, 12, and 13. As such, R1's summary for 10.16.0.0/22, as shown in R3's **show ip ospf database summary 10.16.0.0** command, confirms that by default R1 gave the summary route's Type 3 LSA the best metric among the component subnets.

> **Note:** Although not discussed in depth here, the optional **not-advertise** option on the **area range** command tells the ABR to not advertise the Type 3 LSA for the summary route, making it possible to do the equivalent of Type 3 LSA filtering with the **area range** command.

Manual Summarization at ASBRs

OSPF defines an ASBR as a router that redistributes routes into OSPF from some other routing source. When redistributing the routes, the ASBR creates a Type 5 External LSA for each redistributed subnet, listing the subnet number as the LSID and listing the mask as one of the fields in the LSA. The LSA also lists the ASBR's RID as the advertising router and a cost metric for the route. For the purposes of route summarization, you can think of a Type 5 LSA as working much like a Type 3 LSA, except for routes learned externally.

Chapter 9 discusses external OSPF routes in more depth, including some additional background on Type 5 LSAs. However, to keep the discussion of OSPF route summarization together, this section describes ASBR route summarization, which has many similarities to summarization by an ABR.

If you add the **summary-address** *prefix mask* OSPF subcommand, OSPF will then attempt to summarize the external routes by creating a Type 5 LSA for the summary route, and by no longer advertising the Type 5 LSAs for the subordinate subnets. When looking for potential subordinate subnets inside the summary, the ASBR looks at all routes being redistributed into OSPF from all outside route sources, and if any subordinate subnets exist, the ASBR performs the route summarization.

Notably, this command works very much like the **area range** command on ABRs, with the main exception being that the **summary-address** command cannot explicitly set the metric of the summary route. The list of features is as follows:

- The ASBR compares the summary route's range of addresses with all routes redistributed into OSPF on that ASBR to find any subordinate subnets (subnets that sit inside the summary route range). If at least one subordinate subnet exists, the ASBR advertises the summary route.

- The ASBR does not advertise the subordinate subnets.

- To create the summary, the ASBR actually creates a Type 5 LSA for the summary route.

- The ASBR assigns the summary route the same metric as the lowest metric route amongst all subordinate subnets.

- If no subordinate subnets exist, the ASBR does not advertise the summary.

- Unlike the **area range** command, the **summary-address** command cannot be used to directly set the metric of the summary route.

The **summary-address** OSPF subcommand defines the summary route on the ASBR, with similar syntax and parameters as compared to the **area range** command seen on ABRs. Table 7-2 lists the two commands for comparison and study.

Table 7-2   *OSPF Route Summarization Commands*

Where Used	Command
ASBR	**summary-address** {{*ip-address mask*}	{*prefix mask*}} [**not-advertise**]
ABR	**area** *area-id* **range** *ip-address mask* [**advertise**	**not-advertise**] [**cost** *cost*]

Default Routes and Stub Areas

Enterprises typically use default routes in two different cases:

- To direct remote-site routers at the edge of the Enterprise network to send all packets toward the core of the Enterprise, with the core routers knowing all the more specific routes to Enterprise destination addresses.

- To direct traffic on all Enterprise routers toward an Internet-facing router so that all traffic destined for the Internet eventually arrives at the Enterprise's Internet-connected routers.

Engineers could achieve both of these goals by using route summarization with the **area range** and **summary-address** commands. For example, consider a case in which the goal is to drive all packets destined for Internet hosts to one of two equal Internet routers for an Enterprise, as shown in Figure 7-6. The design shows two ASBRs connected to the Internet. Both ASBRs could learn routes with BGP. Rather than redistribute all BGP routes into the Enterprise, the ASBRs summarize to the ultimate summary, 0.0.0.0/0. The two OSPF ASBRs flood the Type 5 LSA for a summary route–one from ASBR1 and one from ASBR2–throughout the Enterprise. As a result, all OSPF routers choose a default route, with the packets destined for locations in the Internet eventually reaching one of the two ASBRs, which then forwards the packets into the Internet.

To meet the other design goal for using defaults–to get the routers in an area to use default routing to deliver packets to the ABR–the ABR could use the **area range** command to flood a default route into a single area. Again in Figure 7-6, if the design called for the routers in area 1 to use a default route to reach other destinations in the Enterprise, the ABRs connected to area 1, like ABR1, could use the **area 0 range 0.0.0.0 0.0.0.0** command.

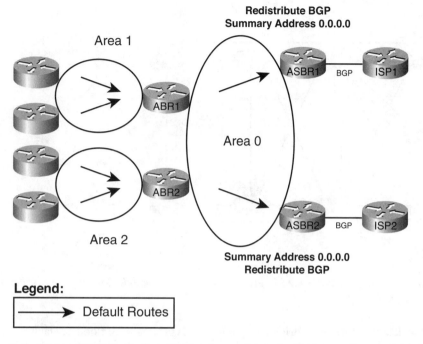

Figure 7-6   *Using ASBR Route Summarization to Advertise Summary Routes*

ABR1 would then advertise a default route into the area, as an LSA type 3, and not advertise any of the other Type 3 LSAs known from area 0. The routers internal to area 1 would use their default route for packets destined to unknown destination addresses, but the ABRs would have full knowledge of the routes inside the Enterprise and know how to forward the packets at that point.

Even though you can use the **summary-address** and **area range** commands, most engineers use other methods to introduce and control default routes inside the OSPF domain. The first tool, the **default-information originate** OSPF subcommand, introduces a default route to be flooded throughout the OSPF domain. As a result, it is most useful for default routing to draw packets toward ASBRs connected to external networks. The other tool, stub areas, focuses on the other common use of default routes, controlling when ABRs flood default routes into a given area. This section examines both topics.

Domain-wide Defaults Using the default-information originate Command

The OSPF subcommand **default-information originate** tells OSPF to create a Type 5 LSA (used for external routes) for a default route–0.0.0.0/0–and flood it like any other Type 5 LSA. In other words, it tells the router to create and flood information about a default route throughout the OSPF domain.

For example, consider a typical single multihomed Internet design, as shown in Figure 7-7. In this case, the Enterprise has two Internet-connected routers, and the engineer wants to use default routing inside the Enterprise to cause all the Enterprise routers to send packets toward either ASBR1 or ASBR2.

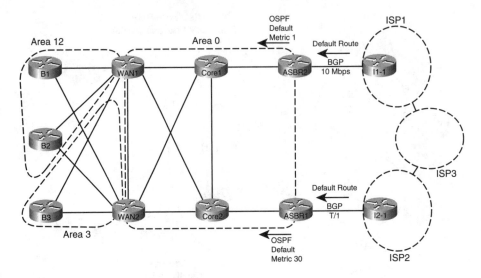

Figure 7-7   *Single Multihomed Internet Design Using Default Routes*

The **default-information originate** command tells the ASBRs to flood a default route into OSPF, but only if the ASBR itself has a default route in its IP routing table. This logic relies on the fact that the ASBRs typically either have a static default route pointing to the connected ISP router, or they learn a default route from the ISP using BGP. (Figure 7-7 each ISP is advertising a default route in this case.) All the routers then learn a default route, based on the Type 5 LSAs for 0.0.0.0/0 as flooded by the ASBRs.

Because a router withdraws its OSPF default route when its own IP route to 0.0.0.0/0 fails, OSPF allows the design in Figure 7-7 to fail over to the other default route. When all is well, both ISP1 and ISP2 advertise a default route to the Enterprise using BGP, so both ASBR1 and ASBR2 have a route to 0.0.0.0/0. As shown in the figure, ASBR2 has been configured to advertise its OSPF default with a lower metric (1) than does ASBR1 (metric 30), so the Enterprise routers will forward traffic to the Internet through ASBR2. However, if ISP1 quits advertising that default with BGP, or BGP fails between ASBR2 and ISP1's I1-1 router, ASBR2 will withdraw its OSPF default route. The only remaining OSPF default route will be the one that leads to ASBR1, making use of the backup default route.

The full command syntax, as shown here, provides several optional parameters that impact its operation:

```
default-information originate [always] [metric metric-value] [metric-type
type-value] [route-map map-name]
```

The following list summarizes the features of the **default-information originate** OSPF subcommand:

■   With all default parameters, it injects a default route into OSPF, as an External Type 2 route, using a Type 5 LSA, with metric 1, but only if a default route exists in that router's routing table.

- With the **always** parameter, the default route is advertised even if there is no default route in the router's routing table.

- The **metric** keyword defines the metric listed for the default route (default 1).

- The **metric-type** keyword defines whether the LSA is listed as external type 1 or external type 2 (default). (Chapter 9's section "Redistribution into OSPF" discusses OSPF external route types.)

- The decision of when to advertise, and when to withdraw, the default route is based on matching the referenced **route-map** with a permit action.

When configured, OSPF will flood the default route throughout the OSPF routing domain, drawing traffic to each ASBR, as shown earlier in Figure 7-6.

Note: The type of external OSPF route (Type 1 or Type 2) is explained more fully in Chapter 9.

Stubby Areas

As mentioned earlier, the two most common reasons to consider using default routes are to drive all Internet-destined traffic toward the Internet-connected routers in the Enterprise and to drive traffic inside an area toward one of the ABRs in that area. This second design choice allows the routers in an area to use default routes for forwarding packets to ABRs, rather than more specific routes. Using default routes inside an area reduces memory consumption and CPU processing time on the routers inside the area, because the routers in that area can have fewer LSAs in their LSDBs.

The OSPF stub router feature provides engineers a very simple way to enable the function of flooding default routes inside an area, with those default routes driving IP packets back toward the ABRs attached to that area. ABRs in stub areas advertise a default route into the stub area. At the same time, the ABR chooses to not advertise external routes (5 LSAs) into the area, or even instead to not advertise interarea routes (in Type 3 LSAs) into the area. As a result, all routers in the stub area can still route to the destinations (based on the default route), but the routers require less memory and processing.

The following list summarizes these features of stub areas for easier study and review:

- ABRs create a default route, using a Type 3 LSA, listing subnet 0.0.0.0 and mask 0.0.0.0, and flood that into the stub area.

- ABRs do not flood Type 5 LSAs into the stub area.

- ABRs may not flood other Type 3 LSAs into the area.

- The default route has a metric of 1 unless otherwise configured using the OSPF subcommand **area** *area-num* **default-cost** *cost*.

- Routers inside stub areas cannot redistribute external routes into the stubby area, because that would require a Type 5 LSA in the area.

■   All routers in the area must be configured to be stubby; if not, neighbor relationships cannot form between potential neighbors based on this mismatched configuration.

Figure 7-8 shows a familiar design in which area 34 will become a stub area. The design shows three external routes and lists three of many internal routes inside area 0. The figure shows ABRs R1 and R2 advertising defaults into area 34.

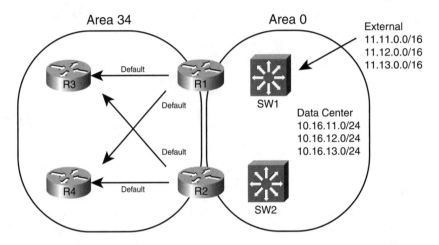

Figure 7-8   *Stubby Area Design*

Figure 7-8 demonstrates the core feature common to all types of stub areas: the ABRs flood a default route into the area. The routers inside the area can then calculate their best default route. Next, the text examines the different types of OSPF areas, before moving on to the details of configuration and verification.

Introducing Stubby Area Types

Even within the realm of stubby areas, four types of stubby areas exist: stub, totally stubby, not-so-stubby areas (NSSA), and totally NSSA.

Two types of stubby areas have the word "totally" as part of the name, and two do not. The differences between those with the word "totally" and those without have to do with whether Type 3 LSAs are flooded into the area. The rules are

■   For all types of stubby areas, the ABR always filters Type 5 (external) LSAs.

■   For totally stubby and totally NSSA areas, the ABR also filters Type 3 LSAs.

■   For stubby and NSSA areas—those without the word "totally" in the name—the ABRs do not filter Type 3 LSAs, advertising Type 3 LSAs as normal.

For example, consider the diagram in Figure 7-8, with area 34 as simply a stub area. As for all types, the ABRs each advertise a default route into area 34. As for all stubby area types, the ABRs filter all Type 5 LSAs, which means that the three Type 5 LSAs for

11.11.0.0/16, 11.12.0.0/16, and 11.13.0.0/16 would not exist in the LSDBs for area 34. Finally, because the area is not a totally stubby area, the ABRs do create and flood Type 3 LSAs for interarea routes as usual, so they flood LSAs for the 10.16.11.0/24, 10.16.12.0/24, and 10.16.13.0/24 subnets listed in the figure.

Next, consider a similar scenario but with a totally stubby area for area 5, as seen in Figure 7-3. As for all stubby area types, the ABRs each advertise a default route into area 5. As for all stubby area types, the ABRs filter all Type 5 LSAs, which means that the three Type 5 LSAs for 11.11.0.0/16, 11.12.0.0/16, and 11.13.0.0/16 would not exist in the LSDBs for area 5. The key difference exists in that the ABRs also would not create and flood Type 3 LSAs for interarea routes as usual, so they would not advertise Type 3 LSAs for the 10.16.11.0/24, 10.16.12.0/24, and 10.16.13.0/24 subnets listed in the figure into area 5.

The other difference in stubby area types relates to whether the name uses NSSA (NSSA or totally NSSA) or not (stubby, totally stubby). Stubby area types that use the NSSA name can redistribute external routes into the area; stubby area types without NSSA in the name cannot.

Configuring and Verifying Stubby Areas

Configuring stub and totally stubby areas requires only three commands, but with at least one command on each router, as listed in Table 7-3:

Table 7-3 *Stub Area Configuration Options*

Action	Configuration Steps
Stubby	Configure **area** *area-id* **stub** on each router in the area
Totally stubby	Configure **area** *area-id* **stub no-summary** command on the ABRs Configure **area** *area-id* **stub**, without the **no-summary** keyword, on all other routers in the area
Set the metric of the default route	Configure **area** *area-id* **default-metric** *metric* on an ABR; can differ from ABR to ABR. Default value is 1.

Note: For totally stubby areas, only the ABRs must have the **no-summary** keyword on the **area** *area-id* **stub no-summary** command. However, including this keyword on internal routers does not cause a problem.

Figure 7-9 shows a more detailed view of area 34 from Figure 7-8, so by making area 34 a stub area, ABRs R1 and R2 will not flood Type 5 LSAs into area 34—other than the Type 3 LSA for the default routes. Example 7-4 shows the configuration on Routers R1, R2, and R3 from Figure 7-9.

Area 34 (Stubby)

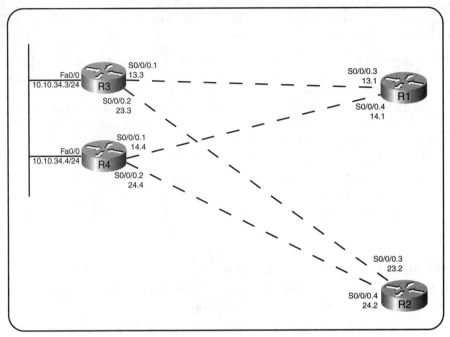

Figure 7-9   *Detailed View of Area 34*

Example 7-4   *Stub Area Configuration*

```
! On Router R1:
router ospf 1
 area 34 stub
 auto-cost reference-bandwidth 1000
!
interface s0/0/0.3 point-to-point
 ip ospf 1 area 34
!
interface s0/0/0.4 point-to-point
  ip ospf 1 area 34
! On Router R2:
router ospf 2
 area 34 stub
 auto-cost reference-bandwidth 1000
!
interface s0/0/0.3 point-to-point
 ip ospf 2 area 34
!
interface s0/0/0.4 point-to-point
 ip ospf 2 area 34
```

```
! On Router R3:
router ospf 3
 area 34 stub
 auto-cost reference-bandwidth 1000
!
interface s0/0/0.1 point-to-point
 ip ospf 1 area 34
 ip ospf 3 cost 500
!
interface s0/0/0.2 point-to-point
 ip ospf 3 area 34
!
interface fa0/0
 ip ospf 3 area 34
```

With the configuration as shown, both R1 and R2 will inject a default route, represented as a Type 3 LSA, with default metric 1. They will also not flood the Type 5 LSAs into area 34. Example 7-5 confirms these facts, showing the Type 3 LSA for the summary, and the absence of Type 5 LSAs in the output of the **show ip ospf database** command on router R3.

Example 7-5 *Evidence of Type 5's Existing, Disappearing, and Defaults Appearing*

```
! Before making Area 34 stubby:


R3#show ip ospf database | begin AS External
                Type-5 AS External Link States

Link ID         ADV Router      Age         Seq#        Checksum Tag
11.11.0.0       7.7.7.7         929         0x80000001  0x00016D 0
12.12.0.0       7.7.7.7         845         0x80000001  0x00E784 0
13.13.0.0       7.7.7.7         835         0x80000001  0x00CE9B 0

! After making area 34 stubby - no output from the next command.


R3#show ip ospf database | begin AS External
R3#


! The database for area 34 now has two Type 3 LSAs for default routes.
R3#show ip ospf database


            OSPF Router with ID (3.3.3.3) (Process ID 3)


                Router Link States (Area 34)
```

```
! Lines omitted for brevity - skipped to "Summary Net" (Type 3) section


                    Summary Net Link States (Area 34)


Link ID          ADV Router        Age         Seq#         Checksum
0.0.0.0          1.1.1.1           692         0x80000001   0x0093A6
0.0.0.0          2.2.2.2           686         0x80000001   0x0075C0
10.10.5.0        1.1.1.1           692         0x8000000E   0x00445C
10.10.5.0        2.2.2.2           686         0x8000000F   0x002477
10.10.12.0       1.1.1.1           692         0x8000000E   0x0054AF
10.10.12.0       2.2.2.2           686         0x8000000E   0x0036C9
! Many Type 3 LSA's omitted for brevity's sake
```

Example 7-5 shows the existence of the Type 5 external LSAs before area 34 became a stubby area, and the disappearance of those same LSAs once it was made a stubby area. The **show ip ospf database** command then shows two LSAs that list default routes, one learned from RID 1.1.1.1 (R1), and one learned from RID 2.2.2.2 (R2).

Example 7-6 continues the verification of how stub areas work with three more commands.

Example 7-6   *Three External Routes Before and None Afterward Changing to Stubby*

```
! Next, R3 confirms it thinks area 34 is a stub area
R3#show ip ospf
 Routing Process "ospf 3" with ID 3.3.3.3
 Start time: 00:00:38.756, Time elapsed: 07:51:19.720
! lines omitted for brevity
    Area 34
        Number of interfaces in this area is 3
        It is a stub area
        Area has no authentication
        SPF algorithm last executed 00:11:21.640 ago
        SPF algorithm executed 18 times
        Area ranges are
        Number of LSA 29. Checksum Sum 0x0D3E01
        Number of opaque link LSA 0. Checksum Sum 0x000000
        Number of DCbitless LSA 0
        Number of indication LSA 0
        Number of DoNotAge LSA 0
        Flood list length 0

! The next command shows all Type 3 (summary) LSAs of prefix 0.0.0.0

R3#show ip ospf database summary 0.0.0.0


            OSPF Router with ID (3.3.3.3) (Process ID 3)
```

```
                    Summary Net Link States (Area 34)


    Routing Bit Set on this LSA
    LS age: 879
    Options: (No TOS-capability, DC, Upward)
    LS Type: Summary Links(Network)
    Link State ID: 0.0.0.0 (summary Network Number)
    Advertising Router: 1.1.1.1
    LS Seq Number: 80000001
    Checksum: 0x93A6
    Length: 28
    Network Mask: /0
          TOS: 0  Metric: 1


    LS age: 873
    Options: (No TOS-capability, DC, Upward)
    LS Type: Summary Links(Network)
    Link State ID: 0.0.0.0 (summary Network Number)
    Advertising Router: 2.2.2.2
    LS Seq Number: 80000001
    Checksum: 0x75C0
    Length: 28
    Network Mask: /0
          TOS: 0  Metric: 1

! The next command lists statistics of the number of LSAs of each type -
! note a total of 0 Type 5 LSAs, but many Type 3

R3#show ip ospf database database-summary


            OSPF Router with ID (3.3.3.3) (Process ID 3)


Area 34 database summary
  LSA Type       Count    Delete    Maxage
  Router         4        0         0
  Network        1        0         0
  Summary Net    24       0         0
  Summary ASBR   0        0         0
  Type-7 Ext     0        0         0
    Prefixes redistributed in Type-7   0
  Opaque Link    0        0         0
  Opaque Area    0        0         0
  Subtotal       29       0         0
```

```
Process 3 database summary
  LSA Type        Count    Delete    Maxage
  Router          4        0         0
  Network         1        0         0
  Summary Net     24       0         0
  Summary ASBR    0        0         0
  Type-7 Ext      0        0         0
  Opaque Link     0        0         0
  Opaque Area     0        0         0
  Type-5 Ext      0        0         0
      Prefixes redistributed in Type-5   0
  Opaque AS       0        0         0
  Non-self        28
  Total           29       0         0
```

Following are the three commands in Example 7-6 in order:

■ **show ip ospf–**Confirms with one (highlighted) line that the router believes that the area is a stub area.

■ **show ip ospf database summary 0.0.0.0–**By definition, this command lists all summary (Type 3) LSAs with prefix 0.0.0.0. It lists two such LSAs, created by R1 and R2 (RIDs 1.1.1.1 and 2.2.2.2, respectively), both with metric 1 (the default setting).

■ **show ip ospf database database-summary–**This command lists statistics about the numbers of and types of LSAs in the database. The counters show 0 Type 5 LSAs, and a few dozen Type 3s–confirming that the area, while stubby, is not totally stubby.

Configuring and Verifying Totally Stubby Areas

Configuring totally stubby areas requires almost no additional effort as compared with stubby areas. As listed earlier in Table 7-3, the only difference for totally stubby configuration versus stubby configuration is that the ABRs include the **no-summary** keyword on the **area stub** command. (**no-summary** refers to the fact that ABRs in totally stubby areas do not create/flood Type 3 summary LSAs.)

Example 7-7 shows another example configuration, this time with area 34 as a totally stubby area. Additionally, the default routes' metrics have been set so that both R3 and R4 will use R1 as their preferred ABR, by setting R2's advertised summary to a relatively high metric (500). Example 7-7 just shows the changes to the configuration shown in Example 7-4.

Example 7-7   *Totally Stubby Area Configuration*

```
! On Router R1:
router ospf 1
 area 34 stub no-summary
 auto-cost reference-bandwidth 1000
```

```
! On Router R2:
router ospf 2
 area 34 stub no-summary
 area 34 default-cost 500
 auto-cost reference-bandwidth 1000
```

The configuration of a totally stubby area reduces the size of the LSDB in area 34, because the ABRs no longer flood Type 3 LSAs into area 34, as shown in Example 7-8. R3 displays its LSDB, listing only two Summary (Type 3) LSAs–the two default routes advertised by the two ABRs, respectively. No other Type 3 LSAs exist, nor do any external (Type 5) or ASBR summary (Type 4) LSAs.

Also, note that the example lists the OSPF routes known to R3. Interestingly, in the topology shown for area 34, R3 learns only three OSPF routes: the two intra-area routes for the subnets between R4 and the two ABRs, plus the best default route. The default route has a metric of 501, based on R3's S0/0/0.1 interface cost plus the cost 1 listed for R1's Type 3 LSA for the default route.

Example 7-8   *Confirmation of the Effects of a Totally Stubby Area*

```
R3#show ip route
Codes: C - connected, S - static, R - RIP, M - mobile, B - BGP
       D - EIGRP, EX - EIGRP external, O - OSPF, IA - OSPF inter area
       N1 - OSPF NSSA external type 1, N2 - OSPF NSSA external type 2
       E1 - OSPF external type 1, E2 - OSPF external type 2
       i - IS-IS, su - IS-IS summary, L1 - IS-IS level-1, L2 - IS-IS level-2
       ia - IS-IS inter area, * - candidate default, U - per-user static route
       o - ODR, P - periodic downloaded static route

Gateway of last resort is 10.10.13.1 to network 0.0.0.0


     10.0.0.0/8 is variably subnetted, 5 subnets, 2 masks
C        10.10.13.0/29 is directly connected, Serial0/0/0.1
O        10.10.14.0/29 [110/657] via 10.10.34.4, 00:57:37, FastEthernet0/0
C        10.10.23.0/29 is directly connected, Serial0/0/0.2
O        10.10.24.0/29 [110/657] via 10.10.34.4, 00:57:37, FastEthernet0/0
C        10.10.34.0/24 is directly connected, FastEthernet0/0
O*IA     0.0.0.0/0 [110/501] via 10.10.13.1, 00:24:35, Serial0/0/0.1


R3#show ip ospf database database-summary


         OSPF Router with ID (3.3.3.3) (Process ID 3)
```

```
! lines omitted for brevity

Process 3 database summary
  LSA Type        Count    Delete    Maxage
  Router          4        0         0
  Network         1        0         0
  Summary Net     2        0         0
  Summary ASBR    0        0         0
  Type-7 Ext      0        0         0
  Opaque Link     0        0         0
  Opaque Area     0        0         0
  Type-5 Ext      0        0         0
      Prefixes redistributed in Type-5   0
  Opaque AS       0        0         0
  Non-self        6
  Total           7        0         0


R3#show ip ospf database ¦ begin Summary
              Summary Net Link States (Area 34)


Link ID        ADV Router       Age        Seq#         Checksum
0.0.0.0        1.1.1.1          1407       0x80000003   0x008FA8
0.0.0.0        2.2.2.2          1506       0x80000004   0x00FF3E
```

Following are the three commands in Example 7-8 in order:

- **show ip route**–It lists a single interarea route–a default route, with destination 0.0.0.0/0. The output also lists this same next-hop information as the gateway of last resort.

- **show ip ospf database database-summary**–The statistics still show no External Type 5 LSAs, just as when the area was stubby, but now shows only 2 Type 3 LSAs, whereas before a few dozen existed.

- **show ip ospf database | begin Summary**–This command shows the output beginning with the Type 3 Summary LSAs. It lists two default route LSAs: one from R1 and one from R2.

Examples 7-6 and 7-8 demonstrate the key differences between stub (they do see Type 3 LSAs) and totally stubby areas (which do not see Type 3 LSAs). Next, this section looks at the different types of not-so-stubby areas.

The Not-So-Stubby Area (NSSA)

Stub and totally stubby areas do not allow external routes to be injected into a stubby area–a feature that originally caused some problems. The problem is based on the fact that stub areas by definition should never learn a Type 5 LSA, and OSPF injects external routes into OSPF as Type 5 LSAs. These two facts together mean that a stubby area could not normally have an ASBR that was injecting external routes into the stub area.

The not-so-stubby area (NSSA) option for stubby areas overcomes the restriction on external routes. The solution itself is simple: Because stubby areas can have no Type 5 LSAs, later OSPF RFCs defined a newer LSA type (Type 7) that serves the same purpose as the Type 5 LSA, but only for external routes in stubby areas. So, an NSSA area can act just like a stub area, except that routers can inject external routes into the area.

Figure 7-10 shows an example, with four steps. The same stubby area 34 from the last few figures still exists; it does not matter at this point whether area 34 is totally stubby or simply stubby.

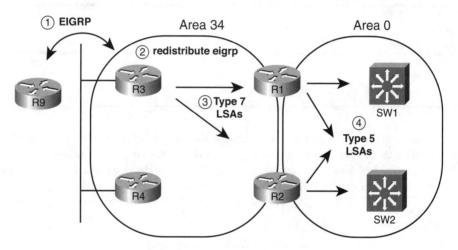

Figure 7-10   *External Routes in an NSSA Area (34)*

The steps labeled in the figure are as follows:

Step 1.   ASBR R3 learns routes from some external source of routing information, in this case, EIGRP from R9.

Step 2.   An engineer configures route redistribution using the **redistribute** command, taking the routes learned with EIGRP, and injecting them into OSPF.

Step 3.   R3 floods Type 7 LSAs throughout stub area 34.

Step 4.   ABRs R1 and R2 then create Type 5 LSAs for the subnets listed in the Type 7 LSAs, and flood these Type 5 LSAs into other areas, like area 0.

Configuring NSSA works much like the configuration of stubby areas. For totally NSSA areas, configure **area** *x* **nssa no-summary** instead of **area** *x* **stub no-summary**. For normal NSSA areas, as with stub areas, omit the **no-summary** keyword. Additionally, normal NSSA areas require that ABRs configure the **default-information-originate** keyword, making the command on ABRs **area** *x* **nssa default-information-orginate**.

Example 7-9 shows a sample with the configuration of a totally NSSA area 34 from the network represented in the last four figures. Note that as with the **area stub** command, the **area nssa** command's **no-summary** option is required only on the ABRs.

Example 7-9 *Totally NSSA Area Configuration and Verification*

```
! On Router R1:
router ospf 1
 area 34 nssa no-summary
! On Router R2:
router ospf 2
 area 34 nssa no-summary
 area 34 default-cost 500
! On Router R3:
router ospf 3
 area 34 nssa
! On Router R4:
router ospf 4
 area 34 nssa
```

The same verification steps and commands can be used for NSSA areas as were shown in the earlier examples for stub areas. In particular, the **show ip ospf** command states that the area is an NSSA area. You can also see Type 7 LSAs in the OSPF LSDB after redistribution has been configured, as shown in Chapter 9.

Stubby Area Summary

Table 7-4 summarizes the key points regarding stubby areas.

Key
Topic

Table 7-4 *OSPF Stubby Area Types*

Area Type	ABRs flood Type 5 External LSAs into the area?	ABRs flood Type 3 Summary LSAs into the area?	Allows redistribution of external LSAs into the stubby area?
Stub	No	Yes	No
Totally stubby	No	No	No
NSSA	No	Yes	Yes
Totally NSSA	No	No	Yes

Note: Both types of totally stubby areas (totally stubby, totally NSSA) are Cisco proprietary.

Exam Preparation Tasks

Planning Practice

The CCNP ROUTE exam expects test takers to review design documents, create implementation plans, and create verification plans. This section provides some exercises that may help you to take a step back from the minute details of the topics in this chapter so that you can think about the same technical topics from the planning perspective.

For each planning practice table, simply complete the table. Note that any numbers in parentheses represent the number of options listed for each item in the solutions in Appendix F, "Completed Planning Practice Tables."

Design Review Table

Table 7-5 lists several design goals related to this chapter. If these design goals were listed in a design document, and you had to take that document and develop an implementation plan, what implementation options come to mind? For any configuration items, a general description can be used, without concern about the specific parameters.

Table 7-5   *Design Review*

Design Goal	Possible Implementation Choices Covered in This Chapter
When using OSPF, prevent the routers in sites for one division of the company from knowing IP routes for subnets in another division. (3)	
The design shows an Enterprise that uses only OSPF. It lists a goal of keeping the LSDBs and routing tables in each area small. (3)	
The design lists a goal of extremely small LS-DBs and IP routing tables on branch office routers—which stub area types work best? (2)	
The design calls for the flooding of a domain-wide default route to draw traffic toward the Internet-connected routers.	

Implementation Plan Peer Review Table

Table 7-6 shows a list of questions that others might ask, or that you might think about, during a peer review of another network engineer's implementation plan. Complete the table by answering the questions.

Table 7-6 *Notable Questions from This Chapter to Consider During an Implementation Plan Peer Review*

Question	Answers
The plan shows a design with area 0, with different ABRs connecting area 0 to areas 1, 2, and 3. The configurations show Type 3 LSA filtering into the nonbackbone areas but not in the opposite direction. Could this configuration filter subnets in area 1 from being seen in area 2?	
The design shows the configuration of Type 3 LSA filtering on an internal router in area 1. Could the filter have any effect?	
The plan shows the configuration of the **area range** command on an ABR. What is the metric for the summary route? And in what conditions will the ABR advertise the summary?	
The plan shows the configuration of the **area 1 stub** command for an area mostly located on the west coast of the USA. The company just bought another company whose sites are also on the west coast. What issues exist if you add links from the acquired company into area 1?	
The plan shows the configuration of the **default-information originate always** command on the one router to which the Internet links connect. What happens to default route when Internet link fails? What happens to packets destined for the Internet during this time?	

Create an Implementation Plan Table

To practice skills useful when creating your own OSPF implementation plan, list in Table 7-7 configuration commands related to the configuration of the following features. You may want to record your answers outside the book, and set a goal to complete this table (and others like it) from memory during your final reviews before taking the exam.

Table 7-7 *Implementation Plan Configuration Memory Drill*

Feature	Configuration Commands/Notes
Filter Type 3 LSAs from being sent into an area.	
Filter the OSPF routes calculated on one router from being added to that one router's routing table.	
Configure route summarization on ABRs.	
Configure route summarization on ASBRs.	
Configure the OSPF domain-wide advertisement of a default route.	
Configure stubby or totally stubby areas.	
Configure NSSA or totally NSSA areas.	

Choose Commands for a Verification Plan Table

To practice skills useful when creating your own OSPF verification plan, list in Table 7-8 all commands that supply the requested information. You may want to record your answers outside the book, and set a goal to complete this table (and others like it) from memory during your final reviews before taking the exam.

Table 7-8 *Verification Plan Memory Drill*

Information Needed	Command(s)
Display all IP routes for subnets in a range, regardless of prefix length.	
Display the contents of an IP prefix list.	
Display details of all Type 3 LSAs known to a router.	
Display details of all Type 5 external LSAs known to a router.	
Display the metric advertised in a summary route created by the **area range** command.	
Display the metric advertised in a summary route created by the **summary-address** command.	
Discover whether a router resides in a stubby area, and if so, which kind.	
Confirm stubby area concepts by looking at the numbers of Type 3 and Type 5 LSAs known to a router.	

Note: Some of the entries in this table may not have been specifically mentioned in this chapter but are listed in this table for review and reference.

Review All the Key Topics

Review the most important topics from inside the chapter, noted with the key topics icon in the outer margin of the page. Table 7-9 lists a reference of these key topics and the page numbers on which each is found.

Key
Topic

Table 7-9 *Key Topics for Chapter 7*

Key Topic Element	Description	Page Number
List	Explanations of the features of the **area range** command	232
List	Explanations of the features of the **summary-address** command	235

Table 7-9   *Key Topics for Chapter 7*

Key Topic Element	Description	Page Number
Table 7-2	Syntax reference for OSPF route summarization commands	236
Table 7-3	Configuration options for stubby areas	241
Table 7-4	Feature summary for stubby areas	250

Complete the Tables and Lists from Memory

Print a copy of Appendix D, "Memory Tables," (found on the CD), or at least the section for this chapter, and complete the tables and lists from memory. Appendix E, "Memory Tables Answer Key," also on the CD, includes completed tables and lists to check your work.

Define Key Terms

Define the following key terms from this chapter, and check your answers in the glossary.

Type 3 LSA Filtering, Stub area, Totally stubby area, Not-so-stubby area, Type 5 External LSA

This chapter covers the following subjects:

Virtual Links: This section examines how engineers can use virtual links to connect separate parts of an area through another area to maintain the requirement that OSPF areas be contiguous.

OSPF over Frame Relay: This section examines the issues related to multipoint Frame Relay designs and configurations, in particular issues related to neighbor discovery or definition, whether the routers use a DR, and issues related to Frame Relay mapping.

CHAPTER 8

OSPF Virtual Links and Frame Relay Operations

This chapter contains two topics that at first glance seem to have little in common. The first topic, OSPF virtual links, gives network designers a tool to overcome an area design issue that occurs from time to time. The second topic, making OSPF work over Frame Relay multipoint interfaces, focuses on the implementation choices with different IOS commands when using OSPF with Frame Relay.

Although unrelated from a technology perspective, these two OSPF topics share that both provide a solution to specific types of problems–problems that occur in a small percentage of OSPF internetworks. Because these features solve particular (but different) problems, rather than include these topics in Chapters 5, 6, or 7–which cover the most central and common OSPF features–we decided to put these less-commonly seen features here in Chapter 8. Hopefully, this separation allowed a little more focus in the other OSPF chapters, while still including these two topics in the book.

"Do I Know This Already?" Quiz

The "Do I Know This Already?" quiz allows you to assess if you should read the entire chapter. If you miss no more than one of these five self-assessment questions, you might want to move ahead to the "Exam Preparation Tasks." Table 8-1 lists the major headings in this chapter and the "Do I Know This Already?" quiz questions covering the material in those headings so that you can assess your knowledge of these specific areas. The answers to the "Do I Know This Already?" quiz appear in Appendix A.

Table 8-1 *"Do I Know This Already?" Foundation Topics Section-to-Question Mapping*

Foundations Topics Section	Questions
Virtual Links	1, 2
OSPF over Frame Relay	3–5

1. Which of the following answers can be verified as true based on the following command output from Router R1?

```
R1#show ip ospf virtual-links
Virtual Link OSPF_VL0 to router 4.4.4.4 is up
  Run as demand circuit
  DoNotAge LSA allowed.
```

```
Transit area 1, via interface FastEthernet0/1, Cost of using 3
```

    a. R1 is configured with an **area 0 virtual-link 4.4.4.4 cost 3** command.

    b. The **ping 4.4.4.4** command on R1 must currently be successful.

    c. R1's Fa0/1 OSPF cost is 3.

    d. 4.4.4.4 is known to R1 based on a Type 1 LSA in area 1.

2. Several links have been broken so that for the next day or two, what was formerly a contiguous area 0 has been broken into two parts. However, both parts of area 0 have working links into area 1 using routers with RID 1.1.1.1 and 2.2.2.2. Which answers list the command on the router with RID 1.1.1.1 to create a virtual link to help solve this temporary problem?

    a. area 0 virtual-link 2.2.2.2

    b. area 1 virtual-link 2.2.2.2

    c. area 0 source-rid 1.1.1.1 dest-rid 2.2.2.2

    d. virtual-link transit-area 1 RID 2.2.2.2

3. Router R1 connects to a Frame Relay cloud using a multipoint subinterface, with ten PVCs associated with the subinterface. What command would make this router not use a DR and require static OSPF neighbor definition?

    a. ip ospf network broadcast

    b. ip ospf network non-broadcast

    c. ip ospf network point-to-multipoint

    d. ip ospf network point-to-multipoint non-broadcast

4. Router R1 connects to a Frame Relay cloud using a multipoint subinterface, with ten PVCs associated with the subinterface. What command would make this router not use a DR, and dynamically discover OSPF neighbors?

    a. ip ospf network broadcast

    b. ip ospf network non-broadcast

    c. ip ospf network point-to-multipoint

    d. ip ospf network point-to-multipoint non-broadcast

5. Ten routers, R1 through R10, connect in a partial mesh over Frame Relay. For the mesh, R1 and R2 have PVCs connected to all other routers, but Routers R3 through R10 act as branch routers, with only two PVCs–one to R1 and one to R2. The routers use IP subnet 10.1.1.0/24, with addresses 10.1.1.1, 10.1.1.2, and so on, through 10.1.1.10, respectively. The routers all use Inverse ARP to learn Frame Relay mapping information. All routers use a multipoint subinterface with network type point-to-multipoint nonbroadcast. A co-worker's implementation plan lists lots of configuration commands related to this design. The design states that all hosts should be able to ping all other hosts. Which commands are required for proper functioning of OSPF in this case? (Choose two.)

    a. **frame-relay map** commands on R3–R10 referencing the other routers in this group.

    b. Nine OSPF **neighbor** commands on each router.

    c. Nine OSPF **neighbor** commands on R1 and R2, with only two such commands on R3–R10.

    d. R1 and R2 with **ip ospf priority 1** commands to ensure they become DR and BDR.

    e. R3–R10 with **ip ospf priority 0** commands to ensure they do not become DR or BDR.

Foundation Topics

Virtual Links

OSPF area design requires the use of a backbone area, area 0, with each area connecting to area 0 through an ABR. However, in some cases two backbone areas exist; in other cases, a nonbackbone area may not have a convenient point of connection to the backbone area, for example:

Case 1.   An existing internetwork needs to add a new area, with a convenient, low-cost connection point with another nonbackbone area. However, that connection does not give the new area any connection to area 0.

Case 2.   Even with a well-designed area 0, a combination of link failures might result in a discontiguous backbone area, essentially creating two backbone areas.

Case 3.   Two companies could merge, each using OSPF. To merge the OSPF domains, one backbone area must exist. It may be more convenient to connect the two networks using links through an existing nonbackbone area, but that design means two backbone areas, which is not allowed.

Figure 8-1 shows an example of each of the first two cases.

The problems in each case have different symptoms, but the problems all stem from the area design requirements: Each area should be contiguous, and each nonbackbone area should connect to the backbone area through an ABR. When the network does not meet these requirements, engineers could simply redesign the areas. However, OSPF provides an alternative tool called an OSPF virtual link.

Understanding OSPF Virtual Link Concepts

An OSPF virtual link allows two ABRs that connect to the same nonbackbone area to form a neighbor relationship through that nonbackbone area, even when separated by many other routers and subnets. This virtual link acts like a virtual point-to-point connection between the two routers, with that link inside area 0. The routers form a neighbor relationship, inside area 0, and flood LSAs over that link.

For example, consider the topology in Figure 8-2, which shows an example of the third of the three cases described in the beginning of this section. In this case, two companies merged. Both companies had a small office in the same city, so for expediency's sake, they connected the two former Enterprise internetworks through a newly combined local sales office in area 1.

Although adding the link between branch offices may be a cost-effective temporary choice, it creates a design problem: Two backbone areas now exist, and OSPF requires that the backbone area be contiguous. To solve this problem, the engineer configures a virtual link between ABRs C1 and C2. The virtual link exists inside area 0, making area 0 contiguous.

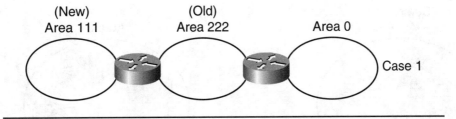

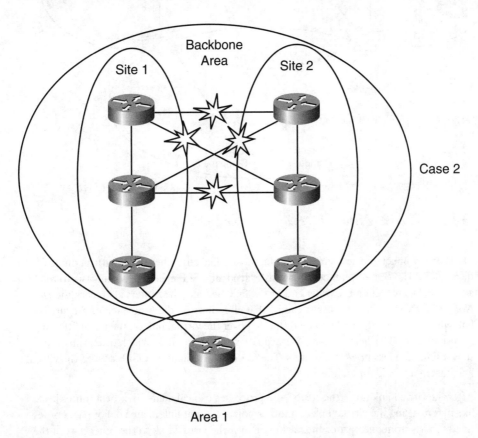

Figure 8-1 *Examples of Area Design Issues*

To define the virtual link, each router configures the other router's RID and a reference to the area through which the virtual link passes (area 1 in this case). The two routers send the usual OSPF message types, encapsulated inside unicast IP packets, with a destination IP address of the router on the other end of the virtual link. Any routers between the two routers that create the virtual link—for instance, the two branch routers in Figure 8-2— just forward these OSPF packets like any other packet. The neighbors on the ends of the virtual link flood their LSDBs to each other so that all routers in both parts of area 0 learn the routes from the other area 0.

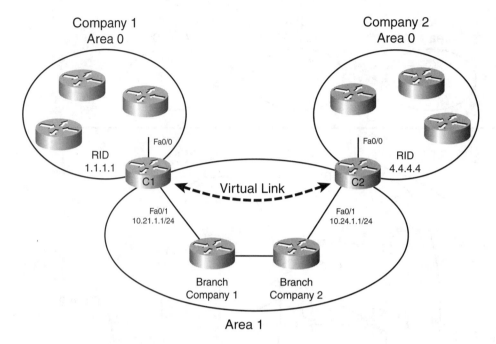

Figure 8-2 *Connecting Two Area 0s with a Virtual Link*

The ABRs connected over a virtual link act mostly like any other ABR, with a couple of differences. The first difference is that ABRs send all OSPF messages as unicasts to the IP address of the router on the other end of the link. Second, the routers also mark the *Do Not Age (DNA)* bit in the LSAs, meaning that all routers on the other side of the virtual link will not expect the LSAs to be reflooded over the virtual link on the usual 30-minute refresh interval. This helps reduce overhead over the virtual link, which often runs over slower links and less-powerful routers. The router also assigns an OSPF cost to the virtual link, just as it would for an interface.

After the virtual link is up, the ABRs' SPF processes can calculate their best routes just like before, using the virtual link as another point-to-point link in area 0. For packets destined to pass from one part of the backbone over the virtual link to the other part of the backbone, the chosen best routes eventually lead the packets to the router with the virtual link. That router, connected to the transit nonbackbone area, has already calculated its next hop based on the LSDB in the transit area (Router C1 and transit area 1 in the example of Figure 8-2). The routers in the transit area choose routes that eventually deliver the packet to the router on the other end of the virtual link (Router C2 in Figure 8-2).

Configuring OSPF Virtual Links with No Authentication

Configuring an OSPF virtual link requires a minor amount of configuration just to get the link working, with several optional configuration items. Most of the optional configuration settings relate to features that would normally be configured on the interface connecting two neighboring routers, but with a virtual link, there is no such interface, so the parameters must be added to the **area virtual-link** command. The following list summarizes the key configuration options on the **area virtual-link** router subcommand:

- The *remote-RID* in the **area** *area-num* **virtual-link** *remote-RID* command refers to the other router's RID.

- The *area-num* in the **area** *area-num* **virtual-link** *remote-RID* command refers to the transit area over which the packets flow between the two routers.

- The transit area over which the two routers communicate must not be a stubby area.

- The optional configuration of OSPF neighbor authentication parameters, normally configured as interface subcommands, must be configured as additional parameters on the **area virtual-link** command.

- The optional configuration of Hello and Dead intervals, normally configured as interface subcommands, must be configured as additional parameters on the **area virtual-link** command.

- The router assigns the virtual link an OSPF cost as if it were a point-to-point link. The router calculates the cost as the cost to reach the router on the other end of the link, as calculated using the transit area's LSDB.

Example 8-1 shows the configuration of a virtual link on Router C1 and Router C2 shown in Figure 8-2. The configuration shows the virtual link, referencing area 1 as the transit area, with each router referring to the other router's RIDs. The configuration also shows the loopback IP addresses on which the ABR's RIDs are based being advertised into OSPF.

Example 8-1 *OSPF Virtual Link Configuration on Routers C1 and C2*

```
! On Router C1:
router ospf 1
 area 1 virtual-link 4.4.4.4
!
interface fastethernet0/0
 ip address 10.1.1.1 255.255.255.0
 ip ospf 1 area 0
!
interface fastethernet0/1
 ip address 10.21.1.1 255.255.255.0
 ip ospf 1 area 1
!
interface loopback 1
 ip address 1.1.1.1 255.255.255.0
 ip ospf 1 area 1

! On Router C2:
router ospf 4
 area 1 virtual-link 1.1.1.1
```

```
!
interface fastethernet0/0
 ip address 10.4.4.4 255.255.255.0
 ip ospf 4 area 0
!
interface fastethernet0/1
 ip address 10.24.1.1 255.255.255.0
 ip ospf 4 area 1
!
interface loopback 1
 ip address 4.4.4.4 255.255.255.0
 ip ospf 4 area 1
```

Verifying the OSPF Virtual Link

To prove whether the virtual link works, a neighbor relationship between C1 and C2 must reach FULL state, resulting in all routers in both parts of area 0 having the same area 0 LSDB. Example 8-2 shows the working neighbor relationship, plus status information for the virtual link with the **show ip ospf virtual-link** command.

Example 8-2 *OSPF Virtual Link Configuration on Routers C1 and C2*

```
C1#show ip ospf virtual-links
Virtual Link OSPF_VL0 to router 4.4.4.4 is up
  Run as demand circuit
  DoNotAge LSA allowed.
  Transit area 1, via interface FastEthernet0/1, Cost of using 3
  Transmit Delay is 1 sec, State POINT_TO_POINT,
  Timer intervals configured, Hello 10, Dead 40, Wait 40, Retransmit 5
    Hello due in 00:00:02
    Adjacency State FULL (Hello suppressed)
    Index 1/2, retransmission queue length 0, number of retransmission 0
    First 0x0(0)/0x0(0) Next 0x0(0)/0x0(0)
    Last retransmission scan length is 0, maximum is 0
    Last retransmission scan time is 0 msec, maximum is 0 msec
!
! next, note that the neighbor reaches FULL state, with no DR elected.

C1#show ip ospf neighbor

Neighbor ID     Pri   State         Dead Time   Address      Interface
4.4.4.4          0    FULL/  -          -        10.24.1.1    OSPF_VL0
2.2.2.2          1    FULL/DR     00:00:35      10.21.1.2    FastEthernet0/1
```

```
C1#show ip ospf neighbor detail 4.4.4.4
 Neighbor 4.4.4.4, interface address 10.24.1.1
    In the area 0 via interface OSPF_VL0
    Neighbor priority is 0, State is FULL, 6 state changes
    DR is 0.0.0.0 BDR is 0.0.0.0
    Options is 0x32 in Hello (E-bit, L-bit, DC-bit)
    Options is 0x72 in DBD (E-bit, L-bit, DC-bit, O-bit)
    LLS Options is 0x1 (LR)
    Neighbor is up for 00:00:21
    Index 1/2, retransmission queue length 0, number of retransmission 0
    First 0x0(0)/0x0(0) Next 0x0(0)/0x0(0)
    Last retransmission scan length is 0, maximum is 0
   Last retransmission scan time is 0 msec, maximum is 0 msec
```

The only new command in the example, **show ip ospf virtual-links**, details some items unique to virtual links. In particular, the first highlighted portion shows the assignment of a name to the link (VL0); if multiple were configured, each would have a different number. This virtual link name/number is then referenced inside the LSDB. It also shows that the routers both allow the use of the Do Not Age (DNA) bit, so periodic reflooding will not occur over this virtual link. It lists a cost of 3; as it turns out, each of the three interfaces between Router C1 and C2 have an OSPF cost of 1, so C1's area 1 cost to reach C2 is 3. The output also confirms that the routers have reached a fully adjacent state and is suppressing the periodic Hello messages.

The familiar **show ip ospf neighbor** command lists a few new items as well. Note that the interface refers to the virtual link "OSPF VL0" instead of the interface, because there is no interface between the neighbors. It also lists no dead timer, because the neighbors choose to not use the usual Hello/Dead interval process over a virtual link. (Instead, if all the transit area's routes to reach the router on the other router of the link fail, the virtual link fails.) Finally, the **show ip ospf neighbor detail 4.4.4.4** command shows the interesting phrase "In the area 0 via interface OSPF VL0," confirming that the neighborship does indeed exist in area 0.

Note: OSPF does not require that the RID IP address range be advertised as a route in OSPF. As a result, the RID listed in the **area virtual-link** command may not be pingable, but the virtual link still works.

Configuring Virtual Link Authentication

Because virtual links have no underlying interface on which to configure authentication, authentication is configured on the **area virtual-link** command itself. Table 8-2 shows the variations of the command options for configuring authentication on virtual links. Note that the configuration shown in Table 8-2 may be typed in one longer **area virtual-link** command, as shown in the table, or the authentication type and key can be configured on separate **area virtual-link** commands. Regardless, IOS stores two different **area virtual-link** commands into the running-config: one command that enables the type of authentication, and one that lists the authentication key, as shown in upcoming Example 8-3.

Table 8-2 *Configuring OSPF Authentication on Virtual Links*

Type (Name)	Type (Number)	Command Syntax for Virtual Links
none	0	**area** *num* **virtual-link** *router-id* **authentication null**
clear text	1	**area** *num* **virtual-link** *router-id* **authentication authentication-key** *key-value*
MD5	2	**area** *num* **virtual-link** *router-id* **authentication message-digest message-digest-key** *key-num* **md5** *key-value*

Example 8-3 shows a modified version of the configuration shown in Example 8-2, now with MD5 authentication configured on both C1 and C2.

Example 8-3 *OSPF Virtual Link Configuration on Routers C1 and C2*

```
! On Router C1 - configuring the authentication type and key
router ospf 1
  area 1 virtual-link 4.4.4.4 authentication message-digest message-digest-key 1
md5 fred
! On Router C2 - configuring the authentication type and key
router ospf 4
  area 1 virtual-link 1.1.1.1 authentication message-digest message-digest-key 1
md5 fred
!
! The router separated the authentication type and authentication key
! into two separate commands.
C2#show running-config
! line omitted for brevity
router ospf 4
  area 1 virtual-link 1.1.1.1 authentication message-digest
  area 1 virtual-link 1.1.1.1 message-digest-key 1 md5 fred

C2#show ip ospf virtual-links
Virtual Link OSPF_VL0 to router 1.1.1.1 is up
! lines omitted for brevity
  Message digest authentication enabled
    Youngest key id is 1
```

This concludes the discussion of OSPF virtual links. As mentioned in the introduction of this chapter, the chapter now changes focus completely to discuss OSPF issues when using Frame Relay.

OSPF over Multipoint Frame Relay

To form OSPF neighbor relationships on LANs and point-to-point WAN interfaces, OSPF simply needs to be enabled on the interface, and the neighboring routers must agree to a set of parameters (as summarized in Chapter 5, Table 5-5.) However, when using Frame Relay in certain configurations, engineers must do more implementation planning and use additional configuration commands to make OSPF work. Additionally, the people monitoring and operating the network must also understand several differences in how OSPF works in such cases and be ready to interpret the output of **show** commands.

The issues described in this section of the chapter arise when the IP subnetting and Frame Relay design places more than two WAN routers into a single subnet. Such a design requires multipoint logic, either configured on the physical serial interface or on a multipoint subinterface.

This section begins by reviewing the IP subnetting design issues that can lead to the broader OSPF issues over Frame Relay. Next, this section examines the issues of running OSPF over Frame Relay, concentrating on the concepts. This final part of this section ends with several OSPF configuration examples using multipoint Frame Relay.

IP Subnetting Design over Frame Relay

When planning the subnets to use over a Frame Relay WAN, the design engineer has several options. The simplest and most obvious choice uses a single subnet for every PVC (as seen throughout the examples in Chapters 5, 6, and 7), with all routers using point-to-point subinterfaces associated with each single PVC. Most companies who still use Frame Relay today still use such a subnetting design.

In some cases, a shortage of IP addresses may make a design engineer choose to use fewer WAN subnets, with less waste. Many companies use private IP addresses inside their Enterprise internetwork–often times specifically class A network 10.0.0.0–and most companies do not have a shortage of IP addresses and subnets available. However, using one subnet per PVC does consume more IP addresses than the alternative–to put more than two routers into a Frame Relay WAN subnet. You get the advantage of fewer IP addresses consumed in the WAN but the penalty of more configuration and complexity with the OSPF implementation.

For example, consider the two internetworks shown in Figure 8-3. On the left, four routers connect in a full mesh of PVCs, whereas on the right, the four routers use a partial mesh. In each case, assume each router uses their s0/0/0 interface to connect to the cloud.

First, consider the differences in IP addressing for the one-subnet-per-PVC choice and the single-subnet choice. The single-subnet design could use just one subnet–for instance, subnet 10.1.1.0/29, with usable address 10.1.1.1–10.1.1.6 (subnet broadcast 10.1.1.7). With four routers, the subnet contains enough IP addresses for each router, plus two additional addresses. Conversely, with a single-subnet-per-PVC, the design would require six subnets,

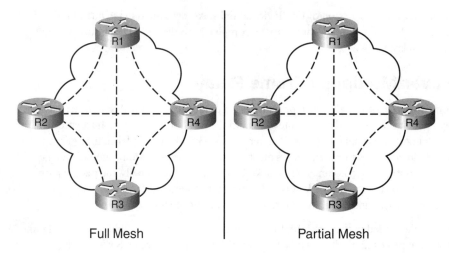

Full Mesh   Partial Mesh

Figure 8-3   *Sample Full and Partial Mesh Frame Relay*

each of which consumes four numbers: subnet number, two usable IP addresses, and a subnet broadcast address. For example, the design could use subnets 10.1.1.0/30, 10.1.1.4/30, 10.1.1.8/30, 10.1.1.12/30, 10.1.1.16/30, and 10.1.1.20.0/30 for a range of consumed numbers of 10.1.1.0–10.1.1.23.

Sample Configuration Using Physical Interfaces

Ignoring OSPF for now, to implement such a design on the internetwork shown in Figure 8-3, a somewhat short configuration could be used on each router. Example 8-4 shows the configuration, with the IP addresses being defined on the physical serial interfaces on each router.

Example 8-4   *OSPF over Point-to-Point Frame Relay Subinterfaces*

```
! Router R1
interface S0/0/0
 encapsulation frame-relay
 ip address 10.2.123.1 255.255.255.248
! Router R2
interface S0/0/0
 encapsulation frame-relay
 ip address 10.2.123.2 255.255.255.248
! Router R3
interface S0/0/0
 encapsulation frame-relay
 ip address 10.2.123.3 255.255.255.248
! Router R4
interface S0/0/0
 encapsulation frame-relay
 ip address 10.2.123.4 255.255.255.248
```

This brief configuration works in part because of many default settings. IOS enables Frame Relay Inverse ARP (InARP) by default, so all four routers learn of the other routers' IP address/DLCI mappings dynamically. All PVCs learned on the interface will be associated with the physical interface.

As a result, after creating this configuration, with a working Frame Relay network, the four routers can **ping** each other in every case for which a PVC exists between the two routers. In other words, in the full mesh case, all four routers should ping the other three routers' IP addresses in the 10.2.123.0/29 subnet. In the partial mesh case, the R2/R3 pair cannot ping each other.

The ping problem between R2 and R3 demonstrates some key concepts related to how Frame Relay mapping works. InARP allows the routers to learn the IP address of any router on the other end of a PVC, but R2/R3 do not have a PVC connecting them in the partial mesh side of Figure 8-3, so InARP does not learn the mapping. Then, when R2 (10.2.123.2) wants to send a packet to 10.2.123.3 (R3), R2 looks at its Frame Relay mapping information and does not find 10.2.123.3. As a result, R2 discards the packet because it does not know what DLCI to use to forward the packet.

Sample Configuration Using Multipoint Subinterfaces

The same effects occur with a valid alternate configuration using a multipoint subinterface, both in the full and partial mesh cases. When using subinterfaces, IOS needs a command under a Frame Relay subinterface that associates each PVC with that subinterface: either a **frame-relay interface-dlci** command or **frame-relay map** command. The **frame-relay interface-dlci** command just associates the DLCI with the subinterface, relying on Frame Relay InARP to discover mappings. The second command (**frame-relay map**) statically configures that mapping, while also associating the DLCI with the subinterface.

Example 8-5 shows an alternative configuration on Router R1, using a multipoint subinterface. All four routers could mimic the same configuration, but that configuration is not shown in the example.

Example 8-5 *OSPF over Multipoint Frame Relay Subinterfaces*

```
! Router R1
interface S0/0/0
 encapsulation frame-relay
!
interface S0/0/0.1 multipoint
 ip address 10.1.123.1 255.255.255.248
 frame-relay interface-dlci 102
 frame-relay interface-dlci 103
 frame-relay interface-dlci 104
```

This configuration on R1, with similar configuration on the other three routers, has the same results as those with Example 8-4. When a full mesh exists, all routers should be pingable. With a partial mesh, all routers should be pingable, except those with no PVC between the two routers (R2/R3 in this case).

With those background details in mind, the chapter now examines the challenges that arise when trying to use multipoint.

OSPF Challenges When Using Multipoint

Next, consider OSPF over both the full and partial meshes as described in the last few pages. As it turns out, if you enabled OSPF on the interfaces, but do not add OSPF configuration, OSPF does not form neighborships in either case.

> **Note:**   Rather than repeat the long phrase "on physical interfaces or on multipoint interfaces" many times in the coming pages, the rest of this chapter simply refers to both as "multipoint interfaces," because more than one destination may be reachable through these types of interfaces.

The default OSPF network type on multipoint interfaces–the nonbroadcast network type–prevents OSPF from working without further configuration. Additionally, depending on the configuration you add to make OSPF work, the network may appear to be working in that the correct routes are learned, but packets cannot be forwarded. Worse yet, packet forwarding could work when testing, but later, when the DR in that subnet failed, packet forwarding could fail, even though paths exist over different PVCs.

To avoid such pitfalls, this section examines the issues. To understand the issues, an engineer needs to know the answer to three questions related to OSPF over Frame Relay multipoint interfaces:

- Do the routers attempt to discover neighbors by sending and receiving multicast OSPF Hello messages, or do the neighbors require static definition?

- Do the routers attempt to elect a DR/BDR?

- Does a partial mesh exist or full mesh?

The next few pages examine these topics one at a time.

Neighbor Discovery or Static Neighbor Definition

The OSPF network type–a per-interface setting–defines whether a router attempts to discover OSPF neighbors on an interface. When the router attempts discovery, it sends multicast (224.0.0.5) OSPF Hello messages out the interface.

The first potential problem occurs when a Frame Relay configuration oversight causes the dynamic OSPF neighbor discovery process to fail. When a router needs to send a broadcast or multicast over Frame Relay, the router must actually send a copy of the packet over each PVC instead, because the Frame Relay network does not have the ability to replicate the broadcast or multicast packet. Routers do send the multicast OSPF Hellos for any PVCs listed in **frame-relay interface-dlci** commands, and for any DLCIs listed in **frame-relay map** commands if the **broadcast** keyword was included. However, if the **frame-relay map** command omits the **broadcast** keyword, that router will not replicate the OSPF multicasts, or any other broadcast or multicast frames for that DLCI.

Alternatively, some OSPF network types tell a router to not attempt automatic discovery of neighbors. In such a case, the router should be configured with the **neighbor** *ip-address* OSPF router subcommand. This command overcomes the issue with neighbor discovery.

The actions to take for the issues related to neighbor discover are somewhat straightforward:

■   If the configured network type allows for neighbor discovery using Hellos, and you use InARP, the neighbors should be discovered.

■   If the configured network type allows for neighbor discovery, and you use **frame-relay map**, ensure that the **broadcast** keyword is included.

■   If the configured network type does not allow for neighbor discovery, statically configure neighbors.

The upcoming samples show cases of using network types that dynamically discover neighbors and cases that show static definition of neighbors.

To Use a Designated Router, or Not

IOS has several available OSPF network types for Frame Relay, some of which tell the router to try to elect a DR/BDR. The reasoning is that when choosing a subnet design like those shown in Figure 8-3, with a single subnet that includes more than two Frame Relay routers, the design looks like a LAN from a Layer 3 perspective. Other options for OSPF network types tell the routers to not elect a DR/BDR.

A potential issue exists when using a DR over Frame Relay. The issue relates to whether the Frame Relay partial mesh includes the right PVCs to support the OSPF messages that flow in the presence of a DR/BDR. As you may recall from Chapter 6, "OSPF Topology, Routes, and Convergence," when a DR exists, all OSPF routers must send and receive OSPF messages with the DR, with messages to the DR being sent to the 224.0.0.6 all-DR's multicast address. Additionally, the DR sends messages to the 224.0.0.5 all-SPF router's multicast address, with these messages intended for all OSPF routers in the subnet. For the same reason, all routers should send and receive messages with the BDR, in case it takes over for the DR. However, two DROther routers do not need to send each other OSPF messages.

For a Frame Relay partial mesh to work when also using an OSPF DR, a PVC must exist between any two routers that need to perform database exchange directly with each other. In short, the following PVCs must exist:

■   Between the DR and every other router in the subnet

■   Between the BDR and every other router in the subnet

For example, consider the partial mesh shown in Figure 8-4, which mirrors the partial mesh seen on the right side of Figure 8-3. In this case, R1 acts as DR, and R2 as BDR. OSPF actually works fine in this design, until the fated day when R1's serial link fails. When it fails, R2 takes over as DR, but R3 has no way to send and receive OSPF messages with R2. As a result, R3 will no longer learn routes that pass over the WAN.

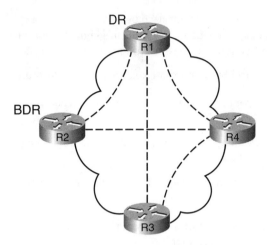

Figure 8-4   *Poor Choices of BDR in a Partial Mesh*

To deal with this particular issue with a partial mesh, either avoid using a DR at all by changing the OSPF network type on all routers in the subnet, or restrict the role of DR/BDR to routers with PVCs connected to all other routers in a subnet. For example, R1 and R4 in Figure 8-4 have three PVCs, one each to the other three routers. By configuring the routers so that R2 and R3 refuse to become DR or BDR, you can avoid the case of a poor choice of DR/BDR.

Summarizing the key points about the issues in this section:

Key Topic

- If using a network type that requires a DR/BDR, restrict the role of DR and BDR to routers that have a PVC connecting to all other routers.

- Configure the OSPF network type to avoid using a DR/BDR.

Mapping Issues with a Partial Mesh

The last issue with OSPF over multipoint Frame Relay topologies relates to the Layer 2 mapping, either created by InARP or statically configured with **frame-relay map** commands. This mapping on a router lists each neighbor's IP address, and that router's DLCI used to reach that router. InARP learns this mapping for each router on the other end of a PVC, but not for other routers where no PVC exists. For example, in Figure 8-4, R2 and R3 would not learn mapping for each other with InARP. Similarly, when configuring the **frame-relay map** command, many engineers think only of statically creating mappings for neighboring routers on the other end of each PVC. In short, the mapping in both cases matches the partial mesh.

OSPF multipoint interfaces have problems when the Frame Relay mapping matches the partial mesh but does not include mapping to every other router in the subnet–even those routers where no PVC exists. The best way to describe the problem is to start with an example, as seen in Figure 8-5. The figure shows the same old partial mesh, with some IP addresses and DLCIs shown.

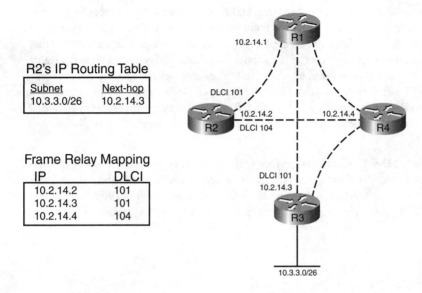

Figure 8-5 *Frame Relay Mapping Issues*

When OSPF works over this Frame Relay WAN, the next-hop address of the learned routes will list the IP address of a router in that WAN subnet–*even if no PVC connects to that next-hop router*. In this case, R2's route for 10.3.3.0/26 lists R3, 10.2.14.3, as next hop. When R2 attempts to add a Frame Relay header to the packet, and assign a DLCI, R2 must have a mapping between that next-hop address (10.2.14.3) and the DLCI to use to reach that next hop. However, no such Frame Relay mapping exists on R2, because R2 was relying on InARP–and InARP works only directly over a PVC and not indirectly.

To solve the problem, R2 needs a mapping for next hop 10.2.14.3 to use a DLCI to another router, allowing that other router to use IP routing to forward the packet to R3. For example, R2 could use DLCI 101, the PVC connecting R2 to R1. By doing so, R2 will encapsulate forwarded packets inside a frame with DLCI 101, sending the packet to R1. R1 will then use IP routing to forward the packet on to R3. Similarly, R3 could use a command that statically mapped 10.2.14.2, R2's IP address, to DLCI 101, which is R3's DLCI used for its PVC to R1.

Summarizing the issue and the solution to this problem:

> For any routers without a direct PVC, statically configure a IP-address-to-DLCI mapping with the other router's next-hop IP address, and a DLCI that does connect to a router that has PVCs with each of the two routers

Key
Topic

Configuring and Verifying OSPF Operations on Frame Relay

The concepts related to the issues of running OSPF over Frame Relay can require a bit of thought about things that many of us can ignore when working with a typical OSPF network. Thankfully, the implementation choices are a little more straightforward. When the design dictates more than two routers per subnet over Frame Relay, you need to configure Frame Relay to use either physical interfaces or multipoint subinterfaces. In those cases, only four OSPF network types exist. Then, the choice of OSPF network type answers two big questions: Will the routers try and elect a DR, and will they try to discover neighbors? From there, the rest of the implementation plan flows from the issues already discussed in this chapter.

For reference, Table 8-3 summarizes the four OSPF network types available on serial interfaces that use Frame Relay, either the physical interface or a multipoint subinterface. Note that the setting is per interface and can be set with the **ip ospf network** *type* interface subcommand; the first column in the table lists the exact keyword according to this command.

Key Topic

Table 8-3 *OSPF Network Types*

Interface Type	Uses DR/BDR?	Dynamic Discovery of Neighbors?	Default Hello Interval	Cisco Proprietary?
broadcast	Yes	Yes	10	Yes
nonbroadcast	Yes	No	30	No
point-to-multipoint	No	Yes	30	No
point-to-multipoint nonbroadcast	No	No	30	Yes

All the upcoming examples use the same network diagram as shown in Figure 8-6. After the figure, the text moves on to the examples showing this internetwork configured with three options for network type on Frame Relay serial and multipoint subinterfaces: nonbroadcast, point-to-multipoint, and point-to-multipoint nonbroadcast. (This chapter does not include a sample of using network type broadcast, because the LAN-based examples in Chapter 5 all use a default of network type broadcast.)

Note: The following samples all use multipoint subinterfaces. Also, for each example, all four routers use the same OSPF network type. However, note that IOS has no mechanism to prevent routers from using different interface types or different OSPF network types, but such inconsistency can cause problems and be very difficult to operate. Configurations that mix OSPF network types in the same subnet are outside the scope of this book.

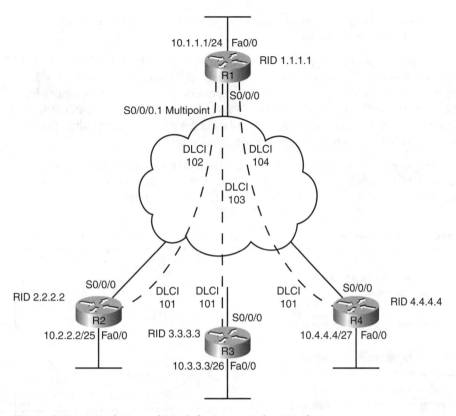

Figure 8-6 *Sample Partial Mesh for Frame Relay Configuration*

Using Network Type Nonbroadcast (NBMA)

By using the (default) network type setting of nonbroadcast, all four routers will elect a DR and BDR. They also will not attempt to multicast Hellos to discover each other, so they need to configure each other in an OSPF **neighbor** command, as follows:

```
neighbor next-hop-IP [cost cost-value]|[priority priority-value]
```

To statically configure an OSPF neighbor, simply use the **neighbor** command in OSPF configuration mode, one command per neighbor. The command references the IP address of the neighbor, specifically the IP address in the subnet to which both the local and neighboring router connect. Also, OSPF requires only this command for two routers connected to the same PVC; routers not connected with a PVC cannot become OSPF neighbors, so no **neighbor** command is required. So, in the design shown in Figure 8-6, router pairs R2-R3, R3-R4, and R2-R4 will not define each other as neighbors with the **neighbor** command.

Next, consider the issue of election of a DR/BDR. The section "To Use a Designated Router, or Not" earlier in this chapter discussed that if a DR is indeed elected, you need to restrict routers so that only routers with PVCs to all other routers are allowed to become DR or BDR. In Figure 8-6, only R1 meets the requirement, so the configuration must limit only R1 to become the DR and simply not use a BDR. (Given the design, a failure of R1 would prevent any further communication on the WAN anyway, so the lack of a BDR does not make the problem worse.)

The OSPF priority defines the priority when choosing a DR and BDR. Configured with the **ip ospf priority** *value* interface subcommand, the higher number (ranges from 0–255) wins. Also, a priority of 0 has special meaning: it prevents that router from becoming the DR or BDR. By configuring OSPF priority of 0 on routers that do not have a PVC connected to each other router (such as R2, R3, and R4 in this case), the other routers (R1 in this case) will be the only routers eligible to become the DR.

Example 8-6 begins by showing the required configuration, defining neighbors and setting the OSPF priority on R2, R3, and R4 to 0. The example shows just R1 and R2; R3's and R4's configuration mirror R2's, other than the IP address settings.

Example 8-6 *OSPF over Multipoint Frame Relay Subinterfaces–Default Configuration*

```
! First, R1's configuration
R1#show running-config int s0/0/0.1
Building configuration...

Current configuration : 169 bytes
!
interface Serial0/0/0.1 multipoint
 ip address 10.2.123.1 255.255.255.248
 frame-relay interface-dlci 102
 frame-relay interface-dlci 103
 frame-relay interface-dlci 104
end


R1#show running-config | begin router ospf
router ospf 1
 network 10.0.0.0 0.255.255.255 area 0
 router-id 1.1.1.1
 neighbor 10.2.123.2
 neighbor 10.2.123.3
 neighbor 10.2.123.4
! Next, R2's configuration
R2#show running-config interface s0/0/0.1
Building configuration...

Current configuration : 113 bytes
!
interface Serial0/0/0.1 multipoint
 ip address 10.2.123.2 255.255.255.248
 frame-relay interface-dlci 101
 ip ospf priority 0
end
```

```
R2#show running-config | begin router ospf
router ospf 2
 network 10.0.0.0 0.255.255.255 area 0
 router-id 2.2.2.2
 neighbor 10.2.123.1

R2#show ip ospf interface s0/0/0.1
Serial0/0/0.1 is up, line protocol is up
  Internet Address 10.2.123.2/29, Area 0
  Process ID 2, Router ID 2.2.2.2, Network Type NON_BROADCAST, Cost: 64
  Transmit Delay is 1 sec, State DROTHER, Priority 0
  Designated Router (ID) 1.1.1.1, Interface address 10.2.123.1
  No backup designated router on this network
  Timer intervals configured, Hello 30, Dead 120, Wait 120, Retransmit 5
```

Example 8-6 shows the configuration of three neighbors on router R1 (R2, R3, and R4), plus one neighbor on R2 (R1). It does not show the explicit configuration of the OSPF network type because each router uses the default for multipoint subinterfaces of non-broadcast. However, the **show ip ospf interface** command at the end of the output confirms the network type on the multipoint subinterface of R2.

The priority configuration results in R1 becoming DR, and none of the other routers being willing to even become BDR. R1 omits an **ip ospf priority** command, defaulting to 1, while R2 shows an **ip ospf priority 0** command, removing itself from consideration as DR or BDR. The output at the bottom of the page again confirms the result on R2, with its own priority of 0, the result of RID 1.1.1.1 (R1) as DR, but with no BDR elected.

Note: You can also attempt to configure a neighboring router's OSPF priority with the **neighbor** *address* **priority** *priority-value* command.

Although the configuration shown in Example 8-6 takes care of the particulars of defining neighbors and of influencing the choice of DR/BDR, it does not, however, include the configuration for the Frame Relay mapping issue with a partial mesh. All four routers need mapping to the other three router's IP addresses in their common Frame Relay subnet. In this particular case, R1 learns all the mappings with InARP, because it has a PVC connected to all the other routers. However, R2, R3, and R4 have learned all OSPF routes but cannot forward traffic to each other because they have not learned the mappings.

Example 8-7 shows the background regarding this issue, along with an example solution on R2 using **frame-relay map** commands. Note that comments inside the example show the progression of proof and changes to solve the problem.

Example 8-7   *The Need for* `frame-relay map` *Commands*

```
! First, R2 has routes for the LAN subnets off R1, R3, and R4, each referring
! to their respective routers as the next-hop IP address
R2#show ip route ospf
     10.0.0.0/8 is variably subnetted, 5 subnets, 5 masks
O       10.4.4.0/27 [110/65] via 10.2.123.4, 00:03:52, Serial0/0/0.1
O       10.3.3.0/26 [110/65] via 10.2.123.3, 00:06:02, Serial0/0/0.1
O       10.1.1.0/24 [110/65] via 10.2.123.1, 00:06:12, Serial0/0/0.1


! Next, R2 successfully pings R1's LAN IP address

R2#ping 10.1.1.1

Type escape sequence to abort.
Sending 5, 100-byte ICMP Echos to 10.1.1.1, timeout is 2 seconds:
!!!!!
Success rate is 100 percent (5/5), round-trip min/avg/max = 4/4/4 ms

! Next, R2 fails when pinging R3's LAN IP address

R2#ping 10.3.3.3

Type escape sequence to abort.
Sending 5, 100-byte ICMP Echos to 10.3.3.3, timeout is 2 seconds:
.....
Success rate is 0 percent (0/5)


! R2 has mapping only for 10.2.123.1 in the Frame Relay subnet
R2#show frame-relay map
Serial0/0/0.1 (up): ip 10.2.123.1 dlci 101(0x65,0x1850), dynamic,
              broadcast,
              CISCO, status defined, active


! Next, the engineer adds the mapping for R3 and R4, with DLCI 101 as the
! PVC, which connects to R1


R2#configure terminal
Enter configuration commands, one per line.  End with CNTL/Z.
R2(config)#int s0/0/0.1
R2(config-subif)#frame-relay map ip 10.2.123.3 101 broadcast
R2(config-subif)#frame-relay map ip 10.2.123.4 101 broadcast
R2(config-subif)#^Z
!
! Not shown, similar mapping configured on R3 and R4
```

```
! R2 now has the necessary mappings
R2#show frame-relay map
Serial0/0/0.1 (up): ip 10.2.123.4 dlci 101(0x65,0x1850), static,
                    broadcast,
                    CISCO, status defined, active
Serial0/0/0.1 (up): ip 10.2.123.3 dlci 101(0x65,0x1850), static,
                    broadcast,
                    CISCO, status defined, active
Serial0/0/0.1 (up): ip 10.2.123.1 dlci 101(0x65,0x1850), dynamic,
                    broadcast,
                    CISCO, status defined, active

! Same ping now works

R2#ping 10.3.3.3

Type escape sequence to abort.
Sending 5, 100-byte ICMP Echos to 10.3.3.3, timeout is 2 seconds:
!!!!!
Success rate is 100 percent (5/5), round-trip min/avg/max = 8/8/8 ms
```

Although the example demonstrates the original problem and then the solution, it does also demonstrate a particularly difficult challenge for a verification plan. Before adding the mapping, OSPF appeared to be working on R2, because R2 had learned all the routes it should have learned. However, packet forwarding failed due to the lack of the correct Frame Relay mappings. When reviewing verification plans for the exam, take extra care when using Frame Relay, and do not rely solely on seeing OSPF routes as proof that connectivity exists between two routers.

Using Network Type Point-to-Multipoint

Network type *point-to-multipoint* tells routers to act oppositely compared to the nonbroadcast type: to not elect a DR/BDR and to dynamically discover neighbors. Both options allow the routers to simply not configure additional commands. As a result, the only configuration requirement, beyond enabling OSPF on the multipoint subinterface or physical serial interface, is to configure any static Frame Relay mappings if a partial mesh exists.

Example 8-8 shows a completed OSPF configuration on Routers R1 and R2 in Figure 8-6. All the routers change their network type using the **ip ospf network point-to-multipoint** interface subcommand. The other big change as compared to using the nonbroadcast network type (as seen in Examples 8-6 and 8-7) is the absence of configuration. (Example 8-8 does show all OSPF-related configuration on R1 and R2.) As with Example 8-6, the example omits the R3 and R4 configuration, but the configuration follows the same conventions as on R2. Also, note that the routers without PVCs to each other router still require the **frame-relay map** commands (included in the example) for the same reasons as shown in Example 8-7.

Example 8-8   *Configuring Multipoint OSPF Using Network Type Point-to-Multipoint*

```
! First, R1's configuration
R1#show run int s0/0/0.1
Building configuration...

Current configuration : 169 bytes
!
interface Serial0/0/0.1 multipoint
 ip address 10.2.123.1 255.255.255.248
 frame-relay interface-dlci 102
 frame-relay interface-dlci 103
 frame-relay interface-dlci 104
 ip ospf network point-to-multipoint
end
R1#show run | begin router ospf
router ospf 1
 network 10.0.0.0 0.255.255.255 area 0
 router-id 1.1.1.1
```
```
! Next, on R2:
R2#show run int s0/0/0.1
Building configuration...

Current configuration : 169 bytes
!
interface Serial0/0/0.1 multipoint
 ip address 10.2.123.2 255.255.255.248
 frame-relay interface-dlci 101
 frame-relay map ip 10.2.123.3 101 broadcast
 frame-relay map ip 10.2.123.4 101 broadcast
 ip ospf network point-to-multipoint
end
R2#show run | begin router ospf
router ospf 1
 network 10.0.0.0 0.255.255.255 area 0
 router-id 2.2.2.2
```

Example 8-9 confirms a few details about the operation with the point-to-multipoint network type. Taken from R1, the **show ip ospf interfaces S0/0/0.1** command confirms the network type, and it also confirms full adjacency with the other three routers. Also, compared to the same command on Router R2 near the end of Example 8-6, note that this command does not even mention the concept of a DR nor BDR, because this network type does not expect to use a DR/BDR.

Example 8-9   *Confirming the Operation of Network Type Point-to-Multipoint*

```
! First, R1's configuration
R1#show ip ospf interface s0/0/0.1
Serial0/0/0.1 is up, line protocol is up
  Internet Address 10.2.123.1/29, Area 0
  Process ID 1, Router ID 1.1.1.1, Network Type POINT_TO_MULTIPOINT, Cost: 64
  Transmit Delay is 1 sec, State POINT_TO_MULTIPOINT
  Timer intervals configured, Hello 30, Dead 120, Wait 120, Retransmit 5
    oob-resync timeout 120
    Hello due in 00:00:23
  Supports Link-local Signaling (LLS)
  Cisco NSF helper support enabled
  IETF NSF helper support enabled
  Index 4/4, flood queue length 0
  Next 0x0(0)/0x0(0)
  Last flood scan length is 1, maximum is 1
  Last flood scan time is 0 msec, maximum is 0 msec
  Neighbor Count is 3, Adjacent neighbor count is 3
    Adjacent with neighbor 2.2.2.2
    Adjacent with neighbor 4.4.4.4
    Adjacent with neighbor 3.3.3.3
  Suppress hello for 0 neighbor(s)
```

Using Network Type Point-to-Multipoint Nonbroadcast

OSPF network type *point-to-multipoint nonbroadcast* tells routers to act like the similarly named point-to-multipoint type by not electing a DR/BDR. However, the difference lies in neighbor discovery–the keyword "nonbroadcast" implies that the routers cannot broadcast (or multicast) to discover neighbors.

The configuration uses a mix of the commands seen for the nonbroadcast and point-to-multipoint network types. Essentially, the configuration of priority for the purpose of influencing the DR/BDR election can be ignored, because no DR/BDR will be elected. However, the routers need **neighbor** commands to predefine neighbors. Also, regardless of network type, for those routers without direct PVCs, Frame Relay mapping must be added.

This particular OSPF network type does have some design advantages if the design also uses multipoint subinterfaces. The required **neighbor** commands also have an optional **cost** parameter so that the cost associated with each neighbor can be different. With point-to-multipoint, the router considers the dynamically discovered neighbors to be reachable with a cost equal to the cost of the associated multipoint subinterface, so the cost cannot be set per neighbor.

Example 8-10 shows the configurations on R1 and R2 for this case, with the configuration of R3 and R4 mirroring R2s.

Example 8-10   *Configuring Multipoint OSPF Using Network Type Point-to-Multipoint Nonbroadcast*

```
! First, R1's configuration
R1#show run int s0/0/0.1
Building configuration...

Current configuration : 169 bytes
!
interface Serial0/0/0.1 multipoint
 ip address 10.2.123.1 255.255.255.248
 frame-relay interface-dlci 102
 frame-relay interface-dlci 103
 frame-relay interface-dlci 104
 ip ospf network point-to-multipoint non-broadcast

end
R1#show run | begin router ospf
router ospf 1
 network 10.0.0.0 0.255.255.255 area 0
 router-id 1.1.1.1
 neighbor 10.2.123.2
 neighbor 10.2.123.3
 neighbor 10.2.123.4
```

```
! Next, on R2:
R2#show run int s0/0/0.1
Building configuration...

Current configuration : 169 bytes
!
interface Serial0/0/0.1 multipoint
 ip address 10.2.123.2 255.255.255.248
 frame-relay interface-dlci 101
 frame-relay map ip 10.2.123.3 101 broadcast
 frame-relay map ip 10.2.123.4 101 broadcast
 ip ospf network point-to-multipoint non-broadcast

end
R2#show run | begin router ospf
router ospf 1
 network 10.0.0.0 0.255.255.255 area 0
 router-id 2.2.2.2
 neighbor 10.2.123.1
```

Exam Preparation Tasks

Planning Practice

The CCNP ROUTE exam expects test takers to review design documents, create implementation plans, and create verification plans. This section provides some exercises that may help you to take a step back from the minute details of the topics in this chapter so that you can think about the same technical topics from the planning perspective.

For each planning practice table, simply complete the table. Note that any numbers in parentheses represent the number of options listed for each item in the solutions in Appendix F, "Completed Planning Practice Tables."

Design Review Table

Table 8-4 lists several design goals related to this chapter. If these design goals were listed in a design document, and you had to take that document and develop an implementation plan, what implementation options come to mind? For any configuration items, a general description can be used, without concern about the specific parameters.

Table 8-4 *Design Review*

Design Goal	Possible Implementation Choices Covered in This Chapter
A merger design plan shows two companies with OSPF backbone areas. How can the two areas 0 be connected? (2)	
The subnetting design over Frame Relay calls for a set of 20 routers to use a single WAN subnet. What Frame Relay interface types make sense?	
The design shows 20 routers connected to Frame Relay, in a partial mesh, with one subnet. What OSPF network type would avoid the use of DR/BDR? (2)	
The design shows 20 routers connected to Frame Relay, in a full mesh, with one subnet. What OSPF network type would allow dynamic neighbor discovery? (2)	

Implementation Plan Peer Review Table

Table 8-5 shows a list of questions that others might ask, or that you might think about, during a peer review of another network engineer's implementation plan. Complete the table by answering the questions.

Table 8-5 *Notable Questions from This Chapter to Consider During an Implementation Plan Peer Review*

Question	Answers
The subnetting design over Frame Relay calls for a set of 20 routers to use a single WAN subnet. What three general issues exist that requires extra configuration?	
The plan shows a virtual link between R1 and R2, through area 99, with the connection using R1's Fa0/0 interface. The configuration shows MD5 authentication configuration as interface subcommands on Fa0/0. Will those commands apply to the virtual link?	
The plan shows a sample OSPF configuration with five routers, Frame Relay connected, with one subnet, each using multipoint subinterfaces. A full mesh exists. The configuration shows network type point-to-multipoint nonbroadcast. What OSPF configuration is needed beyond the enabling of OSPF on the interfaces?	
Using the same scenario as the previous row but with network type nonbroadcast, and a partial mesh, answer the same questions.	

Create an Implementation Plan Table

To practice skills useful when creating your own OSPF implementation plan, list in Table 8-6 configuration commands related to the configuration of the following features. You may want to record your answers outside the book and set a goal to complete this table (and others like it) from memory during your final reviews before taking the exam.

Table 8-6 *Implementation Plan Configuration Memory Drill*

Feature	Configuration Commands/Notes
Create a virtual link through transit area X.	
Configure MD5 authentication on a virtual link.	
Configure clear-text authentication on a virtual link.	
Configure null authentication on a virtual link.	
Configure the OSPF network type on a Frame Relay multipoint interface.	
Statically configure OSPF neighbors.	
Influence OSPF priority of the local router.	
Influence OSPF priority of a neighboring router.	
Add static Frame Relay mappings.	

Choosing Commands for a Verification Plan Table

To practice skills useful when creating your own OSPF verification plan, list in Table 8-7 all commands that supply the requested information. You may want to record your answers outside the book and set a goal to complete this table (and others like it) from memory during your final reviews before taking the exam.

Table 8-7 *Verification Plan Memory Drill*

Information Needed	Command(s)
Display the name and status of a virtual link.	
Display the RID of a neighbor on a virtual link.	
Display the OSPF authentication type and youngest key for MD5 authentication on a Virtual Link.	
Display the OSPF network type for an interface.	
Display a router's own OSPF priority.	
Display the mapping of neighbor IP address and Frame Relay DLCI.	
Display neighbors known on an interface.	

Author's note: Some of the entries in this table may not have been specifically mentioned in this chapter but are listed in this table for review and reference.

Review All the Key Topics

Review the most important topics from inside the chapter, noted with the key topics icon in the outer margin of the page. Table 8-8 lists a reference of these key topics and the page numbers on which each is found.

Key Topic

Table 8-8 *Key Topics for Chapter 8*

Key Topic Element	Description	Page Number
List	Summary of options on the **area virtual-link** command	263
Table 8-2	Summary of OSPF authentication methods and commands for virtual links	266
List	Recommendations related to multipoint Frame Relay and either neighbor discovery or neighbor definition	271
List	Recommendations related to multipoint Frame Relay when a DR is elected	272
Paragraph	Recommendation with a partial mesh in multipoint Frame Relay regarding static Frame Relay mapping	273
Table 8-3	List of OSPF network types used for Frame Relay physical interfaces and multipoint subinterfaces	274

Complete the Tables and Lists from Memory

Print a copy of Appendix D, "Memory Tables," (found on the CD), or at least the section for this chapter, and complete the tables and lists from memory. Appendix E, "Memory Tables Answer Key," also on the CD, includes completed tables and lists to check your work.

Define Key Terms

Define the following key terms from this chapter, and check your answers in the glossary.

Virtual Link, OSPF network type, Full mesh, Partial mesh, Frame Relay mapping, Frame Relay Inverse ARP (InARP), Multipoint subinterface

This chapter covers the following subjects:

Route Redistribution Basics: This section discusses the reasons why designers might choose to use route redistribution, and how routing protocols redistribute routes from the IP routing table.

Redistribution in EIGRP: This section discusses the mechanics of how IOS redistributes routes from other sources into EIGRP.

Redistribution in OSPF: This section discusses the mechanics of how IOS redistributes routes from other sources into OSPF.

CHAPTER 9

Basic IGP Redistribution

This chapter begins Part 4 of this book: "Path Control." Path control refers to a general class of tools and protocols that Layer 3 devices use to learn, manipulate, and use IP routes. EIGRP and OSPF certainly fit into that category.

The three chapters in Part 4 examine path control features that go beyond the base function of learning IP routes. In particular, Chapter 9, "Basic IGP Redistribution," and Chapter 10, "Advanced IGP Redistribution," examine how routers can exchange routes between routing protocols through route redistribution. Chapter 9 begins by discussing the mechanics of what happens when the routes are redistributed. Chapter 10 then goes further to discuss how to also filter and summarize routes when redistributing–yet another path control function–and discusses some issues and solutions when multiple routers redistribute the same routes. Finally, Chapter 11, "Policy-Based Routing and IP Service Level Agreement," discusses a few smaller path control topics, including IP Service-Level Agreement (SLA) and Policy-Based Routing (PBR).

"Do I Know This Already?" Quiz

The "Do I Know This Already?" quiz allows you to assess if you should read the entire chapter. If you miss no more than one of these eight self-assessment questions, you might want to move ahead to the "Exam Preparation Tasks." Table 9-1 lists the major headings in this chapter and the "Do I Know This Already?" quiz questions covering the material in those headings so that you can assess your knowledge of these specific areas. The answers to the "Do I Know This Already?" quiz appear in Appendix A.

Table 9-1 *"Do I Know This Already?" Foundation Topics Section-to-Question Mapping*

Foundations Topics Section	Questions
Route Redistribution Basics	1–2
Redistribution into EIGRP	3–5
Redistribution into OSPF	6–8

1. Which of the following answers is the least likely reason for an engineer to choose to use route redistribution?

   a. To exchange routes between merged companies

    b.   To give separate control over routing to different parts of one company

    c.   To support multiple router vendors

    d.   To knit together an OSPF area if the area becomes discontiguous

2. For a router to successfully redistribute routes between OSPF and EIGRP, which of the following are true? (Choose two.)

    a.   The router must have one routing protocol configured, but configuration for both routing protocols is not necessary.

    b.   The router must have at least one working link connected to each routing domain.

    c.   The **redistribute** command must be configured under EIGRP to send the routes to OSPF.

    d.   The **redistribute** command should be configured under OSPF to take routes from EIGRP into OSPF.

3. Process EIGRP 1 is redistributing routes from process OSPF 2. Which two of the following methods may be used to set the metrics of the redistributed routes? (Choose 2)

    a.   Let the metrics default.

    b.   Set the metric components using the **redistribute** command's **metric** keyword.

    c.   Set the metric components using the **default-metric** router subcommand.

    d.   Set the integer (composite) metric using the **redistribute** command's **metric** keyword.

4. Examine the following excerpt from the **show ip eigrp topology 10.2.2.0/24** command on router R1. Which answer can be verified as definitely true based on this output?

```
External data:
  Originating router is 10.1.1.1
  AS number of route is 1
  External protocol is OSPF, external metric is 64
  Administrator tag is 0 (0x00000000)
```

    a.   R1 is the router that redistributed the route.

    b.   R1's metric to reach subnet 10.2.2.0/24 is 64.

    c.   The route was redistributed on a router that has a **router ospf 1** command configured.

    d.   R1 is redistributing a route to prefix 10.2.2.0/24 into OSPF.

5. Router R1 has a connected route for 10.1.1.0/24 off interface Fa0/0. Interface Fa0/0 has been enabled for OSPF due to a **router ospf 1** and **network 10.0.0.0 0.0.0.255 area 0** command. R1 also has EIGRP configured, with the **redistribute ospf 1 metric 1000 100 10 1 1500** command configured under EIGRP. Which one of the following is true?

    a.   R1 will not redistribute 10.1.1.0/24 into EIGRP, because R1 knows it as a connected route and not as an OSPF route.

    b.   For any OSPF routes redistributed into EIGRP, the metric components include a value equivalent to 1 Mbps of bandwidth.

    c.   For any OSPF routes redistributed into EIGRP, the metric components include a value equivalent to 100 microseconds of delay.

    d.   No subnets of network 10.0.0.0 will be redistributed due to the omission of the **subnets** parameter.

6. Process OSPF 1 is redistributing routes from process OSPF 2. Which of the following methods may be used to set the metrics of the redistributed routes? (Choose two.)

    a.   Let the metrics default.

    b.   Use each redistributed route's OSPF metric using the **redistribute** command's **metric transparent** keywords.

    c.   Set the metric using the **default-metric** router subcommand.

    d.   Redistribution is not allowed between two OSPF processes.

7. Examine the following excerpt from the **show ip ospf database asbr-summary** command on router R1 (RID 1.1.1.1). Which answer can be verified as definitely true based on this output?

```
LS Type: Summary Links (AS Boundary Router)
Link State ID: 9.9.9.9 (AS Boundary Router address)
Advertising Router: 3.3.3.3
LS Seq Number: 8000000D
Checksum: 0xE43A
Length: 28
Network Mask: /0
      TOS: 0   Metric: 100
```

    a.   The output describes the contents of a Type 5 LSA.

    b.   3.3.3.3 identifies a router as being the router performing redistribution.

    c.   R1's metric for its best route to reach the router with RID 9.9.9.9 is 100.

    d.   The router with RID 3.3.3.3's metric for its best route to reach the router with RID 9.9.9.9 is 100.

8. Router R1 sits inside OSPF area 1. Router R2 redistributes an E1 route into OSPF for prefix 2.2.2.0/24, with external metric 20. Router R22 redistributes an E2 route for the same prefix/length, external metric 10. Under what conditions will R1 choose as its best route the route through R22?

    a.   R1 will always choose the route through R22.

    b.   As long as R1's best internal OSPF cost to reach R22 is less than 10.

    c.   As long as R1's best internal OSPF cost to reach R22 is less than 20.

    d.   R1 will never choose the route through R22 if the E1 route through R2 is available.

Foundation Topics

Route Redistribution Basics

Most internetworks use a single IGP to advertise and learn IP routes. However, in some cases, more than one routing protocol exists inside a single enterprise. Also, in some cases, the routes learned with an IGP must then be advertised with BGP, and vice versa. In such cases, engineers often need to take routing information learned by one routing protocol and advertise those routes into the other routing protocol–a function provided by the IOS route redistribution feature.

This section examines the basics of route redistribution.

The Need for Route Redistribution

The potential need for route redistribution exists when a route learned through one source of routing information, most typically one routing protocol, needs to be distributed into a second routing protocol domain. For example, two companies might merge, with one company using EIGRP and the other using OSPF. The engineers could choose to immediately migrate away from OSPF to instead use EIGRP exclusively, but that migration would take time and potentially cause outages. Route redistribution allows those engineers to connect a couple of routers to both routing domains, and exchange routes between the two routing domains, with a minimal amount of configuration and with little disruption to the existing networks.

Figure 9-1 shows just such a case, with R1 performing redistribution by using its knowledge of subnet 1 from the EIGRP domain and advertising a route for subnet 1 into the OSPF domain. Note that the opposite should also occur, with the OSPF domain's subnet 2 being redistributed into the EIGRP domain.

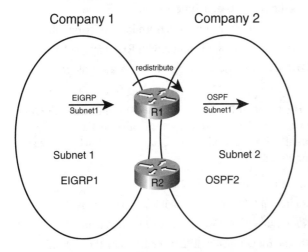

Figure 9-1 *Typical Use of Redistribution*

The main technical reason for needing redistribution is straightforward: An internetwork uses more than one routing protocol, and the routes need to be exchanged between those routing domains, at least temporarily. The business reasons vary widely but include the following:

- Mergers when different IGPs are used.

- Mergers when the same IGP is used.

- Momentum (The Enterprise has been using multiple routing protocols a long time.)

- Different company divisions under separate control for business or political reasons.

- Connections between partners.

- To allow multivendor interoperability (OSPF on non-Cisco, EIGRP on Cisco, for instance).

- Between IGPs and BGP when BGP is used between large segments of a multinational company.

- Layer 3 WAN (MPLS).

The list begins with two entries for mergers just to make the point that even if both merging companies use the same IGP, redistribution may still be useful. Even if both companies use EIGRP, they probably use a different AS number in their EIGRP configuration (with the **router eigrp** *asn* command). In such a case, to have all routers exchange routing information with EIGRP, all the former company's routers would need to migrate to use the same ASN as the first company. Such a migration may be simple, but it still requires disruptive configuration changes in a potentially large number of routers. Redistribution could be used until a migration could be completed.

Although useful as an interim solution, many permanent designs use redistribution as well. For example, it could be that a company has used different routing protocols (or different instances of the same routing protocol) in different divisions of a company. The network engineering groups may remain autonomous, and manage their own routing protocol domains, using redistribution to exchange routes at a few key connecting points between the divisions. Similarly, partner companies have separate engineering staffs, and want autonomy for managing routing, but also need to exchange routes for key subnets to allow the partnership's key applications to function. Figure 9-2 depicts both of these cases.

The last two cases in the previous list each relate to BGP in some way. First, some large corporations actually use BGP internal to the company's internetwork, redistributing routes from IGPs. Each large autonomous division of the company can design and configure their respective routing protocol instance, redistribute into BGP, and then redistribute out of BGP into other divisions. Also, when an Enterprise uses an MPLS VPN service, the MPLS provider's provider edge (PE) router typically redistributes customer routes with BGP inside the MPLS provider's MPLS network. Figure 9-3 shows samples of both these cases. In each of these cases, a given prefix/length (subnet/mask) is typically distributed into BGP at one location, advertised over a BGP domain, and redistributed back into some IGP.

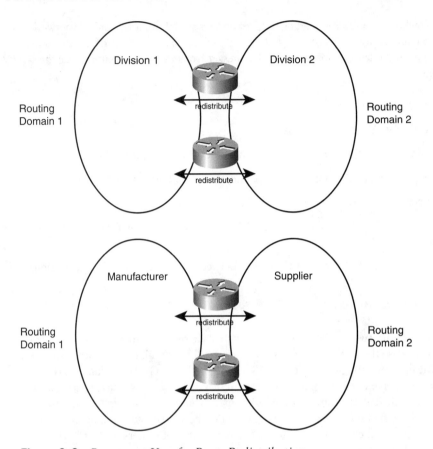

Figure 9-2   *Permanent Uses for Route Redistribution*

Note: Although Enterprises often use BGP to exchange routes with ISPs, redistribution is often not used. Chapter 13, "External BGP," discusses the issues and alternatives for how to advertise Enterprise routes into BGP.

Redistribution Concepts and Processes

Route redistribution requires at least one router to do the following:

Key Topic

Step 1.   Use at least one working physical link with each routing domain.

Step 2.   A working routing protocol configuration for each routing domain.

Step 3.   Additional redistribution configuration for each routing protocol, specifically the **redistribute** command, which tells the routing protocol to take the routes learned by another source of routing information and to then advertise those routes.

The first two steps do not require any new knowledge or commands, but the third step represents the core of the redistribution logic and requires some additional background

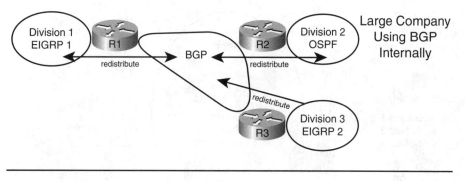

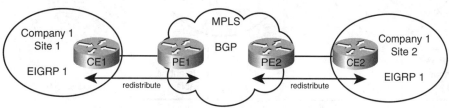

Figure 9-3   *Using Redistribution to Pass Routes Using BGP*

information. To appreciate the third step, Figure 9-4 shows an example router, RD1, that has completed Steps 1 and 2. RD1 uses EIGRP on the left, OSPF on the right, and has learned some routes with each routing protocol (Steps 1 and 2). However, no redistribution has been configured yet.

The goal for redistribution in this case is to have EIGRP advertise about subnets 11, 12, and 13, which exist inside the OSPF domain, and have OSPF advertise about subnets 1, 2, and 3, which exist inside the EIGRP domain. To do that, EIGRP must put topology information about subnets 11, 12 and 13 into its EIGRP topology table, and OSPF must put topology information about subnets 1, 2, and 3 into its topology table. However, OSPF's topology table has a lot of different information in it compared to EIGRP's topology table. OSPF has LSAs, and EIGRP does not. EIGRP lists the components of the composite metric and the neighbor's reported distance (RD)–but OSPF does not. In short, EIGRP and OSPF differ significantly for the contents of their topology tables.

Because the details of various routing protocols' topology tables differ, the redistribution process does not use the topology tables when redistributing routes. Instead, redistribution uses the one table that both routing protocols understand: the IP routing table. Specifically, the IOS **redistribute** command takes routes from the IP routing table and passes those routes to a routing protocol for redistribution. The **redistribute** command, configured inside a routing protocol configuration mode, redistributes routes into that routing protocol from some other source. Figure 9-5 spells it out with an example, which focuses on the internal logic of Router RD1 as shown in Figure 9-4.

Starting on the left of the figure, RD1's EIGRP 1 process configuration lists the **redistribute ospf 2** command. This command tells RD1 to look in the IP routing table, take all OSPF routes added to the IP routing table by the OSPF 2 process on RD1, and put those routes into EIGRP's topology table. Conversely, the **redistribute eigrp 1** command

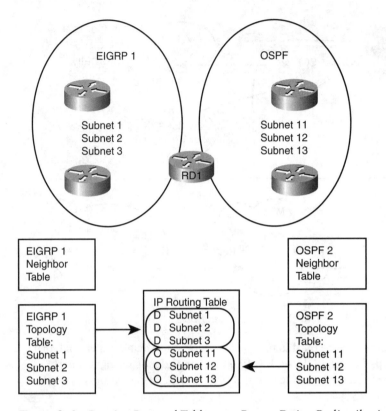

Figure 9-4   *Routing Protocol Tables on a Router Doing Redistribution*

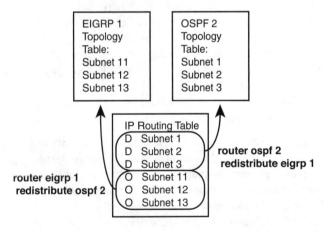

Figure 9-5   *Mutual Redistribution Between OSPF and EIGRP on Router RD1*

configured on the OSPF process tells RD1 to take IP routes from the IP routing table, if learned by EIGRP process 1, and add those routes to OSPF 2's topology table.

The process works as shown in Figure 9-5, but the figure leaves out some important details regarding the type of routes and the metrics used. For EIGRP, the EIGRP topology table needs more than the integer metric value held by the IP routing table–it needs values for the components of the EIGRP composite metric. EIGRP can use default settings that define the metric components for all routes redistributed into EIGRP, or the engineer can set the metric components in a variety of ways, as covered in several locations later in this chapter.

Like EIGRP, OSPF treats the redistributed routes as external routes. OSPF creates an LSA to represent each redistributed subnet–normally a Type 5 LSA, but when redistributed into an NSSA area, the router instead creates a Type 7 LSA. In both cases, OSPF needs an integer metric to assign to the external route's LSA; the redistribution configuration should include the OSPF cost setting, which may or may not match the metric listed for the route in the redistributing router's IP routing table.

The last concept before moving on to the configuration options is that the **redistribute** command tells the router to take not only routes learned by the source routing protocol, but also connected routes on interfaces enabled with that routing protocol–including passive interfaces. Example 9-1 later in this chapter demonstrates this concept.

Redistribution into EIGRP

This section looks at the specifics of how EIGRP performs redistribution–that is, how EIGRP takes routes from other routing sources, such as OSPF, and advertises them into EIGRP. Before moving into the specifics, however, note that the redistribution as discussed in this chapter does not include any filtering or summarization. In real life, engineers often use both route filtering and route summarization at the redistribution point on a router. For the sake of making the underlying concepts clear, this chapter focuses on the mechanics of redistribution, without filtering, or summarization, or any other changes to the redistributed routes. Chapter 10 then looks at the fun options for manipulating routes at the redistribution point.

This section begins with a couple of short discussions of reference information. The first topic summarizes the parameters of the main configuration command, the EIGRP **redistribute** command, and its parameters. Next, the baseline configuration used in the upcoming samples is listed, including all EIGRP and OSPF configuration, but no redistribution configuration. With those details listed for reference, the rest of this section examines the configuration of redistribution into EIGRP.

EIGRP **redistribute** Command Reference

First, for reference, the following lines show the generic syntax of the **redistribute** command when used as a **router eigrp** subcommand. Note that the syntax differs slightly depending on the routing protocol into which routes will be redistributed. Following that, Table 9-2 lists the options on the command with a brief description.

```
redistribute protocol [process-id ¦ as-number] [metric bw delay reliability load
mtu ] [match {internal ¦ nssa-external ¦ external 1 ¦ external 2}]  [tag tag-
value] [route-map name]
```

Table 9-2 *Parameters of the EIGRP* redistribute *Command*

Option	Description
protocol	The source of routing information. Includes **RIP, OSPF, EIGRP, IS-IS, BGP, connected,** and **static.**
process-id, as-number	If redistributing a routing protocol that uses a process ID or ASN on the **router** global config command, use this parameter to refer to that process or ASN value.
metric	A keyword after which follows the four metric components (bandwidth, delay, reliability, link load), plus the MTU associated with the route.
match	If redistributing from OSPF, this keyword lets you match internal OSPF routes, external (by type), and NSSA external routes, essentially filtering which routes are redistributed.
tag	Assigns a unitless integer value to the routes redistributed by this command—tags which can be later matched by other routers using a route-map.
route-map	Apply the logic in the referenced route-map to filter routes, set metrics, and set route tags.

Baseline Configuration for EIGRP Redistribution Examples

The best method to see the results of redistribution is to use examples, so this section explains the sample internetwork used in the upcoming EIGRP redistribution examples. Figure 9-6 shows the sample internetwork. In this case, the EIGRP domain on the left uses subnets of class B network 172.30.0.0, and the OSPF domain on the right uses subnets of class B network 172.16.0.0. Note that all OSPF subnets reside in area 0 in this example internetwork, although that is not a requirement.

The internetwork uses a single router (RD1) to perform redistribution, just to avoid some interesting issues that occur when multiple routers redistribute the same routes. (Chapter 10 discusses these issues in some depth.) Example 9-1 shows the configuration on RD1, listing the IP addresses of the four active serial interfaces shown in Figure 9-6, plus the complete but basic EIGRP and OSPF configuration—but without any redistribution configured yet.

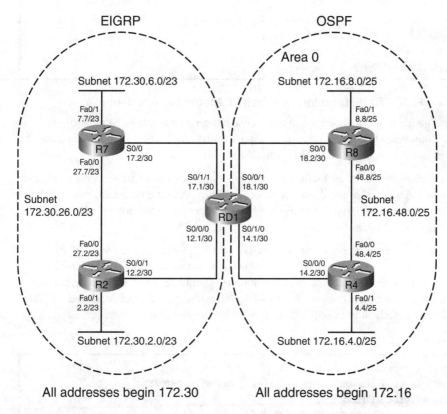

Figure 9-6 *Sample Internetwork Used for Redistribution Examples*

Example 9-1 *Configuration on Router RD1 Before Adding Redistribution Configuration*

```
interface Serial0/0/0
 ip address 172.30.12.1 255.255.255.252
 clock rate 1536000
!
interface Serial0/0/1
 ip address 172.16.18.1 255.255.255.252
 clock rate 1536000
!
interface Serial0/1/0
 ip address 172.16.14.1 255.255.255.252
 clock rate 1536000
!
interface Serial0/1/1
 ip address 172.30.17.1 255.255.255.252
 clock rate 1536000
!
router eigrp 1
 network 172.30.0.0
 no auto-summary
```

```
 !
 router ospf 2
  router-id 1.1.1.1
  network 172.16.0.0 0.0.255.255 area 0
```

Configuring EIGRP Redistribution with Default Metric Components

For the internetwork of Figure 9-6, a reasonable design goal would be to redistribute EIGRP routes into OSPF, and OSPF routes into EIGRP. This section examines the case of redistributing the routes into EIGRP from OSPF.

First, consider the EIGRP **redistribute** command. For those unfamiliar with the command, it may not be obvious of the direction of redistribution. A better command name might have been "take-routes-from," because the first parameter after the command tells IOS from where to get the routes.

For example, consider the configuration in Example 9-2, which was added to RD1's existing configuration in Example 9-1. The configuration uses only required parameters, namely a reference to the source from which routes should be redistributed. Because the configuration places this command in EIGRP configuration mode, the command tells IOS to redistribute the routes into EIGRP 1, from OSPF 2 in this case.

Example 9-2   *Minimal Configuration for Redistribution from OSPF into EIGRP*

```
RD1#configure terminal
Enter configuration commands, one per line.  End with CNTL/Z.
RD1(config)#router eigrp 1
RD1(config-router)#redistribute ospf 2
RD1(config-router)#^Z
```

IOS does accept the configuration; unfortunately, IOS does not actually redistribute routes from OSPF into EIGRP in this case. EIGRP does not have a default setting for the metric components to use when redistributing into EIGRP from OSPF. To confirm these results, examine the output in Example 9-3, which lists **show** command output from RD1 when configured as shown in the previous example. Note that RD1's EIGRP topology table lists only routes for class B network 172.30.0.0, which all sit inside the EIGRP domain; none of the routes from class B network 172.16.0.0, which exist inside the OSPF domain, have been added to RD1's EIGRP topology table.

Example 9-3   *Redistribution Did Not Work on RD1*

```
RD1#show ip eigrp topology
IP-EIGRP Topology Table for AS(1)/ID(172.30.17.1)

Codes: P - Passive, A - Active, U - Update, Q - Query, R - Reply,
       r - reply Status, s - sia Status

P 172.30.17.0/30, 1 successors, FD is 2169856
       via Connected, Serial0/1/1
P 172.30.26.0/23, 2 successors, FD is 2172416
       via 172.30.12.2 (2172416/28160), Serial0/0/0
```

```
              via 172.30.17.2 (2172416/28160), Serial0/1/1
P 172.30.2.0/23, 1 successors, FD is 2172416
              via 172.30.12.2 (2172416/28160), Serial0/0/0
              via 172.30.17.2 (2174976/30720), Serial0/1/1
P 172.30.6.0/23, 1 successors, FD is 2172416
              via 172.30.17.2 (2172416/28160), Serial0/1/1
              via 172.30.12.2 (2174976/30720), Serial0/0/0
P 172.30.12.0/30, 1 successors, FD is 2169856
              via Connected, Serial0/0/0
```

To complete the configuration of redistribution into EIGRP, Router RD1 needs to set the
metric values. EIGRP can set the metrics for redistributed routes in three ways, as summarized in Table 9-3.

Table 9-3 *Methods of Setting EIGRP Metrics When Redistributing into EIGRP*

Function	Command
Setting the default for all **redistribute** commands	The **default-metric** *bw delay reliability load mtu* EIGRP subcommand
Setting the component metrics applied to all routes redistributed by a single **redistribute** command	The **metric** *bw delay reliability load mtu* parameters on the **redistribute** command
Setting different component metrics to different routes from a single route source	Use the **route-map** parameter on the **redistribute** command, matching routes and setting metric components.

Note: EIGRP does have a default metric when redistributing from another EIGRP
process, in which case it takes the metric from the source of the routing information. In all
other cases, the metric must be set using one of the methods in Table 9-3.

If the metrics do not matter to the design, which is likely when only a single redistribution
point exists as in Figure 9-6, either of the first two methods listed in Table 9-3 is reasonable. The first method, using the **default-metric** command in EIGRP configuration mode,
sets the metric for all routes redistributed into EIGRP, unless set by one of the other methods. Alternatively, the second method, which uses additional parameters on the
redistribute command, sets the metric for all routes redistributed because of that one
redistribute command. Finally, if the **redistribute** command also refers to a route map, the
route map can use the set metric command to set the metric components for routes
matched by the route map clause, overriding the metric settings in the **default-metric**
command or with the **metric** keyword on the **redistribute** command.

Example 9-4 shows the addition of the **default-metric 1000 33 255 1 1500** command to
RD1's configuration. This command sets the bandwidth to 1000 (Kbps), the delay to 33
(tens-of-microseconds, or 330 microseconds), reliability to 255 (a value between 1–255,

255 is best), load to 1 (a value between 1–255, 1 is best), and MTU of 1500. Note that even though EIGRP ignores the last three parameters by default when calculating integer metrics, you still must configure these settings for the commands to be accepted.

Example 9-4 *Redistributed Routes in RD1*

```
RD1#configure terminal
Enter configuration commands, one per line.  End with CNTL/Z.
RD1(config)#router eigrp 1
RD1(config-router)#default-metric 1000 33 255 1 1500
RD1(config-router)#^Z
```

Because this example uses a single **redistribute** command for the EIGRP 1 process, you could have used the **redistribute ospf 2 metric 1000 33 255 1 1500** command and ignored the **default-metric** command to achieve the same goal.

Verifying EIGRP Redistribution

As shown earlier in Figure 9-5, redistribution takes routes from the routing table and places the correct information for those subnets into the redistributing router's topology table. The redistributing router then advertises the routes from its topology table as it would for other routes. To verify that redistribution works, Example 9-5 shows the proof that RD1 indeed created entries in its EIGRP topology table for the five subnets in the OSPF domain.

Example 9-5 *Verifying RD1 Added EIGRP Topology Data for Five OSPF Subnets*

```
RD1#show ip eigrp topology
IP-EIGRP Topology Table for AS(1)/ID(172.30.17.1)


Codes: P - Passive, A - Active, U - Update, Q - Query, R - Reply,
       r - reply Status, s - sia Status


! Note - all lines for class B network 172.30.0.0 have been omitted for brevity
P 172.16.48.0/25, 1 successors, FD is 2568448
         via Redistributed (2568448/0)
P 172.16.18.0/30, 1 successors, FD is 2568448
         via Redistributed (2568448/0)
P 172.16.14.0/30, 1 successors, FD is 2568448
         via Redistributed (2568448/0)
P 172.16.8.0/25, 1 successors, FD is 2568448
         via Redistributed (2568448/0)
P 172.16.4.0/25, 1 successors, FD is 2568448
         via Redistributed (2568448/0)
RD1#show ip eigrp topology 172.16.48.0/25
IP-EIGRP (AS 1): Topology entry for 172.16.48.0/25
  State is Passive, Query origin flag is 1, 1 Successor(s), FD is 2568448
```

```
Routing Descriptor Blocks:
172.16.18.2, from Redistributed, Send flag is 0x0
    Composite metric is (2568448/0), Route is External
    Vector metric:
      Minimum bandwidth is 1000 Kbit
      Total delay is 330 microseconds
      Reliability is 255/255
      Load is 1/255
      Minimum MTU is 1500
      Hop count is 0
    External data:
      Originating router is 172.30.17.1 (this system)
      AS number of route is 2
      External protocol is OSPF, external metric is 65
      Administrator tag is 0 (0x00000000)
```

The **show** command output lists several interesting facts, including

■   On Router RD1, which performed the redistribution, the EIGRP topology table lists
    the outgoing interface as "via redistributed."

■   All the redistributed routes have the same feasible distance (FD) calculation
    (2568448), because all use the same component metrics per the configured **default-
    metric** command.

■   RD1's two connected subnets in the OSPF 2 domain–subnets 172.16.14.0/30 and
    172.16.18.0/30–were also redistributed, even though these routes are connected
    routes in RD1's routing table.

■   The output of the **show ip eigrp topology 172.16.48.0/25** command confirms the
    component metrics match the values configured on the **default-metric** command.

■   The bottom of the output of the **show ip eigrp topology 172.16.48.0/25** command
    lists information about the external source of the route, including the routing source
    (OSPF) and that source's metric for the route (65). It also lists the phrase "(this sys-
    tem)," meaning that the router on which the command was issued (RD1 in this case)
    redistributed the route.

The third item in the list–the fact that RD1 redistributed some connected routes–bears
further consideration. The **redistribute ospf 2** command tells EIGRP to redistribute routes
learned by the OSPF 2 process. However, it also tells the router to redistribute connected
routes for interfaces on which process OSPF 2 has been enabled. Back in Example 9-1, the
configuration on RD1 lists a **network 172.16.0.0 0.0.255.255 area 0** command, enabling
OSPF 2 on RD1's S0/0/1 and S0/1/0 interfaces. As such, the redistribution process also redistributed those routes.

Stated more generally, when the **redistribute** command refers to another IGP as the routing source, it tells the router to redistribute the following:

Key Topic

■ All routes in the routing table learned by that routing protocol

■ All connected routes of interfaces on which that routing protocol is enabled

Although Example 9-5 shows the evidence that Router RD1 added the topology data to its EIGRP topology database, it did not show any routes. Example 9-6 shows the IP routing tables on both RD1 and Router R2, a router internal to the EIGRP domain. R2's routes forward the packets toward the redistributing router, which in turn has routes from the OSPF domain with which to forward the packet to the destination subnet.

Example 9-6   *Verification of IP Routes on RD1 and R2*

```
! First, on RD1
RD1#show ip route 172.16.0.0
Routing entry for 172.16.0.0/16, 5 known subnets
  Attached (2 connections)
  Variably subnetted with 2 masks
  Redistributing via eigrp 1


O        172.16.48.0/25 [110/65] via 172.16.18.2, 00:36:25, Serial0/0/1
                          [110/65] via 172.16.14.2, 00:36:25, Serial0/1/0
C        172.16.18.0/30 is directly connected, Serial0/0/1
C        172.16.14.0/30 is directly connected, Serial0/1/0
O        172.16.8.0/25 [110/65] via 172.16.18.2, 00:36:25, Serial0/0/1
O        172.16.4.0/25 [110/65] via 172.16.14.2, 00:36:25, Serial0/1/0
! Next, on Router R2
R2#show ip route
Codes: C - connected, S - static, R - RIP, M - mobile, B - BGP
       D - EIGRP, EX - EIGRP external, O - OSPF, IA - OSPF inter area
       N1 - OSPF NSSA external type 1, N2 - OSPF NSSA external type 2
       E1 - OSPF external type 1, E2 - OSPF external type 2
       i - IS-IS, su - IS-IS summary, L1 - IS-IS level-1, L2 - IS-IS level-2
       ia - IS-IS inter area, * - candidate default, U - per-user static route
       o - ODR, P - periodic downloaded static route

Gateway of last resort is not set

     172.16.0.0/16 is variably subnetted, 5 subnets, 2 masks
D EX    172.16.48.0/25 [170/3080448] via 172.30.12.1, 00:25:15, Serial0/0/1
D EX    172.16.18.0/30 [170/3080448] via 172.30.12.1, 00:25:15, Serial0/0/1
D EX    172.16.14.0/30 [170/3080448] via 172.30.12.1, 00:25:15, Serial0/0/1
D EX    172.16.8.0/25 [170/3080448] via 172.30.12.1, 00:25:15, Serial0/0/1
D EX    172.16.4.0/25 [170/3080448] via 172.30.12.1, 00:25:15, Serial0/0/1
     172.30.0.0/16 is variably subnetted, 5 subnets, 2 masks
D       172.30.17.0/30 [90/2172416] via 172.30.27.7, 00:25:15, FastEthernet0/0
```

```
C        172.30.26.0/23 is directly connected, FastEthernet0/0
C        172.30.2.0/23 is directly connected, FastEthernet0/1
D        172.30.6.0/23 [90/30720] via 172.30.27.7, 00:25:15, FastEthernet0/0
C        172.30.12.0/30 is directly connected, Serial0/0/1
```

Beginning with the output for R2, in the second half of the example, R2 knows routes for all five subnets in class B network 172.16.0.0, listing all as external EIGRP routes. The routes all use R2's link connected to RD1. Also, note that the administrative distance (AD) is set to 170, rather than the usual 90 for EIGRP routes. EIGRP defaults to use AD 90 for internal routes and AD 170 for external routes. Chapter 10 shows cases in which this default helps prevent routing loops when multiple redistribution points exist.

RD1 has routes for all routes in the OSPF domain as well, but as either connected or OSPF-learned routes.

Redistribution into OSPF

As you might expect, OSPF redistribution has several similarities and differences as compared to redistribution into EIGRP. Unlike EIGRP, OSPF does have useful default metrics for redistributed routes, but OSPF does use the same general methods to configure metrics for redistributed routes. Like EIGRP, OSPF flags redistributed routes as being external. Unlike EIGRP, OSPF creates LSAs to represent each external route, and OSPF must then apply some much different logic than EIGRP to calculate the best route to each external subnet.

This section examines the OSPF redistribution process and configuration. It also discusses background on three OSPF LSA Types—Types 4, 5, and 7—all created to help OSPF distribute information so that routers can calculate the best route to each external subnet.

OSPF **redistribute** Command Reference

First, for reference, the following lines show the generic syntax of the **redistribute** command when used as a **router ospf** subcommand. Note that the syntax differs slightly depending on the routing protocol into which routes will be redistributed. Following that, Table 9-4 lists the options on the command with a brief description:

```
redistribute protocol [process-id ¦ as-number] [metric metric-value]
[metric-type type-value] [match {internal ¦ external 1 ¦ external 2 ¦
nssa-external}] [tag tag-value] [route-map map-tag] [subnets]
```

Table 9-4 *Parameters on the OSPF* redistribute *Command*

Key Topic

Option	Description
protocol	The source of routing information. Includes **RIP**, **OSPF**, **EIGRP**, **IS-IS**, **BGP**, **connected**, and **static**.
process-id, as-number	If redistributing a routing protocol that uses a process-id or ASN on the **router** global config command, use this parameter to refer to that process or ASN value.

Table 9-4 *Parameters on the OSPF* **redistribute** *Command*

Option	Description
metric	Defines the cost metric assigned to routes redistributed by this command, unless overridden by a referenced route map.
metric-type {1 | 2}	Defines the external metric type for the routes redistributed by this command: **1** (E1 routes) or **2** (E2 routes).
match	If redistributing from another OSPF process, this keyword lets you match internal OSPF routes, external (by type), and NSSA external routes, essentially filtering which routes are redistributed.
tag	Assigns a unitless integer value to the routes redistributed by this command—a tag that can be later matched by other routers using a route-map.
route-map	Apply the logic in the referenced route-map to filter routes, set metrics, and set route tags.
subnets	Redistribute subnets of classful networks. Without this parameter, only routes for classful networks are redistributed. (This behavior is unique to the OSPF **redistribute** command.)

Configuring OSPF Redistribution with Minimal Parameters

The **redistribute** subcommand under **router ospf** has many optional settings. To better appreciate some of these settings, this section first examines the results when using all defaults, using as few parameters as possible. Following the discussion of the behavior with defaults, the next examples add the parameters that complete the redistribution configuration.

Redistribution into OSPF uses the following defaults:

- When taking from BGP, use a default metric of 1.

- When taking from another OSPF process, take the source route's metric.

- When taking from all other sources, use a default metric of 20.

- Create a Type 5 LSA for each redistributed route (external) if not inside an NSSA area; create a Type 7 LSA if inside an NSSA area.

- Use external metric type 2.

- Redistribute only routes of classful (class A, B, and C) networks, and not routes for subnets.

To demonstrate OSPF redistribution, this section uses an example that uses the same inter-network shown in Figure 9-6, including the baseline configuration shown in Example 9-1, and the EIGRP redistribution configuration shown in Examples 9-2 and 9-4. Essentially, the upcoming OSPF examples begin with Router RD1 including all the configurations seen in all the earlier examples in this chapter. According to those examples, OSPF has been correctly configured on the routers on the right side of Figure 9-6, EIGRP has been configured on the left, and the configuration of redistribution of OSPF routes into EIGRP has been completed. However, no redistribution into OSPF has been configured yet.

For perspective, before showing the redistribution into OSPF, Example 9-7 reviews the OSPF configuration, along with **show** commands listing RD1's IP routing table entries and its OSPF LSDB.

Example 9-7 *Router RD1 Routing Protocol Configuration, Before Redistribution into OSPF*

```
RD1#show run
! lines omitted for brevity
router eigrp 1
 redistribute ospf 2
 network 172.30.0.0
 default-metric 1000 33 255 1 1500
 no auto-summary
!
router ospf 2
 router-id 1.1.1.1
 log-adjacency-changes
 network 172.16.0.0 0.0.255.255 area 0

RD1#show ip route 172.30.0.0
Routing entry for 172.30.0.0/16, 5 known subnets
  Attached (2 connections)
  Variably subnetted with 2 masks
  Redistributing via eigrp 1

C       172.30.17.0/30 is directly connected, Serial0/1/1
D       172.30.26.0/23 [90/2172416] via 172.30.17.2, 01:08:50, Serial0/1/1
                       [90/2172416] via 172.30.12.2, 01:08:50, Serial0/0/0
D       172.30.2.0/23 [90/2172416] via 172.30.12.2, 01:08:50, Serial0/0/0
D       172.30.6.0/23 [90/2172416] via 172.30.17.2, 01:08:50, Serial0/1/1
C       172.30.12.0/30 is directly connected, Serial0/0/0
RD1#show ip ospf database

            OSPF Router with ID (1.1.1.1) (Process ID 2)


               Router Link States (Area 0)
```

```
Link ID          ADV Router       Age        Seq#         Checksum Link count
1.1.1.1          1.1.1.1          1425       0x80000007   0x007622 4
4.4.4.4          4.4.4.4          1442       0x8000000D   0x00B1E9 4
8.8.8.8          8.8.8.8          1466       0x80000006   0x00640E 4


                 Net Link States (Area 0)


Link ID          ADV Router       Age        Seq#         Checksum
172.16.48.4      4.4.4.4          1442       0x80000004   0x007E07
! The following occurs on OSPF internal router R4

R4#show ip route 172.30.0.0
% Network not in table
```

The output in Example 9-7 shows several important points relative to the upcoming redistribution configuration. First, by design, the EIGRP domain contains subnets of network 172.30.0.0; router RD1 knows routes for five subnets in this range. RD1 has four LSAs: three Type 1 Router LSAs (one each for routers RD1, R4, and R8), plus one Type 2 network LSAs (because only one subnet, 172.16.48.0/25, has elected a DR). Because the design for this internetwork puts all OSPF routers in area 0, no Type 3 summary LSAs exist in RD1's LSDB. Also, because no routers have redistributed external routes into OSPF yet, no Type 5 external nor Type 7 NSSA external routes are listed, either.

By adding the **redistribute eigrp 1** command in OSPF configuration mode, OSPF tries to redistribute routes from EIGRP–but with no success. The reason is that by omitting the **subnets** parameter, OSPF will only redistribute routes for entire classful subnets, and only if such a route is listed in the IP routing table. Example 9-8 shows the results.

Example 9-8   *Redistributing into OSPF from EIGRP 1, all Default Settings*

```
RD1#configure terminal
Enter configuration commands, one per line.  End with CNTL/Z.
RD1(config)#router ospf 2
RD1(config-router)#redistribute eigrp 1
% Only classful networks will be redistributed
RD1(config-router)#^Z
RD1#
RD1#show ip ospf database

            OSPF Router with ID (1.1.1.1) (Process ID 2)


                 Router Link States (Area 0)


Link ID          ADV Router       Age        Seq#         Checksum Link count
1.1.1.1          1.1.1.1          6          0x80000008   0x007A1B 4
```

```
4.4.4.4          4.4.4.4          1782      0x8000000D  0x00B1E9  4
8.8.8.8          8.8.8.8          1806      0x80000006  0x00640E  4


                 Net Link States (Area 0)


Link ID          ADV Router       Age       Seq#        Checksum
172.16.48.4      4.4.4.4          1782      0x80000004  0x007E07
```

IOS even mentions that only classful routes will be redistributed. As seen in Example 9-7, no route exists for the exact class B network prefix of 172.30.0.0/16, and by default, OSPF does not redistribute any subnets inside that range, as noted in the informational message in Example 9-8. So, the OSPF database on Router RD1 remains unchanged.

By changing the configuration to use the **redistribute eigrp 1 subnets** command, OSPF indeed redistributes the routes, as shown in Example 9-9.

Example 9-9 *Redistributing from EIGRP into OSPF, with Subnets*

```
RD1#configure terminal
Enter configuration commands, one per line.  End with CNTL/Z.
RD1(config)#router ospf 2
RD1(config-router)#redistribute eigrp 1 subnets
RD1(config-router)#^Z
RD1#
May 12 12:49:48.735: %SYS-5-CONFIG_I: Configured from console by console
RD1#show ip ospf database
! omitting the Type 1 and 2 LSA output for brevity


                 Type-5 AS External Link States


Link ID          ADV Router       Age       Seq#        Checksum Tag
172.30.2.0       1.1.1.1          3         0x80000001  0x008050  0
172.30.6.0       1.1.1.1          3         0x80000001  0x005478  0
172.30.12.0      1.1.1.1          3         0x80000001  0x0005C3  0
172.30.17.0      1.1.1.1          3         0x80000001  0x00CDF5  0
172.30.26.0      1.1.1.1          3         0x80000001  0x007741  0
! The following occurs on router R4
R4#show ip route 172.30.0.0
Routing entry for 172.30.0.0/16, 5 known subnets
  Variably subnetted with 2 masks

O E2    172.30.17.0/30 [110/20] via 172.16.14.1, 00:01:10, Serial0/0/0
O E2    172.30.26.0/23 [110/20] via 172.16.14.1, 00:01:11, Serial0/0/0
O E2    172.30.2.0/23 [110/20] via 172.16.14.1, 00:01:11, Serial0/0/0
O E2    172.30.6.0/23 [110/20] via 172.16.14.1, 00:01:11, Serial0/0/0
O E2    172.30.12.0/30 [110/20] via 172.16.14.1, 00:01:11, Serial0/0/0
```

After adding the **subnets** option, router RD1 redistributes the five routes from the EIGRP domain. Of particular interest:

■ If you look back to Example 9-7's **show ip route** command output from Router RD1, you see three EIGRP-learned routes, plus two connected routes, inside the EIGRP domain. Example 9-9's two **show** commands in Example 9-9 confirm that OSPF redistributes the three EIGRP-learned routes, plus the two connected subnets on which EIGRP is enabled (172.30.12.0/30 and 172.30.17.0/30).

■ The **show ip ospf database** command in Example 9-9 lists R1 (RID 1.1.1.1) as the advertising router of the five new Type 5 LSAs, because RD1 (with RID 1.1.1.1) created each Type 5 LSA.

■ Per OSPF internal router R4's **show ip route 172.30.0.0** command at the end of Example 9-9, the external metric type is indeed E2, meaning external type 2.

■ Per that same command on router R4, the metric for each route is 20. The reasoning is that the default metric is 20 when redistributing from EIGRP into OSPF, and with an E2 route, internal OSPF costs are not added to the cost of the route.

That last point regarding the external route type requires a little more discussion. OSPF defines external routes as either an external type 1 (E1) or external type 2 (E2) route. By default, the OSPF **redistribute** command creates Type 2 routes, noting this external route type in the Type 5 LSA. The difference between the two lies in how OSPF calculates the metrics for E1 and E2 routes.

The next section completes the discussion of how OSPF can set the metrics when redistributing routes–or more specifically, the metric as listed in the Type 5 LSA created for that subnet. Following that, the text takes a detailed look at how OSPF calculates the best route for E2 routes. Later, a different section titled "Redistributing into OSPF as E1 Routes" discusses the same subject, but for E1 routes.

Setting OSPF Metrics on Redistributed Routes

As mentioned earlier, no matter the source of the redistributed route, OSPF has a default metric to use. However, OSPF can set the metrics for redistributed routes using the same options used for EIGRP. Table 9-5 summarizes the defaults and metric setting options for redistribution into OSPF.

Key
Topic

Table 9-5 *Summary of Metric Values When Redistributing into OSPF*

Function	Command or Metric Values
Default if no metric configuration exists	Cost 1 for routes learned from BGP.
	If redistributed from another OSPF process, use the source route's OSPF cost.
	Cost 20 for all other route sources.
Setting the default for all **redistribute** commands	The **default-metric** *cost* OSPF subcommand.

Table 9-5 *Summary of Metric Values When Redistributing into OSPF*

Function	Command or Metric Values
Setting the metric for one route source	The **metric** *cost* parameters on the **redistribute** command.
Setting different metrics for routes learned from a single source	Use the **route-map** parameter on the **redistribute** command.

LSAs and Metrics for External Type 2 Routes

To appreciate how OSPF calculates the possible routes for each E2 route, you need to take a moment to think about the Type 5 LSA in more detail. First, by definition, the router that performs the redistribution into OSPF becomes an autonomous system border router (ASBR) because it injects external routes into OSPF. For each such route, that ASBR creates a Type 5 LSA for that subnet. The Type 5 LSA includes the following fields:

- **LSID:** The subnet number

- **Mask:** The subnet mask

- **Advertising router:** The RID of the ASBR injecting the route

- **Metric:** The metric as set by the ASBR

- **External Metric Type:** The external metric type, either 1 or 2

When created, the ASBR floods the Type 5 LSA throughout the area. Then, if any ABRs exist, the ABRs flood the Type 5 LSAs into any normal (nonstubby) areas. (Note that ABRs must not forward Type 5 LSAs into any type of stubby area, instead relying on default routes.) Figure 9-7 shows a sample flooding of the Type 5 LSA for EIGRP subnet 172.30.27.0/23 as an E2 route.

When flooded, OSPF has little work to do to calculate the metric for an E2 route, because by definition, the E2 route's metric is simply the metric listed in the Type 5 LSA. In other words, the OSPF routers do not add any internal OSPF cost to the metric for an E2 route.

Because routers ignore internal cost when calculating E2 external route metrics, whenever an alternative route can be calculated, the metrics tie. For example, in Figure 9-7, Router R4 has two possible physical routes to ASBR RD1–one directly to RD1, and one through R8. The cost for both routes to external subnet 172.30.26.0/23 will be 20, because that is the cost RD1 assigned to the route (actually, the Type 5 LSA) when redistributing the route.

To avoid loops, OSPF routers use a tiebreaker system to allow a router to choose a best external route. The logic differs slightly depending on whether the router in question resides in the same area as the ASBR (intra-area), or in a different area (interarea), as discussed in under the next two headings.

Determining the Next-Hop for Type 2 External Routes–Intra-area

When a router finds multiple routes for the same E2 destination subnet, it chooses the best route based on the lowest cost to reach any ASBR(s) that advertised the lowest E2 metric. For example, if five ASBRs all advertised the same subnet as an E2 route, and two ASBRs

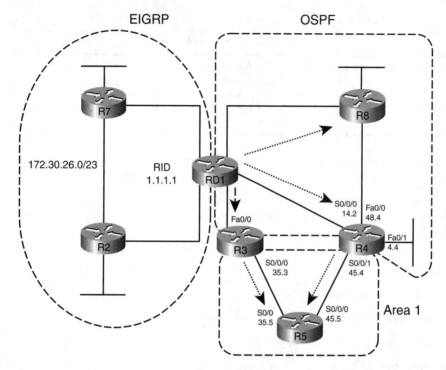

Figure 9-7   *Flooding of Type 5 LSAs*

advertised a metric of 10, and the other three advertised a metric of 20, either of the first two ASBRs could be used. Then, the router calculates its lowest cost route to reach the ASBR and uses the next-hop IP address and outgoing interface listed in that route.

The following list spells out the mechanics of the calculation used to break the tie when multiple equal-cost E2 routes exist for a particular subnet:

Key Topic

Step 1.   Find the advertising ASBR(s) as listed in the Type 5 LSA(s) for Type 5 LSAs.

Step 2.   Calculate the lowest cost route to reach any of the ASBR(s) based on the intra-area LSDB topology.

Step 3.   Use the outgoing interface and next hop based on the best route to reach the ASBR (as chosen at Step 2).

Step 4.   The route's metric is unchanged–it is still simply the value listed in the Type 5 LSA.

For example, use Router R4 in Figure 9-7 as an example and the E2 route for 172.30.26.0/23. Before using these four steps, R4 calculated two possible routes for 172.16.26.0/23: an E2 route directly to RD1, and another route through R8. Both routes use metric 20 in this case, so the routes tie. Because of the tie, R4 proceeds with these steps as follows:

Step 1.   R4 looks in the Type 5 LSA, and sees RID 1.1.1.1 (RD1) is the advertising ASBR.

Step 2.   R4 then looks at its area 0 LSDB entries, including the Type 1 LSA for RID 1.1.1.1, and calculates all possible area 0 routes to reach 1.1.1.1.

Step 3.   R4's best route to reach RID 1.1.1.1 happens to be through its S0/0/0 interface, to next-hop RD1 (172.16.14.1), so R4's route to 172.16.26.0/23 uses these details.

Step 4.   The route lists metric 20, as listed in the Type 5 LSA.

Figure 9-8 shows the interface costs Router R4 will use, based on its LSDB, to calculate the cost for two possible routes to reach ASBR RD1. Again using subnet 172.30.26.0/23 as an example, RD1 first looks at the Type 5 external LSA and sees RID 1.1.1.1 as the advertising ASBR. R4 then calculates the costs based on its intra-area LSDB—but we can perform the equivalent by adding the interface costs seen in Figure 9-8. Example 9-10 lists the external Type 5 LSAs, highlighting subnet 172.30.26.0/23, and the interface costs on both R4 and R8 as seen in the figure.

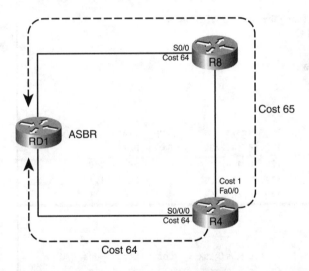

Figure 9-8   *R4's Cost to Reach ASBR RD1*

Example 9-10   *Verifying OSPF External Routes–Intra-area*

```
R4#show ip ospf database | begin Ext
               Type-5 AS External Link States

Link ID          ADV Router       Age        Seq#         Checksum Tag
172.30.2.0       1.1.1.1          189        0x80000002   0x007E51 0
172.30.6.0       1.1.1.1          189        0x80000002   0x005279 0
172.30.12.0      1.1.1.1          189        0x80000002   0x0003C4 0
172.30.17.0      1.1.1.1          189        0x80000002   0x00CBF6 0
172.30.26.0      1.1.1.1          189        0x80000002   0x007542 0

R4#show ip ospf database external 172.30.26.0
```

```
                OSPF Router with ID (4.4.4.4) (Process ID 4)


                   Type-5 AS External Link States

Routing Bit Set on this LSA
LS age: 175
Options: (No TOS-capability, DC)
LS Type: AS External Link
Link State ID: 172.30.26.0 (External Network Number )
Advertising Router: 1.1.1.1
LS Seq Number: 80000001
Checksum: 0x7741
Length: 36
Network Mask: /23
      Metric Type: 2 (Larger than any link state path)
      TOS: 0
      Metric: 20
      Forward Address: 0.0.0.0
      External Route Tag: 0


R4#show ip ospf interface brief
Interface   PID   Area        IP Address/Mask    Cost   State  Nbrs F/C
Se0/0/0     4     0           172.16.14.2/30     64     P2P    1/1
Fa0/1       4     0           172.16.4.4/25      1      DR     0/0
Fa0/0       4     0           172.16.48.4/25     1      DR     1/1
Se0/0/1     4     1           172.16.45.4/25     64     P2P    1/1
! Next output occurs on R8

R8#show ip ospf interface brief
Interface   PID   Area        IP Address/Mask    Cost   State  Nbrs F/C
Fa0/1       8     0           172.16.8.8/25      1      DR     0/0
Se0/0       8     0           172.16.18.2/30     64     P2P    1/1
Fa0/0       8     0           172.16.48.8/25     1      BDR    1/1
```

Determining the Next-hop for Type 2 External Routes–Interarea

When a router exists in a different area than the ASBR, the issues remain the same, but the tie-breaker calculation of choosing the least cost route to reach the ASBR changes. If a router finds multiple routes to reach a single E2 subnet, some or all may tie based on metric, because the metric is based solely on the external cost as defined by the ASBR. (If multiple ASBRs redistribute routes for the same prefix, each ASBR can assign a different metric.) A router then chooses the best route based on the least-cost route to reach an ASBR that has advertised the lowest E2 cost for the subnet.

When the ASBR is in a different area, the calculation of the cost to reach the ASBR requires more information, and even an additional LSA type, as compared with the intra-area calculation. To calculate their best route to reach the ASBR, a router in another area adds the cost to reach an ABR between the areas, plus that ABR's cost to reach the ASBR. To make more sense of that concept, Figure 9-9 shows a portion of Figure 9-7, with costs highlighted, assuming the OSPF reference bandwidth is also using default settings.

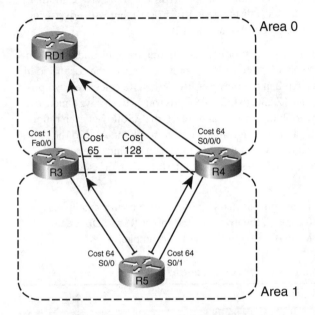

Figure 9-9   *R5's Cost to Reach ASBR RD1*

R5 has two possible routes shown in Figure 9-9 to reach ASBR RD1. On the left, the path through R3 has a total cost of 65. To the right, the router through ABR R4 has a total cost of 128. R5 then chooses the route through R3 as the best route based on the least cost to reach the ASBR.

For humans, when you have a figure and know all costs, the calculation of the costs of the two routes is simple. However, for routers, the calculation occurs in two parts:

Step 1.   Calculate the cost to reach the ABR, based on the local area's topology database.

Step 2.   Add the cost from the ABR to the ASBR, as listed in a Type 4 LSA.

ABRs create this new type of LSA—the Type 4 Summary ASBR LSA—to support the logic mentioned at Step 2. The Type 4 ASBR LSA lists the RID of the ASBR, and the RID of the ABR that created and flooded the Type 4 LSA. Most importantly, the Type 4 LSA lists that ABR's cost to reach the ASBR. In effect, the LSA makes an announcement like this: "I am ABR X, I can reach ASBR Y, and my cost to reach that ASBR is Z." In short, it allows the second part of the computation.

ABRs create Type 4 LSAs in reaction to receiving an external LSA from some ASBR. When an ABR forwards a Type 5 LSA into an area, the ABR looks at the RID of the ASBR that created the Type 5 LSA. The ABR then creates a Type 4 LSA listing that ASBR, and the cost to reach that ASBR, flooding that Type 4 LSA into the neighboring areas.

For example, using Figure 9-9 again, R3 would create and flood a Type 4 Summary ASBR LSA into area 1. R3's Type 4 LSA lists ASBR 1.1.1.1 (RD1), ABR 3.3.3.3 (itself), and cost 1 (R3's cost to reach 1.1.1.1). Similarly, in that same example, ABR R4 would create another Type 4 ASBR Summary LSA. This LSA also lists ASBR 1.1.1.1 (RD1), but with advertising ABR 4.4.4.4 (R4), and lists cost 64 (R4's cost to reach 1.1.1.1).

R5, internal to area 1, then calculates the cost for each competing route by adding R5's intra-area cost to reach the respective ABRs (Step 1 in the previous list), to the cost listed in the corresponding Type 4 LSAs (Step 2 in the previous list). When R5 calculates two possible routes to reach external subnet 172.30.26.0/23, R5 finds routes both have a metric of 20, so R5 tries to break the tie by looking at the cost to reach the ASBR over each route. To do so, R5 examines each route, adding its intra-area cost to reach the ABR to the ABR's cost to reach the ASBR (as listed in the Type 4 LSA). In this case, R5 finds the route through R3 has the lower cost (65), so R5 uses outgoing interface s0/0 for its route to 172.30.26.0/23.

Example 9-11 lists the **show** command output that demonstrates the same example. Again focusing on R5's route for 172.30.26.0/23, the example first shows R5's LSDB, beginning with the Summary ASBR LSAs. More discussion follows the example.

Example 9-11 *Redistributing from EIGRP into OSPF, with Subnets*

```
R5#show ip ospf database | begin ASB
                Summary ASB Link States (Area 1)


Link ID         ADV Router      Age          Seq#         Checksum
1.1.1.1         3.3.3.3         956          0x8000000D   0x00E43A
1.1.1.1         4.4.4.4         1044         0x8000000B   0x00439A


                Type-5 AS External Link States


Link ID         ADV Router      Age          Seq#         Checksum Tag
172.30.2.0      1.1.1.1         1185         0x8000000B   0x006C5A 0
172.30.6.0      1.1.1.1         1185         0x8000000B   0x004082 0
172.30.12.0     1.1.1.1         1185         0x8000000B   0x00F0CD 0
172.30.17.0     1.1.1.1         1185         0x8000000B   0x00B9FF 0
172.30.26.0     1.1.1.1         1185         0x8000000B   0x00634B 0

R5#show ip ospf database asbr-summary


            OSPF Router with ID (5.5.5.5) (Process ID 5)


            Summary ASB Link States (Area 1)


  Routing Bit Set on this LSA
```

```
 LS age: 984
 Options: (No TOS-capability, DC, Upward)
 LS Type: Summary Links(AS Boundary Router)
 Link State ID: 1.1.1.1 (AS Boundary Router address)
 Advertising Router: 3.3.3.3
 LS Seq Number: 8000000D
 Checksum: 0xE43A
 Length: 28
 Network Mask: /0
       TOS: 0  Metric: 1


 LS age: 1072
 Options: (No TOS-capability, DC, Upward)
 LS Type: Summary Links(AS Boundary Router)
 Link State ID: 1.1.1.1 (AS Boundary Router address)
 Advertising Router: 4.4.4.4
 LS Seq Number: 8000000B
 Checksum: 0x439A
 Length: 28
 Network Mask: /0
       TOS: 0  Metric: 64

R5#show ip ospf border-routers
OSPF Process 5 internal Routing Table
Codes: i - Intra-area route, I - Inter-area route

i 4.4.4.4 [64] via 172.16.45.4, Serial0/1, ABR, Area 1, SPF 6
I 1.1.1.1 [65] via 172.16.35.3, Serial0/0, ASBR, Area 1, SPF 6
i 3.3.3.3 [64] via 172.16.35.3, Serial0/0, ABR, Area 1, SPF 6

R5#show ip route 172.30.0.0
Routing entry for 172.30.0.0/16, 5 known subnets
  Variably subnetted with 2 masks


O E2    172.30.17.0/30 [110/20] via 172.16.35.3, 05:48:42, Serial0/0
O E2    172.30.26.0/23 [110/20] via 172.16.35.3, 05:48:42, Serial0/0
O E2    172.30.2.0/23 [110/20] via 172.16.35.3, 05:48:42, Serial0/0
O E2    172.30.6.0/23 [110/20] via 172.16.35.3, 05:48:42, Serial0/0
O E2    172.30.12.0/30 [110/20] via 172.16.35.3, 05:48:42, Serial0/0
```

The **show ip ospf database | begin ASB** command's output lists two Type 4 LSAs. (The command itself lists the summary of R5's OSPF LSDB, beginning with the section that lists Type 4 LSAs.) Both Type 4 LSAs list ASBR RD1's RID of 1.1.1.1 as the LSID, but they each list different advertising routers: 3.3.3.3 (R3) and 4.4.4.4 (R4). In that same command, the output lists five Type 5 LSAs for the five subnets in the EIGRP domain, each with advertising router 1.1.1.1 (RD1).

The next command, **show ip ospf database asbr-summary**, lists the same two Type 4 LSAs seen in the previous command, but in detail. The first lists ASBR 1.1.1.1 (RD1), with ABR 3.3.3.3 (R3), and a cost of 1. The second lists ASBR 1.1.1.1, but with ABR 4.4.4.4 (R4), and a cost of 64. The costs list the respective ABR's cost to reach ASBR 1.1.1.1.

The third command, **show ip ospf border-routers**, lists a line for every ABR and ASBR known to the local router. It lists whether the router is inside the same area or in another area, the RID of the ABR or ASBR, and this router's best route to reach each ABR and ASBR. This command essentially shows the answer to the question "which route to ASBR 1.1.1.1 is best." Finally, the last command lists R5's IP route for 172.30.26.0, with the same next-hop and outgoing interface information as seen in the entry for RID 1.1.1.1 in the output of the **show ip ospf border-routers** command.

Redistributing into OSPF as E1 Routes

OSPF's external metric type feature allows engineers a design tool for influencing the choice of best route. E2 routes work well when the design needs to choose the best route based on the external metric–in other words, the metric as perceived outside the OSPF domain. E2 routes ignore the internal OSPF cost (except when breaking ties for best route), so when OSPF compares two E2 routes for the same subnet, that first choice to pick the lowest-metric route is based on the external metric only.

OSPF routers calculate the metrics of E1 routes by adding the internal cost to reach the ASBR to the external cost defined on the redistributing ASBR. As a result, engineer can influence the choice of routes based on the combination of the external and internal OSPF cost simply by redistributing a route as an E1 route instead of as an E2 route. To take advantage of this feature, the **redistribute** command simply needs to set the metric type.

Example 9-12 shows the simple change to the redistribution configuration on RD1 (as shown earlier in Example 9-9) to make all routes redistributed from EIGRP into OSPF be E1 routes. The example also lists output from R4 demonstrating the metric, which is based on the (default) external metric (20) plus R4's best internal metric to reach ASBR 1.1.1.1 (64).

Example 9-12   *Redistributing from EIGRP into OSPF, with Subnets*

```
RD1#conf t
Enter configuration commands, one per line.  End with CNTL/Z.
RD1(config)#router ospf 2
RD1(config-router)#redistribute eigrp 1 subnets metric-type 1
RD1(config-router)#^Z
RD1#
! Moving to router R4
R4#show ip route 172.30.0.0
Routing entry for 172.30.0.0/16, 5 known subnets
  Variably subnetted with 2 masks


O E1    172.30.17.0/30 [110/84] via 172.16.14.1, 00:00:06, Serial0/0/0
O E1    172.30.26.0/23 [110/84] via 172.16.14.1, 00:00:06, Serial0/0/0
```

```
O E1    172.30.2.0/23 [110/84] via 172.16.14.1, 00:00:06, Serial0/0/0
O E1    172.30.6.0/23 [110/84] via 172.16.14.1, 00:00:06, Serial0/0/0
O E1    172.30.12.0/30 [110/84] via 172.16.14.1, 00:00:06, Serial0/0/0

R4#show ip ospf border-routers

OSPF Process 4 internal Routing Table
Codes: i - Intra-area route, I - Inter-area route

i 1.1.1.1 [64] via 172.16.14.1, Serial0/0/0, ASBR, Area 0, SPF 16
i 3.3.3.3 [65] via 172.16.14.1, Serial0/0/0, ABR, Area 0, SPF 16
i 3.3.3.3 [128] via 172.16.45.5, Serial0/0/1, ABR, Area 1, SPF 8
```

Note that for routers in a different area than the ASBR, the calculation of metric follows the same general logic used when breaking ties for E2 routes. Generally, the computation adds three items:

Key Topic

■ The best intra-area cost to reach the ABR (per that area's LSDB)

■ The cost from that ABR to the ASBR (per Type 4 LSA)

■ The external cost for the route (per Type 5 LSA)

For example, Figure 9-9 shows that R5's best cost to reach ASBR RD1 was out S0/0, to R3 next, with cost 65. Adding the external cost of 20, R5's best route will have a metric of 85. R5 calculates that cost by adding the following:

■ The intra-area cost to ABR R3 (64), by analyzing the area 1 LSDB entries

■ R3's cost to reach ASBR 1.1.1.1, as listed in its Type 4 LSA (1)

■ The external cost as listed in the Type 5 LSA (20)

A Brief Comparison of E1 and E2 Routes

OSPF defines two types of external routes to give network designers two slightly different tools with which to calculate the best route to reach destination external to OSPF. For E1 routes, both the external cost and internal OSPF cost matters to the choice of best route. For E2 routes, only the external cost matters to the choice of best route (unless a tie needs to be broken.)

The benefits of the different external route types apply mostly to when multiple ASBRs advertise the same subnet. For example, imagine two ASBRs, ASBR1 and ASBR2, between OSPF and another routing domain. If the goal is to always send traffic through ASBR1, you could use E2 routes and set the metric for ASBR1's redistributed routes to a lower metric than ASBR2. Because routers ignore the internal metrics when calculating the E2 metrics, then every router will choose ASBR1 as the better ASBR. Conversely, if the goal were to balance the traffic, and make each router pick the closest ASBR, both ASBRs could set the same metric to their redistributed routes, but make the routers Type E1. As a result, routers closer to each ASBR choose best routes based on the lower OSPF internal costs.

Also, note that for a given prefix/length, OSPF always prefers an E1 route over an E2 route.

External Routes in NSSA Areas

Routes may be redistributed into OSPF on any OSPF router, with a few exceptions. The router may be internal to Area 0, like router RD1 in the many examples earlier in this chapter. It can also be an ABR connected to several areas. It can be a router internal to a nonbackbone area as well.

Of the four types of stubby areas, two do not allow redistribution into the area, and two do allow redistribution–even though none of the stubby area types allow Type 5 LSAs. OSPF does not allow routers in stubby and totally stubby areas to inject external routes. However, routers in not-so-stubby areas–NSSA areas–can redistribute routes, while still holding to the restriction of having no Type 5 LSAs.

OSPF supports the injection of external routes into NSSA areas by defining the Type 7 AS External LSA. This LSA type essentially replaces the Type 5 LSA's role, but only inside the NSSA area. Figure 9-10 shows a conceptual view.

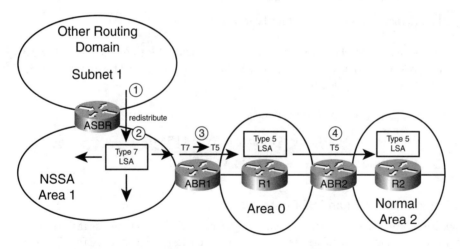

Figure 9-10 *Process of Adding and Converting Type 7 LSAs*

Following the steps in the figure:

Step 1.   The ASBR attached to NSSA area 1 redistributes a route for subnet 1, creating a Type 7 LSA.

Step 2.   The ASBR floods the Type 7 LSA throughout NSSA area 1.

Step 3.   ABR1 converts the Type 7 LSA to a Type 5 LSA when forwarding into other areas (area 0 in this case).

Step 4.   ABR2, connected to another normal area, forwards the Type 5 LSA for subnet 1 into normal area 2.

Example 9-13 demonstrates the concept using area 1 from Figures 9-7 and 9-9. Area 1 has been converted to be an NSSA area. R5 has been configured to redistribute connected routes. This feature allows a router to inject connected routes into a routing domain without having to enable the routing protocol on the corresponding interfaces. In this case, R5 will redistribute subnet 10.1.1.0/24, a connected route added by R5 using interface loopback0.

Example 9-13 *Redistributing from EIGRP into OSPF, with Subnets*

```
! R5's new configuration here:
interface loopback0
 ip address 10.1.1.1 255.255.255.0
router ospf 5
 area 1 nssa
 redistribute connected subnets

R5#show ip ospf database | begin Type-7
                Type-7 AS External Link States (Area 1)


Link ID          ADV Router        Age       Seq#       Checksum Tag
10.1.1.0         5.5.5.5           26        0x80000001 0x00E0A6 0


R5#show ip ospf database nssa-external


            OSPF Router with ID (5.5.5.5) (Process ID 5)


                Type-7 AS External Link States (Area 1)


  LS age: 69
  Options: (No TOS-capability, Type 7/5 translation, DC)
  LS Type: AS External Link
  Link State ID: 10.1.1.0 (External Network Number )
  Advertising Router: 5.5.5.5
  LS Seq Number: 80000001
  Checksum: 0xE0A6
  Length: 36
  Network Mask: /24
        Metric Type: 2 (Larger than any link state path)
        TOS: 0
        Metric: 20
        Forward Address: 172.16.45.5
        External Route Tag: 0
! Moving to router R8
R8#show ip ospf database | begin Type-7


R8#show ip ospf database | begin External
```

```
             Type-5 AS External Link States

Link ID          ADV Router      Age       Seq#        Checksum Tag
10.1.1.0         4.4.4.4         263       0x80000001  0x009302 0
172.30.2.0       1.1.1.1         1655      0x8000000E  0x00665D 0
172.30.6.0       1.1.1.1         1655      0x8000000E  0x003A85 0
172.30.12.0      1.1.1.1         1655      0x8000000E  0x00EAD0 0
172.30.17.0      1.1.1.1         1655      0x8000000E  0x00B303 0
172.30.26.0      1.1.1.1         1655      0x8000000E  0x005D4E 0
```

The example begins with configuration on R5, followed by **show** commands on both Router R5 and R8. In particular, the **show ip ospf database | begin Type-7** command on R5 skips output until the heading for Type 7 LSAs, listing one such LSA. The LSA lists the subnet number (10.1.1.0) as the LSID, and the ASBR's RID (5.5.5.5, or R5). The next command, show detailed output from the **show ip ospf database nssa-external** command on R5 shows the details in the Type 7 LSA, including the LSA cost of 20–the same default used when injecting routes as Type 5 LSAs.

The second half of the output, on Router R8, starts with another **show ip ospf database | begin Type-7** command—the same exact command seen earlier in the example on R5. The null output in this command confirms that R8 has no Type 7 LSAs. However, the final command in the example confirms that R8 does have a Type 5 external LSA for subnet 10.1.1.0, with a listing of R4 (4.4.4.4) as the advertising router. This LSA does not list R5's RID of 5.5.5.5 as the advertising router, because R5 did not create this Type 5 LSA. Instead, R4 created this Type 5 LSA when R4 reacted to learning the Type 7 LSA inside area 1.

Finally, Example 9-14 shows a few interesting items about the IP routing table with NSSA areas. Routers inside the NSSA area use a different code in the output of **show ip route** to denote NSSA external routes as compared with normal external routes. The example shows R4's IP routing table, which lists an N2 route. This means that it is external Type 2, but inside an NSSA area, and using a Type 7 AS external LSA. The second part of the example shows R8's route for the same subnet. Because R8 is inside a non-NSSA area, R8 knows of subnet 10.1.1.0/24 because of a type 5 LSA, so R8 lists the route as an E2 route.

Example 9-14   *Redistributing from EIGRP into OSPF, with Subnets*

```
! R4's output here:
R4#show ip route
Codes: C - connected, S - static, R - RIP, M - mobile, B - BGP
       D - EIGRP, EX - EIGRP external, O - OSPF, IA - OSPF inter area
       N1 - OSPF NSSA external type 1, N2 - OSPF NSSA external type 2
       E1 - OSPF external type 1, E2 - OSPF external type 2
       i - IS-IS, su - IS-IS summary, L1 - IS-IS level-1, L2 - IS-IS level-2
       ia - IS-IS inter area, * - candidate default, U - per-user static route
       o - ODR, P - periodic downloaded static route

Gateway of last resort is not set
```

```
! lines omitted for brevity

     10.0.0.0/24 is subnetted, 1 subnets
O N2    10.1.1.0 [110/20] via 172.16.45.5, 00:10:54, Serial0/0/1
! R8, in area 0, next
R8#show ip route | begin 10.0.0.0
     10.0.0.0/24 is subnetted, 1 subnets
O E2    10.1.1.0 [110/20] via 172.16.48.4, 00:10:24, FastEthernet0/0
```

Exam Preparation Tasks

Planning Practice

The CCNP ROUTE exam expects test takers to review design documents, create implementation plans, and create verification plans. This section provides some exercises that may help you to take a step back from the minute details of the topics in this chapter so that you can think about the same technical topics from the planning perspective.

For each planning practice table, simply complete the table. Note that any numbers in parentheses represent the number of options listed for each item in the solutions in Appendix F, "Completed Planning Practice Tables."

Design Review Table

Table 9-6 lists several design goals related to this chapter. If these design goals were listed in a design document, and you had to take that document and develop an implementation plan, what implementation options come to mind? For any configuration items, a general description can be used, without concern about the specific parameters.

Table 9-6 *Design Review*

Design Goal	Possible Implementation Choices Covered in This Chapter
A design shows Router R1 as being connected to both an EIGRP and OSPF routing domain, with all external EIGRP routes using a particular set of component EIGRP metrics. How can these metrics be set? (3)	
A design shows Router R1 as being connected to two different EIGRP domains, with redistribution planned. Can the design cause the routers to calculate metrics based on both the metric assigned when redistributing and the internal EIGRP topology?	
The same design as in the previous row is shown, except describe whether or not the design can cause the routers to calculate metrics based solely on the metric components assigned when redistributing.	

Table 9-6 *Design Review*

Design Goal	Possible Implementation Choices Covered in This Chapter
A design shows Router R1 as being connected to two different OSPF domains, with redistribution planned, and all routes calculated by including internal and external OSPF distance.	
The same design as in the previous row is shown, except that all external route metrics are based solely on external metrics.	

Implementation Plan Peer Review Table

Table 9-7 shows a list of questions that others might ask, or that you might think about, during a peer review of another network engineer's implementation plan. Complete the table by answering the questions.

Table 9-7 *Notable Questions from This Chapter to Consider During an Implementation Plan Peer Review*

Question	Answer
A design shows Router R1 as being connected to both an EIGRP and OSPF routing domain. What default metrics will be used by the **redistribute** command for each routing protocol, if not set in R1's configuration?	
A plan shows redistribution between two EIGRP domains. What must be done to use the source route's original component metrics?	
A plan shows redistribution between two OSPF domains. What must be done to use the source route's original metric?	
The plan shows the **redistribute eigrp 2** command to redistribute from EIGRP 2 into OSPF. What other optional parameters are required to ensure redistribution of 10.1.1.0/24 from EIGRP?	
R1 has two connected interfaces in the EIGRP 2 domain and knows dozens of EIGRP routes. The plan shows the **redistribute eigrp 2 subnets** under an OSPF process. What else must be done to redistribute the two connected subnets inside the EIGRP domain?	

Create an Implementation Plan Table

To practice skills useful when creating your own implementation plan, list in Table 9-8 configuration commands related to the configuration of the following features. You may want to record your answers outside the book and set a goal to complete this table (and others like it) from memory during your final reviews before taking the exam.

Table 9-8 *Implementation Plan Configuration Memory Drill*

Feature	Configuration Commands/Notes
Configuring redistribution into EIGRP from OSPF. (List all parameters you can recall.)	
Configuring redistribution into OSPF from EIGRP. (List all parameters you can recall.)	
Setting default metrics for all **redistribute** commands, redistributing into EIGRP.	
Setting default metrics for all **redistribute** commands, redistributing into OSPF.	

Choosing Commands for a Verification Plan Table

To practice skills useful when creating your own verification plan, list in Table 9-9 all commands that supply the requested information. You may want to record your answers outside the book and set a goal to complete this table (and others like it) from memory during your final reviews before taking the exam.

Table 9-9 *Verification Plan Memory Drill*

Information Needed	Command(s)
Display a brief version of the EIGRP topology table, listing external routes.	
Display the EIGRP topology table, including notations identifying external routes.	
For external EIGRP routes, display the source of the route, external metric, and IP address of the router that redistributed the route.	
Identify external EIGRP-learned IP routes.	
Display a brief version of the OSPF topology table, listing Type 5 External LSAs.	
Display all OSPF Type 4 LSAs.	
Display all OSPF Type 5 LSAs.	
Display all OSPF Type 7 LSAs.	
Display the external route type for an OSPF external route.	
Display OSPF cost for each interface, briefly.	

Table 9-9   *Verification Plan Memory Drill*

Information Needed	Command(s)
On an internal router, display any same-area ABRs' costs to reach any ASBRs.	
On an internal router, display that router's best cost to reach an ASBR.	
Display the metric for all currently best external OSPF routes.	

Note: Some of the entries in this table may not have been specifically mentioned in this chapter but are listed in this table for review and reference.

Review all the Key Topics

Review the most important topics from inside the chapter, noted with the key topics icon in the outer margin of the page. Table 9-10 lists a reference of these key topics and the page numbers on which each is found.

Key Topic

Table 9-10   *Key Topics for Chapter 9*

Key Topic Element	Description	Page Number
List	Requirements for redistribution in a router	294
Table 9-2	Parameters on the EIGRP **redistribute** command	298
Table 9-3	Commands and options to set metrics when redistributing into EIGRP	301
List	Rules from what is redistributed from an IGP	304
Table 9-4	Parameters on the OSPF **redistribute** command	305
List	Defaults of the OSPF **redistribute** command	306
Table 9-5	Commands and options to set metrics when redistributing into OSPF	310
List	Tiebreaker rules for choosing the best E2 routes	312
List	Rules for calculating the metric of an interarea E1 route	319

Complete the Tables and Lists from Memory

Print a copy of Appendix D, "Memory Tables," (found on the CD), or at least the section for this chapter, and complete the tables and lists from memory. Appendix E, "Memory Tables Answer Key," also on the CD, includes completed tables and lists to check your work.

Define Key Terms

Define the following key terms from this chapter, and check your answers in the glossary.

Redistribution, External route, Type 4 Summary ASBR LSA, Type 5 External LSA, Type 7 AS External LSA, External Type 1, External Type 2

This chapter covers the following subjects:

Redistribution with Route Maps and Distribution Lists: This section focuses on the functions available using route maps and distribute lists on the same router that performs redistribution into either EIGRP or OSPF.

Issues with Multiple Redistribution Points: This section examines the domain loop problem that can occur when multiple routers redistribute routes between the same two routing domains. This section also examines various solutions, including the setting of large metrics, setting the administrative distance, and using route tags.

CHAPTER 10

Advanced IGP Redistribution

This chapter progresses past the basic mechanics of route redistribution (Chapter 9, "Basic IGP Redistribution") to examine two major topics. The first part of this chapter looks at the methods by which a router can manipulate the routes being redistributed beyond the settings of the metrics. This manipulation includes the filtering of routes and the setting of other values that can be associated with a route during the redistribution process.

The second part of the chapter examines a variety of design issues that occur when multiple redistribution points exist between routing domains. Many designs use multiple redistribution points for redundancy and even for load sharing. This redundancy creates some additional complexity. (This complexity has long been a favorite topic for the CCIE Routing lab exam.) This chapter also shows methods of dealing with the design issues, including the manipulation of metrics, administrative distance, and route tags.

"Do I Know This Already?" Quiz

The "Do I Know This Already?" quiz allows you to assess if you should read the entire chapter. If you miss no more than one of these eight self-assessment questions, you might want to move ahead to the "Exam Preparation Tasks." Table 10-1 lists the major headings in this chapter and the "Do I Know This Already?" quiz questions covering the material in those headings so that you can assess your knowledge of these specific areas. The answers to the "Do I Know This Already?" quiz appear in Appendix A.

Table 10-1   *"Do I Know This Already?" Foundation Topics Section-to-Question Mapping*

Foundations Topics Section	Questions
Redistribution with route maps and distribute lists	1-4
Issues with multiple redistribution points	5-8

1. Router R1 has been configured with the **redistribute ospf 1 route-map fred** command under **router eigrp 1**. The route map named fred needs to be configured to match routes to determine which routes are redistributed into EIGRP. Which of the following answers lists an item that cannot be matched by route map fred?

   a. Subnet number

   b. Next-hop router IP address of the route

   c.   Whether the route is an E1 or E2 route

   d.   The route's tag

   e.   The number of router hops between the router and the subnet

2. Router R1 refers to route-map fred when redistributing from EIGRP into OSPF. The entire route-map is listed next. Which of the following answers must be true based on the configuration as shown?

```
route-map fred deny 10
 match ip address one
route-map fred deny 20
 match ip address two
route-map fred permit 100
```

   a.   The third route map clause will allow any routes not already filtered by the first two clauses.

   b.   Routes permitted by ACL "two" will be redistributed.

   c.   Routes denied by ACL "one" will be redistributed.

   d.   All routes will be filtered.

3. On Router R1, process EIGRP 1 is redistributing routes from process OSPF 2, calling route-map fred with the **redistribute ospf 2 route-map fred** command. R1 has learned intra-area routes for 10.1.1.0/24 and 10.1.2.0/24 in part due to the Type 2 LSAs known for each subnet. The route map filters route 10.1.1.0/24 and allows 10.1.2.0/24 through. Which of the following commands on router R1 list subnet 10.1.1.0/24? (Choose two.)

   a.   show ip route

   b.   show ip eigrp topology

   c.   show ip ospf database

   d.   show ip eigrp topology 10.1.1.0/24

4. Router R1 is redistributing between two OSPF processes. Given the configuration shown, which includes all commands in the route map named fred, which of the following answers is true regarding the redistribution into OSPF process 1?

```
router ospf 1
 redistribute ospf 2 external 2 route-map fred
!
route-map fred permit 10
 match ip address 1
 set metric-type type-1
```

   a.   No routes are redistributed because a route cannot be both E1 and E2.

   b.   Only OSPF E2 routes in the OSPF 2 domain will be considered for redistribution.

   c.   Inside the OSPF 2 domain, any formerly E2 routes will become E1 routes.

   d.   Routes permitted by ACL 1 will be redistributed, regardless of whether the routes are E1 or E2 routes.

5. Which of the following is not true regarding IOS default settings for administrative distance?

    a. EIGRP internal: 90

    b. OSPF external: 110

    c. EIGRP external: 90

    d. RIP: 120

    e. OSPF internal: 110

6. A network includes a RIPv2 domain, an EIGRP domain, and an OSPF domain. Each pair of routing domains has multiple routers redistributing routes between the pair of domains. The design requires that the redistribution configuration avoid matching based on prefix/length because of the trouble in maintaining such configurations. Which one of the following tools can be used in all three routing domains to attempt to prevent domain loops? (This book uses the term *domain loop* to refer to the long routes that might be chosen for routes when redistribution exists–for example, a route may forward packets from the EIGRP domain, to the OSPF domain, back to EIGRP, and then to subnet X in the RIP domain.)

    a. Setting route tags

    b. Setting the default administrative distance differently for internal and external routes

    c. Setting administrative distance differently per route

    d. Setting metrics much higher for all external routes than for all internal routes

7. A co-worker is developing an implementation plan for a design that uses OSPF 2 and RIPv2 routing domains, with two routers redistributing between the two domains. The co-worker asks your help in choosing how to prevent domain loops by setting administrative distance. (This chapter uses the term *domain loop* to refer to the long routes that might be chosen for routes when redistribution exists–for example, a route may forward packets from the EIGRP 1 domain, to OSPF2, back to EIGRP 1, and then to subnet X in the RIP domain.) Assuming all other related settings use defaults, which of the following would solve the domain loop problem?

    a. The **distance ospf intra-area 80 inter-area 80** OSPF subcommand

    b. The **distance ospf external 80** OSPF subcommand

    c. The **distance ospf intra-area 180 inter-area 180** OSPF subcommand

    d. The **distance ospf external 180** OSPF subcommand

8. Router R1 sets a route tag for subnet 10.1.1.0/24 when redistributing from OSPF into EIGRP. Which of the following unit is assigned to the route tag?

    a. Kilobits/second.

    b. Tens of microseconds.

    c. Cost.

    d. Hop count.

    e. No unit is assigned.

Foundation Topics

Redistribution with Route Maps and Distribute Lists

In some cases, a redistribution design calls for all routes to be redistributed, all with the same metric, and all with the same external route type (if applicable). However, in other cases, the metrics may need to be set differently for different routes. Additionally, some designs require that only a subset of the routes should be redistributed, for instance, when only a few key subnets need to be exposed for connections from a partner. And with routing protocols that have different types of external routes, such as OSPF and IS-IS, the design may or may not allow all redistributed routes to be of the same external route type.

All these features require a tool by which IOS can identify the routes that need to be treated differently, whether given different metrics, filtered, and assigned a different external route type. IOS provides such a feature by allowing a reference to a **route-map** from the **redistribute** command. In particular, the route-map can perform the following:

Key Topic

- Identify the subset of the routes to filter or change based on the route's prefix/length, plus many other factors.

- Make filtering choices about which routes are redistributed, and which are not.

- Set the metric to different values based on information matchable by the route-map.

- Set the type of External route for different redistributed routes, for example, OSPF Type 1 for some routes, Type 2 for others.

- Set a route tag, a unitless integer value that can later be matched with a **route-map** at another redistribution point.

This section examines the mechanics of using the **redistribute... route-map** command option to filter routes and set the metrics, along with a few other small features.

> **Note:** Chapter 4's section "Filtering by Using route-maps" describes the logic behind the **route-map** command, so this chapter simply reviews the logic as needed. Refer to Chapter 4, "EIGRP Route Summarization and Filtering," for more detail on route maps.

Overview of Using route-maps with Redistribution

The **redistribute** command has two mechanisms that allow filtering of routes:

- The **match {internal | external 1 | external 2 | nssa-external}** parameters

- The **route-map** *map-name* option

Of these two options, the first applies only when redistributing from OSPF, and matches routes solely based on the types of routes listed here. However, the **route-map** referenced by the **redistribute** command has many options for identifying routes by matching various facts about the route.

To identify the routes, route-maps use the **match** subcommand. The **match** command can refer to ACLs and prefix-lists to match anything matchable by those tools, plus match other facts more directly. Table 10-2 lists the **match** command options that matter when using route-maps for IGP redistribution.

Key Topic

match Command	Description
match interface *interface-type interface-number* [... *interface-type interface-number*]	Looks at outgoing interface of routes
*__match ip address__ {[*access-list-number* | *access-list-name*] | **prefix-list** *prefix-list-name*}	Examines route destination prefix and prefix length
* **match ip next-hop** {*access-list-number* | *access-list-name*}	Examines route's next-hop address
* **match ip route-source** {*access-list-number* | *access-list-name*}	Matches advertising router's IP address
match metric *metric-value* [**+-** deviation]	Matches route's metric, or a range (plus/minus the configured deviation)
match route-type {**internal** | **external** [**type-1** | **type-2**] | **level-1** | **level-2**}	Matches route type
match tag *tag-value* [...*tag-value*]	Matches the route tag, which requires that another router has earlier set the tag

* Can reference multiple numbered and named ACLs on a single **match** command.

A route-map referenced by the **redistribute** command always attempts to filter routes. If the route-map matches a particular route with a particular route-map clause, and the action in that clause is **permit**, then the route is redistributed. However, if the first route-map clause matched by a route has a **deny** action, the route is filtered-in other words, not redistributed. In short, the logic matches the same logic as described in Chapter 4 for route-maps referenced by the **distribute-list** command. (Chapter 4 shows how to filter routes inside EIGRP, without redistributing.)

Additionally, for routes not filtered by the route-map, the route-map can set other values (like the route's metric) using the aptly-named **set** command. Table 10-3 lists the various route-map **set** subcommands that can be used to set the values used for routes redistributed into IGPs.

set Command	Description
set metric *metric-value*	Sets the route's metric for OSPF, RIP, and IS-IS
set metric *bandwidth delay reliability loading mtu*	Sets the EIGRP route's metric values
set metric-type {type–1 | type–2}	Sets type of route for OSPF
set tag *tag-value*	Sets the unitless tag value in the route

Filtering Redistributed Routes with Route Maps

As usual, the best way to understand the configuration, and the methods to verify the results, is to use an example. In this case, the same internetwork used throughout Chapter 9 is used, but with some more routes added. Figure 10-1 shows some of the detail of the internetwork.

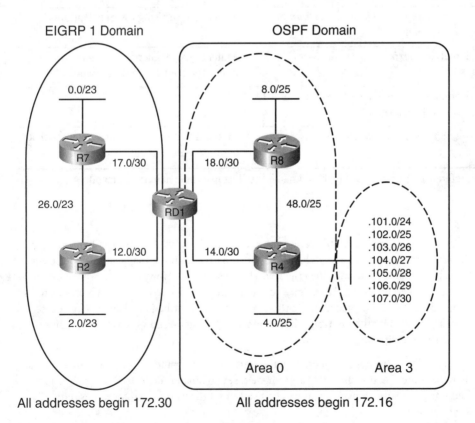

Figure 10-1 *Sample Internetwork Used for Redistribution Route Map Examples*

The internetwork has been preconfigured with mainly defaults, as follows:

- EIGRP works well on the left side of Figure 10-1.

- OSPF works well on the right side.

- Mutual redistribution has been configured on router RD1, with no filtering.

- All routes use these metric settings: EIGRP (1500 10 255 1 1500), OSPF (20).

Example 10-1 shows the routing protocol configuration on Router RD1 at the beginning of the example.

Example 10-1   *Initial Configuration–Mutual Redistribution, No Filtering*

```
RD1#show run
! lines omitted for brevity
router eigrp 1
 redistribute ospf 2
 network 172.30.0.0
 default-metric 1500 10 255 1 1500
 auto-summary
!
router ospf 2
 router-id 1.1.1.1
 log-adjacency-changes
 redistribute eigrp 1 subnets
 network 172.16.0.0 0.0.255.255 area 0
```

Configuring Route Filtering with Redistribution

The configuration shown in Example 10-1 shows mutual redistribution with no filtering. The next example extends that same configuration to now use a **route-map** that should filter routes being redistributed from OSPF process 2 into EIGRP AS 1. Any routes not mentioned in Table 10-4, but shown in Figure 10-1, should be redistributed.

Table 10-4   *Parameters Used in Route Filtering Example*

Prefixes	Action
172.16.101.0/24	deny
172.16.102.0/25	permit
172.16.103.0/26	
172.16.104.0/27	deny
172.16.105.0/28	
172.16.106.0/29	permit
172.16.107.0/30	

The route-map simply needs to match the routes to be filtered with a route-map clause that has a **deny** action and match the routes to not be filtered with a clause with a **permit** action. Example 10-2 shows two such potential solutions, with **route-map** names option1 and option2. The general style of the two options, both of which work, is as follows:

■ **Option 1:** Begin with a match of the routes to be filtered, using extended IP ACLs, with a **deny** action so the routes are filtered. Then use a **permit** clause with no **match** command at all, matching and allowing through all remaining routes.

■ **Option 2:** Begin with a match of the routes to be allowed, matching with prefix lists, with a **permit** action. Then use the implicit deny all at the end of the route-map to filter unwanted routes.

Example 10-2 *Redistribution Filtering Configuration Example*

```
! This ACL matches subnet 172.16.101.0, with mask 255.255.255.0
ip access-list extended match-101
 permit ip host 172.16.101.0 host 255.255.255.0

! This ACL matches subnets 172.16.104.0 and 172.16.105.0, with masks
! 255.255.255.224 and 255.255.255.240, respectively.
ip access-list extended match-104-105
 permit ip host 172.16.104.0 host 255.255.255.224
 permit ip host 172.16.105.0 host 255.255.255.240
!
! This prefix list matches the five subnets in area 0
ip prefix-list match-area0-permit seq 5 permit 172.16.14.0/30
ip prefix-list match-area0-permit seq 10 permit 172.16.18.0/30
ip prefix-list match-area0-permit seq 15 permit 172.16.8.0/25
ip prefix-list match-area0-permit seq 20 permit 172.16.4.0/25
ip prefix-list match-area0-permit seq 25 permit 172.16.48.0/25
!
! This prefix list matches the two sets of two area 3 subnets that will
! be permitted to be redistributed
ip prefix-list match-area3-permit seq 5 permit 172.16.102.0/23 ge 25 le 26
ip prefix-list match-area3-permit seq 10 permit 172.16.106.0/23 ge 29 le 30

! The first alternative route-map:
route-map option1 deny 10
 match ip address match-101
!
```

```
route-map option1 deny 20
 match ip address match-104-105
!
route-map option1 permit 100

! The second alternative route-map:
route-map option2 permit 10
 match ip address prefix-list match-area3-permit
!
route-map option2 permit 20
 match ip address prefix-list match-area0-permit

! Finally, the configuration shows the enablement of option 1.
router eigrp 1
 redistribute ospf 2 route-map option1
```

Route-map option1 takes the approach of denying the redistribution of some routes, and then allowing the rest through. The last clause in this route map, with sequence number 100, does not have a **match** command at all, meaning that it will match any and all routes. The **permit** action on this last clause overrides the implied deny all at the end of the route-map.

The ACLs referenced by **route-map option1** show some particular interesting features for matching routes. With an extended ACL, IOS compares the source IP address parameter to the subnet number of the route and the destination IP address to the subnet mask of the route. For example, the **permit ip host 172.16.101.0 host 255.255.255.0** command matches the specific route for subnet 172.16.101.0, specifically with mask 255.255.255.0.

Route-map option2 takes the opposite approach compared to option1, for no other reason than to just show an alternative. It uses two different prefix lists to match the routes—one for subnets in area 0, all of which are redistributed, another for subnets in area 3 that should be allowed through the redistribution process. Alternatively, all routes could have been matched with a single prefix list, with a single **permit** clause in the option2 route-map.

Finally, the very end of the example shows the syntax of the **redistribute** command, with **route-map option1** enabled.

Verifying Redistribution Filtering Operations

The redistribution process takes routes from the IP routing table of a router and adds the appropriate entries to the destination routing protocol's topology table. The filtering process prevents some of the routes from being added to the topology table, so an examination of the destination routing protocol's topology table shows whether the filtering worked correctly. Additionally, the routing tables of other routers in the destination routing domain can be checked.

A good redistribution verification plan should check that the correct routes are filtered and confirm that no extra routes are filtered. In a production environment, that work might be laborious. With the example shown in Figure 10-1 and Example 10-2, verification takes a little less time due to the relatively small number of routes and that the subnets in the OSPF domain all begin with 172.16.

Example 10-3 shows an abbreviated version of the EIGRP topology table on Router RD1. The **show ip route 172.16.0.0** command lists the 12 OSPF subnets that currently exist in the OSPF domain (as shown in Figure 10-1). The **show ip eigrp topology | include 172[.]16** command lists only routes that include text "172.16," listing only nine subnets–and omitting the three subnets that should have been filtered, which confirms that the filtering worked.

Note: The brackets in the **show ip eigrp topology | include 172[.]16** command tell IOS to treat the period as a literal, searching for the text "172.16" in the command output, instead of treating the period as a wildcard in an IOS regular expression.

Example 10-3 *Verifying Redistribution Filtering*

```
RD1#show ip route 172.16.0.0
Routing entry for 172.16.0.0/16, 12 known subnets
  Attached (2 connections)
  Variably subnetted with 7 masks
  Redistributing via eigrp 1

O       172.16.48.0/25 [110/65] via 172.16.18.2, 03:25:56, Serial0/0/1
                          [110/65] via 172.16.14.2, 03:24:09, Serial0/1/0
C       172.16.18.0/30 is directly connected, Serial0/0/1
C       172.16.14.0/30 is directly connected, Serial0/1/0
O       172.16.8.0/25 [110/65] via 172.16.18.2, 03:25:56, Serial0/0/1
O       172.16.4.0/25 [110/65] via 172.16.14.2, 03:24:49, Serial0/1/0
O IA    172.16.104.0/27 [110/65] via 172.16.14.2, 03:24:44, Serial0/1/0
O IA    172.16.105.0/28 [110/65] via 172.16.14.2, 03:24:44, Serial0/1/0
O IA    172.16.106.0/29 [110/65] via 172.16.14.2, 03:24:44, Serial0/1/0
O IA    172.16.107.0/30 [110/65] via 172.16.14.2, 03:24:44, Serial0/1/0
O IA    172.16.101.0/24 [110/65] via 172.16.14.2, 03:24:44, Serial0/1/0
O IA    172.16.102.0/25 [110/65] via 172.16.14.2, 03:24:44, Serial0/1/0
O IA    172.16.103.0/26 [110/65] via 172.16.14.2, 03:24:44, Serial0/1/0


RD1#show ip eigrp topology | include 172[.]16
P 172.16.48.0/25, 1 successors, FD is 1709056
P 172.16.18.0/30, 1 successors, FD is 1709056
P 172.16.14.0/30, 1 successors, FD is 1709056
```

```
P 172.16.8.0/25, 1 successors, FD is 1709056
P 172.16.4.0/25, 1 successors, FD is 1709056
P 172.16.106.0/29, 1 successors, FD is 1709056
P 172.16.107.0/30, 1 successors, FD is 1709056
P 172.16.102.0/25, 1 successors, FD is 1709056
P 172.16.103.0/26, 1 successors, FD is 1709056
```

Besides examining the topology tables on the router doing the redistribution, a **show ip route** command on other routers inside the EIGRP domain, like R2, could be used to confirm the presence and absence of the routes according to the plan. However, the routing table on the redistributing router will list the routes as learned from the original routing domain.

Any ACLs or prefix lists used to match packets can also be used as a gauge to tell if the correct statements matched routes. The **show ip access-list** *[number/name]* and **show ip prefix-list detail** *[name]* commands list counters that increment each time IOS matches a route for redistribution. Particularly when first using the ACL or prefix list, these commands can confirm which statements have been matched. The counters do increment each time the router considers whether to redistribute a route. In particular, when a route fails, and the redistributing router removes the route from the routing table, and then later adds the route to the routing table again, the counters for matching the ACL or prefix list will increment. Example 10-4 shows an example of each command, and the appropriate counters.

Example 10-4   *Verifying Redistribution Filtering*

```
RD1#show access-list
Extended IP access list match-101
    10 permit ip host 172.16.101.0 host 255.255.255.0 (1 match)
Extended IP access list match-104-105
    10 permit ip host 172.16.104.0 host 255.255.255.224 (1 match)
    20 permit ip host 172.16.105.0 host 255.255.255.240 (1 match)
RD1#show ip prefix-list detail match-area0-permit
ip prefix-list match-area0-permit:
   count: 5, range entries: 0, sequences: 5 - 25, refcount: 3
   seq 5 permit 172.16.14.0/30 (hit count: 6, refcount: 1)
   seq 10 permit 172.16.18.0/30 (hit count: 5, refcount: 1)
   seq 15 permit 172.16.8.0/25 (hit count: 4, refcount: 2)
   seq 20 permit 172.16.4.0/25 (hit count: 3, refcount: 3)
   seq 25 permit 172.16.48.0/25 (hit count: 2, refcount: 2)
```

Setting Metrics when Redistributing

Setting a different metric for different redistributed routes requires only a minor amount of additional configuration. The redistributing router still needs a route-map and still needs to match the routes. Additionally, to set the metric for routes matched by a particular clause, the route-map needs the **set metric** route-map subcommand. When redistributing into EIGRP, this command has five parameters (bandwidth, delay, reliability, load, and MTU). When redistributing into OSPF or RIP, a single integer metric is used.

Configuring the Metric Settings

Continuing with the same internetwork shown in Figure 10-1, and with the same filtering goals summarized earlier in Table 10-4, Table 10-5 further defines the goals from redistribution from OSPF into EIGRP in this internetwork. The same routes will be filtered, but now the metrics of the allowed routes will be set differently as listed in the table.

Table 10-5 *Parameters Used in Metric and Tag Setting Example*

Prefix	Action	Metric (Bandwidth, delay, reliability, load, MTU)
172.16.101.0	deny	N/A
172.16.102.0	permit	1000 44 255 1 1500
172.16.103.0		
172.16.104.0	deny	N/A
172.16.105.0		
172.16.106.0	permit	100 4444 255 1 1500
172.16.107.0		
All others	permit	1500 10 255 1 1500

The requirements in Table 10-5 list three different sets of metrics for the redistributed routes. To implement this design, the route-map needs at least three clauses: one for each set of routes for which the metric should differ. The example route-maps listed earlier in Example 10-2 do not happen to separate the three groups of allowed routes into different route-map clauses, so a new route-map will be used. Example 10-5 shows the new configuration. Note that it does make use of one of the old IP prefix-lists, namely **match-area0-permit**.

Example 10-5 *Route-map to Set Metrics According to Table 10-5*

```
! First, two new prefix lists are added - one to match subnets 102 and 103,
! and another to match subnets 106 and 107.


ip prefix-list match-102-103 seq 5 permit 172.16.102.0/23 ge 25 le 26
!
ip prefix-list match-106-107 seq 5 permit 172.16.106.0/23 ge 29 le 30

! The following is a repeat of the prefix list that matches the five routes
! in area 0
ip prefix-list match-area0-permit seq 5 permit 172.16.14.0/30
ip prefix-list match-area0-permit seq 10 permit 172.16.18.0/30
```

```
ip prefix-list match-area0-permit seq 15 permit 172.16.8.0/25
ip prefix-list match-area0-permit seq 20 permit 172.16.4.0/25
ip prefix-list match-area0-permit seq 25 permit 172.16.48.0/25


! A new route map to filter and set metrics, with three clauses


route-map set-metric permit 10
 match ip address prefix-list match-area0-permit
!
route-map set-metric permit 20
 match ip address prefix-list match-102-103
 set metric 1000 44 255 1 1500
!
route-map set-metric permit 30
 match ip address prefix-list match-106-107
 set metric 100 4444 255 1 1500


!
router eigrp 1
 default-metric 1500 10 255 1 1500
 redistribute ospf 2 route-map set-metric
```

The new route-map has three explicitly configured clauses, two of which explicitly set the metric values using the **set metric** command. However, the first clause (sequence number 10), which matches routes for the five subnets inside area 0, does not use a **set metric** command to set the metric. Instead, because this route map clause omits the **set metric** command, routes that match this clause use the **metric** keyword on the **redistribute** command, or if not listed, the metrics as defined by the **default-metric** EIGRP subcommand. In this case, because the **redistribute** command does not list a **metric** keyword, routes matched by this clause (sequence number 10) use the metric values listed in the **default-metric** command.

Verifying the Metric Settings

Verifying the metrics again requires an examination of the EIGRP topology table. In this case, Example 10-6 displays a couple of views of RD1's EIGRP topology table, focusing on routes to 172.16.102.0/25 and 172.16.106.0/29. The configuration in Example 10-5 earlier set the metrics to different values, and next the output in Example 10-6 shows the differences:

Example 10-6 *Verifying Metrics as Set During Redistribution*

```
RD1#show ip eigrp topology 172.16.102.0/25
IP-EIGRP (AS 1): Topology entry for 172.16.102.0/25
  State is Passive, Query origin flag is 1, 1 Successor(s), FD is 1709056
```

```
        Routing Descriptor Blocks:
        172.16.14.2, from Redistributed, Send flag is 0x0
            Composite metric is (2571264/0), Route is External
            Vector metric:
                Minimum bandwidth is 1000 Kbit
                Total delay is 440 microseconds
                Reliability is 255/255
                Load is 1/255
                Minimum MTU is 1500
                Hop count is 0
            External data:
                Originating router is 172.30.17.1 (this system)
                AS number of route is 2
                External protocol is OSPF, external metric is 65
                Administrator tag is 0 (0x00000000)


RD1#show ip eigrp topology 172.16.104.0/25
% IP-EIGRP (AS 1): Route not in topology table


RD1#show ip eigrp topo 172.16.106.0/29
IP-EIGRP (AS 1): Topology entry for 172.16.106.0/29
  State is Passive, Query origin flag is 1, 1 Successor(s), FD is 1709056
  Routing Descriptor Blocks:
  172.16.14.2, from Redistributed, Send flag is 0x0
        Composite metric is (26737664/0), Route is External
        Vector metric:
            Minimum bandwidth is 100 Kbit
            Total delay is 44440 microseconds
            Reliability is 255/255
            Load is 1/255
            Minimum MTU is 1500
            Hop count is 0
        External data:
            Originating router is 172.30.17.1 (this system)
            AS number of route is 2
            External protocol is OSPF, external metric is 65
            Administrator tag is 0 (0x00000000)
!
RD1#show ip prefix-list detail match-102-103
ip prefix-list match-102-103:
    count: 1, range entries: 1, sequences: 5 - 5, refcount: 2
    seq 5 permit 172.16.102.0/23 ge 25 le 26 (hit count: 14, refcount: 1)
```

Although you could use variations of the **show ip route** command to verify the new metrics, because the redistribution process sets the EIGRP component metrics, the **show ip eigrp topology** command displays much more useful verification information.

Setting the External Route Type

When redistributing into OSPF, IOS automatically sets the external route type to external Type 2 (E2). When redistributing into OSPF, IOS can set the type to E1 or E2 by using the **set metric-type {type-1 | type-2}** route-map subcommand. When a **redistribute** OSPF subcommand references such a route-map, the routes matched by the route-map clause with the **set metric-type** command will be designated as that external type in the Type 5 LSA created for that subnet.

Note that the **redistribute** command also allows the **match {internal | external 1 | external 2 | nssa-external}** parameters, but these parameters do not set the type or route. Instead, these parameters match existing routes as part of the process of deciding which routes to redistribute.

Redistribution Filtering with the **distribute-list** Command

Using a route-map as referenced on the **redistribute** command provides many features. You can filter routes, assign different metrics for different routes, and assign external route types. You can even assign route tags as discussed later in the section "Preventing Domain Loops by Filtering on Route-tag Using Distribute Lists." However, if the plan calls for route filtering only when redistributing, but none of the other functions supplied by a route-map are needed, and you can match all the routes with a single ACL or prefix list, then IOS supports a second style of route filtering configuration using the **distribute-list** command.

This book has reviewed two uses of the **distribute-list** command in earlier chapters (Chapters 4 and 8), both of which show how to filter routes inside a single routing domain. For example, Chapter 4 shows how to filter EIGRP routes using the **distribute-list** command, both for routing updates received in and for routing updates sent out by a router. The **distribute-list** command refers to the direction, and to either an ACL or IP prefix-list, allowing the routes matched with a permit and filtering routes matched with a deny action.

The **distribute-list** command can be configured to refer to the routing process from which routes are redistributed and cause the router to filter routes taken from that process. To do so, the command must use the **out** direction, and it must refer to the routing process from which routes are redistributed. For example, **distribute-list 1 out ospf 2**, configured under an EIGRP process, tells EIGRP to apply ACL 1 to routes redistributed from the OSPF 2 process. For another example, under an OSPF process, the **distribute-list prefix fred out eigrp 1** command tells OSPF to apply IP prefix list fred to routes redistributed from the EIGRP 1 process.

Finally, one note about internals of how this command works. The filtering takes place as the routes are redistributed. As a result, routes filtered by the **distribute-list** command prevent the routes from being added to the topology table of the destination routing protocol. So, the same verification commands seen in earlier examples, with focus on the topology tables, can be used to show whether the filtering worked. Also, the counters in the **show ip access-list** and **show ip prefix-list detail** commands also increment to show whether the filtering worked.

Issues with Multiple Redistribution Points

The use of a single router to redistribute routes means that a single failure could cause hosts in different routing domains to fail. The redistributing router could simply fail, or interfaces or links on that router could fail. To avoid that single point of failure, most redistribution designs call for a minimum of two routers performing redistribution, particularly in cases where the redistribution function will be somewhat permanent.

The existence of two or more redistribution points between the same two routing domains introduces some complexity and caveats. The issues revolve around the concept that a route in one domain can be advertised into another domain, and then back into the original routing domain. In fact, the CCIE Routing and Switching exam has included such tricky redistribution issues as a central part of the exam for many years.

Figure 10-2 shows one of the issues when using multiple redistribution points. In this case, the arrowed lines show the best route from a router in domain 2 to reach a subnet also in domain 2. However, the route actually passes through domain 1.

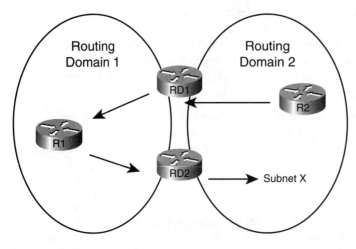

Figure 10-2   *A Domain Loop*

Figure 10-2 shows the long route that goes from R2, through RD1, to R1, back into routing domain 2 through RD2. This long route occurs because of the routing advertisements that flow in the opposite direction: advertised by RD2 into routing domain 1 and then by RD1 back into routing domain 2. The problem occurs when the twice-redistributed route for subnet X is redistributed back into the original domain with a relatively low metric. The twice-redistributed route then has a better metric than the route that was advertised only internal to that routing domain.

This section examines how to prevent this "domain loop" problem when using multiple redistribution points. Interestingly, this problem does not occur, at least with default settings, when EIGRP is one of the two routing protocols. So this section begins with examples of RIP and OSPF redistribution, showing how to prevent this domain looping problem, and then showing why EIGRP accomplishes this same feat with default settings.

Note: I know of no industry standard name for the problem shown in Figure 10-2. For the duration of this chapter, I refer to it simply as the *domain loop* problem.

Preventing Routing Domain Loops with Higher Metrics

One easy method of preventing the domain loop problem is to assign purposefully high metric values when redistributing routes. For example, consider the case shown in Figure 10-3, with a RIP domain on the left, and OSPF on the right. In this case, the two routers doing the redistribution (RD1 and RD2) assign OSPF metric 500 when redistributing routes into OSPF, and metric 5 when redistributing routes into RIP.

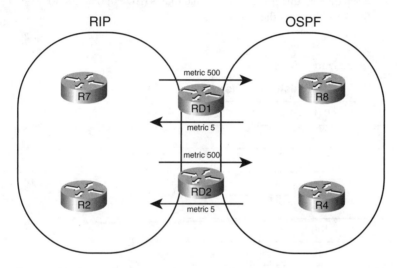

Figure 10-3   *Defeating Domain Loops by Using Very Large Metrics*

First, focus on routes inside the RIP domain. This design prevents the domain loop problem–routes that send packets from the RIP domain, into OSPF, and back again–if the normal intra-domain RIP routes never exceed a hop count of 4. Then, all routes redistributed from RIP into OSPF, and then back into RIP, will at least have a metric of 5. As a result, the route advertisements that looped back into the RIP domain will always have less desirable metrics than the RIP advertisements from within the RIP domain.

The same concept applies to OSPF. For routes completely internal to the OSPF domain, if the highest cost is 499, then the redistribution of external routes as metric 500 makes prevents the domain loop. For example, a subnet that exists in the OSPF domain could be advertised into RIP by RD1, and then re-advertised by RD2 back into the OSPF domain–but with a metric that begins at 500. Again, assuming all the normal OSPF routes that were not reintroduced as external routes have a cost of less than 500, the domain loop problem is defeated.

Note that OSPF actually defeats the domain loop problem without using the higher metrics. OSPF always prefers internal routes over E1 routes, and E1 routes over E2 routes, before even considering the metrics.

Preventing Routing Domain Loops with Administrative Distance

Each router associates an *administrative distance* (AD) with every route it considers to be added to the routing table. When a router must consider multiple routes from different sources for the exact same prefix/length, the first item considered by the router is not the metric, but rather the AD. The lower the AD, the better the route.

Note that the AD is a local setting on a router and cannot be advertised to neighboring routers.

Each routing source has a default AD according to IOS. In some cases, a given routing source has different defaults for different types of routes inside that routing source. For example, EIGRP has a separate setting for EIGRP internal routes (AD 90) than EIGRP external routes (AD 170). Table 10-6 lists the default settings.

Key Topic

Table 10-6 *Default Administrative Distances*

Route Type	Administrative Distance
Connected	0
Static	1
EIGRP summary route	5
eBGP	20
EIGRP (internal)	90
IGRP	100
OSPF	110
IS-IS	115
RIP	120
On-Demand Routing (ODR)	160
EIGRP (external)	170
iBGP	200
Unreachable	255

EIGRP Default AD Defeats Loop from EIGRP to OSPF to EIGRP

The default AD settings for EIGRP takes care of the domain loop problem when redistributing between EIGRP and OSPF. First, consider an EIGRP and OSPF domain with two redistribution points (Routers RD1 and RD2), as shown in Figure 10-4. The figure shows a general idea of route advertisements for subnet X, which exists in the EIGRP domain. (Note: to reduce clutter, the figure shows only route advertisements that affect router RD2's logic; the same issue exists on both redistributing routers.)

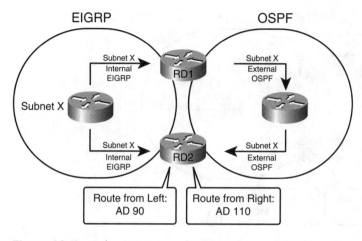

Figure 10-4   *Subnet X: Internal EIGRP, External OSPF, on Router RD2*

Router RD2 hears about a route for subnet X as an internal EIGRP route (default AD 90) on the left. RD2 also hears about the subnet as an external OSPF route on the right (default AD 110). As a result, RD2 will do a couple of things that are important to this discussion:

■ RD2 considers the internal EIGRP route as the best route, because of the lower AD, and places that route in its own IP routing table.

■ RD2 does not redistribute a route for subnet X, from OSPF back to EIGRP, because RD2 does not have an OSPF route for subnet X.

The second point is particularly important but easily missed. Remember that routers use the IP routing table as the basis for route redistribution. Both RD1 and RD2 redistribute routes in both directions between both domains. However, a route must be in the routing table before it can be redistributed. Because RD2's route for subnet X will list its EIGRP route, RD2's redistribution from OSPF into EIGRP will not redistribute a route for subnet X. Because RD2 will not advertise a route for subnet X from OSPF back into EIGRP, the domain loop has been prevented.

EIGRP Default AD Defeats Loop from OSPF to EIGRP to OSPF

The reverse case–routes taken from OSPF, advertised into EIGRP, and then advertised back into OSPF–is the more interesting possible domain loop case. However, the default EIGRP AD settings still defeat the domain loop issue. Figure 10-5 shows an example similar to Figure 10-4, but this time with subnet Y in the OSPF domain. As before, the focus of the figure is on the routing advertisements that reach Router RD2, with other details omitted to reduce clutter.

In this case, Router RD2 hears about a route for subnet Y as an external EIGRP route (default AD 170) and an internal OSPF route (default AD 110). As a result, RD2 chooses the OSPF internal route as the best route and adds that to RD2's routing table. Because RD2 does not have an EIGRP route for subnet Y, RD2 will not redistribute a route for subnet Y from EIGRP into OSPF, again defeating the domain loop problem.

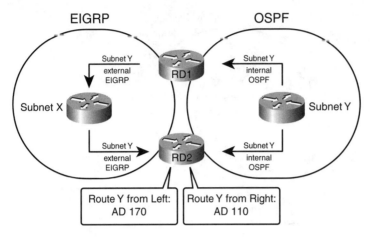

Figure 10-5 *Avoiding Domain Loops from OSPF to EIGRP to OSPF*

Setting AD per Route Source for Internal and External Routes

The reason that the default EIGRP AD settings work well can be summarized generically as follows:

> For each of the two routing protocols, the AD used for internal routes for one routing protocol is better than the AD used for external routes by the other routing protocol.

When comparing EIGRP's and OSPF's defaults, both of the generic criteria are met:

- EIGRP internal AD 90 < OSPF external AD 110

- OSPF internal AD 110 < EIGRP external AD 170

Likewise, when redistributing between EIGRP and RIP:

- EIGRP internal AD 90 < RIP external AD 120

- RIP internal AD 120 < EIGRP external AD 170

Note: RIP does not have a concept of internal and external routes; the preceding references refer to internal routes as routes that exist inside the RIP domain, and external as routes that exist outside the RIP domain.

When redistributing between OSPF and RIP, the default AD settings do not defeat the domain loop problem. However, IOS supports the definition of different AD settings for all routing protocols. With EIGRP, the internal and external AD settings can be overridden, although the defaults work well for the preventing of domain loops. OSPF can be configured to use a different AD for external routes, intra-area routes, and interarea routes. RIP, which does not have a concept of internal and external routes, can only be set with a single AD value. Table 10-7 shows the router subcommands to set the AD values, per route category.

Routing Protocol	Command
RIP	distance *ad-value*
EIGRP	distance eigrp *internal-ad external-ad*
OSPF	distance ospf {external *ad-value*} {intra-area *ad-value*} {inter-area *ad-value*}

To defeat the OSPF-RIP domain loop problem by setting AD, just configure the AD for OSPF external routes using the **distance ospf external** *ad-value* command in OSPF configuration mode. The actual AD value does not matter much, but it should be higher than RIP's AD on that same router. For example, the **distance ospf external 130** command in OSPF configuration mode results in the following, assuming all other AD values default:

■ RIP internal AD 120 < OSPF external AD 130

■ OSPF internal AD 110 < RIP external AD 120

Domain Loop Problems with More than Two Routing Domains

With only two routing domains, the domain loop solutions seen so far–setting higher metrics and setting AD—can deal with the domain loop problems. However, with three or more routing domains, setting metrics and AD values does not always solve the domain loop problem. In particular, problems can occur when three or more routing domains connect in sequence, as shown in Figure 10-6.

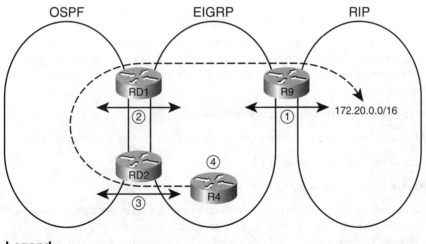

Figure 10-6 *Inefficient Routing with Looped Routing Advertisements*

The steps noted in the figure are as follows:

Step 1.   Router R9 advertises a route for network 172.20.0.0/16 from the RIP domain into the EIGRP domain where the route is treated with (default) AD 170 as an external route.

Step 2.   Router RD1 redistributes this EIGRP external route into OSPF where it is treated as an E2 route, AD 110, by default.

Step 3.   Router RD2 uses the AD 110 E2 route, rather than the AD 170 EIGRP external route, as its best route for 172.20.0.0/16. As a result, RD2 can then redistribute that OSPF route back into EIGRP as an external route.

Step 4.   Router R4 learns of two external routes for 172.20.0.0/16, and the routes tie based on AD (170). R4 may have a better EIGRP metric through RD2, depending on the metrics used at redistribution, preferring this long route through the OSPF domain as shown.

This is just one example case for such problems, but the problem exists because the obviously better route and the longer domain loop route are both external routes. The two competing routes tie on AD as a result. In the earlier cases, with only two routing domains, this problem does not occur.

Several solutions exist for such problems. None of the solutions require a lot of extra configuration, other than that some of the solutions require ACLs or prefix lists that match the prefixes from the various routing domains. The next three sections address each option, namely: using per-route AD settings, filtering routes based on prefix/length, and using route tags.

Using Per-route Administrative Distance Settings

As seen in Table 10-7, you can use the **distance** router subcommand to set the AD value per routing protocol, per type (internal and external). The **distance** command also supports another syntax in which the router sets the AD for individual routes based on the following criteria:

■   The router that advertised the routing information

■   Optionally, for the prefixes/lengths of the routes as matched by a referenced ACL

The syntax of the command in this case is

```
distance distance ip-adv-router wc mask [acl-number-or-name]
```

In this command, the required parameters match the neighboring router that advertises a route. The router with the **distance** command configured compares the advertising router's IP address to the range of addresses implied by the *ip-adv-router* and *wc-mask* parameters of the command, as if these were parameters in an ACL. For routes advertised by a matching neighbor, that router then applies the AD listed in the command.

Optionally, the **distance** command can also refer to an ACL. If included, that router compares the ACL to the prefix/length of each route learned from any matched neighbors and uses the listed AD only for routes permitted by the ACL.

For example, consider the problem in Figure 10-6. Assuming the design calls for all hosts to have reachability to 172.20.0.0/16, the route must be redistributed by R9 into the EIGRP domain. For the best availability, this route should be redistributed from EIGRP into OSPF at both redistribution points (RD1 and RD2). The unfortunate long route choice by Router R4 in the figure occurs at what is listed as Step 3 in that figure, with Router RD2 using AD to determine that its external OSPF route for 172.20.0.0/16 (AD 110) is better than its EIGRP external route (AD 170) for that same prefix.

One solution would be to cause RD2 to use a higher AD–specifically higher than the 170 AD used for EIGRP external routes–for prefix 172.20.0.0/16 as learned with OSPF. A **distance** command on RD2 could solve the problem.

Upcoming Examples 10-7 and 10-8, plus Figure 10-7, demonstrate both the domain loop problem in this same case, along with the solution. First, Figure 10-7 shows a more de-tailed topology for reference. (Note that unlike several other examples in this chapter and in Chapter 9, this example shows EIGRP on the right, and OSPF on the left.) Then, Example 10-7 shows the relevant configuration and a few related **show** commands on Router RD2 before using the **distance** command to prevent the problem. This example shows Router R4 using the longer path through the OSPF domain on the left. Finally, Example 10-8 shows the configuration of the **distance** command and resulting solution.

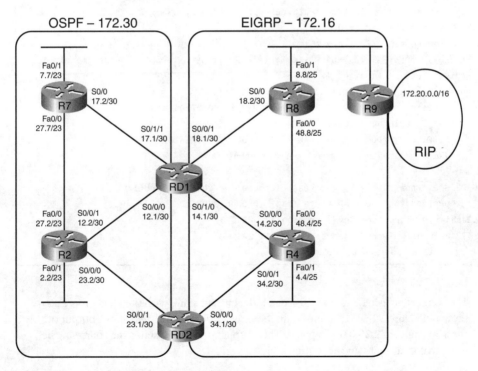

Figure 10-7 *Detailed View of Internetwork*

Example 10-7   *Long Route from RD2, into OSPF, for 172.20.0.0/16*

```
! The following is the routing protocol configuration on RD2
router eigrp 1
 redistribute ospf 2 metric 1000 200 255 1 1500
 network 172.16.0.0
 no auto-summary
!
router ospf 2
 router-id 3.3.3.3
 log-adjacency-changes
 redistribute eigrp 1 subnets
 network 172.30.0.0 0.0.255.255 area 0


! Next, the long route for 172.20.0.0/16 is listed. This route goes from
! RD2 back into the OSPF domain; interface S0/0/1 connects to router R2.
RD2#show ip route | include 172.20.0.0
O E2 172.20.0.0/16 [110/20] via 172.30.23.2, 00:06:57, Serial0/0/1


! Next, the source of this routing information is listed under the
! text "Known via". RD2's current route is learned by OSPF.
RD2#show ip route 172.20.0.0
Routing entry for 172.20.0.0/16
  Known via "ospf 2", distance 110, metric 20, type extern 2, forward metric 128
  Redistributing via eigrp 1
  Advertised by eigrp 1 metric 1000 200 255 1 1500
  Last update from 172.30.23.2 on Serial0/0/1, 00:07:04 ago
  Routing Descriptor Blocks:
  * 172.30.23.2, from 1.1.1.1, 00:07:04 ago, via Serial0/0/1
      Route metric is 20, traffic share count is 1


! RD2 does know a working (successor) route for the same prefix,
! but prefers the lower-AD route (110) through OSPF.
RD2#show ip eigrp topology | section 172.20.0.0
P 172.20.0.0/16, 1 successors, FD is 2611200
        via Redistributed (2611200/0)
```

The comments inside Example 10-7 detail the current state, with the longer route, as shown in Figure 10-6. Most important, note the "Known via..." text in the output of the **show ip route 172.20.0.0** command. This output specifically states the source of the route that is currently in the routing table.

Next, Example 10-8 shows the configuration on RD2 to solve this problem by setting RD2's AD for that specific route and additional **show** commands.

Example 10-8 *Configuring Per-Route AD on Router RD2*

```
RD2#conf t
Enter configuration commands, one per line.  End with CNTL/Z.
RD2(config)#router ospf 2
RD2(config-router)# distance 171 1.1.1.1 0.0.0.0 match-172-20
RD2(config-router)#!
RD2(config-router)#ip access-list standard match-172-20
RD2(config-std-nacl)# permit host 172.20.0.0
RD2(config-std-nacl)#^Z
RD2#

! Now the best route for 172.20.0.0 is known from EIGRP 1.
RD2#show ip route 172.20.0.0
Routing entry for 172.20.0.0/16
  Known via "eigrp 1", distance 170, metric 3635200, type external
  Redistributing via ospf 2, eigrp 1
  Advertised by ospf 2 subnets
  Last update from 172.16.34.2 on Serial0/0/0, 00:08:01 ago
! lines omitted for brevity


! The next command lists the matching logic of the distance command.
RD2#show ip protocols ¦ section ospf
Routing Protocol is "ospf 2"
  Outgoing update filter list for all interfaces is not set
  Incoming update filter list for all interfaces is not set
  Router ID 172.30.23.1
  It is an autonomous system boundary router
  Redistributing External Routes from,
    eigrp 1, includes subnets in redistribution
  Number of areas in this router is 1. 1 normal 0 stub 0 nssa
  Maximum path: 4
  Routing for Networks:
    172.30.0.0 0.0.255.255 area 0
 Reference bandwidth unit is 100 mbps
  Routing Information Sources:
    Gateway         Distance      Last Update
    1.1.1.1              171      00:00:35
    2.2.2.2              110      00:00:35
    7.7.7.7              110      00:00:35
  Distance: (default is 110)
    Address          Wild mask       Distance  List
    1.1.1.1          0.0.0.0              171   match-172-20
  Redistributing: ospf 2, eigrp 1
```

The configuration, although short, has one possibly counterintuitive twist. The IP address of the neighboring router, referenced in the **distance** command in OSPF configuration mode, will be compared to the *OSPF RID of the OSPF router that owns the LSA.* In this case, Router RD1 creates the Type 5 LSA for 172.20.0.0, and RD1's RID happens to be 1.1.1.1. RD2's **distance 171 1.1.1.1 0.0.0.0 match-172-20** command tells OSPF to look for LSAs owned by exactly RID 1.1.1.1, and if the prefix is permitted by the match-172-20 ACL, apply AD 171 to this route.

The **show ip route 172.20.0.0** command verifies that Router RD1 now prefers its AD 170 EIGRP route for 172.20.0.0/16. The highlighted portions of this command now refers to routing source EIGRP 1, with the outgoing interface of S0/0/0, which connects RD2 into the EIGRP domain. Because RD2 no longer has an OSPF route for 172.20.0.0/16, RD2 will not redistribute such an OSPF route back into EIGRP, defeating the domain loop problem.

Note: A complete solution requires all redistributing routers to perform this kind of configuration, for all such routes from the third routing domain.

Although this example shows the OSPF version of the **distance** command, one notable difference exists between the OSPF version and the RIP and EIGRP **distance** commands. When used as a RIP or EIGRP subcommand, the **distance** command matches the interface IP address of the neighboring router that advertises the route.

Preventing Domain Loops by Filtering on Subnet While Redistributing

The next tool prevents domain loops by filtering the routes based on prefix. Figure 10-8 shows the idea from a redistribution design perspective.

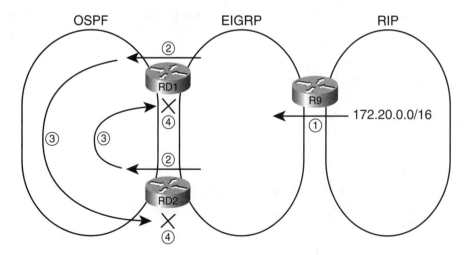

Figure 10-8   *Preventing Domain Loops with Route Filtering*

Following are the steps as listed in the figure:

Step 1.   Router R9 advertises a route for network 172.20.0.0/16 from the RIP domain into the EIGRP domain.

Step 2.   Routers RD1 and RD2 both redistribute this EIGRP external route into OSPF.

Step 3.   Both RD1 and RD2 flood the route advertisement for the OSPF external route throughout the OSPF domain.

Step 4.   Both RD1 and RD2 apply a route-map to their redistribution from OSPF into EIGRP, filtering routes with prefix 172.20.0.0.

The configuration itself uses the same methods and commands as included earlier in the section "Filtering Redistributed Routes with Route Maps."

Interestingly, this design does prevent the long routes, as shown earlier in Figure 10-6, but it does leave the possibility of a long route on a redistributing router. For example, if using all default AD settings, RD2 still learns an OSPF (default AD 110) route for 172.20.0.0 from RD1, so it may choose as best route the OSPF route through RD1 as the best route. Setting the AD for OSPF external routes to something larger than EIGRP's external AD of 170 would prevent this particular problem as well.

Preventing Domain Loops by Filtering on route-tag Using Distribute Lists

Route tags, the last tool shown in this chapter for preventing the domain loop problem, has a much broader use than just preventing redistribution problems.

A route tag is a unitless 32-bit integer that most routing protocols can assign to any given route. The assignment of a tag occurs when some IOS function adds the tag–for instance, it can be assigned by a route-map referenced by a routing protocol **distribute-list** or **redistribute** command. That tag follows the route advertisement, even through the redistribution process. At some later point in the flooding of routing information, other IOS tools, typically other route-maps, can match routes with a given route tag to make a decision.

In some cases, the idea of a route tag creates a mental block because it has no one specific purpose. The network engineer chooses the purpose of any particular route tag; the purpose has not been predetermined by a particular protocol. The folks that created the routing protocol provided us all with a nice, convenient place to add the equivalent of a post-it note to each route; it's up to us to decide what the note means.

Figure 10-9 shows one common use of route tags other than for solving the domain loop problem. In the figure, one large company that uses EIGRP (the middle of the figure) bought two smaller companies, both of whom use OSPF. The larger company wants to connect both small companies into the larger network, but they want to prevent hosts in the two smaller companies from knowing routes to the other smaller company. The figure shows only left-to-right advertisements of routes to reduce the clutter.

The two routers on the left each redistribute routes from the smaller companies into the EIGRP. The routers apply a route tag of 1 to each route from OSPF domain 1, and a tag of 2 to routes redistributed from OSPF domain 2. The actual numbers do not matter, as long as they are unique. On the right, the routers know that the routes from OSPF domain 1

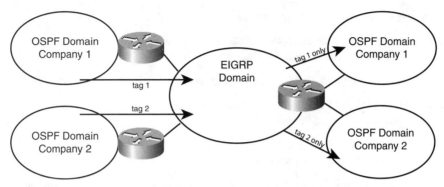

Key Topic   **Figure 10-9**   *Using Route Tags to Determine Routing Domain Origin*

have route tag 1, and only these routes should be redistributed into the other part of
OSPF domain 1. So, when redistributing into OSPF domain 1, the route-map makes a
comparison of the route tag (command **match tag 1**) and allows only those routes. Similarly, when redistributing into OSPF domain 2, the **match tag 2** command would be used,
redistributing only routes with tag 2.

To use route tags to prevent domain loop problems, you can use the following strategy:

Key Topic

■   Choose and set a tag value that identifies routes taken from domain X and advertised
    into domain Y.

■   When redistributing in the opposite direction (from domain Y into domain X), match
    the tag value and filter routes with that tag.

For example, consider the case shown in Figure 10-10. The figure shows the usual RD1
and RD2 between two routing domains, with EIGRP on the right in this case and OSPF on
the left. The engineer then planned to use route tag 11 to mean "routes taken from EIGRP
and redistributed into OSPF." The figure shows one direction of potential loops: From
EIGRP through RD1, through OSPF, and back to EIGRP through RD2. However, the same
concept would apply to the other direction.

The first step (noted with a circled 1 in the figure) is the usual redistribution, but with a
route-map that tags all routes redistributed from EIGRP into OSPF with tag 11. RD2
learns these routes with OSPF. At Step 2, RD2 tries to redistribute the routes but chooses
to filter all routes that have a tag value of 11. As a result, none of the routes learned from
EIGRP are re-advertised back into EIGRP. Example 10-9 shows configuration that matches
Figure 10-10.

Example 10-9   *RD1 and RD2 Configuration with Route Tags to Prevent Domain Loops*

```
! The following is the routing protocol configuration on RD1
router ospf 2
 router-id 3.3.3.3
 log-adjacency-changes
 redistribute eigrp 1 subnets route-map set-tag-11
 network 172.30.0.0 0.0.255.255 area 0
```

```
!
route-map set-tag-11 permit 10
 set tag 11
! The following is the routing protocol configuration on RD2
router eigrp 1
 redistribute ospf 2 metric 1000 200 255 1 1500 route-map stop-tag-11
 network 172.16.0.0
 no auto-summary
!
route-map stop-tag-11 deny 10
 match tag 11
!
route-map stop-tag-11 permit 20
```

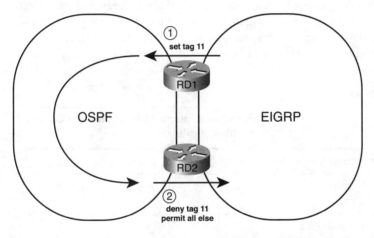

Figure 10-10 *Using Route Tags to Prevent Domain Loop Problems*

First, note that the configuration does rely on a couple of default route-map actions that bear some review. In the set-tag-11 route-map on RD1, only one route-map clause exists, and that clause has no **match** commands. A route-map clause with no **match** commands matches all routes, so all routes are assigned tag 11. In the stop-tag-11 route-map on RD2, the first clause lists a **deny** action, meaning that all routes matched by that clause (all with tag 11) are filtered. All other routes, for example those routes for subnets native to the OSPF domain, match the second clause (line number 20), because that second clause does not have a **match** command.

Example 10-9 shows the configuration that tags routes coming from EIGRP into OSPF and then filters routes with that same tag as they go from OSPF into EIGRP. For a complete solution, the reverse case would also need to be configured, using a different route tag value.

Exam Preparation Tasks

Planning Practice

The CCNP ROUTE exam expects test takers to review design documents, create implementation plans, and create verification plans. This section provides some exercises that may help you to take a step back from the minute details of the topics in this chapter so that you can think about the same technical topics from the planning perspective.

For each planning practice table, simply complete the table. Note that any numbers in parentheses represent the number of options listed for each item in the solutions in Appendix F, "Completed Planning Practice Tables."

Design Review Table

Table 10-8 lists several design goals related to this chapter. If these design goals were listed in a design document, and you had to take that document and develop an implementation plan, what implementation options come to mind? For any configuration items, a general description can be used, without concern about the specific parameters.

Table 10-8 *Design Review*

Design Goal	Possible Implementation Choices Covered in This Chapter
Filter routes when redistributing. (2)	
Set different metrics for different routes redistributed from one routing source.	
Set some OSPF routes as E1, and some as E2, when redistributed from one routing source.	
The design shows multiple redistribution points with two routing domains, with a need to prevent domain loops. (3)	
The design shows multiple redistribution points with more than two routing domains, and a need to prevent domain loops. (2)	

Implementation Plan Peer Review Table

Table 10-9 shows a list of questions that others might ask, or that you might think about, during a peer review of another network engineer's implementation plan. Complete the table by answering the questions.

Table 10-9   *Notable Questions from This Chapter to Consider During an Implementation Plan Peer Review*

Question	Answer
A design shows an OSPF and EIGRP routing domain, with multiple redistributing routers, with no obvious configuration to prevent routing domain loops. What default AD values exist, and do they prevent any problems?	
The same question as the previous row, except with RIP and OSPF domains.	
The same question as the previous row, except with RIP and EIGRP domains.	
A plan shows redistribution between EIGRP and OSPF on two routers. The configuration for OSPF on one router lists **redistribute eigrp 1 subnets** and **distribute-list 1 out**. Will this configuration attempt to filter routes? Is a route-map option required to filter when redistributing?	
A partially complete plan shows three different routing domains, with multiple redistribution points between each pair of routing domains. The configuration shows large ACLs matching various subnets and setting AD per-route using the **distance** command. What alternative method might be easier to maintain as the network changes?	

Create an Implementation Plan Table

To practice skills useful when creating your own implementation plan, list in Table 10-10 configuration commands related to the configuration of the following features. You may want to record your answers outside the book and set a goal to complete this table (and others like it) from memory during your final reviews before taking the exam.

Table 10-10   *Implementation Plan Configuration Memory Drill*

Feature	Configuration Commands/Notes
Filtering routes on redistribution from OSPF into EIGRP, allowing only routes permitted by ACL 1 (2 methods).	
Filtering routes on redistribution from EIGRP into OSPF, allowing only routes permitted by prefix list barney (2 methods).	
Configuring the route map that will set metric components to 1000, 200, 255, 1, and 150, for routes permitted by ACL 1, and filter all other routes.	
Set OSPF's administrative distance for all internal routes to 110, and all external routes to 180.	

Table 10-10 *Implementation Plan Configuration Memory Drill*

Feature	Configuration Commands/Notes
Set EIGRP's administrative distance for routes learned from neighbor 1.1.1.1 to 190, only for subnets between 10.1.0.0 – 10.1.255.255.	

Choose Commands for a Verification Plan Table

To practice skills useful when creating your own verification plan, list in Table 10-11 all commands that supply the requested information. You may want to record your answers outside the book and set a goal to complete this table (and others like it) from memory during your final reviews before taking the exam.

Table 10-11 *Verification Plan Memory Drill*

Information Needed	Command
Confirm that OSPF routes were redistributed from the IP routing table into that same router's EIGRP topology table.	
Display the number of matches in an ACL used for redistribution filtering.	
Display the number of matches in an IP prefix list used for redistribution filtering.	
Display the configuration of a route map.	
Display the component metrics of a route redistributed into EIGRP.	
Confirm the absence or presence of a route that could have been redistributed from OSPF into EIGRP.	
Confirm the absence or presence of a route that could have been redistributed from EIGRP into OSPF.	
Display an IP route's administrative distance.	
Display the administrative distance settings for EIGRP.	
Display the administrative distance settings for OSPF.	

Note: Some of the entries in this table may not have been specifically mentioned in this chapter but are listed in this table for review and reference.

Review all the Key Topics

Review the most important topics from inside the chapter, noted with the key topics icon in the outer margin of the page. Table 10-12 lists a reference of these key topics and the page numbers on which each is found.

Table 10-12   *Key Topics for Chapter 10*

Key Topic Element	Description	Page Number
List	A summary of functions that can be performed by a route-map referenced by a **redistribute** command	332
Table 10-2	The **match** route-map subcommands applicable to OSPF and EIGRP redistribution	333
Table 10-3	The **set** route-map subcommands applicable to OSPF and EIGRP redistribution	334
Table 10-6	Default administrative distance settings in IOS	346
Figure 10-4	Conceptual view of how default EIGRP administrative distance prevents domain loops–EIGRP internal versus OSPF external	347
Figure 10-9	Example use of route tags for purpose other than preventing domain loops	356
List	Recommendations for how to use route tags to prevent the domain loop problem	356
Figure 10-10	Example of how to prevent domain loops using route tags	357

Complete the Tables and Lists from Memory

Print a copy of Appendix D, "Memory Tables," (found on the CD), or at least the section for this chapter, and complete the tables and lists from memory. Appendix E, "Memory Tables Answer Key," also on the CD, includes completed tables and lists to check your work.

Define Key Terms

Define the following key terms from this chapter, and check your answers in the glossary.

Domain loop, administrative distance, route tag

This chapter covers the following subjects:

Policy-Based Routing: This section describes the IOS Policy-Based Routing (PBR) feature, which allows a router to make packet forwarding decisions on criteria other than the packet's destination address as matched with the IP routing table.

IP Service Level Agreement: This section gives a general description of the IP Service Level Agreement (IP SLA) feature, with particular attention to how it can be used to influence when a router uses a static route and when a router uses PBR.

CHAPTER 11

Policy-Based Routing and IP Service Level Agreement

The term *path control* has many fine shades of meaning, depending on the context. The broadest typical use of the term refers to any and every function that influences where a router forwards a packet. With that definition, path control includes practically every topic in this book. In other cases, the term *path control* refers to tools that influence the contents of the routing table, most typically referring to routing protocols.

This chapter examines two path control topics that fit only into the broader definition of the term. The first, Policy-Based Routing (PBR), also sometimes called simply Policy Routing, influences the IP data plane, changing the forwarding decision a router makes, but without first changing the IP routing table. The second tool, IP Service-Level Agreement (SLA), monitors network health and reachability. The router can then choose when to use routes, and when to ignore routes, based on the status determined by IP SLA.

"Do I Know This Already?" Quiz

The "Do I Know This Already?" quiz allows you to assess if you should read the entire chapter. If you miss no more than one of these six self-assessment questions, you might want to move ahead to the "Exam Preparation Tasks." Table 11-1 lists the major headings in this chapter and the "Do I Know This Already?" quiz questions covering the material in those headings so that you can assess your knowledge of these specific areas. The answers to the "Do I Know This Already?" quiz appear in Appendix A.

Table 11-1 *"Do I Know This Already?" Foundation Topics Section-to-Question Mapping*

Foundations Topics Section	Questions
Policy-Based Routing	1-3
IP Service-Level Agreement	4-6

1. Policy-Based Routing (PBR) has been enabled on Router R1's interface F0/0. Which of the following is true regarding how PBR works? (Choose two.)

   a. Packets entering F0/0 will be compared based on the PBR route map.

   b. Packets exiting F0/0 will be compared based on the PBR route map.

   c. IOS ignores the PBR forwarding directions when the packet matches a route map **deny** clause.

    d. IOS ignores the PBR forwarding directions when the packet matches a route map **permit** clause.

2. Examine the following configuration on Router R1. R1's **show ip route 172.16.4.1** command lists a route with outgoing interface S0/1/1. Host 172.16.3.3 uses telnet to connect to host 172.16.4.1. What will Router R1 do with the packets generated by host 172.16.3.3 because of the telnet, assuming the packets enter R1's F0/0 interface? (Choose two.)

```
interface Fastethernet 0/0
 ip address 172.16.1.1 255.255.255.0
 ip policy route-map Q2
!
route-map Q2 permit
 match ip address 101
 set interface s0/0/1
!
access-list 101 permit tcp host 172.16.3.3 172.16.4.0 0.0.0.255
```

    a. The packet will be forwarded out S0/0/1, or not at all.

    b. The packet will be forwarded out S0/0/1 if it is up.

    c. The packet will be forwarded out S0/1/1 if it is up.

    d. The packet will be forwarded out S0/1/1 if it is up, or if it is not up, out s0/0/1.

    e. The packet will be forwarded out S0/0/1 if it is up, or if it is not up, out s0/1/1.

3. The following output occurs on Router R2. Which of the following statements can be confirmed as true based on the output from R2?

```
R2# show ip policy
Interface       Route map
Fa0/0           RM1
Fa0/1           RM2
S0/0/0          RM3
```

    a. R2 will forward all packets that enter Fa0/0 per the PBR configuration.

    b. R2 will use route map RM2 when determining how to forward packets that exit interface Fa0/1.

    c. R2 will consider using PBR for all packets exiting S0/0/0 per route map RM3.

    d. R2 will consider using PBR for all packets entering S0/0/0 per route map RM3.

4. Which of the following are examples of traffic that can be created as part of an IP Service-Level Agreement operation? (Choose two.)

    a. ICMP Echo

    b. VoIP (RTP)

    c. IPX

    d. SNMP

5. The following configuration commands exist only in an implementation plan document. An engineer does a copy/paste of these commands into configuration mode on Router R1. Which of the following answers is most accurate regarding the results?

```
ip sla 1
icmp-echo 1.1.1.1 source-ip 2.2.2.2
ip sla schedule 1 start-time now life forever
```

    a. The SLA operation will be configured but will not start until additional commands are used.

    b. The SLA operation is not completely configured so it will not collect any data.

    c. The SLA operation is complete and working, collecting data into the RTTMON MIB.

    d. The SLA operation is complete and working but will not store the data in the RTTMON MIB without more configuration.

6. The following output occurs on Router R1. IP SLA operation 1 uses an ICMP echo operation type, with default frequency of 60 seconds. The operation pings from address 1.1.1.1 to address 2.2.2.2. Which of the following answers is true regarding IP SLA and object tracking on R1?

```
R1# show track
Track 2
  IP SLA 1 state
  State is Up
    3 changes, last change 00:00:03
  Delay up 45 secs, down 55 secs
  Latest operation return code: OK
  Latest RTT (millisecs) 6
  Tracked by:
   STATIC-IP-ROUTING 0
```

    a. The tracking return code fails immediately after the SLA operation results in an ICMP echo failure three times.

    b. The tracking return code fails immediately after the SLA operation results in an ICMP echo failure one time.

    c. After the tracking object fails, the tracking object moves back to an up state 45 seconds later in all cases.

    d. After moving to a down state, the tracking object moves back to an OK state 45 seconds after the SLA operation moves to an OK state.

Foundation Topics

Policy-Based Routing

When a packet arrives at the incoming interface of a router, the router's data plane processing logic takes several steps to process the packet. The incoming packet actually arrives encapsulated inside a data link layer frame, so the router must check the incoming frame's Frame Check Sequence (FCS) and discard the frame if errors occurred in transmission. If the FCS check passes, the router discards the incoming frame's data link header and trailer, leaving the Layer 3 packet. Finally, the router does the equivalent of comparing the destination IP address of the packet with the IP routing table, matching the longest-prefix route that matches the destination IP address.

Note: Most routers today default to use Cisco Express Forwarding (CEF), which causes the router to match the destination of IP packets with the CEF table, instead of the IP routing table. IOS derives the CEF table from the information in the IP routing table, with much faster table lookup as compared with using the routing table directly.

Policy-Based Routing (PBR) overrides the router's natural destination-based forwarding logic. PBR intercepts the packet after de-encapsulation on the incoming interface, before the router performs the CEF table lookup. PBR then chooses how to forward the packet using criteria other than the usual matching of the packet's destination address with the CEF table.

PBR chooses how to forward the packet by using matching logic defined through a route map, which in turn typically refers to an IP ACL. That same route map also defines the forwarding instructions–the next-hop IP address or outgoing interface–for packets matched by the route map. Figure 11-1 shows the general concept, with PBR on interface F0/0 overriding the usual routing logic, forwarding packets out three different outgoing interfaces.

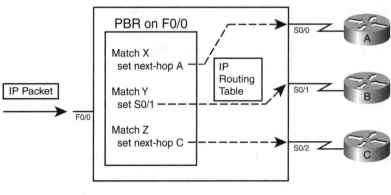

Figure 11-1 *PBR Concepts*

To perform the actions shown in Figure 11-1, the engineer configures two general steps:

Step 1.   Create a route map with the logic to match packets, and choose the route, as shown on the left side of the figure.

Step 2.   Enable the route map for use with PBR, on an interface, for packets entering the interface.

The rest of this section focuses on the configuration and verification of PBR.

Matching the Packet and Setting the Route

To match packets with a route map enabled for PBR, you use the familiar route-map **match** command. However, you have two **match** command options to use:

```
match ip address
match length min max
```

The **match ip address** command uses the same familiar logic as seen in several other chapters of this book. This command can reference standard and extended ACLs. Any item matchable by an ACL can be matched in the route map. The **match length** command allows you to specify a range of lengths, in bytes.

When a route map clause (with a permit action) matches a packet, the **set** command defines the action to take regarding how to forward the packet. The four **set** command options define either the outgoing interface or the next-hop IP address, just like routes in the IP routing table. Table 11-2 lists the options, with some explanations.

Table 11-2   *Choosing Routes Using the PBR* **set** *Command*

Key Topic

Command	Comments
set ip next-hop *ip-address*[...*ip-address*]	Next-hop addresses must be in a connected subnet; forwards to the first address in the list for which the associated interface is up.
set ip default next-hop *ip-address*[...*ip-address*]	Same logic as previous command, except policy routing first attempts to route based on the routing table.
set interface *interface-type interface-number* [... *interface-type interface-number*]	Forwards packets using the first interface in the list that is up.
set default interface *interface-type interface-number* [... *interface-type interface-number*]	Same logic as previous command, except policy routing first attempts to route based on the routing table.

Note that two of the commands allow the definition of a next-hop router, and two allow the definition of an outgoing interface. The other difference in the commands relates to whether the command includes the **default** keyword. The section "How the **default** Keyword Impacts Logic Ordering" later in this chapter describes the meaning of the **default** keyword.

After the route map has been configured with all the clauses to match packets, and set their outgoing interface or next-hop address, the only remaining step requires the **ip policy route-map** *name* command to enable PBR for packets entering an interface.

PBR Configuration Example

To tie the concepts together, Figure 11-2 shows a sample internetwork to use in a PBR example. In this case, EIGRP on R1 chooses the upper route to reach the subnets on the right, because of the higher bandwidth on the upper link (T1) as compared with the lower link (64 Kbps).

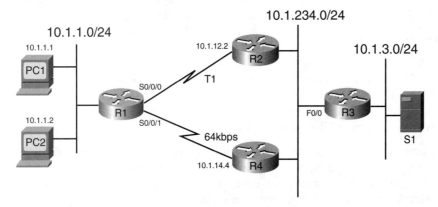

Figure 11-2 *Network Used in PBR Example*

For this example, the PBR configuration matches packets sent from PC2 on the left to server S1 in subnet 10.1.3.0/24 on the right. PBR on R1 routes these packets out S0/0/1 to R4. These packets will be routed over the lower path–out R1's S0/0/1 to R4–instead of through the current through R2, as listed in R1's IP routing table.

Example 11-1 *R1 PBR Configuration*

```
interface Fastethernet 0/0
 ip address 10.1.1.9 255.255.255.0
 ip policy route-map PC2-over-low-route
!
route-map PC2-over-low-route permit
 match ip address 101
 set ip next-hop 10.1.14.4
!
access-list 101 permit ip host 10.1.1.2 10.1.3.0 0.0.0.255
```

The configuration enables PBR with F0/0's **ip policy route-map PC2-over-low-route** command. The referenced route map matches packets that match ACL 101; ACL 101 matches packets from PC2 only, going to subnet 10.1.3.0/24. The route-map clause uses a permit action, which tells IOS to indeed apply PBR logic to these matched packets. (Had the

route-map command listed a deny action, IOS would simply route the packet as normal—it would not filter the packet.) Finally, for packets matched with a permit action, the router forwards the packet based on the **set ip next-hop 10.1.14.4** command, which tells R1 to forward the packet to R4 next.

Note that for each packet entering F0/0, PBR either matches the packet with a route map permit clause, or matches the packet with a route map deny clause. All route maps have an implicit deny clause at the end that matches all packets not already matched by the route map. PBR processes packets that match a permit clause using the defined **set** command. For packets matched by a deny clause, PBR lets the packet go through to the normal IP routing process.

To verify the results of the policy routing, Example 11-2 shows two **traceroute** commands: one from PC1 and one from PC2. Each shows the different paths. (Note that the output actually comes from a couple of routers configured to act as hosts PC1 and PC2 for this example.)

Example 11-2   *Confirming PBR Results Using* **traceroute**

```
! First, from PC1 (actually, a router acting as PC1):
PC1# trace 10.1.3.99
Type escape sequence to abort.
Tracing the route to 10.1.3.99

  1 10.1.1.9 4 msec 0 msec 4 msec
  2 10.1.12.2 0 msec 4 msec 4 msec
  3 10.1.234.3 0 msec 4 msec 4 msec
  4 10.1.3.99 0 msec *  0 msec
! Next, from PC2
PC2# trace 10.1.3.99

Type escape sequence to abort.
Tracing the route to 10.1.3.99

  1 10.1.1.9 4 msec 0 msec 4 msec
  2 10.1.14.4 8 msec 4 msec 8 msec
  3 10.1.234.3 8 msec 8 msec 4 msec
  4 10.1.3.99 4 msec *  4 msec
```

The output differs only in the second router in the end-to-end path—R2's 10.1.12.2 address as seen for PC1's packet and 10.1.14.4 as seen for PC2's packet.

The verification commands on the router doing the PBR function list relatively sparse information. The **show ip policy** command just shows the interfaces on which PBR is enabled and the route map used. The **show route-map** command shows overall statistics for the number of packets matching the route map for PBR purposes. The only way to verify the types of packets that are policy routed is to use the **debug ip policy** command, which can be dangerous on production routers, given its multiple lines of output per packet, or to use **traceroute**. Example 11-3 lists the output of the **show** and **debug** commands on Router R1 with the **debug** output being for a single policy routed packet.

Example 11-3 *Verifying PBR on Router R1*

```
R1# show ip policy
Interface        Route map
Fa0/0            PC2-over-low-route

R1# show route-map
route-map PC2-over-low-route, permit, sequence 10
  Match clauses:
    ip address (access-lists): 101
  Set clauses:
    ip next-hop 10.1.14.4
  Policy routing matches: 12 packets, 720 bytes
R1# debug ip policy
*Sep 14 16:57:51.675: IP: s=10.1.1.2 (FastEthernet0/0), d=10.1.3.99, len 28,
policy match
*Sep 14 16:57:51.675: IP: route map PC2-over-low-route, item 10, permit
*Sep 14 16:57:51.675: IP: s=10.1.1.2 (FastEthernet0/0), d=10.1.3.99 (Serial0/0/1),
len 28, policy routed
*Sep 14 16:57:51.675: IP: FastEthernet0/0 to Serial0/0/1 10.1.14.4
```

How the **default** Keyword Impacts PBR Logic Ordering

The example in the previous section showed a **set** command that did not use the **default** keyword. However, the inclusion or omission of this keyword significantly impacts how PBR works. This parameter in effect tells IOS whether to apply PBR logic *before* trying to use normal destination-based routing, or whether to first try to use the normal destination-based routing, relying on PBR's logic only if the destination-based routing logic fails to match a nondefault route.

First, consider the case in which the **set** command omits the **default** parameter. When IOS matches the associated PBR route map permit clause, IOS applies the PBR logic first. If the **set** command identifies an outgoing interface that is up, or a next-hop router that is reachable, IOS uses the PBR-defined route. However, if the PBR route (as defined in the **set** command) is not working–because the outgoing interface is down or the next hop is unreachable using a connected route–then IOS next tries to route the packet using the normal destination-based IP routing process.

Next, consider the case in which the **set** command includes the **default** parameter. When IOS matches the associated PBR route map permit clause, IOS applies the normal destination-based routing logic first, with one small exception: it ignores any default routes. So, the router first tries to route the packet as normal, but if no nondefault route matches the packet's destination address, then the router forwards the packet as directed in the **set** command.

For example, for the configuration shown in Example 11-1, by changing the **set** command to **set ip default next-hop 10.1.14.4**, R1 would have first looked for (and found) a working route through R2, and forwarded packets sent by PC2 over the link to R2. Summarizing:

- Omitting the **default** parameter gives you logic like this: "Try PBR first, and if PBR's route does not work, try to route as usual."

- Including the **default** parameter gives you logic like this: "Try to route as usual while ignoring any default routes, but if normal routing fails, use PBR."

Additional PBR Functions

Primarily, PBR routes packets received on an interface, but using logic other than matching the destination IP address and the CEF table. This section briefly examines three additional PBR functions.

Applying PBR to Locally Created Packets

In some cases, it may be useful to use PBR to process packets generated by the router itself. However, PBR normally processes packets that enter the interface(s) on which the **ip policy route-map** command has been configured, and packets generated by the router itself do not actually enter the router through some interface. To make IOS process locally created packets using PBR logic, configure the **ip local policy route-map** *name* global command, referring to the PBR route map at the end of the command.

The section "Configuring and Verifying IP SLA" later in this chapter shows an example use of this command. IP SLA causes a router to create packets, so applying PBR to such packets can influence the path taken by the packets.

Setting IP Precedence

Quality of service (QoS) refers to the entire process of how the network infrastructure can choose to apply different levels of service to different packets. For example, a router may need to keep delay and jitter (delay variation) low for VoIP and Video over IP packets, because these interactive voice and video calls only work well when the delay and jitter are held very low. So, the router might let VoIP packets bypass a long queue of data packets that might be waiting to exit an interface, giving the voice packet better (lower) delay and jitter.

Most QoS designs mark each packet with a different value inside the IP header, for the purpose of identifying groups of packets–a service class–that should get a particular QoS treatment. For instance, all VoIP packets could be marked with a particular value so that the router can then find those marked bits, know that the packet is a VoIP packet due to that marking, and apply QoS accordingly.

Although the most commonly used QoS marking tool today is Class-Based Marking, in the past, PBR was one of the few tools that could be used for this important QoS function of marking packets. PBR still supports marking; however, most modern QoS designs ignore PBR's marking capabilities.

Before discussing PBR's marking features, a little background about the historical view of the IP header's type of service (ToS) byte is needed. The IP header originally defined a ToS byte whose individual bits have been defined in a couple of ways over the years. One such definition used the first three bits in the ToS byte as a three-bit IP Precedence (IPP) field, which could be used for generic QoS marking, with the higher values generally implying a better QoS treatment. Back in the 1990s, the ToS byte was redefined as the Differentiated Services (DS) byte, with the first six bits defined as the Differentiated Service Code Point (DSCP). Most QoS implementations today revolve around setting the DSCP field.

PBR supports setting the older QoS marking fields—the IP Precedence (IPP) and the entire ToS byte—using commands **set ip precedence** *value* and **set ip tos** *value*, respectively, in the route map. To configure packet marking, configure PBR as normal, but add a **set** command that defines the field to be marked and the value.

PBR with IP SLA

Besides matching a packet's length, or matching a packet with an ACL, PBR can also react to some dynamic measurements of the health of the IP network. To do so, PBR relies on the IP Service-Level Agreement (IP SLA) tool. In short, if the IP SLA tool measures the network's current performance, and the performance does not meet the defined threshold, PBR chooses to not use a particular route. The second half of this chapter discusses IP SLA, with the section "Configuring and Verifying IP SLA" demonstrating how PBR works with IP SLA.

IP Service-Level Agreement

The IOS IP Service-Level Agreement (IP SLA) feature measures the ongoing behavior of the network. The measurement can be as simple as using the equivalent of a ping to determine if an IP address responds, or as sophisticated as measuring the jitter (delay variation) of VoIP packets that flow over a particular path. To use IP SLA, an engineer configures IP SLA operations on various routers, and the routers will then send packets, receive responses, and gather data about whether a response was received, and the specific characteristics of the results, such as delay and jitter measurements.

IP SLA primarily acts as a tool to test and gather data about the network. Network management tools can then collect that data and report whether the network reached SLAs for the network. Many network management tools support the ability to configure IP SLA from the management tools' graphical interfaces. When configured, the routers gather the results of the operations, storing the statistics in the IOS RTTMON MIB. Management applications can later gather the statistics from this MIB on various routers and report on whether the business SLAs were met based on the gathered statistics. For example, you can use the Cisco Works Internetwork Performance Monitor (IPM) feature to configure and monitor the data collected using IP SLA operations.

So, why bother with a pure network management feature in this book focused on IP routing? Well, you can configure static routes and PBR to use IP SLA operations, so that if the operation shows a failure of a particular measurement or reduced performance of the measurement below a configured threshold, the router stops using either the static route or PBR logic. This combination of features provides a means to control when the static and PBR paths are used and when they are ignored.

This section begins with discussion of IP SLA as an end to itself. Following that, the topic of SLA object tracking is added, along with how to configure static routes and PBR to track IP SLA operations so IOS knows when to use, and when to ignore, these routes.

Understanding IP SLA Concepts

IP SLA uses the concept of an *operation*. Each operation defines a type of packet that the router will generate, the destination and source address, and other characteristics of the packet. The configuration includes settings about the time-of-day when the router should be sending the packets in a particular operation, the types of statistics that should be gathered, and how often the router should send the packets. Also, you can configure a router with multiple operations of different types.

For example, a single IP SLA operation could define the following:

■ Use ICMP echo packets.

■ Measure the end-to-end round trip response time (ICMP echo).

■ Send the packets every 5 minutes, all day long.

Note: For those of you who have been around IOS for a while, IP SLA may sound familiar. IP SLA has origins in earlier IOS features, including the *Response Time Reporter (RTR)* feature. The RTR feature uses the **rtr** command and uses the term *probe* to refer to what IP SLA refers to as an *operation*.

All the SLA operations rely on the router sending packets and some other device sending packets back. Figure 11-3 shows the general idea and provides a good backdrop to discuss some related issues.

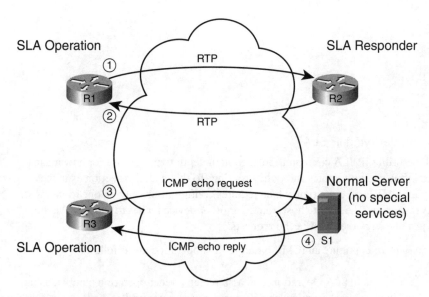

Figure 11-3 *Sending and Receiving Packets with IP SLA*

An IP SLA operation can cause the router to send packets to any IP address, whether on a router or a host. When sending to a host, as in the bottom part of the figure, the host does not need any special software or configuration–instead, the host just acts as normal. That means that if an SLA operation sends packets to a host, the router can only use operation types that send packets that the host understands. For instance, the router could use ICMP echo requests, TCP connection requests, or even HTTP GET requests to a web server, because the server should try to respond to these requests.

The operation can also send packets to another router, which gives IP SLA a wider range of possible operation types. If the operation sends packets to which the remote router would normally respond, like ICMP echo requests, the other router needs no special configuration. However, IP SLA supports the concept of the IP SLA responder, as noted in Figure 11-3 for R2. By configuring R2 as an IP SLA responder, it responds to packets that a router would not normally respond to, giving the network engineer a way to monitor network behavior without having to place devices around the network just to test the network.

For example, the operation could send Real-time Transport Protocol (RTP) packets–packets that have the same content as VoIP–as shown in Figure 11-3 as Step 1. Then the IP SLA responder function on R2 can reply back as if a voice call exists between the two routers, as shown in Step 2 of that figure.

A wide range of IP SLA operations exist. The following list summarizes the majority of the available operation types, just for perspective:

- ICMP (echo, jitter)

- RTP (VoIP)

- TCP connection (establishes TCP connections)

- UDP (echo, jitter)

- DNS

- DHCP

- HTTP

- FTP

Configuring and Verifying IP SLA

This book describes IP SLA configuration in enough depth to get a sense for how it can be used to influence static routes and policy routing. To that end, this section examines the use of an ICMP echo operation, which requires configuration only on one router, with no IP SLA responder. The remote host, router, or other device replies to the ICMP Echo Requests just like any other ICMP echo requests.

The general steps to configure an ICMP-based IP SLA operation are as follows:

Key
Topic

Step 1.   Create the IP SLA Operation, and assign it an integer operation number, using the **ip sla** *sla-ops-number* global configuration command.

Step 2. Define the operation type and the parameters for that operation type. For ICMP echo, you define the destination IP address or hostname, and optionally, the source IP address or hostname, using the **icmp-echo** {*destination-ip-address* | *destination-hostname*} [**source-ip** {*ip-address* | *hostname*} | **source-interface** *interface-name*] SLA operation subcommand.

Step 3. (Optional) Define a (nondefault) frequency that the operation should send the packets, in seconds, using the **frequency** *seconds* IP SLA subcommand.

Step 4. Schedule when the SLA will run, using the **ip sla schedule** *sla-ops-number* [**life** {**forever** | *seconds*}] [**start-time** {*hh:mm*[:*ss*] [*month day* | *day month*] | **pending** | **now** | **after** *hh:mm:ss*}] [**ageout** *seconds*] [**recurring**] global command.

Example 11-4 shows the process of configuring an ICMP Echo operation on Router R1 from Figure 11-2. The purpose of the operation is to test the PBR route through R4. In this case, the operation will be configured as shown in Figure 11-4, with the following criteria:

- Send ICMP Echo Requests to server S1 (10.1.3.99).

- Use source address 10.1.1.9 (R1's F0/0 IP address).

- Send these packets every 60 seconds.

- Start the operation immediately, and run it forever.

- Enable PBR for locally generated packets, matching the IP SLA operation with the PBR configuration so that the SLA operation's packets flow over the lower route.

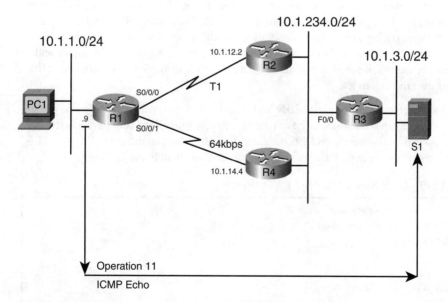

Figure 11-4 *Concept of IP SLA Operation on R1*

Example 11-4 *Configuring an ICMP Echo Operation on Router R1*

```
R1# conf t
Enter configuration commands, one per line.  End with CNTL/Z.
R1(config)# ip sla 11
R1(config-ip-sla)#icmp?
icmp-echo  icmp-jitter

R1(config-ip-sla)# icmp-echo 10.1.3.99 source-ip 10.1.1.9
R1(config-ip-sla)# frequency 60
R1(config-ip-sla)# exit
R1(config)# ip sla schedule 11 start-time now life forever

! Changes to the PBR configuration below
R1(config)# access-list 101 permit ip host 10.1.1.9 host 10.1.3.99
R1(config)# ip local policy route-map PC2-over-low-route
R1(config)# end
```

First, focus on the pure IP SLA configuration, located from the beginning of the example up through command **ip sla schedule**. The configuration creates IP SLA operation 11. The parameters on the **icmp-echo** command act as if you used an extended ping from the command line, specifying both the source and destination IP address. The last command directly related to IP SLA, the **ip sla schedule** command, enables the operation now, and runs the operation until the network engineer takes some action to disable it, in some cases by removing the operation with the **no ip sla** *sla-ops-number* command.

The last two commands in the example show a change to the earlier PBR configuration so that the SLA operation's packets flow over the lower route. The **ip local policy PC2-over-low-route** global command tells R1 to process packets generated by R1, including the IP SLA operation packets, using PBR. The addition of the **access-list 101** command to the configuration shown earlier in Example 11-1 makes the route map match the source and destination address of the SLA operation. That former route map's **set** command sent the packets over the link to R4.

IP SLA supports a couple of particularly useful verification commands: **show ip sla configuration** and **show ip sla statistics**. The first command confirms all the configuration settings for the operation, and the second lists the current statistics for the operation. Example 11-5 shows examples of each on R1, after the configuration shown in Example 11-4.

Example 11-5 *Verification of an IP SLA Operation*

```
R1# show ip sla configuration
IP SLAs Infrastructure Engine-II
Entry number: 11
Owner:
Tag:
Type of operation to perform: echo
Target address/Source address: 10.1.3.99/10.1.1.9
```

```
Type Of Service parameter: 0x0
Request size (ARR data portion): 28
Operation timeout (milliseconds): 5000
Verify data: No
Vrf Name:
Schedule:
    Operation frequency (seconds): 60   (not considered if randomly scheduled)
    Next Scheduled Start Time: Start Time already passed
    Group Scheduled : FALSE
    Randomly Scheduled : FALSE
    Life (seconds): Forever
    Entry Ageout (seconds): never
    Recurring (Starting Everyday): FALSE
    Status of entry (SNMP RowStatus): Active
Threshold (milliseconds): 5000 (not considered if react RTT is configured)
Distribution Statistics:
    Number of statistic hours kept: 2
    Number of statistic distribution buckets kept: 1
    Statistic distribution interval (milliseconds): 20
History Statistics:
    Number of history Lives kept: 0
    Number of history Buckets kept: 15
    History Filter Type: None
Enhanced History:

R1# show ip sla statistics 11
IPSLAs Latest Operation Statistics

IPSLA operation id: 11
        Latest RTT: 8 milliseconds
Latest operation start time: *19:58:08.395 UTC Mon Sep 14 2009
Latest operation return code: OK
Number of successes: 22
Number of failures: 0
Operation time to live: Forever
```

The highlighted lines in the output of the **show ip sla configuration** command correspond to the values explicitly configured in Example 11-4. The more interesting output
exists in the output of the **show ip sla statistics 11** command, which lists the statistics
only for operation 11. In this case, 22 intervals have passed, showing 22 ICMP Echo Requests as successful with no failures. It also lists the latest round trip time (RTT). Finally, it
lists the return code of the most recent operation (OK in this case)—a key value used by
SLA tracking.

Tracking SLA Operations to Influence Routing

As previously mentioned, you can configure both static routes and PBR to be used only when an SLA operation remains successful. The configuration to achieve this logic requires the configuration of a tracking object and cross references between the static route, PBR, and IP SLA, as shown in Figure 11-5.

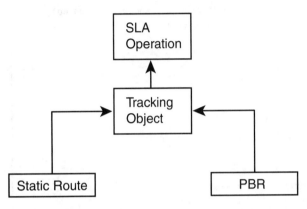

Key
Topic   **Figure 11-5**   *Configuration Relationships for Path Control Using IP SLA*

The tracking object looks at the IP SLA operation's most recent return code to then determine the tracking state as either "up" or "down." Depending on the type of SLA operation, the return code may be a simple toggle, with "OK" meaning that the last operation worked. The tracking object would then result in an "up" state if the SLA operation resulting in an "OK" return code. Other SLA operations that define thresholds have more possible return codes. The tracking operation results in an "up" state if the IP SLA operation is within the configured threshold.

One of the main reasons that IOS requires the use of this tracking object is so that the routes do not flap. Route flapping occurs when a router adds a route to the routing table, then quickly removes it; conditions change, so the router soon adds the route to the table again; and so on. If a static route tracked the IP SLA object directly, the SLA object's return code could change each time the operation ran, causing a route flap. The tracking object concept provides the ability to set a delay of how soon after a tracking state change the tracking object should change state. This feature gives the engineer a tool to control route flaps.

This section shows how to configure a tracking object for use with both a static route and with PBR.

Configuring a Static Route to Track an IP SLA Operation

To configure a static route to track an IP SLA, you need to configure the tracking object and then configure the static route with the **track** keyword. To do so, use these steps:

Key
Topic   **Step 1.**   Use the **track** *object-number* **ip sla** *sla-ops-number* [**state** | **reachability**] global command.

Step 2.   (Optional) Configure the delay to regulate flapping of the tracking state by using the **delay {down** *seconds* | **up** *seconds*} command in tracking configuration mode.

Step 3.   Configure the static route with the **ip route** *destination mask* {*interface* | *next-hop*} **track** *object-number* global command.

Example 11-6 shows the configuration of tracking object 2, using the same design shown in Figure 11-2 and 11-4. In this case, the configuration adds a static route for subnet 10.1.234.0/24, the LAN subnet to which R2, R3, and R4 all connect. EIGRP chooses a route over R1's S0/0/0 as its best route, but this static route uses S0/0/1 as the outgoing interface.

Example 11-6   *Configuring a Static Route with Tracking IP SLA*

```
R1# conf t
Enter configuration commands, one per line.  End with CNTL/Z.
R1(config)# track 2 ip sla 11 state
R1(config-track)# delay up 90 down 90
R1(config-track)# exit
R1(config)# ip route 10.1.234.0 255.255.255.0 s0/0/1 track 2
R1(config)# end
```

The configuration begins with the creation of the tracking object number 2. As with IP SLA operation numbers, the number itself is unimportant, other than that the **ip route** command refers to this same number with the **track 2** option at the end of the command. The tracking object's delay settings have been made at 90 seconds.

The **show track** command lists the tracking object's configuration plus many other details. It lists the current tracking state, the time in this state, the number of state transitions, and the other entities that track the object (in this case, a static route).

Example 11-7 shows what happens when the IP SLA operation fails, causing the static route to be removed. The example starts with the configuration shown in Example 11-6, along with the SLA operation 11 as configured in Example 11-4. The following list details the current operation and what happens sequentially in the example:

Step 1.   Before the text seen in Example 11-7, the current IP SLA operation already sends packets using PBR, over R1's link to R4, using source IP address 10.1.1.9 and destination 10.1.3.99 (server S1).

Step 2.   At the beginning of the next example, because the IP SLA operation is working, the static route is in R1's IP routing table.

Step 3.   An ACL is configured on R4 (not shown) so that the IP SLA operation fails.

Step 4.   A few minutes later, R1 issues a log message stating that the tracking object changed state from up to down.

Step 5.   The example ends with several commands that confirm the change in state for the tracking object, and confirmation that R1 now uses the EIGRP learned route through R2.

Note: This example uses the **show ip route ... longer-prefixes** command because this command lists only the route for 10.1.234.0/24, which is the route that fails over in the example.

Example 11-7   *Verifying Tracking of Static Routes*

```
! Next - Step 2 Step 2 Step 2 Step 2
R1# show ip route 10.1.234.0 255.255.255.0 longer-prefixes
! Legend omitted for brevity

      10.0.0.0/8 is variably subnetted, 7 subnets, 2 masks
S        10.1.234.0/24 is directly connected, Serial0/0/1
R1# show track
Track 2
   IP SLA 11 state
   State is Up
     1 change, last change 01:24:14
   Delay up 90 secs, down 90 secs
   Latest operation return code: OK
   Latest RTT (millisecs) 7
   Tracked by:
     STATIC-IP-ROUTING 0
!

! Next, Step 3 Step 3 Step 3
! Not shown - SLA Operations packets are now filtered by an ACL on R4
! Sometime later...
!

! Next - Step 4 Step 4 Step 4 Step 4
R1#
*Sep 14 22:55:43.362: %TRACKING-5-STATE: 2 ip sla 11 state Up->Down

! Final Step - Step 5 Step 5 Step 5 Step 5
R1# show track
Track 2
   IP SLA 11 state
   State is Down
   2 changes, last change 00:00:15
   Delay up 90 secs, down 90 secs
   Latest operation return code: No connection
   Tracked by:
     STATIC-IP-ROUTING 0
R1# show ip route 10.1.234.0 255.255.255.0 longer-prefixes
! Legend omitted for brevity
```

```
      10.0.0.0/8 is variably subnetted, 7 subnets, 2 masks
D        10.1.234.0/24 [90/2172416] via 10.1.12.2, 00:00:25, Serial0/0/0
```

Configuring PBR to Track an IP SLA

To configure PBR to use object tracking, use a modified version of the **set** command in the route map. For instance, the earlier PBR configuration used the following **set** command:

```
set ip next-hop 10.1.14.4
```

Instead, use the **verify-availability** keyword, as shown in this command:

```
set ip next-hop verify-availability 10.1.14.4 1 track 2
```

When the tracking object is up, PBR works as configured. When the tracking object is down, PBR acts as if the **set** command does not exist. That means that the router will still attempt to route the packet per the normal destination-based routing process.

The output of the related verification commands does not differ significantly when comparing the configuration of tracking for static routes versus PBR. The **show track** command lists "ROUTE-MAP" instead of "STATIC-IP-ROUTING," but the details of the **show track**, **show ip sla statistics**, and object tracking log message seen in Example 11-7, remain the same.

Exam Preparation Tasks

Planning Practice

The CCNP ROUTE exam expects test takers to review design documents, create implementation plans, and create verification plans. This section provides some exercises that may help you to take a step back from the minute details of the topics in this chapter so that you can think about the same technical topics from the planning perspective.

For each planning practice table, simply complete the table. Note that any numbers in parentheses represent the number of options listed for each item in the solutions in Appendix F, "Completed Planning Practice Tables."

Design Review Table

Table 11-5 lists several design goals related to this chapter. If these design goals were listed in a design document, and you had to take that document and develop an implementation plan, what implementation options come to mind? You should write a general description; specific configuration commands are not required.

Table 11-5 *Design Review*

Design Goal	Possible Implementation Choices Covered in This Chapter
The design calls for traffic destined for one server in subnet 10.1.1.0/24 to be sent over a different route than the IGP-learned route for 10.1.1.0/24. (2)	
Same requirement as the previous row, except that only a subset of the source hosts should have their packets take a different route than the IGP-learned route.	
The design requires that a static route be used, but only when a particular database server is reachable.	

Implementation Plan Peer Review Table

Table 11-6 shows a list of questions that others might ask, or that you might think about, during a peer review of another network engineer's implementation plan. Complete the table by answering the questions.

Create an Implementation Plan Table

To practice skills useful when creating your own implementation plan, list in Table 11-7 all configuration commands related to the configuration of the following features. You may want to record your answers outside the book and set a goal to complete this table (and others like it) from memory during your final reviews before taking the exam.

Table 11-6 *Notable Questions from This Chapter to Consider During an Implementation Plan Peer Review*

Question	Answers
A plan lists two PBR route maps–one that uses the **default** keyword in its **set** command, and the other that does not. What is the fundamental difference?	
A plan shows a route map enabled for policy routing, and the route map matches some packets with a deny route-map clause. What does IOS do with those packets?	
The plan document shows a PBR route map with the command **set ip dscp ef**. Does PBR support marking? And can it mark DSCP?	
The plan shows an IP SLA operation number 5, with a static route configured with the **track 5** parameters. What issues might exist with the linkages between these commands?	
The IP SLA configuration shows an IP SLA operation that uses ICMP Echo, with the destination IP address of a server. What must be done on the server to support this operation?	
Same scenario as the previous row, except the destination address is on a router.	
Same scenario as the previous row, except the operation generates RTP packets to measure voice jitter.	

Table 11-7 *Implementation Plan Configuration Memory Drill*

Feature	Configuration Commands/Notes
Configure the matching logic in a PBR route map (two options).	
Configure the next-hop IP address in a PBR route map (two options).	
Configure the outgoing interface in a PBR route map (two options).	
Enable PBR on an interface.	
Enable PBR for packets created by the router.	

Choose Commands for a Verification Plan Table

To practice skills useful when creating your own verification plan, list in Table 11-8 all commands that supply the requested information. You may want to record your answers outside the book and set a goal to complete this table (and others like it) from memory during your final reviews before taking the exam.

Table 11-8 *Verification Plan Memory Drill*

Information Needed	Command
List interfaces on which PBR is enabled and the route-map used.	
Display the configuration of a route map.	
Generate debug messages for each packet that matches PBR.	
Display the configuration of an SLA operation.	
Show the measurements from an SLA operation.	
Display the status of a tracking object.	

Note: Some of the entries in this table may not have been specifically mentioned in this chapter, but are listed in this table for review and reference.

Review all the Key Topics

Review the most important topics from inside the chapter, noted with the key topics icon in the outer margin of the page. Table 11-9 lists a reference of these key topics and the page numbers on which each is found.

Table 11-9 *Key Topics for Chapter 10*

Key Topic Element	Description	Page Number
Figure 1-1	PBR concepts	366
Table 11-2	List of PBR **set** commands to define the route	367
List	Comparisons of PBR logic when including/omitting the **set** command's **default** keyword	371
Figure 1-3	IP SLA concepts	373
List	Configuration checklist for IP SLA	374
Figure 11-5	Configuration relationships for IP SLA and object tracking	378
List	Configuration checklist for object tracking	378

Complete the Tables and Lists from Memory

Print a copy of Appendix D, "Memory Tables," (found on the CD), or at least the section for this chapter, and complete the tables and lists from memory. Appendix E, "Memory Tables Answer Key," also on the CD, includes completed tables and lists to check your work.

Definitions of Key Terms

Define the following key terms from this chapter, and check your answers in the glossary.

Policy-Based Routing, IP Service-Level Agreement, tracking object, path control, ToS, IP Precedence, SLA Operation

This chapter covers the following subjects:

The Basics of Internet Routing and Addressing: This section reviews the use of public and private IP addresses in the Internet, both in theory and practice.

Introduction to BGP: This section introduces several basic concepts about BGP, including the concept of autonomous system numbers (ASN), path attributes (PA), and both internal and external BGP.

Outbound Routing Toward the Internet: This section examines the options and tradeoffs for how to influence outbound routes from an Enterprise toward the Internet.

CHAPTER 12

Internet Connectivity and BGP

Enterprises almost always use some IGP routing protocol. Sure, Enterprises could instead choose to exclusively use static routes throughout their internetworks, but they typically do not. Using an IGP requires much less planning, configuration, and ongoing effort compared to using static routes. Routing protocols take advantage of new links without requiring more static route configuration, and the routing protocols avoid the misconfiguration issues likely to occur when using a large number of static routes.

Similarly, when connecting to the Internet, Enterprises can use either static routes or a routing protocol, namely Border Gateway Protocol (BGP). However, the decision to use BGP instead of static routes does not usually follow the same logic that leads engineers to almost always use an IGP inside the Enterprise. BGP might not be necessary or even useful in some cases. To quote Jeff Doyle, author of two of the most respected books on the subject of IP routing, "Not as many internetworks need BGP as you might think" (from his book Routing TCP/IP, Volume II).

This chapter examines the facts, rules, design options, and some perspectives on Internet connectivity for Enterprises. Along the way, the text examines when static routes may work fine, how BGP might be useful in some cases, and the cases for which BGP can be of the most use. Chapter 13, "External BGP," discusses the configuration and verification of BGP for basic operation, but with no overt attempt to influence BGP's choice of best paths. Chapter 14, "Internal BGP and BGP Route Filtering," then discusses the need for Internal BGP (iBGP), along with BGP route filtering. Finally, Chapter 15, "BGP Path Control," completes this book's coverage of BGP by examining the tools by which BGP can be made to choose different routes, and some basic configuration to manipulate the choices of best route.

This chapter begins with a section that reviews some CCNA-level topics from the perspective of Enterprise connectivity to the Internet. In particular, this first section examines public and private IPv4 addressing, NAT, and how the Internet uses the public IPv4 address space. Next, the chapter introduces BGP as a routing protocol, emphasizing that most Enterprises choose to use BGP when needing to influence the choice of best route. The final section of this chapter examines different design categories for Internet connections, emphasizing the path control options gained by using BGP in those designs.

"Do I Know This Already?" Quiz

The "Do I Know This Already?" quiz allows you to assess if you should read the entire chapter. If you miss no more than one of these seven self-assessment questions, you might want to move ahead to the "Exam Preparation Tasks." Table 12-1 lists the major headings in this chapter and the "Do I Know This Already?" quiz questions covering the material in those headings so that you can assess your knowledge of these specific areas. The answers to the "Do I Know This Already?" quiz appear in Appendix A.

Table 12-1 *"Do I Know This Already?" Foundation Topics Section-to-Question Mapping*

Foundations Topics Section	Questions
The Basics of Internet Routing and Addressing	1–2
Introduction to BGP	3–5
Outbound Routing Toward the Internet	6, 7

1. Which of the following are considered private IPv4 addresses? (Choose two.)

    a. 192.16.1.1

    b. 172.30.1.1

    c. 225.0.0.1

    d. 127.0.0.1

    e. 10.1.1.1

2. Class C network 200.1.1.0/24 was allocated to an ISP that operated primarily in Asia. That ISP then assigned this entire Class C network to one of its Asian customers. Network 200.1.2.0/24 has yet to be assigned to any ISP. Which of the following is most likely to be true?

    a. 200.1.2.0/24 could be assigned to any registrar or ISP in the world.

    b. 200.1.2.0/24 will be assigned in the same geography (Asia) as 200.1.1.0/24.

    c. 200.1.2.0/24 cannot be assigned as public address space.

    d. Routers inside North American ISPs increase their routing table size by 1 as a result of the customer with 200.1.1.0/24 connecting to the Internet.

3. Router R1, in ASN 11, learns a BGP route from BGP peer R22 in ASN 22. R1 and then uses BGP to advertise the route to R2, also in ASN 11. What ASNs would you see in the BGP table on R2 for this route?

    a. 22

    b. 11

    c. 1

    d. None

4. Which of the following are most likely to be used as an ASN by a company that has a registered public 16-bit ASN? (Choose two.)

   a. 1

   b. 65,000

   c. 64,000

   d. 64,550

5. Which of the following statements is true about a router's eBGP peers that is not also true about that same router's iBGP peers?

   a. The eBGP peer neighborship uses TCP.

   b. The eBGP peer uses port 180 (default).

   c. The eBGP peer uses the same ASN as the local router.

   d. The eBGP peer updates its AS_Path PA before sending updates to this router.

6. Which of the following is the primary motivation for using BGP between an Enterprise and its ISPs?

   a. To influence the choice of best path (best route) for at least some routes

   b. To avoid having to configure static routes

   c. To allow redistribution of BGP routes into the IGP routing protocol

   d. To monitor the size of the Internet BGP table

7. The following terms describe various design options for Enterprise connectivity to the Internet. Which of the following imply that the Enterprise connects to two or more ISPs? (Choose two.)

   a. Single Homed

   b. Dual Homed

   c. Single Multihomed

   d. Dual Multihomed

Foundation Topics

The Basics of Internet Routing and Addressing

The original design for the Internet called for the assignment of globally unique IPv4 addresses for all hosts connected to the Internet. The idea is much like the global telephone network, with a unique phone number, worldwide, for all phone lines, cell phones, and the like.

To achieve this goal, the design called for all organizations to register and be assigned one or more public IP networks (Class A, B, or C). Then, inside that organization, each address would be assigned to a single host. By using only the addresses in their assigned network number, each company's IP addresses would not overlap with other companies. As a result, all hosts in the world would have globally unique IP addresses.

The assignment of a single classful network to each organization actually helped keep Internet routers' routing tables small. The Internet routers could ignore all subnets used inside each company, and instead just have a route for each classful network. For instance, if a company registered and was assigned Class B network 128.107.0.0/16, and had 500 subnets, the Internet routers just needed one route for that whole Class B network.

Over time, the Internet grew tremendously. It became clear by the early 1990s that something had to be done, or the growth of the Internet would grind to a halt. At the then-current rate of assigning new networks, all public IP networks would soon be assigned, and growth would be stifled. Additionally, even with routers ignoring the specific subnets, the routing tables in Internet routers were becoming too large for the router technology of that day. (For perspective, more than 2 million public Class C networks exist, and two million IP routes in a single IP routing table would be considered quite large–maybe even too large–for core routers in the Internet even today.)

To deal with these issues, the Internet community worked together to come up with both some short-term and long-term solutions to two problems: the shortage of public addresses and the size of the routing tables. The short-term solutions to these problems included

- Reduce the number of wasted public IP addresses by using classless IP addressing when assigning prefixes—assigning prefixes/lengths instead of being restricted to assigning only Class A, B, and C network numbers.

- Reduce the need for public IP addresses by using Port Address Translation (PAT, also called NAT overload) to multiplex more than 65,000 concurrent flows using a single public IPv4 address.

- Reduce the size of IP routing tables by making good choices for how address blocks are allocated to ISPs and end users, allowing for route summarization on a global scale.

This section examines some of the details related to these three points, but this information is not an end to itself for the purposes of this book. The true goal is to understand outbound routing (from the Enterprise to the Internet), and the reasons why you may or may not need to use a dynamic routing protocol such as Border Gateway Protocol (BGP) between the Enterprise and the Internet.

Public IP Address Assignment

The Internet Corporation for Assigned Network Numbers (ICANN, www.icann.org) owns the processes by which public IPv4 (and IPv6) addresses are allocated and assigned. A related organization, the Internet Assigned Numbers Authority (IANA, www.iana.org) carries out many of ICANN policies. These organizations define which IPv4 addresses can be allocated to different geographic regions, in addition to managing the development of the Domain Name System (DNS) naming structure and new Top Level Domains (TLD), such as .com.

ICANN works with several other groups to administer a public IPv4 address assignment strategy that can be roughly summarized as follows:

Step 1. ICANN and IANA group public IPv4 addresses by major geographic region.

Step 2. IANA allocates those address ranges to Regional Internet Registries (RIR).

Step 3. Each RIR further subdivides the address space by allocating public address ranges to National Internet Registries (NIR) or Local Internet Registries (LIR). (ISPs are typically LIRs.)

Step 4. Each type of Internet Registry (IR) can assign a further subdivided range of addresses to the end user organization to use.

Figure 12-1 shows an example that follows the same preceding four-step sequence. In this example, a company in North America needs a subnet with six hosts, so the ISP assigns a /29 prefix (198.133.219.16/29). Before that happens, however, the process gave this company's ISP (NA-ISP1, an ISP in North America) the right to assign that particular prefix.

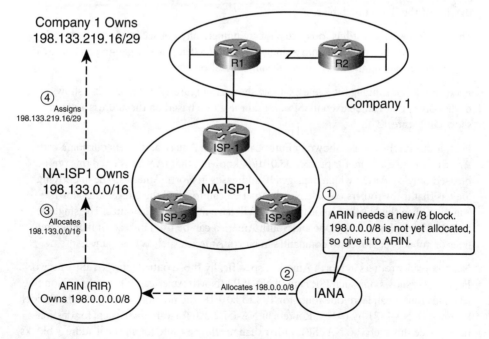

Figure 12-1 *Conceptual View of Public IPv4 Address Assignment*

The process starts with ICANN and IANA. These organizations maintain a set of currently unallocated public IPv4 addresses. (See http://www.iana.org/numbers/, and look for the IPv4 addresses link, to see the current list.) When ARIN, the RIR for North America, notices that it is running out of IPv4 address space, ARIN requests a new public address block. IANA examines the request, finds a currently unallocated public address block (Step 1 in the figure), and allocates the block to ARIN (Step 2 in the figure).

Next, an ISP named NA-ISP1 (shorthand for North American ISP number 1) asks ARIN for a prefix assignment for a /16 sized address block. After ARIN ensures that NA-ISP1 meets some requirements, ARIN assigns a prefix of 198.133.0.0/16 (Step 3 in the figure). Then, when Company1 becomes a customer of NA-ISP1, NA-ISP1 can assign a prefix to Company 1 (198.133.219.16/29 in this example, Step 4).

Although the figure shows the process, the big savings for public addresses occurs because the user of the IP addresses can be assigned a group much smaller than a single Class C network. In some cases, companies only need one public IP address; in other cases, they may need only a few, as with Company1 in Figure 12-1. This practice allows IRs to assign the right-sized address block to each customer, reducing waste.

Internet Route Aggregation

Although the capability to assign small blocks of addresses helped extend the IPv4 public address space, this practice also introduced many more public subnets into the Internet, driving up the number of routes in Internet routing tables. At the same time, the number of hosts connected to the Internet, back in the 1990s, was increasing at a double-digit rate–per month. Internet core routers could not have kept up with the rate of increase in the size of the IP routing tables.

The solution was, and still is today, to allocate numerically consecutive addresses–addresses that can be combined into a single route prefix/length—by geography and by ISP. These allocations significantly aid route summarization.

For example, continuing the same example shown in Figure 12-1, Figure 12-2 shows some of the routes that can be used in ISPs around the globe based on the address assignment shown in Figure 12-1.

First, focus on the routers shown in Europe and South America. Routers outside North America can use a route for prefix 198.0.0.0/8, knowing that IANA assigned this prefix to be used only by ARIN, which manages IP addresses in North America. The underlying logic is that if the routers outside North America can forward the packet into North America, then the North American routers will have more specific routes. The single route for 198.0.0.0/8 shown in Europe and South America can be used instead of literally millions of subnets deployed to companies in North America such as Company1.

Next, consider routers in North America, specifically those outside the NA-ISP1 network. Figure 12-2 shows one such ISP, named NA-ISP2 (North American ISP number 2), on the left. This router can learn one route for 198.133.0.0/16, the portion of the 198.0.0.0/8 block assigned to NA-ISP1 by IANA. Routers in NA-ISP2 can forward all packets for destinations inside this prefix to NA-ISP1, rather than needing a route for all small address blocks

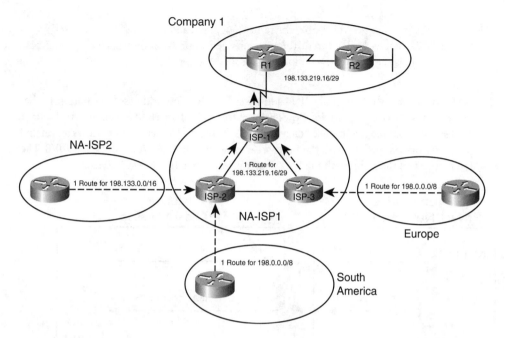

Figure 12-2 *IPv4 Global Route Aggregation Concepts*

assigned to individual Enterprises such as Company1. This significantly reduces the number of routes required on NA-ISP2 routers.

Finally, inside NA-ISP1, its routers need to know to which NA-ISP1 router to forward packets to for that particular customer. So, the routes listed on NA-ISP1's routers lists a prefix of 198.133.219.16/29. As a result, packets are forwarded toward router ISP-1 (located inside ISP NA-ISP1), and finally into Company 1.

The result of the summarization inside the Internet allows Internet core routers to have a much smaller routing table–on the order of a few hundred thousand routes instead of a few tens of millions of routes. For perspective, website www.potaroo.net, a website maintained by Geoff Huston, who has tracked Internet growth for many years, lists statistics for 300,000 BGP routes in Internet routers back in August 2009.

The Impact of NAT/PAT

Although classless public IP address assignment does help extend the life of the IPv4 address space, NAT probably has a bigger positive impact because it enables an Enterprise to use such a small number of public addresses. NAT allows an Enterprise to use private IP addresses for each host, plus a small number of public addresses. As packets pass through a device performing NAT–often a firewall, but it could be a router–the NAT function translates the IP address from the private address (called an *inside local* address by NAT) into a public address (called an *inside global* address).

Note: For the purposes of this book, the terms NAT, PAT, and NAT overload are used synonymously. There is no need to distinguish between static NAT, dynamic NAT without overload, and dynamic NAT with overload (also called PAT).

NAT reduces the need for public IPv4 addresses to only a few addresses per Enterprise because of how NAT can multiplex flows using different TCP or UDP port numbers. Figure 12-3 shows a sample that focuses on a router performing NAT. The figure shows an Enterprise network on the left, with the Enterprise using private Class A network 10.0.0.0/8. The Internet sits on the right, with the NAT router using public IP address 200.1.1.2.

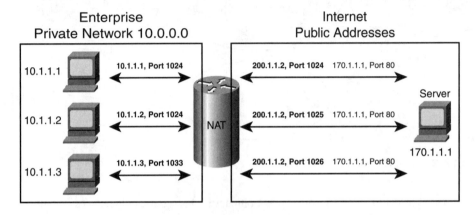

Enterprise
Private Network 10.0.0.0

Internet
Public Addresses

Dynamic NAT Table, With Overloading

Inside Local	Inside Global
10.1.1.1:1024	200.1.1.2:1024
10.1.1.2:1024	200.1.1.2:1025
10.1.1.3:1033	200.1.1.2:1026

Figure 12-3 *IPv4 Global Route Aggregation Concepts*

The figure shows how the Enterprise, on the left, can support three flows with a single public IP address (200.1.1.2). The NAT feature dynamically builds its translation table, which tells the router what address/port number pairs to translate. The router reacts when a new flow occurs between two hosts, noting the source IP address and port number of the Enterprise host on the left, and translating those values to use the public IP address (200.1.1.2) and an unused port number in the Internet. Note that if you collected the traffic using a network analyzer on the right side of the NAT router, the IP addresses would include 200.1.1.2 but not any of the network 10.0.0.0/8 addresses. Because the combination of the IP address (200.1.1.2 in this case) and port number must be unique, this one IP address can support 2^{16} different concurrent flows.

Private IPv4 Addresses and Other Special Addresses

When allocating the public IPv4 address space, IANA/ICANN restricts themselves in several ways. Of course, the private IP address ranges cannot be assigned to any group for use in the public Internet. Additionally, several other number ranges inside the IPv4 address space, as summarized in RFC 3330, are reserved for various reasons. Tables 12-2 and 12-3 list the private addresses and other reserved values, respectively, for your reference.

Table 12-2   *Private IP Address Reference*

Number of Classful Networks	Range of Classful Networks	Prefix for Entire Range
(1) Class A:	10.0.0.0	10.0.0.0/8
(16) Class B:	172.16.0.0 through 172.31.0.0	172.16.0.0/12
(256) Class C:	192.168.0.0 through 192.168.255.0	192.168.0.0/16

Table 12-3 lists other reserved ranges of IPv4 addresses that IANA will not allocate in the public Internet.

Table 12-3   *Reserved Values in IPv4 Address Range (RFC 3330)*

Value or Range	Reason
0.0.0.0/8	Used for self-identification on a local subnet.
127.0.0.0/8	Loopback testing.
169.254.0.0/16	This "link local" block is used for default IPv4 address assignment when DHCP process fails.
192.0.2.0/24	Reserved for use in documentation and example code.
192.88.99.0/24	Used for IPv6 to IPv4 relay (6to4 relay) (RFC 3068).
198.18.0.0/15	Benchmark testing for Internet devices (RFC 2544).

In summary, every Enterprise that connects to the Internet must use at least one public IP address, and often several public IP addresses. Although some companies do have a large public IPv4 address block–often obtained before the shortage of public IPv4 addresses in the early to mid-1990's–most companies have a small address block, which then requires the use of NAT/PAT. These details have some impact on whether BGP is useful in a given case.

Introduction to BGP

Border Gateway Protocol (BGP) advertises, learns, and chooses the best paths inside the global Internet. When two ISPs connect, they typically use BGP to exchange routing information. Collectively, the ISPs of the world exchange the Internet's routing table using BGP. And Enterprises sometimes use BGP to exchange routing information with one or more ISPs, allowing the Enterprise routers to learn Internet routes.

One key difference when comparing BGP to the usual IGP routing protocols is BGP's robust best path algorithm. BGP uses this algorithm to choose the best BGP path (route) using rules that extend far beyond just choosing the route with the lowest metric. This more complex best path algorithm gives BGP the power to let engineers configure many different settings that influence BGP best path selection, allowing great flexibility in how routers choose the best BGP routes.

BGP Basics

BGP, specifically BGP Version 4 (BGPv4), is the one routing protocol in popular use today that was designed as an Exterior Gateway Protocol (EGP) instead of as an Interior Gateway Protocol (IGP). As such, some of the goals of BGP differ from those of an IGP such as OSPF or EIGRP, but some of the goals remain the same.

First, consider the similarities between BGP and various IGPs. BGP does need to advertise IPv4 prefixes, just like IGPs. BGP needs to advertise some information so that routers can choose one of many routes for a given prefix as the currently best route. As for the mechanics of the protocol, BGP does establish a neighbor relationship before exchanging topology information with a neighboring router.

Next, consider the differences. BGP does not require neighbors to be attached to the same subnet. Instead, BGP routers use a TCP connection (port 179) between the routers to pass BGP messages, allowing neighboring routers to be on the same subnet, or to be separated by several routers. (It is relatively common to see BGP neighbors who do not connect to the same subnet.) Another difference lies in how the routing protocols choose the best route. Instead of choosing the best route just by using an integer metric, BGP uses a more complex process, using a variety of information, called BGP *path attributes*, which are exchanged in BGP routing updates much like IGP metric information.

Table 12-4 summarizes some of these key comparison points.

Table 12-4   *Comparing OSPF and EIGRP Logic to BGP*

OSPF/EIGRP	BGP
Forms neighbor relationship before sending routing information	Same.
Neighbors typically discovered using multicast packets on the connected subnets	Neighbor IP address is explicitly configured and may not be on common subnet.
Does not use TCP	Uses a TCP connection between neighbors (port 179).

Table 12-4 *Comparing OSPF and EIGRP Logic to BGP*

OSPF/EIGRP	BGP
Advertises prefix/length	Advertises prefix/length, called *Network Layer Reachability Information (NLRI.)*
Advertises metric information	Advertises a variety of path attributes (PA) that BGP uses instead of a metric to choose the best path.
Emphasis on fast convergence to the truly most efficient route	Emphasis on scalability; may not always choose the most efficient route.
Link state (OSPF) or distance vector (EIGRP) logic	Path vector logic (similar to distance vector).

BGP ASNs and the AS_SEQ Path Attribute

BGP uses BGP path attributes (PA) for several purposes. PAs define information about a path, or route, through a network. Some BGP PAs describe information that can be useful in choosing the best BGP route, using the best path algorithm; BGP also uses some other PAs for other purposes besides choosing the best path. This chapter focuses on one particular PA that routers use when choosing the best path, and using this PA to help prevent loops. Later, in Chapter 15, the text explores PAs in more detail, in the context of how to use those PAs as a tool to achieve some design goal.

By default, if no BGP PAs have been explicitly set, BGP routers use the BGP AS_PATH (autonomous system path) PA when choosing the best route among many competing routes. The AS_Path PA itself has many subcomponents, only some of which matter to the depth of the CCNP coverage of the topic. However, the most obvious component of AS_Path, the AS_Seq (AS Sequence), can be easily explained with an example when the concept of an autonomous system number (ASN) has been explained.

The integer BGP ASN uniquely identifies one organization that considers itself autonomous from other organizations. Each company whose Enterprise network connects to the Internet can be considered to be an autonomous system and can be assigned a BGP ASN. (IANA/ICANN also assigns globally unique ASNs.) Additionally, each ISP has an ASN, or possibly several, depending on the size of the ISP.

When a router uses BGP to advertise a route, the prefix/length is associated with a set of PAs, including the AS_Path. The AS_Path PA associated with a prefix/length lists the ASNs that would be part of an end-to-end route for that prefix as learned using BGP. In a way, the AS_Path implies information like this: "If you use this path (route), the path will go through this list of ASNs."

BGP uses the AS_Path to perform two key functions:

- Choose the best route for a prefix based on the shortest AS_Path (fewest number of ASNs listed).

- Prevent routing loops.

Key Topic

An example can help demonstrate the concept. This example, and some others in this chapter, use the design shown in Figure 12-4. This network has five ASNs: three ISPs and two customers.

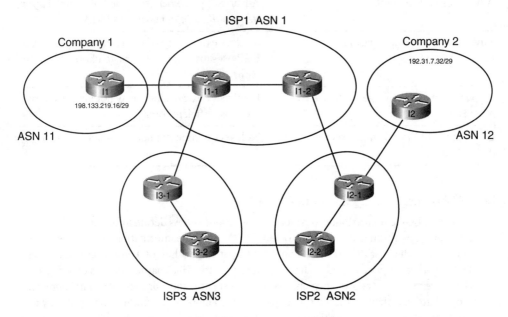

Figure 12-4 *Sample Portion of the Internet*

Figure 12-4 shows only a couple of routers in each ISP, and it also does not bother to show much of the Enterprise networks for the two companies. However, the diagram does show enough detail to demonstrate some key BGP concepts. For the sake of discussion, assume each line between routers represents some physical medium that is working. Each router will use BGP, and each router will form BGP neighbor relationships with the routers on the other end of each link. For example, ISP1's I1-2 router will have a BGP neighbor relationship with Routers I1-1 and with I2-1.

With that in mind, consider Figure 12-5, which shows the advertisement of BGP updates for prefix 192.31.7.32/29 to the other ASNs: The figure shows four steps, as follows:

Step 1. I2, in ASN 12, advertises the route outside ASN 12. So, I2 adds its own ASN (12) to the AS_Path PA when advertising the route.

Step 2. The routers inside ASN 2, when advertising the route outside ASN 2, add their own ASN (2) to the AS_Path PA when advertising the route. Their advertised AS_Path is then (12,2).

Step 3. Router I3-1, inside ASN 3, had previously learned about the route for 192.31.7.32/29 from ASN 2, with AS_Path (12,2). So, I3-1 advertises the route to ASN 1, after adding its own ASN (3) to the AS_Path so that the AS_Path (12, 2, 3).

Step 4.   Similarly, Router I1-1, inside ASN 1, advertises the route to ASN3. Because ASN 3 is a different ASN, I1-1 adds its own ASN (1) to the AS_Path PA so that the AS_Path lists ASNs 12, 2, and 1.

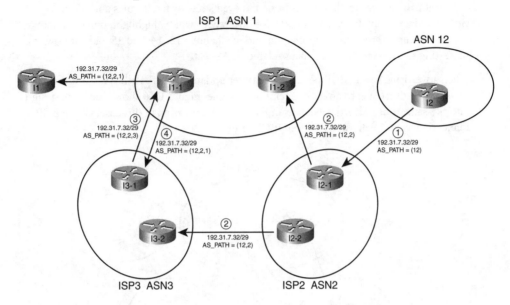

Figure 12-5   *Advertisement of NLRI to Demonstrate AS_Path*

Now, step back from the details, and consider the two alternative routes learned collectively by the routers in ASN 1:

- 192.31.7.32/29, AS_Path (12,2)

- 192.31.7.32/29, AS_Path (12,2,3)

Because the BGP path selection algorithm uses the shortest AS_Path, assuming no other PAs have been manipulated, the routers in ASN 1 use the first of the two paths, sending packets to ASN 2 next, and not using the path through ASN 3. Also, as a result, note the advertisement from ASN 1 into ASN 11 lists an AS_Path that reflects the best path selection of the routers inside ASN 1, with the addition of ASN 1 to the end of the AS_Path of the best route (12,2,1).

BGP routers also prevent routing loops using the ASNs listed in the AS_Path. When a BGP router receives an update, and a route advertisement lists an AS_Path with its own ASN, the router ignores that route. The reason is that because the route has already been advertised through the local ASN, to believe the route and then advertise it further might cause routing loops.

Internal and External BGP

BGP defines two classes of neighbors (peers): internal BGP (iBGP) and external BGP (eBGP). These terms use the perspective of a single router, with the terms referring to whether a BGP neighbor is in the same ASN (iBGP) or a different ASN (eBGP).

A BGP router behaves differently in several ways depending on whether the peer (neighbor) is an iBGP or eBGP peer. The differences include different rules about what must be true before the two routers can become neighbors, different rules about which routes the BGP best path algorithm chooses as best, and even some different rules about how the routers update the BGP AS_Path PA. These differences will be highlighted in the context of other features throughout this chapter and in Chapters 13, 14, and 15, but for now, it is interesting to examine the differences related to AS_Path.

When advertising to an eBGP peer, a BGP router updates the AS_Path PA, but it does not do so when advertising to an iBGP peer. For example, Figure 12-6 shows the same design, with the same route advertisement, as in Figure 12-5. However, in this case, all the BGP connections have been listed as either iBGP or eBGP.

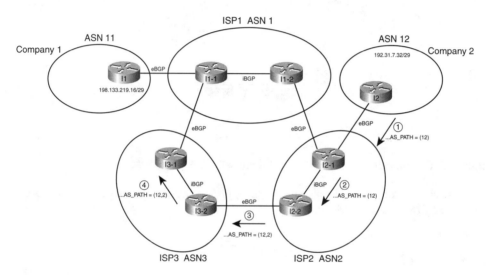

Figure 12-6   *iBGP, eBGP, and Updating AS_Path for eBGP Peers*

The figure highlights the route advertisement from ASN 12, over the lower path through ASN 2 and 3. Note that at Step 1, Router I2, advertising to an eBGP peer, adds its own ASN to the AS_Path. At Step 2, Router I2-1 is advertising to an iBGP peer (I2-2), so it does not add its own ASN (2) to the AS_Path. Then, at Step 3, Router I2-2 adds its own ASN (2) to the AS_Path before sending an update to eBGP peer I3-2, and so on.

Public and Private ASNs

For the Internet to work well using BGP, IANA administers the assignment of ASNs much like it does with IP address prefixes. One key reason why ASNs must be assigned as unique values is that if ASNs are duplicated, the BGP loop prevention process can actually prevent parts of the Internet from learning about a route. For example, consider Figure 12-7, with the same design as in the last few figures—but this time with a duplicate ASN.

In this figure, both ISP1 and Company 1 use ASN 12. The example BGP updates begin as in Figures 12-5 and 12-6, with Company 1 advertising its prefix. Routers inside ISP1 re-

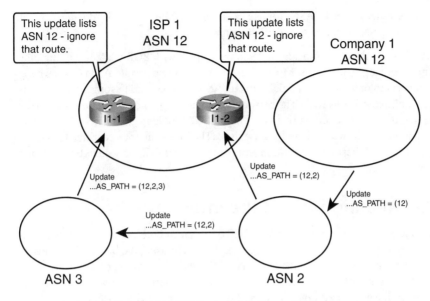

Figure 12-7 *Duplicate ASN (12) Preventing Route Advertisement*

Key
Topic

ceive BGP updates that list the same prefix used by Company 1, but both Updates list an
AS_Path that includes ASN 12. Because ISP1 thinks it uses ASN 12, ISP1 thinks that these
BGP Updates should be ignored as part of the BGP loop prevention process. As a result,
customers of ISP1 cannot reach the prefixes advertised by routers in Company 1.

To prevent such issues, IANA controls the ASN numbering space. Using the same general
process as for IPv4 addresses, ASNs can be assigned to different organizations. The 16-bit
BGP ASN implies a decimal range of 0 through 65,535. Table 12-5 shows some of the details of IANA's current ASN assignment conventions.

Table 12-5 *16-Bit ASN Assignment Categories from IANA*

Key
Topic

Value or Range	Purpose
0	Reserved
1 through 64,495	Assignable by IANA for public use
64,496 through 64,511	Reserved for use in documentation
64,512 through 65,534	Private use
65,535	Reserved

Like the public IPv4 address space has suffered with the potential for complete depletion
of available addresses, the public BGP ASN space has similar issues. To help overcome this
issue, the ASN assignment process requires that each AS justify whether it truly needs a
publicly unique ASN or whether it can just as easily use a private ASN. Additionally, RFC

5398 reserves a small range of ASNs for use in documentation so that the documents can avoid the use of ASNs assigned to specific organizations.

Private ASNs allow the routers inside an AS to participate with BGP, while using the same ASN as many other organizations. Most often, an AS can use a private AS in cases where the AS connects to only one other ASN. (Private ASNs can be used in some cases of connecting to multiple ASNs as well.) The reason is that with only one connection point to another ASN, loops cannot occur at that point in the BGP topology, so the need for unique ASNs in that part of the network no longer exists. (The loops cannot occur due to the logic behind the BGP best path algorithm, coupled with that BGP only advertises the best path for a given prefix.)

Outbound Routing Toward the Internet

The single biggest reason to consider using BGP between an Enterprise and an ISP is to influence the choice of best path (best route). The idea of choosing the best path sounds appealing at first. However, because the majority of the end-to-end route exists inside the Internet, particularly if the destination is 12 routers and a continent away, it can be a challenge to determine which exit point from the Enterprise is actually a better route.

As a result, Enterprises typically have two major classes of options for outbound routing toward the Internet: default routing and BGP. Using default routes is perfectly reasonable, depending on the objectives. This section examines the use of default routes toward the Internet, and some of the typical Enterprise BGP designs and how they can be used to influence outbound routes toward the Internet.

Comparing BGP and Default Routing for Enterprises

Chapter 4, "EIGRP Route Summarization and Filtering," section "Default Routing to the Internet Router," introduced the concept of using default routes on branch office routers, with static routes and redistribution on the WAN edge routers. With this design, the branch router could use a default static route pointing toward the core of the network. The WAN edge routers then needed static routes for the subnets at each branch, with the WAN edge routers advertising these branch subnets into the core using an IGP.

The branch office default routing design results in less processing on the routers, less memory consumption, and no IGP overhead on the link between the branch and WAN distribution routers. In particular, the branch routers can have a single or a few default routes, instead of potentially hundreds of routes for specific prefixes, all with the same next-hop information.

The same general concept of using defaults and static routes at Enterprise branches can be applied to the Enterprise network and its connections to one or a few ISPs. Similar to a branch router, an entire Enterprise often has only a few connections to the Internet. If one of those connections is considered better than the others, then all packets sent from the Enterprise toward the Internet would normally follow that one Internet link, for all Internet destinations. Likewise, the ISPs, similar to WAN distribution routers in this analogy, could configure static routes for the Enterprise's public IP address prefix and then use BGP in the Internet to advertise those routes. Figure 12-8 shows the general idea.

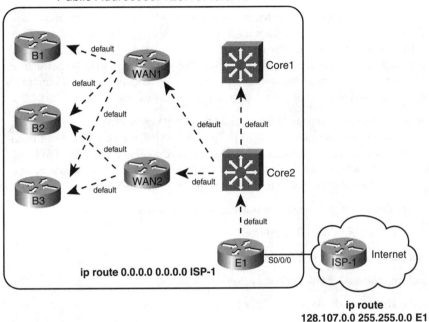

Company 1 Enterprise Network -
Public Addresses: 128.107.0.0/16

ip route 0.0.0.0 0.0.0.0 ISP-1

ip route
128.107.0.0 255.255.0.0 E1

Figure 12-8   *Use of Static Default into the Internet*

Although the Enterprise could choose to use BGP in this case, such a decision is not automatic. First, the alternative of using static routes, as shown in the figure, does not require a lot of work. The Enterprise network engineer just needs to configure a default route and advertise it throughout the Enterprise; the dashed lines in the figure represent the advertisement of the default route with the Enterprise's IGP. (See Chapter 4's section "Default Routing to the Internet Router," and Chapter 7, "OSPF Route Summarization, Filtering, and Default Routing," section "Domain-wide Defaults Using the **default-information originate** Command," for a review of how to flood the static route inside an EIGRP or OSPF domain, respectively.)

In addition to the configuration on the Enterprise router (E1), the ISP network engineer has to configure static routes for that Enterprise's public IP address range, and redistributing those routes into BGP and advertising throughout the Internet. The figure shows a static route for Company 1's 128.107.0.0/16 public address range. Additionally, this prefix would need to be injected into BGP for advertising into the rest of the Internet.

Instead of using static default routes, you could enable BGP between E1 and ISP-1. Running BGP could mean that the Enterprise router requires significant memory and more processing power on the router. The design may also require other Enterprise routers besides the Internet-connected routers to know the BGP routes, requiring additional routers to have significant CPU and memory. Finally, although you can configure BGP to choose one route over another using PAs, the advantage of choosing one path over another may not be significant. Alternatively, you could ask the ISP to advertise only a default route with BGP.

Now that you have seen a few of the reasons why you may be fine using static routes instead of BGP, consider why you might want to use BGP. First, it makes most sense to use BGP when you have at least two Internet connections. Second, BGP becomes most useful when you want to choose one outbound path over another path for particular destinations in the Internet. In short, when you have multiple Internet connections, and you want to influence some packets to take one path and some packets to take another, consider BGP.

The rest of this chapter examines different cases of Internet connectivity and weighs the reasons why you might choose to use BGP. For this discussion, the perspective of the Enterprise network engineer will be used. As such, outbound routing is considered to be routes that direct packets from the Enterprise toward the Internet, and inbound routing refers to routes that direct packets into the Enterprise from the Internet.

To aid in the discussion, this section examines four separate cases:

Key Topic

- Single homed (1 link per ISP, 1 ISP)

- Dual homed (2+ links per ISP, 1 ISP)

- Single multihomed (1 link per ISP, 2+ ISPs)

- Dual multihomed (2+ links per ISP, 2+ ISPs)

Note: The terms in the preceding list may be used differently depending on what book or document you read. For consistency, this book uses these terms in the same way as the Cisco authorized ROUTE course associated with the ROUTE exam.

Single Homed

The single-homed Internet design uses a single ISP, with a single link between the Enterprise and the ISP. With single-homed designs, only one possible next-hop router exists for any and all routes for destinations in the Internet. As a result, no matter what you do with BGP, all learned routes would list the same outgoing interface for every route, which minimizes the benefits of using BGP.

Single-homed designs often use one of two options for routing to and from the Internet:

- Use static routes (default in the Enterprise, and a static for the Enterprise's public address range at the ISP).

- Use BGP, but only to exchange a default (ISP to Enterprise) and a route for the Enterprise's public prefix (Enterprise to ISP).

The previous section, "Comparing BGP and Defaults for Enterprises," already showed the main concepts for the first option. For the second option, the concept still uses the IGP's mechanisms to flood a default throughout the Enterprise, causing all packets to go toward the Internet facing router. Instead of static routes, however, the following must happen:

- The ISP router uses BGP to advertise a default route to the Enterprise.

- You must configure the IGP on the Enterprise's Internet-facing router to flood a default route (typically only if the default route exists in that router's routing table).

- You must configure BGP on the Enterprise router and advertise the Enterprise's public prefix toward the ISP.

Both options—using static defaults and BGP learned defaults—have some negatives. Some packets for truly nonexistent destinations flow through the Enterprise to the Internet-facing router (E1 in the example of Figure 12-8), and over the link to the Internet, before being discarded for lack of a matching route. For example, if the Enterprise used private network 10.0.0.0/8 internally, packets destined for addresses in network 10.0.0.0/8 that have not yet been deployed will match the default route and be routed to the Internet.

To avoid wasting this bandwidth by sending packets unnecessarily, a static route for 10.0.0.0/8, destination null0, could be added to the Internet-facing router but not advertised into the rest of the Enterprise. (This type of route is sometimes called a *discard route*.) This route would prevent the Internet-facing router from forwarding packets destined for network 10.0.0.0/8 into the Internet.

Dual Homed

The dual-homed design has two (or more) links to the Internet, but with all links connecting to a single ISP. This type of design can use a pair of routers, two pairs, or a combination, as shown in the three cases in Figure 12-9.

Comparing the dual-homed case to the single-homed design, the second link gives the Enterprise a choice. The Enterprise router(s) could choose between one of two links, and in the case with two Enterprise routers, the choice of a different link also means the choice of sending packets to a different router.

Each of the cases shown in Figure 12-9 is interesting, but the case with two Enterprise routers provides the most ideas to consider. When considering whether to use BGP in this case, and if so, how to use it, first think about whether you want to influence the choice of outbound route. The common cases when using defaults works well, ignoring BGP, are:

- To prefer one Internet connection over another for all destinations, but when the better ISP connection fails, all traffic re-routes over the secondary connection.

- To treat both Internet connections as equal, sending packets for some destinations out each path. However, when one fails, all traffic re-routes over the one still-working path.

The text now examines each option, in order, including a discussion of how to choose the best outbound routing using both partial and full BGP updates.

Preferring One Path over Another for All Destinations

When the design calls for one of the two Internet connections to always be preferred, regardless of destination, BGP can be used, but it is not required. With a goal of preferring one path over another, the routers can use default routes into the Internet.

To demonstrate the concept, Figure 12-10 shows a dual-homed design, this time with two routers (E1 and E2) connected to the Internet. Each router has a single link into the single ISP. (Using the terminology from the ROUTE class, dual homed means two or more links

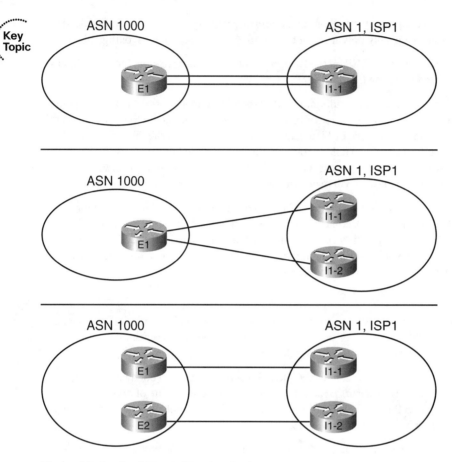

Figure 12-9 *Dual-Homed Design Options*

but to a single ISP; dual multihomed means two or more links each to two or more different ISPs.) Figure 12-10 shows the routes that result from using default routes to forward all traffic toward Router E1.

Figure 12-10 shows that all routers forward the Internet-destined packets toward Router E1, because this router has the faster Internet connection to ISP1 (100 Mbps in this case). Again in this example, the other connection from Router E2 to ISP1 uses a 10 Mbps link.

To make this design work, with failover, both E1 and E2 need to advertise a default route into the Enterprise, but the route advertised by the primary router (E1) needs to have metrics set so that it is always the better of the two routes. For example, with EIGRP, E1 can configure a static default route with Router I1-1 as the next hop, but with very high bandwidth and very low delay upon redistribution into EIGRP. Conversely, E2 can create a default for Router I1-2 as the next-hop router, but with a low bandwidth but high delay. Example 12-1 shows the configuration of the static default route on both E1 and E2, with the **redistribute** command setting the metrics.

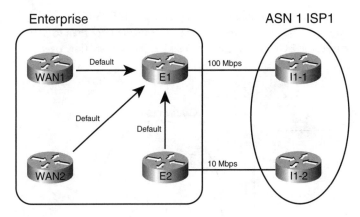

Figure 12-10 *Dual-Homed Design, Using Defaults to Favor One Link*

Example 12-1 *Default Routing on Router E1*

```
! Configuration on router E1 - note that the configuration uses
! a hostname instead of I1-1's IP address
ip route 0.0.0.0 0.0.0.0 I1-1
router eigrp 1
 redistribute static metric 100000 1 255 1 1500
! Configuration on router E2 - note that the configuration uses
! a hostname instead of I1-2's IP address
ip route 0.0.0.0 0.0.0.0 I1-2
router eigrp 1
 redistribute static metric 10000 100000 255 1 1500
```

Note: With EIGRP as the IGP, do not forget that the delay setting must be set higher to avoid cases where some routers forward packets toward the secondary Internet router (E2). The reason is that EIGRP uses constraining bandwidth, so a high setting of bandwidth at the redistribution point on E1 may or may not cause more remote routers to use that route.

A slightly different approach can be taken in other variations of the dual-homed design, as seen back in Figure 12-9. The first two example topologies in that figure show a single router with two links to the same ISP. If the design called to using one link as the preferred link, and the engineer decided to use default routes, that one router would need two default routes. To make one route be preferred, that static default route would be assigned a better administrative distance (AD) than the other route. For example, the commands **ip route 0.0.0.0 0.0.0.0 I1-1 3** and **ip route 0.0.0.0 0.0.0.0 I1-2 4** could be used on Router E1 in Figure 12-9, giving the route through I1-1 a lower AD (3), preferring that route. If the link to I1-1 failed, the other static default route, through I1-2, would be used.

Choosing One Path over Another Using BGP

The big motivation to use BGP occurs when you want to influence which link is used for certain destinations in the Internet. To see such a case, consider Figure 12-11, which adds

Company 3 to the design. In this case, Company 3 uses prefix 192.135.250.0/28 as its public address range. Company 3 may be located closer to I1-2 inside ISP1 than to Router I1-1, and in such cases, the BGP design calls for making the packets flow over the route as shown.

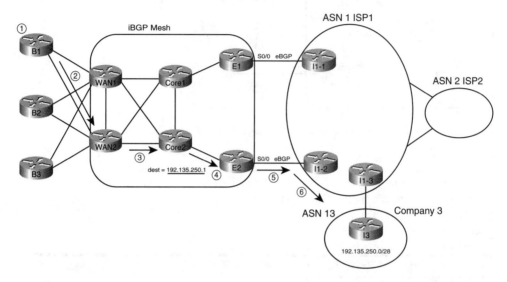

Figure 12-11   *Preferring One Outbound Link over Another*

Two notable actions must take place for this design to work, beyond the basic configuration of the eBGP peers as shown. First, the engineers at the Enterprise and ISP must agree as to how to make BGP specify a prefix as being best reached through a particular link. In this particular case, the routes advertised by I1-2 for prefix for 192.135.250.0/28 must have BGP PA settings that appear better than those learned from I1-1. In this case, you cannot just rely on the default of checking the AS_Path length, because the AS_Path length should tie, because I1-1 and I1-2 are in the same ASN. So when planning with the engineers of ISP1, the Enterprise network engineer must discuss what kinds of prefixes that might work better through I1-1, which would be better through I1-2, and how the ISP might set PA values to which the Enterprise routers (E1 and E2) can react. (Chapter 15 discusses some of the options to influence the outbound routes.)

The second big consideration occurs inside the Enterprise network with a need to run BGP between multiple routers. So far in this chapter, the Enterprise routers all used default routes to send packets to the Internet-facing routers, and only those routers knew Internet routes. However, for the design of Figure 12-11 to work, E1 and E2 must communicate BGP routes using an iBGP connection. And because packet forwarding between E1 and E2 goes through other routers (such as Core1 and Core2), those routers typically also need to run BGP. You might even decide to run BGP on the WAN routers as well. By doing so, the core routers know the best BGP routes; for instance, they all know that the better route for Company 3's 192.135.250.0/28 public address space is through E2, so the packet is forwarded to E2. The following list outlines the logic matching Figure 12-11:

Step 1.   A host at Branch B1 sends a packet to 192.135.250.1.

Step 2.   Router B1 matches its default route, forwarding the packet to Router WAN2.

Step 3.   WAN2 matches its iBGP-learned route for 192.135.250.0/28, forwarding to Core2.

Step 4.   Core2 matches its iBGP-learned route for 192.135.250.0/28, forwarding to E2.

Step 5.   E2 matches its eBGP-learned route for 192.135.250.0/28, forwarding to I1-2.

Step 6.   The routers in ISP1 forward the packet to Router I3, in Company 3.

The routers in the core of the Enterprise need to run BGP because without it, routing loops can occur. For example, if WAN1, WAN2, Core1, and Core2 did not use BGP, and relied on default routes, their default would drive packets to either E1 or E2. Then, E1 or E2 might send the packets right back to Core1 or Core2. (Note that there is no direct link between E1 and E2.) Figure 12-12 shows just such a case.

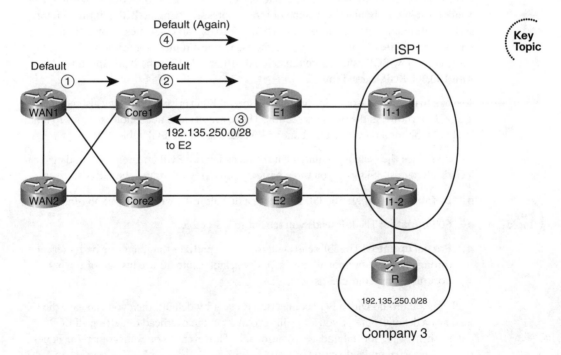

Figure 12-12   *A Routing Loop Without BGP in the Enterprise Core*

In this case, both E1 and E2 know that E2 is the best exit point for packets destined to 192.135.250.0/28 (from Figure 12-11). However, the core routers use default routes, with WAN1 and Core1 using defaults that send packets to E1. Following the numbers in the figure

Step 1.   WAN1 gets a packet destined for 192.135.250.1 and forwards the packet to Core1 based on its default route.

Step 2.   Core1 gets the packet and has no specific route, so it forwards the packet to E1 based on its default route.

Step 3.   E1's BGP route tells it that E2 is the better exit point for this destination. To send the packet to E2, E1 forwards the packet to Core1.

Step 4.   Core1, with no knowledge of the BGP route for 192.135.250.0/28, uses its default route to forward the packet to E1, so the packet is now looping.

A mesh of iBGP peerings between at least E1, E2, Core1, and Core2 would prevent this problem.

Partial and Full BGP Updates

Unfortunately, Enterprise routers must pay a relatively large price for the ability to choose between competing BGP routes to reach Internet destinations. As previously mentioned, the BGP table in the Internet core is at approximately 300,000 routes as of the writing of this chapter in 2009. To make a decision to use one path instead of another, an Enterprise router must know about at least some of those routes. Exchanging BGP information for such a large number of routes consumes bandwidth. It also consumes memory in the routers and requires some processing to choose the best routes. Some samples at Cisco.com show BGP using approximately 70 MB of RAM for the BGP table on a router with 100,000 BGP-learned routes.

To make matters a bit worse, in some cases, several Enterprise routers may also need to use BGP, as shown in the previous section. Those routers also need more memory to hold the BGP table, and they consume bandwidth exchanging the BGP table.

To help reduce the memory requirements of receiving full BGP updates (BGP updates that include all routes), ISPs give you three basic options for what routes the ISP advertises:

■   **Default route only:** The ISP advertises a default route with BGP, but no other routes.

■   **Full updates:** The ISP sends you the entire BGP table.

■   **Partial updates:** The ISP sends you routes for prefixes that might be better reached through that ISP, but not all routes, plus a default route (to use instead of the purposefully omitted routes as needed).

If all you want to do with a BGP connection is use it by default, then you can have the ISP send just a default route. If you are willing to take on the overhead of getting all BGP routes, then asking for full updates is reasonable. However, if you want something in between, the partial updates option is useful.

BGP partial updates give you the benefit of choosing the best routes for some destinations, while limiting the bandwidth and memory consumption. With partial updates, the ISP advertises routes for prefixes that truly are better reached through a particular link. However, for prefixes that may not be any better through that link, the ISP does not advertise those prefixes with BGP. Then the Enterprise routers can use the better path based on the routes learned with BGP, and use a default route for the prefixes not learned with BGP. For example, previously in Figure 12-11, Router I1-2 could be configured to only advertise routes for those such as 192.135.250.0/28, from Company 3 in that figure–in other words, only routes for which Router I1-2 had a clearly better route than the other ISP1 routers.

Single Multihomed

A single-multihomed topology means a single link per ISP, but multiple (at least 2) ISPs. Figure 12-13 shows a couple of single-multihomed designs, each with two ISPs:

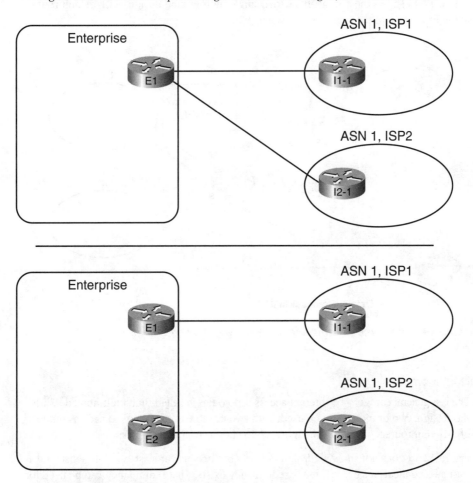

Figure 12-13 *Single-Multihomed Designs*

The single-multihomed design has some similarities with both the single-homed and dual-homed designs previously seen in this section. The single-multihomed design on the top of the figure, which uses a single router, acts like the single-homed design for default routes in the Enterprise. This design can flood a default route throughout the Enterprise, drawing traffic to that one router, because only one router connects to the Internet. With the two-router design on the lower half of Figure 12-13, defaults can still be used in the

Enterprise to draw traffic to the preferred Internet connection (if one is preferred) or to balance traffic across both.

The single-multihomed design works like the dual-homed design in some ways because two (or more) links connect the Enterprise to the Internet. With two links, the Internet design might call for the use of defaults, always preferring one of the links. The design engineer might also choose to use BGP, learn either full or partial updates, and then favor one connection over another for some of the routes.

Figure 12-14 shows these concepts with a single-multihomed design, with default routes in the Enterprise to the one Internet router (E1).

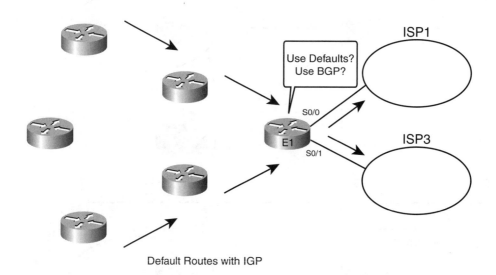

Figure 12-14 *Outbound Routing with a Single-Multihomed Design*

Dual Multihomed

The last general category of Internet access topologies is called dual multihomed. With this design, two or more ISPs are used, with two or more connections to each. A number of different routers can be used. Figure 12-15 shows several examples.

Figure 12-15 does not show all design options, but because at least two ISPs exist, and at least two connections per ISP, much redundancy exists. That redundancy can be used for backup, but most often, BGP is used to make some decisions about the best path to reach various destinations.

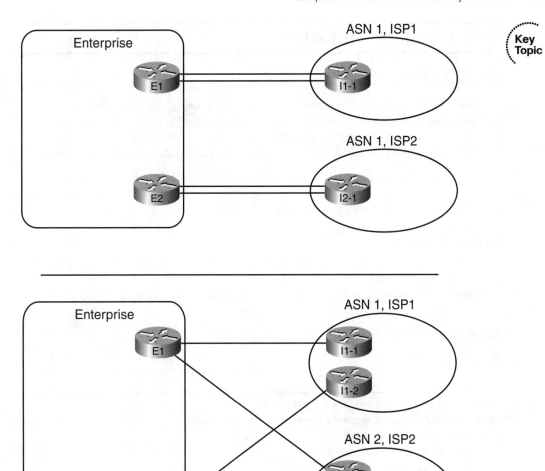

Key
Topic

Figure 12-15 *Dual-Multihomed Options*

Exam Preparation Tasks

Planning Practice

The CCNP ROUTE exam expects test takers to review design documents, create implementation plans, and create verification plans. This section provides some exercises that may help you to take a step back from the minute details of the topics in this chapter so that you can think about the same technical topics from the planning perspective.

For each planning practice table, simply complete the table. Note that any numbers in parentheses represent the number of options listed for each item in the solutions in Appendix F, "Completed Planning Practice Tables."

Design Review Table

Table 12-5 lists several design goals related to this chapter. If these design goals were listed in a design document, and you had to take that document and develop an implementation plan, what implementation options come to mind? You should write a general description; specific configuration commands are not required.

Table 12-5   *Design Review*

Design Goal	Possible Implementation Choices Covered in This Chapter
A design shows a single router connected to the Internet as part of a single-homed Internet design. It lists sections for Enterprise routing toward the Internet-facing router(s) in the Enterprise, and another section for choosing routes on the Internet-facing router into the Internet. List the reasonable options.	
Use the same criteria as the previous item in this table, except the single Enterprise router connected to the Internet now has two links to the same ISP (dual homed).	
Use the same criteria as the previous item, except use two routers with one link each to the same ISP (dual homed).	
Same criteria as previous row, but with a single multihomed with two routers.	

Implementation Plan Peer Review Table

Table 12-6 shows a list of questions that others might ask, or that you might think about, during a peer review of another network engineer's implementation plan. Complete the table by answering the questions.

Table 12-6 *Notable Questions from This Chapter to Consider During an Implementation Plan Peer Review*

Question	Answers
The plan shows a single router in a dual-homed Internet design, with the router using BGP over each link to that same ISP. What criteria would impact your choice of accepting only default routes, or partial updates, or full updates, using BGP in this case? (3)	
The plan shows four Enterprise routers with BGP configuration, with two of those routers with links to two different ISPs. Which connections are eBGP? iBGP?	

Create an Implementation Plan Table

This chapter does not focus on implementation or verification, but it did review one concept about static routes, as listed in Table 12-7.

Table 12-7 *Implementation Plan Configuration Memory Drill*

Feature	Configuration Commands/Notes
Configuring multiple static default routes, each with different administrative distance settings	

Review all the Key Topics

Review the most important topics from inside the chapter, noted with the Key Topics icon in the outer margin of the page. Table 12-8 lists a reference of these key topics and the page numbers on which each is found.

Table 12-8 *Key Topics for Chapter 12*

Key Topic Element	Description	Page Number
Figure 12-1	Public IP Address Assignment model	391
Table 12-4	Comparisons of OSPF and EIGRP to BGP	396
List	Two key functions for BGP AS_Path	397
Figure 12-5	BGP process to update AS_Path when advertising NLRI	399
Figure 12-7	Demonstration of how AS_Path can be used to prevent loops	401
Table 12-5	16-bit BGP ASN assignment ranges	401

Table 12-8   *Key Topics for Chapter 12*

Key Topic Element	Description	Page Number
List	Description of terms single homed, dual homed, single multi-homed, and dual multihomed	404
Figure 12-9	Common dual-homed designs	406
Figure 12-12	Example routing loop due to lack of iBGP in the Enterprise core	409
List	Three options for the routes received from an ISP	410
Figure 12-15	Common dual-multihomed options	413

Complete the Tables and Lists from Memory

Print a copy of Appendix D, "Memory Tables," (found on the CD), or at least the section for this chapter, and complete the tables and lists from memory. Appendix E, "Memory Tables Answer Key," also on the CD, includes completed tables and lists to check your work.

Define Key Terms

Define the following key terms from this chapter, and check your answers in the glossary.

public IP address, private IP address, Network Address Translation (NAT), Port Address Translation (PAT), AS Sequence, Path Attribute (PA), AS path, public ASN, private ASN, default route, single homed, dual homed, single multihomed, dual multihomed, Autonomous System Number (ASN)

This chapter covers the following subjects:

External BGP for Enterprises: This section examines the required configuration for external BGP connections, plus a few optional but commonly used configuration settings. It also examines the commands used to verify that eBGP works.

Verifying the BGP Table: This section discusses the contents of the BGP table, particularly the routes learned using eBGP connections.

Injecting Routes into BGP for Advertisement to the ISPs: This section shows how you can configure an eBGP router to advertise the public IP address range used by an Enterprise.

CHAPTER 13

External BGP

BGP configuration differs slightly when comparing the configuration of an External BGP (eBGP) peer and an Internal BGP (iBGP) peer. Many small differences in operation exist as well.

This chapter focuses on external BGP configuration and verification. The chapter begins with a discussion of the fundamentals of BGP configuration that applies to both internal and external peers. It then discusses the reasons why eBGP peers may or may not benefit from additional optional configuration settings.

After the eBGP neighborships have been established, the BGP routers exchange routes. The chapter examines the verification commands used to see the BGP routes learned from eBGP neighbors by examining the BGP table. The chapter closes with a discussion of how to configure the **network** command and to configure route redistribution to make a BGP router advertise an Enterprise's public IP prefix to its eBGP peers.

Chapter 14, "Internal BGP and BGP Route Filtering," discusses the particulars of iBGP configuration and verification, plus BGP route filtering (for both iBGP and eBGP).

"Do I Know This Already?" Quiz

The "Do I Know This Already?" quiz allows you to assess if you should read the entire chapter. If you miss no more than one of these eight self-assessment questions, you might want to move ahead to the "Exam Preparation Tasks." Table 13-1 lists the major headings in this chapter and the "Do I Know This Already?" quiz questions covering the material in those headings so you can assess your knowledge of these specific areas. The answers to the "Do I Know This Already?" quiz appear in Appendix A.

Table 13-1 *"Do I Know This Already?" Foundation Topics Section-to-Question Mapping*

Foundations Topics Section	Questions
External BGP for Enterprises	1–4
Verifying the BGP Table	5–7
Injecting Routes into BGP for Advertisement to the ISPs	8

1. Enterprise Router R1, in ASN 1, connects to ISP Router I1, ASN 2, using eBGP. The single serial link between the two routers uses IP addresses 10.1.1.1 and 10.1.1.2, respectively. Both routers use their S0/0 interfaces for this link. Which of the following commands would be needed on R1 to configure eBGP? (Choose two.)

   a. router bgp 2

   b. router bgp 1

   c. neighbor 10.1.1.2 remote-as 2

   d. neighbor 10.1.1.2 update-source 10.1.1.1

   e. neighbor 10.1.1.2 update-source S0/0

2. Enterprise Router R1, in ASN 1, connects to ISP Router I1, ASN 2, using eBGP. There are two parallel serial links between the two routers. The implementation plan calls for each router to base their BGP TCP connection on their respective loopback1 interfaces, with IP addresses 1.1.1.1 and 2.2.2.2, respectively. Which of the following commands would not be part of a working eBGP configuration on Router R1?

   a. router bgp 1

   b. neighbor 2.2.2.2 remote-as 2

   c. neighbor 2.2.2.2 update-source loopback1

   d. neighbor 2.2.2.2 multihop 2

3. The following output, taken from a **show ip bgp** command on Router R1, lists two neighbors. In what BGP neighbor state is neighbor 1.1.1.1?

Neighbor	V	AS	MsgRcvd	MsgSent	TblVer	InQ	OutQ	Up/Down	State/PfxRcd
1.1.1.1	4	1	60	61	26	0	0	00:45:01	0
2.2.2.2	4	3	153	159	26	0	0	00:38:13	1

   a. Idle

   b. Opensent

   c. Active

   d. Established

4. The following output was taken from the **show ip bgp** command on Router R2. In this case, which of the following commands are most likely to already be configured on R2? (Choose two.)

```
BGP router identifier 11.11.11.11, local AS number 11
...
Neighbor    V   AS   MsgRcvd   MsgSent   TblVer   InQ   OutQ   Up/Down   State/PfxRcd
1.1.1.1     4    1        87        87        0     0      0   00:00:06  Idle (Admin)
2.2.2.2     4    3       173       183       41     0      0   00:58:47         2
```

    a. router bgp 11

    b. neighbor 1.1.1.1 remote-as 11

    c. neighbor 2.2.2.2 prefix-limit 1

    d. neighbor 1.1.1.1 shutdown

5. Which of the following answers is most true about the BGP Update message?

    a. It lists a set of path attributes, along with a list of prefixes that use those PAs.

    b. It lists a prefix/length, plus the PA settings for that prefix.

    c. It lists withdrawn routes, but never in the same Update message as newly advertised routes.

    d. A single Update message lists at most a single prefix/length.

6. The following output occurs on Router R1. Which of the following cannot be determined from this output?

```
R1# show ip route 180.1.1.0 255.255.255.240
Routing entry for 180.1.1.0/28
  Known via "bgp 2", distance 20, metric 0
  Tag 3, type external
  Last update from 192.168.1.2 00:10:27 ago
  Routing Descriptor Blocks:
  * 192.168.1.2, from 192.168.1.2, 00:10:27 ago
      Route metric is 0, traffic share count is 1
      AS Hops 2
      Route tag 3
```

    a. The type of BGP peer (iBGP or eBGP) that advertised this route to R1

    b. R1's ASN

    c. The next-hop router's ASN

    d. The AS_Path length

7. The following line of output was extracted from the output of the **show ip bgp** command on Router R1. Which of the following can be determined from this output?

```
Network              Next Hop            Metric LocPrf Weight Path
*   130.1.1.0/28        1.1.1.1                              0 1 2 3 4 i
```

   a. The route is learned from an eBGP peer.

   b. The route has no more than three ASNs in the AS_Path.

   c. The route is the best route for this prefix.

   d. None of these facts can be positively determined by this output.

8. Router R1 has eBGP connections to I1 and I2, routers at the same ISP. The company that owns R1 can use public address range 130.1.16.0/20. The following output lists all the IP routes in R1's routing table within this range. Which of the following answers would cause R1 to advertise the 130.1.16.0/20 prefix to its eBGP peers? (You should assume default settings for any parameters not mentioned in this question.)

```
R1# show ip route 130.1.16.0 255.255.240.0 longer-prefixes
! lines omitted...
O        130.1.16.0/24 [110/3] via 10.5.1.1, 00:14:36, FastEthernet0/1
O        130.1.17.0/24 [110/3] via 10.5.1.1, 00:14:36, FastEthernet0/1
O        130.1.18.0/24 [110/3] via 10.5.1.1, 00:14:36, FastEthernet0/1
```

   a. Configure R1 with the **network 130.1.16.0 mask 255.255.240.0** command.

   b. Configure R1 with the **network 130.1.16.0 mask 255.255.240.0 summary-only** command.

   c. Redistribute from OSPF into BGP, filtering so that only routes in the 130.1.16.0/20 range are redistributed.

   d. Redistribute from OSPF into BGP, filtering so that only routes in the 130.1.16.0/20 range are redistributed, and create a BGP summary for 130.1.16.0/20.

Foundation Topics

External BGP for Enterprises

Some of the core operational concepts of BGP mirror those of EIGRP and OSPF. BGP first forms a neighbor relationship with peers. BGP then learns information from its neighbors, placing that information in a table–the BGP table. Finally, BGP analyzes the BGP table to choose the best working route for each prefix in the BGP table, placing those routes into the IP routing table.

This section discusses external BGP (eBGP), focusing on two of the three aspects of how a routing protocol learns routes: forming neighborships and exchanging the reachability or topology information that is stored in the BGP table. First, this section examines the baseline configuration of eBGP peers (also called neighbors), along with several optional settings that may be needed specifically for eBGP connections. This configuration should result in working BGP neighborships. Then, this section examines the BGP table, listing the prefix/length and path attributes (PA) learned from the Internet, and the IP routing table.

eBGP Neighbor Configuration

At a minimum, a router participating in BGP needs to configure the following settings:

- The router's own ASN (**router bgp** *asn* global command)

- The IP address of each neighbor and that neighbor's ASN (**neighbor** *ip-address* **remote-as** *remote-asn* BGP subcommand)

Key
Topic

For example, consider a typical multihomed Enterprise Internet design, as shown in Figure 13-1. In this case, the following design requirements have already been decided, but you must then determine the configuration, knowing the information in the following list and the figure:

- The Enterprise uses ASN 11.

- The connection to ISP1 (two T-1's) is considered the primary connection, with the connection to ISP3 (one T-1) being secondary.

- ISP1 advertises a default route, plus full updates.

- ISP1 uses ASN 1.

- ISP3 advertises a default route, plus partial updates that includes only ISP3's local customers.

- ISP3 uses ASN 3.

- Each ISP uses the IP address of its lowest-numbered interface for its peer relationships.

For Router E1, the BGP configuration requires only three commands, at least to configure BGP to the point where E1 will form neighborships with the two other routers. (Note that this chapter continues to change and add to this configuration when introducing new concepts.) The example also shows the configuration on Routers I1-1 and I3-1 added

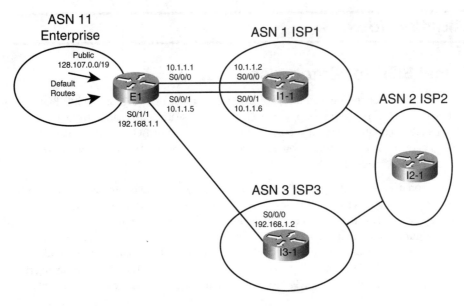

Figure 13-1   *Sample Single Multihomed Design*

solely to support the neighbor connections to E1; other BGP configuration on these routers is not shown.

Example 13-1   *BGP Configuration on E1: Neighborships Configured*

```
! Configuration on router E1
router bgp 11
 neighbor 10.1.1.2 remote-as 1
 neighbor 192.168.1.2 remote-as 3
! Next commands are on I1-1
router bgp 1
 neighbor 10.1.1.1 remote-as 11
! Next commands are on I3-1
router bgp 3
 neighbor 192.168.1.1 remote-as 11
```

The gray portions of the output highlight the configuration of the local ASN and the neighbors' ASNs – parameters that must match for the neighborships to form. First, E1 configures its own ASN as 11 by using the **router bgp 11** command. The other routers must refer to ASN 11 on the **neighbor** commands that refer to E1; in this case I1-1 refers to ASN 11 with its **neighbor 10.1.1.1 remote-as 11** command. Conversely, I1-1's local ASN (1) on its **router bgp 1** global command must match what E1 configures in a **neighbor** command, in this case with E1's **neighbor 10.1.1.2 remote-as 1** command.

Requirements for Forming eBGP Neighborships

Routers must meet several requirements to become BGP neighbors:

- A local router's ASN (on the **router bgp** *asn* command) must match the neighboring router's reference to that ASN with its **neighbor remote-as** *asn* command.

- The BGP router IDs of the two routers must not be the same.

- If configured, MD5 authentication must pass.

- Each router must be part of a TCP connection with the other router, with the remote router's IP address used in that TCP connection matching what the local router configures in a BGP **neighbor remote-as** command.

Consider the first two items in this list. First, the highlights in Example 13-1 demonstrate the first of the four requirements. Next, the second requirement in the list requires only a little thought if you recall the similar details about router IDs (RID) with EIGRP and OSPF. Like EIGRP and OSPF, BGP defines a 32-bit router ID, written in dotted-decimal notation. And like EIGRP and OSPF, BGP on a router chooses its RID the same general way, by using the following steps, in order, until a BGP RID has been chosen:

- **Configured:** Use the setting of the **bgp router-id** *rid* router subcommand.

- **Highest Loopback:** Choose the highest numeric IP address of any up/up loopback interface, at the time the BGP process initializes.

- **Highest other interface:** Choose the highest numeric IP address of any up/up non-loopback interface, at the time the BGP process initializes.

The third requirement in the list, the MD5 authentication check, occurs only if authentication has been configured on at least one of the two routers, using the **neighbor** *neighbor-ip* **password** *key* command. If two BGP neighbors configure this command, referring to the other routers' IP address, while configuring a matching MD5 authentication key value, the authentication passes. If both omit this command, then no authentication occurs, and the neighbor can still work. However, if the keys do not match, or if only one router configures authentication, then authentication fails.

The fourth neighbor requirement–that the IP addresses used for the neighbor TCP connection match–requires a more detailed discussion. BGP neighbors first form a TCP connection; later, BGP messages flow over that connection, which allows BGP routers to know when the messages arrived at the neighbor, and when they did not.

A BGP router creates the TCP connection by trying to establish a TCP connection to the address configured in the **neighbor** *neighbor-ip* **remote-as** command. However, IOS does not require the BGP configuration to explicitly state the source address that router uses when establishing this TCP connection, and if not explicitly configured, IOS picks an IP address on the local router. By default, IOS chooses its BGP source IP address for a given neighbor as the interface IP address of the outgoing interface of the route used to forward packets to that neighbor. That's a lot of words to fight through, and much more easily seen with a figure, such as Figure 13-2, which focuses on the eBGP connection between E1 and I1-1 shown in Figure 13-1.

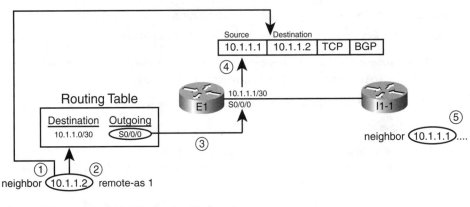

Figure 13-2 *A Default Choice for Update Source*

A description of the steps in logic shown in the figure follows:

Step 1.   E1 finds the **neighbor 10.1.1.2** command, so E1 sends the BGP messages for this neighbor inside packets with destination IP address 10.1.1.2.

Step 2.   E1 looks in the IP routing table for the route that matches destination 10.1.1.2.

Step 3.   The route matched in Step 2 lists S0/0/0 as outgoing interface.

Step 4.   E1's interface IP address for S0/0/0 is 10.1.1.1, so E1 uses 10.1.1.1 as its source IP address for this BGP peer.

Step 5.   The **neighbor** command on the other router, I1-1, must refer to E1's source IP address (10.1.1.1 in this case).

Now, consider again the last of the four requirements to become neighbors. Restated, for proper operation, the BGP update source on one router must match the IP address configured on the other router's **neighbor** command, and vice versa. As shown in Figure 13-2, E1 uses update source 10.1.1.1, with I1-1 configuring the **neighbor 10.1.1.1**... command. Conversely, I1-1 uses 10.1.1.2 as its update source for this neighbor relationship, with E1 configuring a matching **neighbor 10.1.1.2** command.

Note: The update source concept applies per neighbor.

Issues When Redundancy Exists Between eBGP Neighbors

In many cases, a single Layer 3 path exists between eBGP neighbors. For example, a single T1, or single T3, or maybe a single MetroE Virtual Private Wire Service (VPWS) path exists between the two routers. In such cases, the eBGP configuration can simply use the interface IP addresses on that particular link. For example, in Figure 13-1, a single serial link exists between Routers E1 and I3-1, and they can reasonably use the serial link's IP addresses, as shown in Example 13-1.

However, when redundant Layer 3 paths exist between two eBGP neighbors, the use of interface IP addresses for the underlying TCP connection can result in an outage when only one of the two links fails. BGP neighborships fail when the underlying TCP connection fails. TCP uses a concept called a *socket*, which consists of a local TCP port number and an IP address. That IP address must be associated with a working interface (an interface whose state is line status up, line protocol up, per the **show interfaces** command). If the interface whose IP address is used by BGP were to fail, then the TCP socket would fail, closing the TCP connection. As a result, the BGP neighborship can only be up when the associated interfaces also happens to be up.

Two alternative solutions exist in this case. One option would be to configure two **neighbor** commands on each router, one for each of the neighbor's interface IP addresses. This solves the availability issue, because if one link fails, the other neighborship can remain up and working. However, in this case, both neighborships exchange BGP routes, consuming bandwidth and more memory in the BGP table.

The preferred option, which uses loopback interfaces as the TCP connection endpoints, solves the availability problem while avoiding the extra overhead. The two routers each configure a loopback interface and IP address, and use those loopback IP addresses as the source of their single BGP TCP connection. If one of the multiple links fails, the loopback interface does not fail. As long as the two routers have working routes to reach each other's loopback IP addresses, the TCP connection does not fail.

Configuring eBGP peers to use a loopback interface IP address with BGP requires several steps, as follows:

Step 1. Configure an IP address on a loopback interface on each router.

Step 2. Tell BGP on each router to use the loopback IP address as the source IP address using the **neighbor... update-source** *interface-id* command.

Key Topic

Step 3. Configure the BGP **neighbor** command on each router to refer to the other router's loopback IP address at the neighbor IP address in the **neighbor** *neighbor-ip* **remote-as** command.

Step 4. Make sure each router has IP routes so that they can forward packets to the loopback interface IP address of the other router.

Step 5. Configure eBGP multihop using the **neighbor... ebgp-multihop** *hops* command.

The first three steps in the list require configuration on both the routers. Figure 13-3 shows the details related to the first three steps, focusing on Router E1's use of its loopback1 interface (based on Figure 13-1).

The fourth step in the list is an overt reminder that for TCP to work, both routers must be able to deliver packets to the IP address listed in the **neighbor** commands. Because the **neighbor** commands now refer to loopback IP addresses, the routers cannot rely on connected routes for forwarding the packets. To give each router a route to the other router's loopback, you can run an instance of an IGP to learn the routes, or just configure static routes. If using static routes, make sure to configure the routes so that all redundant paths would be used (as seen in upcoming Example 13-2). If using an IGP, make sure the configuration allows the two routers to become IGP neighbors over all redundant links as well.

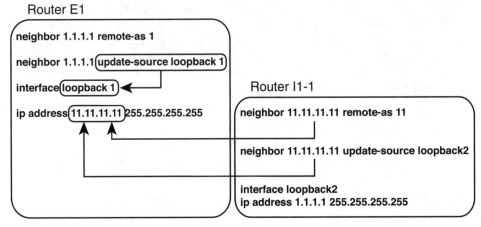

Figure 13-3   *Using Loopbacks with Update Source for eBGP*

eBGP Multihop Concepts

The fifth configuration step for using loopback IP addresses with eBGP peers refers to a feature called *eBGP multihop*. By default, when building packets to send to an eBGP peer, IOS sets the IP Time-To-Live (TTL) field in the IP header to a value of 1. With this default action, the eBGP neighborship fails to complete when using loopback interface IP addresses. The reason is that when the packet with TTL=1 arrives at the neighbor, the neighbor discards the packet.

The logic of discarding the BGP packets may be a bit surprising, so an example can help. For this example, assume the default action of TTL=1 is used and that eBGP multihop is not configured yet. Router E1 from Figure 13-1 is trying to establish a BGP connection to I1-1, using I1-1's loopback IP address 1.1.1.1, as shown in Figure 13-3. The following occurs with the IP packets sent by E1 when attempting to form a TCP connection for BGP to use:

Step 1.   E1 sends a packet to destination address 1.1.1.1, TTL=1.

Step 2.   I1-1 receives the packet. Seeing that the packet is not destined for the receiving interface's IP address, I1-1 passes the packet off to its own IP forwarding (IP routing) logic.

Step 3.   I1-1's IP routing logic matches the destination (1.1.1.1) with the routing table and finds interface loopback 2 as the outgoing interface.

Step 4.   I1-1's IP forwarding logic decrements TTL by 1, decreasing TTL to 0, and as a result, I1-1 discards the packet.

In short, the internal IOS packet forwarding logic decrements the TTL before giving the packet to the loopback interface, meaning that the normal IP forwarding logic discards the packet.

Configuring the routers with the **neighbor ebgp-multihop 2** command, as seen in upcoming Example 13-2, solves the problem. This command defines the TTL that the router will use when creating the BGP packets (2 in this case). As a result, the receiving router will decrement the TTL to 1, so the packet will not be discarded.

Configuring for eBGP Redundancy and Authentication

To pull these optional configuration steps together, Example 13-2 shows a new configuration for E1 and I1-1 (as compared with Example 13-1). In this case:

- Both routers use BGP authentication, with authentication key **fred**.

- Two Layer 3 paths exist between E1 and I1-1, so the configuration uses all the steps required to make both routers use the loopback interfaces listed in Figure 13-3.

- Both routers use eBGP multihop. (Otherwise, the neighborships would fail.)

- Both routers use static routes to provide reachability to the loopback interfaces, with two routes each, one using each redundant path.

Example 13-2 *Broader eBGP Configuration Example*

```
! Configuration on router E1
interface loopback 1
 ip address 11.11.11.11 255.255.255.255
!
ip route 1.1.1.1 255.255.255.255 s0/0/0
ip route 1.1.1.1 255.255.255.255 s0/0/1
!
router bgp 11
 neighbor 1.1.1.1 remote-as 1
 neighbor 1.1.1.1 update-source loopback 1
 neighbor 1.1.1.1 ebgp-multihop 2
 neighbor 1.1.1.1 password fred
! Next commands are on I1-1
interface loopback 2
 ip address 1.1.1.1 255.255.255.255
!
ip route 11.11.11.11 255.255.255.255 s0/0/0
ip route 11.11.11.11 255.255.255.255 s0/0/1
!
router bgp 1
 neighbor 11.11.11.11 remote-as 11
 neighbor 11.11.11.11 update-source loopback 2
 neighbor 11.11.11.11 ebgp-multihop 2
 neighbor 11.11.11.11 password fred
```

Besides listing the various configuration commands, this example is also the first in this chapter that demonstrates how to configure multiple settings for a single BGP neighbor. The IOS BGP **neighbor** command has many options. To set those options for a single neighbor, the command begins with **neighbor** *neighbor-ip-address*, followed by the parameters. So, instead of one **neighbor** command with a large number of parameters, the configuration includes several **neighbor** commands, each listing the IP address of the same neighbor, but each listing a different set of parameters. In this case, each router now uses four **neighbor** commands: one to define the remote ASN, one for the update source, one to enable eBGP multihop, and one for the authentication key.

BGP Internals and Verifying eBGP Neighbors

Similar to OSPF, the BGP neighbor relationship goes through a series of states over time. Although the Finite State Machine (FSM) for BGP neighbor states has many twists and turns, particularly for handling exceptions, retries, and failures, the overall process works as follows:

Step 1.   A router tries to establish a TCP connection with the IP address listed on a **neighbor** command, using well-known destination port 179.

Step 2.   When the three-way TCP connection completes, the router sends its first BGP message, the BGP *Open* message, which generally performs the same function as the EIGRP and OSPF Hello messages. The Open message contains several BGP parameters, including those that must be verified before allowing the routers to become neighbors.

Step 3.   After an Open message has been sent and received and the neighbor parameters match, the neighbor relationship is formed, and the neighbors reach *established* state.

Table 13-2 lists the various BGP states. If all works well, the neighborship reaches the final state: *established*. When the neighbor relationship (also called a BGP peer or BGP peer connection) reaches the established state, the neighbors can send BGP Update messages, which list PAs and prefixes. However, if neighbor relationship fails for any reason, then the neighbor relationship can cycle through all the states listed in Table 13-2 while the routers periodically attempt to bring up the neighborship.

Table 13-2   *BGP Neighbor States*

State	Typical Reasons
Idle	The BGP process is either administratively down or awaiting the next retry attempt.
Connect	The BGP process is waiting for the TCP connection to be completed. You cannot determine from this state information whether the TCP connection can complete.
Active	The TCP connection has been completed, but no BGP messages have been sent to the peer yet.
Opensent	The TCP connection exists, and a BGP Open message has been sent to the peer, but the matching Open message has not yet been received from the other router.
Openconfirm	An Open message has been both sent to and received from the other router. The next step is to receive a BGP Keepalive message (to confirm all neighbor-related parameters matched) or BGP Notification message (to learn there is some mismatch in neighbor parameters).

Table 13-2 *BGP Neighbor States*

State	Typical Reasons
Established	All neighbor parameters match, the neighbor relationship works, and the peers can now exchange Update messages.

Verifying eBGP Neighbor Status

The two most common commands to display a BGP neighbor's status are **show ip bgp summary** and **show ip bgp neighbors** [*neighbor-id*]. Interestingly, most people use the first of these commands because it supplies a similar amount of information, 1 line per neighbor, as do the familiar **show ip eigrp neighbors** and **show ip ospf neighbor** commands. The **show ip bgp neighbors** command lists a large volume of output per neighbor, which, although useful, usually contains far too much information for the verification of the current neighbor state. Examples 13-3 and 13-4 show samples of the output of each of these two commands on Router E1, respectively, based on the configuration shown in Example 13-2, with some description following each example.

Example 13-3 *Summary Information with the* **show ip bgp summary** *Command*

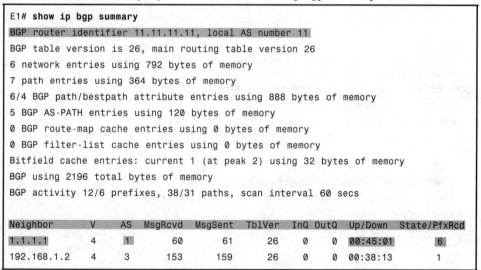

```
E1# show ip bgp summary
BGP router identifier 11.11.11.11, local AS number 11
BGP table version is 26, main routing table version 26
6 network entries using 792 bytes of memory
7 path entries using 364 bytes of memory
6/4 BGP path/bestpath attribute entries using 888 bytes of memory
5 BGP AS-PATH entries using 120 bytes of memory
0 BGP route-map cache entries using 0 bytes of memory
0 BGP filter-list cache entries using 0 bytes of memory
Bitfield cache entries: current 1 (at peak 2) using 32 bytes of memory
BGP using 2196 total bytes of memory
BGP activity 12/6 prefixes, 38/31 paths, scan interval 60 secs


Neighbor        V     AS  MsgRcvd  MsgSent  TblVer  InQ OutQ  Up/Down   State/PfxRcd
1.1.1.1         4      1       60       61      26    0    0  00:45:01             6
192.168.1.2     4      3      153      159      26    0    0  00:38:13             1
```

The first line in the summary lists the local router's BGP RID (11.11.11.11), along with the local router's ASN (11). The rest of the summary focuses on statistics for the BGP table entries. The bottom of the output lists a heading line (highlighted in the output), plus one line per neighbor, with two neighbors in this case. The Neighbor column lists the IP address as defined on the local router's **neighbor** command and not the neighbor's BGP RID. Other notable information includes the neighbor's ASN (as configured on the local router's **neighbor remote-as** command), the time spent in the current state, and an interesting heading: State/PfxRcd.

This final heading, State/PfxRcd, either lists the BGP neighbor state, as summarized in Table 13-2, or the number of prefixes received (PfxRcd) from that neighbor. A numeric value under this heading implies a neighbor state of established, because the peers must be in established state before Updates can be sent. If the peer is not in an established state, the value in this heading lists the text name of the current BGP state.

Example 13-4 shows a sample of the **show ip bgp neighbors 1.1.1.1** command on router E1, which displays information about the connection to Router I1-1 in Figure 13-1. This command lists several facts not seen in the shorter **show ip bgp summary** command output in Example 13-3. The example highlights some of those key items, with the following comments referring to those highlighted items, in order:

■   The neighbor is an eBGP neighbor (external link).

■   The neighbor's BGP RID (1.1.1.1).

■   The current state (Established) is explicitly listed.

■   Route refresh is enabled (as referenced in Chapter 14's section titled "Clearing BGP Neighbors").

■   The eBGP multihop setting (2 hops).

■   Local and remote TCP socket information (IP addresses and port numbers).

Example 13-4   *Detailed Information with the* **show ip bgp neighbors** *Command*

```
E1# show ip bgp neighbors 1.1.1.1
BGP neighbor is 1.1.1.1, remote AS 1, external link
  BGP version 4, remote router ID 1.1.1.1
  BGP state = Established, up for 00:45:08
  Last read 00:00:02, last write 00:00:38, hold time is 180, keepalive interval
is 60 seconds
  Neighbor capabilities:
    Route refresh: advertised and received(new)
    Address family IPv4 Unicast: advertised and received
  Message statistics:
    InQ depth is 0
    OutQ depth is 0

                             Sent       Rcvd
    Opens:                      2          2
    Notifications:              0          0
    Updates:                   16         12
    Keepalives:                43         47
    Route Refresh:              0          0
    Total:                     61         61
  Default minimum time between advertisement runs is 30 seconds
```

```
  For address family: IPv4 Unicast
   BGP table version 26, neighbor version 26/0
   Output queue size : 0
   Index 1, Offset 0, Mask 0x2
   1 update-group member
                                        Sent        Rcvd
   Prefix activity:                      — —         — —
      Prefixes Current:                   6           6 (Consumes 312 bytes)
      Prefixes Total:                    19           7
      Implicit Withdraw:                 11           0
      Explicit Withdraw:                  2           1
      Used as bestpath:                 n/a           5
      Used as multipath:                n/a           0

                                      Outbound    Inbound
   Local Policy Denied Prefixes:       — — —       — — — ·
      AS_PATH loop:                      n/a          2
      Total:                              0           2
   Number of NLRIs in the update sent: max 3, min 1

   Address tracking is enabled, the RIB does have a route to 1.1.1.1
   Connections established 2; dropped 1
   Last reset 00:45:10, due to Peer closed the session
   External BGP neighbor may be up to 2 hops away.
   Transport(tcp) path-mtu-discovery is enabled
Connection state is ESTAB, I/O status: 1, unread input bytes: 0
Connection is ECN Disabled, Minimum incoming TTL 0, Outgoing TTL 2
Local host: 11.11.11.11, Local port: 179
Foreign host: 1.1.1.1, Foreign port: 28995
Connection tableid (VRF): 0

Enqueued packets for retransmit: 0, input: 0  mis-ordered: 0 (0 bytes)

Event Timers (current time is 0x8217A0):
Timer          Starts      Wakeups           Next
Retrans          49           0              0x0
TimeWait          0           0              0x0
AckHold          49          46              0x0
SendWnd           0           0              0x0
KeepAlive         0           0              0x0
GiveUp            0           0              0x0
PmtuAger          0           0              0x0
DeadWait          0           0              0x0
Linger            0           0              0x0
ProcessQ          0           0              0x0
```

```
iss: 2070882650   snduna: 2070884280   sndnxt: 2070884280      sndwnd:   15890
irs: 3327995414   rcvnxt: 3327996693   rcvwnd:        16156  delrcvwnd:     228

SRTT: 300 ms, RTTO: 306 ms, RTV: 6 ms, KRTT: 0 ms
minRTT: 0 ms, maxRTT: 300 ms, ACK hold: 200 ms
Status Flags: passive open, gen tcbs
Option Flags: nagle, path mtu capable, md5
IP Precedence value : 6

Datagrams (max data segment is 516 bytes):
Rcvd: 98 (out of order: 0), with data: 50, total data bytes: 1278
Sent: 99 (retransmit: 0, fastretransmit: 0, partialack: 0, Second Congestion: 0),
with data: 50, total data bytes: 1629
 Packets received in fast path: 0, fast processed: 0, slow path: 0
 fast lock acquisition failures: 0, slow path: 0
E1# show tcp brief
TCB          Local Address         Foreign Address          (state)
66D27FE0     192.168.1.1.179       192.168.1.2.16489        ESTAB
66D27378     11.11.11.11.179       1.1.1.1.28995            ESTAB
```

Note that the end of the example shows another command that you can use to confirm the TCP socket details of the underlying TCP connection: **show tcp brief**.

Administratively Controlling Neighbor Status

Interestingly, Cisco IOS provides a means by which network operations personnel can administratively disable any BGP neighbor. To do so, the operator would enter BGP configuration mode and issue the **neighbor** *neighbor-ip* **shutdown** command. This command brings down the current neighbor to an idle state. Later, when the BGP connection should be brought up, the operator should repeat the process, but with the **no** version of the command (**no neighbor** *neighbor-ip* **shutdown**).

These commands can be particularly useful to try in lab when learning BGP. Teamed with the **debug ip bgp** command, you can bring down neighbors and see the somewhat-readable BGP messages. These messages list the BGP states from Table 13-2. It also shows the information inside the Open messages. Example 13-5 shows a sample, with the debug messages that note a state transition highlighted. The output also lists the **show ip bgp summary** command, with the administratively idle state created by the **neighbor 1.1.1.1 shutdown** BGP configuration command on Router E1.

Example 13-5 *BGP Shutdown and BGP Neighbor State Transitions*

```
E1# debug ip bgp
BGP debugging is on for address family: IPv4 Unicast
E1# conf t
```

```
Enter configuration commands, one per line.  End with CNTL/Z.
E1(config)# router bgp 11
E1(config-router)# neighbor 1.1.1.1 shutdown
E1(config-router)#


*Aug 11 20:23:01.335: BGPNSF state: 1.1.1.1 went from nsf_not_active to
nsf_not_active
*Aug 11 20:23:01.335: BGP: 1.1.1.1 went from Established to Idle
*Aug 11 20:23:01.335: %BGP-5-ADJCHANGE: neighbor 1.1.1.1 Down Admin. Shutdown


E1(config-router)# do show ip bgp summary
! lines omitted for brevity


Neighbor       V   AS   MsgRcvd   MsgSent   TblVer   InQ   OutQ   Up/Down    State/PfxRcd
1.1.1.1        4    1        87        87        0     0      0   00:00:06   Idle (Admin)
192.168.1.2    4    3       173       183       41     0      0   00:58:47              1


E1(config-router)# no neighbor 1.1.1.1 shutdown
E1(config-router)#
*Aug 11 20:23:26.571: BGP: 1.1.1.1 went from Idle to Active
*Aug 11 20:23:26.571: BGP: 1.1.1.1 open active, local address 11.11.11.11
*Aug 11 20:23:26.575: BGP: 1.1.1.1 read request no-op
*Aug 11 20:23:26.575: BGP: 1.1.1.1 went from Active to OpenSent
*Aug 11 20:23:26.575: BGP: 1.1.1.1 sending OPEN, version 4, my as: 11, holdtime
180 seconds
*Aug 11 20:23:26.579: BGP: 1.1.1.1 send message type 1, length (incl. header) 45
*Aug 11 20:23:26.583: BGP: 1.1.1.1 rcv message type 1, length (excl. header) 26
*Aug 11 20:23:26.587: BGP: 1.1.1.1 rcv OPEN, version 4, holdtime 180 seconds
*Aug 11 20:23:26.587: BGP: 1.1.1.1 rcv OPEN w/ OPTION parameter len: 16
*Aug 11 20:23:26.587: BGP: 1.1.1.1 rcvd OPEN w/ optional parameter type 2
(Capability) len 6
*Aug 11 20:23:26.587: BGP: 1.1.1.1 OPEN has CAPABILITY code: 1, length 4
*Aug 11 20:23:26.587: BGP: 1.1.1.1 OPEN has MP_EXT CAP for afi/safi: 1/1
*Aug 11 20:23:26.587: BGP: 1.1.1.1 rcvd OPEN w/ optional parameter type 2
(Capability) len 2
*Aug 11 20:23:26.587: BGP: 1.1.1.1 OPEN has CAPABILITY code: 128, length 0
*Aug 11 20:23:26.587: BGP: 1.1.1.1 OPEN has ROUTE-REFRESH capability(old) for all
address-families
*Aug 11 20:23:26.587: BGP: 1.1.1.1 rcvd OPEN w/ optional parameter type 2
(Capability) len 2
*Aug 11 20:23:26.587: BGP: 1.1.1.1 OPEN has CAPABILITY code: 2, length 0
*Aug 11 20:23:26.587: BGP: 1.1.1.1 OPEN has ROUTE-REFRESH capability(new) for all
address-families
BGP: 1.1.1.1 rcvd OPEN w/ remote AS 1
*Aug 11 20:23:26.587: BGP: 1.1.1.1 went from OpenSent to OpenConfirm
*Aug 11 20:23:26.591: BGP: 1.1.1.1 went from OpenConfirm to Established
*Aug 11 20:23:26.591: %BGP-5-ADJCHANGE: neighbor 1.1.1.1 Up
*Aug 11 20:23:26.603: BGP_Router: unhandled major event code 128, minor 0
```

BGP Message Summary

So far, this chapter has mentioned three of the four BGP messages. For reference, Table 13-3 lists the four BGP messages, with comparisons to EIGRP messages for perspective.

Table 13-3 *BGP Message Types*

Message	Purpose	Similarity with EIGRP
Open	Used to establish a neighbor relationship and exchange basic parameters, including ASN and MD5 authentication values.	Hello
Keepalive	Sent on a periodic basis to maintain the neighbor relationship. The lack of receipt of a Keepalive message within the negotiated Hold timer causes BGP to bring down the neighbor connection.	Hello
Update	Used to exchange PAs and the associated prefix/length (NLRI) that use those attributes.	Update
Notification	Used to signal a BGP error; typically results in a reset to the neighbor relationship.	No direct equivalent

Verifying the BGP Table

When an Enterprise router has established its eBGP neighbor relationships, that router can advertise and learn routes using BGP. To learn routes, an Enterprise BGP router does not need additional configuration beyond the configuration of eBGP neighbors as discussed in the first section of this chapter. To advertise routes to eBGP peers, particularly the public IP address prefix(es) used by that Enterprise, the Enterprise BGP router needs some additional configuration, as discussed in the upcoming section "Injecting Routes into BGP for Advertisement to the ISPs."

The BGP table plays a key role in the process of learning and using routing information with BGP. A router stores all learned BGP prefixes and PAs in its BGP table. The router will later choose which route for each prefix is the best BGP route. The router can then advertise its BGP table to its neighbors, advertising only the best route for each prefix.

This section begins with a brief examination of the BGP Update process by which BGP neighbors exchange routing information. Next, the text looks at the various **show** commands that can be used to examine and confirm the contents of the BGP table.

The BGP Update Message

When a BGP neighborship reaches the established state, those neighbors begin sending BGP Update messages to each other. The router receiving an Update places those learned prefixes into its BGP table, regardless of whether the route appears to be the best route. Like EIGRP and OSPF, BGP puts all learned routing information into its table, and then BGP processes all such potential routes to choose the best route for each prefix.

The BGP Update message itself can be revealing about the motivations behind BGP. Figure 13-4 shows the format of the Update message.

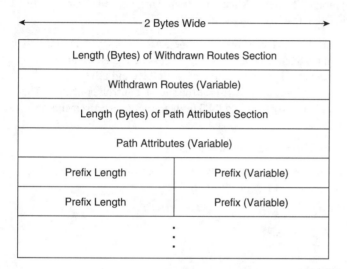

Figure 13-4 *Format of the BGP Update Message*

Interestingly, the format of the Update message tells us something about the nature of BGP as a *Path Vector* algorithm. The message lists a set of PAs and then a potentially long list of prefixes that use that set of PAs. So, you might view the BGP Update message as focusing on advertising paths, or a set of PAs, along with the associated list of prefixes that use the advertised path. (Both are important, of course.) Then, because BGP uses the information in the combined set of PAs to make a decision of which path is best, its underlying logic is called *path vector*.

Note: BGP also uses the term Network Layer Reachability Information (NLRI) to describe the IP prefix and length. This book uses the more familiar term *prefix*.

BGP uses the Update message to both announce and withdraw routes. For example, when a router realizes that a route in the router's BGP table has failed, that router withdraws that route by sending a BGP Update to its neighbors, listing the prefix in the list of withdrawn routes. When a router receives an Update that lists a prefix as withdrawn, that router knows that the route has failed. (Note the field near the top of the Update message that lists withdrawn routes.) That same Update message may contain other announced prefixes later in the Update message.

Examining the BGP Table

One of the key tasks in a BGP verification plan should be to examine the prefixes in the BGP table and confirm that the right prefixes have been learned from the expected neighbors. The BGP table should hold all learned prefixes, from each neighbor, except for any prefixes filtered by an inbound BGP filter. For example, in a router configured a **neighbor route-map in** command, the local router would first filter the routes and then add the allowed routes into the BGP table. (Chapter 14's section "Route Filtering and Clearing BGP Peers" discusses the filtering and its impact on the BGP table.)

As an example, consider Figure 13-5, which shows the same basic topology as Figure 13-1 but with only the information pertinent to the upcoming discussions listed in the figure. In this case, five prefixes exist somewhere in the Internet, with ISP1 and ISP3 learning these prefixes from ISP2. An additional prefix exists at the site of a customer of ISP3. The design calls for the following actions by ISP1 and ISP3 in their eBGP advertisements to the Enterprise:

■ ISP1 should supply a default route plus full BGP updates.

■ ISP3 should supply a default route plus partial BGP updates that include only ISP3's customers' prefixes (for example, 192.135.250.0/28).

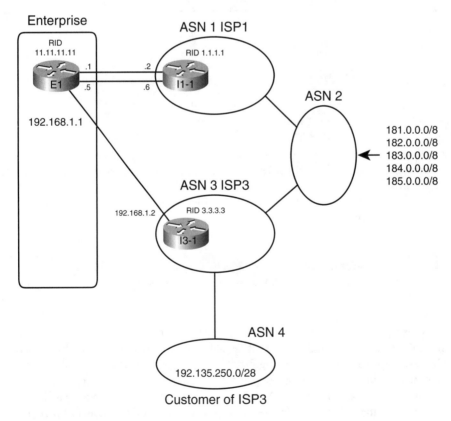

Figure 13-5 *Three Prefixes to be Advertised to E1*

The **show ip bgp** lists the entirety of the BGP routing table. Example 13-6 shows a sample from Router E1. Note that the configuration of this network is based on Example 13-2, with Routers E1 and I1-1 still using their loopback interfaces in their **neighbor** commands.

Example 13-6 *E1's BGP Table with Routes Learned from the ISPs*

```
E1# show ip bgp
BGP table version is 78, local router ID is 11.11.11.11
Status codes: s suppressed, d damped, h history, * valid, > best, i - internal,
              r RIB-failure, S Stale
Origin codes: i - IGP, e - EGP, ? - incomplete

   Network          Next Hop            Metric LocPrf Weight Path
*  0.0.0.0          192.168.1.2              0           0 3 i
*>                  1.1.1.1                  0           0 1 i
*> 181.0.0.0/8      1.1.1.1                              0 1 2 111 111 i
*> 182.0.0.0/8      1.1.1.1                              0 1 2 222 i
*> 183.0.0.0/8      1.1.1.1                              0 1 2 i
*> 184.0.0.0/8      1.1.1.1                              0 1 2 i
*> 185.0.0.0/8      1.1.1.1                              0 1 2 i
*  192.135.250.0/28 1.1.1.1                              0 1 2 3 4 i
*>                  192.168.1.2                          0 3 4 i
```

First, examine the overall format and the headings in the output of the **show ip bgp** command. The Network column lists the prefix/length (NLRI). The Next Hop heading lists the next-hop IP address that would be used for the route. Then, skipping over to the far right, the Path heading lists the AS_Path PA. (Note that it is difficult to see the beginning of the AS_Path, but the weight [another PA] for each route is 0 in this case, so the next number after the 0, in this case, is the beginning of the AS_Path.)

Next, focus on the last two lines of output from the **show ip bgp** command. Each of the last two lines describes a different route to reach 192.135.250.0/28–one with next-hop 1.1.1.1 (router I1-1) and one with next-hop 192.168.1.2 (router I3-1). Because the second of these two lines does not list a prefix (under the heading "Network"), the output implies that this line is just another route for the prefix listed on the previous line. Next, examine the highlighted AS_Path values at the end of each of these lines. For the route through I1-1 (1.1.1.1), the AS_Path lists ASNs 1, 2, 3, and 4. Similarly, the AS_Path for the other route lists only ASNs 3 and 4.

Note: BGP **show** commands list the AS_Path with the first-added ASN on the right and the last-added ASN on the left. BGP uses this convention because when BGP adds an ASN to the AS_Path, BGP prepends the ASN to the list, causing the new ASN to show up as the leftmost ASN in the AS_Path.

Continuing to focus on the final two lines of the **show ip bgp** output, examine the far left part of the output, and note that the second of these two lines has a > highlighted. Per the legend at the top of the command output, the > denotes the chosen best route. In this case, none of the routers inside the various ISPs set PAs for the purpose of influencing the best path choice, so the first used BGP best path decision is the shortest AS_Path. As a result, the path through ISP3, ASN 3, is best, having only 2 ASNs, compared to the path through ISP1, ASN 1, with four ASNs.

You can confirm that all E1's BGP table entries were learned using eBGP, rather than iBGP, by the absence of the letter "i" in the third column. Immediately after the *>, a space appears in the output. If a route was learned with iBGP, an "i" would appear in this third character position. By implication, all the routes in Example 13-6 are eBGP routes due to the absence of the letter i in the third character of possible output.

Finally, taking a broader view of the output of the **show ip bgp** command, consider which prefixes have two known routes and which have only one. Then, consider the design requirements listed before Example 13-6: I1-1 would advertise all prefixes, plus a default, but I3-1 would advertise only partial updates plus a default. As such, I3-1 did not advertise the prefixes that begin 181 through 185, by design, resulting in Router E1 only learning one route for each of these prefixes.

E1 chose the route through I3-1 as the best route for prefix 192.135.250.0/28. Example 13-7 shows the details of the IP routing table entry for this route.

Example 13-7   *E1's IP Route for 192.135.250.0/28*

```
E1# show ip route 192.135.250.0 255.255.255.240
Routing entry for 192.135.250.0/28
  Known via "bgp 11", distance 20, metric 0
  Tag 3, type external
  Last update from 192.168.1.2 00:10:27 ago
  Routing Descriptor Blocks:
  * 192.168.1.2, from 192.168.1.2, 00:10:27 ago
      Route metric is 0, traffic share count is 1
      AS Hops 2
      Route tag 3
```

The output of the **show ip route 192.135.250.0 255.255.255.240** command lists the source of the route (BGP process 11), the next-hop router (192.168.1.2), and the AS Path length (AS Hops 2). The output also confirms that the route is an external (eBGP) route.

Most of the remaining details in the BGP table relate to BGP PAs, which are discussed in more detail in Chapter 15, "BGP Path Control."

Viewing Subsets of the BGP Table

When accepting full or partial BGP updates, the sheer number of BGP table entries can be much too large for the **show ip bgp** command to be useful. The command could list thousands, or even hundreds of thousands, of prefixes. In practice, you need to be comfortable with a variety of options on the **show ip bgp** command, each listing a different part of the BGP table.

For example, you will likely want to look at BGP table entries for specific prefixes, including the default route prefix of 0.0.0.0/0. Additionally, you may want to see routes per neighbor, and see which routes were heard from that neighbor–and which of those routes passed through any inbound route filters to make it into the BGP table. Finally, to verify whether neighboring ISPs sent full or partial updates, you can look at counters for the number of prefixes learned from each neighbor. Although you probably will never know the exact number of prefixes to expect, you should see a significant difference in the number of prefixes learned from a neighbor sending full updates as compared to a neighbor sending partial updates.

Table 13-4 summarizes some of the key command options that can supply these subsets of information.

Table 13-4 *Verification Commands for eBGP-Learned Routes*

Verification Step	Command
List possible default routes.	**show ip bgp 0.0.0.0 0.0.0.0**
List possible routes, per prefix.	**show ip bgp** *prefix [subnet-mask]*
List routes learned from one neighbor, before any inbound filtering is applied.	**show ip bgp neighbors** *ip-address* **received-routes**
List routes learned from a specific neighbor that passed any inbound filters.	**show ip bgp neighbors** *ip-address* **routes**
Lists routes advertised to a neighbor after applying outbound filtering.	**show ip bgp neighbors** *ip-address* **advertised-routes**
List the number of prefixes learned per neighbor.	**show ip bgp summary**

Example 13-8 shows a few samples of these commands on Router E1 from Figures 13-1 and 13-5. The configuration remains unchanged since Example 13-2.

Example 13-8 *Command Samples from Table 13-4*

```
E1# show ip bgp 0.0.0.0 0.0.0.0
BGP routing table entry for 0.0.0.0/0, version 75
Paths: (2 available, best #2, table Default-IP-Routing-Table)
  Advertised to update-groups:
      1
  3
    192.168.1.2 from 192.168.1.2 (3.3.3.3)
      Origin IGP, metric 0, localpref 100, valid, external
```

```
  1
     1.1.1.1 from 1.1.1.1 (1.1.1.1)
       Origin IGP, metric 0, localpref 100, valid, external, best

E1# show ip bgp 192.135.250.0
BGP routing table entry for 192.135.250.0/28, version 78
Paths: (2 available, best #2, table Default-IP-Routing-Table)
  Advertised to update-groups:
       1
  1 2 3 4
     1.1.1.1 from 1.1.1.1 (1.1.1.1)
       Origin IGP, localpref 100, valid, external
  3 4
     192.168.1.2 from 192.168.1.2 (3.3.3.3)
       Origin IGP, localpref 100, valid, external, best


E1# show ip bgp summary
BGP router identifier 11.11.11.11, local AS number 11
BGP table version is 78, main routing table version 78
7 network entries using 924 bytes of memory
9 path entries using 468 bytes of memory
8/5 BGP path/bestpath attribute entries using 1184 bytes of memory
7 BGP AS-PATH entries using 168 bytes of memory
0 BGP route-map cache entries using 0 bytes of memory
0 BGP filter-list cache entries using 0 bytes of memory
Bitfield cache entries: current 1 (at peak 2) using 32 bytes of memory
BGP using 2776 total bytes of memory
BGP activity 7/0 prefixes, 53/44 paths, scan interval 60 secs


Neighbor        V    AS MsgRcvd MsgSent   TblVer  InQ OutQ Up/Down  State/PfxRcd
1.1.1.1         4     1     186     189       78    0    0 00:53:33           7
192.168.1.2     4     3     161     199       78    0    0 00:51:48           2
```

The first command, **show ip bgp 0.0.0.0 0.0.0.0**, displays details about the default routes in the BGP table. The output lists three lines per route, with the AS_Path on the first line. Working through the highlighted portions of the output, in this case, the AS_Path is either 3 or 1, because the ISP routers each originated the route, and those neighboring ASNs are ASN 1 and ASN 3. The output also lists the next-hop address of the route (192.168.1.2 and 1.1.1.1) and the neighbor's BGP RID (I1-1's is 1.1.1.1 and I3-1's is 3.3.3.3). Finally, instead of the > seen in the output of **show ip bgp**, this command simply lists the term "best" for the best route.

The next command, **show ip bgp 192.135.250.0**, looks much like the first. In this case, with no subnet mask listed in the command, IOS displays information for any prefix 192.135.250.0 regardless of prefix length. The output again lists three lines per route beginning with the AS_Path values (as highlighted).

The final command listed earlier in Table 13-4, **show ip bgp summary**, lists the number of prefixes received from each neighbor on the far right side. Also, you can see the amount of memory used for the prefixes (listed as network entries) and for different PAs.

The rest of the commands from Table 13-4 focus on displaying information relative to whether BGP filtering has yet occurred. The first, **show ip bgp neighbors** *neighbor-ip* **received-routes**, lists routes received from the neighbor before inbound BGP filtering. The second, **show ip bgp neighbors** *neighbor-ip* **routes**, lists routes received from that neighbor that passed through any inbound filtering. These commands are particularly useful when verifying the results of any configured BGP filters or route maps. The section "Displaying the Results of BGP Filtering" in Chapter 14 discusses the information in these commands and an extra configuration requirement to use the **received-routes** option.

Injecting Routes into BGP for Advertisement to the ISPs

So far, this chapter has focused on configuring eBGP peers and the routes learned by Enterprise routers from eBGP peers at ISPs. These outbound routes let the Enterprise routers forward packets toward the Internet.

At the same time, the ISPs need to learn routes for the Enterprise's public IP address space. This chapter assumes that the choice to use BGP has already been made, so using BGP to advertise the Enterprise's public IP address range makes good sense. This short final major section of this chapter examines the options for advertising these routes. In particular, this section looks at two options:

■ BGP **network** command

■ Redistribution from an IGP

Injecting Routes Using the network Command

The BGP **network** router subcommand differs significantly from the **network** command used by IGPs. For OSPF and EIGRP, the **network** command lists parameters that the router then compares to all its interface IP addresses. If matched, the router enables the IGP routing protocol on those interfaces. BGP does not use the **network** command to enable BGP on interfaces–in fact, BGP has no concept of being enabled on interfaces at all. For a point of comparison, note that the **show ip ospf interface** and **show ip eigrp interfaces** commands identify the enabled interfaces for OSPF and EIGRP, respectively, but no such equivalent BGP command even exists.

The BGP **network** command does cause a comparison to occur, but the comparison occurs between the **network** command's parameters and the *contents of that router's IP routing table*, as follows:

Look for a route in the router's current IP routing table that exactly matches the parameters of the **network** command; if a route for that exact prefix/length exists, put the equivalent prefix/length into the local BGP table.

Note: The preceding statement, and the remaining logic in this section, assumes a BGP default setting of **no auto-summary**. The effect of reversing this setting to **auto-summary** is described in the upcoming section "The Effect of **auto-summary** on the BGP **network** Command."

For example, the Enterprise shown earlier on the left side of both Figures 13-1 and 13-5 might use a private address range and use NAT to translate to use public addresses. For example, the Enterprise might use private Class A network 10.0.0.0 for all private address needs and public address block 128.107.0.0/19 for public addresses. Enterprise Router E1 would then need to advertise the public prefix (128.107.0.0/19) to its ISPs, but not the private address range. Example 13-9 shows an example.

Example 13-9 *E1's Configuration of a* **network** *Command to Advertise Prefixes with eBGP*

```
router bgp 11
 network 128.107.0.0 mask 255.255.224.0
E1# sh ip bgp
BGP table version is 9, local router ID is 11.11.11.11
Status codes: s suppressed, d damped, h history, * valid, > best, i - internal,
              r RIB-failure, S Stale
Origin codes: i - IGP, e - EGP, ? - incomplete

   Network          Next Hop          Metric LocPrf Weight Path
*  0.0.0.0          192.168.1.2            0             0 3 i
*>                  1.1.1.1                0             0 1 i
*> 128.107.0.0/19   10.1.1.66              3         32768 i
*> 181.0.0.0/8      1.1.1.1                             0 1 2 111 111 i
*> 182.0.0.0/8      1.1.1.1                             0 1 2 222 i
*> 183.0.0.0/8      1.1.1.1                             0 1 2 i
*> 184.0.0.0/8      1.1.1.1                             0 1 2 i
*> 185.0.0.0/8      1.1.1.1                             0 1 2 i
*  192.135.250.0/28 1.1.1.1                             0 1 2 3 4 i
*>                  192.168.1.2                          0 3 4 i
```

The **network 128.107.0.0 mask 255.255.224.0** command lists both the subnet number and mask. It adds this prefix to the BGP table only if the exact prefix with that same mask exists in Router E1's routing table. In this case, such a route existed, so the **show ip bgp** command output that follows now lists 128.107.0.0/19 in the BGP table.

In some cases, the Internet-connected router may not have a single route for the entire public prefix. For example, with such a large range of public addresses as 128.107.0.0/19, the Enterprise will most likely have broken that range into subnets, and the Enterprise router may not have a route for the entire range. For example, Router E1 might see routes for 128.107.1.0/24, 128.107.2.0/24, and so on but no route for 128.107.0.0/19.

When a router knows routes only for subsets of the prefix that needs to be advertised, an additional step is needed when using the **network** command. For instance, the **network 128.107.0.0 mask 255.255.224.0** command will not add this prefix to the BGP table even if routes for subsets of this range exist, such as 128.107.1.0/24. So, either configure a static route for the entire range, with outgoing interface null0, on the Internet facing router, or use IGP route summarization to create a summary route for the entire prefix with IGP.

Note: The static route for 128.107.0.0/19 to null0—a discard route—is not meant to be advertised to other routers. It's only purpose is to enable the operation of the **network** command. This discard route should not cause routing problems on the local router, because of the more specific routes for subnets inside the same range of addresses.

Finally, the **network** command examples in this section use the **mask** parameter, but if omitted, IOS assumes a classful network mask. For example, a **network 9.0.0.0** command assumes a Class A default mask of 255.0.0.0, and the **network 128.1.0.0** command assumes a Class B default mask of 255.255.0.0.

The Effect of auto-summary on the BGP network Command

As of Cisco IOS version 12.3 mainline, BGP defaults to a setting of **no auto-summary**, and the previous section's discussion of the **network** command assumed this default setting. However, if the configuration is changed to **auto-summary**, then IOS makes a small change in how it interprets the **network** command.

The change in logic occurs only when the **network** command omits its **mask** parameter; there is no difference in logic if the **mask** parameter is explicitly configured. When the **network** command refers to a Class A, B, or C network, with no **mask** parameter configured, and with **auto-summary** configured, the router adds a route for that classful network to the BGP table:

■   If the exact classful route is in the IP routing table

or

■   If any subset routes of that classful network are in the routing table

In summary, of the two actions in the list, the first occurs regardless of the **auto-summary** setting, and the second occurs only if **auto-summary** is configured.

For example, with **network 9.0.0.0** configured, regardless of the **auto-summary** setting, if a route to 9.0.0.0/8 exists, the router adds 9.0.0.0/8 to the BGP table. However, if the **network 9.0.0.0** (without the mask parameter) and the **auto-summary** commands were both configured, and if only a subset route exists (for example, 9.1.1.0/24), but no route for exactly 9.0.0.0/8 exists, then the router still adds a route for the classful network (9.0.0.0/8) to the BGP table. This second example demonstrates the additional logic that occurs with the **auto-summary** command configured.

Injecting Routes Using Redistribution

Instead of using a BGP **network** command to add routes to the BGP table, the Enterprise BGP routers can instead redistribute routes from an IGP into BGP. The end goals are the same:

■ Inject the public address range, but not the private IP address range, into the BGP table.

■ Advertise one route for the public address range, instead of any individual subnets of the range.

The Enterprise routers that run BGP often already run the IGP as well and have learned routes for either the entire public range as one route or with subset routes. If a single route exists for the entire public range, for example the 128.107.0.0/19 range used in the last several examples, then the engineer simply needs to add a **redistribute** command to the BGP configuration to redistribute that route, and only that route, into BGP. If only subset routes exist, one of several additional steps need to be taken to meet the design goal to inject one route for the entire public address range.

Example 13-10 shows the majority of the work in a case for which Router E1 has three subset routes in the 128.107.0.0/19 range: 128.107.1.0/24, 128.107.2.0/24, and 128.107.3.0/24. However, E1 does not have a single route for the entire 128.107.0.0/19 public prefix. The example shows the redistribution configuration, all of which uses the same familiar redistribution commands shown in Chapters 9 and 10. The configuration matches prefixes in the public range and redistributes them into BGP.

Example 13-10 *Redistributing OSPF into BGP, but for Public Range Only*

```
router bgp 11
 redistribute ospf 1 route-map only-128-107
!
route-map only-128-107 permit
 match ip address prefix 128-107
!
ip prefix-list 128-107 permit 128.107.0.0/19 le 32

E1# show ip route 128.107.0.0 255.255.224.0 longer-prefixes
! Legend omitted for brevity

Gateway of last resort is 1.1.1.1 to network 0.0.0.0

     128.107.0.0/24 is subnetted, 3 subnets
O       128.107.3.0 [110/3] via 10.1.1.66, 00:05:26, FastEthernet0/0
O       128.107.2.0 [110/3] via 10.1.1.66, 00:05:26, FastEthernet0/0
O       128.107.1.0 [110/3] via 10.1.1.66, 00:05:36, FastEthernet0/0

E1# show ip bgp 128.107.0.0/19 longer-prefixes
BGP table version is 11, local router ID is 11.11.11.11
Status codes: s suppressed, d damped, h history, * valid, > best, i - internal,
```

```
          r RIB-failure, S Stale
Origin codes: i - IGP, e - EGP, ? - incomplete


   Network          Next Hop          Metric LocPrf Weight Path
*> 128.107.1.0/24   10.1.1.66              3          32768 ?
*> 128.107.2.0/24   10.1.1.66              3          32768 ?
*> 128.107.3.0/24   10.1.1.66              3          32768 ?
```

The two **show** commands following the configuration list the IP routes that should match the redistribution configuration, and the resulting BGP table entries. The **show ip route 128.107.0.0 255.255.224.0 longer-prefixes** command lists all three IP routes in the public address range in this case. The **show ip bgp 128.107.0.0/19 longer-prefixes** command shows the same range, listing the three BGP table entries created by the **redistribute ospf** command. These BGP table entries list the same next-hop IP addresses listed in the OSPF routes in the IP routing table, with the same metrics.

Left as is, this configuration results in Router E1 advertising all three BGP routes to the ISPs. However, to reach the goal of advertising only a single route for the entire public prefix 128.107.0.0/19, another step must be taken, typically one of the following:

■ Use IGP route summarization to create the route for the entire prefix.

■ Configure a null static route (a discard route) for the entire prefix on the Internet-connected router.

■ Configure BGP route summarization to make BGP advertise only the entire prefix.

The first two would cause router E1 to list a route for the entire public prefix–128.107.0.0/19 in this case–in its IP routing table. The redistribution configuration could then be changed so that only that exact prefix would be redistributed. (For example, removing the **le 32** parameter from the **ip prefix-list 128-107 permit 128.107.0.0/19 le 32** command would make this command match only the exact route.)

The third option would be to use BGP route summarization, telling Router E1 that when any subset routes of 128.107.0.0/19 exists in the BGP table, advertise only 128.107.0.0/19 but none of the subset routes. Example 13-11 shows this last option.

Example 13-11 *The BGP* **aggregate-address** *Command to Advertise the Entire Public IP Address Prefix*

```
E1# conf t
Enter configuration commands, one per line.  End with CNTL/Z.
E1(config)# router bgp 11
E1(config-router)#aggregate-address 128.107.0.0 255.255.224.0 summary-only
E1(config-router)#^Z


E1# show ip bgp 128.107.0.0/19 longer-prefixes
BGP table version is 15, local router ID is 11.11.11.11
```

```
Status codes: s suppressed, d damped, h history, * valid, > best, i - internal,
              r RIB-failure, S Stale
Origin codes: i - IGP, e - EGP, ? - incomplete

   Network          Next Hop          Metric LocPrf Weight Path
*> 128.107.0.0/19   0.0.0.0                         32768 i
s> 128.107.1.0/24   10.1.1.66              3        32768 ?
s> 128.107.2.0/24   10.1.1.66              3        32768 ?
s> 128.107.3.0/24   10.1.1.66              3        32768 ?
```

Note that with the addition of the **aggregate-address** command, the BGP table now also has a route for 128.107.0.0/19, which will be advertised to E1's neighbors at the two ISPs. Also, the **summary-only** keyword in the **aggregate-address** command tells IOS to suppress the advertisement the subset routes, as noted by the code "s" beside the other three routes listed at the end of the example.

Exam Preparation Tasks

Planning Practice

The CCNP ROUTE exam expects test takers to review design documents, create implementation plans, and create verification plans. This section provides some exercises that may help you to take a step back from the minute details of the topics in this chapter so that you can think about the same technical topics from the planning perspective.

For each planning practice table, simply complete the table. Note that any numbers in parentheses represent the number of options listed for each item in the solutions in Appendix F, "Completed Planning Practice Tables."

Design Review Table

Table 13-5 lists several design goals related to this chapter. If these design goals were listed in a design document, and you had to take that document and develop an implementation plan, what implementation options come to mind? You should write a general description; specific configuration commands are not required.

Table 13-5 *Design Review*

Design Goal	Possible Implementation Choices Covered in This Chapter
The plan shows the use of public prefix 200.1.1.0/26 by an Enterprise. What methods should I consider adding to my implementation plan for advertising that prefix to my ISPs using BGP? (2)	

Implementation Plan Peer Review Table

Table 13-6 shows a list of questions that others might ask, or that you might think about, during a peer review of another network engineer's implementation plan. Complete the table by answering the questions.

Table 13-6 *Notable Questions from This Chapter to Consider During an Implementation Plan Peer Review*

Question	Answers
The plan shows Enterprise Router R1, with two parallel Layer 3 paths to ISP Router R2, with a need for BGP. What options exist for high availability eBGP peering? (2) Which is better?	

Table 13-6 *Notable Questions from This Chapter to Consider During an Implementation Plan Peer Review*

Question	Answers
The implementation plan shows an Enterprise router with an eBGP connection to an ISP router, using a loopback interface as Update source. What other feature must be configured to make the eBGP connection work?	
Router R1 connects via eBGP to Router I1 at ISP1. R1 has routes for 130.1.1.0/24 and 130.1.2.0/24 in its routing table. The design claims the company uses 130.1.0.0/21 as its public range. What methods can be used to advertise one route for the entire range to the eBGP peer? (2)	

Create an Implementation Plan Table

This chapter does not focus on implementation or verification, but it did review one concept about static routes, as listed in Table 13-7.

Table 13-7 *Implementation Plan Configuration Memory Drill*

Feature	Configuration Commands/Notes
Configure an eBGP connection as follows: local AS 1, remote AS 2, remote router uses 1.1.1.1 for BGP peering, with 1.1.1.1 being an IP address on a common link between the routers.	
Configure an eBGP connection as follows: local AS 1, remote AS 2, local uses loopback1 (1.1.1.1), remote uses loopback2 (2.2.2.2).	
Add to the previous row the configuration to use MD5 authentication, key "barney."	
Administratively disable the neighbor configured in the previous two items in this table	
Re-enable the neighbor that was disabled in the previous row of this table.	
Cause the advertisement of IGP-learned prefix 130.1.1.0/24 to the neighbor configured in this table, without redistribution.	
Repeat the task in the previous row of this table, but this time with route redistribution, assuming OSPF process 1 is used for the IGP.	

Choose Commands for a Verification Plan Table

To practice skills useful when creating your own verification plan, list in Table 13-8 all commands that supply the requested information. You may want to record your answers outside the book and set a goal to complete this table (and others like it) from memory during your final reviews before taking the exam.

Table 13-8 *Verification Plan Memory Drill*

Information Needed	Commands
Display a single-line neighbor status for each iBGP neighbors.	
Display the number of prefixes learned from a neighbor. (List where the information is located.)	
Display the number of prefixes advertised to a neighbor. (List where the information is located.)	
Display the local and neighbor ASN.	
Display the number of eBGP hops allowed.	
List the current TCP ports used for BGP connections.	
List all prefixes in the BGP table.	
List all the best routes in the BGP table.	
Find the AS_Path for each BGP Table entry. (Describe how.)	
Determine if a particular BGP table entry is iBGP-learned. (Describe how.)	
Display one-line entries for all BGP table entries with a given prefix/length, plus any subnets inside that ranges.	
List possible default routes.	
List possible routes per prefix.	
List routes learned from one neighbor, which passed any inbound filters.	
List routes learned from one neighbor before any inbound filtering is applied.	
Display routes suppressed and added to the BGP table due to BGP route summarization (aggregation).	

Note: Some of the entries in this table may not have been specifically mentioned in this chapter but are listed in this table for review and reference.

Review all the Key Topics

Review the most important topics from inside the chapter, noted with the Key Topics icon in the outer margin of the page. Table 13-9 lists a reference of these key topics and the page numbers on which each is found.

Table 13-9 *Key Topics for Chapter 13*

Key Topic Element	Description	Page Number
List	Minimal eBGP configuration checklist	423
List	Required plus commonly used optional eBGP configuration command checklist	425
List	Rules for how a router chooses its BGP Router ID	425
Figure 13-2	Diagram of how the **router bgp** and **neighbor remote-as** commands on neighboring routers refer to ASNs	426
List	eBGP Configuration checklist including use of loopbacks as Update source and eBGP Multihop	427
Figure 13-3	Diagram of how the configuration matches on two BGP neighbors when using loopbacks	428
Table 13-2	BGP neighbor states	430
Table 13-3	BGP Messages	436
Table 13-4	Commonly used **show** commands to display eBGP-learned routes	441

Complete the Tables and Lists from Memory

Print a copy of Appendix D, "Memory Tables," (found on the CD), or at least the section for this chapter, and complete the tables and lists from memory. Appendix E, "Memory Tables Answer Key," also on the CD, includes completed tables and lists to check your work.

Define Key Terms

Define the following key terms from this chapter, and check your answers in the glossary.

eBGP multihop, Update Source (BGP), Established (BGP State), Open, Update, Active (BGP state), BGP Table

This chapter covers the following subjects:

Internal BGP Between Internet-Connected Routers: This section examines the need for iBGP peering inside an Enterprise, and both the required and the commonly used optional configuration settings.

Avoiding Routing Loops When Forwarding Toward the Internet: This section discusses the issues that occur when the Internet-connected routers may forward packets to each other through routers that do not use BGP, and how such a design requires some means to supply BGP-learned routes to the internal Enterprise routers.

Route Filtering and Clearing BGP Peers: This section gives a brief description of the options for filtering the contents of BGP Updates, along with explaining some operational issue related to the BGP **clear** command.

Internal BGP and BGP Route Filtering

Outbound routing is simple with a single Internet-connected router. The Enterprise IGP could flood a default route throughout the Enterprise funneling all Internet traffic toward the one Internet-connected router. That router could then choose the best route to any and all Internet destinations it learned with eBGP.

With two (or more) Internet-connected routers in a single Enterprise, additional issues arise, in particular, issues related to outbound routing. These issues require the use of BGP between Enterprise routers; in some cases, the design may require BGP even on Enterprise routers that do not peer with routers at the various ISPs. This chapter examines the scenarios in which using iBGP makes sense, and shows the related configuration and verification commands.

Chapter 14 begins focusing on the issues that occur when an Enterprise uses a pair of Internet-connected routers. In particular, the examples use the sample network shown in Figure 14-1. This design uses the same ISPs and ISP routers as in Chapter 13, "External BGP," with familiar IP address ranges but with a few different links. The design now also shows two of the core routers (actually Layer 3 switches) inside the Enterprise–routers that do not directly connect to any ISP. Figure 14-1 shows the design that will be referenced throughout the chapter.

Note: Figure 14-1 shows the IP addresses as just the last octet of the address; in these cases, the first three octets are 10.1.1.

The first section of this chapter focuses on concepts, configuration, and verification of the iBGP connection between E1 and E2 in the figure. The second major section of this chapter, "Avoiding Routing Loops when Forwarding Toward the Internet," examines the need for iBGP on routers internal to the Enterprise, such as Routers Core1 and Core2 in the figure. The final section of this chapter examines the process of filtering both iBGP and eBGP routing updates.

"Do I Know This Already?" Quiz

The "Do I Know This Already?" quiz allows you to assess if you should read the entire chapter. If you miss no more than one of these eight self-assessment questions, you might want to move ahead to the "Exam Preparation Tasks." Table 14-1 lists the major headings in this chapter and the "Do I Know This Already?" quiz questions covering the material in

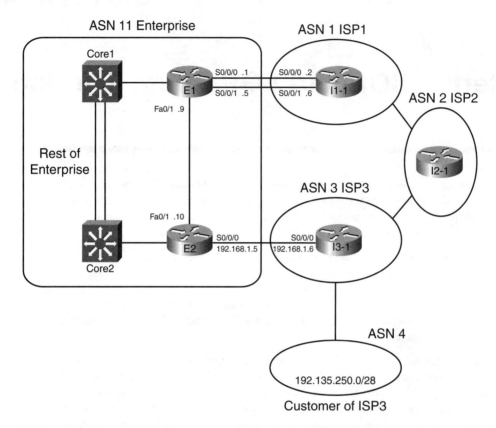

Figure 14-1 *Dual Internet Router Design Used Throughout Chapter 14*

those headings so that you can assess your knowledge of these specific areas. The answers to the "Do I Know This Already?" quiz appear in Appendix A.

Table 14-1 *"Do I Know This Already?" Foundation Topics Section-to-Question Mapping*

Foundations Topics Section	Questions
Internal BGP Between Internet-Connected Routers	1–4
BGP Synchronization and iBGP Meshes	5
Route Filtering and Clearing BGP Peers	6–8

1. R1 in ASN 1 with loopback1 address 1.1.1.1 needs to be configured with an iBGP connection to R2 with loopback2 IP address 2.2.2.2. The connection should use the loopbacks. Which of the following commands is required on R1?

   a. neighbor 1.1.1.1 remote-as 1

   b. neighbor 2.2.2.2 remote-as 2

    c. neighbor 2.2.2.2 update-source loopback1

    d. neighbor 2.2.2.2 ibgp-multihop 2

    e. neighbor 2.2.2.2 ibgp-mode

2. The following output occurred as a result of the **show ip bgp** command on Router R1. The output shows all BGP table entries on R1. How many iBGP-learned routes exist on this router?

```
*>i181.0.0.0/8        10.100.1.1           0     100     0 1 2 111 112 i
*>i182.0.0.0/8        10.100.1.1           0     100     0 1 2 222 i
*>i183.0.0.0/8        10.100.1.1           0     100     0 1 2 i
*>i184.0.0.0/8        10.100.1.1           0     100     0 1 2 i
*> 192.135.250.0/28 192.168.1.6                           0 3 4 i
```

    a. 1

    b. 2

    c. 3

    d. 4

    e. 5

3. The following output on Router R1 lists details of a BGP route for 190.1.0.0/16. Which of the following is true based on this output? (Choose 2)

```
R1# show ip bgp 190.1.0.0/16
BGP routing table entry for 190.1.0.0/16, version 121
Paths: (1 available, best #1, table Default-IP-Routing-Table)
  Advertised to update-groups:
      1
  1 2 3 4
    1.1.1.1 from 2.2.2.2 (3.3.3.3)
      Origin IGP, metric 0, localpref 100, valid, internal, best
```

    a. R1 has a **neighbor 1.1.1.1** command configured.

    b. R1 has a **neighbor 2.2.2.2** command configured.

    c. The **show ip bgp** command lists a line for 190.1.0.0/16 with both an > and an i on the left.

    d. R1 is in ASN 1.

4. A company uses Routers R1 and R2 to connect to ISP1 and ISP2, respectively, with Routers I1 and I2 used at the ISPs. R1 peers with I1 and R2; R2 peers with I2 and R1. Assuming as many default settings as possible are used on all four routers, which of the following is true about the next-hop IP address for routes R1 learns over its iBGP connection to R2?

    a. The next hop is I2's BGP RID.

    b. The next hop is I2's IP address used on the R2-I2 neighbor relationship.

    c. The next hop is R2's BGP RID.

    d. The next hop is R2's IP address used on the R1–R2 neighbor relationship.

5. A company uses Routers R1 and R2 to connect to ISP1 and ISP2, respectively, with Routers I1 and I2 used at the ISPs. R1 peers with I1 and R2; R2 peers with I2 and R1. R1 and R2 do not share a common subnet, relying on other routers internal to the Enterprise for IP connectivity between the two routers. Which of the following could be used to prevent potential routing loops in this design? (Choose 2)

    a. Using an iBGP mesh inside the Enterprise core

    b. Configuring default routes in the Enterprise pointing to both R1 and R2

    c. Redistributing BGP routes into the Enterprise IGP

    d. Tunneling the packets for the iBGP connection between R1 and R2

6. R1 is currently advertising prefixes 1.0.0.0/8, 2.0.0.0/8, and 3.0.0.0/8 over its eBGP connection to neighbor 2.2.2.2 (R2). An engineer configures a prefix list (fred) on R1 that permits only 2.0.0.0/8 and then enables the filter with the **neighbor R2 prefix-list fred out** command. Upon exiting configuration mode, the engineer uses some **show** commands on R1, but no other commands. Which of the following is true in this case?

    a. The **show ip bgp neighbor 2.2.2.2 received-routes** command lists the three original prefixes.

    b. The **show ip bgp neighbor 2.2.2.2 advertised-routes** command lists the three original prefixes.

    c. The **show ip bgp neighbor 2.2.2.2 routes** command lists the three original prefixes.

    d. The **show ip bgp neighbor 2.2.2.2 routes** command lists only 2.0.0.0/8.

    e. The **show ip bgp neighbor 2.2.2.2 advertised-routes** command lists only 2.0.0.0/8.

7. Which of the following three BGP filtering methods enabled with the **neighbor** command will filter BGP prefixes based on the prefix and prefix length? (Choose 3)

    a. A **neighbor distribute-list out** command, referencing a standard ACL

    b. A **neighbor prefix-list out** command

    c. A **neighbor filter-list out** command

    d. A **neighbor distribute-list out** command, referencing an extended ACL

    e. A **neighbor route-map out** command

8. Which of the following commands causes a router to bring down BGP neighbor relationships? (Choose 2)

    a. clear ip bgp *

    b. clear ip bgp 1.1.1.1

    c. clear ip bgp * soft

    d. clear ip bgp 1.1.1.1 out

Foundation Topics

Internal BGP Between Internet-Connected Routers

When an Enterprise uses more than one router to connect to the Internet, and those routers use BGP to exchange routing information with their ISPs, those same routers need to exchange BGP routes with each other as well. The BGP neighbor relationships occur inside that Enterprise—inside a single AS—making these routers iBGP peers.

This first major section of Chapter 14 begins with a look at why two Internet-connected routers need to have an iBGP neighbor relationship. Then, the text looks at various iBGP configuration and verification commands. Finally, discussion turns to a common issue that occurs with next-hop reachability between iBGP peers, with an examination of the options to overcome the problem.

Establishing the Need for iBGP with Two Internet-Connected Routers

Two Internet-connected routers in an Enterprise need to communicate BGP routes to each other because these routers may want to forward IP packets to the other Internet-connected router, which in turn would forward the packet into the Internet. With an iBGP peer connection, each Internet-connected router can learn routes from the other router and decide if that other router has a better route to reach some destinations in the Internet. Without that iBGP connection, the routers have no way to know if the other router has a better BGP path.

For example, consider Figure 14-2, which shows two such cases. The figure shows a topology that uses the following design options, as agreed upon with ISP1 and ISP3:

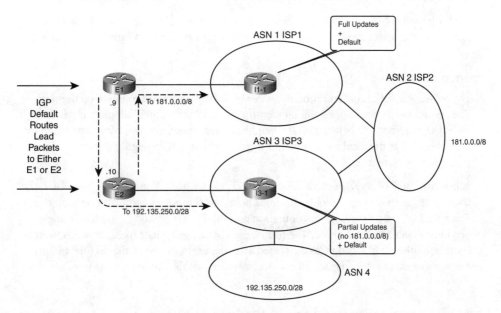

Figure 14-2   *Choosing the Best Routes from ASN 11 to 181.0.0.0/8 and 192.135.250.0/28*

- ISP1 sends full routing updates and a default route.

- ISP3 sends partial updates and a default route.

First, consider the eBGP routing updates, particularly for the two prefixes highlighted in the figure. Both ISP1 and ISP3 know routes for 181.0.0.0/8, but ISP3's agreement with the Enterprise is that ISP3 sends partial updates. This usually means ISP3 sends updates for prefixes in its own ASN plus prefixes for customers attached to its ASN, such as 192.135.250.0/28 in this case. ISP1, however, sends full updates, so E1 learns an eBGP route for both 181.0.0.0/8 and 192.135.250.0/28, but Router E2 only learns an eBGP route for 192.135.250.0/28.

Next, take a closer look at the routes for 181.0.0.0/8, both on E1 and E2. Only E1 learns an eBGP route for 181.0.0.0/8; E2 does not, because of ISP3's partial updates. If E1 and E2 did not use iBGP between each other, E2 would never know that E1 had a good route for 181.0.0.0/8. So, without an iBGP connection, packets destined to hosts in 181.0.0.0/8 if they arrived at E2 would be sent to ISP3 because of E2's default route learned from ISP3. However, if E1 and E2 form an iBGP neighbor relationship, E2 would know a route for 181.0.0.0/8 through E1 and would choose this route as its best route and would forward such packets to E1. Then E1 would forward the packets to ISP1, as shown in the figure.

Finally, take a closer look at the routes for 192.135.250.0/28 on both E1 and E2. If none of the ISPs changed the default PA settings for these routes, both E1 and E2 would choose the route through E2 as the better route, due to the shorter AS_Path length (two ASNs away through ISP3 versus four ASNs away through ISP1). Without iBGP between E1 and E2, E1 would not learn of this better route through E2, so any packets destined to 192.135.250.0/28 that reach E1 would be forwarded to ISP1. With iBGP, E1 would know of E2's better route and forward the packets toward E2, as shown in the figure.

For both prefixes, iBGP allowed both routers in the same ASN to reach the same conclusion about the better router through which to send packets for each Internet destination.

Configuring iBGP

The most basic iBGP configuration differs only slightly compared to eBGP configuration. The configuration does not explicitly identify an eBGP versus an iBGP peer. Instead, for iBGP, the neighbor's ASN listed on the **neighbor... remote-as** *neighbor-asn* command lists the same ASN as the local router's **router bgp** command. eBGP **neighbor remote-as** commands list a different ASN.

When two iBGP peers share a common physical link, such as E1 and E2 in Figure 14-2, the iBGP configuration simply requires a single **neighbor remote-as** command on each router. Example 14-1 shows the BGP configuration on both Router E1 and E2 with this single **neighbor** command highlighted. The rest of the configuration lists the commands used to configure other BGP settings (as described after the example). Note that Figure 14-1 in the introduction to this chapter shows more detail about the eBGP peers as well.

Example 14-1 *BGP Configuration on E1: Neighborships Configured*

```
! Configuration on router E1
router bgp 11
 no synchronization
 bgp log-neighbor-changes
 aggregate-address 128.107.0.0 255.255.224.0 summary-only
 redistribute ospf 1 route-map only-128-107
 neighbor 1.1.1.1 remote-as 1
 neighbor 1.1.1.1 password fred
 neighbor 1.1.1.1 ebgp-multihop 2
 neighbor 1.1.1.1 update-source Loopback1
 neighbor 10.1.1.10 remote-as 11
 no auto-summary
!
! Next, static routes so that the eBGP neighbor packets can reach
! I1-1's loopback interface address 1.1.1.1
ip route 1.1.1.1 255.255.255.255 Serial0/0/0
ip route 1.1.1.1 255.255.255.255 Serial0/0/1
!
ip prefix-list 128-107 seq 5 permit 128.107.0.0/19 le 32
!
route-map only-128-107 permit 10
 match ip address prefix-list 128-107 Neighbor 192.168.1.2 remote-as 3
```

```
! Now, on router E2
router bgp 11
 no synchronization
 bgp log-neighbor-changes
 network 128.107.32.0
 aggregate-address 128.107.0.0 255.255.224.0 summary-only
 redistribute ospf 1 route-map only-128-107
 neighbor 10.1.1.9 remote-as 11
 neighbor 192.168.1.6 remote-as 3
 neighbor 192.168.1.6 password barney
 no auto-summary
!
ip prefix-list 128-107 seq 5 permit 128.107.0.0/19 le 32
!
route-map only-128-107 permit 10
 match ip address prefix-list 128-107 Neighbor 192.168.1.2 remote-as 3
```

Only the four highlighted configuration commands are required for the E1-E2 iBGP peering. Both refer to the other router's IP address on the FastEthernet link between the two routers, and both refer to ASN 11. The two routers then realize the neighbor is an iBGP neighbor because the neighbor's ASN (11) matches the local router's ASN, as seen on the **router bgp 11** command.

The example also lists the rest of the BGP configuration. Focusing on Router E1, the configuration basically matches the configuration of Router E1 from the end of Chapter 13, except that E1 has only one eBGP peer (I1-1) in this case instead of two eBGP peers. The configuration includes the eBGP peer connection to I1-1, using loopback interfaces (1.1.1.1 on I1-1 and 11.11.11.11 on E1). The eBGP peers need to use eBGP multihop because of the use of the loopbacks, and they use MD5 authentication as well. Finally, the configuration shows the redistribution of the Enterprise's public address range of 128.107.0.0/19 by redistributing from OSPF and summarizing with the **aggregate-address** BGP subcommand.

E2's configuration lists the same basic parameters, but with a few differences. E2 does not use a loopback for its peer connection to I3-1, because only a single link exists between the two routers. As a result, E2 also does not need to use eBGP multihop.

Refocusing on the iBGP configuration, Example 14-1 uses the interface IP addresses of the links between Routers E1 and E2. However, often the Internet-connected routers in an Enterprise do not share a common subnet. For example, the two routers may be in separate buildings in a campus for the sake of redundancy. The two routers may actually be in different cities, or even different continents. In such cases, it makes sense to configure the iBGP peers using a loopback IP address for the TCP connection so that a single link failure does not cause the iBGP peer connection to fail. For example, in Figure 14-1, if the FastEthernet link between E1 and E2 fail, the iBGP connection defined in Example 14-1, which uses the interface IP addresses of that link, would fail even though a redundant IP path exists between E1 and E2.

The configuration to use loopback interfaces as the update source mirrors that same configuration for eBGP peers, except that iBGP peers do not need to configure the **neighbor... ebgp-multihop** command. One difference between iBGP and eBGP is that IOS uses the low TTL of 1 for eBGP connections by default but does not for iBGP connections. So, for iBGP connections, only the following steps are required to make two iBGP peers use a loopback interface:

Step 1.   Configure an IP address on a loopback interface on each router.

Step 2.   Configure each router to use the loopback IP address as the source IP address, for the neighborship with the other router, using the **neighbor... update-source** *interface-id* command.

Step 3.   Configure the BGP **neighbor** command on each router to refer to the other router's loopback IP address as the neighbor IP address in the **neighbor** *neighbor-ip* **remote-as** command.

Step 4.   Make sure each router has IP routes so that they can forward packets to the loopback interface IP address of the other router.

Example 14-2 shows an updated iBGP configuration for Routers E1 and E2 to migrate to use a loopback interface. In this case, E1 uses loopback IP address 10.100.1.1/32 and E2 uses 10.100.1.2/32. OSPF on each router has already been configured with a **network 10.0.0.0 0.255.255.255 area 0** command (not shown), which then causes OSPF to advertise routes to reach the respective loopback interface IP addresses.

Example 14-2 *iBGP Configuration to Use Loopbacks as the Update Source*

```
! Configuration on router E1
interface loopback 0
 ip address 10.100.1.1 255.255.255.255
router bgp 11
 neighbor 10.100.1.2 remote-as 11
 neighbor 10.100.1.2 update-source loopback0
! Configuration on router E2
interface loopback 1
 ip address 10.100.1.2 255.255.255.255
router bgp 11
 neighbor 10.100.1.1 remote-as 11
 neighbor 10.100.1.1 update-source loopback1
```

The highlighted portions of the output link the key values together for the E1's definition of its loopback as the update source and E2's reference of that same IP address on its **neighbor** command. The **neighbor 10.100.1.2 update-source loopback0** command on E1 tells E1 to look to interface loopback0 for its update source IP address. Loopback0's IP address on E1 has IP address 10.100.1.1. Then, E2's **neighbor** commands for Router E1 all refer to that same 10.100.1.1 IP address, meeting the requirement that the update source on one router matches the IP address listed on the other router's **neighbor** command.

Verifying iBGP

iBGP neighbors use the same messages and neighbor states as eBGP peers. As a result, the same commands in Chapter 13 for BGP neighbor verification can be used for iBGP peers. Example 14-3 shows a couple of examples, using Router E1's iBGP neighbor relationship with E2 (10.100.1.2) based on the configuration in Example 14-2.

Example 14-3 *Verifying iBGP Neighbors*

```
E1# show ip bgp summary
BGP router identifier 11.11.11.11, local AS number 11
BGP table version is 190, main routing table version 190
11 network entries using 1452 bytes of memory
14 path entries using 728 bytes of memory
11/7 BGP path/bestpath attribute entries using 1628 bytes of memory
7 BGP AS-PATH entries using 168 bytes of memory
0 BGP route-map cache entries using 0 bytes of memory
0 BGP filter-list cache entries using 0 bytes of memory
Bitfield cache entries: current 3 (at peak 4) using 96 bytes of memory
BGP using 4072 total bytes of memory
BGP activity 31/20 prefixes, 100/86 paths, scan interval 60 secs


Neighbor        V     AS MsgRcvd MsgSent   TblVer  InQ OutQ Up/Down   State/PfxRcd
1.1.1.1         4      1     339     344      190    0    0 00:28:41            7
10.100.1.2      4     11      92     132      190    0    0 01:02:04            3
```

```
E1# show ip bgp neighbors 10.100.1.2
BGP neighbor is 10.100.1.2, remote AS 11, internal link
  BGP version 4, remote router ID 10.100.1.2
  BGP state = Established, up for 01:02:10
  Last read 00:00:37, last write 00:00:59, hold time is 180, keepalive interval
is 60 seconds
  Neighbor capabilities:
    Route refresh: advertised and received(new)
    Address family IPv4 Unicast: advertised and received
! lines omitted for brevity
```

Key Topic

The **show ip bgp summary** command lists E1's two neighbors. As with eBGP peers, if the last column (the State/PfxRcd column) lists a number, then the neighbor has reached established state, and BGP Update messages can be sent. The output can distinguish between an iBGP or eBGP neighbor but only by comparing the local router's ASN (in the first line of output) to the ASN listed in each line at the bottom of the output.

The **show ip bgp neighbors 10.100.1.2** command lists many details specifically for the neighbor. In particular, it states that the neighbor is an iBGP neighbor with the phrase "internal link," as highlighted in the output.

Examining iBGP BGP Table Entries

To better understand the BGP table with two (or more) Internet-connected routers inside the same company, start with one prefix, and compare the BGP table entries on the two routers for that one prefix. By examining several such examples, you can appreciate more about the benefits and effects of these iBGP neighborships.

This section examines the BGP tables on Routers E1 and E2, focusing on the prefixes highlighted in Figure 14-2–namely, prefixes 181.0.0.0/8 and 192.135.250.0/28. To make reading the output of the **show** commands a little more obvious, Figure 14-3 collects some key pieces of information into a single figure. This figure shows the two BGP neighbor relationships on each router, showing the update source and neighbor IP address of each BGP neighbor relationship. It also lists the BGP RID of the routers.

Examples 14-4 and 14-5 compare the output on Routers E2 and E1 for prefix 181.0.0.0/8. Example 14-4 lists output on Router E2, listing the BGP table entries for prefix 181.0.0.0/8. Remember, the design calls for ISP3 to only send partial updates, so E2 has not received an eBGP route for 181.0.0.0/8 from I3-1. However, E1 has indeed learned of that prefix from I1-1 (ISP1), and E1 has already advertised prefix 181.0.0.0/8 to E2.

Note: Several BGP routes seen in the examples in this chapter originate in ASNs not shown in the figure. The figure shows enough of the topology to understand the first few ASNs in the AS_Path for these routes.

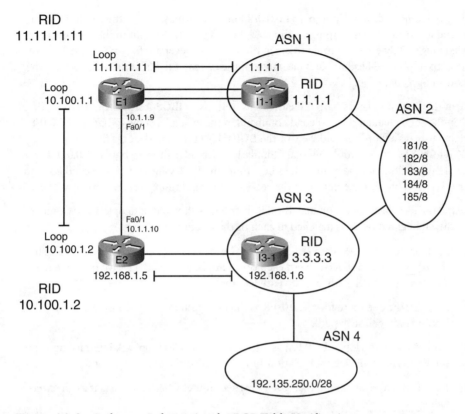

Figure 14-3 *Reference Information for BGP Table Verification*

Example 14-4 *Notations of iBGP Learned Routes in the* **show ip bgp** *Command*

```
E2# show ip bgp 181.0.0.0/8 longer-prefixes
BGP table version is 125, local router ID is 10.100.1.2
Status codes: s suppressed, d damped, h history, * valid, > best, i - internal,
              r RIB-failure, S Stale
Origin codes: i - IGP, e - EGP, ? - incomplete

   Network          Next Hop          Metric LocPrf Weight Path
*>i181.0.0.0/8      1.1.1.1              0    100      0 1 2 111 112 i

E2# show ip bgp 181.0.0.0/8
BGP routing table entry for 181.0.0.0/8, version 121
Paths: (1 available, best #1, table Default-IP-Routing-Table)
  Advertised to update-groups:
        1
  1 2 111 111
    1.1.1.1 from 10.100.1.1 (11.11.11.11)
      Origin IGP, metric 0, localpref 100, valid, internal, best
```

The first command, **show ip bgp 181.0.0.0/8 longer-prefixes**, lists output with the same general format as the **show ip bgp** command, but it limits the output to the prefixes in the listed range. Only one such route exists in this case. The legend information at the top of the output, plus the headings and meanings of the different fields, is the same as with the **show ip bgp** command.

Next, the first command's output denotes this route as an iBGP-learned route with code "i" in the third character. The second command in the example, **show ip bgp 181.0.0.0/8**, which displays a more detailed view of the BGP table entry and denotes this route as iBGP-learned with the word "internal." Similarly, the briefer **show ip bgp 181.0.0.0/8** command output lists this one route as E2's best route by displaying a > in the second column, whereas the more verbose output in the second command simply lists this route as "best."

Next, consider these same commands on Router E1, as shown in Example 14-5. Comparing the highlighted fields as matched in each of the examples:

■   Both list the same AS_Path (1, 2, 111, 112) because iBGP peers do not add ASNs to the AS_Path when advertising to each other. So, both E1 and E2 have the same perspective on the AS_Path and AS_Path length.

■   Both list the one route for 181.0.0.0/8 as the best path in part because each has learned only one such path.

■   Both list a Next_Hop (a BGP PA) as 1.1.1.1, which is I1-1's loopback interface used in the E1 to I1-1 BGP neighbor relationship (also called the BGP neighbor ID).

■   E2 lists the route as an internal (iBGP-learned) route, whereas E1 lists it as an external route.

Example 14-5   *Router E1's* **show** *Commands for BGP Routes for 181.0.0.0/8*

```
E1# show ip bgp 181.0.0.0/8 longer-prefixes
BGP table version is 190, local router ID is 11.11.11.11
Status codes: s suppressed, d damped, h history, * valid, > best, i - internal,
              r RIB-failure, S Stale
Origin codes: i - IGP, e - EGP, ? - incomplete


   Network          Next Hop            Metric LocPrf Weight Path
*> 181.0.0.0/8      1.1.1.1                            0 1 2 111 112 i

E1# show ip bgp 181.0.0.0/8
BGP routing table entry for 181.0.0.0/8, version 181
Paths: (1 available, best #1, table Default-IP-Routing-Table)
  Advertised to update-groups:
        2
  1 2 111 111, (received & used)
    1.1.1.1 from 1.1.1.1 (1.1.1.1)
      Origin IGP, localpref 100, valid, external, best
```

The output from these examples confirms that E1 learned the eBGP route for 181.0.0.0/8, advertised it to E2, and E2 chose to use that iBGP learned route as its best route to reach 181.0.0.0/8.

Next, consider the route for 192.135.250.0/28, a route learned in the full BGP updates from ISP1's Router I1-1 and in the partial BGP updates from ISP3's Router I3-1. After exchanging this route using their iBGP peering, both E1 and E2 should see two possible routes: an eBGP route learned from their one connected ISP and the iBGP route learned from each other. Again assuming that the ISPs have not made any attempt to set PA values to influence the best path choice, and knowing that neither E1 nor E2 have configured BGP to influence the best path choice, the route through E2 should be best because of the shorter AS_Path.

Example 14-6 shows the output of the **show ip bgp** command on both E1 and E2, again for comparison. Note that the command used in the examples, **show ip bgp 192.135.250.0/28 longer-prefixes**, is used because it lists only the routes for that prefix, rather than the full BGP table displayed by **show ip bgp**, but the format of the output is almost identical.

Example 14-6   *Comparing BGP Routes for 192.135.250.0/28 on E1 and E2*

```
! First, on E1:
E1# show ip bgp 192.135.250.0/28 longer-prefixes
BGP table version is 26, local router ID is 128.107.9.1
Status codes: s suppressed, d damped, h history, * valid, > best, i - internal,
              r RIB-failure, S Stale
Origin codes: i - IGP, e - EGP, ? - incomplete


   Network          Next Hop          Metric LocPrf Weight Path
*  192.135.250.0/28 1.1.1.1                            0 1 2 3 4 i
*>i                 192.168.1.6            0    100    0 3 4 i
! Next, on E2:
E2# show ip bgp 192.135.250.0/28 longer-prefixes
BGP table version is 25, local router ID is 10.100.1.2
Status codes: s suppressed, d damped, h history, * valid, > best, i - internal,
              r RIB-failure, S Stale
Origin codes: i - IGP, e - EGP, ? - incomplete


   Network          Next Hop          Metric LocPrf Weight Path
*> 192.135.250.0/28 192.168.1.6                       0 3 4 i
```

First, E1 lists two routes for this prefix, one external and one internal. The output identifies external routes by the absence of an "i" in the third character, whereas the output lists an "i" in the third character for internal routes. In this case, E1's internal route, with Next_Hop 192.168.1.6, is E1's best route, as was shown back in Figure 14-2. E1 chose this iBGP route because of the shorter AS_Path length; the AS_Path is highlighted at the end of each line.

E2's output in the second half of Example 14-6 lists only a single route–its eBGP route for 192.135.250.0/28. That only one route appears, rather than two, is a good example of the effect of two rules about how BGP operates:

■ Only advertise the best route in any BGP Update.

■ Do not advertise iBGP-learned routes to iBGP peers.

E2's output lists a single route for 192.135.250.0/28—its external route learned from ISP3—because E1 chooses not to advertise a route for 192.135.250.0/28 over the iBGP connection. If you look back at E1's output, E1's best route for this prefix is its internal route; so, if E1 were to advertise any route for this prefix to E2, E1 would advertise this internal route, because it is E1's best BGP route for that prefix. However, the second rule–do not advertise iBGP-learned routes to iBGP peers–prevents E1 from advertising this route back to E2. (Logically speaking, it makes no sense for E1 to tell E2 about a route when E2 is the router that originally advertised the route to E1 in the first place—a concept much like Split Horizon, although technically the term does not apply to BGP.) As a result, E2 lists a single route for 192.135.250.0/28.

Note that if the route for 192.135.250.0/28 through ISP3 failed, then E1 would start using the route through ISP1 as its best route. E1 would then advertise that best route to E2 that could then forward traffic through E1 for destinations in 192.135.250.0/28.

Understanding Next-Hop Reachability Issues with iBGP

With IGPs, the IP routes added to the IP routing table list a next-hop IP address. With few exceptions, the next-hop IP address exists in a connected subnet. For example, the E1-E2 iBGP connection uses loopback interfaces 10.100.1.1 (E1) and 10.100.1.2 (E2). E1's OSPF-learned route to reach 10.100.1.2 lists outgoing interface Fa0/1, next-hop 10.1.1.10–an address in the LAN subnet that connects E1 and E2. (See Figure 14-3 a few pages back for reference.)

Examples 14-5 and 14-6 also happened to show two examples of iBGP-learned routes and their next-hop addresses. The next-hop addresses were not in connected subnets; the next-hop addresses were not even IP addresses on a neighboring router. The two examples were as follows; again, it may be helpful to refer to the notations in Figure 14-3:

■ Example 14-4: E2's route for 181.0.0.0/8 lists next-hop address 1.1.1.1, a loopback interface IP address on I1-1.

■ Example 14-6: E1's route for 192.135.250.0/28 lists next-hop address 192.168.1.6, which is I3-1's interface IP address on the link between E2 and I3-1.

In fact, in the case of Example 14-4, the output of the **show ip bgp 181.0.0.0/8** command on E2 listed the phrase "1.1.1.1 from 10.100.1.1 (11.11.11.11)". This phrase lists the next hop (1.1.1.1) of the route, the neighbor from which the route was learned (10.100.1.1 or E1) and the neighbor's BGP RID (11.11.11.11, as listed in Figure 14-3).

BGP advertises these particular IP addresses as the next-hop IP addresses because of a default behavior for BGP. By default, when a router advertises a route using eBGP, the advertising router lists its own update-source IP address as the next-hop address of the route. In other words, the next-hop IP address is the IP address of the eBGP neighbor, as listed on the **neighbor remote-as** command. However, when advertising a route to an iBGP peer, the advertising router (by default) does not change the next-hop address. For example, when I1-1 advertises 181.0.0.0/8 to E1, because it is an eBGP connection, I1-1 sets its own IP address (1.1.1.1)–specifically the IP address I1-1 uses on its eBGP peer connection to E1—as the next-hop. When E1 advertises that same route to iBGP peer E2, E1 does not change the next-hop address of 1.1.1.1, so router E2's iBGP-learned route lists 1.1.1.1 as the next-hop address.

The IP routing process can use routes whose next-hop addresses are not in connected subnets as long as each router has an IP route that matches the next-hop IP address. So, engineers must understand these rules about how BGP sets the next-hop address and ensure each router can reach the next-hop address listed in the BGP routes. Two main options exist to ensure reachability to these next-hop addresses:

■   Create IP routes so that each router can reach these next-hop addresses that exist in other ASNs.

■   Change the default iBGP behavior with the **neighbor next-hop-self** command.

The text now examines each of these two options in more detail.

Ensuring Routes Exist to the Next-Hop Address

Routers can still forward packets using routes whose next-hop addresses are not in connected subnets. To do so, when forwarding packets, the router performs a recursive route table lookup. For example, for packets arriving at E2 with a destination of 181.0.0.1, the following would occur:

Step 1.   E2 would match the routing table for destination address 181.0.0.1, matching the route for 181.0.0.0/8, with next hop 1.1.1.1.

Step 2.   E2 would next look for its route matching destination 1.1.1.1–the next-hop of the first route–and forward the packet based on that route.

So, no matter the next-hop IP address listed in the routing table, as long as a working route exists to reach that next-hop IP address, the packet can be forwarded. Figure 14-4 shows the necessary routes in diagram form using two examples. E1 has a route to 192.135.250.0/28 with next hop 192.168.1.6; two arrowed lines show the required routes on Routers E1 and E2 for forwarding packets to this next-hop address. Similarly, the dashed lines also show the necessary routes on E2 and E1 for next-hop address 1.1.1.1, the next-hop IP address for their routes to reach 181.0.0.0/8.

Two easily implemented solutions exist to add routes for these nonconnected next-hop IP addresses: Either add static routes or use an IGP between the Enterprise and the ISPs for the sole purpose of advertising these next-hop addresses.

Using neighbor... next-hop-self to Change the Next-Hop Address

The second option for dealing with these nonconnected next-hop IP addresses changes the iBGP configuration so that a router changes the next-hop IP address on iBGP-advertised routes. This option simply requires the **neighbor** *neighbor-ip* **next-hop-self** com-

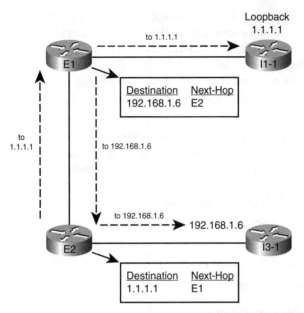

Key
Topic **Figure 14-4**   *Ensuring Routes Exist for Next-Hop Addresses in Other ASNs*

mand to be configured for the iBGP neighbor relationship. A router with this command configured advertises iBGP routes with its own update-source IP address as the next-hop IP address. And because the iBGP neighborship already relies on a working route for these update source IP addresses, if the neighborship is up, then IP routes already exist for these next-hop addresses.

For example, on the iBGP connection from E1 to E2, E1 would add the **neighbor 10.100.1.2 next-hop-self** command, and E2 would add the **neighbor 10.100.1.1 next-hop-self** command. When configured, E1 advertises iBGP routes with its update source IP address (10.100.1.1) as the next-hop address. E2 likewise advertises routes with a next-hop address of 10.100.1.2. Example 14-7 shows E2's BGP table, with a few such examples highlighted, after the addition of these two configuration commands on the respective routers.

Example 14-7   *Seeing the Effects of* **next-hop-self** *from Router E2*

```
E2#show ip bgp
BGP table version is 76, local router ID is 10.100.1.2
Status codes: s suppressed, d damped, h history, * valid, > best, i - internal,
              r RIB-failure, S Stale
Origin codes: i - IGP, e - EGP, ? - incomplete

   Network          Next Hop        Metric LocPrf Weight Path
*> 0.0.0.0          192.168.1.6          0             0 3 i
*  i               10.100.1.1           0    100      0 1 i
*  i128.107.0.0/19  10.100.1.1           0    100      0 i
*>                  0.0.0.0                        32768 i
```

```
 s> 128.107.1.0/24    10.1.1.77              2         32768 ?
 s> 128.107.2.0/24    10.1.1.77              2         32768 ?
 s> 128.107.3.0/24    10.1.1.77              2         32768 ?
 *>i181.0.0.0/8       10.100.1.1             0    100      0 1 2 111 112 i
 *>i182.0.0.0/8       10.100.1.1             0    100      0 1 2 222 i
 *>i183.0.0.0/8       10.100.1.1             0    100      0 1 2 i
 *>i184.0.0.0/8       10.100.1.1             0    100      0 1 2 i
 *>i185.0.0.0/8       10.100.1.1             0    100      0 1 2 i
 *> 192.135.250.0/28 192.168.1.6                            0 3 4 i
```

This completes the discussion of iBGP configuration and operation as related to the routers actually connected to the Internet. The next section continues the discussion of iBGP but with a focus on some particular issues with routing that may require iBGP on routers other than the Internet-connected routers.

Avoiding Routing Loops when Forwarding Toward the Internet

A typical Enterprise network design uses default routes inside the Enterprise, as advertised by the IGP, to draw all Internet traffic toward one or more Internet-connected routers. The Internet-connected routers then forward the traffic into the Internet.

However, as discussed in Chapter 12, "Internet Connectivity and BGP," in the section "Choosing One Path over Another Using BGP," routing loops can occur when the Internet-connected routers do not have a direct connection to each other. For example, if the Internet-connected routers sit on opposite sides of the country, the two routers may be separated by several other internal routers in the Enterprise because they do not have a direct link.

To show a simple example, the same Enterprise network design shown in all previous figures in this chapter can be changed slightly by just disabling the FastEthernet link between the two routers, as shown in Figure 14-5.

Figure 14-5 shows an example of the looping problem. The figure uses the same general criteria as the other examples in this chapter, so that E1's best route for 192.135.250.0/28 points to Router E2 as the next hop. E1's best route for the next-hop IP address for its route to 192.135.250.0/28–regardless of whether using **next-hop self** or not–sends the packet back toward the Enterprise core. However, some (or possibly all) of the Enterprise routers internal to the Enterprise, such as WAN1 and Core1, use a default that sends all packets toward Router E1. Per the steps in the figure, the following happens for a packet destined to 192.135.250.1:

Step 1.   WAN1 sends the packet using its default route to Core1.

Step 2.   Core1 sends the packet using its default route to E1.

Step 3.   E1 matches its BGP route for 192.135.250.0/28, with next hop E2 (10.100.1.2); the recursive lookup on E1 matches a route for 10.100.1.2 with next hop Core1, so E1 sends the packet back to Core1.

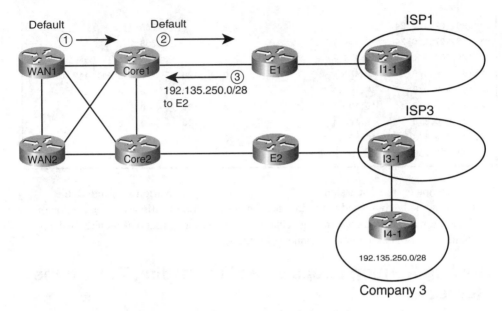

Figure 14-5 *Routing Loop for Packets Destined to 192.135.250.1*

At this point, Steps 2 and 3 repeat until the packet's TTL mechanism causes one of the routers to discard the packet.

The lack of knowledge about the best route for subnet 192.135.250.0/28, particularly on the routers internal to the Enterprise, causes this routing loop. To avoid this problem, internal routers, such as Core1 and Core2, need to know the best BGP routes. Two solutions exist to help these internal routers learn the routes:

■ Run BGP on at least some of the routers internal to the Enterprise (such as Core1 and Core2 in Figure 14-5).

■ Redistribute BGP routes into the IGP (not recommended).

Both solutions solve the problem by giving some of the internal routers the same best-path information already known to the Internet-connected routers—for example, if Core1 knew a route for 192.135.250.0/28, and that route caused the packets to go to Core2 next and then on to Router E2, the loop could be avoided. This section examines both solutions briefly.

Note: The BGP Confederations and BGP Route Reflector features, which are outside the scope of this book, can be used instead of a full mesh of iBGP peers.

Using an iBGP Mesh

To let the internal routers in the Enterprise learn the best BGP routes, one obvious solution is to just run BGP on these routers as well. The not so obvious part relates to the implementation choice of what routers need to be iBGP peers with each other. Based on the topology shown in Figure 14-5, at first glance, the temptation might be to run BGP on E1, E2, Core1, and Core2, but use iBGP peers as shown in Figure 14-6.

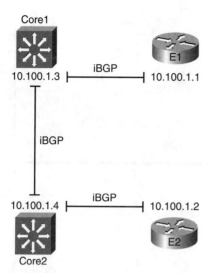

Core1
10.100.1.3

iBGP

E1
10.100.1.1

iBGP

iBGP

10.100.1.4

Core2

iBGP

10.100.1.2

E2

Figure 14-6 *Partial Mesh of iBGP Peers*

The iBGP peers shown in the figure actually match the kinds of IGP neighbor relationships you might expect to see with a similar design. With an IGP routing protocol, each router would learn routes and tell its neighbor so that all routers would learn all routes. Unfortunately, with this design, not all the routers learn all the routes because of the following feature of iBGP:

When a router learns routes from an iBGP peer, that router does not advertise the same routes to another iBGP peer.

Key Topic

Note: This particular iBGP behavior helps prevent BGP routing loops.

Because of this feature, to ensure that all four routers in ASN 11 learn the same BGP routes, a full mesh of iBGP peers must be created. By creating an iBGP peering between all routers inside ASN 11, they can all exchange routes directly and overcome the restriction. In this case, six such neighborships exist: one between each pair of routers.

The configuration itself does not require any new commands that have not already been explained in this book. However, for completeness, Example 14-8 shows the configuration on both E1 and Core1. Note that all configuration related to iBGP has been included, and the routers use the loopback interfaces shown in Figure 14-6.

Example 14-8 *iBGP Configuration for the Full Mesh Between E1, E2, Core, and Core2–E1 and Core1 Only*

```
! First, E1's configuration
router bgp 11
 neighbor 10.100.1.2 remote-as 11
 neighbor 10.100.1.2 update-source loopback0
```

```
 neighbor 10.100.1.2 next-hop-self
!
 neighbor 10.100.1.3 remote-as 11
 neighbor 10.100.1.3 update-source loopback0
 neighbor 10.100.1.3 next-hop-self
!
 neighbor 10.100.1.4 remote-as 11
 neighbor 10.100.1.4 update-source loopback0
 neighbor 10.100.1.4 next-hop-self
! Next, Core1's configuration
interface loopback0
 ip address 10.100.1.3 255.255.255.255
!
router bgp 11
 neighbor 10.100.1.1 remote-as 11
 neighbor 10.100.1.1 update-source loopback0
!
 neighbor 10.100.1.2 remote-as 11
 neighbor 10.100.1.2 update-source loopback0
!
 neighbor 10.100.1.4 remote-as 11
 neighbor 10.100.1.4 update-source loopback0
```

The configurations on E1 and Core1 mostly match. The commonly used commands simply define the neighbor's ASN (**neighbor... remote-as**) and list the local router's BGP update source interface (**neighbor... update-source**). However, note that the engineer also configured E1–the Internet-connected router–with the **neighbor... next-hop-self** command. In this case, the Internet-connected routers want to set their own update-source IP addresses as the next hop for any routes. However, the engineer purposefully chose not to use this command on the two internal routers (Core1 and Core2) because the eventual destination of these packets will be to make it to either E1 or E2 and then out to the Internet. By making the next-hop router for all iBGP-learned routes an address on one of the Internet-connected routers, the packets will be correctly forwarded.

For perspective, Example 14-9 shows Core1's BGP table after adding the configuration shown in Example 14-8, plus the equivalent configuration in E2 and Core2. Focusing on the routes for 181.0.0.0/8 and 192.135.250.0/28 again, note that E1 and E2 had already agreed that E1's route for 181.0.0.0/8 was best and that E2's route for 192.135.250.0/28 was best. As a result, Core1 knows only one route for each of these destinations, as shown in the example. Also, the next-hop addresses for each route refer to the correct of the two Internet-connected routers: 10.100.1.1 (E1) for the route to 181.0.0.0/8 and 10.100.1.2 (E2) for the route to 192.135.250.0/28.

Example 14-9 *BGP Table on Router Core1*

```
Core-1# show ip bgp
BGP table version is 10, local router ID is 10.100.1.3
Status codes: s suppressed, d damped, h history, * valid, > best, i - internal,
              r RIB-failure, S Stale
Origin codes: i - IGP, e - EGP, ? - incomplete

   Network          Next Hop        Metric LocPrf Weight Path
r i0.0.0.0          10.100.1.2           0    100      0 3 i
r>i                 10.100.1.1           0    100      0 1 i
* i128.107.0.0/19   10.100.1.2           0    100      0 i
*>i                 10.100.1.1           0    100      0 i
*>i181.0.0.0/8      10.100.1.1           0    100      0 1 2 111 112 i
*>i182.0.0.0/8      10.100.1.1           0    100      0 1 2 222 i
*>i183.0.0.0/8      10.100.1.1           0    100      0 1 2 i
*>i184.0.0.0/8      10.100.1.1           0    100      0 1 2 i
*>i185.0.0.0/8      10.100.1.1           0    100      0 1 2 i
*>i192.135.250.0/28 10.100.1.2           0    100      0 3 4 i
```

IGP Redistribution and BGP Synchronization

You can also redistribute BGP routes into the IGP to solve the routing loop problem. This solution prevents the routing loop by giving the internal Enterprise routers knowledge of the best exit point for each known Internet destination.

Although it solves the problem, particularly when just learning with lab gear at home, re-distribution of BGP routes into an IGP is generally not recommended. This redistribution requires a relatively large amount of memory and a relatively large amount of processing by the IGP with the much larger number of routes to process. Redistributing the number of routes in the full Internet BGP table could crash the IGP routing protocols.

Note: BGP consumes less memory and uses less CPU for a large number of routes as compared to the equivalent number of routes advertised by an IGP, particularly when compared to OSPF. So using the iBGP mesh may cause internal routers to learn all the same routes but without risk to the IGP.

Although not recommended, the idea of redistributing eBGP-learned Internet routes into the Enterprise IGP needs to be discussed as a backdrop to discuss a related BGP feature called *synchronization* or *sync*. The term refers to the idea that the iBGP-learned routes must be synchronized with IGP-learned routes for the same prefix before they can be used. In other words, if an iBGP-learned route is to be considered to be a usable route, then that same prefix must be in the IP routing table and learned using some IGP protocol such as EIGRP or OSPF. More formally, the synchronization features tells a BGP router the following:

Do not consider an iBGP-learned route as "best" unless the exact prefix was learned via an IGP and is currently in the IP routing table.

For companies, such as the Enterprise shown in Figure 14-5, the combination of redistributing eBGP routes into an IGP, and configuring synchronization on the two routers that run BGP (E1 and E2), prevents the routing loop shown in that figure. Again using prefix 192.135.250.0/28 as an example (see Figure 14-5), E2 again learned this prefix with eBGP. E1 learns this same prefix through its iBGP neighborship with E2, and both agree that E2's BGP route is best.

When E2 has successfully redistributed prefix 192.135.250.0/28 into the Enterprise's IGP (OSPF in the examples in this chapter), E1, with sync enabled, thinks like this:

> I see an IGP route for 192.135.250.0/28 in my IP routing table, so my iBGP route for that same prefix is safe to use.

However, if for some reason the redistribution does not result in an IGP route for 192.135.250.0/28, then E1 thinks as follows:

> I do not see an IGP-learned route for 192.135.250.0/28 in my IP routing table, so I will not consider the iBGP route through E2 to be usable.

In this second case, E1 uses its eBGP-learned route through I1-1, which defeats the routing loop caused at Step 3 of Figure 14-5.

Later IOS versions default to disable synchronization because most sites avoid redistributing routes from BGP into an IGP when using BGP for Internet routes, instead preferring iBGP meshes (or alternatives) to avoid these routing black holes. The setting is applied to the entire BGP process, with the **synchronization** command enabling synchronization and the **no synchronization** command (default) disabling it.

Note: The suggestion to avoid redistribution from BGP into an IGP generally applies to cases in which BGP is used to exchange Internet routes. However, BGP can be used for other purposes as well, including the implementation of Multiprotocol Label Switching (MPLS). Redistribution from BGP into an IGP when using BGP for MPLS is reasonable and commonly done.

Route Filtering and Clearing BGP Peers

BGP allows the filtering of BGP Update messages on any BGP router. The router can filter updates per neighbor for both inbound and outbound Updates on any BGP router.

After adding a new BGP filter to a router's configuration, the BGP neighbor relationships must be reset or cleared to cause the filter to take effect. The IOS BGP **clear** command tells the router specifically how to reset the neighborship. This section also examines the variations on the BGP **clear** command, including the more disruptive hard reset options and the less disruptive soft reset options.

BGP Filtering Overview

BGP filtering works generally like IGP filtering, particularly like EIGRP. Similar to EIGRP, BGP Updates can be filtered on any router, without the restrictions that exist for OSPF with various area design issues. The filtering can examine the prefix information about each router and both the prefix and prefix length information, in either direction (in or out), on any BGP router.

The biggest conceptual differences between BGP and IGP filtering relate to what BGP can match about a prefix to make a choice of whether to filter the route. EIGRP focuses on matching the prefix/length. BGP can also match the prefix/length but can also match the large set of BGP Path Attributes (PA). For example, a filter could compare a BGP route's AS_Path PA and check to see if the first ASN is 4, that at least three ASNs exist, and that the AS_Path does not end with 567. The matching of routes based on their PA settings has no equivalent with any of the IGPs.

The biggest configuration difference between BGP and IGP filtering, beside the details of matching BGP PAs, has to do with the fact that the filters must apply to specific neighbors with BGP. With EIGRP, the filters can be applied to all outbound updates from EIGRP, or all inbound updates into EIGRP, using a single EIGRP **distribute-list** command. BGP configuration does not allow filtering of all inbound or outbound updates. Instead, the BGP filtering configuration enables filters per neighbor (using a **neighbor** command), referencing the type of BGP filter, the filter number or name, and the direction (in or out). So, a router could literally use the same filter for all BGP Updates sent by a router, but the configuration would require a **neighbor** command for each neighbor that enabled the same filter.

The ROUTE course and exam focus on Enterprise routing topics, whereas BGP filtering—especially the more detailed filtering with BGP PAs—is used most frequently by ISP network engineers. As a result, CCNP ROUTE appears to cover BGP filtering very lightly, at least compared to IGP filtering.

This section does briefly describe the BGP filtering commands, showing a few samples just for perspective. Table 14-2 summarizes the BGP filtering options and commands, along with the fields in the BGP Update message that can be matched with each type. Following the table, the text shows an example of how an Enterprise might apply an outbound and inbound filter based on prefix/length.

Table 14-2 *BGP Filtering Tools*

BGP Subcommand	Commands Referenced by neighbor Command	What Can Be Matched
neighbor distribute-list (standard ACL)	**access-list, ip access-list**	Prefix, with WC mask
neighbor distribute-list (extended ACL)	**access-list, ip access-list**	Prefix and prefix length, with WC mask for each
neighbor prefix-list	**ip prefix-list**	Exact or "first *N*" bits of prefix, plus range of prefix lengths

Table 14-2 *BGP Filtering Tools*

BGP Subcommand	Commands Referenced by neighbor Command	What Can Be Matched
neighbor filter-list	ip as-path access-list	AS_PATH contents; all NLRI whose AS_PATHs are matched considered to be a match
neighbor route-map	route-map	Prefix, prefix length, AS_PATH, and/or any other PA matchable within a BGP route map

Inbound and Outbound BGP Filtering on Prefix/Length

Enterprises that choose to use BGP benefit from both learning routes from the connected ISPs and advertising the Enterprise's public prefix to the same ISPs. However, when the eBGP connections to the various ISPs come up, the Enterprise BGP routers advertise all the best routes in each router's BGP table over the eBGP connection. As a result, the ISPs could learn a best route that causes one ISP to send packets to the Enterprise, with the Enterprise then forwarding the packet out to another ISP. In such a case, the Enterprise AS would be acting as a *transit AS*; in other words, an AS through which packets go through, rather than being the destination or source of the packet.

The Enterprise engineers can, and probably should, make an effort to filter inappropriate routes sent to the ISP over the eBGP peer connections with the goal of preventing the Enterprise AS from becoming a transit AS. Additionally, the Enterprise can filter all private IP address ranges, in case any such address ranges get into the Enterprise BGP router's BGP table.

As an example, consider Figure 14-7, with the now-familiar prefix 192.135.250.0/28. As seen in earlier examples, both E1 and E2 learn this prefix, and both agree that the best route from ASN 11 (the Enterprise) toward this prefix is through E2. The figure shows the BGP routing updates as dashed lines.

E1's best route for 192.135.250.0/28 lists E2 as the next-hop router, so without any filtering in place, E1 then advertises prefix 192.135.250.0/28 to Router I1-1 in ISP1. I1-1 may be configured to filter this prefix. (In the examples throughout Chapters 13 and 14, router I1-1 was indeed configured to filter such prefixes.) However, if the Enterprise did not filter this prefix when advertising to ISP1, and ISP1 did not filter it, then ISP1 might choose the route through ASN 11 as its best route, making ASN 11 a transit AS for this prefix and consuming the Enterprise's Internet bandwidth.

Typically, an Enterprise would use outbound filtering on its eBGP neighborships, filtering all routes except for the known public prefixes that need to be advertised into the Internet. Example 14-10 shows just such a case, using the **neighbor prefix-list** command. The example also highlights a particularly useful command, **show ip bgp neighbor** *neighbor-id* **advertised-routes**, which shows the post-filter BGP update sent to the listed neighbor. The example shows the BGP Update before adding the filter, after adding the filter, and then after clearing the peer connection to router I1-1.

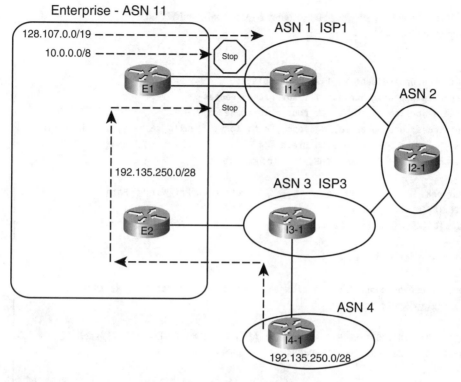

Figure 14-7   *The Need for Enterprise BGP Filtering*

Example 14-10   *Filtering to Allow Only Public Prefix 128.107.0.0/19 Outbound*

```
! The next command occurs before filtering is added.
E1# show ip bgp neighbor 1.1.1.1 advertised-routes
BGP table version is 16, local router ID is 128.107.9.1
Status codes: s suppressed, d damped, h history, * valid, > best, i - internal,
              r RIB-failure, S Stale
Origin codes: i - IGP, e - EGP, ? - incomplete

   Network           Next Hop          Metric LocPrf Weight Path
*>  128.107.0.0/19   0.0.0.0                           32768 i
*>i192.135.250.0/28  10.100.1.2             0    100       0 3 4 i


Total number of prefixes 2

! Next, the filtering is configured.
E1# configure terminal
Enter configuration commands, one per line.  End with CNTL/Z.

E1(config)#ip prefix-list only-public permit 128.107.0.0/19
E1(config)#router bgp 11
```

```
E1(config-router)#neighbor 1.1.1.1 prefix-list only-public out
E1(config-router)#^Z
E1#


! Next, the Update sent to I1-1 is displayed.
E1# show ip bgp neighbor 1.1.1.1 advertised-routes
BGP table version is 16, local router ID is 128.107.9.1
Status codes: s suppressed, d damped, h history, * valid, > best, i - internal,
              r RIB-failure, S Stale
Origin codes: i - IGP, e - EGP, ? - incomplete


   Network          Next Hop        Metric LocPrf Weight Path
*> 128.107.0.0/19   0.0.0.0                        32768 i
*>i192.135.250.0/28 10.100.1.2          0    100      0 3 4 i


Total number of prefixes 2

! Next, the peer connection is cleared, causing the filter to take effect.
E1# clear ip bgp 1.1.1.1
E1#
*Aug 17 20:19:51.763: %BGP-5-ADJCHANGE: neighbor 1.1.1.1 Down User reset
*Aug 17 20:19:52.763: %BGP-5-ADJCHANGE: neighbor 1.1.1.1 Up


! Finally, the Update is displayed with the filter now working.
E1# show ip bgp neighbor 1.1.1.1 advertised-routes
BGP table version is 31, local router ID is 128.107.9.1
Status codes: s suppressed, d damped, h history, * valid, > best, i - internal,
              r RIB-failure, S Stale
Origin codes: i - IGP, e - EGP, ? - incomplete


   Network          Next Hop        Metric LocPrf Weight Path
*> 128.107.0.0/19   0.0.0.0                        32768 i

Total number of prefixes 1
```

Example 14-10 shows an interesting progression if you just read through the example start to finish. To begin, the **show ip bgp 1.1.1.1 advertised-routes** command lists the routes that E1 has advertised to neighbor 1.1.1.1 (Router I1-1) in the past. Then, the configuration shows a prefix-list that matches only 128.107.0.0/19, with a permit action; all other prefixes will be denied by the implied deny all at the end of each prefix list. Then, the **neighbor 1.1.1.1 prefix-list only-public out** BGP subcommand tells BGP to apply the prefix list to filter outbound routes sent to I1-1.

The second part of the output shows an example of how BGP operates on a Cisco router, particularly how BGP requires that the neighbor be cleared before the newly configured filter takes effect. Router E1 has already advertised two prefixes to this neighbor:

128.107.0.0/19 and 192.135.250.0/28, as seen at the beginning of the example. To make the filtering action take effect, the router must be told to clear the neighborship with router I1-1. The **clear ip bgp 1.1.1.1** command tells E1 to perform a hard reset of that neighbor connection, which brings down the TCP connection, and removes all BGP table entries associated with that neighbor. The neighbor (I1-1, using address 1.1.1.1) also removes its BGP table entries associated with Router E1. After the neighborship recovers, E1 resends its BGP Update to Router I1-1–but this time with one less prefix, as noted at the end of the example with the output of the **show ip bgp neighbor 1.1.1.1 advertised-routes** command.

This same filtering action could have been performed with several other configuration options: using the **neighbor distribute-list** or **neighbor route-map** commands. The **neighbor distribute-list** command refers to an IP ACL, which tells IOS to filter routes based on matching the prefix (standard ACL) or prefix/length (extended ACL). The **neighbor route-map** command refers to a route-map that can use several matching options to filter routes, keeping routes matched with a route-map permit clause and filtering routes matched with a route-map deny clause. Example 14-11 shows two such options just for comparison's sake.

Example 14-11   *Alternatives to the Configuration in Example 14-10*

```
! First option - ACL 101 as a distribute-list
access-list 101 permit ip host 128.107.0.0 host 255.255.224.0
router bgp 11
 neighbor 1.1.1.1 distribute-list 101 out

! Second option: Same prefix list as Example 14-10, referenced by a route map
ip prefix-list only-public seq 5 permit 128.107.0.0/19
!
route-map only-public-rmap permit 10
 match ip address prefix-list only-public
!
router bgp 11
 neighbor 1.1.1.1 route-map only-public-rmap out
```

Clearing BGP Neighbors

As noted in Example 14-10 and the related explanations, IOS does not cause a newly configured BGP filter to take effect until the neighbor relationship is cleared. The neighborship can be cleared in several ways, including reloading the router and by administratively disabling and re-enabling the BGP neighborship using the **neighbor shutdown** and **no neighbor shutdown** configuration commands. However, IOS supports several options on the **clear ip bgp** exec command for the specific purpose of resetting BGP connections. This section examines the differences in these options.

Each variation on the **clear ip bgp...** command either performs a hard reset or soft reset of one or more BGP neighborships. When a hard reset occurs, the local router brings down the neighborship, brings down the underlying TCP connection, and removes all BGP table entries learned from that neighbor. Both the local and neighboring router reacts just like it does for any failed BGP neighborship by removing its BGP table entries learned over that neighborship. With a soft reset, the router does not bring down the BGP neighborship or the underlying TCP connection. However, the local router re-sends outgoing Updates, ad justed per the outbound filter and reprocesses incoming Updates per the inbound filter, which adjusts the BGP tables based on the then-current configuration.

Table 14-3 lists many of the variations on the **clear ip bgp** command, with a reference as to whether it uses hard or soft reset.

Table 14-3   *BGP* clear *Command Options*

Command	Hard or Soft	One or All Neighbors	Direction (in or out)
clear ip bgp *	Hard	all	both
clear ip bgp *neighbor-id*	Hard	one	both
clear ip bgp *neighbor-id* out	Soft	one	out
clear ip bgp *neighbor-id* soft out	Soft	one	out
clear ip bgp *neighbor-id* in	Soft	one	in
clear ip bgp *neighbor-id* soft in	Soft	one	in
clear ip bgp * soft	Soft	all	both
clear ip bgp *neighbor-id* soft	Soft	one	both

The commands listed in the table should be considered as pairs. In the first pair, both commands perform a hard reset. The first command uses a * instead of the neighbor IP address, causing a hard reset of all BGP neighbors, while the second command resets that particular neighbor.

The second pair of commands performs soft resets for a particular neighbor but only for outgoing updates, making these commands useful when a router changes its outbound BGP filters. Both commands do the same function; two such commands exist in part because of the history of the BGP implementation in the IOS. When issued, these two commands cause the router to reevaluate its existing BGP table and create a new BGP Update for that neighbor. The router builds that new Update based on the existing configuration, so any new or changed outbound filters affect the contents of the Update. The router sends the new BGP Update, and the neighboring router receives the new Update and adjusts its BGP table as a result.

The third pair of commands performs soft resets for a particular neighbor, but only for incoming updates, making these commands useful when a router changes its inbound BGP filters. However, unlike the two previous commands in the table, these two commands do have slightly different behavior and need a little more description.

The **clear ip bgp** *neighbor-id* **soft in** command, the older command of the two, works only if the configuration includes the **neighbor** *neighbor-id* **soft-reconfiguration inbound** BGP configuration command for this same neighbor. This configuration command causes the router to retain the received BGP Updates from that neighbor. This consumes extra memory on the router, but it gives the router a copy of the original pre-filter Update received from that neighbor. Using that information, the **clear ip bgp** *neighbor-id* **soft in** tells IOS to reapply the inbound filter to the cached received Update, updating the local router's BGP table.

The newer version of the **clear ip bgp** command, namely the **clear ip bgp** *neighbor-id* **in** command (without the **soft** keyword), removes the requirement for the **neighbor** *neighbor-id* **soft-reconfiguration inbound** configuration command. Instead, the router uses a newer BGP feature, the *route refresh* feature, which essentially allows a BGP router to ask its neighbor to re-send its full BGP Update. The **clear ip bgp** *neighbor-id* **in** command tells the local router to use route refresh feature to ask the neighbor to re-send its BGP Update, and then the local router can apply its current inbound BGP filters, updating its BGP table.

Example 14-12 shows a sample of how to confirm whether a router has the route refresh capability. In this case, both the local router (E1 from Figure 14-5) and the neighbor (I1-1 from Figure 14-5) have route refresh capability. As a result, E1 can perform a soft reset inbound without the need to consume the extra memory with the **neighbor soft-reconfiguration inbound** configuration command.

Example 14-12 *Alternatives to the Configuration in Example 14-10*

```
E1# show ip bgp neighbor 1.1.1.1
BGP neighbor is 1.1.1.1,  remote AS 1, external link
  BGP version 4, remote router ID 1.1.1.1
  BGP state = Established, up for 00:04:21
  Last read 00:00:20, last write 00:00:48, hold time is 180, keepalive interval
is 60 seconds
  Neighbor capabilities:
    Route refresh: advertised and received(new)
! Lines omitted for brevity
```

The last pair of commands in Table 14-3 do a soft reset both inbound and outbound at the same time, either for all neighbors (the * option) or for the single neighbor listed in the **clear** command.

Displaying the Results of BGP Filtering

To verify and troubleshoot filtering configurations, you need to see both the results before and after the filter. IOS provides several **show** commands that allow you to do exactly that. For instance, Example 14-10 shows several cases of the **show ip bgp neighbor advertised-routes** command that shows the post-filter BGP Updates sent by a router. Figure 14-8 summarizes these commands, showing how they can be used to display the pre- and post-filter BGP table contents. The figure shows Router E1, with inbound filtering

for Updates received from Router I3-1 and outbound filtering of BGP Updates sent to
Router I1-1.

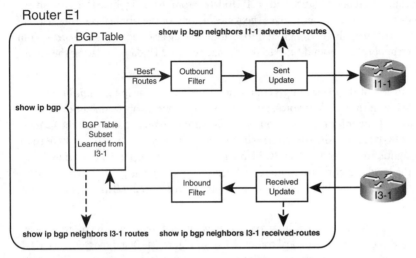

Router E1

**Key
Topic**   **Figure 14-8**   show *Commands Related to BGP Filtering*

The commands for displaying inbound updates, at the bottom of the figure, display output in the same format as the **show ip bgp** command. These commands restrict the contents to either exactly what has been received from that one neighbor (the **show ip bgp
neighbors received-routes** command) or what has been received and passed through any
inbound filter (the **show ip bgp neighbors routes** command).

One of the two commands helpful for the inbound direction, namely the **show ip bgp
neighbor received-routes** command, requires the configuration of the BGP subcommand
neighbor soft-reconfiguration inbound. As a result, to see the pre-filter BGP Update received from a neighbor, a router must configure this extra command, which causes the
router to use more memory to store the inbound Update. (A router cannot use the BGP
route refresh option just to get another copy of the incoming Update to list in this command.) However, when learning in a lab, the extra memory should not pose a problem.

Of the two commands for outbound filtering, the post-filter command is somewhat obvious, but there is no command to specifically display a pre-filter view of the BGP Update
sent to a neighbor. However, BGP advertises the best route for each prefix in the BGP
table, within certain restrictions. Those restrictions include that BGP will not advertise
iBGP-learned routes to an iBGP peer, and a router will not advertise the best route back to
the same neighbor that advertised that route. So, to see the pre-filter BGP table entries,
use the **show ip bgp** command, look for all the best routes, and then consider the additional rules. Use the **show ip bgp neighbor advertised-routes** to display the post-filter
BGP Update for a given neighbor.

Example 14-13 shows the output of these commands on E1. In this case, E1 has already
been configured with an inbound filter that filters inbound prefixes 184.0.0.0/8 and

185.0.0.0/8. (The filter configuration is not shown.) As a result, the post-filter output lists five prefixes, and the pre-filter output lists seven prefixes. The example also shows the error message when soft-reconfiguration is not configured.

Example 14-13   *Displaying the BGP Table Pre- and Post-Inbound Filter*

```
E1# show ip bgp neighbors 1.1.1.1 routes
BGP table version is 78, local router ID is 11.11.11.11
Status codes: s suppressed, d damped, h history, * valid, > best, i - internal,
              r RIB-failure, S Stale
Origin codes: i - IGP, e - EGP, ? - incomplete


   Network          Next Hop          Metric LocPrf Weight Path
*> 0.0.0.0          1.1.1.1                0          0 1 i
*> 181.0.0.0/8      1.1.1.1                           0 1 2 111 111 i
*> 182.0.0.0/8      1.1.1.1                           0 1 2 222 i
*> 183.0.0.0/8      1.1.1.1                           0 1 2 i
*  192.135.250.0/28 1.1.1.1                           0 1 2 3 4 i


Total number of prefixes 5
E1# show ip bgp neighbors 1.1.1.1 received-routes
% Inbound soft reconfiguration not enabled on 1.1.1.1


E1# configure terminal
Enter configuration commands, one per line.  End with CNTL/Z.
E1(config)#router bgp 11
E1(config-router)#neighbor 1.1.1.1 soft-reconfiguration inbound
E1(config-router)#^Z
E1#
E1# show ip bgp neighbors 1.1.1.1 received-routes
BGP table version is 78, local router ID is 11.11.11.11
Status codes: s suppressed, d damped, h history, * valid, > best, i - internal,
              r RIB-failure, S Stale
Origin codes: i - IGP, e - EGP, ? - incomplete


   Network          Next Hop          Metric LocPrf Weight Path
*> 0.0.0.0          1.1.1.1                0          0 1 i
*> 181.0.0.0/8      1.1.1.1                           0 1 2 111 111 i
*> 182.0.0.0/8      1.1.1.1                           0 1 2 222 i
*> 183.0.0.0/8      1.1.1.1                           0 1 2 i
*> 184.0.0.0/8      1.1.1.1                           0 1 2 i
*> 185.0.0.0/8      1.1.1.1                           0 1 2 i
*  192.135.250.0/28 1.1.1.1                           0 1 2 3 4 i


Total number of prefixes 7
```

Exam Preparation Tasks

Planning Practice

The CCNP ROUTE exam expects test takers to review design documents, create implementation plans, and create verification plans. This section provides some exercises that may help you to take a step back from the minute details of the topics in this chapter so that you can think about the same technical topics from the planning perspective.

For each planning practice table, simply complete the table. Note that any numbers in parentheses represent the number of options listed for each item in the solutions in Appendix F, "Completed Planning Practice Tables."

Design Review Table

Table 14-4 lists several design goals related to this chapter. If these design goals were listed in a design document, and you had to take that document and develop an implementation plan, what implementation options come to mind? You should write a general description; specific configuration commands are not required.

Table 14-4   *Design Review*

Design Goal	Possible Implementation Choices Covered in This Chapter
The plan shows a typical single-multihomed design with two routers connected to 2 ISPs. How will you ensure next-hop reachability? (2)	
The plan shows the same design as the last item. The two Enterprise Internet-connected routers do not have a direct link between each other. What methods discussed in this chapter can be used to prevent packet loops in the Enterprise core? (2)	
The plan shows the same design as the previous items but with public range 200.1.1.0/24 being the only public address range used by the Enterprise. How can the Enterprise avoid becoming a transit AS?	

Implementation Plan Peer Review Table

Table 14-5 shows a list of questions that others might ask, or that you might think about, during a peer review of another network engineer's implementation plan. Complete the table by answering the questions.

Table 14-5 *Notable Questions from This Chapter to Consider During an Implementation Plan Peer Review*

Question	Answers
The plan shows a typical single-multihomed design with two routers (R1 and R2) connected to 2 ISPs. Will R1 and R2 be BGP neighbors? Why?	
The plan shows the same design as the previous item. What configuration setting must be used to ensure the routers are iBGP rather than eBGP peers?	
The plan calls for filtering all prefixes except the 200.1.1.0/24 public address range when advertising the any eBGP peers. Which **neighbor** command options exist for filtering based on the prefix/length? (3)	

Create an Implementation Plan Table

This chapter does not focus on implementation or verification, but it did review one concept about static routes, as listed in Table 14-6.

Table 14-6 *Implementation Plan Configuration Memory Drill*

Feature	Configuration Commands/Notes
Configure an iBGP peer.	
Advertise the local router's Update source IP address as the next-hop address to iBGP peers.	
Configure an iBGP mesh with peers 1.1.1.1, 2.2.2.2, 3.3.3.3.	
Enable BGP synchronization.	
Configure filtering of routes sent to eBGP peer 9.9.9.9, using a prefix list to allow only 200.1.1.0/24.	
Configure filtering of routes sent to eBGP peer 9.9.9.9, using an ACL to allow only 200.1.1.0/24.	

Choosing Commands for a Verification Plan Table

To practice skills useful when creating your own verification plan, list in Table 14-7 all commands that supply the requested information. You may want to record your answers outside the book and set a goal to complete this table (and others like it) from memory during your final reviews before taking the exam.

Table 14-7 *Verification Plan Memory Drill*

Information Needed	Commands
Display a single-line neighbor status for all iBGP neighbors.	
Determine if a particular BGP table entry is iBGP-learned.	
Determine the next-hop IP address of an iBGP learned route.	
Identify the neighbor from which a BGP route was learned.	
Display one-line entries for all BGP table entries with a given prefix/length, plus any subnets inside that ranges.	
Display BGP routes learned from a neighbor, before being processed by an inbound filter.	
The same as the previous item, but after applying the inbound filter.	
Display BGP routes sent to a neighbor but after applying the outbound filter.	
Display whether a neighbor can perform BGP route refresh.	

Note: Some of the entries in this table may not have been specifically mentioned in this chapter but are listed in this table for review and reference.

Review all the Key Topics

Review the most important topics from inside the chapter, noted with the Key Topics icon in the outer margin of the page. Table 14-8 lists a reference of these key topics and the page numbers on which each is found.

Table 14-8   *Key Topics for Chapter 14*

Key Topic Element	Description	Page Number
List	Configuration steps for iBGP peer using a loopback as Update source.	462
Text	Paragraph about the default behavior of eBGP and iBGP peers regarding the setting of the next-hop IP address.	464
Figure 14-4	eBGP next-hop default behavior.	470
Text	iBGP behavior regarding not forwarding iBGP learned routes.	473
Figure 14-7	Preventing an Enterprise from becoming a Transit AS.	479
Table 14-3	Options on the BGP **clear** command.	482
Figure 14-8	Reference for BGP filtering verification commands.	484

Complete the Tables and Lists from Memory

Print a copy of Appendix D, "Memory Tables," (found on the CD), or at least the section for this chapter, and complete the tables and lists from memory. Appendix E, "Memory Tables Answer Key," also on the CD, includes completed tables and lists to check your work.

Definitions of Key Terms

Define the following key terms from this chapter, and check your answers in the glossary.

BGP synchronization, iBGP Mesh, Next-hop self, BGP soft reset, BGP hard reset

This chapter covers the following subjects:

BGP Path Attributes and Best Path Algorithm: This section describes the BGP Path Attributes that have an impact on the BGP best path algorithm–the algorithm BGP uses to choose the best BGP route for each destination prefix.

Influencing an Enterprise's Outbound Routes: This section shows how to use the BGP features that influence the BGP best path algorithm.

Influencing an Enterprise's Inbound Routes with MED: This section shows how to use the MultiExit Discriminator BGP feature that influences the BGP best path algorithm for inbound routes.

BGP Path Control

IGPs choose the best route based on some very straightforward concepts. RIP uses the least number of router hops between a router and the destination subnet. EIGRP uses a formula based on a combination of the constraining bandwidth and least delay. And OSPF uses lowest cost but with that cost typically calculated based on bandwidth.

BGP uses a much more detailed process to choose the best BGP route. BGP does not consider router hops, bandwidth, or delay when choosing the best route to reach each subnet. Instead, BGP defines several items to compare about the competing routes, in a particular order. Some of these comparisons use BGP features that can be set based on the router configuration, allowing network engineers to then influence which path BGP chooses as the best path.

BGP's broader set of tools allow much more flexibility when influencing the choice of best route. This BGP best path process also requires only simple comparisons by the router to choose the best route for a prefix. Although the detail of the BGP best path selection process requires more work to understand, that complexity gives engineers additional design and implementation options, and gives engineers many options to achieve their goals when working with the large interconnected networks that comprise the Internet.

Chapter 15 completes the BGP coverage in this book by examining the topic of BGP Path Control, including BGP Path Attributes (PA), the BGP Best Path selection process, along with a discussion of how to use four different features to influence the choice of best path by setting BGP PA values.

"Do I Know This Already?" Quiz

The "Do I Know This Already?" quiz allows you to assess if you should read the entire chapter. If you miss no more than one of these eight self-assessment questions, you might want to move ahead to the "Exam Preparation Tasks." Table 15-1 lists the major headings in this chapter and the "Do I Know This Already?" quiz questions covering the material in those headings so you can assess your knowledge of these specific areas. The answers to the "Do I Know This Already?" quiz appear in Appendix A.

Table 15-1 *"Do I Know This Already?" Foundation Topics Section-to-Question Mapping*

Foundations Topics Section	Questions
BGP Path Attributes and Best Path Algorithm	1–3

Table 15-1   *"Do I Know This Already?" Foundation Topics Section-to-Question Mapping*

Foundations Topics Section	Questions
Influencing an Enterprise's Outbound Routes	4–5
Influencing an Enterprise's Inbound Routes with MED	6

1. An engineer is preparing an implementation plan in which the configuration needs to influence BGP's choice of best path. Which of the following is least likely to be used by the configuration in this implementation plan?

   a.   Weight

   b.   Origin code

   c.   AS_Path

   d.   Local_Pref

2. Router R1 learns two routes with BGP for prefix 200.1.0.0/16. Comparing the two routes, route 1 has a longer AS_Path Length, bigger MED, bigger Weight, and smaller Local Preference. Which of the following is true about Router R1's choice of best path for this prefix?

   a.   Route 1 is the best route.

   b.   Route 2 is the best route.

   c.   The routes tie as best, but one will be picked to be placed in the routing table based on tiebreakers.

   d.   Neither route is considered best.

3. Router R1 learns two routes with BGP for prefix 200.1.0.0/16. Comparing the two routes, route 1 has a shorter AS_Path Length, smaller MED, the same Weight, and smaller Local Preference. Which of the following is true about Router R1's choice of best path for this prefix?

   a.   Route 1 is the best route.

   b.   Route 2 is the best route.

   c.   The routes tie as best, but one will be picked to be placed in the routing table based on tiebreakers.

   d.   Neither route is considered best.

4. An engineer has been told to create an implementation plan to influence the choice of best BGP route on a single router using the Weight feature. The sole Enterprise Internet-connected router, Ent1, has neighbor relationships with Routers ISP1 and ISP2, which reside inside two different ISPs. The goal is to prefer all routes learned from ISP1 over ISP2 using Weight. Which of the following answers lists a configuration step that would not be useful for achieving these goals? (Choose two.)

    a. Configuring the **neighbor weight** command on Ent1.

    b. Having the ISPs configure the **neighbor route-map out** command on ISP1 and ISP2, with the route map setting weight.

    c. Configuring the **set weight** command inside a route map on Router Ent1.

    d. Configuring a prefix list to match all class C networks.

5. An Enterprise router, Ent1, displays the following excerpt from the **show ip bgp** command. ENT1 has an eBGP connection to an ISP router with address 3.3.3.3 and an iBGP connection to a router with address 4.4.4.4. Which of the following is most likely to be true?

```
   Network            Next Hop           Metric LocPrf Weight Path
*>                    3.3.3.3                 0              0 1 1 1 1 2 18 i
```

    a. The Enterprise likely uses ASN 1.

    b. The neighboring ISP likely uses ASN 1.

    c. The route has been advertised through ASN 1 multiple times.

    d. Router Ent1 will add another ASN to the AS_Path before advertising this route to its iBGP peer (4.4.4.4).

6. The following line of output was gathered on Enterprise Router Ent1 using the command **show ip route**. Which of the following answers is most likely to be true, based on this output?

```
B        128.107.0.0 [20/10] via 11.11.11.11, 00:02:18
```

    a. This router has set the Weight of this route to 10.

    b. This router's BGP table lists this route as an iBGP route.

    c. This router's MED has been set to 10.

    d. This router's BGP table lists an AS_Path length of 10 for this route.

Foundation Topics

BGP Path Attributes and Best Path Algorithm

BGP supports a wide variety of Path Attributes. Some of the PAs exist solely to be used as part of the litany of options in the BGP best path algorithm, some have nothing to do with the BGP best path algorithm, and some impact the best path algorithm as well as being used for other purposes. For example, the Local Preference PA exists to give control to a single AS regarding their outbound routes from an AS-wide perspective. Conversely, the BGP Next_Hop PA provides BGP a place to list the next-hop IP address for a path, but it does not provide a useful means for engineers to set different values for the purpose of influencing the best path choice.

The term *BGP best path algorithm* refers to the process by which BGP on a single router examines the competing BGP paths (routes) in its BGP table, for a single prefix, choosing one route as the best route. The best path algorithm has many steps, but it eventually results in the choice of a single route for each prefix as that router's best BGP path.

The initial major section of this chapter examines the BGP PAs used by the BGP best path algorithm, the BGP best path algorithm itself, and some related topics.

BGP Path Attributes

BGP Path Attributes define facts about a particular route or path through a network. Each PA defines something different about the path, so to truly understand BGP PAs, you need to examine each PA. This section begins by reviewing a few PAs that should now be familiar to you if you have read the preceding BGP chapters, and then this section introduces a few new PAs.

BGP uses the *Autonomous System Path* (AS_Path) PA for several purposes, as already seen in Chapters 12, 13, and 14. This particular PA lists the ASNs in the end-to-end path. BGP uses the AS_Path PA as its primary loop-prevention tool: When an eBGP peer receives an Update, if its own ASN is already in the received AS_Path, then that route has already been advertised into the local ASN and should be ignored. In addition to loop prevention, the BGP best path algorithm uses the AS_Path PA to calculate the AS_Path length, which the algorithm considers as one of its many steps.

BGP also defines the *next-hop IP address* (Next_Hop) of a route as a PA. BGP may advertise one of several different IP addresses as a route's Next_Hop, depending on several factors. To support such features, BGP needs to list the Next_Hop IP address for each path (route), and BGP defines this concept in the Next_Hop PA. The best path algorithm includes a check related to the Next_Hop IP address of the route.

Table 15-2 lists these two PAs, plus a few more PAs, and a related BGP feature (Weight) that is not a PA but is used by Cisco BGP best path implementation. The table lists the PAs in the same order that they will be considered by the BGP best path algorithm. The table also describes each feature listed in the table, relative to whether it is most useful to influence outbound routes (away from the Enterprise) and inbound routes (toward the Enterprise).

Table 15-2   *BGP Path Attributes That Affect the BGP Best Path Algorithm*

PA	Description	Enterprise Route Direction (Typical)
NEXT_HOP	Lists the next-hop IP address used to reach a prefix.	N/A
Weight[1]	A numeric value, range 0 through $2^{16} - 1$, set by a router when receiving Updates, influencing that one router's route for a prefix. Not advertised to any BGP peers.	Outbound
Local Preference (LOCAL_PREF)	A numeric value, range 0 through $2^{32} - 1$, set and communicated throughout a single AS for the purpose of influencing the choice of best route for all routers in that AS.	Outbound
AS_PATH (length)	The number of ASNs in the AS_Path PA.	Outbound, Inbound
ORIGIN	Value implying the route was injected into BGP; I (IGP), E (EGP), or ? (incomplete information).	Outbound
Multi Exit Discriminator (MED)	Set and advertised by routers in one AS, impacting the BGP decision of routers in the other AS. Smaller is better.	Inbound

[1]Weight is not a BGP PA; it is a Cisco-proprietary feature that acts somewhat like a PA.

The short descriptions in the table can be helpful for review when doing your final preparation study, but the table does not hold enough information to truly appreciate how an engineer might use these PAs effectively. The second and third major sections of this chapter examine most of these PAs and how to influence the best path choice with each.

To find the current settings of the features in Table 15-2, you can use commands like **show ip bgp** and **show ip bgp** *prefix/length*. However, picking the values out of the clutter in the output of the **show ip bgp** command can be a challenge. Figure 15-1 shows a sample of this command's output and some notations on where to find the various PA settings.

The examples throughout this chapter include examples of these commands, along with the PA settings as changed by various route maps.

Overview of the BGP Best Path Algorithm

The BGP best path algorithm follows the steps shown in shorthand form in Table 15-3. The table lists steps 0 through 8, a short descriptive phrase, and a notation about the criteria for one value to be better than another.

R3 #show ip bgp
BGP table version is 12, local router ID is 3.3.3.3
Status codes: s suppressed, d damped, h history, * valid, > best, i - internal,
            r RIB-failure, S stale
Origin codes: i - IGP, e - EGP, ? - incomplete

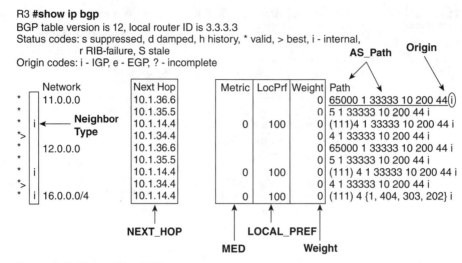

	Network		Next Hop		Metric	LocPrf	Weight	Path
*	11.0.0.0		10.1.36.6				0	65000 1 33333 10 200 44 (i)
*			10.1.35.5				0	5 1 33333 10 200 44 i
*	i ← **Neighbor Type**		10.1.14.4		0	100	0	(111)4 1 33333 10 200 44 i
*>			10.1.34.4				0	4 1 33333 10 200 44 i
*	12.0.0.0		10.1.36.6				0	65000 1 33333 10 200 44 i
*			10.1.35.5				0	5 1 33333 10 200 44 i
*	i		10.1.14.4		0	100	0	(111) 4 1 33333 10 200 44 i
*>			10.1.34.4				0	4 1 33333 10 200 44 i
*	i	16.0.0.0/4	10.1.14.4		0	100	0	(111) 4 {1, 404, 303, 202} i

AS_Path   Origin

NEXT_HOP   LOCAL_PREF

        MED   Weight

Comments: To Discover Other Details...
Neighbor Type: No Letter Means "EBGP"
IGP Metric: **show ip route** *next-hop-address*
RID: **show ip bgp** *nlri*

Key Topic

Figure 15-1 *Finding PA Settings in the Output of the* **show ip bgp** *Command*

Key Topic

Table 15-3 *BGP Decision Process Plus Mnemonic: N WLLA OMNI*

Step	Mnemonic Letter	Short Phrase	Which Is Better?
0	N	Next hop: reachable?	If no route to reach Next_Hop, router cannot use this route.
1	W	Weight	Bigger.
2	L	LOCAL_PREF	Bigger.
3	L	Locally injected routes	Locally injected is better than iBGP/eBGP learned.
4	A	AS_PATH length	Smaller.
5	O	ORIGIN	Prefer I over E. Prefer E over ?
6	M	MED	Smaller.
7	N	Neighbor Type	Prefer eBGP over iBGP.
8	I	IGP metric to Next_Hop	Smaller.

Note: The step numbering of the BGP best path steps does not exist in the BGP RFCs. The steps are numbered in this book for easier reference. Because the RFCs do not dictate a particular step numbering, other references likely use different step numbers; do not be concerned about memorizing the step numbers.

Starting with a Step 0 may seem odd, but it helps make an important point about the logic listed at this step. Some BGP best path references include the logic in this step as a best path step, and some just list this same information as a side note. Regardless, the step 0 concept is important. For step 0, a router looks at the BGP route and compares the Next_Hop IP address to the IP routing table.

If that router does not have a matching IP route for the BGP route's Next_Hop IP address, then that router will not know how to forward packets for that particular prefix, using that particular route. To avoid using such a route, at Step 0, the BGP best path algorithm removes such routes from consideration. BGP then uses the following eight steps, in order, until one best route is chosen for a given prefix.

If a router still did not determine a best route when finishing Step 8, the router takes several other small steps to break the tie. At this point, the competing routes are considered to be just as good as each other. However, unlike IGPs, BGP needs to choose one and only one route as best, in part because BGP advertises only the best routes to its neighbors. In such cases, BGP breaks the tie with these additional steps, which would be considered Steps 9-11:

Step 9. Oldest (longest-known) eBGP route

Step 10. Lowest neighbor BGP RID

Step 11. Lowest neighbor IP address

Taking a more detailed view of the entire best path algorithm, BGP begins by choosing the oldest known route for a given prefix as the best route. It then takes the next longest-known route for that same prefix and compares the two routes using the best path algorithm. The router eventually chooses one of the two BGP routes as the best path (route). If another route exists for the same prefix, the router repeats the process, using the winner of the previous comparisons and the new route, choosing one of those as the better route. The process continues until all routes have been considered, with one route being listed as best in the BGP table.

For example, if Router R1 were considering two routes for prefix 181.0.0.0/8, it would first make sure that both routes had reachable Next_Hop IP addresses. The router would then compare the weight settings, choosing the route with the bigger weight. If they tied on weight, the router would prefer the route with a bigger Local_Pref. If again a tie, the router would prefer the one route that was injected into BGP locally (using the **network** command or using route redistribution). If neither or both routes were locally injected, the router moves on to AS_Path length, and so on, until the router chooses one of the two as the better route.

As soon as one of the steps determines a best route, the comparison of those two routes stops.

Perspectives on the Core 8 Best Path Steps

Some of the BGP best path steps purposefully give the engineer a tool for influencing the choice of best path, whereas other steps have a different purpose, often simply being a side effect of some BGP feature. So, when an engineer starts building a BGP implementation plan, only a subset of the core 8 BGP best path steps need be considered, as follows:

- Weight (Step 1)

- Local_Pref (Step 2)

- AS_Path Length (Step 4)

- MED (often called metric) (Step 6)

Because the ROUTE exam focuses on the more practical aspects of BGP for Enterprises, it gives much more attention to these four features and less attention to the other BGP best path steps. This chapter describes each of these four features to some depth in the context of best path selection. However, before focusing on these four items, it can be helpful to see a small glimpse into the meaning of the other steps, which can be helpful as you work to memorize the steps in the BGP best path algorithm.

Step 3 compares the source from which the routes were added to the BGP table. When the BGP best path algorithm compares two routes at this step, if one were injected into BGP locally, and the other were not (it was learned from a BGP peer), the router chooses the route that was injected locally. Chapter 13, "External BGP," section "Injecting Routes into BGP for Advertisement to the ISPs," describes the two ways to locally inject these routes, the **network** command and redistribution from an IGP.

Step 5 refers to the BGP Origin PA. The Origin PA attempts to identify the source from *outside BGP* from which the route was injected into BGP. The three Origin code values are

- **I:** Injected from an IGP (using a **network** command)

- **E:** Injected from Exterior Gateway Protocol (EGP)

- **?:** Undetermined

Although the original intent of the Origin PA is to identify the source from which BGP learned the route, routers can also set the Origin PA as part of a strategy to influence the BGP best path.

Step 7 refers to the Neighbor type: iBGP or eBGP. Remembering that BGP compares two routes at a time, if one is learned with eBGP, and the other with iBGP, the router chooses the eBGP route as best. Using this feature to influence the best path choice would be difficult, because the ASN in which a router resides is fixed by the BGP design.

Finally, Step 8 refers to the IGP metric to the Next_Hop address. At this step, the router compares the metrics of the IP routes for each Next_Hop IP address and chooses the BGP route with the lower IGP metric to its Next_Hop. (If an IGP-learned route is not used, for example, if both use connected routes, BGP considers the metrics to tie.) It is conceivable that an engineer might tune the IGP to manipulate BGP's best path choice, but this step is so far into the algorithm that the earlier and more flexible settings would be much better options.

Memorization Tips for BGP Best Path

This short section suggests a mnemonic tool to help you memorize Steps 0 through 8 of the BGP best path algorithm. Feel free to skim this section for now, or ignore it entirely–there is no requirement that you memorize the best path algorithm using the mnemonics in this section. (However, you may want to at least review upcoming Figure 15-2, which gives a good visual reference for some of the information summarized in Table 15-3.) But you should plan on memorizing the list at some point before the exam, even if you ignore the mnemonic device.

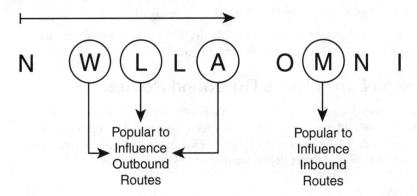

Figure 15-2 *BGP Best Path Mnemonics*

First, if you refer back to the BGP best path algorithm as listed in table 15-3, you see that the second column lists a single-letter mnemonic letter. These letters match the first letter of the description in the third column of that table. Then, take these initial letters and group them as follows:

- N

- WLLA

- OMNI

The N is listed separately because it represents the "is the next-hop reachable" logic of Step 0 and is somewhat separate from the other steps.

The mnemonic groups the eight main steps as two sets of four letters for a couple of reasons. Both sets can be pronounced, even if they don't spell words. It should be easier to memorize as two sets of four. And maybe most important, the first set of four letters, representing Steps 1 through 4, include all the features that engineers typically use to influence outbound routes from the Enterprise:

- **WLLA:** Refers to the three steps that an engineer might use to influence outbound routes: Weight, Local_Pref, and AS_Path length. (Additionally, the second L, in WLLA for Step 3, represents the "Locally injected routes" choice.)

■ **OMNI:** As listed in Table 15-3, the letters represent Origin (I or ?), MED, neighbor type (eBGP over iBGP), and IGP metric to Next-hop.

So, if you can memorize N WLLA OMNI, by the time you've read this chapter you can probably pick out which of those correlate to the four bigger topics later in this chapter: Weight, Local_Pref, AS_Path length, and MED. Hopefully with a little more study, you can memorize the rest of the list.

Figure 15-2 shows the mnemonic letters in graphical form just as another aid in memorizing the steps. It also shows a reminder of which features are most likely to be used to influence outbound routes from the Enterprise, and the one setting (MED) most likely to be used to influence inbound routes into the Enterprise.

The rest of this chapter focuses on a deeper explanation of the four best path steps that engineers typically use to influence the choice of best path.

Influencing an Enterprise's Outbound Routes

This section examines three different features that can influence the outbound routes from an Enterprise: Weight, the Local_Pref PA, and AS_Path length. The topics are listed in the order used by the BGP best path algorithm (Steps 1, 2, and 4). It also introduces the concept of a Routing Table Manager (RTM) function on a router.

Influencing BGP Weight

A Cisco router can use the BGP Weight, on that single router, to influence that one router's choice of outbound route. To do so, when a router receives a BGP Update, that router can set the Weight either selectively, per route, using a route map, or for all routes learned from a single neighbor. The router's best path algorithm then examines the Weight of competing routes, choosing the route with the bigger Weight.

The Cisco-proprietary Weight settings configured on a single router can influence only that one router because the Weight cannot be communicated to other neighboring BGP routers. So, to use the Weight, a router must be configured to examine incoming Updates to set the Weight. The Weight cannot simply be learned in a received Update because that Update message does not support a field in which to communicate the Weight setting.

Table 15-4 summarizes some of the key facts about BGP administrative Weight. Following the table, the text first explains a sample internetwork and its existing configuration, a configuration that begins with configurations that do not set any values that influence the choice of best paths. The next section shows how to set the Weight using the **neighbor route-map in** command, which allows a router to set different Weights for different routes. The second example shows how to set the Weight for all routes learned from a neighbor, using the **neighbor weight** command.

Table 15-4   *Key Features of Administrative Weight*

Feature	Description
Is it a PA?	No; Cisco proprietary feature

Table 15-4 *Key Features of Administrative Weight*

Feature	Description
Purpose	Identifies a single router's best route
Scope	Set on inbound route Updates; influences only that one router's choice
Range	0 through 65,535 ($2^{16} - 1$)
Which is best?	Bigger values are better
Default	0 for learned routes, 32,768 for locally injected routes
Defining a new default	Not supported
Configuration	**neighbor route-map** (per prefix)
	neighbor weight (all routes learned from this neighbor)

Note: For those of you memorizing using the N WLLA OMNI mnemonic, Weight is the W in WLLA.

Sample Internetwork Used in the Weight Examples

Figure 15-3 shows a sample Internetwork used to demonstrate setting the Weight. The figure shows a single Enterprise and a single Enterprise router. The following design requirements have already been met by the configuration in Router E1 and in the ISP routers:

- E1 and I1-1 uses loopback IP addresses (11.11.11.11 and 1.1.1.1) for their neighborship.

- E1 and I3-1 use interface IP addresses for their neighborship.

- None of the routers have attempted to change any settings that can impact the choice of best path.

Next, to have some routes to manipulate with the upcoming examples, the ISP routers each advertise BGP routes for the same five prefixes. Figure 15-4 shows five such prefixes that both ISPs advertise to E1.

Just to get a little deeper understanding of the best path algorithm before getting into the Weight configuration, consider the original configuration state of the sample internetwork, with no attempt to influence E1's choice of best path. The best path for four of the five prefixes will be obvious. Prefixes 181.0.0.0/8 and 182.0.0.0/8 have a shorter AS_Path through ISP1, and 184.0.0.0/8 and 185.0.0.08 have a shorter AS_Path through ISP3. Only 183.0.0.0/8 is in question because its AS_Path length for the competing routes is equal. Example 15-1 shows the output of the **show ip bgp 176.0.0.0/4 longer-prefixes** command, which lists all five of the BGP prefixes listed in Figure 15-4, confirming the results. (Prefix 176.0.0.0/4 implies a range of values whose first octets are in the range 176 through 191, which includes the routes listed in Example 15-1.)

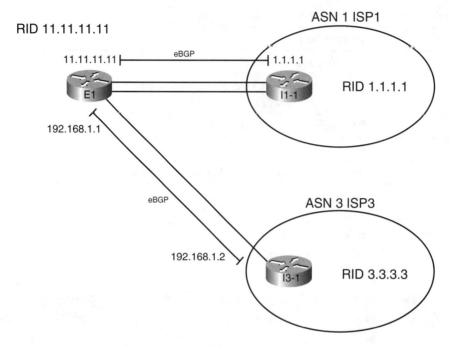

Figure 15-3   *Sample Internetwork for BGP Weight Examples*

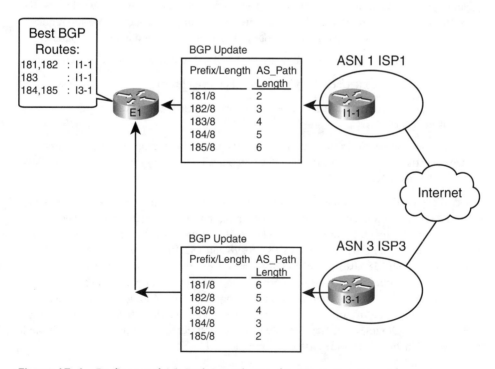

Figure 15-4   *Prefixes and AS_Path Lengths Used in Upcoming Examples*

Example 15-1 *BGP Configuration on E1: Neighborships Configured*

```
E1# show ip bgp 176.0.0.0/4 longer-prefixes
BGP table version is 41, local router ID is 128.107.9.1
Status codes: s suppressed, d damped, h history, * valid, > best, i - internal,
              r RIB-failure, S Stale
Origin codes: i - IGP, e - EGP, ? - incomplete

   Network          Next Hop            Metric LocPrf Weight Path
*  181.0.0.0/8      192.168.1.2              0             0 3 2 50 51 52 1811 i
*>                  1.1.1.1                  0             0 1 1811 i
*  182.0.0.0/8      192.168.1.2              0             0 3 2 50 51 1822 i
*>                  1.1.1.1                  0             0 1 2 1822 i
*  183.0.0.0/8      192.168.1.2              0             0 3 2 50 1833 i
*>                  1.1.1.1                  0             0 1 2 50 1833 i
*> 184.0.0.0/8      192.168.1.2              0             0 3 2 1844 i
*                   1.1.1.1                  0             0 1 2 50 51 1844 i
*> 185.0.0.0/8      192.168.1.2              0             0 3 1855 i
*                   1.1.1.1                  0             0 1 2 50 51 52 1855 i
```

First, consider the best path algorithm on Router E1 for 181.0.0.0/8. E1 knows two BGP routes for 181.0.0.0/8, as expected. The one listed as the best path has 1.1.1.1 (I1-1) as Next_Hop. The following list outlines the best path logic:

Step 0.   The Next_Hop of each is reachable. (Otherwise the neighbors would not be up.)

Step 1.   The Weight ties (both 0).

Step 2.   The Local_Pref ties (unset, so no value is listed; defaults to 100).

Step 3.   Neither route is locally injected; both are learned using BGP, so neither is better at this step.

Step 4.   AS_Path length is shorter for the route through I1-1 (1.1.1.1).

Next, consider the example of the route to 183.0.0.0/8. E1 currently lists the path through I1-1 (1.1.1.1) as best, but the best path decision actually falls all the way to Step 9. For completeness' sake, E1's best path logic runs as follows:

Step 0.   The Next_Hop of each is reachable (otherwise the neighbors would not be up)

Step 1.   The Weight ties (both 0).

Step 2.   The Local_Pref ties (unset, defaults to 100).

Step 3.   Neither route is locally injected.

Step 4.   AS_Path length is 4 in both cases.

Step 5.   Both Origin codes are i.

Step 6.   MED, listed under the Metric column, ties (0).

Step 7.   Neighbor type for each neighbor is eBGP.

Step 8.   IGP metric does not apply, because neither uses IGP routes. (The routes from E1 to 1.1.1.1 are static routes.)

Step 9.   The route learned from 1.1.1.1 is the oldest route.

Although you may believe the claims at Step 9, the output in Example 15-1 does not explicitly state that fact. However, when IOS lists output in the variations of the **show ip bgp** command, the oldest route for each prefix is listed last, and the newest (most recently learned) is listed first. Example 15-2 confirms this logic, and confirming how Step 9 works in this case. Example 15-2 clears peer 1.1.1.1 (I1-1), making E1's route through 192.168.1.2 (I3-1) become the oldest known route for 183.0.0.0/8:

Example 15-2   *Clearing Neighbors to Force a* New Route

```
E1# clear ip bgp 1.1.1.1
E1#
*Aug 24 11:30:41.775: %BGP-5-ADJCHANGE: neighbor 1.1.1.1 Down User reset
*Aug 24 11:30:43.231: %BGP-5-ADJCHANGE: neighbor 1.1.1.1 Up
E1# show ip bgp 176.0.0.0/4 longer-prefixes
BGP table version is 47, local router ID is 128.107.9.1
Status codes: s suppressed, d damped, h history, * valid, > best, i - internal,
              r RIB-failure, S Stale
Origin codes: i - IGP, e - EGP, ? - incomplete

   Network          Next Hop            Metric LocPrf Weight Path
*> 181.0.0.0/8      1.1.1.1                  0             0 1 1811 i
*                   192.168.1.2              0             0 3 2 50 51 52 1811 i
*> 182.0.0.0/8      1.1.1.1                  0             0 1 2 1822 i
*                   192.168.1.2              0             0 3 2 50 51 1822 i
*  183.0.0.0/8      1.1.1.1                  0             0 1 2 50 1833 i
*>                  192.168.1.2              0             0 3 2 50 1833 i
*  184.0.0.0/8      1.1.1.1                  0             0 1 2 50 51 1844 i
*>                  192.168.1.2              0             0 3 2 1844 i
*  185.0.0.0/8      1.1.1.1                  0             0 1 2 50 51 52 1855 i
*>                  192.168.1.2              0             0 3 1855 i
```

After the hard reset of peer 1.1.1.1, E1's oldest-known route for 183.0.0.0/8 is the route through 192.168.1.2, listed second (last). That E1 now chooses this route as best is another confirmation that E1's best path decision fell to Step 9.

Setting the BGP Administrative Weight Using a Route Map

The **neighbor** *neighbor-ip* **route-map in** BGP subcommand tells a router to apply the route map to all BGP Updates received from the listed neighbor. Such route maps *always attempt to filter routes*. The router allows routes first matched in a permit clause and filters (discards) routes first matched with a deny clause.

BGP route maps can also be used to change the PAs of routes by using the **set** command. For example, a router could use a **neighbor 1.1.1.1 route-map fred in** command. The route map could contain permit clauses that cause some routes to not be filtered. In those same route map clauses, the inclusion of commands such as **set weight 100** and **set local-preference 200** can be used to set items such as the Weight or Local_Pref of a route. (Although you can configure a **set** command in a route map deny clause, the set has no effect because the deny clause filters the route.)

Example 15-3 shows a sample configuration that sets the Weight for prefix 181.0.0.0/8 as learned from I3-1 (neighbor ID 192.168.1.2). As shown in Examples 15-1, E1's original best route for this prefix is through I1-1 (1.1.1.1), due to the shorter AS_Path length at Step 4 of the best path algorithm. By setting the Weight higher on the route learned from I3-1, E1 now chooses the route through I3-1.

Example 15-3 *Setting the Weight to 50 for 181/8, as Learned from I3-1*

```
E1# conf t
Enter configuration commands, one per line.  End with CNTL/Z.
E1(config)# ip prefix-list match-181 permit 181.0.0.0/8
E1(config)# route-map set-weight-50 permit 10
E1(config-route-map)# match ip address prefix-list match-181
E1(config-route-map)# set weight 50
E1(config-route-map)# route-map set-weight-50 permit 20
E1(config-route-map)# router bgp 11
E1(config-router)# neighbor 192.168.1.2 route-map set-weight-50 in
E1(config-router)# ^Z
E1#
E1# clear ip bgp 192.168.1.2 soft
E1# show ip bgp 176.0.0.0/4 longer-prefixes
BGP table version is 48, local router ID is 128.107.9.1
Status codes: s suppressed, d damped, h history, * valid, > best, i - internal,
              r RIB-failure, S Stale
Origin codes: i - IGP, e - EGP, ? - incomplete

   Network          Next Hop            Metric LocPrf Weight Path
*  181.0.0.0/8      1.1.1.1                  0             0 1 1811 i
*>                  192.168.1.2              0            50 3 2 50 51 52 1811 i
*> 182.0.0.0/8      1.1.1.1                  0             0 1 2 1822 i
*                   192.168.1.2              0             0 3 2 50 51 1822 i
*  183.0.0.0/8      1.1.1.1                  0             0 1 2 50 1833 i
*>                  192.168.1.2              0             0 3 2 50 1833 i
*  184.0.0.0/8      1.1.1.1                  0             0 1 2 50 51 1844 i
*>                  192.168.1.2              0             0 3 2 1844 i
*  185.0.0.0/8      1.1.1.1                  0             0 1 2 50 51 52 1855 i
*>                  192.168.1.2              0             0 3 1855 i

! The next command lists the pre-route-map received Update
E1# show ip bgp neigh 192.168.1.2 received-routes ¦ include 181
*  181.0.0.0/8      192.168.1.2              0             0 3 2 50 51 52 1811 i
```

```
! The next command shows the post-route-map received Update
E1# show ip bgp neigh 192.168.1.2 routes ¦ incl 181
*> 181.0.0.0/8     192.168.1.2          0          50 3 2 50 51 52 1811 i
```

The configuration uses a single-line IP prefix list that matches exactly prefix 181.0.0.0/8, and a 2-clause route map. The first route-map clause, a permit clause, matches 181.0.0.0/8. The permit action allows the route through the filter. The **set weight 50** command then sets the weight.

The second **route-map** clause, also with a permit action, matches the rest of the prefixes in the Update because there is no **match** command. The permit action allows these routes through the filter. Without clause 20, this route map would have matched all other routes with the route map's implied deny clause at the end of every route map, filtering all other routes learned from 192.168.1.2 except 181.0.0.0/8.

The configuration also includes a **neighbor 192.168.1.2 route-map set-weight-50 in** command to enable the route map for incoming updates from Router I3-1. The example also shows that the neighbor must be cleared, in this case with a soft reset of the **clear ip bgp 192.168.1.2 soft** command which causes the route map logic to take effect.

Examining the results of this change, note that E1 now thinks the better route is through I3-1 (192.168.1.2). The output lists the new weight of 50, with the route through I1-1 (1.1.1.1) using the default weight of 0. With weight, bigger is better.

Finally, the last two commands in the example show the pre-route-map received update (with the **received-routes** option) and the post-route-map results of the received update (with the **routes** option). The received Update does not include Weight because it is Cisco-proprietary, so E1 initially assigned the Weight to its default value (0). After applying the route map, E1 now lists a Weight of 50.

Setting Weight Using the **neighbor weight** Command

Alternatively, the weight can be set for all routes learned from a neighbor using the **neighbor weight** command. Example 15-4 shows this configuration added to E1, setting the Weight for all routes learned from I1-1 (1.1.1.1) to 60. As a result, E1's route for 181.0.0.0/8 switches back to using the route through 1.1.1.1 (I1-1).

Example 15-4   *Setting the Weight to 60 for All Routes Learned from I1-1*

```
E1# conf t
Enter configuration commands, one per line.  End with CNTL/Z.
E1(config)# router bgp 11
E1(config-router)# neighbor 1.1.1.1 weight 60
E1(config-router)#^Z
E1# clear ip bgp 1.1.1.1 soft
```

```
E1# show ip bgp 176.0.0.0/4 longer-prefixes
BGP table version is 54, local router ID is 128.107.9.1
Status codes: s suppressed, d damped, h history, * valid, > best, i - internal,
              r RIB-failure, S Stale
Origin codes: i - IGP, e - EGP, ? - incomplete

   Network          Next Hop        Metric LocPrf Weight Path
*> 181.0.0.0/8      1.1.1.1              0          60 1 1811 i
*                   192.168.1.2          0          50 3 2 50 51 52 1811 i
*> 182.0.0.0/8      1.1.1.1              0          60 1 2 1822 i
*                   192.168.1.2          0           0 3 2 50 51 1822 i
*> 183.0.0.0/8      1.1.1.1              0          60 1 2 50 1833 i
*                   192.168.1.2          0           0 3 2 50 1833 i
*> 184.0.0.0/8      1.1.1.1              0          60 1 2 50 51 1844 i
*                   192.168.1.2          0           0 3 2 1844 i
*> 185.0.0.0/8      1.1.1.1              0          60 1 2 50 51 52 1855 i
*                   192.168.1.2          0           0 3 1855 i
```

The **neighbor weight** command does not use an in or out direction because Weight can only be set on input. The configuration results in all routes learned from 1.1.1.1 (I1-1) having a Weight of 60, as noted in the Weight column of the **show ip bgp** output.

Setting the Local Preference

The BGP Local Preference (Local_Pref) PA gives the routers inside a single AS a value that they can set per-route, advertise to all iBGP routers inside the AS, so that all routers in the AS agree about which router is the best exit point for packets destined for that prefix. By design, the Local_Pref can be set by routers as they receive eBGP routes by using an inbound route map. The routers then advertise the Local_Pref in iBGP updates. As a result, all the routers in the same AS can then make the same choice of which route is best, agreeing as to which router to use to exit the AS for each prefix.

As with the discussion of Weight, this section begins with a description of a sample scenario. Following that, a sample Local_Pref configuration is shown, using a route-map to set Local_Pref for routes advertised into an Enterprise. Table 15-5 summarizes some of the key features of Local_Pref as demonstrated in the upcoming pages.

Table 15-5   *Key Features of Local_Pref*

Key
Topic

Feature	Description
PA?	Yes
Purpose	Identifies the best exit point from the AS to reach a given prefix
Scope	Throughout the AS in which it was set; not advertised to eBGP peers
Range	0 through 4,294,967,295 ($2^{32} - 1$)
Which is best?	Higher values are better

Table 15-5 *Key Features of Local_Pref*

Feature	Description
Default	100
Changing the default	Using the **bgp default local-preference <0-4294967295>** BGP sub-command
Configuration	Via **neighbor route-map** command; **in** option is required for updates from an **eBGP** peer

Note: For those of you memorizing using the N WLLA OMNI mnemonic, Local_Pref is the first L in WLLA.

Sample Internetwork Used in the Local_Pref and AS_Path Length Examples

Figure 15-5 shows a sample Internetwork used to demonstrate setting both Local_Pref, and later, AS_Path Length. The figure shows a single Enterprise with two Internet-connected routers. A full iBGP mesh exists with these two routers plus two routers internal to the Enterprise. Two eBGP neighborships exist, one with ISP1, and one with ISP3. (Note in particular that unlike Figure 15-3, E1 does not have a neighborship with router I3-1 in this case.) The following design requirements have already been met by the initial configuration in all routers shown in the figure:

■ E1 and I1-1 uses loopback IP addresses (11.11.11.11 and 1.1.1.1) for their neighborship.

■ E2 and I3-1 use interface IP addresses for their neighborship.

■ None of the routers have attempted to change any settings that can impact the choice of best path, and Weight settings in the previous examples have been removed.

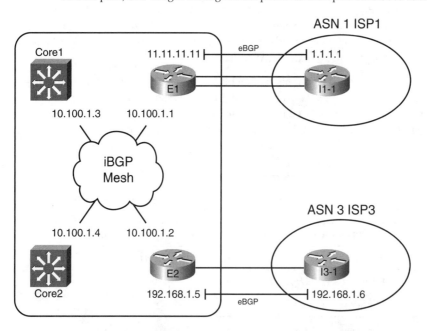

Figure 15-5 *Sample Internetwork for BGP Local_Pref and AS_Path Length Examples*

As with the Weight example, both ISPs advertise the same five prefixes, with different AS_Paths so that the routers have some prefixes to manipulate. Figure 15-6 shows five such prefixes that both ISPs advertise to E1 and E2. Note that this example network uses the same five prefixes, prefix lengths, and As_Path values as the previous Weight examples in this chapter.

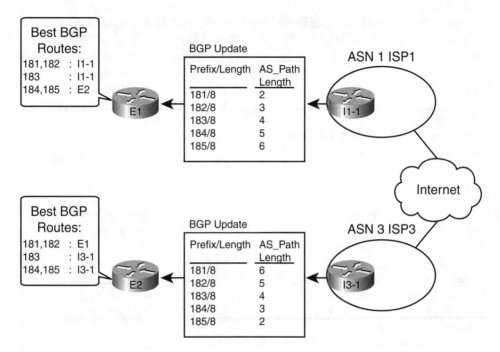

Figure 15-6 *Prefixes and AS_Path Lengths Used in Upcoming Examples*

Before showing the example of how to set the Local_Pref and how it impacts the routes, it is helpful to look at the best BGP routes on the Enterprise routers before any PAs have been changed. Example 15-5 shows the relevant BGP table entries on E1, E2, and Core1 with no attempt to influence E1's choice of best path. The best path for four of the five prefixes will be obvious, but the output listed in the commands requires some review. Prefixes 181.0.0.0/8 and 182.0.0.0/8 have a shorter AS_Path through ISP1, so E1 and E2 will agree that E1's path, through ISP1, is best. Similarly, 184.0.0.0/8 and 185.0.0.08 have a shorter AS_Path through ISP3, so both E1 and E2 agree that E2's path is best for these prefixes. Again, 183.0.0.0/8 ties on AS_Path length.

Example 15-5 *BGP Tables on E1, E2, and Core1, with No Changes to Settings That Affect Best Path*

```
! First, on router E1
E1# show ip bgp 176.0.0.0/4 longer-prefixes
BGP table version is 15, local router ID is 128.107.9.1
Status codes: s suppressed, d damped, h history, * valid, > best, i - internal,
```

```
                 r RIB-failure, S Stale
Origin codes: i - IGP, e - EGP, ? - incomplete


   Network            Next Hop          Metric LocPrf Weight Path
*> 181.0.0.0/8        1.1.1.1               0            0 1 1811 i
*> 182.0.0.0/8        1.1.1.1               0            0 1 2 1822 i
* i183.0.0.0/8        10.100.1.2            0     100    0 3 2 50 1833 i
*>                    1.1.1.1               0            0 1 2 50 1833 i
*>i184.0.0.0/8        10.100.1.2            0     100    0 3 2 1844 i
*                     1.1.1.1               0            0 1 2 50 51 1844 i
*>i185.0.0.0/8        10.100.1.2            0     100    0 3 1855 i
*                     1.1.1.1               0            0 1 2 50 51 52 1855 i
```

```
! Next, on router E2
E2# show ip bgp 176.0.0.0/4 longer-prefixes
! legend omitted for brevity


   Network            Next Hop          Metric LocPrf Weight Path
*>i181.0.0.0/8        10.100.1.1            0     100    0 1 1811 i
*                     192.168.1.6           0            0 3 2 50 51 52 1811 i
*>i182.0.0.0/8        10.100.1.1            0     100    0 1 2 1822 i
*                     192.168.1.6           0            0 3 2 50 51 1822 i
* i183.0.0.0/8        10.100.1.1            0     100    0 1 2 50 1833 i
*>                    192.168.1.6           0            0 3 2 50 1833 i
*> 184.0.0.0/8        192.168.1.6           0            0 3 2 1844 i
*> 185.0.0.0/8        192.168.1.6           0            0 3 1855 i
```

```
! Next, on router Core1
Core1# show ip bgp 176.0.0.0/4 longer-prefixes
! legend omitted for brevity


   Network            Next Hop          Metric LocPrf Weight Path
*>i181.0.0.0/8        10.100.1.1            0     100    0 1 1811 i
*>i182.0.0.0/8        10.100.1.1            0     100    0 1 2 1822 i
*>i183.0.0.0/8        10.100.1.1            0     100    0 1 2 50 1833 i
* i                   10.100.1.2            0     100    0 3 2 50 1833 i
*>i184.0.0.0/8        10.100.1.2            0     100    0 3 2 1844 i
*>i185.0.0.0/8        10.100.1.2            0     100    0 3 1855 i
```

First, pay close attention to the LocPrf column of output in the example. This column lists the Local_Pref settings of each route. Some list a (default) value of 100, and some list nothing. As it turns out, because Updates received from eBGP peers do not include the Local_Pref PA, IOS lists a null value for Local_Pref for eBGP-learned routes by default. However, Updates from iBGP peers do include the Local_Pref. Because this network does not have any configuration that attempts to set Local_Pref yet, the routers advertise their default Local_Pref value of 100 over the iBGP connections.

Also note that when comparing the output on both E1 and E2, the output lists a single eBGP route, but not the alternative iBGP route through the other Internet-connected router in the Enterprise. For example, E2 lists a single route for 184.0.0.0/8 and 185.0.0.0/8, through I3-1 (192.168.1.6). The reason that E2 does not list an alternative route through E1 is that E1's best route for these prefixes, as seen near the top of the example, is E1's iBGP-learned route through E2 (10.100.1.2). BGP does not allow a router to advertise iBGP-learned routes to iBGP peers, so E1 will not advertise routes for 184.0.0.0/8 or 185.0.0.0/8 to router E2.

Finally, for prefix 183.0.0.0/8, both E1 and E2 tie on the As_Path length. In this case, all best path choices tie until Step 7, which prefers eBGP routes over iBGP routes. E1 prefers its eBGP route for 183.0.0.0/8 through ISP1's Router I1-1, and E2 prefers its eBGP route through ISP3's Router I3-1.

Setting the BGP Local_Pref Using a Route Map

To set the Local_Pref, a router can use the **neighbor** *neighbor-ip* **route-map in** BGP sub-command. Typically, a router uses this command with the inbound direction for routes received from eBGP peers. Then, with no additional configuration required, the router then advertises the Local_Pref to any iBGP peers.

To show the Local_Pref configuration and results, start with the sample network shown in the previous section. The configuration will now be changed to set the Local_Pref for two different prefixes for Updates received on E1 from I1-1, as shown in Figure 15-7. Note that the figure reinforces the idea that BGP does not include the Local_Pref PA in eBGP Updates but will in iBGP Updates.

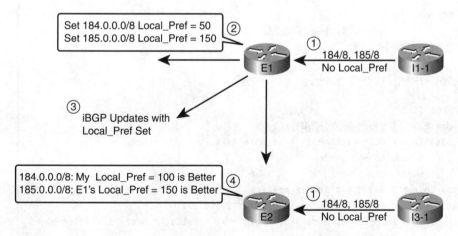

Figure 15-7   *Example Local_Pref Settings for the Upcoming Example*

The figure shows a series of steps, as follows:

Step 1.   I1-1 and I3-1 advertise the prefixes into the Enterprise but with no Local_Pref set because the connections are eBGP peers.

Step 2. E1 sets the Local_Pref for routes learned from I1-1: 184.0.0.0/8 (50) and 185.0.0.0/8 (150).

Step 3. E1 includes the Local_Pref settings in its iBGP Updates to Core1, Core2, and E2.

Step 4. E2 realizes that E1's route for 185.0.0.0/8, Local_Pref 150, is better than E2's eBGP route for this prefix, which E2 assigned default Local_Pref 100. Conversely, E1's advertised route for 184.0.0.0/8, Local_Pref 50, is worse than E2's eBGP route for that same prefix, with assigned default Local_Pref 100.

Example 15-6 shows the configuration on router E1 to assign the Local_Pref values shown in Figure 15-7. The example also shows the results on E1 and E2. Note that the configuration differs only slightly as compared with the configuration for administrative Weight as shown in Example 15-3, the only substantive difference being the **set local-preference** route map command rather than the **set weight** command.

Example 15-6 *Configuring Local_Pref on Router E1 (Step 2 per Figure 15-7)*

```
E1# show running-config
! only pertinent portions shown
ip prefix-list match-184 seq 5 permit 184.0.0.0/8
!
ip prefix-list match-185 seq 5 permit 185.0.0.0/8
!
route-map set-LP-150 permit 10
 match ip address prefix-list match-185
 set local-preference 150
!
route-map set-LP-150 permit 15
 match ip address prefix-list match-184
 set local-preference 50
!
route-map set-LP-150 permit 20
!
router bgp 11
 neighbor 1.1.1.1 route-map set-LP-150 in
! The clearing of BGP neighbor I1-1 is done next, but not shown.
! Next, E1's Updated BGP Table


E1# show ip bgp 176.0.0.0/4 longer-prefixes
BGP table version is 29, local router ID is 128.107.9.1
Status codes: s suppressed, d damped, h history, * valid, > best, i - internal,
              r RIB-failure, S Stale
Origin codes: i - IGP, e - EGP, ? - incomplete

   Network          Next Hop          Metric LocPrf Weight Path
*> 181.0.0.0/8      1.1.1.1               0           0 1 1811 i
*> 182.0.0.0/8      1.1.1.1               0           0 1 2 1822 i
```

```
* i183.0.0.0/8       10.100.1.2              0    100      0 3 2 50 1833 i
*>                   1.1.1.1                 0             0 1 2 50 1833 i
*>i184.0.0.0/8       10.100.1.2              0    100      0 3 2 1844 i
*                    1.1.1.1                 0    50       0 1 2 50 51 1844 i
*> 185.0.0.0/8       1.1.1.1                 0    150      0 1 2 50 51 52 1855 i

E1# show ip bgp 185.0.0.0/8
BGP routing table entry for 185.0.0.0/8, version 7
Paths: (1 available, best #1, table Default-IP-Routing-Table)
  Advertised to update-groups:
        1
  1 2 50 51 52 1855, (received & used)
    1.1.1.1 from 1.1.1.1 (1.1.1.1)
      Origin IGP, metric 0, localpref 150, valid, external, best

! The next output occurs on router E2
E2# show ip bgp 185.0.0.0/8 longer-prefixes
! heading lines omitted

   Network          Next Hop         Metric LocPrf Weight Path
*>i185.0.0.0/8      10.100.1.1            0   150      0 1 2 50 51 52 1855 i
*                   192.168.1.6           0            0 3 1855 i
```

Example 15-6's output shows E1's BGP table entries, now with updated Local_Pref values as compared with Example 15-5. E1 now uses its eBGP route, Next_Hop 1.1.1.1, for prefix 185.0.0.0/8 because of the higher Local_Pref.

The end of the example shows E2 with two possible routes for 185.0.0.0/8. The following list outlines E2's BGP best path logic in this case:

Step 0. The two routes both have reachable Next_Hop IP addresses.

Step 1. Both have Weight 0 (tie).

Step 2. The iBGP route through 10.100.1.1 (E1) has a bigger (better) Local_Pref (150 versus 100) that the route through 192.168.1.6 (I3-1), so it is the better route.

Also, note that both the **show ip bgp longer-prefixes** command's briefer output, and the **show ip bgp 185.0.0.0/8** commands more verbose output, both identify the Local_Pref value. However, the longer command output does not list the Weight value.

IP Routes Based on BGP Best Paths

Some of the complexity related to BGP occurs around the BGP functions created by BGP PAs, including their use by the best path algorithm. When the BGP best path algorithm has gotten through this complexity and chosen a best route for a prefix, the router then tries to add that route to the IP routing table. However, rather than add the BGP route to the IP routing table directly, BGP actually gives that best BGP route to another process for consideration: The IOS *Routing Table Manager (RTM)*.

The IOS RTM chooses the best route among many competing sources. For example, routes may be learned by an IGP, BGP, or even as connected or static routes. IOS collects the best such route for each prefix and feeds those into the RTM function. The RTM then chooses the best route. Figure 15-8 shows the general idea:

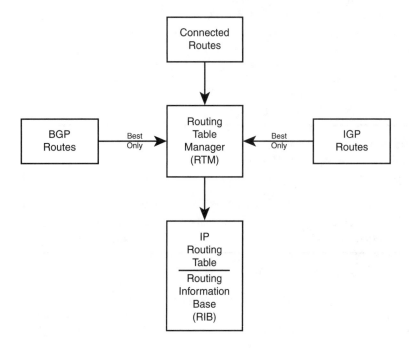

Figure 15-8   *Routing Table Manager Concept*

Among its tasks, RTM uses the concept of Administrative Distance (AD) to choose the best route among these different sources. Table 15-6 repeats the list of default AD values as shown earlier in Table 10-6 from Chapter 10, "Advanced IGP Redistribution," but with highlights for the two BGP-related default values:

Table 15-6   *Default Administrative Distances*

Route Type	Administrative Distance
Connected	0
Static	1
EIGRP summary route	5
eBGP	20
EIGRP (internal)	90

Table 15-6 *Default Administrative Distances*

Route Type	Administrative Distance
IGRP	100
OSPF	110
IS-IS	115
RIP	120
On-Demand Routing (ODR)	160
EIGRP (external)	170
iBGP	200
Unreachable	255

For the most part, an Enterprise router should not see cases in which a prefix learned with BGP has also been learned as a connected or IGP-learned route. (Conversely, these issues occur more often when implementing MPLS VPNs with BGP/IGP redistribution.) However, it can happen, and when it does, the **show ip bgp rib-failures** command can be helpful. This command lists routes for which BGP has chosen the route as best, but the RTM function has not placed the route into the Routing Information Base (RIB), which is simply another name for the IP routing table.

Example of a BGP RIB Failure

To show an example of a RIB failure, imagine that an Enterprise engineer needed to do some testing, so the engineer just picked an IP address range to use. The engineer tries to avoid problems by not using network 10.0.0.0, which is used throughout the Enterprise. So rather than choosing another private network, the engineer then chooses public range 185.0.0.0/8. After changing the lab configuration a few hundred times, a route for 185.0.0.0/8 leaks into the OSPF topology database.

Keep in mind that at the end of the previous example, E1 had chosen its eBGP route for 185.0.0.0/8 as its best route, and E2 had chosen its iBGP route as its best route for 185.0.0.0/8. Example 15-7 shows the results, based on RTM's comparisons of the AD values.

Example 15-7 *Example with the RTM and RIB Failures*

```
! First, E1's IP Routing table for 185.0.0.0/8
E1# show ip route 185.0.0.0 255.0.0.0 longer-prefixes
Codes: C - connected, S - static, R - RIP, M - mobile, B - BGP
       D - EIGRP, EX - EIGRP external, O - OSPF, IA - OSPF inter area
       N1 - OSPF NSSA external type 1, N2 - OSPF NSSA external type 2
       E1 - OSPF external type 1, E2 - OSPF external type 2
       i - IS-IS, su - IS-IS summary, L1 - IS-IS level-1, L2 - IS-IS level-2
       ia - IS-IS inter area, * - candidate default, U - per-user static route
       o - ODR, P - periodic downloaded static route
```

```
Gateway of last resort is 1.1.1.1 to network 0.0.0.0


B     185.0.0.0/8 [20/0] via 1.1.1.1, 00:25:11
! Next, E2's IP Routing table
E2# show ip route 185.0.0.0 255.0.0.0 longer-prefixes
! Legend omitted for brevity


Gateway of last resort is 192.168.1.6 to network 0.0.0.0


O     185.0.0.0/8 [110/2] via 10.1.1.77, 00:15:44, FastEthernet0/0


E2# show ip bgp rib-failure
Network          Next Hop                       RIB-failure    RIB-NH Matches
185.0.0.0/8      10.100.1.1              Higher admin distance              n/a
```

The first command shows that E1, with an eBGP route, actually adds its route to the IP
routing table. The route lists a code of B, meaning BGP. The output lists the eBGP default
AD of 20, which is a better default AD than OSPF's 110. RTM added this BGP route to the
IP routing table on E1 because of eBGP's better AD.

E2 currently lists its iBGP route through E1 as its current best BGP route for 185.0.0.0/8
because of the higher Local_Pref configured in Example 15-6. However, after giving this
route to the RTM, RTM instead choose the lower-AD OSPF route (AD 110) rather than
the higher-AD iBGP route (AD 200).

Finally, the **show ip bgp rib-failure** command lists one line for each best BGP route that
the RTM does not place into the IP routing table. In this case, this command on Router E2
lists the route for 185.0.0.0/8, with the reason listed.

BGP and the maximum-paths Command

Like the IGP protocols, BGP supports the **maximum-paths** *number-of-paths* subcommand, but BGP uses significantly different logic than the IGPs. Unlike the IGP routing
protocols, BGP truly needs to pick one route, and only one route, as the best path for a
given prefix/length. In effect, the BGP best path algorithm already breaks the ties for
"best" route for each prefix, so from BGP's perspective, one route for each prefix is always
best.

BGP does allow multiple BGP routes for a prefix to be considered to tie, at least for the
purpose of adding multiple routes to the IP routing table. The conditions are as follows:

> If the BGP best path algorithm does not choose a best path by Step 8 (per the num-
> bering in this book), the routes which still tie for being best path will be allowed
> into the IP routing table, up to the number defined by the BGP **maximum-paths**
> *number-of-paths* router subcommand.

The section "Overview of the BGP Best Path Algorithm" earlier in this chapter lists the
best path steps, including the tiebreaker steps that allow routes to be considered by the
maximum-paths command.

Increasing the Length of the AS_Path Using AS_Path Prepend

Step 4 of the BGP best path algorithm examines the length of the AS_Path PA. The length of the AS_Path may appear to be obvious: Just add the number of ASNs listed in the AS_Path. However, some BGP features outside the scope of this book actually impact the AS_Path length calculation as well. However, for the purposes of this book, AS_Path length is simply the number of ASNs listed in the AS_Path.

The AS_Path prepend tool gives engineers a means to increase the length of an AS_Path by adding ASNs to the AS_Path, while not impacting the loop prevention role of the AS_Path PA. By increasing the length of an AS_Path, a route is less likely to become the best route. By adding ASNs that already exist inside a particular route's AS_Path, the feature does not inadvertently prevent a route from being ignored due to AS_Path loop prevention.

For example, using the design shown most recently in Figures 15-5, 15-6, and 15-7, imagine that the Enterprise considers ISP1 to be the better ISP, but they do not want to send all traffic through ISP1. So, the Enterprise network engineers could make the following type of implementation choice:

Make the AS_Paths received from ISP3 be 2 ASNs longer.

By making such a choice, when an AS_Path through ISP1 is better, or when it's a tie on AS_Path between ISP1 and ISP3, or when the AS_Path through ISP1 is even slightly longer than through ISP3, the routers can still choose their routes through ISP1. Only when the AS_Path (before prepending) is at least 2 ASNs shorter through ISP3 can the ISP3 path be chosen.

Note: For those of you memorizing using the N WLLA OMNI mnemonic, AS_Path Length is the A in WLLA.

Figure 15-9 shows the mechanics of how an Enterprise router would prepend the AS_Path for routes received by Router E2 from ISP3, namely Router I3-1. Looking specifically at the route for 185.0.0.0/8, in this case, I3-1 has not changed the AS_Path and advertised the route with AS_Path (3, 1855). At Step 2, Router E2 prepends ASN 3–twice–making the AS_Path length 4. At Step 3, E2 advertises the route to its iBGP peers–peers that may now prefer to the other route for this prefix through Router E1.

The configuration itself requires only a little additional work compared to the other examples. As shown in Figure 15-9, Router E2 could use an inbound route map, using the **set as-path prepend 3 3** command to add the two ASNs. (The router sending the Update, ISP3's Router I3-1 in this case, could instead use an outbound route map.) Example 15-8 shows the configuration on E2 to add the ASNs at ingress into E2. (Note that all configuration for changing the Weight and Local_Pref, and the extra OSPF route for 185.0.0.0/8 shown in Example 15-6, have been removed before gathering the output in this example.)

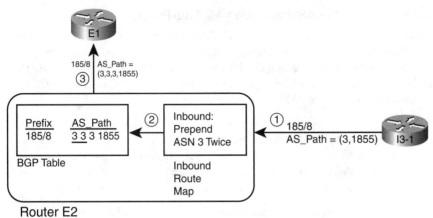

Key Topic

Figure 15-9 *Prepending Two ASNs to an AS_Path*

Example 15-8 *Prepending Additional ASNs to the AS_Path*

```
! First, E2's new configuration
route-map add-two-asns permit 10
 set as-path prepend 3 3
router bgp 11
 neighbor 192.168.1.6 route-map add-two-asns in
!
! Next, note the AS_Path values all start with 3, 3, 3
E2# show ip bgp 176.0.0.0/4 longer-prefixes
BGP table version is 41, local router ID is 10.100.1.2
Status codes: s suppressed, d damped, h history, * valid, > best, i - internal,
              r RIB-failure, S Stale
Origin codes: i - IGP, e - EGP, ? - incomplete


   Network          Next Hop         Metric LocPrf Weight Path
*>i181.0.0.0/8      10.100.1.1            0    100      0 1 1811 i
*                   192.168.1.6          0             0 3 3 3 2 50 51 52 1811 i
*>i182.0.0.0/8      10.100.1.1           0    100      0 1 2 1822 i
*                   192.168.1.6          0             0 3 3 3 2 50 51 1822 i
*>i183.0.0.0/8      10.100.1.1           0    100      0 1 2 50 1833 i
*                   192.168.1.6          0             0 3 3 3 2 50 1833 i
*  i184.0.0.0/8     10.100.1.1           0    100      0 1 2 50 51 1844 i
*>                  192.168.1.6          0             0 3 3 3 2 1844 i
*> 185.0.0.0/8      192.168.1.6          0             0 3 3 3 1855 i
```

Note: When using AS_Path prepending, do not prepend just any ASN. BGP still uses the AS_Path for loop avoidance, so using an ASN already in the AS_Path, like the ASN of the most recently added ASN (for example, ASN 3 in this case), or the local ASN (for example, ASN 11 in this case), makes the most sense.

Although presented here as a tool for influencing outbound routes, As_Path prepending can also be used to influence the inbound routes as well.

Influencing an Enterprise's Inbound Routes with MED

An Enterprise has reasonably good control over its outbound IP routes. The engineers can configure BGP to set and react to Weight, Local_Pref, and AS_Path length, manipulating each to choose a different outgoing link or different router through which to forward packets to the Internet.

An Enterprise has much less control over inbound routes: routes for packets coming back toward the Enterprise. First, these inbound routes exist on routers that the Enterprise does not own. Even if an ISP or set of ISPs can be convinced by engineers at the Enterprise to make their routes toward an Enterprise take a particular path, technical issues may prevent the design from being implemented. In particular, if the Enterprise's public IP address range is summarized, the companies that use addresses in that range may have competing goals, so no policy can be applied to influence the best route.

However, several tools exist that allow some control over the last ASN hop between an ISP and their Enterprise customer. This book examines one such tool, called Multi-Exit Discriminator (MED), originally worked for a dual-homed design–that is, with a single ISP but with multiple links to that ISP. MED was later expanded to support dual-multihomed designs (2+ ASNs, 2+ links), relying on the concept that ISPs would work together. This section examines the dual-homed case, with a single ISP.

MED Concepts

The name Multi Exit Discriminator actually describes its function to a great degree. With a dual-homed design, at least two links exist between the Enterprise and the ISP. The Enterprise can announce to the ISP a value (MED) that tells the ISP which path into the Enterprise is best. As a result, the ISP can discriminate between the multiple exit points from that ISP to the Enterprise.

Because MED lets the Enterprise ASN tell just the neighboring ASN which link into the Enterprise to use, engineers typically use MED when advertising an Enterprise's public IP address space. Those inbound routes into the Enterprise from the ISP typically consist of either one, or a few, public IP address ranges.

For example, consider a new network design as shown in Figure 15-10. In this case, the Enterprise uses the same 128.107.0.0/19 public address range used in Chapters 13 and 14. The Enterprise connects only to ASN 1 with a total of four physical links and three BGP neighbors.

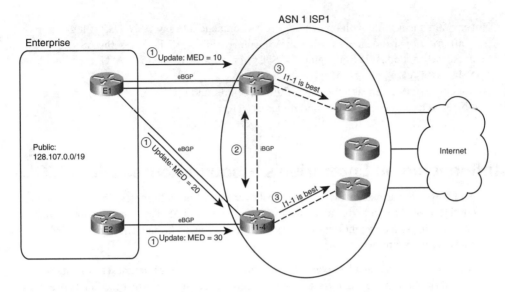

Figure 15-10   *Example of Using MED*

MED uses smallest-is-best logic. As a result, the figure shows a design in which the Enterprise engineer prefers the top BGP neighborship as the best path to use for inbound routes (MED 10), the middle link next (Med 20), and the bottom connection last (MED 30). Following the steps in the figure:

Step 1.   E1 and E2 advertise 128.107.0.0/19, setting MED with an outbound route map, to various settings: MED 10 sent by E1 to I1-1, MED 20 sent by E1 to I1-4, and MED 30 sent by E2 to I1-4.

Step 2.   I1-1 and I1-4 have an iBGP connection, so they learn each other's routes and agree as to which route wins based on MED.

Step 3.   I1-1 and I1-4 also tell the other routers inside ISP1, causing all inbound traffic to funnel toward router I1-1.

Note that Routers I1-1 and I1-4 in this example could have chosen a better route based on all the earlier best path steps. However, a brief analysis of the steps tells us that unless someone makes an effort to override the effects of MED, these routers' best path algorithms will use MED. Assuming the Enterprise and ISP agree to rely on MED, the earlier Best Path steps should not matter. Here's why:

Step 1.   **Weight:** Needs to be set locally, so if relying on MED, the ISP simply chooses to not set the Weight for received Updates from the Enterprise.

Step 2.   **Local_Pref:** Again, this takes overt effort to match and set the Local_Pref, so if relying on MED, the ISP simply chooses to not set the Local_Pref.

Step 3.   **Locally injected?** All these public routes from the Enterprise will be learned with eBGP and not locally injected.

Step 4.   **AS_Path length:** All such routes on the ISP routers should list one ASN–the Enterprise's ASN–so all should tie on this point.

Step 5. Origin: Whatever the Origin is (I or ?), it should tie.

Step 6. MED: None of the other steps determined the best route, so now MED takes effect.

Table 15-7 summarizes the key points about MED.

Table 15-7 *Key Features of MED*

Feature	Description
Is it a PA?	Yes.
Purpose	Allows an AS to tell a neighboring AS the best way to forward packets into the first AS.
Scope	Advertised by one AS into another, propagated inside the AS, but not sent to any other autonomous systems.
Range	0 through 4,294,967,295 ($2^{32} - 1$).
Which is best?	Smaller is better.
Default	0
Configuration	Via **neighbor route-map out** command, using the **set metric** command inside the route map.

Note: For those of you memorizing using the N WLLA OMNI mnemonic, MED is the M in OMNI.

MED Configuration

MED configuration usually occurs on the routers in the AS that wants to control inbound routes from the neighboring AS. As such, in the example design shown in Figure 15-10, Routers E1 and E2 would configure MED. Example 15-9 shows E1's configuration.

Example 15-9 *MED Configuration on Router E1*

```
route-map set-med-to-I1-1 permit 10
 match ip address prefix-list only-public
 set metric 10
!
route-map set-med-to-I1-4 permit 10
 match ip address prefix-list only-public
 set metric 20
!
ip prefix-list only-public permit 128.107.0.0/19
!
```

```
router bgp 11
  neighbor 1.1.1.1 route-map set-med-I1-1 out
  neighbor 192.168.1.2 route-map set-med-I1-4 out
```

Both the configuration and the **show ip bgp** command output refers to MED as metric.
Note that the route map in Example 15-9 uses the **set metric** command, rather than **set
med** (which does not exist). And as shown in I1-1's output for the **show ip bgp** command
in Example 15-10, the output lists MED under the heading metric. In particular, note that
even the **show ip route** command lists the MED value in brackets as the metric for the
BGP route.

Example 15-10 *BGP Table and IP Routing Table on Router I1-1*

```
I1-1# show ip bgp 128.107.0.0/19
BGP routing table entry for 128.107.0.0/19, version 13
Paths: (1 available, best #1, table Default-IP-Routing-Table)
Flag: 0x820
  Not advertised to any peer
  11, (aggregated by 11 128.107.9.1), (received & used)
    11.11.11.11 from 11.11.11.11 (128.107.9.1)
      Origin IGP, metric 10, localpref 100, valid, external, atomic-aggregate, best

I1-1# sh ip bgp 128.107.0.0/19 longer-prefixes
BGP table version is 13, local router ID is 1.1.1.1
Status codes: s suppressed, d damped, h history, * valid, > best, i - internal,
              r RIB-failure, S Stale
Origin codes: i - IGP, e - EGP, ? - incomplete


   Network          Next Hop          Metric LocPrf Weight Path
*> 128.107.0.0/19   11.11.11.11          10          0 11 i

I1-1# show ip route 128.107.0.0 255.255.224.0 longer-prefixes
! Legend omitted for brevity

Gateway of last resort is not set

    128.107.0.0/19 is subnetted, 1 subnets
B      128.107.0.0 [20/10] via 11.11.11.11, 00:02:18
```

Exam Preparation Tasks

Planning Practice

The CCNP ROUTE exam expects test takers to review design documents, create implementation plans, and create verification plans. This section provides some exercises that may help you to take a step back from the minute details of the topics in this chapter so that you can think about the same technical topics from the planning perspective.

For each planning practice table, simply complete the table. Note that any numbers in parentheses represent the number of options listed for each item in the solutions in Appendix F.

Design Review Table

Table 15-8 lists several design goals related to this chapter. If these design goals were listed in a design document, and you had to take that document and develop an implementation plan, what implementation options come to mind? You should write a general description; specific configuration commands are not required.

Table 15-8 *Design Review*

Design Goal	Possible Implementation Choices Covered in This Chapter
Influence outbound route from an Enterprise toward prefixes in the Internet (3).	
Influence outbound route from an Enterprise toward prefixes in the Internet so that multiple Internet-connected Enterprise routers make the same choice based on the same information (2).	
Influence inbound routes into the Enterprise from the neighboring AS (2).	

Implementation Plan Peer Review Table

Table 15-9 shows a list of questions that others might ask, or that you might think about, during a peer review of another network engineer's implementation plan. Complete the table by answering the questions.

Table 15-9   *Notable Questions from This Chapter to Consider During an*
Implementation Plan Peer Review

Question	Answers
A plan shows two Enterprise routers, R1 and R2, connected to two different ISPs, with iBGP between R1 and R2. The plan shows R1 setting Weight for routes learned from an ISP. Will R2 react to those settings? Why or why not?	
A plan shows two Enterprise routers, R1 and R2, connected to two different ISPs, with iBGP between R1 and R2. The plan shows R1 setting Local_Pref for routes learned from an ISP. Will R2 react to those settings? Why or why not?	
The Plan calls for the use of BGP Weight, but the incomplete plan lists no configuration yet. What configuration alternatives exist? (2)	
The Plan calls for the use of BGP Local Preference, but the incomplete plan lists no configuration yet. What configuration alternatives exist?	
A plan shows two Enterprise routers, R1 and R2, connected to different ISPs. The plan calls for using MED to influence inbound routes. Which configuration options exist?	
A plan shows the use of BGP Weight, Local Preference, AS_Path prepending, and MED to influence the best path algorithm. Which of these can be set and advertised to eBGP peers?	

Create an Implementation Plan Table

This chapter does not focus on implementation or verification, but it did review one concept about static routes, as listed in Table 15-10.

Table 15-10   *Implementation Plan Configuration Memory Drill*

Feature	Configuration Commands/Notes
Configure a route map that sets Weight.	
Enable a route map to set BGP weight.	
Enable a router to set BGP weight for all routes received from a neighbor.	
Configure a route map that sets BGP Local Preference.	
Enable a route map to set BGP Local Preference.	
Configure a route map that prepends ASNs to an AS_Path.	
Enable a route map to perform AS_Path prepending.	
Configure a route map that sets MED.	
Enable a route map to set MED.	

Choose Commands for a Verification Plan Table

To practice skills useful when creating your own BGP verification plan, list in Table 15-11 all commands that supply the requested information. You may want to record your answers outside the book and set a goal to complete this table (and others like it) from memory during your final reviews before taking the exam.

Table 15-11 *Verification Plan Memory Drill*

Information Needed	Commands
Display the BGP table, including the chosen best path for each prefix. (State how to identify the best paths.)	
List 1 line per BGP route but for the prefixes within a range.	
Identify a BGP table entry's BGP Weight. (Specify where to find output.)	
Identify a BGP table entry's BGP Local Preference. (Specify where to find output.)	
Identify a BGP table entry's AS_Path length. (Specify where to find output.)	
Identify a BGP table entry's MED. (Specify where to find output.) (4 methods)	
Display routes received from a neighbor before being processed by an inbound filter.	
The same as the previous item but after applying the outbound filter.	
Display BGP routes sent to a neighbor but after applying the outbound filter.	
Display BGP best paths that were not added to the IP routing table.	

Note: Some of the entries in this table may not have been specifically mentioned in this chapter but are listed in this table for review and reference.

Review all the Key Topics

Review the most important topics from inside the chapter, noted with the Key Topics icon in the outer margin of the page. Table 15-12 lists a reference of these key topics and the page numbers on which each is found.

Table 15-12   *Key Topics for Chapter 15*

Key Topic Element	Description	Page Number
Table 15-2	BGP path attributes that affect the BGP Best Path algorithm	495
Figure 15-1	Figure showing the location of BGP PA information in the output of **show ip bgp**	496
Table 15-3	Summary of BGP Best Path algorithm	496
List	Four items commonly set for the purpose of influencing the BGP best path decision	498
Table 15-4	Reference Table for BGP Weight	500
Table 15-5	Reference Table for BGP Local_Pref	507
Figure 15-7	Example of how Local_Pref influences best path choice	511
Figure 15-9	Example of how AS_Path Prepending works	518
Table 15-7	Reference Table for BGP MED	521

Complete the Tables and Lists from Memory

Print a copy of Appendix D, "Memory Tables," (found on the CD), or at least the section for this chapter, and complete the tables and lists from memory. Appendix E, "Memory Tables Answer Key," also on the CD, includes completed tables and lists to check your work.

Define Key Terms

Define the following key terms from this chapter, and check your answers in the glossary.

BGP Weight, Local Preference, AS_Path Prepending, Multi Exit Discriminator, Best Path algorithm, Routing Table Manager, RIB Failure, path attribute

This chapter covers the following subjects:

Global Unicast Addressing, Routing, and Subnetting: This section introduces the concepts behind unicast IPv6 addresses, IPv6 routing, and how to subnet using IPv6, all in comparison to IPv4.

IPv6 Global Unicast Address Assignment: This section examines how global unicast addresses can be assigned to hosts and other devices.

Survey of IPv6 Addressing: This section examines all types of IPv6 addresses.

Configuring IPv6 Addresses on Cisco Routers: This section shows how to configure and verify static IPv6 addresses on Cisco routers.

CHAPTER 16

IP Version 6 Addressing

IP Version 6 (IPv6), the replacement protocol for IPv4, is well known for a couple of reasons. IPv6 provides the ultimate solution for the problem of running out of IPv4 addresses in the global Internet by using a 128-bit address–approximately 10^{38} total addresses, versus the mere (approximate) 4×10^9 total addresses in IPv4. However, many articles over the years have discussed when, if ever, would a mass migration to IPv6 take place. IPv6 has been the ultimate long-term solution for more than 10 years, in part because the interim IPv4 solutions, including NAT/PAT, have thankfully delayed the day in which we truly run out of public unicast IP addresses.

As more IPv6 deployments continue to emerge, Cisco has steadily added more and more IPv6 content to its certification exams. CCNA now includes basic IPv6 concepts and configuration, with this version of the CCNP ROUTE exam examining IPv6 to greater depth than its predecessor BSCI exam. In particular, ROUTE includes the basic concepts, configuration, and verification of most of the router-based tools needed to deploy IPv6 in the Enterprise. As with most of the other topics, ROUTE's coverage of IPv6 does not include all skills and knowledge to plan an Enterprise IPv6 deployment, but it does include enough to take an IPv6 design plan and make a good start on developing an IPv6 implementation and verification plan.

Part VI of this book includes three chapters. This chapter examines the concepts around IPv6 addressing, and how to configure and verify those addresses on Cisco routers. Chapter 17, "IPv6 Routing Protocols and Redistribution," looks at IPv6 routing protocols, as well as route redistribution and static routing. Both these chapters focus on pure IPv6, essentially ignoring issues related to migration from IPv4 and coexistence with IPv4. The final chapter in this part, Chapter 18, "IPv4 and IPv6 Coexistence," looks at the migration and coexistence issues.

"Do I Know This Already?" Quiz

The "Do I Know This Already?" quiz allows you to assess if you should read the entire chapter. If you miss no more than one of these eight self-assessment questions, you might want to move ahead to the "Exam Preparation Tasks." Table 16-1 lists the major headings in this chapter and the "Do I Know This Already?" quiz questions covering the material in those headings so you can assess your knowledge of these specific areas. The answers to the "Do I Know This Already?" quiz appear in Appendix A.

Table 16-1 *"Do I Know This Already?" Foundation Topics Section-to-Question Mapping*

Foundations Topics Section	Questions
Global Unicast Addressing, Routing, and Subnetting	1–2
IPv6 Global Unicast Address Assignment	3–4
Survey of IPv6 Addressing	5–6
Configuring IPv6 Addresses on Cisco Routers	7–8

1. Which of the following is the shortest valid abbreviation for FE80:0000:0000:0000:0010:0000:0000:0123?

    a. FE80::10::123

    b. FE8::1::123

    c. FE80:0:0:0:10::123

    d. FE80::10:0:0:123

2. An ISP has assigned prefix 3000:1234:5678::/48 to Company1. Which of the following terms would typically be used to describe this type of public IPv6 prefix?

    a. Subnet prefix

    b. ISP prefix

    c. Global routing prefix

    d. Registry prefix

3. Which of the following answers lists either a protocol or function that can be used by a host to dynamically learn its own IPv6 address? (Choose two.)

    a. Stateful DHCP

    b. Stateless DHCP

    c. Stateless autoconfiguration

    d. Neighbor Discovery Protocol

4. Which of the following is helpful to allow an IPv6 host to learn the IP address of a default gateway on its subnet?

    a. Stateful DHCP

    b. Stateless RS

    c. Stateless autoconfiguration

    d. Neighbor Discovery Protocol

5. Which of the following answers lists a multicast IPv6 address?

    a. 2000::1:1234:5678:9ABC

    b. FD80::1:1234:5678:9ABC

    c.   FE80::1:1234:5678:9ABC

    d.   FF80::1:1234:5678:9ABC

6. Router R1 has two LAN interfaces and three serial interfaces enabled for IPv6. All the interfaces use link local addresses automatically generated by the router. Which of the following could be the link local address of R1's interface S0/0?

    a.   FEA0::200:FF:FE11:0

    b.   FE80::200:FF:FE11:1111

    c.   FE80::0213:19FF:FE7B:0:1

    d.   FEB0::211:11FF:FE11:1111

7. Router R1 has the following configuration. Assuming R1's F0/0 interface has a MAC address of 0200.0011.1111, what IPv6 addresses will R1 list for interface F0/0 in the output of the **show ipv6 interface brief** command?

```
interface f0/0
 ipv6 address 2345:0:0:8::1/64
```

    a.   2345:0:0:8::1

    b.   2345:0:0:8:0:FF:FE11:1111

    c.   FE80::FF:FE11:1111

    d.   FE80:0:0:8::1

8. Router R1 lists the following output from a **show** command. Which of the following is true about R1?

```
R1# show ipv6 interface f0/0
FastEthernet0/0 is up, line protocol is up
  IPv6 is enabled, link-local address is FE80::213:19FF:FE12:3456
  No Virtual link-local address(es):
  Global unicast address(es):
    2000::4:213:19FF:FE12:3456, subnet is 2000:0:0:4::/64 [EUI]
  Joined group address(es):
  FF02::1
  FF02::2
  FF02::1:FF12:3456
```

    a.   R1's solicited node multicast address is FF02::1:FF12:3456.

    b.   R1's 2000::4:213:19FF:FE12:3456 address is a global unicast with all 128 bits statically configured.

    c.   Address FF02::2 is R1's solicited node multicast.

    d.   R1's solicited node multicast, not listed in this output, would be FF02::213:19FF:FE12:3456.

Foundation Topics

The world has changed tremendously over the last 10–20 years as a result of the growth and maturation of the Internet and networking technologies in general. As recently as 1990, a majority of the general public did not know about nor use global networks to communicate, and when businesses needed to communicate, those communications mostly flowed over private networks. During the 1990s, the public Internet grew to the point where people in most parts of the world could connect to the Internet; many companies connected to the Internet for a variety of applications, with the predominate applications being email and web. During the first decade of the 21st century, the Internet has grown further to billions of addressable devices with the majority of people on the planet having some form of Internet access. With that pervasive access came a wide range of applications and uses, including voice, video, collaboration, and social networking, with a generation that has grown up with this easily accessed global network.

The eventual migration to IPv6 will likely be driven by the need for more and more IP addresses. Practically every mobile phone supports Internet traffic, requiring the use of an IP address. Most new cars have the capability to acquire and use an IP address, along with wireless communications, allowing the car dealer to contact the customer when the car's diagnostics detect a problem with the car. Some manufacturers have embraced the idea that all their appliances need to be IP-enabled.

Although the two biggest reasons why networks might migrate from IPv4 to IPv6 are the need for more addresses and mandates from government organizations, at least IPv6 includes some attractive features and migration tools. Some of those advantages are

- **Address assignment features:** IPv6 supports a couple of methods for dynamic address assignment, including DHCP and Stateless Autoconfiguration.

- **Built-in support for address renumbering:** IPv6 supports the ability to change the public IPv6 prefix used for all addresses in an Enterprise, using the capability to advertise the current prefix with a short timeout and the new prefix with a longer lease life.

- **Built-in support for mobility:** IPv6 supports mobility such that IPv6 hosts can move around the Internetwork and retain their IPv6 address without losing current application sessions.

- **Provider independent and dependent public address space:** ISPs can assign public IPv6 address ranges (dependent), or companies can register their own public address space (independent).

- **Aggregation:** IPv6's huge address space makes for much easier aggregation of blocks of addresses in the Internet, making routing in the Internet more efficient.

- **No need for NAT/PAT:** The huge public IPv6 address space removes the need for NAT/PAT, which avoids some NAT-induced application problems and makes for more efficient routing.

- **IPsec:** Unlike IPv4, IPv6 requires that every IPv6 implementation support IPsec. IPv6 does not require that each device use IPsec, but any device that implements IPv6 must also have the ability to implement IPsec.

- **Header improvements:** Although it might seem like a small issue, the IPv6 header actually improves several things compared to IPv4. In particular, routers do not need to recalculate a header checksum for every packet, reducing per-packet overhead. Additionally, the header includes a flow label that allows for easy identification of packets sent over the same single TCP or UDP connection.

- **No broadcasts:** IPv6 does not use Layer 3 broadcast addresses, instead relying on multicasts to reach multiple hosts with a single packet.

- **Transition tools:** As covered in Chapter 18, the IPv6 has many rich tools to help with the transition from IPv4 to IPv6.

This list includes many legitimate advantages of IPv6 over IPv4, but the core difference, and the main topic of this chapter, is IPv6 addressing. The first two sections of this chapter examine one particular type of IPv6 addresses, global unicast addresses, which have many similarities to IPv4 addresses–particularly public IPv4 addresses. The third section broadens the discussion to include all types of IPv6 addresses, and protocols related to IPv6 address assignment, default router discovery, and neighbor discovery. The final section looks at the router configuration commands for IPv6 addressing.

Global Unicast Addressing, Routing, and Subnetting

The original Internet design called for all organizations to register and be assigned one or more public IP networks (Class A, B, or C). By registering to use a particular public network number, the company or organization using that network was assured by the numbering authorities that no other company or organization in the world would be using the same addresses. As a result, all hosts in the world would have globally unique IP addresses.

From the perspective of the Internet infrastructure, in particular the goal of keeping Internet routers' routing tables from getting too large, assigning an entire network to each organization helped to some degree. The Internet routers could ignore all subnets as defined inside an Enterprise, instead having a route for each classful network. For instance, if a company registered and was assigned Class B network 128.107.0.0/16, the Internet routers just needed one route for that whole network.

Over time, the Internet grew tremendously. It became clear by the early 1990s that something had to be done, or the growth of the Internet would grind to a halt when all the public IP networks were assigned, and no more existed. Additionally, the IP routing tables in Internet routers were becoming too large for the router technology of that day. So, the Internet community worked together to come up with both some short-term and long-term solutions to two problems: the shortage of public addresses and the size of the routing tables.

The short-term solutions included a much smarter public address assignment policy, in which public addresses were not assigned as only Class A, B, and C networks, but as smaller subdivisions (prefixes), reducing waste. Additionally, the growth of the Internet routing tables was reduced by smarter assignment of the actual address ranges based on geography. For example, assigning the class C networks that begin with 198 to only a particular ISP in a particular part of the world allowed other ISPs to use one route for 198.0.0.0/8–in other words, all addresses that begin with 198–rather than a route for each of the 65,536 different Class C networks that begin with 198. Finally, NAT/PAT achieved amazing results by allowing a typical home or small office to consume only one public IPv4 address, greatly reducing the need for public IPv4 addresses.

IPv6 provides the long-term solution to both problems (address exhaustion and Internet routing table size). The sheer size of IPv6 addresses takes care of the address exhaustion issue. The address assignment policies already used with IPv4 have been refined and applied to IPv6, with good results for keeping the size of IPv6 routing tables smaller in Internet routers. This section provides a general discussion of both issues, in particular how *global unicast* addresses, along with good administrative choices for how to assign IPv6 address prefixes, aid in routing in the global Internet. This section concludes with a discussion of subnetting in IPv6.

Global Route Aggregation for Efficient Routing

By the time the Internet community started serious work to find a solution to the growth problems in the Internet, many people already agreed that a more thoughtful public address assignment policy for the public IPv4 address space could help keep Internet routing tables much smaller and more manageable. IPv6 public address assignment follows these same well-earned lessons.

Note: The descriptions of IPv6 global address assignment in this section provides a general idea about the process. The process may vary from one RIR to another, and one ISP to another, based on many other factors.

The address assignment strategy for IPv6 is elegant, but simple, and can be roughly summarized as follows:

■   Public IPv6 addresses are grouped (numerically) by major geographic region.

■   Inside each region, the address space is further subdivided by ISPs inside that region.

■   Inside each ISP in a region, the address space is further subdivided for each customer.

The same organizations handle this address assignment for IPv6 as for IPv4. The Internet Corporation for Assigned Network Numbers (ICANN, www.icann.org) owns the process, with the Internet Assigned Numbers Authority (IANA) managing the process. IANA assigns one or more IPv6 address ranges to each Regional Internet Registries (RIR), of which there are five at the time of publication, roughly covering North America, Central/South America, Europe, Asia/Pacific, and Africa. These RIRs then subdivide their assigned address space into smaller portions, assigning prefixes to different ISPs and other smaller registries, with the ISPs then assigning even smaller ranges of addresses to their customers.

The IPv6 global address assignment plan results in more efficient routing, as shown in Figure 16-1. The figure shows a fictitious company (Company1) which has been assigned an IPv6 prefix by a fictitious ISP, NA-ISP1 (meaning for North American ISP number 1).

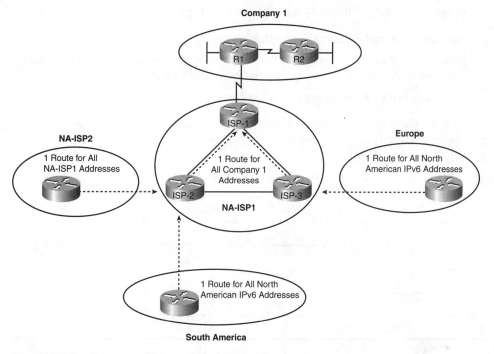

Figure 16-1   *Conceptual View of IPv6 Global Routes*

As shown in the figure, the routers installed by ISPs in other major geographies of the world can have a single route that matches all IPv6 addresses in North America. Although there might be hundreds of ISPs operating in north America, and hundreds of thousands of Enterprise customers of those ISPs, and tens of millions of individual customers of those ISPs, all the public IPv6 addresses can be from one (or a few) very large address blocks–requiring only one (or a few) routes on the Internet routers in other parts of the world. Similarly, routers inside other ISPs in North America (for example, NA-ISP2, meaning North American ISP number 2 in the figure), can have one route that matches all address ranges assigned to NA-ISP2. And the routers inside NA-ISP1 just need to have one route that matches the entire address range assigned to Company1, rather than needing to know about all the subnets inside Company1.

Besides keeping the routers' routing table much smaller, this process also results in fewer changes to Internet routing tables. For example, if NA-ISP1 signed a service contract with another Enterprise customer, NA-ISP1 could assign another prefix inside the range of addresses already assigned to NA-ISP1 by ARIN. The routers outside NA-ISP1's network–the majority of the Internet–do not need to know any new routes, because their existing routes already match the address range assigned to the new customer. The NA-ISP2 routers (another ISP) already have a route that matches the entire address range assigned to NA-ISP1, so they do not need any more routes. Likewise, the routers in ISPs in Europe and South America already have a route that works as well.

Conventions for Representing IPv6 Addresses

IPv6 conventions use 32 hexadecimal numbers, organized into 8 quartets of 4 hex digits separated by a colon, to represent a 128-bit IPv6 address, for example:

2340:1111:AAAA:0001:1234:5678:9ABC:1111

Each hex digit represents 4 bits, so if you want to examine the address in binary, the conversion is relatively easy if you memorize the values shown in Table 16-2.

Table 16-2 *Hexadecimal/Binary Conversion Chart*

Hex	Binary	Hex	Binary
0	0000	8	1000
1	0001	9	1001
2	0010	A	1010
3	0011	B	1011
4	0100	C	1100
5	0101	D	1101
6	0110	E	1110
7	0111	F	1111

Writing or typing 32 hexadecimal digits, although more convenient writing or typing 128 binary digits, can still be a pain. To make things a little easier, two conventions allow you to shorten what must be typed for an IPv6 address:

■ Omit the leading 0s in any given quartet.

■ Represent one or more consecutive quartets of all hex 0s with "::" but only for one such occurrence in a given address.

Note: For IPv6, a quartet is one set of 4 hex digits in an IPv6 address. There are 8 quartets in each IPv6 address.

For example, consider the following address. The bold digits represent digits in which the address could be abbreviated.

FE00:**0000:0000:**0001:**0000:0000:0000:00**56

This address has two different locations in which one or more quartets have 4 hex 0s, so two main options exist for abbreviating this address–using the :: abbreviation in one or the other location. The following two options show the two briefest valid abbreviations:

FE00::1:0:0:0:56

FE00:0:0:1::56

In particular, note that the "::" abbreviation, meaning "one or more quartets of all 0s," cannot be used twice because that would be ambiguous. So, the abbreviation FE00::1::56 would not be valid.

Conventions for Writing IPv6 Prefixes

IPv6 prefixes represent a range or block of consecutive IPv6 addresses. Just like routers use IPv4 subnets in IPv4 routing tables to represent ranges of consecutive addresses, routers use IPv6 prefixes to represent ranges of consecutive IPv6 addresses as well. The concepts mirror those of IPv4 addressing when using a classless view of the IPv4 address. Figure 16-2 reviews both the classful and classless view of IPv4 addresses, compared to the IPv6 view of addressing and prefixes.

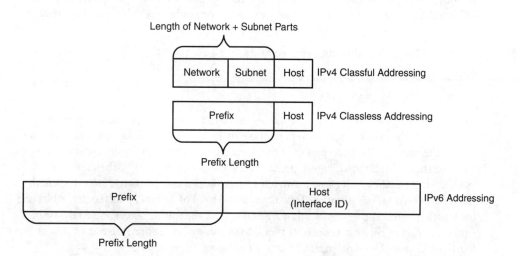

Figure 16-2 *IPv4 Classless and Classful Addressing, IPv6 Addressing*

First, for perspective, compare the classful and classless view of IPv4 addresses. Classful IPv4 addressing means that the class rules always identify part of the address as the network part. For example, the written value 128.107.3.0/24 (or 128.107.3.0 255.255.255.0) means 16 network bits (because the address is in a class B network), 8 host bits (because the mask has 8 binary 0s), leaving 8 subnet bits. The same value, interpreted with classless rules, means prefix 128.107.3.0, prefix length 24. Classless addressing and classful addressing just give slightly different meaning to the same numbers.

IPv6 uses a classless view of addressing, with no concept of classful addressing. Like IPv4, IPv6 prefixes list some prefix value, a slash, and then a numeric prefix length. Like IPv4 prefixes, the last part of the number, beyond the length of the prefix, will be represented by binary 0's. And finally, IPv6 prefix numbers can be abbreviated with the same rules as IPv6 addresses.

Note: IPv6 prefixes are often called IPv6 subnets as well. This book uses these terms interchangeably.

For example, consider the following IPv6 address that is assigned to a host on a LAN:

    2000:1234:5678:9ABC:1234:5678:9ABC:1111/64

This value represents the full 128-bit IP address–there are no opportunities to even abbreviate this address. However, the /64 means that the prefix (subnet) in which this address resides is the subnet that includes all addresses that begin with the same first 64 bits as the address. Conceptually, it is the same logic as an IPv4 address, for example, address 128.107.3.1/24 is in the prefix (subnet) whose first 24 bits are the same values as address 128.107.3.1.

As with IPv4, when writing or typing a prefix, the bits past the end of the prefix length are all binary 0s. In the IPv6 address previously shown, the prefix in which the address resides would be

    2000:1234:5678:9ABC:0000:0000:0000:0000/64

Which, when abbreviated, would be

    2000:1234:5678:9ABC::/64

Next, one last fact about the rules for writing prefixes before seeing some examples and moving on. If the prefix length is not a multiple of 16, then the boundary between the prefix and the interface ID (host) part of the address is inside a quartet. In such cases, the prefix value should list all the values in the last quartet in the prefix part of the value. For example, if the address just shown with a /64 prefix length instead had a /56 prefix length, the prefix would include all of the first 3 quartets (a total of 48 bits), plus the first 8 bits of the fourth quartet. The next 8 bits (last 2 hex digits) of the fourth octet should now be binary 0s, as part of the host portion of the address. So, by convention, the rest of the fourth octet should be written, after being set to binary 0s, as follows:

    2000:1234:5678:9A00::/56

The following list summarizes some key points about how to write IPv6 prefixes.

- The prefix has the same value as the IP addresses in the group for the number of bits in the prefix length.

- Any bits after the prefix length number of bits are binary 0s.

- The prefix can be abbreviated with the same rules as IPv6 addresses.

- If the prefix length is not on a quartet boundary, write down the value for the entire quartet.

Examples can certainly help in this case. Table 16-3 shows several sample prefixes, their format, and a brief explanation.

Table 16-3 *Example IPv6 Prefixes and Their Meanings*

Prefix	Explanation	Incorrect Alternative
2000::/3	All addresses whose first 3 bits are equal to the first 3 bits of hex number 2000 (bits are 001).	2000/3 (omits ::) 2::/3 (omits the trailing 0s in the first quartet)
2340:1140::/26	All addresses whose first 26 bits match the listed hex number.	2340:114::/26 (omits trailing 0 in the second quartet)
2340:1111::/32	All addresses whose first 32 bits match the listed hex number.	2340:1111/32 (omits ::)

Note which options are not allowed. For example, 2::/3 is not allowed instead of 2000::/3, because it omits the rest of the quartet, and a device could not tell if 2::/3 means "hex 0002" or "hex 2000".

Now that you understand a few of the conventions about how to represent IPv6 addresses and prefixes, a specific example can show how IANA's IPv6 global unicast IP address assignment strategy can allow the easy and efficient routing shown in Figure 16-1.

Global Unicast Prefix Assignment Example

IPv6 standards reserve the range of addresses inside the 2000::/3 prefix as global unicast addresses. This address range includes all IPv6 addresses that begin with binary 001, or as more easily recognized, all IPv6 addresses that begin with a 2 or 3. IANA assigns global unicast IPv6 addresses as public and globally unique IPv6 addresses, as discussed using the example previously shown in Figure 16-1, allowing hosts using those addresses to communicate through the Internet without the need for NAT. In other words, these addresses fit the purest design for how to implement IPv6 for the global Internet.

Figure 16-3 shows an example set of prefixes that could result in a company (Company1) being assigned a prefix of 2340:1111:AAAA::/48.

The process starts with IANA, who owns the entire IPv6 address space and assigns the rights to *registry prefix* to one of the RIRs (ARIN in this case, in North America). For the purposes of this chapter, assume that IANA assigns prefix 2340::/12 to ARIN. This assignment means that ARIN has the rights to assign any IPv6 addresses that begin with the first 12 bits of hex 2340 (binary value 0010 0011 0100). For perspective, that's a large group of addresses: 2^{116} to be exact.

Next, NA-ISP1 asks ARIN for a prefix assignment. After ARIN ensures that NA-ISP1 meets some requirements, ARIN might assign *ISP prefix* 2340:1111::/32 to NA-ISP1. This too is a large group: 2^{96} addresses to be exact. For perspective, this one address block may

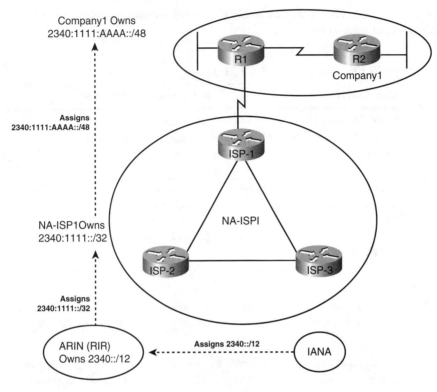

Key Topic **Figure 16-3** *Example IPv6 Prefix Assignment in the Internet*

well be enough public IPv6 addresses for even the largest ISPs, without that ISP ever needing another IPv6 prefix.

Finally, Company1 asks its ISP, NA-ISP1, for the assignment of an IPv6 prefix. NA-ISP1 assigns Company1 the site prefix 2340:1111:AAAA::/48, which is again a large range of addresses: 2^{80} in this case. A little later in this section the text shows what Company1 could do with that prefix, but first, examine Figure 16-4, which presents the same concepts as in Figure 16-1, but now with the actual prefixes shown.

The figure shows the perspectives of routers outside North America, routers from another ISP in North America, and other routers in the same ISP. Routers outside North America can use a route for prefix 2340::/12, knowing the IANA assigned this prefix to be used only by ARIN. This one route could match all IPv6 addresses assigned in North America. Routers in NA-ISP2, an example alternative ISP in North America, need one route for 2340:1111::/32, the prefix assigned to NA-ISP1. This one route could match all packets destined for all customers of NA-ISP1. Inside NA-ISP1, its routers need to know to which NA-ISP1 router to forward packets to for that particular customer (named ISP-1 in this case), so the routes inside NA-ISP1's routers lists a prefix of 2340:1111:AAAA::/48.

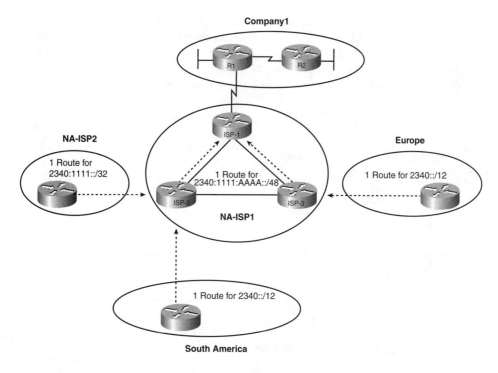

Figure 16-4 *IPv6 Global Routing Concepts*

Note: The /48 prefix assigned to a single company is called either a *global routing prefix* or a *site prefix*.

Subnetting Global Unicast IPv6 Addresses Inside an Enterprise

The original IPv4 Internet design called for each organization to be assigned a classful network number, with the Enterprise subdividing the network into smaller address ranges by subnetting the classful network. This same concept of subnetting carries over from IPv4 to IPv6, with the Enterprise subnetting its assigned global unicast prefix into smaller prefixes.

To better understand the IPv6 subnetting, you can draw on either classful or classless IPv4 addressing concepts, whichever you find most comfortable. From a classless perspective, you can view the IPv6 addresses as follows:

■   The prefix assigned to the Enterprise by the ISP (the global routing prefix) acts like the prefix assigned for IPv4.

■   The Enterprise engineer extends the prefix length, borrowing host bits, to create a subnet part of the address with which to identify individual subnets.

■   The remaining part of the addresses on the right, called either the interface ID or host part, works just like the IPv4 host part, uniquely identifying a host inside a subnet.

Key
Topic

For example, Figure 16-5 shows a more detailed view of the Company1 Enterprise network shown in several of the previous figures in this chapter. The design concepts behind how many subnets are needed with IPv6 are identical as with IPv4–a subnet is needed for each VLAN, and for each serial link, with the same options for subnets with Frame Relay. In this case, two LANs and two serial links exist, so Company1 needs four subnets.

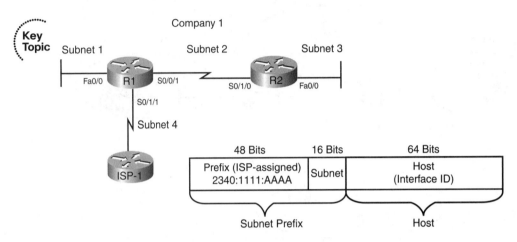

Figure 16-5 *Company1–Needs Four Subnets*

The figure also shows how the Enterprise engineer extended the length of the prefix as assigned by the ISP (/48) to /64, thereby creating a 16-bit subnet part of the address structure. To create this extra 16-bit subnet field, the engineer uses the same concept as with IPv4 when choosing a subnet mask by borrowing bits from the host field of an IPv4 address. In this case, think of the original host field (before subnetting) as having 80 bits, because the site prefix is 48-bits long, leaving 80 bits. The design in Figure 16-5 borrows 16 bits for the subnet field, leaving a measly 64 bits for the host field.

A bit of math about the design choices can help provide some perspective on the scale of IPv6. The 16-bit subnet field allows for 2^{16}, or 65,536, subnets–overkill for all but the very largest organizations or companies. (There are no worries about a zero or broadcast subnet in IPv6!) The host field is seemingly even more overkill: 2^{64} hosts per subnet, which is more than 1,000,000,000,000,000,000 addresses per subnet. However, there is a good reason for this large host or interface ID part of the address because it allows one of the automatic IPv6 address assignment features to work well, as covered later in the section "Assigning IPv6 Global Unicast IP Addresses."

Figure 16-6 takes the concept to the conclusion, assigning the specific four subnets to be used inside Company1. Note that the figure shows the subnet fields and prefix lengths (64 in this case) in bold.

Note: The subnet numbers in Figure 16-6 could be abbreviated slightly, removing the three leading 0s from the last shown quartets. The figure includes the leading 0s to show the entire subnet part of the prefixes.

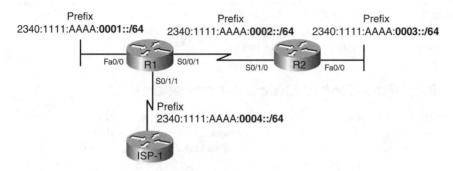

Figure 16-6 *Company1–4 Subnets Assigned*

Figure 16-6 just shows one option for subnetting the prefix assigned to Company1. However, any number of subnet bits could be chosen if the host field retained enough bits to number all hosts in a subnet. For example, a /112 prefix length could be used, extending the /48 prefix by 64 bits (4 hex quartets). Then, for the design in Figure 16-6, you could choose the following four subnets:

2340:1111:AAAA::0001:0000/112

2340:1111:AAAA::0002:0000/112

2340:1111:AAAA::0003:0000/112

2340:1111:AAAA::0004:0000/112

By using global unicast IPv6 addresses, Internet routing can be very efficient; Enterprises can have plenty of IP addresses and plenty of subnets with no requirement for NAT functions to conserve the address space.

Prefix Terminology

Before wrapping up this section, a few new terms need to be introduced. The process of global unicast IPv6 address assignment examines many different prefixes with many different prefix lengths. The text scatters a couple of more specific terms, but for easier study, Table 16-4 summarizes the four key terms with some reminders of what each means.

Table 16-4 *Example IPv6 Prefixes and Their Meanings*

Term	Assignment	Example from Chapter 16
Registry prefix	By IANA to an RIR	2340::/12
ISP prefix	By an RIR to an ISP[1]	2340:1111/32
Site prefix or global routing prefix	By an ISP or registry to a customer (site)	2340:1111:AAAA/48
Subnet prefix	By an Enterprise engineer for each individual link	2340:1111:AAAA:0001/64

Table 16-4   *Example IPv6 Prefixes and Their Meanings*

[1]Although an RIR can assign a prefix to an ISP, an RIR may also assign a prefix to other Internet registries, which might subdivide and assign additional prefixes, until eventually an ISP and then their customers are assigned some unique prefix.

Assigning IPv6 Global Unicast Addresses

This section still focuses on global unicast IPv6 addresses but now examines the topic of how a host, router interface, or other device knows what global unicast IPv6 address to use. Also, hosts (and sometimes routers) also need to know a few other facts that can be learned at the same time as learning their IPv6 address. So, this section also discusses how hosts can get all the following relevant information that lets them use their global unicast addresses:

- IP address

- IP subnet mask (prefix length)

- Default router IP address

- DNS IP address(es)

IPv6 actually has four major options for IPv6 global unicast address assignment. This section looks at these options in the same order as listed in Table 16-5. Each method can use dynamic processes or static configuration, and each method can differ in terms of how a host or router gathers the other pertinent information (such as DNS IP addresses). Table 16-5 summarizes these main methods for easier review.

Table 16-5   *Summary of IPv6 Address Assignment for Global Unicast Addresses*

Method	Dynamic or static	Prefix and length learned from...	Host learned from...	Default router learned from...	DNS addresses learned from...
Stateful DHCP	Dynamic	DHCP Server	DHCP Server	Router, using NDP	(Stateful) DHCP Server
Stateless autoconfig	Dynamic	Router, using NDP	Derived from MAC	Router, using NDP	Stateless DHCP
Static configuration	Static	Local config	Local config	Router, using NDP	Stateless DHCP
Static config with EUI-64	Static	Local config	Derived from MAC	Router, using NDP	Stateless DHCP

The rest of this section develops more detail about the topics in the table. Some of the processes work much like IPv4, and some do not. Regardless, as you work through the material, keep in mind one key fact about how IPv6 protocols approach the address assignment process:

> IPv6 address assignment processes may split the IPv6 address assignment into two parts: the prefix/length assignment and the host (interface ID) assignment.

Stateful DHCP for IPv6

IPv6 hosts can use stateful DHCP to learn and lease an IP address and corresponding prefix length (mask), and the DNS IP address(es). The concept works basically like DHCP for IPv4; the host sends a (multicast) packet searching for the DHCP server. When a server replies, the DHCP client sends a message asking for a lease of an IP address, and the server replies, listing an IPv6 address, prefix length, and DNS IP addresses. (Note that Stateful DHCPv6 does not supply the default router information, instead relying on Neighbor Discovery Protocol between the client and local routers.) The names and formats of the actual DHCP messages have changed quite a bit from IPv4 to IPv6, so DHCPv4 and DHCPv6 actually differ in detail, but the basic process remains the same. (The term DHCPv4 refers to the version of DHCP used for IPv4, and the term DHCPv6 refers to the version of DHCP used for IPv6.)

DHCPv4 servers retain *state information* about each client, such as the IP address leased to that client, and the length of time for which the lease is valid. In other words, DHCPv4 tracks the current state of DHCP clients. DHCPv6 servers happen to have two operational modes: stateful, in which the server does track state information, and stateless, in which the server does not track any state information. Stateful DHCPv6 servers fill the same role as the older DHCPv4 servers, whereas stateless DHCPv6 servers fill a different purpose as one part of the stateless autoconfiguration process. (Stateless DHCP, and its purpose, is covered in the upcoming section "Finding the DNS IP Addresses Using Stateless DHCP.")

One difference between DHCPv4 and stateful DHCPv6 is that IPv4 hosts send IP broadcasts to find DHCP servers, whereas IPv6 hosts send IPv6 multicasts. IPv6 multicast addresses have a prefix of FF00::/8, meaning that if the first 8 bits of an address are binary 11111111, or FF in hex. The multicast address FF02::1:2 (longhand FF02:0000:0000:0000:0000:0000:0001:0002) has been reserved in IPv6 to be used by hosts to send packets to an unknown DHCP server, with the routers working to forward these packets to the appropriate DHCP server.

Stateless Autoconfiguration

The second of the two options for dynamic IPv6 address assignment uses a built-in IPv6 feature called *stateless autoconfiguration* as the core tool. Stateless autoconfiguration allows a host to automatically learn the key pieces of addressing information–prefix, host, and prefix length–plus the default router IP address and DNS IP addresses. To learn or derive all these pieces of information, stateless autoconfiguration actually uses the following functions:

Step 1. IPv6 Neighbor Discovery Protocol (NDP), particularly the router solicitation and router advertisement messages, to learn the prefix, prefix length, and default router

Key
Topic

Step 2. Some math to derive the interface ID (host ID) portion of the IPv6 address, using a format called EUI-64

Step 3. Stateless DHCP to learn the DNS IPv6 addresses

This section examines all three topics in order.

Learning the Prefix/Length and Default Router with NDP Router Advertisements

The IPv6 Neighbor Discovery Protocol (NDP) has many functions. One function allows IPv6 hosts to multicast a message that asks all routers on the link to announce two key pieces of information: the IPv6 addresses of routers willing to act as a default gateway and all known IPv6 prefixes on the link. This process uses ICMPv6 messages called a Router Solicitation (RS) and a Router Advertisement (RA).

For this process to work, before a host sends an RS message on a LAN, some router connected to that same LAN must already be configured for IPv6. The router must have an IPv6 address configured, and it must be configured to route IPv6 traffic. At that point, the router knows it can be useful as a default gateway, and it knows at least one prefix that can be useful to any clients on the LAN.

For example, Figure 16-7 shows a subset of the internetwork seen in Figures 16-5 and 16-6, with the same IPv6 addresses and subnets used. Router R1's Fa0/0 has already been configured with an IPv6 address (2340:1111:AAAA:1:213:19FF:FE7B:5004/64) and has been configured to route IPv6 with the **ipv6 unicast-routing** global command.

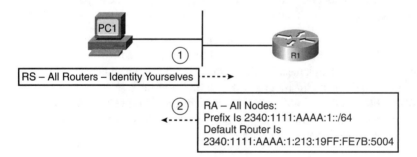

Figure 16-7 *Example NDP RS/RA Process to Find the Default Routers*

In the figure, host PC1, using stateless autoconfig, sends the RS message as an IPv6 multicast message destined to all IPv6 routers on the local link. The RS asks all routers to respond to the questions "What IPv6 prefix(s) is used on this subnet?" and "What is the IPv6 address(s) of any default routers on this subnet?" The figure also shows R1's response (RA), listing the prefix (2340:1111:AAAA:1::/64), and with R1's own IPv6 address as a potential default router.

Note: IPv6 allows for multiple prefixes and multiple default routers to be listed in the RA message; Figure 16-7 just shows one of each for simplicity's sake. One router's RA would include IPv6 addresses and prefixes advertised by other routers on the link as well.

IPv6 does not use broadcasts. In fact, there is no such thing as a subnet broadcast address, a networkwide broadcast address, or an equivalent of the all-hosts 255.255.255.255 broadcast IPv4 address. Instead, IPv6 makes use of multicast addresses. By defining a different multicast IPv6 address for different functions, an IPv6 host that has no need to participate in a particular function can simply ignore those particular multicasts, reducing the impact to the host.

For example, the RS message needs to be received and processed only by routers, so the RS message's destination IP address is FF02::2, which IPv6 reserves for use only by IPv6 routers. IPv6 defines that routers send RA messages to a multicast address intended for use by all IPv6 hosts on the link (FF02::1); routers do not forward these messages to other links. As a result, not only does the host that sent the RS message learn the information, all other hosts on the link learn the details as well. Table 16-6 summarizes some of the key details about the RS/RA messages.

Table 16-6   *Details of the RS/RA Process*

Message	RS	RA
Multicast destination	FF02::2	FF02::1
Meaning of Multicast address	All routers on this link	All IPv6 nodes on this link

Calculating the Interface ID Using EUI-64

Earlier in the chapter, Figure 16-5 shows the format of an IPv6 global unicast address with the second half of the address called the host ID or interface ID. The value of the interface ID portion of a global unicast address can be set to any value if no other host in the same subnet attempts to use the same value.

To automatically create a guaranteed-unique interface ID, IPv6 defines a method to calculate a 64-bit interface ID derived from that host's MAC address. Because the burned-in MAC address should be literally globally unique, the derived interface ID should also be globally unique as well.

The EUI-64 process takes the 6-byte (48-bit) MAC address and expands it into a 64-bit value. To do so, IPv6 fills in 2 more bytes into the middle of the MAC address. IPv6 separates the original MAC address into two 3-byte halves and inserts hex FFFE in between the halves to form the Interface ID field of the IPv6 address. The conversion also requires flipping the seventh bit inside the IPv6 address, resulting in a 64-bit number that conforms to a convention called the EUI-64 format. The process is shown in Figure 16-8.

Although it may seem a bit convoluted, it works. Also, with a little practice, you can look at an IPv6 address and quickly notice the FFFE late in the address and then easily find the two halves of the corresponding interface's MAC address.

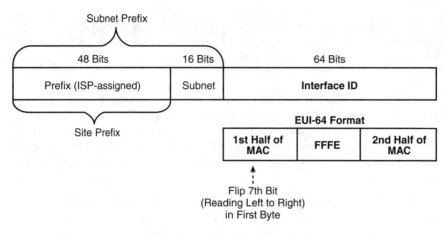

Key
Topic **Figure 16-8** *IPv6 Address Format with Interface ID and EUI-64*

For example, the following two lines list a host's MAC address, and corresponding EUI-64 format Interface ID, assuming the use of an address configuration option that uses the EUI-64 format:

0034:5678:9ABC

0234:56FF:FE78:9ABC

Note: To change the seventh bit (left-to-right) in the example, hex 00 converts to binary 00000000, change the seventh bit to 1 (00000010), convert back to hex, for hex 02 as the first two digits.

At this point in the stateless autoconfig process, a host knows its full IPv6 address and prefix length, plus a local router to use as default gateway. The next section discusses how to complete the process using stateless DHCP.

Finding the DNS IP Addresses Using Stateless DHCP

Although the DHCP server function for IPv4 does not explicitly use the word "stateful" in its name, IPv4 DHCP servers keep state information about DHCP clients. The server keeps a record of the leased IP addresses, and when the lease expires. The server typically re-leases the addresses to the same client before the lease expires, and if no response is heard from a DHCP client in time to renew the lease, the server releases that IP address back into the pool of usable IP addresses–again keeping that state information. The server also has configuration of the subnets in use and a pool of addresses in most subnets from which the server can assign IP addresses. It also serves other information, such as the default router IP addresses in each subnet, and the DNS server IP addresses.

The IPv6 stateful DHCP server, as previously discussed in the section "Stateful DHCP for IPv6", follows the same general idea. However, for IPv6, this server's name includes the word stateful, to contrast it with the stateless DHCP server function in IPv6.

The stateless DHCP server function in IPv6 solves one particular problem: It supplies the DNS server IPv6 address(es) to clients. Because all hosts typically use the same small number of DNS servers, the stateless DHCP server does not need to keep track of any state information. An engineer simply configures the stateless DHCP server to know the IPv6 addresses of the DNS servers, and the servers tells any host or other device that asks, keeping no record of the process.

Hosts that use stateless autoconfig also use stateless DHCP to learn the DNS server IPv6 addresses.

Table 16-7 summarizes some of the key features of stateful and stateless DHCPv6.

Table 16-7 *Comparing Stateless and Stateful DHCPv6 Services*

Feature	Stateful DHCP	Stateless DHCP
Remembers IPv6 address (state information) of clients that make requests	Yes	No
Assigns IPv6 address to client	Yes	No
Supplies useful information, such as DNS server IP addresses	Yes	Yes
Most useful in conjunction with stateless autoconfiguration	No	Yes

Static IPv6 Address Configuration

Two options exist for static configuration of IPv6 addresses. For one option, you configure the entire 128-bit IPv6 address, and for the other, you just configure the 64-bit prefix and tell the device to use an EUI-64 calculation for the interface ID portion of the address. Both options result in the host or router interface knowing its full 128-bit IPv6 address and prefix length.

When a host uses either form of static IPv6 address configuration, the host does not need to statically configure the other key pieces of information (default router and DNS IP addresses). The host can use the usual NDP process to discover any default routers and stateless DHCP to discover the DNS IPv6 addresses.

When a router uses static IPv6 address configuration, it may still use stateless DHCP to learn the DNS IP addresses. The upcoming section "Configuring IPv6 Addresses on Cisco Routers" shows several examples of this configuration.

Survey of IPv6 Addressing

So far, this chapter has focused on the IPv6 addresses that most closely match the concept of IPv4 addresses: the global unicast IPv6 address. This section now takes a broader look at IPv6 addressing, including some concepts that can be tied to older IPv4 concepts, and some that are unique to IPv6.

This section begins with a brief overview of IPv6 addressing. It then looks at unicast IPv6 addresses, along with a brief look at some of the commonly used multicast addresses. This section ends with a discussion of a couple of related protocols, namely Neighbor Discovery Protocol (NDP) and Duplicate Address Detection (DAD).

Overview of IPv6 Addressing

The whole concept of global unicast addressing does have many similarities as compared with IPv4. If viewing IPv4 addresses from a classless perspective, both IPv4 and IPv6 global unicast addresses have two parts: subnet plus host for IPv4 and prefix plus interface ID for IPv6. The format of the addresses commonly list a slash followed by the prefix length–a convention sometimes referred to as *CIDR notation*, and other times as *prefix notation*. Subnetting works much the same, with a public prefix assigned by some numbering authority, and the Enterprise choosing subnet numbers, extending the length of the prefix to make room to number the subnets.

IPv6 addressing, however, includes several other types of unicast IPv6 addresses beside the global unicast address. Additionally, IPv6 defines other general categories of addresses, as summarized in this list.

- **Unicast:** Like IPv4, hosts and routers assign these IP addresses to a single interface for the purpose of allowing that one host or interface to send and receive IP packets.

- **Multicast:** Like IPv4, these addresses represent a dynamic group of hosts, allowing a host to send one packet that is then delivered to every host in the multicast group. IPv6 defines some special-purpose multicast addresses for overhead functions (such as NDP). IPv6 also defines ranges of multicast addresses for application use.

- **Anycast:** This address type allows the implementation of a nearest server among duplicate servers concept. This design choice allows servers that support the exact same function to use the exact same unicast IP address. The routers then forward a packet destined for such an address to the nearest server that is using the address.

Two big differences exist when comparing general address categories for IPv4 and IPv6. First, IPv6 adds the formal concept of Anycast IPv6 addresses as shown in the preceding list. IPv4 does not formally define an Anycast IP address concept, although a similar concept may be implemented in practice. Second, IPv6 simply has no Layer 3 broadcast addresses. For example, all IPv6 routing protocols send Updates either to Unicast or Multicast IPv6 addresses, and overhead protocols such as NDP make use of multicasts as well. In IPv4, ARP still uses broadcasts, and older routing protocols such as RIP-1 also used broadcasts. With IPv6, there is no need to calculate a subnet broadcast address (hoorah!) and no need to make hosts process overhead broadcast packets meant only for a few devices in a subnet.

Finally, note that IPv6 hosts and router interfaces typically have at least two IPv6 addresses and may well have more. Hosts and routers typically have a Link Local type of IPv6 address (as described in the upcoming section "Link Local Unicast Addresses"). A router may or may not have a global unicast address, and may well have multiple. IPv6 simply allows the configuration of multiple IPv6 addresses with no need for or concept of secondary IP addressing.

Unicast IPv6 Addresses

IPv6 supports three main types of unicast addresses: link local, global unicast, and unique local. This section takes a brief look at link local and unique local addresses.

Unique Local IPv6 Addresses

Unique local unicast IPv6 addresses have the same function as IPv4 RFC 1918 private addresses. RFC 4193 states that these addresses should be used inside a private organization, and should not be advertised into the Internet. Unique local unicast addresses begin with hex FD (FD00::/8), with the format shown in Figure 16-9.

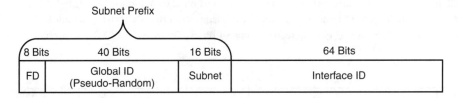

Figure 16-9   *Unique Local Address Format*

To use these addresses, an Enterprise engineer would choose a 40-bit global ID in a pseudo-random manner rather than asking for a registered public prefix from an ISP or other registry. To form the complete prefix, the chosen 40 bits would be combined with the initial required 8 bits (hex FD) to form a 48-bit site prefix. The engineer can then use a 16-bit subnet field to create subnets, leaving a 64-bit Interface ID. The interface ID could be created by static configuration or by the EUI-64 calculation.

This type of unicast address gives the engineer the ability to create the equivalent of an IPv4 private address structure, but given the huge number of available public IPv6 addresses, it may be more likely that engineers plan to use global unicast IP addresses throughout an Enterprise.

Link Local Unicast Addresses

IPv6 uses link local addresses for sending and receiving IPv6 packets on a single subnet. Many such uses exist; here's just a small sample:

■   Used as the source address for RS and RA messages for router discovery (as previously shown in Figure 16-7)

■   Used by Neighbor Discovery (the equivalent of ARP for IPv6)

■   As the next-hop IPv6 address for IP routes

By definition, routers use a link local scope for packets sent to a link local IPv6 address. The term *link local* scope means exactly that–the packet should not leave the local link, or local subnet if you will. When a router receives a packet destined for such a destination address, the router does not forward the packet.

The link local IPv6 addresses also help solve some chicken-and-egg problems because each host, router interface, or other device can calculate its own link local IPv6 address without needing to communicate with any other device. So, before sending the first packets, the host can calculate its own link local address, so the host has an IPv6 address to use when doing its first overhead messages. For example, before a host sends an NDP RS (router solicitation) message, the host will have already calculated its link local address, which can be used as the source IPv6 address on the RS message.

Link local addresses come from the FE80::/10 range, meaning the first 10 bits must be 1111 1110 10. An easier range to remember is that all hex link local addresses begin FE8, FE9, FEA, or FEB. However, practically speaking, for link local addresses formed automatically by a host (rather than through static configuration), the address always starts FE80, because the automatic process sets bits 11-64 to binary 0s. Figure 16-10 shows the format of the link local address format under the assumption that the host or router is deriving its own link local address, therefore using 54 binary 0s after the FE80::/10 prefix.

10 Bits	54 Bits	64 Bits
FE80/10 1111111010	All 0s	Interface ID

Figure 16-10 *Link Local Address Format*

IPv6 Unicast Address Summary

You may come across a few other types of IPv6 addresses in other reading. For example, earlier IPv6 RFCs defined the Site Local address type, which was meant to be used like IPv4 private addresses. However, this address type has been deprecated (RFC 3879). Also, the IPv6 migration and coexistence tools discussed in Chapter 18 use some conventions for IPv6 unicast addresses such that IPv4 addresses are imbedded in the IPv6 address.

Additionally, it is helpful to know about other special unicast addresses. An address of all hex 0s, written ::/128, represents an unknown address. This can be used as a source IPv6 address in packets when a host has no suitable IPv6 address to use. The address ::1/128, representing an address of all hex 0s except a final hex digit 1, is a loopback address. Packets sent to this address will be looped back up the TCP/IP stack, allowing for easier software testing. (This is the equivalent of IPv4's 127.0.0.1 loopback address.)

Table 16-8 summarizes the IPv6 unicast address types for easier study.

Table 16-8 *Common IPv6 Unicast Address Types*

Type of Address	Purpose	Prefix	Easily Seen Hex Prefix(es)
Global unicast	Unicast packets sent through the public Internet	2000::/3	2 or 3
Unique local	Unicast packets inside one organization	FD00::/8	FD

Table 16-8 *Common IPv6 Unicast Address Types*

Type of Address	Purpose	Prefix	Easily Seen Hex Prefix(es)
Link local	Packets sent in the local subnet	FE80::/10	FE8*
Site local	Deprecated; originally meant to be used like private IPv4 addresses	FEC0::/10	FEC, FED, FEE, FEF
Unspecified	An address used when a host has no usable IPv6 address	::/128	N/A
Loopback	Used for software testing, like IPv4's 127.0.0.1	::1/128	N/A

*IPv6 RFCs define the FE80::/10 prefix, which technically means that the first three hex digits could be FE8, FE9, FEA, or FEB. However, bit positions 11-64 of link local addresses should be 0, so in practice, link local addresses should always begin with FE80.

Multicast and Other Special IPv6 Addresses

IPv6 supports multicasts on behalf of applications and multicasts to support the inner workings of IPv6. To aid this process, IPv6 defines ranges of IPv6 addresses and an associated scope, with the scope defining how far away from the source of the packet that the network should forward a multicast.

All IPv6 multicast addresses begin with FF::/8 – in other words, with FF as the first two digits. Multicasts with a link local scope, like most of the multicast addresses referenced in this chapter, begin with FF02::/16; the 2 in the fourth hex digit identifies the scope as link local. A fourth digit of hex 5 identifies the broadcast as site local scope, with those multicasts beginning with FF05::/16.

For reference, Table 16-9 lists some of the more commonly seen IPv6 multicast addresses. Of particular interest are the addresses chosen for use by RIP, OSPF, and EIGRP, which somewhat mirror the multicast addresses each protocol uses for IPv4. Note also that all but the last two entries have link local scope.

Table 16-9 *Common Multicast Addresses*

Purpose	IPv6 Address	IPv4 Equivalent
All IPv6 nodes on the link	FF02::1	subnet broadcast address
All IPv6 routers on the link	FF02::2	N/A
OSPF messages	FF02::5, FF02::6	224.0.0.5, 224.0.0.6

Table 16-9 *Common Multicast Addresses*

Purpose	IPv6 Address	IPv4 Equivalent
RIP-2 messages	FF02::9	224.0.0.9
EIGRP messages	FF02::A	224.0.0.10
DHCP relay agents (routers that forward to the DHCP server)	FF02::1:2	N/A
DHCP servers (site scope)	FF05::1:3	N/A
All NTP servers (site scope)	FF05::101	N/A

Layer 2 Addressing Mapping and Duplicate Address Detection

As with IPv4, any device running IPv6 needs to determine the data link layer address used by devices on the same link. IPv4 uses Address Resolution Protocol (ARP) on LANs and Inverse ARP (InARP) on Frame Relay. IPv6 defines a couple of new protocols that perform the same function. These new functions use ICMPv6 messages and avoid the use of broadcasts, in keeping with IPv6's avoidance of broadcasts. This section gives a brief explanation of each protocol.

Neighbor Discovery Protocol for Layer 2 Mapping

When an IPv6 host or router needs to send a packet to another host or router on the same LAN, the host/router first looks in its neighbor database. This database contains a list of all neighboring IPv6 addresses (addresses in connected links) and their corresponding MAC addresses. If not found, the host or router uses the Neighbor Discovery Protocol (NDP) to dynamically discover the MAC address.

Figure 16-11 shows a sample of such a process, using the same host and router seen earlier in Figure 16-8.

The process acts like the IPv4 ARP process, just with different details. In this case, PC1 sends a multicast message called a Neighbor Solicitation (NS) ICMP message, asking R1 to reply with R1's MAC address. R1 sends a Neighbor Advertisement (NA) ICMP message, unicast back to PC1, listing R1's MAC address. Now PC1 can build a data link frame with R1's MAC listed as the destination address and send encapsulated packets to R1.

The NS message uses a special multicast destination address called a *solicited node multicast* address. On any given link, the solicited node multicast address represents all hosts with the same last 24 bits of their IPv6 addresses. By sending packets to the solicited node multicast address, the packet reaches the correct host, but it may also reach a few other hosts–which is fine. (Note that packets sent to a solicited node multicast address have a link local scope.)

The solicited node multicast address begins with FF02::1:FF00:0/104. The final 24 bits (6 hex digits) of the address is formed by adding the last 24 bits of the IPv6 address to which the message is being sent. This convention allows convenient use of LAN multicast addresses, which begin with hex 01005E hex, followed by one additional binary 0, and then

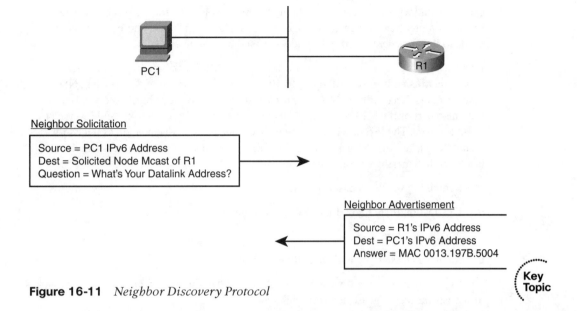

Neighbor Solicitation

Source = PC1 IPv6 Address
Dest = Solicited Node Mcast of R1
Question = What's Your Datalink Address?

Neighbor Advertisement

Source = R1's IPv6 Address
Dest = PC1's IPv6 Address
Answer = MAC 0013.197B.5004

Figure 16-11   *Neighbor Discovery Protocol*

an additional 23 bits–in this case taken from the low order 23 bits of the IPv6 address. All IPv6 listen for frames sent to their own solicited node multicast address, so that when a host or router receives such a multicast, the host can realize that it should reply. For example, in this case, based on R1's IPv6 address previously seen in Figure 16-7:

■ R1's IPv6 address: 2340:1111:AAAA:1:213:19FF:FE7B:5004

■ R1's solicited node address: FF02::1:FF7B:5004

Note: The corresponding Ethernet multicast MAC address would be 0100.5E7B.5004.

Duplicate Address Detection (DAD)

When an IPv6 interface first learns an IPv6 address, or when the interface begins working after being down for any reason, the interface performs duplicate address detection (DAD). The purpose of this check is to prevent hosts from creating problems by trying to use the same IPv6 address already used by some other host on the link.

To perform such a function, the interface uses the same NS message shown in Figure 16-11 but with small changes. To check its own IPv6 address, a host sends the NS message to the solicited node multicast address based on its own IPv6 address. If some host sends a reply, listing the same IPv6 address as the source address, the original host has found that a duplicate address exists.

Inverse Neighbor Discovery

The ND protocol discussed in this section starts with a known neighbor's IPv6 address and seeks to discover the link layer address used by that IPv6 address. On Frame Relay networks, and with some other WAN data link protocols, the order of discovery is reversed. A router begins with knowledge of the neighbor's link layer address and instead needs to dynamically learn the IPv6 address used by that neighbor.

IPv4 solves this discovery problem on LANs using ARP, and the reverse problem over Frame Relay using Inverse ARP (InARP). IPv6 solves the problem on LANs using ND, and now for Frame Relay, IPv6 solves this problem using Inverse Neighbor Discovery (IND). IND, also part of the ICMPv6 protocol suite, defines an Inverse NS (INS) and Inverse NA (INA) message. The INS message lists the known neighbor link layer address (DLCI for Frame Relay), and the INS asks for that neighboring device's IPv6 addresses. The details inside the INS message include the following:

■ Source IPv6: IPv6 unicast of sender

■ Destination IPv6: FF02::1 (all IPv6 hosts multicast)

■ Link layer addresses

■ Request: Please reply with your IPv6 address(es)

The IND reply lists all the IPv6 addresses. As with IPv4, the **show frame-relay map** command lists the mapping learned from this process.

Configuring IPv6 Addresses on Cisco Routers

Most IPv6 implementation plans make use of both static IPv6 address configuration and dynamic configuration options. As is the case with IPv4, the plan assigns infrastructure devices with static addresses, with client hosts using one of the two dynamic methods for address assignment.

IPv6 addressing includes many more options than IPv4, and as a result, many more configuration options exist. A router interface can be configured with a static global unicast IPv6 address, either with or without using the EUI-64 option. Although less likely, a router could be configured to dynamically learn its IPv6 address with either stateful DHCP or stateless autoconfig. The router interface could be configured to either not use a global unicast address, instead relying solely on its link local address, or to borrow another interface's address using the IPv6 unnumbered feature.

This section summarizes the address configuration commands and shows several examples of configuration and verification commands for IPv6. To that end, Table 16-10 summarizes the IPv6 configuration commands and their meanings.

Table 16-10 *Router IOS IPv6 Configuration Command Reference*

Command	Description
ipv6 address *address/length*	Static configuration of the entire IPv6 unicast address.
ipv6 address *prefix/length* **eui-64**	Static configuration of the first 64 address bits; the router derives the last 64 bits with EUI-64.
ipv6 address autoconfig	Router uses stateless autoconfig to find address.

Table 16-10 *Router IOS IPv6 Configuration Command Reference*

Command	Description
ipv6 address dhcp	Router uses stateful DHCP to find address.
ipv6 unnumbered *interface-type number*	Uses the same IPv6 unicast address as the referenced interface.
ipv6 enable	Enables IPv6 on the interface, but results in only a link local address.
ipv6 address *address* **link-local**	Overrides the automatically created link local address. The configured value must conform to the FE80::/10 prefix.
ipv6 address *address/length* **anycast**	Designates that the unicast address is an anycast.

Note: All the interface subcommands in Table 16-10 enable IPv6 on the interface, which means the router derives an IPv6 link local address for the interface. The description shows what the command does in addition to enabling IPv6.

Configuring Static IPv6 Addresses on Routers

The configuration examples in this section use the internetwork shown in Figure 16-12. The figure shows a diagram you might see in an implementation plan, with the five IPv6 subnet numbers shown over the five links. The interface ID of each interface is then abbreviated, or shown as eui-64, as a reminder of whether to configure the whole 128-bit address or to rely on the EUI-64 feature.

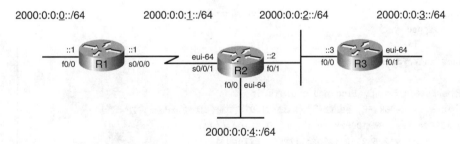

Figure 16-12 *Sample IPv6 Address Planning Diagram*

Example 16-1 shows the configuration process on Router R2, which uses EUI-64 on two interfaces, and a complete IPv6 address on another. Also, note that the configuration includes the **ipv6 unicast-routing** global configuration command, which enables the router to route IPv6 traffic. (The addresses can be configured without also configuring **ipv6 unicast-routing**, but without this command, the router acts more like an IPv6 host, and it will not forward IPv6 packets until this command has been configured.)

Example 16-1   *R2's IPv6 Configuration*

```
R2# show running-config
! lines omitted for brevity

interface FastEthernet0/0
 ipv6 address 2000:0:0:4::/64 eui-64
!
interface FastEthernet0/1
 ipv6 address 2000:0:0:2::2/64
!
interface Serial0/0/1
 ipv6 address 2000:0:0:1::/64 eui-64
!
!
R2# show ipv6 interface brief
FastEthernet0/0              [up/up]
    FE80::213:19FF:FE7B:5004
    2000::4:213:19FF:FE7B:5004
FastEthernet0/1              [up/up]
    FE80::213:19FF:FE7B:5005
    2000:0:0:2::2
Serial0/0/0                  [administratively down/down]
    unassigned
Serial0/0/1                  [up/up]
    FE80::213:19FF:FE7B:5004
    2000::1:213:19FF:FE7B:5004
Serial0/1/0                  [administratively down/down]
    unassigned
Serial0/1/1                  [administratively down/down]
    unassigned

R2# show interfaces fa0/0

FastEthernet0/0 is up, line protocol is up
  Hardware is Gt96k FE, address is 0013.197b.5004 (bia 0013.197b.5004)
  MTU 1500 bytes, BW 100000 Kbit/sec, DLY 100 usec,
     reliability 255/255, txload 1/255, rxload 1/255
! lines omitted for brevity
```

The **ipv6 address** commands both enable IPv6 on the associated interfaces and define either the prefix (with the **eui-64** option) or the entire address. The **show** commands listed after the configuration confirm the IPv6 addresses. Of particular note

■   All three interfaces now have link local addresses that begin FE80.

■   F0/1 has the address exactly as configured.

- S0/0/1 and F0/0 have the configured prefixes (2000:0:0:1 and 2000:0:0:4, respectively), but with EUI-64 derived interface-IDs.

- S0/0/1 uses Fa0/0's MAC address (as shown in the **show interfaces f0/0** command) when forming its EUI-64.

On this last point, whenever IOS needs a MAC address for an interface, and that interface does not have a built-in MAC address, the router uses the MAC address of the lowest-numbered LAN interface on the router–in this case, F0/0. The following list shows the derivation of the last 64 bits (16 digits) of R2's IPv6 interface IDs for its global unicast IPv6 addresses on F0/0 and S0/0/1:

Step 1. Use F0/0's MAC Address: 0013.197B.5004.

Step 2. Split and insert FFFE: 0013:19FF:FE7B:5004.

Step 3. Invert bit 7: Hex 00 = 00000000 binary, flip for 00000010, and convert back to hex 02, resulting in 0213:19FF:FE7B:5004.

Multicast Groups Joined by IPv6 Router Interfaces

Next, consider the deeper information held in the **show ipv6 interface f0/0** command on Router R2, as shown in Example 16-2. Not only does it list the same link local and global unicast addresses, but it lists other special addresses as well.

Example 16-2 *All IPv6 Addresses on an Interface*

```
R2# show ipv6 interface f0/0
FastEthernet0/0 is up, line protocol is up
  IPv6 is enabled, link-local address is FE80::213:19FF:FE7B:5004
  No Virtual link-local address(es):
  Global unicast address(es):
    2000::4:213:19FF:FE7B:5004, subnet is 2000:0:0:4::/64 [EUI]
  Joined group address(es):
    FF02::1
    FF02::2
    FF02::1:FF7B:5004
  MTU is 1500 bytes
  ICMP error messages limited to one every 100 milliseconds
  ICMP redirects are enabled
  ICMP unreachables are sent
  ND DAD is enabled, number of DAD attempts: 1
  ND reachable time is 30000 milliseconds (using 22807)
  ND advertised reachable time is 0 (unspecified)
  ND advertised retransmit interval is 0 (unspecified)
  ND router advertisements are sent every 200 seconds
  ND router advertisements live for 1800 seconds
  ND advertised default router preference is Medium
  Hosts use stateless autoconfig for addresses.
```

The three joined multicast groups should be somewhat familiar after reading this chapter. The first multicast, FF02::1, represents all IPv6 devices, so router interfaces must listen for packets sent to this address. FF02::2 represents all IPv6 routers, so again, R2 must listen for packets sent to this address. Finally, the FF02::1:FF beginning value is the range for an address' solicited node multicast address, used by several functions, including the duplicate address detection (DAD) and neighbor discovery (ND).

Connected Routes and Neighbors

The third example shows some new concepts with the IP routing table. Example 16-3 shows R2's current IPv6 routing table that results from the configuration shown in Example 16-1. Note that no IPv6 routing protocols have been configured, and no static routes have been configured.

Example 16-3 *Connected and Local IPv6 Routes*

```
R2# show ipv6 route
IPv6 Routing Table - Default - 7 entries
Codes: C - Connected, L - Local, S - Static, U - Per-user Static route
       B - BGP, M - MIPv6, R - RIP, I1 - ISIS L1
       I2 - ISIS L2, IA - ISIS interarea, IS - ISIS summary, D - EIGRP
       EX - EIGRP external
       O - OSPF Intra, OI - OSPF Inter, OE1 - OSPF ext 1, OE2 - OSPF ext 2
       ON1 - OSPF NSSA ext 1, ON2 - OSPF NSSA ext 2
C   2000:0:0:1::/64 [0/0]
       via Serial0/0/1, directly connected
L   2000::1:213:19FF:FE7B:5004/128 [0/0]
       via Serial0/0/1, receive
C   2000:0:0:2::/64 [0/0]
       via FastEthernet0/1, directly connected
L   2000:0:0:2::2/128 [0/0]
       via FastEthernet0/1, receive
C   2000:0:0:4::/64 [0/0]
       via FastEthernet0/0, directly connected
L   2000::4:213:19FF:FE7B:5004/128 [0/0]
       via FastEthernet0/0, receive
L   FF00::/8 [0/0]
       via Null0, receive
```

First, the IPv6 routing table lists the expected connected routes, but a new type of route–a "local" route–designated by an L in the output of the **show ipv6 route** command. The connected routes occur for any unicast IPv6 addresses on the interface that happen to have more than link local scope. So, R2 has routes for subnets 2000:0:0:1::/64, 2000:0:0:2::/64, and 2000:0:0:4::/64, but no connected subnets related to R2's link local addresses. The Local routes, all /128 routes, are essentially host routes for the router's unicast IPv6 addresses. These local routes allow the router to more efficiently process packets directed to the router itself, rather than for packets directed toward connected subnets.

The IPv6 Neighbor Table

The IPv6 neighbor table replaces the IPv4 ARP table, listing the MAC address of other devices that share the same link. Example 16-4 shows a **debug** that lists messages during the NDP process, a ping to R3's F0/0 IPv6 address, and the resulting neighbor table entries on R2.

Example 16-4   *Creating Entries and Displaying the Contents of R2's IPv6 Neighbor Table*

```
R2# debug ipv6 nd
  ICMP Neighbor Discovery events debugging is on
R2# ping 2000:0:0:2::3

Type escape sequence to abort.
Sending 5, 100-byte ICMP Echos to 2000:0:0:2::3, timeout is 2 seconds:
!!!!!
Success rate is 100 percent (5/5), round-trip min/avg/max = 0/0/4 ms
R2#
*Sep  2 17:07:25.807: ICMPv6-ND: DELETE -> INCMP: 2000:0:0:2::3
*Sep  2 17:07:25.807: ICMPv6-ND: Sending NS for 2000:0:0:2::3 on FastEthernet0/1
*Sep  2 17:07:25.807: ICMPv6-ND: Resolving next hop 2000:0:0:2::3 on interface
FastEthernet0/1
*Sep  2 17:07:25.811: ICMPv6-ND: Received NA for 2000:0:0:2::3 on FastEthernet0/1
from 2000:0:0:2::3
*Sep  2 17:07:25.811: ICMPv6-ND: Neighbour 2000:0:0:2::3 on FastEthernet0/1 : LLA
0013.197b.6588

R2# undebug all
All possible debugging has been turned off

R2# show ipv6 neighbors
IPv6 Address                            Age Link-layer Addr State Interface
2000:0:0:2::3                             0 0013.197b.6588  REACH Fa0/1
FE80::213:19FF:FE7B:6588                  0 0013.197b.6588  REACH Fa0/1
```

The example shows the entire NDP process by which R2 discovers R3's Fa0/0 MAC address. The example begins with a **debug ipv6 nd** command, which tells R2 to issue messages related to NDP messages. The **ping 2000:0:0:2::3** command that follows tells IOS to use IPv6 ping R3's F0/0 address—but R2 does not know the corresponding MAC address. The debug output that follows shows R2 sending an NS, with R3 replying with an NA message, listing R3's MAC address.

The example ends with the output of the **show ipv6 neighbor** command, which lists the neighbor table entries for both R3's IPv6 addresses.

Stateless Autoconfiguration

The final example in this section demonstrates stateless autoconfiguration using two routers, R2 and R3. In Example 16-5, R2's F0/1 configuration will be changed, using the

ipv6 address autoconfig subcommand on that interface. This tells R2 to use stateless autoconfig process, with R2 learning its prefix from Router R3. R2 then builds the rest of its IPv6 address using EUI-64.

Example 16-5 *Using Stateless Autoconfig on Router R2*

```
R2# conf t
Enter configuration commands, one per line.  End with CNTL/Z.
R2(config)# interface fa0/1
R2(config-if)# no ipv6 address
R2(config-if)# ipv6 address autoconfig
R2(config-if)#^Z

R2# show ipv6 interface brief
FastEthernet0/0              [up/up]
    FE80::213:19FF:FE7B:5004
    2000::4:213:19FF:FE7B:5004
FastEthernet0/1              [up/up]
    FE80::213:19FF:FE7B:5005
    2000::2:213:19FF:FE7B:5005
Serial0/0/0                  [administratively down/down]
    unassigned
Serial0/0/1                  [up/up]
    FE80::213:19FF:FE7B:5004
    2000::1:213:19FF:FE7B:5004
Serial0/1/0                  [administratively down/down]
    unassigned
Serial0/1/1                  [administratively down/down]
    unassigned

R2# show ipv6 router
Router FE80::213:19FF:FE7B:6588 on FastEthernet0/1, last update 0 min
  Hops 64, Lifetime 1800 sec, AddrFlag=0, OtherFlag=0, MTU=1500
  HomeAgentFlag=0, Preference=Medium
  Reachable time 0 (unspecified), Retransmit time 0 (unspecified)
  Prefix 2000:0:0:2::/64 onlink autoconfig
    Valid lifetime 2592000, preferred lifetime 604800
```

Starting with the configuration, the **no ipv6 address** command actually removes all configured IPv6 addresses from the interface and also disables IPv6 on interface F0/1. Then, the **ipv6 address autoconfig** command again enables IPv6 on F0/1 and tells R2 to use stateless autoconfig.

The **show** commands confirm that R2 does indeed learn its IPv6 address: 2000:0:0:2:0213:19FF:FE7B:5005. The **show ipv6 router** command, which lists the cached contents of any received RA messages, lists the information received from R3's RA message, including R3's link local address (used to identify the routers) and R3's advertised prefix (2000:0:0:2::/64).

Exam Preparation Tasks

Planning Practice

The CCNP ROUTE exam expects test takers to review design documents, create implementation plans, and create verification plans. This section provides some exercises that may help you to take a step back from the minute details of the topics in this chapter so that you can think about the same technical topics from the planning perspective.

For each planning practice table, simply complete the table. Note that any numbers in parentheses represent the number of options listed for each item in the solutions in Appendix F.

Design Review Table

Table 16-11 lists several design goals related to this chapter. If these design goals were listed in a design document, and you had to take that document and develop an implementation plan, what implementation options come to mind? You should write a general description; specific configuration commands are not required.

Table 16-11 *Design Review*

Design Goal	Possible Implementation Choices Covered in This Chapter
An IPv6 design suggests that all client hosts should dynamically learn their IPv6 addresses. Which tools can be used? (2)	
A plan shows the use of stateless autoconfiguration. What functions should we expect the IPv6 DHCP server to perform?	

Implementation Plan Peer Review Table

Table 16-12 shows a list of questions that others might ask, or that you might think about, during a peer review of another network engineer's implementation plan. Complete the table by answering the questions.

Table 16-12   *Notable Questions from This Chapter to Consider During an Implementation Plan Peer Review*

Question	Answers
An implementation plan states that router IPv6 address should be assigned as obvious values, using the lowest numbers in the range per each assigned prefix. What configuration methods could be used to configure these low address values?	
A plan calls for the use of stateless autoconfig for client hosts. What must be configured on the routers to support this process?	

Create an Implementation Plan Table

To practice skills useful when creating your own implementation plan, list in Table 16-13 all configuration commands related to the configuration of the following features. You may want to record your answers outside the book, and set a goal to complete this table (and others like it) from memory during your final reviews before taking the exam.

Table 16-13   *Implementation Plan Configuration Memory Drill*

Feature	Configuration Commands/Notes
Configure the full global unicast address on an interface.	
Configure the unicast IPv6 prefix on an interface, and let the router add the interface ID.	
Configure an interface to find its unicast IPv6 address using stateless autoconfig.	
Configure an interface to enable IPv6 and use another interface's IPv6 address as needed.	
Enable IPv6 on an interface and do not configure a unicast IPv6 address.	
Configure the link local address of an interface.	

Choose Commands for a Verification Plan Table

To practice skills useful when creating your own verification plan, list in Table 16-14 all commands that supply the requested information. You may want to record your answers outside the book, and set a goal to be able to complete this table (and others like it) from memory during your final reviews before taking the exam.

Note: Some of the entries in this table may not have been specifically mentioned in this chapter but are listed in this table for review and reference.

Table 16-14   *Verification Plan Memory Drill*

Information Needed	Commands
All IPv6 routes	
A single line per IPv6 address	
Detailed information about IPv6 on an interface, including multicast addresses	
The MAC address used by an interface	
The MAC addresses of neighboring IPv6 hosts	
The information learned from another router in an RA message	

Review all the Key Topics

Review the most important topics from inside the chapter, noted with the Key Topics icon in the outer margin of the page. Table 16-15 lists a reference of these key topics and the page numbers on which each is found.

Table 16-15   *Key Topics for Chapter 16*

Key Topic Element	Description	Page Number
Figure 16-1	Conceptual view of IPv6 global routes	535
List	Rules for abbreviating IPv6 addresses	536
List	Rules about how to write IPv6 prefixes	538
Figure 16-3	IPv6 public prefix assignment concepts	540
List	IPv6 subnetting process	541
Figure 16-5	IPv6 subnetting concepts	542
List	Three steps used by the stateless autoconfig feature	545
Figure 16-8	IPv6 Address format when using EUI-64	548
Table 16-7	Comparisons of Stateful and Stateless DHCP	549
List	IPv6 address types (unicast, multicast, and anycast)	550
Figure 16-10	Link local address format	552
Table 16-9	Address types and prefixes	552
Figure 16-11	NDP concepts	555

Complete the Tables and Lists from Memory

Print a copy of Appendix D, "Memory Tables," (found on the CD), or at least the section for this chapter, and complete the tables and lists from memory. Appendix E, "Memory Tables Answer Key," also on the CD, includes completed tables and lists to check your work.

Define Key Terms

Define the following key terms from this chapter, and check your answers in the glossary.

global unicast address, link local address, unique local address, stateful DHCP, stateless DHCP, stateless autoconfig, Neighbor Discovery Protocol (NDP), Neighbor Solicitation (NS), Neighbor Advertisement (NA), Router Solicitation (RS), Router Advertisement (RA), solicited node multicast address, duplicate address detection (DAD), inverse neighbor discovery

This chapter covers the following subjects:

RIP Next Generation (RIPng): This section compares and contrasts IPv4's RIPv2 and IPv6's RIPng routing protocols and shows how to configure RIPng.

EIGRP for IPv6: This section compares and contrasts EIGRP for IPv4 and for IPv6 and shows how to configure EIGRP for IPv6.

OSPF Version 3: This section compares and contrasts OSPFv2, which applies to IPv4, and OSPFv3, which applies to IPv6, along with how to configure OSPFv3.

IPv6 IGP Redistribution: This section compares and contrasts IPv4 and IPv6 IGP redistribution concepts and configuration.

IPv6 Static Routes: This short section shows the syntax of the **ipv6 route** command and how you can use it to configure static IPv6 routes.

CHAPTER 17

IPv6 Routing Protocols and Redistribution

IPv6 uses an updated version of the three popular IGPs (RIP, EIGRP, and OSPF) to exchange routes inside an Enterprise. Additionally, updates to the BGP Version 4 standard, called multiprotocol extensions for BGP-4 (RFC 4760), allow the exchange of IPv6 routing information in the Internet.

As you might imagine, these updated routing protocols have many features in common with their IPv4 cousins. This chapter examines each of the three IPv6 IGPs, with an eye toward the similarities and differences between the IPv4 and IPv6 versions of each IGP protocol. This chapter also examines IPv6 route redistribution between IPv6 IGPs and static IPv6 routes.

Note that as in Chapter 16, "IP Version 6 Addressing," this chapter also discusses the issues of native support of IPv6, ignoring the transition and translation features discussed in Chapter 18, "IPv4 and IPv6 Coexistence."

"Do I Know This Already?" Quiz

The "Do I Know This Already?" quiz allows you to assess if you should read the entire chapter. If you miss no more than one of these eight self-assessment questions, you might want to move ahead to the "Exam Preparation Tasks." Table 17-1 lists the major headings in this chapter and the "Do I Know This Already?" quiz questions covering the material in those headings so that you can assess your knowledge of these specific areas. The answers to the "Do I Know This Already?" quiz appear in Appendix A.

Table 17-1 *"Do I Know This Already?" Foundation Topics Section-to-Question Mapping*

Foundations Topics Section	Questions
RIP Next Generation (RIPng)	1–2
EIGRP for IPv6	3–4
OSPF Version 3	5–6
IPv6 IGP Redistribution	7
IPv6 Static Routes	8

1. Which of the following features work the same in both RIP-2 and RIPng? (Choose three.)

   a. Distance Vector Logic

   b. Uses UDP

   c. Uses RIP-specific authentication

   d. Maximum useful metric of 15

   e. Automatic route summarization

2. Router R1 currently has no configuration related to IPv6 or IPv4. The following configuration exists in a planning document, intended to be used to copy/paste into Router R1 to enable RIPng and IPv6 on interfaces F0/0 and S0/0/0. No other related configuration exists. Which of the following is true about RIPng on R1 after this configuration has been pasted into R1?

```
ipv6 unicast-routing
interface f0/0
ipv6 rip one enable
ipv6 address 2000::1/64
interface s0/0/0
ipv6 address 2001::/64 eui-64
ipv6 rip one enable
```

   a. RIPng will be enabled on no interfaces.

   b. RIPng will be enabled on one interface.

   c. RIPng will be enabled on two interfaces.

   d. RIPng will advertise about prefixes connected to S0/0/0 and F0/0, but only send Updates on one interface.

3. Router R1 currently has no configuration related to IPv6 or IPv4. The following configuration exists in a planning document intended to be used to copy/paste into Router R1 to enable EIGRP for IPv6 on interfaces F0/0 and S0/0/0. No other related configuration exists. Assuming F0/0 and S0/0/0 reach an up/up state, which of the following is true about EIGRP for IPv6 on R1 after this configuration has been pasted into R1?

```
ipv6 router eigrp 1
ipv6 unicast-routing
interface f0/0
ipv6 address 2000::1/64
ipv6 eigrp 1
interface s0/0/0
ipv6 address 2001::/64 eui-64
ipv6 eigrp 1
```

    a. EIGRP works on F0/0 and S0/0/0 without further configuration.

    b. EIGRP works with the addition of one command: a **no shutdown** command in EIGRP router configuration mode.

    c. EIGRP works with the addition of one command: an **eigrp router-id** command in EIGRP router configuration mode.

    d. EIGRP for IPv6 needs at least two more configuration commands before it works on R1.

4. Router R1 connects to Router R2 over an Ethernet LAN with both routers using their F0/0 interfaces. R1 learns a route from R2 using EIGRP for IPv6. That route lists F0/0 as the outgoing interface with R2 as the next hop. The configuration excerpt shows all relevant configuration on R2's F0/0 interface. Which of the following is true about R1's route?

```
interface f0/0
mac-address 1111.1111.1111
ipv6 address 2000::/64 eui-64
ipv6 address 2001::1/64
```

    a. The next hop is 2000::1311:11FF:FE11:1111

    b. The next hop is FE80::1311:11FF:FE11:1111

    c. The next hop is FE80::5111:11FF:FE11:1111

    d. The next hop is 2001::1

5. Which of the following are true of both OSPFv2 and OSPFv3? (Choose two.)

    a. The method of choosing an OSPF router ID

    b. Verification checks that must be validated before two routers can become OSPF neighbors

    c. Support for route tags

    d. Support for multiple instances per interface

6. Router R1 currently has no configuration related to IPv6 or IPv4. The following configuration exists in a planning document, intended to be used to copy/paste into Router R1 to enable OSPFv3 on interfaces F0/0 and S0/0/0. No other related configuration exists. Assuming F0/0 and S0/0/0 reach an up/up state, which of the following is true about OSPFv3 on R1 after this configuration has been pasted into R1?

```
ipv6 router ospf 1
ipv6 unicast-routing
interface f0/0
ipv6 address 2000::1/64
ipv6 ospf 1 area 1
interface s0/0/0
ipv6 address 2001::/64 eui-64
ipv6 ospf 1 area 0
```

    a. OSPF works on F0/0 and S0/0/0 without further configuration.

    b. OSPF works with the addition of one command: a **no shutdown** command in OSPF router configuration mode.

    c. OSPF works with the addition of one command: an **router-id** command in OSPF router configuration mode.

    d. OSPFv3 needs at least two more configuration commands before it works on R1.

7. The following output occurs on Router R1, which runs both EIGRP for IPv6 and OSPFv3, with redistribution from EIGRP into OSPF configured with the **redistribute eigrp 1 metric 25** command. Interface S0/0/1 has been enabled for EIGRP ASN 1. Which of the following should be true of redistribution in this case?

```
D    2000::/64 [90/1422516]
        via FE80::213:19FF:FE7B:5026, Serial0/0/1
C    2000:0:0:1::/64 [0/0]
        via Serial0/0/1, directly connected
L    2000::1:213:19FF:FE7B:5004/128 [0/0]
        via Serial0/0/1, receive
```

    a. Route 2000::/64 will be redistributed.

    b. Route 2000:0:0:1::/64 will be redistributed.

    c. Route 2000:1:213:19FF:FE7B:5004/128 will be redistributed.

    d. No routes will be redistributed because of the omission of the **subnets** parameter of the **redistribute** command.

8. Router R1 has been configured with an **ipv6 route 2000::/64 S0/0/0 64** command. Which of the following does the 64 at the end of the command represent?

    a. Metric

    b. Administrative distance

    c. Timeout (seconds)

    d. Prefix length

    e. Interface ID

Foundation Topics

To support IPv6, all the IPv4 routing protocols had to go through varying degrees of changes, with the most obvious being that each had to be changed to support longer addresses and prefixes. The actual messages used to send and receive routing information have changed in some cases, using IPv6 headers instead of IPv4 headers, and using IPv6 addresses in those headers. In particular, like their IPv4 versions, each IPv6 IGP uses IPv6 multicast addresses—for example, RIPng sends routing updates to the IPv6 destination address FF02::9 instead of the old RIP-2 IPv4 224.0.0.9 address. Also, the routing protocols typically advertise their link-local IP address as the next hop in a route.

Even with these changes, each IPv6 IGP has more similarities than differences compared to their respective IPv4 cousins. For example, RIPng, based on RIP-2, is still a Distance Vector protocol, with hop count as the metric and 15 hops as the longest valid route (16 is infinity). OSPF Version 3 (OSPFv3), created specifically to support IPv6, uses Link State logic like OSPFv2, uses cost as the metric, and retains the LSA types—but there are some changes to how the LSAs work. However, most of the core OSPF operational concepts remain the same.

Table 17-2 lists the IPv6 routing protocols and their new RFCs (as appropriate).

Table 17-2   *Updates to Routing Protocols for IPv6*

Routing Protocol	Full Name	RFC
RIPng	RIP Next Generation	2080
OSPFv3	OSPF Version 3	5340
MP-BGP4	Multiprotocol BGP-4	4760
EIGRP for IPv6	EIGRP for IPv6	Proprietary

This chapter examines the three IGPs, the redistribution between the IGPs, and static IPv6 routes.

RIP Next Generation (RIPng)

Routing Information Protocol (RIP) began life as one of the earliest efforts in the field of dynamic IP routing protocols. It eventually became the first dynamic routing protocol for the emerging IP protocol back in the 1970s. Later, in the mid-1990s, the RIP Version 2 (RIP-2) specifications enhanced RIP, with the original version becoming known as RIP Version 1, or simply RIP-1.

Also in the mid-1990s, the process of defining IPv6 was drawing toward completion, at least for the original IPv6 standards. To support IPv6, the IETF committees defined a new version of RIP to support IPv6. But rather than number this updated flavor of RIP as RIP Version 3, the creators chose to number this new protocol as version 1, treating it like a new protocol. However, no one bothered to put "version 1" in the name, simply calling it

RIP Next Generation (RIPng), or even simply RIP. To date, no new version of RIPng has been defined, making the original RIPng still the most recent version of the protocol.

Note: For you Star Trek TV show fans, yes, the name in part came from "Star Trek: The Next Generation."

RIPng–Theory and Comparisons to RIP-2

The RIPng RFC states that the protocol uses many of the same concepts and conventions as the original RIP-1 specification, also drawing on some RIP-2 concepts. However, knowing that many of you might not remember a lot of details about RIP-2, particularly because RIP-2 is included in the CCNA certification rather than CCNP, Table 17-3 lists a variety of facts about RIP-2 and RIPng.

Key
Topic

Table 17-3 *Comparing RIP-2 to RIPng*

Feature	RIP-2	RIPng
Advertises routes for...	IPv4	IPv6
RIP messages use these Layer 3/4 protocols	IPv4, UDP	IPv6, UDP
UDP Port	520	521
Use Distance Vector	Yes	Yes
Default Administrative distance	120	120
Supports VLSM	Yes	Yes
Can perform automatic summarization	Yes	N/A
Uses Split Horizon	Yes	Yes
Uses Poison Reverse	Yes	Yes
30 second periodic full updates	Yes	Yes
Uses triggered updates	Yes	Yes
Uses Hop Count metric	Yes	Yes
Metric meaning infinity	16	16
Supports route tags	Yes	Yes
Multicast Update destination	224.0.0.9	FF02::9
Authentication	RIP-specific	uses IPv6 AH/ESP

The overall operation of RIPng closely matches RIP-2. In both, routers send periodic full updates with all routes, except for routes omitted due to Split Horizon rules. No neighbor relationships occur; the continuing periodic Updates, on a slightly-variable 30 second period, also serve the purpose of confirming that the neighboring router still works. The metrics work exactly the same. When a router ceases to see a route in received updates, ceases to receive updates, or receives a poisoned (metric 16) route, it reacts to converge, but relatively slowly compared to EIGRP and OSPF.

Some differences relate specifically to IPv6. First, the messages themselves list IPv6 prefixes/lengths, rather than subnet/mask. In RIP-1 and RIP-2, RIP encapsulated RIP Update messages inside an IPv4 and UDP header; with IPv6, the encapsulation uses IPv6 packets, again with a UDP header. Some small differences in the Update message format exist as well, with the most obvious difference being that the updates list IPv6 prefixes and prefix lengths.

The last difference of note is that because IPv6 supports authentication using the IPsec Authentication Header (AH), RIPng does not natively support authentication, instead relying on IPsec.

Configuring RIPng

RIPng uses a new command style for the basic configuration, but most of the optional features and verification commands look much like the commands used for RIP for IPv4. This section first takes a look at the basic RIPng configuration, accepting as many defaults as possible.

The big difference between RIP-2 and RIPng configuration is that RIPng discards the age-old RIP **network** command in deference to the **ipv6 rip** *name* **enable** interface subcommand, which enables RIPng on the interface. Another difference relates to the routing of IPv4 and IPv6: IOS routes IPv4 by default (due to a default global configuration command of **ip routing**), but IOS does not route IPv6 by default (a default of **no ipv6 unicast-routing**). Finally, RIPng allows multiple RIPng processes on a single router, so IOS requires that each RIPng process is given a text name that identifies each RIPng process for that one router–another difference compared to RIP-2.

The following list shows the basic configuration steps for RIPng, including steps to enable IPv6 routing and enabling IPv6 on the interfaces.

Step 1.   Enable IPv6 routing with the **ipv6 unicast-routing** global command.

Step 2.   Enable RIPng using the **ipv6 router rip** *name* global configuration command. The name must be unique on a router but does not need to match neighboring routers.

Step 3.   Enable IPv6 on the interface, typically with one of these two methods:

    A. Configure an IPv6 unicast address on each interface using the **ipv6 address** *address/prefix-length* [**eui-64**] interface command.

    B. Configure the **ipv6 enable** command, which enables IPv6 and causes the router to derive its link local address.

Step 4.   Enable RIP on the interface with the **ipv6 rip** *name* **enable** interface subcommand (where the name matches the **ipv6 router rip** *name* global configuration command).

Key Topic

> **Note:** For a complete discussion of options for enabling IPv6 on an interface, as men-
> tioned at Step 3, refer to Chapter 16's Table 16-11.

The list includes just a few straightforward configuration commands, but a few subtle interactions also exist. The list shows steps related directly to RIPng (Steps 2 and 4), plus
other steps related to making IPv6 itself work (Steps 1 and 3). The list also pairs two sets
of dependent steps with each other, as follows:

■   Step 2 relies on Step 1 because IOS rejects the command at Step 2 (**ipv6 router rip**
     name) if the command at Step 1 (**ipv6 unicast-routing**) has been omitted.

■   Step 4 relies on Step 3 because IOS rejects the command at Step 4 if IPv6 has not yet
     been enabled on the interface, either statically as mentioned at Step 3 or with one of
     the other methods listed in Chapter 16's Table 16-11.

Finally, note that although the **ipv6 rip** *process-name* **enable** interface subcommand (Step
4) refers to the process name configured at Step 2 (the **ipv6 router rip** *process-name*
command), IOS creates the RIP process in reaction to the **ipv6 rip** *process-name* **enable**
interface subcommand if that RIPng process name does not yet exist. In other words, if
you followed the previous steps in order, but forgot to do Step 2, the command at Step 4
causes IOS to automatically create the command at Step 2.

As with RIP-1 and RIP-2, for any interface on which RIPng has been enabled, the RIP
process does three main actions. First, it starts sending RIP updates on that interface. It
also starts processing any RIP updates received on that interface. Finally, it advertises
about the connected routes on that interface. In particular, because IPv6 allows the configuration of multiple IPv6 unicast addresses on an interface, RIP advertises about most
IPv6 unicast prefixes associated with the interface. The notable exceptions are that RIP
does not advertise about any link local addresses, nor does RIP advertise about the local
host routes–routes with a /128 prefix length–created for each interface IPv6 address. In
short, RIP advertises all routable subnets associated with the interface.

Figure 17-1 shows a sample internetwork with IPv6 global unicast IPv6 subnets shown.
The sample internetwork uses addressing values that are both memorable and make for
shorter IPv6 addresses when abbreviated. All the subnets use /64 prefix length, with quartets 2, 3, and 4 composed of all 0 values. The interface ID portion of each address uses all
hex 0's in the first three quartets (quartets 5, 6, and 7 in the overall address), with the final
digit in the final quartet used to identify each router. This last digit matches the name of
each router in most cases.

For example, all R1's IPv6 addresses' last four octets are 0000:0000:0000:0001. R1's
S0/0/0.3 subinterface, which connects with a PVC to Router R3, uses a prefix of
2003:0000:0000:0000::/64, making the entire IPv6 address on this interface, when abbreviated, 2003::1/64–a convenient value for sifting through all the output in the upcoming
examples.

Example 17-1 shows the RIPng configuration on Router R1 in this design. The RIP process
name is fred.

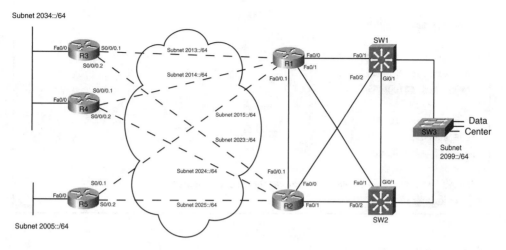

Figure 17-1 *Sample Internetwork for IPv6 Routing Protocol Configuration*

Example 17-1 *Configuring IPv6 Routing and Routing Protocols on R1*

```
R1# show running-config
! The output is edited to remove lines not pertinent to this example.
! Next, step 1's task: enable IPv6 routing
ipv6 unicast-routing
!
! Next, on 5 interfaces, steps 3 and 4: configuring an IPv6 address,
! and enable RIPng, process "fred".
interface FastEthernet0/0.1
 ipv6 address 2012::1/64
 ipv6 rip fred enable
!
interface FastEthernet0/0.2
 ipv6 address 2017::1/64
 ipv6 rip fred enable
!
interface FastEthernet0/1.18
 ipv6 address 2018::1/64
 ipv6 rip fred enable
!
interface Serial0/0/0.3
 ipv6 address 2013::1/64
```

```
 ipv6 rip fred enable
!
interface Serial0/0/0.4
 ipv6 address 2014::1/64
 ipv6 rip fred enable
!
interface Serial0/0/0.5
 ipv6 address 2015::1/64
 ipv6 rip fred enable
!
! Next, step 2's task, creating the RIPng process named "fred"
ipv6 router rip fred
```

Verifying RIPng

The **show** commands related to RIPng have the same general kinds of information as seen with RIP-2. However, some of the commands used to get to the same piece of information differ, and of course, some obvious differences exist due to the different IPv6 address structure. Table 17-4 lists a cross-reference comparing all commands related to RIP that begin either **show ip** or **show ipv6**. It also lists the similar **debug** commands used to display RIP routing information.

Table 17-4 *Comparing Verification Commands:* **show ip** *and* **show ipv6**

Function	IPv4	IPv6
All routes	... route	... route
All RIP learned routes	... route rip	... route rip
Details on the routes for a specific prefix	... route *subnet mask*	... route *prefix/length*
Interfaces on which RIP is enabled	... protocols	... protocols
List of routing information sources	... protocols	... rip next-hops
Debug that displays sent and received Updates	debug ip rip	debug ipv6 rip

The most notable differences occur with the information seen with IPv4 in the **show ip protocols** command. The **show ip protocols** command displays a wide variety of information for IPv4 RIP, whereas the IPv6 commands spread the information over a couple of different commands, as listed in Table 17-4. Example 17-2 shows a sampling of the commands, taken from Router R3 in Figure 17-1. The explanatory comments are listed within the example in this case. Note that Router R3 used a RIPng process name of barney.

Example 17-2   *IPv6 RIPng* show *Commands*

```
! On R3, process name "barney" has two current routes to reach the
! datacenter prefix 2099::/64.


R3# show ipv6 route 2099::/64
Routing entry for 2099::/64
   Known via "rip barney", distance 120, metric 3
   Route count is 2/2, share count 0
   Routing paths:
     FE80::22FF:FE22:2222, Serial0/0/0.2
       Last updated 00:27:12 ago
     FE80::11FF:FE11:1111, Serial0/0/0.1
       Last updated 00:27:10 ago


! Note that the next command lists only RIP-learned routes. It lists
! two next-hops for 2099::64. Note the next-hop information lists
! link-local addresses.
R3# show ipv6 route rip
IPv6 Routing Table - Default - 19 entries
Codes: C - Connected, L - Local, S - Static, U - Per-user Static route
        B - BGP, M - MIPv6, R - RIP, I1 - ISIS L1
        I2 - ISIS L2, IA - ISIS interarea, IS - ISIS summary, D - EIGRP
        EX - EIGRP external
        O - OSPF Intra, OI - OSPF Inter, OE1 - OSPF ext 1, OE2 - OSPF ext 2
        ON1 - OSPF NSSA ext 1, ON2 - OSPF NSSA ext 2
R    2005::/64 [120/3]
      via FE80::11FF:FE11:1111, Serial0/0/0.1
      via FE80::22FF:FE22:2222, Serial0/0/0.2
R    2012::/64 [120/2]
      via FE80::11FF:FE11:1111, Serial0/0/0.1
      via FE80::22FF:FE22:2222, Serial0/0/0.2


! lines omitted for brevity...
R    2099::/64 [120/3]
      via FE80::22FF:FE22:2222, Serial0/0/0.2
      via FE80::11FF:FE11:1111, Serial0/0/0.1


! Unlike show ip protocols, show ipv6 protocols displays little info.
R3# show ipv6 protocols
IPv6 Routing Protocol is "connected"
IPv6 Routing Protocol is "rip barney"
  Interfaces:
    Serial0/0/0.2
    Serial0/0/0.1
    FastEthernet0/0
```

```
      Redistribution:
        None

 ! This command lists the timers displayed for RIP-2 with show ip protocols.
 R3# show ipv6 rip
 RIP process "barney", port 521, multicast-group FF02::9, pid 258
        Administrative distance is 120. Maximum paths is 16
        Updates every 30 seconds, expire after 180
        Holddown lasts 0 seconds, garbage collect after 120
        Split horizon is on; poison reverse is off
        Default routes are not generated
        Periodic updates 57, trigger updates 10
      Interfaces:
        Serial0/0/0.2
        Serial0/0/0.1
        FastEthernet0/0
      Redistribution:
        None


 ! This command lists the equivalent of the information in the
 ! show ip protocols commands' "Routing Information Sources" heading.
 ! Note the link local addresses are listed.
 R3# show ipv6 rip next-hops
  RIP process "barney", Next Hops
   FE80::11FF:FE11:1111/Serial0/0/0.1 [9 paths]
   FE80::44FF:FE44:4444/FastEthernet0/0 [3 paths]
   FE80::22FF:FE22:2222/Serial0/0/0.2 [9 paths]
```

Beyond the information emphasized in the comments inside the example, the next-hop IPv6 addresses in the example need to be scrutinized. RIPng uses the link local IPv6 address as the next-hop IP address. (Reminder: link local addresses begin with FE80.) The **show ipv6 route 2099::/64** and **show ipv6 route** commands early in the example, and the **show ipv6 rip next-hops** command at the end of the example, all show next-hop IP addresses that begin with FE80, confirming that RIP indeed uses link local addresses as next-hop addresses.

To discover which routers use which link local addresses, and make it easier to work with link local addresses, you have a couple of options. First, you can set the MAC address of each LAN interface to something noticeable. For Example 17-2, the routers each used a recognizable MAC: R1 used 0200.1111.1111, R2 used 0200.2222.2222, and so on. Alternatively, you can just configure the link local address with the **ipv6 address** command, using the **link-local** keyword at the end, and make each link local address be more recognizable. Regardless, to find the router whose link local address is listed in the IPv6 routing table, the **show cdp entry** *name* command can be useful because it lists both the IPv4 and IPv6 addresses, including the neighbor's link local address.

EIGRP for IPv6

Cisco originally created EIGRP to advertise routes for IPv4, IPX, and AppleTalk. This original EIGRP architecture easily allowed for yet another Layer 3 protocol, IPv6, to be added. As a result, Cisco did not have to change EIGRP significantly to support IPv6, so many similarities exist between the IPv4 and IPv6 versions of EIGRP.

Note: Many documents, including this chapter, refer to the IPv6 version of EIGRP as EIGRP for IPv6. However, some documents at www.cisco.com also refer to this protocol as EIGRPv6, not because it is the sixth version of the protocol, but because it implies a relationship with IPv6.

As with the previous section "RIP Next Generation (RIPng)," this section begins with a discussion of the similarities and differences between the IPv4 and IPv6 versions of EIGRP. The remaining coverage of EIGRP focuses on the changes to EIGRP configuration and verification in support of IPv6.

EIGRP for IPv4 and IPv6–Theory and Comparisons

For the most part, EIGRP for IPv4 and for IPv6 have many similarities. The following list outlines some of the key differences:

■   EIGRP for IPv6 advertises IPv6 prefixes/lengths, rather than IPv4 subnet/mask information.

■   EIGRP for IPv6 uses the neighbor's link local address as the next-hop IP address; EIGRP for IPv4 has no equivalent concept.

■   EIGRP for IPv6 encapsulates its messages in IPv6 packets, rather than IPv4 packets.

■   Like RIPng and OSPFv3, EIGRP for IPv6 authentication relies on IPv6's built-in authentication and privacy features.

■   EIGRP for IPv4 defaults to use automatic route summarization at the boundaries of classful IPv4 networks; IPv6 has no concept of classful networks, so EIGRP for IPv6 cannot perform any automatic summarization.

■   EIGRP for IPv6 does not require neighbors to be in the same IPv6 subnet as a requirement to become neighbors.

Other than these differences, most of the details of EIGRP for IPv6 works like EIGRP for IPv4. For reference, Table 17-5 compares the features of each.

Table 17-5 *Comparing EIGRP for IPv4 and IPv6*

Key Topic

Feature	EIGRP for IPv4	EIGRP for IPv6
Advertises routes for...	IPv4	IPv6
Layer 3 protocol for EIGRP messages	IPv4	IPv6

Table 17-5   *Comparing EIGRP for IPv4 and IPv6*

Feature	EIGRP for IPv4	EIGRP for IPv6
Layer 3 header protocol type	88	88
UDP Port	N/A	N/A
Uses Successor, Feasible Successor logic	Yes	Yes
Uses Dual	Yes	Yes
Supports VLSM	Yes	Yes
Can perform automatic summarization	Yes	N/A
Uses triggered updates	Yes	Yes
Uses composite metric, default using bandwidth and delay	Yes	Yes
Metric meaning infinity	$2^{32} - 1$	$2^{32} - 1$
Supports route tags	Yes	Yes
Multicast Update destination	224.0.0.10	FF02::A
Authentication	EIGRP-specific	Uses IPv6 AH/ESP

Configuring EIGRP for IPv6

EIGRP for IPv6 follows the same basic configuration style as for RIPng, plus a few additional steps, as follows:

Key Topic

Step 1.   Enable IPv6 routing with the **ipv6 unicast-routing** global command.

Step 2.   Enable EIGRP using the **ipv6 router eigrp** *{1 – 65535}* global configuration command.

Step 3.   Enable IPv6 on the interface, typically with one of these two methods:

A. Configure an IPv6 unicast address on each interface, using the **ipv6 address** *address/prefix-length* [**eui-64**] interface command.

B. Configure the **ipv6 enable** command, which enables IPv6 and causes the router to derive its link local address.

Step 4.   Enable EIGRP on the interface with the **ipv6 eigrp** *asn* interface subcommand (where the asn matches the **ipv6 router eigrp** *asn* global configuration command).

Step 5.   Enable EIGRP for IPv6 with a **no shutdown** command while in EIGRP configuration mode.

Step 6.   If no EIGRP router ID has been automatically chosen, due to not having at least one working interface with an *IPv4* address, configure an EIGRP router ID with the **eigrp router-id** *rid* command in EIGRP configuration mode.

Note: For a complete discussion of options for enabling IPv6 on an interface, as mentioned at Step 3, refer to Chapter 16's Table 16-10.

The first four steps essentially mirror the four steps in the RIPng configuration process previously listed in this chapter. The same interdependencies exist for EIGRP for IPv6 as well; in particular, the command at Step 2 works only if Step 1's command has been configured, and the command at Step 4 fails if the command at Step 3 has not yet been completed.

EIGRP for IPv6 requires Steps 5 and 6, whereas RIPng does not need equivalent steps. First, at Step 5, IOS supports the ability to stop and start the EIGRP process with the **shutdown** and **no shutdown** router mode subcommands. After initial configuration, the EIGRP for IPv6 process starts in shutdown mode, so to make the process start, IOS requires a **no shutdown** command.

Step 6 shows the other difference as compared to RIPng configuration, but this step may or may not be needed. The EIGRP for IPv6 process must have a router ID (RID) before the process works. EIGRP for IPv6 uses the same process as EIGRP for IPv4 for choosing the RID. The EIGRP for IPv6 RID is indeed a 32-bit number, with two of the EIGRP RID decision steps based on IPv4 configuration. The following list defines how EIGRP for IPv6 picks its RID, listed in the order of preference:

Step 1.   Use the configured value (using the **router-id** *a.b.c.d* EIGRP subcommand under the **ipv6 router eigrp** command).

Step 2.   Use the highest IPv4 address on an up/up loopback interface.

Step 3.   Use the highest IPv4 address on an up/up nonloopback interface.

Note that although most installations already have IPv4 addresses configured, it is possible that the EIGRP for IPv6 process cannot derive a RID value. If the router has no working interfaces that have IPv4 addresses, and the EIGRP for IPv6 RID is not explicitly configured, then the EIGRP for IPv6 process simply does not work. So, the six-step configuration process includes a mention of the EIGRP RID; more generally, it may be prudent to configure a RID explicitly as a matter of habit.

After being enabled on an interface, EIGRP for IPv6 performs the same two basic tasks as it does with EIGRP for IPv4: it discovers neighbors and advertises about connected subnets. EIGRP for IPv6 uses the same set of neighbor checks as do routers using EIGRP for IPv4, except that EIGRP for IPv6 does not require that neighboring IPv6 routers have IPv6 addresses in the same subnet. (See Table 2-4 in Chapter 2, "EIGRP Overview and Neighbor Relationships," for the list of neighbor validations performed by EIGRP for IPv4). Also, as with EIGRP for IPv4, EIGRP for IPv6 advertises about any and all connected subnets on the interface, with the exception of the link local addresses and the local routes (the host routes for a router's own interface IPv6 addresses).

Example 17-3 shows a sample configuration on Router R1 from Figure 17-1. All neighboring routers must use the same ASN; ASN 9 will be used in this case.

Example 17-3 *Configuring EIGRP for IPv6 Routing and Routing Protocols on R1*

```
R1# show running-config
! output is edited to remove lines not pertinent to this example
! Configuration step 1: enabling IPv6 routing
ipv6 unicast-routing

! Next, configuration steps 3 and 4, on 5 different interfaces
interface FastEthernet0/0.1
 ipv6 address 2012::1/64
 ipv6 eigrp 9
!
interface FastEthernet0/0.2
 ipv6 address 2017::1/64
 ipv6 eigrp 9
!
interface FastEthernet0/1.18
 ipv6 address 2018::1/64
 ipv6 eigrp 9
!
interface Serial0/0/0.3
 ipv6 address 2013::1/64
 ipv6 eigrp 9
!
interface Serial0/0/0.4
 ipv6 address 2014::1/64
 ipv6 eigrp 9
!
interface Serial0/0/0.5
 ipv6 address 2015::1/64
 ipv6 eigrp 9
!
! Configuration steps 2, 5, and 6
ipv6 router eigrp 9
 no shutdown
 router-id 10.10.34.3
```

Verifying EIGRP for IPv6

The EIGRP for IPv6 **show** commands generally list the same kinds of information as the equivalent commands for EIGRP for IPv4, even more so than RIPng. In most cases, simply use the same **show ip...** commands applicable with IPv4 and EIGRP, and substitute **ipv6** instead of **ip**. Table 17-6 lists a cross-reference comparing the most popular EIGRP-related commands for both versions. Note that the table assumes that the commands begin either **show ip** or **show ipv6** in all but the last row of the table.

Table 17-6   *Comparing EIGRP Verification Commands:* show ip *and* show ipv6...

Function	show ip...	show ipv6...
All routes	... route	... route
All EIGRP learned routes	... route eigrp	... route eigrp
Details on the routes for a specific prefix	... route *subnet mask*	... route *prefix/length*
Interfaces on which EIGRP is enabled, plus metric weights, variance, redistribution, max-paths, admin distance	... protocols	... protocols
List of routing information sources	... protocols ... eigrp neighbors	... eigrp neighbors
Hello interval	... eigrp interfaces detail	... eigrp interfaces detail
EIGRP database	... eigrp topology [all-links]	... eigrp topology [all-links]
Debug that displays sent and received Updates	debug ip eigrp notifications	debug ipv6 eigrp notifications

Example 17-4 shows a few sample **show** commands taken from Router R3 in the internetwork shown in Figure 17-1. The explanatory comments are listed within the example in this case.

Example 17-4   *IPv6 EIGRP* show *Commands*

```
! On R3, as when using RIPng, the next-hop address is the
! link-local address of the next router.


R3# show ipv6 route 2099::/64
Routing entry for 2099::/64
  Known via "eigrp 9", distance 90, metric 2174976, type internal
  Route count is 2/2, share count 0
  Routing paths:
    FE80::22FF:FE22:2222, Serial0/0/0.2
      Last updated 00:24:32 ago
    FE80::11FF:FE11:1111, Serial0/0/0.1
      Last updated 00:07:51 ago


! Note that the next command lists only EIGRP-learned routes. It lists
! two next-hops for 2099::64. Note the next-hop information lists
! link-local addresses.
R3# show ipv6 route eigrp
IPv6 Routing Table - Default - 19 entries
```

```
Codes: C - Connected, L - Local, S - Static, U - Per-user Static route
       B - BGP, M - MIPv6, R - RIP, I1 - ISIS L1
       I2 - ISIS L2, IA - ISIS interarea, IS - ISIS summary, D - EIGRP
       EX - EIGRP external
       O - OSPF Intra, OI - OSPF Inter, OE1 - OSPF ext 1, OE2 - OSPF ext 2
       ON1 - OSPF NSSA ext 1, ON2 - OSPF NSSA ext 2
D   2005::/64 [90/2684416]
     via FE80::11FF:FE11:1111, Serial0/0/0.1
     via FE80::22FF:FE22:2222, Serial0/0/0.2
D   2012::/64 [90/2172416]
     via FE80::22FF:FE22:2222, Serial0/0/0.2
     via FE80::11FF:FE11:1111, Serial0/0/0.1
D   2014::/64 [90/2681856]
     via FE80::11FF:FE11:1111, Serial0/0/0.1
D   2015::/64 [90/2681856]
     via FE80::11FF:FE11:1111, Serial0/0/0.1

! lines omitted for brevity...
D   2099::/64 [90/2174976]
     via FE80::22FF:FE22:2222, Serial0/0/0.2
     via FE80::11FF:FE11:1111, Serial0/0/0.1


! show ipv6 protocols displays less info than its IPv4 cousin.
R3# show ipv6 protocols
IPv6 Routing Protocol is "eigrp 9"
  EIGRP metric weight K1=1, K2=0, K3=1, K4=0, K5=0
  EIGRP maximum hopcount 100
  EIGRP maximum metric variance 1
  Interfaces:
    FastEthernet0/0
    Serial0/0/0.1
    Serial0/0/0.2
  Redistribution:
    None
  Maximum path: 16
  Distance: internal 90 external 170


! This command lists the equivalent of the information in the
! show ip protocols commands' "Routing Information Sources" heading.
! Note the link local addresses are listed.
R3# show ipv6 eigrp neighbors
IPv6-EIGRP neighbors for process 9
H   Address              Interface      Hold Uptime   SRTT  RTO  Q   Seq
                                        (sec)         (ms)       Cnt Num
1   Link-local address:  Se0/0/0.2      14 01:50:51    3    200  0   82
```

```
        FE80::22FF:FE22:2222
0   Link-local address:     Se0/0/0.1          13 01:50:52   14   200  0   90
        FE80::11FF:FE11:1111


! The next command lists the EIGRP topology database, including
! feasible distance calculations, reported distance, and listing
! all successor and feasible successor routes.
R3# show ipv6 eigrp topology
IPv6-EIGRP Topology Table for AS(9)/ID(10.10.34.3)

Codes: P - Passive, A - Active, U - Update, Q - Query, R - Reply,
       r - reply Status, s - sia Status

P 2005::/64, 2 successors, FD is 2684416
        via FE80::11FF:FE11:1111 (2684416/2172416), Serial0/0/0.1
        via FE80::22FF:FE22:2222 (2684416/2172416), Serial0/0/0.2
P 2012::/64, 2 successors, FD is 2172416
        via FE80::11FF:FE11:1111 (2172416/28160), Serial0/0/0.1
        via FE80::22FF:FE22:2222 (2172416/28160), Serial0/0/0.2
P 2013::/64, 1 successors, FD is 2169856
        via Connected, Serial0/0/0.1

! lines omitted for brevity
P 2099::/64, 2 successors, FD is 2174976
        via FE80::11FF:FE11:1111 (2174976/30720), Serial0/0/0.1
        via FE80::22FF:FE22:2222 (2174976/30720), Serial0/0/0.2


! Finally, the link-local address of neighbor R1 is identified.
R3# show cdp entry R1
-------------------
Device ID: R1
Entry address(es):
  IP address: 10.10.13.1
  IPv6 address: 2013::1 (global unicast)
  IPv6 address: FE80::11FF:FE11:1111 (link-local)
Platform: Cisco 1841,  Capabilities: Router Switch IGMP
Interface: Serial0/0/0.1,  Port ID (outgoing port): Serial0/0/0.3
! lines omitted for brevity
```

The most notable fact listed in the example is that the output confirms that little difference exists with the **show** commands for EIGRP for IPv4 versus IPv6. The main differences relate to the **show ip protocols/show ipv6 protocols** commands and that EIGRP for IPv6 uses a link-local IP address for the next hop of each route.

OSPF Version 3

The original OSPF, created to exchange routing information for IPv4, began life as Version 1 and was later enhanced as Version 2. The original OSPFv2 RFC (1247) made draft standard status in 1991. Although some changes and additions have occurred in OSPFv2 over the years, the OSPF many companies have used for a long time is OSPFv2.

To support IPv6, an IETF working group took the OSPFv2 standard and made changes to the protocol to support IPv6, resulting in the new protocol named OSPF Version 3 (OSPFv3). OSPFv3 does advertise IPv6 prefixes, but it does not advertise IPv4 prefixes, so in most OSPF shops that begin migration to IPv6, the routers run OSPFv2 for IPv4 support and OSPFv3 for IPv6 support, just like a network running EIGRP for IPv4 would then add configuration for EIGRP for IPv6.

As with the earlier sections about RIPng and EIGRP for IPv6, this section first examines the similarities and differences between the IPv6 version of OSPF and the earlier IPv4 version. It then looks at the OSPFv3 configuration and finally OSPFv3 verification.

Comparing OSPFv2 and OSPFv3

Because OSPFv2 should already be somewhat familiar to you after reading Part 3 of this book, this section summarizes the similarities and differences, and then explains some of the differences briefly. To that end, Table 17-7 summarizes a wide variety of OSPF features, comparing OSPFv2 and OSPFv3.

Table 17-7 *Comparing OSPFv2 and OSPFv3*

Feature	OSPFv2	OSPFv3
Advertises routes for...	IPv4	IPv6
OSPF messages use this layer 3 protocol	IPv4	IPv6
IP Protocol Type	89	89
Uses Link State logic	Yes	Yes
Supports VLSM	Yes	Yes
Process to choose RID, compared to OSPFv2	Same	Same
LSA flooding and aging compared to OSPFv2	Same	Same
Area structure compared to OSPFv2	Same	Same
Packet types and uses compared to OSPFv3 (Table 6-4)	Same	Same
LSA flooding and aging compared to OSPFv2	Same	Same
RID based on highest up/up loopback IPv4 address, or highest other IPv4 interface address?	Yes	Yes
32-bit LSID	Yes	Yes

Table 17-7 *Comparing OSPFv2 and OSPFv3*

Feature	OSPFv2	OSPFv3
Uses interface cost metric, derived from interface bandwidth	Yes	Yes
Metric meaning infinity	$2^{16} - 1$	$2^{16} - 1$
Supports route tags	Yes	Yes
Elects DR based on highest priority, then highest RID	Yes	Yes
Periodic reflooding every...	30 minutes	30 minutes
Multicast–all SPF routers	224.0.0.5	FF02::5
Multicast–All Designated routers	224.0.0.6	FF02::6
Authentication	OSPF-specific	Uses IPv6 AH/ESP
Neighbor checks compared to OSPFv2 (table 5-5)	Same	Same, except no "same subnet" check
Multiple instances per interface	No	Yes

Some of the comparisons in the table require further explanation:

Key Topic

- The multicast addresses used by OSPFv3 of course differ, but they keep similar numbers compared to OSPFv2.

- OSPF uses IPv6's inherent IPsec capabilities, rather than defining a separate authentication process.

- As with RIPng and EIGRP for IPv6, OSPFv3 does not require neighboring routers to be in the same subnet as a requirement for becoming neighbors. However, OSPFv3 does follow all other neighbor verification checks as compared with OSPFv2, as summarized in Table 5-5 in Chapter 5, "OSPF Overview and Neighbor Relationships."

- Support for multiple *instances* of OSPF on a single link, whereas OSPFv2 supports only a single instance per link.

- OSPF uses the neighbor's link local IPv6 address as the next-hop IP address.

- The RID is still based on IPv4 addresses, not IPv6 addresses. Like EIGRP for IPv6, a router must have a RID before OSPFv3 will work.

Other differences exist as well, particularly when examining the details listed in the OSPFv3 LSDB. However, keeping to a scope that includes general concepts, configuration, and verification, this chapter does not get into those details.

Configuring OSPFv3

OSPFv3 configuration requires no new steps and few changes syntactically when compared to the newer style of OSPFv2 configuration discussed in Chapter 5's section "Enabling OSPF Neighbor Discovery on LANs." That section explained how to configure OSPF using the interface **ip ospf area** interface subcommand to enable OSPF on an interface, rather than relying on the indirect reference made by OSPFv2's **network** router subcommand. With OSPFv3, only one configuration style is supported, using the similar **ipv6 ospf area** command to enable OSPFv3 on an interface. IOS does not support a **network** command for OSPFv3.

The basic OSPFv3 configuration matches the newer style of OSPFv2 configuration, except for substituting **ipv6** instead of **ip** in the configuration commands. The following list shows the basic configuration steps, including the assignment of an IPv6 address to the interface.

Step 1.   Enable IPv6 routing with the **ipv6 unicast-routing** global command.

Step 2.   Create an OSPFv3 routing process using the **ipv6 router ospf** *process-id* global configuration command.

Step 3.   Enable IPv6 on the interface, typically by configuring static IPv6 addresses as follows:

    A. Configure an IPv6 unicast address on each interface, using the **ipv6 address** *address/prefix-length* [**eui-64**] interface command.

    B. Configure the **ipv6 enable** command, which enables IPv6 and causes the router to derive its link local address.

Step 4.   Enable OSPFv3 on the interface with the **ipv6 ospf** *process-id* **area** *area-number* interface subcommand.

Step 5.   If no OSPF router ID has been automatically chosen, due to not having at least one working interface with a IPv4 address, configure an OSPF router ID with the **router-id** *rid* command in OSPFv3 configuration mode.

Note: for a complete discussion of options for enabling IPv6 on an interface, as mentioned at Step 3, refer to Chapter 16's Table 16-10.

Note: Unlike a new EIGRP for IPv6 routing process, a newly created OSPFv3 routing process defaults to an administratively enabled state. As a result, the previous configuration checklist does not include the **no shutdown** OSPFv3 subcommand. However, the router mode subcommands **shutdown** and **no shutdown** can be used to disable and re-enable the OSPFv3 routing process.

To be complete, Example 17-5 lists the OSPFv3 configuration on Router R1 from Figure 17-2. Figure 17-2 shows the area design used for the configuration.

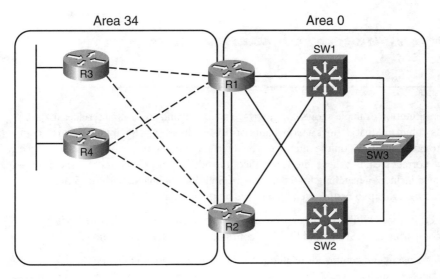

Figure 17-2 *Area Design Used for Example 17-5*

Example 17-5 *Configuring IPv6 Routing and Routing Protocols on R1*

```
R1# show running-config
! output is edited to remove lines not pertinent to this example
! Step 1: Enable IPv6 routing
ipv6 unicast-routing
!
! On five interfaces, do steps 3 and 4: configure static IPv6 addresses,
! and enable OSPFv3 process 5, in the appropriate areas
interface FastEthernet0/0.1
 ipv6 address 2012::1/64
 ipv6 ospf 5 area 0
!
interface FastEthernet0/0.2
 ipv6 address 2017::1/64
 ipv6 ospf 5 area 0
!
interface FastEthernet0/1.18
 ipv6 address 2018::1/64
 ipv6 ospf 5 area 0
!
interface Serial0/0/0.3
 ipv6 address 2013::1/64
 ipv6 ospf 5 area 34
!
interface Serial0/0/0.4
 ipv6 address 2014::1/64
 ipv6 ospf 5 area 34
```

```
! Steps 2 and 5 - creating the OSPFv3 process, and defining the RID
ipv6 router ospf 5
 router-id 1.1.1.1
```

The configuration example shows two interface subcommands on each interface: an **ipv6 address** command that defines a global unicast IPv6 address, plus the **ipv6 ospf area** command to enable OSPFv3 on the interface. The interface subcommands place each interface into the correct area. But these interface subcommands have no effect unless the configuration also includes a matching **ipv6 router ospf 5** global command, with the 5 in this case matching the **ipv6 ospf 5 area** commands on the interfaces.

Beyond this basic OSPFv3 configuration, many of the optional OSPF features match when comparing the OSPFv2 and OSPFv3 configuration as well, for example:

■ The concept and commands related to OSPF stub areas are literally identical, using commands such as **area 34 stub**. (See Table 7-3 for a reminder of the commands for OSPFv2.)

■ Like OSPFv2, OSPFv3 can only summarize routes on ABRs and ASBRs, using the similar command **area *x* range** *ipv6-prefix/length* router subcommand, with the only difference being that the command lists an IPv6 prefix rather than an IPv4 subnet and mask.

■ Like OSPFv2, OSPFv3 uses the concept of OSPF interface types as configured with the **ipv6 ospf network** *type* interface subcommand. These types dictate whether OSPFv3 attempts to elect a DR, and whether routers need to configure neighbors with the **ipv6 ospf neighbor** interface subcommand, with the same issues seen with OSPFv2.

Verifying OSPFv3

Most of the **show** commands for OSPFv3 have similar output compared to the OSPFv2 versions of the commands. The biggest differences exist in the output related to the OSPF database, both due to the changes in LSA terminology, the addition of new LSA types, and that some LSDB information is located with a different LSA type when comparing OSPFv2 and OSPFv3. Table 17-8 lists a cross-reference comparing the key commands related to both OSPFv2 and OSPFv3, with the second column listing the parameters after **show ip**, and the third column listing parameters after **show ipv6**.

Table 17-8   *Comparing OSPF Verification Commands:* **show ip** *and* **show ipv6**...

Function	show ipv4...	show ipv6...
All OSPF-learned routes	... route ospf	... route ospf
Router ID, Timers, ABR, SPF statistics	... ospf	... ospf
List of routing information sources	... protocols ... ospf neighbor	... ospf neighbor

Table 17-8 *Comparing OSPF Verification Commands:* **show ip** *and* **show ipv6...**

Function	show ipv4...	show ipv6...
Interfaces assigned to each area	... **protocols** ... **ospf interface brief**	... **protocols** ... **ospf interface brief**
OSPF interfaces–costs, state, area, number of neighbors	... **interface brief**	... **interface brief**
Detailed information about OSPF interfaces	... **ospf interface**	... **ospf interface**
Displays summary of OSPF database	... **ospf database**	... **ospf database**

The first verification example focuses on some of the differences between OSPFv2 and OSPFv3 for the display of neighbor status. Example 17-6 shows output from Router R3, as shown in Figures 17-1 and 17-2. The output highlights the only noticeable difference between the output of the **show ip ospf neighbor** and **show ipv6 ospf neighbor** commands: OSPFv2 displays the interface IP address of neighbors, but OSPFv3 displays an interface ID. OSPFv3 routers create a locally significant interface ID, using that in LSAs that describe the intra-area topology, rather than using neighbor IPv4 addresses to describe the topology. OSPFv3 separates the topology information from the Layer 3 addressing information, so OSPFv3 uses the interface ID concept to identify how a router reaches a particular neighbor.

Example 17-6 *IPv6 OSPFv3 Interface IDs on Router R3*

```
! On R3, IPv4 OSPFv2 neighbors are listed, with interface IPv4 addresses.
R3# show ip ospf neighbor

Neighbor ID     Pri   State        Dead Time   Address       Interface
2.2.2.2          0    FULL/  -     00:00:31    10.10.23.2    Serial0/0/0.2
1.1.1.1          0    FULL/  -     00:00:31    10.10.13.1    Serial0/0/0.1
4.4.4.4          1    FULL/DR      00:00:39    10.10.34.4
FastEthernet0/0

! On R3, IPv6 OSPFv3 neighbors are listed, with interface IDs.
R3# show ipv6 ospf neighbor

Neighbor ID     Pri   State        Dead Time   Interface ID  Interface
2.2.2.2          1    FULL/  -     00:00:36    19            Serial0/0/0.2
1.1.1.1          1    FULL/  -     00:00:35    19            Serial0/0/0.1
4.4.4.4          1    FULL/DR      00:00:34    3
FastEthernet0/0

! Next, the LSA for R3 (RID 3.3.3.3) lists its own interface ID and
! the neighbor interface ID, for each link.
R3# show ipv6 ospf database router adv-router 3.3.3.3

       OSPFv3 Router with ID (3.3.3.3) (Process ID 5)
```

```
                    Router Link States (Area 34)


  LS age: 996
  Options: (V6-Bit, E-Bit, R-bit, DC-Bit)
  LS Type: Router Links
  Link State ID: 0
  Advertising Router: 3.3.3.3
  LS Seq Number: 80000007
  Checksum: 0xDC04
  Length: 72
  Number of Links: 3

     Link connected to: another Router (point-to-point)
       Link Metric: 64
       Local Interface ID: 17
       Neighbor Interface ID: 19
       Neighbor Router ID: 2.2.2.2

     Link connected to: another Router (point-to-point)
       Link Metric: 64
       Local Interface ID: 16
       Neighbor Interface ID: 19
       Neighbor Router ID: 1.1.1.1

     Link connected to: a Transit Network
       Link Metric: 1
       Local_Interface ID: 3
       Neighbor (DR) Interface ID: 3
       Neighbor (DR) Router ID: 4.4.4.4
```

Example 17-7 displays the output of a few other IPv6 **show** command, just for perspective. The **show ipv6 ospf interface brief** command lists the same kind of information shown in the similar **show ip ospf interface brief** command, but again listing the interface ID as new information. The **show ipv6 protocols** command lists much sparser information as compared to the similar **show ip protocols** command. Note that both commands identify which OSPFv3 interfaces have been assigned to each area.

Example 17-7 *Finding Interfaces and Areas for OSPFv3, on Router R3*

```
R1# show ipv6 protocols
IPv6 Routing Protocol is "connected"
IPv6 Routing Protocol is "ospf 1"
  Interfaces (Area 34):
    Serial0/0/0.1
    Serial0/0/0.2
```

```
      FastEthernet0/0
   Redistribution:
     None
R1# show ipv6 ospf interface brief
Interface    PID   Area            Intf ID    Cost   State  Nbrs F/C
Se0/0/0.1    1     34              19         64     P2P    1/1
Se0/0/0.2    1     34              19         64     P2P    1/1
Fa0/0        1     34              3          1      BDR    1/1
```

IPv6 IGP Redistribution

IPv6 routing protocols can perform route redistribution, much like IPv4 route redistribution (as detailed in Chapter 9, "Basic IGP Redistribution," and Chapter 10, "Advanced IGP Redistribution"). This section shows a few examples to confirm those similarities and compares IPv4 and IPv6 route redistribution.

The following list summarizes some of those key similarities between both IPv4 and IPv6 route redistribution:

Key Topic

■ Redistribution takes routes from the IP routing table, not from the topology tables and databases controlled by the source routing protocol.

■ Route maps can be applied when redistributing for the purpose of filtering routes, setting metrics, and setting route tags.

■ IPv6 routing protocols use the same default administrative distances, with the same basic mechanisms to override those defaults.

■ The same basic mechanisms exist in IPv6 to defeat routing loop problems: administrative distance, route tags, and filtering.

■ The routing protocols use the same default administrative distance (AD) settings for internal and external routes.

■ The redistribution configuration uses practically the same syntax with the same commands.

Some differences do exist, both in configuration and in concept, as follows:

■ Any matching done with distribution lists or route maps would use IPv6 prefix lists and IPv6 ACLs, which match based on IPv6 prefix and length.

■ The IPv6 version of the **redistribute** command takes only routes learned from an IGP but by default does not take connected routes on interfaces enabled for that IGP. To also redistribute those connected routes, the **redistribute** command must include the **include-connected** parameter. When an IPv4 routing protocol redistributes from an IGP, it always attempts to take both the IGP-learned routes and the connected routes for interfaces enabled for that IGP.

■ Unlike OSPFv2, OSPFv3 does not require a **subnets** parameter on the **redistribute** command, because IPv6 does not maintain the IPv4 concept of classful networks and the subnets inside those classful networks.

■ IPv6 redistribution ignores the "local" routes in the IPv6 routing table (the /128 host routes for a router's own interface IPv6 addresses). IPv4 has no equivalent concept.

Redistributing without Route Maps

As with IPv4 redistribution, IPv6 redistribution can be done without applying a route map. The first redistribution example shows such a case, with router R2 performing the redistribution. In this case, R2 redistributes routes learned from an OSPF domain on the right, into a RIP domain on the left, without applying a route map. Figure 17-3 shows the two routing domains and the IPv6 subnets used.

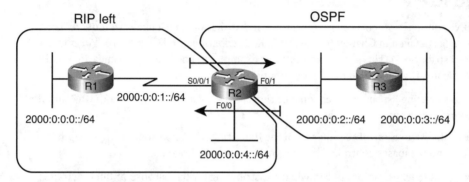

Figure 17-3 *Redistribution Plan*

Example 17-8 shows the redistribution configuration on Router R2, which takes routes from OSPF process number 5 and redistributes them into RIP process "left." The example begins with a **show ipv6 route** command on R2 to list the routes that could be redistributed, and ends with those routes being seen on Router R1.

Example 17-8 *Redistributing from OSPF into RIP, with Default Metrics*

```
R2# show ipv6 ospf interface brief
Interface    PID   Area          Intf ID    Cost   State Nbrs F/C
Fa0/1        5     0             4          1      BDR   1/1


R2# show ipv6 route
IPv6 Routing Table - Default - 9 entries
Codes: C - Connected, L - Local, S - Static, U - Per-user Static route
       B - BGP, M - MIPv6, R - RIP, I1 - ISIS L1
       I2 - ISIS L2, IA - ISIS interarea, IS - ISIS summary, D - EIGRP
       EX - EIGRP external
       O - OSPF Intra, OI - OSPF Inter, OE1 - OSPF ext 1, OE2 - OSPF ext 2
       ON1 - OSPF NSSA ext 1, ON2 - OSPF NSSA ext 2
R    2000::/64 [120/2]
      via FE80::213:19FF:FE7B:5026, Serial0/0/1
C    2000:0:0:1::/64 [0/0]
```

```
             via Serial0/0/1, directly connected
L    2000::1:213:19FF:FE7B:5004/128 [0/0]
             via Serial0/0/1, receive
C    2000:0:0:2::/64 [0/0]
             via FastEthernet0/1, directly connected
L    2000:0:0:2::2/128 [0/0]
             via FastEthernet0/1, receive
O    2000:0:0:3::/64 [110/2]
             via FE80::213:19FF:FE7B:6588, FastEthernet0/1
C    2000:0:0:4::/64 [0/0]
             via FastEthernet0/0, directly connected
L    2000::4:213:19FF:FE7B:5004/128 [0/0]
             via FastEthernet0/0, receive
L    FF00::/8 [0/0]
             via Null0, receive


R2# configure terminal
Enter configuration commands, one per line.  End with CNTL/Z.
R2(config)# ipv6 router rip left
R2(config-rtr)# redistribute ospf 5 include-connected
R2(config-rtr)# ^Z
R2#
```

```
! The next command is executed on router R1
R1# show ipv6 route rip
IPv6 Routing Table - Default - 8 entries
Codes: C - Connected, L - Local, S - Static, U - Per-user Static route
       B - BGP, M - MIPv6, R - RIP, I1 - ISIS L1
       I2 - ISIS L2, IA - ISIS interarea, IS - ISIS summary, D - EIGRP
       EX - EIGRP external
       O - OSPF Intra, OI - OSPF Inter, OE1 - OSPF ext 1, OE2 - OSPF ext 2
       ON1 - OSPF NSSA ext 1, ON2 - OSPF NSSA ext 2
R    2000:0:0:2::/64 [120/2]
         via FE80::213:19FF:FE7B:5004, Serial0/0/0
R    2000:0:0:3::/64 [120/3]
         via FE80::213:19FF:FE7B:5004, Serial0/0/0
R    2000:0:0:4::/64 [120/2]
         via FE80::213:19FF:FE7B:5004, Serial0/0/0
```

The brief configuration shows both the simplicity and one difference in the IPv4 and IPv6 redistribution configuration. First, the redistribution function works with only the **redistribute ospf 5** command, which takes routes from R2's OSPF 5 process. However, the **redistribute** command has the **include-connected** keyword, which tells RIP to not only take the OSPF-learned routes for 2000:0:0:3::/64, but also the connected route for 2000:0:0:2::/64, the connected route off R2's F0/1 interface. The beginning of the example lists a **show ipv6 ospf interface brief** command, which lists that only F0/1 has been enabled for OSPF.

The **show ipv6 route rip** command on R1, at the end of the example, shows that R2 indeed redistributed the two routes from the OSPF side of Figure 17-3.

Redistribution into RIPng uses a metric as taken from the IPv6 routing table by default. In this case, the output from R1 at the end of the example lists the two redistributed routes with metrics 2 and 3. You can see from the earlier output in the example that R2's metric for its OSPF route to 2000:0:0:3::/64 was 2, so R3's metric is now listed as 3.

Using RIPng's default action to take the integer metric from the source IGP worked in this case, but in most cases, the metric should be set via configuration. OSPF metrics will often be more than the maximum usable RIP metric of 15, making these routes instantly unusable in RIP. Redistributing from EIGRP into RIP would not work either, given the relatively large integer metrics calculated by EIGRP. So when redistributing into RIP, change the configuration to set the metric. For instance, using the command **redistribute ospf 5 include-connected metric 3** would have set the default metric for all redistributed routes and avoided such problems.

Redistributing with Route Maps

IPv6 redistribution can also call route maps, for all the usual reasons: setting metrics for different routes, filtering routes, and setting route tags, to name a few. To demonstrate the configuration, Example 17-9 shows another example, using the same design in Figure 17-3. In this case, Router R2 redistributes RIP routes into OSPF, with the following criteria:

- Redistribute only LAN subnets, with OSPF metric 200.

- Filter all other subnets.

Example 17-9 shows the configuration on R2 and the resulting OSPF routes on R3.

Example 17-9   *Redistributing from RIP into OSPF, Using a Route Map*

```
R2# show run
! unrelated lines omitted
ipv6 router ospf 5
 router-id 2.2.2.2
 redistribute rip left route-map only-RIP-lan include-connected
!
ipv6 router rip left
 redistribute ospf 5 metric 3 include-connected
!
ipv6 prefix-list rip-to-ospf seq 5 permit 2000::/64
ipv6 prefix-list rip-to-ospf seq 10 permit 2000:0:0:4::/64
!
route-map only-RIP-lan permit 10
 match ipv6 address prefix-list rip-to-ospf
 set metric 200

R3# show ipv6 route ospf
IPv6 Routing Table - Default - 7 entries
Codes: C - Connected, L - Local, S - Static, U - Per-user Static route
```

```
    B - BGP, M - MIPv6, R - RIP, I1 - ISIS L1
    I2 - ISIS L2, IA - ISIS interarea, IS - ISIS summary, D - EIGRP
    EX - EIGRP external
    O - OSPF Intra, OI - OSPF Inter, OE1 - OSPF ext 1, OE2 - OSPF ext 2
    ON1 - OSPF NSSA ext 1, ON2 - OSPF NSSA ext 2
OE2 2000::/64 [110/200]
    via FE80::213:19FF:FE7B:5005, FastEthernet0/0
OE2 2000:0:0:4::/64 [110/200]
    via FE80::213:19FF:FE7B:5005, FastEthernet0/0
```

First, the configuration shows an IPv6 prefix list and a route map that uses a **match ipv6** command that refers to the prefix list. The prefix list works just like an IPv4 prefix list, other than matching with the IPv6 prefix format rather than IPv4. The route map works with the same logic as well, in this case referencing the IPv6 prefix list with the **match ipv6 address prefix rip-to-ospf** command. The route map matches the two LAN subnets in the RIP domain with the first route map clause and sets the metric to 200. The implied deny clause at the end of the route map matches all other routes, which makes R2 filter all other routes from being redistributed into OSPF. As a result, the serial IPv6 subnet, 2000:0:0:1::/64, is filtered by the redistribution process.

The **show ipv6 route ospf** command on R3 at the end of the example confirms that R3 learned routes for both LAN subnets in the RIP domain but no other routes. Of particular interest, note that OSPFv3 lists the route as OSPF external Type 2, because just like OSPFv2, OSPFv3 defaults to redistribute routes as external Type 2 routes. Note also that the output lists metrics for each route as 200, because R2 set the metric to 200, and OSPF does not add anything to the metric of E2 routes.

Static IPv6 Routes

IPv6 supports the configuration of static routes with similar syntax compared to the **ip route** command used to configured IPv4 static routes. The syntax of the **ipv6 route** command matches the **ip route** command, other than that the IPv6 destination is represented as prefix/length, and any next-hop IP address is an IPv6 address, of course. The generic syntax is

```
ipv6 route prefix/length {outgoing-interface [next-hop-address] ¦
next-hop-address} [admin-distance] [tag tag-value]
```

The parameters use the same concepts as the same parameters used for IPv4. However, with IPv6, a few interesting differences exist. First, when using the next-hop IP address, you can use any address on the neighboring router, including the neighbor's link local IPv6 address. Second, if using a link local address as the next-hop address, then you must configure both the outgoing interface and the link local address.

Example 17-10 shows such a case, with a static route configured on Router R3 in Figure 17-4. R3 adds a static route for R1's LAN prefix, 2000::/64, using R2 as next hop, specifically R2's F0/1 link local address as next hop.

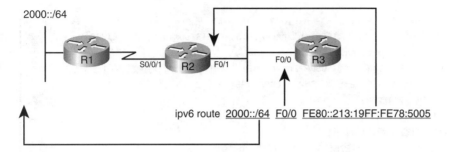

Figure 17-4   *Static IPv6 Route on Router R3*

Example 17-10   *Static Route on R3, with Link Local Next-Hop Address*

```
R3# conf t
Enter configuration commands, one per line.  End with CNTL/Z.
R3(config)# ipv6 route 2000::/64 FE80::213:19FF:FE7B:5005
% Interface has to be specified for a link-local nexthop

R3(config)# ipv6 route 2000::/64 f0/0 FE80::213:19FF:FE7B:5005
R3(config)# ^Z
R3# show ipv6 route
IPv6 Routing Table - Default - 7 entries
Codes: C - Connected, L - Local, S - Static, U - Per-user Static route
       B - BGP, M - MIPv6, R - RIP, I1 - ISIS L1
       I2 - ISIS L2, IA - ISIS interarea, IS - ISIS summary, D - EIGRP
       EX - EIGRP external
       O - OSPF Intra, OI - OSPF Inter, OE1 - OSPF ext 1, OE2 - OSPF ext 2
       ON1 - OSPF NSSA ext 1, ON2 - OSPF NSSA ext 2
S   2000::/64 [1/0]
     via FE80::213:19FF:FE7B:5005, FastEthernet0/0
C   2000:0:0:2::/64 [0/0]
     via FastEthernet0/0, directly connected
L   2000:0:0:2::3/128 [0/0]
     via FastEthernet0/0, receive
C   2000:0:0:3::/64 [0/0]
     via FastEthernet0/1, directly connected
L   2000::3:213:19FF:FE7B:6589/128 [0/0]
     via FastEthernet0/1, receive
OE2 2000:0:0:4::/64 [110/200]
     via FE80::213:19FF:FE7B:5005, FastEthernet0/0
L   FF00::/8 [0/0]
     via Null0, receive
R3# show ipv6 route 2000::/64
Routing entry for 2000::/64
  Known via "static", distance 1, metric 0
```

```
Backup from "ospf 1 [110]"
Route count is 1/1, share count 0
Routing paths:
  FE80::213:19FF:FE7B:5005, FastEthernet0/0
    Last updated 00:11:50 ago
```

The example shows a static route that uses a multiaccess interface as the outgoing interface, so using both the outgoing interface (F0/0) and the next-hop address in the **ipv6 route** command prevents ambiguity. Also, note that IPv6 routers do not actually have a route that matches the neighbor's link local address. As a result, the **ipv6 route** command must supply the outgoing interface as well, so the local router (R3 in this case) knows on which interface to use NDP to discover how to reach this neighboring IPv6 address. The example shows an attempt to configure the **ipv6 route** command with only R2's next-hop link local address, but R3 rejects the command. When both the outgoing interface (F0/0) has been listed, plus R2's link local address as next hop, R3 accepts the command and adds this static route to its IPv6 routing table.

Finally, the output of the **show ipv6 route 2000::/64** command at the end of the example lists some information not seen in the equivalent IPv4 command. The output reveals some insight into the operation of the routing table manager (RTM), which chooses the best route for a prefix among many sources. In this case, the static route for 2000::/64 used a default administrative distance of 1. The routers in this design were also still configured as they were at the end of Example 17-9, with RIP on the left of the figure, OSPF on the right, and redistribution between the two. So, R3 still has an OSPF route for 2000::/64, with default administrative distance 110. The output of this command lists not only the static route, but also the backup route, with a worse administrative distance, in this case the OSPF-learned route. When configuring a floating static route–a static route with a high administrative distance so that the route will not be used until the IGP routes have all failed–this command can be useful to confirm that this backup route is known to IOS.

Exam Preparation Tasks

Planning Practice

The CCNP ROUTE exam expects test takers to review design documents, create implementation plans, and create verification plans. This section provides some exercises that may help you to take a step back from the minute details of the topics in this chapter so that you can think about the same technical topics from the planning perspective.

For each planning practice table, simply complete the table. Note that any numbers in parentheses represent the number of options listed for each item in the solutions in Appendix F, "Completed Practice Planning Tables."

Implementation Plan Peer Review Table

Table 17-9 shows a list of questions that others might ask, or that you might think about, during a peer review of another network engineer's implementation plan. Complete the table by answering the questions.

Table 17-9   *Notable Questions from This Chapter to Consider During an Implementation Plan Peer Review*

Question	Answers
A RIPng implementation plan lists two neighboring routers with unicast IPv6 addresses 2000::1/64 and 2001::2/64, respectively. Will this cause a neighborship issue?	
Same issues as in the previous row, but the plan uses EIGRP for IPv6.	
A plan shows a planned config for a new router, with no IPv4 addresses, IPv6 addresses on all interfaces, and EIGRP for IPv6 configuration. What potential issues should you look for in the configuration? (3)	
Same scenario as the previous row, but with OSPFv3.	
The plan shows an EIGRP for IPv6 and OSPFv3 domain with mutual redistribution. The configuration shows a **redistribute eigrp 1** command under the OSPF process. What kinds of routes should be redistributed? Which kinds will not?	

Create an Implementation Plan Table

To practice skills useful when creating your own implementation plan, list in Table 17-10 all configuration commands related to the configuration of the following features. You may want to record your answers outside the book, and set a goal to complete this table (and others like it) from memory during your final reviews before taking the exam.

Table 17-10 *Implementation Plan Configuration Memory Drill*

Feature	Configuration Commands/Notes
Assuming IPv6 routing and IPv6 addresses have already been configured, configure RIPng.	
Assuming IPv6 routing and IPv6 addresses have already been configured and no IPv4 addresses exist on the router, configure EIGRP for IPv6.	
Assuming IPv6 routing and IPv6 addresses have already been configured and no IPv4 addresses exist on the router, configure OSPFv3.	
Configure RIPng to redistribute routes from OSPF process 1 including subnets, and connected interfaces.	

Choose Commands for a Verification Plan Table

To practice skills useful when creating your own EIGRP verification plan, list in Table 17-11 all commands that supply the requested information. You may want to record your answers outside the book, and set a goal to complete this table (and others like it) from memory during your final reviews before taking the exam.

Table 17-11 *Verification Plan Memory Drill*

Information Needed	Commands
All IPv6 routes	
Details about a given IPv6 prefix	
All routes within a given range of IPv6 addresses	
All RIP-learned IPv6 routes	
All next-hop IPv6 addresses used by RIP routes	
The interfaces on which RIP is enabled	
All EIGRP-learned IPv6 routes	
All EIGRP neighbors	
Summary of the EIGRP topology table	
OSPF router ID and SPF statistics	
List of OSPF neighbors	
All OSPF-learned IPv6 routes	
Interfaces enabled for OSPF and their assigned areas	
OSPF costs per interface	
Summary of the OSPF database	

Note: Some of the entries in this table may not have been specifically mentioned in this chapter but are listed in this table for review and reference.

Review all the Key Topics

Review the most important topics from inside the chapter, noted with the Key Topics icon in the outer margin of the page. Table 17-12 lists a reference of these key topics and the page numbers on which each is found.

Table 17-12   *Key Topics for Chapter 17*

Key Topic Element	Description	Page Number
Table 17-3	Comparisons between RIP-2 and RIPng	574
List	Configuration steps for RIPng	575
Table 17-5	Comparisons between EIGRP for IPv4 and EIGRP for IPv6	581
List	Configuration steps for EIGRP for IPv6	582
List	Decision process for choosing an EIGRP for IPv6 router ID	583
Table 17-7	Comparisons between EIGRP for IPv4 and EIGRP for IPv6	588
List	Additional explanations of key differences between OSPFv3 and OSPFv2	589
List	Configuration steps for OSPFv3	590
List	Similarities and differences with IPv4 and IPv6 redistribution	595

Complete the Tables and Lists from Memory

Print a copy of Appendix D, "Memory Tables," (found on the CD), or at least the section for this chapter, and complete the tables and lists from memory. Appendix E, "Memory Tables Answer Key," also on the CD, includes completed tables and lists to check your work.

Define Key Terms

Define the following key terms from this chapter, and check your answers in the glossary.

RIP Next Generation, OSPF Version 3, EIGRP for IPv6

This chapter covers the following subjects:

IPv4 and IPv6 Migration and Coexistence Concepts: This section introduces the three main branches of coexistence tools: dual stacks, tunnels, and protocol translation.

Static Point-to-Point IPv6 Tunnels: This section explains the concepts behind IPv6 point-to-point tunnels, their differences, and the configuration of each.

Dynamic Multipoint IPv6 Tunnels: This section explains the concepts behind IPv6 multipoint tunnels, their differences, and the configuration of each.

CHAPTER 18

IPv4 and IPv6 Coexistence

Most of the barriers for a migration to IPv6 have been removed. The IPv6 protocol set has been complete for more than a decade. Many products, including the most common client and server operating systems, support IPv6. Cisco routers have supported IPv6 long enough that IPv6 support exists in the most commonly deployed IOS versions. The product support means that IPv6 deployment should not be inhibited by the availability of IPv6 in commonly used software. Additionally, the Internet's support for IPv6 is growing. Barriers do still exist, but IPv6 adoption may have finally reached the point of gathering momentum worldwide.

Although the tools exist, the process of migrating billions of IPv4-based computers and devices to IPv6–devices under the control of millions of organizations and maybe billions of individual people–will not happen overnight. In the real world, the migration from IPv4 to IPv6 will probably take a generation to complete–arguably, it has been in progress for a decade already. Knowing that the migration would take years, the creators of IPv6 wisely planned for coexistence tools that allow both a single Enterprise, and the Internet, to use both IPv4 and IPv6 at the same time, coexisting peacefully.

This chapter discusses the three major categories of migration and coexistence tools for IPv6: dual stacks, tunneling, and protocol translation. However, the majority of the chapter examines four different options for tunneling IPv6 over IPv4 networks.

"Do I Know This Already?" Quiz

The "Do I Know This Already?" quiz allows you to assess if you should read the entire chapter. If you miss no more than one of these nine self-assessment questions, you might want to move ahead to the "Exam Preparation Tasks." Table 18-1 lists the major headings in this chapter and the "Do I Know This Already?" quiz questions covering the material in those headings so that you can assess your knowledge of these specific areas. The answers to the "Do I Know This Already?" quiz appear in Appendix A.

Table 18-1 *"Do I Know This Already?" Foundation Topics Section-to-Question Mapping*

Foundations Topics Section	Questions
IPv4 and IPv6 Migration and Coexistence Concepts	1–3
Static Point-to-Point IPv6 Tunnels	4–6
Dynamic Multipoint IPv6 Tunnels	7–9

1. An enterprise has plans to start adding IPv6 support. For the first year, the IPv6 will be in small pockets spread around the existing large IPv4 network, with occasional IPv6 traffic while applications teams test IPv6-enabled servers and applications. Which of the following tools would be most appropriate?

   a. Native IPv6

   b. Point-to-point tunnels

   c. Multipoint tunnels

   d. NAT-PT

2. An enterprise has plans to start adding IPv6 support. The initial deployment requires support from some IPv6-only devices that need to access servers that support only IPv4. Which of the following tools would be most appropriate?

   a. Native IPv6

   b. Point-to-point tunnels

   c. Multipoint tunnels

   d. NAT-PT

3. A client host uses IPv4 to communicate with one server and IPv6 to communicate with another. Which of the following IPv6 coexistence features is likely at work on the host?

   a. Native IPv6

   b. Point-to-point tunnels

   c. Multipoint tunnels

   d. NAT-PT

   e. Dual stacks

4. The following configuration exists on a router on one end of an IPv6 tunnel. Which type of tunnel is created by this configuration?

```
interface loopback 1
 ip address 1.1.1.1 255.255.255.255
interface tunnel 2
 ipv6 address 2000::1/64
 tunnel source loopback 1
 tunnel destination 2.2.2.2
 tunnel mode ipv6ip
 ipv6 eigrp 1
```

   a. Automatic 6to4

   b. Manually configured tunnel

   c. ISATAP

   d. GRE

5. An engineer is reviewing another engineer's sample configuration for a GRE tunnel used to pass IPv6 traffic. The tunnel has not yet been configured on the router. Which of the following commands is not required for the configuration to pass IPv6 traffic?

- **a.** tunnel source
- **b.** tunnel destination
- **c.** tunnel mode
- **d.** All these commands are required.

6. Which of the following IPv6 tunneling mechanisms support IPv6 IGP routing protocols? (Choose two.)

- **a.** Automatic 6to4
- **b.** Manually configured tunnel
- **c.** ISATAP
- **d.** GRE

7. The following configuration exists on a router on one end of an IPv6 tunnel. Although the configuration added so far is correct, the configuration is incomplete. Which type of tunnel is most likely to be intended by the network engineer?

```
interface loopback 1
 ip address 192.168.1.1 255.255.255.255
interface tunnel 2
 ipv6 address 2002:C0A8:101::1/64
 tunnel source loopback 1
```

- **a.** Automatic 6to4
- **b.** Manually configured tunnel
- **c.** ISATAP
- **d.** GRE

8. The answers each list a tunnel method and two consecutive IPv6 address quartets. Which answers identify a tunneling method that relies on an IPv4 address to be embedded into an IPv6 address, within the correct quartets listed? (Choose two.)

- **a.** Automatic 6to4, quartets 2 and 3
- **b.** Automatic 6to4, quartets 7 and 8
- **c.** ISATAP, quartets 2 and 3
- **d.** ISATAP, quartets 7 and 8

9. Router R1 uses MAC address 1111.1111.1111 for its Fa0/0 interface. An engineer sees the following configuration in the output of a **show running-config** command. Then, the engineer issues a **show ipv6 interface brief** command. What global unicast IPv6 address does this command display for interface tunnel 1?

```
interface loopback 1
 ip address 192.168.1.1 255.255.255.255
interface tunnel 1
 tunnel source loopback 1
 tunnel destination 192.168.1.2
 tunnel mode ipv6ip isatap
 ipv6 address 2000::/64 eui-64
```

a. 2000::1311:11FF:FE11:1111

b. 2000::C0A5:101

c. 2000:C0A5:101::

d. 2000::5EFE:C0A8:101

Foundation Topics

IPv4 and IPv6 Migration and Coexistence Concepts

Most Enterprises do not move from having no formal IPv6 support to creating a full native IPv6 implementation on all routers, hosts, servers, and other devices. In the real world, some Enterprise networks will begin with several locations that need consistent and working IPv6 support. Other companies may begin with a small set of people who want to experiment with IPv6 in anticipation of the day in which IT will take advantage of IPv6. Eventually, IPv6 may well become the predominate traffic in the Enterprise, and one day, IPv4 may go away altogether, but that day may be decades away. As a result, IPv4 and IPv6 will likely coexist in a given internetwork for a very long time.

During this possibly long migration, three main classes of tools may be used to allow IPv4 to continue to work well, while supporting IPv6:

- Dual IPv4/IPv6 stacks (*dual stacks*)

- Tunneling

- NAT Protocol Translator (NAT-PT)

This section looks at each type of tool in succession.

IPv4/IPv6 Dual Stacks

The term *dual stacks* means that the host or router uses both IPv4 and IPv6 at the same time. For hosts, this means that the host has both an IPv4 and IPv6 address associated with each NIC, that the host can send IPv4 packets to other IPv4 hosts, and that the host can send IPv6 packets to other IPv6 hosts. For routers, it means that in addition to the usual IPv4 IP addresses and routing protocols, the routers would also have IPv6 addresses and routing protocols configured as discussed in Chapters 16, "IP Version 6 Addressing," and 17, "IPv6 Routing Protocols and Redistribution." To support both IPv4 and IPv6 hosts, the router could then receive and forward both IPv4 packets and IPv6 packets.

Note: Although not used as often today, the general term *protocol stack* refers to the layers in a protocol suite, with a protocol stack referring to the implementation of all layers of that protocol on a computer. Historical examples include Novell Netware, AppleTalk, and IBM SNA protocol stacks.

The hosts using dual stacks follow the same general process of using DNS to resolve a name into an IP address. The DNS requests can return either an IPv4 address or an IPv6 address. The dual stack host can then choose to use IPv4 to communicate with an IPv4 host or IPv6 to communicate with an IPv6 host.

To support dual stack hosts, routers need to forward both IPv4 and IPv6 packets. To forward IPv6 packets to the various destinations, the design engineer can use one of two general approaches:

- **Native IPv6:** Configure IPv6 on most or all routers, on most or all production interfaces, making all routers use a dual stack.

- **IPv6 tunnels:** Configure some routers with IPv6, others without IPv6, and tunnel the IPv6 packets over the IPv4 network by encapsulating IPv6 packets inside IPv4 packets.

Configuring native IPv6 simply means that you configure IPv6 as discussed in detail in Chapters 16 and 17, giving each interface one or more IPv6 addresses, enabling IPv6 routing protocols, and so on. Assuming an IPv4 network already exists, the engineer could build and execute an implementation plan to configure native IPv6 by enabling IPv6 on the same interfaces as IPv4, configuring an IPv6 routing protocol, and the routers would be ready to forward both types of packets.

A router that has been configured to forward both IPv4 and IPv6 is a dual stack router. This works well, but it does require the implementation of IPv6 on all routers that might one day receive an IPv6 packet that needs to be forwarded. Alternatively, using tunnels may be more reasonable to support smaller pockets of IPv6 hosts, because tunnels require fewer routers to be configured with IPv6 at all.

From a practical exam-preparation perspective for the CCNP ROUTE exam, the implementation of dual stacks means that you need to configure IPv6 as detailed in Chapters 16 and 17, while leaving the existing IPv4 configuration in place. Therefore, this chapter does not discuss the dual stack option's configuration, instead relying on the detail in Chapters 16 and 17.

Tunneling

Tunneling refers to a process by which one router or host encapsulates the IPv6 packet inside an IPv4 packet. The networking devices forward the IPv4 packet, ignoring the fact that the packet's payload is an IPv6 packet. Some later device or host decapsulates the original IPv6 packet, forwarding it on to the final destination.

From a network design perspective, tunneling IPv6 over IPv4 results in fewer routers needing any IPv6 configuration at all. As such, it allows a quicker migration from no IPv6 support to enough support to get IPv6 packets between two sites. Fewer routers need new configuration, the smaller number of changes means less operational risk, and the end hosts can still forward IPv6 traffic to each other.

This section begins by examining the concepts behind IPv6 tunneling. Then the text more closely examines the two main categories of tunnels: point-to-point tunnels and multipoint tunnels.

General Tunneling Concepts

To appreciate the configuration of the many types of IPv6 tunnels discussed in this chapter, you need a solid understanding of the basics. Throughout this chapter, most examples will be built on a small internetwork that represents a pre-existing IPv4-only Enterprise network. The IPv6 tunneling discussed in this chapter will be built on this simple network, as shown in Figure 18-1.

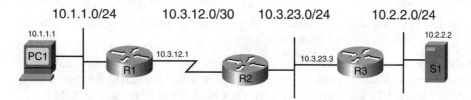

Figure 18-1   *Simple IPv4 Enterprise Network*

Next, consider the case in which an engineer must create an implementation plan to allow PC1 and server S1 to communicate using IPv6. They both may use IPv6 exclusively, or maybe one or both use a dual stack. In either case, for this example, the engineer's task is to ensure delivery of IPv6 packets sent between these two hosts. Additionally, the native mode option–in other words, configuring IPv6 on all three routers and all interface on each router–has been rejected, so IPv6 tunneling will be used.

To configure an IPv6 tunnel, the engineer could enable IPv6 on R1 and R3, and not at all on R2. The configuration on R1 and R3 would not need to enable IPv6 on the inner interfaces at all. Additionally, R1 and R3 would need the configuration related to a point-to-point tunnel. Figure 18-2 shows some of the concepts behind this point-to-point tunnel between R1 and R3.

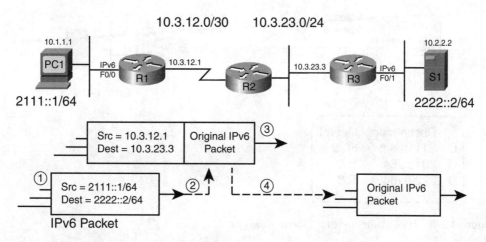

Figure 18-2   *IPv6 Tunneling Encapsulation and De-encapsulation*

Following the steps in Figure 18-2

Step 1.   PC1, acting as an IPv6 host, sends an IPv6 packet to S1, IPv6 address 2222::2. (PC1 would have likely used a DNS process to find S1's IPv6 address at some point prior.)

Step 2. R1 encapsulates the IPv6 packet into an IPv4 packet, with R1's IPv4 address as source IPv4 address, and R3's IPv4 address as the destination IPv4 address.

Step 3. R2 forwards the IPv4 packet to R3, with no knowledge of IPv6.

Step 4. R3 decapsulates the original IPv6 packet, forwarding the IPv6 packet on its IPv6-enabled F0/1 interface, to server S1.

Although the figure and steps show the mechanics of the IPv6 tunnel, with such a small sample network, it may be easier to just natively configure IPv6 on all three routers. However, imagine that the Enterprise has 500 branches, hundreds of servers, and only 10 branches and two servers need IPv6 support. Additionally, the distribution and core layers were rightfully designed with redundancy, so to support 10 branches, 30-40 routers may need IPv6 support added to support IPv6 natively just to cover all possible cases of links or routers failing. Alternatively, a tunnel could be created from each branch router to the new IPv6 server subnet. In such cases, the use of tunneling can give you a much quicker and easier start to the journey toward IPv6.

Point-to-Point IPv6 Tunnels

Some tunnels use a point-to-point concept, whereas others use a multipoint concept. For point-to-point, two devices (and only two) sit at the ends of the tunnel, as did routers R1 and R3 in Figure 18-2. These point-to-point tunnels work like a virtual point-to-point serial link. Figure 18-3 shows these concepts, plus a few other details, using the same underlying network as shown in Figures 18-1 and 18-2.

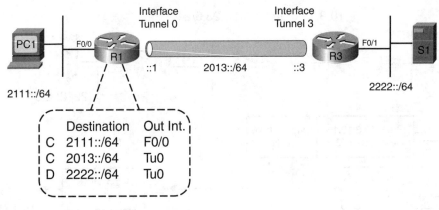

Key Topic **Figure 18-3** *IPv6 Point-to-Point Tunnel Concept*

To create the tunnel shown in the figure, each router configures a type of virtual interface called a *tunnel* interface. The configuration associated with the tunnel interfaces tells IOS the encapsulation details as previously shown in Figure 18-2. In the example of Figure 18-3, R1 uses tunnel interface 0, and R3 uses tunnel interface 3. The tunnel interface numbers can be any integer (up into the low billions), much like choosing loopback interface numbers, with no advantage or disadvantage of using any particular interface number.

The two routers on the ends of the tunnel treat the tunnel interfaces like serial interfaces on a point-to-point serial link, at least from a Layer 3 forwarding perspective. For example, to support IPv6, the engineer would actually enable IPv6 on the tunnel interfaces with the same commands shown in Chapter 16 and configure a routing protocol so that it runs over the tunnel interfaces, as shown in Chapter 17. In this case, Figure 18-3 shows IPv6 addresses assigned to the tunnel interfaces from within the 2013::/64 subnet.

When the configuration is complete, R1 and R3 exchange IPv6 routes and route IPv6 packets over the tunnel interface, which then triggers the encapsulation seen back in Figure 18-2.

Point-to-Multipoint IPv6 Tunnels

Multipoint IPv6 tunnels allow the sending router–the "point" if you will–to use a single tunnel interface to send packets to multiple remote routers. In some ways, a multipoint tunnel works much like a LAN, or even more like a Non-Broadcast Multi-Access (NBMA) network like Frame Relay. Multipoint tunnels still encapsulate the IPv6 packets, but they need additional logic so that the sending router (the "point") knows to which of several remote routers (the "multipoints") to send the encapsulating IPv4 packet.

The biggest leap in logic from point-to-point tunnels to point-to-multipoint tunnels is the logic in how a router chooses which of the many remote tunnel endpoints should receive a particular packet. Multipoint tunnels rely on either the IPv6 packet's destination address, or next-hop information in the IPv6 routing table, to determine which of the multiple remote devices should receive a given packet. This decision happens dynamically on the sending router. In some cases, this dynamic decision process can result in less configuration when adding a new member of the multipoint group. In other cases, the dynamic decision just happens to be how it works, but with no real advantage over point-to-point tunnels.

In all types of multipoint IPv6 tunnels, the tunneling process starts when the router receives an IPv6 packet and then tries to route that packet out the multipoint tunnel interface. This action triggers the logic by which the source router determines how to forward the IPv6 packet, inside an IPv4 packet, to the correct router. Figure 18-4 shows the general idea of how the logic works. In this case, R1 acts as the point–the encapsulating router that must dynamically decide to what IPv4 address to encapsulate and send the IPv6 packet. The figure shows one example of how R1 reacts when it receives an incoming IPv6 packet from the left. Figure 18-4 illustrates the following steps:

Step 1.   R1 receives an IPv6 packet in its LAN interface and decides that the packet should be forwarded out its multipoint tunnel interface.

Step 2.   R1 analyzes the destination IPv6 address (listed as Y in the figure), deriving the tunnel endpoint's IPv4 address (in this case, R9's IPv4 address).

Step 3.   R1 builds an IPv4 packet header, with its own address as source address and using R9's IPv4 address as the destination (as derived at Step 2).

Step 4.   R1 puts the original IPv6 packet into the new IPv4 packet.

Step 5.   The IPv4 routers forward the IPv4 packet to R9.

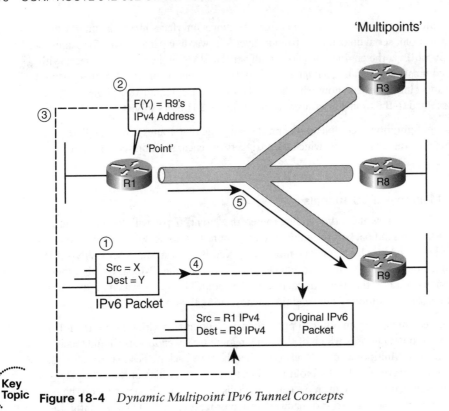

Key
Topic **Figure 18-4**   *Dynamic Multipoint IPv6 Tunnel Concepts*

The particularly interesting part of this process relates to how the encapsulating router (R1 in this case) determines to what IPv4 address to send the IPv4 packet, shown as Step 2 in the figure. Two general options for these dynamic tunnels exist: automatic 6to4 tunnels and ISATAP tunnels. In both cases, the 32-bit IPv4 address of the destination is embedded in the destination IPv6 address. To make the whole process work, the network engineer must plan the IPv6 and IPv4 addresses so that they conform to various rules, so that the sending router can derive the correct destination IPv4 address.

Summary of IPv6 Tunneling Methods

Tunneling IPv6 over IPv4 gives engineers a tool with which to avoid a full native migration to IPv6 on all routers. However, all tunneling methods add more overhead to the routers that perform the tunneling encapsulation and decapsulation. The engineer designing each network needs to weigh the benefits of a full native IPv6 implementation versus a more gradual migration using IPv6 tunnels.

The tunnels themselves also have many pros and cons. Generally, the point-to-point tunnels work best when the IPv6 traffic occurs regularly. In such cases, it should be worth the effort to run an IPv6 IGP over the tunnel. Multipoint tunnels generally work best when the IPv6 traffic occurs infrequently, or even in cases where the traffic volumes are less predictable. Also, the dynamic capabilities of multipoint tunnels allow hosts to form dynamic tunnels with routers, without requiring any additional router configuration.

The more detailed discussion of tunneling in the rest of this chapter more fully develops these pros and cons. For now, Table 18-2 lists the tunneling techniques discussed in more detail inside this chapter, along with some notes that will make more sense as you work through the chapter.

Table 18-2   *Summary of IPv6 Tunneling Options in This Chapter*

Key Topic

Method	Static or Dynamic	Topology	Advantages and Other Notes
Manually Configured	Static	Pt-pt	Acts like a virtual point-to-point link, supporting IPv6 IGPs. Good for more permanent tunnels. Supports IPv6 IGPs. Slightly less overhead than GRE.
GRE	Static	Pt-pt	Generic Routing Encapsulation. Same advantages as previous row, plus it can support other Layer 3 protocols over the same tunnel.
6to4	Dynamic	Mpt	It may require less configuration than all other types when adding a new site. Supports global unicasts, with some extra configuration. Uses second and third quartets to store IPv4 address.
ISATAP	Dynamic	Mpt	It easily supports global unicast addresses for all prefixes. Uses seventh and eighth quartets to store IPv4 address.

NAT Protocol Translation

The migration toward IPv6 typically begins with no IPv6 installed but with pervasive IPv4 support on hosts, routers, and other devices. Next, engineers start adding IPv6 support, typically making hosts dual stacked. To support those hosts, network engineers either configure IPv6 natively in the network, or use some form of tunneling. Eventually, some devices migrate fully to IPv6. Those devices may be new devices that speak only to IPv6 servers. They may be traditional end-user clients that need to communicate only with IPv6-capable servers.

In all these cases, when any pair of hosts communicate, they both support the same protocol, whether IPv4 and IPv6. Because they send and receive either IPv4 packets, or both send and receive IPv6 packets, the network simply needs to deliver those packets. The packets may be encapsulated at some point in its journey, but if the packet left one host as a particular version of IP, the packet received by the other host is the same version.

However, at some time during the migration toward IPv6, the network may need to support the ability for an IPv4-only host to communicate with an IPv6-only host. The IPv6 migration and coexistence RFCs actually make allowance for such a feature, but to do so, something between the two hosts must translate between the two different protocols (IPv4 and IPv6). The solution is the *Network Address Translation–Protocol Translation* (NAT-PT) feature.

NAT-PT gets the first part of its name from the old IPv4 Network Address Translation (NAT) feature. The venerable IPv4 NAT translates the IP addresses inside an IPv4 header, most often changing the Enterprise host's private IPv4 address into a public, Internet-routable IPv4 address. NAT-PT translates both the source and destination IP address, translating between an IPv4 and IPv6 address for both. Not only does NAT-PT translate IP addresses, but also it translates the entire IPv4 and IPv6 header, plus other headers as well, such as TCP, UDP, and ICMP. Figure 18-5 shows an example of the results of NAT-PT on Router R1, with PC1 sending a packet to Server S1, and S1 returning the packet.

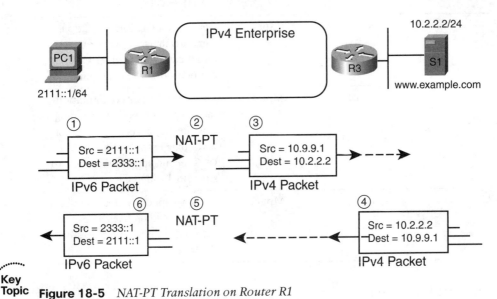

Key Topic

Figure 18-5 *NAT-PT Translation on Router R1*

Following the steps in the figure

Step 1. PC1, an IPv6-only host, sends an IPv6 packet to destination 2333::1, source 2111::1. And 2333::1 actually resides on R1, so the IPv6 network forwards the packet to R1.

Step 2. R1, with NAT-PT configured, listens for packets sent to 2333::1. R1 converts the IPv6 header and other packet headers to IPv4 standards.

Step 3. The IPv4 network forwards the packet to IPv4 host Server S1.

Step 4. S1 sends an IPv4 packet back to what it thinks of as PC1, source IPv4 address 10.2.2.2, destination IPv4 address 10.9.9.1. 10.9.9.1 actually resides on Router R1, so the IPv4 network forwards the IPv4 packet to R1.

Step 5. R1, with NAT-PT configured, listens for IPv4 packets sent to 10.9.9.1. R1 converts the IPv4 header and other packet headers to IPv6 standards.

Step 6.   R1 forwards the IPv6 packet through the IPv6 side of the network to PC1, the IPv6-only host.

For the process in Figure 18-5 to work, NAT-PT must also be heavily involved in DNS flows as well. For example, before the flow in Figure 18-5, PC1 will have sent a DNSv6 request to resolve the name of the server (www.example.com in this case). The router performing NAT-PT must convert the requests between DNSv4 and DNSv6, keeping track of the names and address bindings so that the NAT-PT translation process converts to the correct addresses.

Note: NAT-PT, while interesting, has actually been moved to historic status (RFC 2766). IOS still supports NAT-PT, and the ROUTE course's e-learning component still includes coverage of NAT-PT. However, NAT-PT will likely fade away over time. Protocols meant to replace the function of NAT-PT are under development as of the writing of this book.

This completes the overview of IPv6 coexistence tools. The final two major sections of this chapter examine the various IPv6 tunneling methods in depth.

Static Point-to-Point IPv6 Tunnels

This section examines the configuration and some basic verification for two different types of IPv6 point-to-point tunnels:

- Manually configured tunnels (MCT)

- Generic Routing Encapsulation (GRE) tunnels

Note: The phrase *manually configured tunnels* refers to an RFC standard encapsulation of IPv6 inside IPv4 packets. There is no formal name for this feature, so most documents refer to it as "manually configured tunnels," "manual tunnels," or "configured tunnels." This chapter uses the term manually configured tunnels (MCT) for consistency and easier reference.

MCT and GRE tunnels have many similarities, including the configuration. They both create a virtual point-to-point link between two IPv4 routers for the purpose of supporting the forwarding of IPv6 packets. IPv6 IGP routing protocols can run over these virtual links. To support the IGPs, plus other features, the routers will assign link local addresses on these links and allow the forwarding of IPv6 multicast traffic. Both types allow the configuration of additional security features over the tunnel interfaces. Finally, both require static configuration of both the tunnel source and the tunnel destination IPv4 addresses.

To the depth used for these topics in this book, these two tunneling options have only minor differences. Manually configured tunnels simply conform to the rules about generic IPv6 tunnels outlined in RFC 4213, which defines how to encapsulate IPv6 inside an IPv4 packet, without additional headers. GRE tunnels use a generic encapsulation originally defined by Cisco and later standardized in RFC 2784. GRE uses an additional stub header between the IPv4 and IPv6 header; this extra header includes a protocol type field, which allows a GRE tunnel to carry many passenger protocols. (The passenger protocol is the protocol encapsulated inside another protocol's header.) GRE also supports several transport protocols (transport protocols encapsulate the passenger protocol), although IPv4 typically is the only transport protocol used for tunneling IPv6. GRE's flexibility allows a single GRE tunnel to carry IPv6 plus other traffic as well, whereas manually configured tunnels cannot.

This section examines manually configured tunnels in detail and then compares GRE tunnels to manually configured tunnels.

Manually Configured Tunnels

The main planning task for an implementation plan that includes manually configured tunnels requires a little thought about the tunnel source and destination IPv4 addresses. Other than that, the configuration uses straightforward commands that refer to the key elements in the conceptual drawings in Figures 18-2 and 18-3. However, even though the individual commands are straightforward, the configuration requires several steps. So, this section breaks the configuration into two sections: tunnel configuration steps and IPv6 configuration steps.

Configuring and Verifying a Manually Configured Tunnel

To configure the tunnel, first you need to choose what IPv4 addresses will be used when encapsulating packets (as shown in Figure 18-2). A router's tunnel interface borrows the IPv4 address on some other interface; the router then uses that IPv4 address as the source address when encapsulating packets. Comparing the configuration on the two routers on either end of the tunnel, the two routers must agree to the correct IPv4 addresses: the source address used by one router should match the other router's tunnel destination IPv4 address and vice versa. Finally, for better availability, if any IPv4 redundancy exists between the two routers, the engineer should choose to use loopback interface IPv4 addresses, because the tunnel interface fails if the interface associated with the source IP address fails.

The configuration centers around the configuration of a virtual interface called a tunnel interface. The tunnel interface creates an object that can be configured like an interface, so that additional commands can set parameters for a given tunnel. For instance, the engineer configures the source and destination IPv4 addresses (two different interface subcommands), with another command to configure the tunnel encapsulation (GRE or manually configured tunnel). The following list outlines the steps to configure the tunnel.

Key Topic

Step 1.   Find the tunnel IPv4 addresses planned for the tunnel, and ensure that each router can forward IPv4 packets between the addresses. If using a new loopback interface, create the loopback using the **interface loopback** *number* command, assign it an IPv4 address with the **ip address** command, and confirm that routes for this interface will be advertised by IPv4.

Step 2.   Create a tunnel interface using the **interface tunnel** *number* command, selecting a locally significant integer as the tunnel interface number.

Step 3. Define the source IPv4 address of the tunnel using the **tunnel source** {*interface-type interface-number* | *ipv4-address*} interface subcommand. (This address must be an IPv4 address configured on the local router.)

Step 4. Define the destination IPv4 address for the encapsulation using the **tunnel destination** *ipv4-address* interface subcommand; the address must match the **tunnel source** command on the other router.

Step 5. Define the tunnel as a manually configured tunnel (not GRE), as defined in RFC 4213, using the **tunnel mode ipv6ip** interface subcommand.

For example, consider Figure 18-6, which shows an updated representation of the Enterprise network shown in Figures 18-1, 18-2, and 18-3. In this case, even though no redundancy exists, the engineer plans to use loopback addresses (10.9.9.1 on R1 and 10.9.9.3 on R3). Example 18-1 that follows shows the tunnel configuration on R1 and R3.

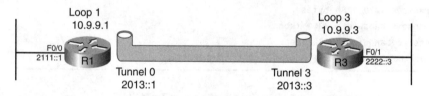

Figure 18-6 *Figure Showing Configuration Items in Example 18-1*

Example 18-1 *Configuring an IPv6IP Tunnel on R1 and R3*

```
R1# conf t
Enter configuration commands, one per line.  End with CNTL/Z.
R1(config)# interface loopback 1
R1(config-if)# ip address 10.9.9.1 255.255.255.255
R1(config-if)# interface tunnel 0
R1(config-if)# tunnel source loopback 1
R1(config-if)# tunnel destination 10.9.9.3
R1(config-if)# tunnel mode ipv6ip
! Next, on router R3
R3# conf t
Enter configuration commands, one per line.  End with CNTL/Z.
R3(config)# interface loopback 3
R3(config-if)# ip address 10.9.9.3 255.255.255.255
R3(config-if)# interface tunnel 3
R3(config-if)# tunnel source loopback 3
R3(config-if)# tunnel destination 10.9.9.1
R3(config-if)# tunnel mode ipv6ip
```

At this point, assuming IPv4 connectivity exists between the two tunnel endpoints, the tunnel interfaces should be up. A quick **show** command, as shown in Example 18-2, confirms the tunnel interface's status on R1, plus a few other interesting tidbits. Beside the tunnel interface being up, the output confirms the source and destination IPv4 addresses.

It also confirms that the tunnel mode uses IPv6 over IP (the word "IP" implying IPv4) to match the **tunnel mode ipv6ip** configuration command.

Example 18-2   *Verification of the Tunnel*

```
R1# show interfaces tunnel0
Tunnel0 is up, line protocol is up
  Hardware is Tunnel
  MTU 17920 bytes, BW 100 Kbit/sec, DLY 50000 usec,
      reliability 255/255, txload 1/255, rxload 1/255
  Encapsulation TUNNEL, loopback not set
  Keepalive not set
  Tunnel source 10.9.9.1 (Loopback1), destination 10.9.9.3
  Tunnel protocol/transport IPv6/IP
  Tunnel TTL 255
  Tunnel transport MTU 1480 bytes
  Tunnel transmit bandwidth 8000 (kbps)
  Tunnel receive bandwidth 8000 (kbps)
! the rest of the output is the typical counter information
```

Configuring and Verifying the Manually Configured Tunnel

The configuration shown in the previous section prepares the tunnel to encapsulate traffic inside IPv4 packets, but it does not complete the configuration. The configuration also needs to enable IPv6 on the routers that create the tunnel, treating the tunnel interfaces just like you would for serial interfaces connected with a leased line.

The configuration steps mirror those discussed at some length in Chapters 16 and 17, so the specific commands will not be discussed here. However, Example 18-3 shows the configuration of both the tunnel and the IPv6 details on R1, with the newly added IPv6 commands highlighted.

Example 18-3   *Completed Tunnel and IPv6 Configuration on Router R1*

```
R1# show running-config
! Only pertinent portions retained
ipv6 unicast-routing
!
interface Loopback1
 ip address 10.9.9.1 255.255.255.255
!
interface Tunnel0
 no ip address
 ipv6 address 2013::1/64
 ipv6 eigrp 1
 tunnel source Loopback1
 tunnel destination 10.9.9.3
 tunnel mode ipv6ip
```

```
!
interface FastEthernet0/0
 ip address 10.1.1.1 255.255.255.0
 ipv6 address 2111::1/64
 ipv6 eigrp 1
!
ipv6 router eigrp 1
 eigrp router-id 1.1.1.1
 no shutdown
```

The new configuration should be somewhat familiar from the last few chapters, but a few items could use some emphasis. First, note that the tunnel interface does indeed have an IPv6 address configured, and EIGRP enabled, just as if it were a physical interface. However, the tunnel interface does not have, nor does it need, an IPv4 address. The tunnel interface needs only a Layer 3 address for the passenger protocols – in other words, the protocols carried as data inside the encapsulating packets. So, only an IPv6 address is needed on the interface. The rest of the highlighted IPv6 configuration uses the same logic discussed in Chapters 16 and 17.

The same verification commands seen in Chapters 16 and 17 can confirm the IPv6 details on the tunnel. Example 18-4 lists the output from a few of these commands, highlighting some of the key details.

Example 18-4 *Verifying IPv6 Works over the Tunnel*

```
R1# show ipv6 interface brief
FastEthernet0/0                [up/up]
    FE80::213:19FF:FE7B:5026
    2111::1
! irrelevant lines omitted for brevity
Loopback1                      [up/up]
    unassigned
Tunnel0                        [up/up]
    FE80::A09:901
    2013::1
R1# show ipv6 interface tunnel0
Tunnel0 is up, line protocol is up
  IPv6 is enabled, link-local address is FE80::A09:901
  No Virtual link-local address(es):
  Global unicast address(es):
    2013::1, subnet is 2013::/64
  Joined group address(es):
    FF02::1
    FF02::2
    FF02::A
    FF02::1:FF00:1
```

```
 FF02::1:FF09:901
 MTU is 1480 bytes
 ICMP error messages limited to one every 100 milliseconds
 ICMP redirects are enabled
 ICMP unreachables are sent
 ND DAD is enabled, number of DAD attempts: 1
 ND reachable time is 30000 milliseconds (using 42194)
 Hosts use stateless autoconfig for addresses.
R1# traceroute ipv6 2222::3

Type escape sequence to abort.
Tracing the route to 2222::3
 1 2013::3 0 msec 4 msec 4 msec
```

The first two commands show how routers create the link local IPv6 addresses for manually configured tunnel interfaces. Routers normally form a serial interface's link local IPv6 address using EUI-64 rules based on the MAC address of the first LAN interface on the router. In this case, the router forms the link local address with a FE80::/96 prefix and then adds the 32-bit tunnel source IPv4 address as the last 32 bits. For example, the first two **show** commands in Example 18-4 list R1's link local address on its tunnel interface: FE80::A09:901. Adding back the leading 0s in the last two quartets, the last two quartets look like this:

   0A09:0901

Converting each pair of hex characters to decimal, you can find the IPv4 address of 10.9.9.1. (Appendix B, "Conversion Tables," includes a hex/decimal conversion table.)

The **show ipv6 interface tunnel0** command lists the usual IPv6 addresses. It lists the link local address, along with the statically configured global unicast address (2013::1). It lists multicast addresses, including EIGRP's FF02::A, and the (highlighted) solicited node multicast address associated with both the link local and the global unicast address on the interface. (When a multicast needs to be sent out a manually configured tunnel's interface, the router encapsulates the IPv6 multicast and forwards it inside a unicast IPv4 packet to the other end of the tunnel.)

The **traceroute ipv6 2222::3** command at the end of the example confirms that IPv6 traffic can pass over the tunnel.

GRE Tunnels

Only one difference exists in the configuration between manually configured tunnels and point-to-point GRE tunnels: the tunnel mode. IOS uses the **tunnel mode ipv6ip** command for manually configured tunnels, which also tells IOS to use the encapsulation as defined in RFC 4213. IOS uses the **tunnel mode gre ip** command to instead configure a GRE tunnel, meaning that IOS uses the RFC 2784 GRE encapsulation. This encapsulation adds the GRE header to the encapsulation. (Also, because IOS defaults to use GRE over IP, you can alternatively just omit the **tunnel mode** command as well.)

The configurations are indeed almost identical. For example, to migrate from the configuration shown in Example 18-3, which shows all of R1's configuration for both the tunnel and IPv6 with a manually configured tunnel, simply use one of the following two options:

■ Issue the **tunnel mode gre ip** command on both routers' tunnel interfaces.

■ Issue the **no tunnel mode ipv6ip** command on both routers' tunnel interfaces, which reverts to the default of GRE over IP.

Key Topic

Note: If the two routers' tunnel modes do not match, the tunnel interfaces can stay up/up, but the routers cannot forward IPv6 packets because of the mismatched encapsulations.

The verification command output looks almost identical as well, but with just a few differences to note. IOS uses a different convention for the link local address created for a GRE tunnel interface. It works as if the tunnel interface is a serial interface, deriving the interface ID using EUI-64 rules and the MAC address of the first LAN interface on the router. The second difference relates to how IOS automatically sets the MTU of the passenger protocols (IPv6 in this case) to 1476 for GRE tunnels; with manually configured tunnels, the passenger MTU was set to 1480. These settings allow space in both modes for the 20-byte additional IPv4 header that encapsulates the packet, plus in the case of GRE, the additional 4-byte GRE header. Example 18-5 highlights some of these minor differences.

Example 18-5 *Verifying GRE over IP Tunnels That Support IPv6*

```
R1# show interfaces tunnel 0
Tunnel0 is up, line protocol is up
Hardware is Tunnel
MTU 17916 bytes, BW 100 Kbit/sec, DLY 50000 usec,
reliability 255/255, txload 1/255, rxload 1/255
Encapsulation TUNNEL, loopback not set
Keepalive not set
Tunnel source 10.9.9.1 (Loopback1), destination 10.9.9.3
Tunnel protocol/transport GRE/IP
Key disabled, sequencing disabled
Checksumming of packets disabled
Tunnel TTL 255
Fast tunneling enabled
Tunnel transport MTU 1476 bytes
Tunnel transmit bandwidth 8000 (kbps)
Tunnel receive bandwidth 8000 (kbps)
! the remaining omitted lines list interface counters
```

Point-to-Point IPv6 Tunnel Summary

Point-to-point IPv6 tunnels give engineers a means to implement IPv6 connectivity without requiring extensive deployment of native IPv6. At the same time, these tunnels act like native IPv6 links, running IPv6 IGPs, using link local addresses, and requiring no static route configuration. The two options in this category have almost no practical difference. Table 18-3 summarizes the key features, with the small differences highlighted in the table.

Table 18-3   *Comparing Manual and GRE IPv6-over-IP Tunnels*

	Manual Tunnels	GRE
RFC	4213	2784
Tunnel mode command	tunnel mode ipv6ip	tunnel mode gre ip
Passenger MTU default	1480	1476
Supports IPv6 IGPs?	Yes	Yes
Forwards IPv6 multicasts?	Yes	Yes
Uses static configuration of tunnel destination?	Yes	Yes
Supports multiple passenger protocols?	No	Yes
Link local based on...	FE80::/96, plus 32 bits from tunnel source IPv4 address	IPv6 EUI-64, using lowest numbered interface's MAC address

Dynamic Multipoint IPv6 Tunnels

Multipoint tunnels give engineers a convenient tool to use when irregular or infrequent IPv6 traffic occurs between sites. The multipoint topology creates the possibility that new sites can join into the tunnel without requiring additional configuration on the existing routers. Additionally, these multipoint tunnels in some cases allow IPv6 hosts to act as tunnel endpoints, allowing a host at a remote site to connect into the Enterprise IPv6 network even if the local router has no knowledge of IPv6. This flexibility and ability to add routers and hosts with potentially no extra configuration makes multipoint IPv6 tunnels a very useful migration tool.

Multipoint tunnels also have some disadvantages. To take advantage of the possibility to limit future configuration changes, IPv6 address planning must follow some additional rules and constraints. These tunnels also do not support IPv6 IGPs, requiring the use of either static routes or multiprotocol BGP. The dynamic forwarding logic requires more work per packet as compared with point-to-point tunnels, which is one of the main reasons multipoint tunnels are best used for less frequent traffic, with point-to-point tunnels best used for more frequent traffic. Finally, the additional addressing rules and considerations require a bit more of a learning curve to become comfortable with these tools, at least as compared with point-to-point tunnels.

This section examines the configuration of two types of multipoint tunnels: automatic 6to4 tunnels, as defined in RFC 3056, and ISATAP tunnels, as defined in RFC 4214.

Automatic 6to4 Tunnels

As previously described in the section "Point-to-Multipoint IPv6 Tunnels," a multipoint tunnel does not explicitly define the tunnel endpoint IPv4 addresses. Instead, the incoming IPv6 packet's destination IPv6 address implies the IPv4 address that a router should use when encapsulating and forwarding the packet. Because the tunnels rely on the IPv6 address to determine the destination IPv4 address for these tunnels, network engineers must spend more time initially planning IPv6 and IPv4 addresses used to deploy IPv6.

The first big planning and design choice when using automatic 6to4 tunnels relates to whether to use global unicast addresses for the end user subnets, or whether to use a special reserved range of addresses (2002::/16). If the Enterprise expects all Internet traffic to/from the Enterprise to remain IPv4-only for the foreseeable future, then the IPv6 addresses used in the Enterprise do not matter much, and the network engineer can take advantage of the 2002::/16 reserved range. Using this range allows new sites to be added to the multipoint tunnel at a later time, without requiring new configuration on the existing routers in a multipoint tunnel. However, if the Enterprise needs to use its registered global unicast site prefix, automatic 6to4 tunnels can still be used, just with a little more configuration effort over time.

This section first examines the case where the Enterprise needs no IPv6 Internet connectivity, using the 2002::/16 reserved range of addresses. Following that, this section examines the same tool, this time using a registered global unicast site prefix.

Using the Automatic 6to4 Prefix for All Devices

RFC 3056 defines a reserved range of IPv6 addresses for use with automatic 6to4 tunnels: 2002::/16. Even though this range appears to come from the range of global unicast IPv6 addresses (2000::/3), IANA reserves the 2002::/16 prefix as a set of addresses that will never be assigned as global unicast addresses.

By starting with the 2002::/16 prefix, a network engineer can then create a /48 prefix:

- The network engineer can assign each tunnel endpoint (router or host) its own /48 prefix, used for all prefixes connected to that local router, by adding the hex version of the router's IPv4 address as bits 17 through 48 (quartets 2 and 3).

- The engineer can allocate /64 prefixes for each required subnet connected to each router by allocating a unique subnet number in the fourth quartet (much like when an Enterprise receives a /48 site prefix from an IPv6 registrar).

Figure 18-7 shows the format of the automatic 6to4 tunnel IPv6 addresses.

2002 : AABB : CCDD : Subnet : : /64
Prefix   4 Octet IPv4 Address

Figure 18-7 *Reserved Automatic 6to4 IPv6 Addresses*

The first half of the address has three major parts, with the second half of the address structure used for the host ID as with most implementations of global unicast addresses. The addresses always begin with a first quartet of 2002. The second and third quartet list the hex version of the IPv4 address for that site–usually the IPv4 address of a loopback interface on a router. (In this case, the hex value AABBCCDD represents 170.187.204.221, found by converting each pair of hex digits to the decimal equivalent.) The fourth quartet can be conveniently used as a subnet field so that the engineer can assign the various subnets connected to each router. The /48 prefix chosen for each router works much like when a registrar gives a company a /48 global unicast prefix, leaving 16 bits for the company to use for subnetting.

For example, consider the case with a multipoint tunnel with three routers, R1, R3, and R4, as shown in Figure 18-8. The figure depicts the planning steps taken by the engineer when using the 2002::/16 prefix for all IPv6 addresses.

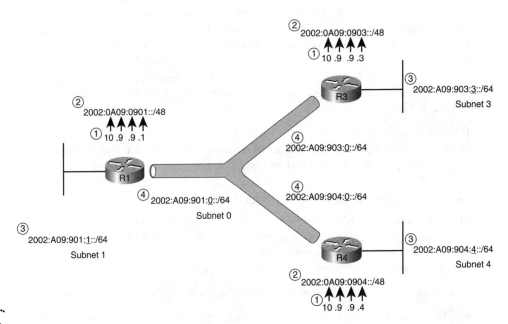

Key Topic **Figure 18-8** *Example Planning Diagram for 2002::/16 Prefixes*

Following the steps in Figure 18-8

Step 1. The engineer chooses an IPv4 address on each router to use as the tunnel endpoints. In this case, he chose loopback IPv4 addresses, which is typical.

Step 2. The engineer then derived the /48 prefix used for allocating subnets off each router by converting each octet of the IPv4 addresses to hex to form the /48 prefix used on each router.

Step 3.   The engineer then allocates the first /64 prefixes, one for each router's LAN subnet. The IPv6 hosts on these LANs use IPv6 addresses from these prefixes.

Step 4.   The engineer picks an IPv6 address to use on each tunnel interface. With automatic 6to4 tunnels, these IPv6 addresses typically come from each router's own prefix, so each router's tunnel IPv6 address will actually be in different IPv6 subnets.

That completes an example of the address planning, but the underlying logic is not yet complete. Multipoint IPv6 tunnels do not support IGP routing protocols, but to trigger the dynamic encapsulation process for the tunnel, the routers must route IPv6 traffic out the tunnel interface. The solution is actually simple: because all the IPv6 addresses start with 2002::/16 (by implementation choice), the engineer plans a static route for prefix 2002::/16, forwarding all packets destined for these special 2002::/16 addresses out the multipoint tunnel interface. This process triggers the tunnel as previously discussed for Figure 18-4.

So, what happens when an IPv6 packet now arrives at one of these routers? With these well-chosen IPv6 address, the following occurs:

Step 1.   The packet's IPv6 destination address begins with 2002, so the router tries to forward the packet out its tunnel interface, triggering the process.

Step 2.   The router notices the tunnel type (automatic 6to4), which tells IOS to encapsulate and send the IPv6 packet to the destination IPv4 address found in quartets 2 and 3.

Configuring the Automatic 6to4 Tunnel

The configuration of the automatic 6to4 tunnel has some similarities and some differences compared to point-to-point tunnels. For the tunnel itself, unlike point-to-point tunnels, the multipoint tunnel configuration does not need a configured **tunnel destination** command, because the destination IPv4 address is instead embedded in the destination IPv6 address. Also, the setting of the **tunnel mode** command differs. Otherwise, the tunnel configuration details remain the same.

Some differences also exist for the IPv6-specific configuration related to the tunnel. An IPv6 IGP is not needed, because the router finds the destination IPv4 address on the other end of the tunnel embedded in the destination IPv6 address in the received packet. Although IPv6 IGPs cannot be configured on the automatic 6to4 tunnel, static IPv6 routes and multiprotocol BGP (for IPv6) can be configured. And even though the tunnel interface must be enabled for IPv6, as with point-to-point tunnels, the IPv6 addresses are not in the same subnet as the other routers' tunnel interfaces.

The following list outlines the steps to configure the automatic 6to4 tunnel and to enable IPv6 forwarding across the tunnel. Note that the steps list the use of a loopback interface because most sites use a loopback, but any interface's IPv4 address may be used.

Step 1.   Configure the planned loopback interface (**interface loopback** *number* global command), and assign the planned IPv4 address. (Ensure that the IPv4 IGP advertises a route for this address.)

Step 2. Create a tunnel interface using the **interface tunnel** *number* command, selecting a locally significant integer as the tunnel interface number.

Step 3. Define the source IPv4 address of the tunnel using the **tunnel source** {*interface-type interface-number* | *ipv4-address*} interface subcommand using the loopback IP address from Step 1.

Step 4. Do NOT define a tunnel destination with the **tunnel destination** interface subcommand.

Step 5. Identify the tunnel as an automatic 6to4 tunnel using the **tunnel mode ipv6ip 6to4** interface subcommand.

Step 6. Enable IPv6 on the tunnel interface, typically with the **ipv6 address** interface subcommand.

Step 7. Complete the normal IPv6 configuration, include defining the LAN interface IPv6 addresses per the planning chart, and enable IPv6 routing with the **ipv6 unicast-routing** command.

Step 8. Define a static route for 2002::16, with outgoing interface of the tunnel interface, using the **ipv6 route 2002::/16 tunnel** *number* global command.

Example 18-6 shows the configuration on Router R1 from Figure 18-8. Note that although not shown, the routers in the figure do exchange IPv4 routes for their respective loopback addresses so that all IPv4 loopbacks in Figure 18-7 are pingable. The routers also use IPv6 addresses on their interfaces, rather than just having IPv6 enabled with the **ipv6 enable** command: 2002:A09:901::1 on R1, 2002:A09:903::3 on R3, and 2002:A09:904::4 on R4.

Example 18-6 *R1 Configuration for an Automatic 6to4 Tunnel*

```
ipv6 unicast-routing
!
interface Loopback1
 ip address 10.9.9.1 255.255.255.255
!
interface Tunnel0
 no ip address
 ipv6 address 2002:a09:901::/128
 tunnel source Loopback1
 tunnel mode ipv6ip 6to4
!
interface FastEthernet0/0
 ip address 10.1.1.1 255.255.255.0
 ipv6 address 2002:A09:901:1::1/64
!
ipv6 route 2002::/16 Tunnel0
```

This configuration defines all the small pieces listed in the configuration checklist, but the configuration does not spell out the underlying logic. Looking at the configuration, along with the design and the knowledge of how automatic 6to4 tunnels work, the following logic occurs in the background:

Step 1.   R1 will have two connected IPv6 routes (F0/0's and tunnel0's) in the 2002::/16 range, plus a static route for the entire 2002::/16 range.

Step 2.   When R1 receives an IPv6 packet, destination in the 2002::/16 range, and the destination is not in one of the connected subnets, R1 will try to forward the packet out tunnel0.

Step 3.   The **tunnel mode ipv6ip 6to4** command tells R1 to look to the 2nd/3rd octets to find the destination IPv4 address, and perform the tunneling.

Also, take another moment to review the configuration in Example 18-6, looking specifically for any configuration on R1 that references anything specific about either R3 or R4 in Figure 18-8. No such specifics exist. R1's logic works without any preconfigured addressing information about R3, and to R4, and to hundreds of future routers, if the engineer plans the IPv6 addresses correctly. So, if this Enterprise decided to enable the automatic tunnel on yet another router, only the configuration in that one new router would need to be changed, but the configuration on R1, R3, and R4 would be unchanged. The rest of the routers would not need any more configuration because the static route for 2002::/16 triggers the routing of IPv6 packets, tunneled in IPv4, to the correct remote routers.

Example 18-7 lists the **show** commands that confirm some of these facts.

Example 18-7   *R1's State When Using the Automatic 6to4 Tunnel*

```
R1# show ipv6 route
IPv6 Routing Table - Default - 5 entries
Codes: C - Connected, L - Local, S - Static, U - Per-user Static route
       B - BGP, M - MIPv6, R - RIP, I1 - ISIS L1
       I2 - ISIS L2, IA - ISIS interarea, IS - ISIS summary, D - EIGRP
       EX - EIGRP external
       O - OSPF Intra, OI - OSPF Inter, OE1 - OSPF ext 1, OE2 - OSPF ext 2
       ON1 - OSPF NSSA ext 1, ON2 - OSPF NSSA ext 2
S   2002::/16 [1/0]
      via Tunnel0, directly connected
LC  2002:A09:901::/128 [0/0]
      via Tunnel0, receive
C   2002:A09:901:1::/64 [0/0]
       via FastEthernet0/0, directly connected
L   2002:A09:901:1::1/128 [0/0]
       via FastEthernet0/0, receive
L   FF00::/8 [0/0]
       via Null0, receive


R1# show ipv6 interface brief
FastEthernet0/0              [up/up]
```

```
    FE80::213:19FF:FE7B:5026
    2002:A09:901:1::1
FastEthernet0/1                 [administratively down/down]
    unassigned
! unrelated lines omitted
Tunnel0                         [up/up]
    FE80::A09:901
    2002:A09:901::


R1# trace 2002:a09:903:3::3

Type escape sequence to abort.
Tracing the route to 2002:A09:903:3::3

  1 2002:A09:903::3 4 msec 4 msec 4 msec
```

The **show ipv6 route** command lists the static route and both connected routes. Note that in this case, the configuration used a /128 prefix length for Tunnel0's IPv6 address, so the connected route shows up on the same line as the local route, both of which have a /128 prefix length. The **show ipv6 interface brief** command confirms the configured IPv6 address from the 2002::/16 range, plus the link local address derived for the Tunnel0 interface. Note that link local address uses an unusual convention–instead of using the usual EUI-64 logic, the link local address starts with FE80::/96, with the last two quartets the same as the tunnel's IPv4 source address. Finally, the **traceroute** command at the end of the example proves the tunnel works.

Using Global Unicasts with Automatic Tunnels

The previous example of automatic 6to4 tunnels assumed that the engineer chose all IPv6 addresses from the reserved 2002::/16 range because no need existed for IPv6 Internet connectivity. This section looks at the same automatic 6to4 concepts but with global unicasts used for the LAN subnets.

The big conceptual difference that occurs when using global unicast addresses relates to when using an assigned global unicast prefix, the second and third quartets are set, are the same for all subnets in the Enterprise, and can no longer be used to store the tunnel destination's IPv4 address. For example, if an Enterprise were assigned 2000:0:1::/48 as a site prefix, then all the subnets at the Enterprise would need to begin 2000:0:1, instead of encoding the IPv4 address of the site in the second and third quartets.

The problem can be overcome, however, through a piece of logic used when the router forwards packets out the tunnel interface after doing a recursive route lookup:

> When the router matches a route with an outgoing 6to4 tunnel interface, but with no next-hop IPv6 address, AND this route was matched due to route recursion, then derive the tunnel's destination IPv4 address based on the previously matched route's next-hop IPv6 address.

Although true, the formal definition is a bit much to work through. So, consider Figure 18-9, which shows a revised version of Figure 18-8. The figure uses the same three routers, same IPv4 loopback addresses, and same IPv6 addresses on the tunnel interfaces. However, for the three LANs, the engineer chose IPv6 prefixes from within the site's 2000:0:1::/48 prefix, essentially making R1's LAN Subnet 1, R3's LAN Subnet 3, and R4's LAN Subnet 4.

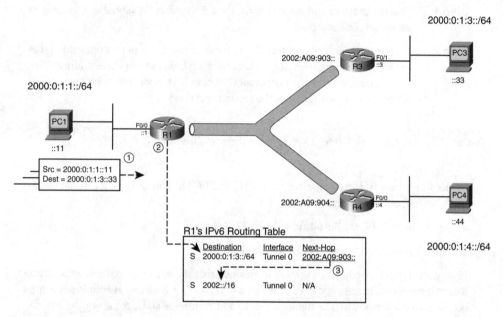

Figure 18-9 *Automatic Tunnels, Using Global Unicast IPv6 Addresses*

The underlying logic hinges on the two static routes in R1's IPv6 routing table, as shown in Figure 18-9. One route is the old route for 2002::/16, whereas the other route, added because of the use of global unicast addresses, matches the prefix for R3's LAN. Following the numbered sequence in the figure

Step 1.   PC1 sends an IPv6 packet to PC3, destination address 2000:0:1:3::33.

Step 2.   R1 compares the destination IPv6 address, matching the first route (destination 2000:0:1:3::/64) with outgoing interface Tunnel0 and next-hop router 2002:A09:903:: (R3's tunnel IPv6 address).

Step 3.   R1 needs to decide how to forward packets to 2002:A09:903::, so R1 performs route recursion to find the matching route for this destination. R1 matches the static route for 2002::/16 with outgoing interface tunnel0 and with no next-hop address listed.

At this point, the usual automatic 6to4 tunnel logic kicks in but based on the first route's next-hop address of 2002:a09:903::.

Summarizing, the differences in planning and configuration for using global unicasts with automatic 6to4 tunnels are

Step 1. Plan the prefixes and addresses for the LANs using the global unicast range assigned to the Enterprise.

Step 2. Configure an additional static route for each remote subnet, configuring the tunnel as outgoing interface and configuring the next-hop IPv6 address. That next-hop must be the remote router's tunnel IPv6 address, which embeds the destination IPv4 address as the second and third octets.

Note: You also can use BGP for IPv6 to learn the route listed in Step 2.

For R1 to forward traffic to the IPv6 hosts PC3 and PC4 in Figure 18-9, R1 would need the following two additional routes:

■ **ipv6 route 2000:0:1:3::/64 tunnel0 2002:a09:903::**

■ **ipv6 route 2000:0:1:4::/64 tunnel0 2002:a09:904::**

Finally, the introduction to this section mentioned that the use of global unicast addresses required more configuration changes. When a new router is added to the multipoint tunnel, each router already on the tunnel needs to add additional static routes or the alternative additional BGP configuration.

IPv6 ISATAP Tunnels

You can use ISATAP–the Intra-site Automatic Tunnel Addressing Protocol–to identify the IPv4 address of the remote site for the purposes of tunneling IPv6 packets. As a result, you can create dynamic multipoint tunnels using ISATAP, in general a concept much like the multipoint tunnels created using automatic 6to4 tunnels.

Comparing ISATAP and Automatic 6to4 Concepts

ISATAP tunnels differ in some ways with automatic 6to4 tunnels. However, ISATAP IPv6 tunnels use concepts that closely match those used by automatic 6to4 tunnels when using global unicast addresses (as previously shown in Figure 18-9). The following list makes some important comparisons between these two options with the items that differ between ISATAP tunnels and automatic 6to4 tunnels highlighted in gray:

Key Topic

1. ISATAP tunnels use global unicast prefixes for user subnets.

2. ISATAP tunnel interfaces use IPv6 addresses that embed the tunnel's destination IPv4 address inside the IPv6 address.

3. The routers need static routes for the destination end-user IPv6 prefixes; the route must list a next-hop IPv6 address, which in turn embeds the tunnel destination IPv4 address.

4. ISATAP tunnel interface IPv6 addresses embed the IPv4 address in the last two quartets.

5. ISATAP tunnels do not use a special reserved range of IPv6 addresses at all, instead using just normal IPv6 unicast prefixes.

6. ISATAP tunnels typically use a single prefix to which all tunnel interfaces connect, so all routers have a connected IPv6 route to that same subnet.

7. ISATAP tunnels can automatically derive the tunnel interface's interface ID by using modified EUI-64 rules.

As usual, an example can help sift through some of the details; Figure 18-10 shows just such an example. The figure is the same as Figure 18-9's automatic 6to4 tunnel example with the same user IPv6 prefixes from the global unicast range. However, the design and configuration has been changed to work with ISATAP tunnels, as follows:

■   The three tunnel interfaces now have IPv6 addresses in common IPv6 subnet 2000:0:1:9::/64. (The actual subnet number is not important; just choose a currently unused IPv6 subnet.)

■   The tunnel interfaces' IPv6 addresses conform to *modified* EUI-64 rules (explained following the figure) embedding the IPv4 address in the last two quartets.

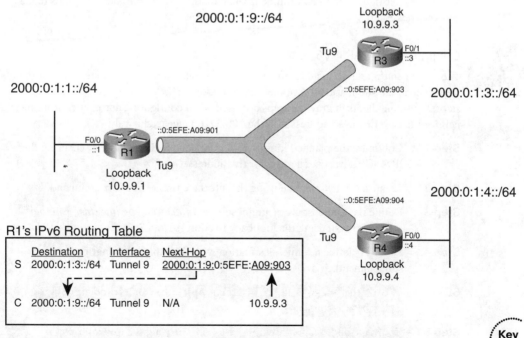

Figure 18-10   *ISATAP Tunnel Example, with Minimal Changes Compared to Figure 18-9*

Key Topic

■ The routers no longer need a route for 2002::/16, instead relying on the connected route created for subnet 2000:0:1:9::/64.

First, examine the four IPv6 global unicast prefixes in the figure. The three LAN-based prefixes match the same ones used in the example of Figure 18-9. The fourth prefix includes all three routers' tunnel interfaces, much like a typical LAN. All three router's tunnel interfaces use an IPv6 address from this same prefix (2000:0:1:9::/64), and each will configure their address using a /64 prefix length.

Next, consider R1's routing logic when it receives an IPv6 packet destined for R3's LAN IPv6 prefix. R1's routing table lists a static route for R3's LAN subnet (2000:0:1:3::/64), with R3's tunnel IPv6 address listed as next hop (2000:0:1:9:0:5EFE:A09:903). When R1 receives an IPv6 packet destined for R3's LAN IPv6 subnet, R1 matches this static route. R1 also notices that the outgoing interface is not only a tunnel, but also an ISATAP tunnel, so R1 derives the tunnel's destination IPv4 address from the last two quartets of the next-hop address of the route (A09:903). (These values convert to 10.9.9.3.) R1 can then encapsulate and send the IPv4 transport packet to 10.9.9.3.

Beyond the detail in Figure 18-10, the only other item that needs some explanation is the format of the ISATAP-defined IPv6 address. The addresses can be configured manually but can also be derived by the router using *modified EUI-64 rules*. The rules work as follows:

Key Topic

■ Configure a 64-bit prefix on the tunnel interface, and use the **eui-64** parameter, telling the router to derive the second half (interface ID) of the address.

■ The router adds 0000:5EFE as quartets 5 and 6.

■ The router finds the tunnel's source IPv4 address, converts it to hex, and adds that as quartets 7 and 8.

Configuring ISATAP IPv6 Tunnels

The overall configuration includes many steps, as usual, but most of the steps mirror the steps seen in the automatic 6to4 tunnel configurations. The following list outlines the steps. It also highlights in gray the steps not used when configuring automatic 6to4 tunnels for the case that used addresses in the 2002::/16 range exclusively.

Key Topic

Step 1. Configure the planned loopback interface and its IPv4 address, ensuring the IPv4 IGP advertises a route for this address.

Step 2. Create a tunnel interface using the **interface tunnel** *number* command.

Step 3. Define the tunnel source (**tunnel source** {*interface-type interface-number* | *ipv4-address*}) using the loopback IP address from Step 1.

Step 4. Do NOT define a tunnel destination with the **tunnel destination** interface subcommand.

Step 5. Identify the tunnel as an ISATAP tunnel using the **tunnel mode ipv6ip isatap** interface subcommand.

Step 6. Configure an IPv6 prefix with EUI-64 option using the **ipv6 address** *prefix/length* **eui-64** interface subcommand.

Step 7.   Complete the normal IPv6 configuration, include defining the LAN interface
IPv6 addresses per the planning chart and enabling IPv6 routing with the **ipv6
unicast-routing** command.

Step 8.   Define static IPv6 routes (using the **ipv6 route** global command) for each destination IPv6 prefix, with an outgoing interface and next-hop address. (The
next-hop should be the destination router's IPv6 address that embeds the IPv4
address as the last two octets.)

Example 18-8 shows the configuration on Routers R1 and R3 from Figure 18-10 with the
tunnel details highlighted.

Example 18-8   *Configuring R1 and R3 for an ISATAP Tunnel per Figure 18-10*

```
! First, on router R1:
R1# show running-config
! only relevant portions shown
ipv6 unicast-routing
!
interface Loopback1
 ip address 10.9.9.1 255.255.255.255
!
interface Tunnel9
 no ip address
 ipv6 address 2000:0:1:9::/64 eui-64
 tunnel source Loopback1
 tunnel mode ipv6ip isatap
!
interface FastEthernet0/0
 ip address 10.1.1.1 255.255.255.0
 ipv6 address 2000:0:1:1::1/64
!
ipv6 route 2000:0:1:3::/64 2000:0:1:9:0:5EFE:A09:903
ipv6 route 2000:0:1:4::/64 2000:0:1:9:0:5EFE:A09:904

! Next, on router R3:

R3# show running-config
! only relevant portions shown
ipv6 unicast-routing
!
interface Loopback3
 ip address 10.9.9.3 255.255.255.255
!
interface Tunnel9
 no ip address
 ipv6 address 2000:0:1:9::/64 eui-64
 tunnel source Loopback3
 tunnel mode ipv6ip isatap
```

```
!
interface FastEthernet0/1
 ip address 10.1.3.3 255.255.255.0
 ipv6 address 2000:0:1:3::3/64
!
ipv6 route 2000:0:1:1::/64 2000:0:1:9:0:5EFE:A09:901
ipv6 route 2000:0:1:4::/64 2000:0:1:9:0:5EFE:A09:904
```

The most important parts of the configurations are the tunnel configuration and the static routes. First, on R1's new tunnel interface (Tunnel 9), the configuration sets the mode to ISATAP (**tunnel mode ipv6ip isatap**). This command, in combination with the **ipv6 address 2000:0:1:9::/64 eui-64** command, tells R1 to use the modified EUI-64 rules to give R1's Tunnel 9 interface an IPv6 address of 2000:0:1:9:0:5EFE:A09:901. R1 derives the last two octets based on the indirect reference made in the **tunnel source loopback 1** command, using loopback 1's IPv4 address (10.9.9.1) to complete Tunnel 9's IPv6 address.

The two static routes on R1 simply define routes to the LAN subnet on each remote router with the important part being the next-hop IPv6 address. The listed addresses exist on R3 and R4, generated by the modified EUI-64 process on those routers.

Example 18-9 shows some supporting verification commands on Router R1.

Example 18-9 *Verifying Tunnel Operation on R1*

```
R1# show ipv6 interface brief
FastEthernet0/0              [up/up]
    FE80::213:19FF:FE7B:5026
    2000:0:1:1::1
! irrelevant interfaces removed
Loopback1                   [up/up]
    unassigned
Tunnel9                     [up/up]
    FE80::5EFE:A09:901
    2000:0:1:9:0:5EFE:A09:901

R1# show ipv6 route
IPv6 Routing Table - Default - 7 entries
Codes: C - Connected, L - Local, S - Static, U - Per-user Static route
       B - BGP, M - MIPv6, R - RIP, I1 - ISIS L1
       I2 - ISIS L2, IA - ISIS interarea, IS - ISIS summary, D - EIGRP
       EX - EIGRP external
       O - OSPF Intra, OI - OSPF Inter, OE1 - OSPF ext 1, OE2 - OSPF ext 2
       ON1 - OSPF NSSA ext 1, ON2 - OSPF NSSA ext 2
C    2000:0:1:1::/64 [0/0]
     via FastEthernet0/0, directly connected
L    2000:0:1:1::1/128 [0/0]
     via FastEthernet0/0, receive
```

```
S    2000:0:1:3::/64 [1/0]
        via 2000:0:1:9:0:5EFE:A09:903
S    2000:0:1:4::/64 [1/0]
        via 2000:0:1:9:0:5EFE:A09:904
C    2000:0:1:9::/64 [0/0]
        via Tunnel9, directly connected
L    2000:0:1:9:0:5EFE:A09:901/128 [0/0]
        via Tunnel9, receive
L    FF00::/8 [0/0]
        via Null0, receive


R1# traceroute
Protocol [ip]: ipv6
Target IPv6 address: 2000:0:1:3::3
Source address: 2000:0:1:1::1
Insert source routing header? [no]:
Numeric display? [no]:
Timeout in seconds [3]:
Probe count [3]:
Minimum Time to Live [1]:
Maximum Time to Live [30]:
Priority [0]:
Port Number [0]:
Type escape sequence to abort.
Tracing the route to 2000:0:1:3::3

  1 2000:0:1:9:0:5EFE:A09:903 0 msec 0 msec 4 msec
```

The example begins with the **show ipv6 interfaces brief** command, which shows the two IPv6 addresses R1 derives. It lists the 2000:0:1:9::5EFE:A09:901 address, derived using the modified EUI-64 rules. It also lists a link local address on the interface, formed not with traditional EUI-64 rules but instead with the same modified EUI-64 rules used for the global unicast address.

The **show ipv6 route** command output highlights the same routes shown in Figure 18-10. It lists the static route for R3's LAN subnet, a route to 2000:0:1:3::/64, with R3's modified EUI-64 IPv6 address as the next hop. The output also shows R1's connected route for the tunnel subnet (2000:0:1:9::/64). Finally, the **traceroute** command at the end confirms that R1 can send packets to R3's LAN IPv6 address (2000:0:1:3::3) from R1's LAN IPv6 address (2000:0:1:1::1).

Multipoint IPv6 Tunnel Summary

Multipoint IPv6 tunnels give engineers a good means to implement IPv6 connectivity for short periods of time. The tunnels can allow easier addition of new sites, with less config-uration on existing routers. These tunnels also support tunneling with IPv6 hosts. How-ever, these tunnels do not support IPv6 IGPs. Also, the extra processing required to forward each IPv6 packet makes this solution most useful as a short-term temporary solution, with native IPv6 and point-to-point tunnels more reasonable for more extended periods of time. Table 18-4 summarizes the key features with the small differences highlighted in the table.

Key
Topic

Table 18-4   *Comparing IPv6 Multipoint Tunnels*

	Automatic 6to4	ISATAP
RFC	3056	4214
Uses a reserved IPv6 address prefix.	Yes (2002::/16)	No
Supports the use of global unicast addresses?	Yes	Yes
Quartets holding the IPv4 destination address.	2/3	7/8
End-user host addresses embed the IPv4 destination?	Sometimes	No
Tunnel endpoints IPv6 addresses embed IPv4 destination.	Sometimes	Yes
Uses modified EUI-64 to form tunnel IPv6 addresses?	No	Yes

Exam Preparation Tasks

Planning Practice

The CCNP ROUTE exam expects test takers to review design documents, create implementation plans, and create verification plans. This section provides some exercises that may help you to take a step back from the minute details of the topics in this chapter so that you can think about the same technical topics from the planning perspective.

For each planning practice table, simply complete the table. Note that any numbers in parentheses represent the number of options listed for each item in the solutions in Appendix F, "Completed Practice Planning Tables."

Design Review Table

Table 18-5 lists several design goals related to this chapter. If these design goals were listed in a design document, and you had to take that document and develop an implementation plan, what implementation options come to mind? You should write a general description; specific configuration commands are not required.

Table 18-5 *Design Review*

Design Goal	Possible Implementation Choices Covered in This Chapter
The design states that an Enterprise needs IPv6 support for most LANs, with a regular high-volume of IPv6 traffic. Would native IPv6, point-to-point tunnels, or multipoint tunnels seem most appropriate?	
The design states that an Enterprise needs IPv6 support for a set small subset of LANs but that their traffic will be regular. Would native IPv6, point-to-point tunnels, or multipoint tunnels seem most appropriate?	
The design states that an Enterprise needs IPv6 support for a set small subset of LANs but that their traffic will be irregular and occasional. Would native IPv6, point-to-point tunnels, or multipoint tunnels seem most appropriate?	
The plan calls for IPv6 tunneling so that new routers, when added to the tunnel, do not require additional configuration on existing routers. What type tunnel would you choose, and what IPv6 address ranges?	

Implementation Plan Peer Review Table

Table 18-6 shows a list of questions that others might ask, or that you might think about, during a peer review of another network engineer's implementation plan. Complete the table by answering the questions.

Table 18-6 *Notable Questions from This Chapter to Consider During an Implementation Plan Peer Review*

Question	Answers
The plan calls for the use of OSPFv3 along with the implementation of IPv6 tunnels. What tunnel types do you expect to find the sample configurations? (2)	
The planning diagrams show multipoint tunnels, with IPv6 addresses that embed an IPv4 address in the last two quartets. What type of tunneling do you expect to see in the sample configurations?	
The plan lists a sample configuration with the command **tunnel mode ipv6ip** under a tunnel interface. What type of tunneling is used in this case?	
Same question as the previous row, but the command listed is **tunnel mode ipv6ip isatap.**	
Same question as the previous row, but the command listed is **tunnel mode gre ip.**	
Same question as the previous row, but the command listed is **tunnel mode ipv6ip 6to4.**	
A plan shows the use of a manually configured tunnel and an ISATAP tunnel. What tunnel sub-command would you expect to see for the point-to-point tunnel, but not the multipoint tunnel?	

Create an Implementation Plan Table

To practice skills useful when creating your own implementation plan, list in Table 18-7 all configuration commands related to the configuration of the following features. You may want to record your answers outside the book and set a goal to complete this table (and others like it) from memory during your final reviews before taking the exam.

Table 18-7 *Implementation Plan Configuration Memory Drill*

Feature	Configuration Commands/Notes
Configure an IPv6 manually configured tunnel using a loopback IPv4 address. Ignore IPv6 addressing and routing configuration.	
Add IPv6 addressing and routing configuration to the previous row's list. Assume EIGRP for IPv6 ASN 1 is preconfigured.	
Configure an IPv6 GRE tunnel using a loopback IPv4 address. Ignore IPv6 addressing and routing configuration.	
Configure an IPv6 automatic 6to4 tunnel using a loopback IPv4 address. Include only IPv6 configuration required for the tunnel to pass IPv6 traffic. Assume all hosts use addresses in the 2002::/16 range.	
List steps to migrate from the automatic 6to4 tunnel from the previous row to a comparable ISATAP tunnel	

Choose Commands for a Verification Plan Table

To practice skills useful when creating your own verification plan, list in Table 18-8 all commands that supply the requested information. You may want to record your answers outside the book and set a goal to complete this table (and others like it) from memory during your final reviews before taking the exam.

Note: Some of the entries in this table may not have been specifically mentioned in this chapter but are listed in this table for review and reference.

Table 18-8 *Verification Plan Memory Drill*

Information Needed	Commands
Tunnel interface status for IPv6.	
Tunnel interface's IPv6 address(es).	
Connected routes related to the tunnel.	
The tunnel source and destination IPv4 addresses.	
Test the tunnel to see if it can pass traffic.	

Review all the Key Topics

Review the most important topics from inside the chapter noted with the Key Topics icon in the outer margin of the page. Table 18-9 lists a reference of these key topics and the page numbers on which each is found.

Table 18-9   *Key Topics for Chapter 10*

Key Topic Element	Description	Page Number
Figure 18-3	Point-to-point IPv6 tunnel concept	614
Figure 18-4	Multipoint IPv6 tunnel concept	616
Table 18-2	Comparisons of four IPv6 tunnel types	617
Figure 18-5	NAT-PT concepts	618
List	Manually configured tunnel configuration checklist	620
List	Configuration differences between GRE and manually configured IPv6 tunnels	625
Table 18-3	Comparisons of manually configured tunnels and GRE tunnels	626
Figure 18-8	Address planning for automatic 6to4 tunnels	628
List	Configuration checklist for automatic 6to4 tunnels	629
List	Comparisons of automatic 6to4 and ISATAP tunnels	634
Figure 18-10	ISATAP tunnel logic	635
List	Modified EUI-64 rules for forming ISATAP IPv6 addresses	636
List	ISATAP tunnel configuration checklist	636
Table 18-4	Comparisons of Automatic 6to4 and ISATAP tunnels	640

Complete the Tables and Lists from Memory

Print a copy of Appendix D, "Memory Tables," (found on the CD), or at least the section for this chapter, and complete the tables and lists from memory. Appendix E, "Memory Tables Answer Key," also on the CD, includes completed tables and lists to check your work.

Define Key Terms

Define the following key terms from this chapter, and check your answers in the glossary.

Dual stacks, Network Address Translation–Protocol Translation (NAT-PT), tunneling, tunnel, tunnel interface, point-to-point tunnel, multipoint tunnel, ISATAP tunnel, ISATAP, automatic 6to4 tunnel, manually configured tunnel, GRE tunnel, Modified EUI-64

This chapter covers the following subjects:

Branch Office Broadband Internet Access: This section introduces some of the issues related to using the Internet as a WAN connectivity option for an Enterprise network.

Broadband Branch Access Configuration: This section generally discusses the configuration of a DSL connection on a router, along with the associated NAT and DHCP configuration.

VPN Configuration: This section generally discusses IPSec VPN and GRE tunnel configuration, particularly the routing aspects as they apply to branch office routers.

CHAPTER 19

Routing over Branch Internet Connections

This chapter discusses routing from the Enterprise branch office perspective, specifically for cases in which the branch uses the Internet for its connectivity back to the rest of the Enterprise network. Such a branch router needs to supply many functions: NAT, DHCP services, firewall, and even dynamic routing when multiple connections exist to the Enterprise. This chapter examines each of these and some basics regarding Internet access technologies as well.

From an exam preparation perspective, this chapter differs from the other 17 technology-focused chapters (Chapters 2 through 18) in this book. For the most part, the other chapters not only introduce some networking topics, the descriptions, figures, and examples go quite deep into the subject. This chapter, however, discusses more generalized concepts and some configuration samples without getting into every command option. Some topics mentioned in this chapter are actually part of the prerequisite CCNA topics, and some fit into other Cisco certifications, such as CCNA Security and CCSP. This chapter attempts to maintain the intended depth and breadth of the exam for this small set of remaining topics.

"Do I Know This Already?" Quiz

The "Do I Know This Already?" quiz allows you to assess if you should read the entire chapter. If you miss no more than one of these six self-assessment questions, you might want to move ahead to the "Exam Preparation Tasks." Table 19-1 lists the major headings in this chapter and the "Do I Know This Already?" quiz questions covering the material in those headings so that you can assess your knowledge of these specific areas. The answers to the "Do I Know This Already?" quiz appear in Appendix A.

Table 19-1 *"Do I Know This Already?" Foundation Topics Section-to-Question Mapping*

Foundations Topics Section	Questions
Branch Office Broadband Internet Access	1-2
Branch Router Configuration for Broadband Access	3-4
VPN Configuration	5

1. Router R1 sits at an Enterprise branch office, using the Internet for its only connectivity back to the rest of the Enterprise. Which of the following is not a benefit of using

an IPsec tunnel for packets sent through the Internet, between R1 and the rest of the Enterprise?

    a. Privacy

    b. Authentication

    c. Allows using an IGP between R1 and the Enterprise

    d. Secure communications

2. Router R1 sits at an Enterprise branch office, using both the Internet and a leased line to another Enterprise router for its two connectivity options back into the rest of the Enterprise network. The engineer planning for this branch decided to use the leased line for all Enterprise traffic, unless it fails, in which case the Internet connection should be used to pass traffic to the Enterprise. Which of the following is most likely to be useful on the branch router? (Choose two.)

    a. IPsec tunnel

    b. GRE tunnel

    c. Floating static route

    d. An IGP

3. Router R1, a branch router, connects to the Internet using DSL. The engineer plans to use a configuration with a dialer interface. The answers list a feature and interface on which the feature could be configured. Which combinations accurately describe the interface under which a feature will be configured?

    a. PPP on the ATM interface

    b. VPI/VCI on the dialer interface

    c. IP address on the ATM interface

    d. CHAP on the dialer interface

4. Router R1, a branch router, connects to the Internet using DSL. Some traffic flows through a GRE and IPsec tunnel, over the DSL connection, and into the core of an Enterprise network. The branch also allows local hosts to communicate directly with public sites in the Internet over this same DSL connection. Which of the following answers defines how the branch NAT config avoids performing NAT for the Enterprise-directed traffic but does perform NAT for the Internet-directed traffic?

    a. By not enabling NAT on the IPsec tunnel interface

    b. By not enabling NAT on the GRE tunnel interface

    c. By configuring the NAT-referenced ACL to not permit the Enterprise traffic

    d. By asking the ISP to perform NAT in the cloud

5. Router R1, a branch router, connects to the Internet using DSL. Some traffic flows through a GRE and IPsec tunnel, over the DSL connection, destined for an Enterprise network. Which of the following answers best describes the router's logic that tells the router, for a given packet, to apply GRE encapsulation to the packet?

   a. When the packet received on the LAN interface is permitted by the ACL listed on the **tunnel gre** *acl* command under the incoming interface

   b. When routing the packet, matching a route whose outgoing interface is the GRE tunnel interface

   c. When routing the packet, matching a route whose outgoing interface is the IPsec tunnel interface

   d. When permitted by an ACL that was referenced in the associated crypto map

Foundation Topics

Branch Office Broadband Internet Access

Many options exist today for private connectivity between an Enterprise branch office and the core of an Enterprise network. These options include leased lines, Frame Relay, MPLS VPNs, and Metro Ethernet. Although each differs in some way, they all share an important characteristic: They provide an inherently private path over which two Enterprise routers can send packets to each other.

Several other public options exist for branch office connectivity. All these options use the Internet for connectivity between the branch office and the core of the Enterprise network. Regardless of the particular physical Internet access technology–typically digital subscriber line (DSL), cable, or wireless broadband–all these options use a public Internet to forward the packets.

The differences between the public Internet and private connectivity mean that the branches need to use several additional functions just to make the connectivity work, plus the branches need to add other functions to make the connection secure. This chapter focuses on the functions required, and how they impact routing between the branch and the rest of the Enterprise.

The branch routing for the Internet-connected branch differs in part depending on the design. Figure 19-1 shows three examples of branch offices of different sizes. The figure labels these branches as small, medium, and large, but frankly, those descriptions are a bit subjective. For the purposes of this chapter, as the size increases, the number of connections or routers increases, and with that, the number of issues to consider also increases.

For the small branch design, most of the implementation challenges fall into two main categories: features needed for communication with hosts in the public Internet, and features needed to support secure communications with hosts in the Enterprise. The first category includes the Internet access details–how to make DSL, cable, and so on work–plus services likely to be required to learn, allocate, and translate the public IP addresses learned from the ISP, such as NAT and DHCP. The second category focuses on virtual private network (VPN) options that allow the Enterprise to trust that a packet comes from a legitimate branch office, and to prevent attackers from reading the contents of the packet as it crosses the Internet.

The rest of this first section of the chapter gives an overview of the various pieces of the puzzle of supporting private Enterprise traffic, over the public Internet, between the branch and the rest of the Enterprise.

Broadband Internet Access Basics

The term *broadband* has been around in the world of networking for a long time. The original meaning related to the frequency bands used by some Layer 1 standards that used a wider (broader) range of frequencies to achieve a higher bit rate. Today, the term broadband has grown to become synonymous with *high speed*.

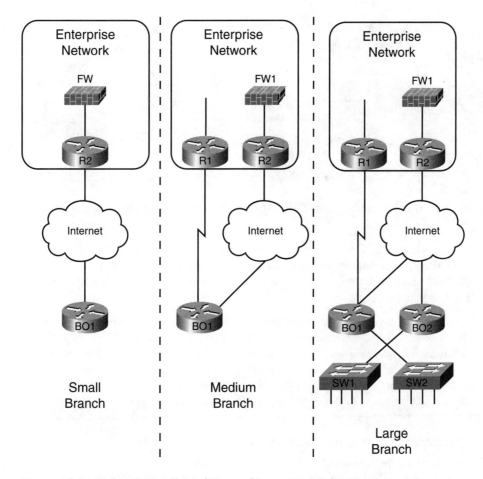

Figure 19-1 *Example Small, Medium, and Large Branch Designs*

The term *broadband Internet access technology* simply refers to a class of high-speed (a relative term) communications methods that allows a device to access some ISP, and in turn the Internet. Today, this term generally refers to (high-speed) cable Internet access, (high-speed) DSL Internet access, and (high-speed) wireless Internet access, with DSL and cable as the most commonly used options.

The hardware used at the branch office for each of these access technologies varies. However, whether a single piece of hardware does all the work, or whether several pieces of hardware combine to do the work, the hardware typically includes an IP router and either a cable modem or DSL modem. Again, like the term broadband, the term *modem* has taken new meaning over the years compared to its original historic use. However, a cable modem or DSL modem sits in the same location as a traditional analog modem, so the term has grown to a broader meaning. For example, Figure 19-2 shows a typical branch office LAN with a router and a cable modem.

Figure 19-2 shows a typical connection at a small office/home office (SOHO) site, with a separate router and cable modem. The router in this case uses two LAN interfaces, routing

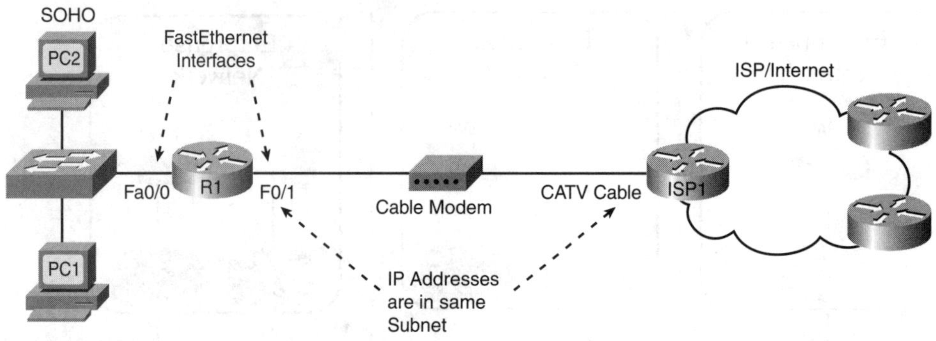

Figure 19-2   *Typical Cabling with Cable Modem at a Small Office/Home Office (SOHO)*

over those interfaces. However, on the LAN interface connected toward the ISP, the router uses a slightly different convention on the Ethernet called *PPP over Ethernet (PPPoE)*. The frames sent by the router still use an Ethernet header, but then include a PPP header, and then an IP header.

The PPP header gives the router and ISP the capability to use PPP features such as the Challenge Handshake Authentication Protocol (CHAP). CHAP allows the ISP to perform authentication, which allows the ISP to confirm the identity of the router that sent the packet. This allows the ISP to check the user's account, make accounting records of the access, and confirm that the customer is not late in paying their high-speed cable bill. (DSL uses a similar protocol, PPP over ATM (PPPoA), also in part to support PPP CHAP.)

Branch Router as DHCP Server and Client

When planning the permanent connection from an Enterprise to the Internet, as discussed at some length in Chapter 12, "Internet Connectivity and BGP," the ISP uses a range of registered public IP addresses. The ISP often assigns this range, or the Enterprise may register a prefix directly. Most Enterprises then use RFC 1918 private IPv4 addresses for most hosts inside the Enterprise. To make the whole package work, the Enterprise must also configure NAT, typically with the port address translation (PAT) feature, to translate between the private and public addresses.

Each Internet-connected branch follows the same public IP addressing model in general, but with some differences. First, the ISP typically assigns one and only one public IP address for the branch site, expecting the branch to use PAT. That public IP address may change over time; even though most broadband Internet access technologies use "always on" logic, the underlying protocols act more like a dial connection that never stops. So, the ISP dynamically assigns the public IP address so that if the subscriber stops using the connection, fails to pay the bill, or cancels the account, the public IP address can be easily and automatically reclaimed into the pool of available addresses.

The IP address assignment process differs slightly for the branch LAN as well. Hosts still learn their IP address, mask, default gateway, and DNS server addresses, but rather than require a separate host at each branch to act as DHCP server, the branch router may act as

DHCP server. Figure 19-3 shows the idea of the branch router learning its public address, plus acting as DHCP server for local LAN hosts.

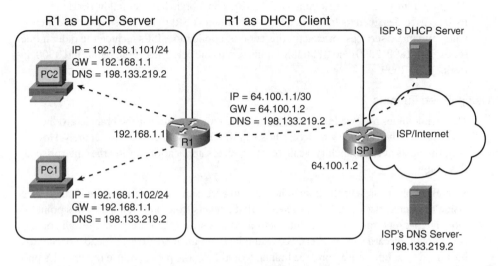

Figure 19-3 *Branch Office Router Acting as DHCP Client and DHCP Server*

As you can see, the two branch hosts both received the appropriate addressing information for private network 192.168.1.0/24. R1 itself learns similar information from the ISP's DHCP server. R1 will use this learned IP address on the interface it uses to connect to the ISP. R1 also adds a default route to its IP routing table, using the ISP1's IP address as next hop–in this case, 64.100.1.2.

Finally, R1 must enable NAT/PAT. As a reminder, the term NAT today refers to all NAT functions, including the port address translation feature. PAT allows a little more than 65,000 concurrent flows to use a single public IP address by using a different TCP or UDP port number for each flow. As a result, this single public IP address should be more than enough for a typical branch office.

Note: Consumer-class products enable by default most of the features described in this section, such as DHCP client, server, and NAT/PAT. Enterprise-class routers typically rely on explicit configuration by a network engineer for these same features.

Branch Office Security

With a permanent Internet connection near the core of the Enterprise network, the Enterprise typically uses one or more border security products. These products include stateful firewalls such as the ASA appliance from Cisco, plus Intrusion Prevention Systems (IPS).

Now that a branch has a connection to the Internet, most Enterprises implement similar features at the branch. Again, for economic reasons, it makes more sense to implement those features on the same router platform already needed for so many other reasons. So, Cisco includes firewall and IPS features in IOS. These features include the older Context

Based Access Control (CBAC) and newer IOS Zone-Based Firewall. Cisco also supplies the IOS IPS feature as well.

Although it may seem that running such features on a branch router might overload the router, Cisco designed its Integrated Services Routers (ISR) to have the power to concurrently run many services for exactly this type of application. ISRs include the older model series 800, 1800, 2800, and 3800 ISR families, plus model series 1900, 2900, and 3900, introduced in 2009.

Using IPsec Tunnels

The technologies reviewed up to this point, when implemented at the branch, give hosts at the branch the capability to access hosts in the Internet, and to do so securely. However, the hosts at the branch typically cannot access applications inside the Enterprise at this point.

Several problems prevent the branch hosts from accessing hosts with private IP addresses inside the Enterprise core. One problem is that packets from branch hosts at this point look like packets from any other Internet-based hosts, and the Enterprise firewall could (and should) discard such packets. For example, if a branch host tries to send a packet to a host inside the Enterprise core, the branch would NAT the packet to use the branch's public IP address. When that packet arrives at the Enterprise's firewall at the company's main Internet connection, the firewall would have no way to know whether the packet came from a legitimate host at the branch. One solution would be to allow packets past the firewall, making the server available to the Internet, and rely on host security to prevent access, but that may be too risky.

To solve this problem, typically the engineer configures a tunnel between the branch and the Enterprise core. Then the branch router directs traffic destined for the Enterprise through the tunnel. For such packets, the branch router will not translate the IP address of the original packet using NAT. Instead, the branch router will encrypt the IP packet and encapsulate the encrypted packet inside another IPv4 header, using public source and destination addresses in this new packet. Then, the branch router can forward this packet through the public Internet, with a device in the Enterprise core receiving and decrypting the packet. That device can tell from additional security headers in the encrypted packet whether it comes from a trusted branch router. Figure 19-4 shows an example of the process.

Following the steps in Figure 19-4:

Step 1.   PC1 creates a packet, with its own 10.99.1.1 address as source, and server S1's 10.1.1.1 IP address as destination. PC1 sends the packet to its default gateway (BO1).

Step 2.   When Router BO1 tries to route the packet toward the Internet, the router's logic tells it to check an ACL. All packets permitted by the ACL go through the tunnel–in this case, all packets destined for 10.0.0.0/8, the private network used by this Enterprise.

Step 3.   Router BO1 encrypts the original packet so that no one in the Internet can read the data.

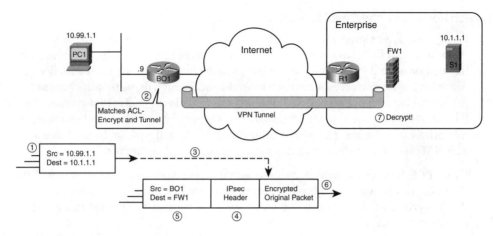

Figure 19-4   *IPsec Tunnel Concept*

Step 4.   Router BO1 adds a security header (IPsec header), which helps the receiver de-crypt the packet, and know that it came from a trusted router.

Step 5.   Router BO1 adds a new IPv4 header, this time with BO1's public IP address as source, and the tunnel destination's public IPv4 address as destination. In this case, the destination is a public IPv4 address used by Firewall FW1.

Step 6.   Router BO1 sends the packet into the Internet, with the various routers for-warding the packet to FW1's public IP address.

Step 7.   Firewall FW1 de-encapsulates and decrypts the original packet, leaving the original packet as described at Step 1. FW1 forwards the packet toward Server S1.

The process of tunneling the packet gives the branch office the logical equivalent of a point-to-point link between the branch router and the firewall. The tunnel logic works like the point-to-point tunnel logic discussed throughout Chapter 18, "IPv4 and IPv6 Coexis-tence," except for two key differences. First, this tunnel uses IPv4 as both the transport protocol and passenger protocol, rather than using IPv4 to transport IPv6 as the passenger protocol. Also, this tunnel uses additional security features, like the encryption shown in Figure 19-4.

IP Security (IPsec) defines the details of how this particular tunnel works. IPsec defines which security standards may be used to encrypt the packet—for example, IPsec allows the use of triple DES (3DES) and Advanced Encryption Standard (AES). IPsec also allows the use of authentication protocols and headers as well, which the firewall can use to ver-ify that the packet came from a legitimate branch office and not some attacker.

Although the security protocols may be interesting, this book does not delve into the de-tails, other than to say that the protocols ensure that the data in the tunnel is private (through encryption) and comes from a legitimate branch (through authentication).

Branch Routing for the Small Branch

Figure 19-1 shows a sample small branch whose only WAN connectivity is to the Internet. It may seem that such a router has no need to be concerned about routing. However, with the addition of an IPsec tunnel from the branch to the Enterprise core, the branch does have a kind of routing decision to make: to send a packet through the tunnel, or to send it to the local ISP after performing NAT. Both actions result in the packet flowing toward the ISP, but one option results in the original packet successfully arriving at the Enterprise, with private IP addresses. The other routing choice results in the packet being changed with NAT and forwarded to an address somewhere in the public Internet.

Figure 19-5 shows an example of such a routing decision, again using branch Router BO1. Host PC1 has two windows open–one using a web-based application with a server inside the Enterprise core, with another web browser window open and connected to the user's favorite public website.

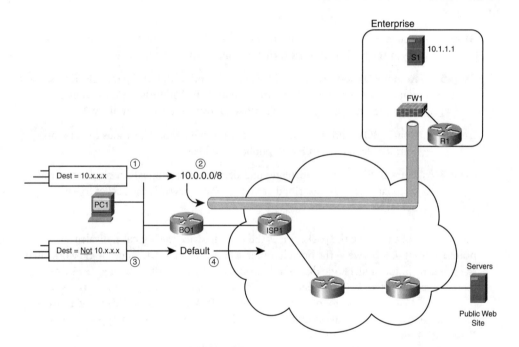

Figure 19-5 *Routing over the IPsec Tunnel or Through the Public Internet*

Following the steps in the Figure 19-5

Step 1. PC1 sends a packet destined to the Enterprise server's 10.x.x.x IP address.

Step 2. Router BO1 uses logic that matches destination addresses in the 10.0.0.0/8 range and directs the packet over the IPsec tunnel. This action results in the encapsulation shown in Figure 19-4 and in the original packet being forwarded into the Enterprise core.

Step 3.   PC1 sends another packet; this one is destined for the public web server's public IP address.

Step 4.   Router BO1 does not match the packet with its IPsec ACL, so BO1 just routes the packet out its Internet connection, after using NAT.

Routing in Medium and Large Branches

The final concept in this broad overview section has to do with routing in medium and large branches, after the branch has a working Internet connection plus an IPsec tunnel. In the medium- and large-branch examples, another private WAN connection exists between the branch and the Enterprise core. So, the branch needs to make choices about when to use routes that use the private connection and when to use routes that use the public connection. Likewise, the routers in the Enterprise need to make good routing choices about how to route packets back to the branch.

Focusing on the branch router's logic, two main options exist: using static routes and using an IGP. Static routes can be used to forward traffic over the private connection and over the IPsec tunnel. However, IPsec does not directly support IGP protocols, because the IPsec tunnel cannot natively forward IPv4 multicasts. To overcome this restriction, you can use a GRE tunnel that actually runs over the IPsec tunnel. GRE supports multicasts by encapsulating them in unicast packets, so GRE supports IGPs. Summarizing, by using GRE, you get the following features:

■   A GRE tunnel acts like a point-to-point link from a Layer 3 perspective.

■   A GRE tunnel supports many passenger protocols, including IPv4.

■   A GRE tunnel encapsulates/forwards broadcasts and multicasts, therefore supporting IPv4 IGPs.

■   Although not mentioned in Chapter 18, GRE tunnels can run through IPsec tunnels.

After configuring a GRE tunnel to run over the IPsec tunnel on a medium or large branch, from a routing perspective, the branch now has two Layer 3 paths to the rest of the Enterprise network: out the GRE tunnel interface and out the private WAN interface. Then you can run an IGP on each, and the branch can choose which path is best using the usual IGP criteria. Figure 19-6 shows an example with a single branch router, a leased line, and a GRE tunnel running through the Internet.

For the network in the figure, branch Router BO1 has two possible outgoing interface choices for any static or IGP-learned route: interface S0/0 (the leased line) or tunnel0 (the GRE tunnel). When a packet arrives at BO1, if the route forwards the packet over tunnel0, the next step in the logic triggers the GRE tunnel logic, encapsulating the packet. Then, that packet matches the IPsec ACL for all packets destined for network 10.0.0.0/8 (in this case) and causes the IPsec process to occur. The IPsec-generated packet can then be routed through the public Internet.

Note: Figure 19-12, in the section "Summary–Branch Routing from PC1 to Enterprise Server S1," shows the encapsulation used to support the design shown in Figure 19-6.

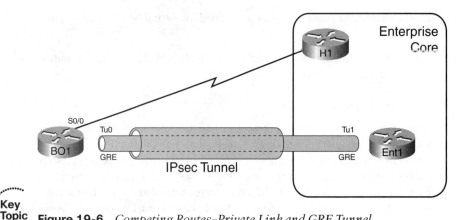

Figure 19-6   *Competing Routes–Private Link and GRE Tunnel*

Next, the text examines the static routing option at the branch, followed by the option to use IGPs and GRE tunnels.

Routing Using Floating Static Routes

A floating static route occurs when the **ip route** command configures a static route in which the command overrides the default AD value of 1. With a higher AD for the static route, the router may consider some other routes for that same prefix as being better. For example, if the IGP learns a route for the same prefix as defined in the static route, the router does not use the static route with the higher AD, instead uses the dynamically learned route with the lower AD. Should the dynamically learned route fail, the router adds the static route back to the IP routing table. The term *floating static* refers to that the route may float in and out of the routing table.

A branch router can use a floating static route directing Enterprise traffic over the Internet, but only using that route when the IGP-learned route over the private link fails. Often, the branch design uses the Internet connection just as a backup for the private link into the Enterprise. To implement such a design, a branch router can use a floating static route for the route over the Internet, only using that route when the IGP-learned route over the private link fails. For example, in Figure 19-6, Router BO1 could use EIGRP over the leased line and configure a floating static route for 10.0.0.0/8 that routes traffic over the Internet connection. Router BO1 would prefer an EIGRP learned, AD 90 route for 10.0.0.0/8 instead, until that route through S0/0 failed.

Note that to use the floating static route option, a GRE tunnel would not be required, because the routers do not need to use an IGP through the Internet.

Dynamic Routing over the GRE Tunnel

If the design engineer decides that the branch router should use both paths into the Enterprise, a somewhat simple solution exists. Simply configure an IGP to run as normal, over both the private WAN connection and over a GRE tunnel. For example, with Figure 19-6, enable EIGRP on the branch Router BO1 on both interface S0/0 and Tu0. The design can then use all the usual tools to manipulate the choice of routes, including tuning the metrics and configuring variance to influence load sharing.

This concludes the overview of branch office routing. The next two major sections of this chapter examine broadband access and IPsec VPNs. These sections go a little deeper on the concepts and show sample configurations for perspective.

Branch Router Configuration for Broadband Access

This section focuses on a branch office router configuration using DSL and the services that must be configured to support Internet traffic. The discussion starts with a little more background about DSL concepts, followed by some sample configurations.

Understanding DSL Concepts

DSL uses the Telco local loop: the phone line that runs between the phone company's nearby facility (called the central office, or CO) and the customer site. In other words, DSL uses the same phone line that runs to most people's homes and to most office buildings. The phone company has used these types of lines for the better part of a century to carry analog electrical signals for voice traffic, but DSL uses other frequency ranges to carry a digital signal for the purpose of sending data.

From the customer premise perspective, the customer can still use the same old analog phones, which still use frequencies below 4000 Hz. The DSL router connects to another RJ-11 socket in the wall, just as if it were just another analog telephone. However, the router sends digital signals at frequencies above 4000 Hz, which does not interfere with the voice traffic. So, both the voice and DSL electrical signals flow over the same cable, at the same time, just at different frequencies.

Note: Although the human voice generates frequencies below 4000 Hz, the human ear can hear some higher frequencies, so some DSL installations require the use of filters on the lines connected to the phones. These filters prevent humans from hearing some of the higher frequency DSL tones.

From the telco perspective, the Telco has to separate the voice and DSL signals. To do so, the Telco uses a device called a DSL Access Multiplexor (DSLAM). It splits the analog signal off to the switch that handles traditional analog voice calls and splits the digital traffic to a router. Figure 19-7 shows these ideas, both for the customer premise and central office.

At Layer 1, the DSL uses digital signals that use some encoding that does not matter to the discussions in this book. However, at Layer 2, DSL uses two different data link protocols: Asynchronous Transfer Mode (ATM) and Point-to-Point Protocol (PPP).

DSL uses ATM in the traditional role of a data link protocol, and PPP for several reasons, but particularly for its CHAP authentication. For DSL, ATM controls the use of the Layer 1 medium so that data can be successfully sent over the link and to the right device. ATM defines the headers used on the link, the data link addresses, and the rules for passing Layer 3 data up and down the protocol stack. For instance, the ATM cell headers enable the DSLAM to know where to send the data received from a customer over a DSL link.

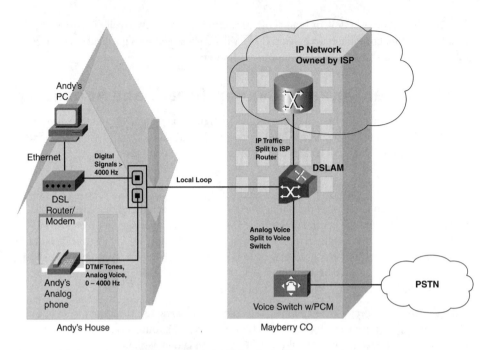

Figure 19-7 *DSL at the Home and the Telco Local Loop*

ATM uses a PVC concept similar to a Frame Relay PVC. With DSL, an ATM PVC would exist between the DSL router at the branch and the ISP router in Figure 19-7. Similar to Frame Relay, an ATM address identifies the PVC, but the address value is local, so the value used by one endpoint may be different than the address used on the other end of the PVC. Frame Relay uses the DLCI as the identifier of a PVC, whereas ATM uses a two-part address, called the Virtual Path Identifier/Virtual Connection Identifier (VPI/VCI).

Frame Relay and ATM differ quite a bit in relation to Layer 2 encapsulation. Frame Relay uses simpler conventions than ATM: When a packet needs to be sent out a Frame Relay interface, the router adds a Frame Relay header and trailer and sends the frame. ATM adds a short extra header to the packet and then performs *segmentation*. The segmentation process breaks the data into 48-byte segments and adds a 5-byte header to each to create ATM *cells*. The cell header holds the VPI/VCI pair, which allows the network to forward the cells to the correct destination end of the PVC. Figure 19-8 shows an example of the encapsulation.

Follow the steps in Figure 19-8:

Step 1.   The router wants to send a packet out the DSL ATM interface. (This logic oc-curs after any tunneling logic and NAT, and works the same whether using IPSec, GRE over IPsec, or the packet is just destined for a public host in the Internet.)

Step 2.   The router, using PPPoA concepts, adds a PPP header.

Step 3.   The router adds another short header (details unimportant here).

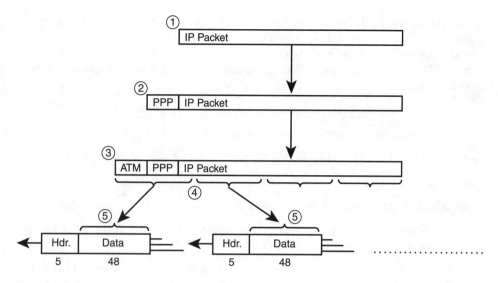

Figure 19-8   *ATM Encapsulation and Segmentation*

Step 4.   The router's segmentation and reassembly (SAR) chip segments the frame from the previous step into 48-byte segments.

Step 5.   The SAR chip encapsulates these segments inside 5-byte cell headers and sends the cells over the DSL link.

The DSLAM then receives the cells and forwards them on to the router. The router at the other end of the PVC reassembles the cells—the finishing touch on the ATM SAR process. The receiving router can then begin interpreting the various headers and de-encapsulate the packet.

Briefly, note that the encapsulation process also adds a PPP header to the IP packet before sending the data over the DSL link. The routers use the PPP header for several reasons, including PPP authentication with CHAP, and for dynamic address assignment and discovery. This convention to use both PPP and ATM protocols together is called PPP over ATM (PPPoA).

Configuring DSL

DSL configuration—even ignoring related services like DHCP and NAT—requires several steps. The goal of this section is to give you a general idea of the configuration by showing one example, just to give you a sense of the configuration pieces.

To appreciate the sample configuration, first consider that DSL is a switched connection. Most people think DSL (and cable) provide an *always on* or leased Internet connection, because typically the user does not need to do anything to start and stop the connection. However, a router can start and stop the DSL connection—or using the traditional terms, the router can dial and hang-up the connection. The idea that DSL routers do something to dial the connection means that the connection is actually switched.

Because cable and DSL connections use switched logic, IOS implements DSL configuration using some older switched network commands, including dialer interfaces and virtual templates. The option used in this section's example, the dialer interface, has been around IOS for a long time as a place to configure the logic and features related to a dialed connection.

The main pieces of the DSL configuration as shown in this section are as follows:

- The configuration creates a dialer interface.

- The Layer 3 and PPP configuration related to DSL is applied to the dialer interface.

- The ATM configuration is applied to the physical ATM interface.

- The ATM interface is linked to the dialer interface.

- An IP route forwards traffic out the dialer interface, which triggers the DSL encapsulation process, as shown in Figure 19-8.

Figure 19-9 shows the configuration, with some notes about the interactions of the various pieces of the configuration.

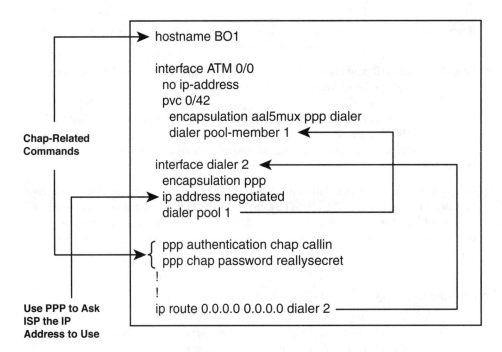

Figure 19-9 *DSL Configuration on Router BO1*

First examine the ATM interface. The configuration defines the VPI/VCI as 0/42; the ISP needs to match this value, or more likely, dictates the value to the customer. The **encapsulation** command defines that PPP will also be used (as shown in Step 2 of Figure 19-8's encapsulation), and it defines the style of ATM header added at Step 3 of that same figure (AAL5MUX). The **encapsulation aal5mux ppp dialer** command's **dialer** parameter defines that this PVC will use the logic of a dialer interface. Finally, the **dialer pool-member 1** command associates the ATM interface with the dialer interface as noted in the figure.

The dialer interface has five subcommands in this case, including three related to PPP. One command tells the router to use PPP to learn its IP address from the ISP (**ip address negotiated**). The **dialer pool 1** command tells the dialer interface that when it needs to signal a new connection, look for interfaces with **dialer pool-member 1** configured, such as interface ATM 0/0.

Finally, the static default route sends traffic out the dialer interface. Packets forwarded out this DSL connection will match this route, causing IOS to try to forward the packet using the dialer interface, triggering the encapsulation and logic described in Figure 19-8.

Configuring NAT

When the branch router receives a packet over the LAN interface, it has several options of how to process the packet. For instance, using the medium-sized branch from Figure 19-1, which has a leased line into the Enterprise plus a DSL Internet connection, the router could do the following:

- Forward the packet out the serial interface, unchanged, to the rest of the Enterprise network.

- Forward the packet out the tunnel, changed somewhat (encrypted, encapsulated, and so on), to the rest of the Enterprise network.

- Forward the packet over the Internet link (the DSL dialer interface), after using NAT to change the source private address to a public address, to some public IP destination address.

Only the third option requires NAT. Thankfully, NAT configuration easily supports the concept of performing NAT for traffic going to Internet destinations and not performing NAT for traffic in the tunnel. Example 19-1 shows a sample configuration, again using Router BO1. This configuration assumes that BO1 was already configured, as shown in Figure 19-9.

Example 19-1   *NAT Configuration for Router BO1*

```
interface fastethernet 0/0
 ip address 10.99.1.9 255.255.255.0
 ip nat inside

interface dialer 2
 ip nat outside
ip nat inside source list local-lan interface dialer2 overload
ip access-list extended local-lan
 permit ip 10.99.1.0 0.0.0.255 any
```

The configuration shows NAT overload, using a single public IP address–namely, dialer2's dynamically learned IP address. ACL local-lan matches all packets whose source IP address is from the branch's local LAN subnet (10.99.1.0/24). The ACL, referenced by the **ip nat inside** global command, tells the router to NAT traffic permitted by this ACL. The traffic going through the tunnel will already be encapsulated in a new IP header, and no longer have a source address from the LAN subnet, so only traffic destined for Internet destinations will have NAT applied. Finally, the interface subcommands **ip nat inside** and **ip nat outside** tell the interfaces on which to attempt the translation.

Configuring DHCP Server

The branch router also may need to act as the DHCP server. If so, the router needs to have a pool of IP addresses appropriate for the local branch LAN. It needs to know the IP addresses of the DNS servers–both inside the Enterprise and the ISP's DNS server. It also needs to assign a default gateway, typically that same branch router's LAN IP address. Example 19-2 continues the same configuration.

Example 19-2   *DHCP Configuration for Router BO1*

```
ip dhcp pool fred
 network 10.99.1.0 255.255.255.0
 default-router 10.99.1.9
 ip dhcp exclude-address 10.99.1.9
 dns-server 10.2.2.2 128.107.2.1
```

Note that no interface configuration is needed on the LAN interface–the router notices the incoming interface of the DHCP request, compares the connected subnets to the pool, and picks a pool that matches the correct address range.

VPN Configuration

Earlier, this chapter introduced the concept of an IPsec VPN between the branch router and another device in the Enterprise core. This VPN, sometimes called a *VPN tunnel*, gives the Enterprise engineer a way to send a packet native to the Enterprise, with private IP addresses, through the Internet. Additionally, the VPN provides privacy (through encryption) and verification that the sender is legitimate (through authentication).

Although extremely useful, the IPsec tunnel unfortunately does not allow IGP traffic to flow directly over the IPsec VPN tunnel. One solution is to also use a GRE tunnel, which does support IGPs because it can encapsulate the IGP's multicasts inside a unicast IP packet. As previously shown in Figure 19-6, GRE solves the problem by routing over the GRE tunnel interface, whose traffic is, in turn, processed by the IPSsec tunnel.

Other alternatives exist for supporting routing over an IPsec tunnel. These options include

■   **Virtual Tunnel Interfaces:** Similar in concept to GRE tunnels but it uses an encapsulation that does not add and extra 4-byte header. (GRE adds such a header.)

■   **Dynamic Multipoint VPN (DMVPN):** Creates a multipoint VPN concept, allowing less configuration to add new sites.

■ **Group Encrypted Transport (GET) VPN:** A more recent addition to IOS, also supporting multipoint VPNs with less configuration to add new sites.

This section shows a sample configuration for both IPsec and GRE tunnels, just to complete the perspectives on the Internet-connected branch router.

Configuring an IPsec VPN

To fully understand the IPsec configuration, you need a deeper understanding of the security protocols than the detail included in this book. However, if you ignore the particulars about security protocols, a sample configuration can reveal some interesting facts about branch routing, which is the focus of this chapter.

Figure 19-10 shows a sample IPsec configuration for Router BO1. Again, this configuration assumes the configuration in the previous examples, plus Figure 19-9, have already occurred.

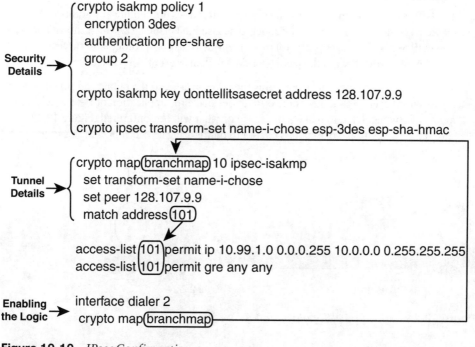

Figure 19-10 *IPsec Configuration*

Focus first on the crypto map (named branchmap) and the dialer interface. The dialer interface enables IPsec with the **crypto map branchmap** command, causing IOS to consider applying IPsec to packets *exiting* Dialer 2. The crypto map causes IOS to only encrypt and tunnel the packets that are matched by ACL 101 in this case. (See the arrows in the figures as to how the crypto map is linked to using ACL 101.) The crypto map also identifies the destination IP address used when the encapsulation takes place (128.107.9.9). This address is the public IP address of the device on the other end of the tunnel; the earlier figures showed that as Router Ent1.

Next, think about a packet received by BO1 over the LAN, in light of ACL 101, and in light of the crypto map processing outbound traffic on interface Dialer 2. The packet arrives in BO1's F0/0 interface. The packet may be processed by a GRE tunnel first, or it may not. Then, some route must route the packet out Dialer 2. At that point, the logic of the commands in Figure 19-10 finally begins.

Continuing with this same packet, the ACL matches packets that were tunneled by GRE, or other packets that come from the LAN and are going toward the rest of the Enterprise. The first line in the ACL matches the packets from the local LAN (10.99.1.0/8) going to another destination in the Enterprise. The second line in the ACL matches all GRE packets. Note that packets destined to some public IP address in the Internet would not match the ACL with a permit action. So, only packets destined for the Enterprise network match ACL 101; only the packets permitted by ACL 101 will be processed by the IPsec tunnel logic.

Configuring GRE Tunnels

The GRE tunnel configuration on the branch router does not require any additional commands as compared with the GRE tunnels discussed in Chapter 18, which showed how to tunnel IPv6 (the passenger protocol) over IPv4 (the transport protocol). In this case, the GRE tunnel carries IPv4 as the passenger protocol, inside an IPv4 packet.

The fact that an IPSec tunnel exists, plus the issues related to the public and private addresses used over the Internet connection, does make the application of the tunnel a bit more challenging. First, to make more sense of what will be configured, Figure 19-11 shows the concepts and parameters related to configuring a GRE tunnel in this case.

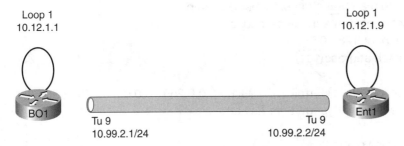

Loop 1
10.12.1.1

Loop 1
10.12.1.9

BO1

Ent1

Tu 9
10.99.2.1/24

Tu 9
10.99.2.2/24

Figure 19-11   *GRE Tunnel Topology and Addresses*

The link that appears as a tunnel between the branch router (BO1) and central site Enterprise router (Ent1) acts like a point-to-point serial link. In the many examples in Chapter 18, this link would have had IPv6 addresses because IPv6 was the passenger protocol. In this case, the tunnel interfaces have IPv4 addresses because IPv4 is the passenger protocol, with the addresses in a new subnet allocated just for this tunnel.

The configuration also uses loopback interfaces, with those interfaces and their IP addresses used as the tunnel endpoints. This configuration means that the new IP packet header created by GRE will use addresses 10.12.1.1 and 10.12.1.9. Finally, any routes learned over the tunnel will list tunnel 9 as an outgoing interface, with next-hop address 10.99.2.2.

Example 19-3 shows a sample configuration, again on Router BO1.

Example 19-3 *GRE Tunnel Configuration*

```
interface tunnel 9
 ip address 10.99.2.1 255.255.255.255
 tunnel source loopback 1
 tunnel destination 10.12.1.9

interface loopback 1
 ip address 10.12.1.1 255.255.255.0

router eigrp 1
 network 10.12.1.1 0.0.0.0
 network 10.99.2.1 0.0.0.0

ip route 10.12.1.9 255.255.255.255 dialer2
```

The tunnel configuration just uses three subcommands: one to define the source IP address (indirectly, as loopback 1's 10.12.1.1), the tunnel destination (10.12.1.9), and the interface's passenger protocol address (IP address 10.99.2.1). The **tunnel mode** command is not needed, because IOS defaults to use IPv4 as the transport protocol, which then allows any of the supported passenger protocols.

The configuration also requires two main branches of logic for routing to work correctly. First, for the tunnel to function, the tunnel destination must be reachable; in this example, a static route was added for this purpose. Additionally, the routers need to exchange routes that will list the tunnel interface as the outgoing interface, which in turn directs packets through the tunnel. The example includes the EIGRP configuration that enables EIGRP on tunnel 9 just as a reminder that one of the primary motivations for bothering with the GRE tunnel is to support IGP routing protocols.

Summary–Branch Routing from PC1 to Enterprise Server S1

To complete the chapter, this section works through an example where a host at the branch sends a packet to a server inside the Enterprise. For the sake of argument, the branch prefers to send this packet over the Internet. It is immaterial whether the branch does not have a private link into the Enterprise, or if the engineer chose to implement routing so that the path through the Internet is currently preferred. The example then gives us a chance to work through the logic when the packet is sent through a GRE tunnel, and an IPsec tunnel, and then out the DSL ATM interface.

Figure 19-12 shows the example. The example begins with the arrival of a packet from PC1, destined from servers S1, 10.1.1.1. The packet has arrived at Router BO1, which has removed the incoming frame's data link header/trailer. The figure picks up the story as BO1 makes its first routing decision about this packet.

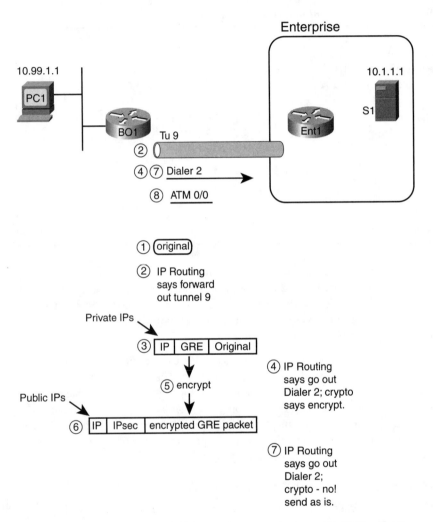

Figure 19-12   *Example of Routing and Encapsulation with GRE over IPsec*

Following are the steps in Figure 19-12:

Step 1.   BO1 has the original packet in memory, source 10.99.1.1 (PC1), destination 10.1.1.1 (S1).

Step 2.   BO1's best route for destination 10.1.1.1 uses outgoing interface tunnel 9. This route may have been learned by an IGP running over this GRE tunnel.

Step 3.   BO1 adds a new IPv4 header and GRE header to the original packet. This new packet as a destination based on BO1's tunnel 9 subcommand **tunnel destination**, per the previous Example 19-3, is address 10.12.1.9.

Step 4.   BO1 routes the packet formed in the previous step. This best route for 10.12.1.9 lists Dialer 2 as the outgoing interface. The crypto map on interface Dialer 2 refers to an ACL, and ACL matches this packet with a permit action. This combination of logic tells BO1 to use IPsec to encrypt this packet for transmission over the IPsec tunnel.

Step 5.   BO1 encrypts the packet that was created in Step 3–in other words, it encrypts the GRE-created packet.

Step 6.   BO1 encapsulates the encrypted data, adding several IPsec headers, plus a new IPv4 header. The new IPv4 header uses BO1's public IPv4 address as source and the configured public IPv4 address of the other end of the IPsec tunnel as destination. Per the example in Figure 19-10, the destination IP address would be 128.107.9.9.

Step 7.   BO1 routes this latest packet, with its destination IP address of 128.107.9.9, matching a route (probably a default route) that lists Dialer 2 (again) as the outgoing interface. However, the crypto map's ACL does not match the packet with a permit action, so BO1 bypasses any further IPsec functions and simply tries to forward the packet.

Step 8.   Forwarding out the dialer interface then causes this DSL-connected router to forward the packet out the underlying ATM interface, which performs the encapsulation and segmentation previously shown in Figure 19-8.

Interestingly, this process drives the branch router to make comparisons to the routing table three separate times when forwarding this data. The most important thing to remember from this example is to get a sense for how the pieces work together and how the steps add additional headers.

Exam Preparation Tasks

Planning Practice

The CCNP ROUTE exam expects test takers to review design documents, create implementation plans, and create verification plans for most topics. However, the CCNP ROUTE exam topics require less depth for the topics in this chapter. For example, the exam topics do not specifically mention the verification task for any of the topics in this chapter, so the chapter does not examine **show** command output.

Because of this key difference, the typical tables at the end of each chapter are not as useful for this chapter. However, some review can be helpful. Table 19-2 lists a series of questions for the purpose of reviewing the content in this chapter. Refer to the same appendix you have been using throughout this book for the suggested answers.

Table 19-2   *Design Review*

Question	Answer
When a branch uses its broadband Internet connection to communicate into the rest of an Enterprise network, what benefits does an IPsec tunnel provide? (3)	
To make the basic broadband connection work, and to support flows from the branch office hosts to/from public websites, what features discussed in this chapter might the router need to configure? (5)	
What method allows a branch to statically route over the IPsec tunnel to the rest of the Enterprise, but only when routes through the private WAN connection fail?	
For what reasons might a network engineer consider also using a GRE tunnel when connecting a branch router, over the Internet, with the rest of the Enterprise network?	
When configuring DSL using dialer interfaces, in what configuration mode are the ATM details configured? PPP details? Layer 3 details?	
A branch router has configured its one LAN interface as a NAT inside interface and its DSL dialer interface as an outside interface. What prevents packets in the IPsec tunnel from being NATted?	
When configuring an IPsec tunnel on a branch router, identify the three main configuration components that link the interface to the matching logic that determines which packets the router processes into the tunnel.	

Note that all the questions assume that a branch office router exists and that it uses some form of broadband access to the Internet.

Review all the Key Topics

Review the most important topics from inside the chapter, noted with the key topics icon in the outer margin of the page. Table 19-3 lists a reference of these key topics and the page numbers on which each is found.

Table 19-3 *Key Topics for Chapter 10*

Key Topic Element	Description	Page Number
Figure 19-3	Branch router's role as DHCP server and client	653
Figure 19-4	IPsec tunnel concepts	655
Figure 19-6	Comparing the competing routes–private and tunnel	658
Figure 19-10	IPsec configuration	665

Define Key Terms

Define the following key terms from this chapter, and check your answers in the glossary.

IPsec, IPsec tunnel, GRE tunnel, Floating static route, Digital Subscriber Line (DSL), Cable, PPP over ATM (PPPoA), PPP over Ethernet (PPPoE), Challenge Handshake Authentication Protocol (CHAP)

CHAPTER 20

Final Preparation

The first 19 chapters of this book cover the technologies, protocols, commands, and features required to be prepared to pass the ROUTE exam. Although these chapters supply the detailed information, most people need more preparation than simply reading the first 19 chapters of this book. This chapter details a set of tools and a study plan to help you complete your preparation for the exams.

This short chapter has two main sections. The first section lists the exam preparation tools useful at this point in the study process. The second section lists a suggested study plan now that you have completed all the preceding chapters in this book.

Note: Appendixes D, E, and F exist as soft-copy appendixes on the CD included in the back of this book.

Tools for Final Preparation

This section lists some information about the available tools and how to access the tools.

Exam Engine and Questions on the CD

The CD in the back of the book includes the Boson Exam Environment (BEE). The BEE is the exam-engine software that delivers and grades a set of free practice questions written by Cisco Press. The BEE supports multiple-choice questions, drag-and-drop questions, and many scenario-based questions that require the same level of analysis as the questions on the ROUTE exam. The installation process has two major steps. The first step is installing the BEE software; the CD in the back of this book has a recent copy of the BEE software, supplied by Boson Software (http://www.boson.com). The second step is activating and downloading the free practice questions. The practice questions written by Cisco Press for the ROUTE exam are not on the CD. Instead, the practice questions must be downloaded from www.boson.com.

Note: The CD case in the back of this book includes the CD and a piece of paper. The paper contains the activation key for the practice questions associated with this book. Do not lose this activation key.

Install the Software from the CD

Following are the steps you should perform to install the software:

Step 1.   Insert the CD into your computer.

Step 2.   From the main menu, click the option to install the Boson Exam Environment (BEE). The software that automatically runs is the Cisco Press software needed to access and use all CD-based features, including the BEE, a PDF of this book, and the CD-only appendixes.

Step 3.   Respond to the prompt windows as you would with any typical software installation process.

The installation process might give you the option to register the software. This process requires that you establish a login at the www.boson.com website. You need this login to activate the exam; therefore, you should register when prompted.

Activate and Download the Practice Exam

After the Boson Exam Environment (BEE) is installed, you should activate the exam associated with this book.

Step 1.   Launch the BEE from the Start menu.

Step 2.   The first time you run the software, you should be asked to either log in or register an account. If you do not already have an account with Boson, select the option to register a new account. You must register to download and use the exam.

Step 3.   After you register or log in, the software might prompt you to download the latest version of the software, which you should do. Note that this process updates the BEE, not the practice exam.

Step 4.   From the Boson Exam Environment main window, click the Exam Wizard button to activate and download the exam associated with this book.

Step 5.   From the Exam Wizard dialog box, select Activate a purchased exam and click the Next button. Although you did not purchase the exam directly, you purchased it indirectly when you bought the book.

Step 6.   In the EULA Agreement window, click Yes to accept the terms of the license agreement and click the Next button. If you do not accept the terms of the license agreement, you cannot install or use the software.

Step 7.   In the Activate Exam Wizard dialog box, enter the activation key from the paper inside the CD holder in the back of the book, and click the Next button.

Step 8.   Wait while the activation process downloads the practice questions. When the exam has been downloaded, the main BEE menu should list a new exam. If you do not see the exam, click the My Exams tab on the menu. You might also need to click the plus sign icon (+) to expand the menu and see the exam.

At this point, the software and practice questions are ready to use.

Activating Other Exams

You need to install the exam software and register only once. Then, for each new exam, you need to complete only a few additional steps. For instance, if you bought this book along with *CCNP SWITCH 642-813 Official Certification Guide* or *CCNP TSHOOT 642-832 Official Certification Guide*, you would need to perform the following steps:

Step 1.   Launch the BEE (if it is not already open).

Step 2.   Perform the preceding Steps 4 through 7 under Activate and Download the Practice Exam.

Step 3.   Repeat Steps 1 and 2 for any exams in other Cisco Press books.

You can also purchase Boson ExSim-Max practice exams that are written and developed by Boson Software's subject-matter experts at www.boson.com. The ExSim-Max practice exams simulate the content on the actual certification exams allowing you to gauge whether you are ready to pass the real exam. When you purchase an ExSim-Max practice exam, you receive an activation key; you can then activate and download the exam by performing the preceding Steps 1 and 2.

The Cisco Learning Network

Cisco provides a wide variety of CCNP preparation tools at a Cisco website called the Cisco Learning Network. This site includes a large variety of exam preparation tools, including sample questions, forums on each Cisco exam, learning video games, and information about each exam.

To reach the Cisco Learning Network, go to learningnetwork.cisco.com, or just search for "Cisco Learning Network." You need to use the login you created at www.cisco.com. If you don't have such a login, you can register for free. To register, simply go to www.cisco.com, click Register at the top of the page, and supply some information.

Memory Tables

Like most Certification Guides from Cisco Press, this book purposefully organizes information into tables and lists for easier study and review. Re-reading these tables can be very useful before the exam. However, it is easy to skim over the tables without paying attention to every detail, especially when you remember having seen the table's contents when reading the chapter.

Instead of simply reading the tables in the various chapters, this book's Appendixes D and E give you another review tool. Appendix D, "Memory Tables," lists partially completed versions of many of the tables from the book. You can open Appendix D (a PDF on the CD that comes with this book) and print the appendix. For review, you can attempt to complete the tables. This exercise can help you focus on the review. It also exercises the memory connectors in your brain; plus it makes you think about the information without as much information, which forces a little more contemplation about the facts.

Appendix E, "Memory Tables Answer Key," also a PDF located on the CD, lists the completed tables to check yourself. You can also just refer to the tables as printed in the book.

Chapter-Ending Review Tools

Chapters 2 through 19 each have several features in the Exam Preparation Tasks section at the end of the chapter. You may have used some of or all these tools at the end of each chapter. It can also be useful to use these tools again as you make your final preparations for the exam.

Suggested Plan for Final Review/Study

This section lists a suggested study plan from the point at which you finish reading through Chapter 19 until you take the ROUTE exam. Certainly, you can ignore this plan, use it as is, or just take suggestions from it.

The plan uses six steps. If following the plan verbatim, you should proceed by part through the steps as previously listed. That is, starting with Part 2 (EIGRP), do the following six steps. Then, for Part 3 (OSPF), do the following six steps, and so on. The steps are as follows:

Step 1.   **Review key topics and DIKTA questions:** You can use the table that lists the key topics in each chapter, or just flip the pages looking for the Key Topics icons. Also, reviewing the DIKTA questions from the beginning of the chapter can be helpful for review.

Step 2.   **Complete memory tables:** Open Appendix D on the CD, and print the entire appendix, or print the tables by major part. Then complete the tables and check your answers in Appendix E, which also appears on the CD.

Step 3.   **Hands-on practice:** Most people practice CCNP configuration and verification before the exam. Whether you use real gear, a simulator, or an emulator, practice the configuration and verification commands.

Step 4.   **Build configuration checklists:** Glance through the Table of Contents, looking for major configuration tasks. Then from memory create your own configuration checklists for the various configuration commands.

Step 5.   **Planning practice:** Even if you use the "Planning Practice" tables when you initially read each chapter, repeat the process, particularly the tables related to interpreting a design and reviewing another engineer's implementation plan.

Step 6.   **Subnetting practice:** If you can no longer do subnetting well and quickly without a subnetting calculator, take some time to get better and faster before going to take the ROUTE exam.

Step 7.   **Use the exam engine to practice:** The exam engine on the CD can be used to study using a bank of 100 unique exam-realistic multiple-choice questions available only with this book.

The rest of this section describes Steps 1, 3, 6, and 7 for which a little more explanation may be helpful.

Step 1: Review Key Topics and DIKTA Questions

This review step focuses on the core facts related to the ROUTE exam. The exam certainly covers other topics as well, but the DIKTA questions and the Key Topics items attempt to focus attention on the more important topics in each chapter.

As a reminder, if you follow this plan after reading the first 19 chapters, working a major part at a time (EIGRP, Chapters 2 through 4, for example) helps you pull each major topic together.

Step 3: Hands-On Practice

Although this book gives you many configuration checklists, specific configuration examples, examples of output, and explanations for the meaning of that output, there is no substitute for hands-on practice. This short section provides a couple of suggestions regarding your efforts at practice from the CLI.

First, most people use one or more of the following options for hands-on skills:

■ **Real gear:** Either purchased (often used), borrowed, or rented

■ **Simulators:** Software that acts like real gear

■ **Emulators:** Software that acts like router hardware, with IOS running inside that environment

First, a few words about finding these tools. For real gear, this book makes no attempt at suggesting how to go about getting, borrowing, or renting gear. However, the topic of what gear to buy for a home Cisco certification lab tends to be a popular topic from time-to-time on my (the author's) blog. Because the blog makes a good place for discussion, but a poor place for reference material, some of the base information about used gear, IOS versions/feature sets, relative to CCNP ROUTE (and other exams) is listed at www.certskills.com. The site also lists a link to the blog as well.

As for emulators, two exist of note. For the general public, a group of three free software offerings cooperate to allow you to run multiple instances of IOS on a PC: Dynagen and Dynamips (see www.dynagen.org) for the emulation, and GNS3 for the graphical interface (see www.gns3.net). Many websites devote attention to how to best use these tools; this book simply mentions the tools and their websites to get you started if interested.

Step 6: Subnetting Practice

This book assumes that you have mastered subnetting and the related math. However, many people who progress through CCNA, and move on to CCNP, follow a path like this:

Step 1.   Learn subnetting conceptually.

Step 2.   Get really good at doing the math quickly.

Step 3.   Pass CCNA.

Step 4.   Don't practice regularly and therefore become a lot slower at doing the subnetting math.

Step 5.   Study for CCNP ROUTE.

Although subnetting should not be assessed as an end to itself on CCNP ROUTE, many questions require that you understand subnetting math and can do that math just as quickly as you did when you passed CCNA. If you are a little slow on doing subnetting math, before you go to the ROUTE exam, try some of the following exercises:

■   Practice finding the subnet number, broadcast address, and range of addresses in a subnet. To do so, pick a number and mask, calculate the values, and use your favorite subnet calculator to check your work. Look at the Cisco Learning Network for a calculator if you don't have one.

■   Use the Cisco Subnetting Game, also at the Cisco Learning Network.

■   Practice choosing the best summary route for a range of subnets. Pick three to four addresses/masks. Calculate the subnet number and range. Then, try to choose the summary (subnet number/mask) that includes those three to four subnets, without including any more subnets than what is required. You can check your math with a subnet calculator as well.

If you like using binary/decimal conversions when you work through these problems, but just need to go faster, check out the Cisco Binary game, also at the Cisco Learning Network.

Step 7: Use the Exam Engine

The exam engine software that currently downloads for this book includes a 100-question database of questions related to the ROUTE exam. The user interface allows you to study, or with a little effort, to simulate a timed exam. This section describes how to use each option.

Study for the ROUTE Exam

Study mode—the default mode of the exam software that ships with the book—gives you an environment in which you can learn the topics as you review the questions. In particular:

■   You can click to see the answers and explanations

■   You see a running counter of the number of questions you got right

■   You can go forwards and backwards between questions

■   You can change answers to questions

■   There is no time limit

As a result, study mode works well when using the questions to learn. To use Study mode, use the following steps:

Step 1.   Click the **Choose Exam** button, which should list the exam under the title **Cisco Press Exams.**

Step 2.   Click the name of the exam once, which should highlight the exam name.

Step 3.   Click the **Load Exam** button.

Step 4.   On the next window, on the left, choose the option labeled **ICND2 Exam.**

Step 5.   Click the **Begin** button on the lower right of the window.

Simulate a ROUTE Exam

To simulate an exam with this software, you need to change the features of the user interface. Making the changes will make the exam software act as follows:

■   You cannot see the answers and explanations

■   You cannot see a running counter of the number of questions you got right

■   You cannot go forwards and backwards between questions

■   You cannot change answers to questions once you have moved on to the next question

■   There is a time limit

To simulate an exam, you have to use the **Custom Exam** option. This option takes a little effort to change some settings. First, to get to the place to change the settings, use the following steps:

Step 1.   Click the **Choose Exam** button, which should list the exam under the title **Cisco Press Exams**, and **CCNP ROUTE.**

Step 2.   Click the name of the exam once, which should highlight the exam name.

Step 3.   Click the **Load Exam** button.

Step 4.   On the next window, on the left, choose the option labeled **Custom Exam.**

Step 5.   Click the **Modify Settings** button on the lower right of the window.

At this point, you will be at a screen where you can customize the exam experience. To do so, you should make the following settings:

■   Check the **randomize question order** option

■   Check the **randomize answer order** option

■   Check the **Timed Test** option

■   Specify a time limit (suggested: 75 minutes)

■   Specify a number of questions (suggested: 60)

■   UnCheck the **Show current score** option

■   Under the **show answers and explanations** pull-down, select **Never**

After making the selections, click **Done**, and then click **Begin** to begin your simulated exam.

Summary

The tools and suggestions listed in this chapter have been designed with one goal in mind: to help you develop the skills required to pass the ROUTE exam. This book has been developed from the beginning to not just tell you the facts, but also help you learn how to apply the facts. No matter what your experience level is leading up when you take the exams, it is our hope that the broad range of preparation tools, and even the structure of the books, can help you pass the exams with ease. I hope you do well on the exam.

Answers to "Do I Know This Already?" Quizzes

Chapter 2

1. B and C. The **network 172.16.1.0 0.0.0.255** command tells IOS to match the first three octets when comparing the interface IP addresses to the configured "172.16.1.0" value. Only two answers match in the first three octets. The other two answers have a 0 in the 3ʳᵈ octet, making the addresses not match the **network** command.

2. D. The **show ip eigrp interfaces** command displays interfaces on which EIGRP has been enabled but omits passive interfaces. Making the interface passive, would omit the interface from the output of this command.

3. D. The **show ip eigrp interfaces detail** command does display a router's EIGRP Hello timer setting for each enabled interface. The other listed commands do not display the timer. Also, EIGRP routers do not have to have matching Hello timers to become neighbors.

4. C. The **show ip eigrp neighbors failure** command is not a valid IOS command. The debug displays messages that state when a neighborship fails due to authentication each time Hellos are exchanged. The **show key chain** command lists the specific keys that are currently valid, allowing you to determine if both routers use the same key values in currently valid keys. The **show clock** command displays the current time-of-day clock setting on a router, allowing you to check the valid times of the various keys versus the two router's clocks.

5. C. The **neighbor 172.16.2.20 fa0/0** command would only be rejected if the IP address (172.16.2.20) is not inside the range of addresses in the subnet (172.16.2.0/26, range 172.16.2.0–172.16.2.63). This command does not impact interface state. The command does disable all EIGRP multicasts, and because the three dynamically discovered neighbors require the EIGRP multicasts, all three neighbors fail. Although 172.16.2.20 is a valid potential neighbor, both routers must be configured with static **neighbor** commands, and we know that 172.16.2.20 was not previously configured with a static **neighbor** command; otherwise, it could not have been a neighbor with R1.

6. A and D. Table 2-4 lists the issues. For EIGRP, Router IDs do not have to be unique for EIGRP routers to become neighbors, and the hold timer does not have to match between the two neighbors. However, making an interface passive disables the processing of all EIGRP messages on the interface, preventing all neighborships. Mismatched IP subnets also prevent neighborships from forming.

7. A. The configuration requires the **ip authentication mode eigrp** *asn* **md5** command, which is currently missing. This command enables MD5-style authentication, rather than the default of no authentication. Adding this one command completes the configuration. Any valid key numbers can be used. Also, the 9 in the **ip authentication key-chain eigrp 9 fred** command refers to the EIGRP ASN, not an authentication type.

8. A. EIGRP forms neighborships only when two routers can communicate directly over a data link. As a result, with Frame Relay, EIGRP neighborships occur only between routers on the ends of a PVC, so in this case, 100 neighborships exist.

Chapter 3

1. B and C. Other than the two listed correct answers, the local router also adds connected routes for which the **network** command matches the corresponding interfaces, so it may not add all connected routes. Also, EIGRP does not add static routes to the EIGRP topology table, unless those routes are redistributed, as discussed in Chapter 9, "Basic IGP Redistribution."

2. B and D. EIGRP sends bandwidth, delay, reliability, load, MTU, and hop-count in the message. The formula to calculate the metric includes bandwidth, delay, reliability, and load.

3. A. EIGRP performs WAN bandwidth control without any explicit configuration, using default settings. Because no **bandwidth** commands have been configured, each subinterface uses the default 1544 Kbps setting. For S0/0.1, WAN bandwidth control divides the 1544 by 3 (515 Kbps), and then takes the (default) WAN bandwidth of 50 percent, meaning about 250 Kbps for each of the three DLCIs. For the two subinterfaces with one PVC, the default 1544 is multiplied by the 50 percent default WAN bandwidth, meaning that each could use about 750 Kbps.

4. A. This command lists all successor and feasible successor routes. The output states that two successors exist, and only two routes (listed with the "via..." text) exist. So, no feasible successor routes exist.

5. A and C. By default, the metric weights cause EIGRP to consider bandwidth and delay in the metric calculation, so changing either bandwidth or delay impacts the calculation of the feasible distance and reported distance, and impacts choice of feasible successor routes. Offset lists also change the metric, which in turn can change whether a route is an FS route. Link loading would impact the metrics, but not without changing the metric weights to nonrecommended values. Finally, variance impacts which routes end up in the IP routing table, but it is not considered by EIGRP when determining which routes are FS routes.

6. C and E. The EIGRP metric calculation treats bandwidth and delay differently. For bandwidth, EIGRP takes the lowest bandwidth, in Kbps, which is in this case 500 Kbps. For delay, EIGRP takes the cumulative delay, which is 20100 per the various **show interfaces** commands. However, the **show interfaces** command uses a unit of microseconds, and the interface **delay** command, and the EIGRP metric formula uses a unit of tens-of-microseconds, making the delay that feeds into the formula be 2010.

7. C and E. R1, as a stub router with the **connected** option, still advertises routes, but only routes for connected subnets. R1 announces its stub attribute to R2, so R2 chooses to not send Query messages to R1, knowing that R1 cannot be a transit router for other subnets anyway.

8. B. Of the five options, the **show ip route eigrp all-links** and **show ip eigrp topology all-learned** are not valid commands. Both **show ip eigrp topology** and **show ip route eigrp** can show at most successor and feasible successor routes. However, **show ip eigrp topology all-links** shows also nonfeasible successor routes, making it more likely to show all possible neighbors.

9. D. EIGRP considers only successor and feasible successor routes. Each of those routes must have metrics such that variance * metric is less than the best route's metric; the best route's metric is called the feasible distance (FD).

Chapter 4

1. D and E. The two listed commands correctly configure EIGRP route filtering such that prefixes matched by the ACL's permit clause will be allowed. All other prefixes will be filtered due to the implied deny all at the end of the ACL. The ACL permits numbers in the range 10.10.32.0–10.10.47.255, which leaves 10.10.48.0 and 10.10.60.0 unmatched by the permit clause.

2. B, C, and E. Sequence number 5 matches prefixes from 10.1.2.0–10.1.2.255, with prefix lengths between 25–27, and denies (filters) those prefixes. This results in answer A being incorrect, because the prefix length (/24) is not in the correct range. Clause 15 matches prefixes from 10.2.0.0–10.2.255.255, with prefix length exactly 30, matching answer C. Clause 20 matches only prefix 0.0.0.0 with length /0, so only a default route would match this entry. As a result, 10.0.0.0/8 does not match any of the three clauses.

3. C. When used for route filtering, the route map action (permit or deny) defines the filtering action, and any referenced **match** commands' permit or deny action just defines whether the prefix is matched. By not matching ACL 1 with a permit action, EIGRP does not consider a match to have occurred with clause 10, so it moves to clause 20. The prefix list referenced in clause 20 has a permit action, matching prefixes from 10.10.10.0–10.10.11.255, with prefix lengths from 23–25. Both criteria match the prefix in question, making answer C correct.

4. B and C. Answer A is invalid–the **ge** value must be larger than /24 in this case, so the command is rejected. Answer B implies a prefix length range from 24–28, inclusive. Answer C implies a range from 25–32 inclusive, because no **le** parameter exists to limit the prefix length lower than the full length of an IPv4 subnet mask. The same logic applies with answer D, but with a range from 28–32, so this final list could not match prefix lengths of /27.

5. B. 10.1.0.0/18 implies a range from 10.1.0.0–10.1.63.255, which includes none of the four subnets. 10.1.64.0/18 implies a range from 10.1.64.0–10.1.127.255, which includes all subnets. 10.1.100.0/24 implies range 10.1.100.0–10.1.100.255, which leaves out two of the subnets. Finally, 10.1.98.0/22 does not actually represent a summary–instead, 10.1.96.0/22 represents range 10.1.96.0–10.1.99.255, with 10.1.98.0 as listed in answer D being an IP address in that range. As such, IOS would actually accept the command, and change the parameter from 10.1.98.0 to 10.1.96.0, and would not include the four listed subnets.

6. B. The **ip summary-address** command does reset neighborships, but only on the interface under which it is configured. After those neighborships come up, R1 will advertise the summary route, but none of the subordinate routes inside that summary. The summary route will us a metric equal to the metric of the lowest metric subordinate route, approximately 1,000,000 in this case.

7. B and D. R2 has interfaces only in class A network 10.0.0.0, so the auto-summary setting has no effect. R3 has interfaces in both class A network 10.0.0.0 and class B network 172.16.0.0, so auto-summary causes R3 to summarize all subnets of 172.16.0.0/16 as a summary route when advertising to R2.

8. D. The phrase quoted in the question means that R1 is using its route for class A network 2.0.0.0 to decide where to send packets by default. R1's route for network 2.0.0.0 must have 1.1.1.1 as its next-hop router. This phrase occurs when EIGRP has learned a route for class A network 2.0.0.0 that has been flagged as a candidate default route by another router. The router flagging a route as a candidate default route, using the **ip default-network** command, does not actually use the route as its default route.

9. C and E. With the suggested configuration style, the static route must first be configured statically, as shown in answer A. Then, either this route must be redistributed as a static route into EIGRP (answer B), or pulled into EIGRP by virtue of the **network 0.0.0.0** EIGRP subcommand (answer D). The other two options have no effect on default route creation and advertisement.

Chapter 5

1. A and D. The wildcard mask is used for matching the prefix only, and not the prefix length. As such, 172.16.1.0 0.0.0.255 matches all addresses that begin with 172.16.1, and 172.16.0.0 0.0.255.255 matches all addresses that begin 172.16. Also, OSPF reviews the **network** command with the most specific wildcard masks (wildcard masks with the most binary 0's) first, so an interface IP address beginning with 172.16.1 matches the command that references area 8.

2. D. ABRs, by definition, connect the backbone area to one or more nonbackbone areas. To perform this function, a router must have at least one interface assigned to the backbone area, and at least one interface assigned to a nonbackbone area.

3. B and C. First, for the two correct answers: **show ip ospf interface brief** explicitly lists all OSPF-enabled interfaces that are not passive. **show ip protocols** lists either the details of the configured **network** commands, or if configured using the **ip ospf area** command, it lists the interfaces on which OSPF is enabled. This command also lists the passive interfaces, so armed with interface IP address information, the list of OSPF-enabled nonpassive interfaces could be derived. Of the three wrong answers, **show ip ospf database** does not list enough detail to show the OSPF-enabled interfaces. **show ip route ospf** lists only routes learned with OSPF, so if no routes use a particular OSPF-enabled interface as an outgoing interface, this command would not indirectly identify the interface. Finally, an interface may be OSPF-enabled but with no neighbors reachable on the interface, so the **show ip ospf neighbor** command may not identify all OSPF-enabled interfaces.

4. B and C. On a LAN, the non-DR routers form fully adjacent neighborships with only the DR and BDR, giving R1 two neighbors in the FULL state. The other two neighbors settle into the 2WAY state.

5. C and D. The **show ip ospf interface** command displays a router's OSPF Hello Interval setting for each enabled interface. The other listed commands do not display the timer. Also, OSPF routers do need to have matching Hello timers to become neighbors, so the neighborship would fail.

6. B and D. The **area 0 authentication** command tells R1 to use simple text password authentication on all interfaces in area 0 unless overridden by an interface subcommand. So, R1 must have configured the **ip ospf authentication message-digest** on its Fa0/0 interface, enabling MD5 authentication instead. The other correct answer is the command that correctly configures the MD5 authentication key. Of the two incorrect answers that list an authentication key, **ip ospf authentication-key** defines the clear-text key, and the other is not a valid IOS command.

7. E. Table 5-5 in Chapter 5 lists the issues. For OSPF, Router IDs must be unique; the interfaces must not be passive; the dead timers must match; and the primary IP addresses must be in the same subnet, with the same subnet mask. However, the process IDs, found on the **router ospf** *process-id* command, do not have to match.

8. A. Frame Relay is a Layer 2 service and as such does not participate in customer routing protocols. Because the design uses a separate subnet per PVC, and one point-to-point subinterface per PVC/subnet, OSPF will use a point-to-point network type. That means that the two routers on either end of a PVC will become neighbors, and become fully adjacent, meaning the central site router will have 100 fully adjacent neighborships.

Chapter 6

1. D. As an ABR connected to areas 0 and 2, ABR2 will have LSDB entries for both area 0 and area 2. In Area 0, ABR2 learns Type 1 LSAs from the four routers internal to area 0, plus ABR1, and plus 1 for the area 0 Type 1 LSA ABR2 creates for itself. In area 2, ABR2 learns 1 each for the five routers internal to area 2, plus the 1 Type 1 LSA ABR2 created for itself inside area 2. The total is 12.

2. E. OSPF creates a Type 2 LSA for a subnet when the router interface connected to the subnet calls for the election of a designated router (DR), and at least two routers have discovered each other and elected a DR. Then, the DR creates and floods the Type 2 LSA. IOS by default does not elect a DR on point-to-point topologies. It does on router LAN interfaces. One answer states that one router only exists in the subnet, so it does not actually find a second router and elect a DR. In the other case, a DR and BDR have been elected, but the router described in the answer is the BDR, not the DR. So, none of the other answers is correct.

3. C. Each ABR, by definition, creates a single Type 3 LSA to represent a subnet known in one area to be advertised into another area. Assuming 10.100.0.0 is a subnet in area 0, both ABR1 and ABR2 would advertise a Type 3 LSA into area 100. The **show ip ospf database summary** command specifically lists type 3 network summary LSAs.

4. C. The Database Description (DD) packet lists a short LSA header but not the entire LSA. The Link State Request (LSR) packet asks the neighbors for a copy of an LSA. The Link State Update (LSU) holds the LSAs. LSAck simply acknowledges received LSAs, and Hello is used for neighbor discovery and neighbor state maintenance.

5. B and D. Because the subnet was stable before R5 arrived, the other routers will have elected a DR and BDR. OSPF does not preemptively elect a new DR nor BDR, so R5 will be neither (DROther). As a result, R5's messages to the DR will be sent to the 224.0.0.6 all-DR-routers multicast address, and the DR's messages directed to R5 will be sent to the 224.0.0.5 all-SPF-router address.

6. E. R1, internal to area 1, can use LSAs only in the area 1 LSDB. R2's Type 1 LSA exists only in area 2's LSDB. The Type 2 LSA for subnet 10.1.1.0/24, if one exists, also only exists in area 2's LSDB. R1 will use ABR1's Type 1 LSA in area 1 to calculate the possible intra-area routes inside area 1, but R1 will use ABR1's Type 1 LSA in area 1. Finally, the Type 3 LSA, created for 10.1.1.0/24, and flooded into area 1, is also needed to calculate the metric.

7. A and B. OSPF builds the SPF tree based on the topology information Type 1 and Type 2 LSAs. Changes therefore require another SPF run. Changes to the other LSA types do not require an SPF calculation.

8. A and B. Because none of the interfaces have a **bandwidth** command configured, the only commands that can influence the OSPF cost are the **auto-cost reference-bandwidth** router subcommand and the **ip ospf cost** interface subcommand. To give the output shown in the question, either the interface cost could be set directly on all three interfaces listed. Alternatively, the reference-bandwidth could be set (in router

configuration mode) to cause one of the interface costs to be as shown in the output, with the other two interfaces having their costs set directly.

For the wrong answers, the **ip ospf cost interface s0/0/0.1** router subcommand does not exist—instead, it is an interface subcommand. An auto-cost of 64700, used as the numerator in the ref-bw/bandwidth cost calculation, does not result in any of the three listed interface costs.

For the two correct answers, with a default bandwidth of 1544 (Kbps) on the serial subinterfaces, a reference bandwidth of 1000 (Mbps) implies the math 1,000,000 / 1544, for an Interface cost of 647. With a default bandwidth of 100,000 Kbps (100 Mbps) on Fa0/0, a reference bandwidth of 2000 (MBps) implies math of 2,000 / 100 = 20.

9. A, B, and C. OSPF uses Types 1, 2, and 3 for calculating routes internal to the OSPF domain. OSPF uses types 4, 5, and 7 for external routes redistributed into the OSPF domain, as discussed in Chapter 9, "Basic IGP Redistribution."

Chapter 7

1. C. The output lists all B1's routes for subnets within the range of 10.1.0.0–10.1.255.255, whose prefix lengths are longer than /16. One answer lists subnet 10.2.2.0/24, which is not in this range, so the output cannot be used to confirm nor deny whether the subnet was filtered. B1's route for 10.1.2.0/24 is an intra-area route by virtue of not listing an IA code by the route; Type 3 LSA filtering only filters Type 3 LSAs, which routers use to calculate interarea routes, so the output tells us nothing about any filtering of 10.1.2.0/24. The output shows a single interarea route for 10.1.3.0/24, so at least one ABR has flooded a Type 3 LSA for this route. Additionally, the output confirms that at least one ABR flooded a type 3 LSA for 10.1.3.0/24, or the output would not show an IA route for 10.1.3.0/24. So, the type 3 LSA for 10.1.3.0/24 was not filtered by both ABRs.

2. C. When referenced from a distribute list, OSPF filters routes from being added to that router's IP routing table but has no impact on the flow of LSAs. As such, neither A nor B is correct. An OSPF **distribute-list** command does attempt to filter routes from being added to the IP routing table by OSPF, so the two answers that mention the IP routing table might be correct. Sequence number 5 matches prefixes from 10.1.2.0–10.1.2.255, with prefix lengths between 25–27, and denies (filters) those prefixes. So, the prefix list will match 10.1.2.0/26 with the first line, with a deny action. The 10.1.2.0/24 subnet does not match the first line of the prefix list, but it does match the third line, the match all line, with a permit action. Because 10.1.2.0/26 is matched by a deny clause, this route is indeed filtered, so it is not added to R1's IP routing table. 10.1.2.0/24, matched with a permit clause, is allowed and would be in the IP routing table.

3. A. When referenced from an **area filter-list** command, OSPF filters Type 3 LSAs created on that router, preventing them from being flooded into area 1 (per the configuration command). As an ABR, R1 would calculate intra-area routes to these area 0 subnets, so this filtering will have no effect on R1's routes. Sequence number 5

matches prefixes from 10.1.2.0–10.1.2.255, with prefix lengths between 25–27, and denies (filters) those prefixes. So, the prefix list will match 10.1.2.0/26 with the first line, with a deny action. The 10.1.2.0/24 subnet does not match the first line of the prefix list because the prefix length does not match, but it does match the third line, the match all line, with a permit action. By matching subnet 10.1.2.0/26 with a deny action, the filter-list does prevent R1 from flooding a Type 3 LSA for that subnet. By matching 10.1.2.0/24 with a permit action, R1 does not filter the Type 3 LSA for that subnet.

4. B and D. The **area range** command does not cause a failure in neighborships. Because at least one intra-area subordinate subnet of 10.1.0.0/16 exists in R1, R1 both creates a summary route for 10.1.0.0/16 and stops advertising LSAs for the (three) subordinate subnets. By default, the metric of the summary is the metric of the lowest-metric component subnet.

5. D. The **show ip ospf database summary** command lists only Type 3 LSAs. The **summary-address** command creates Type 5 LSAs on ASBRs, ruling out one answer. The output does not specify whether the LSA was created as a summary route; all references to the word "summary" refer to Type 3 Summary LSAs. If created by an **area range** command, the metric defaults to be the best metric of all subordinate subnets, but it may also be explicitly set, ruling out another of the possible answers. In short, this LSA may represent a route summarized by the **area range** command, but that fact cannot be proved or disproved by the output as shown..

6. B. Without the **always** parameter, the **default-information originate** command generates an LSA for a default route, with prefix 0.0.0.0/0, but only if its own IP routing table has a route for 0.0.0.0/0. It does not flag another LSA as being used as a candidate default route.

7. C and D. Both types of NSSA stubby areas allow the redistribution of external routes into the area, but these routes are advertised as Type 7 LSAs. As a totally NSSA area, the ABR should flood no Type 5 LSAs into the area and flood no Type 3 LSAs into the area, except for the Type 3 LSAs used to advertise the default route into the area. As such, a router internal to a totally stubby are should see zero Type 5 LSAs, and a small number of Type 3 LSAs for the default route(s) advertised by the ABR(s).

8. B. The **stub** keyword means either a stub area or totally stubby. The **no-summary** command means the area is totally stubby.

Chapter 8

1. D. The answer with **area 0 virtual-link 4.4.4.4 cost 3** is incorrect because the show command output lists a transit area of 1, but the answer's **area** parameter refers to area 0 as the transit area. (There is also no **cost** parameter on the **area virtual-link** command.) The RID of the router on the other end of the virtual link, 4.4.4.4 per the **show** command output, does not have to be pingable for the virtual link to work. The cost of the virtual link is 3, but that cost is calculated as the cost to reach the other router through the transit area, so the command output listed with the question can-

not be used to predict Fa0/1's OSPF interface cost alone. However, because the output lists area 1 as the transit area, and because the neighbor RID is listed as 4.4.4.4, R1 will use the area 1 LSDB entries to calculate the cost to reach 4.4.4, a process that will include the area 1 Type 1 LSA for RID 4.4.4.4.

2. B. The **area virtual-link** command defines the virtual link, with the transit area—the area through which the virtual link passes—listed as the first parameter. The other parameter is the RID of the other router. Two of the wrong answers are not IOS commands.

3. D. Of the four types listed, only point-to-multipoint nonbroadcast does not use a DR but does require the static definition of neighbors.

4. C. Of the four types listed, only point-to-multipoint does not use a DR and dynamically discovers neighbors.

5. A and C. For routers to use their OSPF routes in a multipoint design, each router needs mapping to each other router in the Frame Relay subnet. In this case, R3–R10 all need **frame-relay map** commands to define the mapping to other routers with which they do not have a PVC. This network type requires static definition of neighbors, but the neighbor relationships match the PVC topology, so R3–R10 need only two **neighbor** commands. This OSPF network type does not use a DR, so the **ip ospf priority** commands have no effect and would be unnecessary.

Chapter 9

1. D. The three incorrect answers list typical reasons for using route redistribution. The correct answer—the least likely reason among the answers for using route redistribution—lists a problem for which an OSPF virtual link is often used. Route redistribution could be attempted to solve a problem with a discontiguous OSPF area, but the redistribution completely changes the LSAs that would have otherwise been known and could have negative impacts on route summaries and cause routing loops, and have other problems as well.

2. B and D. For a router to redistribute routes between two routing protocols, the router must have both routing protocols configured, have a working link into each routing domain, and configure **redistribute** commands under each routing process. The **redistribute** command, issued in routing protocol configuration mode, pulls routes into that routing process, from another routing process as referenced on the **redistribute** command.

3. B and C. Because the metrics come from a different routing protocol than EIGRP, the metric must be set. The metric must be set with five components; EIGRP will then use those components as it would for an internal route. The metric components may be set as listed in the two correct answers, plus using a route-map as referenced by the **redistribute** command.

4. C. This output is the external data section of a detailed view of an EIGRP topology table entry for an external route. This output confirms that this route was redistributed into EIGRP. If R1 were the redistributing router, the output would include the phrase "(this system)"; this example does not include that notation. The output means that on the router that did the redistribution, the route was redistributed from OSPF process 1, and the OSPF metric was 64. R1's metric is not based on the OSPF metric of the route.

5. B. The **redistribute ospf** command will attempt to redistribute OSPF routes and connected routes from interfaces on which OSPF is enabled. The metric components include 1000 Kbps (or 1 Mbps), 100 tens-of-microseconds (or 1000 microseconds), 10 for the loading, 1 for the reliability, and 1500 for MTU. The EIGRP version of the **redistribute** command does not include a **subnets** option.

6. A and C. Because the routes come from OSPF and feed into OSPF, the metrics can be set with the usual tools, or the metric can default. When taking routes from OSPF into another OSPF process, the default metric is taken from the source route's OSPF cost. Alternatively, the metric can be set for all routes, regardless of the route source, using the **default-metric** OSPF subcommand. The **metric transparent** keywords cannot be used for an OSPF **redistribute** command.

7. D. This command lists the output of Type 4 Summary ASBR LSAs. The LSID identifies the redistributing ASBR (9.9.9.9). The advertising router is the ABR that created and flooded the LSA (3.3.3.3), and the metric is the ABR's best metric route to reach the ASBR.

8. D. Routers add internal and external costs for E1 routes and use only external costs for E2 routes, so the cost for the route through R22 will always be lower. However, for a given prefix/length, OSPF always prefers intra-area routes first, then interarea, then E1, and finally, E2, all regardless of metric.

Chapter 10

1. E. Because OSPF does not use hop count as a metric, the information about the number of hops is not available in OSPF routes in the IP routing table. The other answers list items that can be matched with the route map **match** subcommand.

2. A. The deny clauses in the route map mean that the route map will filter routes matched by that clause. The permit or deny action of the referenced ACLs just defines whether the route is matched. So, routes permitted by ACL "two" will be matched and then filtered due to the route-map clause deny action. Routes denied by ACL "one" simply do not match the route map clause numbered 10; such routes may or may not be redistributed depending on the next two clauses. Clause number 100 does not have a **match** command, meaning it matches all routes not otherwise matched, with a permit action, allowing these routes to be redistributed.

3. A and C. The problem states that R1 has learned OSPF intra-area routes for 10.1.1.0/24, so **show ip route** will display that subnet. As an intra-area route based on a Type 2 LSA, the **show ip ospf database** command lists the summary of the LSAs, including the 10.1.1.0 subnet number for that Type 2 LSA. However, because the redistribution filtering discards subnet 10.1.1.0/24, this value will not be included in the EIGRP topology table.

4. B. The **external 2** parameters on the **redistribute** command act as matching logic; only routes from the source routing protocol (in this case OSPF 2) that match this extra logic will be considered for redistribution by this **redistribute** command. The **set metric-type type-1** route-map subcommand sets the route type as it is injected into the destination routing protocol (in this case OSPF 1); this logic is not used for matching the source routes. The routes permitted by ACL 1 will be redistributed, but only those that are also E2 routes from the (source) OSPF 2 domain. The redistribute function will not change the attributes of routes inside a single routing domain, but only in the destination routing domain (OSPF 1), so the configuration has no effect on the OSPF 2 routes that remain in OSPF 2.

5. C. EIGRP, by default, sets a different AD for internal (90) and external (170) routes. The rest of the answers are accurate regarding default settings.

6. A. All the answers list reasonable options in some cases, but the only feature listed that is useful with all three routing protocols is the route tag feature. RIPv2 does not support the concept of differentiating between internal and external routes, so the two answers that suggest setting administrative distance (AD) based on the route type (internal or external) could not be used in all three routing domains, as required by the question. All three routing protocols support setting route tags and setting the AD per route; however, because RIPv2 cannot match based on the route type (internal/external), the option to set the route tags is the only option that applies to all three routing domains.

7. D. AD can be used to prevent the domain loop problem with two routing domains by making each routing protocol's AD for internal routes be better (lower) than the other routing protocol's AD for external routes. RIP uses AD 120 for all routes, with no distinction of internal or external. As such, OSPF's internal default AD settings of 110 meet the requirement that OSPF's internal AD (110) is better than RIP's external (120). However, RIP's default of 120 is not better than OSPF's default for externals (110), so the **distance ospf external 180** command changes that setting to meet both requirements. The three wrong answers, while syntactically valid, do not help meet the requirements.

8. E. Route tags are unitless integers that can be given to a route and even passed between different routing protocols by routers that perform redistribution.

Chapter 11

1. A and C. PBR supports processing packets on an interface, for the inbound direction only. The referenced route map causes PBR to attempt policy routing of packets that match a permit clause in the route map.

2. B and E. Packets created by Telnet use TCP, so the packet will match ACL 101 with a permit action. So, PBR will match the only route map clause shown in the configuration, with that permit route map clause listing a **set** command. The **set** command lists S0/0/1 as the outgoing interface, and without a **default** parameter. So, Router R1 will first attempt to forward the packet based on the **set** command (interface S0/0/1), but if the interface is down, then try to forward based on the IP routing table (interface S0/1/1).

3. D. The output from the **show ip policy** command shows the interfaces on which PBR has been enabled, and the name of the route map enabled for PBR on each interface. For the purposes of this question, the output tells us the interfaces on which PBR has been enabled. Two answers mention packets exiting the interface, so these answers cannot be correct, because PBR applies to packets entering an interface. For the two interfaces that mention inbound packets, one suggests that all packets will be forwarded per the PBR configuration; some may not be forwarded per PBR, depending on the configuration of the route map. The correct answer specifically mentions that PBR will consider all packets with PBR, which is the more accurate statement about PBR operations.

4. A and B. The IP SLA feature focuses on IP traffic, so IOS does not include Novell's older IPX protocol as part of IP SLA. IP SLA uses SNMP MIBs to store statistics, but it does not use SNMP as an operation.

5. C. The three lines shown create the operation number (first command), define the operation (second command), and start the operation (third command). All commands are correct. After the operation is started, IP SLA stores the data in the RTTMON MIB–no additional configuration necessary.

6. D. The up timers on the tracking object defines how long to wait, when in a down state, after seeing the IP SLA object transition to an OK state. Similarly, the down timer defines how long to wait, when in an OK state, after seeing the IP SLA object move to a down state, before moving the tracking object to a down state.

Chapter 12

1. B and E. The private IPv4 address space consists of Class A network 10.0.0.0, Class B networks 172.16.0.0–172.31.0.0, and the 256 Class C networks that begin 192.168.

2. B. ICANN and IANA manage the assignment of public IPv4 address space such that large address blocks (often called CIDR blocks) exist in a particular geography or

are assigned to particular ISPs. As such, Internet routers can more easily create summary routes to help keep the routing table small in the Internet. 200.1.2.0/24 would likely also be allocated to some registrar, ISP, or customer in Asia. Because of the large route summaries, in this case possibly a summary for 200.0.0.0/8, routers in North America would not see an increase in the size of their routing tables.

3. A. The router in ASN 22, R22, advertises the BGP update with (at least) 22 in the AS_Path Path Attribute (PA). When R1 advertises the route to R2, also in ASN 11, R1 does not add an ASN. As a result, R2's AS_Path has at least ASN 22 and not ASN 11.

4. A and C. The public range of 16-bit BGP ASNs is 1 through 64,495.

5. D. The question asks which answers are true about the eBGP peer but also not true about an iBGP peer. Both iBGP and eBGP use TCP port 179. An eBGP peer uses a different ASN than the local router, by definition, making that answer incorrect. The correct answer refers to the fact that an eBGP peer adds its own ASN to the BGP AS_Path PA before sending routing information to another router, whereas iBGP peers do not.

6. A. Although using BGP does avoid some static configuration at the Enterprise and the ISP, the primary reason to consider using BGP in the Enterprise is to influence and react to Path Attributes for the purpose of choosing the best path. Typically, engineers do not redistribute BGP routes into the IGP due to scalability problems. And although it may be interesting to monitor the size of the Internet BGP table, it is not a primary motivation for choosing to use BGP on a router.

7. C and D. The terms "homed" makes reference to a single homed ISP, and "multi-homed" to multiple ISPs. The terms "single" and "dual" refer to the number of connections to each ISP.

Chapter 13

1. B and C. The **router bgp** command lists the local ASN, and the **neighbor remote-as** command lists the neighbor's ASN. Because the neighbor relationship uses the IP addresses on the common link, the routers do not need to identify the update source interface, because each will default to use their S0/0 interfaces (in this case) as the update source.

2. D. Three of the commands list valid commands. The **neighbor 2.2.2.2 multihop 2** command is syntactically incorrect; it should be **neighbor 2.2.2.2 ebgp-multihop 2**.

3. D. The **show ip bgp** command lists the BGP neighbor state in the last column of output, listing the literal state, unless in an established state. In that state, the output lists the number of prefixes learned from the neighbor, so a numeric value implies an established state.

4. A and D. The output lists R2's local ASN as ASN 11, a value that is configured in the **router bgp** *asn* command. The line for neighbor 1.1.1.1 lists that router's ASN as 1, so a **neighbor 1.1.1.1 remote-as 1** command should exist on R2 instead of the **neighbor 1.1.1.1 remote-as 11** command. The state for neighbor 1.1.1.1 lists "Idle (Admin)," implying that the **neighbor 1.1.1.1 shutdown** command has been configured. The other answer lists a nonexistent command.

5. A. The BGP Update message lists a set of PAs, plus any prefixes/lengths that use those PAs. It can also list withdrawn routes in the same Update message as newly advertised routes. It can also list multiple prefixes in a single Update message.

6. C. The "Known via" text refers to the local router's (R1's) **router bgp** command, which identifies the local router's ASN. The rest of the output does not identify the neighboring ASN, nor the rest of the AS_Path details. It does list that the route is external, with the text "type external", and the AS Hops (which is the AS_Path length).

7. A. The third character in each line for each router is either blank, meaning the route is an eBGP route, or an "i," meaning an iBGP-learned route. The contents of the AS_Path can be determined (1, 2, 3, 4), but the answer about AS_Path does not suggest 4 ASNs. The best route for each prefix has a ">" in the second character, and this route does not.

8. D. The **network** command will take the route from the IP routing table and put the equivalent into the BGP table, if that exact route exists. The output does not show a route for 130.1.16.0/20, so the **network 130.1.16.0 mask 255.255.240.0** command does not match a specific route. The other answer with a **network** command is syntactically incorrect. Redistribution without aggregation would redistribute the three routes, but all three subordinate routes would be advertised into eBGP. By also using BGP route summarization, a single route for 130.1.16.0/20 can be advertised.

Chapter 14

1. C. R1 needs to be configured with **router bgp 1**, **neighbor 2.2.2.2 remote-as 1**, and **neighbor 2.2.2.2 update-source loopback1**. The **neighbor 2.2.2.2 ibgp-multihop 2** and **neighbor 2.2.2.2 ibgp-mode** commands are simply unsupported commands. The **neighbor 1.1.1.1 remote-as 1** command has correct syntax and is used as a command in R2's configuration but not on R1. The **neighbor 2.2.2.2 remote-as 2** command has correct syntax but with the wrong ASN (2 instead of 1).

2. D. The small letter "i" in the third character position implies the route was learned with iBGP. Of the five lines, four have an "i" in the third column.

3. B and C. The line reading "1.1.1.1 from 2.2.2.2..." implies the BGP RID of the neighbor is 1.1.1.1, with neighbor ID–the IP address on the local router's **neighbor** command–of 2.2.2.2. The end of the output shows that the route is internal (iBGP learned) and is best, so both the > and i will be displayed for this route by the **show ip bgp** command. Finally, the output does not identify the local ASN, although it does list the AS_Path of the route (1, 2, 3, 4).

4. B. By default, when a router advertises an iBGP route, it leaves the Next-Hop PA unchanged. By default, R2's next hop for routes learned from I2 will be I2's IP address used on the R2–I2 neighbor relationship.

5. A and C. The Enterprise core routers need to know which exit point (R1 or R2) is best; the correct answers supply those routes to the routers internal to the company. Note that redistribution from BGP into the IGP is not recommended, but it does defeat this particular problem.

6. B. The **show ip bgp neighbors 2.2.2.2 advertised-routes** command does list the post-outbound-filter BGP Update; however, the user did not issue a **clear** command, so the filter has not yet taken effect. As such, the output still lists the original three prefixes as if the filter had not yet been applied.

7. B, D, and E. The **neighbor distribute-list out** command refers to an ACL, but for the ACL to match on both prefix and prefix length, the ACL must be an extended ACL. The **neighbor filter-list** command refers to an AS-path filter and cannot match based on prefix/length.

8. A and B. The router resets the BGP neighborship when performing a hard reset of the peer. See Table 14-3 in the chapter for a list of several variations of the **clear** command and whether they perform a hard or soft reset.

Chapter 15

1. B. Weight and Local_Pref were created for the purpose of giving engineers tools to influence the BGP best path choice. AS_Path was created for loop avoidance, but AS_Path length can also be manipulated (for instance, with AS_Path prepend) to influence the best path choice. Although the Origin PA can be changed by configuration for the purpose of influencing the best path decision, the intent of this PA is to identify the source from which the route was introduced into BGP. Additionally, the best path algorithm considers the Origin PA after the other PAs listed in the answers, making Origin the least useful of these answers for influencing path choice.

2. A. Of the items listed in the question, Weight is the first one considered in the best path algorithm, with a bigger weight being better. As a result, Route 1 is the better route of the two.

3. B. Of the items listed in the question, Weight is the first one considered in the best path algorithm, and it is a tie. The next item considered, Local Preference, uses bigger-is-better logic, so Route 2 will be considered best.

4. B and D. Weight, a Cisco-proprietary feature of BGP on Cisco routers, cannot be transmitted in a BGP Update, so setting Weight on an outbound route map at the ISPs will have no effect. Also, the goals call for setting Weight for all routes from an ISP to the same number, so creating a prefix list to match a subset of reachable prefixes, in this case all class C networks, is not useful. However, two methods of configuring Weight do exist: the **neighbor weight** command and configuring an inbound route map with a **set weight** command in the route map.

5. B. The output shows the results of AS_Path prepending. The repetitive 1's cannot mean that the route has been advertised into and out of the same ASN repeatedly because loop prevention would have prevented such an advertisement. With AS_Path prepending, the neighboring ASN typically adds its own ASN to the end of the AS_Path (as listed on the left of the output).

6. C. The command lists the administrative distance as the first number inside the square brackets and the MED values as the second number in brackets. The AD of 20 implies an eBGP route instead of iBGP. The output says nothing about the Weight or AS_Path length.

Chapter 16

1. D. Inside a quartet, any leading 0s can be omitted, and one sequence of one or more quartets of all 0s can be replaced with "::". The correct answer replaces the longer three-quartet sequence of 0s with ::.

2. C. The name of the prefix generally represents the group to which the prefix is given, with the exception of the term *global routing*. IANA assigns a prefix to a registry (registry prefix). The registry may assign a subset of that range as a prefix to an ISP (ISP prefix). That ISP then subdivides that range of addresses into prefixes and assigns a prefix to one of its customers (site prefix, also called global routing prefix). The Enterprise network engineers then further subdivides the range, often with prefix length 64, into subnet prefixes.

3. A and C. IPv6 supports stateful DHCP, which works similarly to IPv4's DHCP protocol to dynamically assign the entire IP address. Stateless autoconfiguration also allows for the assignment by finding the prefix from some nearby router and calculating the Interface ID using EUI-64 format. Stateless DHCP simply supplies the DNS server IP addresses, and NDP supplies Layer 2 mapping information.

4. D. Stateless autoconfiguration only helps a host learn and form its own IP address, but it does not help the host learn a default gateway. Stateless RS is not a valid term or feature. Neighbor Discovery Protocol (NDP) is used for several purposes, including the same purpose as ARP in IPv4, plus to learn configuration parameters such as a default gateway IP address.

5. D. Global unicast addresses begin with 2000::/3, meaning the first three bits match the value in hex 2000. Similarly, unique local addresses match FD00::/8, and link local addresses match FE80::/10 (values that begin with FE8, FE9, FEA, and FEB hex). Multicast IPv6 addresses begin FF00::/8, meaning the first two hex digits are F.

6. B. When created automatically, link local addresses begin FE80::/64, because after the prefix of FE80::/10, the device builds the next 54 bits as binary 0s. Statically assigned link local addresses simply need to conform to the FE80::/10 prefix. As a result, only two answers are candidates with a beginning quartet of FE80. Of these, only one has only hex 0s in the second, third, and fourth quartets, making answer B the only valid answer.

7. A and C. The **ipv6 address** command does not list an **eui-64** parameter, so R1 does not form its global unicast address using the EUI-64 format. However, it does form its link local address using EUI-64. The **show ipv6 interface brief** command lists both the global unicast and link local addresses in its output.

8. A. The group addresses listed in the output are the all IPv6 hosts address (FF02::1), the all IPv6 routers address (FF02::2), and the solicited node address that is based on R1's global unicast address (FF02::1:FF12:3456). Also, R1's global unicast address is listed correctly in answer B, but the "[EUI]" notation implies that R1 derived the interface ID portion using EUI-64 conventions.

Chapter 17

1. A, B, and D. RIP-2 and RIPng both use UDP, both use Distance Vector logic, and both use the same metric, with the same maximum (15) and same metric that means infinity (16). RIPng does not perform automatic route summarization because IPv6 has no concept of a classful network. RIPng also uses the built-in IPv6 authentication mechanisms, rather than a RIP-specific authentication such as RIP-2.

2. B. That the configuration will be copied/pasted into a router means that the order of the commands matters. In this case, that the **ipv6 rip one enable** command precedes the **ipv6 address** command on interface f0/0 means that IOS will reject the first of these commands, therefore not enabling RIPng on F0/0. The correct order listed under S0/0/0 means that RIPng will be enabled on S0/0/0. As a result, RIPng on R1 will advertise about S0/0/0's connected IPv6 prefixes, and send Updates on S0/0/0, but will do nothing related for F0/0.

3. D. Because the question states that no IPv4 configuration exists, EIGRP for IPv6 cannot derive a 32-bit EIGRP router ID. Before EIGRP will work, R1 needs to define an EIGRP router ID (using the **eigrp router-id** command) and enable EIGRP using the **no shutdown** router subcommand.

4. B. EIGRP uses the link local address as the next hop for routing protocols. Based on R2's MAC address, R2's link local address on F0/0 will be FE80::1311:11FF:FE11:1111. This value is derived by splitting the MAC, inserting FFFE, and flipping bit 7, making the initial hex 11 become hex 13.

5. A and C. OSPFv3 supports multiple OSPF instances per interface, whereas OSPFv2 does not. Also, each version requires a different set of requirements be met before becoming neighbors, most notably that OSPFv3 does not require neighboring OSPFv3 routers to be in the same subnet.

6. C. Because the question states that no IPv4 configuration exists, OSPFv3 cannot derive a 32-bit OSPF router ID. Before OSPFv3 works, R1 needs to define an OSPF router ID (using the OSPF **router-id** command).

7. A. The **redistribute** command does not have a **subnets** option for IPv6 because OSPFv3 has no concept of IPv6 classful networks nor their subnets. As configured, the **redistribute** command redistributes only EIGRP-learned routes. If the **include-connected** parameter had been included, the connected route for 2000:0:0:1::/64 would have also been redistributed. Local routes are never redistributed.

8. B. The only configurable item after the interface that does not first list a keyword is the administrative distance parameter.

Chapter 18

1. C. Native IPv6 makes the most sense when the IPv6 deployment is pervasive, with traffic loads heavy or at least steady. Point-to-point tunnels work best when IPv6 is needed in only a subset of sites but also when the traffic should be somewhat regular or with higher volume. Multipoint tunnels also work well when IPv6 is needed in a subset of sites, but it is more appropriate when the traffic is more occasional and lower volume. Finally, NAT-PT is useful when an IPv4-only host needs to communicate with an IPv6-only host.

2. D. Native IPv6 makes the most sense when the IPv6 deployment is pervasive, with traffic loads heavy or at least steady. Point-to-point tunnels work best when IPv6 is needed in only a subset of sites, but also when the traffic should be somewhat regular or with higher volume. Multipoint tunnels also work well when IPv6 is needed in a subset of sites, but it is more appropriate when the traffic is more occasional and lower volume. Finally, NAT-PT is useful when an IPv4-only host needs to communicate with an IPv6-only host.

3. E. Dual stacks means that the host runs both IPv4 and IPv6. A host must run both if the host is to send packets of each protocol. The host may use a multipoint tunnel, but the other three answers list features applicable to routers, but not hosts.

4. B. A manually configured tunnel explicitly defines the destination IPv4 address, as does a GRE IPv6 tunnel. The other two types listed in the answer do not. Additionally, a manually configured tunnel uses mode **ipv6ip**, whereas GRE tunnels use mode **gre**.

5. C. IOS defaults to use GRE encapsulation mode on tunnel interfaces, so the **tunnel mode** command is not required. The mode will default to GRE. The **tunnel source** and **tunnel destination** commands are required.

6. B and D. The two point-to-point tunneling methods—manually configured tunnel and GRE—support IPv6 IGPs. The two multipoint tunneling methods—automatic 6to4 and ISATAP—do not.

7. A. An automatic 6to4 tunnel does not use a **tunnel destination** command on the tunnel interface; ISATAP tunnels also do not use this command. However, automatic 6to4 tunnels use IPv6 addresses that begin 2002::/16 and have the tunnel's source IPv4 address imbedded as the second and third octets of the IPv6 address, whereas ISATAP tunnels do not. Because C0A8:101 hex equals 192.168.1.1 in dotted decimal, this configuration represents the almost completed configuration for an automatic 6to4 tunnel.

8. A and D. ISATAP uses a modified EUI-64 format, which adds the IPv4 address, in hex, into quartets 7 and 8. Automatic 6to4 tunnels use address range 2002::/16, with the next two quartets (second and third quartets) used to store the hex version of an IPv4 address.

9. D. The combination of the configured eui-64 parameter on the **ipv6 address** command, and the tunnel mode of **isatap**, tells the router to use modified EUI-64 rules. These rules start with the configured 64 bit prefix (2000::/64 in this case), adding 0000:5EFE as the fifth and sixth quartets. The last two quartets are taken from the **tunnel source** command's referenced IPv4 address. In this case, 192.168.1.1 converts to C0A8:0101, making the last answer correct.

Chapter 19

1. C. IPsec tunnels make for more secure communications, including encryption and authentication. However, it does not support IGP communications across the tunnel.

2. A and C. An IPsec tunnel would be useful to allow the packet to pass over the Internet and into the Enterprise. The GRE tunnel would only be needed if an IGP is also needed, and for this design, an IGP is not required. Instead, a floating static default route would work fine, with the static route sending traffic over the IPsec tunnel but only when the private leased line fails.

3. D. The ATM details, like VPI/VCI, will be configured under the ATM interface. PPP (including CHAP) and Layer 3 details will be configured under the dialer interface.

4. C. The NAT configuration acts only on packets permitted by a referenced ACL. As a result, the ACL can permit packets destined for the Internet, performing NAT on those packets. The ACL also denies packets going to the Enterprise, meaning that the router does not apply NAT to those packets.

5. B. As for the correct answer, the process of routing a packet out a GRE tunnel interface triggers the GRE encapsulation action. As for the incorrect answers: There is no **tunnel gre** *acl* command. There is no IPsec tunnel interface. Finally, one answer refers to logic that would describe a router's logic when determining whether to encapsulate a packet into an IPsec tunnel.

Conversion Tables

This appendix lists two conversion tables for reference when studying:

- Hex-to-decimal
- Decimal-to-binary

Use these tables for learning; however, such tables will not be available on the exam.

Table B-1 *Hex-to-Decimal Conversion Table*

Hex	Decimal
0	0
1	1
2	2
3	3
4	4
5	5
6	6
7	7
8	8
9	9
A	10
B	11
C	12
D	13
E	14
F	15

Table B-2   *Binary-to-Decimal Conversion Table*

Decimal Value	Binary Value	Decimal Value	Binary Value	Decimal Value	Binary Value	Decimal Value	Binary Value
0	00000000	32	00100000	64	01000000	96	01100000
1	00000001	33	00100001	65	01000001	97	01100001
2	00000010	34	00100010	66	01000010	98	01100010
3	00000011	35	00100011	67	01000011	99	01100011
4	00000100	36	00100100	68	01000100	100	01100100
5	00000101	37	00100101	69	01000101	101	01100101
6	00000110	38	00100110	70	01000110	102	01100110
7	00000111	39	00100111	71	01000111	103	01100111
8	00001000	40	00101000	72	01001000	104	01101000
9	00001001	41	00101001	73	01001001	105	01101001
10	00001010	42	00101010	74	01001010	106	01101010
11	00001011	43	00101011	75	01001011	107	01101011
12	00001100	44	00101100	76	01001100	108	01101100
13	00001101	45	00101101	77	01001101	109	01101101
14	00001110	46	00101110	78	01001110	110	01101110
15	00001111	47	00101111	79	01001111	111	01101111
16	00010000	48	00110000	80	01010000	112	01110000
17	00010001	49	00110001	81	01010001	113	01110001
18	00010010	50	00110010	82	01010010	114	01110010
19	00010011	51	00110011	83	01010011	115	01110011
20	00010100	52	00110100	84	01010100	116	01110100
21	00010101	53	00110101	85	01010101	117	01110101
22	00010110	54	00110110	86	01010110	118	01110110
23	00010111	55	00110111	87	01010111	119	01110111
24	00011000	56	00111000	88	01011000	120	01111000
25	00011001	57	00111001	89	01011001	121	01111001
26	00011010	58	00111010	90	01011010	122	01111010
27	00011011	59	00111011	91	01011011	123	01111011
28	00011100	60	00111100	92	01011100	124	01111100
29	00011101	61	00111101	93	01011101	125	01111101
30	00011110	62	00111110	94	01011110	126	01111110
31	00011111	63	00111111	95	01011111	127	01111111

Table B-2 *Binary-to-Decimal Conversion Table*

Decimal Value	Binary Value	Decimal Value	Binary Value	Decimal Value	Binary Value	Decimal Value	Binary Value
128	10000000	160	10100000	192	11000000	224	11100000
129	10000001	161	10100001	193	11000001	225	11100001
130	10000010	162	10100010	194	11000010	226	11100010
131	10000011	163	10100011	195	11000011	227	11100011
132	10000100	164	10100100	196	11000100	228	11100100
133	10000101	165	10100101	197	11000101	229	11100101
134	10000110	166	10100110	198	11000110	230	11100110
135	10000111	167	10100111	199	11000111	231	11100111
136	10001000	168	10101000	200	11001000	232	11101000
137	10001001	169	10101001	201	11001001	233	11101001
138	10001010	170	10101010	202	11001010	234	11101010
139	10001011	171	10101011	203	11001011	235	11101011
140	10001100	172	10101100	204	11001100	236	11101100
141	10001101	173	10101101	205	11001101	237	11101101
142	10001110	174	10101110	206	11001110	238	11101110
143	10001111	175	10101111	207	11001111	239	11101111
144	10010000	176	10110000	208	11010000	240	11110000
145	10010001	177	10110001	209	11010001	241	11110001
146	10010010	178	10110010	210	11010010	242	11110010
147	10010011	179	10110011	211	11010011	243	11110011
148	10010100	180	10110100	212	11010100	244	11110100
149	10010101	181	10110101	213	11010101	245	11110101
150	10010110	182	10110110	214	11010110	246	11110110
151	10010111	183	10110111	215	11010111	247	11110111
152	10011000	184	10111000	216	11011000	248	11111000
153	10011001	185	10111001	217	11011001	249	11111001
154	10011010	186	10111010	218	11011010	250	11111010
155	10011011	187	10111011	219	11011011	251	11111011
156	10011100	188	10111100	220	11011100	252	11111100
157	10011101	189	10111101	221	11011101	253	11111101
158	10011110	190	10111110	222	11011110	254	11111110
159	10011111	191	10111111	223	11011111	255	11111111

Route Exam Updates

Over time, reader feedback allows Cisco Press to gauge which topics give our readers the most problems when taking the exams. To assist readers with those topics, the authors created new materials clarifying and expanding upon those troublesome exam topics. As mentioned in the introduction, the additional content about the exam is contained in a PDF document on this book's companion website, at http://www.ciscopress.com/title/9781587202537.

This appendix is intended to provide you with updated information if Cisco makes minor modifications to the exam upon which this book is based. When Cisco releases an entirely new exam, the changes are usually too extensive to provide in a simple update appendix. In those cases, you might need to consult the new edition of the book for the updated content.

This appendix attempts to fill the void that occurs with any print book. In particular, this appendix does the following:

- Mentions technical items that might not have been mentioned elsewhere in the book
- Covers new topics if Cisco adds new content to the exam over time
- Provides a way to get up-to-the-minute current information about content for the exam

Always Get the Latest at the Companion Website

You are reading the version of this appendix that was available when your book was printed. However, given that the main purpose of this appendix is to be a living, changing document, it is important that you look for the latest version online at the book's companion website. To do so:

Step 1   Browse to http://www.ciscopress.com/title/9781587202537.

Step 2   Select the Appendix option under the More Information box.

Step 3   Download the latest "Appendix C" document.

> **Note**   Note that the downloaded document has a version number. Comparing the version of this print Appendix C (Version 1.0) with the latest online version of this appendix, you should do the following:
>
> - Same version—Ignore the PDF that you downloaded from the companion website.
>
> - Website has a later version—Ignore this Appendix C in your book and read only the latest version that you downloaded from the companion website.

Technical Content

The current version of this appendix does not contain any additional technical coverage.

Index

J - K - L

W - X - Y - Z

informIT.com THE TRUSTED TECHNOLOGY LEARNING SOURCE

PEARSON

InformIT is a brand of Pearson and the online presence for the world's leading technology publishers. It's your source for reliable and qualified content and knowledge, providing access to the top brands, authors, and contributors from the tech community.

Addison-Wesley   Cisco Press   EXAM/CRAM   IBM Press.   QUE   PRENTICE HALL   SAMS | Safari Books Online

LearnIT at InformIT

Looking for a book, eBook, or training video on a new technology? Seeking timely and relevant information and tutorials? Looking for expert opinions, advice, and tips? **InformIT has the solution.**

- Learn about new releases and special promotions by subscribing to a wide variety of newsletters.
  Visit **informit.com/newsletters**.

- Access FREE podcasts from experts at **informit.com/podcasts**.

- Read the latest author articles and sample chapters at **informit.com/articles**.

- Access thousands of books and videos in the Safari Books Online digital library at **safari.informit.com**.

- Get tips from expert blogs at **informit.com/blogs**.

Visit **informit.com/learn** to discover all the ways you can access the hottest technology content.

Are You Part of the **IT** Crowd?

Connect with Pearson authors and editors via RSS feeds, Facebook, Twitter, YouTube, and more! Visit **informit.com/socialconnect**.

informIT.com THE TRUSTED TECHNOLOGY LEARNING SOURCE   **PEARSON**

Try Safari Books Online FREE

Get online access to 5,000+ Books and Videos

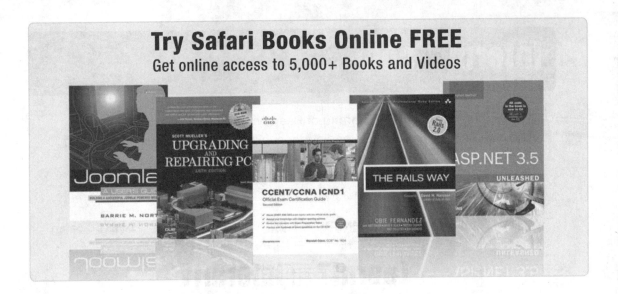

FREE TRIAL—GET STARTED TODAY!
www.informit.com/safaritrial

Find trusted answers, fast

Only Safari lets you search across thousands of best-selling books from the top technology publishers, including Addison-Wesley Professional, Cisco Press, O'Reilly, Prentice Hall, Que, and Sams.

Master the latest tools and techniques

In addition to gaining access to an incredible inventory of technical books, Safari's extensive collection of video tutorials lets you learn from the leading video training experts.

WAIT, THERE'S MORE!

Keep your competitive edge

With Rough Cuts, get access to the developing manuscript and be among the first to learn the newest technologies.

Stay current with emerging technologies

Short Cuts and Quick Reference Sheets are short, concise, focused content created to get you up-to-speed quickly on new and cutting-edge technologies.

GO FURTHER, FASTER.
BECOME CERTIFIED.

Stop thinking about your potential.
Realize it. Take your training, skills
and knowledge to the next level. Get
Cisco Certified through Pearson VUE.

Take your Cisco Career Certification exam at
one of more than 4,400 conveniently located
Pearson VUE® Authorized Test Centers
worldwide to experience a no-hassle test
experience. To register at a test center near
you, simply visit PearsonVUE.com/Cisco.

PEARSON
VUE

Copyright © 2009 Pearson Education, Inc. or its affiliate(s). All rights reserved. PearsonVUE.com.

FREE Online Edition

Your purchase of **CCNP ROUTE 642-902 Official Certification Guide** includes access to a free online edition for 45 days through the Safari Books Online subscription service. Nearly every Cisco Press book is available online through Safari Books Online, along with more than 5,000 other technical books and videos from publishers such as Addison-Wesley Professional, Exam Cram, IBM Press, O'Reilly, Prentice Hall, Que, and Sams.

SAFARI BOOKS ONLINE allows you to search for a specific answer, cut and paste code, download chapters, and stay current with emerging technologies.

Activate your FREE Online Edition at www.informit.com/safarifree

> **STEP 1:** Enter the coupon code: CMNJZAA.

> **STEP 2:** New Safari users, complete the brief registration form. Safari subscribers, just log in.

If you have difficulty registering on Safari or accessing the online edition, please e-mail customer-service@safaribooksonline.com

 Addison Wesley   Adobe Press   ALPHA   Cisco Press   FT Press FINANCIAL TIMES   IBM Press   lynda.com   Microsoft Press   New Riders

 O'REILLY   Peachpit Press   PRENTICE HALL   que   Redbooks   SAMS   SAS Publishing   Sun   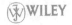 WILEY